W9-BST-932

Worlds of History

A Comparative Reader

Worlds of History

A Comparative Reader

Third Edition

Kevin Reilly
Raritan Valley College

Bedford/St. Martin's
Boston • New York

To those who taught me to think historically: Eugene Meehan, Donald Weinstein, and Peter Stearns; and to the memory of Warren Susman and Traian Stoianovich

For Bedford/St. Martin's

Publisher for History: Mary V. Dougherty
Director of Development for History: Jane Knetzger
Senior Developmental Editor: Louise Townsend
Cover Design: Donna Lee Dennison
Cover Art: J. H. Wilner, *Rice Harvest* (20th c.) Coll. Manu Sassonian, New York, N.Y., U.S.A. © Manu Sassonian/Art Resource, N.Y. Qing Dynasty (1644–1912). *Harvesting Tea Leaves*. From a series of paintings depicting tea curing. Qing dynasty, 19th c. © Scala/Art Resource, N.Y.

President: Joan E. Feinberg
Editorial Director: Denise B. Wydra
Director of Marketing: Karen Melton Soeltz
High School Marketing Manager: Daniel McDonough
Director of Editing, Design, and Production: Marcia Cohen
Assistant Director of Editing, Design, and Production: Elise S. Kaiser
Manager, Publishing Services: Emily Berleth

Library of Congress Control Number: 2006927524

    3 4 5 6   13 12 11 10

For information, write: Bedford/St. Martin's, 75 Arlington Street, Boston, MA 02116   (617-399-4000)

ISBN-10: 0-312-54558-4
ISBN-13: 978-0-312-54558-1

Acknowledgments
Acknowledgments and copyrights are continued at the back of the book on pages 1081–89, which constitutes a continuation of the copyright page.

Preface

Teaching introductory world history to college students for more than thirty-five years has helped me appreciate three enduring truths that provide the framework for this book. The first is that any introductory history course must begin by engaging with the students, as they sit before us in their remarkable diversity. The second is that world history requires a wide lens; it embraces all, the entire past, the whole world. The third is that students need to learn to think historically, critically, and independently, and realize that the subject matter of history can teach them how. With these truths in mind, I have constructed chapters in *Worlds of History* that pique student interest, teach broad trends and comparative experiences, and develop what today we call "critical thinking skills" and the Romans used to call "habits of mind."

The primary and secondary source selections in this reader address specific topics that I believe can imbue a general understanding of world history while helping students develop critical thinking skills. The reader's format helps students (and instructors) make sense of the overwhelming richness and complexity of world history. First, the reader has a **topical organization** that is also chronological, with each chapter focusing on an engaging topic within a particular time period. I am convinced that students are generally more interested in topics than eras, and that an appreciation of period and process can be taught by concentrating on topics. Into these topical chapters I've woven a **comparative approach,** examining two or more cultures at a time. In some chapters students can trace parallel developments in separate regions, such as the role of women in ancient China, India, and the Greco-Roman world in Chapter 5, or the rise of capitalism and industrialization in Latin America, India, Europe, and Japan in Chapter 21. In other cases students examine the enduring effects of contact and exchange between cultures, as in Chapter 11 on Mongol and Viking raiding and settlements from the tenth to the fourteenth centuries or Chapter 19 on the scientific revolution in Europe, the Americas, and Asia.

A wealth of **pedagogical tools** helps students unlock the readings and hone their critical thinking skills. Each chapter begins with "**Historical Context,**" an introduction to the chapter's topic that sets the stage for directed comparisons among the readings. A separate "**Thinking Historically**" section follows, exploring a particular critical thinking skill — reading primary and secondary sources or distinguishing causes of change — that ties to the chapter's selections. These skills build students' capacity to analyze, synthesize, and interpret one step at a time. A set of "**Reflections**" that both summarizes and extends the chapter's lessons concludes each chapter.

The reader's twenty-eight chapters should correspond to general survey texts and to most instructors' syllabi. Understanding that some variation might exist, I have included a correlation chart in the **Instructor's Re-source Manual** that matches each reading in this text with related chapters in more than a dozen of the most widely used survey texts. The manual, available at **bedfordstmartins.com/reilly** as well as in a one-volume print version, provides the rationale for the selection and organization of the readings, suggestions for teaching with the documents, and information about additional resources, including films and Internet sites.

NEW TO THIS EDITION

While I am continually testing selections in my own classroom, I appreciate input from readers and adopters, and I want to thank them for their many suggestions. Having incorporated some of this feedback, I think those who have used the reader previously will find the third edition even more geographically and topically comprehensive, interesting, and accessible to students. Twenty-five to 30 percent new documents on regions and topics from Latin America to Polynesia and from genocide to women in politics in the twentieth century have allowed me to introduce fresh material into each volume. In addition, I have included two new chapters: Chapter 12: "The Black Death" offers an in-depth look at this momentous event in Afro-Eurasian history; Chapter 26, "Religion and Politics: Israel, Palestine, and the West" provides a compelling and troubling look at contemporary conflict in the Middle East and its historic antecedents. Finally, I have also included five new "Thinking Historically" exercises: "Distinguishing Historical Understanding from Moral Judgments," "Considering Cause and Effect," "Understanding and Explaining the Unforgivable," "Evaluating Grand Theories," and "Making Use of the Unexpected."

Another exciting substantive change to this edition is the inclusion of more visuals as documents and increased emphasis on their importance as historical evidence. Eight chapters incorporate visual evidence, including Egyptian wall paintings, Fayum portraits of women, images of the Black Death, illustrations of humans and the environment, contrasting views of Amerindians, Japanese images of Westernization, World War I propaganda posters, and "Global Snapshots" of the world's energy use, population, and wealth.

Two more changes to this edition of *Worlds of History* I hope have made the reader even more accessible. Improved and new maps in almost every chapter — for example, "The Expansion of Islam to 750" in Chapter 7, and "U.S. Involvement in Central America" in Chapter 25 — will help students locate the regions and cultures under consideration. A running pronunciation guide at the base of the page that sounds out difficult-to-pronounce terms and names for readers should help students discuss the sources with greater confidence.

I am not a believer in change for its own sake; when I have a successful way of teaching a subject, I am not disposed to jettison it for something new. Consequently, many of my most satisfying changes are incremental: a better translation of a document or the addition of a newly discovered source. In some cases I have been able to further edit a useful source, retaining its muscle, but providing room for a precious new find. I begin each round of revision with the conviction that the book is already as good as it can get. And I end each round with the surprising discovery that it is much better than it was.

ACKNOWLEDGMENTS

A book like this cannot be written without the help and advice, even if sometimes unheeded, of a vast army of colleagues and friends. I consider myself enormously fortunate to have met and known such a large group of gifted and generous scholars and teachers during my years with the World History Association. Some were especially helpful in the preparation of this new edition. They include Jean Berger, *University of Wisconsin–Fox Valley*; Fred Bilenkis, *John Jay College, CUNY*; John Bohstedt, *University of Tennessee, Knoxville*; James Burns, *Springside School*; James Chrismer, *Chaminade Preparatory School*; Jason Freitag, *Ithaca College*; Helen Grady, *Springside School*; Jesse Hingson, *Georgia College*; Theodore Kallman, *San Joaquin Delta College*; Andrew J. Kirkendall, *Texas A&M University*; Mel Maskin, *Bronx High School of Science*; Leonora Neville, *The Catholic University of America*; Colin Ramsay, *Lemon Bay High School*; Lauren Ristvet, *Georgia State University*; Fulian Patrick Shan, *Grand Valley State University*; Anthony J. Steinhoff, *University of Tennessee-Chattanooga*; and Stephen Tallackson, *Purdue University Calumet*.

Over the years I have benefited from the suggestions of innumerable friends and fellow world historians. Among them: Michael Adas, *Rutgers University*; Jerry Bentley, *University of Hawaii*; David Berry, *Essex County Community College*; Edmund (Terry) Burke III, *UC Santa Cruz*; Catherine Clay, *Shippensburg University*; Philip Curtin, *Johns Hopkins University*; S. Ross Doughty, *Ursinus College*; Ross Dunn, *San Diego State University*; Marc Gilbert, *North Georgia College*; Steve Gosch, *University of Wisconsin at Eau Claire*; Gregory Guzman, *Bradley University*; Brock Haussamen, *Raritan Valley College*; Allen Howard, *Rutgers University*; Sarah Hughes, *Shippensburg University*; Stephen Kaufman, *Raritan Valley College*; Karen Jolly, *University of Hawaii*; Maghan Keita, *Villanova University*; Pat Manning, *University of Pittsburgh*; John McNeill, *Georgetown University*; William H. McNeill, *University of Chicago*; Gyan Prakash, *Princeton University*; Robert Rosen, *UCLA*; Heidi Roupp, *Aspen High School*; John

Russell-Wood, *Johns Hopkins University*; Lynda Shaffer, *Tufts University*; Robert Strayer, *UC Santa Cruz*; Robert Tignor, *Princeton University*; and John Voll, *Georgetown University*.

I also want to thank the people at Bedford/St. Martin's. Joan Feinberg and Denise Wydra remained involved and helpful throughout, as did Mary Dougherty, Katherine Meisenheimer, and Jane Knetzger. Amy Leathe provided invaluable help in reviewing the previous edition, and Holly Dye developed the instructor's manual and companion Web site for the book. I want to thank my production managers, Nancy Benjamin, for her project management, and Emily Berleth, for overseeing the entire production process (some thirty-five years after she first made me an author). I would also like to thank Mary Sanger for copyediting, Billy Boardman and Donna Dennison for the cover design, and Jenna Bookin Barry for advertising and promotion. Finally, it was a pleasure to work with senior developmental editor Louise Townsend. Rarely is an editor so knowledgeable in a field as vast as world history, so vigorous and insightful in her comments and suggestions, and so ready and able to do more.

While writing this book, memories of my own introduction to history and critical thinking came flooding back to me. I was blessed at Rutgers in the 1960s with teachers I still aspire to emulate. Eugene Meehan taught me how to think and showed me that I could. Traian Stoianovich introduced me to the world and an endless range of historical inquiry. Warren Susman lit up a room with more life than I ever knew existed. Donald Weinstein guided me as a young teaching assistant to listen to students and talk with them rather than at them. And Peter Stearns showed me how important and exciting it could be to understand history by making comparisons. I dedicate this book to them.

Finally, I want to thank my own institution, Raritan Valley College, for nurturing my career, allowing me to teach whatever I wanted, and entrusting me with some of the best students one could encounter anywhere. I could not ask for anything more. Except, of course, a loving wife like Pearl.

							Kevin Reilly

Introduction

You have here twenty-eight lessons in world history, each of which deals with a particular historical period and topic from human origins to the present day. Some of the topics are narrow and specific, covering events such as the First Crusade or the Arab-Israeli crisis in detail, while others are broad and general, such as the spread of universal religions or westernization and nationalism in the modern world.

As you learn about historical periods and topics, you will also be learning to explore history by analyzing primary and secondary sources systematically. The "Thinking Historically" exercises in each chapter encourage habits of mind that I associate with my own study of history. They are not necessarily intended to turn you into historians but, rather, to give you skills that will help you in all of your college courses and throughout your life. For example, the first chapter leads you to become more perceptive about time, the passage of time, measuring time, the time between events, all of which are useful throughout life. Similarly, a number of chapters help you in various ways to distinguish between fact and opinion and otherwise to build critical thinking, clearly abilities as necessary at work, on a jury, in the voting booth, and in discussions with friends as they are in the study of history.

World history is nothing less than everything ever done or imagined, so we cannot possibly cover it all. In his famous novel *Ulysses*, James Joyce imagines the thoughts and actions of a few friends on a single day in Dublin, June 16, 1904. The book runs almost a thousand pages. Obviously, there were many more than a few people in Dublin on that particular day, countless other cities in the world, and infinitely more days than that one particular day in world history. So we are forced to choose among different places and times in our study of the global past.

In this reader our choices do include some particular moments in time, like the one in 195 B.C.E., when Roman women demonstrated against the Oppian Law that forbade them from buying certain luxury goods or Lakota Indian Luther Standing Bear's experience in the 1880s at a white-run boarding school, but our attention will be directed toward much longer periods as well. And while we will visit particular places in time like Republican Rome in the second century B.C.E. or the boarding school, typically we will study more than one place at a time by using a comparative approach.

Comparisons can be enormously useful in studying world history. When we compare the religious origins of Christians and Buddhists, and the raiding and trading of Vikings and Mongols, or capitalism in England and Japan and genocide in Guatemala and Rwanda, we learn about the general and the specific at the same time. My hope is that by comparing some of the various *worlds* of history, a deeper and more nuanced understanding of our global past will emerge. With that understanding, we are better equipped to make sense of the world today and to confront whatever the future holds.

Contents

3. Identity in Caste and Territorial Societies

Greece and India, 1000–300 B.C.E.   66

Ancient Greece and India developed with different ideas of society. Does who we are depend on where we are or who we know? While finding out, we explore the relationship between facts and opinions, sources and interpretations.

4. Classical Civilizations and Empires

China and Rome, 300 B.C.E.–300 C.E. 108

Two thousand years ago the Chinese Han dynasty and the Roman Empire spanned Eurasia. In comparing these ancient empires, we seek to understand more about ancient empires, empires in general, and the course of change in ancient societies. A good comparison can lead us to consider new questions and topics, and generate new comparisons as well.

HISTORICAL CONTEXT   *108*

THINKING HISTORICALLY
Making Comparisons   *111*

Reflections   *152*

5. Women in Classical Societies

India, China, and the Mediterranean,
500 B.C.E.–500 C.E. 154

The experiences of women varied greatly over time both within and among the classical cultures of India, China, and the Greco-Roman world. The written and visual documents in this chapter allow us to explore the differences and similarities. At the same time we also examine both moments and processes in the history of women in classical antiquity to understand two different ways of thinking about the past.

HISTORICAL CONTEXT   *154*

THINKING HISTORICALLY
Considering Historical Moment and Historical Process   *154*

6. From Tribal to Universal Religion
Hindu-Buddhist and Judeo-Christian Traditions, 1000 B.C.E.–100 C.E.   187

Two religious traditions transformed themselves into universal religions at about the same time in two different parts of Asia as each became part of a more connected world. Their holy books reveal the changes as well as the desire to hold on to the tried and true.

7. Encounters and Conversions: Monks, Merchants, and Monarchs
Expansion of Salvation Religions, 400 B.C.E.–1400 C.E.   221

Christianity, Buddhism, and later, Islam, spread far across Eurasia often along the same routes in the first thousand years of the Common Era. To understand their success, we explore the evolution of religions in a larger context.

8. Medieval Civilizations

European, Islamic, and Chinese Societies,
600–1400 C.E.   268

Three great civilizations spanned Eurasia between 500 and 1500. Of the three, China and Islam were the strongest, Europe the weakest. But their differences can be best understood by looking separately at the social structure, economy, politics, and culture of each.

HISTORICAL CONTEXT   268

THINKING HISTORICALLY
Distinguishing Social, Economic, Political, and Cultural Aspects   268

9. Love and Marriage

Medieval Europe, India, and Japan, 400–1200 C.E.   301

Love and marriage make the world go 'round today, but not a thousand years ago. Love meant different things to different people in Europe, India, and Japan, and we use cultural comparisons to find out how and why.

HISTORICAL CONTEXT   *301*

THINKING HISTORICALLY
Analyzing Cultural Differences   *302*

Reflections   *335*

10. The First Crusade

Muslims, Christians, and Jews during the First Crusade,
1095–1099 C.E.   337

The First Crusade initiated a centuries-long struggle and dialogue between Christians and Muslims that would have a lasting impact on both. Wars are windows on cultures, but they also make moving narratives. Using the selections here, put together your own version of the story.

HISTORICAL CONTEXT   *337*

THINKING HISTORICALLY
Analyzing and Writing Narrative   *339*

11. Raiders of Steppe and Sea: Vikings and Mongols

Eurasia and the Atlantic, 750–1350 C.E.   *375*

From the late ninth through the tenth century, waves of Viking ships attacked across Europe; a few centuries later beginning in 1200, the Mongols swept across Eurasia, conquering all in their path and creating the largest empire the world had ever seen. What was the impact of these raiding peoples on settled societies and vice versa? In considering this question and the violent and destructive nature of these "barbarian" raids, we will consider the relationship of morality to history.

12. The Black Death

Afro-Eurasia, 1346–1350 C.E.   *422*

The pandemic plague ravaged the population of Afro-Eurasia, killing about one-third of the population of Europe and Egypt. In this chapter, looking at both written and visual evidence, we examine the impact of the plague in various locales while also contemplating its causes and the relation between cause and effect.

13. On Cities

European, Chinese, Islamic, and Mexican Cities,
1000–1550 C.E.   455

What did increasing urbanization from the medieval period on mean for those who lived in cities and those who did not? Wandering through some of the great cities of medieval Europe, China, and the Islamic world, we attempt to answer this question while also considering the validity and merits of one historian's famous comparative thesis about urbanization.

HISTORICAL CONTEXT   455

THINKING HISTORICALLY
Evaluating a Comparative Thesis   455

14. Ecology, Technology, and Science

Europe, Asia, Oceania, and Africa, 500–1550 C.E.   *493*

Since the Middle Ages, the most significant changes have occurred in the fields of ecology, technology, and science. In this chapter we read and assess three grand theories about the origins of our technological transformation and of our environmental problems, drawing on written and visual primary source evidence to develop our conclusions.

HISTORICAL CONTEXT   *493*

THINKING HISTORICALLY
Evaluating Grand Theories   *494*

15. Overseas Expansion in the Early Modern Period

China and Europe, 1400–1600   *539*

Both China and Europe set sail for global expansion in the fifteenth century, but China's explorations ended just as Europe's began. What were the factors that led to their similar efforts yet different outcomes? We examine primary and secondary sources in search of clues.

HISTORICAL CONTEXT   *539*

THINKING HISTORICALLY
Reading Primary and Secondary Sources   *542*

16. Atlantic World Encounters
Europeans, Americans, and Africans, 1500–1750   *580*

*European encounters with Africans and Americans were similar in some ways,
yet markedly different in others. The cultural clash created a new Atlantic world
that both integrated and divided these indigenous peoples. We compare primary
sources, including visual evidence, to understand these first contacts and conflicts.*

HISTORICAL CONTEXT   *580*

THINKING HISTORICALLY
Comparing Primary Sources   *581*

17. State and Religion
Asian, Islamic, and Christian States, 1500–1800   *626*

*In this chapter, we view the relationship between religion and political author-
ity through the prism of Chinese, Japanese, South Asian, and Western experience in the early modern period. By examining the competing and sometimes
cooperating dynamics between church and state in the past, we explore the*

history of an issue much debated in our own time and gain new insights into church-state relations today.

18. Gender and Family
China, Southeast Asia, Europe, and "New Spain," 1600–1750   660

With the blinds drawn on the domestic lives of our ancestors, one might assume their private worlds were uneventful and everywhere the same. By comparing different cultures we see historical variety in family and economic life and the roles of both men and women.

19. The Scientific Revolution

Europe, the Ottoman Empire, China, Japan,
and the Americas, 1600–1800					697

The scientific revolution of the seventeenth and eighteenth centuries occurred
in Europe, but had important roots in Asia, and its consequences reverberated
throughout the world. In this chapter we seek to understand what changed and
how. How "revolutionary" was the scientific revolution and how do we distin-
guish between mere change and "revolutionary" change?

HISTORICAL CONTEXT					697

THINKING HISTORICALLY
Distinguishing Change from Revolution					698

Reflections					728

20. Enlightenment and Revolution

Europe and the Americas, 1650–1850					731

The eighteenth-century Enlightenment applied scientific reason to politics, but
reason meant different things to different people and societies. What were the
goals of the political revolutions produced by the Enlightenment? A close read-
ing of the period texts reveals disagreement and shared dreams.

HISTORICAL CONTEXT					731

THINKING HISTORICALLY
Close Reading and Interpretation of Texts					732

21. Capitalism and the Industrial Revolution
Europe and the World, 1750–1900   765

Modern society has been shaped dramatically by capitalism and the industrial revolution, but these two forces are not the same. Which one is principally responsible for the creation of our modern world: the economic system of the market or the technology of the industrial revolution? Distinguishing different "causes" allows us to gauge their relative effects and legacies.

HISTORICAL CONTEXT   765

THINKING HISTORICALLY
Distinguishing Causes of Change   766

22. Colonized and Colonizers
Europeans in Africa and Asia, 1850–1930   811

Colonialism resulted in a world divided between the colonized and the colonizers, a world in which people's identities were defined by their power relationships with others who looked and often spoke differently. The meeting of strangers and their forced adjustment to predefined roles inspired a number of great literary works that we look to in this chapter for historical guidance.

HISTORICAL CONTEXT   811

THINKING HISTORICALLY
Using Literature in History   813

23. Nationalism and Westernization
Japan, India, and the Americas, 1880–1930   *846*

Western colonialism elicited two often conflicting responses among the colonized — the assertion of national independence and the desire to imitate Western power or culture. Exploring these sometimes contradictory movements through the visual and written sources in this chapter reveals much about the historical process and helps us appreciate the struggles of peoples torn between different ideals.

24. World War I and Its Consequences
Europe and the Soviet Union, 1914–1920   884

The First World War brutally ended an era — the world would never be the same after such death and destruction. We read historical accounts and analyze images from the era so that we can begin to understand the war's far-reaching chain of causes and consequences.

HISTORICAL CONTEXT   884

THINKING HISTORICALLY
Understanding Causes and Consequences   886

Reflections   918

25. World War II and Genocide
Europe, Japan, China, Rwanda,
and Guatemala, 1931–1994   921

The rise of fascism in Europe and Asia led to world war and genocide. Although we hope another world war will not occur, the legacy of World War II's genocide and of the mass killings that preceded it earlier in the century lives on in contemporary genocides around the globe. How could (how can) people allow their governments, armies, families, and friends to commit such unspeakable acts? How does the unforgivable happen?

HISTORICAL CONTEXT   921

THINKING HISTORICALLY
Understanding and Explaining the Unforgivable   923

26. Religion and Politics
Israel, Palestine, and the West, 1896 to the Present   959

The conflict between Israel and Palestine allows us to study the role of religion and politics in a particular place at a particular time, but the conflict is one whose impact can be felt not just across the Middle East but throughout the world. Learning to make use of new and unexpected information and ideas found in historical documents can provide a fresh take on seemingly intractable conflicts.

HISTORICAL CONTEXT   959

THINKING HISTORICALLY
Making Use of the Unexpected   960

27. Women's World
1950 to the Present   1007

The lives of women in the modern world are as diverse as those of men. Can you find any patterns in these personal accounts and stories? Can you develop any theories about women's lives in the modern world?

HISTORICAL CONTEXT   1007

THINKING HISTORICALLY
Constructing Theory   1008

28. Globalization and Planetary Health
1960 to the Present   1044

Globalization is a word with many meanings and a process with many causes. What are the forces most responsible for the shrinking of the world into one global community? Do the forces of globalization unite or divide us? What are the environmental effects of these forces? We undertake the study of process to answer these questions.

List of Maps

Worlds of History

A Comparative Reader

Prehistory and the Origins of Patriarchy

Gathering, Agricultural, and Urban Societies, 20,000–3000 B.C.E.

HISTORICAL CONTEXT

Men control more of the world's income, wealth, and resources; enjoy more opportunities, freedoms, and positions of power; and exercise greater control over the bodies, wishes, and lives of others than do women. In most of the world, men dominate, parents prefer sons to daughters, and most people—even women—associate maleness with strength, energy, reason, science, and the important public sphere. A system of male rule—"patriarchy"—seems as old as humanity itself. But is it? This chapter will ask if patriarchy is natural or historical. If patriarchy did not always exist, did it have a historical beginning, middle, and, therefore, potentially a historical end? If patriarchy had human causes, can humans also create a more equal world?

The selections in this chapter span the three types of societies known to human history: hunting and gathering (the earliest human lifestyle), agricultural and pastoral (beginning about ten thousand years ago), and urban (beginning about five thousand years ago). Thus, we can speak of the agricultural revolution (8000 B.C.E.) and the urban revolution (3000 B.C.E.) as two of the most important changes in human history. These events drastically transformed the way people earned a living and led to increased populations, greater productivity, and radically changed lifestyles.

How did the lives of men and women change with these revolutions? How did the relationships between men and women change? As people settled in agricultural villages, and later in cities, economic and social differences between groups became more marked. Did differences between the sexes increase as well? Did men and women have relatively equal power before the development of agriculture and the rise of cities? Did patriarchy originate as part of the transition from agricultural to urban society, or did men always have more power?

THINKING HISTORICALLY
Thinking about History in Stages

To answer these questions, one must think of early human history in broad periods or stages. History does not develop in neat compartments, however, one clearly distinguished from the other. Historians must organize and analyze disparate events and developments that occur over time in order to make sense of them. This chapter follows a widely accepted division of early history into the hunting-gathering, agricultural/pastoral, and urban stages. You might reflect on how this system of structuring the past makes history more intelligible; you might also consider the shortcomings of such a system. What challenges to the idea of historical stages do the readings in the chapter pose? On balance, does organizing history into stages make it easier or more difficult to understand complex changes, such as evolving gender roles?

1

NATALIE ANGIER

Furs for Evening, But Cloth Was the Stone Age Standby

The female "Venus" statues discussed in the following article date back over 20,000 years and are the earliest sculptures of humans. Archaeologists have long considered them symbols of fertility, given their exaggerated depiction of the female anatomy. As *New York Times* science writer Natalie Angier reports, some archaeologists have recently begun to reinterpret these "Venuses," emphasizing the detailed clothing and reconsidering what these costumes might reveal

Natalie Angier, "Furs for Evening, But Cloth Was the Stone Age Standby," *New York Times*, December 15, 1999, p. F1.

about the role of women in hunting and gathering societies. What conclusions do archaeologists draw from these new interpretations? What conclusions might you draw from these statues about the roles of women and their relative status in prehistoric society?

Thinking Historically

Grouping prehistory into the hunting-gathering, agricultural/pastoral, and urban stages emphasizes how early people sustained themselves. Archaeologists and historians also divide prehistory into eras defined by the tools that humans developed. They also call the age of hunters and gatherers the Old Stone Age, or Paleolithic era, because of the rough stone tools and arrow points that humans fashioned in this period. The age of agriculture is called the New Stone Age, or Neolithic era, because of the use of more sophisticated stone tools. The urban age is often called the Bronze Age because city people began to smelt tin and copper to make bronze tools. Angier's article asks us to reconsider the importance of these designations by highlighting what Dr. Elizabeth Wayland Barber has termed "the string revolution." What is the string revolution, and what was its significance? According to Angier, how might the string revolution prompt us to reconsider stages of prehistory?

Ah, the poor Stone Age woman of our kitschy imagination. When she isn't getting bonked over the head with a club and dragged across the cave floor by her matted hair, she's hunched over a fire, poking at a roasting mammoth thigh while her husband retreats to his cave studio to immortalize the mammoth hunt in fresco. Or she's Raquel Welch, saber-toothed sex kitten, or Wilma Flintstone, the original Soccer Mom. But whatever her form, her garb is the same: some sort of animal pelt, cut nasty, brutish, and short.

Now, according to three anthropologists, it is time to toss such hidebound clichés of Paleolithic woman on the midden heap of prehistory. In a new analysis of the renowned "Venus" figurines, the hand-size statuettes of female bodies carved from 27,000 to 20,000 years ago, the researchers have found evidence that the women of the so-called upper Paleolithic era were far more accomplished, economically powerful, and sartorially gifted than previously believed.

As the researchers see it, subtle but intricate details on a number of the figurines offer the most compelling evidence yet that Paleolithic women had already mastered a revolutionary skill long thought to have arisen much later in human history: the ability to weave plant fibers into cloth, rope, nets, and baskets.

And with a flair for textile production came a novel approach to adorning and flaunting the human form. Far from being restricted to a wardrobe of what Dr. Olga Soffer, one of the researchers, calls "smelly animal hides," Paleolithic people knew how to create fine fabrics that very likely resembled linen. They designed string skirts, slung low on the hips or belted up on the waist, which artfully revealed at least as much as they concealed. They wove elaborate caps and snoods for the head, and bandeaux for the chest—a series of straps that amounted to a cupless brassiere. [See Figure 1.1.]

"Some of the textiles they had must have been incredibly fine, comparable to something from Donna Karan or Calvin Klein," said Dr. Soffer, an archaeologist with the University of Illinois in Urbana-Champaign.

Archaeologists and anthropologists have long been fascinated by the Venus figurines and have theorized endlessly about their origin and purpose. But nearly all of that speculation has centered on the exaggerated body parts of some of the figurines: the huge breasts, the bulging thighs and bellies, the well-defined vulvas. Hence, researchers have suggested that the figurines were fertility fetishes, or prehistoric erotica, or gynecology primers.

"Because they have emotionally charged thingies like breasts and buttocks, the Venus figurines have been the subject of more spilled ink than anything I know of," Dr. Soffer said. "There are as many opinions on them as there are people in the field."

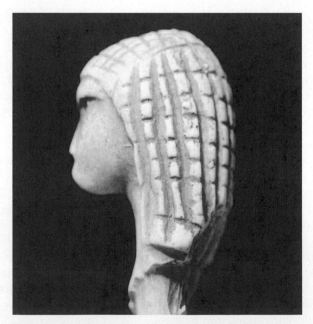

Figure 1.1   The Venus of Brassempouy, France.
Source: Steve Holland, University of Illinois.

In their new report, which will be published in the spring in the journal *Current Anthropology*, Dr. Soffer and her colleagues, Dr. James M. Adovasio and Dr. David C. Hyland of the Mercyhurst Archaeological Institute at Mercyhurst College in Erie, Pa., point out that voluptuous body parts notwithstanding, a number of the figurines are shown wearing items of clothing. And when they zeroed in on the details of those carved garments, the researchers saw proof of considerable textile craftsmanship, an intimate knowledge of how fabric is woven.

"Scholars have been looking at these things for years, but unfortunately, their minds have been elsewhere," Dr. Adovasio said. "Most of them didn't recognize the clothing as clothing. If they noticed anything at all, they misinterpreted what they saw, writing off the bandeaux, for example, as tattoos or body art." [See Figure 1.2.]

Scrutinizing the famed Venus of Willendorf, for example, which was discovered in lower Austria in 1908, the researchers paid particular attention to the statuette's head. The Venus has no face to speak of, but detailed coils surround its scalp. Most scholars have interpreted the coils as a kind of paleo-coiffure, but Dr. Adovasio, an authority on

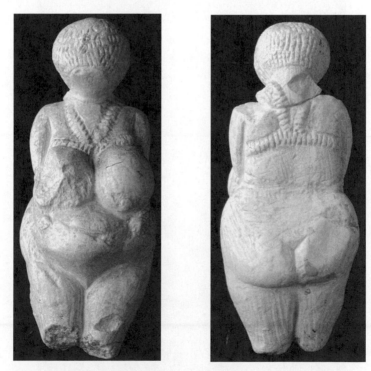

Figure 1.2   The Venus of Kostenki (Russia), wearing a woven bandeau.

Source: Bill Wiegand, University of Illinois.

textiles and basketry, recognized the plaiting as what he called a "radially sewn piece of headgear with vertical stem stitches."

Willendorf's haberdashery "might have looked like one of those woven hats you see on Jamaicans on the streets of New York," he said, adding, "These were cool things."[See Figure 1.3.]

On the Venus of Lespugue, an approximately 25,000-year-old figurine from southwestern France, the anthropologists noticed a "remarkable" degree of detail lavished on the rendering of a string skirt, with the tightness and angle of each individual twist of the fibers carefully delineated. The skirt is attached to a low-slung hip belt and tapers in the back to a tail, the edges of its hem deliberately frayed.

"That skirt is to die for," said Dr. Soffer, who, before she turned to archaeology, was in the fashion business. "Though maybe it's an acquired taste."

Figure 1.3   The Venus of Willendorf
Source: Visual Arts Library (London)/Alamy.

To get an idea of what such an outfit might have looked like, she said, imagine a hula dancer wrapping a 1930s-style beaded curtain around her waist. "We're not talking protection from the elements here," Dr. Soffer said. "This would have been ritual wear, if it was worn at all, a way of communicating with higher powers."

Other anthropologists point out that string skirts, which appear in Bronze-Age artifacts and are mentioned by Homer, may have been worn at the equivalent of a debutantes' ball, to advertise a girl's coming of age. In some parts of Eastern Europe, the skirts still survive as lacy elements of folk costumes.

The researchers presented their results earlier this month at a meeting on the importance of perishables in prehistory that was held at the University of Florida in Gainesville. "One of the most common reactions we heard was, 'How could we have missed that stuff all these years?'" Dr. Adovasio said.

Dr. Margaret W. Conkey, a professor of anthropology at the University of California at Berkeley, and co-editor, with Joan Gero, of *Engendering Archaeology* (Blackwell Publishers, 1991) said, "They're helping us to look at old materials in new ways, to which I say bravo!"

Not all scholars had been blinded by the Venusian morphology. Dr. Elizabeth Wayland Barber, a professor of archaeology and linguistics at Occidental College in Los Angeles, included in her 1991 volume *Prehistoric Textiles* a chapter arguing that some Venus figurines were wearing string skirts. The recent work from Dr. Soffer and her colleagues extends and amplifies on Dr. Barber's original observations.

The new work also underscores the often neglected importance of what Dr. Barber has termed the "string revolution." Archaeologists have long emphasized the invention of stone and metal tools in furthering the evolution of human culture. Even the names given to various periods in human history and prehistory are based on heavyweight tools: the word *Paleolithic*—the period extending from about 750,000 years ago to 15,000 years ago—essentially means "Old Stone Age." And duly thudding and clanking after the Paleolithic period were the Mesolithic and Neolithic, or Middle and New Stone Age, the Bronze Age, the Iron Age, the Industrial Age.

But at least as central to the course of human affairs as the invention of stone tools was the realization that plant products could be exploited for purposes other than eating. The fact that some of the Venus figurines are shown wearing string skirts, said Dr. Barber, "means that the people who made them must also have known how to make twisted string."

With the invention of string and the power to weave, people could construct elaborate yet lightweight containers in which to carry, store, and cook food. They could fashion baby slings to secure an infant snugly against its mother's body, thereby freeing up the woman to work and wander. They could braid nets, the better to catch prey animals without the risk of hand-to-tooth combat. They could lash together wooden logs or planks to build a boat.

"The string revolution was a profound event in human history," Dr. Adovasio said. "When people started to fool around with plants and plant byproducts, that opened vast new avenues of human progress."

In the new report, the researchers argue that women are likely to have been the primary weavers and textile experts of prehistory, and may have even initiated the string revolution in the first place — although men undoubtedly did their share of weaving when it came to making hunting and fishing nets, for example. They base that conclusion on modern crosscultural studies, which have found that women constitute the great bulk of the world's weavers, basketry makers, and all-round mistresses of plant goods.

But while vast changes in manufacturing took the luster off the textile business long ago, with the result that such "women's work" is now accorded low status and sweatshop wages, the researchers argue that weaving and other forms of fiber craft once commanded great prestige. By their estimate, the detailing of the stitches shown on some of the Venus figurines was intended to flaunt the value and beauty of the original spinsters' skills. Why else would anybody have bothered etching the stitchery in a permanent medium, if not to boast, whoa! Check out these wefts!

"It's made immortal in stone," Dr. Soffer said. "You don't carve something like this unless it's very important."

The detailing of the Venusian garb also raises the intriguing possibility that the famed little sculptures, which rank right up there with the Lascaux cave paintings in the pantheon of Western art, were hewn by women — moonlighting seamstresses, to be precise. "It's always assumed that the carvers were men, a bunch of guys sitting around making their zaftig Barbie dolls," Dr. Soffer said. "But maybe that wasn't the case, or not always the case. With some of these figurines, the person carving them clearly knew weaving. So either that person was a weaver herself, or he was living with her. He's got an adviser."

Durable though the Venus figurines are, Dr. Adovasio and his coworkers are far more interested in what their carved detailing says about the role of perishables in prehistory. "The vast bulk of what humans made was made in media that hasn't survived," Dr. Adovasio said. Experts estimate the ratio of perishable objects to durable objects generated in the average culture is about 20 to 1.

"We're reconstructing the past based on 5 percent of what was used," Dr. Soffer said.

Because many of the items that have endured over the millennia are things like arrowheads and spear points, archaeologists studying the Paleolithic era have generally focused on the ways and means of that noble savage, a.k.a. Man the Hunter, to the exclusion of other members of the tribe.

"To this day, in Paleolithic studies we hear about Man the Hunter doing such boldly wonderful things as thrusting spears into woolly mammoths, or battling it out with other men," Dr. Adovasio said. "We've emphasized the activities of a small segment of the population—healthy young men—at the total absence of females, old people of either sex, and children. We've glorified one aspect of Paleolithic life ways at the expense of all the other things that made that life way successful."

Textiles are particularly fleeting. The oldest examples of fabric yet discovered are some carbonate-encrusted swatches from France that are about 18,000 years old, while pieces of cordage and string dating back 19,000 years have been unearthed in the Near East, many thousands of years after the string and textile revolution began.

In an effort to study ancient textiles in the absence of textiles, Dr. Soffer, Dr. Adovasio, and Dr. Hyland have sought indirect signs of textile manufacture. They have pored over thousands of ancient fragments of fired and unfired clay, and have found impressions of early textiles on a number of them, the oldest dating to 29,000 B.C.E. But the researchers believe that textile manufacture far predates this time period, for the sophistication of the stitchery rules out its being, as Dr. Soffer put it, "what you take home from Crafts 101." Dr. Adovasio estimates that weaving and cord-making probably goes back to the year 40,000 B.C.E. "at a minimum," and possibly much further.

Long before people had settled down into towns with domesticated plants and animals, then, while they were still foragers and wanderers, they had, in a sense, tamed nature. The likeliest sort of plants from which they extracted fibers were nettles. "Nettle in folk tales and mythology is said to have magic properties," Dr. Soffer said. "In one story by the Brothers Grimm, a girl whose two brothers have been turned into swans has to weave them nettle shirts by midnight to make them human again." The nettles stung her fingers, but she kept on weaving.

But what didn't make it into Grimms' was that when the girl was done with the shirts, she took out a chisel, and carved herself a Venus figurine.

MARJORIE SHOSTAK

From Nisa: The Life and Words of a !Kung Woman

Marjorie Shostak, a writer and photographer, interviewed Nisa, a woman of the hunting-gathering !Kung people of the Kalahari Desert of Southern Africa. (The exclamation point at the beginning of !Kung indicates one of the clicking sounds used in their language.) From these interviews, which took place between 1969 and 1971, Shostak compiled Nisa's story in Nisa's own words.

As you read Nisa's account of her early adulthood, consider how it is similar to, and how it is different from, that of a young woman growing up today in modern society. If Nisa is typical of women in her world, do !Kung women have more or less authority, prestige, or power than women in your own society?

Finally, what does Nisa's story tell us about women in hunting-gathering societies?

Thinking Historically

Keep in mind that Nisa exists in the late twentieth century. When we think of stages of history, we are abstracting the human past in a way that vastly oversimplifies what happened but allows us to draw important conclusions. We know hunting and gathering did not end ten thousand years ago when agriculture first began. Hunters and gatherers still live in the world today—in places like the Arctic, the Amazon, and the Kalahari. That is why we use Nisa's account, which we are lucky to have. We have no vivid first-person accounts from those ancient hunters and gatherers—writing was not invented until the first cities developed five thousand years ago. So we generalize from Nisa's experience because we know that in some ways her life is like that of our hunting-gathering ancestors. But there are ways in which it is not. At the very least, the hunters and gatherers in the world today have been pushed by farmers and city people into the most remote parts of the globe—like the Kalahari Desert.

Using a contemporary of ours, like Nisa, as a kind of representative of our most distant ancestors is clearly a strange thing to do. Does

Marjorie Shostak, *Nisa: The Life and Words of a !Kung Woman* (Cambridge: Harvard University Press, 1981), 51, 56–59, 61–62, 89–90, 132–38.

it work? What precautions should we take when using a contemporary account as evidence of life in the Paleolithic Era?

One time, my father went hunting with some other men and they took dogs with them. First they saw a baby wildebeest and killed it. Then, they went after the mother wildebeest and killed that too. They also killed a warthog.

As they were coming back, I saw them and shouted out, "Ho, ho, Daddy's bringing home meat! Daddy's coming home with meat!" My mother said, "You're talking nonsense. Your father hasn't even come home yet." Then she turned to where I was looking and said, "Eh-hey, daughter! Your father certainly has killed something. He *is* coming with meat."

I remember another time when my father's younger brother traveled from far away to come and live with us. The day before he arrived he killed an eland. He left it in the bush and continued on to our village. When he arrived, only mother and I were there. He greeted us and asked where his brother was. Mother said, "Eh, he went to look at some tracks he had seen near a porcupine hole. He'll be back when the sun sets." We sat together the rest of the day. When the sun was low in the sky, my father came back. My uncle said, "Yesterday, as I was coming here, there was an eland—perhaps it was just a small one—but I spent a long time tracking it and finally killed it in the thicket beyond the dry water pan. Why don't we get the meat and bring it back to the village?" We packed some things, left others hanging in the trees, and went to where the eland had died. It was a huge animal with plenty of fat. We lived there while they skinned the animal and the meat into strips to dry. A few days later we started home, the men carrying the meat on sticks and the women carrying it in their karosses.

At first my mother carried me on her shoulder. After a long way, she set me down and I started to cry. She was angry, "You're a big girl. You know how to walk." It was true that I was fairly big by then, but I still wanted to be carried. My older brother said, "Stop yelling at her, she's already crying," and he picked me up and carried me. After a long time walking, he also put me down. Eventually, we arrived back at the village.

We lived, eating meat; lived and lived. Then, it was finished. . . .

When adults talked to me, I listened. When I was still a young girl with no breasts, they told me that when a young woman grows up, her parents give her a husband and she continues to grow up next to him.

When they first talked to me about it, I said, "What kind of thing am I that I should take a husband? When I grow up, I won't marry. I'll just lie by myself. If I married, what would I be doing it for?"

My father said, "You don't know what you're saying. I, I am your father and am old; your mother is old, too. When you marry, you will gather food and give it to your husband to eat. He also will do things for you. If you refuse, who will give you food? Who will give you things to wear?"

I said, "There's no question about it, I won't take a husband. Why should I? As I am now, I'm still a child and won't marry." I said to my mother, "You say you have a man for me to marry? Why don't you take him and set him beside Daddy? You marry him and let them be co-husbands. What have I done that you're telling me I should marry?"

My mother said, "Nonsense. When I tell you I'm going to give you a husband, why do you say you want me to marry him? Why are you talking to me like this?"

I said, "Because I'm only a child. When I grow up and you tell me to take a husband, I'll agree. But I haven't passed through my childhood yet and I won't marry!" . . .

When I still had no breasts, when my genitals still weren't developed, when my chest was without anything on it, that was when a man named Bo came from a distant area and people started talking about marriage. Was I not almost a young woman?

One day, my parents and his parents began building our marriage hut. The day we were married, they carried me to it and set me down inside. I cried and cried and cried. Later, I ran back to my parents' hut, lay down beside my little brother, and slept, a deep sleep like death.

The next night, Nukha, an older woman, took me into the hut and stayed with me. She lay down between Bo and myself, because young girls who are still children are afraid of their husbands. So, it is our custom for an older woman to come into the young girl's hut to teach her not to be afraid. The woman is supposed to help the girl learn to like her husband. Once the couple is living nicely together and getting along, the older woman leaves them beside each other.

That's what Nukha was supposed to do. Even the people who saw her come into the hut with me thought she would lay me down and that once I fell asleep, she would leave and go home to her husband.

But Nukha had within her clever deceit. My heart refused Bo because I was a child, but Nukha, she liked him. That was why, when she laid me down in the hut with my husband, she was also laying me down with her lover. She put me in front and Bo was behind. We stayed like that for a very long time. As soon as I was asleep, they started to make love. But as Bo made love to Nukha, they knocked into me. I kept waking up as they bumped me, again and again.

I thought, "I'm just a child. I don't understand about such things. What are people doing when they move around like that? How come Nukha took me into my marriage hut and laid me down beside my husband, but when I started to cry, she changed places with me and lay down next to him? Is he hers? How come he belongs to her yet Mommy and Daddy said I should marry him?"

I lay there, thinking my thoughts. Before dawn broke, Nukha got up and went back to her husband. I lay there, sleeping, and when it started getting light, I went back to my mother's hut.

The next night, when darkness sat, Nukha came for me again. I cried, "He's your man! Yesterday you took me and brought me inside the hut, but after we all lay there, he was with you! Why are you now bringing me to someone who is yours?" She said, "That's not true, he's not mine. He's *your* husband. Now, go to your hut and sit there. Later, we'll lie down."

She brought me to the hut, but once inside, I cried and cried and cried. I was still crying when Nukha lay down with us. After we had been lying there for a very long time, Bo started to make love to her again. I thought, "What is this? What am I? Am I supposed to watch this? Don't they see me? Do they think I'm only a baby?" Later, I got up and told them I had to urinate. I passed by them and went to lie down in mother's hut and stayed there until morning broke.

That day, I went gathering with my mother and father. As we were collecting mongongo nuts and klaru roots, my mother said, "Nisa, as you are, you're already a young woman. Yet, when you go into your marriage hut to lie down, you get up, come back, and lie down with me. Do you think I have married you? No, I'm the one who gave birth to you. Now, take this man as your husband, this strong man who will get food, for you and for me to eat. Is your father the only one who can find food? A husband kills things and gives them to you; a husband works on things that become your things; a husband gets meat that is food for you to eat. Now, you have a husband, Bo; he has married you."

I said, "Mommy, let me stay with you. When night sits, let me sleep next to you. What have you done to me that I'm only a child, yet the first husband you give me belongs to Nukha?" My mother said, "Why are you saying that? Nukha's husband is not your husband. Her husband sits elsewhere, in another hut."

I said, "Well . . . the other night when she took me and put me into the hut, she laid me down in front of her; Bo slept behind. But later, they woke me up, moving around the way they did. It was the same last night. Again, I slept in front and Bo behind and again, they kept bumping into me. I'm not sure exactly what they were doing, but that's why tonight, when night sits, I want to stay with you and sleep next to you. Don't take me over there again."

My mother said, "Yo! My daughter! They were moving about?" I said. "Mm. They woke me while I was sleeping. That's why I got up and came back to you." She said, "Yo! How horny that Bo is! He's screwing Nukha! You are going to leave that man, that's the only thing I will agree to now."

My father said, "I don't like what you've told us. You're only a child, Nisa, and adults are the ones responsible for arranging your marriage. But when an adult gives a husband and that husband makes love to someone else, then that adult hasn't done well. I understand what you have told us and I say that Bo has deceived me. Therefore, when Nukha comes for you tonight, I will refuse to let you go. I will say, 'My daughter won't go into her marriage hut because you, Nukha, you have already taken him for a husband.' "

We continued to talk on our way back. When we arrived at the village, I sat down with my parents. Bo walked over to our marriage hut, then Nukha went over to him. I sat and watched as they talked. I thought, "Those two, they were screwing! That's why they kept bumping into me!"

I sat with Mother and Father while we ate. When evening came, Nukha walked over to us. "Nisa, come, let me take you to your hut." I said, "I won't go." She said, "Get up. Let me take you over there. It's your hut. How come you're already married but today you won't make your hut your home?"

That's when my mother, drinking anger, went over to Nukha and said, "As I'm standing here, I want you to tell me something. Nisa is a child who fears her husband. Yet, when you took her to her hut, you and her husband had sex together. Don't you know her husband should be trying to help bring her up? But that isn't something either of you are thinking about!"

Nukha didn't say anything, but the fire in my mother's words burned. My mother began to yell, cursing her, "Horny, that's what you are! You're no longer going to take Nisa to her husband. And, if you ever have sex with him again, I'll crack your face open. You horny woman! You'd screw your own father!"

That's when my father said, "No, don't do all the talking. You're a woman yet, how come you didn't ask me? I am a man and I will do the talking now. You, you just listen to what I say. Nisa is my child. I also gave birth to her. Now, you are a woman and will be quiet because I am a man."

Then he said, "Nukha, I'm going to tell you something. I am Gau and today I'm going to pull my talk from inside myself and give it to you. We came together here for this marriage, but now something very bad has happened, something I do not agree to at all. Nisa is no longer going to go from here, where I am sitting, to that hut over there, that hut which you have already made your own. She is no longer going to look for anything for herself near that hut."

He continued, "Because, when I agree to give a man to my daughter, then he is only for my daughter. Nisa is a child and her husband isn't there for two to share. So go, take that man, he's already yours. Today my daughter will sit with me; she will sit here and sleep here. Tomorrow I will take her and we will move away. What you have already done to this marriage is the way it will remain."

Nukha didn't say anything. She left and went to the hut without me. Bo said, "Where's Nisa? Why are you empty, returning here alone?" Nukha said, "Nisa's father refused to let her go. She told him that you had made love to me and that's what he just now told me. I don't know what to do about this, but I won't go back to their hut again." Bo said, "I have no use for that kind of talk. Get the girl and come back with her." She said, "I'm not going to Gau's hut. We're finished with that talk now. And when I say I'm finished, I'm saying I won't go back there again."

She left and walked over to her own hut. When her husband saw her, he said, "So, you and Bo are lovers! Nisa said that when you took her to Bo, the two of you . . . how exactly *did* Bo reward you for your help?" But Nukha said, "No, I don't like Bo and he's not my lover. Nisa is just a child and it is just a child's talk she is talking."

Bo walked over to us. He tried to talk but my father said, "You, be quiet. I'm the one who's going to talk about this." So Bo didn't say anything more, and my father talked until it was finished.

The next morning, very early, my father, mother, and aunt packed our things and we all left. We slept in the mongongo groves that night and traveled on until we reached another water hole where we continued to live.

We lived and lived and nothing more happened for a while. After a long time had passed, Bo strung together some trade beads made of wood, put them into a sack with food, and traveled the long distance to the water hole where we were living.

It was late afternoon; the sun had almost left the sky. I had been out gathering with my mother, and we were coming back from the bush. We arrived in the village and my mother saw them, "Eh-hey, Bo's over there. What's he doing here? I long ago refused him. I didn't ask him to come back. I wonder what he thinks he's going to take away from here?"

We put down our gatherings and sat. We greeted Bo and his relatives — his mother, his aunt, Nukha, and Nukha's mother. Bo's mother said, "We have come because we want to take Nisa back with us." Bo said, "I'm again asking for your child. I want to take her back with me."

My father said, "No, I only just took her from you. That was the end. I won't take her and then give her again. Maybe you didn't hear me the first time? I already told you that I refused. Bo is Nukha's husband and my daughter won't be with him again. An adult woman does not make love to the man who marries Nisa."

Then he said, "Today, Nisa will just continue to live with us. Some day, another man will come and marry her. If she stays healthy and her eyes stand strong, if God doesn't kill her and she doesn't die, if God stands beside her and helps, then we will find another man to give to her."

That night, when darkness set, we all slept. I slept beside mother. When morning broke, Bo took Nukha, her mother, and the others and they left. I stayed behind. They were gone, finally gone.

We continued to stay at that water hole, eating things, doing things, and just living. No one talked further about giving me another husband, and we just lived and lived and lived.

ELISE BOULDING

Women and the Agricultural Revolution

Because women were the foragers or gatherers in hunting-gathering societies (while men were normally the hunters), women probably developed agriculture. The earliest form of agriculture was horticulture, a simple process of planting seeds with a digging stick and tending the plants in a garden. Sociologist Elise Boulding imagines how the planting of wild einkorn, a wheatlike grain of the ancient Middle East, must have transformed the lives of men and women about ten thousand years ago. How might this early agriculture or horticulture have contributed to women's power or prestige?

Thinking Historically

Boulding draws a distinction between the early horticultural stage of agriculture and the later agriculture that depended on animal-drawn plows. How did this later stage of agriculture change the roles of men and women?

Is agriculture one stage for the history of women, or are there two stages? How does our idea of stages of history depend on what we are studying?

Elise Boulding, *The Underside of History: A View of Women Through Time* (Boulder, CO: Westview Press, 1976; Rev. ed., Sage, 1992), 114–17, 118–19.

There is some disagreement about whether the domestication of animals or plants came first. In fact, both were probably happening at the same time. There is evidence from campfire remains as long ago as 20,000 B.C.E. that women had discovered the food value of einkorn, a kind of wild wheat that grows all through the fertile crescent.[1] An enterprising Oklahoma agronomist, Professor Jack Harlan of the University of Oklahoma, noticed several years ago, on an expedition to eastern Turkey, how thick these stands of wild einkorn grew. He tried harvesting some, and once he had resorted to a nine-thousand-year-old flint sickle blade set in a new wooden handle (he tried to use his bare hands first, with disastrous results), he was able to come away with an excellent harvest. After weighing what he had reaped, he estimated that a single good stand of einkorn would feed a family for a whole year. He also found that the grains had 50 percent more protein than the wheat we use now in North America for bread flour. Einkorn grains are found everywhere on the ancient home-base sites of the fertile crescent, either as roasted hulls in cooking hearths, or as imprints in the mud-and-straw walls of the earliest preagriculture huts.

It would be inevitable that grains from sheaves of einkorn carried in from a distant field would drop in well-trodden soil just outside the home base, or perhaps in a nearby pile of refuse. When the band returned the following year to this campsite—perhaps a favorite one, since not all campsites were revisited—there would be a fine stand of einkorn waiting for them right at their doorstep. We might say that the plants taught the women how to cultivate them. Planting, however, was quite a step beyond just leaving some stalks at the site where they were picked, to seed themselves for the next year. There was less reason for deliberate planting as long as bands were primarily nomadic and there was plenty of game to follow. But in time there was a premium on campsites that would have abundant grain and fruit and nuts nearby, and then there was a point in scattering extra grain on the ground near the campsite for the next year. Because of the construction of the seed, einkorn easily plants itself, so it was a good plant for initiating humans into agriculture.

Gradually, bands lengthened their stays at their more productive home bases, harvesting what had been "planted" more or less intentionally, and letting the few sheep they had raised from infancy graze on nearby hills. One year there would be such a fine stand of wheat at their favorite home base, and so many sheep ambling about, that a band would decide just to stay for a while, not to move on that year.

If any one band of nomads could have anticipated what lay in store for humankind as a result of that fateful decision (made separately by

---

[1]The Tigris-Euphrates river valley, so called because it forms a crescent of highly fertile land between the Persian Gulf and the uplands near the Mediterranean Sea. [Ed.]

thousands of little bands over the next ten thousand years), would they after all have moved on? While it may have been a relief not to be on the move, they in fact exchanged a life of relative ease, with enough to eat and few possessions, for a life of hard work, enough to eat, and economic surplus. As [archaeologist V. Gordon] Childe says, "a mild acquisitiveness could now take its place among human desires."

Successful nomads have a much easier life than do farmers. Among the !Kung bushmen today, the men hunt about four days a week and the women only need to work two-and-a-half days at gathering to feed their families amply for a week. (At that, meat is a luxury item, and most of the nourishment comes from nuts and roots.) The rest of their time is leisure, to be enjoyed in visiting, creating, and carrying out rituals, and just "being."

The First Settlements

For better or worse, the women and the men settled down. They settled in the caves of Belt and Hotu to a prosperous life of farming and herding on the Caspian. They settled in Eynan, Jericho, Jarmo, Beidha, Catal Huyuk, Hacilar, Arpachiyah, and Kherokitia in Cyprus, and in uncounted villages that no archaeologist's shovel has touched. These places were home-base sites first, some going back thousands of years. By 10,000 B.C.E. Eynan had fifty houses, small stone domes, seven meters in diameter, around a central area with storage pits. This was probably preagricultural, still a hunting and gathering band, but a settled one. The village covered two thousand square meters. Each hut had a hearth, and child and infant burials were found under some of the floors. Three successive layers of fifty stone houses have been found at the same site, so it must have been a remarkably stable site for a settlement.

What was life like, once bands settled down? This was almost from the start a woman's world. She would mark out the fields for planting, because she knew where the grain grew best, and would probably work in the fields together with the other women of the band. There would not be separate fields at first, but as the former nomads shifted from each sleeping in individual huts to building houses for family groups of mother, father, and children, a separate family feeling must have developed and women may have divided the fields by family groups.

Their fire-hardened pointed digging sticks, formerly used in gathering, now became a multipurpose implement for planting and cultivating the soil. At harvest time everyone, including the children, would help bring in the grain. The women also continued to gather fruit and nuts, again with the help of the children. The children watched the sheep and goats, but the women did the milking and cheese making. Ethnologists who have studied both foraging and agricultural societies comment on the change in the way of life for children that comes with agriculture. Whereas in foraging societies they have no responsibilities beyond feeding themselves and learning the hunting and foraging skills they will need, and therefore they have much leisure, it is very common in agricultural societies to put children to work at the age of three, chasing birds from the food plots. Older children watch the animals, and keep them out of the planted areas.

The agriculture practiced by these first women farmers and their children, producing enough food for subsistence only, must be distinguished from that agriculture which developed out of subsistence farming and which produced surpluses and fed nonfarming populations in towns. The first type is commonly called horticulture and is carried out with hand tools only. The second is agriculture proper, and involves intensive cultivation with the use of plow and (where necessary) irrigation. In areas like the hilly flanks of the fertile crescent in the Middle East, horticulture moved fairly rapidly into agriculture as it spread to the fertile plains. As we shall see, trading centers grew into towns and cities needing food from the countryside. Women and children could not unaided produce the necessary surpluses, and by the time the digging stick had turned into an animal-drawn plow, they were no longer the primary workers of the fields.

The simpler form of farming continued in areas where the soil was less fertile, and particularly in the tropical forest areas of Africa. Here soils were quickly exhausted, and each year the village women would enlist the men in helping to clear new fields which were then burned over in the slash-and-burn pattern which helped reconstitute the soils for planting again. The slash-and-burn pattern of horticulture has continued into this century, since it is a highly adaptive technique for meager tropical soils. Where the simple horticultural methods continued to be used, women continued as the primary farmers, always with their children as helpers. In a few of these societies women continued also in the positions of power; these are usually the tribes labeled by ethnologists as matrilocal. Not many tribes have survived into the twentieth century with a matrilocal pattern, however, though traces of matrilineal descent reckoning are not infrequent.

The first women farmers in the Zagros foothills were very busy. Not only did they tend the fields and do the other chores mentioned above, they also probably built the round stone or mud-brick houses in the first villages. The frequency with which women construct shelters in foraging societies has already been cited.

Women also began to spend more time on making tools and containers. No longer needing to hold the family possessions down to what they could carry, women could luxuriate in being able to choose larger and heavier grinding stones that crushed grain more efficiently. They could make containers to hold food stores that would never have to go on the road. They ground fine stone bowls, made rough baskets, and in the process of lining their baskets with mud accidentally discovered that a mudlined basket placed in the hearth would come out hardened—the first pottery. [Archaeologist] Sonja Cole suggests that pottery was invented in Khartoum in Africa about 8000 B.C.E., spreading northwest to the Mediterranean, but the same process probably happened over and over again as people became more sedentary.

The evidence from food remains in these early villages, 10,000 to 6000 B.C.E., indicates that men were still hunting, to supplement the agriculture and modest domestic herds. This means that they were not around very much. When they were, they probably shared in some of the home-base tasks.

Evidence from some of the earliest village layouts suggests that adults lived in individual huts, women keeping the children with them. Marriage agreements apparently did not at first entail shared living quarters. As the agricultural productivity of the women increased, and the shift was made to dwellings for family units, husband-wife interaction probably became more frequent and family living patterns more complex.

With the accumulation of property, decisions about how it was to be allocated had to be made. The nature of these agreements is hardly to be found in the archaeological record, so we must extrapolate from what we know of the "purest" matrilineal tribes of the recent past.

The senior woman of a family and her daughters and sons formed the property-holding unit for the family. The senior woman's *brother* would be the administrator of the properties. His power, whether over property or in political decision making, would be derivative from his status as brother (usually but not always the oldest) to the senior woman in a family. This role of the brother, so important in present-day matrilineal societies, may not have been very important in the period we are now considering, between 12,000 and 8000 B.C.E.

4

GERDA LERNER

The Urban Revolution:
Origins of Patriarchy

Often called "the rise of civilization," the urban revolution ushered in many changes five thousand years ago. The city societies or city-states that developed in Mesopotamia, Egypt, and the Indus River Valley after 3000 B.C.E. gave rise to the first kings, temples, priests, and social classes, as well as to writing, laws, metallurgy, warfare, markets, and private property. With the city-state came patriarchy, the assertion of male power, and the subordination of women—the signs of which were clear in Sumer and Mesopotamia, both ruled by assemblies of men or kings. Mesopotamian law codes favored men: Women could be divorced, punished, or sold into slavery for adultery, while men could not. Laws also required that women wear veils, restricted women's freedom of movement, and treated women as the property of fathers or husbands.

People in ancient Egypt worshiped their kings as gods. Cities worshiped Sky Father Gods. One Egyptian creation myth describes the great god Ra emerging from the waters of Nun and creating the Egyptian universe from his own body. A Mesopotamian creation story, the *Enuma Elish*, recounts a primordial battle between the male god Marduk and the mother goddess Tiamat: Marduk splits Tiamat's heart with his arrow and then cracks her dead body in half like a shellfish, her hollowed-out form becoming heaven and earth.

In this selection, *The Creation of Patriarchy*, the author, modern historian Gerda Lerner, gives considerable attention to the way in which religious ideas changed as city-based states replaced the world of small Neolithic villages. At the beginning of the selection, Lerner notes the impact of urban social classes and patriarchy. Because cities legislated the rule of the rich and powerful classes above the poor and slaves, there were periods in which some women—the wives and daughters of wealthy and powerful men—benefited at the expense of other women. Eventually, though, city law curtailed the freedom of all women, rich and poor. Despite these restrictions, some women continued to play a role in popular religion. What was that role? How important do you think it was?

Gerda Lerner, *The Creation of Patriarchy* (Oxford: Oxford University Press, 1986), 141–45.

What do you think of the author's comparison of Ishtar and the Virgin Mary? Does this comparison suggest that Christianity was more patriarchal? Do we live in a patriarchy today? What would suggest the presence of patriarchy in modern society? What would suggest its absence?

Thinking Historically

Any stage theory of history depends on a series of broad generalizations. We might distinguish two here. First, Lerner suggests that cities, archaic states, kings, gods, militarism, and patriarchy are all related, that they appeared at about the same time as part of the same process of change. Notice how Lerner links some of these elements, one to the other. Which of these couplings is persuasive?

Second, notice the absence of specific dates in this selection. The kinds of evidence Lerner uses here cannot be dated very precisely. She uses phrases like "the first half of the third millennium B.C.," which would mean between 3000 and 2500 B.C.E. When would you date the origins of patriarchy? Notice the time lag between the imposition of patriarchal laws and the slower process of replacing goddesses with gods. How does Lerner account for this time lag?

Do you think religion would be slower to change than law or social custom? Could the worship of Ishtar have been representative of an earlier, more agricultural, religious tradition?

... In Mesopotamian societies the institutionalization of patriarchy created sharply defined boundaries between women of different classes, although the development of the new gender definitions and of the customs associated with them proceeded unevenly. The state, during the process of the establishment of written law codes, increased the property rights of upper-class women, while it circumscribed their sexual rights and finally totally eroded them. The lifelong dependency of women on fathers and husbands became so firmly established in law and custom as to be considered "natural" and god-given. In the case of lower-class women, their labor power served either their families or those who owned their families' services. Their sexual and reproductive capacities were commodified, traded, leased, or sold in the interest of male family members. Women of all classes had traditionally been excluded from military power and were, by the turn of the first millennium B.C., excluded from formal education, insofar as it had become institutionalized.

Yet, even then, powerful women in powerful roles lived on in cultic service, in religious representation, and in symbols. There was a considerable time lag between the subordination of women in patriarchal society and the declassing of the goddesses. As we trace below changes in the position of male and female god figures in the pantheon of the gods in a period of over a thousand years, we should keep in mind that the power of the goddesses and their priestesses in daily life and in popular religion continued in force, even as the supreme goddesses were dethroned. It is remarkable that in societies which had subordinated women economically, educationally, and legally, the spiritual and metaphysical power of goddesses remained active and strong.

We have some indication of what practical religion was like from archaeological artifacts and from temple hymns and prayers. In Mesopotamian societies the feeding of and service to the gods was considered essential to the survival of the community. This service was performed by male and female temple servants. For important decisions of state, in warfare, and for important personal decisions one would consult an oracle or a diviner, who might be either a man or a woman. In personal distress, sickness, or misfortune the afflicted person would seek the help of his or her household-god and, if this was of no avail, would appeal to any one of a number of gods or goddesses who had particular qualities needed to cure the affliction. If the appeal were to a goddess, the sick person also required the intercession and good services of a priestess of the particular goddess. There were, of course, also male gods who could benefit one in case of illness, and these would usually be served by a male priest.

For example, in Babylonia a sick man or woman would approach the Ishtar temple in a spirit of humility on the assumption that the sickness was a result of his or her transgression. The petitioner would bring appropriate offerings: food, a young animal for sacrifice, oil, and wine. For the goddess Ishtar such offerings quite frequently included images of a vulva, the symbol of her fertility, fashioned out of precious lapis lazuli stone. The afflicted person would prostrate himself before the priestess and recite some appropriate hymns and prayers. A typical prayer contained the following lines:

> Gracious Ishtar, who rules over the universe,
> Heroic Ishtar, who creates humankind,
> who walks before the cattle, who loves the shepherd . . .
> You give justice to the distressed, the suffering you give
>   them justice.
> Without you the river will not open,
> the river which brings us life will not be closed,
> without you the canal will not open,
> the canal from which the scattered drink,
> will not be closed . . . Ishtar, merciful lady . . .
> hear me and grant me mercy.

Mesopotamian men or women, in distress or sickness, humbled themselves before a goddess-figure and her priestly servant. In words reflecting the attitude of slave toward master, they praised and worshiped the goddess's power. Thus, another hymn to Ishtar addresses her as "mistress of the battle field, who pulls down the mountains"; "Majestic one, lioness among the gods, who conquers the angry gods, strongest among rulers, who leads kings by the lead; you who open the wombs of women . . . mighty Ishtar, how great is your strength!" Heaping praise upon praise, the petitioner continued:

> Where you cast your glance, the dead awaken, the sick arise;
> The bewildered, beholding your face, find the right way.
> I appeal to you, miserable and distraught,
> tortured by pain, your servant,
> be merciful and hear my prayer! . . .
> I await you, my mistress; my soul turns toward you.
> I beseech you: Relieve my plight.
> Absolve me of my guilt, my wickedness, my sin,
> forget my misdeeds, accept my plea!

We should note that the petitioners regarded the goddess as all-powerful. In the symbol of the goddess's vulva, fashioned of precious stone and offered up in her praise, they celebrated the sacredness of female sexuality and its mysterious life-giving force, which included the power to heal. And in the very prayers appealing to the goddess's mercy, they praised her as mistress of the battlefield, more powerful than kings, more powerful than other gods. Their prayers to the gods similarly extolled the god's virtues and listed his powers in superlatives. My point here is that men and women offering such prayers when in distress must have thought of women, just as they thought of men, as capable of metaphysical power and as potential mediators between the gods and human beings. That is a mental image quite different from that of Christians, for example, who in a later time would pray to the Virgin Mary to intercede with God in their behalf. The power of the Virgin lies in her ability to appeal to God's mercy; it derives from her motherhood and the miracle of her immaculate conception. She has no power for herself, and the very sources of her power to intercede separate her irrevocably from other women. The goddess Ishtar and other goddesses like her had power in their own right. It was the kind of power men had, derived from military exploits and the ability to impose her will on the gods or to influence them. And yet Ishtar was female, endowed with a sexuality like that of ordinary women. One cannot help but wonder at the contradiction between the power of the goddesses and the increasing societal constraints upon the lives of most women in Ancient Mesopotamia.

Unlike the changes in the social and economic status of women, which have received only tangential and scattered attention in Ancient Mesopotamian studies, the transition from polytheism to monotheism and its attendant shift in emphasis from powerful goddesses to a single male god have been the subject of a vast literature. The topic has been approached from the vantage point of theology, archaeology, anthropology, and literature. Historical and artistic artifacts have been interpreted with the tools of their respective disciplines; linguistic and philosophical studies have added to the richness of interpretation. With Freud and Jung and Erich Fromm, psychiatry and psychology have been added as analytic tools, focusing our attention on myth, symbols, and archetypes. And recently a number of feminist scholars from various disciplines have discussed the period and the subject from yet another vantage point, one which is critical of patriarchal assumptions.

Such a richness and diversity of sources and interpretations makes it impossible to discuss and critique them all within the confines of this volume. I will therefore focus, as I have done throughout, on a few analytic questions and discuss in detail a few models which, I believe, illustrate larger patterns.

Methodologically, the most problematic question is the relation between changes in society and changes in religious beliefs and myths. The archaeologist, art historian, and historian can record, document, and observe such changes, but their causes and their meaning cannot be given with any kind of certainty. Different systems of interpretation offer varying answers, none of which is totally satisfying. In the present case it seems to me most important to record and survey the historical evidence and to offer a coherent explanation, which I admit is somewhat speculative. So are all the other explanations including, above all, the patriarchal tradition.

I am assuming that Mesopotamian religion responded to and reflected social conditions in the various societies. Mental constructs cannot be created from a void; they always reflect events and concepts of historic human beings in society. Thus, the existence of an assembly of the gods in "The Epic of Gilgamesh" has been interpreted as indicating the existence of village assemblies in pre-state Mesopotamian society. Similarly, the explanation in the Sumerian Atrahasis myth that the gods created men in order that men might serve them and relieve them of hard work can be regarded as a reflection of social conditions in the Sumerian city-states of the first half of the third millennium B.C.E., in which large numbers of people worked on irrigation projects and in agricultural labor centered on the temples. The relation between myth and reality is not usually that direct, but we can assume that no people could invent the concept of an assembly of the gods if they had not at some time experienced and known a like institution on earth. While we cannot say with certainty that certain political and economic changes "caused" changes in religious beliefs and myths, we cannot help but notice a pattern in the changes of religious beliefs in a number of societies, following upon or concurrent with certain societal changes.

My thesis is that, just as the development of plow agriculture, coinciding with increasing militarism, brought major changes in kinship and in gender relations, so did the development of strong kingships and of archaic states bring changes in religious beliefs and symbols. The observable pattern is: first, the demotion of the Mother-Goddess figure and the ascendance and later dominance of her male consort/son; then his merging with a storm-god into a male Creator-God, who heads the pantheon of gods and goddesses. Wherever such changes occur, the power of creation and of fertility is transferred from the Goddess to the God.

REFLECTIONS

A historical stage is a specific example of a larger process that historians call *periodization*. Dividing history into periods is one way historians make the past comprehensible. Without periodization, history would be a vast, unwieldy continuum, lacking points of reference, form, intelligibility, and meaning.

One of the earliest forms of historical periodization—years of reign—was a natural system of record keeping in the ancient cities dominated by kings. Each kingdom had its own list of kings, and each marked the current date by numbering the years of the king's reign. Some ancient societies periodized their history according to the years of rule of local officials or priesthoods. In the ancient Roman Republic, time was figured according to the terms of the elected consuls. The ancient Greeks used four-year periods called Olympiads, beginning with the first Olympic games in 776 B.C.E.

The ancient Greeks did not use "B.C." or "B.C.E.," of course. The periodization of world history into B.C. ("before Christ") and A.D. (*anno Domini*, "the Year of Our Lord" or "after Christ") did not come until the sixth century A.D., when a Christian monk named Dionysius Exiguus hit upon a way to center Christ as the major turning point in history. We use a variant of this system in this text, when designating events "B.C.E." for "before the common era" or "C.E." for "of the common era." This translation of "B.C." and "A.D." avoids the Christian bias of the older system but preserves its simplicity. A common dating system can be used worldwide to delineate time and coordinate different dynastic calendars.

All systems of periodization implicitly claim to designate important transitions in the past. The periodization of Dionysius inscribed the Christian belief that Christ's life, death, and resurrection fundamentally changed world history: Because Christ died to atone for the sins of humankind, only those who lived after Christ's sacrifice could be saved when they died. Few other systems of periodization made such a sweeping claim, though, of course, most people today—even many non-Christians—use it because of its convenience. Muslims count the years from a year one A.H. (*anno Hegire*, designating the year of the prophet Muhammad's escape from Mecca to Medina) in 622 A.D. of the Christian calendar, and Jews date the years from a Biblical year one.

Millennia, centuries, and decades are useful periods for societies that count in tens and (after the spread of Indian numerals) use the zero. While such multiples are only mathematical, some historians use them for rough periodization, to distinguish between the 1950s and the 1960s or between the eighteenth and nineteenth centuries, for example, as if there were a genuine and important transition between one period and the other. Sometimes historians "stretch" the boundaries of centuries or decades in order to account for earlier or later changes. For example, some historians speak of "the long nineteenth century," embracing the period from the French Revolution in 1789 to the First World War in 1914, on the grounds that peoples' lives were transformed in 1789 rather than in 1800 and in 1914 rather than in 1900. Similarly, the "sixties," as a term for American society and culture during the Vietnam War era, often means the period from about 1963 to about 1975, since civil rights and antiwar activity became significant a few years after the beginning of the decade and the war continued until 1975.

Characterizing and defining a decade or century in chronological terms is only one method of periodization, however. Processes can also be periodized. In this chapter we have periodized world history by process. All of world history can be divided into three periods—hunting-gathering, agricultural/pastoral, and urban. These are overlapping and continuing periods, and we can date only the beginning of the agricultural/pastoral and the urban periods, at about ten thousand and five thousand years ago, respectively. None of these periods has ended, as there are still hunters and gatherers as Nisa's story shows, and many farmers and pastoralists in the world. Still, the periodization is useful, because both the agricultural/pastoral revolution and the urban revolution brought about widespread and permanent changes.

We have also tried to locate patriarchy in a historical period, suggesting that it was a product of the urban revolution. We have not attempted to periodize changes in patriarchy over the course of the last five thousand years, but we could investigate this as well. Many people would say that patriarchy has been declining in recent decades. Is this a valid view, or is it a view specific to North America? If patriarchy is a product of cities and if the world is becoming more urban, can patriarchy be declining globally? What forces do you see bringing a decline or end to patriarchy?

To periodize something like the history of patriarchy would require a good deal of knowledge about the history of male and female relations over the course of the last five thousand years. That is a tall order for anyone. But you can get a sense of how the historian goes about periodizing and a feeling for its value if you periodize something you know a lot about. You might start, for instance, with your own life. Think of the most important change or changes in your life. How have these changes divided your life into certain periods? Outline your autobiography by marking these periods as parts or chapters of the story of your life so far. As you review these periods of your life, recognize how periodization must be grounded in reality. Defining these periods may help you understand yourself better.

To gain a sense of how periodization is imposed on reality, imagine how a parent or good friend would periodize your life. How would you periodize your life ten or twenty years from now? How would you have done it five years ago?

2

The Urban Revolution and "Civilization"

Mesopotamia and Egypt, 3500–1000 B.C.E.

HISTORICAL CONTEXT

The urban revolution that began approximately five thousand years ago produced a vast complex of new inventions, institutions, and ideas in cities that dominated surrounding farms and pastures. The first selection in this chapter surveys the wide range of innovations in these earliest civilizations.

The term *civilization* has to be used cautiously. Especially when the idea of civilization is used as a part of a stage theory of human history, we tend to assume that technological advancement means moral advancement. For instance, one hundred years ago scholars described ancient history as the progression from "savagery" to "barbarism" to "civilization."

It would be a shame to throw out the word *civilization* because it has been written more often with an axe than with a pen. The fact remains that the ancient cities created new ways of life for better or worse that were radically different from the world of agricultural villages. If we discard the word *civilization* as too overburdened with prejudice, we will have to find another one to describe that complex of changes. The term *civilization* comes from the Latin root word for city, *civitas,* from which we also get *civic, civilian,* and *citizen.* But, as the first reading argues, cities also created social classes, institutionalized inequalities, and calls to arms; most civilizations created soldiers as well as civilians.

Note: Pronunciations of difficult-to-pronounce terms will be given throughout the book. The emphasis goes on the syllables appearing in all capitals. [Ed.]

29

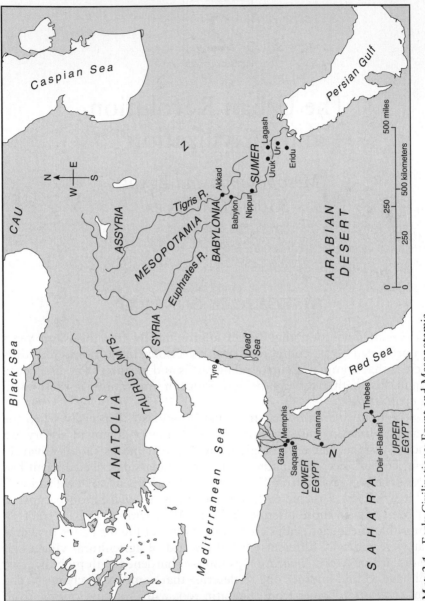

Map 2.1   Early Civilizations: Egypt and Mesopotamia.

The earliest cities, the small city-states on the Tigris and Euphrates*
in ancient Sumer, included King Gilgamesh's Uruk, which is recounted
in the second reading. Later cities, like Hammurabi's† Babylon, united
Sumerian city-states and upriver pastoral kingdoms into giant empires
(see Map 2.1). The third reading presents excerpts from Hammurabi's
law code.

The ancient Egyptian empire depended less on cities than on the
power of the king or pharaoh, but life along the Nile was magnified in
the pharaoh's residence city and in his future home in the City of the
Dead.

As you examine these selections, consider the overall transformation of the urban revolution in both Mesopotamia and Egypt. Note
also the differences between Mesopotamian and Egyptian civilizations.

THINKING HISTORICALLY
Distinguishing Primary and Secondary Sources

For some historians, the "age of cities" is the beginning of history because cities invented writing. The period before city building and the
creation of writing systems thus is often called "prehistory."

Our knowledge of ancient cities is enormously enhanced by ancient
writings, art, and artifacts which we call primary sources. These would
include literature, law codes, and inscriptions, but also sculpture, mu-
rals, building remains, tools, and weapons, indeed virtually anything
from the time and place being studied. Secondary sources differ: They
are written after the fact. History books or historical interpretations are
secondary sources. They are secondary in that they rely on primary
sources for information. Historians read, study, and interpret primary sources to compose secondary sources. In this chapter you will
read one secondary source and examine three primary sources to help
you learn ways to discern sources and extrapolate information from
them.

---

*TY gruhs and yu FRAY teez
†ha muh RAH bee

KEVIN REILLY

Cities and Civilization

This selection from a college textbook is an obvious secondary source. You know it is a secondary source because it was written long after the events described by a modern historian—me.

From my perspective, this selection does two things. First, it explores the wide range of changes brought about by the urban revolution, from particulars like writing and money and metallurgy to abstractions like social class, visual acuity, and anonymity. After you read the selection, you might make a list of all of the inventions and new phenomena of cities. You will likely be surprised by the great number of ideas, institutions, and activities that originated in the first cities. You might also find it interesting to place pluses and minuses next to the items on your list to help you determine whether "civilization" (city life) was, on balance, beneficial or harmful.

Second, the selection compares the "civilizations" of Mesopotamia and Egypt. According to the selection, what are the chief differences between Mesopotamian and Egyptian civilization? What accounts for these differences?

Thinking Historically

To get a feel for the differences between a primary source and a secondary source, try to determine what primary sources might lead to some of these interpretations. Choose a sentence or two that appear specific enough to be based on a primary source. What kind of source could lead to such an interpretation? Conversely, find interpretations in this selection that *could not* possibly derive from a primary source and ask yourself, why not? Finally, consider what kind of non-written sources and evidence inform this account.

Kevin Reilly, *The West and the World: A History of Civilization*, 2nd ed. (New York: Harper & Row, 1989), 48–54, 56, 58, 60.

The Urban Revolution: Civilization and Class

The full-scale urban revolution occurred not in the rain-watered lands that first turned some villages into cities, but in the potentially more productive river valleys of Mesopotamia around 3500 B.C.E. Situated along the Tigris and Euphrates rivers, large villages like Eridu, Erech, Lagash, Kish, and later Ur and Babylon built irrigation systems that increased farm production enormously. Settlements like these were able to support five thousand, even ten thousand people, and still allow something like 10 percent of the inhabitants to work full-time at non-farming occupations.

A change of this scale was a revolution, certainly the most important revolution in human living since the invention of agriculture five thousand years earlier. The urban revolution was prepared by a whole series of technological inventions in agricultural society. Between 6000 and 3000 B.C.E. people not only learned how to harness the power of oxen and the wind with the plow, the wheeled cart, and the sailboat; they also discovered the physical properties of metals, learned how to smelt copper and bronze, and began to work out a calendar based on the movements of the sun. River valleys like those of the Tigris and Euphrates were muddy swamps that had to be drained and irrigated to take advantage of the rich soil deposits. The dry land had literally to be built by teams of organized workers.

Therefore, cities required an organizational revolution that was every bit as important as the technological one. This was accomplished under the direction of the new class of rulers and managers—probably from the grasslands—who often treated the emerging cities as a conquered province. The work of irrigation itself allowed the rulers ample opportunity to coerce the inhabitants of these new cities. Rain knows no social distinctions. Irrigated water must be controlled and channeled.

It is no wonder then that the first cities gave us our first kings and our first class societies. In Mesopotamia, along the Nile of Egypt, in China, and later in Middle America the king is usually described as the founder of cities. These kings were able to endow their control with religious sanction. In Egypt and America the king was god. In Mesopotamia a new class of priests carried out the needs of the king's religion of control.

In some cities the new priesthood would appoint the king. In others, the priests were merely his lieutenants. When they were most loyal, their religion served to deify the king. The teachings of the new class of Mesopotamian priests, for instance, were that their god had created the people solely to work for the king and make his life easier. But even when the priesthood attempted to wrest some of the king's power from him, the priests taught the people to accept the divided society, which benefited king and priesthood as providers of a natural god-given order. The priesthood, after all, was responsible for measuring time, bounding space, and predicting seasonal events. The mastery of people was easy for those who controlled time and space.

The priesthood was only one of the new classes that insured the respectability of the warrior-chieftain turned king. Other palace intellectuals—scribes (or writers), doctors, magicians, and diviners—also struggled to maintain the king's prestige and manage his kingdom. This new class was rewarded, as were the priests, with leisure, status, and magnificent buildings, all of which further exalted the majesty of the king and his city.

Beneath the king, the priesthood, and the new class of intellectuals-managers was another new class charged with maintaining the king's law and order. Soldiers and police were also inventions of the first cities. Like the surrounding city wall, the king's military guard served a double function: it provided defense from outside attack and an obstacle to internal rebellion.

That these were the most important classes of city society can be seen from the physical remains of the first cities. The archeologist's spade has uncovered the monumental buildings of these classes in virtually all of the first cities. The palace, the temple, and the citadel (or fort) are, indeed, the monuments that distinguish cities from villages. Further, the size of these buildings and the permanency of their construction (compared with the small, cheaply built homes of the farmers) attest to the fundamental class divisions of city society.

Civilization: Security and Variety

The most obvious achievements of the first civilizations are the monuments—the pyramids, temples, palaces, statues, and treasures—that were created for the new ruling class of kings, nobles, priests, and their officials. But civilized life is much more than the capacity to create monuments.

Civilized life is secure life. At the most basic level this means security from the sudden destruction that village communities might suffer. Civilized life gives the feeling of permanence. It offers regularity, stability, order, even routine. Plans can be made. Expectations can be realized. People can be expected to act predictably, according to the rules.

The first cities were able to attain stability with walls that shielded the inhabitants from nomads and armies, with the first codes of law that defined human relationships, with police and officials who enforced the laws, and with institutions that functioned beyond the lives of their particular members. City life offered considerably more permanence and security than village life.

Civilization involves more than security, however. A city that provided only order would be more like a prison than a civilization. The first cities provided something that the best-ordered villages lacked. They provided far greater variety: More races and ethnic groups were speaking more languages, engaged in more occupations, and living a greater variety of lifestyles. The abundance of choice, the opportunities for new sensations, new experiences, knowledge—these have always been the appeals of city life. The opportunities for growth and enrichment were far greater than the possibilities of plow and pasture life.

Security plus variety equals creativity. At least the possibility of a more creative, expressive life was available in the protected, semipermanent city enclosures that drew, like magnets, foreign traders and diplomats, new ideas about gods and nature, strange foods and customs, and the magicians, ministers, and mercenaries of the king's court. Civilization is the enriched life that this dynamic urban setting permitted and the human creativity and opportunity that it encouraged. At the very least, cities made even the most common slave think and feel a greater range of things than the tightly knit, clannish agricultural village allowed. That was (and still is) the root of innovation and creativity—of civilization itself.

The variety of people and the complexity of city life required new and more general means of communication. The villager knew everyone personally. Cities brought together people who often did not even speak the same language. Not only law codes but written language itself became a way to bridge the many gaps of human variety. Cities invented writing so that strangers could communicate, and so that those communications could become permanent—remembered publicly, officially recorded. [Writer and philosopher Ralph Waldo] Emerson was right when he said that the city lives by memory, but it was the official memory that enabled the city to carry on its business or religion beyond the lifetime of the village elders. Written symbols that everyone could recognize became the basis of laws, invention, education, taxes, accounting, contracts, and obligations. In short, writing and records made it possible for each generation to begin on the shoulders of its ancestors. Village life and knowledge often seemed to start from scratch. Thus, cities cultivated not only memory and the past, but hope and the future as well. City civilizations invented not only history and record keeping but also prophecy and social planning.

Writing was one city invention that made more general communication possible. Money was another. Money made it possible to deal with anyone just as an agreed-upon public language did. Unnecessary in the village climate of mutual obligations, money was essential in the city society of strangers. Such general media of communication as writing and money vastly increased the number of things that could be said and thought, bought and sold. As a consequence, city life was more impersonal than village life, but also more dynamic and more exciting.

The "Eye" and "I"

[Communication theorist] Marshall McLuhan has written that "civilization gave the barbarian an eye for an ear." We might add that civilization also gave an "I" for an "us." City life made the "eye" and the "I" more important than they had been in the village. The invention of writing made knowledge more visual. The eye had to be trained to recognize the minute differences in letters and words. Eyes took in a greater abundance of detail: laws, prices, the strange cloak of the foreigner, the odd type of shoes made by the new craftsworker from who-knows-where, the colors of the fruit and vegetable market, and elaborate painting in the temple, as well as the written word. In the village one learned by listening. In the city seeing was believing. In the new city courts of law an "eyewitness account" was believed to be more reliable than "hearsay evidence." In some villages even today, the heard and the spoken are thought more reliable than the written and the seen. In the city, even spoken language took on the uniformity and absence of emotion that is unavoidable in the written word. Perhaps emotions themselves became less violent. "Civilized" is always used to mean emotional restraint, control of the more violent passions, and a greater understanding, even tolerance, of the different and foreign.

Perhaps empathy (the capacity to put yourself in someone else's shoes) increased in cities—so full of so many different others that had to be understood. When a Turkish villager was recently asked, "What would you do if you were president of your country?" he stammered: "My God! How can you ask such a thing? How can I . . . I cannot . . . president of Turkey . . . master of the whole world?" He was completely unable to imagine himself as president. It was as removed from his experience as if he were master of the world. Similarly, a Lebanese villager who was asked what he would do if he were editor of a newspaper accused the interviewer of ridiculing him, and frantically waved the interviewer on to another question. Such a life was beyond his comprehension. It was too foreign to imagine. The very variety of city life must have increased the capacity of the lowest commoner to imagine, empathize, sympathize, and criticize.

The oral culture of the village reinforced the accepted by saying and singing it almost monotonously. The elders, the storytellers, and the minstrels must have had prodigious memories. But their stories changed only gradually and slightly. The spoken word was sacred. To say it differently was to change the truth. The written culture of cities taught "point of *view*." An urban individual did not have to remember everything. That was done permanently on paper. Knowledge became a recognition of different interpretations and the capacity to look up things. The awareness of variety meant the possibility of criticism, analysis, and an ever-newer synthesis. It is no wonder that the technical and scientific knowledge of cities increased at a geometric rate compared with the knowledge of villages. The multiplication of knowledge was implicit in the city's demand to recognize difference and variety. Civilization has come to mean that ever-expanding body of knowledge and skill. Its finest achievements have been that knowledge, its writing, and its visual art. The city and civilization (like the child) are to be seen and not heard.

It may seem strange to say that the impersonal life of cities contributed greatly to the development of personality—the "I" as well as the "eye." Village life was in a sense much more personal. Everything was taken personally. Villagers deal with each other not as "the blacksmith," "the baker," "that guy who owes me a goat," or "that no-good bum." They do not even "deal" with each other. They know each other by name and family. They love, hate, support, and murder each other because of who they are, because of personal feelings, because of personal and family responsibility. They have full, varied relationships with each member of the village. They do not merely buy salt from this person, talk about the weather with this other person, and discuss personal matters with only this other person. They share too much with each other to divide up their relationships in that way.

City life is a life of separated, partial relationships. In a city you do not know about the butcher's life, wife, kids, and problems. You do not care. You are in a hurry. You have too many other things to do. You might discuss the weather—but while he's cutting. You came to buy meat. Many urban relationships are like that. There are many business, trading, or "dealing" relationships because there are simply too many people to know them all as relatives.

The impersonality of city life is a shame in a way. (It makes it easier to get mugged by someone who does not even hate you.) But the luxurious variety of impersonal relationships (at least some of the time) provides the freedom for the individual personality to emerge. Maybe that is why people have often dreamed of leaving family and friends (usually for a city) in the hope of "finding themselves." Certainly, the camaraderie and community of village life had a darker side of surveillance and conformity. When everything was known about everyone, it was difficult for the individual to find his or her individuality. Family ties and village custom were often obstacles to asserting self-identity. The city offered its inhabitants a huge variety of possible relationships and personal identities. The urban inhabitant was freer than his village cousin to choose friends, lovers, associates, occupation, housing, and lifestyle. The city was full of choices that the village could not afford or condone. The village probably provided more security in being like everyone else and doing what was expected. But the city provided the variety of possibilities that could allow the individual to follow the "inner self" and cultivate inner gardens.

The class divisions of city society made it difficult for commoners to achieve an effective or creative individuality. But the wealthy and powerful—especially the king—were able to develop models of individuality and personality that were revolutionary. No one before had ever achieved such a sense of the self, and the model of the king's power and freedom became a goal for the rest of the society. The luxury, leisure, and opportunity of the king was a revolutionary force. In contrast to a village elder, the king could do whatever he wanted. Recognizing that, more and more city inhabitants asked, "Why can't we?" City revolutions have continually extended class privilege and opportunities ever since.

Once a society has achieved a level of abundance, once it can offer the technological means, the educational opportunities, the creative outlets necessary for everyone to lead meaningful, happy, healthy lives, then classes may be a hindrance. Class divisions were, however, a definite stimulus to productivity and creativity in the early city civilizations. The democratic villagers preferred stability to improvement. As a result, their horizons were severely limited. They died early, lived precipitously, and suffered without much hope. The rulers of the first cities discovered the possibilities of leisure, creation, and the good life. They invented heaven and utopia—first for themselves. Only very gradually has the invention of civilization, of human potential, sifted down to those beneath the ruling class. In many cases, luxury, leisure, freedom, and opportunity are still the monopolies of the elite. But once the powerful have exploited the poor enough to establish their own paradise on earth and their own immortality after death, the poor also have broader horizons and plans.

Mesopotamian and Egyptian Civilizations: A Tale of Two Rivers

Experts disagree as to whether Mesopotamian or Egyptian civilization is older. Mesopotamian influence in Egypt was considerable enough to suggest slightly earlier origins, but both had evolved distinct civilizations by 3000 B.C.E. Indeed, the difference between the two civilizations attests to the existence of multiple routes to civilized life. In both cases, river valleys provided the necessary water and silt for an agricultural surplus large enough to support classes of specialists who did not have to farm. But the differing nature of the rivers had much to do with the different types of civilization that evolved.

The Egyptians were blessed with the easier and more reliable of the two rivers. The Nile overflowed its banks predictably every year on the parched ground in the summer after August 15, well after the harvest had been gathered, depositing its rich sediment, and withdrawing by early October, leaving little salt or marsh, in time for the sowing of winter crops. Later sowings for summer crops required only simple canals that tapped the river upstream and the natural drainage of the Nile Valley. Further, transportation on the Nile was simplified by the fact that the prevailing winds blew from the north, while the river flowed from the south, making navigation a matter of using sails upstream and dispensing with them coming downstream.

The Euphrates offered none of these advantages as it cut its way through Mesopotamia. The Euphrates flowed high above the flood plain (unlike the neighboring Tigris) so that its waters could be used, but it flooded suddenly and without warning in the late spring, after the summer crops had been sown and before the winter crops could be harvested. Thus, the flooding of the Euphrates offered no natural irrigation. Its waters were needed at other times, and its flooding was destructive. Canals were necessary to drain off water for irrigation when the river was low, and these canals had to be adequately blocked, and the banks reinforced, when the river flooded. Further, since the Euphrates was not as easily navigable as the Nile, the main canals had to serve as major transportation arteries as well.

In Mesopotamia the flood was the enemy. The Mesopotamian deities who ruled the waters, Nin-Girsu and Tiamat, were feared. The forces of nature were often evil. Life was a struggle. In Egypt, on the other hand, life was viewed as a cooperation with nature. Even the Egyptian god of the flood, Hapi, was a helpful deity, who provided the people's daily bread. Egyptian priests and philosophers were much more at ease with their world than were their Mesopotamian counterparts. And, partly because of their different experiences with their rivers, the Mesopotamians developed a civilization based on cities, while the Egyptians did not. From the first Sumerian city-states on the lower Euphrates to the later northern Mesopotamian capital of Babylon, civilization was the product and expression of city life. Egyptian civilization, in contrast, was the creation of the pharaoh's court rather than of cities. Beyond the court, which was moved from one location to another, Egypt remained a country of peasant villages.

A prime reason for Egypt's lack of urbanization was the ease of farming on the banks of the Nile. Canal irrigation was a relatively simple process that did not demand much organization. Small market towns were sufficient for the needs of the countryside. They housed artisans, shopkeepers, the priests of the local temple, and the agents of the pharaoh, but they never swelled with a large middle class and never developed large-scale industry or commerce.

In Sumer, and later in Mesopotamia, the enormous task of fighting the Euphrates required a complex social organization with immediate local needs. Only communal labor could build and maintain the network of subsidiary canals for irrigation and drainage. Constant supervision was necessary to keep the canals free of silt, to remove salt deposits, to maintain the riverbanks at flood-time, and to prevent any farmer from monopolizing the water in periods of drought. Life on the Euphrates required cooperative work and responsibility that never ceased. It encouraged absolute, administrative control over an area larger than the village, and it fostered participation and loyalty to an irrigated area smaller than the imperial state. The city-state was the political answer to the economic problems of Sumer and Mesopotamia.

The religious practices in the Euphrates Valley reflected and supported city organization. Residents of each local area worshiped the local god while recognizing the existence of other local gods in a larger Sumerian, and eventually Mesopotamian, pantheon of gods. The priests of the local temple supervised canal work, the collection of taxes, and the storage of written records, as well as the proper maintenance of religious rituals. Thus, religious loyalty reinforced civic loyalty. Peasant and middle-class Sumerians thought of themselves as citizens of their particular city, worshipers of their particular city god, subjects of their particular god's earthly representative, but not as Sumerian nationals. By contrast, the Egyptian peasant was always an Egyptian, a subject of the pharaoh, but never a citizen.

The local, civic orientation of Mesopotamian cities can be seen in the physical structure of the capital city of Sumer, the city of Ur. Like other cities on the Euphrates, Ur was surrounded by a wall. It was dominated by the temple of Nannar, the moon-god who owned the city, and the palace complex beneath the temple. The residential areas were situated outside of the sacred Temenos, or temple compound, but within the walls, between the river and the main canal. The well-excavated remains of Ur of the seventeenth century B.C.E. show a residential street plan that looks like many Middle Eastern cities of today. A highly congested area of winding alleys and broad streets sheltered one- and two-story houses of merchants, shopkeepers, tradespeople, and occasional priests and scribes that suggest a large, relatively prosperous middle class. Most houses were built around a central courtyard that offered shade throughout the day, with mud-brick, often even plastered, outside walls that protected a number of interior rooms from the sun and the eyes of the tax inspector. The remains of seventeenth-century Ur show both the variety and the density of modern city life. There are specialized districts throughout the city. Certain trades have their special quarters: a bakers' square, probably special areas for the dyers, tanners, potters, and metalworkers. But life is mixed together as well. Subsidiary gods have temples outside the Temenos. Small and large houses are jumbled next to each other. There seems to be a slum area near the Temenos, but there are small houses for workers, tenant farmers, and the poor throughout the city. And no shop or urban professional is more than a short walking distance away. The entire size of the walled city was an oval that extended three-quarters of a mile long and a half a mile wide.

A well-excavated Egyptian city from roughly the same period (the fourteenth century B.C.E.) offers some striking contrasts. Akhetaton, or Tell el Amarna, Pharaoh Akhenaton's capital on the Nile, was not enclosed by walls or canals. It merely straggled down the eastern bank of the Nile for five miles and faded into the desert. Without the need for extensive irrigation or protection, Tell el Amarna shows little of the crowded, vital density of Ur. Its layout lacks any sense of urgency. The North Palace of the pharaoh is a mile and a half north of the temple complex and offices, which are three and a half miles from the official pleasure garden. The palaces of the court nobility and the large residences of the court's officials front one of the two main roads that parallel the river, or they are situated at random. There is plenty of physical space (and social space) between these and the bunched villages of workers' houses. The remains suggest very little in the way of a middle class or a merchant or professional class beyond the pharaoh's specialists and retainers. Life for the wealthy was, judging from the housing, more luxurious than at Ur, but for the majority of the population, city life was less rich. In many ways, the pharaoh's court at Tell el Amarna was not a city at all.

6

From The Epic of Gilgamesh

The Epic of Gilgamesh is the earliest story written in any language. It also serves as a primary source for the study of ancient Mesopotamia—the land between the two great rivers, the Tigris and Euphrates.

Gilgamesh was an ancient king of Sumer, who lived about 2700 B.C.E. Since *The Epic* comes from a thousand years later, we can assume Sumerians kept telling this tale about King Gilgamesh for some time before it was written down. In Sumer, writing was initially used

The Epic of Gilgamesh, trans. N. K. Sanders (London: Penguin Books, 1972), 61–69, 108–13.

by temple priests to keep track of property and taxes. Soon, however, writing was used to preserve stories and to celebrate kings.

The more you know about the Sumerian people, the more information you will be able to mine from your source. In the previous secondary selection, you read some historical background that will help you make sense of this story. Look in *The Epic* for evidence of the urban revolution discussed in the previous selection. What is the meaning of the story of the taming of Enkidu by the harlot? Does Enkidu also tame Gilgamesh? What two worlds do Enkidu and Gilgamesh represent?

Do the authors or listeners of *The Epic* think city life is better than life in the country? According to *The Epic*, what are the advantages of the city? What problems does it have?

What does the story of the flood tell you about life in ancient Mesopotamia? Would you expect the ancient Egyptians to tell a similar story?

Thinking Historically

Reading a primary source differs markedly from reading a secondary source. Primary sources were not written with you or me in mind. It is safe to say that the author of *The Epic of Gilgamesh* never even imagined our existence. For this reason, primary sources are a bit difficult to access. Reading a primary source usually requires some intensive work. You have to keep asking yourself, why was this story told? How would a story like this help or teach people at that time? That is, you must put yourself in the shoes of the original teller and listener.

Primary sources offer us a piece of the past. No historian is in your way explaining things. With your unique perspective, you have an advantage over the intended audience: You can ask questions about the source that the author and original audience never imagined or, possibly, would not have dared ask.

Ask a question for which this primary source can provide an answer, then find the answer.

Prologue: Gilgamesh King in Uruk

I will proclaim to the world the deeds of Gilgamesh. This was the man to whom all things were known; this was the king who knew the countries of the world. He was wise, he saw mysteries and knew secret things, he brought us a tale of the days before the flood. He went on a long journey, was weary, worn-out with labor; returning he rested, he engraved on a stone the whole story.

When the gods created Gilgamesh they gave him a perfect body. Shamash the glorious sun endowed him with beauty, Adad the god of the storm endowed him with courage, the great gods made his beauty perfect, surpassing all others, terrifying like a great wild bull. Two thirds they made him god and one third man.

In Uruk he built walls, a great rampart, and the temple of blessed Eanna for the god of the firmament Anu, and for Ishtar the goddess of love. Look at it still today: the outer wall where the cornice runs, it shines with the brilliance of copper; and the inner wall, it has no equal. Touch the threshold; it is ancient. Approach Eanna the dwelling of Ishtar, our lady of love and war, the like of which no latter-day king, no man alive can equal. Climb upon the wall of Uruk; walk along it, I say; regard the foundation terrace and examine the masonry; is it not burnt brick and good? The seven sages laid the foundations.

The Coming of Enkidu

Gilgamesh went abroad in the world, but he met with none who could withstand his arms till he came to Uruk. But the men of Uruk muttered in their houses, "Gilgamesh sounds the tocsin for his amusement, his arrogance has no bounds by day or night. No son is left with his father, for Gilgamesh takes from all, even the children; yet the king should be a shepherd to his people. His lust leaves no virgin to her lover, neither the warrior's daughter nor the wife of the noble; yet this is the shepherd of the city, wise, comely, and resolute."

The gods heard their lament, the gods of heaven cried to the Lord of Uruk, to Anu the god of Uruk: "A goddess made him, strong as a savage bull, none can withstand his arms. No son is left with his father, for Gilgamesh takes them all; and is this the king, the shepherd of his people? His lust leaves no virgin to her lover, neither the warrior's daughter nor the wife of the noble." When Anu had heard their lamentation the gods cried to Aruru, the goddess of creation, "You made him, O Aruru, now create his equal; let it be as like him as his own reflection, his second self, stormy head for stormy heart. Let them contend together and leave Uruk in quiet."

So the goddess conceived an image in her mind, and it was of the stuff of Anu of the firmament. She dipped her hands in water and pinched off clay, she let it fall in the wilderness, and noble Enkidu* was created. There was virtue in him of the god of war, of Ninurta himself. His body was rough; he had long hair like a woman's; it waved like the hair of Nisaba, the goddess of corn. His body was covered with matted hair like Samuqan's, the god of cattle. He was innocent of mankind; he knew nothing of cultivated land.

*EHN kee doo

Enkidu ate grass in the hills with the gazelle and lurked with wild beasts at the water-holes; he had joy of the water with the herds of wild game. But there was a trapper who met him one day face to face at the drinking-hole, for the wild game had entered his territory. On three days he met him face to face, and the trapper was frozen with fear. He went back to his house with the game that he had caught, and he was dumb, benumbed with terror. His face was altered like that of one who has made a long journey. With awe in his heart he spoke to his father: "Father, there is a man, unlike any other, who comes down from the hills. He is the strongest in the world, he is like an immortal from heaven. He ranges over the hills with wild beasts and eats grass; he ranges through your land and comes down to the wells. I am afraid and dare not go near him. He fills in the pits which I dig and tears up my traps set for the game; he helps the beasts to escape and now they slip through my fingers."

His father opened his mouth and said to the trapper, "My son, in Uruk lives Gilgamesh; no one has ever prevailed against him, he is strong as a star from heaven. Go to Uruk, find Gilgamesh, extol the strength of this wild man. Ask him to give you a harlot, a wanton from the temple of love; return with her, and let her woman's power overpower this man. When next he comes down to drink at the wells she will be there, stripped naked; and when he sees her beckoning he will embrace her, and then the wild beasts will reject him."

So the trapper set out on his journey to Uruk and addressed himself to Gilgamesh saying, "A man unlike any other is roaming now in the pastures; he is as strong as a star from heaven and I am afraid to approach him. He helps the wild game to escape; he fills in my pits and pulls up my traps." Gilgamesh said, "Trapper, go back, take with you a harlot, a child of pleasure. At the drinking-hole she will strip, and when he sees her beckoning he will embrace her and the game of the wilderness will surely reject him."

Now the trapper returned, taking the harlot with him. After a three days' journey they came to the drinking-hole, and there they sat down; the harlot and the trapper sat facing one another and waited for the game to come. For the first day and for the second day the two sat waiting, but on the third day the herds came; they came down to drink and Enkidu was with them. The small wild creatures of the plains were glad of the water, and Enkidu with them, who ate grass with the gazelle and was born in the hills; and she saw him; the savage man, come from far-off in the hills. The trapper spoke to her: "There he is. Now, woman, make your breasts bare, have no shame, do not delay but welcome his love. Let him see you naked, let him possess your body. When he comes near uncover yourself and lie with him; teach him, the savage man, your woman's art, for when he murmurs love to you the wild beasts that shared his life in the hills will reject him."

She was not ashamed to take him, she made herself naked and welcomed his eagerness; as he lay on her murmuring love she taught him the woman's art. For six days and seven nights they lay together, for Enkidu had forgotten his home in the hills; but when he was satisfied he went back to the wild beasts. Then, when the gazelle saw him, they bolted away; when the wild creatures saw him they fled. Enkidu would have followed, but his body was bound as though with a cord, his knees gave way when he started to run, his swiftness was gone. And now the wild creatures had all fled away; Enkidu was grown weak, for wisdom was in him, and the thoughts of a man were in his heart. So he returned and sat down at the woman's feet, and listened intently to what she said. "You are wise, Enkidu, and now you have become like a god. Why do you want to run wild with the beasts in the hills? Come with me. I will take you to strong-walled Uruk, to the blessed temple of Ishtar and of Anu, of love and of heaven: there Gilgamesh lives, who is very strong, and like a wild bull he lords it over men."

When she had spoken Enkidu was pleased; he longed for a comrade, for one who would understand his heart. "Come, woman, and take me to that holy temple, to the house of Anu and of Ishtar, and to the place where Gilgamesh lords it over people. I will challenge him boldly, I will cry out aloud in Uruk, 'I am the strongest here, I have come to change the old order, I am he who was born in the hills, I am he who is strongest of all.'"

She said, "Let us go, and let him see your face. I know very well where Gilgamesh is in great Uruk. O Enkidu, there all the people are dressed in their gorgeous robes, every day is holiday, the young men and the girls are wonderful to see. How sweet they smell! All the great ones are roused from their beds. O Enkidu, you who love life, I will show you Gilgamesh, a man of many moods; you shall look at him well in his radiant manhood. His body is perfect in strength and maturity; he never rests by night or day. He is stronger than you, so leave your boasting. Shamash the glorious sun has given favors to Gilgamesh, and Anu of the heavens, and Enlil, and Ea the wise has given him deep understanding. I tell you, even before you have left the wilderness, Gilgamesh will know in his dreams that you are coming."

Now Gilgamesh got up to tell his dream to his mother, Ninsun, one of the wise gods. "Mother, last night I had a dream. I was full of joy, the young heroes were round me and I walked through the night under the stars of the firmament, and one, a meteor of the stuff of Anu, fell down from heaven. I tried to lift it but it proved too heavy. All the people of Uruk came round to see it, the common people jostled and the nobles thronged to kiss its feet; and to me its attraction was like the love of woman. They helped me, I braced my forehead and I raised it with thongs and brought it to you, and you yourself pronounced it my brother."

Then Ninsun, who is well-beloved and wise, said to Gilgamesh, "This star of heaven which descended like a meteor from the sky; which you tried to lift, but found too heavy, when you tried to move it it would not budge, and so you brought it to my feet; I made it for you, a goad and spur, and you were drawn as though to a woman. This is the strong comrade, the one who brings help to his friend in his need. He is the strongest of wild creatures, the stuff of Anu; born in the grasslands and the wild hills reared him; when you see him you will be glad; you will love him as a woman and he will never forsake you. This is the meaning of the dream."

Gilgamesh said, "Mother, I dreamed a second dream. In the streets of strong-walled Uruk there lay an axe; the shape of it was strange and the people thronged round. I saw it and was glad. I bent down, deeply drawn towards it; I loved it like a woman and wore it at my side." Ninsun answered, "That axe, which you saw, which drew you so powerfully like love of a woman, that is the comrade whom I give you, and he will come in his strength like one of the host of heaven. He is the brave companion who rescues his friend in necessity." Gilgamesh said to his mother, "A friend, a counsellor has come to me from Enlil, and now I shall befriend and counsel him." So Gilgamesh told his dreams; and the harlot retold them to Enkidu.

And now she said to Enkidu, "When I look at you you have become like a god. Why do you yearn to run wild again with the beasts in the hills? Get up from the ground, the bed of a shepherd." He listened to her words with care. It was good advice that she gave. She divided her clothing in two and with the one half she clothed him and with the other herself; and holding his hand she led him like a child to the sheepfolds, into the shepherds' tents. There all the shepherds crowded round to see him, they put down bread in front of him, but Enkidu could only suck the milk of wild animals. He fumbled and gaped, at a loss what to do or how he should eat the bread and drink the strong wine. Then the woman said, "Enkidu, eat bread, it is the staff of life; drink the wine, it is the custom of the land." So he ate till he was full and drank strong wine, seven goblets. He became merry, his heart exulted and his face shone. He rubbed down the matted hair of his body and anointed himself with oil. Enkidu had become a man; but when he had put on man's clothing he appeared like a bridegroom. He took arms to hunt the lion so that the shepherds could rest at night. He caught wolves and lions and the herdsmen lay down in peace; for Enkidu was their watchman, that strong man who had no rival.

He was merry living with the shepherds, till one day lifting his eyes he saw a man approaching. He said to the harlot, "Woman, fetch that man here. Why has he come? I wish to know his name." She went and called the man saying, "Sir, where are you going on this weary journey?" The man answered, saying to Enkidu, "Gilgamesh has gone into the marriage-house and shut out the people. He does strange things in

Uruk, the city of great streets. At the roll of the drum work begins for the men, and work for the women. Gilgamesh the king is about to celebrate marriage with the Queen of Love, and he still demands to be first with the bride, the king to be first and the husband to follow, for that was ordained by the gods from his birth, from the time the umbilical cord was cut. But now the drums roll for the choice of the bride and the city groans." At these words Enkidu turned white in the face. "I will go to the place where Gilgamesh lords it over the people, I will challenge him boldly, and I will cry aloud in Uruk, 'I have come to change the old order, for I am the strongest here.'"

Now Enkidu strode in front and the woman followed behind. He entered Uruk, that great market, and all the folk thronged round him where he stood in the street in strong-walled Uruk. The people jostled; speaking of him they said, "He is the spit of Gilgamesh." "He is shorter." "He is bigger of bone." "This is the one who was reared on the milk of wild beasts. His is the greatest strength." The men rejoiced: "Now Gilgamesh has met his match. This great one, this hero whose beauty is like a god, he is a match even for Gilgamesh."

In Uruk the bridal bed was made, fit for the goddess of love. The bride waited for the bridegroom, but in the night Gilgamesh got up and came to the house. Then Enkidu stepped out, he stood in the street and blocked the way. Mighty Gilgamesh came on and Enkidu met him at the gate. He put out his foot and prevented Gilgamesh from entering the house, so they grappled, holding each other like bulls. They broke the doorposts and the walls shook, they snorted like bulls locked together. They shattered the doorposts and the walls shook. Gilgamesh bent his knee with his foot planted on the ground and with a turn Enkidu was thrown. Then immediately his fury died. When Enkidu was thrown he said to Gilgamesh, "There is not another like you in the world. Ninsun, who is as strong as a wild ox in the byre, she was the mother who bore you, and now you are raised above all men, and Enlil has given you the kingship, for your strength surpasses the strength of men." So Enkidu and Gilgamesh embraced and their friendship was sealed.

The Story of the Flood

"You know the city Shurrupak, it stands on the banks of Euphrates? That city grew old and the gods that were in it were old. There was Anu, lord of the firmament, their father, and warrior Enlil their counsellor, Ninurta the helper, and Ennugi watcher over canals; and with them also was Ea. In those days the world teemed, the people multiplied, the world bellowed like a wild bull, and the great god was aroused by the clamour. Enlil heard the clamour and he said to the gods in council, 'The uproar of mankind is intolerable and sleep is no longer possible by reason of the babel.' So the gods agreed to exterminate mankind. Enlil did this, but Ea because of his oath warned me in a dream. He whispered their words to my house of reeds, 'Reed-house, reed-house! Wall, O wall, hearken reed-house, wall reflect; O man of Shurrupak, son of Ubara-Tutu; tear down your house and build a boat, abandon possessions and look for life, despise worldly goods and save your soul alive. Tear down your house, I say, and build a boat. These are the measurements of the barque as you shall build her: let her beam equal her length, let her deck be roofed like the vault that covers the abyss; then take up into the boat the seed of all living creatures.'

"When I had understood I said to my lord, 'Behold, what you have commanded I will honour and perform, but how shall I answer the people, the city, the elders?' Then Ea opened his mouth and said to me, his servant, 'Tell them this: I have learnt that Enlil is wrathful against me, I dare no longer walk in his land nor live in his city; I will go down to the Gulf to dwell with Ea my lord. But on you he will rain down abundance, rare fish and shy wild-fowl, a rich harvest-tide. In the evening the rider of the storm will bring you wheat in torrents.'

"In the first light of dawn all my household gathered round me, the children brought pitch and the men whatever was necessary. On the fifth day I laid the keel and the ribs, then I made fast the planking. The ground-space was one acre, each side of the deck measured one hundred and twenty cubits, making a square. I built six decks below, seven in all, I divided them into nine sections with bulkheads between. I drove in wedges where needed, I saw to the punt-poles, and laid in supplies. The carriers brought oil in baskets, I poured pitch into the furnace and asphalt and oil; more oil was consumed in caulking, and more again the master of the boat took into his stores. I slaughtered bullocks for the people and every day I killed sheep. I gave the shipwrights wine to drink as though it were river water, raw wine and red wine and oil and white wine. There was feasting then as there is at the time of the New Year's festival; I myself anointed my head. On the seventh day the boat was complete.

"Then was the launching full of difficulty; there was shifting of ballast above and below till two thirds was submerged. I loaded into her all that I had of gold and of living things, my family, my kin, the beast of the field both wild and tame, and all the craftsmen. I sent them on board, for the time that Shamash had ordained was already fulfilled when he said 'In the evening, when the rider of the storm sends down the destroying rain, enter the boat and batten her down.' The time was fulfilled, the evening came, the rider of the storm sent down the rain. I looked out at the weather and it was terrible, so I too boarded the boat and battened her down. All was now complete, the battening and the caulking; so I handed the tiller to Puzur-Amurri the steersman, with the navigation and the care of the whole boat.

"With the first light of dawn a black cloud came from the horizon; it thundered within where Adad, lord of the storm, was riding. In front over hill and plain Shullat and Hanish, heralds of the storm, led on. Then the gods of the abyss rose up; Nergal pulled out the dams of the nether waters, Ninurta the war-lord threw down the dykes, and the seven judges of hell, the Annunaki, raised their torches, lighting the land with their livid flame. A stupor of despair went up to heaven when the god of the storm turned daylight to darkness, when he smashed the land like a cup. One whole day the tempest raged, gathering fury as it went, it poured over the people like the tides of battle; a man could not see his brother nor the people be seen from heaven. Even the gods were terrified at the flood, they fled to the highest heaven, the firmament of Anu; they crouched against the walls, cowering like curs. Then Ishtar the sweet-voiced Queen of Heaven cried out like a woman in travail: 'Alas the days of old are turned to dust because I commanded evil; why did I command this evil in the council of all the gods? I commanded wars to destroy the people, but are they not my people, for I brought them forth? Now like the spawn of fish they float in the ocean.' The great gods of heaven and of hell wept, they covered their mouths.

"For six days and six nights the winds blew, torrent and tempest and flood overwhelmed the world, tempest and flood raged together like warring hosts. When the seventh day dawned the storm from the south subsided, the sea grew calm, the flood was stilled; I looked at the face of the world and there was silence, all mankind was turned to clay. The surface of the sea stretched as flat as a roof-top; I opened a hatch and the light fell on my face. Then I bowed low, I sat down and I wept, the tears streamed down my face, for on every side was the waste of water. I looked for land in vain, but fourteen leagues distant there appeared a mountain, and there the boat grounded; on the mountain of Nisir the boat held fast, she held fast and did not budge. One day she held, and a second day on the mountain of Nisir she held fast and did not budge. A third day, and a fourth day she held fast on the mountain and did not budge; a fifth day and a sixth day she held fast on the mountain. When the seventh day dawned I loosed a dove and let her go. She flew away, but finding no resting-place she returned. Then I loosed a swallow, and she flew away but finding no resting-place she returned. I loosed a raven, she saw that the waters had retreated, she ate, she flew around, she cawed, and she did not come back. Then I threw everything open to the four winds, I made a sacrifice and poured out a libation on the mountain top. Seven and again seven cauldrons I set up on their stands, I heaped up wood and cane and cedar and myrtle. When the gods smelled the sweet savour, they gathered like flies over the sacrifice. Then, at last, Ishtar also came, she lifted her necklace with the jewels of heaven that once Anu had made to please her. 'O you gods here present, by the lapis lazuli round my neck I shall remember these days as I remember the jewels of my throat; these last days I shall not forget. Let all the gods gather round the sacrifice, except Enlil. He shall not approach this offering, for without reflection he brought the flood; he consigned my people to destruction.'

"When Enlil had come, when he saw the boat, he was wrath and swelled with anger at the gods, the host of heaven, 'Has any of these mortals escaped? Not one was to have survived the destruction.' Then the god of the wells and canals Ninurta opened his mouth and said to the warrior Enlil, 'Who is there of the gods that devise without Ea? It is Ea alone who knows all things.' Then Ea opened his mouth and spoke to warrior Enlil, 'Wisest of gods, hero Enlil, how could you so sense-lessly bring down the flood?

> Lay upon the sinner his sin,
> Lay upon the transgressor his transgression,
> Punish him a little when he breaks loose,
> Do not drive him too hard or he perishes;
> Would that a lion had ravaged mankind
> Rather than the flood,
> Would that a wolf had ravaged mankind
> Rather than the flood,
> Would that famine had wasted the world
> Rather than the flood,
> Would that pestilence had wasted mankind
> Rather than the flood.

It was not I that revealed the secret of the gods; the wise man learned it in a dream. Now take your counsel what shall be done with him.'

"Then Enlil went up into the boat, he took me by the hand and my wife and made us enter the boat and kneel down on either side, he standing between us. He touched our foreheads to bless us saying, 'In time past Utnapishtim was a mortal man; henceforth he and his wife shall live in the distance at the mouth of the rivers.' Thus it was that the gods took me and placed me here to live in the distance, at the mouth of the rivers."

From Hammurabi's Code

King Hammurabi of Babylon conquered the entire area of Mesopotamia (including Sumer) between 1793 and 1750 B.C.E. His law code provides us with a rare insight into the daily life of ancient urban society.

Law codes give us an idea of a people's sense of justice and notions of proper punishment. This selection includes only parts of Hammurabi's Code, so we cannot conclude that if something is not mentioned here it was not a matter of legal concern. We can, however, deduce much about Babylonian society from the laws mentioned in this essay.

What do these laws tell us about class divisions or social distinctions in Babylonian society? What can we learn from these laws about the roles of women and men? Which laws or punishments seem unusual today? What does that difference suggest to you about ancient Babylon compared to modern society?

Thinking Historically

As a primary source, law codes are extremely useful. They zero in on a society's main concerns, revealing minutiae of daily life in great detail. But, for a number of reasons, law codes cannot be viewed as a precise reflection of society.

We cannot assume, for instance, that all of Hammurabi's laws were strictly followed or enforced, nor can we assume that for our own society. If there was a law against something, we can safely assume that some people obeyed it and some people did not. (That is, if no one engaged in the behavior, there would be no need for the law.) Therefore, law codes suggest a broad range of behaviors in a society.

While laws tell us something about the concerns of the society that produces them, we cannot presume that all members of society share the same concerns. Recall that, especially in ancient society, laws were written by the literate, powerful few. What evidence do you see of the upper-class "patrician" composition of Babylonian law in this code?

Finally, if an ancient law seems similar to our own, we cannot assume that the law reflects motives, intents, or goals similar to our own laws. Laws must be considered within the context of the society in which they were created. Notice, for instance, the laws in Hammurabi's Code that may seem, by our standards, intended to protect women. On closer examination, what appears to be their goal?

"Hammurabi's Code," from C. H. Johns, *Babylonian and Assyrian Laws, Contracts and Letters* (Library of Ancient Inscriptions) (New York: Charles Scribner's Sons, 1904), 33–35.

Theft

6. If a man has stolen goods from a temple, or house, he shall be put to death; and he that has received the stolen property from him shall be put to death.

8. If a patrician has stolen ox, sheep, ass, pig, or goat, whether from a temple, or a house, he shall pay thirtyfold. If he be a plebeian, he shall return tenfold. If the thief cannot pay, he shall be put to death.

14. If a man has stolen a child, he shall be put to death.

15. If a man has induced either a male or female slave from the house of a patrician, or plebeian, to leave the city, he shall be put to death.

21. If a man has broken into a house he shall be killed before the breach and buried there.

22. If a man has committed highway robbery and has been caught, that man shall be put to death.

23. If the highwayman has not been caught, the man that has been robbed shall state on oath what he has lost and the city or district governor in whose territory or district the robbery took place shall restore to him what he has lost.

Family

128. If a man has taken a wife and has not executed a marriage-contract, that woman is not a wife.

129. If a man's wife be caught lying with another, they shall be strangled and cast into the water. If the wife's husband would save his wife, the king can save his servant.

130. If a man has ravished another's betrothed wife, who is a virgin, while still living in her father's house, and has been caught in the act, that man shall be put to death; the woman shall go free.

131. If a man's wife has been accused by her husband, and has not been caught lying with another, she shall swear her innocence, and return to her house.

138. If a man has divorced his wife, who has not borne him children, he shall pay over to her as much money as was given for her bride-price and the marriage-portion which she brought from her father's house, and so shall divorce her.

139. If there was no bride-price, he shall give her one mina of silver, as a price of divorce.

140. If he be a plebeian, he shall give her one-third of a mina of silver.

148. If a man has married a wife and a disease has seized her, if he is determined to marry a second wife, he shall marry her. He shall not divorce the wife whom the disease has seized. In the home they made together she shall dwell, and he shall maintain her as long as she lives.

149. If that woman was not pleased to stay in her husband's house, he shall pay over to her the marriage-portion which she brought from her father's house, and she shall go away.

153. If a man's wife, for the sake of another, has caused her husband to be killed, that woman shall be impaled.

154. If a man has committed incest with his daughter, that man shall be banished from the city.

155. If a man has betrothed a maiden to his son and his son has known her, and afterward the man has lain in her bosom, and been caught, that man shall be strangled and she shall be cast into the water.

156. If a man has betrothed a maiden to his son, and his son has not known her, and that man has lain in her bosom, he shall pay her half a mina of silver, and shall pay over to her whatever she brought from her father's house, and the husband of her choice shall marry her.

186. If a man has taken a young child to be his son, and after he has taken him, the child discovers his own parents, he shall return to his father's house.

188, 189. If a craftsman has taken a child to bring up and has taught him his handicraft, he shall not be reclaimed. If he has not taught him his handicraft that foster child shall return to his father's house.

Assault

195. If a son has struck his father, his hands shall be cut off.

196. If a man has knocked out the eye of a patrician, his eye shall be knocked out.

197. If he has broken the limb of a patrician, his limb shall be broken.

198. If he has knocked out the eye of a plebeian or has broken the limb of a plebeian's servant, he shall pay one mina of silver.

199. If he has knocked out the eye of a patrician's servant, or broken the limb of a patrician's servant, he shall pay half his value.

200. If a patrician has knocked out the tooth of a man that is his equal, his tooth shall be knocked out.

201. If he has knocked out the tooth of a plebeian, he shall pay one-third of a mina of silver.

Liability

229. If a builder has built a house for a man, and has not made his work sound, and the house he built has fallen, and caused the death of its owner, that builder shall be put to death.

230. If it is the owner's son that is killed, the builder's son shall be put to death.

231. If it is the slave of the owner that is killed, the builder shall give slave for slave to the owner of the house.

232. If he has caused the loss of goods, he shall render back whatever he has destroyed. Moreover, because he did not make sound the house he built, and it fell, at his own cost he shall rebuild the house that fell.

237. If a man has hired a boat and a boatman, and loaded it with corn, wool, oil, or dates, or whatever it be, and the boatman has been careless, and sunk the boat, or lost what is in it, the boatman shall restore the boat which he sank, and whatever he lost that was in it.

238. If a boatman has sunk a man's boat, and has floated it again, he shall pay half its value in silver.

251. If a man's ox be a gorer, and has revealed its evil propensity as a gorer, and he has not blunted its horn, or shut up the ox, and then that ox has gored a free man, and caused his death, the owner shall pay half a mina of silver.

252. If it be a slave that has been killed, he shall pay one-third of a mina of silver.

8

Advice to the Young Egyptian: "Be a Scribe"

Writing was a hallmark of the urban revolution five thousand years ago. Egyptian society, like Mesopotamian, prospered through written laws, records, and knowledge. Urban societies required many occupations that had not existed in the agricultural village, but foremost among these was the writer, or scribe. Sometimes a priest, often an official, the scribe, by virtue of his ability to read and write, provided the glue that held complex societies together.

Excavations of ancient Egypt have unearthed many papyri like these from the 20th Dynasty (twelfth century B.C.E.) that urge young Egyptians to become scribes. Because these papyri often contain spelling mistakes and other errors, archaeologists have concluded they are probably writing exercises for future scribes. How would the assignment to copy

Miriam Lichtheim, *Ancient Egyptian Literature: A Book of Readings, Volume II: The New Kingdom* (Berkeley: University of California Press, 1976), 169–72.

these paragraphs help train writers in ancient Egypt? What do these papyri tell you about the life of the scribe in ancient Egypt?

Thinking Historically

These paragraphs tell us about other occupations besides that of the scribe. What, according to the papyri, were some of the other occupations common in ancient Egypt? How accurate do you think the descriptions of these occupations are? This document is sometimes called "the satire on the trades." Why would it be called that? How might you use this document to argue that Egyptian society was reasonably fair and egalitarian for the ancient world? How might you use this document to argue that Egyptian society was a deeply divided class society? Which do you think it was?

All Occupations Are Bad Except That of the Scribe

See for yourself with your own eye. The occupations lie before you.

The washerman's day is going up, going down. All his limbs are weak, (from) whitening his neighbors' clothes every day, from washing their linen.

The marker of pots is smeared with soil, like one whose relations have died. His hands, his feet are full of clay; he is like one who lives in the bog.

The cobbler mingles with vats. His odor is penetrating. His hands are red with madder,[1] like one who is smeared with blood. He looks behind him for the kite, like one whose flesh is exposed.

The watchman prepares garlands and polishes vase-stands. He spends a night of toil just as one on whom the sun shines.

The merchants travel downstream and upstream. They are as busy as can be, carrying goods from one town to another. They supply him who has wants. But the tax collectors carry off the gold, that most precious of metals.

The ships' crews from every house (of commerce), they receive their loads. They depart from Egypt for Syria, and each man's god is with him. (But) not one of them says: "We shall see Egypt again!"

The carpenter who is in the shipyard carries the timber and stacks it. If he gives today the output of yesterday, woe to his limbs! The shipwright stands behind him to tell him evil things.

His outworker who is in the fields, his is the toughest of all the jobs. He spends the day loaded with his tools, tied to his tool-box. When he returns home at night, he is loaded with the tool-box and the timbers, his drinking mug, and his whetstones.

The scribe, he alone, records the output of all of them. Take note of it!

[1]A plant used to make red dye. [Ed.]

The Misfortunes of the Peasant

Let me also expound to you the situation of the peasant, that other tough occupation. [Comes] the inundation and soaks him———, he attends to his equipment. By day he cuts his farming tools; by night he twists rope. Even his midday hour he spends on farm labor. He equips himself to go to the field as if he were a warrior. The dried field lies before him; he goes out to get his team. When he has been after the herdsman for many days, he gets his team and comes back with it. He makes for it a place in the field. Comes dawn, he goes to make a start and does not find it in its place. He spends three days searching for it; he finds it in the bog. He finds no hides on them; the jackals have chewed them. He comes out, his garment in his hand, to beg for himself a team.

When he reaches his field he finds [it] "broken up." He spends time cultivating, and the snake is after him. It finishes off the seed as it is cast to the ground. He does not see a green blade. He does three plowings with borrowed grain. His wife has gone down to the merchants and found nothing for "barter." Now the scribe lands on the shore. He surveys the harvest. Attendants are behind him with staffs, Nubians with clubs. One says (to him): "Give grain." "There is none." He is beaten savagely. He is bound, thrown in the well, submerged head down. His wife is bound in his presence. His children are in fetters. His neighbors abandon them and flee. When it's over, there's no grain.

If you have any sense, be a scribe. If you have learned about the peasant, you will not be able to be one. Take note of it!

Be a Scribe

The scribe of the army and commander of the cattle of the house of Amun, Nebmare-nakht, speaks to the scribe Wenemdiamun, as follows. Be a scribe! Your body will be sleek; your hand will be soft. You will not flicker like a flame, like one whose body is feeble. For there is not the bone of a man in you. You are tall and thin. If you lifted a load to carry it, you would stagger, your legs would tremble. You are lacking in strength; you are weak in all your limbs; you are poor in body.

Set your sight on being a scribe; a fine profession that suits you. You call for one; a thousand answer you. You stride freely on the road. You will not be like a hired ox. You are in front of others.

I spend the day instructing you. You do not listen! Your heart is like an [empty] room. My teachings are not in it. Take their ["meaning"] to yourself!

The marsh thicket is before you each day, as a nestling is after its mother. You follow the path of pleasure; you make friends with revellers. You have made your home in the brewery, as one who thirsts for beer. You sit in the parlor with an idler. You hold the writings in contempt. You visit the whore. Do not do these things! What are they for? They are of no use. Take note of it!

The Scribe Does Not Suffer Like the Soldier

Furthermore. Look, I instruct you to make you sound; to make you hold the palette freely. To make you become one whom the king trusts; to make you gain entrance to treasury and granary. To make you receive the ship-load at the gate of the granary. To make you issue the offerings on feast days. You are dressed in fine clothes; you own horses. Your boat is on the river; you are supplied with attendants. You stride about inspecting. A mansion is built in your town. You have a powerful office, given you by the king. Male and female slaves are about you. Those who are in the fields grasp your hand, on plots that you have made. Look, I make you into a staff of life! Put the writings in your heart, and you will be protected from all kinds of toil. You will become a worthy official.

Do you not recall the (fate of) the unskilled man? His name is not known. He is ever burdened [like an ass carrying] in front of the scribe who knows what he is about.

Come, [let me tell] you the woes of the soldier, and how many are his superiors: the general, the troop-commander, the officer who leads, the standard-bearer, the lieutenant, the scribe, the commander of fifty, and the garrison-captain. They go in and out in the halls of the palace, saying: "Get laborers!" He is awakened at any hour. One is after him as (after) a donkey. He toils until the Aten sets in his darkness of night. He is hungry, his belly hurts; he is dead while yet alive. When he receives the grain-ration, having been released from duty, it is not good for grinding.

He is called up for Syria. He may not rest. There are no clothes, no sandals. The weapons of war are assembled at the fortress of Sile. His march is uphill through mountains. He drinks water every third day; it is smelly and tastes of salt. His body is ravaged by illness. The enemy comes, surrounds him with missiles, and life recedes from him. He is told: "Quick, forward, valiant soldier! Win for yourself a good name!" He does not know what he is about. His body is weak, his legs fail him. When victory is won, the captives are handed over to his majesty, to be taken to Egypt. The foreign woman faints on the march; she hangs herself [on] the soldier's neck. His knapsack drops, another grabs it while he is burdened with the woman. His wife and children are in their village; he dies and does not reach it. If he comes out alive, he is worn out from marching. Be he at large, be he detained, the soldier suffers. If he leaps and joins the deserters, all his people are imprisoned. He dies on the edge of the desert, and there is none to perpetuate his name. He suffers in death as in life. A big sack is brought for him; he does not know his resting place.

Be a scribe, and be spared from soldiering! You call and one says: "Here I am." You are safe from torments. Every man seeks to raise himself up. Take note of it!

9

Images of Ancient Egypt

Thanks to the preservative dry climate and the ancient Egyptian interest in illustrating books of papyrus and painting the interiors of pyramids, temples, and tombs, we have excellent visual primary sources on the daily life of ancient Egypt. The first two images are from a papyrus called Hunefer's *Book of the Dead*. Hunefer was a royal official of the 13th century B.C.E. Like other wealthy or powerful Egyptians, Hunefer had a version of the *Book of the Dead*, with all its prayers and incantations, prepared especially for him.

In Figure 2.1, Hunefer's mummy is prepared to enter the afterlife. His wife and daughter dab their heads with dirt. Three priests administer the rituals. The priest on the far left, dressed in a lion skin, burns incense and readies the food offerings. Two others prepare the important ceremony of opening the mummy's mouth so that it can breathe and eat. Anubis, the jackal-headed god of death, holds the mummy. Behind him we can read an enlarged version of Hunefer's tombstone, which will be placed in front of his tomb, a miniature image of which we see on the far right.

In Figure 2.2 we see Hunefer led by Anubis, about to be judged. In the center of the frame Hunefer's heart is weighed against a feather. If his heart is lighter than the feather he will be admitted to the presence of Osiris and enter the afterlife. If not, his heart will be devoured by the demon Ammut, whose crocodile head is turned to the ibis-headed god Thoth, standing to the right of the scales and writing the verdict. In that case, his existence will end forever. Fortunately, Hunefer's artist assures him of a happy ending. Thoth conducts Hunefer to Osiris seated on a throne, behind his four sons standing on a lotus leaf and in front of his wife, the goddess Isis, and her sister. What do these

Book of the Dead of Hunefer Thebes, Egypt, 19th Dynasty, around 1275 B.C.E.

images tell you about Egyptian society? How do they compare to your own ideas of death?

Egyptians also celebrated life. Figures 2.3 and 2.4 are representative of countless paintings from Egyptian tombs that were made to ensure the deceased a happy immortality. In this case, we see images from a vineyard and a bakery. What do these images tell you about Egyptian society?

Thinking Historically

Reading primary sources, whether they be words or images, is always tricky. Unlike secondary sources, they were not written, painted, or left for us. The assumptions and intentions of the writer or artist may be very different from our own, and so we may misunderstand the meaning or purpose of a work.

Entering an Egyptian tomb today, one cannot help being overwhelmed by the beauty of the paintings. Their vitality can be breathtaking. To the modern viewer, especially in museums where paintings and papyrus are torn from their original setting, they appear to us as beautiful works of art. And so they are. But for the ancient Egyptians, these images were more than representations, more than art. They were the things depicted. The food that was displayed was food for the deceased in the afterlife; the people painted on the walls were there to provide and serve. The pictures were intended to be more vital than we can imagine. Are visual images more or less reliable as primary sources than written words? What visuals add to our understanding? How might they mislead us?

Images are different from written words in another way. You are able to make sense of these images from Hunefer's *Book of the Dead* because primary and secondary texts enable us to provide a summary of the story behind them. But the Egyptian artist and viewer knew that story, and hundreds of subplots, by heart. Imagine "reading" the images the way an ancient Egyptian viewer would have. Would the difference between your modern interpretation and the Egyptian viewer's interpretation be similar to the difference between seeing a movie and reading the book? And if "the book" was the wisdom of the ages as everyone knew it, and images could be real, what sort of movie would that be?

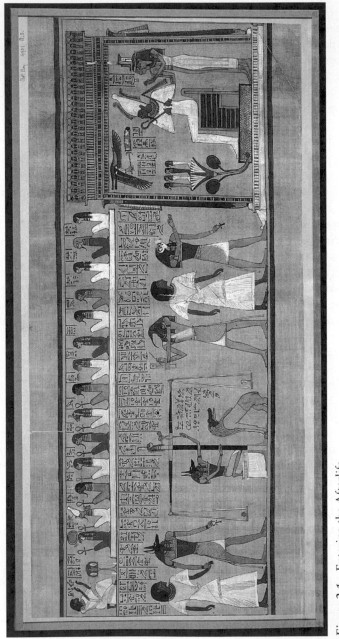

Figure 2.1 Entering the Afterlife.
Source: © The Trustees of The British Museum.

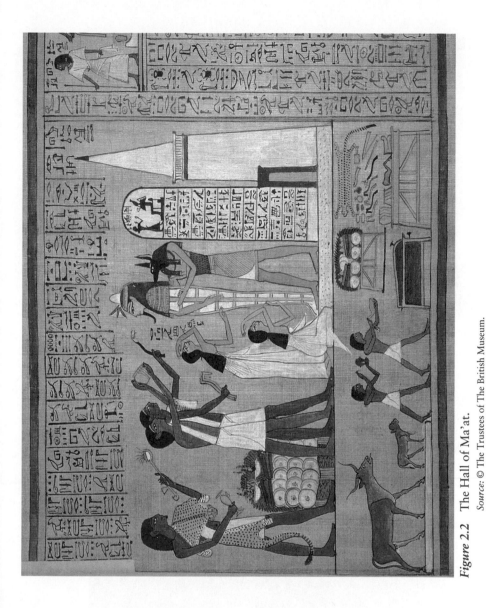

Figure 2.2   The Hall of Ma'at.

Figure 2.3 Making Wine.
Source: The Image Works.

Figure 2.4 Making Bread.
Source: The Image Works.

REFLECTIONS

To focus our subject in a brief chapter we have examined Mesopotamia and Egypt almost exclusively. This enabled us to observe the beginnings of the urban revolution in Mesopotamia and one of the most spectacular and best preserved of ancient civilizations in Egypt. The city-states of Mesopotamia and the territorial state of Egypt were the two extremes of ancient civilization. City-states packed most people tightly within their walls. Eighty percent of Mesopotamians lived within city walls by 2800 B.C.E. By contrast, less than 10 percent of Egyptians lived in cities—if we can call their unwalled settlements, palace compounds, and pyramid construction sites "cities" at all. The lesser role of cities in Egypt has led some historians to drop the term "urban revolution" for "the rise of civilization." Other historians, objecting to the moralistic implications of the term "civilization," prefer "the rise of complex societies." "Complex" is not a very precise term, but it would refer to the appearance of social classes, the mixing of different populations, a multilayered governmental structure with rulers, officials, and ordinary people, and numerous specialists who are not full-time farmers or herders. More specifically, we might include kings, priests, writing, wheels, monumental building, markets, and money.

If we broaden our view, however, to include the "complex societies" of South Asia, China, and the Americas, cities—even city-states—pop up like mushrooms after a spring rain. Along the Indus River in Pakistan dozens of small and midsize cities formed independent clones of Harappa and Mohenjodaro. These numerous cities seem to have enjoyed the independence of city-states since there is no evidence of kings, soldiers, or warfare along the Indus. Instead of being bound to a territorial sovereign, these cities and dozens of others in what is today Iran, Afghanistan, India, and surrounding areas communicated and traded with each other in a web of economic interactions.

Territorial states, more like Egypt than Mesopotamia, integrated the Yellow River valley of northern China and the settlements of the high Andes in South America, but they also constructed large cities as administrative and spiritual centers. In Mexico, early civilizations were centered in cities: the Zapotec at Monte Alban, the Toltec at Teotihuacan, the Aztec at Tenochtitlan, and the Mayan at numerous ceremonial and residential centers. Cities defined the complex societies of the Americas more than wheels (used only for toys) and writing, which remained highly pictorial in Mexico, and, in the Andes, a matter of reading colored strings where the place of knots signified meaning like an ancient system of digital computing.

Thus, a larger lens raises more questions than we have allowed in our brief examination of Mesopotamia and Egypt. How important were such "urban inventions" as kings, soldiers, warfare, wheels, and writing if they did not exist everywhere cities were created? Further, how important were cities in the creation of the complex lives we have lived for the last five thousand years?

We might also ask the larger question: Has the urban revolution improved our lives? The belief that it has lies behind the use of the word *civilization*. Though the root of the word is the same as city, civil, and civilian, the word *civilization* came into the modern vocabulary of historians and social scientists in the nineteenth century. At this time anthropologists were working to distinguish stages of history and to illustrate the differences between what were then called "primitive" peoples and people of the modern world whom anthropologists considered "civilized." Thus, they contended there had been three stages of history that could be summarized, in chronological order, as savagery, barbarism, and civilization. By the early twentieth century, in the work of the great prehistorian V. Gordon Childe, these terms stood for hunting-gathering, agricultural, and urban societies.

The belief that the world of the anthropologists and the "moderns" of the nineteenth and twentieth centuries was more civilized than the pre-urban world that they studied was more than a bit presumptuous. But this presumption continues today, in the popular mythology of "country bumpkins" who lack the manners and savoir faire of their city cousins. Interestingly, it was also the assumption of the earliest founders of cities. *The Epic of Gilgamesh* tells of the need of the city to tame the wild Enkidu so that he can take his place in:

> . . . ramparted Uruk,
> Where fellows are resplendent in holiday clothing,
> Where every day is set for celebration.

There are many reasons to be skeptical of the so-called achievements of city life: increased inequality, suppression of women, slavery, organized warfare, conscription, heavy taxation, forced labor, to name some of the most obvious. But our museums are full of the art and artifacts that testify to what the ancients meant by "civilization." The pyramids of Egypt and of Mexico and the ziggurats of Mesopotamia are among the wonders of the world. Does it matter that the great pyramids of Egypt were built from the forced labor of thousands to provide a resting place for a single person and that people were entombed alive in order to serve him? We can view the pyramids today as a remarkable achievement of engineering and organization while still condemning the manner of their execution. We can admire the art in the tombs, thrill to the revealing detail of ancient Egyptian life, marvel at the persistence of vivid colors mixed almost five thousand years ago, and treasure the art for what it reveals of the world of its creators, while we still detest its purpose.

We can do this because these monuments have become something different for us than what they were for the ancients. They have become testaments to human achievement, regardless of the cost. These ancient city-based societies were the first in which humans produced abundant works of art and architecture, which still astound us in their range, scope, and design.

The significance of the urban revolution was that it produced things that lasted beyond their utility or meaning—thanks to new techniques in stone cutting and hauling; baking brick, tile, and glass; and smelting tin, copper, and bronze—as a legacy for future generations. Even three thousand years ago, Egyptian engineers studied the ancient pyramids to understand a very distant past, 1,500 years before, and to learn, adapt, revive, or revise ancient techniques. In short, the achievement of the urban revolution is that it made knowledge cumulative, so that each generation could stand on the shoulders of its predecessors.

3

Identity in Caste and Territorial Societies

Greece and India, 1000–300 B.C.E.

HISTORICAL CONTEXT

Both India and Greece developed ancient city-based civilizations within a thousand years of the urban revolution. In India that civilization was concentrated on the Indus River valley in what is today Pakistan. (See Map 3.1.) In Greece the Minoan civilization on the island of Crete was followed by the Mycenaean civilization on the mainland. (See Map 3.2.) But both ancient Indian and ancient Greek civilizations were transformed by new peoples from the grasslands of Eurasia, who settled in both areas between 1500 and 1000 B.C.E. Called by later generations the Aryans in India and the Dorians in Greece, these pastoral peoples arrived with horses, different customs, and new technologies. The Aryans came with chariots (as had the early Mycenaeans), while the Dorians, somewhat later, brought iron tools and weapons.

Despite the similar origins of the newcomers and the similar urban experience of the lands in which they settled, Aryan India and Dorian Greece developed in significantly different ways. As William H. McNeill writes in the first selection, by the year 500 B.C.E. Indian and Greek civilizations had found entirely different ways of organizing and administering their societies. And these differences had profound effects on the subsequent history of Indian and European society.

THINKING HISTORICALLY

Interpreting Primary Sources in Light of a Secondary Source

In Chapter 2, we distinguished between primary and secondary sources. Similarly, we begin here with a secondary source, or an interpretation. We then turn, as we did in the last chapter, to a series of primary sources. But while the last chapter focused on recognizing and distinguishing primary from secondary sources, here we concentrate on the relationship of the primary sources to the secondary interpretation — how one affects our reading of the other.

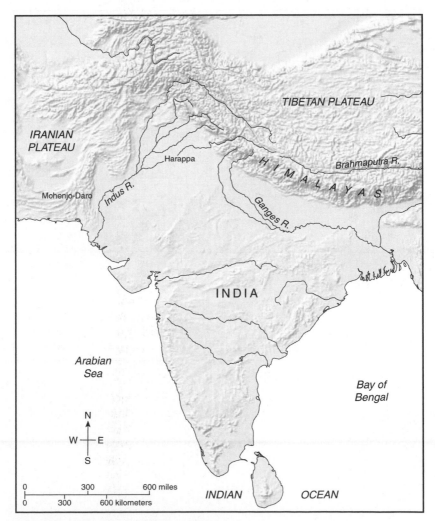

Map 3.1   Indus River Valley, c. 500 B.C.E.

In this chapter, the primary sources were chosen to illustrate points made in the introductory interpretation. This provides an opportunity to understand the interpretation in some detail and with some degree of subtlety. The primary sources do not give you enough material to argue that McNeill is right or wrong, but you will be able to flesh out some of the meaning of his interpretation. You might also reflect more generally on the relationship of sources and interpretations. You will be asked how particular sources support or even contradict the interpretation. You will consider the relevance of sources for other interpretations, and you will imagine what sort of sources you might seek for evidence.

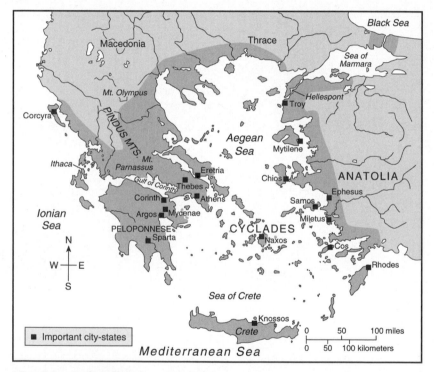

Map 3.2   Archaic Greece, c. 750–500 B.C.E.

10

WILLIAM H. McNEILL
Greek and Indian Civilization

William H. McNeill is one of the leading world historians in the United States. In this selection from his college textbook *A World History*, he compares the different ways in which Indian and Greek civilizations of the classical age (by around 500 B.C.E.) organized themselves. He distinguishes between Indian *caste* and Greek *territorial sovereignty*. These concepts are complex but useful to distinguish between two of the basic ways societies organize and identify themselves. As you read, try to define what each term means. McNeill argues that caste and territorial sovereignty had enormously different effects on the subsequent development of Indian and European society. What were some of these different effects?

Thinking Historically

As you read this secondary source or historical interpretation, consider what sort of primary sources might have led McNeill to this view or support his interpretation. Notice especially that in the first half of the selection, McNeill mentions specific ancient Indian writings: These are obvious primary sources for his interpretation. Not having read McNeill's primary sources, can you imagine what in them would lead to this interpretation?

Less of McNeill's interpretation of Greece is included in this selection and, consequently, there is no mention of primary sources. In this chapter, you will read a number of Greek primary sources, but at this point can you speculate about what types of sources would demonstrate the Greek idea of territorial sovereignty?

Keep in mind that caste and territorial sovereignty are modern terms not known or used by the ancients; therefore, you will not find them in the primary sources that follow. What words might the ancient Indians or Greeks have used to denote these concepts?

William H. McNeill, *A World History*, 2nd ed. (New York: Oxford University Press, 1971), 78–83, 88, 90, 95, 99–100.

Caste

A modern caste is a group of persons who will eat with one another and intermarry, while excluding others from these two intimacies. In addition, members of any particular caste must bear some distinguishing mark, so that everyone will know who belongs and who does not belong to it. Definite rules for how to behave in the presence of members of other castes also become necessary in situations where such contacts are frequent. When an entire society comes to be organized on these principles, any group of strangers or intruders automatically becomes another caste, for the exclusive habits of the rest of the population inevitably thrust the newcomers in upon themselves when it comes to eating and marrying. A large caste may easily break into smaller groupings as a result of some dispute, or through mere geographical separation over a period of time. New castes can form around new occupations. Wanderers and displaced individuals who find a new niche in society are automatically compelled to eat together and marry one another by the caste-bound habits of their neighbors.

How or when Indian society came to be organized along these lines remains unclear. Perhaps the Indus civilization itself was built upon something like the caste principle. Or perhaps the antipathy between Aryan invaders and the dark-skinned people whom they attacked lay at the root of the caste system of later India. But whatever the origins of caste, three features of Indian thought and feeling were mobilized to sustain the caste principle in later times. One of these was the idea of ceremonial purity. Fear of contaminating oneself by contact with a member of a lower, "unclean" caste gave Brahmans and others near the top of the pyramid strong reasons for limiting their association with low-caste persons.

From the other end of the scale, too, the poor and humble had strong reasons for clinging to caste. All but the most miserable and marginal could look down upon somebody, a not unimportant psychological feature of the system. In addition, the humbler castes were often groups that had only recently emerged from primitive forest life. They naturally sought to maintain their peculiar customs and habits, even in the context of urban or mixed village life, where men of different backgrounds and different castes lived side by side. Other civilized societies usually persuaded or compelled newcomers to surrender their peculiar ways, and assimilated them in the course of a few generations to the civilized population as a whole. In India, on the contrary, such groups were able to retain their separate identities indefinitely by preserving their own peculiar customs within the caste framework, generation after generation.

The third factor sustaining the caste principle was theoretical: the doctrine of reincarnation and of "varna." The latter declared that all men were naturally divided into four castes: the Brahmans who prayed, the Kshatriyas* who fought, the Vaisyas† who worked, and the Sudras who performed unclean tasks. Official doctrine classified the first three castes as Aryan, the last as non-Aryan, and put much stress on caste rank, from Brahmans at the top to Sudras at the bottom. Reality never corresponded even remotely to this theory. There were hundreds if not thousands of castes in India, rather than the four recognized in Brahmanical teaching. But apparent injustices and anomalies disappeared when the doctrine of reincarnation was combined with the doctrine of varna. The idea of reincarnation, indeed, gave logical explanation and justification to the system by explaining caste as a divinely established institution, hereditary from father to son, and designed to reward and punish souls for their actions in former lives. This undoubtedly helped to stabilize the confused reality. A man of unblemished life, born into the lowest caste, could hope for rebirth higher up the ladder. Conversely, a man of high caste who failed to conform to proper standards could expect rebirth in a lower caste. A man even risked reincarnation as a worm or beetle, if his misbehavior deserved such a punishment.

Clearly, the caste system as observed today did not exist in ancient India. Yet modern castes are the outgrowth of patterns of social organization that are as old as the oldest records. Early Buddhist stories, for instance, reveal many episodes turning upon caste distinctions, and passages in the *Rig Veda*‡ and other ancient writings imply caste-like practices and attitudes. By 500 B.C.E. we can at least be sure that the seeds from which the modern caste organization of society grew had already sprouted luxuriantly on Indian soil.

Caste lessened the significance of political, territorial administration. Everyone identified himself first and foremost with his caste. But a caste ordinarily lacked both definite internal administration and distinct territorial boundaries. Instead, members of a particular caste mingled with men of other castes, observing the necessary precautions to prevent contamination of one by the other. No king or ruler could command the undivided loyalty of people who felt themselves to belong to a caste rather than to a state. Indeed, to all ordinary caste members, rulers, officials, soldiers, and tax collectors were likely to seem mere troublesome outsiders, to be neglected whenever possible

*KSHAH tree uh
†VYS yuh
‡rihg VAY dah

and obeyed only as far as necessary. The fragile character of most Indian states resulted in large part from this fact. A striking absence of information about war and government is characteristic of all early Indian history; and this, too, presumably reflects Indian peoples' characteristic emotional disengagement from the state and from politics. . . .

The Vedas and Brahmanas

Our knowledge of Aryan religion derives from the Vedas. The Vedas, used as handbooks of religious ritual, consist of songs that were recited aloud during sacrifices, together with other passages instructing the priests what to do during the ceremony. In course of time, the language of the Vedas became more or less unintelligible, even to priests. A great effort was thereupon made to preserve details of accent and pronunciation, by insisting on exact memorization of texts from master to pupil across the generations. Every jot and tittle of the inherited verses was felt to matter, since a misplaced line or mispronounced word could nullify a whole sacrifice and might even provoke divine displeasure.

Preoccupation with correctness of detail speedily shifted emphasis from the gods of the Aryan pantheon to the act of worship and invocation itself. Aryan priests may also have learned about magical powers claimed by priests of the Indus civilization. At any rate, some Brahmans began to argue that by performing rituals correctly they could actually compel the gods to grant what was asked of them. Indeed, proper sacrifice and invocation created the world of gods and men anew, and stabilized afresh the critical relation between natural and supernatural reality. In such a view, the importance and personalities of the separate gods shrank to triviality, while the power and skill of the priesthood was greatly magnified. These extravagant priestly claims were freely put forward in texts called Brahmanas. These were cast in the form of commentaries on the Vedas, purportedly explaining what the older texts really meant, but often changing meanings in the process.

The Upanishads and Mysticism

Priestly claims to exercise authority over gods and men were never widely accepted in ancient India. Chiefs and warriors might be a bit wary of priestly magic, but they were not eager to cede to the priests the primacy claimed by the Brahmanas. Humbler ranks of society also objected to priestly presumption. This is proved by the fact that a rival type of piety took hold in India and soon came to constitute the most distinctive element in the whole religious tradition of the land. Another body of oral literature, the Upanishads,* constitutes our evidence of this religious development. The Upanishads are not systematic treatises nor do they agree in all details. Yet they do express a general consensus on important points.

First of all, the Upanishads conceive the end of religious life in a radically new way. Instead of seeking riches, health, and long life, a wise and holy man strives merely to escape the endless round of rebirth. Success allows his soul to dissolve into the All from whence it had come, triumphantly transcending the suffering, pain, and imperfection of existence.

In the second place, holiness and release from the cycle of rebirths were attained not by obedience to priests nor by observance of ceremonies. The truly holy man had no need of intermediaries and, for that matter, no need of gods. Instead, by a process of self-discipline, meditation, asceticism, and withdrawal from the ordinary concerns of daily life, the successful religious athlete might attain a mystic vision of Truth — a vision which left the seer purged and happy. The nature and content of the mystic vision could never be expressed in words. It revealed Truth by achieving an identity between the individual soul and the Soul of the universe. Such an experience, surpassing human understanding and ordinary language, constituted a foretaste of the ultimate bliss of self-annihilation in the All, which was the final goal of wise and holy life. . . .

While India worked its way toward the definition of a new and distinctive civilization on one flank of the ancient Middle East, on its other flank another new civilization was also emerging: the Greek. The principal stages of early Greek history closely resemble what we know or can surmise about Indian development. But the end product differed fundamentally. The Greeks put political organization into territorial states above all other bases of human association, and attempted to explain the world and man not in terms of mystic illumination but through laws of nature. Thus despite a similar start, when fierce "tamers of horses" — like those of whom Homer[1] later sang — overran priest-led agricultural societies, the Indian and Greek styles of civilization diverged strikingly by 500 B.C.E. . . .

The self-governing city-states created by Greeks on the coast of Asia Minor had . . . great . . . importance in world history. For by inventing the city-state or *polis* (hence our word "politics"), the Greeks of Ionia established the prototype from which the whole Western world derived its penchant for political organization into territorially defined

---

*oo PAH nee shahdz
[1]Greek poet c. 800 B.C.E.; author of *The Iliad* and *The Odyssey*. [Ed.]

sovereign units, i.e., into states. The supremacy of territoriality over all other forms of human association is neither natural nor inevitable, as the Indian caste principle may remind us. . . .

Dominance of the Polis in Greek Culture

So powerful and compelling was the psychological pull of the polis that almost every aspect of Greek cultural activity was speedily caught up in and — as it were — digested by the new master institution of Greek civilization. Religion, art, literature, philosophy, took shape or acquired a new accent through their relationship with the all-engulfing object of the citizens' affection. . . .

Despite the general success of the polis ordering of things, a few individuals fretted over the logical inconsistencies of Greek religion and traditional world view. As trade developed, opportunities to learn about the wisdom of the East multiplied. Inquiring Greeks soon discovered that among the priestly experts of the Middle East there was no agreement about such fundamental questions as how the world was created or why the planets periodically checked their forward movement through the heavens and went backward for a while before resuming their former motion. It was in Ionia that men first confronted this sort of question systematically enough to bother recording their views. These, the first philosophers, sought to explain the phenomena of the world by imaginative exercise of their power of reason. Finding conflicting and unsupported stories about the gods to be unsatisfactory, they took the drastic step of omitting the gods entirely, and boldly substituted natural law instead as the ruling force of the universe. To be sure, the Ionian philosophers did not agree among themselves when they sought to describe how the laws of nature worked, and their naive efforts to explain an ever wider range of phenomena did not meet with much success.

Nevertheless, their attempts at using speculative reason to explain the nature of things marked a major turning point in human intellectual development. The Ionian concept of a universe ruled not by the whim of some divine personality but by an impersonal and unchangeable law has never since been forgotten. Throughout the subsequent history of European and Middle Eastern thought, this distinctively Greek view of the nature of things stood in persistent and fruitful tension with the older, Middle Eastern theistic explanation of the universe. Particular thinkers, reluctant to abandon either position entirely, have sought to reconcile the omnipotence of the divine will with the unchangeability of natural law by means of the most various arguments. Since, however, the two views are as logically incompatible with one another as were the myths from which the Ionian philosophers started, no formulation or reconciliation ever attained lasting and universal consent. Men always had to start over again to reshape for themselves a more satisfactory metaphysic and theology. Here, therefore, lay a growing point for all subsequent European thought which has not yet been exhausted.

Indeed, the recent successes of natural science seem to have vindicated the Ionian concept of natural law in ways and with a complexity that would have utterly amazed Thales* (d. c. 546 B.C.E.) or any of his successors, who merely voiced what turned out to be amazingly lucky guesses. How did they do it? It seems plausible to suggest that the Ionians hit upon the notion of natural law by simply projecting the tight little world of the polis upon the universe. For it was a fact that the polis was regulated by law, not by the personal will or whim of a ruler. If such invisible abstractions could govern human behavior and confine it to certain roughly predictable paths of action, why could not similar laws control the natural world? To such a question, it appears, the Ionians gave an affirmative answer, and in doing so gave a distinctive cast to all subsequent Greek and European thought.

Limitations of the Polis

It would be a mistake to leave the impression that all facets of Greek life fitted smoothly and easily into the polis frame. The busy public world left scant room for the inwardness of personal experience. Striving for purification, for salvation, for holiness, which found such ample expression in the Indian cultural setting, was almost excluded. Yet the Greeks were not immune from such impulses. Through the ancient mystery religions, as well as through such an association as the "Order" founded by Pythagoras,† the famous mathematician and mystic (d. c. 507 B.C.E.), they sought to meet these needs. But when such efforts took organized form, a fundamental incompatibility between the claims of the polis to the unqualified loyalty of every citizen and the pursuit of personal holiness quickly became apparent. This was illustrated by the stormy history of the Pythagorean Order. Either the organized seekers after holiness captured the polis, as happened for a while in the city of Croton in southern Italy, or the magistrates of the polis persecuted the Order, as happened in Pythagoras' old age. There seemed no workable ground of compromise in this, the earliest recorded instance of conflict between church and state in Western history.

The fundamental difference between Greek and Indian institutions as shaped by about 500 B.C.E. was made apparent by this episode. The loose federation of cultures allowed by the caste principle in India experienced

*THAY leez
†py THAG uhr ahs

no difficulty at all in accommodating organized seekers after holiness such as the communities of Buddhist monks. By contrast, the exclusive claim upon the citizens' time, effort, and affection which had been staked out by the Greek polis allowed no sort of corporate rival.

Enormous energies were tapped by the polis. A wider segment of the total population was engaged in cultural and political action than had been possible in any earlier civilized society, and the brilliant flowering of classical Greek civilization was the consequence. Yet the very intensity of the political tie excluded ranges of activity and sensitivity that were not compatible with a territorial organization of human groupings, and sowed seeds of civil strife between the Greek cities which soon proved disastrous. But every achievement involves a surrender of alternatives: It is merely that the Greek achievement, by its very magnitude, casts an unusually clear light upon what it also excluded.

11

From the Rig Veda:
Sacrifice as Creation

As McNeill discusses in the previous selection, the Vedas are the writings of the ancient Brahman priests in India. They cover a wide variety of religious subjects and concerns: ritual, sacrifice, hymns, healing, incantations, allegories, philosophy, and the problems of everyday life. In general, the earliest Vedas (like the Rig Veda) focus more on the specifics of ritual and sacrifice, reflecting the needs and instructions of the priests during the Aryan conquest. The last of the Vedas (like the Upanishads) are more philosophical and speculative.

This selection is from the Rig Veda. What happened when Purusha was sacrificed? What is the meaning of this first sacrifice? How does this story support the role of priests?

Thinking Historically

Consider how this primary source supports the division of Indian society into castes, as McNeill discusses in the previous selection. How does this story suggest that the people who wrote the Rig Veda thought the division of society into four castes was pretty basic? Can

"Rig Veda," 10.90, in *Sources of Indian Tradition*, 2nd ed., ed. and rev. Ainslie T. Embree (New York: Columbia University Press, 1988), 18–19.

you deduce from this source which of the four castes was most likely the originator of the story? Does this support anything else that Mc-Neill said in his interpretation?

Thousand-headed Purusha, thousand-eyed, thousand-footed — he, having pervaded the earth on all sides, still extends ten fingers beyond it.

Purusha alone is all this — whatever has been and whatever is going to be. Further, he is the lord of immortality and also of what grows on account of food.

Such is his greatness; greater, indeed, than this is Purusha. All creatures constitute but one-quarter of him, his three-quarters are the immortal in the heaven.

With his three-quarters did Purusha rise up; one-quarter of him again remains here. With it did he variously spread out on all sides over what eats and what eats not.

From him was Virāj born, from Virāj the evolved Purusha. He, being born, projected himself behind the earth as also before it.

When the gods performed the sacrifice with Purusha as the oblation, then the spring was its clarified butter, the summer the sacrificial fuel, and the autumn the oblation.

The sacrificial victim, namely, Purusha, born at the very beginning, they sprinkled with sacred water upon the sacrificial grass. With him as oblation, the gods performed the sacrifice, and also the Sādhyas [a class of semidivine beings] and the rishis [ancient seers].

From that wholly offered sacrificial oblation were born the verses [ṛc] and the sacred chants; from it were born the meters [chandas]; the sacrificial formula was born from it.

From it horses were born and also those animals who have double rows [i.e., upper and lower] of teeth; cows were born from it, from it were born goats and sheep.

When they divided Purusha, in how many different portions did they arrange him? What became of his mouth, what of his two arms? What were his two thighs and his two feet called?

His mouth became the brāhman; his two arms were made into the rajanya; his two thighs the vaishyas; from his two feet the shūdra was born.

The moon was born from the mind, from the eye the sun was born; from the mouth Indra and Agni, from the breath [prāna] the wind [vāyu] was born.

From the navel was the atmosphere created, from the head the heaven issued forth; from the two feet was born the earth and the quarters (the cardinal directions) from the ear. Thus did they fashion the worlds.

Seven were the enclosing sticks in this sacrifice, thrice seven were the fire-sticks made when the gods, performing the sacrifice, bound down Purusha, the sacrificial victim.

With this sacrificial oblation did the gods offer the sacrifice. These were the first norms [*dharma*] of sacrifice. These greatnesses reached to the sky wherein live the ancient Sādhyas and gods.

From the Upanishads: Karma and Reincarnation

The idea of karma (cause and effect, appropriate consequences) appears in the earliest Upanishads. Karma meant: "As you sow, so shall you reap." Good karma would be enhanced; bad karma would lead to more bad karma. The universe was a system of complete justice in which all people got what they deserved. The idea that the soul might be reborn in another body may have been an even older idea, but in the Upanishads it combined easily with the idea of karma. That a good soul was reborn in a higher life, or a bad soul in a lower, was perhaps a more material, less subtle, version of the justice of karma. The idea of reincarnation, or the transmigration of souls, united justice with caste.

What effect would these ideas have on people? In what ways would these ideas aid people in gaining a sense of power over their lives? How might these ideas be tools of control? What does "morality" mean in this tradition?

Thinking Historically

How does the idea of karma presented in this primary source support McNeill's interpretation of the importance of the caste system in India? Would the idea of reincarnation make caste organization stronger or weaker?

According as one acts, according as one conducts himself, so does he become. The doer of good becomes good. The doer of evil becomes evil. One becomes virtuous by virtuous action, bad by bad action.

Brihad Aranyaka, IV:4:5–6, in *The Thirteen Principal Upanishads*, ed. and trans. R. E. Hume (Bombay: Oxford University Press, 1954), 140–41. *Chandogya*, V:10:7, in Hume, quoted in *The Hindu Tradition: Readings in Oriental Thought*, ed. Ainslee T. Embree (New York: Vintage, 1966, copyright renewed 1994), 62–63.

But people say: "A person is made not of acts, but of desires only."
In reply to this I say: As is his desire, such is his resolve; as is his resolve, such the action he performs; what action (*karma*) he performs,
that he procures for himself.

On this point there is this verse: —

Where one's mind is attached — the inner self
Goes thereto with action, being attached to it alone.

   Obtaining the end of his action,
   Whatever he does in this world,
   He comes again from that world
   To this world of action.

— So the man who desires.

Now the man who does not desire. — He who is without desire, who
is freed from desire, whose desire is satisfied, whose desire is the Soul —
his breaths do not depart. Being very Brahman, he goes to Brahman.

Accordingly, those who are of pleasant conduct here — the
prospect is, indeed, that they will enter a pleasant womb, either the
womb of a Brahman, or the womb of a Kshatriya, or the womb of a
Vaishya. But those who are of stinking conduct here — the prospect is,
indeed, that they will enter a stinking womb, either the womb of a dog,
or the womb of a swine, or the womb of an outcaste (*candāla*).

$$13$$

From the Upanishads:
Brahman and Atman

In this selection *Brahman* does not refer to priests or to a specific god.
In the late Vedas, or Upanishads, Brahman is all divinity, and all is
Brahman. Even the individual soul or *atman* can be one with the universal Brahman, "as the Father of Svetaketu demonstrates to his son
through the examples of a banyan tree and salt water." How would
ideas like these challenge the caste system?

Chandogya Upanishad, in *The Upanishads*, trans. Juan Mascaro (Harmondsworth: Penguin
Press, 1965), 113–14.

Thinking Historically

McNeill suggests that the Upanishads expressed a religious vision that challenged the power of priests, sacrifice, and caste. How does this selection from the Upanishads support that interpretation?

Great is the Gayatri, the most sacred verse of the Vedas; but how much greater is the Infinity of Brahman! A quarter of his being is this whole vast universe: the other three quarters are his heaven of Immortality. (3.12.5)

There is a Light that shines beyond all things on earth, beyond us all, beyond the heavens, beyond the highest, the very highest heavens. This is the Light that shines in our heart. (3.13.7)

All this universe is in the truth Brahman. He is the beginning and end and life of all. As such, in silence, give unto him adoration.

Man in truth is made of faith. As his faith is in this life, so he becomes in the beyond: with faith and vision let him work.

There is a Spirit that is mind and life, light and truth and vast spaces. He contains all works and desires and all perfumes and all tastes. He enfolds the whole universe, and in silence is loving to all.

This is the Spirit that is in my heart, smaller than a grain of rice, or a grain of barley, or a grain of mustard-seed, or a grain of canary-seed, or the kernel of a grain of canary-seed. This is the Spirit that is in my heart, greater than the earth, greater than the sky, greater than heaven itself, greater than all these worlds.

He contains all works and desires and all perfumes and all tastes. He enfolds the whole universe and in silence is loving to all. This is the Spirit that is in my heart, this is Brahman. (3.14)

"Bring me a fruit from this banyan tree."
"Here it is, father."
"Break it."
"It is broken, Sir."
"What do you see in it?"
"Very small seeds, Sir."
"Break one of them, my son."
"It is broken, Sir."
"What do you see in it?"
"Nothing at all, Sir."
Then his father spoke to him: "My son, from the very essence in the seed which you cannot see comes in truth this vast banyan tree.

Believe me, my son, an invisible and subtle essence is the Spirit of the whole universe. That is Reality. That is Atman. THOU ART THAT."

"Explain more to me, father," said Svetaketu.

"So be it, my son.

Place this salt in water and come to me tomorrow morning."

Svetaketu did as he was commanded, and in the morning his father said to him: "Bring me the salt you put into the water last night."

Svetaketu looked into the water, but could not find it, for it had dissolved.

His father then said: "Taste the water from this side. How is it?"

"It is salt."

"Taste it from the middle. How is it?"

"It is salt."

"Taste it from that side. How is it?"

"It is salt."

"Look for the salt again and come again to me."

The son did so, saying: "I cannot see the salt. I only see water."

His father then said: "In the same way, O my son, you cannot see the Spirit. But in truth he is here.

An invisible and subtle essence is the Spirit of the whole universe. That is Reality. That is Truth. THOU ART THAT." (6.12–14)

14

From the Bhagavad Gita: Caste and Self

The *Bhagavad Gita** is the best-known work in Hindu religious liter-ature. It is part of a larger epic called the *Mahabharata*,† a story of two feuding families that may have had its origins in the Aryan inva-sion of 1500 B.C.E. The *Bhagavad Gita* is a philosophical interlude that interrupts the story just before the great battle between the two families. It poses some fundamental questions about the nature of life, death, and proper religious behavior. It begins as the leader of one of the battling armies, Arjuna, asks why he should fight his friends and relatives on the other side. The answer comes from none other than the god Krishna, who has taken the form of Arjuna's charioteer.

*BUH guh vahd GEE tuh
†mah hah BAH rah tah

Bhagavad Gita, trans. Barbara Stoler Miller (New York: Bantam Books, 1986), 31–34, 52, 86–87.

What is Krishna's answer? What will happen to the people Arjuna kills? What will happen to Arjuna? What would happen to Arjuna if he refused to fight the battle? What does this selection tell you about Hindu ideas of life, death, and the self?

Thinking Historically

In some ways this work reconciles the conflict in the Upanishads between caste and *atman*. Performing the *dharma,* or duty, of caste is seen as a liberating act. Would the acceptance of this story support or challenge the caste system? Does this primary source support McNeill's interpretation of Indian society?

Lord Krishna

You grieve for those beyond grief,
and you speak words of insight;
but learned men do not grieve
for the dead or the living.

Never have I not existed,
nor you, nor these kings;
and never in the future
shall we cease to exist.

Just as the embodied self
enters childhood, youth, and old age,
so does it enter another body;
this does not confound a steadfast man.

Contacts with matter make us feel
heat and cold, pleasure and pain.
Arjuna, you must learn to endure
fleeting things — they come and go!

When these cannot torment a man,
when suffering and joy are equal
for him and he has courage,
he is fit for immortality.

Nothing of nonbeing comes to be,
nor does being cease to exist;
the boundary between these two
is seen by men who see reality.

Indestructible is the presence
that pervades all this;

no one can destroy
this unchanging reality.

Our bodies are known to end,
but the embodied self is enduring,
indestructible, and immeasurable;
therefore, Arjuna, fight the battle!

He who thinks this self a killer
and he who thinks it killed,
both fail to understand;
it does not kill, nor is it killed.

It is not born,
it does not die;
having been,
it will never not be;
unborn, enduring,
constant, and primordial,
it is not killed
when the body is killed.

Arjuna, when a man knows the self
to be indestructible, enduring, unborn,
unchanging, how does he kill
or cause anyone to kill?

As a man discards
worn-out clothes
to put on new
and different ones,
so the embodied self
discards
its worn-out bodies
to take on other new ones.

Weapons do not cut it,
fire does not burn it,
waters do not wet it,
wind does not wither it.

It cannot be cut or burned;
it cannot be wet or withered;
it is enduring, all-pervasive,
fixed, immovable, and timeless.

It is called unmanifest,
inconceivable, and immutable;

since you know that to be so,
you should not grieve!

If you think of its birth
and death as ever-recurring,
then too, Great Warrior,
you have no cause to grieve!

Death is certain for anyone born,
and birth is certain for the dead;
since the cycle is inevitable,
you have no cause to grieve!

Creatures are unmanifest in origin,
manifest in the midst of life,
and unmanifest again in the end.
Since this is so, why do you lament!

Rarely someone
sees it,
rarely another
speaks it,
rarely anyone
hears it —
even hearing it,
no one really knows it.

The self embodied in the body
of every being is indestructible;
you have no cause to grieve
for all these creatures, Arjuna!

Look to your own duty;
do not tremble before it;
nothing is better for a warrior
than a battle of sacred duty.

The doors of heaven open
for warriors who rejoice
to have a battle like this
thrust on them by chance.

If you fail to wage this war
of sacred duty,
you will abandon your own duty
and fame only to gain evil.

People will tell
of your undying shame,

and for a man of honor
shame is worse than death.

> In this next passage from the *Bhagavad Gita*, Krishna reveals a deeper
> meaning to his message to Arjuna. Not only must Arjuna act like a war-
> rior because that is his caste, but he must also act without regard to the
> consequences of his action. What does Krishna seem to mean by this?
> How does one do "nothing at all even when he engages in action"?

Abandoning attachment to fruits
of action, always content, independent,
he does nothing at all
even when he engages in action.

He incurs no guilt if he has no hope,
restrains his thought and himself,
abandons possessions,
and performs actions with his body only.

Content with whatever comes by chance,
beyond dualities, free from envy,
impartial to failure and success,
he is not bound even when he acts.

When a man is unattached and free,
his reason deep in knowledge,
acting only in sacrifice,
his action is wholly dissolved.

When devoted men sacrifice
to other deities with faith,
they sacrifice to me, Arjuna,
however aberrant the rites.

I am the enjoyer
and the lord of all sacrifices;
they do not know me in reality,
and so they fail.

Votaries of the gods go to the gods,
ancestor-worshippers go to the ancestors,
those who propitiate ghosts go to them,
and my worshippers go to me.

The leaf or flower or fruit or water
that he offers with devotion,
I take from the man of self-restraint
in response to his devotion.

Whatever you do — what you take,
what you offer, what you give,
what penances you perform —
do as an offering to me, Arjuna!

You will be freed from the bonds of action,
from the fruit of fortune and misfortune;
armed with the discipline of renunciation,
your self liberated, you will join me.

I am impartial to all creatures,
and no one is hateful or dear to me;
but men devoted to me are in me,
and I am within them.

If he is devoted solely to me,
even a violent criminal
must be deemed a man of virtue,
for his resolve is right.

His spirit quickens to sacred duty,
and he finds eternal peace;
Arjuna, know that no one
devoted to me is lost.

If they rely on me, Arjuna,
women, commoners, men of low rank,
even men born in the womb of evil,
reach the highest way.

How easy it is then for holy priests
and devoted royal sages —
in this transient world of sorrow,
devote yourself to me!

Keep me in your mind and devotion,
sacrifice to me, bow to me,
discipline yourself toward me,
and you will reach me!

15

ARISTOTLE

The Athenian Constitution: Territorial Sovereignty

The process of establishing political authority based on the territorial state was not achieved at one particular moment in history. Much of Greek history (indeed much of world history since the Greeks) witnessed the struggle of territorial authority over family, blood, and kinship ties.

The process of replacing kinship and tribal alliances with a territorial "politics of place" can, however, be seen in the constitutional reforms attributed to the Athenian noble Cleisthenes* in 508 B.C.E. Cleisthenes was not a democrat; his reform of Athenian politics was probably intended to win popular support for himself in his struggle with other noble families. But the inadvertent results of his reforms were to establish the necessary basis for democracy: a territorial state in which commoners as citizens had a stake in government. A description of those reforms is contained in a document called "The Athenian Constitution," discovered in Egypt only a hundred years ago and thought to have been written by the philosopher Aristotle (384–322 B.C.E.) around 330 B.C.E.

Modern scholars doubt that Cleisthenes created the *demes*† (local neighborhoods) that were the basis of his reforms. Some existed earlier. But by making the *demes* the root of political organization, he undoubtedly undercut the power of dominant families. As *demes* were given real authority, power shifted from relatives to residents. Also, as Cleisthenes expanded the number of citizens, the *deme* structure became more "*deme*-ocratic."

Notice how the constitutional reform combined a sense of local, residential identity with citizenship in a larger city-state by tying city, country, and coastal *demes* together in each new "tribe." Why were these new tribes less "tribal" than the old ones? What would be the modern equivalent of these new tribes? Was democracy possible without a shift from kinship to territorial or civic identity? Was it inevitable?

*KLYS thuh neez
†deems

Aristotle, "The Athenian Constitution," in *Aristotle, Politics, and the Athenian Constitution*, trans. John Warrington (London: David Campbell Publishers, 1959).

Thinking Historically

Territorial sovereignty is something we take for granted. It means the law of the land. Regardless of the beliefs of our parents or ancestors, we obey the law of the territory. In the United States, we are bound to observe the law of the nation and the law of the state and municipal ordinances. We do not take our own family law with us when we move from one town or state or country to another. When we go to Japan, we are bound by Japanese law, even if we are not Japanese. In the modern world, sovereignty, ultimate authority, is tied to territory. Because this is so obvious to us in modern society, it is difficult to imagine that this was not always the case.

Historians have to acknowledge that things they and their societies take for granted may not have always existed; rather, they have developed throughout history. McNeill's interpretation of the essential difference between India and Greece makes such a leap. Many people have pointed out the unique Athenian invention of democracy. But McNeill recognized that the Athenians invented democracy because they had already invented something more fundamental — territorial sovereignty, politics, government, citizenship. How does "The Athenian Constitution" support McNeill's interpretation?

The overthrow of the Peisistratid tyranny left the city split into two actions under Isagoras and Cleisthenes respectively. The former, a son of Tisander, had supported the tyrants; the latter was an Alcmaeonid. Cleisthenes, defeated in the political clubs, won over the people by offering citizen rights to the masses. Thereupon Isagoras, who had fallen behind in the race for power, once more invoked the help of his friend Cleomenes and persuaded him to exorcise the pollution; that is, to expel the Alcmaeonidae, who were believed still to be accursed. Cleisthenes accordingly withdrew from Attica with a small band of adherents, while Cleomenes proceeded to drive out seven hundred Athenian families. The Spartan next attempted to dissolve the Council and to set up Isagoras with three hundred of his supporters as the sovereign authority. The Council, however, resisted; the populace flew to arms; and Cleomenes with Isagoras and all their forces took refuge in the Acropolis, to which the people laid siege and blockaded them for two days. On the third day it was agreed that Cleomenes and his followers should withdraw. Cleisthenes and his fellow exiles were recalled.

The people were now in control, and Cleisthenes, their leader, was recognized as head of the popular party. This was not surprising; for the Alcmaeonidae were largely responsible for the overthrow of the tyrants, with whom they had been in conflict during most of their rule.

... The people, therefore, had every grounds for confidence in Cleisthenes. Accordingly, three years after the destruction of the tyranny, in the archonship of Isagoras, he used his influence as leader of the popular party to carry out a number of reforms. (A) He divided the population into ten tribes instead of the old four. His purpose here was to intermix the members of the tribes so that more persons might have civic rights; and hence the advice "not to notice the tribes," which was tendered to those who would examine the lists of the clans. (B) He increased the membership of the Council from 400 to 500, each tribe now contributing fifty instead of one hundred as before. His reason for not organizing the people into *twelve* tribes was to avoid the necessity of using the existing division into trittyes, which would have meant failing to regroup the population on a satisfactory basis. (C) He divided the country into thirty portions — ten urban and suburban, ten coastal, and ten inland — each containing a certain number of demes. These portions he called trittyes, and assigned three of them by lot to each tribe in such a way that each should have one portion in each of the three localities just mentioned. Furthermore, those who lived in any given deme were to be reckoned fellow demesmen. This arrangement was intended to protect new citizens from being shown up as such by the habitual use of family names. Men were to be officially described by the names of their demes; and it is thus that Athenians still speak of one another. Demes had now supplanted the old naucraries,[1] and Cleisthenes therefore appointed Demarchs whose duties were identical with those of the former Naucrari. He named some of the demes from their localities, and others from their supposed founders; for certain areas no longer corresponded to named localities. On the other hand, he allowed everyone to retain his family and clan and religious rites according to ancestral custom. He also gave the ten tribes names which the Delphic oracle had chosen out of one hundred selected national heroes.

---

[1]Forty-eight subdivisions of the old four tribes, each responsible for one galley of the Athenian navy. [Ed.]

16

THUCYDIDES

The Funeral Oration of Pericles

The most famous statement of Greek loyalty to the city-state is the following account of the funeral speech of the Athenian statesman Pericles in the classic *History of the Peloponnesian War* by the ancient historian Thucydides.* The speech eulogized the Athenian soldiers who had died in the war against Sparta in 431 B.C.E.

Notice the high value placed on loyalty to Athens and service to the state. Here is the origin of patriotism. Pericles also insists that Athens is a democratic city-state. He praises Athenian freedom as well as public service. Could there be a conflict between personal freedom and public service? If so, how would Pericles resolve such a conflict? You might also notice that Pericles is praising Athenian citizen-soldiers who died defending not their home but the empire. Could there be a conflict between Athenian democracy and the ambitious empire?

Thinking Historically

Are the sentiments that Pericles expresses a consequence of territorial sovereignty? Could such sentiments be expressed in defense of caste? Notice how Pericles speaks of ancestors, family, and parents. Do his words suggest any potential conflict between family ties and loyalty to the state? How is Pericles able to convince his audience of the priority of the state over kinship ties? How does this primary source provide evidence for McNeill's interpretation?

I will speak first of our ancestors, for it is right and seemly that now, when we are lamenting the dead, a tribute should be paid to their memory. There has never been a time when they did not inhabit this land, which by their valour they have handed down from generation to generation, and we have received from them a free state. But if they were worthy of praise, still more were our fathers, who added to their inheritance, and after many a struggle transmitted to us their sons this great

*thoo SIH duh deez

The History of Thucydides, Book II, trans. Benjamin Jowett (New York: Tandy-Thomas, 1909).

empire. And we ourselves assembled here today, who are still most of us in the vigour of life, have carried the work of improvement further, and have richly endowed our city with all things, so that she is sufficient for herself both in peace and war. Of the military exploits by which our various possessions were acquired, or of the energy with which we or our fathers drove back the tide of war, Hellenic or Barbarian [non-Greek], I will not speak: for the tale would be long and is familiar to you. But before I praise the dead, I should like to point out by what principles of action we rose to power, and under what institutions and through what manner of life our empire became great. For I conceive that such thoughts are not unsuited to the occasion, and that this numerous assembly of citizens and strangers may profitably listen to them.

Our form of government does not enter into rivalry with the institutions of others. We do not copy our neighbours, but are an example to them. It is true that we are called a democracy, for the administration is in the hands of the many and not of the few. But while the law secures equal justice to all alike in their private disputes, the claim of excellence is also recognised; and when a citizen is in any way distinguished, he is preferred to the public service, not as a matter of privilege, but as the reward of merit. Neither is poverty a bar, but a man may benefit his country whatever be the obscurity of his condition. There is no exclusiveness in our public life, and in our private intercourse we are not suspicious of one another, nor angry with our neighbour if he does what he likes; we do not put on sour looks at him which, though harmless, are not pleasant. While we are thus unconstrained in our private intercourse, a spirit of reverence pervades our public acts; we are prevented from doing wrong by respect for the authorities and for the laws, having an especial regard to those which are ordained for the protection of the injured as well as to those unwritten laws which bring upon the transgressor of them the reprobation of the general sentiment.

And we have not forgotten to provide for our weary spirits many relaxations from toil; we have regular games and sacrifices throughout the year; our homes are beautiful and elegant; and the delight which we daily feel in all these things helps to banish melancholy. Because of the greatness of our city the fruits of the whole earth flow in upon us; so that we enjoy the goods of other countries as freely as of our own.

Then, again, our military training is in many respects superior to that of our adversaries. Our city is thrown open to the world, and we never expel a foreigner or prevent him from seeing or learning anything of which the secret if revealed to an enemy might profit him. We rely not upon management or trickery, but upon our own hearts and hands. And in the matter of education, whereas they from early youth are always undergoing laborious exercises which are to make them brave, we live at ease, and yet are equally ready to face the perils which they face. And here is the proof. . . .

If then we prefer to meet danger with a light heart but without laborious training, and with a courage which is gained by habit and not enforced by law, are we not greatly the gainers? Since we do not anticipate the pain, although, when the hour comes, we can be as brave as those who never allow themselves to rest; and thus too our city is equally admirable in peace and in war. For we are lovers of the beautiful, yet simple in our tastes, and we cultivate the mind without loss of manliness. Wealth we employ, not for talk and ostentation, but when there is a real use for it. To avow poverty with us is no disgrace; the true disgrace is in doing nothing to avoid it. An Athenian citizen does not neglect the state because he takes care of his own household; and even those of us who are engaged in business have a very fair idea of politics. We alone regard a man who takes no interest in public affairs, not as a harmless, but as a useless character; and if few of us are originators, we are all sound judges of policy. The great impediment to action is, in our opinion, not discussion, but the want of that knowledge which is gained by discussion preparatory to action. For we have a peculiar power of thinking before we act and of acting too, whereas other men are courageous from ignorance but hesitate upon reflection. And they are surely to be esteemed the bravest spirits who, having the clearest sense both of the pains and pleasures of life, do not on that account shrink from danger. In doing good, again, we are unlike others; we make our friends by conferring, not by receiving favours. Now he who confers a favour is the firmer friend, because he would fain by kindness keep alive the memory of an obligation; but the recipient is colder in his feelings, because he knows that in requiting another's generosity he will not be winning gratitude but only paying a debt. We alone do good to our neighbours, not upon a calculation of interest, but in the confidence of freedom and in a frank and fearless spirit.

To sum up: I say that Athens is the school of Hellas, and that the individual Athenian in his own person seems to have the power of adapting himself to the most varied forms of action with the utmost versatility and grace. This is no passing and idle word, but truth and fact; and the assertion is verified by the position to which these qualities have raised the state. For in the hour of trial Athens alone among her contemporaries is superior to the report of her. No enemy who comes against her is indignant at the reverses which he sustains at the hands of such a city; no subject complains that his masters are unworthy of him. And we shall assuredly not be without witnesses; there are mighty monuments of our power which will make us the wonder of this and of succeeding ages; we shall not need the praises of Homer or of any other panegyrist whose poetry may please for the moment, although his representation of the facts will not bear the light of day. For we have compelled every land and every sea to open a path for our valour, and have everywhere planted eternal memorials of our friendship and of our enmity. Such is the city of whose sake these men nobly fought and died; they could not bear the thought that she might be taken from them; and every one of us who survive should gladly toil on her behalf.

I have dwelt upon the greatness of Athens because I want to show you that we are contending for a higher prize than those who enjoy none of these privileges, and to establish by manifest proof the merit of these men whom I am now commemorating. Their loftiest praise has been already spoken. For in magnifying the city I have magnified them, and men like them whose virtues made her glorious. And of how few Hellenes can it be said as of them, that their deeds when weighed in the balance have been found equal to their fame! . . . They resigned to hope their unknown chance of happiness; but in the fact of death they resolved to rely upon themselves alone. And when the moment came they were minded to resist and suffer, rather than to fly and save their lives; they ran away from the word of dishonour, but on the battlefield their feet stood fast, and in an instant, at the height of their fortune, they passed away from the scene, not of their fear, but of their glory.

Such was the end of these men; they were worthy of Athens, and the living need not desire to have a more heroic spirit, although they may pray for a less fatal issue. The value of such a spirit is not to be expressed in words. Any one can discourse to you forever about the advantages of a brave defence, which you know already. But instead of listening to him I would have you day by day fix your eyes upon the greatness of Athens, until you become filled with the love of her; and when you are impressed by the spectacle of her glory, reflect that this empire has been acquired by men who knew their duty and had the courage to do it, who in the hour of conflict had the fear of dishonour always present to them, and who, if ever they failed in an enterprise, would not allow their virtues to be lost to their country, but freely gave their lives to her as the fairest offering which they could present at her feast. The sacrifice which they collectively made was individually repaid to them; for they received again each one of himself a praise which grows not old, and the noblest of all sepulchres — I speak not of that in which their remains are laid, but of that in which their glory survives, and is proclaimed always and on every fitting occasion both in word and deed. For the whole earth is the sepulchre of famous men; not only are they commemorated by columns and inscriptions in their own country, but in foreign lands there dwells also an unwritten memorial of them, graven not on stone but in the hearts of men. Make them your examples, and, esteeming courage to be freedom and freedom to be happiness, do not weigh too nicely the perils of war. The unfortunate who has no hope of a change for the better has less reason to throw away his life than the prosperous who, if he survives, is always liable to a change for the worse, and to whom any accidental fall makes the most serious difference. To a man of spirit, cowardice and disaster coming together are far more bitter than death striking him unperceived at a time when he is full of courage and animated by the general hope.

Wherefore I do not now commiserate the parents of the dead who stand here; I would rather comfort them. You know that your life has been passed amid manifold vicissitudes; and that they may be deemed fortunate who have gained most honour, whether an honourable death like theirs, or an honourable sorrow like yours, and whose days have been so ordered that the term of their happiness is likewise the term of their life. I know how hard it is to make you feel this, when the good fortune of others will too often remind you of the gladness which once lightened your hearts. And sorrow is felt at the want of those blessings, not which a man never knew, but which were a part of his life before they were taken from him. Some of you are of an age at which they may hope to have other children, and they ought to bear their sorrow better; not only will the children who may hereafter be born make them forget their own lost ones, but the city will be doubly a gainer. She will not be left desolate, and she will be safer. For a man's counsel cannot have equal weight or worth, when he alone has no children to risk in the general danger. To those of you who have passed their prime, I say: Congratulate yourselves that you have been happy during the greater part of your days; remember that your life of sorrow will not last long, and be comforted by the glory of those who are gone. For the love of honour alone is ever young, and not riches, as some say, but honour is the delight of men when they are old and useless.

To you who are the sons and brothers of the departed, I see that the struggle to emulate them will be an arduous one. For all men praise the dead, and, however pre-eminent your virtue may be, hardly will you be thought, I do not say to equal, but even to approach them. The living have their rivals and detractors, but when a man is out of the way, the honour and good-will which he receives is unalloyed. And, if I am to speak of womanly virtues to those of you who will henceforth be widows, let me sum them up in one short admonition: To a woman not to show more weakness than is natural to her sex is a great glory, and not to be talked about for good or for evil among men.

I have paid the required tribute, in obedience to the law, making use of such fitting words as I had. The tribute of deeds has been paid in part; for the dead have been honourably interred, and it remains only that their children should be maintained at the public charge until they are grown up; this is the solid prize with which, as with a garland, Athens crowns her sons living and dead, after a struggle like theirs. For where the rewards of virtue are greatest, there the noblest citizens are enlisted in the service of the state. And now, when you have duly lamented, everyone his own dead, you may depart.

PLATO

From The Republic

This selection is from one of the world's most famous books of philosophy. Two events dominated the early life of Plato (428–348 B.C.E.), turning him away from the public life he was expected to lead. Plato was born in the shadow of the Peloponnesian War, which ended with the defeat of Athens in his twenty-third year. Disillusioned with the postwar governments, especially the democracy that condemned his teacher Socrates in 399 B.C.E., Plato forsook the political arena for a life of contemplation.

Plato's philosophical books, called dialogues because of the way they develop ideas from discussion and debate, follow Plato's teacher Socrates around the city-state of Athens. Often they begin, like *The Republic*, with a view of Socrates and other Athenian citizens enjoying the public spaces and festivals of the city. Notice in this introduction how territorial sovereignty creates public places and public activities.

Thinking Historically

Plato was neither a democrat nor politically active. Nevertheless, his life and his philosophy exemplify a commitment to the world of what McNeill calls "territorial sovereignty."

A primary source can support a particular viewpoint by espousing it, as Plato espouses the benefits of living in a territorial state or thinking about government. But a source can also provide clues about the

Plato, *The Republic of Plato*, trans. F. M. Cornford (London: Oxford University Press, 1941), 2–3, 177–79, 227–35.

society from which it comes. What clues in Plato's text show that his life and the lives of the people around him are shaped by the city-state?

Chapter 1

SOCRATES. I walked down to the Piraeus yesterday with Glaucon, the son of Ariston, to make my prayers to the goddess. As this was the first celebration of her festival, I wished also to see how the ceremony would be conducted. The Thracians, I thought, made as fine a show in the procession as our own people, though they did well enough. The prayers and the spectacle were over, and we were leaving to go back to the city, when from some way off Polemarchus, the son of Cephalus, caught sight of us starting homewards and sent his slave running to ask us to wait for him. The boy caught my garment from behind and gave me the message.

I turned around and asked where his master was.

There, he answered; coming up behind. Please wait.

Very well, said Glaucon; we will.

A minute later Polemarchus joined us, with Glaucon's brother, Adeimantus, and Niceratus, the son of Nicias, and some others who must have been at the procession.

Socrates, said Polemarchus, I do believe you are starting back to town and leaving us.

You have guessed right, I answered.

Well, he said, you see what a large party we are?

I do.

Unless you are more than a match for us, then, you must stay here.

Isn't there another alternative? said I; we might convince you that you must let us go.

How will you convince us, if we refuse to listen?

We cannot, said Glaucon.

Well, we shall refuse; make up your minds to that.

Here Adeimantus interposed: Don't you even know that in the evening there is going to be a torch-race on horseback in honour of the goddess?

On horseback! I exclaimed; that is something new. How will they do it? Are the riders going to race with torches and hand them on to one another?

Just so, said Polemarchus. Besides, there will be a festival lasting all night, which will be worth seeing. We will go out after dinner and look on. We shall find plenty of young men there and we can have a talk. So please stay, and don't disappoint us.

It looks as if we had better stay, said Glaucon.

Well, said I, if you think so, we will.
Accordingly, we went home with Polemarchus.

At the home of Polemarchus, the participants meet a number of other
old friends. After the usual greetings and gossip, the discussion begins
in response to Socrates' question, what is justice?

Each of the participants poses an idea of justice that Socrates challenges. Then Socrates outlines an ideal state that would be based on
absolute justice. In the following selection he is asked how this ideal
could ever come about.

Aside from the specifics of Socrates' argument, notice the way in
which public issues, for Socrates, are passionate personal concerns.

Chapter 18

But really, Socrates, Glaucon continued, if you are allowed to go on like
this, I am afraid you will forget all about the question you thrust aside
some time ago; whether a society so constituted can ever come into existence, and if so, how. No doubt, if it did exist, all manner of good things
would come about. I can even add some that you have passed over. Men
who acknowledged one another as fathers, sons, or brothers and always
used those names among themselves would never desert one another; so
they would fight with unequalled bravery. And if their womenfolk went
out with them to war, either in the ranks or drawn up in the rear to in-
timidate the enemy and act as a reserve in case of need, I am sure all this
would make them invincible. At home, too, I can see many advantages
you have not mentioned. But, since I admit that our commonwealth
would have all these merits and any number more, if once it came into existence, you need not describe it in further detail. All we have now to do
is to convince ourselves that it can be brought into being and how.

This is a very sudden onslaught, said I; you have no mercy on my shilly-
shallying. Perhaps you do not realize that, after I have barely escaped the
first two waves, the third, which you are now bringing down upon me, is
the most formidable of all. When you have seen what it is like and heard my
reply, you will be ready to excuse the very natural fears which made me
shrink from putting forward such a paradox for discussion.

The more you talk like that, he said, the less we shall be willing to
let you off from telling us how this constitution can come into existence; so you had better waste no more time.

Well, said I, let me begin by reminding you that what brought us to
this point was our inquiry into the nature of justice and injustice.

True; but what of that?

Merely this: suppose we do find out what justice is, are we going to demand that a man who is just shall have a character which exactly corresponds in every respect to the ideal of justice? Or shall we be satisfied if he comes as near to the ideal as possible and has in him a larger measure of that quality than the rest of the world?

That will satisfy me.

If so, when we set out to discover the essential nature of justice and injustice and what a perfectly just and a perfectly unjust man would be like, supposing them to exist, our purpose was to use them as ideal patterns: we were to observe the degree of happiness or unhappiness that each exhibited, and to draw the necessary inference that our own destiny would be like that of the one we most resembled. We did not set out to show that these ideals could exist in fact.

That is true.

Then suppose a painter had drawn an ideally beautiful figure complete to the last touch, would you think any the worse of him, if he could not show that a person as beautiful as that could exist?

No, I should not.

Well, we have been constructing in discourse the pattern of an ideal state. Is our theory any the worse, if we cannot prove it possible that a state so organized should be actually founded?

Surely not.

That, then, is the truth of the matter. But if, for your satisfaction, I am to do my best to show under what conditions our ideal would have the best chance of being realized, I must ask you once more to admit that the same principle applies here. Can theory ever be fully realized in practice? Is it not in the nature of things that action should come less close to truth than thought? People may not think so; but do you agree or not?

I do.

Then you must not insist upon my showing that this construction we have traced in thought could be reproduced in fact down to the last detail. You must admit that we shall have found a way to meet your demand for realization, if we can discover how a state might be constituted in the closest accordance with our description. Will not that content you? It would be enough for me.

And for me too.

Then our next attempt, it seems, must be to point out what defect in the working of existing states prevents them from being so organized, and what is the least change that would effect a transformation into this type of government — a single change if possible, or perhaps two; at any rate let us make the changes as few and insignificant as may be.

By all means.

Well, there is one change which, as I believe we can show, would bring about this revolution — not a small change, certainly, nor an easy one, but possible.

What is it?

I have now to confront what we called the third and greatest wave. But I must state my paradox, even though the wave should break in laughter over my head and drown me in ignominy. Now mark what I am going to say.

Go on.

Unless either philosophers become kings in their countries or those who are now called kings and rulers come to be sufficiently inspired with a genuine desire for wisdom; unless, that is to say, political power and philosophy meet together, while the many natures who now go their several ways in the one or the other direction are forcibly debarred from doing so, there can be no rest from troubles, my dear Glaucon, for states, nor yet, as I believe, for all mankind; nor can this commonwealth which we have imagined ever till then see the light of day and grow to its full stature. This it was that I have so long hung back from saying; I knew what a paradox it would be, because it is hard to see that there is no other way of happiness either for the state or for the individual.

Socrates, exclaimed Glaucon, after delivering yourself of such a pronouncement as that, you must expect a whole multitude of by no means contemptible assailants to fling off their coats, snatch up the handiest weapon, and make a rush at you, breathing fire and slaughter. If you cannot find arguments to beat them off and make your escape, you will learn what it means to be the target of scorn and derision.

Well, it was you who got me into this trouble.

Yes, and a good thing too. However, I will not leave you in the lurch. You shall have my friendly encouragement for what it is worth; and perhaps you may find me more complaisant than some would be in answering your questions. With such backing you must try to convince the unbelievers.

I will, now that I have such a powerful ally.

In arguing that philosophers should be kings, Plato (or Socrates) was parting ways with the democratic tradition of Athens. Like other conservative Athenians, he seems to have believed that democracy degenerated into mob rule. The root of this antidemocratic philosophy was the belief that the mass of people was horribly ignorant and only the rare philosopher had true understanding. Plato expressed this idea in one of the most famous passages in the history of philosophy: the parable of the cave.

Next, said I, here is a parable to illustrate the degrees in which our nature may be enlightened or unenlightened. Imagine the condition of

men living in a sort of cavernous chamber underground, with an entrance open to the light and a long passage all down the cave. Here
they have been from childhood, chained by the leg and also by the
neck, so that they cannot move and can see only what is in front of
them, because the chains will not let them turn their heads. At some
distance higher up is the light of a fire burning behind them; and between the prisoners and the fire is a track with a parapet built along it,
like the screen at a puppet-show, which hides the performers while they
show their puppets over the top.

I see, said he.

Now behind this parapet imagine persons carrying along various
artificial objects, including figures of men and animals in wood or stone
or other materials, which project above the parapet. Naturally, some of
these persons will be talking, others silent.

It is a strange picture, he said, and a strange sort of prisoners.

Like ourselves, I replied; for in the first place prisoners so confined
would have seen nothing of themselves or of one another, except the
shadows thrown by the firelight on the wall of the Cave facing them,
would they?

Not if all their lives they had been prevented from moving their
heads.

And they would have seen as little of the objects carried past.

Of course.

Now, if they could talk to one another, would they not suppose
that their words referred only to those passing shadows which they
saw?

Necessarily.

And suppose their prison had an echo from the wall facing them?
When one of the people crossing behind them spoke, they could only
suppose that the sound came from the shadow passing before their
eyes.

No doubt.

In every way, then, such prisoners would recognize as reality nothing but the shadows of those artificial objects.

Inevitably.

Now consider what would happen if their release from the chains
and the healing of their unwisdom should come about in this way. Suppose one of them was set free and forced suddenly to stand up, turn his
head, and walk with eyes lifted to the light; all these movements would
be painful, and he would be too dazzled to make out the objects whose
shadows he had been used to see. What do you think he would say, if
someone told him that what he had formerly seen was meaningless illusion, but now, being somewhat nearer to reality and turned towards
more real objects, he was getting a truer view? Suppose further that he

were shown the various objects being carried by and were made to say, in reply to questions, what each of them was. Would he not be perplexed and believe the objects now shown him to be not so real as what he formerly saw?

Yes, not nearly so real.

And if he were forced to look at the firelight itself, would not his eyes ache, so that he would try to escape and turn back to the things which he could see distinctly, convinced that they really were clearer than these other objects now being shown to him?

Yes.

And suppose someone were to drag him away forcibly up the steep and rugged ascent and not let him go until he had hauled him out into the sunlight, would he not suffer pain and vexation at such treatment, and, when he had come out into the light, find his eyes so full of its radiance that he could not see a single one of the things that he was now told were real?

Certainly he would not see them all at once.

He would need, then, to grow accustomed before he could see things in that upper world. At first it would be easiest to make out shadows, and then the images of men and things reflected in water, and later on the things themselves. After that, it would be easier to watch the heavenly bodies and the sky itself by night, looking at the light of the moon and stars rather than the Sun and the Sun's light in the daytime.

Yes, surely.

Last of all, he would be able to look at the Sun and contemplate its nature, not as it appears when reflected in water or any alien medium, but as it is in itself in its own domain.

No doubt.

And now he would begin to draw the conclusion that it is the Sun that produces the seasons and the course of the year and controls everything in the visible world, and moreover is in a way the cause of all that he and his companions used to see.

Clearly he would come at last to that conclusion.

Then if he called to mind his fellow prisoners and what passed for wisdom in his former dwelling-place, he would surely think himself happy in the change and be sorry for them. They may have had a practice of honouring and commending one another, with prizes for the man who had the keenest eye for the passing shadows and the best memory for the order in which they followed or accompanied one another, so that he could make a good guess as to which was going to come next. Would our released prisoner be likely to covet those prizes or to envy the men exalted to honour and power in the Cave? Would he not feel like Homer's Achilles, that he would far sooner "be on earth as a hired servant in the house of a landless man" or endure anything rather than go back to his old beliefs and live in the old way?

Yes, he would prefer any fate to such a life.

Now imagine what would happen if he went down again to take his former seat in the Cave. Coming suddenly out of the sunlight, his eyes would be filled with darkness. He might be required once more to deliver his opinion on those shadows, in competition with the prisoners who had never been released, while his eyesight was still dim and unsteady; and it might take some time to become used to the darkness. They would laugh at him and say that he had gone up only to come back with his sight ruined; it was worth no one's while even to attempt the ascent. If they could lay hands on the man who was trying to set them free and lead them up, they would kill him.

Yes, they would.

Every feature in this parable, my dear Glaucon, is meant to fit our earlier analysis. The prison dwelling corresponds to the region revealed to us through the sense of sight, and the firelight within it to the power of the Sun. The ascent to see the things in the upper world you may take as standing for the upward journey of the soul into the region of the intelligible; then you will be in possession of what I surmise, since that is what you wish to be told. Heaven knows whether it is true; but this, at any rate, is how it appears to me. In the world of knowledge, the last thing to be perceived and only with great difficulty is the essential Form of Goodness. Once it is perceived, the conclusion must follow that, for all things, this is the cause of whatever is right and good; in the visible world it gives birth to light and to the lord of light, while it is itself sovereign in the intelligible world and the parent of intelligence and truth. Without having had a vision of this Form no one can act with wisdom, either in his own life or in matters of state.

So far as I can understand, I share your belief.

Then you may also agree that it is no wonder if those who have reached their height are reluctant to manage the affairs of men. Their souls long to spend all their time in that upper world — naturally enough, if here once more our parable holds true. Nor, again, is it at all strange that one who comes from the contemplation of divine things to the miseries of human life should appear awkward and ridiculous when, with eyes still dazed and not yet accustomed to the darkness, he is compelled, in a law court or elsewhere, to dispute about the shadows of justice or the images that cast those shadows, and to wrangle over the notions of what is right in the minds of men who have never beheld Justice itself.

It is not at all strange.

No; a sensible man will remember that the eyes may be confused in two ways — by a change from light to darkness or from darkness to light; and he will recognize that the same thing happens to the soul. When he sees it troubled and unable to discern anything clearly, instead of laughing thoughtlessly, he will ask whether, coming from a brighter existence, its unaccustomed vision is obscured by the darkness, in which case he will think its condition enviable and its life a happy one; or whether, emerging from the depths of ignorance, it is dazzled by excess of light. If so, he will rather feel sorry for it; or, if he were inclined to laugh, that would be less ridiculous than to laugh at the soul which has come down from the light.

That is a fair statement.

If this is true, then, we must conclude that education is not what it is said to be by some, who profess to put knowledge into a soul which does not possess it, as if they could put sight into blind eyes. On the contrary, our own account signifies that the soul of every man does possess the power of learning the truth and the organ to see it with; and that, just as one might have to turn the whole body round in order that the eye should see light instead of darkness, so the entire soul must be turned away from this changing world, until its eye can bear to contemplate reality and that supreme splendour which we have called the Good. Hence there may well be an art whose aim would be to effect this very thing, the conversion of the soul, in the readiest way; not to put the power of sight into the soul's eye, which already has it, but to ensure that, instead of looking in the wrong direction, it is turned the way it ought to be.

Yes, it may well be so.

It looks, then, as though wisdom were different from those ordinary virtues, as they are called, which are not far removed from bodily qualities, in that they can be produced by habituation and exercise in a soul which has not possessed them from the first. Wisdom, it seems, is certainly the virtue of some diviner faculty, which never loses its power, though its use for good or harm depends on the direction towards which it is turned. You must have noticed in dishonest men with a reputation for sagacity the shrewd glance of a narrow intelligence piercing the objects to which it is directed. There is nothing wrong with their power of vision, but it has been forced into the service of evil, so that the keener its sight, the more harm it works.

Quite true.

And yet if the growth of a nature like this had been pruned from earliest childhood, cleared of those clinging overgrowths which come of gluttony and all luxurious pleasure and, like leaden weights charged with affinity to this mortal world, hang upon the soul, bending its vision downwards; if, freed from these, the soul were turned round towards true reality, then this same power in these very men would see the truth as keenly as the objects it is turned to now.

Yes, very likely.

Is it not also likely, or indeed certain after what has been said, that a state can never be properly governed either by the uneducated who know nothing of truth or by men who are allowed to spend all their days in the pursuit of culture? The ignorant have no single mark before their eyes at which they must aim in all the conduct of their own lives and of affairs of state; and the others will not engage in action if they can help it, dreaming that, while still alive, they have been translated to the Islands of the Blest.

Quite true.

It is for us, then, as founders of a commonwealth, to bring compulsion to bear on the noblest natures. They must be made to climb the ascent to the vision of Goodness, which we called the highest object of knowledge; and, when they have looked upon it long enough, they must not be allowed, as they now are, to remain on the heights, refusing to come down again to the prisoners or to take any part in their labours and rewards, however much or little these may be worth.

Shall we not be doing them an injustice, if we force on them a worse life than they might have?

You have forgotten again, my friend, that the law is not concerned to make any one class specially happy, but to ensure the welfare of the commonwealth as a whole. By persuasion or constraint it will unite the citizens in harmony, making them share whatever benefits each class can contribute to the common good; and its purpose in forming men of that spirit was not that each should be left to go his own way, but that they should be instrumental in binding the community into one.

True, I had forgotten.

You will see, then, Glaucon, that there will be no real injustice in compelling our philosophers to watch over and care for the other citizens. We can fairly tell them that their compeers in other states may quite reasonably refuse to collaborate: there they have sprung up, like a self-sown plant, in despite of their country's institutions; no one has fostered their growth, and they cannot be expected to show gratitude for a care they have never received. "But," we shall say, "it is not so with you. We have brought you into existence for your country's sake as well as for your own, to be like leaders and king-bees in a hive; you have been better and more thoroughly educated than those others and hence you are more capable of playing your part both as men of thought and as men of action. You must go down, then, each in his turn, to live with the rest and let your eyes grow accustomed to the darkness. You will then see a thousand times better than those who live there always; you will recognize every image for what it is and know what it represents, because you have seen justice, beauty, and goodness in their reality; and so you and we shall find life in our commonwealth no mere dream, as it is in most existing states, where men live fighting one another about shadows and quarrelling for power, as if that were a great prize; whereas in truth government can be at its best and free from dissension only where the destined rulers are least desirous of holding office."

Quite true.

Then will our pupils refuse to listen and to take their turns at sharing in the work of the community, though they may live together for most of their time in a purer air?

No; it is a fair demand, and they are fair-minded men. No doubt, unlike any ruler of the present day, they will think of holding power as an unavoidable necessity.

Yes, my friend; for the truth is that you can have a well-governed society only if you can discover for your future rulers a better way of life than being in office; then only will power be in the hands of men who are rich, not in gold, but in the wealth that brings happiness, a good and wise life. All goes wrong when, starved for lack of anything good in their own lives, men turn to public affairs hoping to snatch from thence the happiness they hunger for. They set about fighting for power, and this internecine conflict ruins them and their country. The life of true philosophy is the only one that looks down upon offices of state; and access to power must be confined to men who are not in love with it; otherwise rivals will start fighting. So whom else can you compel to undertake the guardianship of the commonwealth, if not those who, besides understanding best the principles of government, enjoy a nobler life than the politician's and look for rewards of a different kind?

There is indeed no other choice.

REFLECTIONS

Caste and territorial sovereignty were alternate but equally effective systems of social organization in the ancient world. Both worked. Both allocated jobs and rewards, arranged marriages and created families, assured the peace and fought wars. Neither was necessarily more just, tyrannical, expensive, or arbitrary. Yet each system created its own complex world of ideas and behavior.

Caste and territorial sovereignty were not the only bases for identity in the ancient world. In many societies, a person's identity was based on family ties of a different sort than caste. In China, the family lineage, constituting many generations of relatives, was particularly important. Almost every society in human history organized itself around families to a certain extent, and most societies also had a sense of multiple family units called clans or tribes. The Indian caste system was only one variant of these multifamily systems, and some non-Indian societies had divisions resembling castes.

Family, clan, and tribe are still important determinants of identity in the modern world. In some societies, the authority of a tribal leader, clan elder, or family patriarch rivals that of the state. Nevertheless, the modern world is made up of states. We live according to the law of the land, not that of kinship. In the United States, one obeys the laws of the United States, regardless of who one knows. If the police pull you over for driving through a red light, you do not say that your father gave you permission or your uncle ordered you to drive through red lights. In the territory of the United States, you obey the laws of the United States and the particular state in which you find yourself. When a citizen of the United States goes to Canada, he or she must obey the laws of Canada. This is the world of states, of territorial sovereignty.

One of the major transitions in human history in the last five thousand years has been the rise of territorial sovereignty and the supplanting of the authority of the law of the state over the rule of family, clan, tribe, and caste. This is what developed in ancient Greece twenty-five hundred years ago. It did not occur completely and finally with Cleisthenes or even with the rise of Greek democracy in the fifth century B.C.E. Tribal alliances reasserted themselves periodically in Greece and elsewhere, in the Middle Ages and in modern society. The establishment of territorial sovereignty and ultimately of civil society, where political parties replaced tribes, was gradual and interrupted and is still continuing. Aristotle tells us that after Cleisthenes, Greeks took new surnames based on their new civic "tribes." That would have ended the rule of the old family-based tribes, but we know the old tribal names did not disappear. A thorough transition would mean that political parties would express entirely civic goals without a trace of tribal identity, but that too is a process that still continues. In modern Ireland, for instance, one of the political parties, Finn Gael, means literally the tribe of the Gael. In the wake of the U.S. invasion of Iraq in 2003, many Americans have learned how difficult it is to impose a system of territorial sovereignty on a society where tribal identities are strong.

India today is also a modern state in which the law of the land applies to all regardless of caste, family, or tribe. In fact, recent Indian governments have outlawed discrimination based on caste, and created affirmative action programs on behalf of Dahlits, the outcastes or untouchables. Nevertheless, Indian newspapers still run matrimonial ads that specify caste, though international Web sites often do not.

Modern society encourages us to be many things. Family and caste can still play a role. Religion, ethnicity, national origin, even race are given an importance in modern society that was often absent or irrelevant in ancient societies. But with the civic society produced by territorial sovereignty comes not only citizenship but also a range of chosen identities based on career, education, job, hobbies, friends, and a wide range of living possibilities. These choices can sometimes overwhelm. Sometimes the indelibility of family, caste, or birth can seem a comfort. But over the long term of history, the range and choice of identities seem likely to increase, and more and more of them will likely be voluntary rather than stamped on the birth certificate.

4

Classical Civilizations
and Empires

China and Rome,
300 B.C.E.–300 C.E.

HISTORICAL CONTEXT

Both China and Rome expanded from small states to large empires around 200 B.C.E. (See Maps 4.1 and 4.2.) Each empire ruled at least fifty million people in an area of over one and a half million square miles. Both regimes managed to fund and field enormous armies, tax and control competitors for power in their own aristocracies, and convert millions to their cultural ideas. After the second century C.E., however, both empires became increasingly vulnerable to the nomadic peoples on their frontiers whom they called "barbarians."

This simultaneous development of the two great empires of the classical age did not occur without contact or mutual interaction. During this period the great Silk Road developed across central Asia, Roman senators complained of the price of Chinese silks, and Roman coins were found throughout China. Nevertheless, these two great empires developed largely independently of each other. The Greek roots of Roman civilization were well developed in the Roman Republic of the last centuries B.C.E., and Han China continued the traditions of earlier Chinese dynasties stretching back a thousand years. For these reasons, a comparison of the two great empires broadens our understanding of the possibilities, and limits, of life in the classical age two thousand years ago.

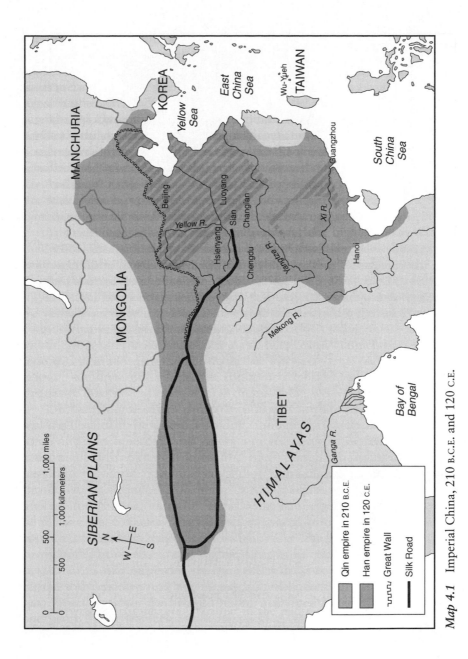

Map 4.1 Imperial China, 210 B.C.E. and 120 C.E.

Qin empire in 210 B.C.E.

Han empire in 120 C.E.

Great Wall

Silk Road

SIBERIAN PLAINS

MONGOLIA

MANCHURIA

KOREA

Yellow Sea

East China Sea

TAIWAN

Wu-Yüeh

Beijing

Luoyang

Yellow R.

Sian

Changian

Hsienyang

Chengdu

Yangtze R.

Xi R.

Guangzhou

South China Sea

Hanoi

Mekong R.

TIBET

HIMALAYAS

Ganga R.

Bay of Bengal

1,000 miles

1,000 kilometers

500

500

0

0

N

E

W

S

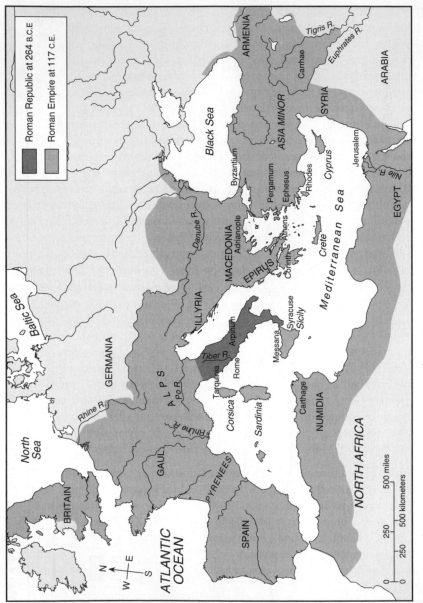

Map 4.2 The Roman Empire, 264 B.C.E. and 117 C.E.

Legend:
- Roman Republic at 264 B.C.E
- Roman Empire at 117 C.E.

ATLANTIC OCEAN

N
W — E
S

North Sea

Baltic Sea

BRITAIN

GERMANIA

GAUL

Rhine R.

PYRENEES

SPAIN

ALPS

Po R.

Rhône R.

Corsica

Sardinia

Tarquinia

Tiber R.

Rome

Arpinum

Messana

Carthage

NUMIDIA

NORTH AFRICA

Danube R.

ILLYRIA

MACEDONIA

EPIRUS

Adrianople

Athens

Corinth

Syracuse

Sicily

Mediterranean Sea

Crete

Black Sea

Byzantium

Pergamum

Ephesus

Rhodes

Cyprus

ASIA MINOR

ARMENIA

Carrhae

Tigris R.

Euphrates R.

SYRIA

ARABIA

Jerusalem

Nile R.

EGYPT

0   250   500 miles
0   250   500 kilometers

THINKING HISTORICALLY
Making Comparisons

"Compare and contrast" is one of the most common types of exam instructions and is not limited to history courses. Students know that the instruction asks them to find similarities and differences. Even when one is asked simply to "compare" two things, the process usually involves looking for similarities and differences because likenesses have no meaning except in reference to those things which are not alike. To understand something, perhaps even to *see* it, we must first perceive how it is different from other things.

In our daily lives, when we encounter something new, we sift through our memory for similarities and differences. We learn through a process of almost instinctively going back and forth between those things that are similar and those that are different. When we try to be more systematic, however, we might focus on similarities and differences separately. We might notice and list similarities first because generally differences make more sense in terms of similarities, rather than vice versa. For example, if we want to buy a car we begin with those that have a similar appeal, price range, or features, and then examine the differences. We wouldn't start with cars that were radically different and then look for similarities.

Historians also generally begin with cases that are similar, as we have here with our comparison of the Chinese Han and Roman empires. Given all of the similarities mentioned in the first paragraph of this chapter, it becomes interesting to ask about the differences. There would not be much point in beginning with two different entities, say the Chinese Han Empire and medieval Albania, and asking how, despite their differences, they were similar. The chances are that any similarities we discovered would be too general (they both had agriculture), coincidental, or meaningless (they both later became communist).

Ultimately, we compare to understand more than we might learn from examining each case in isolation. In comparing the ancient Chinese and Roman empires, we might seek to understand more about ancient empires, the course of change in ancient societies, or empires in general. Almost invariably, by comparison we also learn something about each of the things compared: in this case China and Rome. Often a good comparison also leads us to new questions, new topics, and new comparisons as well.

S. A. M. ADSHEAD

China and Rome Compared

In this selection a modern historian of China compares the Chinese Han dynasty with the Roman Empire. You will have to read carefully because his analysis is quite dense. He uses a complex vocabulary and covers a wide range of factors—from food to social classes to writing and roads. How, according to the author, were these two empires similar? How were they different? Which of these factors (showing similarities or differences) would you judge to be the most important, and why? In addition, can you think of any similarities or differences between Rome and China that are not mentioned in this reading? If so, how important are they?

Thinking Historically

The easiest way to make a comparison is to list the similarities in one column and the differences in another. You might do this for Rome and China, according to Adshead. Thus in the similarities column, you might begin with such items as empire, 1.5 million square miles, conquered aristocracies, and so on. After you have listed as many items as you can in each column, it might be useful to ask yourself what relation exists between the similarities and differences.

Notice that Adshead begins with similarities and then turns to differences. As we said in the introduction, this is a standard procedure, because differences are only meaningful in terms of some assumed or recognized similarities. Generally, we assume that the similarities are more important than the differences. The differences are mere variations on the larger similarity. Here, however, Adshead says that the differences between Rome and China are greater than the similarities. What might he mean? Are Adshead's differences more important? Are the similarities more superficial? Return to your list of similarities and differences and decide.

This section examines first the similarities between Han China and the classical, pre-Constantinian Roman empire and second, the differences. The conclusion will be that the differences outweighed the similarities.

S. A. M. Adshead, *China in World History*, 3rd ed. (London: Macmillan and New York: St. Martin's, 2000), 4–7, 9–16, 17–19.

Similarities

These may be divided into origin, organization and outcome.

Origin

Both the Han and Roman empires began in the third century BC with the military expansion of conservative, relatively unideological aristocratic states on the western peripheries of their respective civilized zones. The Roman republic was not a full member of the Hellenistic world; the duchy of Ch'in[1] was an outsider in the Chou confederacy. Both expansions were based on a combination of political stability, abundant rural manpower nourished by advanced agriculture, and disciplined infantry, which was pitted against political instability, artificial urban growth and over-specialized military technology. Both were directed first against mercantile rivals: Carthage, the emporium of tin and silver in the West and Ch'i, the emporium of salt and iron in the East; and then against colonial frontiers: the Hellenistic east and Gaul, Ch'u and Wu-yueh. In both cases conquest was followed by civil war. It ended in the elimination of the aristocracies which had organized the expansion and the establishment of bureaucracies which disguised their novelty by archaizing their ideology and exaggerating their continuity. Thus the neotraditionalist refoundation of the republic by Augustus was paralleled by Han-Wu-ti' *feng* and *shan* sacrifices in imitation of the sage rulers of antiquity. In both cases the *novi homines*[2] of the bureaucracy came to be supplied by men from the defeated but more educated east, freedmen, from Greece and scholars from Honan, through the patronage of aggressive and colourful empress-dowagers: Agrippina in the West, empress-dowager Teng in the East.

Organization

In terms of organization the Han and Roman empires had much in common, both problems and solutions. The Roman empire under Hadrian covered 1,763,000 square miles; the Han empire towards the end of the second century AD covered 1,532,000 square miles. Both faced similar problems of distance and time in administering an area half the size of the United States with a technology in which nothing went faster than a horse. Both sought a solution in the cultural solidarity of elites: the spontaneous coordination produced by the shared values, institutions,

---

[1]Duchy of Ch'in (256–206 B.C.E.). Unified China in 221 B.C.E. by conquering the larger Chou confederacy (1050–256 B.C.E.). [Ed.]

[2]Latin for "new men." Usually refers to a newly created class of powerful or wealthy men. In this case, Adshead means new recruits to the bureaucracies. [Ed.]

vocabulary and reactions of, on the one hand, the classical *paedeia**
and, on the other, the Confucian *wen-yen*.[3] Both empires relied on this
solidarity as their foundation, both built roads to foster it and facilitate
military flexibility, and both constructed great walls to give that flexibility time to operate and to avoid the costly continuous mass mobilization
which might destroy culturalism by militarism. In both empires, the
dominant element of the army was the infantry; the dominant colour of
the culture, literary, with poetry giving way to prose. In both the army
was opposed by cavalry enemies, the Iranian cataphract[4] and the Hsu-
ing-nu light horseman, and in both the culture of the elite was challenged by barbarians, *sectaries*,[5] soldiers, and peasants in varying degrees of alienation from it. In both the challenge was for a long time
contained by political skill, social flexibility, economic prosperity and
cultural syncretism, underpinned by military effectiveness. When the
system needed reconstruction, the Severi of 193–235, provincial lawyers
turned soldiers, populists and patrons of exotic religions, were closely
paralleled by Ts'ao Ts'ao and the Wei dynasty of 184–265, outsiders
from a eunuch background, meritocrats, founders of military colonies,
and friends of unorthodox, new-style philosophy.

Outcome

Despite reconstruction, by the Severi and the tetrarchy and by the Wei
and the Chin, the long-term outcome was the same: the rise of barbarism and religion; the collapse of the too-costly superstructure in one
half of the empire; its survival, reformed, in the other. Both the Roman
and the Han empires collapsed in their north-western halves through a
mixture of institutional hypertrophy, military pronunciamentos, ecclesiastical non-cooperation, and barbarian invasions. Both survived in
slightly new forms in their south-eastern halves with a new capital and
the establishment of a foreign, previously "sectarian," ecumenical religion which gradually conquered the north-west as well. In the northwest, the leaders of the invading barbarian armies, often ex-imperial
foederati,[6] set up kingdoms but, except in the vicinity of the *limes*,[7]
there was no serious linguistic change. In both China and the West, society ruralized and centred itself upon self-contained aristocratic es-

*py DEE oh
[3]*Paedeia* and *wen-yen* are names for the educational systems of Rome and China, respectively. *Paedeia* or *paideia* refers to humanistic Greek culture; *wen-yen* refers to humanistic
Confucian education. [Ed.]
[4]Heavily armed horsemen. [Ed.]
[5]Members of religious sects, especially Christians and Buddhists. [Ed.]
[6]Allies of Rome by treaty (*foedus*). [Ed.]
[7]Roman frontier or wall at Roman boundary. [Ed.]

tates, lay and monastic which, with their immunities, vassals, retainers, "guests," and servants, were more sociological than economic units. In both, a new superstructure, a medieval civilization with deeper roots and firmer foundations than its antique predecessor, was eventually constructed, but in neither was it built on the old plan or centred on the segment of the old system which had survived in the south-east. Neither Constantinople nor Nanking were to be a basis for the medieval world.

Differences

These may be grouped as contrasts of foundation, architectonics, and decay which paralleled the similarities of origin, organization, and outcome, qualified their genuineness, and limited their significance.

Foundation

. . . In the Roman west, the principal crop was wheat or its relatives barley and oats. In Han China, on the other hand, although wheat and rice were known, the principal crop was millet. Millet is a less palatable grain than wheat, but it had a higher productivity in pre-modern conditions in both quantity sown and area sown. Before the nineteenth century, the ratio of wheat harvested to wheat sown was seldom more than 6:1, while the rate for millet was 10:1. Similarly, while the average pre-modern yield of wheat was 6 quintals a hectare, that of millet was 12 quintals a hectare.

The original difference in productivity was compounded by the difference of natural milieu. In the Roman west, grain was grown on light downland soils which, to maintain their nitrogen content and hence fertility, required fallowing in alternate years. In China, on the other hand, grain was grown on the porous loess[8] of the north-west hills which, because of its permeability by the chemicals of the air and subsoil, was self-renewing and did not require either fallowing or manuring. The amount of arable land under grain at any one time in China was thus double that in Rome.

By the Han period, a higher percentage of [China's] arable acreage was irrigated than in the Roman west, and a larger proportion of the irrigation was by large-scale macrohydraulic means than elsewhere. . . . If this advantage be added to those of millet yields and the absence of fallowing, then average Chinese grain yields would have been eight times those of the Roman west. The two societies had different nutritional bases.

---

[8]Wind-blown dusty but fertile soil of northern China. [Ed.]

A corollary of this greater intensity of Chinese grain farming was a difference in the role of animal husbandry between China and the Roman west. The difference was not as pronounced as it was later to become, but already the two societies were oriented in different directions. Because of the self-renewal of the loess, Chinese arable farming did not require animals for manure; because it did not need to lie fallow there were no unsown fields free for temporary stocking; and because farms could be smaller thanks to the higher grain yields, there was less marginal land for permanent pasture and less need for ploughing animals. Thus, though China and Europe shared the same domestic animals—cows, horses, sheep, goats, pigs—and, as we shall see, China in antiquity used the horse more efficiently than did the West, in China animals were ancillary while in Europe they were essential. True, in antiquity, animals, in particular horses, were much fewer in Europe than they subsequently became (why could Pheidippides[9] not find a mount between Athens and Sparta?), while the opposite was true in China, but already the Chinese farmer was oriented to pure arablism in contrast to the European farmer who was oriented to a mixture of arablism and pastoralism.

This difference, in turn, contributed to others: different attitudes to space (the pastoralist can never have too much of it); to mobility (the pastoralist has both ends and means for it); to energy (the pastoralist will be lavish with it so long as it is non-human); to nomadic pastoralism (the mixed farmer can compromise, the pure arablist cannot); to food (the pastoralist will structure his meal round a main course of meat where the arablist will blend a collection of vegetable dishes); and even to human relations generally (the pastoralist is a herder whereas the arablist is a grower). In *Pilgrim's Regress*, C. S. Lewis[10] called the Jews the "shepherd people": it would be an appropriate name for all westerners. Chinese regalia never included the sword. Even more significant is that Chinese official insignia never included the shepherd's crook, the pastoral staff.

Chinese agriculture was further differentiated from Roman by China's superiority in metallurgy in antiquity, particularly iron. Needham[11] has shown that while the West could not liquify and cast iron until the fourteenth century AD, so that all ancient and medieval iron in the West was low-carbon wrought iron, China produced cast-iron hoes, ploughshares, picks, axes, and swords from the fourth century BC. This metallurgical superiority affected both agriculture and war. The Chinese arable farmer, in addition to his other advantages,

[9]Greek hero who, according to legend, ran the twenty-six miles from Marathon to Athens to announce the Greek victory over the Persians. Aspiring "marathon" runners should also know he collapsed and died after announcing the news. [Ed.]

[10]Twentieth-century English Christian writer. [Ed.]

[11]Joseph Needham was a famous scholar of Chinese science. [Ed.]

had more and better iron implements than his Roman counterpart. If China clung to infantry where Constantinople switched to cavalry, it was partly because the Chinese footsoldier was better armed and was better able to cope with his equestrian opponent than the Roman legionary. For example, it is doubtful if Roman artisans could have produced the precision-made bronze trigger mechanism required for the Chinese cross-bow. Consequently the Han never suffered a Carrhae or an Adrianople.[12] The capacity to cast iron, in turn, raised the level of steel production both in quantity and quality. Wrought iron is low in carbon, cast iron is high in carbon, and steel lies in between. For premodern siderurgy it was easier to decarbonize than recarbonize. So, by the Han period, the Chinese, starting with cast iron, could produce considerable quantities of good steel by what was, in essence, the Bessemer process of oxygenation, i.e., liquifying the iron while simultaneously blowing away part of the carbon; while the West, starting with wrought iron, could only produce limited amounts of poor steel by heating the iron in charcoal. The Damascus and Toledo blades,[13] which were later to so impress the Crusaders, were the products of transplanted Chinese technology and when Pliny the Younger spoke admiringly of Seric iron, he was probably thinking of Chinese steel.

Intellectual technology.   All four primary civilizations shared the primary human tool of articulate speech. Western Eurasia, East Asia, and Amerindia all possessed the basic tool for higher organization: a system of writing. In China and the West, but not in Amerindia, writing was sufficiently old and diffused to constitute the necessary vehicle for education: a literary tradition. As between China and the West, however, there was significant differences in all three intellectual techniques; speech, writing, and literary tradition.

Languages, one might assume are born equal. Each can express the full range of human consciousness and each is completely translatable into every other: as Leonardo Bruni[14] put it: "Nothing is said in Greek that cannot be said in Latin." All languages are equal vehicles of speech and writing, prose and poetry, even though one may think, with Robert Frost, that poetry is what gets lost in translation. The Chomskyan hypothesis of a single transformational grammar or syntactic structure governing all languages supports the assumption of linguistic equivalence. Yet, it may be argued, at a more superficial level, languages are not equal and the inequality may have implications for the thought

---

[12]In the Battle of Carrhae in 53 B.C.E. the Romans suffered a serious defeat at the hands of the Parthians whose calvary and archery tactics overwhelmed the Roman soldiers. The Battle of Adrianople in 378 C.E. against the Huns was the beginning of the end for the Roman Empire. [Ed.]

[13]Muslim steel made in Syrian and Spanish cities. [Ed.]

[14]Leonardo Bruni (c. 1370–1444) was a leading humanist and historian from Tuscany.

expressed in them. In particular one may consider whether or not the different sound/meaning ratio in Chinese as compared to the Indo-European languages influenced thought patterns in China and the West. Chinese, it has been said, "is exceptionally rich in homophones," or, to put it another way, it operates with a "poverty of sounds." Thus modern Mandarin uses only 1280 sounds to express what must be presumed to be the same gamut of meaning as the phoneme-rich Indo-European languages. Although archaic and ancient Chinese, the languages of Confucius and the middle ages, may have had a wider phonological range than Mandarin, economy in phonemes seems to be an original and basic characteristic of Chinese speech. The effect has been a wider indeterminacy of meaning *vis-à-vis* sound, a greater dependence on context and audience to establish signification, and a bias in favour of nuance, indirection, allusion and paradigm, as compared to the cruder, more direct, less allusive, more syntagmatic[15] languages of the West. The medium does not prescribe the content of the message. It may be that nothing is said in Chinese that cannot be said in English, and vice versa: but it does determine the level of articulation, the degree of thematization, the place on the implicit/explicit scale. In this sense, the Chinese language with its peculiar sound/meaning ratio was an invitation both to the collective introversion which Jung[16] found characteristic of the eastern mind and to the protocol thinking which Granet[17] ascribed to the Chinese. . . .

Signification, already depotentiated by the sound/meaning ratio, was further beclouded by the accommodating but unresponsive script. The alphabet was an arithmetic tailored exactly to sound and significance; the *tzu*[18] were an algebra which could mean everything or nothing. Once again the medium smothered the message.

By the beginning of the Christian era, both China and the West possessed a body of literature and a tradition of study which was, on one hand, a vehicle of education and, on the other, both a means and end of government. Both the Han and the Roman empires, as we saw above, were founded upon a *paedeia*. The character of the *paedeias*, however, were different. The Chinese tradition was paradigmatic, introverted to concepts, ethical; the Western tradition was syntagmatic, extraverted to things, metaphysical. In both cultures there was a certain transition from mythology to philosophy, but it had been made to different degrees and in opposite directions. In Greece the concrete myth-

[15]Ordered into a collection of statements or propositions (usually logically ordered). [Ed.]

[16]Carl Jung was a Swiss student of Sigmund Freud who generalized about cultural traits. [Ed.]

[17]Marcel Granet was an early twentieth-century French scholar of Chinese civilization. [Ed.]

[18]Chinese characters. [Ed.]

ology of Homer and Hesiod was overlaid by the equally concrete pre-Socratic cosmologies, and both gods and cosmologies were eventually subsumed in the mathematical *Dieu cosmique* of orthodox Platonism or the transcendent *Dieu inconnu*[19] of gnosticism. Concrete paradigm was replaced by concrete syntagmata and then by abstract syntagmata. There was a complete transition from mythology to philosophy. In China, *per contra*, the concrete mythology of the Shang and the early Chou was dissolved by, on the one hand, historicization (conversion of gods to heroes and dynastic founders, an inverse Euhemerism[20]) and, on the other, ritualization (absorption of myth in liturgy), leaving only abstractions like *t'ien, tao,* and *te*[21] behind. Paradigm was reinforced by theoretical abstraction and practical concreteness and philosophy's problem was not the structure of the cosmos but the method of elucidating the paradigms. There was only a partial transition from mythology to philosophy.

The Chinese *paideia*, more than the Western, was centred on form rather than content. It was a communications system rather than a body of doctrine. The *Shih-ching*[22] provided the model for poetry, the *Shu-ching*[23] for prose, and poetry was preferred to prose as being more highly formalized. In both China and the West, the past was a prototype for the present, but where Alexander the Great used the model of Achilles to assert his personality and break continuity, the Han emperors used the model of the sage-emperors to conceal theirs and buttress it. History was understood not, as in Thucydides, as tragedy or pathology, but, as in the *Ch'un-ch'iu*, as annals where morality taught by example. In the *Li-chi*, ethics were reduced to protocol and the *I-ching* provided not an actual cosmology but a repository of concepts for all possible cosmologies.

Similarly, Confucius (author of *Lun-yu*) and Lao-tzu* (author of *Tao-te ching*) had no doctrine to teach, no wisdom to impart. They

---

[19]*Dieu cosmique* and *dieu inconnu*: literally "cosmic god" of science and "unknown god" of gnosticism. The argument is that Greek philosophy led to the idea of a governing god of the universe and that later religious mystics, for whom the visible world was less "real," believed the world was run by an unknown or invisible god. [Ed.]

[20]Euhemerus (ca. 300 B.C.E.) was a Greek philosopher who argued that the gods were once heroic people who had been turned into mythical beings and that mythological stories were elaborations of actual events. This process of rationalizing mythology is called euhemerism. It is sometimes used more broadly for an extremely rational, debunking, or nonreligious attitude. Here, however, Adshead uses it literally, suggesting that Chinese philosophers did just the opposite: turning gods into real people and treating myths as if they were real and abstractions as if they were concrete. [Ed.]

[21]*T'ien* means heaven, god, or nature. *Tao* means the "way" as in the way of nature. *Te* means power or virtue. Adshead's point is that Chinese retained abstractions while the Greeks looked for specific and concrete origins for abstract concepts. [Ed.]

[22]The first and classic collection of Chinese poetry. [Ed.]

[23]The classic collection of documents, or history. [Ed.]

*low TZOO

were concerned not to advance views, but to define the conditions for any views: linguistic reform in the one case, the recognition of the inadequacy of language in the other. They defined the conditions for debate, not as a modern philosopher to clear the ground for argument, but because for them to settle the medium was to settle the message: the categories of thought are thought, thought and reality are isomorphic, and all thought needs are the proper paradigms, the little red book of reality. This tradition was in marked contrast with that of the West where, whether in Indian cosmology, Zoroastrian ethical prophecy, Greek empiricism and logic, or Old Testament theocentrism, there was a recognition of the duality of paradigm and syntagma and the primacy of the latter. In this major intellectual contrast with China, all the minor contrasts within the West—the one and the many, metaphysics and ethics, rationalism and religion, science and intentionality analysis—were swallowed up.

Architectonics

In addition to the contrast of physical and intellectual foundations between China and the West, there was also a contrast in architectonics. The social and political structures erected on the foundations differed in ground plan, spatial relations, and decor.

Ground plans.   The Roman empire was laid out like an amp[h]itheatre around the arena of the Mediterranean. Rome itself was the imperial box, the older coastal provinces were the stalls, the new inland *limes* provinces were the heavily buttressed upper circle. The internal differentiation was between, on the one hand, upper and lower, *limes* and city, and on the other, sun and shade, the old urbanization of the east, the new urbanization of the west. The Han empire, *per contra*, was laid out like a wheel. The region of the two imperial capitals, Ch'ang-an and Lo-yang, formed the hub; the converging valleys of the Wei, the Fen, the Ching, the Lo, the Han, and the Huang-ho formed the spokes. The internal differentiation was between centre and circumference, capital and provinces. Both empires in antiquity were centrally planned, but Rome in a series of concentric circles, China in a series of radiating lines. The Roman empire was the work of a city state which sought to stabilize its dominion by universalizing cities, city life, institutions, and values. It tended therefore to homogenization, a general rise in the level of urbanization, a Conrad Hilton civilization[24] of everywhere-similar fora, basilicas, theatres, baths, circuses, and insulae. The Chinese em-

---

[24]Adshead means a civilization that spreads the same hotels (Hiltons), buildings, foods, and chain-culture everywhere. [Ed.]

pire, on the other hand, was the work of a bureaucratic territorial state which sought to stabilize its dominion by monopolizing for the court capital resources, amenities, protection, and prestige. It tended therefore to heterogenization, to a fall in the general level of urbanization following the unification of the empire and a growing disparity between the lifestyles of court and country. Both empires lived by and for cultural glamour and conspicuous consumption but in the one case they were diffused, in the other concentrated.

Spatial relations. A comparison of the extent and character of the communications systems of the two areas suggests that Han China was less integrated than the Roman empire. According to Needham, the Roman empire under Hadrian covered 1,763,000 square miles and had 48,500 miles of road, an average of 27.5 miles of road per 1000 square miles of territory. Han China, on the other hand, covered 1,532,000 square miles and had 22,000 miles of road, an average of only 14.35 miles of road per 1000 square miles of territory. Moreover, while for Han China, roads were the essence of the communications system, for Rome they were only an adjunct to the Mediterranean whose sea lanes will have at least doubled the total length of routes. Needham suggests that the greater use of rivers and canals for transportation in China as compared to Europe counterbalanced the advantage of the Mediterranean. This may be true for the later periods of Chinese history, the T'ang and the Sung, for example, when the Grand Canal had been completed, but it is doubtful for the Han. Neither the Yellow River nor its tributaries, in whose valleys Chinese civilization was then centred, are good for navigation and most Han hydraulic activity was for irrigation, not communication. Like the Achaemenid empire, Han China was a road state on a plateau, and this in itself ensured inferiority in spatial integration to a Mediterranean empire, since in pre-modern conditions land transport was twenty to forty times more expensive than water transport. . . .

Decor. Even allowing for accidents of survival, it is difficult not to conclude from the archaeological remains that Han China was a less splendid society than Imperial Rome. The Great Wall no doubt is a stupendous monument, though most of its imposing appearance dates from Ming rather than Han times, but it stands by itself, and though Chinese cities had impressive walls, they did not contain the monumental public buildings of the Classical West—the amphitheatres, aqueducts, arches, basilicas, baths, circuses, theatres, and temples. Rome was a federation of city states, Han China was a swollen court; but in addition, the difference between their towns was rooted in different options for building materials and different conceptions of what a house was for. The fundamental options of Rome and, following her, Europe generally, were for stone, diffusion of heat by hypocausts or multiple fireplaces, and durability. A house was a capital investment, perhaps the prototype of all fixed capital investment, an assertion of culture in the face of nature. The fundamental Chinese options, on the other hand, were for wood, concentration of heat at the *k'ang* or heated divan, and repairability. A house was a charge on income, an extension of consumer non-durables, an adaptation of culture to nature. In the West, buildings were in principle winter palaces, exclusions of weather, permanent embodiments of hearth and family. In China, buildings were in principle summer houses, modifications of weather, makeshift additions to the real home which was the loess cave or the family tomb. The one option produced monumentality and splendour, the other convenience and harmony. . . .

Decay

Finally, besides these contrasts of foundations and architectonics, there was a contrast between the two empires in the pattern of their decay. Although there were superficial similarities between the fall of the Roman empire and the fall of the Han empire, there were more profound differences which in the end made the two episodes more unlike than like: differences in health, pathology, and prognosis.

The body politic of the Han was healthier than that of the Roman empire. With its superior physical technology in arable farming and metallurgy and its lower degree of urbanization, intercommunication and luxury building, the Han world did not suffer from irremediable contradictions between superstructure and base, state and society. Frictions there were, no doubt, but they were adjustable without cataclysm. In the Roman body politic, on the other hand, with its more primitive physical technology yet more grandiose and more parasitic sociology, there were such contradictions, especially after the Illyrian emperors, in response to the military mutinies and barbarian invasions of the mid-third century, doubled the army and multiplied fortifications without sufficient provision for increased agricultural productivity behind the front. . . .

Both the Han and the Roman empires were the work of elites—educated, civilian, and urban. Both coexisted with and were threatened by non-elites: barbarians beyond the frontier, sectaries outside the *paedeia*, soldiers separated from the civilian community, and peasants below the level of urbanization. . . . All four non-elites—barbarians, sectaries, soldiers, and peasants—played some part in the fall of the Roman empire: it was a social revolution.

In China on the other hand, under the Han and its successor states down to 400 A.D., the San-kuo and the Chin, pathology came from within the elite. It came from the aristocracy of great families, the equivalent, *mutatis mutandis*[25] of the senatorial aristocracy of the Western empire or the *pronoia*-holding[26] magnates of medieval Byzantium. These people, the Ma, the Tou, the Liang, the Wang, the Ssu-ma, who as a Chin catch-phrase put it "share the world," were not primarily a landed aristocracy though they owned estates and, especially, the newly invented watermill. Rather their substance consisted in men: *k'o*, literally guests, that is clients, retainers, tenants, servants, and slaves. For their *k'o*, as evidence of their power and prestige, patrons sought exemption from tax lists and muster rolls and thus weakened the fiscal and military foundations of the central government. The Han empire rested on a base of tax-paying and conscription-bearing free farmers. A vicious circle began: the more privileges for *k'o*, the greater the fiscal and draft pressures on the remaining free farmers, the greater the temptation to escape such freedom by commendation and an increase in the number of *k'o*. The Han empire died slowly by financial and military asphyxiation.

[25]After the same changes. [Ed.]

[26]*Pronoia* were land grants made to nobility by the Byzantine or Eastern Roman emperor. [Ed.]

19

CONFUCIUS

From The Analects

Confucius (551–479 B.C.E.) was a son of a low-level noble family in China who, despite some political success in his early years, spent most of his later life teaching and looking for a governmental appointment. His *Analects*, a collection of sayings or teachings compiled by his students, touch on all of his major concerns: filial piety (or respect of sons for fathers), virtuous conduct, governance by good example, tradition, rites, music, and dance. Confucius, the person and model, and Confucianism, the school or writings known as *wen-yen*, had an enormous impact on Chinese thought and culture.

The Analects of Confucius, http://classics.mit.edu//Confucius/analects.html.

What kind of society would ideas like these encourage? In the previous reading, Adshead writes that both the Chinese and the Romans solved the problem of ruling vast empires by increasing the "cultural solidarity of elites: the spontaneous coordination produced by the shared values, institutions, vocabulary, and reactions of, on the one hand, the classical *paedeia* and, on the other, the Confucian *wen-yen*." How would these Confucian *wen-yen* (writings) do what Adshead suggests?

Thinking Historically

A common response that people have when they read writings like this from a famous philosopher or religious figure is to nod in agreement, reflect on the wisdom, and speculate about the similarities among great philosophies. On a second or third reading, we might find more matters of difference and disagreement. We might be more struck by the differences between Confucius and other classical writers: whether Jesus, Plato, or Plutarch or Cicero. What similarities do you see between Confucius and Plato or some other philosophers you have read? After you read Plutarch (selection 20), we will ask how the writings of Confucius and Plutarch are similar and different, and how those differences reflect differences between Chinese and Roman cultures.

Section 1

Part 1

The Master said, "Is it not pleasant to learn with a constant perseverance and application?

"Is it not delightful to have friends coming from distant quarters?

"Is he not a man of complete virtue, who feels no discomposure though men may take no note of him?"

The philosopher Yu said, "They are few who, being filial and fraternal, are fond of offending against their superiors. There have been none, who, not liking to offend against their superiors, have been fond of stirring up confusion.

"The superior man bends his attention to what is at the root. That being established, all practical courses naturally grow up. Filial piety and fraternal submission, are they not the root of all benevolent actions?"

The Master said, "Fine words and an insinuating appearance are seldom associated with true virtue."

The philosopher Tsang said, "I daily examine myself on three points: whether, in transacting business for others, I may have been not faithful; whether, in intercourse with friends, I may have been not sincere; whether I may have not mastered and practiced the instructions of my teacher."

The Master said, "To rule a country of a thousand chariots, there must be reverent attention to business, and sincerity; economy in expenditure, and love for men; and the employment of the people at the proper seasons."

The Master said, "A youth, when at home, should be filial, and, abroad, respectful to his elders. He should be earnest and truthful. He should overflow in love to all, and cultivate the friendship of the good. When he has time and opportunity, after the performance of these things, he should employ them in polite studies."

Tsze-hsia said, "If a man withdraws his mind from the love of beauty, and applies it as sincerely to the love of the virtuous; if, in serving his parents, he can exert his utmost strength; if, in serving his prince, he can devote his life; if, in his intercourse with his friends, his words are sincere: although men say that he has not learned, I will certainly say that he has."

The Master said, "If the scholar be not grave, he will not call forth any veneration, and his learning will not be solid.

"Hold faithfulness and sincerity as first principles.

"Have no friends not equal to yourself.

"When you have faults, do not fear to abandon them."

The philosopher Tsang said, "Let there be a careful attention to perform the funeral rites to parents, and let them be followed when long gone with the ceremonies of sacrifice; then the virtue of the people will resume its proper excellence." . . .

Part 4

The Master said, "It is virtuous manners which constitute the excellence of a neighborhood. If a man in selecting a residence does not fix on one where such prevail, how can he be wise?"

The Master said, "Those who are without virtue cannot abide long either in a condition of poverty and hardship, or in a condition of enjoyment. The virtuous rest in virtue; the wise desire virtue."

The Master said, "It is only the truly virtuous man, who can love, or who can hate, others."

The Master said, "If the will be set on virtue, there will be no practice of wickedness."

The Master said, "Riches and honors are what men desire. If they cannot be obtained in the proper way, they should not be held. Poverty and meanness are what men dislike. If they cannot be avoided in the proper way, they should not be avoided." . . .

Part 9

The subjects of which the Master seldom spoke were profitableness, and also the appointments of Heaven, and perfect virtue.

A man of the village of Ta-hsiang said, "Great indeed is the philosopher K'ung! His learning is extensive, and yet he does not render his name famous by any particular thing."

The Master heard the observation, and said to his disciples, "What shall I practice? Shall I practice charioteering, or shall I practice archery? I will practice charioteering."

The Master said, "The linen cap is that prescribed by the rules of ceremony, but now a silk one is worn. It is economical, and I follow the common practice.

"The rules of ceremony prescribe the bowing below the hall, but now the practice is to bow only after ascending it. That is arrogant. I continue to bow below the hall, though I oppose the common practice."

There were four things from which the Master was entirely free. He had no foregone conclusions, no arbitrary predeterminations, no obstinacy, and no egoism. . . .

Section 3

Part 13

Tsze-lu asked about government. The Master said, "Go before the people with your example, and be laborious in their affairs."

He requested further instruction, and was answered, "Be not weary in these things."

Chung-kung, being chief minister to the head of the Chi family, asked about government. The Master said, "Employ first the services of your various officers, pardon small faults, and raise to office men of virtue and talents."

Chung-kung said, "How shall I know the men of virtue and talent, so that I may raise them to office?" He was answered, "Raise to office those whom you know. As to those whom you do not know, will others neglect them?"

Tsze-lu said, "The ruler of Wei has been waiting for you, in order with you to administer the government. What will you consider the first thing to be done?"

The Master replied, "What is necessary is to rectify names."

"So! indeed!" said Tsze-lu. "You are wide of the mark! Why must there be such rectification?"

The Master said, "How uncultivated you are, Yu! A superior man, in regard to what he does not know, shows a cautious reserve.

"If names be not correct, language is not in accordance with the truth of things. If language be not in accordance with the truth of things, affairs cannot be carried on to success.

"When affairs cannot be carried on to success, proprieties and music do not flourish. When proprieties and music do not flourish, punishments will not be properly awarded. When punishments are not properly awarded, the people do not know how to move hand or foot.

"Therefore a superior man considers it necessary that the names he uses may be spoken appropriately, and also that what he speaks may be carried out appropriately. What the superior man requires is just that in his words there may be nothing incorrect." . . .

Part 15

The Duke Ling of Wei asked Confucius about tactics. Confucius replied, "I have heard all about sacrificial vessels, but I have not learned military matters." On this, he took his departure the next day.

When he was in Chan, their provisions were exhausted, and his followers became so ill that they were unable to rise.

Tsze-lu, with evident dissatisfaction, said, "Has the superior man likewise to endure in this way?" The Master said, "The superior man may indeed have to endure want, but the mean man, when he is in want, gives way to unbridled license."

20

PLUTARCH

On Education

Plutarch (46 C.E.–120 C.E.) was born in Greece but taught philosophy in Rome and wrote widely on morality, literature, and history. He is known best for his biographies of Greeks and Romans, which he presented as parallel lives from which he drew moral lessons.

No Greek or Roman shaped Mediterranean culture in the way that Confucius influenced Chinese and East Asian culture. Nevertheless, Plutarch's interest in morality and education offers points of comparison

Adapted from Oliver J. Thatcher, ed., *The Library of Original Sources*, vol. III: *The Roman World* (Milwaukee: University Research Extension Co., 1907), 370–91.

with Confucius. In what ways was Plutarch's moral and educational phi-
losophy similar to that of Confucius? In what ways was it different?
What do those differences say about the differences between Roman and
Chinese culture?

Thinking Historically

One way to draw out a comparison of two major thinkers like
Plutarch and Confucius is to list the key concerns and to note the
words used by each. You have already read, and we have already
listed, some of Confucius's main concerns. You might compose a similar list for Plutarch noting also any key words you see repeated. How
do these two lists compare?

Although Plutarch does not represent Roman or Greco-Roman
thought as thoroughly as Confucius stands for China, his work was
part of what Adshead calls the classical *paedeia* (taught morality) that
increased the cultural solidarity of elites. How might these ideas have
helped Greek and Roman upper classes identify with their counterparts in the broader empire?

Adshead also suggests that the "sound/meaning ratio" in Chinese
(a high percentage of homophones, or sounds that could convey a
number of different meanings) made Chinese less explicit than Greek,
Latin, or other Indo-European languages. The wider range of
phonemes (distinct sounds units) in Indo-European languages, according to Adshead, tends to make Greek and Latin speakers more precise
or blunt, less evasive or poetic. Does your reading of Plutarch and
Confucius support this judgment? Compare Confucius and Plutarch
to Plato or Thucydides (in Chapter 3). Whose writing is more syntagmatic (organized in a logical order of statements)?

1. THE COURSE that ought to be taken for the training of freeborn
children, and the means whereby their manners may be rendered virtuous,
will, with the reader's permission, be our present subject.

2. We should begin with their very procreation. I would therefore, in
the first place, advise those who desire to become the parents of famous
and eminent children, that they keep not company with all women that
they light on; I mean such as harlots, or concubines. For such children as
are blemished in their birth, either by the father's or the mother's side, are
liable to be pursued, as long as they live, with the indelible infamy of their
base extraction, . . .

[Discussion of birth and childhood follows.]

8. In brief therefore I say (and what I say may justly challenge the re-
pute of an oracle rather than of advice), that the one chief thing in that mat-

ter—which comprises the beginning, middle, and end of all—is good education and regular instruction; and that these two afford great help and assistance toward the attainment of virtue and felicity. For all other good things are but human and of small value, such as will hardly recompense the industry required to the getting of them. It is, indeed, a desirable thing to be well-descended; but the glory belongs to our ancestors. Riches are valuable; but they are the goods of Fortune, who frequently takes them from those that have them, and carries them to those that never so much as hoped for them. Yes, the greater they are, the fairer mark they are for those to aim at who design to make our bags their prize; I mean evil servants and accusers. But the weightiest consideration of all is, that riches may be enjoyed by the worst as well as the best of men. Glory is a thing deserving respect, but unstable; beauty is a prize that men fight to obtain, but, when obtained, it is of little continuance; health is a precious enjoyment, but easily impaired; strength is a thing desirable, but apt to be the prey of disease and old age. And, in general, let any man who values himself upon strength of body know that he makes a great mistake; for what indeed is any proportion of human strength, if compared to that of other animals, such as elephants and bulls and lions? But learning alone, of all things in our possession, is immortal and divine. And two things there are that are most peculiar to human nature, reason and speech; of which two, reason is the master of speech, and speech is the servant of reason, impregnable against all assaults of fortune, not to be taken away by false accusation, nor impaired by sickness, nor enfeebled by old age. For reason alone grows youthful by age; and time, which decays all other things before it carries them away with it, leaves learning alone behind. Whence the answer seems to me very remarkable, which Stilpo, a philosopher of Megara, gave to Demetrius, who, when he leveled that city to the ground and made the citizens slaves, asked Stilpo whether he had lost anything. Nothing, he said, for war cannot plunder virtue. To this saying that of Socrates also is very agreeable; who, when Gorgias (as I take it) asked him what his opinion was of the king of Persia, and whether he judged him happy, returned answer, that he could not tell what to think of him, because he knew not how he was furnished with virtue and learning—as judging human felicity to consist in those endowments, and not in those which are subject to fortune. . . .

11. In the next place, the exercise of the body must not be neglected; but children must be sent to schools of gymnastics, where they may have sufficient employment that way also. This will conduce partly to a more handsome carriage, and partly to the improvement of their strength. For the foundation of a vigorous old age is a good constitution of the body in childhood. Wherefore, as it is expedient to provide those things in fair weather which may be useful to the mariners in a storm, so is it to keep good order and govern ourselves by rules of temperance in youth, as the best provision we can lay in for age. Yet must they husband their strength, so as not to become dried up (as it were) and destitute of strength to follow their studies. For, according to Plato, sleep and weariness are enemies to the arts.

But why do I stand so long on these things? I hasten to speak of that which is of the greatest importance, even beyond all that has been spoken of; namely, I would have boys trained for the contests of wars by practice in the throwing of darts, shooting of arrows, and hunting of wild beasts. For we must remember in war the goods of the conquered are proposed as rewards to the conquerors. But war does not agree with a delicate habit of body, used only to the shade; for even one lean soldier that has been used to military exercises shall overthrow whole troops of mere wrestlers who know nothing of war. But, somebody may say, while you profess to give precepts for the education of all free-born children, why do you carry the matter so as to seem only to accommodate those precepts to the rich, and neglect to suit them also to the children of poor men and plebeians? To which objection it is no difficult thing to reply. For it is my desire that all children whatsoever may partake of the benefit of education alike; but if yet any persons, by reason of the narrowness of their estates, cannot make use of my precepts, let them not blame me that give them for Fortune, which disabled them from making the advantage by them they otherwise might. Though even poor men must use their utmost endeavor to give their children the best education; or, if they cannot, they must bestow upon them the best that their abilities will reach. Thus much I thought fit here to insert in the body of my discourse, that I might the better be enabled to annex what I have yet to add concerning the right training of children. . . .

17. And in sum, it is necessary to restrain young men from the conversation of debauched persons, lest they take infection from their evil examples. This was taught by Pythagoras in certain enigmatical sentences, which I shall here relate and expound, as being greatly useful to further virtuous inclinations. Such are these: *Taste not of fish that have black tails*; that is, converse not with men that are smutted with vicious qualities. *Stride not over the beam of the scales*; wherein he teaches us the regard we ought to have for justice, so as not to go beyond its measures. *Sit not on a phoenix*, wherein he forbids sloth, and requires us to take care to provide ourselves with the necessaries of life. *Do not strike hands with every man*; he means we ought not to be over hasty to make acquaintances or friendships with others. *Wear not a tight string*; that is, we are to labor after a free and independent way of living, and to submit to no fetters. *Stir not up the fire with a sword*; signifying that we ought not to provoke a man more when he is angry already (since this is a most unseemly act), but we should rather comply with him while his passion is in its heat. *Eat not your heart*; which forbids to afflict our souls, and waste them with vexatious cares. *Abstain from beans*; that is, keep out of public offices, for anciently the choice of the officers of state was made by beans. *Put not food in a chamber-pot*; wherein he declares that elegant discourse ought not to be put into an impure mind; for discourse is the food of the mind, which is rendered unclean by the foulness of the man who receives it. *When men are arrived at the goal, they should not turn back*; that is, those who are near

the end of their days, and see the period of their lives approaching, ought to entertain it contentedly, and not to be grieved at it. . . .

18. These counsels which I have now given are of great worth and importance; what I have now to add touches certain allowances that are to be made to human nature. Again, therefore, I would not have fathers of an over-rigid and harsh temper, but so mild as to forgive some slips of youth, remembering that they themselves were once young. . . .

I will add a few words more, and put an end to these advices. The chief thing that fathers are to look to is that they themselves become effectual examples to their children, by doing all those things which belong to them and avoiding all vicious practices, which in their lives, as in a glass, their children may see enough to give them an aversion to all ill words and actions. For those that chide children for such faults as they themselves fall into unconsciously accuse themselves, under their children's names. And if they are altogether vicious in their own lives, they lose the right of reproaching their very servants, and much more do they forfeit it towards their sons. Yes, what is more than that, they make themselves even counselors and instructors to them in wickedness. For where old men are impudent, there of necessity must the young men be so too. Wherefore we are to apply our minds to all such practices as may conduce to the good breeding of our children. And here we may take example from Eurydice of Hierapolis, who, although she was an Illyrian, and so thrice a barbarian, yet applied herself to learning when she was well advanced in years, that she might teach her children. Her love towards her children appears evidently in this Epigram of hers, which she dedicated to the Muses:

> Eurydice to the Muses here doth raise
> This monument, her honest love to praise;
> Who her grown sons that she might scholars breed,
> Then well in years, herself first learned to read.

And thus have I finished the precepts which I designed to give concerning this subject. But that they should all be followed by any one reader is rather, I fear, to be wished than hoped. And to follow the greater part of them, though it may not be impossible to human nature, yet will need a concurrence of more than ordinary diligence joined with good fortune.

21

G. E. R. LLOYD

Chinese and Greco-Roman Innovation

In this selection, a modern historian of ideas compares the Chinese and Greco-Roman paths to invention. He focuses on three areas — warfare, agriculture, and civil engineering. His point is not to determine which society was more advanced; they excelled in different areas. He focuses, instead, on how ideas were applied to new technologies in both societies. The different methods of turning ideas into inventions tell us far more about how differently the two societies functioned. What were the different routes to innovation in China and the Greco-Roman world? What does that tell us about the difference between Chinese and Roman societies?

Thinking Historically

Lloyd focuses on a much narrower field than did Adshead. The subject of how a society innovates is minuscule compared to the range of issues compared by Adshead. Yet Lloyd's attempt to answer this simple question in two societies leads to a larger understanding about those two societies. What is that larger understanding?

Notice also that Lloyd's method of comparing is different from Adshead's. He does not list similarities and then list differences. Instead he chooses an action (or three) that all societies must perform: inventing new techniques (in warfare, agriculture, and civil engineering). Then he asks how these two societies did it. Do you find either of these methods preferable? Does Lloyd's method lead you to add another difference between Rome and China to Adshead's list?

I shall consider each of three main subject areas, first warfare, then agriculture, then civil engineering, though it will be immediately apparent that there is some overlap between that third area and the other two. These three, between them, certainly do not cover everything that might be discussed under the heading of the practical applications of theory: but they will give us some idea of the scope of the problems.

G. E. R. Lloyd, *The Ambitions of Curiosity* (Cambridge: Cambridge University Press, 2002), 72–73, 74–76, 77, 79, 80–82, 84–86, 88, 91–92, 94–97.

WARFARE is a subject that no state, no ruler, can afford to ignore. But ideas about the aims and methods of waging war, and about the winning of battles, have varied enormously, as also has the attention paid to improving the efficiency of armies whether by employing better tactics or better weaponry. Both the Greeks and the Chinese were conscious of certain differences between their own ideas, techniques, and practices, and those of the foreign peoples with whom they were familiar. Contacts with other peoples were one source of influence on Greek and Chinese battle tactics themselves. We are told by Vitruvius that certain types of siege engines that came into general use in the Greco-Roman world originated among Tyrian and Carthaginian engineers. The Chinese derived their horses (used first in chariots, then in cavalry engagements) from the people of the steppes.

At the same time efficiency was not the sole criterion, at least, in Greece. For the Greeks, the use of the bow was thought inferior—morally—to fighting hand to hand with spear, sword, and shield. From Homer onwards, the individual's performance in battle was a crucial factor in the moral evaluation of the man. The *Iliad* is organised around the consecutive *aristeia*, deeds of valour, of the Greek heroes who take centre stage in turn in the absence of Achilles. But even when victory in battle depended, as it later did, on the disciplined manoeuvring of the heavy-armed troops—the hoplites—in the massed formation of the phalanx, playing one's part there was the prime test of courage, *andreia*, literally manhood.

Evidence of the increasing complexity of warfare begins already in Herodotus and more especially Thucydides. Thucydides refers to the development of the trireme, the ship on which victory at sea for long depended. In his accounts of the various sieges that took place during the Peloponnesian war, he refers at one point to a primitive kind of flame-thrower. Not much later, in the fourth century BCE, we have our first extant specialist Greek military treatise, the *poliorketika*—siege-warfare—of Aeneas Tacticus, part (it seems) of a series of works he wrote on military matters, the rest of which have not survived. . . .

A comparison between these Chinese and Greco-Roman works yields immediately several points of similarity and two important contrasts. Both Aeneas and *Sunzi* stress the importance of experience, of military intelligence (knowledge of the enemy's strength, whereabouts and intentions) and especially of morale. Both describe the use of spies; both devote attention to the problems of passwords and signalling; both describe various tricks or ploys to gain a psychological or tactical advantage over the enemy.

But for *Sunzi*[1] the supreme skill of the commander consists in securing victory with a minimum of cost, indeed if possible without

[1]Sunzi or Sun Tzu, author of *The Art of War*, c. 500 B.C.E.

having to fight a battle. The idea is that you so manoeuvre your troops that the enemy comes to realise the hopelessness of his own position and surrenders without an engagement. For *Sunzi* the value of victory is seriously diminished if the enemy's land is destroyed or his population decimated: the prime prize is to take over and occupy the territory of the vanquished more or less unharmed. . . .

A second major difference lies in the preoccupation, throughout the pages of Aeneas, with the possibility that the city being defended may be betrayed by disaffected elements in the population who disagreed with the policies of those in command. He gives advice on the dangers of having a lot of poor people, or debtors, in the defending army, and on how to counter the plots of would-be revolutionaries. Considerable sections of the work are devoted to guarding against the possibility of the city-gates being opened *from within*. The problems posed by *political* disagreements, among the *citizen* body, on the conduct of the war, just do not figure in our Chinese texts, for all that disagreements between *generals* often do.

The second type of text that has come down to us on the Greco-Roman side deals with military weaponry. Archimedes' reputation as a practical genius depended partly on the stories of the engines he devised to repel the forces of Marcellus besieging Syracuse: but our evidence there is second-hand and anecdotal. However, Philo, Vitruvius, and Hero all deal with the construction and improvement of the various types of catapults—scorpions and ballistae—designed to hurl bolts or stones, in both torsion and non-torsion varieties. Starting with the arrow-shooting *gastraphetes*, or cross-bow, these underwent considerable developments from the early fourth century BCE, as did other types of weapons and siege-engines (battering-rams, for example, and "tortoises" designed to protect attacking forces and so on). . . .

On the Chinese side, the emphasis is not so much on experimental research to prove a mathematical formula setting out the relevant proportionalities. On the other hand, there is a deep concern with what will work and with efficient performance. The main Chinese weapon was the cross-bow, introduced maybe as early as 400 BCE, an extremely powerful weapon, once equipped with an efficient trigger mechanism and once the problems of arming it were overcome. . . .

We could certainly not claim that Greco-Roman engineers were less ingenious, less curious, less inventive, in their attempts to improve weapons of war, than their Chinese counterparts. Indeed the Greeks went further than the Chinese in their admittedly only partially successful efforts to reduce the problems to mathematical terms. Yet where the Chinese had a net advantage was in the organisations that existed for exploiting and implementing new ideas once they were proposed. Although the success of Chinese advisers in gaining the ear of rulers obviously varied, what rulers and advisers alike shared was an intense concern for every aspect of the art of war and a sense of the need to explore any possibility of an advantage and a determination to do so.

These comments will prove relevant also to the next domain we have to consider, namely AGRICULTURE. Every society, large or small, must be concerned with ensuring an adequate food-supply and most call on considerable collective knowledge of the relevant local ecological conditions to achieve that end. In hunting, fishing, herding, sowing, and planting, once certain methods and techniques prove to be effective, there may be little incentive—indeed possibly great risk—in trying to change them. Experimenting with new crops has always been a dangerous business, has it not? In the domain of agriculture, in other words, the forces of conservatism have generally been particularly strong. Departure from tried and tested methods has, accordingly, to be motivated either by necessity—say the need to feed an increasing population—or by some perceived desirable end, the acquisition of wealth or prestige. . . .

We may begin with two fundamental differences in the perception of the importance of agriculture in our two ancient civilisations. First, for the ancient Chinese, agriculture came under the auspices of important divinities and culture heroes, Shennong, the tutelary deity or spirit of agriculture, Hou Ji, the Lord of Millet, and Yu the Great. Of course the Greeks had Demeter, the Romans Ceres. But they did not combine the role of corn goddesses with presiding over technological skills, which were the province, rather, of Athena and in a different way of Prometheus. Yu the Great was responsible for taming the flood, for land clearance, for inaugurating agriculture itself. Flood stories in Greece or the ancient Near East, by contrast, did not culminate in the celebration of the activities of a hero-figure whose efforts *countered* the flood and so enabled agriculture to begin.

The second important difference relates to the role of the Prince or Emperor himself, who in China was personally in charge of agriculture and presided over agricultural activities season by season. Thus he inaugurated the ploughing of the fields every year, just as the Queen started the picking of the mulberry leaves for the silkworms. In *Huainanzi*[2] the ruler does not just sacrifice to the appropriate deities at the appropriate moments of the year: he oversees each and every important agricultural activity. If he fails in his duty, the consequences this text predicts are dire, the failure of crops, drought, unseasonable rains, floods, fire, disease, and not just "natural" calamities but others, such as the invasions of barbarians and the proliferation of bandits. To be sure, the Romans had a ruler—Cincinnatus—who came from

[2]A second century B.C.E. Chinese philosophical classic that deals with agriculture, among other things.

ploughing the fields to rule. But even though Columella, in reporting that story, nostalgically approves of the connection between ruling and agriculture, that just points to their normal dissociation in Roman eyes.

Agriculture, one may say, had a far higher ideological profile in China than in the Greco-Roman world, and this is reflected in the amount of literature devoted to the subject. Agricultural topics are discussed in texts from the third to the first centuries BCE in the *Zhouli*, *Guanzi*, and *Lüshi chunqiu*, for example sections defining the responsibilities of the many different types of officials concerned, planning the most efficient use of the available land of different types, specifying what should be done in each season and stressing the importance of the care of agricultural implements. Specialist treatises begin not much later, as well as monographs dealing with particular crops and the vast *bencao* literature dealing with medicinal plants, pharmacopoeia in other words.

Ancient China suffered, we know, from time to time, from terrible famines, brought about by floods or drought or crop failures of one kind or another. Nevertheless the increase of yields by crop rotation, by large-scale irrigation works, by hybridising strains of corn and rice, by manuring, was impressive. New devices for harrowing, ridging, seed-drilling, rolling, were introduced, and the design of the plough underwent considerable modification. These advances came, in the main, from the peasant-farmers themselves, rather than from the members of the literate elite who wrote the treatises. The latter were not, on the whole, themselves innovators: yet they *recorded* the innovations that were made, and, given the prestige and imperial support their writings often enjoyed, this helped to ensure the diffusion of those innovations.

In the Greco-Roman world, too, we have extensive extant writings, ranging from didactic poems such as Hesiod's *Works and Days*, through general works discussing household and estate management, such as Xenophon's *Economica*, to specialist treatises dealing with plants and plant uses (as by Theophrastus) or with agriculture as a whole. Those last go back to the fifth century BCE, though our chief extant examples are from Latin writers of the second century BCE to the first century CE, the works of Cato, Varro and Columella. Some of the mechanical devices useful in agriculture, meanwhile, are described in other treatises as well, in Vitruvius, for example, or in Pliny's encyclopedic *Natural History*. These devices include most notably the mills and presses used in the manufacture of oil and wine, the water-wheel, water-lifting devices, and even such complex machines as the Gallic corn-harvester: the machine is very effective, but the terrain must be level; the design is close to that first adopted when the combine harvester came to be reinvented in modern times—not that the Gallic antecedent was known to the reinventors.

Some of these Greek and Roman machines exhibit a considerable sophistication, and those that employ the screw in its various forms (screw-presses or the Archimedean screw) depend on an understanding of the geometrical principles involved, as well as the all-important empirical know-how necessary to manufacture screws. Although the Greeks and Romans missed out on some simple devices, such as the wheel-barrow, in other areas they exhibit both curiosity and inventiveness.

Yet one key difference marks the Greco-Roman literature out from the Chinese. This is that the specialist agricultural treatises are mainly addressed to private estate-owners—to give individual rich landlords the information they needed for the profitable running of their estates. They could be the audience of Chinese works too, but in China the prime target was often grander—to provide the Emperor with the wherewithal to ensure the prosperity of all under his control. True, Vitruvius does address his "architectural" treatise to Augustus, and his hopes of thereby securing favour and employment are strictly comparable to those of many Chinese writers who presented memorials to the throne with similar ambitions. Yet Vitruvius writes first and foremost as an architect-engineer, not as an agronomist. He entertains no general expectation that the mechanical devices for use in agriculture that he describes will forthwith be taken up and exploited right across the Roman empire. Indeed in the case of the water-wheel, we can confirm from the archaeological record that its diffusion through the Greco-Roman world was both slow and limited in extent.

At this point the factor that many would invoke to explain the technological weaknesses in the Greco-Roman world is the widespread dependence on slave labour, often represented as the chief factor inhibiting the search for and exploitation of labour-saving devices. Their relevance to the problem must certainly be granted, but should not be exaggerated, for three main reasons.

First, slaves, while expendable, still involved their owners in the expense of their upkeep and were far from necessarily always cheaper than machines. That depended crucially on the outlay needed for the machines.

Moreover, secondly, as between the Greco-Roman world and China, although chattel slaves were not common in China, the use of other types of unfree labour, such as conscripts, certainly was. I shall come back to this when considering civil engineering in the next section.

Thirdly, in the domain of agriculture itself, the existence of slaves will hardly be enough to explain the slow diffusion of mechanical devices, for the simple reason that they were everywhere present throughout the Greco-Roman world. If we ask why the water-wheel was not immediately exploited, once the principle had been discovered, or why the Gallic combine harvester was never used in antiquity outside Gaul, then the existence of slaves *by itself* hardly provides the whole answer, since it offers no discriminating factor. Among the other considerations we have to add is the one we noted before, the lack of state structures taking overall responsibility for agricultural production. In the Greco-Roman world this meant that decisions concerning the running of estates, about the use of slaves or of machines, rested with individual landlords and their perception of where their private profits—or prestige—lay.

The third main subject area I identified is what I called CIVIL ENGINEERING, where there are obvious overlaps with military engineering (as in the siege-engines mentioned before) and with agriculture—insofar as irrigation projects, for example, in China especially, could involve considerable problems of planning and construction.

On the Greek side, the chief large-scale projects undertaken in the early classical period related to the building of cities and particularly to their embellishment, with public buildings, theatres, gymnasia, and especially temples. Much remains unclear about how precisely the "architects" in charge worked, the extent to which they made use of models or plans, how they made the often very subtle adjustments on site to produce the effects they did, as for example in connection with entasis (the curvature of columns and entablatures). But here is certainly an example where major works were undertaken on a corporate basis, not (as was usually the case in the running of estates) for private profit, but rather for public prestige.

Moreover considerable mechanical devices came to be deployed in connection with monumental building. Vitruvius describes how the problems of transporting large blocks of marble were overcome, reporting the devices used by Chersiphron and his son Metagenes in this connection in the construction of the classical temple of Artemis at Ephesus. One such consisted essentially in a pair of rollers between which the marble block was suspended, enabling it to be dragged along. That suggests that already in the sixth century BCE considerable ingenuity was being brought to bear to surmount the difficulties, as there was also in connection with lifting devices, where Vitruvius provides evidence of the development of elaborate cranes, especially those using compound pulleys.

Here is another instance where we can be sure that the theoretical principles involved attracted attention and study. We can infer that from the stories about Archimedes. When he was challenged by King Hiero about his claim to be able to move the whole earth, he is said to have arranged a demonstration in which, with a system of compound pulleys, he dragged a fully laden merchant ship across land single-handed. The story is preposterous, but we can still see it as useful evidence for an *interest* in exploring the extrapolations of mechanical devices. Similarly the potential applications of the lever and related devices are the subject of elaborate discussions in Hero and Pappus.

The second main area where more than just a private individual's interests were at stake, was in the matter of the delivery of water-supplies to cities. This culminated in the vast networks of aqueducts that served Rome, feats of great engineering skill and again the topic of much ancient discussion. It is clear that those responsible never solved satisfactorily the problem of measuring the quantities of water delivered from sluice gates or openings of different apertures set at different angles to the flow of water: rather they used very rough-and-ready rules of thumb, not precise methods of calculation. While the major aqueducts were Roman achievements, the supply of water to the *polis* of Samos had already been the subject of another, different feat of engineering in the sixth century BCE, when Eupalinus constructed a tunnel through the mountain behind the city to achieve this end. As an inspection of the site reveals, he was confident enough of his technique to start tunnelling from both ends simultaneously. The theory of how to do this by using geometrical methods is set out in Hero's *Dioptra*. But it is now abundantly clear that Eupalinus did not proceed by triangulation, but used dead reckoning with sights set up in a straight line over the top of the mountain.

On the Chinese side, the construction of elaborate temples took second place to that of massive tombs. Many of them, we are told, were equipped with complex devices to deter anyone who might try to enter. These included stones that dropped into place automatically to block an entrance if a door was forced, and cross-bows that fired, again automatically, if anyone attempted to pass. The construction of the tombs themselves (sited always after extensive geomantic investigations) is one of the two most vivid illustrations of the Chinese ability to plan and carry out massive projects of civil engineering. In the case of the first Emperor's tomb, outside modern Xian, guarded by the famous terracotta warriors, we are told by Sima Qian (*Shiji Histories*) that 700,000 conscripts worked on it. All who had been involved in its construction and provision with treasure were subsequently executed—so they had no chance to divulge its secrets.

The second main illustration of those same Chinese capabilities is provided by vast irrigation projects, again involving the marshalling of immense labour forces and demonstrating extraordinary skills in overcoming practical difficulties. The most famous of these is the project started by Li Bing, around 270 BCE, and continued by his son Zhengguo. They divided the river Min north of Chengdu and thereby solved at a stroke both the problem of the recurrent flooding to which the river was liable, and that of providing water to irrigate vast stretches of what is now the province of Sichuan. One uncontrollable river was thereby turned into two controllable ones. To achieve this dual aim, Li Bing had to overcome the problems of the seasonal variations in the quantities of water in the river, and those of silting, over and above the main one of dividing the main channel of the river into two. Although theory, in the sense of applied physical theory, was not much involved, here, even so, practical ingenuity of the highest order was displayed.

Grand generalisations about the development of technology in China or in the Greco-Roman world inevitably fall foul of the actual diversities we find between periods and across fields. To have any pretensions to comprehensiveness, my rapid survey of just these three main areas would need to be supplemented by a review of such other domains as transport, navigation, time-keeping devices, astronomical and geological instruments (such as Zhang Heng's famous second-century CE water-driven armillary and his seismoscope): metallurgy, the applications of pneumatics, catoptrics, and acoustics, not to mention such other fields as pharmaceutics which involve non-mechanical applications of theory. But while recognising that I have had to be selective, I shall now ask how far we can answer the principal questions I posed at the outset. What part did theorists play in the advances in technology that were made, in these three fields at least? How far did they manifest an interest in applying their theoretical ideas to practical problems? To what extent did the actual advances we can identify happen without any theoretical input at all? Should all these questions be answered differently for China and for the Greco-Roman world, and if so, what was responsible for the differences?

We may use the last question as a point of entry for suggesting answers to the others. There is, I argued, a far greater similarity between China and the Greco-Roman world than the contrasting stereotypes of practical Chinese and impractical, head-in-the-clouds Greeks would allow for. Many members of the Chinese literate elite were as reluctant to get their hands dirty as were many educated Greeks or Romans.

Against the stereotype of the theoretically oriented, impractical, Greeks, a considerable body of counter-evidence can be adduced. Some of the mechanical devices recorded in the literature are, to be sure, no more than toys, exhibiting a certain ingenuity but of no practical consequence. Such are the ball rotated by steam described by Hero of Alexandria in *Pneumatics* (drastically misnamed his "steam engine"), and many of his pneumatic and hydraulic devices, designed to amuse diners at a symposium, or to impress religious worshippers, as in his idea for temple doors that open automatically when a fire is lit on an altar. That was no practical proposition, but plenty of his other gadgets can be made to work. One such device is a water-pump incorporating one-way valves that was used as a fire-extinguisher. Even though Pappus amazingly included the gadgets of the "wonder-workers" among what he calls the "most necessary" parts of the mechanical arts, not all Greek mechanics was like that. Improvements in weapons of war, in lifting devices using compound pulleys, in the development of applications of the screw in oil and wine presses and in water-lifting devices, all owe something to the researches of Greek and Roman theorists.

It is certainly the case that many of the actual technological advances we can trace in both civilisations cannot now be assigned to named inventors—nor maybe could they ever have been. Many, probably most, were the work of anonymous individuals or groups directly engaged in the business of food-producing and processing, of fighting battles or whatever. Yet both civilisations produced a considerable technical literature devoted to the description and analysis of practical problems. If the driving force was often necessity, many gifted individuals saw the opportunity (and took it) to make a reputation for themselves and were duly celebrated for their achievements, as hydraulic engineers, builders, inventors, whether in the military or the civil domain. While some texts content themselves with recording the devices used, some individuals and groups (the Mohists, Li Bing, Zhang Heng, Archimedes, the Alexandrian engineers, Hero) evidently engaged in more or less sustained investigations into the problems on their own account.

Yet certain differences may be detected, first in the nature of the theoretical discussions to be found in that literature, and then, more fundamentally, in the matter of the structures that existed for the implementation of new ideas.

On the first score, two features appear particularly striking, first the Greek predilection for geometrical idealisations, and second the Chinese focus on exploring the propensities of things, *shi*. I have remarked before that in such fields as statics, Greek geometrical analysis led both to a successful isolation of the key factors in play, and to the bonus that the results could be presented in the form of axiomatic-deductive demonstrations. . . .

On the Chinese side, geometrisation was not the route that theoretical analysis of these questions took, though that cannot be put down to an alleged Chinese lack of interest in geometry as such. . . . But over a range of technological problems, the Chinese interest is less in attempting to *master* the materials they worked with, than in getting those materials to work *for* them. Li Bing's success would be better described not as overcoming the river Min, but as getting it to cooperate with his aims. Similarly, in warfare, the goal of the Chinese strategist was not to annihilate the enemy, but to have him do what you want—surrender. The means to this end was the exploitation of the potentialities of the situation, from the lie of the land to the disposition and morale of your own and the enemy forces. Both the early military classics, *Sunzi* and *Sun Bin*, have chapters devoted to *shi*, understanding and using the propensities of things, and as François Jullien has shown, the concept plays a similar role, as the focus of interest and theoretical elaboration, across a variety of fields where the goal is effect.

Different emphases, such as these, may, then, be found in the *motifs* given prominence, when Chinese, or when Greek or Latin, authors discuss the keys to the solution of practical problems. But there are far more marked differences, between the two civilisations, in the matter of the exploitation of whatever new ideas the theorists and others proposed.

The exceptional nature of the Ptolemies' support for their military engineers just highlights the contrast with the *norm* in the Greco-Roman world. Where, in that world, civic or state interests *were* at stake—in temple building or in the construction of aqueducts—there we find great projects seen through to successful completion. But that was the *norm* in China, increasingly so after the unification of the empire under Qin Shi Huang Di, with the systematic engagement of the Emperor himself (and so of all his many officials under him) in agriculture, in warfare, in the welfare of all under heaven. It was not that the Emperor sought to ensure the prosperity of his people *solely* in a spirit of disinterested magnanimity. Rather, that prosperity had often been, and continued to be, taken as a sign of his virtue and of his mandate from heaven. So where the Roman agronomists (for example) targeted private landowners whose desire for greater efficiency was driven largely by the profit motive, many of the Chinese—not unmoved by profit themselves of course, despite Mencius—were further influenced by the ideal of the welfare of the empire as a whole. But that was not just in a spirit of idealism, but also one of self-interest, for the apparently altruistic ideal of the welfare of the empire coincided with the egoistic one of a secure job in the imperial service.

22

The Salt and Iron Debates

The Chinese state, as selection 21 points out, was much more centralized than the Roman Empire. One of the great centralizers was the Han dynasty Emperor Wu (r. 140–87 B.C.E.). He sent large armies to drive the nomadic Xiongnu* out of Chinese territory and into central Asia, increased domestic and foreign trade, and introduced a system of government bureaus, staffed by graduates of his newly created Confucian Academy. To pay for the greater costs of defense and government administration and services, Emperor Wu initiated government monopolies on salt and iron. The central control of iron production (performed by conscripts and convicts) and the manufacture of iron weapons and tools (everything from cooking pots and scissors to

*zhee yong NOO

"The Debate on Salt and Iron," trans. Pat Ebrey, in *Chinese Civilization: A Sourcebook*, ed. Pat Ebrey (New York: The Free Press, 1993), 60–63.

farm tools and salt drills) were particularly profitable for the government. In addition, Emperor Wu established licenses for the production and sale of alcoholic beverages and set up bureaus to purchase grain when the price was low and sell it when the price was high, called the system of "equable marketing."

In 86 B.C.E. Emperor Wu's successor called a conference to investigate the economic problems of the people. In 81, debate was held between government ministers and the "learned men" who were mainly Confucian scholars. This is part of the record of that debate. What was the disagreement between the government ministers and the "learned men" regarding the salt and iron monopolies? What signs do you see that the Chinese economy and society had become centralized?

Thinking Historically

Our tendency in reading a debate is to notice where the two sides disagree. It is also useful, however, to notice where they agree. What assumptions do the government ministers and Confucians share in this debate? What does that agreement tell you about Han China?

Other comparisons might usefully be drawn from this selection. Since you have read some of Confucius, you might compare the ideas of the Master with the ideas of these Confucian scholars. How similar or different are these two sets of ideas? How might you explain that similarity or difference?

You might also usefully relate this reading to the previous one. Lloyd discusses innovation. What Chinese innovations are discussed in this selection? How do you imagine the Romans might have struggled with the same sort of problems?

In 81 B.C. an imperial edict directed the chancellor and chief minister to confer with a group of wise and learned men about the people's hardships.

The learned men responded: We have heard that the way to rule lies in preventing frivolity while encouraging morality, in suppressing the pursuit of profit while opening the way for benevolence and duty. When profit is not emphasized, civilization flourishes and the customs of the people improve.

Recently, a system of salt and iron monopolies, a liquor excise tax, and an equable marketing system have been established throughout the country. These represent financial competition with the people which undermines their native honesty and promotes selfishness. As a result, few among the people take up the fundamental pursuits [agriculture] while many flock to the secondary [trade and industry]. When artificiality thrives, simplicity declines; when the secondary flourishes, the basic decays. Stress on the secondary makes the people decadent; emphasis on the basic keeps them unsophisticated. When the people are unsophisticated, wealth abounds; when they are extravagant, cold and hunger ensue.

We desire that the salt, iron, and liquor monopolies and the system of equable marketing be abolished. In that way the basic pursuits will be encouraged, and the people will be deterred from entering secondary occupations. Agriculture will then greatly prosper. This would be expedient.

The minister: The Xiongnu rebel against our authority and frequently raid the frontier settlements. To guard against this requires the effort of the nation's soldiers. If we take no action, these attacks and raids will never cease. The late emperor had sympathy for the long-suffering of the frontier settlers who live in fear of capture by the barbarians. As defensive measures, he therefore built forts and beacon relay stations and set up garrisons. When the revenue for the defense of the frontier fell short, he established the salt and iron monopolies, the liquor excise tax, and the system of equable marketing. Wealth increased and was used to furnish the frontier expenses.

Now our critics wish to abolish these measures. They would have the treasury depleted and the border deprived of funds for its defense. They would expose our soldiers who defend the frontier passes and walls to hunger and cold, since there is no other way to supply them. Abolition is not expedient.

The learned men: Confucius observed, "The ruler of a kingdom or head of a family does not worry about his people's being poor, only about their being unevenly distributed. He does not worry about their being few, only about their being dissatisfied." Thus, the emperor should not talk of much and little, nor the feudal lords of advantage and harm, nor the ministers of gain and loss. Instead they all should set examples of benevolence and duty and virtuously care for people, for then those nearby will flock to them and those far away will joyfully submit to their authority. Indeed, the master conqueror need not fight, the expert warrior needs no soldiers, and the great commander need not array his troops.

If you foster high standards in the temple and courtroom, you need only make a bold show and bring home your troops, for the king who practices benevolent government has no enemies anywhere. What need can he then have for expense funds?

The minister: The Xiongnu are savage and cunning. They brazenly push through the frontier passes and harass the interior, killing provincial officials and military officers at the border. Although they have long deserved punishment for their lawless rebellion, Your Majesty has taken pity on the financial exigencies of the people and has not wished to expose his officers to the wilderness. Still, we cherish the goal of raising a great army and driving the Xiongnu back north.

I again assert that to do away with the salt and iron monopolies and equable marketing system would bring havoc to our frontier military policies and would be heartless toward those on the frontier. Therefore this proposal is inexpedient.

The learned men: The ancients honored the use of virtue and discredited the use of arms. Confucius said, "If the people of far-off lands do not submit, then the ruler must attract them by enhancing his refinement and virtue. When they have been attracted, he gives them peace."

At present, morality is discarded and reliance is placed on military force. Troops are raised for campaigns and garrisons are stationed for defense. It is the long-drawn-out campaigns and the ceaseless transportation of provisions that burden our people at home and cause our frontier soldiers to suffer from hunger and cold.

The establishment of the salt and iron monopolies and the appointment of financial officers to supply the army were meant to be temporary measures. Therefore, it is expedient that they now be abolished.

The minister: The ancient founders of our country laid the groundwork for both basic and secondary occupations. They facilitated the circulation of goods and provided markets and courts to harmonize the various demands. People of all classes gathered and goods of all sorts were assembled, so that farmers, merchants, and workers could all obtain what they needed. When the exchange of goods was complete, everyone went home. The *Book of Changes* says, "Facilitate exchange so that the people will not be over-worked." This is because farmers are deprived of tools, and without merchants, desired commodities are unavailable. When farmers lack tools, grain is not planted, just as when valued goods are unavailable, wealth is exhausted.

The salt and iron monopolies and the equable marketing system are intended to circulate accumulated wealth and to regulate consumption according to the urgency of need. It is inexpedient to abolish them.

The learned men: If virtue is used to lead the people, they will return to honesty, but if they are enticed with gain, they will become vulgar. Vulgar habits lead them to shun duty. Vulgar habits lead them to shun duty and chase profit; soon they throng the roads and markets. Laozi said, "A poor country will appear to have a surplus." It is not that it possesses abundance, but that when wishes multiply the people become restive. Hence, a true king promotes the basic and discourages the secondary. He restrains the people's desires through the principles of ritual and duty and arranges to have grain exchanged for other goods. In his markets merchants do not circulate worthless goods nor artisans make worthless implements.

The purpose of merchants is circulation and the purpose of artisans is making tools. These matters should not become a major concern of the government.

The minister: Guanzi[1] said: "If a country possesses fertile land and yet its people are underfed, the reason is that there are not enough tools. If it possesses rich natural resources in its mountains and seas and yet the people are poor, the reason is that there are not enough artisans and merchants." The scarlet lacquer and pennant feathers from the kingdoms of Long and Shu; the leather goods, bone, and ivory from Jing and Yang; the cedar, catalpa, bamboo, and reeds from Jiangnan; the fish, salt, felt, and furs from Yan and Qi; the silk yarn, linen, and hemp cloth from Yan and You—all are needed to maintain our lives or be used in our funerals. We depend upon merchants for their distribution and on artisans for their production. For such reasons the ancient sages built boats and bridges to cross rivers; they domesticated cattle and horses to travel over mountains and plains. By penetrating to remote areas, they were able to exchange all kinds of goods for the benefit of the people.

Thus, the former emperor set up iron officials to meet the farmers' needs and started the equable marketing system to assure the people adequate goods. The bulk of the people look to the salt and iron monopolies and the equable marketing system as their source of supply. To abolish them would not be expedient.

The learned men: If a country possesses a wealth of fertile land and yet its people are underfed, the reason is that merchants and workers have prospered while agriculture has been neglected. Likewise, if a country possesses rich natural resources in its mountains and seas and yet its people are poor, the reason is that the people's necessities have not been attended to while luxuries have multiplied. A spring cannot fill a leaking cup; the mountains and seas cannot satisfy unlimited desires. This is why [the ancient emperor] Pan Geng practiced communal living, [the ancient emperor] Shun concealed the gold, and [the Han dynasty founder] Gaozu prohibited merchants and shopkeepers from becoming officials. Their purpose was to discourage habits of greed and to strengthen the spirit of sincerity. Now, even with all of the discriminations against commerce, people still do evil. How much worse it would be if the ruler himself were to pursue profit!

The *Zuo Chronicle* says: "When the feudal lords take delight in profit, the officers become petty; when the officers are petty, the gentle-

---

[1]Guan Zhong, a famous minister of the seventh century B.C. noted for his economic policies.

men become greedy; when the gentlemen are greedy, the common people steal." Thus to open the way for profit is to provide a ladder for the people to become criminals!

The minister: Formerly the feudal lords in the commanderies and kingdoms sent in the products of their respective regions as tribute. Transportation was troublesome and disorganized and the goods often of such bad quality as not to be worth the transport cost. Therefore, transport officers were appointed in every commandery and kingdom to assist in speeding the delivery of tribute and taxes from distant regions. This was called the equable marketing system. A receiving bureau was established at the capital for all the commodities. Because goods were bought when prices were low and sold when prices were high, the government suffered no loss and the merchants could not speculate for profit. This was called the balancing standard.

The balancing standard safeguards the people from unemployment; the equable marketing system distributes their work fairly. Both of these measures are intended to even out goods and be a convenience for the people. They do not provide a ladder for the people to become criminals by opening the way to profit!

The learned men: The ancients in placing levies and taxes on the people would look for what they could provide. Thus farmers contributed their harvest and the weaving women the products of their skill. At present the government ignores what people have and exacts what they lack. The common people then must sell their products cheaply to satisfy the demands of the government. Recently, some commanderies and kingdoms ordered the people to weave cloth. The officials caused the producers various difficulties and then traded with them. They requisitioned not only the silk from Qi and Tao and the broadcloth from Shu and Han, but also the ordinary cloth people make. These were then nefariously sold at "equable" prices. Thus the farmers suffered twice over and the weavers were doubly taxed. Where is the equability in this marketing?

The government officers busy themselves with gaining control of the market and cornering commodities. With the commodities cornered, prices soar and merchants make private deals and speculate. The officers connive with the cunning merchants who are hoarding commodities against future need. Quick traders and unscrupulous officials buy when goods are cheap in order to make high profits. Where is the balance in this standard?

The equable marketing system of antiquity aimed at bringing about fair division of labor and facilitating transportation of tribute. It was surely not for profit or commodity trade.

23

CICERO

Against Verres

Marcus Tullius Cicero* (106–43 B.C.E.) was one of the great orators and statesmen of the late Roman Republic. He was admired especially for the legal arguments he made for or against other Romans, usually public figures, brought before the courts. In this oration, Cicero spoke against a corrupt governor of Sicily, Caius Verres.† Cicero contrasted his own career as a Roman governor with that of Verres. What does Cicero's criticism of Verres, and his brief autobiography, tell you about Roman governance?

Thinking Historically

Like any primary source, this document is only a small piece of the past. In this case, it is a small part of one of many speeches Cicero wrote against Verres, and Cicero spoke about many other figures in many other cases. He also wrote volumes of letters, political philosophy, and diverse orations. Cicero was one of perhaps four million Romans when he prosecuted Verres in 70 B.C.E. Consequently, we must be very careful in generalizing from such a small fragment from the period. Nevertheless, a careful reading reveals certain facts about Roman society that are indisputable and certain facts that are highly likely. What are some of these?

If you compare this single source from Rome with the single source from China in selection 22, what conclusions can you draw about the different systems of government in Rome and China?

. . . At the height of the summer, governors of Sicily are accustomed to move around. This is because they feel that the best season for inspecting their province is the time when the grain is on the threshing-floor. For that is when the workers are all gathered together, so that the size

*SIH suh roh
†KY uhs   VEHR uhs

Cicero, "Against Verres" (II, 5), from *On Government*, trans. Michael Grant (London: Penguin, 1993), 29–31, 32–34, 45–46, 82–85.

of the slave households can be reliably estimated, and the sort of work they are doing can be most easily seen. Yet at this time of year, when all other governors travel about, this novel type of commander, Verres, instead remained stationary, and had a camp set up for him at the city of Syracuse, and indeed in its most agreeable section. Precisely at the entrance of the harbour, where the gulf turns in from the sea-coast towards the city, he pitched a series of pavilions; they were constructed of fine linen, stretched on poles. Moving out of the governor's residence—the former palace of King Hiero[1]—he established himself on this new site so completely that, throughout all this time, it was impossible for anyone to catch a glimpse of him in the outside world.

Moreover, the only people allowed into this new dwelling of his were people whose job it was to share, or minister to, his sensualities. Here flocked all the women with whom he had had relations (and the number of them, at Syracuse, is past belief). Here assembled, also, the people whom Verres deemed worthy to be his friends—worthy, that is to say, to share the life of revelry in which he indulged. And Verres's son, too, by now a grown man, spent his time with men and women of the same type. His own character might incline him to be different from his father. But habit and upbringing made him his father's true son, all the same. . . .

Dressed in a purple Greek cloak and a tunic down to the ankles, Verres spent all this period having a good time with his women. However, while he was thus engaged, the absence of the chief magistrate from the Forum, the lack of any legal decisions and hearings, caused no one to feel in any way offended or displeased. Where Verres was staying, on the coast, there resounded a constant din of female voices and vocalists. In the Forum, on the other hand, laws and lawsuits had ceased to exist. But nobody minded. Men did not worry at all because, with Verres away, the law and the courts were suspended. On the contrary, his absence, they felt, was sparing them violence and brutality, and the savage, unprovoked plundering of their possessions. . . .

Next came his behavior when he had become a grown man. . . . I shall . . . only refer . . . to two recent matters, which will enable you to form your own idea about the rest of what was happening.

One was an entirely notorious fact, known to all the world: so well known that, during the consulships of Lucius Licinius Lucullus and Marcus Aurelius Cotta, every plainest rustic, from any country town, who came to Rome on legal business was aware of it. This fact that everyone learnt was that every single decision which Verres pronounced as city praetor had been made on the prompting of the prostitute Chelidon, and according to her wishes. A second matter that everyone knew about was this. Verres had, by this time, left the city, in his

---

[1]Hiero II, king of Syracuse (270–215 B.C.E.).

military commander's cloak. He had already offered his vows relating to his period of office and the welfare of the state. And yet time after time he got himself carried back to the city in a litter after darkness had fallen, in order to commit adultery with a woman who had a husband; though she was also available to everyone else. It was a proceeding entirely opposed to morality, to the auspices, to every principle of religion and human behaviour.

Heavens above, what different attitudes men have from one another, and what different intentions! Take my own case. If it is not true that I, when assuming the offices with which the Roman people has up to now honoured me, have felt the most solemn obligation to carry out my duties with the utmost conscientiousness, then, gentlemen, I will feel obliged, voluntarily, to sacrifice all the goodwill that you and our country have been kind enough to lavish upon my plans and hopes for the future! When I was elected quaestor,[2] I felt that the post had not only been conferred on me, but was a solemn trust committed into my hands. When I was carrying out the duties of my quaestorship in Sicily, I was convinced that all men's eyes were turned upon myself, and myself alone. It seemed to me that my own person, and my office, were set upon a stage, acting before an audience which was nothing less than the whole of the world. And so I denied myself all the amenities which are permitted to the incumbents of such offices, not only for the gratification of out-of-the-way tastes but even to satisfy the most orthodox and indispensable requirements. . . . Now I am an aedile elect.

In return for the labour and worry . . . I shall be the recipient of certain privileges. I shall have the right to speak early in the Senate. I shall be entitled to wear a purple-bordered toga, and sit in a curule chair.[3] I shall be permitted a portrait bust, as my memorial for later generations. And yet, over and above all these things, gentlemen—as I hope for the favour of all the gods in heaven—I must assure you of something else. Certainly, I am very happy that the Roman people has honoured me with this post. And yet my happiness is overtaken by a feeling of consuming anxiety. What I am anxious about is that men should not just think that I was given this office because it had to go to one or another of the candidates. What I want is that they should believe that the people came to a correct decision, and that the appointment went to the right man.

But, in contrast, Verres, consider yourself. I do not propose to talk about the circumstances of your election as praetor. But think of the moment when your election was announced, when the crier declared that you had been invested with this high office, by the votes of the entire Assembly, its senior and junior sections alike. I cannot see how, on

---

[2]A comparatively junior rung on the official ladder.
[3]An ivory folding seat, reserved for senior, "curule" officials.

that occasion, the very sound of the crier's voice could have failed to in-spire you with a feeling that a share in the government of your country had been entrusted into your hands—so that for this one, forthcoming, year at least you would have to keep away from the houses of prosti-tutes! . . .

Let me now tell you, also, of Verres's novel scheme for extracting loot—which he was the first man ever to devise. The normal practice had been that all communities should make provision for their own fleet's costs, comprising food and pay and all other such expenditure. This was done by supplying their commander with the necessary sum. Let us bear in mind that he, for his part, was never likely to venture to incur the danger that he would be charged with misappropriation by people in Rome. For it was his obligation to submit accounts to his fellow-citizens. Thus his conduct of his duties at all times involved not only work but personal risk. This, I repeat, was the invariable practice, not only in Sicily but in every other of our provinces as well. Indeed, it even applied to the pay and expenses of our Italian allies, and of the Latins too, during the period when we used to employ them as auxiliary troops.

Verres, however, was the first man, ever since our imperial rule began, to have ordered that all these funds should be counted out by the provincial communities, to himself in person, and looked after by individuals who were his own nominees. Now, why you chose to intro-duce this innovation, changing a custom that was so longstanding and universal, must be perfectly clear to all. It must be clear enough, too, why, although it would have been so manifestly convenient to leave the handling of the money in other hands, you nevertheless preferred to do nothing of the kind; and why you were willing to take over, personally, a function which was not only tiresome and troublesome but made you the object of suspicions of the most disagreeable nature.

Other schemes for making money, too, were set on foot by Verres. In this connection you should note, gentlemen, how many opportunities of the kind the naval situation alone supplied, quite apart from anything else. For cities were only too ready to pay Verres to exempt them from the requirement of providing sailors. Enlisted men could secure dis-charge for a fee. Then the pay they would have been due to receive would be diverted by Verres to himself, while at the same time he would fail to hand over to all the rest the pay to which they were entitled. . . .

Concerning the torments inflicted on other Roman citizens I prefer just to offer a general, comprehensive description, rather than consider-ing them one by one. While Verres was governor, the prison built at Syracuse by the cruel despot Dionysius I, and known as the Stone Quarries, was the place where Roman citizens had to live. If the thought or sight of any of them caused Verres displeasure, the man was immediately thrown into the Quarries. I can see, gentlemen, that this makes you all very angry.

. . . Verres, how you could have had the nerve to use that place of confinement for foreign malefactors and criminals and pirates and enemies of Rome to incarcerate Roman citizens, in substantial numbers. It is remarkable that the prospect of your future trial never occurred to you, nor the thought of a gathering such as this, at which such a mass of listeners are staring at you with censorious, hostile gaze. How strange that the greatness of the Roman people never entered your mind or presented itself to your imagination, not to speak, as I said, of this great concourse that you might have to face. That you would never again have to appear before their eyes, never re-enter the Forum of the Roman nation, never again be obliged to submit to the authority of our laws and our courts, was surely more than you could have hoped for. . . .

If it had been some monarch, or foreign people or nation, that had treated Roman citizens in this way, we should surely be taking official measures to punish those responsible, and dispatch our armies against them. For we could not possibly have endured such a disgraceful slur upon the honour of Rome without exacting vengeance and punishment. Remember all those important wars upon which our ancestors embarked, because Roman citizens were said to have been insulted, Roman ship-masters placed under arrest, Roman traders subjected to robbery. Yet I, on this occasion, am not complaining because these merchants were arrested, I am not declaring it unendurable that they were robbed. My accusation is that, after their ships and slaves and trading goods had been taken away from them, they were hurled into prison, and in that prison, although Roman citizens, they were killed.

My theme, then, is the brutal execution of that multitude of Roman citizens. And I am speaking about it in Rome itself, before this vast gathering of Romans. I am speaking to a jury composed of senators, members of the most eminent body in the state. I am speaking in the Forum of our Roman people. Yet, if my audience were Scythians instead, what I am saying would move even their barbarian hearts. For so magnificent is our empire, so greatly is the name of Rome respected among all the nations of the world, that it is not felt permissible for any man whatsoever to treat our citizens with such savagery. . . .

REFLECTIONS

We have compared Han China and ancient Rome on many topics. We began by noting that their empires straddled Eurasia about the same time, that they were a similar size with about the same number of people, that they were both based on agricultural technologies that supported emperors, large land-owning classes, and soldiers, and exploited subordinate populations. In selection 18, Adshead laid out these and other broad similarities and then explored a wide range of differences. Some of these differences seem to have been more important than others in making China different from Rome: using a language based on characters, perhaps, more than eating rice. Some differences seem quite profound in their effects. Both Adshead and Lloyd, in selection 21, contrasted Chinese and Greco-Roman thinking patterns and both related different modes of thinking to different types of social organizations.

The idea that different cultures think differently—not just think about different things, but actually think differently—is a periodic theory of anthropologists and social scientists. The French philosopher Lucien Levy-Bruhl wrote *How Natives Think* in 1910 to argue that "natives" had a "pre-logical mentality" of "mystical participation." Most historians and philosophers since have been wary of the implied prejudice in the idea that "natives" do not think logically and of the falsity of the assumption that their behavior is not practical. Levy-Bruhl was dismissed by many later social scientists as a representative of the European colonial attitude toward colonized peoples. Nevertheless, Levy-Bruhl had a profound influence in the development in the twentieth century of the sociology of knowledge, a field of philosophy and social science that explored the ways in which the social position of the knower shaped what was known. The intellectual debate flared recently with the publication of sociologist Marshall Sahlins's *How "Natives" Think: About Captain Cook, For Example* (1996) in which he argued that "natives" thought differently and that scholars who said otherwise were the ones who imposed a distinctly Western emphasis on logic and reason on others in the world who thought differently.

Han China, of course, was nothing like a "primitive" society. Yet the debate about logical/scientific versus symbolic/associational thinking that is raised by Adshead and Lloyd echoes the early debate that gave birth to the sociology of knowledge. In considering the possibility of deep human differences in thought or behavior, one always has to be careful of easy generalizations that fit current prejudices. In the 1950s and 1960s, after World War II, when China was struggling just to feed its population and the Japanese economy exported only cheap toys, social scientists argued that the social consciousness of Confucian cultures led them to become communist or collectivist, but prevented them from becoming capitalist or prosperous. Then, when Japan, Korea, and Taiwan became economic powerhouses in the 1980s, social scientists compared the advantages of the Confucian "Asian tigers" with the presumed cultural inhibitions of the slower economies of India and Southeast Asia. Inevitably, we construct our historical comparisons to understand how we have arrived at where we are. The problem of constructing a good comparison begins with the problem of knowing where we are.

5

Women in Classical Societies

India, China, and the Mediterranean, *500* B.C.E. – *500* C.E.

HISTORICAL CONTEXT

In Chapter 1 we saw how the earliest city societies or "civilizations," which emerged about five thousand years ago, often created patriarchies where fathers ruled families, kings ruled societies, priests administered for gods, and state officials, soldiers, and police preserved laws favoring men. The patriarchies that developed in the ancient world continued through the classical age down to the recent past, if not the present.

Nevertheless, not all patriarchies were alike. Some allowed women greater freedom or autonomy. Yet, they did have one thing in common—change. In the thousand years between 500 B.C.E. and 500 C.E. the roles of women did not remain constant in any society or civilization.

Historians call this period the "classical age" because it produced some of the enduring works of a number of the world's major civilizations, some of which we read in Chapters 3 and 4. In this chapter, we will read more of these works, partly to savor their authors' vision and insights and to understand the reasons for their wide acclaim. But we will also use these writings as windows on classical social life. We will ask specifically what they tell us about the comparative and changing roles of women in the classical age.

THINKING HISTORICALLY
Considering Historical Moment and Historical Process

We can think of history as moment or process. Most popular history attempts to capture a moment. Plays, movies, even our own imagina-

154

tions usually try to capture moments: what it was like to live in ancient Rome, witness the assassination of Caesar or the preaching of Jesus. The appeal of a good primary source is that it can immerse us in its particular historical moment. In the previous two chapters we also used primary sources to compare two moments in different cultures—Rome with China, Greece with India, for instance—as if these moments could stand in for the whole history of a culture or civilization.

We also study history to understand how things change: How did the Roman Empire decline? How did Christianity spread? This is the study of history as process. Here we must also use primary sources (since that is, by definition, all we have of the past), but since each one represents only a particular moment we have to either examine it for evidence of change or gather many to see the changes that occurred from one moment to the next.

In this chapter we will be studying both historical moments and historical processes in the history of women in classical antiquity. We will read the efforts of historians to understand the process of change in women's history during this period. And we will examine primary sources—written and visual—that reflect moments of that past. We will also be comparing one document with another. But in addition to comparing a document from Rome, for instance, with one from China, we will also be considering how each document might reflect a particular stage or period in the longer process of the history of its civilization and of the history of women generally. We do this to understand and practice two different ways of thinking about the past.

24

SARAH SHAVER HUGHES
AND BRADY HUGHES

Women in the Classical Era

Sarah and Brady Hughes are modern historians. This selection is part of their essay on the history of women in the ancient world. They write here of the classical era in India, China, Greece, and Rome. All of these were patriarchal societies, but how were they different? The authors also mention later Greek Hellenistic society and pre-Roman Etruscan society. How do these two societies round out your understanding of women in the classical era? What seem to be the conditions or causes that improved the status of women in some societies and periods?

Thinking Historically

Notice that from the first sentence, the authors are interested in understanding the historical process, specifically how the role of women changed over time. In what societies do they see change? Did the roles of women improve or decline in these societies during this period? How do the authors use primary sources to show change?

India

Women's rights deteriorated after the Vedic* period (1600–800 B.C.E.). No one has been able to prove why this happened. Scholarly interest has focused on women's exclusion from performing Hindu rituals, which was in effect by 500 B.C.E. . . . Julia Leslie thinks that women's exclusion resulted from intentional mistranslation of the Vedas by male scholars, as the rituals became more complicated and as the requirement for property ownership was more rigorously enforced at a time when women could not own property.

*VAY dihk

Sarah Shaver Hughes and Brady Hughes, "Women in Ancient Civilizations," in *Women's History in Global Perspective*, vol. II, ed. Bonnie G. Smith (Urbana: University of Illinois Press, published with the American Historical Association, 2005), 26–30 minus deletions and 36–40 minus deletions.

The falling age of marriage for Indian women is another illustration of their loss of rights. In 400 B.C.E. about sixteen years was a normal age for a bride at marriage; between 400 B.C.E. and 100 C.E. it fell to pre-puberty; and after 100 C.E. pre-puberty was favored. These child marriages also affected women's religious roles. Because girls married before they could finish their education, they were not qualified to perform ritual sacrifices. Furthermore, wives' legal rights eroded. As child wives, they were treated as minors. Then their minority status lengthened until they were lifetime minors as wards of their husbands. Finally, women were prohibited any independence and were always under men's control: their fathers, husbands, or sons. By 100 C.E. Hindu texts defined women with negative characteristics, stating, for example, that women would be promiscuous unless controlled by male relatives. While Indian women were losing their independence, Indian men continued to glorify their wives and mothers. A wife was the essence of the home, a man was not complete without a wife, and sons were expected to respect their mothers more than their fathers. As Romila Thapar sums up these contradictions, "The symbol of the woman in Indian culture has been a curious intermeshing of low legal status, ritual contempt, sophisticated sexual partnership, and deification."

One of the causes for this deterioration of women's rights and independence was the increasing rigidity of Hinduism under the influence of the Brahmans. By 600 B.C.E. sects were springing up that opposed Brahman power and ostentatiously omitted some of the Hindu essentials, such as priests, rituals and ceremonies, animal sacrifices, and even caste distinctions. Jainism and Buddhism are two of the sects that have survived. They were especially attractive to women. Jainism, the older religion, gained prominence with the efforts of its last prophet, Mahavira, who lived at the end of the sixth century B.C.E. Jains sought to live without passion and to act "correctly." One could achieve liberation only by living within a monastery or nunnery. Women who sought to join a nunnery found that the Jains had no membership restrictions. Many women entered and found new and exciting roles that were for the first time open to them. . . .

Mahavira's contemporary, Gautama Siddhartha* (the Buddha), began the religion that eventually spread throughout Asia. Among studies of Buddhist women, the early years have been a focus of interest. While Buddhism had no priests, it relied on celibate monks, who were initially homeless, except in the monsoon season, and had to beg for their necessities as they spread their ideas. The Buddha was reluctant to allow women to become nuns. He refused even the women in

*GAW tah moh   sih DAHR thah

his family who sought to become nuns until he was reminded repeatedly by his aunt and his disciple Ananda of his stated principle that anyone could attain enlightenment. The Buddha then reluctantly accepted women followers, and they, like monks, eventually lived in their own self-governing celibate monasteries. . . .

China

. . . For Chinese women the ideas of Confucius (551–479 B.C.E.) have been most influential. There is little mention of women in his *Analects*. His neo-Confucian interpreters corrected this omission, however. They made explicit men's desire for a woman's subordination to her family, her husband, and her sons. For example, Lieh Nu Chuan (also known as Liu Hsiang, 80–87 B.C.E.) wrote *The Biographies of Eminent Chinese Women*, in which he included 125 biographies of women from the peasant class to the emperor's wife, taken from prehistoric legends to the early years of the Han dynasty.

Although the purpose of these biographical sketches was to provide moral instruction in the passive ideals of Confucian womanhood, translator Albert Richard O'Hara's analysis of the women's actions reveals their influence on events that were important to them. The traditional Chinese interpretation of the genre is evident in one of the best-known biographies, that of the widowed mother of Mencius (Meng K'o, or Meng-tzu), whose stern supervision and self-sacrifice were shown to have shaped her son's character and philosophy. This tale drives home the point that a woman's highest ambitions should be fulfilled indirectly through the talents of her sons. Pan Chao,[1] a female scholar in the first century C.E., wrote *The Seven Feminine Virtues* as a Confucian manual for girls' behavior. Its prescriptions of humility, meekness, modesty, and hard work continued to be copied by generations of young women until the twentieth century. . . .

Occasionally, imperial women seized power to govern when acting as regent for an underage emperor. Usually regents exercised this power cautiously behind the scenes because there was much opposition to women's open governance. Two famous empresses ruled openly, however, and sought to transfer royal descent to their own natal families. The first, Empress Lu, violated every canon of Confucian femininity. The widow of Gaodi, the first Han emperor (ruled 202–195 B.C.E.), Empress Lu acted swiftly and brutally to eliminate competitors at court during the near-fifteen years of her rule as regent for her son, her grandson, and another adopted infant grandson. By retaining power

---

[1]Ban Zhao in selection 26. [Ed.]

until her death in 181 B.C.E., she expected that her own nephews would succeed her. Instead, a civil war over the succession ended the period of peaceful prosperity, low taxes, and lessened punishment for crimes that had made her reign popular with the Chinese people. . . .

Greece

Classical Greece has long been admired for its political theories, philosophy, science, and the arts. Until recently, Greek social history was largely ignored. Slavery, homosexuality, and subordination of women are topics once dismissed as insignificant but now recognized as important to understanding the culture. In the classical period there were actually many "Greeces," with distinct societies developing in the city-states of Athens, Sparta, and Thebes. Gender patterns varied considerably among these cities. Sparta's aristocratic women, for example, were often left alone to acquire wealth and some autonomy when their mercenary husbands soldiered elsewhere. To some Athenian men such as Aristotle, Spartan women were thought to be despicable, licentious, greedy, and the reason for Sparta's decline.

Aristotle and other Athenian men dominate the discourse from classical Greece. Their male descriptions tell how Athenian society secluded elite women, denigrated and exploited them, and made them the legal dependents of men. Because no women's writings survive, only indirect evidence suggests how Athenian wives escaped their lives of hard work in the isolated, dark rooms that their husbands imagined necessary to preserve their chastity. But as drawn on vases, groups of Athenian women read to one another, spun and wove, shared child care, or talked. Women are shown in public processions and getting water from wells. Bits of documentary records show respectable married women earning their livings as wet nurses, farm workers, and retail vendors. Most records reveal the lives of privileged women, yet many Athenian women were slaves. Exposure of unwanted female babies was one internal source of slaves, for the rescuer of such an infant became her owner. Athenian enslavement of females was exceptional in its celebration of prostitution in literary and artistic records. One explanation for the large number of slave sex workers may be the Athenians' desire to attract sailors and merchants to their port.

Research on women in the Hellenistic period concentrates on Greek women living in Egypt. These women were much more assertive and influential than their sisters in either contemporary Greece or later Rome. Women in the ruling Ptolemaic family often actually ruled Egypt, some as regents, others as queens. Cleopatra VII (69–30 B.C.E.), one of the best-known women in ancient history, guided her country from a tributary position in the Roman Empire into a partnership with

Marc Antony that might have led to Egypt's domination of the eastern Mediterranean. Non-elite women had unusual freedom. They owned property (including land), participated in commerce, produced textiles, were educated, and enjoyed careers as artists, poets, and farmers. But some women were slaves. . . .

Rome

As late as the sixth century B.C.E., Rome was dominated by its northern neighbors, the Etruscans. Although no body of Etruscan literature exists, scholars have sought evidence of women's lives from inscriptions and art found in their tombs. Upper-class Etruscan women were more autonomous and privileged than contemporary Greek women. Paintings of husbands and wives feasting together horrified Greek males, who only allowed prostitutes to attend their banquets. Etruscan women were not restricted to their homes as Greek women were and attended the games at gymnasiums. In Italy, all women left votive statues of women in sacred places, probably as a fertility offering, but only Etruscan statues included a nursing child, suggesting an affection for children that paralleled the affectionate touching between couples occasionally shown in their art. Finally, Etruscan women had personal names, in contrast to Greek women, who were known first as their fathers' daughters and later as their husbands' wives.

The Romans did not duplicate the autonomy of women in Etruscan society. Roman women legally were constrained within a highly patriarchal agricultural system organized around clans. A father could kill or sell his children into slavery without fear of legal action. Husbands could kill their wives if they were caught in adultery. Women did not speak in public meetings. They could not buy and sell property without their male relatives' approval. Legally treated as minors, women were first the responsibility of their fathers, then of their husbands, and finally of appointed guardians. Rome was a warrior society and a male republic. Men even dominated the state religion, with the exception of the six Vestal Virgins who served as priestesses. Roman society remained staunchly male until conquests brought wealth to Italy in the second century B.C.E. Changes that accompanied the booty of empire gave women a measure of economic and marital independence that is illustrated by the loosening of legal restrictions against women's property ownership.

The paterfamilias, the oldest male in the family, had complete *manus* (legal control) over his children. In marriage, manus passed from the paterfamilias to the new husband. Among other things, that meant the husband then controlled all of his wife's property. Before the first century B.C.E. some Roman marriages were made without transferring manus to the husband; the wife and her property would remain under her father's control, whose approval was theoretically required for the daughter to buy or sell property. Susan Treggiari explains how this enabled many women to gain control over their property:

> Given ancient expectation of life, it is probable that many women were fatherless for a relatively long period of their married lives. The pattern . . . for the middle ranks of Roman society is that girls married in their late teens and men in their mid- to late twenties. If expectation of life at birth is put between twenty and thirty, then 46 percent of fifteen-year-olds had no father left alive. The percentage grows to 59 percent of twenty-year-olds and 70 percent of twenty-five-year-olds. So there is about a 50 percent chance that a woman was already fatherless at the time of her first marriage.

Upon a father's death, manus was transferred to a guardian, and women began to choose as their guardians men who agreed with them. By the later years of the Roman Republic, therefore, many women bought and sold land as they pleased. Rome's expansion contributed to this change as it fueled a growing market in real and personal property.

In the third century B.C.E., Rome began two centuries of conquests that eventually placed most of the land surrounding the Mediterranean under Roman administration or in the hands of client states. Roman wives farmed while citizen-soldiers of the Republic were on campaigns, sometimes for more than a decade. Successful wars enriched a Roman elite who accumulated estates worked by male and female slaves as small farmers sold their lands and moved to the city with their wives and children. Elite Romans, both men and women, possessed large estates, luxurious urban houses, much rental property, and many slaves. By 50 B.C.E., Rome had a population of approximately one million. Slaves poured into Italy after successful campaigns, when the defeated enemy was enslaved. As the Romans conquered country after country, they brutalized the captured women, enslaving many. Ruling queens in subdued countries were inevitably replaced with either indigenous male elites or Roman officials. Queen Boudicca of Britain, for example, led a revolt that ended in her death in the first century C.E. Queen Zenobia of Palmyra's invasion of the empire in the third century C.E. was so well organized that Roman authors praised her. Cleopatra of Egypt committed suicide when her plan to make Egypt a regional partner of Rome failed.

Roman women did not publicly speak in the Forum (where men debated civic affairs), with the notable exception of Hortensia in 43 B.C.E. She was the spokesperson for a demonstration of wealthy women who protested taxation without representation for civil wars they did not support. Elite women usually indirectly influenced political decisions through networks of politicians' wives. During the civil wars of the first century B.C.E., wives of some tyrants even made temporary political decisions. On a wider scale, middle-class and elite women took advantage of the turmoil at the end of the Republic to acquire businesses, as analysis of Pompeii shows. Prostitution flowered in Rome with the inflow of slaves, both male and female. A small part of the elite lived in the self-indulgent luxury that became famous in literature. In a brief period of two generations at the end of the first century B.C.E., Roman elite women eschewed children and family responsibilities for a glamorous and self-absorbed life of parties and lovers. In this period men and women were openly adulterous. This "café society" flourished in the chaos of civil wars that nearly destroyed the prestige of the elite and killed or exiled many of them.

This era of chaos ended during the reign of the emperor Augustus (ruled 27 B.C.E.–14 C.E.), who sought to stabilize Roman society in part by reducing women's freedoms. Women were criticized for adultery, wearing too much makeup, having immodest dress and conduct, and especially for refusing to have children. Augustus procured laws that intended to remove control of marriage and reproduction from the family and allow the state to regulate marriage and reproduction. He attempted to penalize women between the ages of twenty and fifty and men over the age of twenty-five who did not marry and have children by denying them the right to inherit wealth. Furthermore, women were not to be released from male guardianship until they had three children. The Augustan laws made the state the regulator of private behavior and attempted to raise the birthrate of citizens while accepting some of the social changes that had modified the patriarchal society of the old Roman Republic. Augustus sought political support from conservative males by decreasing the autonomy of women who had less political influence than men.

Comparing Women's Status in Various Societies

As discussed earlier, the major literate civilizations of the ancient world were patriarchal. Later records from preliterate societies of the ancient period indicate that women in such societies could be more independent and have a higher status (for example, in many Southeast Asian and African societies). An appearance of universal subordination of women results from focusing only on early literate civilizations while ignoring the lives of women in nonliterate societies.

In the twentieth century, individual choice in personal relationships has replaced family selection of spouses in many societies, although arranged marriages persist in some cultures. In the ancient patriarchal world, however, the family chose spouses for their daughters and sons. Women lived with few civil rights in male-dominated societies. In inter-

preting ancient women's lives, scholars are faced with two contradictory images. The harsh portrayal is that women were sold by their fathers or brothers to husbands who abused them and that they were
considered to have the intellectual capacity of a child, perpetually dependent on a male. Alternatively, some documents reveal women who
were loved by their parents, husbands, and children. These women
could use the love and affection of their male relatives to gain personal
advantages that society would legally deny them. More likely, both explanations accurately reflect aspects of women's lives. Women negotiated a daily balance of gender power in personal relationships, often ignoring disadvantageous laws or ritual regulations, but those laws and
regulations could also fall with terrible force on any woman in the ancient patriarchal world.

R. K. NARAYAN

From The Ramayana

The Ramayana is a classic Indian epic that originated as an oral tradition between 1500 and 400 B.C.E., and was first recorded in the first
century C.E. by the poet Valmiki. The poem celebrates the virtues of
Prince Rama and his wife Sita, who eventually came to be worshiped
as deities in the Hindu pantheon. Exiled from his father's kingdom,
Rama goes to live in the forest, and Sita, a dutiful and devoted wife,
follows him. Sita is abducted by Ravana, an evil king who holds her
prisoner in his kingdom. Rama eventually defeats Ravana with the
help of the god Hanuman and brings his beloved Sita back to his own
kingdom, which he rightfully regains. But before Rama can fully accept Sita as his queen, she must prove that she has remained loyal to
him during her captivity.

There are innumerable versions and variations on this basic story,
which is divided into distinct episodes, two of which you will read
here. The first selection, the story of Ahalya and Gautama, serves as a
prologue to the main tale of Rama and Sita, and focuses on female
loyalty. We skip over the main body of the epic and pick up at the end

R. K. Narayan, *The Ramayana* (Harmondsworth: Penguin Books, 1977), 20–22, 161–64.

of the story in the second selection, in which Sita proves her fidelity to
Rama. The assurance of a wife's loyalty to her husband was (and still
is) an important requirement in patriarchal societies in which men preserve their family lines by ensuring the legitimacy of their sons.

How are the stories of Ahalya and Gautama and of Rama and Sita
similar? Why are the women punished? What seem to be the lessons
of these stories? What do these stories reveal about classical Indian
ideas of women, sexuality, and chastity?

Thinking Historically

In the previous selection, Sarah and Brady Hughes made a distinction
between Vedic and post-Vedic Indian history. In which period would
you place this story of Rama and Sita? Any document represents a
moment in history. Yet this story has been told in many versions over
the centuries. This version is by the modern Indian novelist R. K.
Narayan. Does it then reflect modern Indian values? Narayan writes
about his modern Indian audience in the introduction: "Everyone of
whatever age, outlook, education, or station in life knows the essential
part of the epic and adores the main figures in it—Rama and Sita."
Narayan based his version on an eleventh-century C.E. version. What
does the continued appeal of this story suggest about the history of
patriarchy in India?

While passing over slightly raised ground beside the walls of the fort,
Rama noticed a shapeless slab of stone, half buried vertically in the
ground; when he brushed past, the dust of his feet fell on it, and transformed it, that very instant, into a beautiful woman. As the woman did
obeisance and stood aside respectfully, Viswamithra introduced her to
Rama. "If you have heard of Sage Gautama, whose curse resulted in
great Indra's body being studded with a thousand eyes, all over. . . .
This lady was his wife, and her name is Ahalya." And he told Rama her
story.

Ahalya's Story

Brahma once created, out of the ingredients of absolute beauty, a
woman, and she was called Ahalya (which in the Sanskrit language
means non-imperfection). God Indra, being the highest god among the
gods, was attracted by her beauty and was convinced that he alone was
worthy of claiming her hand. Brahma, noticing the conceit and pre-
sumptuousness of Indra, ignored him, sought out Sage Gautama, and
left him in charge of the girl. She grew up in his custody, and when the

time came the sage took her back to Brahma and handed her over to him.

Brahma appreciated Gautama's purity of mind and heart (never once had any carnal thought crossed his mind), and said, "Marry her, she is fit to be your wife, or rather you alone deserve to be her husband." Accordingly, she was married, blessed by Brahma and other gods. Having spent her childhood with Gautama, Ahalya knew his needs and so proved a perfect wife, and they lived happily.

Indra, however, never got over his infatuation for Ahalya, and often came in different guises near to Gautama's *ashram*, waiting for every chance to gaze and feast on Ahalya's form and figure; he also watched the habits of the sage and noticed that the sage left his ashram at the dawn of each day and was away for a couple of hours at the river for his bath and prayers. Unable to bear the pangs of love any more, Indra decided to attain the woman of his heart by subterfuge. One day, hardly able to wait for the sage to leave at his usual hour, Indra assumed the voice of a rooster, and woke up the sage, who, thinking that the morning had come, left for the river. Now Indra assumed the sage's form, entered the hut, and made love to Ahalya. She surrendered herself, but at some stage realized that the man enjoying her was an imposter; but she could do nothing about it. Gautama came back at this moment, having intuitively felt that something was wrong, and surprised the couple in bed. Ahalya stood aside filled with shame and remorse; Indra assumed the form of a cat (the most facile animal form for sneaking in or out) and tried to slip away. The sage looked from the cat to the woman and was not to be deceived. He arrested the cat where he was with these words:

"Cat, I know you; your obsession with the female is your undoing. May your body be covered with a thousand female marks, so that in all the worlds, people may understand what really goes on in your mind all the time." Hardly had these words left his lips when every inch of Indra's body displayed the female organ. There could be no greater shame for the proud and self-preening Indra.

After Indra slunk away, back to his world, Gautama looked at his wife and said, "You have sinned with your body. May that body harden into a shapeless piece of granite, just where you are. . . ." Now in desperation Ahalya implored, "A grave mistake has been committed. It is in the nature of noble souls to forgive the errors of lesser beings. Please . . . I am already feeling a weight creeping up my feet. Do something . . . please help me. . . ."

Now the sage felt sorry for her and said, "Your redemption will come when the son of Dasaratha, Rama, passes this way at some future date. . . ."

"When? Where?" she essayed to question, desperately, but before the words could leave her lips she had become a piece of stone.

Indra's predicament became a joke in all the worlds at first, but later proved noticeably tragic. He stayed in darkness and seclusion and could never appear before men or women. This caused much concern to all the gods, as his multifarious duties in various worlds remained suspended, and they went in a body to Brahma and requested him to intercede with Gautama. By this time, the sage's resentment had vanished. And he said in response to Brahma's appeal, "May the thousand additions to Indra's features become eyes." Indra thereafter came to be known as the "thousand-eyed god."

Viswamithra concluded the story and addressed Rama. "O great one, you are born to restore righteousness and virtue to mankind and eliminate all evil. At our yagna, I saw the power of your arms, and now I see the greatness of the touch of your feet."

Rama said to Ahalya, "May you seek and join your revered husband, and live in his service again. Let not your heart be burdened with what is past and gone."

On their way to Mithila, they stopped to rest at Gautama's hermitage, and Viswamithra told the sage, "Your wife is restored to her normal form, by the touch of Rama's feet. Go and take her back, her heart is purified through the ordeal she has undergone." All this accomplished, they moved on, leaving behind the scented groves and forest, and approached the battlemented gates of Mithila City.

[The epic goes on to tell the story of Sita's abduction by the evil King Ravana. Rama defeats Ravana, and Sita is brought back home.]

Conclusion

After the death of Ravana, Rama sent Hanuman as his emissary to fetch Sita. Sita was overjoyed. She had been in a state of mourning all along, completely neglectful of her dress and appearance, and she immediately rose to go out and meet Rama as she was. But Hanuman explained that it was Rama's express wish that she should dress and decorate herself before coming to his presence.

A large crowd pressed around Rama. When Sita eagerly arrived, after her months of loneliness and suffering, she was received by her husband in full view of a vast public. She felt awkward but accepted this with resignation. But what she could not understand was why her lord seemed preoccupied and moody and cold. However, she prostrated herself at his feet, and then stood a little away from him, sensing some strange barrier between herself and him.

Rama remained brooding for a while and suddenly said, "My task is done. I have now freed you. I have fulfilled my mission. All this effort has been not to attain personal satisfaction for you or me. It was to vindicate the honour of the Ikshvahu race and to honour our ancestors' codes and values. After all this, I must tell you that it is not customary to admit back to the normal married fold a woman who has resided all alone in a stranger's house. There can be no question of our living together again. I leave you free to go where you please and to choose any place to live in. I do not restrict you in any manner."

On hearing this, Sita broke down. "My trials are not ended yet," she cried. "I thought with your victory all our troubles were at an end . . . ! So be it." She beckoned to Lakshmana and ordered, "Light a fire at once, on this very spot."

Lakshmana hesitated and looked at his brother, wondering whether he would countermand the order. But Rama seemed passive and acquiescent. Lakshmana, ever the most unquestioning deputy, gathered faggots and got ready a roaring pyre within a short time. The entire crowd watched the proceedings, stunned by the turn of events. The flames rose to the height of a tree; still Rama made no comment. He watched. Sita approached the fire, prostrated herself before it, and said, "O Agni, great god of fire, be my witness." She jumped into the fire.

From the heart of the flame rose the god of fire, bearing Sita, and presented her to Rama with words of blessing. Rama, now satisfied that he had established his wife's integrity in the presence of the world, welcomed Sita back to his arms.

Rama explained that he had to adopt this trial in order to demonstrate Sita's purity beyond a shadow of a doubt to the whole world. This seemed a rather strange inconsistency on the part of one who had brought back to life and restored to her husband a person like Ahalya, who had avowedly committed a moral lapse; and then there was Sugreeva's wife, who had been forced to live with Vali, and whom Rama commended as worthy of being taken back by Sugreeva after Vali's death. In Sita's case Ravana, in spite of repeated and desperate attempts, could not approach her. She had remained inviolable. And the fiery quality of her essential being burnt out the god of fire himself, as he had admitted after Sita's ordeal.

BAN ZHAO

Lessons for Women

Just as the epic poem *The Ramayana* created ideals for men, and women in India, the teachings of Confucius (561–479 B.C.E.) provided the Chinese and other Asian peoples with ideals of private and public conduct. Confucius's teachings emphasized the importance of filial piety, or the duty of children to serve and obey their parents, as well as to exercise restraint and treat others as one would like to be treated (see selection 19 for excerpts from Confucius's *Analects*). Ban Zhao* (45–116 C.E.) (Pan Chao in selection 24) was the leading female Confucian scholar of classical China. Born into a literary family and educated by her mother, she was married at the age of fourteen. After her husband's death she finished writing her brother's history of the Han dynasty and served as imperial historian to Emperor Han Hedi (r. 88–105 C.E.) and as an advisor to the Empress-Dowager Deng.

Ban Zhao is best remembered, however, for her *Lessons for Women*, which she wrote to fill a gap in Confucian literature. With their emphasis on the responsibilities of the son to the father and on the moral example of a good ruler, the writings of Confucius virtually ignored women. Ban Zhao sought to rectify that oversight by applying Confucian principles to the moral instruction of women. In what ways would Ban Zhao's *Lessons* support Chinese patriarchy? In what ways might they challenge the patriarchy or make it less oppressive for women? What similarities are there between the Confucian and Indian ideas of women's proper role?

Thinking Historically

This text came from a particular historical moment—in fact a moment that we can date with greater accuracy and assurance than any of the Confucian writings. Still, there are two reasons why we might be persuaded that it speaks for a longer period of Chinese history than its single moment of appearance. One reason is that, like *The Ramayana*, it is a classic text that has been retold for generations. We can imagine that its message was continually reinforced in the

*bahn ZHOW

Pan Chao: Foremost Woman Scholar of China, trans. Nancy Lee Swann (New York: Century Co., 1932), 82–90.

retelling. Second, there are clues in the text itself that these ideas are not entirely new. What are those clues?

This may seem to be a very patriarchal text. Yet it is written by a woman. How do you account for that? Some have said that Ban Zhao was actually modifying Confucian patriarchal values by stressing the bond between husband and wife rather than the traditional Confucian bond between father and son or parents and daughter-in-law. Can you see any evidence of such emphasis in the text of the document?

I, the unworthy writer, am unsophisticated, unenlightened, and by nature unintelligent, but I am fortunate both to have received not a little favor from my scholarly Father, and to have had a cultured mother and instructresses upon whom to rely for a literary education as well as for training in good manners. More than forty years have passed since at the age of fourteen I took up the dustpan and the broom in the Cao family.[1] During this time with trembling heart I feared constantly that I might disgrace my parents, and that I might multiply difficulties for both the women and the men of my husband's family. Day and night I was distressed in heart, but I labored without confessing weariness. Now and hereafter, however, I know how to escape from such fears.

Being careless, and by nature stupid, I taught and trained my children without system. Consequently I fear that my son Gu may bring disgrace upon the Imperial Dynasty by whose Holy Grace he has unprecedentedly received the extraordinary privilege of wearing the Gold and the Purple, a privilege for the attainment of which by my son, I a humble subject never even hoped. Nevertheless, now that he is a man and able to plan his own life, I need not again have concern for him. But I do grieve that you, my daughters, just now at the age for marriage, have not at this time had gradual training and advice; that you still have not learned the proper customs for married women. I fear that by failure in good manners in other families you will humiliate both your ancestors and your clan. I am now seriously ill, life is uncertain. As I have thought of you all in so untrained a state, I have been uneasy many a time for you. At hours of leisure I have composed . . . these instructions under the title, "Lessons for Women." In order that you may have something wherewith to benefit your persons, I wish every one of you, my daughters each to write out a copy for yourself.

From this time on every one of you strive to practice these lessons.

---

[1] Her husband's family. [Ed.]

Humility

On the third day after the birth of a girl the ancients observed three customs: first to place the baby below the bed; second to give her a potsherd[2] with which to play; and third to announce her birth to her ancestors by an offering. Now to lay the baby below the bed plainly indicated that she is lowly and weak, and should regard it as her primary duty to humble herself before others. To give her potsherds with which to play indubitably signified that she should practice labor and consider it her primary duty to be industrious. To announce her birth before her ancestors clearly meant that she ought to esteem as her primary duty the continuation of the observance of worship in the home.

These three ancient customs epitomize woman's ordinary way of life and the teachings of the traditional ceremonial rites and regulations. Let a woman modestly yield to others; let her respect others; let her put others first, herself last. Should she do something good, let her not mention it; should she do something bad let her not deny it. Let her bear disgrace; let her even endure when others speak or do evil to her. Always let her seem to tremble and to fear. When a woman follows such maxims as these then she may be said to humble herself before others.

Let a woman retire late to bed, but rise early to duties; let her not dread tasks by day or by night. Let her not refuse to perform domestic duties whether easy or difficult. That which must be done, let her finish completely, tidily, and systematically. When a woman follows such rules as these, then she may be said to be industrious.

Let a woman be correct in manner and upright in character in order to serve her husband. Let her live in purity and quietness of spirit, and attend to her own affairs. Let her love not gossip and silly laughter. Let her cleanse and purify and arrange in order the wine and the food for the offerings to the ancestors. When a woman observes such principles as these, then she may be said to continue ancestral worship.

No woman who observes these three fundamentals of life has ever had a bad reputation or has fallen into disgrace. If a woman fails to observe them, how can her name be honored; how can she but bring disgrace upon herself?

Husband and Wife

The Way of husband and wife is intimately connected with Yin and Yang and relates the individual to gods and ancestors. Truly it is the great principle of Heaven and Earth, and the great basis of human rela-

---

[2]A piece of broken pottery. [Ed.]

tionships. Therefore the "Rites"[3] honor union of man and woman; and in the "Book of Poetry"[4] the "First Ode" manifests the principle of marriage. For these reasons the relationship cannot but be an important one.

If a husband be unworthy, then he possesses nothing by which to control his wife. If a wife be unworthy, then she possesses nothing with which to serve her husband. If a husband does not control his wife, then the rules of conduct manifesting his authority are abandoned and broken. If a wife does not serve her husband, then the proper relationship between men and women and the natural order of things are neglected and destroyed. As a matter of fact the purpose of these two[5] is the same.

Now examine the gentlemen of the present age. They only know that wives must be controlled, and that the husband's rules of conduct manifesting his authority must be established. They therefore teach their boys to read books and study histories. But they do not in the least understand that husbands and masters must also be served, and that the proper relationship and the rites should be maintained. Yet only to teach men and not to teach women — is that not ignoring the essential relation between them? According to the "Rites," it is the rule to begin to teach children to read at the age of eight years, and by the age of fifteen years they ought then to be ready for cultural training. Only why should it not be that girls' education as well as boys' be according to this principle?

Respect and Caution

As Yin and Yang are not of the same nature, so man and woman have different characteristics. The distinctive quality of the Yang is rigidity; the function of the Yin is yielding. Man is honored for strength; a woman is beautiful on account of her gentleness. Hence there arose the common saying: "A man though born like a wolf may, it is feared, become a weak monstrosity; a woman though born like a mouse may, it is feared, become a tiger."

Now for self-culture nothing equals respect for others. To counteract firmness nothing equals compliance. Consequently it can be said that the Way of respect and acquiescence is woman's most important principle of conduct. So respect may be defined as nothing other than holding on to that which is permanent; and acquiescence nothing other

---

[3]*The Classic of Rites.* [Ed.]
[4]*The Classic of Odes.* [Ed.]
[5]The controlling of women by men, and the serving of men by women. [Ed.]

than being liberal and generous. Those who are steadfast in devotion know that they should stay in their proper places; those who are liberal and generous esteem others, and honor and serve them.

If husband and wife have the habit of staying together, never leaving one another, and following each other around within the limited space of their own rooms, then they will lust after and take liberties with one another. From such action improper language will arise between the two. This kind of discussion may lead to licentiousness. But of licentiousness will be born a heart of disrespect to the husband. Such a result comes from not knowing that one should stay in one's proper place.

Furthermore, affairs may be either crooked or straight; words may be either right or wrong. Straightforwardness cannot but lead to quarreling; crookedness cannot but lead to accusation. If there are really accusations and quarrels, then undoubtedly there will be angry affairs. Such a result comes from not esteeming others, and not honoring and serving them.

If wives suppress not contempt for husbands, then it follows that such wives rebuke and scold their husbands. If husbands stop not short of anger, then they are certain to beat their wives. The correct relationship between husband and wife is based upon harmony and intimacy, and conjugal love is grounded in proper union. Should actual blows be dealt, how could matrimonial relationship be preserved? Should sharp words be spoken, how could conjugal love exist? If love and proper relationship both be destroyed, then husband and wife are divided.

Womanly Qualifications

A woman ought to have four qualifications: (1) womanly virtue; (2) womanly words; (3) womanly bearing; and (4) womanly work. Now what is called womanly virtue need not be brilliant ability, exceptionally different from others. Womanly words need be neither clever in debate nor keen in conversation. Womanly appearance requires neither a pretty nor a perfect face and form. Womanly work need not be work done more skillfully than that of others.

To guard carefully her chastity; to control circumspectly her behavior; in every motion to exhibit modesty; and to model each act on the best usage, this is womanly virtue.

To choose her words with care; to avoid vulgar language; to speak at appropriate times; and not to weary others with much conversation, may be called the characteristics of womanly words.

To wash and scrub filth away; to keep clothes and ornaments fresh and clean; to wash the head and bathe the body regularly, and to keep the person free from disgraceful filth, may be called the characteristics of womanly bearing.

With whole-hearted devotion to sew and to weave; to love not gossip and silly laughter; in cleanliness and order to prepare the wine and food for serving guests, may be called the characteristics of womanly work.

These four qualifications characterize the greatest virtue of a woman. No woman can afford to be without them. In fact they are very easy to possess if a woman only treasures them in her heart. The ancients had a saying: "Is love afar off? If I desire love, then love is at hand!" So can it be said of these qualifications.

Implicit Obedience

Whenever the mother-in-law says, "Do not do that," and if what she says is right, unquestionably the daughter-in-law obeys. Whenever the mother-in-law says, "Do that," even if what she says is wrong, still the daughter-in-law submits unfailingly to the command. Let a woman not act contrary to the wishes and the opinions of parents-in-law about right and wrong; let her not dispute with them what is straight and what is crooked. Such docility may be called obedience which sacrifices personal opinion. Therefore the ancient book, "A Pattern for Women," says: "If a daughter-in-law who follows the wishes of her parents-in-law is like an echo and shadow, how could she not be praised?"

$$\boxed{27}$$

ARISTOPHANES

From Lysistrata

Lysistrata* is often considered the best play of the comic Athenian playwright Aristophanes.† Written in the midst of the Peloponnesian War (431–404 B.C.E.), which concluded with the capitulation of Athens and the end of the Athenian golden age, Aristophanes imagines the women of Athens, Sparta, and other Greek city-states coming together

*lih sih STRAH tuh
†air ih STAH fuh neez

Aristophanes, *Lysistrata*, trans. Douglas Parker (New York: Signet, 2001), 55–58.

to force their husbands to make peace by means of a sex strike. The successful strategy of the women follows the plan of the Athenian Lysistrata to refuse sexual intercourse with their husbands or anyone else until the war is ended. Aristophanes suggests that their motive is partly personal—their men are gone and some of their sons are dead. But the play also allows Aristophanes to use women's voices to express misgivings about the war. In this selection, from midway in the play, Lysistrata berates the male politicians for the war and their ineptitude.

Nothing like this happened, of course. But even an overtly farcical and comical play reflects something of the world that produced it. What does the play tell you about the role of women in Athens or in other Greek city-states? How do the lives of Greek women compare to the lives of women in China or India?

Thinking Historically

Lysistrata appeared at a critical moment in the Athenian Peloponnesian War with Sparta, after the annihilation of the Athenian expeditionary forces in Sicily in 413 B.C.E. but before the overthrow of the Athenian constitution in 411. The play prefigures the domestic collapse that followed the external disaster. This was a moment of crisis for Greek politics. But was it also one for women? We do not know. It is interesting that Greek women were generally more independent in Sparta than Athens, and enjoyed greater autonomy in the Hellenistic period that followed the Peloponnesian War than in the Athenian golden age. A moment of crisis is likely to suggest such extreme, though admittedly impossible or improbable, solutions, but what evidence do you see in this selection that Athenian women may have had long-lasting sources of power that had not just appeared overnight?

COMMISSIONER   Might I ask where you women conceived this concern about War and Peace?

LYSISTRATA   *Loftily.* We shall explain.

COMMISSIONER   *Making a fist.* Hurry up, and you won't get hurt.

LYSISTRATA   Then *listen.* And do try to keep your hands to yourself.

COMMISSIONER   *Moving threateningly toward her.* I can't. Righteous anger forbids restraint, and decrees . . .

KLEONIKE   *Brandishing her chamber pot.* Multiple fractures?

COMMISSIONER   *Retreating.* Keep those croaks for yourself, you old crow! *To Lysistrata.* All right, lady, I'm ready. Speak.

KYSISTRATA   I shall proceed: When the War began, like the prudent, dutiful wives that we are, we tolerated you men, and endured your actions in silence. (Small wonder—you wouldn't let us say boo.) You were not precisely the answer to a matron's prayer—we knew you too well, and found out more.

Too many times, as we sat in the house, we'd hear that you'd done it again—manhandled another affair of state with your usual staggering incompetence. Then, masking our worry with a nervous laugh, we'd ask you, brightly, "How was the Assembly today, dear? Anything in the minutes about Peace?" And my husband would give his stock reply. "What's that to you? Shut up!" And I did.

KLEONIKE   *Proudly. I* never shut up!

COMMISSIONER   I trust you were shut up. Soundly.

LYSISTRATA   Regardless, *I* shut up. And then we'd learn that you'd passed another decree, fouler than the first, and we'd ask again: "Darling, how *did* you manage anything so idiotic?" And my husband, with his customary glare, would tell me to spin my thread, or else get a clout on the head. And of course he'd quote from Homer: Yᵉ *menne must husband yᵉ warre.*[1]

COMMISSIONER   Apt and irrefutably right.

LYSISTRATA   *Right*, you miserable misfit? To keep us from giving advice while you fumbled the City away in the Senate? Right, indeed!

But this time was really too much: Wherever we went, we'd hear you engaged in the same conversation:

"What Athens needs is a Man." "But there isn't a Man in the country." "You can say that again."

There was obviously no time to lose. We women met in immediate convention and passed a unanimous resolution: To work in concert for safety and Peace in Greece. We have valuable advice to impart, and if you can possibly deign to emulate our silence, and take your turn as audience, we'll rectify you—we'll straighten you out and set you right.

COMMISSIONER   *You'll* set *us* right? You go too far. I cannot permit such a statement to . . .

LYSISTRATA   Shush.

COMMISSIONER   I categorically decline to shush for some confounded woman, who wears—as a constant reminder of congenital inferiority, an injunction to public silence—a veil!

Death before such dishonor!

---

[1] From *The Iliad*—"Men must wage war."

LYSISTRATA   *Removing her veil.* If that's the only obstacle . . .
I feel you need a new panache, so take the veil, my dear Commissioner, and drape it thus—and SHUSH!

As she winds the veil around the startled Commissioner's head, Kleonike and Myrrhine, with carding-comb and wool-basket, rush forward and assist in transforming him into a woman.

KLEONIKE   Accept, I pray, this humble comb.

MYRRHINE   Receive this basket of fleece as well.

LYSISTRATA   Hike up your skirts, and card your wool, and gnaw your beans—and stay at home! While we rewrite Homer:
      Y WOMEN *must WIVE y* warre!*[2]

To the Chorus of Women, as the Commissioner struggles to remove his new outfit.
   Women, weaker vessels, arise!
   Put down your pitchers.
   It's our turn, now. Let's supply our friends with some moral support.

The Chorus of Women dances to the same tune as the Men, but with much more confidence.

CHORUS OF WOMEN   *Singly.*
   Oh, yes! I'll dance to bless their success.
   Fatigue won't weaken my will. Or my knees.
   I'm ready to join in any jeopardy.
      with girls as good as *these*!
   Tutte. A tally of their talents
   convinces me they're giants
   of excellence. To commence:
   there's Beauty, Duty, Prudence, Science,
   Self-Reliance, Compliance, Defiance,
   and Love of Athens in balanced alliance
      with Common Sense!

[2]Women must wage war!

28

LIVY

Women Demonstrate against the Oppian Law

In 215 B.C.E., after suffering a disastrous defeat by Hannibal of Carthage in the Second Punic War, Rome desperately needed to raise money to replenish its armies. Roman citizens met the emergency with various taxes and sacrifices, among them the Oppian law, which prohibited women from buying certain luxury goods and limited the amount of gold they could possess, passing the remainder on to the state.

Twenty years later, the crisis a dim memory, Roman women demonstrated to bring an end to the Oppian law. The moment of confrontation in 195 B.C.E. offers a window into gender relations in the Roman republic. Livy* (64 or 59 B.C.E.–17 C.E.), a Roman historian writing at the beginning of the first century C.E., provides us with the following account of the women's protest. What does the debate tell you about the relative power and position of women in this period? Do the women seem to be more or less powerful than the women of classical India, China, or Greece?

Thinking Historically

While this source and the much earlier *Lysistrata* both deal with women's protests, Livy was a historian, not a playwright. The women's protest against the Oppian law actually happened in 195 B.C.E. Cato† and Valerius actually gave these speeches. How did Cato think the lives of women had changed by 195 B.C.E.? How was Valerius's idea of women's history different from Cato's? Which of these interpretations of change comes closest to that of the modern historians in the first selection? Which interpretation do you think came closer to Livy's? Why do you think all of these authors are so interested in historical change? What were (or are) the political implications of emphasizing change or continuity?

*LIH vee
†KAY toh

Maureen B. Fant, trans., in Mary R. Lefkowitz and Maureen B. Fant, *Women's Lives in Greece and Rome*, 2nd ed. (Baltimore: The Johns Hopkins Press, 1982), 143–47.

Among the troubles of great wars, either scarcely over or yet to come, something intervened which, while it can be told briefly, stirred up enough excitement to become a great battle. Marcus Fundanius and Lucius Valerius, the tribunes of the people, brought a motion to repeal the Oppian law before the people. Gaius Oppius had carried this law as tribune at the height of the Punic War, during the consulship of Quintus Fabius and Tiberius Sempronius. The law said that no woman might own more than half an ounce of gold nor wear a multicoloured dress nor ride in a carriage in the city or in a town within a mile of it, unless there was a religious festival. The tribunes, Marcus and Publius Junius Brutus, were in favour of the Oppian law and said that they would not allow its repeal. Many noble men came forward hoping to persuade or dissuade them; a crowd of men, both supporters and opponents, filled the Capitoline Hill. The matrons, whom neither counsel nor shame nor their husbands' orders could keep at home, blockaded every street in the city and every entrance to the Forum. As the men came down to the Forum, the matrons besought them to let them, too, have back the luxuries they had enjoyed before, giving as their reason that the republic was thriving and that everyone's private wealth was increasing with every day. This crowd of women was growing daily, for now they were even gathering from the towns and villages. Before long they dared go up and solicit the consuls, praetors, and other magistrates; but one of the consuls could not be moved in the least, Marcus Porcius Cato, who spoke in favour of the law:

"If each man of us, fellow citizens, had established that the right and authority of the husband should be held over the mother of his own family, we should have less difficulty with women in general; now, at home our freedom is conquered by female fury, here in the Forum it is bruised and trampled upon, and, because we have not contained the individuals, we fear the lot. . . .

"Indeed, I blushed when, a short while ago, I walked through the midst of a band of women. Had not respect for the dignity and modesty of certain ones (not them all!) restrained me (so they would not be seen being scolded by a consul), I should have said, "What kind of behaviour is this? Running around in public, blocking streets, and speaking to other women's husbands! Could you not have asked your own husbands the same thing at home? Are you more charming in public with others' husbands than at home with your own? And yet, it is not fitting even at home (if modesty were to keep married women within the bounds of their rights) for you to concern yourselves with what laws are passed or repealed here." Our ancestors did not want women to conduct any—not even private—business without a guardian; they wanted them to be under the authority of parents, brothers, or husbands; we (the gods help us!) even now let them snatch at the government and meddle in the Forum and our assemblies. What are they doing now on the streets and crossroads, if they are not persuading the tribunes to vote for repeal? . . .

"If they are victorious now, what will they not attempt? . . . As soon as they begin to be your equals, they will have become your superiors. . . .

"What honest excuse is offered, pray, for this womanish rebellion? 'That we might shine with gold and purple,' says one of them, 'that we might ride through the city in coaches on holidays and working-days, as though triumphant over the conquered law and the votes which we captured by tearing them from you; that there should be no limit to our expenses and our luxury.' . . .

"The woman who can spend her own money will do so; the one who cannot will ask her husband. Pity that husband—the one who gives in and the one who stands firm! What he refuses, he will see given by another man. Now they publicly solicit other women's husbands, and, what is worse, they ask for a law and votes, and certain men give them what they want. You there, you, are easily moved about things which concern yourself, your estate, and your children; once the law no longer limits your wife's spending, you will never do it by yourself. Fellow citizens, do not imagine that the state which existed before the law was passed will return. A dishonest man is safer never accused than acquitted, and luxury, left alone, would have been more acceptable than it will be now, as when wild animals are first chafed by their chains and then released. I vote that the Oppian law should not, in the smallest measure, be repealed; whatever course you take, may all the gods make you happy with it."

After this, when the tribunes of the people, who had declared that they would oppose the motion to repeal, had added a few remarks along the same lines, Lucius Valerius spoke on behalf of the motion which he himself had brought:

"[Cato] used up more words castigating the women than he did opposing the motion, and he left in some uncertainty whether the women had done the deeds which he reproached on their own or at our instigation. I shall defend the motion, not ourselves, against whom the consul has hurled this charge, more for the words than for the reality of the accusation. He has called this assemblage 'secession' and sometimes 'womanish rebellion,' because the matrons have publicly asked you, in peacetime when the state is happy and prosperous, to repeal a law passed against them during the straits of war. . . .

"What, may I ask, are the women doing that is new, having gathered and come forth publicly in a case which concerns them directly? Have they never appeared in public before this? Allow me to unroll your own *Origines* before you. Listen to how often they have done so —always for the public good. From the very beginning—the reign of Romulus—when the Capitoline had been taken by the Sabines and there was fighting in the middle of the Forum, was not the battle halted by the women's intervention between the two lines? How about this? After the kings had been expelled, when the Volscian legions and their general, Marcius Coriolanus, had pitched camp at the fifth milestone, did not the matrons turn away the forces which would have buried the city? When Rome was in the hands of the Gauls, who ransomed it? Indeed the matrons agreed unanimously to turn their gold over to the public need. Not to go too far back in history, in the most recent war, when we needed funds, did not the widows' money assist the treasury? . . . You say these cases are different. I am not here to say they are the same; it is enough to prove that nothing new has been done. Indeed, as no one is amazed that they acted in situations affecting men and women alike, why should we wonder that they have taken action in a case which concerns themselves? What, after all, have they done? We have proud ears indeed, if, while masters do not scorn the appeals of slaves, we are angry when honourable women ask something of us . . .

"Who then does not know that this is a recent law, passed twenty years ago? Since our matrons lived for so long by the highest standards of behaviour without any law, what risk is there that, once it is repealed, they will yield to luxury? For if the law were an old one, or if it had been passed to restrain feminine licence, there might be reason to fear that repeal would incite them. The times themselves will show you why the law was passed. Hannibal was in Italy, victorious at Cannae. Already he held Tarentum, Arpi, and Capua. He seemed on the verge of moving against Rome. Our allies had gone over to him. We had no reserve troops, no allies at sea to protect the fleet, no funds in the treasury. Slaves were being bought and armed, on condition that the price be paid their owners when the war was over. The contractors had declared that they would provide, on that same day of payment (after the war), the grain and other supplies the needs of war demanded. We were giving our slaves as rowers at our own expense, in proportion to our property rating. We were giving all our gold and silver for public use, as the senators had done first. Widows and children were donating their funds to the treasury. We were ordered to keep at home no more than a certain amount of wrought and stamped gold and silver. . . . To whom is it not clear that poverty and misfortune were the authors of that law of yours, since all private wealth had to be turned over to public use, and that it was to remain in effect only as long as the reason for its writing did? . . .

"Shall it be our wives alone to whom the fruits of peace and tranquility of the state do not come? . . . Shall we forbid only women to wear purple? When you, a man, may use purple on your clothes, will you not allow the mother of your family to have a purple cloak, and will your horse be more beautifully saddled than your wife is garbed? . . .

"[Cato] has said that, if none of them had anything, there would be no rivalry among individual women. By Hercules! All are unhappy and indignant when they see the finery denied them permitted to the wives of the Latin allies, when they see them adorned with gold and purple, when those other women ride through the city and they follow on foot, as though the power belonged to the other women's cities, not to their own. This could wound the spirits of men; what do you think it could do to the spirits of women, whom even little things disturb? They cannot partake of magistracies, priesthoods, triumphs, badges of office, gifts, or spoils of war; elegance, finery and beautiful clothes are women's badges, in these they find joy and take pride, this our forebears called the women's world. When they are in mourning, what, other than purple and gold, do they take off? What do they put on again when they have completed the period of mourning? What do they add for public prayer and thanksgiving other than still greater ornament? Of course, if you repeal the Oppian law, you will not have the power to prohibit that which the law now forbids; daughters, wives, even some men's sisters will be less under your authority—never, while her men are well, is a woman's slavery cast off; and even they hate the freedom created by widowhood and orphanage. They prefer their adornment to be subject to your judgment, not the law's; and you ought to hold them in marital power and guardianship, not slavery; you should prefer to be called fathers and husbands to masters. The consul just now used odious terms when he said 'womanish rebellion' and 'secession.' For there is danger—he would have us believe—that they will seize the Sacred Hill as once the angry plebeians did, or the Aventine. It is for the weaker sex to submit to whatever you advise. The more power you possess, all the more moderately should you exercise your authority."

When these speeches for and against the law had been made, a considerably larger crowd of women poured forth in public the next day; as a single body they besieged the doors of the Brutuses, who were vetoing their colleagues' motion, and they did not stop until the tribunes took back their veto. After that there was no doubt but that all the tribes would repeal the law. Twenty years after it was passed, the law was repealed.

29

Fayum Portraits

Some of the most vivid and best-preserved images of women from antiquity come from the Fayum region of Egypt and date from the first century B.C.E. to the third century C.E. These are the beautifully painted and distinctive mummy portraits of inhabitants of Hellenistic and Roman Egypt, portraits usually painted while the subjects were alive and interred with them after death. The practice of painting tomb portraits in encaustic (that is, with hot pigmented wax) on wooden panels was a fairly common one in the region, and Egypt's extremely dry climate ensured the survival of many of these ancient works.

Figures 5.1 and 5.2 show portraits of women buried in Fayum, while Figure 5.3 depicts one "Ammonius from Antinoe," a young man from a town near Fayum. We do not know their ethnic background, although it is likely that they were either Roman settlers in Egypt or descendants of Egypt's Hellenistic rulers and colonists from Macedonia after Alexander the Great conquered Egypt. What clues *do* these visual sources offer about their subjects?

Sarah and Brady Hughes argue in their selection that Greek women living in Egypt during the Hellenistic period "were much more assertive than their sisters in either contemporary Greece or later Rome" (see page 159) and that even "non-elite women had unusual freedom. They owned property (including land), participated in commerce, produced textiles, were educated, and enjoyed careers as artists, poets and farmers." Do Figures 5.1 and 5.2 appear to support this argument? Why or why not?

Thinking Historically

Consider these images, individually and collectively. How would you describe the subjects' expressions? Content? Anxious? Serene? Fatalistic? Sad? What, if anything, can each tell us about the historical moment in which they were created? What are their limitations as evidence about their subjects? Can/Do these portraits tell us anything meaningful about those who sat for them?

The practice of painting the face of the deceased on a shroud, panel, or actual sarcophagus goes back to the time of the ancient pharaohs. Ammonius is holding an ankh, the ancient Egyptian hieroglyph that symbolized life force and eternal life, and one often carried as a good luck charm or amulet by the Hellenistic and Roman

Figure 5.1   Portrait of a Fayum Woman with Large
Gold Necklace.
Source: The Detroit Institute of Arts, USA, Gift
of Julius H. Haass/The Bridgeman Art Library
International.

inhabitants of Egypt. How do you account for the popularity of ancient Egyptian religious traditions among Egypt's Greco-Roman
populations? What might the ankh and the practice of tomb portrai-
ture tell us about process in the history of women and religion in antiquity?

Figure 5.2 Portrait of a Fayum Woman with White
Earrings.
Source: Louvre, Paris, France, Lauros/Giraudon/
The Bridgeman Art Library International.

Figure 5.3 Portrait of "Ammonius from
Antinoe," with Ankh.
Source: Visual Arts Library (London)/Alamy.

REFLECTIONS

Thirty years ago the historian Joan Kelly ignited the study of women's
history with an essay that asked: "Did Women Have a Renaissance?"
Questioning whether the great eras in men's history were also great
eras for women, she found that men's achievements often came at the
expense of women. We have seen how the urban revolution fit this pattern. The rise of cities, the creation of territorial states, the invention of
writing, and the development of complex societies, all beginning about
five thousand years ago, accompanied the development of patriarchal
institutions and ideas. Similarly, the rise of classical cultures, cities, and
states about twenty-five hundred years ago seems to have cemented patriarchy.

Chinese classical culture may have been the most patriarchal. In
China, the rise of the state undermined feudal nobilities where women's
role depended more on family status than gender. In India, too, the
state formation of the post-Vedic period may have undercut earlier matrilineal societies.

Roman and Greek women were affected differently by the rise of the state. The establishment of civil society in fifth-century Greece certainly undermined the power of familial clans and tribes, and with them the prestige and power of well-connected women. Most city-states confined women to the domestic sphere while male citizens controlled the public business of government. Nevertheless, the women of Sparta were less cloistered than the women of Athens, and the women of Rome enjoyed greater use of the public outdoors as early as 195 B.C.E.

Thus, if we compare China, India, and both Greece and Rome as a single "Mediterranean" society, the fortunes of women deteriorated during the classical period in China and India, but improved in the Mediterranean. The protest of Roman women against the Oppian law in 195 B.C.E. went far beyond the possibilities, if not the feared fantasies, of the classical Greeks. The upper-class Roman women Livy knew could own and inherit property and run businesses. All Roman women in the first century had access to the street, the marketplace, and other public spaces. They could not, however, participate in politics except informally as influential wives, mothers, and courtesans. Women would have to wait almost another two thousand years to vote and hold office.

In this chapter we see that capturing the moment and assessing change are not mutually exclusive. Nor are comparison and understanding change. We can compare how different societies change over the same period, and that knowledge can very usefully lead us to more sophisticated questions. What enabled Roman women, especially in the Empire, to achieve rights and liberties that were not available before or elsewhere? Was there a connection between the rights of women in the Empire and the loss of the rights that ordinary men had enjoyed in the earlier Republic? What Roman or Mediterranean social or cultural institutions lessened the patriarchal pressures that prevailed in other urban-based states? What was the impact of Christianity for Roman women? We will explore at least the last of these in the next chapter.

6

From Tribal
to Universal Religion

Hindu-Buddhist and Judeo-Christian
Traditions, 1000 B.C.E.–100 C.E.

HISTORICAL CONTEXT

From 1000 B.C.E. to 100 C.E. two major religious traditions, one centered in the Middle East and the other in northern India, split into at least four major religious traditions, so large that today they are embraced by a majority of the inhabitants of the world. Each of the two original traditions, Hinduism and Judaism, were in 1000 B.C.E. highly restricted in membership. Neither sought converts but instead ministered to members of their own tribe and castes. This chapter explores how these two essentially inward-looking religions created universal religions, open to all. It is a story not only of the emergence of Christianity and Buddhism but also of the development of modern Judaic and Hindu religions.

Remarkably, both of these traditions moved from tribal to universal religions; even more remarkable are the common elements, given their different routes along that path. While Hinduism cultivated a psychological approach to spiritual enlightenment out of a priestly religion of obligation, Judaism developed an abiding faith in historical providence from a disastrous history.

As you read the selections in this chapter, notice over the course of the first millennium B.C.E. how both core religions created new faiths and the reform of the old. Notice also the fundamentally different ways these two great religious traditions changed. Finally, observe how the later offspring religions, Buddhism and Christianity, preached ideas that were already current, but not dominant, in the "parental" traditions.

THINKING HISTORICALLY
Detecting Change in Primary Sources

Understanding how religions change or evolve is especially difficult because of the tendency of religious adherents to emphasize the timelessness of their truths. Fortunately, religious commitment and belief do not require a denial of historical change. Indeed, many adherents have found strength in all manifestations of the sacred — the specific and historical as well as the universal and eternal.

Whether motives are primarily religious or secular, however, the historical study of religion offers a useful window on understanding large-scale changes in human behavior. Since religions tend to conserve, repeat, and enshrine, change is more gradual than in many other aspects of human thought and behavior: fashion, say, or technology. Thus, when religions develop radically new ideas or institutions, we can learn much about human resistance and innovation by studying the circumstances.

Because religions typically prefer conservation over innovation, changes are often grafted on to old formulations. Historians who want to understand when and how change occurred must sometimes discover and unmask new ideas and ways of doing things that have been assimilated into the tradition.

The easiest way to see change in primary sources is to compare a number of them composed in different historical periods. However, sometimes we are able to see examples of change in a single document. A written source may, for instance, originate in more than one oral account and the writer may combine them both even though one is later than the other and they represent different ideas. A manuscript might also pick up errors or updates as it is rewritten for the next generation. We will see examples of both of these changes and others in the documents in this chapter.

30

Svetasvatara Upanishad

In Chapter 3 selections from the Hindu Vedas* and Upanishads† help introduce some basic ideas in Hinduism: the belief that animals and human castes were created out of the primal sacrifice of the god Purusha in the Vedas, the complementary ideas of karma and reincarnation in the Upanishads, and, lastly, the identification of Brahman and *atman* (self and God) also in the Upanishads.

Take a look at the same selections again to understand the changing nature of Hinduism from the earliest Vedas to the latest Upanishads. For example, we see in selection 11 the interest of the Aryan invaders of India in defining and justifying caste differences and the supremacy of the Brahman priests as masters of sacrifice, prayers, rituals, and sacred hymns.

The authors of the Upanishads were less interested in sacrifice and priestly rituals and more absorbed by philosophical questions. Thus, selection 12 on karma and reincarnation spells out the idea of justice and a philosophy of nature that reflects the interests of a later settled society. Finally, selection 13 on the identity of Brahman and *atman* reflects an even more meditative Upanishad that virtually ignores the role of priests. This meditative tradition may have existed in early Hinduism, but there is far more evidence of its expression in the Upanishads (after 800 B.C.E.) than in the earlier Vedas.

The *Svetasvatara*‡ Upanishad selection included here reflects an additional step along the path from the religion of priests, sacrifice, and caste obligation to individualized spirituality. Here the idea of the transmigration of souls from one body to another in an endless cycle of reincarnations — an idea that developed after the Vedas — is challenged by the idea that the individual who seeks Brahman might break out of the wheel of life. How would this idea of escaping reincarnation diminish the power of Brahman priests? How does it minimize the importance of caste and karma?

*VAY duhz
†oo PAH nee shahdz
‡sveh tah SVAH tah ruh

Svetasvatara Upanishad in *The Upanishads: The Breath of the Eternal*, trans. Swami Prabhavananda and Frederick Manchester (Hollywood: The Vedanta Society of Southern California, 1948; New York: Mentor Books, 1957), 118–21.

189

Thinking Historically

Recognizing changes in the Hindu tradition is more difficult than in the Judaic tradition. The literature of Judaism is full of historical references: names of historical figures and even dates. Hindu sacred literature, as you can tell from this brief introduction, shows virtually no interest in historical names and dates. Because time in India was conceived as cyclical, rather than linear, and the cycles of the Indian time scheme were immense, determining the exact time an event occurred was less important in Hindu thought than understanding its eternal meaning.

Consequently, our analysis of the changes in Hinduism is more logical than chronological. We can therefore speak of a long-term historical process even though we cannot date each step.

The oldest of the thirteen universally recognized Upanishads, all of which were composed between 800 and 400 B.C.E., are the Brihad Aranyaka and the Chandogya (from which selections 12 and 13 on *atman* and Brahman are taken). The *Svetasvatara* is one of the last of the thirteen, composed closer to 400 B.C.E. What is the idea of time suggested by this Upanishad?

This vast universe is a wheel. Upon it are all creatures that are subject to birth, death, and rebirth. Round and round it turns, and never stops. It is the wheel of Brahman. As long as the individual self thinks it is separate from Brahman, it revolves upon the wheel in bondage to the laws of birth, death, and rebirth. But when through the grace of Brahman it realizes its identity with him, it revolves upon the wheel no longer. It achieves immortality.

He who is realized by transcending the world of cause and effect, in deep contemplation, is expressly declared by the scriptures to be the Supreme Brahman. He is the substance, all else the shadow. He is the imperishable. The knowers of Brahman know him as the one reality behind all that seems. For this reason they are devoted to him. Absorbed in him, they attain freedom from the wheel of birth, death, and rebirth.

The Lord supports this universe, which is made up of the perishable and the imperishable, the manifest and the unmanifest. The individual soul, forgetful of the Lord, attaches itself to pleasure and thus is bound. When it comes to the Lord, it is freed from all its fetters.

Mind and matter, master and servant — both have existed from beginningless time. The Maya which unites them has also existed from beginningless time. When all three — mind, matter, and Maya — are known as one with Brahman, then is it realized that the Self is infinite and has no part in action. Then is it revealed that the Self is all.

Matter is perishable. The Lord, the destroyer of ignorance, is imperishable, immortal. He is the one God, the Lord of the perishable and of all souls. By meditating on him, by uniting oneself with him, by identifying oneself with him, one ceases to be ignorant.

Know God, and all fetters will be loosed. Ignorance will vanish. Birth, death, and rebirth will be no more. Meditate upon him and transcend physical consciousness. Thus will you reach union with the lord of the universe. Thus will you become identified with him who is One without a second. In him all your desires will find fulfillment.

The truth is that you are always united with the Lord. But you must *know* this. Nothing further is there to know. Meditate, and you will realize that mind, matter, and Maya (the power which unites mind and matter) are but three aspects of Brahman, the one reality.

Fire, though present in the firesticks, is not perceived until one stick is rubbed against another. The Self is like that fire: It is realized in the body by meditation on the sacred syllable OM.[1]

Let your body be the stick that is rubbed, the sacred syllable OM the stick that is rubbed against it. Thus shall you realize God, who is hidden within the body as fire is hidden within the wood.

Like oil in sesame seeds, butter in cream, water in the river bed, fire in tinder, the Self dwells within the soul. Realize him through truthfulness and meditation.

Like butter in cream is the Self in everything. Knowledge of the Self is gained through meditation. The Self is Brahman. By Brahman is all ignorance destroyed.

To realize God, first control the outgoing senses and harness the mind. Then meditate upon the light in the heart of the fire — meditate, that is, upon pure consciousness as distinct from the ordinary consciousness of the intellect. Thus the Self, the Inner Reality, may be seen behind physical appearance.

Control your mind so that the Ultimate Reality, the self-luminous Lord, may be revealed. Strive earnestly for eternal bliss.

With the help of the mind and the intellect, keep the senses from attaching themselves to objects of pleasure. They will then be purified by the light of the Inner Reality, and that light will be revealed.

The wise control their minds, and unite their hearts with the infinite, the omniscient, the all-pervading Lord. Only discriminating souls practice spiritual disciplines. Great is the glory of the self-luminous being, the Inner Reality.

Hear, all ye children of immortal bliss, also ye gods who dwell in the high heavens: Follow only in the footsteps of the illumined ones,

---

[1]Sacred symbol for God and the sound chanted in meditation. [Ed.]

and by continuous meditation merge both mind and intellect in the eternal Brahman. The glorious Lord will be revealed to you.

Control the vital force. Set fire to the Self within by the practice of meditation. Be drunk with the wine of divine love. Thus shall you reach perfection.

Be devoted to the eternal Brahman. Unite the light within you with the light of Brahman. Thus will the source of ignorance be destroyed, and you will rise above karma.

Sit upright, holding the chest, throat, and head erect. Turn the senses and the mind inward to the lotus of the heart. Meditate on Brahman with the help of the syllable OM. Cross the fearful currents of the ocean of worldliness by means of the raft of Brahman — the sacred syllable OM.

With earnest effort hold the senses in check. Controlling the breath, regulate the vital activities. As a charioteer holds back his restive horses, so does a persevering aspirant hold back his mind.

Retire to a solitary place, such as a mountain cave or a sacred spot. The place must be protected from the wind and rain, and it must have a smooth, clean floor, free from pebbles and dust. It must not be damp, and it must be free from disturbing noises. It must be pleasing to the eye and quieting to the mind. Seated there, practice meditation and other spiritual exercises.

As you practice meditation, you may see in vision forms resembling snow, crystals, smoke, fire, lightning, fireflies, the sun, the moon. These are signs that you are on your way to the revelation of Brahman.

As you become absorbed in meditation, you will realize that the Self is separate from the body and for this reason will not be affected by disease, old age, or death.

31

Buddhism: Gotama's Discovery

Gotama Siddhartha* (c. 563–483 B.C.E.), known to history as the Buddha, was the son of a Hindu Kshatriya prince in northern India. This selection tells a traditional story about his youth. Because his father was warned by "Brahman soothsayers" that young Gotama would leave his home to live among the seekers in the forest, his father kept the boy distracted in the palace, the sufferings of people outside hidden from him. This selection begins when the prince, or *raja*, finally agrees to let Gotama tour outside the palace.

What does Gotama discover? What seems to be the meaning of these discoveries for him? How is his subsequent thought or behavior similar to that of other Hindus in the era? How is the message of this story similar to the lessons of the Upanishads, especially the *Svetasvatara* Upanishad?

Thinking Historically

None of the stories we have of the Buddha was written during his lifetime. For some four hundred years, stories of the Buddha were passed by word of mouth before they were put into writing. Can you see any signs in this story that it was memorized and told orally? When the stories were finally written down, some were no doubt more faithful to the Buddha's actual words and experience than others. What elements in this story would most likely reflect the historical experience of Gotama? What parts of the story would most likely be added later by people who worshiped the Buddha?

Now the young lord Gotama, when many days had passed by, bade his charioteer make ready the state carriages, saying: "Get ready the carriages, good charioteer, and let us go through the park to inspect the pleasaunce." "Yes, my lord," replied the charioteer, and harnessed the state carriages and sent word to Gotama: "The carriages are ready, my lord; do now what you deem fit." Then Gotama mounted a state carriage and drove out in state into the park.

*GAH tah mah   sih DAHR thah

"The Life of Gotama the Buddha," trans. E. H. Brewster, in Clarence H. Hamilton, *Buddhism* (1926; reprint, New York: Routledge, 1952).

Now the young lord saw, as he was driving to the park, an aged man as bent as a roof gable, decrepit, leaning on a staff, tottering as he walked, afflicted and long past his prime. And seeing him Gotama said: "That man, good charioteer, what has he done, that his hair is not like that of other men, nor his body?"

"He is what is called an aged man, my lord."

"But why is he called aged?"

"He is called aged, my lord, because he has not much longer to live."

"But then, good charioteer, am I too subject to old age, one who has not got past old age?"

"You, my lord, and we too, we all are of a kind to grow old; we have not got past old age."

"Why then, good charioteer, enough of the park for today. Drive me back hence to my rooms."

"Yea, my lord," answered the charioteer, and drove him back. And he, going to his rooms, sat brooding sorrowful and depressed, thinking, "Shame then verily be upon this thing called birth, since to one born old age shows itself like that!"

Thereupon the rāja sent for the charioteer and asked him: "Well, good charioteer, did the boy take pleasure in the park? Was he pleased with it?"

"No, my lord, he was not."

"What then did he see on his drive?"

(And the charioteer told the rāja all.)

Then the rāja thought thus: We must not have Gotama declining to rule. We must not have him going forth from the house into the homeless state. We must not let what the brāhman soothsayers spoke of come true.

So, that these things might not come to pass, he let the youth be still more surrounded by sensuous pleasures. And thus Gotama continued to live amidst the pleasures of sense.

Now after many days had passed by, the young lord again bade his charioteer make ready and drove forth as once before. . . .

And Gotama saw, as he was driving to the park, a sick man, suffering and very ill, fallen and weltering in his own water, by some being lifted up, by others being dressed. Seeing this, Gotama asked: "That man, good charioteer, what has he done that his eyes are not like others' eyes, nor his voice like the voice of other men?"

"He is what is called ill, my lord."

"But what is meant by ill?"

"It means, my lord, that he will hardly recover from his illness."

"But am I too, then, good charioteer, subject to fall ill; have I not got out of reach of illness?"

"You, my lord, and we too, we are all subject to fall ill; we have not got beyond the reach of illness."

"Why then, good charioteer, enough of the park for today. Drive me back hence to my rooms." "Yea, my lord," answered the charioteer, and drove him back. And he, going to his rooms, sat brooding sorrowful and depressed, thinking: Shame then verily be upon this thing called birth, since to one born decay shows itself like that, disease shows itself like that.

Thereupon the rāja sent for the charioteer and asked him: "Well, good charioteer, did the young lord take pleasure in the park and was he pleased with it?"

"No, my lord, he was not."

"What did he see then on his drive?"

(And the charioteer told the rāja all.)

Then the rāja thought thus: We must not have Gotama declining to rule; we must not have him going forth from the house to the homeless state; we must not let what the brāhman soothsayers spoke of come true.

So, that these things might not come to pass, he let the young man be still more abundantly surrounded by sensuous pleasures. And thus Gotama continued to live amidst the pleasures of sense.

Now once again, after many days . . . the young lord Gotama . . . drove forth.

And he saw, as he was driving to the park, a great concourse of people clad in garments of different colours constructing a funeral pyre. And seeing this he asked his charioteer: "Why now are all those people come together in garments of different colours, and making that pile?"

"It is because someone, my lord, has ended his days."

"Then drive the carriage close to him who has ended his days."

"Yea, my lord," answered the charioteer, and did so. And Gotama saw the corpse of him who had ended his days and asked: "What, good charioteer, is ending one's days?"

"It means, my lord, that neither mother, nor father, nor other kinsfolk will now see him, nor will he see them."

"But am I too then subject to death, have I not got beyond reach of death? Will neither the rāja, nor the ranee, nor any other of my kin see me more, or shall I again see them?"

"You, my lord, and we too, we are all subject to death; we have not passed beyond the reach of death. Neither the rāja, nor the ranee, nor any other of your kin will see you any more, nor will you see them."

"Why then, good charioteer, enough of the park for today. Drive me back hence to my rooms."

"Yea, my lord," replied the charioteer, and drove him back.

And he, going to his rooms, sat brooding sorrowful and depressed, thinking: Shame verily be upon this thing called birth, since to one born the decay of life, since disease, since death shows itself like that!

Thereupon the rāja questioned the charioteer as before and as before let Gotama be still more surrounded by sensuous enjoyment. And thus he continued to live amidst the pleasures of sense.

Now once again, after many days . . . the lord Gotama . . . drove forth.

And he saw, as he was driving to the park, a shaven-headed man, a recluse, wearing the yellow robe. And seeing him he asked the charioteer, "That man, good charioteer, what has he done that his head is unlike other men's heads and his clothes too are unlike those of others?"

"That is what they call a recluse, because, my lord, he is one who has gone forth."

"What is that, 'to have gone forth'?"

"To have gone forth, my lord, means being thorough in the religious life, thorough in the peaceful life, thorough in good action, thorough in meritorious conduct, thorough in harmlessness, thorough in kindness to all creatures."

"Excellent indeed, friend charioteer, is what they call a recluse, since so thorough is his conduct in all those respects, wherefore drive me up to that forthgone man."

"Yea, my lord," replied the charioteer and drove up to the recluse. Then Gotama addressed him, saying, "You master, what have you done that your head is not as other men's heads, nor your clothes as those of other men?"

"I, my lord, am one who has gone forth."

"What, master, does that mean?"

"It means, my lord, being thorough in the religious life, thorough in the peaceful life, thorough in good actions, thorough in meritorious conduct, thorough in harmlessness, thorough in kindness to all creatures."

"Excellently indeed, master, are you said to have gone forth since so thorough is your conduct in all those respects." Then the lord Gotama bade his charioteer, saying: "Come then, good charioteer, do you take the carriage and drive it back hence to my rooms. But I will even here cut off my hair, and don the yellow robe, and go forth from the house into the homeless state."

"Yea, my lord," replied the charioteer, and drove back. But the prince Gotama, there and then cutting off his hair and donning the yellow robe, went forth from the house into the homeless state.

Now at Kapilavatthu, the rāja's seat, a great number of persons, some eighty-four thousand souls, heard of what prince Gotama had done and thought: Surely this is no ordinary religious rule, this is no common going forth, in that prince Gotama himself has had his head shaved and has donned the yellow robe and has gone forth from the house into the homeless state. If prince Gotama has done this, why then should not we also? And they all had their heads shaved and donned the yellow robes; and in imitation of the Bodhisat [Buddha] they went forth from the house into the homeless state. So the Bodhisat went forth from the house into the homeless state. So the Bodhisat went up on his rounds through the villages, towns, and cities accompanied by that multitude.

Now there arose in the mind of Gotama the Bodhisat, when he was meditating in seclusion, this thought: That indeed is not suitable for me that I should live beset. 'Twere better were I to dwell alone, far from the crowd.

So after a time he dwelt alone, away from the crowd. Those eighty-four thousand recluses went one way, and the Bodhisat went another way.

Now there arose in the mind of Gotama the Bodhisat, when he had gone to his place and was meditating in seclusion, this thought: Verily, this world had fallen upon trouble — one is born, and grows old, and dies, and falls from one state, and springs up in another. And from the suffering, moreover, no one knows of any way to escape, even from decay and death. O, when shall a way of escape from this suffering be made known — from decay and from death?

32

The Buddha's First Sermon

This is said to be the Buddha's first sermon, delivered shortly after he achieved enlightenment. It contains the essence of Buddhist thought: the four noble truths, the eightfold path, and the middle way. The middle way is the course between the extremes of the pursuit of pleasure and the pursuit of pain. It is defined by an eightfold path, eight steps to a peaceful mind. The four noble truths might be summarized as the following:

1. Life is sorrow.
2. Sorrow is the result of selfish desire.
3. Selfish desire can be destroyed.
4. It can be destroyed by following the eightfold path.

The Buddhist Tradition in India, China and Japan, ed. William Theodore de Bary (New York: Random House, 1969), 16–17.

What do these ideas mean? What was considered the value of a "middle way"? In what ways did the eightfold path offer a spiritual discipline? What answers did the four noble truths provide?

Thinking Historically

Notice how the tone and style of this document are different from the preceding one. Which source reads more like the report of a witness or someone close to the events described? Which reads more like an idealization or myth? Why is it likely that a report would be written before an idealization or myth?

Thus I have heard. Once the Lord was at Vrānasī, at the deer park called Iwipatana. There he addressed the five monks:

There are two ends not to be served by a wanderer. What are these two? The pursuit of desires and of the pleasure which springs from desire, which is base, common, leading to rebirth, ignoble, and unprofitable; and the pursuit of pain and hardship, which is grievous, ignoble, and unprofitable. The Middle Way of the Tathāgata avoids both these ends. It is enlightened, it brings clear vision, it makes for wisdom, and leads to peace, insight, enlightenment, and Nirvāna. What is the Middle Way? . . . It is the Noble Eightfold Path — Right Views, Right Resolve, Right Speech, Right Conduct, Right Livelihood, Right Effort, Right Mindfulness, and Right Concentration. This is the Middle Way. . . .

And this is the Noble Truth of Sorrow. Birth is sorrow, age is sorrow, disease is sorrow, death is sorrow; contact with the unpleasant is sorrow, separation from the pleasant is sorrow, every wish unfulfilled is sorrow — in short all the five components of individuality are sorrow.

And this is the Noble Truth of the Arising of Sorrow. It arises from craving, which leads to rebirth, which brings delight and passion, and seeks pleasure now here, now there — the craving for sensual pleasure, the craving for continued life, the craving for power.

And this is the Noble Truth of the Stopping of Sorrow. It is the complete stopping of that craving, so that no passion remains, leaving it, being emancipated from it, being released from it, giving no place to it.

And this is the Noble Truth of the Way which Leads to the Stopping of Sorrow. It is the Noble Eightfold Path — Right Views, Right Resolve, Right Speech, Right Conduct, Right Livelihood, Right Effort, Right Mindfulness, and Right Concentration.

33

Buddhism and Caste

This story, part of the Buddhist canon that was written between one hundred and four hundred years after his death, tells of a confrontation between the Buddha and Brahmans, members of the Hindu priestly caste. This encounter would have been common. Why would it be important? How would you expect most Brahmans to react to the Buddha's opposition to caste? Would some Brahmans be persuaded by the Buddha's arguments? How and why would the appeal of Buddhism be more universal than Hinduism?

Thinking Historically

Notice the mention of Greece and the dialogue style of this selection. If, as some scholars have suggested, there may be Greek influence here, which Greek writer would they be referring to? How might this Greek influence help us find an approximate date for this writing?

Once when the Lord was staying at Sāvatthī there were five hundred brāhmans from various countries in the city . . . and they thought: "This ascetic Gautama preaches that all four classes are pure. Who can refute him?"

At that time there was a young brāhman named Assalāyana in the city . . . a youth of sixteen, thoroughly versed in the Vedas . . . and in all brāhmanic learning. "He can do it!" thought the brāhmans, and so they asked him to try; surrounded by a crowd of brāhmans, he went to the Lord, and, after greeting him, sat down and said:

"Brāhmans maintain that only they are the highest class, and the others are below them. They are white, the others black; only they are pure, and not the others. Only they are the true sons of Brahmā, born from his mouth, born of Brahmā, creations of Brahmā, heirs of Brahmā. Now what does the worthy Gautama say to that?"

"Do the brāhmans really maintain this, Assalāyana, when they're born of women just like anyone else, of brāhman women who have their periods and conceive, give birth and nurse their children, just like any other women?"

The Buddhist Tradition in India, China and Japan, ed. William Theodore de Bary (New York: Random House, 1969), 49–51.

"For all you say, this is what they think. . . ."

"Have you ever heard that in the lands of the Greeks and Kambojas and other peoples on the borders there are only two classes, masters and slaves, and a master can become a slave and vice versa?"

"Yes, I've heard so."

"And what strength or support does that fact give to the brāhmans' claim?"

"Nevertheless, that is what they think."

"Again if a man is a murderer, a thief, or an adulterer, or commits other grave sins, when his body breaks up on death does he pass on to purgatory if he's a kshatriya,[1] vaishya,[2] or shūdra,[3] but not if he's a brāhman?"

"No, Gautama. In such a case the same fate is in store for all men, whatever their class."

"And if he avoids grave sin, will he go to heaven if he's a brāhman, but not if he's a man of the lower classes?"

"No, Gautama. In such a case the same reward awaits all men, whatever their class."

"And is a brāhman capable of developing a mind of love without hate or ill-will, but not a man of the other classes?"

"No, Gautama. All four classes are capable of doing so."

"Can only a brāhman go down to a river and wash away dust and dirt, and not men of the other classes?"

"No, Gautama, all four classes can."

"Now suppose a king were to gather together a hundred men of different classes and to order the brāhmans and kshatriyas to take kindling wood of sāl, pine, lotus, or sandal, and light fires, while the low-class folk did the same with common wood. What do you think would happen? Would the fires of the high-born men blaze up brightly . . . and those of the humble fail?"

"No, Gautama. It would be alike with high and lowly. . . . Every fire would blaze with the same bright flame." . . .

"Suppose there are two young brāhman brothers, one a scholar and the other uneducated. Which of them would be served first at memorial feasts, festivals, and sacrifices, or when entertained as guests?"

"The scholar, of course; for what great benefit would accrue from entertaining the uneducated one?"

"But suppose the scholar is ill-behaved and wicked, while the uneducated one is well-behaved and virtuous?"

"Then the uneducated one would be served first, for what great benefit would accrue from entertaining an ill-behaved and wicked man?"

---

[1]kuh SHAH tree uh   Warrior. [Ed.]
[2]VAH eesh uh   Free peasant, artisan, or producer. [Ed.]
[3]SHOO druh   Serf. [Ed.]

"First, Assalāyana, you based your claim on birth, then you gave up birth for learning, and finally you have come round to my way of thinking, that all four classes are equally pure!"

At this Assalāyana sat silent . . . his shoulders hunched, his eyes cast down, thoughtful in mind, and with no answer at hand.

$$34$$

The Bible: History, Laws, and Psalms

Just as the caste-based Hinduism of ancient Aryan tribes gave rise to universal Buddhism after 500 B.C.E., so did the Judaism of the tribe of Abraham give birth to universalist Christianity. Judaism was already an ancient religion by the time of Jesus. It traced its roots back (perhaps two thousand years) to Abraham himself who, according to tradition, made a contract (or covenant) with God to worship him and him alone.

This commitment to one god, and one god only, was to mark the ancient Jews as unique. No other people in the ancient world were monotheistic. The people of Mesopotamia, Egypt, India, and the Mediterranean accepted various ancestral and natural gods. Only the Egyptians for a brief moment (around 1300 B.C.E.) preached the singularity of god, in this case the sun god Aton, but that was soon renounced. Since such a belief was unusual, the descendants of Abraham had difficulty accepting it. In their wanderings throughout the land of the Tigris and Euphrates rivers, from Abraham's native Ur to Egypt, the Jews came into contact with many different religious beliefs; some were even tempted by foreign gods. (See Map 6.1.) However, by around 1300 B.C.E., Abraham's descendants escaped Egyptian domination, crossed the Red Sea, and with the help of Moses renewed their covenant with God in the Ten Commandments. Even then, stories were told of Jews who worshiped the Golden Calf and other idols and of the displeasure of the God of Abraham. "I am a jealous God," he told his people. "Thou shall not take other gods before you."

Such is the story told in the books of the Hebrew Bible, written after the Jews settled in Jerusalem and the surrounding area sometime

Gen. 1:1–2:25, 17:1–14; Exod. 19:1–20:18; Lev. 1:1–9; Ps. 23:1–6; Amos 5:21–24. All biblical selections are from the King James Version.

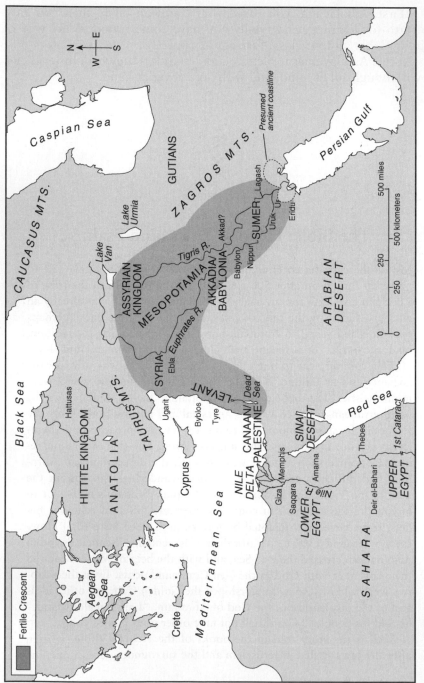

Map 6.1 The Ancient Near East, 4000–1000 B.C.E.

202

after 1000 B.C.E. They wrote of their history since the time of Abraham, and even of the ages before the patriarch, stretching back to the beginning of the world. By about 900 B.C.E., in the heyday of Jewish kingship, Kings Saul, David, and Solomon ruled large parts of what is today Israel, Palestine, and Jordan. The book we know as the Old Testament included their histories, the laws of the two Jewish kingdoms Judah and Israel, and various other writings (songs, psalms, and philosophy).

As you read these first selections from the Bible (Genesis, Exodus, Leviticus, and Psalms), note how they are similar to, and different from, the Vedas and Upanishads of Hinduism. How, for instance, is the story of the beginning of the world different from the sacrifice of Purusha? Why is an understanding of history more important to the Jews than it was to the Hindus? Compare the role of morality in the religion of Jews and Hindus. In what sense is the morality of Judaism universal and that of Hinduism caste based? How is the Judaic emphasis on morality also different from Buddhist ideas?

Thinking Historically

Since the books of the Hebrew Bible were composed over a long period of time, from about 900 B.C.E. to about 165 B.C.E., we might expect to see changes in emphasis, especially since this period was such a tumultuous one in Jewish history. The immediate descendants of Abraham were a nomadic pastoral people — shepherds, Psalm 23 reminds us, though this beautiful psalm attributed to King David was written in an urban, monarchal stage of Jewish history. Leviticus, too, echoes an earlier pastoral life where animal sacrifice, and the worship by shepherds generally, was still practiced.

When did morality replace sacrifice as the sign of respect to the God of Abraham? Was it around 1300 B.C.E., the traditional date for the reception by Moses of the Ten Commandments? Or is the existence of Leviticus, perhaps five hundred years later, a sign that sacrifice was still practiced? The sentiments of Amos (783–743 B.C.E.) suggest a later rejection not only of animal sacrifice but also of moral obedience that was not truly felt.

When did monotheism (the belief in one god) become unequivocal, unquestioned? Since this was a new idea, there must have been a time when it wasn't held. Some scholars see signs of an earlier polytheism (belief in many gods) in the book of Genesis itself. For instance, in Genesis 3:5 we find, "ye shall be as gods," and in Genesis 3:22, "And the Lord God said: Behold the man has become like one of us."

Certainly the beginning of Genesis is no-nonsense monotheism, majestically so: "In the beginning God created the heaven and the earth." But scholars have pointed out that this opening is followed by another story of origin beginning at Chapter 2, Verse 4, that not only tells the story over again, but does so without the intense declarative monotheism. They date this document at about 850 B.C.E. and the section from 1:1 to 2:3 at about 650 B.C.E. Compare the language in Genesis 1 to 2:3 with the section that begins at 2:4. Using the categories from the previous selection, reporting versus idealizing or myth-making, which selection from Genesis seems more idealized, which more like a report? Which version would probably be closer to the oral story-telling tradition? Which reflects the style of a sophisticated, urban, philosophical culture? Which is more monotheistic: God or Lord God?

If we can see increased emphasis on monotheism from 850 to 650 B.C.E., we might also see in these selections the transition from the religion of a tribe of shepherds to that of a political kingdom. What evidence do you see that a pastoral religion of animal sacrifice became a religion of law, or even internalized morality?

Finally, notice there is no heaven here — no afterlife. God promised Abraham land and prosperity. Even today, a belief in personal immortality is more accepted by Christians than Jews. Still, we will explore the development of that idea in Judaism in the second century B.C.E.

Genesis

Chapter 1

1 In the beginning God created the heaven and the earth. 2 And the earth was without form, and void; and darkness was upon the face of the deep. And the Spirit of God moved upon the face of the waters. 3 And God said, Let there be light: and there was light. 4 And God saw the light, and it was good: and God divided the light from the darkness. 5 And God called the light Day, and the darkness he called Night. And the evening and the morning were the first day.

6 And God said, Let there be a firmament in the midst of the waters, and let it divide the waters. 7 And God made the firmament, and divided the waters which were under the firmament from the waters which were above the firmament: and it was so. 8 And God called the firmament Heaven. And the evening and the morning were the second day.

9 And God said, Let the waters under the heaven be gathered together unto one place, and let the dry land appear: and it was so. 10 And God called the dry land Earth; and the gathering together of the water called he Seas: and God saw it was good. 11 And God said, Let the earth bring forth grass, the herb yielding seed, and the fruit tree

yielding fruit after his kind, whose seed is in itself, upon the earth: and it was so. 12 And the earth brought forth grass, and herb yielding seed after his kind, and the tree yielding fruit, whose seed was in itself, after his kind: and God saw it was good. 13 And the evening and the morning were the third day.

14 And God said, Let there be lights in the firmament of the heaven to divide the day from the night; and let them be for signs, and for seasons, and for days, and years: 15 And let them be for lights in the firmament of the heaven to give light upon the earth: and it was so. 16 And God made two great lights; the greater light to rule the day, and the lesser light to rule the night: he made the stars also. 17 And God set them in the firmament of the heaven to give light upon the earth, 18 And to rule over the day and over the night, and to divide the light from the darkness: and God saw that it was good. 19 And the evening and the morning were the fourth day.

20 And God said, Let the waters bring forth abundantly the moving creatures that hath life, and fowl that may fly above the earth in the open firmament of heaven. 21 And God created great whales, and every living creature that moveth, which the waters brought forth abundantly, after their kind, and every winged fowl after his kind: and God saw that it was good. 22 And God blessed them, saying, Be fruitful, and multiply, and fill the waters in the seas, and let fowl multiply in the earth. 23 And the evening and the morning were the fifth day.

24 And God said, Let the earth bring forth the living creature after his kind, cattle, and creeping thing, and beast of the earth after his kind: and it was so. 25 And God made the beast of the earth after his kind, and cattle after their kind, and every thing that creepeth upon the earth after his kind: and God saw that it was good.

26 And God said, Let us make man in our image, after our likeness: and let them have dominion over the fish of the sea, and over the fowl of the air, and over the cattle, and over all the earth, and over every creeping thing that creepeth upon the earth. 27 So God created man in his own image, in the image of God created he him: male and female created he them. 28 And God blessed them, and God said unto them, Be fruitful, and multiply, and replenish the earth, and subdue it: and have dominion over the fish of the sea, and over the fowl of the air, and over every living thing that moveth upon the earth.

29 And God said, Behold, I have given you every herb bearing seed, which is upon the face of all the earth, and every tree, in which is the fruit of a tree yielding seed; to you it shall be for meat. 30 And to every beast of the earth, and to every fowl of the air, and to every thing that creepeth upon the earth, wherein there is life, I have given every green herb for meat: and it was so. 31 And God saw every thing that he had made, and, behold, it was very good. And the evening and the morning were the sixth day.

Chapter 2

1 Thus the heavens and the earth were finished, and all the host of them. 2 And on the seventh day God ended his work which he had made; and he rested on the seventh day from all his work which he had made. 3 And God blessed the seventh day, and sanctified it: because that in it he had rested from all this work which God created and made.

4 These are the generations of the heavens and of the earth when they were created, in the day that the Lord God made the earth and the heavens. 5 And every plant of the field before it was in the earth, and every herb of the field before it grew: for the Lord God had not caused it to rain upon the earth, and there was not a man to till the ground. 6 But there went up a mist from the earth, and watered the whole face of the ground. 7 And the Lord God formed man of the dust of the ground, and breathed into his nostrils the breath of life; and man became a living soul.

8 And the Lord God planted a garden eastward in Eden; and there he put the man whom he had formed. 9 And out of the ground made the Lord God to grow every tree that is pleasant to the sight, and good for food; and the tree of life also in the midst of the garden, and the tree of knowledge of good and evil. 10 And a river went out of Eden to water the garden; and from thence it was parted, and became into four heads. 11 The name of the first is Pison: that is it which compasseth the whole land of Havilah, where there is gold; 12 And the gold of the land is good: there is bdellium and the onyx stone. 13 And the name of the second river is Gihon: the same is it that compasseth the whole land of Ethiopia. 14 And the name of the third river is Hiddekel: that is it which goeth toward the east of Assyria. And the fourth river is Euphrates. 15 And the Lord God took the man, and put him into the garden of Eden to dress it and to keep it. 16 And the Lord God commanded the man, saying, Of every tree of the garden thou mayest freely eat: 17 But of the tree of the knowledge of good and evil, thou shalt not eat of it: for in the day that thou eatest thereof thou shalt surely die.

18 And the Lord God said, It is not good that the man should be alone; I will make him a help meet for him. 19 And out of the ground the Lord God formed every beast of the field, and every fowl of the air; and brought them unto Adam to see what he would call them: and whatsoever Adam called every living creature, that was the name thereof. 20 And Adam gave names to all cattle, and to the fowl of the air, and to every beast of the field; but for Adam there was not found a help meet for him. 21 And the Lord God caused a deep sleep to fall upon Adam, and he slept; and he took one of his ribs, and closed up the flesh instead thereof. 22 And the rib, which the Lord God had taken from man, made he a woman, and brought her unto the man. 23 And Adam said, This is now bone of my bones, and flesh of my flesh: she

shall be called Woman, because she was taken out of man. 24 Therefore shall a man leave his father and his mother, and shall cleave unto his wife: and they shall be one flesh. 25 And they were both naked, the man and his wife, and were not ashamed.

Chapter 17

1 And when Abram was ninety years old and nine, the Lord appeared to Abram, and said unto him, I am the Almighty God; walk before me, and be thou perfect. 2 And I will make my covenant between me and thee, and will multiply thee exceedingly. 3 And Abram fell on his face: and God talked with him, saying, 4 As for me, behold, my covenant is with thee, and thou shalt be a father of many nations. 5 Neither shall thy name any more be called Abram, but thy name shall be Abraham; for a father of many nations I have made thee. 6 And I will make thee exceeding fruitful, and I will make nations of thee, and kings shall come out of thee. 7 And I will establish my covenant between me and thee and thy seed after thee in their generations, for an everlasting covenant, to be a God unto thee and to thy seed after thee. 8 And I will give unto thee, and to thy seed after thee, the land wherein thou art a stranger, all the land of Canaan, for an everlasting possession; and I will be their God. 9 And God said unto Abraham. Thou shalt keep my covenant therefore, thou, and thy seed after thee in their generations.

10 This is my covenant, which he shall keep, between me and you and thy seed after thee; Every man child among you shall be circumcised.

11 And ye shall circumcise the flesh of your foreskin; and it shall be a token of the covenant betwixt me and you. 12 And he that is eight days old shall be circumcised among you, every man child in your generations, he that is born in the house, or bought with money of any stranger, which is not of thy seed. 13 He that is born in thy house, and he that is bought with thy money, must needs be circumcised: and my covenant shall be in your flesh for an everlasting covenant. 14 And the uncircumcised man child whose flesh of his foreskin is not circumcised, that soul shall be cut off from his people; he hath broken my covenant.

Exodus

Chapter 19

1 In the third month, when the children of Israel were gone forth out of the land of Egypt, the same day came they into the wilderness of Sinai.

2 For they were departed from Rephidim, and were come to the desert of Sinai, and had pitched in the wilderness; and there Israel

camped before the mount. 3 And Moses went up unto God, and the Lord called unto him out of the mountain, saying, Thus shalt thou say to the house of Jacob, and tell the children of Israel; 4 Ye have seen what I did unto the Egyptians, and how I bare you on eagles' wings, and brought you unto myself. 5 Now therefore, if ye will obey my voice indeed, and keep my covenant, then ye shall be a peculiar treasure unto me above all people: for all the earth is mine: 6 And ye shall be unto me a kingdom of priests, and a holy nation. These are the words which thou shalt speak unto the children of Israel.

7 And Moses came and called for the elders of the people, and laid before their faces all these words which the Lord commanded him. 8 And all the people answered together, and said, All that the Lord hath spoken we will do. And Moses returned the words of the people unto the Lord. 9 And the Lord said unto Moses, Lo, I come unto thee in a thick cloud, that the people may hear when I speak with thee, and believe thee for ever. And Moses told the words of the people unto the Lord.

Chapter 20

1 And God spake all these words, saying,

2 I am the Lord thy God, which have brought thee out of the land of Egypt, out of the house of bondage. 3 Thou shalt have no other gods before me.

4 Thou shalt not make unto thee any graven image, or any likeness of any thing that is in heaven above, or that is in the earth beneath, or that is in the water under the earth: 5 Thou shalt not bow down thyself to them, nor serve them: for I the Lord thy God am a jealous God, visiting the iniquity of the fathers upon the children unto the third and fourth generation of them that hate me; 6 And showing mercy unto thousands of them that love me, and keep my commandments.

7 Thou shalt not take the name of the Lord thy God in vain: for the Lord will not hold him guiltless that taketh his name in vain.

8 Remember the sabbath day, to keep it holy. 9 Six days shalt thou labor, and do all thy work: 10 But the seventh day is the sabbath of the Lord thy God: in it thou shalt not do any work, thou, nor thy son, nor thy daughter, nor thy manservant, nor thy maidservant, nor thy cattle, nor thy stranger that is within thy gates: 11 For in six days the Lord made heaven and earth, the sea, and all that in them is, and rested the seventh day: wherefore the Lord blessed the sabbath day, and hallowed it.

12 Honor thy father and thy mother: that thy days may be long upon the land which the Lord thy God giveth thee.

13 Thou shalt not kill.

14 Thou shalt not commit adultery.

15 Thou shalt not steal.

16 Thou shalt not bear false witness against thy neighbor.

17 Thou shalt not covet thy neighbor's house; thou shalt not covet thy neighbor's wife, nor his manservant, nor his maidservant, nor his ox, nor his ass, nor any thing that is thy neighbor's.

18 And all the people saw the thunderings, and the lightnings, and the noise of the trumpet, and the mountain smoking: and when the people saw it, they removed, and stood afar off.

Leviticus

Chapter 1

1 And the Lord called unto Moses, and spake unto him out of the tabernacle of the congregation, saying, 2 Speak unto the children of Israel, and say unto them, If any man of you bring an offering unto the Lord, ye shall bring your offering of the cattle, even of the herd, and of the flock.

3 If his offering be a burnt sacrifice of the herd, let him offer a male without blemish: he shall offer it of his own voluntary will at the door of the tabernacle of the congregation before the Lord. 4 And he shall put his hand upon the head of the burnt offering; and it shall be accepted for him to make atonement for him. 5 And he shall kill the bullock before the Lord: and the priests, Aaron's sons, shall bring the blood, and sprinkle the blood round about upon the altar that is by the door of the tabernacle of the congregation. 6 And he shall flay the burnt offering, and cut it into his pieces. 7 And the sons of Aaron the priest shall put fire upon the altar, and lay the wood in order upon the fire: 8 And the priests, Aaron's sons, shall lay the parts, the head, and the fat, in order upon the wood that is on the fire which is upon the altar: 9 But his inwards and his legs shall he wash in water: and the priest shall burn all on the altar, to be a burnt sacrifice, an offering made by fire, of a sweet savor unto the Lord.

Psalm 23

1 The Lord is my shepherd; I shall not want.

2 He maketh me to lie down in green pastures: He leadeth me beside the still waters.

3 He restoreth my soul: He leadeth me in the paths of righteousness for his name's sake.

4 Yea, though I walk through the valley of the shadow of death, I will fear no evil: for thou art with me; Thy rod and thy staff they comfort me.

5 Thou preparest a table before me in the presence of mine enemies: Thou anointest my head with oil; my cup runneth over.

6 Surely goodness and mercy shall follow me all the days of my life:
And I will dwell in the house of the Lord for ever.

Amos

Chapter 5

21 I hate, I despise your feast days, and I will not delight in your
solemn assemblies.

22 Though you offer me burnt offerings and your meat offerings, I
will not accept them: neither will I regard the peace offerings of your
fat beasts.

23 Take thou away from me the noise of thy songs; for I will not
hear the melody of thy viols.

24 But let judgment run down as waters, and righteousness as a
mighty stream.

$$\boxed{35}$$

The Bible: Prophets and Apocalypse

**The golden days of Jewish kings were not to last. Powerful empires
rose up to challenge and dominate the Jews: the Assyrians in 800
B.C.E., the Babylonians around 600 B.C.E., then the Medes, the Persians, the armies of Alexander the Great, his successor states — ruled
by his generals and their descendants — and then the Romans after 64
B.C.E. The Babylonians were among the worst of the invaders. They
conquered Jerusalem, destroyed the temple, and brought Jews as
hostages to Babylon. In 538 B.C.E. Cyrus, king of the Persians, allowed
Jews to return to Jerusalem and even rebuild the temple. But the Jews
never regained their kingdom or independence (except for brief periods), and the Greek Seleucid* rulers after Alexander proved to be intolerant of non-Greek forms of worship.**

*sel OO sihd

Dan. 12:1–13 King James.

Ironically, it was during this period of conquest and dispersal that Judaism began to develop the elements of a universal religion. The Babylonian destruction of the temple and population transfer made the religion of Yahweh less dependent on place. Virtually all religions of the ancient world were bound to a particular place, usually the sacred temple where the god was thought to reside. Judaism remained a religion of the descendants of Abraham and his son Israel, and the period after 600 B.C.E. was one of intense cultivation of that identity. But much of the Hebrew Bible was composed in exile, as a way of recalling a common history, reaffirming a common identity, predicting a common future. The prophets foresaw a brighter future or explained how the violation of the covenant had brought God's wrath on the people.

One of the great prophets of the exile and the postexile period was Daniel, described as one of the young men who was brought to Babylon by Nebuchadnezzar,* conqueror of Jerusalem in 586 B.C.E. The Book of Daniel begins by recounting that conquest. In Babylon Nebuchadnezzar asked Daniel to reveal the meaning of a dream. You will read his response below.

Daniel is the first to foretell of an apocalyptic end to history and the first to envision personal immortality. Previous prophets had predicted a new independent kingdom of Judah or they had predicted God's punishment of his people, but Daniel prophesied that God would come down to reign on earth forever, judging the living and the dead for all eternity. These ideas — an end to history, the Last Judgment, the Kingdom of God, eternal life or damnation — became more important later in Christianity than in Judaism, where these notions never entered the mainstream. But their appearance in Daniel shows the way in which Judaic ideas became more universal over the course of the first millennium B.C.E. Why would Daniel's ideas open the Judaic tradition to non-Jews or people not descended from Abraham? How would Daniel's prophecy affect his contemporaries? How would it affect you?

Thinking Historically

When did the idea of an afterlife enter Judaism? To answer this question we have to date the Book of Daniel, which is a bit more complex than it would seem. As mentioned, the book is presented as the prophecy of a Daniel who was taken from Jerusalem to Babylon around 586 B.C.E. If there was such a Daniel and he was a prophet, the version we have shows signs of continual updating. In the initial prophecy for Nebuchadnezzar and in similar instances reported throughout the Book of Daniel, the author predicts the string of empires that determined the fate of the Jews from the Babylonian to the

*neh boo kuhd NEH zur

Median to the Persian to the Greek under Alexander to the Seleucid (Alexander's successors). This is the meaning of the gold, silver, bronze, iron, clay sequence. In each case, the prophecy is vague (and sometimes inaccurate) when referring to the Babylonian period but very specific and exact about the period of iron and clay (the Seleucids). When Daniel speaks of the signs of the last days, his veiled references clearly refer to events during the reign of the Seleucid ruler Antiochus IV. He distinctly sees the desecration of the temple by Antiochus as the key event that will bring about God's eternal kingdom. Antiochus, who ruled from 175 to 163 B.C.E., pressured the Jews to accept Greek gods. In 168 B.C.E. he polluted the temple by slaughtering pigs on the altar and then erecting a statue of the Greek god Zeus — the event that Daniel predicts will bring on God's last judgment.

What would be the purpose of putting this prophecy in the writings of someone who had lived hundreds of years earlier? How does the age of Daniel's message give it added impact? When and why would the author of the Book of Daniel have predicted that the end of the world would occur 1290 days after an event in 168 B.C.E.? When and why would he have written "blessed are those who wait 1335 days"?

Daniel

Daniel Interprets the Dream of Nebuchadnezzar (Chapter 2)

Thou, O king, sawest, and behold a great image. This great image, whose brightness was excellent, stood before thee; and the form thereof was terrible.

32 This image's head was of fine gold, his breast and his arms of silver, his belly and his thighs of brass,

33 His legs of iron, his feet part of iron and part of clay.

34 Thou sawest till that a stone was cut out without hands, which smote the image upon his feet that were of iron and clay, and brake them to pieces.

35 Then was the iron, the clay, the brass, the silver, and the gold, broken to pieces together, and became like the chaff of the summer threshing floors; and the wind carried them away, that no place was found for them: and the stone that smote the image became a great mountain, and filled the whole earth.

36 This is the dream; and we will tell the interpretation thereof before the king.

37 Thou, O king, art a king of kings: for the God of heaven hath given thee a kingdom, power, and strength, and glory.

38 And wheresoever the children of men dwell, the beasts of the field and the fowls of the heaven hath he given into thine hand, and hath made thee ruler over them all. Thou art this head of gold.

39 And after thee shall arise another kingdom inferior to thee,[1] and another third kingdom of brass,[2] which shall bear rule over all the earth.

40 And the fourth kingdom[3] shall be strong as iron: forasmuch as iron breaketh in pieces and subdueth all things: and as iron that breaketh all these, shall it break in pieces and bruise.

41 And whereas thou sawest the feet and toes, part of potters' clay, and part of iron, the kingdom shall be divided;[4] but there shall be in it of the strength of the iron, forasmuch as thou sawest the iron mixed with miry clay.

42 And as the toes of the feet were part of iron, and part of clay, so the kingdom shall be partly strong, and partly broken.

43 And whereas thou sawest iron mixed with miry clay, they shall mingle themselves with the seed of men:[5] but they shall not cleave one to another, even as iron is not mixed with clay.

44 And in the days of these kings shall the God of heaven set up a kingdom, which shall never be destroyed: and the kingdom shall not be left to other people, but it shall break in pieces and consume all these kingdoms, and it shall stand for ever.

45 Forasmuch as thou sawest that the stone was cut out of the mountain without hands, and that it brake in pieces the iron, the brass, the clay, the silver, and the gold; the great God hath made known to the king what shall come to pass hereafter: and the dream is certain, and the interpretation thereof sure.

Daniel Sees the End of the Age of Iron and Clay (Chapter 11)

28 Then shall he[6] return into his land[7] with great riches and his heart shall be against the holy covenant;[8] and he shall do exploits, and return to his own land.

---

[1]Media, or Mede, Empire. Iranians who defeated Babylonians and ruled in the Middle East to 550 B.C.E. [Ed.]

[2]Persia, 550–330 B.C.E. [Ed.]

[3]Greek empire of Alexander the Great, 330–323 B.C.E. [Ed.]

[4]The Middle Eastern portion of Alexander's empire was divided after his death in 323 B.C.E. by his generals: Seleucus in Palestine and Syria and Ptolemy in Egypt. The kingdom of the Seleucids (iron) was stronger than the Ptolemy (clay). These two dynasties lasted until conquered by Rome and Persian Parthia. [Ed.]

[5]Probably refers to mixing of peoples and cultures in Alexander's and his successors' empire. [Ed.]

[6]Antiochus IV, the Seleucid emperor from 175 to 161 B.C.E., ruled Palestine, Syria, and Alexander's eastern empire, which included Jerusalem. [Ed.]

[7]Antiochus IV returned to Jerusalem after his first war with Egypt, 170 B.C.E. [Ed.]

[8]Antiochus stole Temple treasures and massacred many Jews, 169 B.C.E. [Ed.]

29 At the time appointed he shall return, and come toward the south;[9] but it shall not be as the former, or as the latter.

30 For the ships of Chittim[10] shall come against him: therefore he shall be grieved, and return, and have indignation against the holy covenant: so shall he do; he shall even return, and have intelligence with them that forsake[11] the holy covenant.

31 And arms shall stand on his part, and they shall pollute the sanctuary of strength, and shall take away the daily sacrifice, and they shall place the abomination that maketh desolate.[12]

32 And such as do wickedly against the covenant shall he corrupt by flatteries: but the people that do know their God shall be strong, and do exploits.

33 And they that understand among the people shall instruct many: yet they shall fall by the sword, and by flame, by captivity, and by spoil, many days.

34 Now when they shall fall, they shall be helped with a little help:[13] but many shall cleave to them with flatteries.[14]

35 And some of them of understanding shall fall, to try them, and to purge, and to make them white, even to the time of the end: because it is yet for a time appointed.

36 And the king shall do according to his will; and he shall exalt himself, and magnify himself above every god,[15] and shall speak marvelous things against the God of gods, and shall prosper till the indignation be accomplished: for that that is determined shall be done.

37 Neither shall he regard the God of his fathers, nor the desire of women, nor regard any god: for he shall magnify himself above all.

38 But in his estate shall he honour the God of forces: and a god whom his fathers knew not shall he honour with gold, and silver, and with precious stones, and pleasant things.

39 Thus shall he do in the most strong holds with a strange god, whom he shall acknowledge and increase with glory: and he shall cause them to rule over many, and shall divide the land for gain.

40 And at the time of the end shall the king of the south[16] push at him: and the king of the north shall come against him like a whirlwind,

---

[9]The second war of Antiochus IV with Egypt in 168 B.C.E. was not successful. [Ed.]

[10]Cyprus. Here it means ships of Romans, generally, who blocked him. [Ed.]

[11]Jews like Jason the high priest, who favored Greek customs. [Ed.]

[12]The army of Antiochus broke down the temple walls, desecrated the interior, and installed Greek statues. [Ed.]

[13]While many Jews chose martyrdom, some received the help of Judas Maccabeus, leader of the opposition to Antiochus. [Ed.]

[14]Some of the followers of Judas Maccabeus were insincere. [Ed.]

[15]Antiochus had himself declared "Epiphanes," or God Manifest. [Ed.]

[16]Ptolemy VI Philometor (Egypt) initiated the third Egyptian war, against Antiochus. [Ed.]

with chariots, and with horsemen, and with many ships; and he shall enter into the countries, and shall overflow and pass over.

41 He shall enter also into the glorious land, and many countries shall be overthrown: but these shall escape out of his hand, even Edom, and Moab, and the chief of the children of Ammon.

42 He shall stretch forth his hand also upon the countries: and the land of Egypt shall not escape.

43 But he shall have power over the treasures of gold and of silver, and over all the precious things of Egypt: and the Libyans and the Ethiopians shall be at his steps.

44 But tidings out of the east and out of the north[17] shall trouble him: therefore he shall go forth with great fury to destroy, and utterly to make away many.

45 And he shall plant the tabernacles of his palace between the seas in the glorious holy mountain;[18] yet he shall come to his end,[19] and none shall help him.

Then Shall Come the End of Days (Chapter 12)

1 And at that time shall Michael[20] stand up, the great prince which standeth for the children of thy people: and there shall be a time of trouble, such as never was since there was a nation even to that same time: and at that time thy people shall be delivered, every one that shall be found written in the book.

2 And many of them that sleep in the dust of the earth shall awake, some to everlasting life, and some to shame and everlasting contempt.

3 And they that be wise shall shine as the brightness of the firmament; and they that turn many to righteousness as the stars for ever and ever.

4 But thou, O Daniel, shut up the words, and seal the book, even to the time of the end: many shall run to and fro, and knowledge shall be increased.

5 Then I Daniel looked, and, behold, there stood other two, the one on this side of the bank of the river, and the other on that side of the bank of the river.

6 And one said to the man clothed in linen, which was upon the waters of the river, How long shall it be to the end of these wonders?

7 And I heard the man clothed in linen, which was upon the waters of the river, when he held up his right hand and his left hand unto

---

[17]Antiochus spent his last year in war with Armenia and Parthia (Persia). [Ed.]
[18]In Palestine. [Ed.]
[19]Antiochus IV died at Tabae in Persia in 163 B.C.E. [Ed.]
[20]Protective angel of Israel. [Ed.]

---

heaven, and sware by him that liveth for ever that it shall be for a time, times, and an half; and when he shall have accomplished to scatter the power of the holy people, all these things shall be finished.

8 And I heard, but I understood not: then said I, O my Lord, what shall be the end of these things?

9 And he said, Go thy way, Daniel: for the words are closed up and sealed till the time of the end.

10 Many shall be purified, and made white, and tried; but the wicked shall do wickedly: and none of the wicked shall understand; but the wise shall understand.

11 And from the time that the daily sacrifice shall be taken away, and the abomination that maketh desolate set up, there shall be a thousand two hundred and ninety days.

12 Blessed is he that waiteth, and cometh to the thousand three hundred and five and thirty days.

13 But go thou thy way till the end be: for thou shalt rest, and stand in thy lot at the end of the days.

36

Christianity: Jesus according to Matthew

The related ideas first enunciated in Daniel — the coming end of the world or the Kingdom of God, the Last Judgment, individual immortality or life after death — were to become central to the branch of Judaism that produced Christianity. Along with Judaic monotheism and the insistence of the prophets (like Amos) on internalized morality, the idea of personal responsibility and eternal salvation or damnation gave Christianity an appeal that would eventually reach far beyond the children of Abraham.

In this selection from the Gospel of Matthew, the evangelist recounts Jesus speaking of the apocalypse and there is a note of urgency here. Like Daniel, Jesus speaks of the signs that the end is at hand. Yet, in the same chapter, sometimes in the same paragraph, Matthew recounts Jesus telling his listeners that there is plenty of time before the end.

Matt. 24:1–41 King James.

What accounts for this apparent contradiction? If you were in the audience listening to Jesus, what idea would motivate you more — the fact that the end of the world is rapidly approaching or that it is generations away? If you were taking notes for the daily newspaper, which message would get the headline? If you were writing a history of Jesus for future generations, which message would you emphasize?

Thinking Historically

Matthew was writing about forty years after Jesus died. If he had been among those who heard Jesus speak, he took a long time to write it down. It is more likely that the author of this gospel is a second-generation evangelist, drawing on an earlier source, now lost. He may have had access to an earlier eyewitness account, or to a collection of sayings of Jesus.

We know that Matthew updated the words of Jesus for the benefit of those Christians living after 70 C.E. Notice, for example, Matthew's reference to Daniel in 24:15: Jesus tells his listeners that when they see the abomination of the temple of which Daniel spoke, they should flee into the mountains to prepare for the end. But we know today that Daniel was speaking of the desecration of the temple by Antiochus IV in 168 B.C.E. Matthew, unaware of the historical context of Daniel and writing after the Roman destruction of the temple in 70 C.E., believed that Roman destruction was the event Daniel was predicting. So Matthew updates the message of Jesus for future generations by including the temple desecration for the readers of his gospel ("whoso readeth, let him understand"). This is one of the ways we know that Matthew was written after 70 C.E. Jesus would not have referred to an event which was for his audience forty years into the future, and expect his audience to understand his reference. In addition to the Daniel reference, which parts of this selection would most likely have been updated by Matthew? Which quotations of Jesus were apt to need updating?

Matthew

Chapter 24

1 And Jesus went out, and departed from the temple: and his disciples came to him for to show him the buildings of the temple. 2 And Jesus said unto them, See ye not all these things? verily I say unto You, There shall not be left here one stone upon another, that shall not be thrown down. 3 And as he sat upon the Mount of Olives, the disciples came unto him privately, saying, Tell us, when shall these things be? and what shall be the sign of thy coming, and of the end of the world?

4 And Jesus answered and said unto them, Take heed that no man deceive you. 5 For many shall come in my name, saying, I am Christ; and shall deceive many. 6 And ye shall hear of wars and rumors of wars: see that ye be not troubled: for all these things must come to pass, but the end is not yet. 7 For nation shall rise against nation, and kingdom against kingdom: and there shall be famines, and pestilences, and earthquakes, in divers places. 8 All these are the beginning of sorrows. 9 Then shall they deliver you up to be afflicted, and shall kill you: and ye shall be hated of all nations for my name's sake. 10 And then shall many be offended, and shall betray one another, and shall hate one another. 11 And many false prophets shall rise, and shall deceive many. 12 And because iniquity shall abound, the love of many shall wax cold. 13 But he that shall endure unto the end, the same shall be saved. 14 And this gospel of the kingdom shall be preached in all the world for a witness unto all nations; and then shall the end come.

15 When ye therefore shall see the abomination of desolation, spoken of by Daniel the prophet, stand in the holy place (whoso readeth, let him understand), 16 Then let them which be in Judea flee into the mountains: 17 Let him which is on the housetop not come down to take any thing out of his house: 18 Neither let him which is in the field return back to take his clothes. 19 And woe unto them that are with child, and to them that give suck in those days! 20 But pray ye that your flight be not in the winter, neither on the sabbath day: 21 For then shall be great tribulation, such as was not since the beginning of the world to this time, no, nor ever shall be. 22 And except those days should be shortened, there should no flesh be saved: but for the elect's sake those days shall be shortened. 23 Then if any man shall say unto you, Lo, here is Christ, or there; believe it not. 24 For there shall arise false Christs, and false prophets, and shall show great signs and wonders; insomuch that, if it were possible, they shall deceive the very elect. 25 Behold, I have told you before. 26 Wherefore if they shall say unto you, Behold, he is in the desert; go not forth: behold he is in the secret chambers; believe it not. 27 For as the lightning cometh out of the east, and shineth even unto the west; so shall also the coming of the Son of man be. 28 For wheresoever the carcass is, there will the eagles be gathered together.

29 Immediately after the tribulation of those days shall the sun be darkened, and the moon shall not give her light, and the stars shall fall from heaven, and the powers of the heavens shall be shaken: 30 And then shall appear the sign of the Son of man in heaven: and then shall all the tribes of the earth mourn, and they shall see the Son of man coming in the clouds of heaven with power and great glory. 31 And he shall send his angels with a great sound of a trumpet, and they shall gather together his elect from the four winds, from one end of heaven to the other. 32 Now learn a parable of the fig tree; When his branch

is yet tender, and putteth forth leaves, ye know that summer is nigh: 33 So likewise ye, when ye shall see all these things, know that it is near, even at the doors. 34 Verily I say unto you, This generation shall not pass, till all these things be fulfilled. 35 Heaven and earth shall pass away, but my words shall not pass away.

36 But of that day and hour knoweth no man, no, not the angels of heaven, but my Father only. 37 But as the days of Noe [Noah] were, so shall also the coming of the Son of man be. 38 For as in the days that were before the flood they were eating and drinking, marrying and giving in marriage, until the day that Noe entered into the ark, 39 And knew not until the flood came, and took them all away; so shall also the coming of the Son of man be. 40 Then shall two be in the field; the one shall be taken, and the other left. 41 Two women shall be grinding at the mill; the one shall be taken, and the other left.

REFLECTIONS

The layers of revision are etched more sharply in Daniel and Matthew than in the Hindu and Buddhist documents because dates, chronology, and time sequences were far more important to the Judeo-Christian tradition. It was, and is, a tradition committed to the belief that God works in time; that there is a beginning, middle, and end to things; and that it is crucially important for humans to know where they are in the providential timeline. A modern skeptic might be bothered by the way the author or authors of Daniel turn history into prophecy. But for the Jews of the 160s B.C.E., the need to get the dates right and be ready for the end of days was far more important than checking who predicted what when.

Ironically, the precise prophecy of Daniel transcended its historical moorings when it was used by the author of Matthew in an effort to update the prophecy of Jesus, and it has been used regularly by every generation since with a different "king of the south" and new supporting cast. But if the Judeo-Christian tradition has left a legacy of apocalyptic warnings and millennial musings, it has also given us the interest and the tools that have shaped this chapter. The need to date, to find the actual words, to peel away the layers of rust that obfuscate an authentic past — that is a fine legacy indeed.

We have seen how Hinduism produced Buddhism and how Judaism generated Christianity, but neither Hinduism nor Judaism ended two thousand years ago. In fact, both "parental" religions underwent profound changes as well. Both became more universal, less dependent on particular places or people, and less limited to caste, region, or tribe.

We saw in the Upanishads how, around 500 B.C.E., Hinduism became almost monotheistic in its worship of Brahman. Similarly, about three hundred years later, Hindu devotional cults that centered on two of the other deities of the Hindu pantheon (Vishnu — especially in his incarnation as Krishna — and Shiva) developed. Reread the last eight stanzas of selection 14 from the *Bhagavad Gita* (written about 200 B.C.E.) to see how the worship of Vishnu/Krishna became enormously appealing to masses of Indian people.

At about the time of Jesus, Judaism also underwent a transformation that has continued until this day. A process that began with the destruction of the first temple and the captivity in Babylon in the sixth century B.C.E. — the development of a Judaism independent of a particular temple or place — was revived after the Romans destroyed the second temple in 70 C.E. The Roman conquest created a much greater diaspora (migration or dispersal) of Jews throughout the world than what the Babylonian conquest had spawned. Among new exiles throughout the world, Judaism became a religion of rabbis (teachers) rather than of temple priests. So great was this transformation of Judaism that one might argue, with Alan Segal in *Rebecca's Children*, that "the time of Jesus marks the birth of not one but two great religions in the West, Judaism and Christianity. . . . So great is the contrast between previous Jewish religious systems and rabbinism."[1]

And yet neither Judaism nor Hinduism became missionary religions; neither sought converts aggressively. Christianity and Buddhism did, however, and that is the subject of the next chapter.

---

[1]Alan F. Segal, *Rebecca's Children: Judaism and Christianity in the Roman World* (Cambridge: Harvard University Press, 1986), 1.

7

Encounters and Conversions: Monks, Merchants, and Monarchs

Expansion of Salvation Religions, 400 B.C.E.–1400 C.E.

HISTORICAL CONTEXT

From their beginnings, Buddhism and Christianity were less tribal and more universal than their parental religions, Hinduism and Judaism, because they offered universal salvation to their followers. The teachings of Jesus and the Buddha emphasized personal religious experience over the dictates of caste, ancestry, and formal law, making their ideas more likely to spread beyond their cultures of origin. Both religions, however, had relatively small followings at the deaths of their founders. How, then, did they win millions of converts within the next few hundred years? Similarly, how did Islam, founded in 622 C.E., spread from the Arabian peninsula to embrace the Berbers of North Africa, the Visigoths of Spain, Syrians, Persians, Turks, Central Asians, Indians, and even the western Chinese by 750 C.E.? What was happening throughout Eurasia that explained these successes? In this chapter we explore how both an array of powerful and charismatic individuals — religious figures, political leaders, and even merchants and traders — and specific economic, political, and social conditions helped to broaden the appeal of the salvation religions and find larger audiences for their gospels.

Religious thinkers loosened the new religions from their parental ties, often changing them as they spread them. St. Paul almost single-handedly separated Jesus from his Jewish roots, presenting him as the Son of God who was sacrificed for the sins of humankind, not just the

Jewish people. Similarly, Mahayana Buddhists taught that Buddha was more than a teacher and spiritual guide whom one could imitate; he was a savior, responsive to prayer and worship. Sufi shaykhs spread Islam in remote rural areas by incorporating local beliefs and practices into Islamic teachings.

Religious leaders weren't the only ones spreading faith; merchants and traders also played a crucial role. The spread of universal faiths and common cultures over great distances owed much to the roads and maritime transport of the Roman and Chinese empires, as well as the Persian, central Asian, and Indian states in between. But it was also a product of the Silk Road, or roads, that connected China with Rome after 100 B.C.E. (see Map 7.1, p. 223). The expansion of the great religious traditions was the work of merchants as well as monks; gods traveled in camel caravans, and holy images were carried on rolls of silk.

Contact alone, however, is not enough to explain why people converted to Christianity, Buddhism, and Islam. The appeals to salvation beyond this world testified to difficult times. Nomadic pastoral peoples undermined the stability of empires already weakened by public debt, class antagonisms, dwindling crop yields, and disease. Populations declined from 200–800 C.E. and did not reach earlier levels again until about 1000 C.E. in Europe and China. People sought spiritual reassurance as well as economic alliances that would protect them in uncertain times. When those in power adopted new religions, it often benefited others to follow their lead, securing a network of influence for new religious movements.

THINKING HISTORICALLY
Studying Religion in Historic Context

In the previous chapter we looked for evidence of change in primary religious documents. In this chapter we take the historical study of religion a step further by examining how religions developed in the larger historical context of political, economic, and social change. Religions evolve not only according to an inner theological dynamic but also in response to changes within the broader society. Our study of the expansion of Buddhism, Christianity, and Islam provides a particularly useful set of questions about the relationship of religion to other historical forces. When we ask how these great salvation religions spread, we must consider how religious ideas are different from other ideas. How are such ideas affected by political, social, and economic forces, and how are these forces affected by religious ideas?

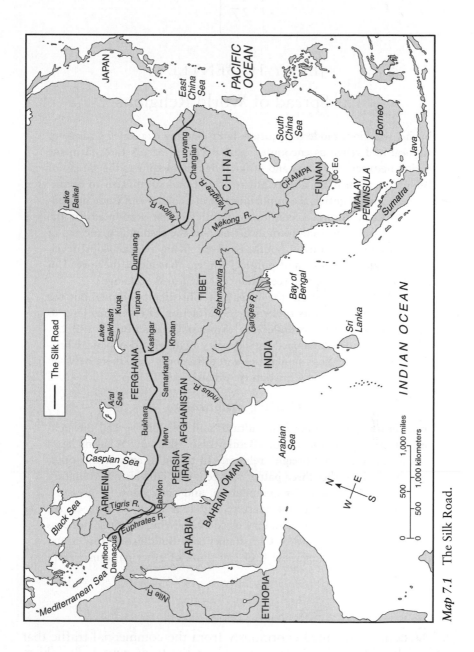

Map 7.1 The Silk Road.

223

37

JERRY H. BENTLEY

The Spread of World Religions

In this selection, modern historian Jerry Bentley examines a range of cultural and religious encounters that occurred across Eurasia in the period between 400 B.C.E. and 400 C.E. He first explores the spread of Buddhism from India northward to China and southward to Southeast Asia, highlighting the importance of merchants and trade in seeding new conversions. According to Bentley, what accounted for the initial resistance to Buddhism in China and the resounding success of Indian ideas and faiths in Southeast Asia? What relationships developed between religious and political leaders that aided the spread of Buddhism? Where do you see instances of cultural exchange?

Bentley then examines the spread of Christianity throughout the Roman Empire, from its rocky start as a faction of rebellious Jews to its eventual legalization under the emperor Constantine in 313 C.E. What specific developments does Bentley highlight to explain Christianity's success? What similarities and differences were there between the way Buddhism and Christianity spread?

Thinking Historically

In addition to describing *how* cultures and religions spread throughout Eurasia during this period, Bentley also asks *why*. What makes a people convert to a "foreign" religion? In trying to answer this question, he distinguishes three patterns of religious conversion: voluntary association, syncretism, or assimilation, and conversion by pressure. Obviously, these categories overlap, and it is often difficult to tell whether a conversion is voluntary or coerced. Which of these patterns best describes the spread of Christianity and Buddhism? How useful do you find these categories? Can you think of other patterns of religious conversion?

. . . Buddhism benefited enormously from the commercial traffic that crossed the silk roads. Once it arrived on the trade routes, Buddhism

Jerry H. Bentley, *Old World Encounters: Cross-Cultural Contacts and Exchanges in Pre-Modern Times* (Oxford: Oxford University Press, 1993), 47–53, 60–64.

found its way very quickly indeed to distant lands. Merchants proved to be an efficient vector of the Buddhist faith, as they established diaspora communities in the string of oasis towns—Merv, Bukhara, Samarkand, Kashgar, Khotan, Kuqa, Turpan, Dunhuang—that served as lifeline of the silk roads through central Asia. (See Map 7.1.) The oases depended heavily on trade for their economic survival, and they quickly accommodated the needs and interests of the merchants whom they hosted. They became centers of high literacy and culture; they organized markets and arranged for lodging, care of animals, and storage of merchandise; and they allowed their guests to build monasteries and bring large contingents of Buddhist monks and copyists into their communities. Before too long—perhaps as early as the first or even the second century B.C.E.—the oasis dwellers themselves converted to Buddhism.

Thus a process of conversion through voluntary association with well-organized foreigners underwrote the first major expansion of Buddhism outside India. Buddhist merchants linked the oases to a large and cosmopolitan world, and the oases became enormously wealthy by providing useful services for the merchants. It is not at all surprising that inhabitants of the small oasis communities would gradually incline toward the beliefs and values of the numerous Buddhist merchants who traveled the silk roads and enriched the oases.

Once established in oasis communities, Buddhism had the potential to spread both to nomadic peoples on the steppes of central Asia and even to China, a land of long-settled civilization with its own long-established cultural traditions. Buddhism realized this potential only partially, however, and only in gradual fashion. As a faith foreign to China and generally despised by Chinese during its early centuries there, Buddhism had a certain attraction for nomadic peoples who themselves had quite difficult relations with the Chinese. In other words, Buddhism exercised a kind of countercultural appeal to nomads who loathed the Chinese, but who also desired and even depended upon trade with China. Yet many nomadic peoples found it difficult to accept Buddhism; they did not have traditions of literacy to accommodate Buddhist moral and theological teachings, and their mobility made it impossible to maintain fixed monastic communities. As a result, many nomadic peoples held to their native shamanist cults, and others turned to Manichaeism[1] or Nestorian Christianity.[2] Meanwhile, some of those

---

[1]man ih KEE ih zuhm   Third-century Persian religion; belief that the body is trapped in darkness searching for the light. [Ed.]

[2]Fifth-century Syrian faith that spread to India, central Asia, and China; belief in the human nature of Jesus. [Ed.]

who adopted Buddhism did so at a very late date. Among the Mongols, for example, Buddhism did not become a popular faith until the sixteenth century. When nomadic peoples became involved in commerce, however, or when they established themselves as rulers of settled lands that they conquered, they frequently adopted Buddhism through a process of conversion through voluntary association. These patterns were quite prominent in central Asia and northern China during the era of the ancient silk roads.

The career of the monk and missionary Fotudeng especially helps to illuminate the voluntary conversion of nomadic peoples to Buddhism. Fotudeng probably came from Kuqa, an oasis town on the Silk Road in modern Xinjiang. He became a priest at an early age, traveled through central Asia, visited Kashmir, and set out to do missionary work in northern China during the early fourth century. He went to Dunhuang in order to improve his Chinese, then continued on to Luoyang about the year 310. There he caught the attention of Shi Le, the ruler of the nomadic Jie people (western allies of the Xiongnu), who controlled most of northern China during the fourth century. Fotudeng realized early on that he would not get very far with Shi Le by lecturing him on fine points of Buddhist philosophy, but he had a reputation for working miracles, which he used to the advantage of his mission. He dazzled Shi Le by producing bright blue lotus blossoms from his monk's begging bowl and by looking into his palm to see the reflection of distant events. Among his more utilitarian talents were rainmaking, healing, and prophecy. Fotudeng helped Shi Le plan military campaigns by foreseeing the outcome and devising clever strategies to ensure success. As a result of his miraculous talents, Fotudeng won widespread fame, and people from distant regions worshipped him. When he died about the year 345, he reportedly had ten thousand disciples and the erection of 893 temples to his credit.

Thus did a process of voluntary conversion help to establish Buddhism in northern China. The nomadic Jie settled in northern China and became deeply engaged in the political and economic affairs of a large and complex world. Fotudeng represented the culture of that larger world and brought talents useful for Jie rulers as they entered its life. He parlayed his personal relationship with Shi Le into official approval for his efforts to spread Buddhist values and even to found Buddhist institutions in northern China. Hence, his work not only illuminates the voluntary conversion of nomadic peoples but also helps to explain the early presence of the Buddhist faith in China.

The establishment of Buddhism in China was an even more difficult and gradual affair than its spread among nomadic peoples. Indeed, it required half a millennium for Buddhism to attract a large popular following in China. There as in Persia, the foreign faith could not immediately attract many followers away from indigenous cultural traditions, in this case principally Confucianism and Daoism. Even in its early years in China, Buddhism encountered determined resistance from Confucian and Daoist quarters. Representatives of the native Chinese traditions charged that Buddhism detracted from the authority of the state, that monasteries were unproductive and useless drags on the economy, that Buddhism itself was a barbarian faith inferior to Chinese traditions, and that the monastic life violated the natural order of society and disrupted family life. Not surprisingly, then, during its early centuries in China, Buddhism remained largely the faith of foreigners: merchants, ambassadors, refugees, hostages, and missionaries. . . .

As an alien cultural tradition that did not resonate in China, Buddhism could easily have experienced the same fate there that it did in Persia: It could have survived in the quarters inhabited by foreign merchants as an expatriate faith, perhaps even for centuries, without attracting much interest from the larger host community. The explanation for Buddhism's remarkable spread as a popular faith in east Asia begins with the voluntary conversion of elites, which enabled the foreign tradition to gain a foothold in Chinese society. In the north, where Buddhism first established its presence in China, voluntary conversion reflected the political interests of ruling elites. In most cases they were nomads, such as the Jie whom Fotudeng served so well, or the Toba rulers of the Northern Wei dynasty (386–534). After an initial period of tension and uncertain relations, it dawned on both Buddhists and rulers that an alliance could serve the interests of both parties. Buddhist monasteries provided ideological and economic support for established ruling houses: They recognized the legitimacy of the Jie and Toba rule; they facilitated long-distance trade, which figured prominently in the local economy; and they served as a conduit for the importation of exotic and luxury goods that symbolized the special status of the ruling elites. Meanwhile, the dynasties patronized the Buddhists in return, participated in their rituals, and protected the interests of their monasteries.

Like the oasis dwellers of central Asia, then, the ruling elites of northern China made common cause with representatives of a foreign cultural tradition who had extensive political and commercial links in the larger world. This sort of voluntary conversion was the only way by which Buddhism could find a place in Chinese society. Buddhists entered China in numbers too small to bring about a massive social transformation by way of pressure or assimilation. Only by winning the favor and protection of elites could the early Buddhists ensure their survival in China. . . .

Meanwhile, as Buddhism found tentative footing in China, both Buddhism and Hinduism attracted the attention of elites and won converts in southeast Asia. As in China, the carriers of Indian cultural traditions were mostly merchants. During the late centuries B.C.E., Indian traders began to sail the seas and visit the coastal towns of southeast Asia. Even during those remote centuries, there was considerable incentive for merchants to embark upon long and often dangerous voyages. According to an ancient Gujarati story, for example, men who went to Java never returned—but if by chance they did return, they brought with them wealth enough to provide for seven generations. By the early centuries C.E., southeast Asian mariners themselves traveled to India as well as to other southeast Asian sites. The resulting networks of trade and communication invigorated not only the economic but also the political and cultural life of southeast Asia.

Among the principal beneficiaries of early trade between India and southeast Asia were the political and cultural traditions of India. Merchants from the subcontinent established diaspora communities, into which they invited Hindu and Buddhist authorities. Local chiefs controlled commerce at the trading sites they ruled, and they quickly became introduced to the larger world of the Indian Ocean. The ruler of an important trading site was no longer a "frog under a coconut shell," as the Malay proverb has it, but, rather, a cultural and commercial broker of some moment. Trade and external alliances enabled local rulers to organize states on a larger scale than ever before in southeast Asia. The first of these well represented in historical sources—though by no means the only early state in southeast Asia—was Funan, founded along the Mekong River in the first century C.E. Through its main port, Oc Eo, Funan carried on trade with China, Malaya, Indonesia, India, Persia, and indirectly with Mediterranean lands. By the end of the second century, similar trading states had appeared in the Malay peninsula and Champa (southern Vietnam).

Indian influence ran so deep in these states that they and their successors for a millennium and more are commonly referred to as the "Indianized states of southeast Asia." Indian traditions manifested their influence in many different ways. In a land previously governed by charismatic individuals of great personal influence, for example, rulers adopted Indian notions of divine kingship. They associated themselves with the cults of Siva, Visnu, or the Buddha, and they claimed both foreign and divine authority to legitimize their rule. They built walled cities with temples at the center, and they introduced Indian music and ceremonies into court rituals. They brought in Hindu and Buddhist advisers, who reinforced the sense of divinely sanctioned rule. They took Sanskrit names and titles for themselves, and they used Sanskrit as the language of law and bureaucracy. Indian influence was so extensive, in fact, that an earlier generation of historians suggested that vast armadas of Indians had colonized southeast Asia—a view now regarded as complete fiction. More recent explanations of the Indianization process place more emphasis on southeast Asian elites who for their own purposes associated themselves as closely as possible with the

Hindu and Buddhist traditions. They certainly found no lack of willing and talented tutors; the quality of Sanskrit literature produced in southeast Asia argues for the presence there of many sophisticated and well-educated representatives of Indian cultural traditions. But high interest in foreign traditions on the part of southeast Asian elites drove the process of Indianization.

By no means did indigenous cultures fade away or disappear. During the early years after their arrival in southeast Asia, Indian traditions worked their influence mostly at the courts of ruling elites, and not much beyond. Over a longer term, however, Indian and native traditions combined to fashion syncretic cultural configurations and to bring about social conversion on a large scale. . . . In any case, though, the voluntary conversion of local elites to Hinduism and Buddhism decisively shaped the cultural development of southeast Asia.

. . .

Of all the religions that established themselves in the Roman empire, . . . none succeeded on such a large scale or over such a long term as Christianity. (See Map 7.2.) Its early experience thus calls for some discussion.

Christianity had many things in common with other religions that became widely popular in the Roman empire. It offered an explanation of the world and the cosmic order, one that endowed history with a sense of purpose and human life with meaning. It addressed the needs and interests of individuals by holding out the prospect of personal immortality, salvation, and perpetual enjoyment of a paradisiacal existence. It established high standards of ethics and morality, well suited to the needs of a complex, interdependent, and cosmopolitan world where peoples of different races and religions intermingled on a systematic basis. It was a religion of the cities, efficiently disseminated throughout the empire along established routes of trade and communication. It welcomed into its ranks the untutored and unsophisticated as well as the more privileged classes. It even shared with the other religions several of its ritual elements, such as baptism and the community meal. In many ways, then, early Christianity reflected the larger cultural world of the early Roman empire.

During its first three centuries, Christianity developed under a serious political handicap. The earliest Christians were associated with parties of rebellious Jews who resisted Roman administration in Palestine. Later Christians, even gentiles, refused to honor the Roman emperor and state in the fashion deemed appropriate by imperial authorities. As a result, Christians endured not only social contempt and scorn but also organized campaigns of persecution. Meanwhile, the Roman state generously patronized many of the empire's pagan cults: in exchange for public honor and recognition, the emperors and other

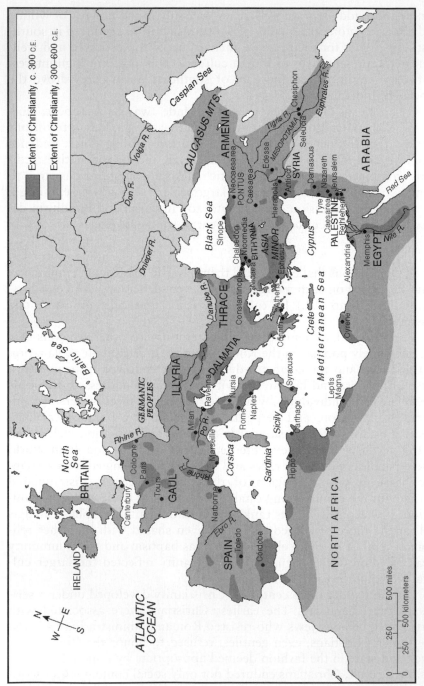

Map 7.2 The Spread of Christianity, 300–600 C.E.

important political figures provided financial sponsorship for rituals, festivals, and other pagan activities.

Nevertheless, Christianity benefited from the work of zealous missionaries who were able to persuade individuals and small groups that the Christians' god possessed awesome and unique powers. They communicated this message most effectively among the popular masses by acquiring a reputation for the working of miracles—healing illnesses, casting out demons, bestowing blessings on the faithful—that demonstrated the powers at their god's disposal. [Historian] Ramsay Mac-Mullen has recently argued, in fact, that fear of pain and punishment, desire for blessings, and belief in miracles were the principal inducements that attracted pagans to Christianity in the period before the conversion of Constantine about the year 312 C.E.

A bit of information survives on one of the more effective of the early Christian missionaries, Gregory the Wonderworker, and it illustrates the importance of miracles for the building of the early Christian community. Gregory had studied with the great Origen,[3] and he wrote several formal theological treatises. For present purposes, though, his significance arises from his work in the Roman province of Pontus (north central Anatolia) during the 240s. Early accounts of his mission record one miracle after another. Gregory's prayers prevented a pagan deity from exercising his powers, but upon request Gregory summoned the deity to his pagan temple, thus demonstrating his superior authority; as a result, the caretaker of the temple converted to Christianity. On several occasions individuals interrupted Gregory's public teaching; each time, Gregory exorcized a demon from the offensive party, provoking widespread amazement and winning converts in the process. Gregory moved boulders, diverted a river in flood, and dried up an inconveniently located lake. By the end of his campaign, Gregory had brought almost every soul of the town of Neocaesarea into the ranks of the Christians, and surrounding communities soon joined the bandwagon. As in the case of Fotudeng in north China, Gregory's reputation as a miracle worker seized the attention of his audiences and helped him to promote his faith among pagans.

Did the conversions brought about by Christian miracle workers represent cases of conversion through voluntary association? To some extent, this interpretation seems plausible, in that converts voluntarily adopted Christianity as the cultural alternative that best reflected the realities of the larger world—for example by offering access to powers not available to others. A reputation for the ability to work miracles helped missionaries to dramatize the benefits and blessings that Christianity promised to individuals and suggested that Christianity possessed

---

[3]Biblical scholar and Christian theologian, c. 185–254. [Ed.]

an unusually effective capacity to explain and control the world. In other ways, however, the winning of early Christian converts differed from the more common pattern of conversion through voluntary association. Converts came from all ranks of society, not just those of merchants, rulers, and others who had extensive dealings with representatives from the larger world. Moreover, until the conversion of the emperor Constantine and the legalization of Christianity, there were some powerful disincentives to conversion, so that potential converts to the new faith had to weigh heavy political, social, and economic risks against the personal and spiritual benefits offered by Christianity.

On balance, then, it seems to me that the category of conversion through voluntary association helps at least in a limited way to explain the early spread of Christianity in the Mediterranean basin. From the viewpoint of Roman society as a whole, however, rather than that of individual citizens, early conversion to Christianity benefited especially from two additional developments that accompanied the process of conversion through voluntary association. In the first place, until the fourth century, Christianity spread largely through a process of syncretism. In the second place, following the conversion of Constantine, Christianity gained state sponsorship, and a process of conversion by political, social, and economic pressure consolidated the new faith as a securely institutionalized church. Both of these developments warrant some attention.

The decline of long-established pagan cults afforded an opportunity for Christianity to extend its influence by way of syncretism. Beginning in the third century, the pagan cults suffered progressively more difficult financial problems as the Roman economy went into serious decline. The Roman state could no longer afford to support the cults on the generous basis of centuries past. Wealthy individuals continued to provide a great deal of aid, but their sponsorship was more erratic and precarious than that of the state.

As the pagan cults failed to provide for the needs and interests of their followers, Christianity offered a meaningful alternative that was the more acceptable for its resemblance to the cults. In their rituals and their assumptions about the natural world, the early Christians very much reflected the larger culture of the late Roman empire. Like devotees of the pagan cults, they offered their sacraments as great mysteries, and there were pagan analogues to many of their rituals, such as the intonation of divine language, the use of special garments and paraphernalia, and even the observance of ceremonies like baptism and a community meal open only to initiates. Christians appropriated the power and authority associated with pagan heroes by emphasizing the virtues of a saint or martyr with similar attributes. Eventually, Christians even baptized pagan philosophy and festivals, which served as new links between pagan and Christian cultures: St. Augustine transformed Neoplatonism into a powerful Christian philosophy, and the birthdate of the unconquered pagan sun god became Christmas, the birthdate also of Jesus. Thus from a very early date, Christianity appealed to Mediterranean peoples partly because of its syncretic capacity: It came in familiar dress, and it dealt with many of the same concerns addressed by the pagan cults.

The conversion of Constantine amplified the effects of syncretism by inaugurating a process of officially sponsored conversion that ultimately resulted in the cultural transformation of the entire Roman empire. Constantine favored Christians from the moment that he consolidated his hold on the imperial throne. In the year 313 he issued his famous edict of toleration, which for the first time recognized Christianity as a legal religion in the Roman empire. At some indeterminate point, Constantine himself converted to Christianity. Constantine's personal example of course did not lead to immediate Christianization of the Roman empire, or even of the army that the emperor directly supervised. In several ways, though, it brought long-term changes that favored the Christians' efforts. It brought immediate material benefits, as Constantine and his successors underwrote the construction of churches and showered Christians with financial support. It also brought an intangible but nonetheless important social benefit: Christianity gained more public respect than it had ever previously enjoyed. As a result, ambitious and reputable individuals of increasing prominence joined Christian ranks—especially because Christians received preferential consideration for high imperial posts. Finally, the legalization of their religion allowed Christians to promote their faith more publicly and more aggressively than ever before. From its earliest days, the Christian community had produced combative and confrontational spokesmen. After Constantine's edict of toleration allowed Christians to promote their faith publicly, they relentlessly attacked the pagan cults, sometimes sparking episodes of personal violence, forcible conversion of individuals, and destruction of pagan temples and images.

State sponsorship provided Christianity with the material and political support required to bring about social conversion on a large scale. Christianity quickly became the official and only legally tolerated religion of the Roman empire: Already by the late fourth century, the emperors had begun to prohibit observance of pagan cults. By no means, however, did the various pagan religions forfeit their claims to cultural allegiance. Pagan spokesmen resisted efforts to destroy their cults, and thanks to syncretism, their values and rituals to some extent survived in Christian dress. Nevertheless, by the late fourth century, Christianity had won a cultural and institutional initiative over paganism that it would never relinquish. . . .

38

Pliny Consults the Emperor Trajan

The inhabitants of an average city of the ancient Mediterranean worshiped dozens of gods, though usually one was thought to be a special guardian of the populace and a protector of the state. Cities of the Roman Empire added deities and cults from conquered and distant territories, creating a bewildering array. General tolerance prevailed. No one cared which gods an individual worshiped. Only Rome, as the capital of the empire, might require worship of a state god, including, at times, the emperor himself. But aside from this matter of loyalty to the state, one's religious convictions were one's own affair.

Christians ran afoul of the law and practice not only by refusing the demonstration of loyalty to the state but also by aggressively denying the validity of all other gods—an attitude that many found distasteful.

Like the Jews, Christians were alternately persecuted and ignored. Roman oppression broke out when Nero blamed Christians for the great fire in Rome in 64 C.E. but then abated under the moderate rule of Trajan.

A brief correspondence between Pliny,* serving as governor of Bithynia (in modern Turkey), and the Emperor Trajan† from about the year 111 C.E. has survived, throwing light on official Roman policy toward Christians of that era. What does Pliny's letter to Trajan tell you about official Roman policy? What do you think of Trajan's answer?

Thinking Historically

Pliny is enforcing policy while at the same time he is personally repelled by the Christians. Try to distinguish these elements in Pliny's mind. What does he see as their legal guilt, and what does he find personally distasteful? How do you explain Pliny's confusion about whether he should punish former Christians? What does Pliny know about the Christians?

Pliny mentions that some of the accused Christians admitted that they had been Christians but were no longer. Were they telling the truth? What do you think?

*PLIH nee
†TRAY juhn

Pliny, Letters 10:96–97, in *Pliny Secundus: Letters and Panegyricus,* Loeb Classical Library, vol. II, trans. Betty Radice (Cambridge: Harvard University Press, 1959), 285, 287, 289, 291, 293.

Pliny to the Emperor Trajan

It is my custom to refer all my difficulties to you, Sir, for no one is better able to resolve my doubts and to inform my ignorance.

I have never been present at an examination of Christians. Consequently, I do not know the nature or the extent of the punishments usually meted out to them, nor the grounds for starting an investigation and how far it should be pressed. Nor am I at all sure whether any distinction should be made between them on the grounds of age, or if young people and adults should be treated alike; whether a pardon ought to be granted to anyone retracting his beliefs, or if he has once professed Christianity, he shall gain nothing by renouncing it; and whether it is the mere name of Christian which is punishable, even if innocent of crime, or rather the crimes associated with the name.

For the moment this is the line I have taken with all persons brought before me on the charge of being Christians. I have asked them in person if they are Christians, and if they admit it, I repeat the question a second and third time, with a warning of the punishment awaiting them. If they persist, I order them to be led away for execution; for, whatever the nature of their admission, I am convinced that their stubbornness and unshakeable obstinacy ought not to go unpunished. There have been others similarly fanatical who are Roman citizens. I have entered them on the list of persons to be sent to Rome for trial.

Now that I have begun to deal with this problem, as so often happens, the charges are becoming more widespread and increasing in variety. An anonymous pamphlet has been circulated which contains the names of a number of accused persons. Among these I considered that I should dismiss any who denied that they were or ever had been Christians when they had repeated after me a formula of invocation to the gods and had made offerings of wine and incense to your statue (which I had ordered to be brought into court for this purpose along with the images of the gods), and furthermore had reviled the name of Christ: none of which things, I understand, any genuine Christian can be induced to do.

Others, whose names were given to me by an informer, first admitted the charge and then denied it; they said that they had ceased to be Christians two or more years previously, and some of them even twenty years ago. They all did reverence to your statue and the images of the gods in the same way as the others, and reviled the name of Christ. They also declared that the sum total of their guilt or error amounted to no more than this: They had met regularly before dawn on a fixed day to chant verses alternately among themselves in honour of Christ as if to a god, and also to bind themselves by oath, not for any criminal purpose, but to abstain from theft, robbery and adultery, to commit no breach of trust and not to deny a deposit when called upon to restore it. After this ceremony it had been their custom to disperse and re-assemble later to take food of an ordinary, harmless kind; but they had in fact given up this practice since my edict, issued on your instructions, which banned all political societies. This made me decide it was all the more necessary to extract the truth by torture from two slave-women, whom they call deaconesses. I found nothing but a degenerate sort of cult carried to extravagant lengths.

I have therefore postponed any further examination and hastened to consult you. The question seems to me to be worthy of your consideration, especially in view of the number of persons endangered; for a great many individuals of every age and class, both men and women, are being brought to trial, and this is likely to continue. It is not only the towns, but villages and rural districts too which are infected through contact with this wretched cult. I think though that it is still possible for it to be checked and directed to better ends, for there is no doubt that people have begun to throng the temples which had been almost entirely deserted for a long time; the sacred rites which had been allowed to lapse are being performed again, and flesh of sacrificial victims is on sale everywhere, though up till recently scarcely anyone could be found to buy it. It is easy to infer from this that a great many people could be reformed if they were given an opportunity to repent.

Trajan to Pliny

You have followed the right course of procedure, my dear Pliny, in your examination of the cases of persons charged with being Christians, for it is impossible to lay down a general rule to a fixed formula. These people must not be hunted out; if they are brought before you and the charge against them is proved, they must be punished, but in the case of anyone who denies that he is a Christian, and makes it clear that he is not by offering prayers to our gods, he is to be pardoned as a result of his repentance however suspect his past conduct may be. But pamphlets circulated anonymously must play no part in any accusation. They create the worst sort of precedent and are quite out of keeping with the spirit of our age.

39

EUSEBIUS

From Life of Constantine

If Christians were persecuted by Roman officials and emperors, and despised by the thoughtful and powerful elite of Roman society, how then did Christianity ever succeed?

Part of the answer lies in the location of these Christians. They were more concentrated in urban than rural areas (the Latin word *pagan* meant "rural" before it meant "unchristian") and managed to gain significant advocates among the powerful elite.

No more powerful spokesman could be found than a Roman emperor, and so a short answer to the question of how Christianity succeeded must be "the Emperor Constantine" (288–337 C.E.). The emperor's historian Eusebius* (260–339 C.E.) recognized both the importance of the emperor and the role of the empire in the success of Christianity in winning the Roman Empire:

> At the same time one universal power, the Roman Empire arose and flourished, while the enduring and implacable hatred of nation against nation was now removed; and as the knowledge of one god and one way of religion and salvation, even the doctrine of Christ, was made known to all mankind; so at the same time the entire dominion of the Roman Empire being invested in a single sovereign, profound peace reigned throughout the world. And thus, by the express appointment of the same God, two roots of blessing, the Roman Empire and the doctrine of Christian piety, sprang up together for the benefit of men.[1]

In 312 C.E., Constantine, who ruled Gaul and Britain, was about to invade Italy and try to gain the throne of the western empire by defeating Maxentius, who ruled Rome. In his *Life of Constantine*, Eusebius, who knew the emperor, tells a story that must have circulated at the time to explain Constantine's support of Christianity.

---

*yoo SAY bee uhs
[1]Eusebius, *Oration in Praise of Constantine*, xv, 4. [Ed.]

P. Schaff and H. Wace, eds. *The Library of Nicene and Post-Nicene Fathers*, vol. I, *Church History, Life of Constantine, Oration in Praise of Constantine* (New York: The Christian Literature Company, 1890), 489–91.

Thinking Historically

What do you think of Eusebius's explanation for Constantine's acceptance of Christianity? What does Constantine's reasoning say about
how people of his day chose their religious beliefs and loyalties? How
would the conversion of the emperor encourage others to become
Christians? What, if anything, might have slowed the advance of
Christianity after 312 C.E.?

Being convinced, however, that he needed some more powerful aid
than his military forces could afford him, on account of the wicked and
magical enchantments which were so diligently practiced by the tyrant
[Maxentius], he sought Divine assistance, deeming the possession of
arms and a numerous soldiery of secondary importance, but believing
the cooperating power of Deity invincible and not to be shaken. He
considered, therefore, on what God he might rely for protection and assistance. While engaged in this enquiry, the thought occurred to him,
that, of the many emperors who had preceded him, those who had
rested their hopes in a multitude of gods, and served them with sacrifices and offerings, had in the first place been deceived by flattering pre-
dictions, and oracles which promised them all prosperity, and at last
had met with an unhappy end, while not one of their gods had stood by
to warn them of the impending wrath of heaven; while one alone who
had pursued an entirely opposite course, who had condemned their
error, and honored the Supreme God during his whole life, had found
him to be the Saviour and Protector of his empire, and the Giver of
every good thing. Reflecting on this, and well weighing the fact that
they who had trusted in many gods had also fallen by manifold forms
of death, without leaving behind them either family or offspring, stock,
name, or memorial among men: while the God of his father had given
to him, on the other hand, manifestations of his power and very many
tokens: and considering farther that those who had already taken arms
against the tyrant, and had marched to the battle-field under the protection of a multitude of gods, had met with a dishonorable end (for
one of them had shamefully retreated from the contest without a blow,
and the other, being slain in the midst of his own troops, became, as it
were, the mere sport of death); reviewing, I say, all these considerations, he judged it to be folly indeed to join in the idle worship of those
who were no gods, and after such convincing evidence, to err from the
truth; and therefore felt it incumbent on him to honor his father's God
alone.

Accordingly he called on Him with earnest prayer and supplications that he would reveal to him who He was, and stretch forth His

right hand to help him in his present difficulties. And while he was thus praying with fervent entreaty, a most marvelous sign appeared to him from heaven, the account of which it might have been hard to believe had it been related by any other person. But since the victorious emperor himself long afterwards declared it to the writer of this history, when he was honored with his acquaintance and society, and confirmed his statement by an oath, who could hesitate to accredit the relation, especially since the testimony of after-time has established its truth? He said that about noon, when the day was already beginning to decline, he saw with his own eyes the trophy of a cross of light in the heavens, above the sun, and bearing the inscription, CONQUER BY THIS. At this sight he himself was struck with amazement, and his whole army also, which followed him on this expedition, and witnessed the miracle.

He said, moreover, that he doubted within himself what the import of this apparition could be. And while he continued to ponder and reason on its meaning, night suddenly came on; then in his sleep the Christ of God appeared to him with the same sign which he had seen in the heavens, and commanded him to make a likeness of that sign which he had seen in the heavens, and to use it as a safeguard in all engagements with his enemies.

At the dawn of day he arose, and communicated the marvel to his friends: and then, calling together the workers in gold and precious stones, he sat in the midst of them, and described to them the figure of the sign he had seen, bidding them represent it in gold and precious stones. And this representation I myself have had an opportunity of seeing. . . .

The emperor constantly made use of this sign of salvation as a safeguard against every adverse and hostile power, and commanded that others similar to it should be carried at the head of all his armies.

These things were done shortly afterwards. But at the time above specified, being struck with amazement at the extraordinary vision, and resolving to worship no other God save Him who had appeared to him, he sent for those who were acquainted with the mysteries of His doctrines, and enquired who that God was, and what was intended by the sign of the vision he had seen.

They affirmed that He was God, the only begotten Son of the one and only God: that the sign which had appeared was the symbol of immortality, and the trophy of that victory over death which He had gained in time past when sojourning on earth. They taught him also the causes of His advent, and explained to him the true account of His incarnation. Thus he was instructed in these matters, and was impressed with wonder at the divine manifestation which had been presented to his sight. Comparing, therefore, the heavenly vision with the interpretation given, he found his judgment confirmed; and, in the persuasion that the knowledge of these things had been imparted to him by Divine teaching, he determined thenceforth to devote himself to the reading of the inspired writings.

40

Buddhism in China:
From The Disposition of Error

When Buddhist monks traveled from India to China they came to a culture with different philosophical and religious traditions. In China, ancestor worship, which did not exist for Indians who believed in reincarnation, was a very important religious tradition. The leading Chinese philosopher was Confucius, who said very little about religion but stressed the need for respect: sons to fathers (filial piety), wives to husbands, children to parents, students to teachers, youngsters to elders, everyone to the emperor, the living to the deceased. More spiritual and meditative was the religion developed by the followers of a contemporary of Confucius, Lao Tze,* whose *Dao De Jing* (The Book of the Way) prescribed the peace that came from an acceptance of natural flows and rhythms. "Practice non-action" was the Daoist method.

The Disposition of Error is a Buddhist guide for converting the Chinese. While the author and date are uncertain, this kind of tract was common under the Southern Dynasties (420–589 C.E.). The author uses a frequently asked questions (FAQ) format that enables us to see what the Chinese—mainly Confucian—objections were to Buddhism, as well as what they considered good Buddhist answers.

What were the main Chinese objections to Buddhism? Why were Buddhist ideas of death such a stumbling block for Chinese Confucians? Were Confucian ideas about care of the body and hair only superficial concerns, or did they reflect basic differences between Confucianism and Buddhism?

*low TSAY

Hung-ming Chi, in Taishō daizōkyō, LII, 1–7, quoted in William Theodore de Bary, ed., *The Buddhist Tradition in India, China and Japan* (New York: Random House, 1969), 132–37.

Thinking Historically

Notice how the Buddhist Mou Tzu answers Chinese questions about Buddhism with both Confucian and Daoist ideas. Which answers do you think were most effective? Would Chinese converts to Buddhism become more Confucian or Daoist? Was conversion to Buddhism a greater challenge to traditional Chinese ideas or behavior?

Why Is Buddhism Not Mentioned in the Chinese Classics?

The questioner said: If the way of the Buddha is the greatest and most venerable of ways, why did Yao, Shun, the Duke of Chou, and Confucius not practice it? In the Five Classics one sees no mention of it. You, sir, are fond of the *Book of Odes* and the *Book of History*, and you take pleasure in rites and music. Why, then, do you love the way of the Buddha and rejoice in outlandish arts? Can they exceed the Classics and commentaries and beautify the accomplishments of the sages? Permit me the liberty, sir, of advising you to reject them.

Mou Tzu said: All written works need not necessarily be the words of Confucius, and all medicine does not necessarily consist of the formulae of [the famous physician] P'ien-ch'üeh. What accords with principle is to be followed, what heals the sick is good. The gentleman-scholar draws widely on all forms of good, and thereby benefits his character. Tzu-kung [a disciple of Confucius] said, "Did the Master have a permanent teacher?" Yao served Yin Shou, Shun served Wu-ch'eng, the Duke of Chou learned from Lü Wang, and Confucius learned from Lao Tzu. And none of these teachers is mentioned in the Five Classics. Although these four teachers were sages, to compare them to the Buddha would be like comparing a white deer to a unicorn, or a swallow to a phoenix. Yao, Shun, the Duke of Chou, and Confucius learned even from such teachers as these. How much less, then, may one reject the Buddha, whose distinguishing marks are extraordinary and whose superhuman powers know no bounds! How may one reject him and refuse to learn from him? The records and teachings of the Five Classics do not contain everything. Even if the Buddha is not mentioned in them, what occasion is there for suspicion?

Why Do Buddhist Monks Do Injury to Their Bodies?

The questioner said: The *Classic of Filial Piety* says, "Our torso, limbs, hair, and skin we receive from our fathers and mothers. We dare not do them injury." When Tseng Tzu was about to die, he bared his hands and feet.[1] But now the monks shave their heads. How this violates the sayings of the sages and is out of keeping with the way of the filially pious! . . .

Mou Tzu said: . . . Confucius has said, "He with whom one may follow a course is not necessarily he with whom one may weigh its merits." This is what is meant by doing what is best at the time. Furthermore, the *Classic of Filial Piety* says, "The kings of yore possessed the ultimate virtue and the essential Way." T'ai-po cut his hair short and tattooed his body, thus following of his own accord the customs of Wu and Yüeh and going against the spirit of the "torso, limbs, hair, and skin" passage.[2] And yet Confucius praised him, saying that his might well be called the ultimate virtue.

Why Do Monks Not Marry?

The questioner said: Now of felicities there is none greater than the continuation of one's line, of unfilial conduct there is none worse than childlessness. The monks forsake wife and children, reject property and wealth. Some do not marry all their lives. How opposed this conduct is to felicity and filial piety! . . .

Mou Tzu said: . . . Wives, children, and property are the luxuries of the world, but simple living and inaction are the wonders of the Way. Lao Tzu has said, "Of reputation and life, which is dearer? Of life and property, which is worth more?" . . . Hsü Yu and Ch'ao-fu dwelt in a tree. Po I and Shu Ch'i starved in Shou-yang, but Confucius praised their worth, saying, "They sought to act in accordance with humanity and they succeeded in acting so." One does not hear of their being ill-spoken of because they were childless and propertyless. The monk practices the Way and substitutes that for the pleasures of disporting himself in the world. He accumulates goodness and wisdom in exchange for the joys of wife and children.

Death and Rebirth

The questioner said: The Buddhists say that after a man dies he will be reborn. I do not believe in the truth of these words. . . .

Mou Tzu said: . . . The spirit never perishes. Only the body decays. The body is like the roots and leaves of the five grains, the spirit is like the seeds and kernels of the five grains. When the roots and leaves

[1]To show he had preserved them intact from all harm.

[2]Uncle of King Wen of the Chou who retired to the barbarian land of Wu and cut his hair and tattooed his body in barbarian fashion, thus yielding his claim to the throne to King Wen.

come forth they inevitably die. But do the seeds and kernels perish? Only the body of one who has achieved the Way perishes. . . .

Someone said: If one follows the Way one dies. If one does not follow the Way one dies. What difference is there?

Mou Tzu said: You are the sort of person who, having not a single day of goodness, yet seeks a lifetime of fame. If one has the Way, even if one dies one's soul goes to an abode of happiness. If one does not have the Way, when one is dead one's soul suffers misfortune.

Why Should a Chinese Allow Himself to Be Influenced by Indian Ways?

The questioner said: Confucius said, "The barbarians with a ruler are not so good as the Chinese without one." Mencius criticized Ch'en Hsiang for rejecting his own education to adopt the ways of [the foreign teacher] Hsü Hsing, saying, "I have heard of using what is Chinese to change what is barbarian, but I have never heard of using what is barbarian to change what is Chinese." You, sir, at the age of twenty learned the way of Yao, Shun, Confucius, and the Duke of Chou. But now you have rejected them, and instead have taken up the arts of the barbarians. Is this not a great error?

Mou Tzu said: . . . What Confucius said was meant to rectify the way of the world, and what Mencius said was meant to deplore one-sidedness. Of old, when Confucius was thinking of taking residence among the nine barbarian nations, he said, "If a gentleman-scholar dwells in their midst, what baseness can there be among them?" . . . The Commentary says, "The north polar star is in the center of heaven and to the north of man." From this one can see that the land of China is not necessarily situated under the center of heaven. According to the Buddhist scriptures, above, below, and all around, all beings containing blood belong to the Buddha-clan. Therefore I revere and study these scriptures. Why should I reject the Way of Yao, Shun, Confucius, and the Duke of Chou? Gold and jade do not harm each other, crystal and amber do not cheapen each other. You say that another is in error when it is you yourself who err.

Why Must a Monk Renounce Worldly Pleasures?

The questioner said: Of those who live in the world, there is none who does not love wealth and position and hate poverty and baseness, none who does not enjoy pleasure and idleness and shrink from labor and fatigue. . . . But now the monks wear red cloth, they eat one meal a day, they bottle up the six emotions, and thus they live out their lives. What value is there in such an existence?

Mou Tzu said: Wealth and rank are what man desires, but if he cannot obtain them in a moral way, he should not enjoy them. Poverty and meanness are what man hates, but if he can only avoid them by departing from the Way, he should not avoid them. Lao Tzu has said, "The five colors make men's eyes blind, the five sounds make men's ears deaf, the five flavors dull the palate, chasing about and hunting make men's minds mad, possessions difficult to acquire bring men's conduct to an impasse. The sage acts for his belly, not for his eyes." Can these words possibly be vain? Liu-hsia Hui would not exchange his way of life for the rank of the three highest princes of the realm. Tuan-kan Mu would not exchange his for the wealth of Prince Wen of Wei. . . . All of them followed their ideas, and cared for nothing more. Is there no value in such an existence?

Does Buddhism Have No Recipe for Immortality?

The questioner said: The Taoists say that Yao, Shun, the Duke of Chou, and Confucius and his seventy-two disciples did not die, but became immortals. The Buddhists say that men must all die, and that none can escape. What does this mean?

Mou Tzu said: Talk of immortality is superstitious and unfounded; it is not the word of the sages. Lao Tzu says, "Even Heaven and earth cannot be eternal. How much the less can man!" Confucius says, "The wise man leaves the world, but humanity and filial piety last forever." I have observed the six arts and examined the commentaries and records. According to them, Yao died, Shun had his [death place at] Mount Ts'ang-wu, Yü has his tomb on K'uai-chi, Po I and Shu Ch'i have their grave in Shou-yang. King Wen died before he could chastise Chou, King Wu died without waiting for King Ch'eng to grow up. We read of the Duke of Chou that he was reburied, and of Confucius that [shortly before his death] he dreamed of two pillars. [As for the disciples of Confucius], Po-yü died before his father, of Tzu Lu it is said that his flesh was chopped up and pickled.

41

From The Lotus Sutra

Buddhist monks won Chinese converts not by confronting the worldly practicality of Confucianism, but by emphasizing the mystical side of Buddhism, which was also found in Chinese Daoism. Still, it is unlikely that a heavily monastic religion like orthodox Buddhism would have swept across the family-centered Confucian cultures of East Asia. Though orthodox monastic Buddhism was successful in the Indian-influenced cultures of Southeast Asia, it was a more accommodative Buddhism, called Mahayana* or "the greater vehicle," that attracted many Chinese, Koreans, and Japanese.

Like Christianity, Mahayana Buddhism promised salvation from the ills of this world. The agents who brought this salvation to masses of people were called bodhisattvas,† enlightened ones who generously stopped at the brink of nirvana so that they could help others.

The Lotus Sutra—a sutra is a preaching, sermon, or other religious writing that Buddhists learn, practice, and repeat—is one of the classic texts of Mahayana Buddhism. While its origins are lost, it was translated into Chinese first in 255 C.E. and frequently thereafter, with greatest effect by Kumarajiva, a Central Asian monk and scholar, in 406 C.E. This selection is a translation of Kumarajiva's popular version. The first half of the selection (from Chapter 25 of the *Sutra*) introduces the bodhisattva named "Perceiver of the World's Sounds." The second half (from the last chapter, 28) tells of the bodhisattva named "Universal Worthy" and the importance of *The Lotus Sutra* itself. According to the *Sutra,* what does a bodhisattva do? How does one gain help from a bodhisattva? What do you think would be the appeal of Mahayana Buddhism?

Thinking Historically

The spread of both Christianity and Mahayana Buddhism suggests the attraction of salvation religions across Eurasia in this period. How were the appeals of Christianity and Mahayana Buddhism similar? How were they different? Did they appeal to the same or different sorts of people? How was the historical context of each expansion similar or different?

---

*mah hah YAH nuh
†boh dee SAHT vuh

The Lotus Sutra, trans. Burton Watson (New York: Columbia University Press, 1993), 298–300, 319–22.

25

The Universal Gateway of the Bodhisattva Perceiver of the World's Sounds

At that time the bodhisattva Inexhaustible Intent immediately rose from his seat, bared his right shoulder, pressed his palms together and, facing the Buddha, spoke these words: "World-Honored One, this Bodhisattva Perceiver of the World's Sounds—why is he called Perceiver of the World's Sounds?"

The Buddha said to Bodhisattva Inexhaustible Intent: "Good man, suppose there are immeasurable hundreds, thousands, ten thousands, millions of living beings who are undergoing various trials and suffering. If they hear of this bodhisattva Perceiver of the World's Sounds and single-mindedly call his name, then at once he will perceive the sound of their voices and they will all gain deliverance from their trials.

"If someone, holding fast to the name of Bodhisattva Perceiver of the World's Sounds, should enter a great fire, the fire could not burn him. This would come about because of this bodhisattva's authority and supernatural power. If one were washed away by a great flood and called upon his name, one would immediately find himself in a shallow place.

"Suppose there were a hundred, a thousand, ten thousand, a million living beings who, seeking for gold, silver, lapis lazuli, seashell, agate, coral, amber, pearls, and other treasures, set out on the great sea. And suppose a fierce wind should blow their ship off course and it drifted to the land of rakshasa demons.[1] If among those people there is even just one who calls the name of Bodhisattva Perceiver of the World's Sounds, then all those people will be delivered from their troubles with the rakshasas. This is why he is called Perceiver of the World's Sounds.

"If a person who faces imminent threat of attack should call the name of Bodhisattva Perceiver of the World's Sounds, then the swords and staves wielded by his attackers would instantly shatter into so many pieces and he would be delivered.

"Though enough yakshas[2] and rakshasas to fill all the thousand-millionfold world should try to come and torment a person, if they hear him calling the name of Bodhisattva Perceiver of the World's Sounds, then these evil demons will not even be able to look at him with their evil eyes, much less do him harm.

"Suppose there is a person who, whether guilty or not guilty, has had his body imprisoned in fetters and chains, cangue and lock. If he calls the name of Bodhisattva Perceiver of the World's Sounds, then all

---

[1]Evil spirits of Hindu mythology. [Ed.]
[2]Native spirits; maybe demons. [Ed.]

his bonds will be severed and broken and at once he will gain deliverance.

"Suppose, in a place filled with all the evil-hearted bandits of the thousand-millionfold world, there is a merchant leader who is guiding a band of merchants carrying valuable treasures over a steep and dangerous road, and that one man shouts out these words: 'Good men, do not be afraid! You must single-mindedly call on the name of Bodhisattva Perceiver of the World's Sounds. This bodhisattva can grant fearlessness to living beings. If you call his name, you will be delivered from these evil-hearted bandits!' When the band of merchants hear this, they all together raise their voices, saying, 'Hail to the Bodhisattva Perceiver of the World's Sounds!' And because they call his name, they are at once able to gain deliverance. Inexhaustible Intent, the authority and supernatural power of the bodhisattva and mahasattva Perceiver of the World's Sounds are as mighty as this!

"If there should be living beings beset by numerous lusts and cravings, let them think with constant reverence of Bodhisattva Perceiver of the World's Sounds and then they can shed their desires. If they have great wrath and ire, let them think with constant reverence of Bodhisattva Perceiver of the World's Sounds and then they can shed their ire. If they have great ignorance and stupidity, let them think with constant reverence of Bodhisattva Perceiver of the World's Sounds and they can rid themselves of stupidity.

"Inexhaustible Intent, the bodhisattva Perceiver of the World's Sounds possesses great authority and supernatural powers, as I have described, and can confer many benefits. For this reason, living beings should constantly keep the thought of him in mind.

"If a woman wishes to give birth to a male child, she should offer obeisance and alms to Bodhisattva Perceiver of the World's Sounds and then she will bear a son blessed with merit, virtue, and wisdom. And if she wishes to bear a daughter, she will bear one with all the marks of comeliness, one who in the past planted the roots of virtue and is loved and respected by many persons. . . . "

28
Encouragements of the Bodhisattva Universal Worthy

At that time Bodhisattva Universal Worthy, famed for his freely exercised transcendental powers, dignity and virtue, in company with great bodhisattvas in immeasurable, boundless, indescribable numbers, arrived from the east. . . .

When [Bodhisattva Universal Worthy] arrived in the midst of Mount Gridhrakuta in the saha world, he bowed his head to the ground in obeisance to Shakyamuni Buddha, circled around him to the right seven times, and said to the Buddha: "World-Honored One, when I was in the land of the Buddha King Above Jeweled Dignity and Virtue, from far away I heard the Lotus Sutra being preached in this saha world. In company with this multitude of immeasurable, boundless hundreds, thousands, ten thousands, millions of bodhisattvas I have come to listen to and accept it. I beg that the World-Honored One will preach it for us. And good men and good women in the time after the Thus Come One[3] has entered extinction—how will they be able to acquire this Lotus Sutra?"

The Buddha said to Bodhisattva Universal Worthy: "If good men and good women will fulfill four conditions in the time after the Thus Come One has entered extinction, then they will be able to acquire this Lotus Sutra. First, they must be protected and kept in mind by the Buddhas. Second, they must plant the roots of virtue. Third, they must enter the stage where they are sure of reaching enlightenment. Fourth, they must conceive a determination to save all living beings. If good men and good women fulfill these four conditions, then after the Thus Come One has entered extinction they will be certain to acquire this sutra."

At that time Bodhisattva Universal Worthy said to the Buddha: "World-Honored One, in the evil and corrupt age of the last five-hundred-year period, if there is someone who accepts and upholds this sutra, I will guard and protect him, free him from decline and harm, see that he attains peace and tranquility, and make certain that no one can spy out and take advantage of his shortcomings. . . .

"Whether that person is walking or standing, if he reads and recites this sutra, then at that time I will mount my six-tusked kingly white elephant and with my multitude of great bodhisattvas will proceed to where he is. I will manifest myself, offer alms, guard and protect him, and bring comfort to his mind. I will do this because I too want to offer alms to the Lotus Sutra. If when that person is seated he ponders this sutra, at that time too I will mount my kingly white elephant and manifest myself in his presence. If that person should forget a single phrase or verse of the Lotus Sutra, I will prompt him and join him in reading and reciting so that he will gain understanding. At that time the person who accepts, upholds, reads, and recites the Lotus Sutra will be able to see my body, will be filled with great joy, and will apply himself with greater diligence than ever. Because he has seen me, he will immediately acquire samadhis and dharanis.[4] These are called the repetition dharani, the hundred, thousand, ten thousand, million repetition dharani,

---

[3]A title for the Buddha. [Ed.]
[4]States of ecstasy and mantras, incantations, and prayers. [Ed.]

and the Dharma sound expedient dharani. He will acquire dharanis such as these.

"World-Honored One, in that later time, in the evil and corrupt age of the last five-hundred-year period, if monks, nuns, laymen believers or laywomen believers who seek out, accept, uphold, read, recite, and transcribe this Lotus Sutra should wish to practice it, they should do so diligently and with a single mind for a period of twenty-one days. When the twenty-one days have been fulfilled, I will mount my six-tusked white elephant and, with immeasurable numbers of bodhisattvas surrounding me and with this body that all living beings delight to see, I will manifest myself in the presence of the person and preach the Law for him, bringing him instruction, benefit, and joy. . . .

If there are those who accept, uphold, read, and recite this sutra, memorize it correctly, understand its principles, and practice it as the sutra prescribes, these persons should know that they are carrying out the practices of Universal Worthy himself. In the presence of immeasurable, boundless numbers of Buddhas they will have planted good roots deep in the ground, and the hands of the Thus Come Ones will pat them on the head.

"If they do no more than copy the sutra, when their lives come to an end they will be reborn in the Trayastrimsha heaven. At that time eighty-four thousand heavenly women, performing all kinds of music, will come to greet them. Such persons will put on crowns made of seven treasures and amidst the ladies-in-waiting will amuse and enjoy themselves. How much more so, then, if they accept, uphold, read, and recite the sutra, memorize it correctly, understand its principles, and practice it as the sutra prescribes. If there are persons who accept, uphold, read, and recite the sutra and understand its principles, when the lives of these persons come to an end, they will be received into the hands of a thousand Buddhas, who will free them from all fear and keep them from falling into the evil paths of existence. Immediately they will proceed to the Tushita heaven, to the place of Bodhisattva Maitreya. Bodhisattva Maitreya possesses the thirty-two features and is surrounded by a multitude of great bodhisattvas. He has hundreds, thousands, ten thousands, millions of heavenly women attendants, and these persons will be reborn in their midst. Such will be the benefits and advantages they enjoy."

42

From the Koran

In the centuries following the expansion of Christianity and Buddhism, a new monotheistic salvation religion, Islam, originated in Arabia and rapidly spread over much of the same area. (See Map 7.3.) The new faith centered on the Koran (or Qu'ran), which is said by Islamic believers, or Muslims, to be the word of God as spoken by the Angel Gabriel to the Prophet Muhammad about 610 C.E. Muhammad then recited these words so that others could memorize them or write them down. After Muhammad's death (632), these writings and memories were gathered together to form the Koran (literally "Recitation").

The chapters (or *surahs*) of the Koran, 114 in all, are organized by length, the longest first. This means that the earliest pieces, which are among the shortest, are found at the end of the book. We begin with an exception to this rule, *surah* 1, "The Opening," followed by numbers 99, 109, and 112. We also include excerpts from the later *surahs,* number 2, "The Cow,"[1] and number 4, "Women." What beliefs do these *surahs* convey? How are they similar to, or different from, other religious writings you have read? Why might Islam be called a salvation religion?

Thinking Historically

The early *surahs* (those with higher numbers) almost certainly reflect the concerns of early Islam. What are these concerns? The later *surahs* (such as 2 and 4) were probably written after Muhammad, threatened by the ruling tribes, had fled Mecca and taken control of the government of Medina. They may even have been written after Muhammad's death when his successors struggled with problems of governance. Judging from these later chapters, what kinds of issues most concerned leaders of the Muslim community?

---

[1]The title "The Cow" refers to verses 67–73 in *surah* 2 of the Koran (not included here), which tell of a dispute between Moses and the Israelites. After Moses tells the Israelites that God wants them to sacrifice a cow, they hesitate by asking a number of questions as to what kind of cow. Muslim meaning is that one should submit to God, not debate his commands.

Chapters 1, 91, 109, and 112: *Approaching the Qu'ran: The Early Revelations,* trans. Michael Sells (Ashland, OR: White Cloud Press, 1999), 42, 108, 128, 136. Chapters 2 and 4: *The New On-Line Translation of the Qur'an,* the Noor Foundation, http://www.islamusa.org/.

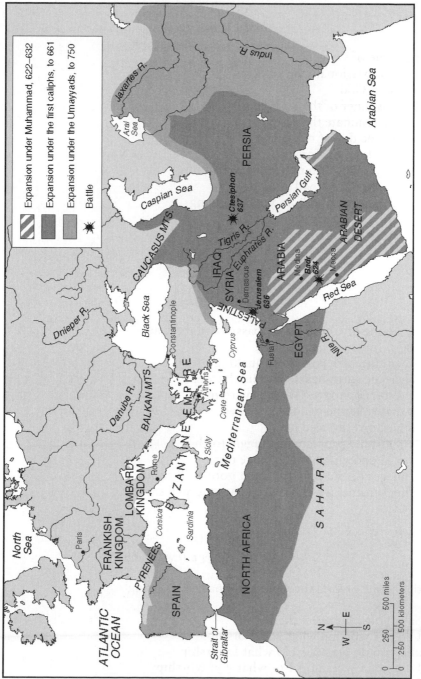

Map 7.3 The Expansion of Islam to 750 C.E.

Expansion under Muhammad, 622–632

Expansion under the first caliphs, to 661

Expansion under the Umayyads, to 750

Battle

North Sea

ATLANTIC OCEAN

FRANKISH KINGDOM

Paris

PYRENEES

SPAIN

Strait of Gibraltar

LOMBARD KINGDOM

Corsica

Sardinia

Rome

Sicily

NORTH AFRICA

SAHARA

Danube R.

BALKAN MTS.

BYZANTINE EMPIRE

Athens

Crete

Mediterranean Sea

Dnieper R.

Black Sea

Constantinople

Cyprus

EGYPT

Nile R.

Fustat

Red Sea

Caucasus Mts.

Caspian Sea

Aral Sea

Jaxartes R.

PERSIA

Indus R.

Ctesiphon 637

Tigris R.

Euphrates R.

IRAQ

SYRIA

Damascus

PALESTINE

Jerusalem 636

ARABIA

Medina

Badr 624

Mecca

ARABIAN DESERT

Persian Gulf

Arabian Sea

N
W E
S

0   250   500 miles
0   250   500 kilometers

251

Surah 1
The Opening

In the name of God
   the Compassionate the Caring
Praise be to God
   lord sustainer of the worlds
the Compassionate the Caring
master of the day of reckoning
To you we turn to worship
   and to you we turn in time of need
Guide us along the road straight
the road of those to whom you are giving
   not those with anger upon them
   not those who have lost the way

Surah 99
The Quaking

In the Name of God the Compassionate the Caring

   When the earth is shaken, quaking
   When the earth bears forth her burdens
   And someone says "What is with her?"
   At that time she will tell her news
   As her lord revealed her
   At that time people will straggle forth
     to be shown what they have done
   Whoever does a mote's weight good will see it
   Whoever does a mote's weight wrong will see it

Surah 109
Those Who Reject the Faith

In the Name of God the Compassionate the Caring

   Say: You who reject the faith
   I do not worship what you worship
   and you do not worship what I worship
   I am not a worshipper of what you worship
   You are not a worshipper of what I worship
   A reckoning for you and a reckoning for me

Surah 112
Sincerity / Unity

In the Name of God the Compassionate the Caring

Version 1
  Say he is God, one
  God forever
  Not begetting, unbegotten,
    and having as an equal none

Version 2
  Say he is God, one
  God the refuge
  Not begetting, unbegotten,
    and having as an equal none

Version 3
  Say he is God, one
  God the rock
  Not begetting, unbegotten,
    and having as an equal none

Surah 2
The Cow

Section 22

177. It is not the sole virtue that you turn your faces to the east or the west but true virtue is theirs, who believe in Allâh, the Last Day, the angels, the Book, and in the Prophets, and who give away their wealth (and substance) out of love for Him, to the near of kin, the orphans, the needy, the wayfarer and to those who ask (in charity) and in ransoming the slaves; and who observe the Prayer, who go on presenting the *Zakât* (the purifying alms) and those who always fulfill their pledges and agreements when they have made one, and those who are patiently persevering in adversity and distress and (steadfast) in times of war. It is these who have proved truthful (in their promises and in their faith) and it is these who are strictly guarded against evil.

178. O you who believe! equitable retaliation has been ordained for you in (the matter of) the slain. (Everyone shall pay for his own crime), the freeman (murderer) for the freeman (murdered), and the slave (murderer) for the slave (murdered), and the female (murderer) for the female (murdered), but who has been granted any remission by his

(aggrieved) brother (or family) then pursuing (of the matter) shall be done with equity and fairness, and the payment (of the blood money) to him (the heir) should be made in a handsome manner. This is an alleviation from your Lord and a mercy. But he who exceeds the limits after this (commandment), for him is a grievous punishment.

179. O people of pure and clear wisdom! your very life lies in (the law of) equitable retaliation, (you have been so commanded) so that you may enjoy security.

180. It has been prescribed for you at the time of death to any one of you, that if the (dying) person is leaving considerable wealth behind, to make a will to his parents and the near of kin to act with equity and fairness. This is an obligation incumbent on those who guard against evil.

181. He who alters it (the will) after he has heard it, (should know that) it is those that alter it who shall bear the burden of sin. Allâh indeed is All-Hearing, All-Knowing.

182. If anyone apprehends that the testator is partial or follows a sinful course there will be no blame on him provided he sets things right (and so brings about reconciliation) between them (the parties concerned under the will). Surely, Allâh is Great Protector, Ever Merciful.

Section 23

183. O you who believe! you are bound to observe fasting as those before you (followers of the Prophets) were bound, so that you may guard against evil.

184. (You are required to fast) for a prescribed number of days. But if anyone of you is sick or is on a journey he shall fast (to make up) the prescribed number in other days. And for those who are able to fast is an expiation (as thanksgiving) the feeding of a poor person (daily for the days of fasting). And he who volunteers (extra) good, (will find that) it is even better for him. And that you observe fasting is better for you, if you only know.

185. The (lunar) month of _Ramadzân_ is that in which the Qur'ân (started to be) revealed as a guidance for the whole of mankind with its clear evidences (providing comprehensive) guidance and the Discrimination (between right and wrong). Therefore he who shall witness the month, should fast (for full month) during it, but he who is sick or is on a journey shall fast (to make up) the prescribed number in other days. Allâh wishes facility for you and does not wish hardship for you. (This facility is given to you) that you may complete the number (of required fasts) and you may exalt the greatness of Allâh for His having guided you, and that you may render thanks (to Him). . . .

187. (Though during Fasting you must abstain from all the urges of nature including the sexual urge) it is made lawful for you on the nights

of the fasts to approach and lie with your wives (for sexual relationship). They are (a sort of) garment for you and you are (a sort of) garment for them. Allâh knows that you have been doing injustice to yourselves (by restricting conjugal relations with your wives even at night), so He turned to you with mercy and provided you relief; now enjoy their company (at night during *Ramadzân*) and seek what Allâh has ordained for you. Eat and drink till the white streak of the dawn becomes distinct to you from the black streak (of the darkness), then complete the fast till nightfall. And you shall not lie with them (your wives) while you perform *I'tikâf* (while you are secluding in the mosque for prayer and devotion to God). These are the limits (imposed) by Allâh so do not approach these (limits). Thus does Allâh explain His commandments for people that they may become secure against evil. . . .

Section 24

190. And fight in the cause of Allâh those who fight and persecute you, but commit no aggression. Surely, Allâh does not love the aggressors.

191. And slay them (the aggressors against whom fighting is made incumbent) when and where you get the better of them, in disciplinary way, and turn them out whence they have turned you out. (Killing is bad but) lawlessness is even worse than carnage. But do not fight them in the precincts of *Masjid al-Harâm* (the Holy Mosque at Makkah) unless they fight you therein. Should they attack you (there) then slay them. This indeed is the recompense of such disbelievers.

192. But if they desist (from aggression) then, behold, Allâh is indeed Great Protector, Ever Merciful.

193. And fight them until persecution is no more and religion is (freely professed) for Allâh. But if they desist (from hostilities) then (remember) there is no punishment except against the unjust (who still persist in persecution). . . .

195. And spend in the cause of Allâh and do not cast yourselves into ruin with your own hands, and do good to others, and verily Allâh loves the doers of good to others.

196. Accomplish the <u>Hajj</u>* (the Greater Pilgrimage to Makkah) and the 'Umrah (the minor pilgrimage) for the sake of Allâh. But if you are kept back, then (offer) whatever sacrifice is easily available, and do not shave your heads (as is prescribed for the Pilgrims) till the offering reaches its destination (in time, or place). And whosoever of you is sick and has an ailment of his head (necessitating shaving before time) then he should make an expiation either by fasting or alms-giving or by making a sacrifice. When you are in peaceful conditions then he, who

*HAH juh

would avail himself of the *'Umrah* (a visit to the *Ka'bah* or a minor *Hajj*) together with the *Hajj* (the Greater Pilgrimage and thus performs *Tammattu'*) should make whatever offering is easily available; and whosoever finds none (for an offering) should fast for three days during (the days of) the pilgrimage and (for) seven (days) when he returns (home)—these are ten complete (days of fasting in all). This is for him whose family does not reside near the *Masjid al-Harâm* (the Holy Mosque at Makkah). Take Allâh as a shield, and know that Allâh is Severe in retribution (if you neglect your duties).

Section 25

197. The months of performing the *Hajj* are well Known; so whoever undertakes to perform the *Hajj* in them (should remember that) there is (to be) no obscenity, nor abusing, nor any wrangling during the (time of) *Hajj*. And whatever good you do Allâh knows it. And take provisions for yourselves. Surely, the good of taking provision is guarding (yourselves) against the evil (of committing sin and begging). Take Me alone as (your) shield, O people of pure and clear wisdom!

198. There is no blame on you that you seek munificence from your Lord (by trading during the time of *Hajj*). When you pour forth (in large numbers) from 'Arafât then glorify Allâh (with still more praises) near *Mash'aral-Harâm* (Holy Mosque in *Muzdalifah*), and remember Him (with gratitude) as He has guided you, though formerly you were certainly amongst the astray. . . .

Surah 4
Women

Section 1

1. O you people! take as a shield your Lord Who created you from a single being. The same stock from which He created the man He created his spouse, and through them both He caused to spread a large number of men and women. O people! regard Allâh with reverence in Whose name you appeal to one another, and (be regardful to) the ties of relationship (particularly from the female side). Verily, Allâh ever keeps watch over you.

2. And give the orphans their property and substitute not (your) worthless things for (their) good ones, nor consume their property mingling it along with your own property, for this indeed is a great sin.

3. And if (you wish to marry them and) you fear that you will not be able to do justice to the orphan girls then (marry them not, rather) marry of women (other than these) as may be agreeable to you, (you

may marry) two or three or four (provided you do justice to them), but if you fear that you will not be able to deal (with all of them) equitably then (confine yourselves only to) one, or (you may marry) that whom your right hands possess (your female captives of war). That is the best way to avoid doing injustice.

4. And give the women their dowers unasked, willingly and as agreed gift. But if they be pleased to remit you a portion thereof, of their own free will, then take it with grace and pleasure.

Section 2

11. Allâh prescribes (the following) law (of inheritance) for your children. For male is the equal of the portion of two females; but if they be all females (two or) more than two, for them is two thirds of what he (the deceased) has left; and if there be only one, for her is the half and for his parents, for each one of the two is a sixth of what he has left, if he (the deceased) has a child; but if he has no child and his parents only be his heirs, then for the mother is one third (and the rest two thirds is for the father); but if there be (in addition to his parents) his brothers (and sisters) then there is one sixth for the mother after (the payment of) any bequest he may have bequeathed or (still more important) of any debt (bequests made by the testator and his debts shall however be satisfied first). Your fathers and your children, you do not know which of them deserve better to benefit from you. (This) fixing (of portions) is from Allâh. Surely, Allâh is All-Knowing, All-Wise.

12. And for you is half of that which your wives leave behind, if they have no child; but if they have a child, then for you is one fourth of what they leave behind, after (the payment of) any bequest they may have bequeathed or (still more important) of any (of their) debt. And for them (your wives) is one fourth of what you leave behind if you have no child; but if you leave a child, then, for them is an eighth of what you leave after (the payment of) any bequest you have bequeathed or (still more important) of any debt. And if there be a man or a woman whose heritage is to be divided and he (or she—the deceased) has no child and he (or she) has (left behind) a brother or a sister then for each one of the twain is a sixth; but if they be more than one then they are (equal) sharers in one third after the payment of any bequest bequeathed or (still more important) of any debt (provided such bequest made by the testator and the debt) shall be without (any intent of) being harmful (to the interests of the heirs). This is an injunction from Allâh, and Allâh is All-Knowing, Most Forbearing.

13. These are the limits (of the law imposed) by Allâh, and who obeys Allâh and His Messenger He will admit them into Gardens served with running streams; therein they shall abide for ever; and that is a great achievement.

14. But whoso disobeys Allâh and His Messenger and transgresses the limits imposed by Him He will make him enter Fire where he shall abide long, and for him is a humiliating punishment.

15. As to those of your women who commit sexual perversity, call in four of you to witness against them, and if they bear witness then confine them to their houses, until death overtakes them or Allâh makes for them a way out.

16. And if two of your males commit the same (act of indecency), then punish them both, so if they repent and amend (keeping their conduct good) then turn aside from them, verily Allâh is Oft-Returning (with compassion), Ever Merciful.

43

Peace Terms with Jerusalem (636)

The expansion of Islam was far more rapid and more forceful than the expansion of Christianity and Buddhism. By 636, Arab armies had conquered many of the lands previously held by the Byzantine and Persian empires. Merchants and holy men would spread the faith even further afield at a later stage. But by 750 an Arab-dominated Muslim government controlled Eurasia from the strait of Gibraltar to the western borders of India and China. (See Map 7.3 on page 251.)

How much of this early expansion was military conquest and how much religious conversion? To help us answer this question, we look at an early peace treaty after the conquest of Jerusalem from the Byzantine (called "Roman") Empire.

As the Arabian force for Judeo-Christian monotheism, Muslims had a strong sentimental attachment to Jerusalem. In the first years of the faith, Muhammad and his followers prayed facing Jerusalem, Al Quds (the Holy City, as it is still called in Arabic). In 624, Mecca was substituted as the *qibla* or direction to face for prayer. At the time of Muhammad's death (632), his followers controlled most of Arabia. His successor (or *caliph*), Abu Bakr (r. 632–634), regained control of

---

"Peace Terms with Jerusalem (636)," in *Islam from the Prophet Muhammad to the Conquest of Constantinople*, ed. and trans. Bernard Lewis, vol. I, *Politics and War* (New York: Harper & Row, 1974), 235–36. Originally published in Al Tabari, *Tarik al-Rusulcwa'l muluk*, Vol. I (Leiden: Brill), 2405–6.

the tribes that tried to withdraw from the alliance after the prophet's death and turned to the conquest of Iraq and Syria. The second caliph, Omar (634–644), negotiated the surrender of the Byzantine forces that controlled Jerusalem after the defeat of Byzantine armies in 636. This document, written by the caliph and directed to the Christian community of Jerusalem, set the terms for continued Christian presence in the city. Many of these terms were continuations of past practice. The *jizya* was a tax or tribute that non-Muslims paid Muslim governments for protection. Jews had been expelled from Jerusalem under Roman administration, a policy continued under the Byzantine Christian administration, and reinstated in this document, though Omar later allowed Jews to reside in the city.

The Muslim sources tell us that the inhabitants of Jerusalem appealed to Omar to take control of Jerusalem. What evidence do you see in these terms that would make that story plausible? What would both sides, Muslim and Christian, seem to gain by these terms?

Thinking Historically

A forceful expansion does not preclude voluntary conversion. There are many stories of Christians, Zoroastrians, and others converting to Islam. What might be some of the reasons why one would convert to Islam before or after the Arab conquest? What might be a reason that Muslims would *not* want people of other religions to convert?

In the name of God the Merciful and the Compassionate.

This is the safe-conduct accorded by the servant of God 'Umar, the Commander of the Faithful, to the people of Aelia [Jerusalem].

He accords them safe-conduct for their persons, their property, their churches, their crosses, their sound and their sick, and the rest of their worship.

Their churches shall neither be used as dwellings nor destroyed. They shall not suffer any impairment, nor shall their dependencies, their crosses, nor any of their property.

No constraint shall be exercised against them in religion nor shall any harm be done to any among them.

No Jew shall live with them in Aelia.[1]

The people of Aelia must pay the *jizya* in the same way as the people of other cities.

---

[1]Aelia Capitolina was the name given to Jerusalem by Roman emperor Hadrian after he suppressed the second Jewish revolt in 132–135 (the first revolt was 66–70). He also expelled Jews from the city and banned them from living there. [Ed.]

They must expel the Romans[2] and the brigands from the city. Those who leave shall have safe-conduct for their persons and property until they reach safety. Those who stay shall have safe-conduct and must pay the *jizya* like the people of Aelia.

Those of the people of Aelia who wish to remove their persons and effects and depart with the Romans and abandon their churches and their crosses shall have safe-conduct for their persons, their churches, and their crosses, until they reach safety.

The country people who were already in the city before the killing of so-and-so may, as they wish, remain and pay the *jizya* the same way as the people of Aelia or leave with the Romans or return to their families. Nothing shall be taken from them until they have gathered their harvest.

This document is placed under the surety of God and the protection [*dhimma*] of the Prophet, the Caliphs and the believers, on condition that the inhabitants of Aelia pay the *jizya* that is due from them.

Witnessed by Khālid ibn al-Walīd, 'Amr ibn al-Āṣ, 'Abd al-Raḥmān ibn 'Awf, Muāwiya ibn Abī Sufyān, the last of whom wrote this document in the year 15 [636].

[2]Byzantine soldiers and officials.

44

From The Glorious Victories of 'Āmda Ṣeyon, King of Ethiopia

The sweeping expansion of Islam in the seventh and eighth centuries did not mean the end of Christian or Buddhist expansion. It did, however, signal a new emphasis on military conflicts, especially between Christian and Muslim states. The Crusaders' struggle over Jerusalem was one of the most well known of those battles (and we will examine it in Chapter 10). But there were many other conflicts on the borders between Christendom and the Muslim world, several

The Glorious Victories of 'Āmda Ṣeyon: King of Ethiopia, trans. G. W. B. Huntingford (London: Oxford University Press, 1965), 53–65.

occurring between the earliest Christian state, Ethiopia, and the surrounding Muslim states of Egypt and Sudan in the north and west and the growing Arab trading colonies on the coast of the eastern horn of Africa (modern Eritrea, Djibouti, and Somalia). In the fourteenth century, Ethiopia became engaged in a series of conflicts with the Muslim areas to its east. This was also the period in which Ethiopian history was first written down in the "Glory of the Kings," which began with Menelik I, by legend the son of the Queen of Sheba and the Biblical King Solomon, whom she met on a visit to Palestine about 1000 B.C.E. *The Glorious Victories of 'Āmda Ṣeyon* is one of these histories.

'Āmda Ṣeyon* was a fourteenth-century Ethiopian monarch who extended the kingdom to something like its present boundaries. This selection describes the battles he waged in 1329. How important is religion in these conflicts? How would you characterize the Christianity of 'Āmda Ṣeyon?

Thinking Historically

When we think of religions moving from one place to another, we sometimes make the mistake of assuming that a fixed set of ideas or practices moves without changing. In fact, when a religion moves, it changes. It constantly adapts to the new circumstances and new environment. In a later section of the history of 'Āmda Ṣeyon, the author refers to the monarch's two queens, the younger and the elder, as well as his courtesans. Clearly, the king's Christianity contained elements of traditional African polygamy or monarchical privilege, or both. Ethiopian Christianity was also unique in its insistence that its rulers were descended from Jewish kings as well as its early conversion to Christianity. What signs of this unique identity do you see in this selection? In what other ways does this Christianity seem different from others you know or have studied? What might account for those differences?

Let us write, with the help of our Lord Jesus Christ, of the power and the victory which God wrought by the hands of 'Āmda Ṣeyon king of Ethiopia, whose throne-name is Gabra Masqal, in the eighteenth year of his reign, and in the year 516 of the Era of Mercy. Let us write then this book trusting in the Father who helps, in the Son who consoles, and in the Holy Spirit who guides and seeks help from the Holy Trinity, "for," says the Apostle James, "if any one lacketh wisdom, let him

*AHM duh   SAY uhn

ask from God, who giveth generously to all, and he shall not be spurned." And so we also seek help from the Father, the Son, and the Holy Spirit, that they may guard us for ever. Amen.

Now the king of Ethiopia, whose name was 'Āmda Ṣeyon, heard that the king of the Rebels had revolted, and in (his) arrogance was unfaithful to him, making himself great, like the Devil who set himself above his creator and exalted himself like the Most High. The king of the Rebels, whose name was Sabradin, was full of arrogance towards his lord 'Āmda Ṣeyon, and said; "I will be king over all the land of Ethiopia; I will rule the Christians according to my law, and I will destroy their churches." And having said this, he arose and set out and came to the land of the Christians, and killed some of them; and those who survived, both men and women, he took prisoner and converted them to his religion. . . .

But the feet cannot become the head, nor the earth the sky, nor the servant the master. That perverse one, the son of a viper, of the seed of a serpent, the son of a stranger from the race of Satan, thought (covetously) of the throne of David and said, "I will rule in Ṣeyon," for pride entered into his heart, as (into) the Devil his father. He said, "I will make the Christian churches into mosques for the Moslems, and I will convert to my religion the king of the Christians together with his people, and I will nominate him governor of one (province), and if he refuses to be converted to my religion I will deliver him to the herdsmen who are called Warjeḥ that they make him a herder of camels. As for the queen Žān Mangeśā, the wife of the king, I will make her work at the mill. And I will make Mar'ādē his capital city my capital also. And I will plant there plants of čāt, because the Moslems love that plant, and (it is) a gift which he sent to the king."

And he gave permission to his soldiers to kill everyone, for the rebellious servant made himself equal to his lord, and vain were his thoughts and vain his words.

Now when the king (of Ethiopia) heard of the Rebel's insults to him, he was very angry, and moved by his wrath sent to him a messenger to tell him, in these words, "Of your truth, did you or did you not burn the churches of God and kill the Christians? And those who survived, did you make them turn to your religion, which is not as the religion of Christ, but (is) that of the Devil your father? Do you not know what I myself formerly accomplished when your brother Ḥaqadin took by force one of my young servants named Te'eyentay? (This is what I did:) . . .

[Āmda Ṣeyon then goes on to describe his glorious military victories over Sabradin's brother and other Moslem armies.]

But I defeated them through the strength of Jesus Christ, and also their master, the son of your brother, by name Darāder. Him I killed; and to you also I will do the same, for I will cast you from your throne, and with the help of God I will cause you to vanish from the earth. If you have killed ten Christians, then I will kill from among your side a thousand Moslems; and if you kill a thousand, then I will kill many thousands through the power of God."

When he heard this from the king's messenger, that accursed and evil man of Satan, the enemy of truth and adversary of the faith of Christ, a stranger to God, far from the glory of the Son, and divorced from the constitution of the Holy Spirit, sent word to the king (of Ethiopia) and said, "I will not come to your place; I will not stand before you (as a supplicant); and if you come against me I will not fear you, because I have more soldiers than you, who can fight with the sword, with the knife, with horses, with the bow, with the shield, with the spear, with the *dembus,* that is, the iron staff, with javelins, and with arrows. If you wish to come against me, come, the road is open. But if you do not come, I will make war on you." . . .

The messengers whom the king had sent to that Rebel returned to him the whole answer of the renegade, that rebel against righteousness. Hearing the insults of the evil man, the king called together (his) commanders . . . telling them to prepare for war. Then he ordered to be brought out from his treasury gold and silver and fine clothing which he had looted, and adorned each of his soldiers, from the (most) senior to the (most) junior; for in his time gold and silver were (as numerous) as stones, and precious raiment (as common) as the leaves of the trees (or) the grass of the field. So having adorned them, he sent them forth to war against the evil Sabradin on the 24th day of Yakātit, saying to them, "May God give you strength and victory, and may He help you." And obeying the king, a detachment from the corps called Takuelā marched out joyfully and in five days came to the headquarters of that Rebel. The greater part however did not arrive because of the badness of the country, and the roughness and even absence of roads. But the detachment which arrived found him ready for war, and they fought with him and forced him out of his residence; and he fled before them. And they defeated him through the power of God. And after this the rest of the king's army arrived, and destroyed the capital of the Rebel's kingdom, and killed a very great number of his soldiers. As for (the Rebel) himself, he fled from them, and they pursued him till sunset; but he escaped them, (going by) a different road. God threw him down from his glory; as it is said in the Book of God, "He humbleth the great, and exalteth the lowly."

Then the army of the king set forth and attacked the camp of the Rebel. They looted the (Rebel) king's treasure houses and (took) gold and silver and fine clothes and jewels without number. They killed men and women, old men and children; the corpses of the slain filled a large space. And those who survived were made prisoners, and there were left none but those who had escaped with that evil man. But the soldiers could not find a place to camp because of the foul smell of the corpses; and they went to another place and made their camp there. Then they sent word to the king saying, "(There is) good news for you, O king, for we have defeated your enemy who set himself up (to rule) over your kingdom. We your soldiers have killed those who remained, even the women and slaves, and have left only those who fled. Also we have looted his treasure-houses, (taking) gold and silver and fine raiment and precious stones and vessels of bronze, iron, tin, and glass without number. All this we have given to the (people) of Šāgurā, of Zaber, and of the Medra Zēgā, according to their ability to carry it. As for him, he has escaped us through his trickery by another road."

The king, hearing that the Rebel had escaped, went into the tabernacle and approached the altar; seizing the horns of the altar he implored mercy of Jesus Christ saying, "Hear the petition of my heart and reject not the prayer of my lips, and shut not the gates of Thy mercy because of my sins, but send me Thy good angel to guide me on my road to pursue mine enemy who has set himself above Thy sheep and above Thy holy name." And having said this, he gave an offering to the church of coloured hangings for the altar, and went out. Then he sent other troops, those called Dāmot, Saqalt, Gondar, and Ḥadyā, cavalry and foot-soldiers, strong and skilled in war, powerful without comparison in warfare and battle; he sent their commander Ṣagā Krestos to Bēgamedr to make war in the land of the renegades who are like Jews, the crucifiers, of Samēn and Waggarā and Ṣalamt and Ṣagadē who were formerly Christian. Because like the Jews, the crucifiers, they denied Christ, he sent troops to destroy and devastate them and subject them to the rule of Christ. . . .

The king set out with the troops which were with him on the 6th day of Magābit, and going by the road of the right came to a country called Dawāro. The governor of this country, by name Ḥaydarā, in his words professed to love the king but in secret had evil designs, like Judas the traitor who sold his Lord. He spoke with two tongues, for he said to that rebel Sabradin, "If he (the king of Ethiopia) comes against you I will come with my soldiers (to you); and if he comes against me, come with your soldiers (to me); we will fight him together and destroy him utterly with his army." The king continued his march and came to Gālā on the 28th day of Miyāzyā; here he celebrated the feast of Easter, the resurrection of Christ, with joy and happiness. Here he left his camp and the queen Mangeśā, and set out to attack the district of Samāryā, where he killed many men, took their women and their livestock, and captured much booty. The next day he left his army secretly and set out on a journey of two days, riding a horse and accompanied by twenty-seven young horsemen unaccustomed to war and battles. He spent the night there with (these) few soldiers, eating no food, drinking no water, not ungirding his loins, and not sleeping. He did not even lie down that night, not from fear, but because of his experience as a soldier; though he trusted not in the number of his horses or his men, nor in the bow and spear, for (as) David said, "The king is not saved by the number of his soldiers, and the horse is a deceit for safety; not in my bow or spear do I trust to be saved." In the same manner Āmda Şeyon did not rely on numbers, and with only a few he was not afraid, but put his trust in God his Lord.

Now when he disappeared his soldiers went from place to place weeping and saying, "Woe unto us, for we know not what has become of our lord (nor) whether he is alive or not." At daylight the king arose and set out on the road, and while on the march met with the soldiers who were seeking him and weeping together. Then the king returned to his camp with much booty. After this, the troops which he had previously sent to make war on the Rebel (Sabradin) returned, and reported how they had fought and defeated (the enemy); and the king forthwith gave thanks to God.

When he learned that the king had been joined by (the rest of) his troops, that Rebel was filled with fear, and not knowing where to turn, for fear had taken possession of him, he sent to the queen saying, "I have done wrong to my lord the king, I have wrought injustice against him, and it is better that I fall into his hands than into the hands of a stranger. I will come myself and surrender to him, that he may do what he will to me." Thereupon the queen went to tell (the king) the whole of the message from that Rebel Sabradin, whose acts, like his name "broken judgement," consist of insults, mad rage, errors, contentions, and arrogance. When the king heard this message which the Rebel had sent to the queen, he was exceedingly angry, and said to the queen, "Do you send him a message and say: 'If you come, or if you do not come, it will not trouble me; but if you go to a distant country I will pursue you through the power of God. And if you go into a cave, or if you (just) run away, I will not leave you alone nor will I return to my capital till I have taken you.'"

Now when he received this message, (Sabradin) set out and came to the king, and stood before him. And the king asked him, saying, "Why have you behaved thus to me? The gifts which you (formerly) sent to me you have given to your servants; and the multitude of goods of silver and gold which I gave to the poor you have taken away. Those who traded with me you have bound in chains; and what is worse, you have aspired to the throne of my kingdom, in imitation of the Devil your father who wished to be the equal of his creator." When that Rebel heard these words of the king he was at a loss for an answer in the greatness of his fear, for he was afraid of the king's presence; and he answered, "Do with me according to your will." And immediately the soldiers who were on the left and right of the king stood forth in anger and said, "This man is not worthy of life, for he has burnt the churches of

God, he has slain Christians, and those whom he did not kill he has compelled to accept his religion. (Moreover) he desired to ascend the high mountain of the kingdom." And some said, "Let us slay him with the edge of the sword"; others said, "Let us stone him to death"; and others again, "Let us burn him with fire that he may disappear from the earth." And they said to the king, "Think not, O king, that he comes to you honestly and freely, for he trusts in his magic art." And so saying, they lifted from his bosom and arm a talisman and revealed the *sena kini* of his magic. Then said the king, "Can your talismans deliver you from my hands in which God has imprisoned you?" And he gave orders for his two hands to be bound with iron chains; he did not wish him to be killed, for he is merciful and forbearing. (Thus) was taken the Rebel in the net which he himself had woven, and in the snare which he himself had set, as said David, "He delved and dug a pit, and hath fallen into the pit which he made himself; his sins shall descend upon the crown of his head. God hath lowered him from his glory, for every one that maketh himself great shall be abased, and he that abaseth himself shall be honoured."

REFLECTIONS

Understanding religion in social and historical context may be particularly difficult for those of us raised in a culture that thinks of religion as belief rather than behavior. For many of us the relationship between individual religious ideas, faith, or belief, on the one hand, and religious social identity, membership, or behavior, on the other hand, is difficult to understand. Inevitably our own religious experiences and cultural background affect how we understand others and their religious beliefs. If we have strong beliefs, we expect intelligent, sensitive people to have similar beliefs. If they do not, we expect them to be easily persuaded when exposed to ideas that we find compelling. This may be a particularly American expectation. American culture, even in its secular forms, is a product of the Protestant reformation and Christian efforts to create a "city on a hill," as a beacon to the world.

Belief has always meant a lot to Christians. Ever since St. Paul organized a church based purely on faith—all you have to do is believe, he said—the particulars of belief have splintered Christianity into a thousand sects. But most religions did not evolve this way. Even other religions that have scriptural authorities—Judaism, Islam, Buddhism, Hinduism, to a certain extent—have devoted less attention to defining doctrine and rooting out heretics than they have to regulating daily life within the larger society. Among them only Islam displays a similar zeal to convert nonbelievers, but there is no set of doctrines, no credo, required of the Muslim besides the profession of faith in God and his Prophet. The schism of Islam between Sunnis and Shi'ites is deep, but it is historical and communal rather than intellectual or doctrinal. Jews, Buddhists, and Hindus do not evangelize and would be hard-pressed to answer if asked by potential recruits what to believe. For most people throughout the history of the world, religion was defined by birth; beliefs came later.

We started the chapter with religious conversion and ended it with religious warfare. A story that began with wandering monks and merchants, sharing ideas and building communities, concludes with armies wiping out women and children. It is hard to believe that soldiers thought they could convert souls by separating them from their bodies.

When did persuasion turn to enforcement? When did religion become the business of soldiers and kings? Perhaps it was when religion became a matter of state. Many early states were concerned with ensuring the proper observance of rituals, but usually only for their own subjects. Most ancient empires that governed foreign peoples allowed their subjects to administer their own religious affairs provided these affairs did not undermine political or social stability. Judaism, for example, did not present a threat to the Roman Empire as long as it remained a national religion in its own territory, and one willing to accept Roman law. When some Jews, called Christians, not only moved about the empire but sought to convert Roman citizens and caused them to neglect Roman gods, the state stepped in.

The combination of state and monotheistic religion could and did result in a potentially lethal intolerance. Indeed, the medieval history of Christian Crusade and Muslim Jihad bristles with battles of true believers. But when did that begin? The initial expansion of Islam has sometimes been seen as the first storm of mounted believers ready to convert or kill all in their path. Increasingly, however, this appears to be an age-old Christian myth. Recent histories argue that the initial seventh-century conquest was driven more by Arab tribal raiding traditions and antiforeign nationalism than it was by religious zeal. Arab armies gained more from the taxes and labor of subject populations than they would from religious equals. Conversions probably came later.

The historian Richard Bulliet shows how the Iranian conversions to Islam only took off a hundred years after the Arab conquest. Between 750 and 850, the percentage of Iranians who were Muslim rose from 10 percent to 90 percent. Clearly the Arab armies that conquered Iran in 648 did not shout "convert or die." Bulliet shows that conversion of Iranians to Islam followed a standard bell curve typical of the adoption of successful consumer products like high-definition televisions. That raises another question. In converting, did people merely choose to join the socially dominant group? Or were ideas and personal religious feelings more important factors?

8

Medieval Civilizations

European, Islamic, and Chinese
Societies, 600–1400 C.E.

HISTORICAL CONTEXT

In the centuries after 200 C.E., an influx of nomadic peoples from the grasslands of Eurasia into the Roman and Han Chinese empires brought an end to the classical civilizations. In their wake, three distinct civilizations developed: European Christian, Islamic (after 622 C.E.), and Chinese. Of the three, the Chinese was most like its preceding classical civilization; in some ways the Sui dynasty (589–618) revived the institutions of the Han. The greatest change occurred in Western Europe, especially the former urban areas of the Roman Empire, some of which virtually disappeared. The area from Byzantium to the Indus River was radically transformed by the rise of Islam, but a foreign observer might have been struck more by the continuity of urban growth and material progress than by the change of faith in Western Asia from the classical to Muslim period.

In any case, these three worlds of Eurasia in the Middle Ages were vastly different from each other. The goal of this chapter is to explore some of those differences.

THINKING HISTORICALLY
Distinguishing Social, Economic, Political, and Cultural Aspects

Comparing civilizations is a daunting undertaking; there are so many variables one must keep in mind. Consequently, when historians compare civilizations, or any social system, they first break them down into parts. Most commonly, historians distinguish between the political, economic, social, and cultural features of a system. The political refers to how a society or civilization is governed, the economic to how it supports itself, the social to how it organizes population groups, including families, and the cultural to how it explains and represents itself, including its religion.

In this chapter, you are asked to be systematic in distinguishing among these features for each of the three main civilizations. We will break them down to compare each part — for example, European and Chinese politics, Muslim and Chinese culture — but also to see how the parts of each civilization make a whole: for example, how Chinese politics and Chinese culture fit together.

$$45$$

Feudalism: An Oath of Homage and Fealty

This primary source is from France, selected to illustrate one of the important institutions of Europe in the Middle Ages: feudalism. This document details the mutual obligation between a feudal lord and his vassal. In this case, the feudal lord is a religious institution, the monastery of St. Mary of Grasse. Acting for the monastery and its lands is the abbot, Leo. The vassal who holds the properties of the monastery as a fief, and in return pledges homage and fealty, is Bernard Atton, viscount of Carcassonne.* The year is 1110.

What exactly does the viscount of Carcassonne promise to do? What is Leo the abbot's responsibility on behalf of the monastery? How new or old does this agreement appear to be? What else does this document tell you about the relationship of lords and vassals in European feudalism?

Thinking Historically

Using the distinctions suggested in the chapter introduction, how would you characterize this agreement? In short, is it an economic, political, social, or cultural agreement? Because it obviously has more

*cahr cas OHN

"Charter of Homage and Fealty of the Viscount of Carcassone, 1110," in D. C. Munro, *Translations and Reprints from the Original Sources of European History*, vol. IV, bk. 3 (Philadelphia: University of Pennsylvania Press, 1897), 18–20.

than one of these elements, how might you argue for each of the four characterizations?

What would be the closest equivalent to this sort of agreement today? Would you characterize the modern equivalent as economic, political, social, or cultural?

In the name of the Lord, I, Bernard Atton, Viscount of Carcassonne, in the presence of my sons, Roger and Trencavel, and of Peter Roger of Barbazan, and William Hugo, and Raymond Mantellini, and Peter de Vietry, nobles, and of many other honorable men, who had come to the monastery of St. Mary of Grasse, to the honor of the festival of the august St. Mary; since lord Leo, abbot of the said monastery, has asked me, in the presence of all those above mentioned, to acknowledge to him the fealty and homage for the castles, manors, and places which the patrons, my ancestors, held from him and his predecessors and from the said monastery as a fief, and which I ought to hold as they held, I have made to the lord abbot Leo acknowledgment and homage as I ought to do.

Therefore, let all present and to come know that I the said Bernard Atton, lord and viscount of Carcassonne, acknowledge verily to thee my lord Leo, by the grace of God, abbot of St. Mary of Grasse, and to thy successors that I hold and ought to hold as a fief, in Carcassonne, the following: . . . Moreover, I acknowledge that I hold from thee and from the said monastery as a fief the castle of Termes in Narbonne; and in Minerve the castle of Ventaion, and the manors of Cassanolles, and of Ferral and Aiohars; and in Le Rogès, the little village of Longville; for each and all of which I make homage and fealty with hands and with mouth to thee my said lord abbot Leo and to thy successors, and I swear upon these four gospels of God that I will always be a faithful vassal to thee and to thy successors and to St. Mary of Grasse in all things in which a vassal is required to be faithful to his lord, and I will defend thee, my lord, and all thy successors, and the said monastery and the monks present and to come and the castles and manors and all your men and their possessions against all malefactors and invaders, at my request and that of my successors at my own cost; and I will give to thee power over all the castles and manors above described, in peace and in war, whenever they shall be claimed by thee or by thy successors.

Moreover I acknowledge that, as a recognition of the above fiefs, I and my successors ought to come to the said monastery, at our own expense, as often as a new abbot shall have been made, and there do homage and return to him the power over all the fiefs described above. And when the abbot shall mount his horse I and my heirs, viscounts of

Carcassonne, and our successors ought to hold the stirrup for the honor of the dominion of St. Mary of Grasse; and to him and all who come with him, to as many as two hundred beasts, we should make the abbot's purveyance in the borough of St. Michael of Carcassonne, the first time he enters Carcassonne, with the best fish and meat and with eggs and cheese, honorably according to his will, and pay the expense of the shoeing of the horses, and for straw and fodder as the season shall require.

And if I or my sons or their successors do not observe to thee or to thy successors each and all the things declared above, and should come against these things, we wish that all the aforesaid fiefs should by that very fact be handed over to thee and to the said monastery of St. Mary of Grasse and to thy successors.

I, therefore, the aforesaid lord Leo, by the grace of God, abbot of St. Mary of Grasse, receive thy homage and fealty for all the fiefs of castles and manors and places which are described above; in the way and with the agreements and understandings written above; and likewise I concede to thee and thy heirs and their successors, the viscounts of Carcassonne, all the castles and manors and places aforesaid, as a fief, along with this present charter, divided through the alphabet. And I promise to thee and thy heirs and successors, viscounts of Carcassonne, under the religion of my order, that I will be a good and faithful lord concerning all those things described above.

Moreover, I, the aforesaid viscount, acknowledge that the little villages of [twelve are listed] with the farmhouse of Mathus and the chateaux of Villalauro and Claromont, with the little villages of St. Stephen of Surlac, and of Upper and Lower Agrifolio, ought to belong to the said monastery, and whoever holds anything there holds from the same monastery, as we have seen and have heard read in the privileges and charters of the monastery, and as was there written.

Made in the year of the Incarnation of the Lord 1110, in the reign of Louis. Seal of [the witnesses named in paragraph one, Bernard Atton and abbot Leo] who has accepted this acknowledgment of the homage of the said viscount.

And I, the monk John, have written this charter at the command of the said lord Bernard Atton, viscount of Carcassonne and of his sons, on the day and year given above, in the presence and witness of all those named above.

46

Manorialism: Duties of a Villein

Manorialism is another term used to describe medieval European civilization. It concerns the life around the manor houses that were the centers of life in the countryside. Manors were owned by feudal lords whose income derived, at least in good part, from the work of free peasants and dependent serfs (*villeins*).*

This document, from England in 1307, delineates the duties required of a villein, John of Cayworth, to the lord of the manor, Battle Abbey. What duties does the abbey require of John of Cayworth? What does he get in return? In what ways is this document similar to the previous one? In what ways is it different?

Thinking Historically

How is the social status of John of Cayworth different from that of Bernard Atton in the previous selection? What would you imagine about the differences in their economic welfare?

What would be the modern equivalent of this document? Would you call that modern equivalent economic, political, social, or cultural? Which word best characterizes this document?

They say that John of Cayworth holds one house and thirty acres of land, and he owes 2 *s.*[1] a year at Easter and Michaelmas, and he owes one cock and two hens at Christmas worth 4 *s.*

And he ought to harrow for two days at the sowing at Lent with one man and his own horse and harrow, the value of the work is 4 *d.*;[2] and he receives from the lord on each day three meals worth 3 *d.*; and the lord will thus lose 1 *d.*; and so this harrowing is worth nothing to the service of the lord.

And he ought to carry the manure of the lord for two days with one cart using his own two oxen, the work to value 8 *s.*, and he receives from the lord three meals of the above value each day; and so the work is worth 3 *d.* clear.

*vih LAYN
[1]Shilling, a British measure of money traditionally worth ½0 of a pound. [Ed.]
[2]Pence, smallest measure of British currency traditionally worth ½2 of a shilling. "d." comes from Roman *denarius*. [Ed.]

"Services Due from a Villein, 1307," in *Customals of Battle Abbey*, ed. S. R. Scargill-Bird (The Camden Society, 1887), 19–23.

And he should find one man for two days to mow the meadow of the lord, who can mow an estimated one acre and a half: the value of mowing one acre is 6 *d.*; and the total is 9 *d.*; and he receives for each day three meals of the above value, and thus the mowing is worth 4 *d.* clear.

And he ought to collect and carry that same hay which he has mowed, the value of the work is 3 *d.* And he has from the lord two meals to one man worth 1½ *d.*; thus the work is worth 1½ *d.* clear.

And he ought to carry the hay of the lord for one day with one cart and three animals of his own, the price of the work is 6 *d.*; and he has from the lord three meals worth 2½ *d.*; and thus the work has a value of 3½ *d.* clear.

And he ought to carry in the autumn beans or oats for two days with one cart and three of his own animals, the price of the work is 12 *d.*; and he has from the lord three meals of the above price for each day, and thus the work is worth 7 *d.* clear.

And he ought to carry wood from the woods of the lord to the manor house for two days in summer with one cart and three of his own animals, the price of the work is 9 *d.*; and he receives from the lord for each day three meals of the above price. And so the work is worth 4 *d.* clear.

And he ought to find one man for two days to cut heath, the price of the work is 4 [*d.*]; and he will have three meals for each day of the above price; and so the lord loses if he receives the work 1 *d.*; and thus that cutting is worth nothing to the work of the lord.

And he ought to carry the heath that he has cut, the price of the work is 5 *d.*; and he receives from the lord three meals of the price of 2½ *d.*; and thus the work is worth 2½ *d.* clear.

And he ought to carry to Battle [Abbey] two times in the summer half a load of grain each time, the price of the work is 4 *d.*; and he will receive in the manor each time one meal worth 2 *d.*; and thus the work is worth 2 *d.* clear.

The sum of the rents, with the price of the chickens is 2 *s.* 4 *d.*; the sum of the value of the work is 2 *s.* 3½ *d.*; owed from the said John per year. . . .

And it must be noted that all the aforesaid villeins may not marry their daughters nor have their sons tonsured, nor can they cut down timber growing on the lands they hold, without the personal approval of the bailiff or servant of the lord, and then for building and no other purpose.

And after the death of any one of the aforesaid villeins the lord will have as a heriot the best animal that he had; if, however, he had no living beast, the lord will have no heriot, as they say.

The sons or daughters of the aforesaid villeins will give to enter the tenement after the death of their ancestors as much as they gave in rent per year.

47

From the Magna Carta

The Magna Carta was a contract between King John of England and his nobles (or "liegemen") in which the king agreed to recognize certain rights and liberties of the nobility. In return the nobles accepted certain obligations to the king. What were some of these rights and obligations? Can you tell from these provisions what some of the nobles' complaints had been? Did the signing of this agreement in 1215 improve the position of the common people, women, or foreigners? What does the document tell you about English society in the early thirteenth century?

Thinking Historically

This is obviously a political document, as it details the mutual obligations of King John and his nobles, the barons. But in addition to political matters, it covers a number of issues that might be considered economic, social, and cultural. Which items would you characterize as falling into one of those categories?

What does the Magna Carta have in common with the other European documents on feudalism and manorialism? What does this commonality tell you about European society in the Middle Ages?

John, by the grace of God, King of England, Lord of Ireland, Duke of Normandy and Aquitaine, and Count of Anjou: To the Archbishops, Bishops, Abbots, Earls, Barons, Justiciaries, Foresters, Sheriffs, Reeves, Ministers, and all Bailiffs and others, his faithful subjects, Greeting. Know ye that in the presence of God, and for the health of Our soul, and the souls of Our ancestors and heirs, to the honor of God, and the exaltation of Holy Church, and amendment of Our Kingdom, by the advice of Our reverend Fathers, Stephen, Archbishop of Canterbury, Primate of all England, and Cardinal of the Holy Roman Church; Henry, Archbishop of Dublin; William of London, Peter of Winchester, Jocelin of Bath and Glastonbury, Hugh of Lincoln, Walter of Worcester, William of Coventry, and Benedict of Rochester, Bishops; Master Pandulph, the Pope's subdeacon and familiar; Brother Aymeric, Master

"Magna Carta," trans. E. P. Cheney, in *Translations and Reprints from the Original Sources of European History*, ed. D. C. Munro, vol. I, bk. 6 (Philadelphia: University of Pennsylvania Press, 1897), 6–15, passim.

of the Knights of the Temple in England; and the noble persons, William Marshal, Earl of Pembroke; William, Earl of Salisbury; William, Earl of Warren; William, Earl of Arundel; Alan de Galloway, Constable of Scotland; Warin Fitz-Gerald, Peter Fitz-Herbert, Hubert de Burgh, Seneschal of Poitou, Hugh de Neville, Matthew Fitz-Herbert, Thomas Basset, Alan Basset, Philip Daubeny, Robert de Roppelay, John Marshal, John Fitz-Hugh, and others, Our liegemen:

1. We have, in the first place, granted to God, and by this Our present Charter confirmed for Us and Our heirs forever — That the English Church shall be free and enjoy her rights in their integrity and her liberties untouched. And that We will this so to be observed appears from the fact that We of Our own free will, before the outbreak of the dissensions between Us and Our barons, granted, confirmed, and procured to be confirmed by Pope Innocent III the freedom of elections, which if considered most important and necessary to the English Church, which Charter We will both keep Ourself and will it to be kept with good faith by Our heirs forever. We have also granted to all the free men of Our kingdom, for Us and Our heirs forever, all the liberties underwritten, to have and to hold to them and their heirs of Us and Our heirs.

2. If any of Our earls, barons, or others who hold of Us in chief by knight's service shall die, and at the time of his death his heir shall be of full age and owe a relief[1] he shall have his inheritance by ancient relief; to wit, the heir or heirs of an earl of an entire earl's barony, £100; the heir or heirs of a baron of an entire barony, £100; the heir or heirs of a knight of an entire knight's fee, 100s. at the most; and he that owes less shall give less, according to the ancient custom of fees.

3. If, however, any such heir shall be under age and in ward, he shall, when he comes of age, have his inheritance without relief or fine.

4. The guardian of the land of any heir thus under age shall take therefrom only reasonable issues, customs, and services, without destruction or waste of men or property; and if We shall have committed the wardship of any such land to the sheriff or any other person answerable to Us for the issues thereof, and he commit destruction or waste, We will take an amends from him, and the land shall be committed to two lawful and discreet men of that fee, who shall be answerable for the issues to Us or to whomsoever We shall have assigned them. And if We shall give or sell the wardship of any such land to anyone, and he commit destruction or waste upon it, he shall lose the wardship, which shall be committed to two lawful and discreet men of that fee, who shall, in like manner, be answerable unto Us as has been aforesaid.

[1]A form of tax. [Ed.]

5. The guardian, so long as he shall have the custody of the land, shall keep up and maintain the houses, parks, fishponds, pools, mills, and other things pertaining thereto, out of the issues of the same, and shall restore the whole to the heir when he comes of age, stocked with ploughs and tillage, according as the season may require and the issues of the land can reasonably bear.

6. Heirs shall be married without loss of station, and the marriage shall be made known to the heir's nearest of kin before it be contracted.

7. A widow, after the death of her husband, shall immediately and without difficulty have her marriage portion and inheritance. She shall not give anything for her marriage portion, dower, or inheritance which she and her husband held on the day of his death, and she may remain in her husband's house for forty days after his death, within which time her dower shall be assigned to her.

8. No widow shall be compelled to marry so long as she has a mind to live without a husband, provided, however, that she give security that she will not marry without Our assent, if she holds of Us, or that of the lord of whom she holds, if she holds of another.

9. Neither We nor Our bailiffs shall seize any land or rent for any debt so long as the debtor's chattels are sufficient to discharge the same; nor shall the debtor's sureties be distrained so long as the debtor is able to pay the debt. If the debtor fails to pay, not having the means to pay, then the sureties shall answer the debt, and, if they desire, they shall hold the debtor's lands and rents until they have received satisfaction of the debt which they have paid for him, unless the debtor can show that he has discharged his obligation to them.

10. If anyone who has borrowed from the Jews any sum of money, great or small, dies before the debt has been paid, the heir shall pay no interest on the debt so long as he remains under age, of whomsoever he may hold. If the debt shall fall into Our hands, We will take only the principal sum named in the bond. . . .

13. The City of London shall have all her ancient liberties and free customs, both by land and water. Moreover, We will and grant that all other cities, boroughs, towns, and ports shall have their liberties and free customs.

14. For obtaining the common counsel of the kingdom concerning the assessment of aids (other than in the three cases aforesaid) or of scutage, We will cause to be summoned, severally by Our letters, the archbishops, bishops, abbots, earls, and great barons; We will also cause to be summoned, generally, by Our sheriffs and bailiffs, all those who hold lands directly of Us, to meet on a fixed day, but with at least forty days' notice, and at a fixed place. In all letters of such summons We will explain the cause thereof. The summons being thus made, the business shall proceed on the day appointed, according to the advice of

those who shall be present, even though not all the persons summoned have come. . . .

16. No man shall be compelled to perform more service for a knight's fee or other free tenement than is due therefrom.

17. Common Pleas shall not follow Our Court, but shall be held in some certain place. . . .

20. A free man shall be amerced[2] for a small fault only according to the measure thereof, and for a great crime according to its magnitude, saving his position; and in like manner a merchant saving his trade, and a villein saving his tillage, if they should fall under Our mercy. None of these amercements shall be imposed except by the oath of honest men of the neighborhood.

21. Earls and barons shall be amerced only by their peers, and only in proportion to the measure of the offense.

22. No amercement shall be imposed upon a clerk's[3] lay property, except after the manner of the other persons aforesaid, and without regard to the value of his ecclesiastical benefice.

23. No village or person shall be compelled to build bridges over rivers except those bound by ancient custom and law to do so. . . .

28. No constable or other of Our bailiffs shall take corn or other chattels of any man without immediate payment, unless the seller voluntarily consents to postponement of payment.

29. No constable shall compel any knight to give money in lieu of castle-guard when the knight is willing to perform it in person or (if reasonable cause prevents him from performing it himself) by some other fit man. Further, if We lead or send him into military service, he shall be quit of castle-guard for the time he shall remain in service by Our command.

30. No sheriff or other of Our bailiffs, or any other man, shall take the horses or carts of any free man for carriage without the owner's consent.

31. Neither We nor Our bailiffs will take another man's wood for Our castles or for any other purpose without the owner's consent. . . .

35. There shall be one measure of wine throughout Our kingdom, and one of ale, and one measure of corn, to wit, the London quarter, and one breadth of dyed cloth, russets, and haberjets[4] to wit, two cells within the selvages. As with measure so shall it also be with weights. . . .

38. In the future no bailiff shall upon his own unsupported accusation put any man to trial without producing credible witnesses to the truth of the accusation.

[2]Fined. [Ed.]
[3]Clergyman. [Ed.]
[4]Types of cloth. [Ed.]

39. No free man shall be taken, imprisoned, disseised,[5] outlawed, banished, or in any way destroyed, nor will We proceed against or prosecute him, except by the lawful judgment of his peers and by the law of the land.

40. To no one will We sell, to none will We deny or delay, right or justice.

41. All merchants shall have safe conduct to go and come out of and into England, and to stay in and travel through England by land and water for purposes of buying and selling, free of illegal tolls, in accordance with ancient and just customs, except, in time of war, such merchants as are of a country at war with Us. If any such be found in Our dominion at the outbreak of war, they shall be attached, without injury to their persons or goods, until it be known to Us or Our Chief Justiciary how Our merchants are being treated in the country at war with Us, and if Our merchants be safe there, then theirs shall be safe with Us.

42. In the future it shall be lawful (except for a short period in time of war, for the common benefit of the realm) for anyone to leave and return to Our kingdom safely and securely by land and water, saving his fealty to Us. Excepted are those who have been imprisoned or outlawed according to the law of the land, people of the country at war with Us, and merchants, who shall be dealt with as aforesaid. . . .

52. If anyone has been disseised or deprived by Us, without the legal judgment of his peers, of lands, castles, liberties, or rights, We will immediately restore the same, and if any dispute shall arise thereupon, the matter shall be decided by judgment of the twenty-five barons mentioned below in the clause for securing the peace. With regard to all those things, however, of which any man was disseised or deprived, without legal judgment of his peers, by King Henry Our Father or Our Brother King Richard, and which remain in Our warranty, We shall have respite during the term commonly allowed to the Crusaders, except as to those matters on which a plea had arisen, or an inquisition had been taken by Our command, prior to Our taking the Cross. Immediately after Our return from Our pilgrimage, or if by chance We should remain behind from it, We will at once do full justice.

[5]Dispossessed. [Ed.]

48

Islam: Sayings Ascribed to the Prophet

For Muslims the Koran was the word of God. Therefore no other writing was comparable. Nevertheless, when Muslims engaged in politics, considered laws, or studied social, economic, cultural, or other issues they could also refer to a body of writing called *hadiths,* or the sayings of the Prophet. These were writings attributed to Muhammad's contemporaries that described the decisions, acts, and the statements of the Prophet of Islam and the religion's first governor. What likely effect would the sayings included here have on the thinking of a devout Muslim? Under what circumstances would he or she be likely to be rebellious?

Thinking Historically

Most of these sayings deal with religion and government. What attitude toward politics do they express? If this selection was all you had to construct a Muslim idea of government, what would it be? How are these political ideas different from those in medieval Europe? What accounts for the differences?

I charge the Caliph[1] after me to fear God, and I commend the community of the Muslims to him, to respect the great among them and have pity on the small, to honor the learned among them, not to strike them and humiliate them, not to oppress them and drive them to unbelief, not to close his doors to them and allow the strong to devour the weak.

The Imams[2] are of Quraysh;[3] the godly among them rulers of the godly, and the wicked among them rulers of the wicked. If Quraysh gives a crop-nosed Ethiopian slave authority over you, hear him and obey him as long as he does not force any of you to choose between his Islam and his neck. And if he does force anyone to choose between his Islam and his neck, let him offer his neck.

---

[1]KAY lihf   Successor to the prophet; supreme authority. [Ed.]

[2]A leader, especially in prayer; clergyman. [Ed.]

[3]An aristocratic trading clan of Mecca; hostile to Muhammad, but after his death regained prominence. That religious leaders come from Quraysh was agreed after victory of the Meccan faction in 661. [Ed.]

Al-Muttaqi, *Kanz al'Ummal,* quoted in *Islam from the Prophet Muhammad to the Capture of Constantinople,* ed. and trans. Bernard Lewis, vol. I (New York: Harper, 1974), 150–51.

279

Hear and obey, even if a shaggy-headed black slave is appointed over you.

Whosoever shall try to divide my community, strike off his head.

If allegiance is sworn to two Caliphs, kill the other.

He who sees in his ruler something he disapproves should be patient, for if anyone separates himself from the community, even by a span, and dies, he dies the death of a pagan.

Obey your rulers, whatever happens. If their commands accord with the revelation I brought you, they will be rewarded for it, and you will be rewarded for obeying them; if their commands are not in accord with what I brought you, they are responsible and you are absolved. When you meet God, you will say, "Lord God! No evil." And He will say, "No evil!" And you will say, "Lord God! Thou didst send us Prophets, and we obeyed them by Thy leave; and Thou didst appoint over us Caliphs, and we obeyed them by Thy leave; and Thou didst place over us rulers, and we obeyed them for Thy sake." And He will say, "You speak truth. They are responsible, and you are absolved."

If you have rulers over you who ordain prayer and the alms tax and the Holy War for God, then God forbids you to revile them and allows you to pray behind them.

If anyone comes out against my community when they are united and seeks to divide them, kill him, whoever he may be.

He who dies without an Imam dies the death of a pagan, and he who throws off his obedience will have no defense on the Day of Judgment.

Do not revile the Sultan, for he is God's shadow on God's earth. Obedience is the duty of the Muslim man, whether he like it or not, as long as he is not ordered to commit a sin. If he is ordered to commit a sin, he does not have to obey.

The nearer a man is to government, the further he is from God; the more followers he has, the more devils; the greater his wealth, the more exacting his reckoning.

He who commends a Sultan in what God condemns has left the religion of God.

49

AL-TANUKHI

A Government Job

Al-Tanukhi* (d. 994) was a judge in Baghdad. In this selection, he relates the story of his great uncle Abu Qasim's† response when he asked him why he gave up a government job. What does Abu Qasim's story tell you about the job of government officials in Muslim Baghdad in the tenth century? How was government in Muslim Baghdad different from government in medieval Europe? How were ideas of government different?

Thinking Historically

This story concerns a political post, but in what ways is the story an economic one as well? Would you say the lesson of the story is political, economic, or religious?

How did you come to repent of being in Government service, Abu Qasim? I once asked, What was the cause?

This was the cause, said my great-uncle. Abu Ali Jubbai (the great Rationalist theologian) used to stay with me when he came to Ahwaz. I was Clerk to the Ahwaz municipality as well as deputy Finance Minister, so that all business used to pass through my hands. I really ran the whole place. Once a year, when the Land Tax collections began, Abu Ali Jubbai used to come to Ahwaz to arrange to have the taxes due from certain persons, who over the years had come to regard themselves as his dependents, added to the Land Tax on his own private estate at Jubba. Everybody treated him with the highest honor and respect whenever he came to town. As a rule he would only stay with me; and I used to settle his business with the Governor. The Governor, of course, was not always a friend of mine, nor was he always a man who realized Abu Ali's position, or else the amount at which his assessment was fixed would have been even lower than it was. But he would always remit at least half or a third of the tax due from him.

*ahl tah NOO kee
†ah BOO   kah SEEM

Judge Muhassin Tanukhi, "Resurrections of Loquacity or Table-talk (10th century)," in Eric Schroeder, *Muhammad's People: A Tale by Anthology* (Portland, ME: Bond Wheelwright Company, 1955), 566–68.

Returning to Jubba, Abu Ali never kept for himself any of the money which in an ordinary case would have been taken in taxes from an estate like his. He used to deduct from the gross amount the sum he was to pay to Government, and then distribute the remainder among the members of his religious following, stipulating in return that each of them should entertain for a whole year one of the poor students who attended his lectures; the actual expense these students put them to was small, not a fifth of the amount due which Abu Ali's high standing had sufficed to get remitted. Then he would go to his own house, and there take out of the revenues of his estate a full tithe, which he used to give in alms among the poor people of his village, Pool, where he maintained his disciples. And he did all this every year.

On one occasion, he was staying with me at the usual season, I had done what he wanted in the matter of his Land Tax, and we were sitting talking in the evening.

Abu Ali, I said to him, are you afraid of the consequences to me in the Hereafter of the profession I am following?

How could I but be anxious, Abu Qasim? he replied. For be sure of this: if you should die employed as you now are, you will never breathe the fragrance of the Garden.

Why not? I asked. How am I guilty? I am only an accountant — I act merely as a copyist, an employee of the Treasury. It may be that somebody will come to me with a grievance, some man whose Land Tax has been unduly raised; and if I reduce it for him and set matters straight, he is only too glad to give me a present. At times perhaps I may appropriate something which really belongs to the Sovereign; but it only represents a share in the booty of the Muslims, to which I have a right.

Abu Qasim, he rejoined, *GOD IS NOT DECEIVED.* Tell me this: is it not you who appoints the land surveyors and sends them out to make their surveys, which are supposed to be accurate? And don't they go out into the country, and raise the acreage figures by ten or twenty per cent, with pen on paper, and then hand in these falsifications of theirs, and do you not make up your assessment registers on the basis of these same falsifications? And then hand over these registers to the Collector's officer, and tell him that unless he produces so much money at the Collector's Office within so many days his hands will be nailed to his feet?

Yes, I admitted.

And then the officer sets out with his escort of soldiers, horse and foot, his despatch riders and speed-up men, and flogs and cuffs and fetters? and all the time he is acting on your instructions. For if you bid him let a man off, or give him time, he does that; whereas if you give no such permission he is merciless until the man pays up.

Yes, said I.

And then the money is deposited at the Collector's Office, and the receipt forms are issued to him from your office, with your mark on them?

Yes, said I.

Then what part of the whole business, asked Abu Ali, is not of your undertaking? What part are you not answerable for? Beware of God, or you are lost. Give up your Government job. Provide for your future.

From such exhortations, from such grave warnings he would not desist until at last I burst into tears.

You are not more highly favored, he then said, nor more highly placed than Ja'far ibn Harb was: he held high office at court, his privileges and rank were almost those of a Vizier; and he was also an orthodox Believer, and a famous scholar, the author of more than one book which is still read. And yet Ja'far, when he was in office, and riding one day in a superb cavalcade, on the very crest of pomp and circumstance, suddenly heard a man reading the verse: *IS NOT THE HOUR YET COME WHEN ALL WHO TRULY BELIEVE MUST BE BROKEN AND CONTRITE OF HEART AT THE VERY MENTION OF GOD AND OF TRUTH REVEALED?* Ay, the hour is come! Ja'far exclaimed. Over and over again he said it, weeping. And he dismounted, and stripped off his dress, and waded into Tigris until the water came up to his neck. Nor did he come out again until he had given away everything he owned to atone for wrongs he had done, in reparations, pious foundations, and alms, doing everything that his system of Belief demanded, or that he thought his duty. Some passer-by, who saw him standing in the water and was told his story, gave him a shirt and a pair of breeches to cover his coming out; and he put them on. He gave himself to study and devotion from then until his death.

After a moment, Abu Ali said to me: Go, and do thou likewise, Abu Qasim. But if you cannot bring yourself to go the whole way, at least repent of being an official.

What Jubbai said made a great impression on me. I resolved that I would repent, that I would give up my job. For some time I conducted my affairs with this in view; and when I saw an opportunity of getting out of Government service, I repented, my mind made up that I would never take public office again.

Egyptian Invitation

This document is an invitation issued by the sultan of Egypt between 1280 and 1290. Egypt had been a part of the Muslim world since the Arab invasion under Omar in 639. Like other Arab dominions, Egypt was ruled by the Umayyad caliphate in Damascus before 747 and then nominally by the Abbasid caliphate in Baghdad after 750. (See Map 7.3.) But other powers created dynasties that effectively ruled Egypt after 868: first Turks, then Persians, then the North African Fatimids (910–1171), followed by the Kurdish Ayyubid dynasty founded in 1174 by Saladin that lasted until the Mongol invasion. The last Ayyubid ruler was murdered in 1250 and was replaced as sultan (political leader) by his Mamluk slave general. The use of purchased or captured non-Muslim slaves as soldiers gave Muslim rulers loyal forces that had no ties to other tribal leaders. Converted to Islam, well trained, and given considerable power and authority, these Mamluk troops and administrators owed everything to the Sultan. Between 1250 and 1517, two dynasties of Mamluks ruled Egypt. At first, Mamluk status was strictly nonhereditary, and their sons were prevented from sharing power. Eventually, however, Mamluk dynasties were grafted onto the tribal structure.

To whom is this invitation addressed? What did the Sultan hope to achieve by issuing it? What does the content of the document tell us about Mamluk Egyptian society? Every society needs soldiers and merchants. Using this document and those you have read from Europe, compare the Mamluk Egyptian method of supplying this need with the method of medieval Europe.

Thinking Historically

The purpose of this invitation is clearly economic. Yet this economic purpose has political, social, and cultural dimensions as well. What are these other dimensions? How is economics related to other aspects of medieval Islamic society?

A decree has been issued, may God exalt the Sultan's exalted command, and may his [the Sultan's] justice keep the subjects in assured protection. He requests the prayers of the people of both east and west

---

Islam from the Prophet Muhammad to the Conquest of Constantinople, ed. and trans. Bernard Lewis, vol. II, *Religion and Society* (New York: Harper & Row, 1974), 166–68.

for his thriving reign, and let all of them be sincere. He offers a genuine welcome to those who come to his realm, as to the garden of Eden, by whatever gate they may choose to enter, from Iraq, from Persia, from Asia Minor, from the Ḥijāz, from India, and from China. Whoever wishes to set forth — the distinguished merchants, the men of great affairs, and the small traders, from the countries enumerated and also those which have not been enumerated — and whoever wishes to enter our realms may sojourn or travel at will and to come to our country of broad lands and leafy shades, then let him, like those whom God has destined for this, make firm resolve on this worthy and beneficial act, and let him come to a country whose inhabitants have no need either of supplies or reserves of food, for it is an earthly paradise for those who dwell in it, and a consolation for those who are far from their own homes, a delight of which the eye does not weary, a place from which one is never driven by excessive cold, for one lives there in perpetual spring and permanent well-being. It is enough to say that one of its descriptions is that it is God's beauty spot on His earth. God's blessing accrues in the baggage of whoever does a good deed by lending or receives a good deed by borrowing. Another of its features is that anyone who comes there hoping for anything, gets what he wants, for it is a land of Islam, with armies whose swords are beyond reproach. For justice has made its lands prosper and has multiplied its inhabitants. The buildings have increased so that it is a land of great cities. The needy is at ease there, and does not fear the violence of the creditors, for demands there are not exacting and deferments easily obtained. The rest of the people and all the merchants have no fear there of any oppression, for justice protects.

Whoever becomes aware of this our decree, among the merchants who live in Yemen and India and China and Sind and elsewhere, let them prepare to travel and come to our country, where they will find the reality better than the word and will see a beneficence beyond the mere fulfillment of their promises and will sojourn in "a fair land under a forgiving Lord" [Qur'ān, xxxv, 15] and in comfort deserving of gratitude (for only the grateful is rewarded) and in security of person and property, and felicity which illuminates their circumstances and fulfills their hopes. They will receive from us all the justice that they expect. Our justice responds to those who call on it, has procedure which will be praised by their way of life, will leave their property to their descendants, and will protect and preserve them so that they will take shelter under its shadow and be protected. Whoever brings merchandise with him, such as spices and other articles imported by the Kārimī[1]

---

[1]An association of merchants in Egypt and Arabia, engaged in the eastern trade.

merchants, will suffer no unjust impost nor be subjected to any burdensome demand, for [our] justice will leave with them what is desirable and remove what is burdensome. If anyone brings [white] male slaves [mamlūk] or slave-girls, he will find their sale price beyond his expectations and [will be accorded] the tolerance in fixing a profitable price which is customarily accorded to those who import such slaves from near and all the more from distant lands; for our desire is directed toward the increase of our troops, and those who import mamlūks have gained a title to our generosity. Let whoever can do so increase his import of mamlūks, and let him know that the purpose in demanding them is to increase the armies of Islam. For thanks to them, Islam today is in glory with flag unfurled and the Sultan al-Manṣūr [Qalawun]. The mamlūk who is thus imported is removed from darkness to light. Yesterday he was blamed for unbelief; today he is praised for faith and fights for Islam against his own tribe and people.

This is our decree for all traveling merchants to whose knowledge it comes, "They seek the bounty of God, while others fight in the cause of God." [Qur'ān, lxxiii, 20] Let them read in it the orders which will ease their task; let them be guided by its star, nourished by its wisdom. Let them mount the neck of the hope which impels them to leave their homes and stretch out their hands in prayer for him who wishes people to come to his country, so that they may benefit from his generosity in all clarity and in all beneficence; and let them take advantage of the occasions for profit, for they are ripe for picking. These true promises are sent to them to confirm their high hopes and reaffirm to them that the noble rescript is valid, by the command of God, in accordance with what the pens have written, and [God is] the best Guarantor.

ICHISADA MIYAZAKI

The Chinese Civil Service Exam System

The Chinese civil service examination system originated fourteen hundred years ago, making it the first in the world. As a device for ensuring government by the brightest young men, regardless of class or social standing, it may also be viewed as one of the world's earliest democratic systems. It was not perfect. Like democratic systems in the West only two hundred years ago, it excluded women. The system also put enormous pressure on young boys of ambitious families.

This selection consists of two passages from a book by a noted modern Japanese historian of China. The first passage concerns the elaborate early preparations for the exams.

What did young boys have to learn? In what ways was their education different from your own? What effects did the examination system have on the goals and values of young people?

Thinking Historically

The Chinese examination system was primarily a political system, a way for the emperor to rule most effectively, employing the most talented administrators. In what sense did this system make China more "democratic" than the political systems of Western Europe or the Muslim world? In what sense was it less so? Did it become more or less democratic over the course of Chinese history? How did its purpose change from the Tang dynasty to the Sung dynasty?

Like any political system, the civil service system had a major impact on other aspects of life — social, economic, and cultural. How did it affect Chinese society, families, class differences, boys and girls? What were the economic effects of the system? How did it influence Chinese cultural values, ideas, and education?

Judging from this excerpt and your readings about Western Europe and the Islamic world, what was the single most important difference between Chinese and Western European civilizations? Between Chinese and Muslim civilization?

Ichisada Miyazaki, *China's Examination Hell*, trans. Conrad Schirokauer (New York: Weatherhill, 1976), 13–17, 111–16, passim.

Preparing for the Examinations

Competition for a chance to take the civil service examinations began, if we may be allowed to exaggerate only a little, even before birth. On the back of many a woman's copper mirror the five-character formula "Five Sons Pass the Examinations" expressed her heart's desire to bear five successful sons. Girls, since they could not take the examinations and become officials but merely ran up dowry expenses, were no asset to a family; a man who had no sons was considered to be childless. People said that thieves warned each other not to enter a household with five or more girls because there would be nothing to steal in it. The luckless parents of girls hoped to make up for such misfortune in the generation of their grandchildren by sending their daughters into marriage equipped with those auspicious mirrors.

Prenatal care began as soon as a woman was known to be pregnant. She had to be very careful then, because her conduct was thought to have an influence on the unborn child, and everything she did had to be right. She had to sit erect, with her seat and pillows arranged in exactly the proper way, to sleep without carelessly pillowing her head on an arm, to abstain from strange foods, and so on. She had to be careful to avoid unpleasant colors, and she spent her leisure listening to poetry and the classics being read aloud. These preparations were thought to lead to the birth of an unusually gifted boy.

If, indeed, a boy was born the whole family rejoiced, but if a girl arrived everyone was dejected. On the third day after her birth it was the custom to place a girl on the floor beneath her bed, and to make her grasp a tile and a pebble so that even then she would begin to form a lifelong habit of submission and an acquaintance with hardship. In contrast, in early times when a boy was born arrows were shot from an exorcising bow in the four directions of the compass and straight up and down. In later times, when literary accomplishments had become more important than the martial arts, this practice was replaced by the custom of scattering coins for servants and others to pick up as gifts. Frequently the words "First-place Graduate" were cast on those coins, to signify the highest dreams of the family and indeed of the entire clan.

It was thought best for a boy to start upon his studies as early as possible. From the very beginning he was instructed almost entirely in the classics, since mathematics could be left to merchants, while science and technology were relegated to the working class. A potential grand official must study the Four Books, the Five Classics, and other Confucian works, and, further, he must know how to compose poems and write essays. For the most part, questions in civil service examinations did not go beyond these areas of competence.

When he was just a little more than three years old, a boy's education began at home, under the supervision of his mother or some other suitable person. Even at this early stage the child's home environment exerted a great effect upon his development. In cultivated families, where books were stacked high against the walls, the baby sitter taught the boy his first characters while playing. As far as possible these were characters written with only a few strokes.

First a character was written in outline with red ink on a single sheet of paper. Then the boy was made to fill it in with black ink. Finally he himself had to write each character. At this stage there was no special need for him to know the meanings of the characters.

After he had learned in this way to hold the brush and to write a number of characters, he usually started on the *Primer of One Thousand Characters*. This is a poem that begins:

Heaven is dark, earth is yellow,
The universe vast and boundless . . .

It consists of a total of two hundred and fifty lines, and since no character is repeated, it provided the student with a foundation of a thousand basic ideograms.

Upon completing the *Primer*, a very bright boy, who could memorize one thing after another without difficulty, would go on to a history text called *Meng Ch'iu* (*The Beginner's Search*) and then proceed to the Four Books and the Five Classics normally studied in school. If rumors of such a prodigy reached the capital, a special "tough examination" was held, but often such a precocious boy merely served as a plaything for adults and did not accomplish much in later life. Youth examinations were popular during the Sung dynasty, but declined and finally were eliminated when people realized how much harm they did to the boys.

Formal education began at about seven years of age (or eight, counting in Chinese style). Boys from families that could afford the expense were sent to a temple, village, communal, or private school staffed by former officials who had lost their positions, or by old scholars who had repeatedly failed the examinations as the years slipped by. Sons of rich men and powerful officials often were taught at home by a family tutor in an elegant small room located in a detached building, which stood in a courtyard planted with trees and shrubs, in order to create an atmosphere conducive to study.

A class usually consisted of eight or nine students. Instruction centered on the Four Books, beginning with the *Analects*, and the process of learning was almost entirely a matter of sheer memorization. With their books open before them, the students would parrot the teacher, phrase by phrase, as he read out the text. Inattentive students, or those who amused themselves by playing with toys hidden in their sleeves, would be scolded by the teacher or hit on the palms and thighs with his fan-shaped "warning ruler." The high regard for discipline was re-flected in the saying, "If education is not strict, it shows that the teacher is lazy."

Students who had learned how to read a passage would return to their seats and review what they had just been taught. After reciting it a hundred times, fifty times while looking at the book and fifty with the book face down, even the least gifted would have memorized it. At first the boys were given twenty to thirty characters a day, but as they became more experienced they memorized one, two, or several hundred each day. In order not to force a student beyond his capacity, a boy who could memorize four hundred characters would be assigned no more than two hundred. Otherwise he might become so distressed as to end by detesting his studies.

Along with the literary curriculum, the boys were taught proper conduct, such as when to use honorific terms, how to bow to superiors and to equals, and so forth — although from a modern point of view their training in deportment may seem somewhat defective, as is suggested by the incident concerning a high-ranking Chinese diplomat in the late Ch'ing dynasty who startled Westerners by blowing his nose with his fingers at a public ceremony.

It was usual for a boy to enter school at the age of eight and to complete the general classical education at fifteen. The heart of the curriculum was the classics. If we count the number of characters in the classics that the boys were required to learn by heart, we get the following figures:

Analects	11,705
Mencius	34,685
Book of Changes	24,107
Book of Documents	25,700
Book of Poetry	39,234
Book of Rites	99,010
Tso Chuan	196,845

The total number of characters a student had to learn, then, was 431,286.

The *Great Learning* and the *Doctrine of the Mean*, which together with the *Analects* and the *Mencius* constitute the Four Books, are not counted separately, since they are included in the *Book of Rites*. And, of course, those were not 431,286 *different* characters: Most of the ideographs would have been used many times in the several texts. Even so, the task of having to memorize textual material amounting to more than 400,000 characters is enough to make one reel. They required exactly six years of memorizing, at the rate of two hundred characters a day.

After the students had memorized a book, they read commentaries, which often were several times the length of the original text, and practiced answering questions involving passages selected as examination topics. On top of all this, other classical, historical, and literary works had to be scanned, and some literary works had to be examined carefully, since the students were required to write poems and essays modeled upon them. Anyone not very vigorous mentally might well become sick of it all halfway through the course.

Moreover, the boys were at an age when the urge to play is strongest, and they suffered bitterly when they were confined all day in a classroom as though under detention. Parents and teachers, therefore, supported a lad, urging him on to "become a great man!" From ancient times, many poems were composed on the theme, "If you study while young, you will get ahead." The Sung emperor Chen-tsung wrote such a one:

> To enrich your family, no need to buy good land:
> Books hold a thousand measures of grain.
> For an easy life, no need to build a mansion:
> In books are found houses of gold.
> Going out, be not vexed at absence of followers:
> In books, carriages and horses form a crowd.
> Marrying, be not vexed by lack of a good go-between:
> In books there are girls and faces of jade.
> A boy who wants to become a somebody
> Devotes himself to the classics, faces the window, and reads.

In later times this poem was criticized because it tempted students with the promise of beautiful women and riches, but that was the very reason it was effective.

Nonetheless, in all times and places students find shortcuts to learning. Despite repeated official and private injunctions to study the Four Books and Five Classics honestly, rapid-study methods were devised with the sole purpose of preparing candidates for the examinations. Because not very many places in the classics were suitable as subjects for examination questions, similar passages and problems were often repeated. Aware of this, publishers compiled collections of examination answers, and a candidate who, relying on these compilations, guessed successfully during the course of his own examinations could obtain a good rating without having worked very hard. But if he guessed wrong he faced unmitigated disaster because, unprepared, he would have submitted so bad a paper that the officials could only shake their heads and fail him. Reports from perturbed officials caused the government to issue frequent prohibitions of the publication of such collections of model answers, but since it was a profitable business with a steady demand, ways of issuing them surreptitiously were arranged, and time and again the prohibitions rapidly became mere empty formalities.

An Evaluation of the Examination System

Did the examination system serve a useful purpose? . . .

The purpose of instituting the examinations, some fourteen hundred years ago under the Sui rulers, was to strike a blow against government by the hereditary aristocracy, which had prevailed until then, and to establish in its place an imperial autocracy. The period of disunion lasting from the third to the sixth century was the golden age of the Chinese aristocracy: during that time it controlled political offices in central and local governments. . . .

The important point in China, as in Japan, was that the power of the aristocracy seriously constrained the emperor's power to appoint officials. He could not employ men simply on the basis of their ability, since any imperial initiative to depart from the traditional personnel policy evoked a sharp counterattack from the aristocratic officials. This was the situation when the Sui emperor, exploiting the fact that he had reestablished order and that his authority was at its height, ended the power of the aristocracy to become officials merely by virtue of family status. He achieved this revolution when he enacted the examination system (and provided that only its graduates were to be considered qualified to hold government office), kept at hand a reserve of such officials, and made it a rule to use only them to fill vacancies in central and local government as they occurred. This was the origin of the examination system.

The Sui dynasty was soon replaced by the T'ang, which for the most part continued the policies of its predecessor. Actually, as the T'ang was in the process of winning control over China, a new group of aristocrats appeared who hoped to transmit their privileges to their descendants. To deal with this problem the emperor used the examination system and favored its *chin-shih*[1] trying to place them in important posts so that he could run the government as he wished. The consequence was strife between the aristocrats and the *chin-shih*, with the contest gradually turning in favor of the latter. Since those who gained office simply through their parentage were not highly regarded, either by the imperial government or by society at large, career-minded aristocrats, too, seem to have found it necessary to enter officialdom through the examination system. Their acceptance of this hard fact meant a real defeat for the aristocracy.

The T'ang can be regarded as a period of transition from the aristocratic government inherited from the time of the Six Dynasties to the purely bureaucratic government of future regimes. The examination

---

[1]Highest degree winners. [Ed.]

system made a large contribution to what was certainly a great advance for China's society, and in this respect its immense significance in Chinese history cannot be denied. Furthermore, that change was begun fourteen hundred years ago, at about the time when in Europe the feudal system had scarcely been formed. In comparison, the examination system was immeasurably progressive, containing as it did a superb idea the equal of which could not be found anywhere else in the world at that time.

This is not to say that the T'ang examination system was without defects. First, the number of those who passed through it was extremely small. In part this was an inevitable result of the limited diffusion of China's literary culture at a time when printing had not yet become practical and hand-copied books were still both rare and expensive, thus restricting the number of men able to pursue scholarly studies. Furthermore, because the historical and economic roots of the new bureaucratic system were still shallow, matters did not always go smoothly and sometimes there were harsh factional conflicts among officials. The development of those conflicts indicates that they were caused by the examination system itself and constituted a second serious defect.

As has been indicated, a master-disciple relationship between the examiner and the men he passed was established, much like that between a political leader and his henchmen, while the men who passed the examination in the same year considered one another as classmates and helped one another forever after. When such combinations became too strong, factions were born.

These two defects of the examination system were eliminated during the Sung regime. For one thing, the number of men who were granted degrees suddenly rose, indicating a similar rise in the number of candidates. This was made possible by the increase in productive power and the consequent accumulation of wealth, which was the underlying reason that Chinese society changed so greatly from the T'ang period to the Sung. A new class appeared in China, comparable to the bourgeoisie in early modern Europe. In China this newly risen class concentrated hard on scholarship, and with the custom of this group, publishers prospered mightily. The classic books of Buddhism and Confucianism were printed; the collected writings of contemporaries and their discourses and essays on current topics were published; and the government issued an official gazette, so that in a sense China entered upon an age of mass communications. As a result learning was so widespread that candidates for the examinations came from virtually every part of the land, and the government could freely pick the best among them to form a reserve of officials.

In the Sung dynasty the system of conducting the examinations every three years was established. Since about three hundred men were selected each time, the government obtained an average of one hundred men a year who were qualified for the highest government positions. Thus the most important positions in government were occupied by *chin-shih*, and no longer were there conflicts between men who differed in their preparatory backgrounds, such as those between *chin-shih* and non–*chin-shih* that had arisen in the T'ang period.

Another improvement made during the Sung period was the establishment of the palace examination as the apex of the normal examination sequence. Under the T'ang emperors the conduct of the examinations was completely entrusted to officials, but this does not mean that emperors neglected them, because they were held by imperial order. It even happened that Empress Wu (r. 684–705) herself conducted the examinations in an attempt to win popularity. . . .

The position of the emperor in the political system changed greatly from T'ang times to Sung. No longer did the emperor consult on matters of high state policy with two or three great ministers deep in the interior of the palace, far removed from actual administrators. Now he was an autocrat, directly supervising all important departments of government and giving instructions about every aspect of government. Even minor matters of personnel needed imperial sanction. Now the emperor resembled the pivot of a fan, without which the various ribs of government would fall apart and be scattered. The creation of the palace examination as the final examination, given directly under the emperor's personal supervision, went hand in hand with this change in his function in the nation's political machinery and was a necessary step in the strengthening of imperial autocracy.

Thus, the examination system changed, along with Chinese society as a whole. Created to meet an essential need, it changed in response to that society's demand. It was most effective in those early stages when, first in the T'ang period, it was used by the emperor to suppress the power of the aristocracy, and then later, in the Sung period, when the cooperation of young officials with the *chin-shih* was essential for the establishment of imperial autocracy. Therefore, in the early Sung years *chin-shih* enjoyed very rapid promotion; this was especially true of the first-place *chin-shih*, not a few of whom rose to the position of chief councilor in fewer than ten years.

52

LIU TSUNG-YUAN

Camel Kuo the Gardener

Liu Tsung-yuan* (773–819) was one of the great writers of the T'ang dynasty (618–907). He was especially loved for his scenes of nature, a topic he uses here for an allegory about government. What is the message of the allegory?

Thinking Historically

Are the ideas of government expressed here more like those of Confucius or Lao Tzu? How do you think Liu Tsung-yuan felt about the civil service system? Can we assume that Chinese government was practiced as the author desired, or that it was not?

How does this view of government differ from that of Western European or Muslim societies? In what sense is it more typically Chinese?

W hatever name Camel Kuo may have had to begin with is not known. But he was a hunchback and walked in his bumpy way with his face to the ground, very like a camel, and so that was what the country folk called him. When Camel Kuo heard them he said, "Excellent. Just the right name for me." — And he forthwith discarded his real name and himself adopted "Camel" also.

He lived at Feng-lo, to the west of Ch'ang-an. Camel was a grower of trees by profession; and all the great and wealthy residents of Ch'ang-an who planted trees for their enjoyment or lived off the sale of their fruit would compete for the favour of his services. It was a matter of observation that when Camel Kuo had planted a tree, even though it was uprooted from elsewhere, there was never a one but lived, and grew strong and glossy, and fruited early and abundantly. Other growers, however they spied on him and tried to imitate his methods, never could achieve his success.

*lee OU   tsung WAHN

Liu Tsung-yuan, "Camel Kuo the Gardener," in *Anthology of Chinese Literature*, ed. and trans. Cyril Birch (New York: Grove Press, 1965), 258–59.

Once, when questioned on the point, Camel replied: "I cannot make a tree live for ever or flourish. What I *can* do is comply with the nature of the tree so that it takes the way of its kind. When a tree is planted its roots should have room to breathe, its base should be firmed, the soil it is in should be old, and the fence around it should be close. When you have it this way, then you must neither disturb it nor worry about it, but go away and not come back. If you care for it like this when you plant it, and neglect it like this *after* you have planted it, then its nature will be fulfilled and it will take the way of its kind. And so all *I* do is avoid harming its growth — I have no power to make it grow; I avoid hindering the fruiting — I have no power to bring it forward or make it more abundant.

"With other growers it is not the same. They coil up the roots and they use fresh soil. They firm the base either too much or not enough. Or if they manage to avoid these faults, then they dote too fondly and worry too anxiously. They inspect the tree every morning and cosset it every night; they cannot walk away from it without turning back for another look. The worst of them will even scrape off the bark to see if it is still living, or shake the roots to test whether they are holding fast. And with all this the tree gets further every day from what a tree should be. This is not mothering but smothering, not affection but affliction. This is why they cannot rival my results: what other skill can I claim?"

"Would it be possible to apply this philosophy of yours to the art of government?" asked the questioner.

"My only art is the growing of trees," said Camel Kuo in answer. "Government is not my business. But living here in the country I have seen officials who go to a lot of trouble issuing orders as though they were deeply concerned for the people; yet all they achieve is an increase of misfortune. Morning and evening runners come yelling, 'Orders from the government: plough at once! Sow right away! Harvest inspection! Spin your silk! Weave your cloth! Raise your children! Feed your livestock!' Drums roll for assembly, blocks are struck to summon us. And we the common people miss our meals to receive the officials and still cannot find the time: how then can we expect to prosper our livelihood and find peace in our lives? This is why we are sick and weary; and in this state of affairs I suppose there may be some resemblance to my profession?"

"Wonderful!" was the delighted cry of the man who had questioned him. "The art I sought was of cultivating trees; the art I found was of cultivating men. Let this be passed on as a lesson to all in office!"

53

FAN ZHONGYAN

Rules for the
Fan Lineage's Charitable Estate

From the time of the Sung dynasty (960–1279), many wealthy Chinese families formed charitable trusts for their descendants. One of the first men to set up such a trust was Fan Zhongyan (989–1052), an important political official.

This selection presents the rules that Fan set down for the way in which his descendants would share the income from his estate. What activities did the lineage support? What other activities would have been left to individual families? Why would lineages be more common among wealthy than poor families?

Thinking Historically

Lineage was both a social and economic organization. What impact would these lineages have on Chinese social life? Would they strengthen or weaken Chinese families? How might they affect Chinese economic life?

How did lineages make Chinese society different from that of Western Europe? Were there similar social institutions in Islamic society? Is there a modern equivalent?

1. One pint of rice per day may be granted for each person whom a branch has certified to be one of its members. (These quantities refer to polished rice. If hulled rice is used, the amount should be increased proportionately.)

2. Children of both sexes over five years of age are counted in the total.

3. Female servants may receive rice if they have borne children by men in the lineage and the children are over fifteen or they themselves are over fifty.

4. One bolt of silk for winter clothing may be granted for each individual, except children between five and ten years of age who may receive half a bolt.

Fan Zhongyan, *Fan Wengzheng gong ji,* in *Chinese Civilization: A Sourcebook,* 2nd ed., ed. and trans. Patricia Buckley Ebrey (New York: The Free Press, 1993), 155–56.

5. Each branch may receive a rice ration for a single slave, but not any silk.

6. Every birth, marriage, death, or other change in the number of lineage members must immediately be recorded.

7. Each branch should make a list of those entitled to grain rations. At the end of the month the manager should examine these requests. He must not make any prior arrangements or exceed the stipulated monthly rations. The manager should also keep his own register in which he records the quantity due each branch based on the number of its members. If the manager spends money wastefully or makes advance payments to anyone, the branches have the authority to require him to pay an indemnity.

8. For the expenses of marrying a daughter, thirty strings of cash may be granted, unless the marriage is a second one, in which case twenty strings may be granted.

9. For the expenses of taking a first wife, twenty strings may be granted (but nothing for a second wife).

10. Lineage members who become officials may receive the regular rice and silk grants and the special grants for weddings and funerals if they are living at home awaiting a post, awaiting selection, or mourning their parents. They may also receive the grants if they leave their families at home while they serve in Sichuan, Gwangdong, or Fujien, or for any other good reason.

11. For the expenses of mourning and funerals in the various branches, if the deceased is a senior member, when mourning begins, a grant of ten strings of cash may be made, and a further fifteen at the time of the burial. For more junior members, the figures are five and ten strings respectively. In the case of low-ranking members or youths under nineteen, seven strings for both expenses; for those under fifteen, three strings; for those under ten, two strings. No grant should be made for children who die before seven, or slaves or servants.

12. If any relatives through marriage living in the district face dire need or unexpected difficulties, the branches should jointly determine the facts and discuss ways to provide assistance from the income of the charitable estate.

13. A stock of rice should be stored by the charitable estate from year to year. The monthly rations and the grants of silk for winter clothing should start with the tenth month of 1050. Thereafter, during each year with a good harvest, two years' worth of grain rations should be hulled and stored. If a year of dearth occurs, no grants should be made except for the rice rations. Any surplus over and above the two years' reserve should be used first for funeral and mourning expenses, then marriage expenses. If there is still a remainder, winter clothes may be issued. However, if the surplus is not very large, the priorities should be discussed, and the amount available divided up and granted in equi-

table proportions. If grants cannot be made to all entitled to them, they should be made first to those who have suffered bereavement, next to those with weddings. In cases where more than one death has occurred at the same time, senior members take precedence over junior ones. Where the relative seniority of those concerned is the same, the grant should be made on the basis of which death or burial took place first. If, after paying out the rations and the allowances for marriages and burials, a surplus still remains, it must not be sold off, but hulled and put into storage for use as rations for three or more years. If there is a danger that the stored grain might go bad, it may be sold off and re-placed with fresh rice after the autumn harvest. All members of the branches of the lineage will carefully comply with the above rules.

Tenth month, 1050. Academician of the Zizheng Hall, Vice-president of the Board of Rites, and Prefect of Hangzhou, Fan. Sealed.

REFLECTIONS

Whatever particular period or region historians work on — in the case of this chapter, medieval Europe, Islam, and China — they also tend to specialize in particular kinds of documents and related aspects of life. They are social historians, or economic historians, or cultural histori-ans. As a matter of fact, most of them would characterize their work even more precisely than that. A particular social historian might prefer to be called a historian of gender or a historian of the family. A politi-cal historian might be a diplomatic historian. A cultural historian might be a historian of religion, or even of medieval Christianity, or of Chris-tian anti-Semitism. As in the sciences, historians are able to dig deeper and learn more by specializing. And, as in any field, the more you spe-cialize, the more you discover you do not know, the more questions you have, and the more you can learn.

All of this begins, however, with some basic categories, like those we have used in this chapter. That is why you were asked to think in terms of political, economic, social, and cultural history.

To pull together and compare some of the characterizations you made from the selections in this chapter, make a chart: Write the names of the three civilizations — European, Islamic, and Chinese — across the top of the page, and the categories social, economic, political, and cultural down the left margin, allowing a quarter page for each. Try to fill in as many of the blocks as you can. You might use more than one characterization for each. For instance, in the box for social aspects of European civilization you would, no doubt, write "feudalism." You might also write "nobles," "monasteries," "fealty and homage," "vas-sals defend," and "sons inherit status." Or your style of observing and characterizing might lead you to such notes as "churches can be land-lords," "lots of witnesses," and "they were very formal." All of these descriptions are correct: Just make sure your comments are about soci-ety, social behavior, social relationships, social organization, or various social elements — class, family, men and women, population, and age. Repeat this exercise with the other three categories. These are by no means exclusive, but try not to use the same words in describing, say, a social and an economic aspect.

After you have filled in as many of the blanks as you can, you can make comparisons in a number of interesting ways. (You have already done some of this, but here you can be more systematic.) First, compare how one category, say society, is different in Europe and Islam, or Eu-rope and China, or China and Islam. You might, for example, say that European society was less centralized than Chinese or Islamic society or that the extended family was more important in China.

After doing the same for economics, politics, and culture, notice how the four categories of any civilization fit together. How does the type of society in medieval Europe, for instance, "fit" medieval Eu-rope's economy? This interaction is what constitutes a civilization. See if you used a word repetitively in characterizing each of the four aspects of a particular civilization. Then try to categorize the civilization as a whole.

Now you are ready to compare each of these civilizations to an-other one. These characterizations may be general, or they may be qualified and later modified, but at the very least you now have a gen-eral starting point for more in-depth analysis of these three great civi-lizations in future chapters.

Love and Marriage

Medieval Europe, India, and Japan,
400–1200 C.E.

HISTORICAL CONTEXT

Love and marriage, love and marriage,
Go together like a horse and carriage.
This I tell ya, brother,
You can't have one without the other.[1]

Despite the lyrics of the song, love and marriage had little to do with each other throughout most of human history. Parents arranged marriages with their own economic needs foremost. Few people had the time to cultivate the idea of romantic love. One group who did, the ancient Greeks, wrote of love as a sickness; its symptoms were sweaty palms, palpitating heart, blushing complexion, and stammering speech. Marriage cured the disease, ending all symptoms, returning the couple to the steady sanity of daily life. But the idea of love as affliction, accident, or attack (symbolized by the random shot of Cupid's arrow) was evidently too enticing to disappear with the end of the classical world. Cultivated in the religious poetry of the Islamic world, ideas of fevered emotional dedication revived in Europe in the Middle Ages.

A thousand years ago, romantic love was experienced by very few people—often members of a leisure class who seemed to have time on their hands. And the set of ideas, feelings, and actions they exhibited might strike modern readers as rather bizarre. We have to look closely to see the roots of one of our favorite modern emotions.

[1]Written by Sammy Cahn and Jimmy Van Heusen.

THINKING HISTORICALLY
Analyzing Cultural Differences

In the previous chapter, we distinguished among the economic, social, political, and cultural aspects of a society. In this chapter we will examine cultural aspects alone. Actually, culture is never alone, any more than are economics, politics, or social behavior. Culture is nothing less than all our thoughts and feelings and the way we express them by the way we walk, talk, dream, and read history books. Even love, a single ingredient of a culture, is related to aspects of behavior, economics, and even politics. Yet we will isolate this one cultural piece—love—to see how its meaning is different in different cultures. We will analyze these differences to understand better the different cultures and also to understand something about the history of love.

KEVIN REILLY

Love in Medieval Europe, India, and Japan

We hesitantly introduce this piece as a secondary source. It might be better called a tertiary source because it is based so much on the work of others and is part of a chapter in a college textbook. Nevertheless, it sets the stage for our discussion about love. The selection begins with the classic argument that romantic love was a product of medieval Europe, originating in the troubadour tradition of southern France around the twelfth century. The story of Ulrich von Liechtenstein, although probably not typical, details all the facets of the new idea of love, as well as the courts of chivalry that developed its code of behavior. What, according to this interpretation, are the elements of romantic love? How is it similar to, or different from, other kinds of love? How does it relate to sex and marriage? How is the medieval Indian tradition of *bhakti* different from European romantic love? How were medieval Hindu ideas of sex different from Christian ideas of sex? How was the Japanese idea of love during the Heian* period (794–1185) different from European romantic love? How was it similar?

*hay AHN

Kevin Reilly, *The West and the World*, 3rd ed. (Princeton, N.J.: Markus Wiener, 1997), 279–80, 282–83, 287–92.

Thinking Historically

Every culture encompasses a wide variety of ideas and behavior at any one time, making it difficult to argue that a certain idea or behavior defines the culture as a whole. Nevertheless, if there were no common- alities there could be no culture. One way to understand what makes one culture different from another is to discount the extreme behavior at the fringes and focus on what most people think or do. But another way is to compare the extremes of one culture with the extremes of another, on the assumption that the extremists of any culture will magnify the culture's main trait. You might think of Ulrich von Liech- tenstein as an extreme example of medieval European ideas of roman- tic love. A question to ask after you read about other societies is: Could there have been an Ulrich elsewhere? Could medieval India or Japan have produced an Ulrich? If not, why not?

Notice also that this selection highlights particular social classes as well as particular cultures. How do cultures and classes interact to form the ideal of romantic love in Europe and something both similar and different in Japan?

In the Service of Woman

In the twelfth century the courtly love tradition of the troubadours traveled north into France and Germany, and it became a guide to be- havior for many young knights.

We are lucky to have the autobiography of one of these romantic knights, a minor noble who was born in Austria about 1200. His name was Ulrich von Liechtenstein, and he called his autobiography, appro- priately enough, *In the Service of Woman.*[1]

At an early age Ulrich learned that the greatest honor and happiness for a knight lay in the service of a beautiful and noble woman. He seems to have realized, at least subconsciously, that true love had to be full of obstacles and frustrations in order to be spiritually ennobling. So at the age of twelve Ulrich chose as the love of his life a princess. She was a perfect choice: Far above him socially, she was also older than Ulrich and already married. Ulrich managed to become a page in her court so that he could see her and touch the same things that she touched. Some- times he was even able to steal away to his room with the very water that she had just washed her hands in, and he would secretly drink it.

By the age of seventeen Ulrich had become a knight and took to the countryside to joust the tournaments wearing the lady's colors. Finally

---

[1]Paraphrased from Martin Hunt, *The National History of Love* (New York: Alfred A. Knopf, 1959), 132–39. Quotations from Hunt.

after a number of victories, Ulrich gained the courage to ask his niece to call on the lady and tell her that he wanted to be a distant, respectful admirer. The princess would have none of it. She told Ulrich's niece that she was repulsed by Ulrich's mere presence, that he was low class and ugly—especially with that harelip of his. On hearing her reply Ulrich was overjoyed that she had noticed him. He went to have his harelip removed, recuperated for six weeks, and wrote a song to the princess. When the lady heard of this she finally consented to let Ulrich attend a riding party she was having, suggesting even that he might exchange a word with her if the opportunity arose. Ulrich had his chance. He was next to her horse as she was about to dismount, but he was so tongue-tied that he couldn't say a word. The princess thought him such a boor that she pulled out a lock of his hair as she got off her horse.

Ulrich returned to the field for the next three years. Finally the lady allowed him to joust in her name, but she wouldn't part with as much as a ribbon for him to carry. He sent her passionate letters and songs that he had composed. She answered with insults and derision. In one letter the princess derided Ulrich for implying that he had lost a finger while fighting for her when he had actually only wounded it slightly. Ulrich responded by having a friend hack off the finger and send it to the lady in a green velvet case. The princess was evidently so impressed with the power that she had over Ulrich that she sent back a message that she would look at it every day—a message that Ulrich received as he had the others—"on his knees, with bowed head and folded hands."

More determined than ever to win his lady's love, Ulrich devised a plan for a spectacular series of jousts, in which he challenged all comers on a five-week trip. He broke eight lances a day in the service of his princess. After such a showing, the princess sent word that Ulrich might at last visit her, but that he was to come disguised as a leper and sit with the other lepers who would be there begging. The princess passed him, said nothing, and let him sleep that night out in the rain. The following day she sent a message to Ulrich that he could climb a rope to her bedroom window. There she told him that she would grant no favors until he waded across the lake; then she dropped the rope so that he fell into the stinking moat.

Finally, after all of this, the princess said that she would grant Ulrich her love if he went on a Crusade in her name. When she learned that he was making preparations to go, she called it off and offered her love. After almost fifteen years Ulrich had proved himself to the princess.

What was the love that she offered? Ulrich doesn't say, but it probably consisted of kisses, an embrace, and possibly even a certain amount of fondling. Possibly more, but probably not. That was not the point. Ulrich had not spent fifteen years for sex. In fact, Ulrich had not spent fifteen years to win. The quest is what kept him going. His real reward was in the suffering and yearning. Within two years Ulrich was after another perfect lady.

Oh yes. We forgot one thing. Ulrich mentions that in the middle of his spectacular five-week joust, he stopped off for three days to visit the wife and kids. He was married? He was married. He speaks of his wife with a certain amount of affection. She was evidently quite good at managing the estate and bringing up the children. But what were these mundane talents next to the raptures of serving the ideal woman? Love was certainly not a part of the "details of crops, and cattle, fleas and fireplaces, serfs and swamp drainage." In fact, Ulrich might expect that his wife would be proud of him if she knew what he was up to. The love of the princess should make Ulrich so much more noble and esteemed in his wife's eyes.

Courtly Love

The behavior of Ulrich von Liechtenstein reflected in exaggerated form a new idea of love in the West. Historians have called it "courtly love" because it developed in the courts of Europe, where noble ladies and knights of "quality" came together. For the first time since the Greeks a man could idealize a woman, but only if he minimized her sexuality. The evidence is overwhelming that these spiritual affairs would ideally never be consummated.

It is difficult for us to understand how these mature lords and ladies could torture themselves with passionate oaths, feats of endurance, fainting spells when they heard their lover's name or voice, in short the whole repertoire of romance, and then refrain from actually consummating that love. Why did they insist on an ideal of "pure love" that allowed even naked embraces but drew the line at intercourse, which they called "false love"? No doubt the Christian antipathy for sex was part of the problem. Earlier Christian monks had practiced a similar type of *agape*, Christianity had always taught that there was a world of difference between love and lust. The tendency of these Christian men to think of their ladies as replicas of the Virgin Mother also made sex inappropriate, if not outright incestuous.

But these lords and ladies were also making a statement about their "class" or good breeding. They were saying (as did Sigmund Freud almost a thousand years later) that civilized people repress their animal lust. They were distinguishing themselves from the crude peasants and soldiers around them who knew only fornication and whoring and raping. They were cultivating their emotions and their sensitivity, and priding themselves on their self-control. They were privileged (as members of the upper class) to know that human beings were capable of loyalty and love and enjoying beauty without behaving like animals. They were telling each other that they were refined, that they had "class." . . .

Further, despite the new romanticized view of the woman (maybe because of it), wives were just as excluded as they had always been. Noble, uplifting love, genuine romantic love, could not be felt for someone who swept the floor any more than it could be felt *by* someone whose life was preoccupied with such trivia. The lords and one of their special ladies, Marie, the countess of Champagne, issued the following declaration in 1174:

> We declare and we hold as firmly established that love cannot exert its power between two people who are married to each other. For lovers give each other everything freely, under no compulsion of necessity, but married people are in duty bound to give in to each other's desires and deny themselves to each other in nothing.[2]

The Court of Love

The proclamation was one of many that were made by the "courts of love" that these lords and ladies established in order to settle lovers' quarrels—and to decide for themselves the specifics of the new morality. . . .

No one did more to formulate these rules than Andreas Capellanus. Andreas not only summarized the numerous cases that came before the court, but he used these decisions to write a manual of polite, courtly love. He called his influential book *A Treatise on Love and Its Remedy*, a title that indicated his debt to Sappho and the Greek romantic idea of love as a sickness. Andreas, however, did not think that he was advocating a "romantic" idea of love. The word was not even used in his day. He considered himself to be a modern twelfth-century Ovid—merely updating the Roman's *Art of Love*. He called himself Andreas the Lover and, like Ovid, considered himself an expert on all aspects of love.

But Andreas only used the same word as Ovid. The similarity ended there. The "aspects" of love that Andreas taught concerned the loyalty of the lovers, courteous behavior, the spiritual benefits of "pure love," the importance of gentleness, the subservience of the man to his lover, and the duties of courtship. There is none of Ovid's preoccupation with the techniques of seduction. Andreas is not talking about sex. In fact, he clearly advises against consummating the relationship.

Ovid made fun of infatuation and silly emotional behavior, but urged his readers to imitate such sickness in order to get the woman in bed. Andreas valued the passionate emotional attachment that Ovid mocked. Sincerity and honesty were too important to Andreas to dream

[2]Andreas, *Tractatus de Amore*, 1:6, 7th Dialogue. Quoted in Hunt, 143–44.

of trickery, deceit, or pretense. Love, for Andreas, was too noble an emotion, too worthy a pursuit, to be put on like a mask. In short, the Roman had been after sexual gratification; the Christian wanted to refine lives and cleanse souls. They both called it love, but Andreas never seemed to realize that they were not talking the same language.

A Medieval Indian Alternative: Mystical Eroticism

Sometimes the best way to understand our own traditions is to study those of a different culture. It is difficult, for instance, for us to see Christian sexual morality as unusual because it has shaped our culture to such a great extent.

There have been alternatives, however. One of the most remarkable was the Indian ecstatic religion of the Middle Ages. Here the erotic played a central role, not as temptation to be shunned but as a source of salvation. Most medieval temple sculpture was erotic. The temples at Khajuraho and Orissa are full of sexual imagery: sensuous nudes and embracing couples. The temple architecture itself suggests fertility and reproduction. The temple sculptures, like the popular story *Gita Govinda* of the twelfth century, tell of the loves of the god Krishna. He is shown scandalizing young women, dancing deliriously, and bathing with scores of admirers. Krishna's erotic appeal is a testament to his charisma. He is "divine in proportion to his superiority as a great lover."

> Worshippers were encouraged to commit excesses during festivals as the surest way to achieve . . . ecstasy, the purging climax of the orgiastic feast, the surmounting of duality.[3]

Among the most popular forms of medieval Hindu worship were the *bhakti* cults, which originated in devotion to Krishna in the *Bhagavad Gita*. *Bhakti* cults underline the difference between Indian and European devotion. While the Christian church discouraged spiritual love that might easily lead to "carnal love," the Indian *bhakti* sects encouraged rituals of ecstasy and sensual love precisely because they obliterated moral distinctions. The ecstatic union with the divine Krishna, Vishnu, or Shiva enabled the worshiper to transcend the limitations of self and confining definitions of good and evil.

Thus, Indian ecstatic religion sought sexual expression as a path to spiritual fulfillment. It is interesting that the word *bhakti* meant sex as well as worship, while we use the word "devotion" to mean worship and love. Hindu eroticism had nothing to do with the private expression of romantic love. In fact, it was the opposite. While romantic love depended

[3]Richard Lannoy, *The Speaking Tree: A Study of Indian Culture and Society* (Oxford: Oxford University Press, 1971), 64.

on the development of the individual personality and the cultivation of individual feelings, *bhakti* depended on the loss of self in the sexual act.

Bhakti cults differed from the European courtly love tradition in one other important respect. They were not expressions of upper-class control. They were popular expressions of religious feeling. In essence they were directed against the dominating *brahman* and *kshatriya* castes because they challenged the importance of caste distinctions altogether. The ecstatic communion with the deity that they preached was open to all, regardless of caste. They appealed even to women and untouchables, as well as to farmers and artisans.

As Christianity did in Europe, popular Hinduism of the Middle Ages replaced a classical formal tradition with a spiritual passion. Ovid's *Art of Love* and the *Kama Sutra* were mechanical, passionless exercises for tired ruling classes. Both India and Europe turned to more emotionally intense religious experiences in the Middle Ages. Perhaps the classical ideals seemed sterile after the spread of salvation religions like Christianity, Buddhism, and revived Hinduism. The similarity between Christian and Hindu emotionalism may be a product of uncertain times, barbarian threats, and diseases that stalked the Eurasian continent. But the differences between Christian courtly love and *bhakti* cults were also profound. In India, sexual passion was an avenue to spiritual salvation. In Christian Europe sexual passion was at best a dead end, and at worst a road to hell.

Polygamy, Sexuality, and Style: A Japanese Alternative

At the same time that feudal Europe was developing a code of chivalry that romanticized love and almost desexualized marriage, the aristocracy of feudal Japan was evolving a code of polygamous sexuality without chivalry and almost without passion. We know about the sexual lives of Japanese aristocrats between 950 and 1050—the apex of the Heian period—through a series of remarkable novels and diaries, almost all of which were written by women. These first classics of Japanese literature, like *The Tale of Genji* and *The Pillow Book*, were written by women because Japanese men were still writing the "more important" but less-informative laws and theological studies in Chinese (just as Europeans still wrote in a Latin that was very different from the everyday spoken language).

When well-born Japanese in the Heian court spoke of "the world" they were referring to a love affair, and the novels that aristocratic women like Murasaki Shikibu or Sei Shonagon had time to compose in the spoken language were full of stories of "the world."

In *The World of the Shining Prince* Ivan Morris distinguishes three types of sexual relationships between men and women of the Heian aristocracy. (Homosexuality among the court ladies was "probably quite common," he writes, "as in any society where women were obliged to live in continuous and close proximity," but male homosexuality among "warriors, priests, and actors" probably became prevalent in later centuries.) The first type of heterosexual relationship was between the male aristocrat and his "principal wife." She was often several years older than her boy-husband and frequently served more as a guardian than as a bride. She was always chosen for her social standing, usually to cement a political alliance between ruling families. Although the match must frequently have been loveless, her status was inviolate; it was strictly forbidden, for instance, for a prince to exalt a secondary wife to principal wife. Upon marriage the principal wife would normally continue to live with her family, visited by her husband at night, until he became the head of his own household on the death or retirement of his father. Then the principal wife would be installed with all of her servants and aides as the head of the north wing of her husband's residence. An aristocratic woman (but never a peasant woman) might also become a secondary wife or official concubine. If she were officially recognized as such (much to the pleasure of her family), she might be moved into another wing of the official residence (leading to inevitable conflicts with the principal wife and other past and future secondary wives), or she might be set up in her own house. The arrangements were virtually limitless. The third and most frequent type of sexual relationship between men and women was the simple (or complex) affair—with a lady at court, another man's wife or concubine, but usually with a woman of a far lower class than the man. Ivan Morris writes of this kind of relationship:

> Few cultured societies in history can have been as tolerant about sexual relations as was the world of *The Tale of Genji*. Whether or not a gentleman was married, it redounded to his prestige to have as many affairs as possible; and the palaces and great mansions were full of ladies who were only too ready to accommodate him if approached in the proper style. From reading the *Pillow Book* we can tell how extremely commonplace these casual affairs had become in court circles, the man usually visiting the girl at night behind her screen of state and leaving her at the crack of dawn.[4]

That emphasis on "the proper style" is what distinguishes the sexuality of medieval Japan from that of ancient Rome, and reminds us of the medieval European's display of form—the aristocracy's mark of "class." Perhaps because the sexuality of the Heian aristocracy was potentially more explosive than the repressed rituals of European chivalry, style was that much more important. Polygamous sexuality could be practiced

---

[4]Ivan Morris, *The World of the Shining Prince: Court Life in Ancient Japan* (Baltimore: Penguin Books, 1969), 237.

without tearing the society apart (and destroying aristocratic dominance in the process) only if every attention were given to style. Listen, for instance, to what the lady of *The Pillow Book* expected from a good lover:

> A good lover will behave as elegantly at dawn as at any other time. He drags himself out of bed with a look of dismay on his face. The lady urges him on: "Come, my friend, it's getting light. You don't want anyone to find you here." He gives a deep sigh, as if to say that the night has not been nearly long enough and that it is agony to leave. Once up, he does not instantly pull on his trousers. Instead he comes close to the lady and whispers whatever was left unsaid during the night. Even when he is dressed, he still lingers, vaguely pretending to be fastening his sash.
>
> Presently he raises the lattice, and the two lovers stand together by the side door while he tells her how he dreads the coming day, which will keep them apart; then he slips away. The lady watches him go, and this moment of parting will remain among her most charming memories.
>
> Indeed, one's attachment to a man depends largely on the elegance of his leave-taking. When he jumps out of bed, scurries about the room, tightly fastens his trouser-sash, rolls up the sleeves of his Court cloak, over-robe, or hunting costume, stuffs his belongings into the breast of his robe and then briskly secures the outer sash—one really begins to hate him.[5]

The stylistic elegance of the lover's departure was one of the principal themes of Heian literature. Perhaps no situation better expressed the mood of the Japanese word *aware* (a word that was used over a thousand times in *The Tale of Genji*), which meant the poignant or the stylishly, even artistically, sorrowful—a style of elegant resignation. The word also suggests the mood of "the lady in waiting" and even the underlying anguish and jealousy of a precariously polygamous existence for the women consorts and writers of the Japanese feudal age. The ladies of the court were trained in calligraphy, poetry, and music; they were dressed in elaborate, colorful silks, painted with white faces and black teeth, and rewarded by sexual attention that always had to be justified by its cultured style. . . .

Aristocracies have behaved in similar ways throughout the world, and throughout history. They demonstrate their "class" or "good breeding" with elaborate rituals that differentiate their world from the ordinary. But the example of aristocratic Heian Japan a thousand years ago points to some of the differences between Japanese and Christian culture. The Japanese developed rituals of courtship and seduction for the leisured few that were sexually satisfying and posed no threat to

---

[5]*The Pillow Book of Sei Shonagon*, trans. Ivan Morris (Baltimore: Penguin Books, 1971), 49–50.

marriage. They were rituals that showed artistic refinement rather than sexual "purity" or chastity. They could be sexual because Japanese culture did not disparage sexuality. Rather it disparaged lack of "taste." The affair did not threaten marriage because the culture did not insist on monogamy. The new sexual interest could be carried on outside or inside the polygamous estate of the Japanese aristocrat. Perhaps the main difference, then, is that the Japanese aristocrat invented stylized sex rather than romantic love.

55

ULRICH VON LIECHTENSTEIN
The Service of Ladies

This selection is drawn from Ulrich von Liechtenstein's own account of his adventures. After over ten years of service, as a page and then a distant admirer, in 1226, Ulrich undertook a spectacular series of jousts to impress and win his lady, the princess. In the course of a five-week itinerary in northern Italy and southern German-speaking areas in which he took on all comers, he claims to have broken three hundred and seven lances. In the first part of this selection he details his preparation for the traveling tournament. In the second part of the selection, he tells of a brief interruption in his jousting for a stop at home. What does this selection tell you about Ulrich's ideas of love and marriage?

Thinking Historically

Sometimes the best entry point for analyzing cultural differences is to begin with the surprising or incomprehensible. If we can refrain from merely dismissing what seems beyond the pale, this can be an opportunity to understand how cultures can be truly different from our own.

Even a moderately careful reading of the two selections from Ulrich's autobiography should evoke some surprise. In the first selection, Ulrich sketches a visual image of himself on horseback that is far from our expectations. Imagine what he must have looked like. Imagine how others must have seen him. Recognizing that this was not some Halloween prank, that others proceeded to joust with him rather than laugh him out of town, we are forced to rethink what his outfit and

Ulrich von Liechtenstein, *The Service of Ladies*, trans. J. W. Thomas (Suffolk, England and Rochester, N.Y.: The Boydell Press, 2004; published by arrangement with University of North Carolina Press, Chapel Hill, 1969), 46–49, 85–86.

presentation meant to him and those in his society. The recognition
that the meaning of an act (like donning women's clothing) could be
vastly different in Europe of the thirteenth century from what it is
today offers the entry to comparative analysis.

We may also note that there are many things in Ulrich's description
of love that are not at all surprising. This may be because they have
become second nature to our own society. Certainly some of the elements of romantic love, which were fresh in Ulrich's day, have become clichés in modern film and television. What do you make of the
elements of this story that are familiar? What do you make of those
that surprise you?

"My service must be God's command.
Now let me tell you what I've planned.
I'll take on woman's dress and name
and thus disguised will strive for fame.
Sweet God protect me and sustain!
I'll travel with a knightly train
up to Bohemia from the sea.
A host of knights shall fight with me.

"This very winter I shall steal
out of the land and shall conceal
my goal from everyone but you.
I'll travel as a pilgrim who
to honor God is bound for Rome
(no one will question this at home).
I'll stop in Venice and shall stay
in hiding till the first of May.

"I'll carefully remain unseen
but deck myself out like a queen;
it should be easy to acquire
some lovely feminine attire
which I'll put on—now hear this last—
and when St. George's day is past,
the morning afterwards, I'll ride
(I pray that God is on my side)

"from the sea to Mestre, near
by Venice. He who breaks a spear
with me to serve, by tourneying,
his lady fair will get a ring

of gold and it will be quite nice.
I'll give it to him with this advice,
that he present it to his love,
the one he's in the service of.

"Messenger, I'll make the trip
so there will never be a slip
and no one possibly can guess
whose form is hid beneath the dress.
For I'll be clad from head to toe
in woman's garb where'er I go,
fully concealed from people's eyes.
They'll see me only in disguise.

"If you would please me, messenger,
then travel once again to her.
Just tell her what I have in mind
and ask if she will be so kind
as to permit that I should fight
throughout this journey as her knight.
It's something she will not repent
and I'll be glad of her assent."

He rode at once to tell her this
and swore upon his hope of bliss
my loyalty would never falter,
that I was true and would not alter.
He told my plan in full detail
and said, "My lady, should you fail
to let him serve and show your trust
in him, it wouldn't seem quite just."

"Messenger," she spoke, "just let
him have this message, don't forget.
This trip, if I have understood
you right, will surely do him good
and he will win a rich reward
in praise from many a lady and lord.
Whether it helps with me or not,
from others he will gain a lot."

The messenger was pleased and sure.
He found me by the river Mur
at Liechtenstein where I was then.
'T was nice to have him there again.

I spoke, "O courtly youth, now tell
me if the lady's feeling well.
For, if my darling's doing fine,
then shall rejoice this heart of mine."

He spoke, "She's fair and happy too;
she bade me bring this word to you
about your journey. If you should
go through with it 't will do you good
and, whether it helps with her or not,
from others you will gain a lot.
She certainly supports your aim
and says that you'll be rich in fame."

I listened to the news he had,
and heart and body both were glad.
It was a joy for me to know
my undertaking pleased her so.
I didn't linger but began
at once to carry out my plan
and was quite happy, I admit,
that he also approved of it.

I soon was ready, I assure
you, to begin my knightly tour.
I started out as pilgrim dressed
and left the land. I thought it best
to take a staff and pouch at least,
for looks (I got them from a priest);
one would have thought me bound for Rome.
I prayed God bring me safely home.

I got to Venice without delay
and found a house in which to stay,
right on the edge of town, a place
where none would ever see my face
who might have recognized me there.
I was as cautious everywhere
and all the winter long I hid.
But let me tell you what I did:

I had some woman's clothing made
to wear throughout the masquerade.
They cut and sewed for me twelve skirts
and thirty fancy lady's shirts.

I bought two braids for my disguise,
the prettiest they could devise,
and wound them with some pearls I got
which didn't cost an awful lot.

I bade the tailors then prepare
three velvet cloaks for me to wear,
all white. The saddles too on which
the master labored, stitch by stitch,
were silver white. As for a king
was made the saddle covering,
long and broad and gleaming white.
The bridles all were rich and bright.

The tailors sewed for every squire
(there were a dozen) white attire.
A hundred spears were made for me
and all as white as they could be.
But I need not continue so,
for all I wore was white as snow
and everything the squires had on
was just as white as any swan.

My shield was white, the helmet too.
I had them make ere they were through
a velvet cover for each steed
as armor. These were white, indeed,
as was the battle cape which I
should wear for jousting by and by,
the cloth of which was very fine.
I was quite pleased to call it mine.

At last I had my horses sent
to me (none knew just where they went)
and got some servants, as I'd planned,
each native to a foreign land.
They carefully did not let slip
a thing about my coming trip
and I took heed that those who came
to serve me never learned my name.

· · ·

They rode toward me with armor on;
I had not waited long to don
a rich and splendid battle dress.

Von Ringenberg with full success
broke off a spear on me. The one
I jousted with when this was done
I knocked down backwards off his horse,
which made him feel ashamed, of course.

The spears I broke then numbered four.
On the field had come no more
with armor on and lance in hand
and so I stopped. At my command
the servants gave six rings away.
I sought the inn where I should stay
and found a pretty hostel there;
I got some other things to wear.

I changed my clothing under guard,
and then the hostel door was barred.
I took with me a servant who
would not say anything, I knew.
We stole away without a sound
and rode with joy to where I found
my dearest wife whom I adore;
I could not ever love her more.

She greeted me just as a good
and loving woman always should
receive a husband she holds dear.
That I had come to see her here
had made her really very pleased.
My visit stilled her grief and eased
her loneliness. We shared our bliss,
my sweet and I, with many a kiss.

She was so glad to see her knight,
and I had comfort and delight
till finally the third day came;
to give me joy was her sole aim.
When dawn appeared it was the third.
I dressed, an early mass was heard,
I prayed God keep me from transgressing,
and then received a friendly blessing.

Right after that I took my leave,
lovingly, you may believe,
and rode with joyful heart to where

I'd left my servants unaware.
I entered Gloggnitz hastily
and found them waiting there for me,
prepared to journey on again.
At once we left the city then.

We rode to Neunkirchen gaily decked
and were received as I'd expect
of those whose manners are refined.
Each knight was courteous and kind
who waited there with spear and shield.
When I came riding on the field
I found them all prepared, adorned
with trappings no one would have scorned.

Nine waited there, not more nor less,
to joust with me, in battle dress.
I saw them and it wasn't long
till I'd donned armor, bright and strong.
The first to come I'd heard much of;
his great desire was ladies' love.
It was Sir Ortold von Graz, a name
already widely known to fame.

All that he wore was of the best.
The good man cut me in the chest
so strong and skilful was his joust;
through shield and armor went the thrust.
When I beheld the wound indeed
and saw that it began to bleed
I hid it quickly with my coat
before the other knights took note.

I broke nine lances there in haste
and found my inn. I dared not waste
much time before I got in bed.
I sent nine rings of golden red
to each of them who with his spear
had earned from me a present here.
My injuries were deftly bound
by a doctor whom my servants found.

$\boxed{56}$

ANDREAS CAPELLANUS

From The Art of Courtly Love

Andreas Capellanus (Andreas the Chaplain) compiled this guide to courtly love between 1184 and 1186. He probably intended his book to update Ovid's *Art of Love,* as discussed in selection 54, but his approach reflects many of the new ideas of love circulating among the upper classes of Europe in the twelfth century. Andreas says that love is suffering, but also that it is wonderful. What does he mean? Compare his ideas about sex and marriage to those of Ulrich von Liechtenstein. The bishop of Paris condemned Andreas's ideas in 1277, but do they seem religious or Christian in any way? Notice the author's attention to passion and proper behavior. How does he combine or balance the two?

Thinking Historically

How unusual are these ideas about love? Do you think that most people in most societies would agree with these ideas or are they unique? How might these ideas be considered European?

Introduction to the Treatise on Love

We must first consider what love is, whence it gets its name, what the effect of love is, between what persons love may exist, how it may be acquired, retained, increased, decreased, and ended, what are the signs that one's love is returned, and what one of the lovers ought to do if the other is unfaithful.

What Love Is

Love is a certain inborn suffering derived from the sight of and excessive meditation upon the beauty of the opposite sex, which causes each one to wish above all things the embraces of the other and by common desire to carry out all of love's precepts in the other's embrace.

That love is suffering is easy to see, for before the love becomes equally balanced on both sides there is no torment greater, since the

---

Andreas Capellanus, *The Art of Courtly Love,* trans. John J. Parry (New York: Columbia University Press, 1990), 28–32, 159–86.

lover is always in fear that his love may not gain its desire and that he is wasting his efforts. He fears, too, that rumors of it may get abroad, and he fears everything that might harm it in any way, for before things are perfected a slight disturbance often spoils them. If he is a poor man, he also fears that the woman may scorn his poverty; if he is ugly, he fears that she may despise his lack of beauty or may give her love to a more handsome man; if he is rich, he fears that his parsimony in the past may stand in his way. To tell the truth, no one can number the fears of one single lover. This kind of love, then, is a suffering which is felt by only one of the persons and may be called "single love." But even after both are in love the fears that arise are just as great, for each of the lovers fears that what he has acquired with so much effort may be lost through the effort of someone else, which is certainly much worse for a man than if, having no hope, he sees that his efforts are accomplishing nothing, for it is worse to lose the things you are seeking than to be deprived of a gain you merely hope for. The lover fears, too, that he may offend his loved one in some way; indeed he fears so many things that it would be difficult to tell them.

That this suffering is inborn I shall show you clearly, because if you will look at the truth and distinguish carefully you will see that it does not arise out of any action; only from the reflection of the mind upon what it sees does this suffering come. For when a man sees some woman fit for love and shaped according to his taste, he begins at once to lust after her in his heart; then the more he thinks about her the more he burns with love, until he comes to a fuller meditation. Presently he begins to think about the fashioning of the woman and to differentiate her limbs, to think about what she does, and to pry into the secrets of her body, and he desires to put each part of it to the fullest use. Then after he has come to this complete meditation, love cannot hold the reins, but he proceeds at once to action; straightway he strives to get a helper to find an intermediary. He begins to plan how he may find favor with her, and he begins to seek a place and a time opportune for talking; he looks upon a brief hour as a very long year, because he cannot do anything fast enough to suit his eager mind. It is well known that many things happen to him in this manner. This inborn suffering comes, therefore, from seeing and meditating. Not every kind of meditation can be the cause of love, an excessive one is required; for a restrained thought does not, as a rule, return to the mind, and so love cannot arise from it.

Between What Persons Love May Exist

Now, in love you should note first of all that love cannot exist except between persons of opposite sexes. Between two men or two women love can find no place, for we see that two persons of the same sex are not at all fitted for giving each other the exchanges of love or for practicing the acts natural to it. Whatever nature forbids, love is ashamed to accept.

What the Effect of Love Is

Now it is the effect of love that a true lover cannot be degraded with any avarice. Love causes a rough and uncouth man to be distinguished for his handsomeness; it can endow a man even of the humblest birth with nobility of character; it blesses the proud with humility; and the man in love becomes accustomed to performing many services gracefully for everyone. O what a wonderful thing is love, which makes a man shine with so many virtues and teaches everyone, no matter who he is, so many good traits of character! There is another thing about love that we should not praise in few words: it adorns a man, so to speak, with the virtue of chastity, because he who shines with the light of one love can hardly think of embracing another woman, even a beautiful one. For when he thinks deeply of his beloved the sight of any other woman seems to his mind rough and rude.

If One of the Lovers Is Unfaithful to the Other

If one of the lovers should be unfaithful to the other, and the offender is the man, and he has an eye to a new love affair, he renders himself wholly unworthy of his former love, and she ought to deprive him completely of her embraces.

But what if he should be unfaithful to his beloved—not with the idea of finding a new love, but because he has been driven to it by an irresistible passion for another woman? What, for instance, if chance should present to him an unknown woman in a convenient place or what if at a time when Venus is urging him on to that which I am talking about he should meet with a little strumpet or somebody's servant girl? Should he, just because he played with her in the grass, lose the love of his beloved? We can say without fear of contradiction that just for this a lover is not considered unworthy of the love of his beloved unless he indulges in so many excesses with a number of women that we may conclude that he is overpassionate. But if whenever he becomes acquainted with a woman he pesters her to gain his end, or if he attains his object as a result of his efforts, then rightly he does deserve to be deprived of his former love, because there is strong presumption that he has acted in this way with an eye toward a new one, especially where he has strayed with a woman of the nobility or otherwise of an honorable estate.

I know that once when I sought advice I got the answer that a true lover can never desire a new love unless he knows that for some definite and sufficient reason the old love is dead; we know from our own experience that this rule is very true. We have fallen in love with a woman of the most admirable character, although we have never had, or hope to have, any fruit of this love. For we are compelled to pine away for love of a woman of such lofty station that we dare not say one word about it, nor dare we throw ourself upon her mercy, and so at length we are forced to find our body shipwrecked. But although rashly and without foresight we have fallen into such great waves in this tempest, still we cannot think about a new love or look for any other way to free ourself.

But since you are making a special study of the subject of love, you may well ask whether a man can have a pure love for one woman and a mixed or common love with another. We will show you, by an unanswerable argument, that no one can feel affection for two women in this fashion. For although pure love and mixed love may seem to be very different things, if you will look at the matter properly you will see that pure love, so far as its substance goes, is the same as mixed love and comes from the same feeling of the heart. The substance of the love is the same in each case, and only the manner and form of loving are different, as this illustration will make clear to you. Sometimes we see a man with a desire to drink his wine unmixed, and at another time his appetite prompts him to drink only water or wine and water mixed; although his appetite manifests itself differently, the substance of it is the same and unchanged. So likewise when two people have long been united by pure love and afterwards desire to practice mixed love, the substance of the love remains the same in them, although the manner and form and the way of practicing it are different. . . .

The Rules of Love

Let us come now to the rules of love, and I shall try to present to you very briefly those rules which the King of Love[1] is said to have proclaimed with his own mouth and to have given in writing to all lovers. . . .

I.   Marriage is no real excuse for not loving.
II.   He who is not jealous cannot love.
III. No one can be bound by a double love.
IV.   It is well known that love is always increasing or decreasing.
V.   That which a lover takes against the will of his beloved has no relish.
VI.   Boys do not love until they arrive at the age of maturity.
VII. When one lover dies, a widowhood of two years is required of the survivor.
VIII. No one should be deprived of love without the very best of reasons.

[1]King Arthur of Britain. [Ed.]

IX. No one can love unless he is impelled by the persuasion of love.

X. Love is always a stranger in the home of avarice.

XI. It is not proper to love any woman whom one should be ashamed to seek to marry.

XII. A true lover does not desire to embrace in love anyone except his beloved.

XIII. When made public love rarely endures.

XIV. The easy attainment of love makes it of little value; difficulty of attainment makes it prized.

XV. Every lover regularly turns pale in the presence of his beloved.

XVI. When a lover suddenly catches sight of his beloved his heart palpitates.

XVII. A new love puts to flight an old one.

XVIII. Good character alone makes any man worthy of love.

XIX. If love diminishes, it quickly fails and rarely revives.

XX. A man in love is always apprehensive.

XXI. Real jealousy always increases the feeling of love.

XXII. Jealousy, and therefore love, are increased when one suspects his beloved.

XXIII. He whom the thought of love vexes, eats and sleeps very little.

XXIV. Every act of a lover ends in the thought of his beloved.

XXV. A true lover considers nothing good except what he thinks will please his beloved.

XXVI. Love can deny nothing to love.

XXVII. A lover can never have enough of the solaces of his beloved.

XXVIII. A slight presumption causes a lover to suspect his beloved.

XXIX. A man who is vexed by too much passion usually does not love.

XXX. A true lover is constantly and without intermission possessed by the thought of his beloved.

XXXI. Nothing forbids one woman being loved by two men or one man by two women.

$\boxed{57}$

KALIDASA
From Shakuntala

Kalidasa (c. 400 C.E.) was one of the greatest Indian dramatists. His play *Shakuntala*, a classic of the Hindu literary tradition, tells the story of a love between a king and a hermit girl. The two fall passionately in love with each other although they have barely exchanged words. Despite their different stations in life, they are equally overcome by *kama*, one of the four great forces in the Hindu culture—the force of love and physical attraction. In this selection from Act 3 (of seven acts), Shakuntala is urged by her friends, Priyamvadā and Anasuya, who say they "don't know what it is to be in love," to write a letter to the king, who overhears their conversation. In what ways is this similar to European ideas of romantic love? In what ways is it different?

Thinking Historically

The description of feelings in this selection might seem overly florid, but the emotions are not unfamiliar to a modern reader. Can you think of a play or film that is similar to this? What is the similarity? Is there any unfamiliar aspect? If you were to present this story to a modern American audience, how might you change it? Why?

PRIYAMVADĀ: Compose a love letter and I'll hide it in a flower. I'll deliver it to his hand on the pretext of bringing a gift from our offering to the deity.

ANASŪYĀ: This subtle plan pleases me. What does Shakuntalā say?

SHAKUNTALĀ: I'll try my friend's plan.

PRIYAMVADĀ: Then compose a poem to declare your love!

SHAKUNTALĀ: I'm thinking, but my heart trembles with fear that he'll reject me.

KING [IN HIDING]: (*delighted*):
> The man whom you fear will reject you
> waits longing to love you, timid girl—
> a suitor may be lucky or cursed,
> but his goodness of fortune always wins.

Kalidasa, *Shakuntala*, Act III, trans. Barbara Stoler Miller, in *Theater of Memory: The Plays of Kalidasa*, ed. Barbara Stoler Miller (New York: Columbia University Press, 1984), 114–18.

BOTH FRIENDS: Why do you devalue your own virtues? Who would keep autumn moonlight from cooling the body by covering it with a bit of cloth?

SHAKUNTALĀ (*smiling*): I'm following your advice. (*She sits thinking*)

KING: As I stare at her, my eyes forget to blink.
    She arches an eyebrow
    struggling to compose the verse—
    the down rises on her cheek,
    showing the passion she feels.

SHAKUNTALĀ: I have thought of a song, but there's nothing I can write it on.

PRIYAMVADĀ: Engrave the letters with your nails on this lotus leaf! It's as delicate as a parrot's breast.

SHAKUNTALĀ (*miming what Priyamvadā described*): Listen and tell me if this makes sense!

BOTH FRIENDS: We're both paying attention.

SHAKUNTALĀ (*sings*):
    I don't know your heart,
    but day and night Love
    violently burns my limbs
    with desire for you, cruel man.

KING (*Having been listening to them, entering suddenly*):
    Love torments you, slender girl,
    but he utterly consumes me—
    daylight makes the moon fade
    when it folds the white lotus.

BOTH FRIENDS (*Looking, rising with delight*): Welcome to the swift success of love's desire!
    (*Shakuntalā tries to rise.*)

KING: Don't strain yourself!
    Limbs on a couch of crushed flowers
    and fragrant tips of lotus stalks
    are too frail from suffering
    to perform ceremonial acts . . .

ANASŪYĀ: We've heard that kings have many loves. Will our beloved friend become a sorrow to her relatives after you've spent your time with her?

KING: Noble lady, enough of this! I may have many wives, but my royal line rests on two foundations: the sea-bound earth and this friend of yours!

BOTH FRIENDS: We are assured.

PRIYAMVADĀ (*casting a glance*): Anasūyā this fawn is looking for its mother. Let's take it to her!
    (*They both begin to leave.*)

SHAKUNTALĀ: Come back! Don't leave me unprotected!

BOTH FRIENDS: The protector of the earth is at your side.

SHAKUNTALĀ: Why have they gone?

KING: Don't be alarmed! A servant worships at your side.

> Shall I set moist winds in motion
> with lotus-leaf fans to cool your pain,
> or put your pale red lotus feet on my lap
> and stroke them, voluptuous girl?

SHAKUNTALĀ: I cannot sin against those I respect! (*standing as if she wants to leave*)

KING: Beautiful Shakuntalā, the day is still hot.

> Why leave this couch of flowers
> and its shield of lotus leaves
> to venture into the heat
> with your frail wan limbs?
> (*Saying this, he forces her to turn around.*)

SHAKUNTALĀ: Puru king, control yourself! Though I'm burning with love I'm not free to give myself to you.

KING: Don't fear your elders! The father of your family knows the law. When he finds out, he will not fault you. Many kings' daughters first marry in secret and their fathers bless them.

SHAKUNTALĀ: Release me! I must ask my friends' advice!

KING: Yes, I shall release you.

SHAKUNTALĀ: When?

KING:

> Only let my thirsting mouth
> gently drink from your lips,
> the way a bee sips nectar
> from a fragile virgin blossom.

58

MIRABAI

Bhakti Poems

Mirabai (b. c. 1550) was one of the great poets of the medieval Indian Bhakti or Hindu devotional tradition. Bhakti philosophers and poets expressed a Hinduism suffused with love for the deity. Typically, Mirabai's religious experience of personal love represented a form of protest against the religious formalism of caste and the authority of Brahmin sacrifice. According to legend, Mirabai refused to consummate her marriage to a king because she had fallen in love with the god Khrishna, who was often pictured as the deep blue "dark Lord" and the lifter of mountains. How is Mirabai's imagery similar to that of medieval European courtly love? How is it different?

Thinking Historically

India was not the only society that produced women who expressed an almost sexual passion toward a god. The great Muslim mystic Rabia al-Adawiyya (b. c. 717) and the Sufis used similar language, and St. Teresa of Avila (1515–1582) is perhaps the best known among Christian devotees who wrote with an almost erotic passion. The Hindu celebration of *kama* and the development of Bhakti Hinduism were particularly Indian. Still, can you think of cases in your own culture where love of a deity faded into, or felt like, love for another person? How about Ulrich's "worship" of the princess? How unique is this Indian cultural form after all?

Colored by Devotion to Krishna

The motif of being dyed with the color of devotion to the Dark Lord is common in bhakti poetry, as is dancing before him. The poison cup refers to an incident when the Rānā tried to poison her, but the only effect was to make her glow with the beauty of Krishna. The "mountain lifter" is a reference to one of Krishna's miracles.

[From Mīrābāī, in Parashurām Caturvedī, Mīrābāī kī Padāvalī, no. 37, trans. by J.S.H. and M.J.]

Poems of Mirabai, trans. John S. Hawley and Mark Juergensmeyer, in *Sources of Indian Tradition*, vol. I, *From the Beginning to 1800*, 2nd ed., ed. Ainslee Embree (New York: Columbia University Press, 1988), 365–69.

I'm colored with the color of dusk, O Rānā
  colored with the color of my Lord.
Drumming out the rhythm on the drums, I danced,
  dancing in the presence of the saints,
    colored with the color of my Lord.
They thought me mad for the Wily One,
  raw for my dear dark love,
    colored with the color of my Lord.
The Rānā sent me a poison cup:
  I didn't look, I drank it up,
    colored with the color of my Lord.
The clever Mountain Lifter is the Lord of Mīrā.
  Life after life he's true—
    colored with the color of my Lord.

Marriage with Krishna

This poem echoes Mīrā's consciousness of having been married to
Krishna in previous births. She is filled with longing for him and is begging him to unite with her now in this life.

[From Mīrābāī, Mīrābāī Kī Padāvalī, no. 51, trans. by J.S.H. and M. J.]

I have talked to you, talked,
  Dark Lifter of Mountains,
About this old love,
  from birth after birth.
Don't go, don't,
  Lifter of Mountains,
Let me offer a sacrifice—myself—
  beloved,
    to your beautiful face.
Come, here in the courtyard,
  Dark Lord,
The women are singing auspicious wedding songs;
My eyes have fashioned
  an altar of pearl tears,
And here is my sacrifice:
  the body and mind
of Mīrā,
  the servant who clings to your feet,
    through life after life,
      a virginal harvest for you to reap.

Life without Krishna

Mīrā's love for Krishna leads to the enmity of her family, but at the same time gives her a refuge to which she can escape.

[From Mīrābāī, *Mīrābāī kī Padāvalī*, no. 42, trans. by J. S. H. and M. J.]

Life without Hari is no life, friend,
And though my mother-in-law fights,
    my sister-in-law teases,
    the *rānā* is angered,
A guard is stationed on the stoop outside,
    and a lock is mounted on the door,
How can I abandon the love I have loved
    in life after life?
Mīrā's Lord is the clever Mountain-Lifter:
    Why would I want anyone else?

The Sound of Krishna's Flute

Muralī is the bamboo flute that is one of Krishna's chief symbols. It is the medium through which Krishna entrances the women of Braj, calling them to love. Sometimes the flute is pictured as a woman herself, with more immediate access to Krishna than has anyone else. So the sound of the flute fills Mīrā with the intense pain of longing for love, a longing that is one of the constant themes of love poetry in the Indian tradition.

[From Mīrābāī, no. 166, trans. by J.S.H. and M. J.]

Muralī sounds on the banks of the Jumna,
Muralī snatches away my mind;
My senses cut away from their moorings—
Dark waters, dark garments, Dark Lord.
I listen close to the sounds of Muralī
And my body withers away—
Lost thoughts, lost even the power to think.
    Mīrā's Lord, clever Mountain-Lifter,
    Come quick, snatch away my pain.

59

MURASAKI SHIKIBU

From The Tale of Genji

The Tale of Genji is, by some measures, the world's first novel. It was written by Murasaki Shikibu, a woman at the Japanese court, probably in the first decade after the year 1000. During the Heian period (794–1185) of Japanese history, women in the Japanese aristocracy differentiated their culture from the Chinese one that had dominated it since the seventh century.

While Japanese men were still using a dated form of Chinese for official documents, women like Lady Murasaki were fashioning the Japanese language into an effective and contemporary medium of communication. As ladies of the court, they also had the experience and leisure for writing intriguing, richly evocative stories.

The Tale of Genji is about Prince Genji—an attractive, talented, and sensitive son of the emperor—and his love interests. This chapter, occurring near the end of the novel, tells of one of Prince Genji's many flirtations. It also reveals much about the culture of the Japanese court. Notice the cultivation of music, dance, and poetry among the court nobility. What, if anything, does this display of sensitivity have to do with ideas of love and marriage? What signs do you see here of the persistence of Chinese culture in Heian Japan?

Also, notice the absence of monogamy in the court. The emperor is married but has taken in turn three consorts: Kokiden, Kiritsubo, and now Fujitsubo. What is the relationship between marriage and sex in this society? What does that tell you about the mores of the time?

Thinking Historically

Would you call this a story of romantic love? In what ways is the love Lady Murasaki describes similar to or different from the love Andreas Capellanus describes in selection 56? What aspects of Heian Japanese culture are different from the culture of medieval Europe? Is the dominant-upper class idea of love in Japan during this period different from that of Europe?

Murasaki Shikibu, *The Tale of Genji*, trans. Arthur Waley (1929; reprint, Garden City, N.Y.: Anchor Books, 1955), 201–10.

About the twentieth day of the second month the Emperor gave a Chinese banquet under the great cherry-tree of the Southern Court. Both Fujitsubo and the Heir Apparent were to be there. Kokiden, although she knew that the mere presence of the Empress was sufficient to spoil her pleasure, could not bring herself to forgo so delightful an entertainment. After some promise of rain the day turned out magnificent; and in full sunshine, with the birds singing in every tree, the guests (royal princes, noblemen, and professional poets alike) were handed the rhyme words which the Emperor had drawn by lot, and set to work to compose their poems. It was with a clear and ringing voice that Genji read out the word "Spring" which he had received as the rhyme-sound of his poem. Next came To no Chujo who, feeling that all eyes were upon him and determined to impress himself favourably on his audience, moved with the greatest possible elegance and grace; and when on receiving his rhyme he announced his name, rank, and titles, he took great pains to speak pleasantly as well as audibly. Many of the other gentlemen were rather nervous and looked quite pale as they came forward, yet they acquitted themselves well enough. But the professional poets, particularly owing to the high standard of accomplishment which the Emperor's and Heir Apparent's lively interest in Chinese poetry had at that time diffused through the Court, were very ill at ease; as they crossed the long space of the garden on their way to receive their rhymes they felt utterly helpless. A simple Chinese verse is surely not much to ask of a professional poet; but they all wore an expression of the deepest gloom. One expects elderly scholars to be somewhat odd in their movements and behaviour, and it was amusing to see the lively concern with which the Emperor watched their various but always uncouth and erratic methods of approaching the Throne. Needless to say a great deal of music had been arranged for. Towards dusk the delightful dance known as the Warbling of Spring Nightingales was performed, and when it was over the Heir Apparent, remembering the Festival of Red Leaves, placed a wreath on Genji's head and pressed him so urgently that it was impossible for him to refuse. Rising to his feet he danced very quietly a fragment of the sleeve-turning passage in the Wave Dance. In a few moments he was seated again, but even into this brief extract from a long dance he managed to import an unrivalled charm and grace. Even his father-in-law who was not in the best of humour with him was deeply moved and found himself wiping away a tear.

"And why have we not seen To no Chujo?" said the Heir Apparent. Whereupon Chujo danced the Park of Willow Flowers, giving a far more complete performance than Genji, for no doubt he knew that he would be called upon and had taken trouble to prepare his dance. It was a great success and the Emperor presented him with a cloak, which everyone said was a most unusual honour. After this the other young noblemen who were present danced in no particular order, but it was now so dark that it was impossible to discriminate between their performances.

Then the poems were opened and read aloud. The reading of Genji's verses was continually interrupted by loud murmurs of applause. Even the professional poets were deeply impressed, and it may well be imagined with what pride the Emperor, to whom at times Genji was a source of consolation and delight, watched him upon such an occasion as this. Fujitsubo, when she allowed herself to glance in his direction, marvelled that even Kokiden could find it in her heart to hate him. "It is because he is fond of me; there can be no other reason," she decided at last, and the verse, "Were I but a common mortal who now am gazing at the beauty of this flower, from its sweet petals not long should I withhold the dew of love," framed itself on her lips, though she dared not utter it aloud.

It was now very late and the banquet was over. The guests had scattered. The Empress and the Heir Apparent had both returned to the Palace—all was still. The moon had risen very bright and clear, and Genji, heated with wine, could not bear to quit so lovely a scene. The people at the Palace were probably all plunged in a heavy sleep. On such a night it was not impossible that some careless person might have left some door unfastened, some shutter unbarred. Cautiously and stealthily he crept towards Fujitsubo's apartments and inspected them. Every bolt was fast. He sighed; here there was evidently nothing to be done. He was passing the loggia of Kokiden's palace when he noted that the shutters of the third arch were not drawn. After the banquet Kokiden herself had gone straight to the Emperor's rooms. There did not seem to be anyone about. A door leading from the loggia into the house was standing open, but he could hear no sound within. "It is under just such circumstances as this that one is apt to drift into compromising situations," thought Genji. Nevertheless he climbed quietly on to the balustrade and peeped. Everyone must be asleep. But no; a very agreeable young voice with an intonation which was certainly not that of any waiting-woman or common person was softly humming the last two lines of the *Oborozuki-yo*.[1] Was not the voice coming towards him? It seemed so, and stretching out his hand he suddenly found that he was grasping a lady's sleeve. "Oh, how you frightened me!" she cried. "Who is it?" "Do not be alarmed," he whispered. "That both of us were not content to miss the beauty of this departing night is proof more clear than the half-clouded moon that we were meant to meet," and as he recited the words he took her gently by the hand and led her into the house, closing the door behind them. Her surprised and puzzled air fascinated him. "There is someone there," she whispered

---

[1]A famous poem by Oye no Chisato (ninth century): "What so lovely as a night when the moon though dimly clouded is never wholly lost to sight!"

tremulously, pointing to the inner room. "Child," he answered, "I am allowed to go wherever I please and if you send for your friends they will only tell you that I have every right to be here. But if you will stay quietly here. . . ." It was Genji. She knew his voice and the discovery somewhat reassured her. She thought his conduct rather strange, but she was determined that he should not think her prudish or stiff. And so because he on his side was still somewhat excited after the doings of the evening, while she was far too young and pliant to offer any serious resistance, he soon got his own way with her.

Suddenly they saw to their discomfiture that dawn was creeping into the sky. She looked, thought Genji, as though many disquieting reflections were crowding into her mind. "Tell me your name," he said. "How can I write you unless you do? Surely this is not going to be our only meeting?" She answered with a poem in which she said that names are of this world only and he would not care to know hers if he were resolved that their love should last till worlds to come. It was a mere quip and Genji, amused at her quickness, answered, "You are quite right. It was a mistake on my part to ask." And he recited the poem: "While still I seek to find on which blade dwells the dew, a great wind shakes the grasses of the level land." "If you did not repent of this meeting," he continued, "you would surely tell me who you are. I do not believe that you want. . . ." But here he was interrupted by the noise of people stirring in the next room. There was a great bustle and it was clear that they would soon be starting out to fetch Princess Koki-den back from the palace. There was just time to exchange fans in token of their new friendship before Genji was forced to fly precipitately from the room. In his own apartments he found many of his gentlemen waiting for him. Some were awake, and these nudged one another when he entered the room as though to say, "Will he never cease these disreputable excursions?" But discretion forbad them to show that they had seen him and they all pretended to be fast asleep. Genji too lay down, but he could not rest. He tried to recall the features of the lady with whom he had just spent so agreeable a time. Certainly she must be one of Kokiden's sisters. Perhaps the fifth or sixth daughter, both of whom were still unmarried. . . . But at present he could think of no way to make sure. She had not behaved at all as though she did not want to see him again. Why then had she refused to give him any chance of communicating with her? In fact he worried about the matter so much and turned it over in his mind with such endless persistency that it soon became evident he had fallen deeply in love with her. Nevertheless no sooner did the recollection of Fujitsubo's serious and reticent demeanour come back to his mind than he realized how incomparably more she meant to him than this light-hearted lady.

That day the after-banquet kept him occupied till late at night. At the Emperor's command he performed on the thirteen-stringed zithern and had an even greater success than with his dancing on the day before. At dawn Fujitsubo retired to the Emperor's rooms. Disappointed in his hope that the lady of last night would somewhere or somehow make her appearance on the scene, he sent for Yoshikiyo and Koremitsu with whom all his secrets were shared and bade them keep watch upon the lady's family. When he returned next day from duty at the Palace they reported that they had just witnessed the departure of several coaches which had been drawn up under shelter in the Courtyard of the Watch. "Among a group of persons who seemed to be the domestic attendants of those for whom the coaches were waiting two gentlemen came threading their way in a great hurry. These we recognized as Shii no Shosho and Uchuben, so there is little doubt that the carriages belonged to Princess Kokiden. For the rest we noted that the ladies were by no means ill-looking and that the whole party drove away in three carriages." Genji's heart beat fast. But he was no nearer than before to finding out which of the sisters it had been. Supposing her father, the Minister of the Right, should hear anything of this, what a to-do there would be! It would indeed mean his absolute ruin. It was a pity that while he was about it he did not stay with her till it was a little lighter. But there it was! He did not know her face, but yet he was determined to recognize her. How? . . . He still had her fan. It was a folding fan with ribs of hinoki-wood and tassels tied in a splice-knot. One side was covered with silverleaf on which was painted a dim moon, giving the impression of a moon reflected in water. It was a device which he had seen many times before, but it had agreeable associations for him, and continuing the metaphor of the "grass on the moor" which she had used in her poem, he wrote on the fan—"Has mortal man ever puzzled his head with such a question before as to ask where the moon goes to when she leaves the sky at dawn?" And he put the fan safely away. . . .

Fugitive as their meeting had been, it had sufficed to plunge the lady whose identity Prince Genji was now seeking to establish into the depths of despair; for in the fourth month she was to become the Heir Apparent's wife. Turmoil filled her brain. Why had not Genji visited her again? He must surely know whose daughter she was. But how should he know which daughter? Besides, her sister Kokiden's house was not a place where, save under very strange circumstances, he was likely to feel at all at his ease. And so she waited in great impatience and distress; but of Genji there was no news.

About the twentieth day of the third month her father, the Minister of the Right, held an archery meeting in which most of the young noblemen and princes were present. It was followed by a wistaria feast. The cherry blossom was for the most part over, but two trees, which the Minister seemed somehow to have persuaded to flower later than all the rest, were still an enchanting sight. He had had his house rebuilt only a short time ago when celebrating the initiation of his grand-daughters, the children of Kokiden. It was now a magnificent building and not a thing in it but was of the very latest fashion. He had invited Genji when he had met him at the Palace only a few days before and was extremely annoyed when he did not appear. . . . It was very late indeed when at last he [Genji] made his appearance at the party. He was dressed in a cloak of thin Chinese fabric, white outside but lined with yellow. His robe was of a deep wine-red colour with a very long train. The dignity and grace with which he carried this fancifully regal attire in a company where all were dressed in plain official robes were indeed remarkable, and in the end his presence perhaps contributed more to the success of the party than did the fragrance of the Minister's boasted flowers. His entry was followed by some very agreeable music. It was already fairly late when Genji, on the plea that the wine had given him a headache, left his seat and went for a walk. He knew that his two stepsisters, the daughters of Kokiden, were in the inner apartments of the palace. He went to the eastern portico and rested there. It was on this side of the house that the wistaria grew. The wooden blinds were raised and a number of ladies were leaning out of the window to enjoy the blossoms. They had hung bright-coloured robes and shawls over the windowsill just as is done at the time of the New Year dancing and other gala days and were behaving with a freedom of allure which contrasted very oddly with the sober decorum of Fujitsubo's household. "I am feeling rather overpowered by all the noise and bustle of the flower-party," Genji explained. "I am very sorry to disturb my sisters, but I can think of nowhere else to seek refuge . . ." and advancing towards the main door of the women's apartments, he pushed back the curtain with his shoulder. . . . A scent of costly perfumes pervaded the room; silken skirts rustled in the darkness. There could be little doubt that these were Kokiden's sisters and their friends. Deeply absorbed, as indeed was the whole of his family, in the fashionable gaieties of the moment, they had flouted decorum and posted themselves at the window that they might see what little they could of the banquet which was proceeding outside. Little thinking that his plan could succeed, yet led on by delightful recollections of his previous encounter, he advanced towards them chanting in a careless undertone the song:

> At Ishikawa, Ishikawa
> A man from Koma [Korea] took my belt away . . .

But for "belt" he substituted "fan" and by this means he sought to discover which of the ladies was his friend. "Why, you have got it wrong! I never heard of *that* Korean," one of them cried. Certainly it was not she. But there was another who though she remained silent seemed to him to be sighing softly to herself. He stole towards the curtain-of-state behind which she was sitting and taking her hand in his at a venture he whispered the poem: "If on this day of shooting my arrow went astray, 'twas that in dim morning twilight only the mark had glimmered in my view." And she, unable any longer to hide that she knew him, answered with the verse: "Had it been with the arrows of the heart that you had shot, though from the moon's slim bow no brightness came, would you have missed your mark?" Yes, it was her voice. He was delighted, and yet . . .

REFLECTIONS

Cultural comparisons, formerly a staple of historical studies, have come under harsh criticism in recent years, and for good reason. The ambitious general histories and philosophical anthropologies written at the beginning of the twentieth century were full of gross generalizations about the "essence" of various cultures and the advantages of one civilization over another. These grand overviews, predating serious empirical studies of African, Asian, and Latin American societies, invariably argued that such "pre-modern," or "traditional," societies lacked some critical cultural attribute honed in Europe that enabled Europeans to conquer the world after 1500. It goes without saying that these sweeping interpretations were written by Europeans and their North American descendants.

The comparative history of love got caught up in the whirlwind with historians and anthropologists, seeking to explain European expansion, industrialization, and modernization, arguing that conjugal love—the nonromantic familial variety—created family units in Europe and America that were different from those in other parts of the world. They saw the Western family as the stimulus of modern society. Still others found the Western practices of dating, mate choosing, and individual decision making unique.

Toward the end of the twentieth century, in a postcolonial age that had grown skeptical of Western claims of objectivity, cultural comparisons were seen for what they often were—thinly veiled exercises in self-aggrandizement and implicit rationales for Western domination. For example, Western scientific racism, in which the reigning Western anthropologists and scientists divided the world by cranial sizes, nose width, or culture-bound intelligence tests (always putting themselves on top), came crashing down, after its rationale was exposed as the foundation for the horrific genocides of World War II. `

There is a growing debate about the strategy of explaining Western growth and dominance by looking for Western traits that non-Western cultures lacked. But whether or not such a strategy is wise, we would

be foolish to stop trying to compare cultures. Cultures are rich reposi-
tories of human thought and behavior; they differ over time and across
the globe; and the process of comparison is essential to learning and
creating knowledge. In any case, historical comparisons should not be
about establishing which culture is better or worse. Culture, almost by
definition, is good for the particular society in which it arises. That
people in different parts of the world have found different ways of dealing with the same human problems should not surprise us. To call some
better than others is meaningless.

What we can learn from cultural comparison is something about
the malleability of human nature and the range of options available to
us. We also learn much about ourselves when we peer at another face
in the mirror. The differences leap out at us over time as well as space.
In some ways, Ulrich's mirror is as foreign as Genji's. In other ways it is
not. Both reflect elements of our own culture, call it European, Western, global, or something else. In response to an age of prejudice and
cultural stereotyping, many well-intentioned people choose to deny or
celebrate cultural differences. A far wiser course is to understand what
these differences reveal about our world and us.

10

The First Crusade

Muslims, Christians, and Jews during the First Crusade, 1095–1099 C.E.

HISTORICAL CONTEXT

In the eleventh century the Seljuk Turks, recently converted to Islam, emerged from the grasslands of central Asia to conquer much of the land held by the weakened Caliphate at Baghdad, the Egyptian Fatimid Caliphate, and the Byzantine Empire. By 1095 the Seljuks controlled the important cities of Baghdad and Jerusalem and threatened to take Constantinople.

Alexius, the Byzantine emperor, appealed to the Roman pope for help and found a receptive audience. Pope Urban II was continuing recent papal efforts to strengthen the Roman church's power over the scattered nobles and princes of European feudal society. He sought to reform the church of abuses such as the sale of church offices, and to bring peace to the fractious countryside, riddled with private armies of knights that fought each other or preyed on Christian peasants. Urban II's efforts to revitalize Christendom found a mission in the Seljuk occupation of Jerusalem, and in 1095 the First Crusade began with his urgent call for Christians to rout the new Muslim occupiers of the Holy Land. (See Map 10.1.)

The Crusades were an important chapter in the religious and military history—or more broadly, the cultural and political history—of both European and Islamic civilizations. They brought large numbers of European Christians and Muslims into contact with each other in a struggle and dialogue that would last for centuries.

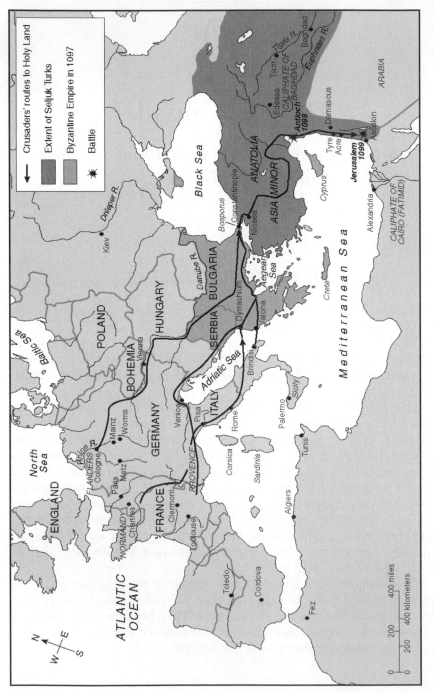

Map 10.1 The First Crusade, 1096–1099.

THINKING HISTORICALLY
Analyzing and Writing Narrative

When most people think of history, they think of narrative—the story itself. Narrative settles on specific details—one at a time—neither indiscriminately nor as examples of general laws, but usually chronologically, as they happen, woven in a chain of cause and effect. The "truth" of narrative is different from that of social science, which aspires to generality. The social scientist writes, "Holy wars among states are a dime a dozen." The narrative historian immerses us in the specific details of the battle: "The Duke's trumpets sounded, the shimmering line swayed forward, the long lances came down to point at the foe, their pennons shadowing the ground before them." A good narrative has the appeal of a good story: It places the reader on the scene, enables us to feel the drama of the moment, to experience what happened as it happened.

In this chapter you will read a number of brief narratives about the Crusades. You will analyze each narrative for what it tells you and to reflect on the way the story conveys that information, and then you will be encouraged to write your own narrative.

Keep in mind that narrative, or storytelling, is only one way of providing information. Storytelling is often considered a low-level skill, less sophisticated than analysis or synthesis. In college classes instructors will often say: "Don't just tell me the story" when they want you to analyze or make comparisons. Most professional historians write analytical books devoted to answering a particular historical question or challenging an interpretation. Generally historians only write narratives for a popular audience, not for each other. But the power of narrative is so strong some have even suggested that we might be hardwired for story telling—that we ought to be aware of how this form of knowing and presenting affects our understanding of historical events.

60

FULCHER OF CHARTRES
Pope Urban at Clermont

The Chronicle of Fulcher of Chartres is one of the few firsthand accounts of the First Crusade. Born in 1059, Fulcher was present at the Council of Clermont, where Pope Urban II issued his call for the First Crusade in 1095. In response to Urban's plea, Fulcher joined the army of Robert of Normandy, Stephen of Blois, and Robert of Flanders. He then joined Baldwin of Boulogne in Edessa (see Map 10.1, p. 338), the first Crusader state, and later visited Jerusalem after its capture by the Crusaders. In 1100 when Baldwin became King of Jerusalem, Fulcher returned to the Holy City to become his chaplain. There he wrote his history from 1101 until about 1128. The reliability of Fulcher's Chronicles, therefore, depends on his important contacts as well as his own observations.

Why, according to Fulcher, did Pope Urban II call the Council of Clermont? What did he hope to accomplish? How important among the pope's concerns was the capture of Jerusalem? How important was strengthening the Church?

Thinking Historically

What indications do you see in Urban's speech that the call to capture Jerusalem was only part of his agenda, perhaps even an afterthought? Fulcher's account of the speech and his section on "events after the council" mainly address the issue of Jerusalem. That emphasis is appropriate in a history of the crusade. A historical narrative must follow a particular thread. If Fulcher was writing a history of church reforms rather than of the First Crusade, what kind of "events after the council" might he have included?

A narrative, or story, is different from an explanation. What do you think were the causes of the First Crusade, based on what you have read so far? How is your answer an explanation rather than a narrative? How would you make your answer more of a narrative?

The First Crusade: The Chronicle of Fulcher of Chartres and Other Source Materials, 2nd ed., ed. Edward Peters (Philadelphia: University of Pennsylvania Press, 1998), 49–55.

I. The Council of Clermont

1. In the year 1095 from the Lord's Incarnation, with Henry reigning in Germany as so-called emperor,[1] and with Philip as king in France, manifold evils were growing in all parts of Europe because of wavering faith. In Rome ruled Pope Urban II, a man distinguished in life and character, who always strove wisely and actively to raise the status of the Holy Church above all things.

2. He saw that the faith of Christianity was being destroyed to excess by everybody, by the clergy as well as by the laity. He saw that peace was altogether discarded by the princes of the world, who were engaged in incessant warlike contention and quarreling among themselves. He saw the wealth of the land being pillaged continuously. He saw many of the vanquished, wrongfully taken prisoner and very cruelly thrown into foulest dungeons, either ransomed for a high price or, tortured by the triple torments of hunger, thirst, and cold, blotted out by a death hidden from the world. He saw holy places violated; monasteries and villas burned. He saw that no one was spared of any human suffering, and that things divine and human alike were held in derision.

3. He heard, too, that the interior regions of Romania, where the Turks ruled over the Christians, had been perniciously subjected in a savage attack.[2] Moved by long-suffering compassion and by love of God's will, he descended the mountains to Gaul, and in Auvergne he called for a council to congregate from all sides at a suitable time at a city called Clermont. Three hundred and ten bishops and abbots, who had been advised beforehand by messengers, were present.

4. Then, on the day set aside for it, he called them together to himself and, in an eloquent address, carefully made the cause of the meeting known to them. In the plaintive voice of an aggrieved Church, he expressed great lamentation, and held a long discourse with them about the raging tempests of the world, which have been mentioned, because faith was undermined.

5. One after another, he beseechingly exhorted them all, with renewed faith, to spur themselves in great earnestness to overcome the Devil's devices and to try to restore the Holy Church, most unmercifully weakened by the wicked, to its former honorable status.

---

[1]Henry IV (1056–1106). Fulcher uses the term "so-called emperor," since Henry was not recognized as rightful emperor by adherents of Gregory VII and Urban II.

[2]This refers to the Seljuk conquest of Anatolia, probably to Manzikert, 1071.

II. *The Decree of Pope Urban in the Council*

1. "Most beloved brethren," he said, "by God's permission placed over the whole world with the papal crown, I, Urban, as the messenger of divine admonition, have been compelled by an unavoidable occasion to come here to you servants of God. I desired those whom I judged to be stewards of God's ministries to be true stewards and faithful, with all hypocrisy rejected.[3]

2. "But with temperance in reason and justice being remote, I, with divine aid, shall strive carefully to root out any crookedness or distortion which might obstruct God's law. For the Lord appointed you temporarily as stewards over His family to serve it nourishment seasoned with a modest savor. Moreover, blessed will you be if at last the Overseer find you faithful.[4]

3. "You are also called shepherds; see that you are not occupied after the manner of mercenaries. Be true shepherds, always holding your crooks in your hands; and sleeping not, guard on every side the flock entrusted to you.

4. "For if through your carelessness or negligence, some wolf seizes a sheep, you doubtless will lose the reward prepared for you by our Lord.[5] Nay, first most cruelly beaten by the whips of the lictors, you afterwards will be angrily cast into the keeping of a deadly place.

5. "Likewise, according to the evangelical sermon, you are the 'salt of the earth.'[6] But if you fail, it will be disputed wherewith it was salted. O how much saltiness, indeed, is necessary for you to salt the people in correcting them with the salt of wisdom, people who are ignorant and panting with desire after the wantonness of the world; so that, unsalted, they might not be rotten with sins and stink whenever the Lord might wish to exhort them.

6. "For if because of the sloth of your management, He should find in them worms, that is, sin, straightway, He will order that they, despised, be cast into the dungheap. And because you could not make restoration for such a great loss, He will banish you, utterly condemned in judgment, from the familiarity of His love.

7. "It behooves saltiness of this kind to be wise, provident, temperate, learned, peace-making, truth-seeking, pious, just, equitable, pure. For how will the unlearned be able to make men learned, the intemper-

---

[3]Reference to I Corinthians 4:1, 2.
[4]Reference to Matthew 24:45, 46.
[5]Reference to John 10:12–16.
[6]Matthew 5:13.

ate make temperate, the impure make them pure? If one despises peace, how will he appease? Or if one has dirty hands, how will he be able to wipe the filth off another one defiled? For it is read, 'If the blind lead the blind, both shall fall into a ditch.'[7]

8. "Set yourselves right before you do others, so that you can blamelessly correct your subjects. If you wish to be friends of God, gladly practice those things which you feel will please Him.

9. "Especially establish ecclesiastical affairs firm in their own right, so that no simoniac heresy will take root among you. Take care lest the vendors and moneychangers, flayed by the scourges of the Lord, be miserably driven out into the narrow streets of destruction.[8]

10. "Uphold the Church in its own ranks altogether free from all secular power. See that the tithes of all those who cultivate the earth are given faithfully to God; let them not be sold or held back.

11. "Let him who has seized a bishop be considered an outlaw. Let him who has seized or robbed monks, clerics, nuns and their servants, pilgrims, or merchants, be excommunicated. Let the robbers and burners of homes and their accomplices, banished from the Church, be smitten with excommunication.

12. "It must be considered very carefully, as Gregory says, by what penalty he must be punished who seizes other men's property, if he who does not bestow his own liberally is condemned to Hell. For so it happened to the rich man in the well-known Gospel, who on that account was not punished because he had taken away the property of others, but because he had misused that which he had received.

13. "And so by these iniquities, most beloved, you have seen the world disturbed too long; so long, as it was told to us by those reporting, that perhaps because of the weakness of your justice in some parts of your provinces, no one dares to walk in the streets with safety, lest he be kidnapped by robbers by day or thieves by night, either by force or trickery, at home or outside.

14. "Wherefore the Truce,[9] as it is commonly called, now for a long time established by the Holy Fathers, must be renewed. In admonition, I entreat you to adhere to it most firmly in your own bishopric. But if anyone affected by avarice or pride breaks it of his own free will, let him be excommunicated by God's authority and by the sanction of the decrees of this Holy Council."

---

[7]Matthew 15:14.

[8]Reference to John 2:15.

[9]Truce of God—Cessation of all feuds from Wednesday evening to Monday morning in every week and during church festivals, ordered by the Church in 1041. This was proclaimed anew at the Council of Clermont.

III. The Pope's Exhortation Concerning
the Expedition to Jerusalem

1. These and many other things having been suitably disposed of, all those present, both clergy and people, at the words of Lord Urban, the Pope, voluntarily gave thanks to God and confirmed by a faithful promise that his decrees would be well kept. But straightway he added that another thing not less than the tribulation already spoken of, but even greater and more oppressive, was injuring Christianity in another part of the world, saying:

2. "Now that you, O sons of God, have consecrated yourselves to God to maintain peace among yourselves more vigorously and to uphold the laws of the Church faithfully, there is work to do, for you must turn the strength of your sincerity, now that you are aroused by divine correction, to another affair that concerns you and God. Hastening to the way, you must help your brothers living in the Orient, who need your aid for which they have already cried out many times.

3. "For, as most of you have been told, the Turks, a race of Persians,[10] who have penetrated within the boundaries of Romania[11] even to the Mediterranean to that point which they call the Arm of Saint George, in occupying more and more of the lands of the Christians, have overcome them, already victims of seven battles, and have killed and captured them, have overthrown churches, and have laid waste God's kingdom. If you permit this supinely for very long, God's faithful ones will be still further subjected.

4. "Concerning this affair, I, with suppliant prayer—not I, but the Lord—exhort you, heralds of Christ, to persuade all of whatever class, both knights and footmen, both rich and poor, in numerous edicts, to strive to help expel that wicked race from our Christian lands before it is too late.

5. "I speak to those present, I send word to those not here; moreover, Christ commands it. Remission of sins will be granted for those going thither, if they end a shackled life either on land or in crossing the sea, or in struggling against the heathen. I, being vested with that gift from God, grant this to those who go.

6. "O what a shame, if a people, so despised, degenerate, and enslaved by demons would thus overcome a people endowed with the trust of almighty God, and shining in the name of Christ! O how many evils will be imputed to you by the Lord Himself, if you do not help those who, like you, profess Christianity!

---

[10]Really Seljuk Turks who conquered lands from east to west by way of Persia.

[11]Fulcher uses the term *Romania* to refer to the Anatolian as well as to the European provinces of the Byzantine Empire, but here, of course, he means the Anatolian. The Seljuks called the state which they founded here *Rum*.

7. "Let those," he said, "who are accustomed to wage private wars wastefully even against Believers, go forth against the Infidels in a battle worthy to be undertaken now and to be finished in victory. Now, let those, who until recently existed as plunderers, be soldiers of Christ; now, let those, who formerly contended against brothers and relations, rightly fight barbarians; now, let those, who recently were hired for a few pieces of silver, win their eternal reward. Let those, who wearied themselves to the detriment of body and soul, labor for a twofold honor. Nay, more, the sorrowful here will be glad there, the poor here will be rich there, and the enemies of the Lord here will be His friends there.

8. "Let no delay postpone the journey of those about to go, but when they have collected the money owed to them and the expenses for the journey, and when winter has ended and spring has come, let them enter the crossroads courageously with the Lord going on before."

IV. The Bishop of Puy and the Events after the Council

1. After these words were spoken, the hearers were fervently inspired. Thinking nothing more worthy than such an undertaking, many in the audience solemnly promised to go, and to urge diligently those who were absent. There was among them one Bishop of Puy, Ademar by name, who afterwards, acting as vicar-apostolic, ruled the whole army of God wisely and thoughtfully, and spurred them to complete their undertaking vigorously.

2. So, the things that we have told you were well established and confirmed by everybody in the Council. With the blessing of absolution given, they departed; and after returning to their homes, they disclosed to those not knowing, what had taken place. As it was decreed far and wide throughout the provinces, they established the peace, which they call the Truce, to be upheld mutually by oath.

3. Many, one after another, of any and every occupation, after confession of their sins and with purified spirits, consecrated themselves to go where they were bidden.

4. Oh, how worthy and delightful to all of us who saw those beautiful crosses, either silken or woven of gold, or of any material, which the pilgrims sewed on the shoulders of their woolen cloaks or cassocks by the command of the Pope, after taking the vow to go. To be sure, God's soldiers, who were making themselves ready to battle for His honor, ought to have been marked and fortified with a sign of victory. And so by embroidering the symbol [of the cross] on their clothing in recognition of their faith, in the end they won the True Cross itself. They imprinted the ideal so that they might attain the reality of the ideal.

5. It is plain that good meditation leads to doing good work and that good work wins salvation of the soul. But, if it is good to mean well, it is better, after reflection, to carry out the good intention. So, it is best to win salvation through action worthy of the soul to be saved. Let each and everyone, therefore, reflect upon the good, that he makes better in fulfillment, so that, deserving it, he might finally receive the best, which does not diminish in eternity.

6. In such a manner Urban, a wise man and reverenced,
Meditated a labor, whereby the world florescenced.

For he renewed peace and restored the laws of the Church to their former standards; also he tried with vigorous instigation to expel the heathen from the lands of the Christians. And since he strove to exalt all things of God in every way, almost everyone gladly surrendered in obedience to his paternal care. . . .

61

Chronicle of Solomon bar Simson

Solomon bar Simson (who is known only from this chronicle) provides the most complete of the Hebrew chronicles of the First Crusade. He takes up the story after Pope Urban II's appeal. Franks and Germans have organized their armies of knights, suppliers, aides, and followers, and have set off for Jerusalem by way of Constantinople. Why did these Crusaders stop at Mainz* and other German cities to murder Jews?

Thinking Historically

This narrative, like the previous selection, includes quotations from speeches. How can you tell that some of these quotations do not contain the exact words that were spoken?

Solomon bar Simson's narrative contains another element that, while absent from modern histories, is found in other narratives of the Crusades and is especially pronounced here. This is not just a narra-

*myntz

"Chronicle of Solomon bar Simson," in *The Jews and the Crusaders: The Hebrew Chronicles of the First and Second Crusades*, ed. and trans. Shlomo Eidelberg (Madison: University of Wisconsin Press, 1977), 21–26.

tive of human action and intention, but it interprets divine action and intention as well. Why is this narrative strategy necessary for this author? If you were writing a narrative of the Crusades today, would you want to tell both of these stories, or only the human one? Why?

I will now recount the event of this persecution in other martyred communities as well—the extent to which they clung to the Lord, God of their fathers, bearing witness to His Oneness to their last breath.

In the year four thousand eight hundred and fifty-six, the year one thousand twenty-eight of our exile, in the eleventh year of the cycle Ranu, the year in which we anticipated salvation and solace, in accordance with the prophecy of Jeremiah: "Sing with gladness for Jacob, and shout at the head of the nations," etc.—this year turned instead to sorrow and groaning, weeping and outcry. Inflicted upon the Jewish People were the many evils related in all the admonitions; those enumerated in Scripture as well as those unwritten were visited upon us.

At this time arrogant people, a people of strange speech, a nation bitter and impetuous, Frenchmen and Germans, set out for the Holy City, which had been desecrated by barbaric nations, there to seek their house of idolatry and banish the Ishmaelites and other denizens of the land and conquer the land for themselves. They decorated themselves prominently with their signs, placing a profane symbol—a horizontal line over a vertical one—on the vestments of every man and woman whose heart yearned to go on the stray path to the grave of their Messiah. Their ranks swelled until the number of men, women, and children exceeded a locust horde covering the earth; of them it was said: "The locusts have no king [yet go they forth all of them by bands]." Now it came to pass that as they passed through the towns where Jews dwelled, they said to one another: "Look now, we are going a long way to seek out the profane shrine and to avenge ourselves on the Ishmaelites, when here, in our very midst, are the Jews—they whose forefathers murdered and crucified him for no reason. Let us first avenge ourselves on them and exterminate them from among the nations so that the name of Israel will no longer be remembered, or let them adopt our faith and acknowledge the offspring of promiscuity."

When the Jewish communities became aware of their intentions, they resorted to the custom of our ancestors, repentance, prayer, and charity. The hands of the Holy Nation turned faint at this time, their hearts melted, and their strength flagged. They hid in their innermost rooms to escape the swirling sword. They subjected themselves to great endurance, abstaining from food and drink for three consecutive days and nights, and then fasting many days from sunrise to sunset, until their skin was shriveled and dry as wood upon their bones. And they cried out loudly and bitterly to God.

But their Father did not answer them; He obstructed their prayers, concealing Himself in a cloud through which their prayers could not pass, and He abhorred their tent, and He removed them out of His sight—all of this having been decreed by Him to take place "in the day when I visit"; and this was the generation that had been chosen by Him to be His portion, for they had the strength and the fortitude to stand in His Sanctuary, and fulfill His word, and sanctify His Great Name in His world. It is of such as these that King David said: "Bless the Lord, ye angels of His, ye almighty in strength, that fulfil His word," etc.

That year, Passover fell on Thursday, and the New Moon of the following month, Iyar, fell on Friday and the Sabbath. On the eighth day of Iyar, on the Sabbath, the foe attacked the community of Speyer and murdered eleven holy souls who sanctified their Creator on the holy Sabbath and refused to defile themselves by adopting the faith of their foe. There was a distinguished, pious woman there who slaughtered herself in sanctification of God's Name. She was the first among all the communities of those who were slaughtered. The remainder were saved by the local bishop without defilement [i.e., baptism], as described above.

On the twenty-third of Iyar they attacked the community of Worms.[1] The community was then divided into two groups; some remained in their homes and others fled to the local bishop seeking refuge. Those who remained in their homes were set upon by the steppe-wolves who pillaged men, women, and infants, children, and old people. They pulled down the stairways and destroyed the houses, looting and plundering; and they took the Torah Scroll, trampled it in the mud, and tore and burned it. The enemy devoured the children of Israel with open maw.

Seven days later, on the New Moon of Sivan—the very day on which the Children of Israel arrived at Mount Sinai to receive the Torah—those Jews who were still in the court of the bishop were subjected to great anguish. The enemy dealt them the same cruelty as the first group and put them to the sword. The Jews, inspired by the valor of their brethren, similarly chose to be slain in order to sanctify the Name before the eyes of all, and exposed their throats for their heads to be severed for the glory of the Creator. There were also those who took their own lives, thus fulfilling the verse: "The mother was dashed in pieces with her children." Fathers fell upon their sons, being slaughtered upon one another, and they slew one another—each man his kin, his wife and children; bridegrooms slew their betrothed, and merciful

---

[1]Town in the Holy Roman Empire (now Germany). [Ed.]

women their only children. They all accepted the divine decree whole-heartedly and, as they yielded up their souls to the Creator, cried out: "Hear, O Israel, the Lord is our God, the Lord is One." The enemy stripped them naked, dragged them along, and then cast them off, sparing only a small number whom they forcibly baptized in their profane waters. The number of those slain during the two days was approximately eight hundred—and they were all buried naked. It is of these that the Prophet Jeremiah lamented: "They that were brought up in scarlet embrace dunghills." I have already cited their names above. May God remember them for good.

When the saints, the pious ones of the Most High, the holy community of Mainz, whose merit served as shield and protection for all the communities and whose fame had spread throughout the many provinces, heard that some of the community of Speyer had been slain and that the community of Worms had been attacked a second time, and that the sword would soon reach them, their hands became faint and their hearts melted and became as water. They cried out to the Lord with all their hearts, saying: "O Lord, God of Israel, will You completely annihilate the remnant of Israel? Where are all your wonders which our forefathers related to us, saying: 'Did You not bring us up from Egypt and from Babylonia and rescue us on numerous occasions?' How, then, have You now forsaken and abandoned us, O Lord, giving us over into the hands of evil Edom so that they may destroy us? Do not remove Yourself from us, for adversity is almost upon us and there is no one to aid us."

The leaders of the Jews gathered together and discussed various ways of saving themselves. They said: "Let us elect elders so that we may know how to act, for we are consumed by this great evil." The elders decided to ransom the community by generously giving of their money and bribing the various princes and deputies and bishops and governors. Then, the community leaders who were respected by the local bishop approached him and his officers and servants to negotiate this matter. They asked: "What shall we do about the news we have received regarding the slaughter of our brethren in Speyer and Worms?" They [the Gentiles] replied: "Heed our advice and bring all your money into our treasury. You, your wives, and your children, and all your belongings shall come into the courtyard of the bishop until the hordes have passed by. Thus will you be saved from the errant ones."

Actually, they gave this advice so as to herd us together and hold us like fish that are caught in an evil net, and then to turn us over to the enemy, while taking our money. This is what actually happened in the end, and "the outcome is proof of the intentions." The bishop assembled his ministers and courtiers—mighty ministers, the noblest in the land—for the purpose of helping us; for at first it had been his desire to save us with all his might, since we had given him and his ministers and servants a large bribe in return for their promise to help us. Ultimately, however, all the bribes and entreaties were of no avail to protect us on the day of wrath and misfortune.

It was at this time that Duke Godfrey [of Bouillon], may his bones be ground to dust, arose in the hardness of his spirit, driven by a spirit of wantonness to go with those journeying to the profane shrine, vowing to go on this journey only after avenging the blood of the crucified one by shedding Jewish blood and completely eradicating any trace of those bearing the name "Jew," thus assuaging his own burning wrath. To be sure, there arose someone to repair the breach—a God-fearing man who had been bound to the most holy of altars—called Rabbi Kalonymos, the *Parnass*[2] of the community of Mainz. He dispatched a messenger to King Henry in the kingdom of Pula, where the king had been dwelling during the past nine years, and related all that had happened.

The king was enraged and dispatched letters to all the ministers, bishops, and governors of all the provinces of his realm, as well as to Duke Godfrey, containing words of greeting and commanding them to do no bodily harm to the Jews and to provide them with help and refuge. The evil duke then swore that he had never intended to do them harm. The Jews of Cologne nevertheless bribed him with five hundred *zekukim* of silver, as did the Jews of Mainz. The duke assured them of his support and promised them peace.

However, God, the maker of peace, turned aside and averted His eyes from His people, and consigned them to the sword. No prophet, seer, or man of wise heart was able to comprehend how the sin of the people infinite in number was deemed so great as to cause the destruction of so many lives in the various Jewish communities. The martyrs endured the extreme penalty normally inflicted only upon one guilty of murder. Yet, it must be stated with certainty that God is a righteous judge, and we are to blame.

Then the evil waters prevailed. The enemy unjustly accused them of evil acts they did not do, declaring: "You are the children of those who killed our object of veneration, hanging him on a tree, and he himself had said: 'There will yet come a day when my children will come and avenge my blood.' We are his children and it is therefore obligatory for us to avenge him since you are the ones who rebel and disbelieve in him. Your God has never been at peace with you. Although He intended to deal kindly with you, you have conducted yourselves improperly before Him. God has forgotten you and is no longer desirous of you since you are a stubborn nation. Instead, He has departed from you and has taken us for His portion, casting His radiance upon us."

[2]Reference to the Greek mountain Parnassus, perhaps meaning "mainstay" of the community. [Ed.]

When we heard these words, our hearts trembled and moved out of their places. We were dumb with silence, abiding in darkness, like those long dead, waiting for the Lord to look forth and behold from heaven.

And Satan—the Pope of evil Rome—also came and proclaimed to all the nations believing in that stock of adultery—these are the stock of Seir[3]—that they should assemble and ascend to Jerusalem so as to conquer the city, and journey to the tomb of the superstition whom they call their god. Satan came and mingled with the nations, and they gathered as one man to fulfill the command, coming in great numbers like the grains of sand upon the seashore, the noise of them clamorous as a whirlwind and a storm. When the drops of the bucket had assembled, they took evil counsel against the people of the Lord and said: "Why should we concern ourselves with going to war against the Ishmaelites dwelling about Jerusalem, when in our midst is a people who disrespect our god—indeed, their ancestors are those who crucified him. Why should we let them live and tolerate their dwelling among us? Let us commence by using our swords against them and then proceed upon our stray path."

The heart of the people of our God grew faint and their spirit flagged, for many sore injuries had been inflicted upon them and they had been smitten repeatedly. They now came supplicating to God and fasting, and their hearts melted within them. But the Lord did as He declared, for we had sinned before Him, and He forsook the sanctuary of Shiloh—the Temple-in-Miniature—which He had placed among His people who dwelt in the midst of alien nations. His wrath was kindled and He drew the sword against them, until they remained but as the flagstaff upon the mountaintop and as the ensign on the hill, and He gave over His nation into captivity and trampled them underfoot. See, O Lord, and consider to whom Thou hast done thus: to Israel, a nation despised and pillaged, Your chosen portion! Why have You uplifted the shield of its enemies, and why have they gained in strength? Let all hear, for I cry out in anguish; the ears of all that hear me shall be seared: How has the staff of might been broken, the rod of glory—the sainted community comparable to fine gold, the community of Mainz! It was caused by the Lord to test those that fear Him, to have them endure the yoke of His pure fear. . . .

[3]An enemy of ancient Israel.

62

ANNA COMNENA
From The Alexiad

Anna Comnena was the daughter of Emperor Alexius (r. 1081–1118) of Byzantium. Threatened on three sides—by the Seljuk Turks to the east, the Norman Kingdom of southern Italy to the west, and rebellions to the north—Alexius appealed for aid to Pope Urban II of Rome in 1095. He expected a mercenary army, but because the pope saw a chance to send a massive force against Muslim occupiers of Jerusalem as well as against those threatening Constantinople, Alexius instead received an uncontrollable ragtag force of Christians and Crusaders that included his Norman enemies, led by Bohemond.

Princess Anna, the emperor's daughter, recalled the story of the First Crusade's appearance in Byzantium some forty years later in her history titled *The Alexiad* after her father. According to Anna, how did Alexius respond to the approach of the Crusader army? Did Alexius fear the Franks more than he feared the Turks?

Thinking Historically

This is a third perspective on the history of the First Crusade—the view of a Christian ally of Rome, more directly threatened than the Roman church by the Muslim armies. Yet, Byzantium and Rome were also at odds. Since 1054, they had accepted a parting of ways, theologically and institutionally. And with the advancing Frankish armies, Anna and Alexius were not sure whether they were facing friend or foe. How does Anna's critical perspective change our idea of the Crusaders? How might her idea of the Franks change our narrative of the early stage of the crusade?

Notice how this narrative combines a sequence of events with generalizations (often about the "race" or nature of the Franks) to explain specific events. Does a narrative history have to include generalizations as well as a sequence of specific events? Can the events alone provide sufficient explanation?

Anna Comnena, *The Alexiad of the Princess Anna Comnena*, trans. Elizabeth A. S. Dawes (London: Routledge & Kegan Paul Ltd., 1967), 247–52. Reprinted in William H. McNeill and Schuyler O. Houser, *Medieval Europe* (Oxford: Oxford University Press, 1971), 135–40.

Before he had enjoyed even a short rest, he heard a report of the approach of innumerable Frankish armies. Now he dreaded their arrival for he knew their irresistible manner of attack, their unstable and mobile character and all the peculiar natural and concomitant characteristics which the Frank retains throughout; and he also knew that they were always agape for money, and seemed to disregard their truces readily for any reason that cropped up. For he had always heard this reported of them, and found it very true. However, he did not lose heart, but prepared himself in every way so that, when the occasion called, he would be ready for battle. And indeed the actual facts were far greater and more terrible than rumour made them. For the whole of the West and all the barbarian tribes which dwell between the further side of the Adriatic and the pillars of Heracles, had all migrated in a body and were marching into Asia through the intervening Europe, and were making the journey with all their household. The reason of this upheaval was more or less the following. A certain Frank, Peter by name, nicknamed Cucupeter, had gone to worship at the Holy Sepulchre and after suffering many things at the hands of the Turks and Saracens who were ravaging Asia, he got back to his own country with difficulty. But he was angry at having failed in his object, and wanted to undertake the same journey again. However, he saw that he ought not to make the journey to the Holy Sepulchre alone again, lest worse things befall him, so he worked out a cunning plan. This was to preach in all the Latin countries that "the voice of God bids me announce to all the Counts in France" that they should all leave their homes and set out to worship at the Holy Sepulchre, and to endeavour wholeheartedly with hand and mind to deliver Jerusalem from the hand of Hagarenes.[1] And he really succeeded. For after inspiring the souls of all with this quasi-divine command he contrived to assemble the Franks from all sides, one after the other, with arms, horses and all the other paraphernalia of war. And they were all so zealous and eager that every highroad was full of them. And those Frankish soldiers were accompanied by an unarmed host more numerous than the sand or the stars, carrying palms and crosses on their shoulders, women and children, too, came away from their countries and the sight of them was like many rivers streaming from all sides, and they were advancing towards us through Dacia generally with all their hosts. Now the coming of these many peoples was preceded by a locust which did not touch the wheat, but made a terrible attack on the vines. This was really a presage as the diviners of the time interpreted it, and meant that this enormous Frankish army would, when it came, refrain from interference in Christian affairs, but fall very heavily upon the barbarian

---

[1]Saracens, who were considered "children of Hagar" (cf. Gen. 16). [Ed.]

Ishmaelites who were slaves to drunkenness, wine, and Dionysus.[2] For this race is under the sway of Dionysus and Eros,[3] rushes headlong into all kind of sexual intercourse, and is not circumcised either in the flesh or in their passions. It is nothing but a slave, nay triply enslaved, to the ills wrought by Aphrodite. For this reason they worship and adore Astarte and Ashtaroth[4] too and value above all the image of the moon, and the golden figure of Hobar[5] in their country. Now in these symbols Christianity was taken to be the corn because of its wineless and very nutritive qualities; in this manner the diviners interpreted the vines and the wheat. However let the matter of the prophecy rest.

The incidents of the barbarians' approach followed in the order I have described, and persons of intelligence could feel that they were witnessing a strange occurrence. The arrival of these multitudes did not take place at the same time nor by the same road (for how indeed could such masses starting from different places have crossed the straits of Lombardy all together?). Some first, some next, others after them and thus successively all accomplished the transit, and then marched through the Continent. Each army was preceded, as we said, by an unspeakable number of locusts; and all who saw this more than once recognized them as forerunners of the Frankish armies. When the first of them began crossing the straits of Lombardy sporadically the Emperor summoned certain leaders of the Roman forces, and sent them to the parts of Dyrrachium and Valona[6] with instructions to offer a courteous welcome to the Franks who had crossed, and to collect abundant supplies from all the countries along their route; then to follow and watch them covertly all the time, and if they saw them making any foraging-excursions, they were to come out from under cover and check them by light skirmishing. These captains were accompanied by some men who knew the Latin tongue, so that they might settle any disputes that arose between them.

Let me, however, give an account of this subject more clearly and in due order. According to universal rumour Godfrey,[7] who sold his country, was the first to start on the appointed road; this man was very rich and very proud of his bravery, courage and conspicuous lineage; for every Frank is anxious to outdo the others. And such an upheaval

---

[2]Anna's account of the beliefs of the Muslims was highly biased. Muhammad forbade his followers to drink intoxicating liquors.

[3]Dionysus was the Greek god associated with wine and revelry; Eros was the patron of lovers, and son of Aphrodite, goddess of love.

[4]Names of the Semitic goddess of fertility.

[5]I.e., Hathor, the Egyptian goddess of love, usually depicted with the head of a cow. (N.B. Idol worship was strictly forbidden by Islamic law.)

[6]Ports on the Adriatic, directly opposite the heel of Italy in modern Albania.

[7]Godfrey of Bouillon, the duke of Lower Lorraine (c. 1060–1100). To raise money for the Crusade, he sold two of his estates, and pledged his castle at Bouillon to the bishop of Liège.

of both men and women took place then as had never occurred within human memory, the simpler-minded were urged on by the real desire of worshipping at our Lord's Sepulchre, and visiting the sacred places; but the more astute, especially men like Bohemund and those of like mind, had another secret reason, namely, the hope that while on their travels they might by some means be able to seize the capital [Constantinople] itself, looking upon this as a kind of corollary. And Bohemund disturbed the minds of many nobler men by thus cherishing his old grudge against the Emperor. Meanwhile Peter, after he had delivered his message, crossed the straits of Lombardy before anybody else with eighty thousand men on foot, and one hundred thousand on horseback, and reached the capital by way of Hungary.[8] For the Frankish race, as one may conjecture, is always very hotheaded and eager, but when once it has espoused a cause, it is uncontrollable.

The Emperor, knowing what Peter had suffered before from the Turks, advised him to wait for the arrival of the other Counts, but Peter would not listen for he trusted the multitude of his followers, so he crossed and pitched his camp near a small town called Helenopolis.[9] After him followed the Normans numbering ten thousand, who separated themselves from the rest of the army and devastated the country round Nicaea, and behaved most cruelly to all. For they dismembered some of the children and fixed others on wooden spits and roasted them at the fire, and on persons advanced in age they inflicted every kind of torture. But when the inhabitants of Nicaea became aware of these doings, they threw open their gates and marched out upon them, and after a violent conflict had taken place they had to dash back inside their citadel as the Normans fought so bravely. And thus the latter recovered all the booty and returned to Helenopolis. Then a dispute arose between them and the others who had not gone out with them, as is usual in such cases, for the minds of those who stayed behind were aflame with envy, and thus caused a skirmish after which the headstrong Normans drew apart again, marched to Xerigordus[10] and took it by assault. When the Sultan[11] heard what had happened, he dispatched Elchanes[12] against them with a substantial force. He came, and recaptured Xerigordus and sacrificed some of the Normans to the sword, and took others captive, at the same time laid plans to catch those who had remained behind with Cucupeter. He placed ambushes in suitable spots so that any coming from the camp in the direction of Nicaea would fall into them unexpectedly and be killed. Besides this, as he knew the Franks' love of money, he sent for two active-minded men

---

[8]Peter's contingent probably numbered about twenty thousand including noncombatants.

[9]I.e., Peter moved his forces across the Bosphorus and into Asia Minor.

[10]A castle held by the Turks.

[11]Qilij Arslan I, ruled 1092–1106.

[12]An important Turkish military commander.

and ordered them to go to Cucupeter's camp and proclaim there that the Normans had gained possession of Nicaea, and were now dividing everything in it. When this report was circulated among Peter's followers, it upset them terribly. Directly [When] they heard the words "partition" and "money" they started in a disorderly crowd along the road to Nicaea, all but unmindful of their military experience and the discipline which is essential for those starting out to battle. For, as I remarked above, the Latin race is always very fond of money, but more especially when it is bent on raiding a country; it then loses its reason and gets beyond control. As they journeyed neither in ranks nor in squadrons, they fell foul of the Turkish ambuscades near the river Dracon and perished miserably. And such a large number of Franks and Normans were the victims of the Ishmaelite sword, that when they piled up the corpses of the slaughtered men which were lying on either side they formed, I say, not a very large hill or mound or a peak, but a high mountain as it were, of very considerable depth and breadth—so great was the pyramid of bones. And later men of the same tribe as the slaughtered barbarians built a wall and used the bones of the dead to fill the interstices as if they were pebbles, and thus made the city their tomb in a way. This fortified city is still standing today with its walls built of a mixture of stones and bones. When they had all in this way fallen prey to the sword, Peter alone with a few others escaped and reentered Helenopolis,[13] and the Turks who wanted to capture him, set fresh ambushes for him. But when the Emperor received reliable information of all this, and the terrible massacre, he was very worried lest Peter should have been captured. He therefore summoned Constantine Catacalon Euphorbenus (who has already been mentioned many times in this history), and gave him a large force which was embarked on ships of war and sent him across the straits to Peter's succour. Directly the Turks saw him land they fled. Constantine, without the slightest delay, picked up Peter and his followers, who were but few, and brought them safe and sound to the Emperor. On the Emperor's reminding him of his original thoughtlessness and saying that it was due to his not having obeyed his, the Emperor's, advice that he had incurred such disasters, Peter, being a haughty Latin, would not admit that he himself was the cause of the trouble, but said it was the others who did not listen to him, but followed their own will, and he denounced them as robbers and plunderers who, for that reason, were not allowed by the Saviour to worship at His Holy Sepulchre. Others of the Latins, such as Bohemund and men of like mind, who had long cherished a desire for the Roman Empire, and wished to win it for themselves, found a pretext in Peter's preaching, as I have said, deceived the more single-

[13]According to other accounts of the battle, Peter was in Constantinople at the time.

minded, caused this great upheaval and were selling their own estates under the pretence that they were marching against the Turks to redeem the Holy Sepulchre.

63

FULCHER OF CHARTRES

The Siege of Antioch

We return here to Fulcher's Chronicles (Book I, Chapters 16 and 17). Antioch, in northern Syria, was the largest and most formidable Muslim-controlled city on the Crusaders' route to Jerusalem. After laying siege to the city for more than two years, the Crusader forces had suffered losses that seriously reduced their strength and morale. After their initial success, what events seem to have caused these reversals? What were the strengths and weaknesses of the Crusader armies?

Thinking Historically

Like the narrative of Solomon bar Simson, this narrative operates on two levels: the human and the divine. Notice how Fulcher attempts to interpret both of these narrative lines, separately and in their interaction. How much of Fulcher's narrative recounts God's work? How much recounts the work of the Crusaders? How does he combine these two threads? Of course, modern historians are normally limited to the human thread. Try to write a narrative that shows how the human Crusaders conquered Antioch.

XVI. The Wretched Poverty of the Christians and the Flight of the Count of Blois

1. In the year of the Lord 1098, after the region all around Antioch had been wholly devastated by the multitude of our people, the strong as well as the weak were more and more harassed by famine.

The First Crusade: The Chronicle of Fulcher of Chartres and Other Source Materials, 2nd ed., ed. Edward Peters (Philadelphia: University of Pennsylvania Press, 1998), 73–75.

2. At that time, the famished ate the shoots of beanseeds growing in the fields and many kinds of herbs unseasoned with salt; also thistles, which, being not well cooked because of the deficiency of firewood, pricked the tongues of those eating them; also horses, asses, and camels, and dogs and rats. The poorer ones ate even the skins of the beasts and seeds of grain found in manure.

3. They endured winter's cold, summer's heat, and heavy rains for God. Their tents became old and torn and rotten from the continuation of rains. Because of this, many of them were covered by only the sky.

4. So like gold thrice proved and purified sevenfold by fire, long predestined by God, I believe, and weighed by such a great calamity, they were cleansed of their sins. For even if the assassin's sword had not failed, many, long agonizing, would have voluntarily completed a martyr's course. Perhaps they borrowed the grace of such a great example from Saint Job, who, purifying his soul by the torments of his body, ever held God fast in mind. Those who fight with the heathen, labor because of God.

5. Granting that God—who creates everything, regulates everything created, sustains everything regulated, and rules by virtue—can destroy or renew whatsoever He wishes, I feel that He assented to the destruction of the heathen after the scourging of the Christians. He permitted it, and the people deserved it, because so many times they cheaply destroyed all things of God. He permitted the Christians to be killed by the Turks, so that the Christians would have the assurance of salvation; the Turks, the perdition of their souls. It pleased God that certain Turks, already predestined for salvation, were baptized by priests. "For those whom He predestined, He also called and glorified."

6. So what then? There were some of our men, as you heard before, who left the siege because it brought so much anguish; others, because of poverty; others, because of cowardice; others, because of fear of death; first the poor and then the rich.

7. Stephen, Count of Blois, withdrew from the siege and returned home to France by sea. Therefore all of us grieved, since he was a very noble man and valiant in arms. On the day following his departure, the city of Antioch was surrendered to the Franks. If he had persevered, he would have rejoiced much in the victory with the rest. This act disgraced him. For a good beginning is not beneficial to anyone unless it be well consummated. I shall cut short many things in the Lord's affairs lest I wander from the truth, because lying about them must be especially guarded against.

8. The siege lasted continuously from this same month of October, as it was mentioned, through the following winter and spring until June. The Turks and Franks alternately staged many attacks and counter-attacks; they overcame and were overcome. Our men, however, triumphed more often than theirs. Once it happened that many of the fleeing Turks fell into the Fernus River, and being submerged in it,

they drowned. On the near side of the river, and on the far side, both forces often waged war alternately.

9. Our leaders constructed castles before the city, from which they often rushed forth vigorously to keep the Turks from coming out [of the city]. By this means, the Franks took the pastures from their animals. Nor did they get any help from Armenians outside the city, although these Armenians often did injury to our men.

XVII. *The Surrender of the City of Antioch*

1. When it pleased God that the labor of His people should be consummated, perhaps pleased by the prayers of those who daily poured out supplications and entreaties to Him, out of His compassion He granted that through a fraud of the Turks the city be returned to the Christians in a secret surrender. Hear, therefore, of a fraud, and yet not a fraud.

2. Our Lord appeared to a certain Turk, chosen beforehand by His grace, and said to him: "Arise, thou who sleepest! I command thee to return the city to the Christians." The astonished man concealed that vision in silence.

3. However, a second time, the Lord appeared to him: "Return the city to the Christians," He said, "for I am Christ who command this of thee." Meditating what to do, he went away to his ruler, the prince of Antioch, and made that vision known to him. To him the ruler responded: "You do not wish to obey the phantom, do you, stupid?" Returning, he was afterwards silent.

4. The Lord again appeared to him, saying: "Why hast thou not fulfilled what I ordered thee? Thou must not hesitate, for I, who command this, am Lord of all." No longer doubting, he discreetly negotiated with our men, so that by his zealous plotting they might receive the city.

5. He finished speaking, and gave his son as hostage to Lord Bohemond, to whom he first directed that discourse, and whom he first persuaded. On a certain night, he sent twenty of our men over the wall by means of ladders made of ropes. Without delay, the gate was opened. The Franks, already prepared, entered the city. Forty of our soldiers, who had previously entered by ropes, killed sixty Turks found there, guards of the tower. In a loud voice, altogether the Franks shouted: "God wills it! God wills it!" For this was our signal cry, when we were about to press forward on any enterprise.

6. After hearing this, all the Turks were extremely terrified. Then, when the redness of dawn had paled, the Franks began to go forward to attack the city. When the Turks had first seen Bohemond's red banner on high, furling and unfurling, and the great tumult aroused on all sides, and the Franks running far and wide through the streets with their naked swords and wildly killing people, and had heard their horns sounding on the top of the wall, they began to flee here and there,

bewildered. From this scene, many who were able fled into the citadel situated on a cliff.

7. Our rabble wildly seized everything that they found in the streets and houses. But the proved soldiers kept to warfare, in following and killing the Turks.

$$64$$

IBN AL-QALANISI
From The Damascus Chronicle

Here we switch to a Muslim view of the events of 1098 and 1099: especially the battles of Antioch, Jerusalem, and Ascalon (modern Ashkelon, Israel). Ibn al-Qalanisi* (d. 1160) was a scholar in Damascus, Syria. How does his account of the battle for Antioch differ from the previous selection by Fulcher of Chartres? How do you resolve these differences?

Thinking Historically

We noticed how the medieval Christian historian provided two historical threads—the human and divine. How does this Muslim account integrate the threads of human action and divine will?

Modern historians restrict their accounts to human action but they seek to include the view of both sides in a conflict. How do you integrate both sides into your narrative? Also, what signs do you see here of a possible second conflict, this one between Muslims?

A.H. 491
(9th December, 1097, to 27th November, 1098)

At the end of First Jumādā (beginning of June, 1098) the report arrived that certain of the men of Antioch among the armourers in the train of the amīr Yāghī Siyān had entered into a conspiracy against Antioch and

---

*IH buhn   ahl kahl ah NEE see

H. A. R. Gibb, *The Damascus Chronicle of the Crusades*, extracted and translated from the *Chronicle of Ibn al-Qalanisi* (Mineola, N.Y.: Dover Publications, 2002), 44–49.

had come to an agreement with the Franks to deliver the city up to them, because of some ill-usage and confiscations which they had formerly suffered at his hands. They found an opportunity of seizing one of the city bastions adjoining the Jabal, which they sold to the Franks, and thence admitted them into the city during the night. At daybreak they raised the battle cry, whereupon Yāghī Siyān took to flight and went out with a large body, but not one person amongst them escaped to safety. When he reached the neighbourhood of Armanāz, an estate near Ma 'arrat Masrīn, he fell from his horse to the ground. One of his companions raised him up and remounted him, but he could not maintain his balance on the back of the horse, and after falling repeatedly he died. As for Antioch, the number of men, women, and children, killed, taken prisoner, and enslaved from its population is beyond computation. About three thousand men fled to the citadel and fortified themselves in it, and some few escaped for whom God had decreed escape.

In Sha'bān (July) news was received that al-Afdal, the commander-in-chief (amīr al-juyūsh), had come up from Egypt to Syria at the head of a strong 'askar.[1] He encamped before Jerusalem, where at that time were the two amīrs Sukmān and Il-Ghāzī, sons of Ortuq, together with a number of their kinsmen and followers and a large body of Turks, and sent letters to them, demanding that they should surrender Jerusalem to him without warfare or shedding of blood. When they refused his demand, he opened an attack on the town, and having set up mangonels[2] against it, which effected a breach in the wall, he captured it and received the surrender of the Sanctuary of David[3] from Sukmān. On his entry into it, he shewed kindness and generosity to the two amīrs, and set both them and their supporters free. They arrived in Damascus during the first ten days of Shawwāl (September), and al-Afdal returned with his 'askar to Egypt.

In this year also the Franks set out with all their forces to Ma'arrat al-Nu'mān,[4] and having encamped over against it on 29th Dhu'l-Hijja (27th November), they opened an attack on the town and brought up a tower and scaling-ladders against it.

Now after the Franks had captured the city of Antioch through the devices of the armourer, who was an Armenian named Fīrūz,[5] on the eve

---

[1]Small military force of slaves and freed men, under Muslim amirs. [Ed.]

[2]A catapult that could hurl large stones as far as four hundred feet to break down a wall. [Ed.]

[3]The Citadel of Jerusalem.

[4]Ma'arrat al-Numān or Ma'arat al-Numān: Syrian city south of Antioch. Conquest of Antioch did not provide enough food so crusaders marched on to this next city on route to Jerusalem. There they massacred the population of 10,000–20,000 and by some accounts cannibalized some of them. [Ed.]

[5]In the text Nairūz.

of Friday, 1st Rajab (night of Thursday 3rd June), and a series of reports were received confirming this news, the armies of Syria assembled in uncountable force and proceeded to the province of Antioch, in order to inflict a crushing blow upon the armies of the Franks. They besieged the Franks until their supplies of food were exhausted and they were reduced to eating carrion; but thereafter the Franks, though they were in the extremity of weakness, advanced in battle order against the armies of Islām, which were at the height of strength and numbers, and they broke the ranks of the Muslims and scattered their multitudes. The lords of the pedigree steeds[6] were put to flight, and the sword was unsheathed upon the footsoldiers who had volunteered for the cause of God, who had girt themselves for the Holy War, and were vehement in their desire to strike a blow for the Faith and for the protection of the Muslims. This befel on Tuesday, the [twenty] sixth of Rajab, in this year (29th June, 1098).

A.H. 492

(28th November, 1098, to 16th November, 1099)

In Muharram of this year (December, 1098), the Franks made an assault on the wall of Ma'arrat al-Nu'mān from the east and north. They pushed up the tower until it rested against the wall, and as it was higher, they deprived the Muslims of the shelter of the wall. The fighting raged round this point until sunset on 14th Muharram (11th December), when the Franks scaled the wall, and the townsfolk were driven off it and took to flight. Prior to this, messengers had repeatedly come to them from the Franks with proposals for a settlement by negotiation and the surrender of the city, promising in return security for their lives and property, and the establishment of a [Frankish] governor amongst them, but dissension among the citizens and the fore-ordained decree of God prevented acceptance of these terms. So they captured the city after the hour of the sunset prayer, and a great number from both sides were killed in it. The townsfolk fled to the houses of al-Ma'arra, to defend themselves in them, and the Franks, after promising them safety, dealt treacherously with them. They erected crosses over the town, exacted indemnities from the townsfolk, and did not carry out any of the terms upon which they had agreed, but plundered everything that they found, and demanded of the people sums which they could not pay. On Thursday 17th Safar (13th January, 1099) they set out for Kafr Tāb.

Thereafter they proceeded towards Jerusalem, at the end of Rajab (middle of June) of this year, and the people fled in panic from their

---

[6]Literally "of the short-haired and swift-paced."

abodes before them. They descended first upon al-Ramla, and captured it after the ripening of the crops. Thence they marched to Jerusalem, the inhabitants of which they engaged and blockaded, and having set up the tower against the city they brought it forward to the wall. At length news reached them that al-Afdal was on his way from Egypt with a mighty army to engage in the Holy War against them, and to destroy them, and to succour and protect the city against them. They therefore attacked the city with increased vigour, and prolonged the battle that day until the daylight faded, then withdrew from it, after promising the inhabitants to renew the attack upon them on the morrow. The townsfolk descended from the wall at sunset, whereupon the Franks renewed their assault upon it, climbed up the tower, and gained a footing on the city wall. The defenders were driven down, and the Franks stormed the town and gained possession of it. A number of the townsfolk fled to the sanctuary [of David], and a great host were killed. The Jews assembled in the synagogue, and the Franks burned it over their heads. The sanctuary was surrendered to them on guarantee of safety on the 22nd of Sha'bān (14th July) of this year, and they destroyed the shrines and the tomb of Abraham. Al-Afdal arrived with the Egyptian armies, but found himself forestalled, and having been reinforced by the troops from the Sāhil,[7] encamped outside Ascalon on 14th Ramadān (4th August), to await the arrival of the fleet by sea and of the Arab levies. The army of the Franks advanced against him and attacked him in great force. The Egyptian army was thrown back towards Ascalon, al-Afdal himself taking refuge in the city. The swords of the Franks were given mastery over the Muslims, and death was meted out to the footmen, volunteers, and townsfolk, about ten thousand souls, and the camp was plundered. Al-Afdal set out for Egypt with his officers, and the Franks besieged Ascalon, until at length the townsmen agreed to pay them twenty thousand dinars as protection money, and to deliver this sum to them forthwith. They therefore set about collecting this amount from the inhabitants of the town, but it befel that a quarrel broke out between the [Frankish] leaders, and they retired without having received any of the money. It is said that the number of the people of Ascalon who were killed in this campaign—that is to say of the witnesses, men of substance, merchants, and youths, exclusive of the regular levies—amounted to two thousand seven hundred souls.

---

[7]The Sāhil was the general name given to the coastal plain and the maritime towns, from Ascalon to Bairūt.

65

RAYMOND OF ST. GILES, COUNT OF TOULOUSE

The Capture of Jerusalem by the Crusaders

The author of this letter or proclamation was the secular military leader chosen by Pope Urban II to lead the crusade. By the time of the capture of Jerusalem in 1099, he was certainly—with the Norman Bohemond and a couple other nobles—among the top military leaders. How does he account for their capture of Jerusalem? How would you explain it? Raymond tells how immediately after conquering Jerusalem, the Crusaders went to meet an Egyptian army (mistakenly identified as Babylonian) at Ascalon. How does Raymond explain their success? How did Ibn al-Qalanisi explain it? How might you explain it?

Thinking Historically

A letter can read much like a historical narrative, as does this one by Raymond of St. Giles. The author clearly wants to tell his readers what has happened. But this letter addressed to the pope, his bishops, and "the whole Christian people" is as much a testament to God's work as it is a history. Why does this make it difficult to construct the human narrative? Which events could you confidently include in your history of the crusade?

To lord Paschal, pope of the Roman church, to all the bishops, and to the whole Christian people, from the archbishop of Pisa, duke Godfrey, now, by the grace of God, defender of the church of the Holy Sepulchre, Raymond, count of St. Giles, and the whole army of God, which is in the land of Israel, greeting.

Multiply your supplications and prayers in the sight of God with joy and thanksgiving, since God has manifested His mercy in fulfilling by our hands what He had promised in ancient times. For after the capture of Nicaea, the whole army, made up of more than three hundred thousand soldiers, departed thence. And, although this army was so

Raymond of St. Giles, Count of Toulouse, "The Capture of Jerusalem by the Crusaders," in D. C. Munro, ed., *Translations and Reprints from the Original Sources of European History,* 4th ed., vol. I, bk. 4 (New York: AMC Press, Inc., 1971), 8–12.

great that it could have in a single day covered all Romania and drunk up all the rivers and eaten up all the growing things, yet the Lord conducted them amid so great abundance that a ram was sold for a penny and an ox for twelve pennies or less. Moreover, although the princes and kings of the Saracens rose up against us, yet, by God's will, they were easily conquered and overcome. Because, indeed, some were puffed up by these successes, God opposed to us Antioch, impregnable to human strength. And there He detained us for nine months and so humbled us in the siege that there were scarcely a hundred good horses in our whole army. God opened to us the abundance of His blessing and mercy and led us into the city, and delivered the Turks and all of their possessions into our power.

Inasmuch as we thought that these had been acquired by our own strength and did not worthily magnify God who had done this, we were beset by so great a multitude of Turks that no one dared to venture forth at any point from the city. Moreover, hunger so weakened us that some could scarcely refrain from eating human flesh. It would be tedious to narrate all the miseries which we suffered in that city. But God looked down upon His people whom He had so long chastised and mercifully consoled them. Therefore, He at first revealed to us, as a recompense for our tribulation and as a pledge of victory, His lance which had lain hidden since the days of the apostles. Next, He so fortified the hearts of the men, that they who from sickness or hunger had been unable to walk, now were endued with strength to seize their weapons and manfully to fight against the enemy.

After we had triumphed over the enemy, as our army was wasting away at Antioch from sickness and weariness and was especially hindered by the dissensions among the leaders, we proceeded into Syria, stormed Barra and Marra, cities of the Saracens, and captured the fortresses in that country. And while we were delaying there, there was so great a famine in the army that the Christian people now ate the putrid bodies of the Saracens.[1] Finally, by the divine admonition, we entered into the interior of Hispania,[2] and the most bountiful, merciful and victorious hand of the omnipotent Father was with us. For the cities and fortresses of the country through which we were proceeding sent ambassadors to us with many gifts and offered to aid us and to surrender their walled places. But because our army was not large and it was the unanimous wish to hasten to Jerusalem, we accepted their pledges and made them tributaries. One of the cities forsooth, which

---

[1]Radulph of Caen, another Crusader chronicler, wrote, "In Ma'arra our troops boiled pagan adults alive in cooking-pots; they impaled children on spits and devoured them grilled." [Ed.]

[2]Probably a metaphor for an extremely fertile Muslim land, as Muslim Spain was known to be. [Ed.]

was on the sea-coast, had more men than there were in our whole army. And when those at Antioch and Laodicea and Archas heard how the hand of the Lord was with us, many from the army who had remained in those cities followed us to Tyre. Therefore, with the Lord's companionship and aid, we proceeded thus as far as Jerusalem.

And after the army had suffered greatly in the siege, especially on account of the lack of water, a council was held and the bishops and princes ordered that all with bare feet should march around the walls of the city, in order that He who entered it humbly in our behalf might be moved by our humility to open it to us and to exercise judgment upon His enemies. God was appeased by this humility and on the eighth day after the humiliation He delivered the city and His enemies to us. It was the day indeed on which the primitive church was driven thence, and on which the festival of the dispersion of the apostles is celebrated. And if you desire to know what was done with the enemy who were found there, know that in Solomon's Porch and in his temple our men rode in the blood of the Saracens up to the knees of their horses.

Then, when we were considering who ought to hold the city, and some moved by love for their country and kinsmen wished to return home, it was announced to us that the king of Babylon had come to Ascalon with an innumerable multitude of soldiers. His purpose was, as he said, to lead the Franks, who were in Jerusalem, into captivity, and to take Antioch by storm. But God had determined otherwise in regard to us.

Therefore, when we learned that the army of the Babylonians was at Ascalon, we went down to meet them, leaving our baggage and the sick in Jerusalem with a garrison. When our army was in sight of the enemy, upon our knees we invoked the aid of the Lord, that He who in our other adversities had strengthened the Christian faith, might in the present battle break the strength of the Saracens and of the devil and extend the kingdom of the church of Christ from sea to sea, over the whole world. There was no delay; God was present when we cried for His aid, and furnished us with so great boldness, that one who saw us rush upon the enemy would have taken us for a herd of deer hastening to quench their thirst in running water. It was wonderful, indeed, since there were in our army not more than 5,000 horsemen and 15,000 foot-soldiers, and there were probably in the enemy's army 100,000 horsemen and 400,000 foot-soldiers. Then God appeared wonderful to His servants. For before we engaged in fighting, by our very onset alone, He turned this multitude in flight and scattered all their weapons, so that if they wished afterwards to attack us, they did not have the weapons in which they trusted. There can be no question how great the spoils were, since the treasures of the king of Babylon were captured. More than 100,000 Moors perished there by the sword. Moreover, their panic was so great that about 2,000 were suffocated at the gate of the city. Those who perished in the sea were innumerable. Many were entangled in the thickets. The whole world was certainly fighting for us, and if many of ours had not been detained in plundering the camp, few of the great multitude of the enemy would have been able to escape from the battle.

And although it may be tedious, the following must not be omitted: On the day preceding the battle the army captured many thousands of camels, oxen, and sheep. By the command of the princes these were divided among the people. When we advanced to battle, wonderful to relate, the camels formed in many squadrons and the sheep and oxen did the same. Moreover, these animals accompanied us, halting when we halted, advancing when we advanced, and charging when we charged. The clouds protected us from the heat of the sun and cooled us.

Accordingly, after celebrating the victory, the army returned to Jerusalem. Duke Godfrey remained there; the count of St. Giles, Robert, count of Normandy, and Robert, count of Flanders, returned to Laodicea. There they found the fleet belonging to the Pisans and to Bohemond. After the archbishop of Pisa had established peace between Bohemond and our leaders, Raymond prepared to return to Jerusalem for the sake of God and his brethren.

Therefore, we call upon you of the Catholic Church of Christ and of the whole Latin church to exult in the so admirable bravery and devotion of your brethren, in the so glorious and very desirable retribution of the omnipotent God, and in the so devoutly hoped-for remission of all our sins through the grace of God. And we pray that He may make you—namely, all bishops, clerks, and monks who are leading devout lives, and all the laity—to sit down at the right hand of God, who liveth and reigneth God for ever and ever. And we ask and beseech you in the name of our Lord Jesus, who has ever been with us and aided us and freed us from all our tribulations, to be mindful of your brethren who return to you, by doing them kindnesses and by paying their debts, in order that God may recompense you and absolve you from all your sins and grant you a share in all the blessings which either we or they have deserved in the sight of the Lord. Amen.

66

IBN AL-ATHIR

The Conquest of Jerusalem

Ibn al-Athir* (1160–1233) was an influential Arab historian who wrote a history of the first three crusades, having witnessed the third himself. The following selection, taken from his work *The Perfect History*, is one of the most authoritative, roughly contemporaneous histories of the First Crusade from the Muslim perspective. What reason does al-Athir give for the Egyptian capture of Jerusalem from the Turks? Why were the Franks successful in wresting Jerusalem and other lands from Muslim control? What is the significance of the poem at the end of the selection?

Thinking Historically

There are always more than two sides to a story, but it is certainly useful to have battle descriptions from two sides of a conflict. In constructing your own narrative of the battle of Jerusalem, you might first look for points of agreement. On what points does Ibn al-Athir agree with other accounts you have read? How else would you decide which elements from each account to include in your narrative?

Taj ad-Daula Tutūsh was the Lord of Jerusalem but had given it as a feoff to the amīr Suqmān ibn Artūq the Turcoman. When the Franks defeated the Turks at Antioch the massacre demoralized them, and the Egyptians, who saw that the Turkish armies were being weakened by desertion, besieged Jerusalem under the command of al-Afdal ibn Badr al-Jamali. Inside the city were Artūq's sons, Suqmān and Ilghazi, their cousin Sunij and their nephew Yaquti. The Egyptians brought more than forty siege engines to attack Jerusalem and broke down the walls at several points. The inhabitants put up a defense, and the siege and fighting went on for more than six weeks. In the end the Egyptians forced the city to capitulate, in Sha'bān 489/August 1096. Suqmān, Ilghazi, and their friends were well treated by al-Afdal, who gave them

*IH buhn   ahl AH tuhr

Francesco Gabrieli, ed., *Arab Historians of the Crusades: Selected and Translated from the Arabic Sources*, ed. and trans. E. J. Costello. Islamic World Series (Berkeley: University of California Press, 1969), 10–12.

large gifts of money and let them go free. They made for Damascus and then crossed the Euphrates. Suqmān settled in Edessa and Ilghazi went on into Iraq. The Egyptian governor of Jerusalem was a certain Iftikhār ad-Daula, who was still there at the time of which we are speaking.

After their vain attempt to take Acre by siege, the Franks moved on to Jerusalem and besieged it for more than six weeks. They built two towers, one of which, near Sion, the Muslims burnt down, killing everyone inside it. It had scarcely ceased to burn before a messenger arrived to ask for help and to bring the news that the other side of the city had fallen. In fact Jerusalem was taken from the north on the morning of Friday 22 Sha'bān 492/July 15, 1099. The population was put to the sword by the Franks, who pillaged the area for a week. A band of Muslims barricaded themselves into the Oratory of David and fought on for several days. They were granted their lives in return for surrendering. The Franks honoured their word, and the group left by night for Ascalon. In the Masjid al-Aqsa the Franks slaughtered more than 70,000 people, among them a large number of Imams and Muslim scholars, devout and ascetic men who had left their homelands to live lives of pious seclusion in the Holy Place. The Franks stripped the Dome of the Rock of more than forty silver candelabra, each of them weighing 3,600 drams, and a great silver lamp weighing forty-four Syrian pounds, as well as a hundred and fifty smaller silver candelabra and more than twenty gold ones, and a great deal more booty. Refugees from Syria reached Baghdād in Ramadan, among them the qadi Abu Sa'd al-Hárawi. They told the Caliph's ministers a story that wrung their hearts and brought tears to their eyes. On Friday they went to the Cathedral Mosque and begged for help, weeping so that their hearers wept with them as they described the sufferings of the Muslims in that Holy City: the men killed, the women and children taken prisoner, the homes pillaged. Because of the terrible hardships they had suffered, they were allowed to break the fast. . . .

It was the discord between the Muslim princes, as we shall describe, that enabled the Franks to overrun the country. Abu l-Muzaffar al-Abiwardi composed several poems on this subject, in one of which he says:

> We have mingled blood with flowing tears, and there is no room left in
> us for pity[?]
> To shed tears is a man's worst weapon when the swords stir up the
> embers of war.
> Sons of Islām, behind you are battles in which heads rolled at your
> feet.
> Dare you slumber in the blessed shade of safety, where life is as soft as
> an orchard flower?

How can the eye sleep between the lids at a time of disasters that
would waken any sleeper?

While your Syrian brothers can only sleep on the backs of their
chargers, or in vultures' bellies!

Must the foreigners feed on our ignominy, while you trail behind you
the train of a pleasant life, like men whose world is at peace?

When blood has been spilt, when sweet girls must for shame hide their
lovely faces in their hands!

When the white swords' points are red with blood, and the iron of the
brown lances is stained with gore!

At the sound of sword hammering on lance young children's hair turns
white.

This is war, and the man who shuns the whirlpool to save his life shall
grind his teeth in penitence.

This is war, and the infidel's sword is naked in his hand, ready to be
sheathed again in men's necks and skulls.

This is war, and he who lies in the tomb at Medina seems to raise his
voice and cry: "O sons of Hashim!

I see my people slow to raise the lance against the enemy: I see the
Faith resting on feeble pillars.

For fear of death the Muslims are evading the fire of battle, refusing to
believe that death will surely strike them."

Must the Arab champions then suffer with resignation, while the
gallant Persians shut their eyes to their dishonour?

67

Letter from a Jewish Pilgrim in Egypt

The following letter was written in 1100 by an anonymous Jewish pilgrim from Alexandria, unable to make his pilgrimage to Jerusalem because of the ongoing war. How does the letter's author regard the
Egyptian Sultan? How does he view the struggle between the Sultan
and the Franks? What does this suggest about the lives of Jews under
Muslim rule during this time period?

"Contemporary Letters on the Capture of Jerusalem by the Crusaders," trans. S. D. Goitein, *Journal of Jewish Studies*, vol. 3, no. 4 (London: Jewish Chronicle Publications, 1952), 162–77.

Thinking Historically

What does this letter add to your understanding of the Crusaders' capture of Jerusalem? How would you write a narrative of the First Crusade that took advantage of Christian, Muslim, and Jewish sources?

In Your name, You Merciful.

If I attempted to describe my longing for you, my Lord, my brother *and cousin,*—may God prolong your days and make permanent your honour, success, happiness, health, and welfare; and . . . subdue your enemies—all the paper in the world would not suffice. My longing will but increase and double, just as the days will grow and double. May *the Creator of the World* presently make us meet together in joy when I return under His guidance to my homeland *and to the inheritance of my Fathers* in complete happiness, *so that we rejoice and be happy through His great mercy and His vast bounty; and thus may be His will!*

You may remember, my Lord, that many years ago I left our country to seek God's mercy and help in my poverty, to behold Jerusalem and return thereupon. However, when I was in Alexandria God brought about circumstances which caused a slight delay. Afterwards, however, "the sea grew stormy," and many armed bands made their appearance in Palestine; "*and he who went forth and he who came had no peace,*" so that hardly one survivor out of a whole group came back to us from Palestine and told us that scarcely anyone could save himself from those armed bands, since they were so numerous and were gathered round . . . every town. There was further the journey through the desert, among [the bedouins] and whoever escaped from the one, fell into the hands of the other. Moreover, mutinies [spread throughout the country and reached] even Alexandria, so that we ourselves were besieged several times and the city was ruined; . . . the end however *was good*, for the Sultan—may God bestow glory upon his victories— conquered the city and caused justice to abound in it in a manner unprecedented in the history of any king in the world; not even a dirham was looted from anyone. Thus I had come to hope that because of his justice and strength God would give the land into his hands, and I should thereupon go to Jerusalem in safety and tranquility. For this reason I proceeded from Alexandria to Cairo, in order to start [my journey] from there.

When, however, God had given Jerusalem, the blessed, into his hands this state of affairs continued for too short a time to allow for making a journey there. The Franks arrived and killed everybody in the city, whether of *Ishmael or of Israel*; and the few who survived the slaughter were made prisoners. Some of these have been ransomed since, while others are still in captivity in all parts of the world.

Now, all of us had anticipated that our Sultan—may God bestow glory upon his victories—would set out against them [the Franks] with his troops and chase them away. But time after time our hope failed. Yet, to this very present moment we do hope that God will give his [the Sultan's] enemies into his hands. For it is inevitable that the armies will join in battle this year; and, if God grants us victory through him [the Sultan] and he conquers Jerusalem—and so it may be, with God's will—I for one shall not be amongst those who will linger, but shall go there to behold the city; and shall afterwards return straight to you—if God wills it. My salvation is in God, for this [is unlike] the other previous occasions [of making a pilgrimage to Jerusalem]. God, indeed, will exonerate me, since at my age I cannot afford to delay and wait any longer; I want to return home under any circumstances, if I still remain alive—whether I shall have seen Jerusalem or have given up the hope of doing it—both of which are possible.

You know, of course, my Lord, what has happened to us in the course of the last five years: the plague, the illnesses, and ailments have continued unabated for four successive years. As a result of this the wealthy became impoverished and a great number of people died *of the plague*, so that entire families perished in it. I, too, was affected with a grave illness, from which I recovered only about a year ago; then I was taken ill the following year so that (on the margin) for four years I have remained. . . . He who has said: *The evil diseases of Egypt* . . . he who hiccups does not live . . . ailments and will die . . . otherwise . . . will remain alive.

REFLECTIONS

The First Crusade (1095–1099) only marks the beginning of a protracted conflict between Christians and Muslims that continued until, perhaps, the eighteenth century. In the Holy Land there were crusades intermittently over the next forty years culminating in what was called the Second Crusade from 1147–1149. Meanwhile, the conquest of Muslims in Spain, which had been equated with the crusade by Pope Urban II, continued, as did frequent crusades into Eastern Europe.

The establishment of Latin kingdoms in Palestine could not be maintained without continual reinforcements, and they were vulnerable to Muslim attack. In 1187 Saladin reconquered most of Palestine, including Jerusalem, for the Muslims, a trauma for the Christians that led to the Third Crusade (1189–1192) and German Crusade

(1197–1198) by which Christians retook settlements on the coast. Popular enthusiasm continued in the Children's Crusade (1212) and the Crusade of the Shepherds (1251). The armies of the Fourth Crusade (1202–1204) were diverted to Constantinople, which they sacked in 1204. A Fifth Crusade (1217–1229) recovered Jerusalem, which was retaken by the Muslims in 1244, leading to crusades initiated by King Louis IX of France. Other crusading armies invaded Egypt, Tunisia, Muslim Spain, northwest Africa, southern France, Poland, Latvia, Germany, Russia, the Mongol Empire, Finland, Bosnia, and Italy, against papal enemies and Eastern Orthodox Christians as well as Muslims. Recent histories of the Crusades have ended their narratives in 1521, 1560, 1588, and 1798, according to Jonathan Riley-Smith who ends the recent *Oxford History of the Crusades* with images of the crusades in twentieth-century wars. Does the imagery of the Crusades still animate our wars?

While Americans, like President George W. Bush, learned the effects of using the term *crusade* in the context of American aspirations in the Middle East, the interference of Western forces in the region is a constant reminder to Muslims of a long history of Western intervention that began with the First Crusade. In Syria, Lebanon, Jordan, Palestine, and Israel one can still see crusader castles looming over the landscape and meet the descendants and coreligionists of the founders of Crusader states. From the perspective of many Muslims, unquestioned U.S. support of Israel, especially in Jerusalem, is a direct continuation of the Crusades. On more than one occasion, leaders of Middle Eastern countries have pictured themselves as a modern-day Saladin, the twelfth-century Kurdish Muslim warrior from Tikrit, Iraq, who retook Jerusalem in 1187, eighty-eight years after the events described by Raymond of St. Giles and Ibn al-Athir.

Writing a narrative of the First Crusade is difficult enough given the many sides to the conflict. Anna Comnena and the orthodox Christians of Byzantium had a very different perspective than the Franks or Roman Christian Crusaders of Western Europe. Nor were Muslims a single force of opposition. The Seljuk Turks had different interests than the Caliph of Baghdad, and, contrary to the opinion of Raymond St. Giles, the Fatimid Egyptian forces at Ascalon were neither Biblical Babylonians nor Abbasids from Baghdad. Then too there were Jews, and those in Germany may have had different interests from those in Egypt, despite an agreement about Christian crusading. Still, there are more sources than we have been able to explore here, and more interpretations than we have been able to include.

After trying your hand at writing a narrative of the First Crusade, you might think of how narratives are constructed. Each story leaves out some information to include other information, lest it read like a phone book. How do you decide whose "numbers" to include? To stimulate your thoughts about narrative choices, you might choose a subject a little closer to home where you have greater knowledge of the primary sources. Try a narrative of your own life up to now. If you dare, ask someone close to you to point out what you missed or over-emphasized.

11

Raiders of Steppe and Sea: Vikings and Mongols

Eurasia and the Atlantic, 750–1350 C.E.

HISTORICAL CONTEXT

Ever since the first urban settlements emerged five thousand years ago, they have been at risk of attack. The domestication of the horse and the development of sailing ships about four thousand years ago increased that risk. Much of ancient history is the story of the conflict between settled peoples and raiders on horseback or sailors on fleet ships. Eventually — between the third and fifth centuries C.E. — the great empires of Rome and Han dynasty China succumbed to raiding nomadic tribes from central Asia. As nomadic peoples settled themselves, new waves of raiders appeared.

In the previous chapter, we explored the impact of the Seljuk Turks who conquered cities in the Middle East that had been taken hundreds of years earlier by Arab armies on horseback. At about the same time as the Turks emerged from central Asia to threaten settlements south of the great Eurasian steppe grasslands, a new force from the north, Viking raiders on sailing ships, burst across the northern seas to attack the coastal enclaves and river cities of Europe and what came to be known in their wake as Russia. As generations oscillated between raiding and trading, new waves of Norsemen explored the edges of known waters to plant new settlements as far west as Iceland, Greenland, and North America. (See Map 11.1.) Who were these people? What did they hope to accomplish? How were they different from the land-raiders who preceded them?

At about the time that the Vikings were becoming farmers and grandfathers, around the year 1200, the Eurasian steppe exploded with its last and largest force of nomadic tribesmen on horseback: the

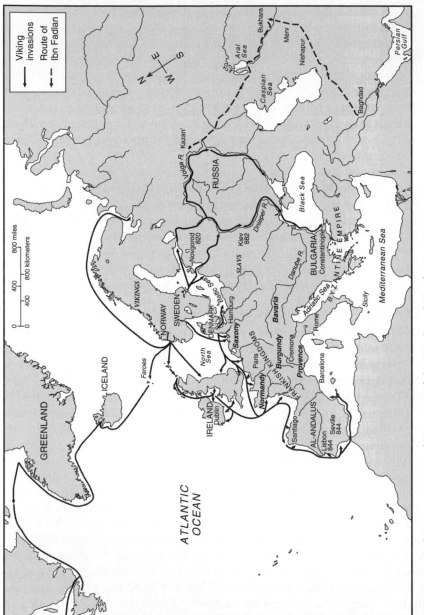

Map 11.1 Viking Invasions and Voyages of the Ninth and Tenth Centuries.

Mongols. Between the election of Chingis [or Genghis] Khan* (c. 1162–1227) as the Khan of Khans in 1206 and the Black Death of 1350 (or the end of the Mongol Yuan dynasty in China in 1368), the Mongols swept across Eurasia and created the largest empire the world had ever seen. (See Map 11.2.) Who were the Mongols? What made them so successful? How were they similar to, and different from, the Norsemen?

What was the impact of these raiding peoples on settled societies? How did they change each other? How did they change themselves? How did they create some of the conditions necessary for the modern world to come into being?

THINKING HISTORICALLY
Distinguishing Historical Understanding from Moral Judgments

The ancient Greeks called non-Greeks "barbarians" (because their languages contained "bar-bar"-like sounds that seemed foreign, untutored, and, thus, uncivilized). Since then the terms *barbarian* and *civilized* have been weighted with the same combination of descriptive and moral meaning. In the nineteenth century it was even fashionable among historians and anthropologists to distinguish between nomadic peoples and settled, urban peoples with the terms *barbarian* and *civilized*. As our first reading (and perhaps modern common sense) makes clear, rural or nomadic people are not necessarily less "moral" than city people; technological development is hardly the same thing as moral development (or the opposite).

What connection, if any, is there between history and morality? Stories of the past are frequently used to celebrate or condemn past individuals or groups. Sometimes we find past behavior shocking or reprehensible. Is it logical or proper to make moral judgments about the past? Can historians find answers to moral questions by studying the past?

Perhaps the place to begin is by recognizing that just as the "is" is different from the "ought," so too the "was" is different from the "should have been." Historians must begin by finding out what was. Our own moral values may lead us to ask certain questions about the past, but the historian's job is only to find out what happened. We will see in the following selections how difficult it has been for past observers to keep their own moral judgments from coloring their

*chihn GIHZ kahn

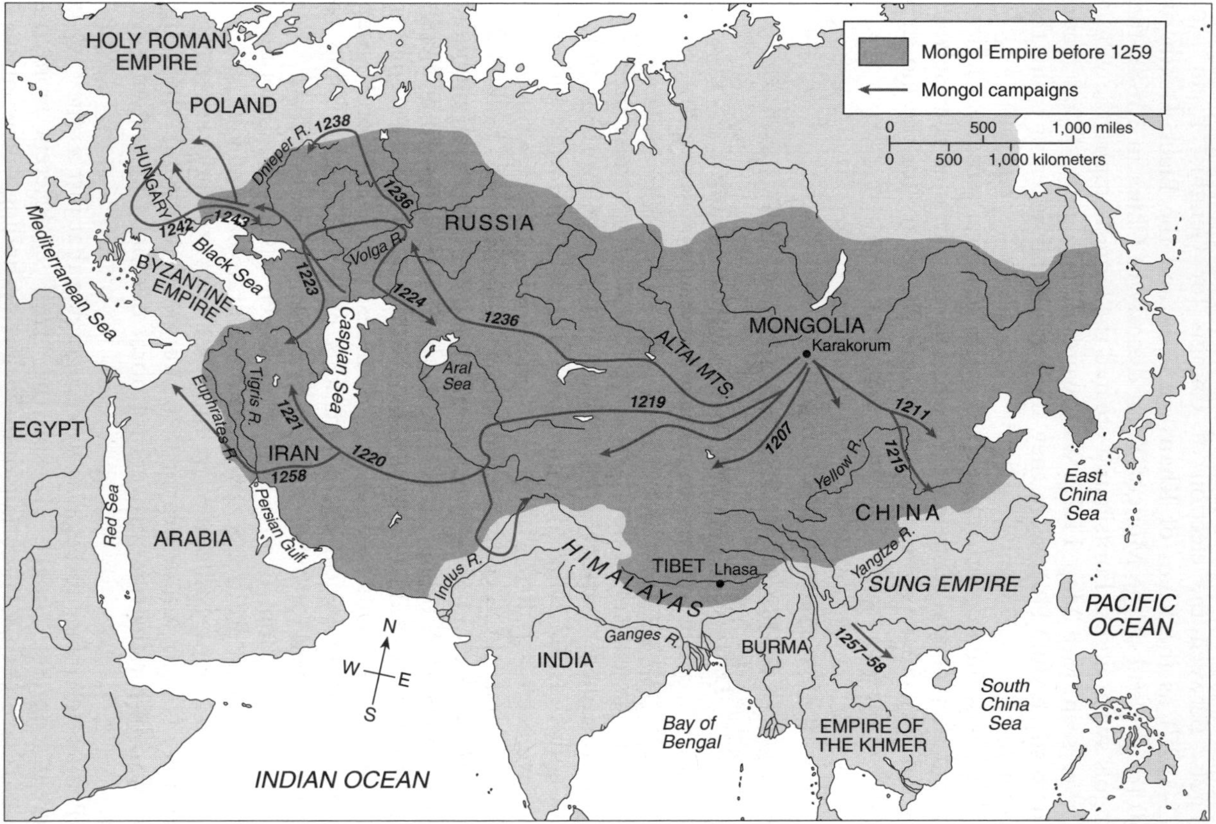
Mongol Empire before 1259
Mongol campaigns
0
500
1,000 miles
0
500
1,000 kilometers
HOLY ROMAN EMPIRE
POLAND
HUNGARY
Dnieper R.
1238
1236
1243
1242
RUSSIA
Volga R.
Black Sea
BYZANTINE EMPIRE
Mediterranean Sea
1223
1224
1236
Caspian Sea
Aral Sea
ALTAI MTS.
MONGOLIA
Karakorum
1219
1211
1207
1215
Yellow R.
EGYPT
Euphrates R.
Tigris R.
1221
IRAN
1220
1258
Persian Gulf
Red Sea
ARABIA
Indus R.
HIMALAYAS
TIBET
Lhasa
CHINA
Yangtze R.
SUNG EMPIRE
East China Sea
PACIFIC OCEAN
N
W
E
S
Ganges R.
INDIA
BURMA
1257–58
South China Sea
Bay of Bengal
EMPIRE OF THE KHMER
INDIAN OCEAN

Map 11.2 Mongol Invasions of the Thirteenth Century.

descriptions of peoples and events they found disagreeable. This part of our study may help us realize how our own moral feelings affect our responses.

Then, assuming we have established the facts fairly, can our moral sentiments legitimately come into play? As "consumers" of history, readers, and thinking people, we cannot avoid making judgments about the past. Under what conditions are such judgments fair, helpful, or appropriate? We will explore this much larger and more complex question in this chapter.

68

GREGORY GUZMAN

Were the Barbarians a Negative or Positive Factor in Ancient and Medieval History?

Gregory Guzman is a modern world historian. In this essay he asks some questions about the peoples who have been called "barbarians." How were the lives of pastoral nomads different from those of settled people? How did the horse shape life on the steppe? How effective were these herders as rulers of settled societies? What were the achievements of the pastoral nomads?

Thinking Historically

Why, according to Guzman, have most histories of the barbarians made them look bad? How have city people or historians let their own prejudices block an appreciation of the achievements of pastoralists?

According to the general surveys of ancient and medieval history found in most textbooks, barbarian peoples and/or primitive savages repeatedly invaded the early Eurasian civilized centers in Europe, the Middle East, India, and China. All accounts of the early history of these four

Gregory Guzman, "Were the Barbarians a Negative or Positive Factor in Ancient and Medieval History?" *The Historian* L (August 1988): 558–72.

civilizations contain recurrent references to attacks by such familiar and famous barbarians as the Hittites, Hyksos, Kassites, Aryans, Scythians, Sarmatians, Hsiung-nu, Huns, Germans, Turks, and Mongols, and they also record the absorption and assimilation of these Inner Asian barbarian hordes into the respective cultures and lifestyles of the more advanced coastal civilizations. The early sources generally equate the barbarians with chaos and destruction. The barbarians are presented as evil and despicable intruders, associated only with burning, pillaging, and slaughtering, while the civilized peoples are portrayed as the good and righteous forces of stability, order, and progress.

But it must be remembered that most of these early sources are not objective; they are blatantly one-sided, biased accounts written by members of the civilized societies. Thus, throughout recorded history, barbarians have consistently received bad press — bad PR to use the modern terminology. By definition, barbarians were illiterate, and thus they could not write their own version of events. All written records covering barbarian-civilized interaction came from the civilized peoples at war with the barbarians — often the sedentary peoples recently defeated and overwhelmed by those same barbarians. Irritated and angered coastal historians tended to record and emphasize only the negative aspects of their recent interaction with the barbarians. These authors tended to condemn and denigrate the way their barbarian opponents looked and to associate them with the devil and evil, rather than to report with objectivity what actually happened. For example, the Roman historian Ammianus Marcellinus, whose description is distorted by hatred and fear, described the barbarians as "two-footed beasts, seemingly chained to their horses from which they take their meat and drink, never touching a plough and having no houses." While living in Jerusalem, St. Jerome also left a vivid description of the Huns who ". . . filled the whole earth with slaughter and panic alike as they flittered hither and thither on their swift horses. . . . They were at hand everywhere before they were expected; by their speed they outstripped rumor, and they took pity neither upon religion nor rank nor age nor wailing childhood. Those who had just begun to live were compelled to die. . . ."

Such reports obviously made the barbarians look bad, while their nomadic habits and practices, which differed from those of the sedentary coastal peoples, were clearly portrayed as inferior and less advanced: the incarnation of evil itself. These horror-filled and biased descriptions were not the accounts of weak and defenseless peoples. Rather, they were written by the citizens of the most advanced and powerful states and empires in Europe, the Middle East, India, and China. The individual barbarian tribes were, nevertheless, able to attack and invade these strong and well-organized civilized states with relative impunity — pillaging and killing almost at will.

Several important questions, not addressed by the ancient and medieval historians, need to be answered here. Who were these barbarians?

Why and how did they manage to repeatedly defeat and overwhelm so easily the wealthiest and most advanced civilizations of the day? And why were they so vehemently condemned and hated in recorded history, if these barbarian Davids were able to consistently defeat such mighty Goliath civilized centers? Since the rich and populous civilized states enjoyed tremendous advantages in the confrontations, why have the barbarians so often been denied the popular role of the underdog?

In the process of answering those questions, this study would like to suggest that maybe the barbarians were not really the "bad guys." While they may not deserve to be called the "good guys," they made a much more positive contribution to human civilization than presented in the grossly distorted written sources. The barbarians deserve much more credit than they have been given, for they created a complex pastoral lifestyle as an alternative to sedentary agriculture, and in that achievement they were not subhuman savages only out to loot, pillage, and destroy. As this study will show, the barbarians played a much more positive and constructive role in the development and diffusion of early human history than that with which they are usually credited.

Before proceeding further, it is necessary to identify these much-maligned barbarians and describe how their way of life and their basic practices differed from those of the sedentary coastal peoples in order to better evaluate the barbarian role and its impact on the history of humanity.

In terms of identity, the barbarians were the steppe nomads of Inner Asia or Central Eurasia. This area represents one of the toughest and most inhospitable places in the world in which to survive. The climate of the interior of the large Eurasian landmass is not moderated by the distant seas, resulting in extremes of climate, of hot and cold, wet and dry. It is an area of ice, forest, desert, and mountains — with bitter winds, dust, and poor soil. Unlike the coastal regions with their dependable moisture and warmth, the soil of Inner Asia was too cold, poor, and dry for agriculture; thus the sedentary urban lifestyle of the coastal civilized centers was not an option in the Eurasian heartland. The people living there had to be tough to endure such a hostile environment, where they constantly fought both nature and other people for survival.

Due to necessity, the people of Inner Asia were nomads, wandering in search of food and pasture, and they became herdsmen, shepherds, and warriors. These steppe nomads, the barbarians of recorded history, were frequently nothing more than migrants looking for new homes; these people needed little encouragement to seek safety, security, and better living conditions in the warm, rich, and fertile coastal civilization centers. Thus the steppe barbarians were not always savage marauders coming only to loot and pillage. Many of the so-called barbarian invaders constituted a surplus population which harsh Inner Asia could not support, or they represented whole tribes being pushed out of their ancestral homeland by stronger tribes behind them. At any rate, these repeated waves of nomadic peoples leaving the steppes soon encountered the coastal civilizations.

These Inner Asian barbarians were more or less harmless outsiders until the horse dramatically changed their lifestyle on the vast steppes. They adopted the pastoral system as the best way of providing for basic needs. The natural pasture provided by the steppe grassland proved ideal for grazing large herds and flocks of animals. Soon their whole life revolved around their animals; they became shepherds, herders, and keepers of beasts. . . .

The dominant feature of this emerging barbarian pastoralism was its mounted nature; it was essentially a horse culture by 1000 B.C. At first small horses were kept only for food and milk, but bigger horses eventually led to riding. Once an accomplished fact, mounted practices dramatically changed the lifestyle of the barbarian steppe peoples. Horseback riding made the tending of scattered herds faster and less tiring, and it enlarged the size of herds while increasing the range of pastoral movement. It also made possible, when necessary, the total migration of entire tribes and clans. Mastery of the horse reduced the vast expanses of steppe pasturage to more manageable proportions. Steppe nomads moved twice a year between traditional winter and summer pastures; the spring and fall were spent moving between the necessary grazing grounds. All peoples and possessions moved with regularity; the nomads became used to living in the saddle, so to speak.

The horse thus became the center of pastoral life on the steppes. The barbarian nomads could literally live off their animals which provided meat, milk, and hides for clothing, coverings, boots, etc. Tools and weapons were made from the bones and sinews, and dried dung was used as fuel. The barbarians ate, sold, negotiated, slept, and took care of body functions in the saddle as indicated in the following quotations: "From their horses, by day and night every one of that nation buys and sells, eats and drinks, and bowed over the narrow neck of the animal relaxes in a sleep so deep as to be accompanied by many dreams." "All the time they let themselves be carried by their horses. In that way they fight wars, participate in banquets, attend public and private business. On their back, they move, stand still, carry on trade, and converse." These mounted practices led to the emergence of the centaur motif in Middle Eastern art, as the civilized people tended to view the horse and rider as one inseparable unit.

Military action also became an integral part of nomadic steppe life. Warfare was simply cavalry action by the pastoral herdsmen who served as soldiers for the duration of the conflict. Steppe military service differed little from the normal, on-the-move pastoral life. Large-scale steppe alliances were hard to organize and even harder to hold together among the independent nomads. Such temporary alliances, called hordes, rose swiftly to great strength and power, but they usually declined and disintegrated just as quickly.

At any rate, these barbarian nomads were tough and hardy warriors. The horse gave them speed and mobility over both the light and heavily armed infantry of the civilized centers, but for this speed and mobility the barbarians gave up any type of defensive armor. They learned to guide their horses with their knees, since both arms needed to be free for the bow and arrow, their primary offensive weapon. By 1000 B.C. the compound bow was in common use by barbarians. This shorter bow could be handled with ease from horseback, and arrows could be shot up to three hundred yards with accuracy. As steppe hunters, all barbarians made excellent archers.

Early civilized armies had no cavalry. The famous Macedonian phalanx and the formidable Roman legions contained only light and heavily armed infantry. At first these brave foot soldiers had no tactical maneuvers to face and contain a barbarian cavalry charge. Even more devastating was the storm of arrows raining down upon them long before they could engage in the traditional hand-to-hand combat. The formidable steppe cavalry thus subjected civilized defenses to continuous pressure. Every nomad with a horse and bow was a potential front-line soldier who was tough, resourceful, and ferocious, whereas only a small percentage of the civilized population was equipped and trained for war. The nomadic lifestyle and the speed of the horse eliminated the need for expensive and heavy metal armor and its accompanying technological skills. Cavalry tactics gave an initial military advantage to the barbarians and the mounted horsemen won most of the early battles. The best defense against barbarian cavalry was an insurmountable obstacle, a wall. Ten- to twenty-foot-high walls of dirt, wood, or stone were built around cities and along some frontiers, i.e., the Great Wall of China. The old statement that Rome fell because China built a wall may not be such a simple overstatement after all.

Since they had the military advantage of cavalry tactics, the steppe nomads attacked and conquered various coastal civilizations with regularity. In a typical conquest, the victorious barbarians were the new military/political rulers. These new rulers possessed strengths obvious to all. The barbarians had vigorous and dynamic leadership; good, able, and charismatic leadership had been needed to organize the independent nomads into an effective horde in the first place. The new rulers had the complete loyalty of their followers; their group identity based on common blood and ancestors resulted in an intense personal and individual allegiance and commitment.

The first century after the initial conquest was usually an era of dynamic leadership, good government, and economic prosperity, as nomadic strengths mixed with the local advances and practices of that civilization. The new ruling family was often a fusion of the best of both sides as the barbarian victors married into the previous ruling dynasty. This brought forth an age of powerful and successful rulers, and produced an era of energetic leadership, good government, low taxes, agricultural revival, and peace. . . .

After this early period of revitalized and dynamic rule, slow decline usually set in. Royal vigor and ability sank as the rulers became soft, both mentally and physically. Without physical exercise and self-discipline, the rulers became overindulgent, instantly acquiring everything they wanted — excessive amounts of food or drink, harems, puppets, and yes-men as advisers. At the same time court rivalries and internal divisiveness began to emerge once the strong unity required for the conquest was no longer needed. A rivalry that often arose was between the ruler and various groups of his followers — his military, his bureaucracy, his harem (especially the queen mothers), his conquered subjects, and his old nomadic supporters. His steppe horsemen began to give first loyalty to their new family land rather than to their individual leader who was now weak, impaired, and soft. Such internal rivalries weakened the central government and led to chaos and civil wars. Thus, a civilized center was ripe for the next series of invasions and conquest by the next group of unified, tough, and well-led barbarians who would, in turn, be assimilated and absorbed in this process of ongoing revitalization of stagnant civilizations.

Despite the usual negative view and definition of barbarians provided by the sedentary civilized peoples, the steppe nomads had developed a complex pastoral and nomadic society. They were tough and hardy horsemen whose cavalry tactics gave them the military advantage for several centuries. The barbarians used this advantage, and their periodic attacks on civilization centers caused destruction, sometimes severe destruction. But the barbarian role in mankind's history was not always negative. The barbarians can and should be viewed as representing a dynamic and vital element in human history for they periodically revived many stagnating coastal civilizations. Many of these sedentary centers flourished, growing rich and powerful. In the process they also became conservative, settled into a fixed routine. Preferring the status quo, they tended to use old answers and ways to face new problems and issues, and as a consequence they lost the vitality and flexibility required for healthy and progressive growth.

The barbarians were active and dynamic. In their conquests of civilized centers, they frequently destroyed and eliminated the old and outdated and preserved and passed on only the good and useful elements. Sometimes, the mounted invaders also introduced new ideas and practices. Some of these new barbarian innovations (horseback riding, archery, trousers, and boots, etc.) fused with the good and useful practices of the sedentary peoples. Old and new practices and processes merged, and provided viable alternatives to the old, outdated civilized ways which had failed or outlived their usefulness. This fusion brought forth dynamic creativity and development. The ongoing encounters with barbarian strangers inevitably fostered innovation and progress in the civilized centers — due to their need to adjust in order to survive. . . .

It can be argued that barbarians also played a positive role in the spread and diffusion of civilization itself. The four major Eurasian civilization centers were separated from each other by deserts, mountains, and the vast expanses of the steppe heartland of Inner Asia. In its early stages each civilization was somewhat isolated from the others. Overland trade and contact was possible only through the barbarian steppe highway which stretched over five thousand miles across Eurasia, from Hungary to Manchuria. There was little early sea contact between the four sedentary centers, as naval travel was longer and more dangerous than the overland routes.

Thus the steppe barbarians were the chief agency through which the ideas and practices of one civilization were spread to another before 1500 A.D. According to [historian] William H. McNeill, there was much conceptual diffusion carried along the steppe highway by the barbarians. Writing originated in the ancient Middle East. The concept, not the form, of writing then spread eastward from the Middle East, as the Indian and Chinese forms and characters were significantly different than Middle Eastern cuneiform. The making and use of bronze and chariots also spread from the Middle East to Europe, India, and China. Chariots were introduced to China, on the eastern end of the steppe highway, a few centuries after their appearance in the Middle East. Needless to say, this type of early cultural diffusion is difficult to document with any degree of certainty, but enough evidence exists to make it highly probable, even if not scientifically provable.

The late medieval period provides even more examples of cultural diffusion via the movement of barbarians along the Inner Asian steppe highway. The great Eurasian *Pax Mongolica* opened the way for much cultural cross-fertilization in the late-thirteenth and early-fourteenth centuries. Chinese inventions like gunpowder and printing made their way to the Middle East and Europe in this period. Records show that Chinese artillerymen accompanied the Mongol armies into the Middle East. Papal envoys like John of Plano Carpini and William of Rubruck traveled to the Mongol capital of Karakorum in the 1240s and 1250s. In the 1280s, Marco Polo brought with him from Kublai Khan's court in China a Mongol princess to be the bride of the Mongol Khan of Persia. . . .

This cultural interaction and exchange between Eurasian coastal civilizations ended with the collapse of the Mongol Khanates in Persia and China in the mid-fourteenth century. The barbarian Mongols, therefore, provided the last period of great cultural cross-fertilization before the modern age.

Historical evidence that exists enables one to argue that the barbarian nomads played an active and positive role in the history of mankind. The barbarian invaders revitalized stagnant and decaying civilizations and were responsible for a certain amount of cultural diffusion between emerging ancient and medieval civilizations. The traditional portrayal of barbarians as mere marauders and destroyers is misleading and incorrect. Unfortunately this is the usual role they are given when historians center their study of the past narrowly on the civilized centers and the biased written sources produced by those peoples. All too often historians tend to adopt and reflect the biases and values of their subjects under study, and thus continue to denigrate and condemn all barbarians without objectively evaluating their real contributions to human development. The study of the steppe nomads, the barbarians, is just as valid a topic for historical analysis as the traditional study of coastal sedentary civilizations. Only by knowing and understanding the pastoral barbarian can historians accurately evaluate the constant interaction between the two lifestyles and come to understand the full picture of humanity's early growth and development in the ancient and medieval periods of Eurasian history.

$$\boxed{69}$$

IBN FADLAN

The Viking Rus

In 921 C.E. the Muslim caliph of Baghdad sent Ibn Fadlan* on a mission to the King of the Bulgars.[1] The Muslim king of the Bulgars may have been looking for an alliance with the caliph of Baghdad against the Khazars, sandwiched between them, just west of the Caspian Sea. North and west of the Bulgars was the area that became Ukraine and Russia. The Volga River, which had its source in the Ural Mountains,

---

*IH buhn   fahd LAHN

[1]These Bulgars, with a Muslim king, had recently been forced north of the Caspian Sea (while other Bulgars moved west to what is today Bulgaria where they were converted to Christianity by Byzantium).

Albert Stanburrough Cook, "Ibn Fadlan's Account of Scandinavian Merchants on the Volga in 922," in *Journal of English and Germanic Philology*, vol. 22, no. 1 (1923): 56–63.

flowed north through this land into the Baltic Sea. In the eighth and ninth centuries this area was inhabited by various tribes, many of which spoke early Slavic languages. At some point these tribes were united under the command of a people called the Rus. The origins of the Rus are disputed, but most experts believe that they were either Vikings or the descendants of Vikings and Slavs.

Ibn Fadlan provides our earliest description of these Rus (or Northmen, as he calls them here), whom he encountered on the Volga near the modern city of Kazan' during his trip to the Bulgar king. (See Map 11.1 on page 376 for his route.) They or their ancestors had sailed downriver from the Baltic Sea on raiding and trading expeditions. What does Ibn Fadlan tell us about these Scandinavian raiders who gave their name to Russia?

Thinking Historically

Notice Ibn Fadlan's moral judgments about the Viking Rus. Notice your own moral judgments. How are Ibn Fadlan's judgments different from your own? What do you think accounts for those differences?

I saw how the Northmen had arrived with their wares, and pitched their camp beside the Volga. Never did I see people so gigantic; they are tall as palm trees, and florid and ruddy of complexion. They wear neither camisoles nor *chaftans*, but the men among them wear a garment of rough cloth, which is thrown over one side, so that one hand remains free. Every one carries an axe, a dagger, and a sword, and without these weapons they are never seen. Their swords are broad, with wavy lines, and of Frankish make. From the tip of the finger-nails to the neck, each man of them is tattooed with pictures of trees, living beings, and other things. The women carry, fastened to their breast, a little case of iron, copper, silver, or gold, according to the wealth and resources, of their husbands. Fastened to the case they wear a ring, and upon that a dagger, all attached to their breast. About their necks they wear gold and silver chains. If the husband possesses ten thousand dirhems, he has one chain made for his wife; if twenty thousand, two; and for every ten thousand, one is added. Hence it often happens that a Scandinavian woman has a large number of chains about her neck. Their most highly prized ornaments consist of small green shells, of one of the varieties which are found in [the bottoms of] ships. They make great efforts to obtain these, paying as much as a dirhem for such a shell, and stringing them as a necklace for their wives.

They are the filthiest race that God ever created. They do not wipe themselves after going to stool, nor wash themselves after a nocturnal pollution, any more than if they were wild asses.

They come from their own country, anchor their ships in the Volga, which is a great river, and build large wooden houses on its banks. In every such house there live ten or twenty, more or fewer. Each man has a couch, where he sits with the beautiful girls he has for sale. Here he is as likely as not to enjoy one of them while a friend looks on. At times several of them will be thus engaged at the same moment, each in full view of the others. Now and again a merchant will resort to a house to purchase a girl, and find her master thus embracing her, and not giving over until he has fully had his will.

Every morning a girl comes and brings a tub of water, and places it before her master. In this he proceeds to wash his face and hands, and then his hair, combing it out over the vessel. Thereupon he blows his nose, and spits into the tub, and, leaving no dirt behind, conveys it all into this water. When he has finished, the girl carries the tub to the man next [to] him, who does the same. Thus she continues carrying the tub from one to another till each of those who are in the house has blown his nose and spit into the tub, and washed his face and hair.

As soon as their ships have reached the anchorage, every one goes ashore, having at hand bread, meat, onions, milk, and strong drink, and betakes himself to a high, upright piece of wood, bearing the likeness of a human face; this is surrounded by smaller statues, and behind these there are still other tall pieces of wood driven into the ground. He advances to the large wooden figure, prostrates himself before it, and thus addresses it: "O my Lord, I am come from a far country, bringing with me so and so many girls, and so and so many pelts of sable" [or, marten]; and when he has thus enumerated all his merchandise, he continues, "I have brought thee this present," laying before the wooden statue what he has brought, and saying: "I desire thee to bestow upon me a purchaser who has gold and silver coins, who will buy from me to my heart's content, and who will refuse none of my demands." Having so said, he departs. If his trade then goes ill, he returns and brings a second, or even a third present. If he still continues to have difficulty in obtaining what he desires, he brings a present to one of the small statues, and implores its intercession, saying: "These are the wives and daughters of our lord." Continuing thus, he goes to each statue in turn, invokes it, beseeches its intercession, and bows humbly before it. If it then chances that his trade goes swimmingly, and he disposes of all his merchandise, he reports: "My lord has fulfilled my desire; now it is my duty to repay him." Upon this, he takes a number of cattle and sheep, slaughters them, gives a portion of the meat to the poor, and carries the rest before the large statue and the smaller ones that surround it, hanging the heads of the sheep and cattle on the large piece of wood which is planted in the earth. When night falls, dogs come and devour it all. Then he who has so placed it exclaims: "I am well pleasing to my lord; he has consumed my present."

If one of their number falls sick, they set up a tent at a distance, in which they place him, leaving bread and water at hand. Thereafter they never approach nor speak to him, nor visit him the whole time, especially if he is a poor person or a slave. If he recovers and rises from his sick bed, he returns to his own. If he dies, they cremate him; but if he is a slave they leave him as he is till at length he becomes the food of dogs and birds of prey.

If they catch a thief or a robber, they lead him to a thick and lofty tree, fasten a strong rope round him, string him up, and let him hang until he drops to pieces by the action of wind and rain.

I was told that the least of what they do for their chiefs when they die, is to consume them with fire. When I was finally informed of the death of one of their magnates, I sought to witness what befell. First they laid him in his grave — over which a roof was erected — for the space of ten days, until they had completed the cutting and sewing of his clothes. In the case of a poor man, however, they merely build for him a boat, in which they place him, and consume it with fire. At the death of a rich man, they bring together his goods, and divide them into three parts. The first of these is for his family; the second is expended for the garments they make; and with the third they purchase strong drink, against the day when the girl resigns herself to death, and is burned with her master. To the use of wine they abandon themselves in mad fashion, drinking it day and night; and not seldom does one die with the cup in his hand.

When one of their chiefs dies, his family asks his girls and pages: "Which one of you will die with him?" Then one of them answers, "I." From the time that he [or she] utters this word, he is no longer free: should he wish to draw back, he is not permitted. For the most part, however, it is the girls that offer themselves. So, when the man of whom I spoke had died, they asked his girls, "Who will die with him?" One of them answered, "I." She was then committed to two girls, who were to keep watch over her, accompany her wherever she went, and even, on occasion, wash her feet. The people now began to occupy themselves with the dead man — to cut out the clothes for him, and to prepare whatever else was needful. During the whole of this period, the girl gave herself over to drinking and singing, and was cheerful and gay.

When the day was now come that the dead man and the girl were to be committed to the flames, I went to the river in which his ship lay, but found that it had already been drawn ashore. Four corner-blocks of birch and other woods had been placed in position for it, while around were stationed large wooden figures in the semblance of human beings. Thereupon the ship was brought up, and placed on the timbers above mentioned. In the mean time the people began to walk to and fro, uttering words which I did not understand. The dead man, meanwhile, lay at a distance in his grave, from which they had not yet removed him. Next they brought a couch, placed it in the ship, and covered it with Greek cloth of gold, wadded and quilted, with pillows of the same material. There came an old crone, whom they call the angel of death, and spread the articles mentioned on the couch. It was she who attended to the sewing of the garments, and to all the equipment; it was she, also, who was to slay the girl. I saw her; she was dark, . . . thickset, with a lowering countenance.

When they came to the grave, they removed the earth from the wooden roof, set the latter aside, and drew out the dead man in the loose wrapper in which he had died. Then I saw that he had turned quite black, by reason of the coldness of that country. Near him in the grave they had placed strong drink, fruits, and a lute; and these they now took out. Except for his color, the dead man had not changed. They now clothed him in drawers, leggings, boots, and a *kurtak* and *chaftan* of cloth of gold, with golden buttons, placing on his head a cap made of cloth of gold, trimmed with sable! Then they carried him into a tent placed in the ship, seated him on the wadded and quilted covering, supported him with the pillows, and, bringing strong drink, fruits, and basil, placed them all beside him. Then they brought a dog, which they cut in two, and threw into the ship; laid all his weapons beside him; and led up two horses which they chased until they were dripping with sweat, whereupon they cut them in pieces with their swords, and threw the flesh into the ship. Two oxen were then brought forward, cut in pieces, and flung into the ship. Finally they brought a cock and a hen, killed them, and threw them in also.

The girl who had devoted herself to death meanwhile walked to and fro, entering one after another of the tents which they had there. The occupant of each tent lay with her, saying, "Tell your master, 'I [the man] did this only for love of you.'"

When it was now Friday afternoon, they led the girl to an object which they had constructed, and which looked like the framework of a door. She then placed her feet on the extended hands of the men, was raised up above the framework, and uttered something in her language, whereupon they let her down. Then again they raised her, and she did as at first. Once more they let her down, and then lifted her a third time, while she did as at the previous times. They then handed her a hen, whose head she cut off and threw away; but the hen itself they cast into the ship. I inquired of the interpreter what it was that she had done. He replied: "The first time she said, 'Lo, I see here my father and mother'; the second time, 'Lo, now I see all my deceased relatives sitting'; the third time, 'Lo, there is my master, who is sitting in Paradise. Paradise is so beautiful, so green. With him are his men and boys. He calls me, so bring me to him.'" Then they led her away to the ship.

Here she took off her two bracelets, and gave them to the old woman who was called the angel of death, and who was to murder her. She also drew off her two anklets, and passed them to the two serving-maids, who were the daughters of the so-called angel of death. Then they lifted her into the ship, but did not yet admit her to the tent. Now men came up with shields and staves, and handed her a cup of strong drink. This she took, sang over it, and emptied it. "With this," so the interpreter told me, "she is taking leave of those who are dear to her." Then another cup was handed her, which she also took, and began a lengthy song. The crone admonished her to drain the cup without lingering, and to enter the tent where her master lay. By this time, as it seemed to me, the girl had become dazed [or, possibly, crazed]; she made as though she would enter the tent, and had brought her head forward between the tent and the ship, when the hag seized her by the head, and dragged her in. At this moment the men began to beat upon their shields with the staves, in order to drown the noise of her outcries, which might have terrified the other girls, and deterred then from seeking death with their masters in the future. Then six men followed into the tent, and each and every one had carnal companionship with her. Then they laid her down by her master's side, while two of the men seized her by the feet and two by the hands. The old woman known as the angel of death now knotted a rope around her neck, and handed the ends to two of the men to pull. Then with a broad-bladed dagger she smote her between the ribs, and drew the blade forth while the two men strangled her with the rope till she died.

The next of kin to the dead man now drew near, and, taking a piece of wood, lighted it, and walked backwards toward the ship holding the stick in one hand, with the other placed upon his buttocks (he being naked), until the wood which had been piled under the ship was ignited. Then the others came up with staves and firewood, each one carrying a stick already lighted at the upper end, and threw it all on the pyre. The pile was soon aflame, then the ship, finally the tent, the man, and the girl, and everything else in the ship. A terrible storm began to blow up, and thus intensified the flames, and gave wings to the blaze.

At my side stood one of the Northmen, and I heard him talking with the interpreter, who stood near him. I asked the interpreter what the Northman had said, and received this answer: "'You Arabs,' he said, must be a stupid set! You take him who is to you the most revered and beloved of men, and cast him into the ground, to be devoured by creeping things and worms. We, on the other hand, burn him in a twinkling, so that he instantly, without a moment's delay, enters into Paradise.' At this he burst out into uncontrollable laughter, and then continued: 'It is the love of the Master [God] that causes the wind to blow and snatch him away in an instant.'" And, in very truth, before an hour had passed, ship, wood, and girl had with the man, turned to ashes.

Thereupon they heaped over the place where the ship had stood something like a rounded hill, and erecting on the centre of it a large birchen post, wrote on it the name of the deceased, along with that of the king of the Northmen. Having done this, they left the spot.

70

BARRY CUNLIFFE

The Western Vikings

The Vikings who sailed down the rivers of Russia to raid, trade, and settle came mainly from eastern Scandinavia — what is today Sweden and Finland. Their cousins in western Scandinavia sailed to the south and west. In this selection from a wide-ranging history of the European Atlantic world, the author, a modern archaeologist, discusses the expansion of Western Vikings — mainly Danes and Norwegians — into the Atlantic. How would you compare the expansion of the Western Vikings with that of the Eastern Vikings into what became Russia?

Thinking Historically

The modern historian lets us hear enough from the medieval victims of the Vikings for us to feel their fear, and his list of destroyed cities and massacred peoples registers the horror they must have unleashed in their era. But Cunliffe also gives us information that enables us to put the Viking attacks in some perspective. What is that information? What perspective on the Vikings does the reading give you?

The Coming of the Northmen

About 790 Beaduheard, the king's reeve at Dorchester in southern Britain, got news that three foreign ships had landed at Portland and, assuming them to be traders, he went to welcome them. He was wrong.

Barry Cunliffe, *Facing the Ocean: The Atlantic and Its Peoples* (Oxford: Oxford University Press, 2001), 482–83, 488–95, 499, 514–16.

They were raiders from Scandinavia and he died for his mistake. The Dorset landing was a foretaste. A few years later, in 793, the raiding began in earnest with the attack on the monastery of St Cuthbert on Lindisfarne: "Never before has such terror appeared in Britain as we have now suffered from a pagan race, nor was it thought that such an inroad from the sea could be made. Behold, the church of St Cuthbert spattered with the blood of the priests of God, despoiled of all its ornaments; a place more venerable than all in Britain is given as prey to pagan people." So wrote the English cleric Alcuin at the court of Charlemagne. Many more raids followed around the coasts of Britain and Ireland. The Franks were soon to suffer, so too the Bretons. By the 840s Viking war bands were exploring further south along the Atlantic coasts. A vast fleet of 150 ships sailed up the Garonne and plundered almost to Toulouse. Then it moved onwards to attack Galicia and Lisbon before sailing into the Guadalquivir. Here, from their base on the Isla Menor, the Vikings pillaged Seville but were severely mauled by the Moors. Those captured were hanged from the city's palm trees, and two hundred Viking heads were sent by the Emir to his allies in Tangier as an effective witness to his military prowess. Undeterred, the Viking force continued through the Straits of Gibraltar harassing the coasts as they sailed to the mouth of the Rhône where, on an island in the Camargue, a base was established for raiding upriver into the heart of France and across the sea to the coasts of Italy. In 861 they returned to their base on the Loire. The expedition had been "at once profitable and honourable."

The Mediterranean venture, while a notable feat, was of little lasting consequence. But meanwhile, in the north, raids and settlement had reached significant proportions. Some indication of what was going on is given by the pained lamentation of Ermentarius, a monk at Noirmoutier, writing in the 860s:

> The number of ships increases, the endless flood of Vikings never ceases to grow bigger. Everywhere Christ's people are the victims of massacre, burning, and plunder. The Vikings overrun all that lies before them, and no one can withstand them. They seize Bordeaux, Périgueux, Limoges, Angoulême, Toulouse; Angers, Tours, and Orleans are made deserts. Ships past counting voyage up the Seine . . . Rouen is laid waste, looted, and burnt; Paris, Beauvais, Meaux are taken, Melun's stronghold is razed to the ground, Chartres occupied, Evreux and Bayeux looted, and every town invested. . . .

Why the Raids of the Northmen Began

The raids of the Danes and Norwegians began in the last decade of the eighth century, and over the next seventy years rose to a devastating crescendo. No single factor was responsible for unleashing the fury, but there can be little doubt that the overseas ventures became possible only after the longship had reached its peak of excellence by the middle of the eighth century. The Scandinavian landscape demanded good shipping. The long Atlantic coastline of Norway, with its deeply indented fjords, was accessible with ease only by sea, while the sounds and islands of Denmark had, for millennia, been bound together by boat. The Baltic, too, was a cradle for navigation — a great inland sea providing ease of access between the extensive littorals and their productive hinterlands, and to the river routes penetrating far south across the North European Plain. Throughout Scandinavia settlements favoured the sea coasts and the inland lakes and waterways. They faced the open water and kept their backs to the forest. Thus communities depended upon ships for their livelihood, their rulers able to maintain their power only by command of the sea. In such a world it is easy to see how the ship became a symbol of authority, honed to perfection to reflect the status of the elite. A ship, either real or symbolic, might also accompany its owner in his burial. . . . By the early years of the ninth century, all the features characteristic of the classic Viking ship had been brought together, creating fast and highly efficient seagoing vessels suitable for carrying men across the ocean in search of land and plunder.

. . . In the course of the eighth century, trade between continental Europe and England developed apace, with well-established links leading northwards to the Baltic. In this way the volume of mercantile traffic in the southern North Sea increased dramatically, while the rulers of Denmark became increasingly aware of the wealth to be had to the south. Through the various traders who visited the Scandinavian ports they would also have learnt the political geography of western Europe — most notably the whereabouts of its rich, isolated monasteries and the distracting factional disputes endemic among its ruling households. To the Scandinavian elite there was much prestige to be had in leading a successful raid: the spoils would enrich the begetters and would bind followers closer to their leader. In the competitive emulation which accompanied the early raiding expeditions the number, intensity, and duration of the raids inevitably escalated.

Another, quite different, factor at work was the desire for new land to settle. With a growing population the narrow coastal zone of Norway was too restricted a territory to provide the social space needed for enterprising sons to establish themselves. The only solution was to find new territories overseas in Britain and Ireland, and further afield on the more remote islands of the north Atlantic. For the most part what was sought was new farmland, like the home territories, where families could set up new farms with plenty of space around for expansion by successive generations. It was this that the north Atlantic could supply in plenty. What England had to offer was rather different but no less acceptable — well-run estates which new Scandinavian lords could leave largely undisturbed, simply taking the profits.

Another incentive to moving overseas was the possibility of setting up merchant colonies emulating those that were so successful in the Baltic and along the eastern coasts of the North Sea. York, already a developing English market, was taken over by the Northmen in 866 and rapidly expanded to become the principal entrepôt in northern Britain, while an entirely new port-of-trade was established at Dublin and soon became a centre for Irish Sea commerce. In all of these ventures the ship was vital.

It would be wrong to give the impression that overseas activities were narrowly focused: trading could soon turn into raiding, while raiding could dissipate itself into settlement. One was never exclusive of the other. This is evocatively summed up in an account of the lifestyle of Svein Asleifarson recorded in the twelfth-century *Orkneyinga Saga*, no doubt referring wistfully to a long-gone era when Vikings behaved like Vikings:

> In the spring he had more than enough to occupy him, with a great deal of seed to sow which he saw to carefully himself. Then when the job was done, he would go off plundering in the Hebrides and in Ireland on what he called his "spring-trip," then back home just after midsummer where he stayed till the cornfields had been reaped and the grain was safely in. After that he would go off raiding again, and never came back till the first month of winter was ended. This he used to call his "autumn trip."

The Vikings in the West: A Brief Progress

. . . *Viking* is the word frequently used by the English sources to describe raiders and settlers from Scandinavia, while the Carolingian sources prefer *Northmen*. Both words include, without differentiation, Danes and Norwegians. Until the mid-ninth century it is possible to make a broad distinction between Norwegians, who settled northern and western Scotland and the Northern and Western Isles and were active in the Irish Sea, and Danes, who raided the North Sea and Channel coasts, but thereafter the distinction becomes blurred.

The progress of the settlement of north-western Britain by the Norwegians is unrecorded, but contact began as early as the seventh century and it is quite likely that the colonization was largely completed during the course of the eighth century. The newly settled areas provided the springboard for attacks on Ireland and the Irish Sea coasts, becoming increasingly widespread and frequent in the period 795–840.

The rich and unprotected monasteries were the target. Iona was attacked three times, in 795, 802, and 806, in the first flush of activity. Thereafter raids thrust further and further south — 821 Wexford, 822 Cork, and 824 the isolated monastery of Skelling Michael in the Atlantic off the Kerry coast. Having picked off the vulnerable coastal communities the attacks then began to penetrate inland, but usually no more than 30 kilometres or so from the safety of navigable water. These early attacks were opportunistic hit-and-run affairs, meeting no significant organized opposition.

Meanwhile in the North Sea the Danes adopted similar tactics. In 820 a massive Danish fleet of two hundred vessels threatened Saxony, and in three successive years, beginning in 834, the great trading port of Dorestad was devastated. Frisia became the immediate focus of contention. In 838 the Danish king Harik demanded of the Frankish king Louis that "The Frisians be given over to him" — a request that was roundly refused. The vulnerability of the coast was vividly brought home when, in 835, the monastery of St-Philibert on the island of Noirmoutier south of the Loire estuary was attacked. England suffered only sporadic raids at first, but these intensified in the 830s. . . .

The events of 840–865 saw the Scandinavians working the full length of the Atlantic zone from the Rhine to Gibraltar and beyond, but they were at their most active and most persistent along the major rivers — the Seine, the Thames, the Loire, and the Garonne — feeding off the cities that owed their wealth and well-being to their command of the river routes. The rivers that brought them their commercial advantage through access to the sea now brought men who sought to take it for themselves.

The 860s saw a change of pace from raid to settlement, accompanied by intensified and co-ordinated opposition by those whose land the Northmen were intent on taking. The Franks were the first to come to terms with the new reality by building fortified bridges across the rivers Seine and Loire, by fortifying towns and monasteries, and by paying tribute to groups of Vikings in return for protection or military services. These tactics protected the heart of the kingdom while leaving the lower reaches of the two rivers to the roving bands of invaders who had now taken up residence in the areas. The strategy kept Frankia free from further incursions until a new wave of attacks began on Paris in 885. . . .

Towards the end of the tenth century, with the rise of a strong dynasty in Denmark under Harald Bluetooth and his son, Sven Forkbeard, a new phase of Viking raiding was initiated, and once more it was the Atlantic coastal regions as far south as Iberia that took the brunt of the attack. England was particularly vulnerable. In 991 Sven Forkbeard led his first raid against the English, his activities culminating in the conquest of the kingdom in 1013. Three years later, after his death, his son Knut was formally recognized as king of England. Dynastic squabbles and claims and counter-claims to the English throne rumbled on throughout the eleventh century, but the failure of the threatened Danish conquest of England to materialize in 1085 was the effective end of the Viking episode. Occasional Norwegian expeditions to the Northern and Western Isles were the last ripples, three centuries after the Viking wave first struck.

The Northmen and the Atlantic Communities

That the impact of the Scandinavians on the Atlantic communities was profound and lasting there can be no doubt, but sufficient will have been said to show that it varied significantly from region to region.

In lightly inhabited or empty lands like the Northern and Western Isles, the Faroes, Iceland, and Greenland, Scandinavian culture was directly transplanted in its entirety and flourished much in the style of the Norwegian homeland, but elsewhere the Scandinavian component fused with indigenous culture. In regions where the local systems were well established and comparatively stable, as in eastern England and the maritime region of France (soon to become Normandy), the new order emerged imperceptibly from the old with little disruption to the social or economic balance, but in other areas, like Ireland, where warfare between rival factions of the elite was endemic, the Scandinavian presence was a catalyst for widespread change. Here the ferocity of the Irish warlords matched their own. For this reason the small enclaves established at harbours around the coast remained small, developing as isolated trading colonies in an otherwise hostile landscape. Apart from certain areas of the north-east, large-scale land-taking and settlement was not possible. Much the same pattern can be seen in south-west Wales.

The Scandinavian settlements of the Irish Sea zone chose good docking facilities, initially to serve as protected anchorages for the vessels of the early raiders, but these quickly developed as trading centres, making the Irish Sea the major focus of exchange in the Scandinavian maritime system. From here ships might go south to Andalucía, north to Iceland and beyond, or around Britain eastwards to the Baltic. In this way the Irish Sea became the hub of a complex network of communications built upon the long-distance exchange systems which had already been established in the preceding centuries.

In Brittany a rather different pattern of interaction emerged. Here the long-term hostility between the Bretons and the Franks provided a situation in which raiding and mercenary activity could profitably be maintained, while the internecine warfare that broke out in both kingdoms in the painful periods when succession was being contested offered the raiders further opportunities for easy intervention.

Throughout this time the Loire formed the focus of Scandinavian activity and Nantes was often in their control, but there is, as yet, little evidence that a major trading enclave developed here. It may simply have been that the political turmoil in the region allowed warfare in its various modes to provide the necessary economic underpinning to sustain Viking society. From the Breton point of view the Scandinavian presence, disruptive though it was, was an important factor in helping to maintain their independence from the Franks.

South of the Loire, Viking military activity was sporadic and superficial, at least in so far as the historical record allows us to judge, but given their interest in trade it is difficult to believe that there were not regular visits by merchants to the Gironde and Garonne and along the Atlantic seaboard of Iberia. In this they would simply have been following the routes plied by their predecessors.

Some measure of the integration of the multifaceted maritime system that emerged is provided by a wreck excavated at Skuldelev in the Danish fjord of Roskilde. It was one of six that had been sunk to block the fjord from seaward attack some time in the late eleventh or early twelfth century. The vessel was a typical Viking longship suitable for carrying fifty to sixty warriors. Dendrochronology has shown that the ship had been built about 1060 at, or in the vicinity of, Dublin. What service it saw as a raiding vessel in the seas around Britain and France we will never know, but its final resting place 2,200 kilometres from the yard in which it had been built is a vivid reminder of the capacity of the sea in bringing the communities of Atlantic Europe ever closer together.

71

Eirik's Saga

Scandinavian seafarers spread out in all directions in the tenth century. While Swedes and Finns sailed down the rivers of Russia to the Black and Caspian seas, Danes conquered and colonized from England down the coast of France into the Mediterranean as far as Italy, North Africa, and Arabia. The Vikings of Norway sailed mainly

"Eirik's Saga," in *The Vinland Sagas: The Norse Discovery of America*, trans. and introduction by Magnus Magnusson and Hermann Palsson (Harmondsworth, Middlesex, England: Penguin Books, 1965), 75–78.

westward, colonizing Iceland, Greenland, and North America (certainly Newfoundland but likely further south). The Norsemen discovered Iceland in about 860 and began settlement some fourteen years later. By 930, Iceland contained the families and retainers of many lords who fled Western Norway to escape the conquering Harald Fairhair.

Eirik the Red (950–1003) came to Iceland with his family in 960 after his father had to flee Norway because of "some killings." In turn, Eirik was exiled from Iceland in 982 after he committed murder in the heat of two quarrels. Exile meant searching for a settlement even further west, leading Eirik to Greenland. While not the first to see or land in Greenland, Eirik established the first colony there.

This excerpt from "Eirik's Saga," written about 1260, insofar as it captures the oral tradition, gives us an idea of Viking thought in the tenth century. Does this account change your idea of Viking society? How? How does it contribute to your understanding of the Viking expansion?

Thinking Historically

How does this internal view of Viking society inevitably change our moral perspective from that of an outsider? How might the religious differences between Ibn Fadlan and this author lead to different moral perspectives?

There was a warrior king called Olaf the White, who was the son of King Ingjald. Olaf went on a Viking expedition to the British Isles, where he conquered Dublin and the adjoining territory and made himself king over them. He married Aud the Deep-Minded, the daughter of Ketil Flat-Nose; they had a son called Thorstein the Red.

Olaf was killed in battle in Ireland, and Aud and Thorstein the Red then went to the Hebrides. There Thorstein married Thurid, the daughter of Eyvind the Easterner; they had many children.

Thorstein the Red became a warrior king, and joined forces with Earl Sigurd the Powerful, together they conquered Caithness, Sutherland, Ross, and Moray, and more than half of Argyll. Thorstein ruled over these territories as king until he was betrayed by the Scots and killed in battle.

Aud the Deep-Minded was in Caithness when she learned of Thorstein's death; she had a ship built secretly in a forest, and when it was ready she sailed away to Orkney. There she gave away in marriage Groa, daughter of Thorstein the Red.

After that, Aud set out for Iceland; she had twenty freeborn men aboard her ship. She reached Iceland and spent the first winter with her brother Bjorn at Bjarnarhaven. Then she took possession of the entire Dales district between Dogurdar River and Skraumuhlaups River, and made her home at Hvamm. She used to say prayers at Kross Hills; she had crosses erected there, for she had been baptized and was a devout Christian.

Many well-born men, who had been taken captive in the British Isles by Vikings and were now slaves, came to Iceland with her. One of them was called Vifil; he was of noble descent. He had been taken prisoner in the British Isles and was a slave until Aud gave him his freedom.

When Aud gave land to members of her crew, Vifil asked her why she did not give him some land like the others. Aud replied that it was of no importance, and said that he would be considered a man of quality wherever he was. She gave him Vifilsdale, and he settled there. He married, and had two sons called Thorbjorn and Thorgeir; they were both promising men, and grew up with their father.

Eirik Explores Greenland

There was a man called Thorvald, who was the father of Eirik the Red. He and Eirik left their home in Jaederen because of some killings and went to Iceland. They took possession of land in Hornstrands, and made their home at Drangar. Thorvald died there, and Eirik the Red then married Thjodhild, and moved south to Haukadale; he cleared land there and made his home at Eirikstead, near Vatnshorn.

Eirik's slaves started a landslide that destroyed the farm of a man called Valthjof, at Valthjofstead; so Eyjolf Saur, one of Valthjof's kinsmen, killed the slaves at Skeidsbrekkur, above Vatnshorn. For this, Eirik killed Eyjolf Saur; he also killed Hrafn the Dueller, at Leikskalar. Geirstein and Odd of Jorvi, who were Eyjolf's kinsmen, took action over his killing, and Eirik was banished from Haukadale.

Eirik then took possession of Brok Island and Oxen Island, and spent the first winter at Tradir, in South Island. He lent his benchboards to Thorgest of Breidabolstead. After that, Eirik moved to Oxen Island, and made his home at Eirikstead. He then asked for his benchboards back, but they were not returned; so Eirik went to Breidabolstead and seized them. Thorgest pursued him, and they fought a battle near the farmstead at Drangar. Two of Thorgest's sons and several other men were killed there.

After this, both Eirik and Thorgest maintained a force of fighting-men at home. Eirik was supported by Styr Thorgrimsson, Eyjolf of Svin Island, Thorbjorn Vifilsson, and the sons of Thorbrand of Alptafjord;

Thorgest was supported by Thorgeir of Hitardale, Aslak of Langadale and his son Illugi, and the sons of Thord Gellir.

Eirik and his men were sentenced to outlawry at the Thorsness Assembly. He made his ship ready in Eiriksbay, and Eyjolf of Svin Island hid him in Dimunarbay while Thorgest and his men were scouring the islands for him.

Thorbjorn Vifilsson and Styr and Eyjolf accompanied Eirik out beyond the islands, and they parted in great friendship; Eirik said he would return their help as far as it lay within his power, if ever they had need of it. He told them he was going to search for the land that Gunnbjorn, the son of Ulf Crow, had sighted when he was driven westwards off course and discovered the Gunnbjarnar Skerries; he added that he would come back to visit his friends if he found this country.

Eirik put out to sea past Snæfells Glacier, and made land near the glacier that is known as Blaserk. From there he sailed south to find out if the country were habitable there. He spent the first winter on Eiriks Island, which lies near the middle of the Eastern Settlement. In the spring he went to Eiriksfjord, where he decided to make his home. That summer he explored the wilderness to the west and gave names to many landmarks there. He spent the second winter on Eiriks Holms, off Hvarfs Peak. The third summer he sailed all the way north to Snæfell and into Hrafnsfjord, where he reckoned he was farther inland than the head of Eiriksfjord. Then he turned back and spent the third winter on Eiriks Island, off the mouth of Eiriksfjord.

He sailed back to Iceland the following summer and put in at Breidafjord. He stayed the winter with Ingolf of Holmlatur. In the spring he fought a battle with Thorgest of Breidabolstead and was defeated. After that a reconciliation was arranged between them.

That summer Eirik set off to colonize the country he had discovered; he named it *Greenland*, for he said that people would be much more tempted to go there if it had an attractive name.

72

The Poetic Edda, Selections from the Havamol

The Poetic Edda constitutes a collection of poems, songs, stories, and proverbs from the rich body of Nordic mythology. In addition to the Edda, there are the Sagas — the historic stories like selection 71 and the epic tales of gods, giants, heroes, and the end of the world. Much of the Sagas have enriched the imaginations of generations from the operas of Richard Wagner to *The Lord of the Rings*. The Edda are shorter and less well known, but more immediately accessible than the grand stories. The Havamol is the part of *The Poetic Edda* that contains an abundance of practical guidance and moral lessons. These poems were part of an oral tradition in northern Europe for centuries before they were written down about the eleventh century. This version was translated from an Icelandic poetic Edda of the thirteenth century. What do these brief poems tell you about the culture and life of the people who told and wrote them?

Thinking Historically

Of all Norse, Viking, or Icelandic literature, the poems of the Havamol most directly express moral values. What do they tell you about the moral values of their authors? The Havamol has sometimes been compared to other books of wisdom literature, including the book of Proverbs in the Hebrew Bible. No single book can represent the ideas of an entire people throughout time and space. However, to the extent that these selections can stand for the ideas of the Vikings, how would you characterize their ideas of morality? What if any of these values do you see reflected in the behavior of the people described by Ibn Fadlan? How were the Vikings different from the barbarians who toppled the Roman and Han empires in the third to sixth centuries?

The Poetic Edda, trans. from the Icelandic with an introduction and notes by Henry Adams Bellows (Princeton, N.J.: Princeton University Press, 1936). Scanned at sacred-texts.com, April–July 2001, available online at http://www.sacred-texts.com/neu/poe/poe04.htm.

1. Within the gates | ere a man shall go,
(Full warily let him watch,)
Full long let him look about him;
For little he knows | where a foe may lurk,
And sit in the seats within.

3. Fire he needs | who with frozen knees
Has come from the cold without;
Food and clothes | must the farer have,
The man from the mountains come.

4. Water and towels | and welcoming speech
Should he find who comes, to the feast;
If renown he would get, | and again be greeted,
Wisely and well must he act.

5. Wits must he have | who wanders wide,
But all is easy at home;
At the witless man | the wise shall wink
When among such men he sits.

34. Crooked and far | is the road to a foe,
Though his house on the highway be;
But wide and straight | is the way to a friend,
Though far away he fare.

35. Forth shall one go, | nor stay as a guest
In a single spot forever;
Love becomes loathing | if long one sits
By the hearth in another's home.

36. Better a house, | though a hut it be,
A man is master at home;
A pair of goats | and a patched-up roof
Are better far than begging.

38. Away from his arms | in the open field
A man should fare not a foot;
For never he knows | when the need for a spear
Shall arise on the distant road.

39. If wealth a man | has won for himself,
Let him never suffer in need;
Oft he saves for a foe | what he plans for a friend,
For much goes worse than we wish.

78. Cattle die, | and kinsmen die,
And so one dies one's self;
One thing now | that never dies,
The fame of a dead man's deeds.

81. Give praise to the day at evening, | to a woman on her pyre,
To a weapon which is tried, | to a maid at wed lock,
To ice when it is crossed, | to ale that is drunk.

82. When the gale blows hew wood, | in fair winds seek the water;
Sport with maidens at dusk, | for day's eyes are many;
From the ship seek swiftness, | from the shield protection,
Cuts from the sword, | from the maiden kisses.

90. The love of women | fickle of will
Is like starting o'er ice | with a steed unshod,
A two-year-old restive | and little tamed,
Or steering a rudderless | ship in a storm,
Or, lame, hunting reindeer | on slippery rocks.

91. Clear now will I speak, | for I know them both,
Men false to women are found;
When fairest we speak, | then falsest we think,
Against wisdom we work with deceit.

92. Soft words shall he speak | and wealth shall he offer
Who longs for a maiden's love,
And the beauty praise | of the maiden bright;
He wins whose wooing is best.

139. I ween that I hung | on the windy tree,
Hung there for nights full nine;
With the spear I was wounded, | and offered I was
To Othin, myself to myself,
On the tree that none | may ever know
What root beneath it runs.

73

From The Secret History
of the Mongols

This Mongol account records the early years of Mongol expansion under Chingis Khan, the founder of the empire. Born Temujin in 1155 or 1167, the young son of a minor tribal chieftain attracted the support of Mongol princes in the years between 1187 and 1206 through a series of decisive military victories over other tribes and competing Mongol claimants to the title of Great Khan.

The Mongols were illiterate before the time of Chingis Khan, who adopted the script of the Uighurs, one of the more literate peoples of the steppe. Thus the *Secret History* was written in Mongolian with Uighur letters. The only surviving version is a fourteenth-century Chinese translation. The author is unknown, but the book provides detailed accounts of the early years of Temujin and ends with the reign of his son and successor, Ogodai, in 1228 — only a year after his father's death.

Because so much about the Mongols was written by their literate enemies, *The Secret History* is an invaluable resource: It is clearly an "insider's" account of the early years of Mongol expansion. While it includes mythic elements — it begins with the augury of the birth of a blue wolf to introduce Chingis Khan — *The Secret History* is, without doubt, an authentic representation of a Mongol point of view.

In this selection, you will read three passages. The first describes a meeting in about 1187 of several tribal leaders who agree that the twenty-year-old Temujin should become Great Khan (Chingis Khan). What do these tribal leaders expect to gain from this alliance under Temujin? What do they offer in return?

The second passage deals with an early Mongol victory in 1202 over the neighboring Tatars, a tribe that Europeans often confused with the Mongols. How merciful or harsh does Chingis Khan seem?

The third passage recounts the story of an important Mongol victory over the Naiman in 1204. What does this section tell you about the sources of Mongol military strength?

How does this "insider's" view of the Mongols provide unique information or a perspective that would be unattainable from non-Mongols?

Adapted by K. Reilly from R. P. Lister, *Genghis Khan* (New York: Barnes & Noble, 1993), 99–100, 136–39, 166–76, 191–93. While this volume is a retelling of the almost indecipherable *The Secret History of the Mongols* in Lister's own words, the selections that follow simplify without contextualizing or explaining the original work. More scholarly editions, trans. and ed. Francis Woodman Cleaves (Cambridge, Mass.: Harvard University Press, 1982) and Paul Kahn (San Francisco: North Point Press, 1984) are less accessible.

Thinking Historically

What moral values does this selection reveal? Do the Mongols think of themselves as "moral" people? Is the author-historian interested in describing what happened objectively, or in presenting an unblemished, sanitized view?

In what ways does this written Mongol history make you more sympathetic to the Mongols? Notice that the "Mongols Conquer the Naiman" passage begins with an account of the Naiman. How fair does the Mongol author seem to be toward the Naiman? Would this be a good source for understanding the Naiman? Do you think the Mongol authors described the Naiman more accurately than Chinese or Europeans described the Mongols?

The Choosing of the Khan

. . . A general council of all the chieftains was called, and the three most notable men among them, Prince Altan, Khuchar, and Sacha Beki, came forward. They addressed Temujin formally, in the following manner:

> We will make you Khan; you shall ride at our head, against our foes.
> We will throw ourselves like lightning on your enemies;
> We will bring you their finest women and girls, their rich tents like palaces.
> From all the peoples and nations we will bring you the fair girls and the high-stepping horses;
> When you hunt wild beasts, we will drive them towards you; we will encircle them, pressing hard at their heels.
>
> If on the day of battle we disobey you,
> Take our flocks from us, our women and children, and cast our worthless heads on the steppe.
> If in times of peace we disobey you,
> Part us from our men and our servants, our wives and our sons;
> Abandon us and cast us out, masterless, on the forsaken earth. . . .

Mongol Conquest of Tatars

. . . Temujin came up against the Tatars at Dalan Namurgas, on the Khalkha, east of Buir Nor, and defeated them in battle. They fell back; the Mongol armies pursued them, slaying and capturing them in large numbers.

The princes, Altan, Khuchar, and Daritai, were less assiduous in the pursuit. Finding a great number of animals roaming the steppes in the absence of their Tatar owners, they followed the usual custom of rounding them up, and collecting anything that took their fancy in the abandoned Tatar camps.

Temujin, having issued a clear order [against looting], could not tolerate their disobedience. He detached portions of his army, placed them under the command of Jebe and Khubilai, and sent them off after the disobedient princes, with orders to take away from them everything they had captured. The outcome was what might have been expected. Prince Altan and Khuchar, retiring in haste with as much of their booty as they could take with them, departed from their allegiance to him. They re-established themselves as independent chieftains, entering into such arrangements with Ong Khan, Jamukha, and other rulers as seemed desirable.

Daritai, however, seeing a little more clearly than the others, submitted to having his booty taken away from him.

Owing to his determined pursuit of the Tatars, Temujin found that he had a very considerable number of Tatar prisoners. They were kept under guard in the Mongol camp, and for the most part they were not greatly perturbed by their situation. Some of the chieftains might expect to be executed, but the lesser men had a reasonable hope of surviving. Some might have to serve as warriors under the Mongols, or even be enslaved, but a slave of talents could always hope to become a warrior again.

Temujin held a council to decide what to do with them. It was a great matter, and nobody was present at this council but his own family. The Khan's intention [was] to wipe out his enemies on a large scale. . . .

Belgutai had . . . made friends among the Tatar prisoners. One of these was Yeke Charan, the principal Tatar leader. . . . When Yeke Charan asked him what decision the family council had come to, Belgutai did not hesitate to tell him.

"We agreed to measure you against the linchpin,"[1] he said.

Yeke Charan told his fellow prisoners of the Khan's decision. Having nothing to lose, they rose up against their guards and fought their way out of the camp, taking with them what weapons they could seize. They gathered themselves together on a hilltop in a tight formation of fierce warriors. Men who are going to be killed whatever happens, and know it, fight well. The destruction of the Tatars, which was in due course accomplished, cost many Mongol lives.

Temujin was remarkably lenient towards Belgutai.

"Because Belgutai revealed the decision of the family council," he said, "Our army suffered great losses. From now on, Belgutai will take

---

[1]This was not an unknown procedure, though it had never been applied on quite such a vast scale. Prisoners were led past the wheel of a wagon. Those who were taller than the linchpin were beheaded; the children, who were smaller, survived to be taken into the Mongol armies when they grew up.

no part in the council. While it is being held, he will remain outside, keeping order in the camp, and he will sit in judgment during that time over the quarrelsome, the thieves, and the liars. When the council is finished and the wine is all drunk, then Belgutai can come in."

He ordered at the same time that Daritai should be banned from the family councils, for disobeying his *yasakh*.[2] . . .

Mongols Conquer the Naiman

When the news was brought to [the Naiman] Tayang Khan that someone claiming to be Ong Khan had been slain at the Neikun watercourse, his mother, Gurbesu, said: "Ong Khan was the great Khan of former days. Bring his head here! If it is really he, we will sacrifice to him."

She sent a message to Khorisu, commanding him to cut the head off and bring it in. When it was brought to her, she recognised it as that of Ong Khan. She placed it on a white cloth, and her daughter-in-law carried out the appropriate rites. . . . A wine-feast was held and stringed instruments were played. Gurbesu, taking up a drinking-bowl, made an offering to the head of Ong Khan.

When the sacrifice was made to it, the head grinned.

"He laughs!" Tayang Khan cried. Overcome by religious awe, he flung the head on the floor and trampled on it until it was mangled beyond recognition.

The great general Kokse'u Sabrakh was present at these ceremonies, and observed them without enthusiasm. It was he who had been the only Naiman general to offer resistance to Temujin and Ong Khan on their expedition against Tayang Khan's brother Buyiruk.

"First of all," he remarked, "you cut off the head of a dead ruler, and then you trample it into the dust. What kind of behaviour is this? Listen to the baying of those dogs: It has an evil sound. The Khan your father, Inancha Bilgei, once said: 'My wife is young, and I, her husband, am old. Only the power of prayer has enabled me to beget my son, this same Tayang. But will my son, born a weakling, be able to guard and hold fast my common and evil-minded people?'

"Now the baying of the dogs seems to announce that some disaster is at hand. The rule of our queen, Gurbesu, is firm; but you, my Khan, Torlukh Tayang, are weak. It is truly said of you that you have no thought for anything but the two activities of hawking and driving game, and no capacity for anything but these."

Tayang Khan was accustomed to the disrespect of his powerful general, but he was stung into making a rash decision.

---

[2]Order, law.

"There are a few Mongols in the east. From the earliest days this old and great Ong Khan feared them, with their quivers; now they have made war on him and driven him to death. No doubt they would like to be rulers themselves. There are indeed in Heaven two shining lights, the sun and the moon, and both can exist there; but how can there be two rulers here on earth? Let us go and gather those Mongols in."

His mother Gurbesu said: "Why should we start making trouble with them? The Mongols have a bad smell; they wear black clothes. They are far away, out there; let them stay there. Though it is true," she added, "that we could have the daughters of their chieftains brought here; when we had washed their hands and feet, they could milk our cows and sheep for us."

Tayang Khan said: "What is there so terrible about them? Let us go to these Mongols and take away their quivers."

"What big words you are speaking," Kokse'u Sabrakh said. "Is Tayang Khan the right man for it? Let us keep the peace."

Despite these warnings, Tayang Khan decided to attack the Mongols. It was a justifiable decision; his armies were stronger, but time was on Temujin's side. Tayang sought allies, sending a messenger to Alakhu Shidigichuri of the Onggut, in the south, the guardians of the ramparts between Qashin and the Khingan. "I am told that there are a few Mongols in the east," he said. "Be my right hand! I will ride against them from here, and we will take their quivers away from them."

[Alakhu Shidigichuri's] reply was brief: "I cannot be your right hand." He in his turn sent a message to Temujin. "Tayang Khan of the Naiman wants to come and take away your quivers. He sent to me and asked me to be his right hand. I refused. I make you aware of this, so that when he comes your quivers will not be taken away."[3]

When he received Alakhu's message Temujin, having wintered near Guralgu, was holding one of his . . . roundups of game on the camel-steppes of Tulkinche'ut, in the east. The beasts had been encircled by the clansmen and warriors; the chieftains were gathered together, about to begin the great hunt.

"What shall we do now?" some of them said to each other. "Our horses are lean at this season."

. . . The snow had only lately left the steppe; the horses had found nothing to graze on during these recent months. Their ribs stuck out and they lacked strength.

The Khan's youngest brother, Temuga, spoke up. . . .

---

[3]Temujin, grateful for this warning, sent him five hundred horses and a thousand sheep. His friendship with Alakhu was valuable to him at a later time.

"How can that serve as an excuse," he said, "that the horses are lean? My horses are quite fat enough. How can we stay sitting here, when we receive a message like that?"

Prince Belgutai spoke. . . .

"If a man allows his quivers to be taken away during his lifetime, what kind of an existence does he have? For a man who is born a man, it is a good enough end to be slain by another man, and lie on the steppe with his quiver and bow beside him. The Naiman make fine speeches, with their many men and their great kingdom. But suppose, having heard their fine speeches, we ride against them, would it be so difficult to take their quivers away from them? We must mount and ride; it is the only thing to do."

Temujin was wholly disposed to agree with these sentiments. He broke off the hunt, set the army in motion, and camped near Ornu'u on the Khalkha. Here he paused for a time while he carried out a swift re-organisation of the army. A count was held of the people; they were divided up into thousands, hundreds, and tens, and commanders of these units were appointed. Also at this time he chose his personal body-guards, the seventy day-guards and eighty night-guards. . . .

Having reorganised the army, he marched away from the mountainside of Ornu'u on the Khalkha, and took the way of war against the Naiman.

The spring of the Year of the Rat [1204] was by now well advanced. During this westward march came the Day of the Red Disc, the sixteenth day of the first moon of summer. On this day, the moon being at the full, the Khan caused the great yak's-tail banner to be consecrated, letting it be sprinkled with fermented mare's milk, with the proper observances.

They continued the march up the Kerulen, with Jebe and Khubilai in the van. When they came on to the Saari steppes, they met with the first scouts of the Naiman. There were a few skirmishes between the Naiman and Mongol scouts; in one of these, a Mongol scout was captured, a man riding a grey horse with a worn saddle. The Naiman studied this horse with critical eyes, and thought little of it. "The Mongols' horses are inordinately lean," they said to each other.

The Mongol army rode out on to the Saari steppes, and began to deploy themselves for the forthcoming battle. . . . Dodai Cherbi, one of the newly appointed captains, put a proposal before the Khan.

"We are short in numbers compared to the enemy; besides this, we are exhausted after the long march, our horses in particular. It would be a good idea to settle in this camp, so that our horses can graze on the steppe, until they have had as much to eat as they need. Meanwhile, we can deceive the enemy by making puppets and lighting innumerable fires. For every man, we will make at least one puppet, and we will burn fires in five places. It is said that the Naiman people are very numerous, but it is rumoured also that their king is a weakling, who has never left his tents. If we keep them in a state of uncertainty about our numbers, with our puppets and our fires, our geldings can stuff themselves till they are fat."

The suggestion pleased Temujin, who had the order passed on to the soldiers to light fires immediately. Puppets were constructed and placed all over the steppe, some sitting or lying by the fires, some of them even mounted on horses.

At night, the watchers of the Naiman saw, from the flanks of the mountain, fires twinkling all over the steppe. They said to each other: "Did they not say that the Mongols were very few? Yet they have more fires than there are stars in Heaven."

Having previously sent to Tayang Khan news of the lean grey horse with the shabby saddle, they now sent him the message: "The warriors of the Mongols are camped out all over the Saari steppes. They seem to grow more numerous every day; their fires outnumber the stars."

When this news was brought to him from the scouts, Tayang Khan was at the watercourse of Khachir. He sent a message to his son Guchuluk.

"I am told that the geldings of the Mongols are lean, but the Mongols are, it seems, numerous. Once we start fighting them, it will be difficult to draw back. They are such hard warriors that when several men at once come up against one of them, he does not move an eyelid; even if he is wounded, so that the black blood flows out, he does not flinch. I do not know whether it is a good thing to come up against such men.

"I suggest that we should assemble our people and lead them back to the west, across the Altai; and all the time, during this retreat, we will fight off the Mongols as dogs do, by running in on them from either side as they advance. Our geldings are too fat; in this march we shall make them lean and fit. But the Mongols' lean geldings will be brought to such a state of exhaustion they will vomit in the Mongols' faces."

On receiving this message, Guchuluk Khan, who was more warlike than his father, said: "That woman Tayang has lost all his courage, to speak such words. Where does this great multitude of Mongols come from? Most of the Mongols are with Jamukha, who is here with us. Tayang speaks like this because fear has overcome him. He has never been farther from his tent than his pregnant wife goes to urinate. He has never dared to go so far as the inner pastures where the knee-high calves are kept." So he expressed himself on the subject of his father, in the most injurious and wounding terms.

When he heard these words, Tayang Khan said: "I hope the pride of this powerful Guchuluk will not weaken on the day when the clash of arms is heard and the slaughter begins. Because once we are committed to battle against the foe, it will be hard to disengage again."

Khorisu Beki, a general who commanded under Tayang Khan, said: "Your father, Inancha Bilgei, never showed the back of a man or the haunch of a horse to opponents who were just as worthy as these. How can you lose your courage so early in the day? We would have done better to summon your mother Gurbesu to command over us. It is a pity that Kokse'u Sabrakh has grown too old to lead us. Our army's discipline has become lax. For the Mongols, their hour has come. It is finished! Tayang, you have failed us." He belted on his quiver and galloped off.

Tayang Khan grew angry. "All men must die," he said. "Their bodies must suffer. It is the same for all men. Let us fight, then."

So, having created doubt and dismay, and lost the support of some of his best leaders, he decided to give battle. He broke away from the watercourse of Khachir, marched down the Tamir, crossed the Orkhon and skirted the eastern flanks of the mountain Nakhu. When they came to Chakirma'ut, Temujin's scouts caught sight of them and brought back the message: "The Naiman are coming!"

The Battle of Chakirma'ut

When the news was brought to Temujin he said: "Sometimes too many men are just as big a handicap as too few."

Then he issued his general battle orders. "We will march in the order 'thick grass,' take up positions in the 'lake' battle order, and fight in the manner called 'gimlet.'"[4] He gave Kasar the command of the main army, and appointed Prince Otchigin to the command of the reserve horses, a special formation of great importance in Mongol warfare.

The Naiman, having advanced as far as Chakirma'ut, drew themselves up in a defensive position on the foothills of Nakhu, with the mountain behind them. . . . The Mongols forced their scouts back on to the forward lines, and then their forward lines back on to the main army, and drove tightly knit formations of horsemen again and again into the Naiman ranks. The Naiman, pressed back on themselves, could do nothing but retreat gradually up the mountain. Many of their men . . . hardly had the chance to fight at all, but were cut down in an immobile mass of men as soon as the Mongols reached them.

Tayang Khan, with his advisers, also retreated up the mountain as the day advanced. From the successive spurs to which they climbed, each one higher than the last, they could see the whole of this dreadful disaster as it took place below them.

Jamukha was with Tayang Khan. . . .

"Who are those people over there," Tayang Khan asked him, "who throw my warriors back as if they were sheep frightened by a wolf, who come huddling back to the sheepfold?"

---

[4]These were the names of various tactical disciplines in which he had drilled his army.

Jamukha said: "My *anda*[5] Temujin has four hounds whom he brought up on human flesh, and kept in chains. They have brows of copper, snouts like chisels, tongues like bradawls, hearts of iron, and tails that cut like swords. They can live on dew, and ride like the wind. On the day of battle they eat the flesh of men. You see how, being set loose, they come forward slavering for joy. Those two are Jebe and Khubilai; those two are Jelmei and Subetai. That is who those four hounds are."

He pointed out to him also the Uru'ut and the Mangqut, who, as Tayang Khan remarked, seemed to bound like foals set loose in the morning, when, after their dams have suckled them, they frisk around her on the steppe. "They hunt down men who carry lances and swords," he said. "Having struck them down, they slay them, and rob them of all they possess. How joyful and boisterous they look, as they ride forward!"

"Who is it coming up there in the rear," Tayang Khan asked him, "who swoops down on our troops like a ravening falcon?"

"That is my *anda* Temujin. His entire body is made of sounding copper; there is no gap through which even a bodkin could penetrate. There he is, you see him? He advances like an eagle about to seize his prey. You said formerly that if you once set eyes on the Mongols you would not leave so much of them as the skin of a lamb's foot. What do you think of them now?"

By this time the chieftains were standing on a high spur. Below them, the great army of the Naiman, Jamukha's men with them, were retreating in confusion, fighting desperately as the Mongols hemmed them in.

"Who is that other chieftain," Tayang asked Jamukha, "who draws ever nearer us, in a dense crowd of men?"

"Mother Hoelun brought up one of her own sons on human flesh. He is nine feet tall; he eats a three-year-old cow every day. If he swallows an armed man whole, it makes no difference to his appetite. When he is roused to anger, and lets fly with one of his *angqu'a* [forked] arrows, it will go through ten or twenty men. His normal range is a thousand yards; when he draws his bow to its fullest extent, he shoots over eighteen hundred yards. He is mortal, but he is not like other mortals; he is more than a match for the serpents of Guralgu. He is called Kasar."

They were climbing high up the mountain now, to regroup below its summit. Tayang Khan saw a new figure among the Mongols.

"Who is that coming up from the rear?" he asked Jamukha.

"That is the youngest son of Mother Hoelun. He is called Otchigin [Odeigin] the Phlegmatic. He is one of those people who go to bed

---

[5]Sworn brother, blood brother, declared ally.

early and get up late. But when he is behind the army, with the reserves, he does not linger; he never comes too late to the battle lines."

"We will climb to the peak of the mountain," Tayang Khan said.

Jamukha, seeing that the battle was lost, slipped away to the rear and descended the mountain, with a small body of men. One of these he sent to Temujin with a message. "Say this to my *anda*. Tayang Khan, terrified by what I have told him, has completely lost his senses. He has retreated up the mountain as far as he can. He could be killed by one harsh word. Let my *anda* take note of this: They have climbed to the top of the mountain, and are in no state to defend themselves any more. I myself have left the Naiman."

Since the evening was drawing on, Temujin commanded his troops in the forefront of the attack to draw back. Bodies of men were sent forward on the wings, east and west, to encircle the summit of Mount Nakhu. There they stood to arms during the night. During the night, the Naiman army tried to break out of the encircling ring. Bodies of horsemen plunged down the mountainside in desperate charges; many fell and were trampled to death, the others were slain. In the first light they were seen lying about the mountain in droves, like fallen trees. Few were left defending the peak; they put up little resistance to the force sent up against them.

74

JOHN OF PLANO CARPINI
History of the Mongols

Chingis Khan united the tribes of the steppe and conquered northern China, capturing Peking by 1215. He then turned his armies against the West, conquering the tribes of Turkestan and the Khorezmian Empire, the great Muslim power of central Asia, by 1222 and sending an army around the Caspian Sea into Russia. In 1226, he turned again to the East, subduing and destroying the kingdom of Tibet before he

John of Plano Carpini, "History of the Mongols," in *Mission to Asia: Narratives and Letters of the Franciscan Missionaries in Mongolia and China in the Thirteenth and Fourteenth Centuries*, trans. a nun of Stanbrook Abbey, ed. Christopher Dawson (1955; reprint, New York: Harper & Row, 1966), 60–69.

died in 1227. One historian, Christopher Dawson, summarizes the career of Chingis Khan this way:

> In spite of the primitive means at his disposal, it is possible that [Chingis Khan] succeeded in destroying a larger portion of the human race than any modern expert in total warfare. Within a dozen years from the opening of his campaign against China, the Mongol armies had reached the Pacific, the Indus, and the Black Sea, and had destroyed many of the great cities in India. For Europe especially, the shock was overwhelming.

European fears intensified in 1237 as the principal Mongol armies under Batu Khan systematically destroyed one Russian city after another. In April 1241, one Mongol army destroyed a combined force of Polish and German armies, while another defeated the Hungarian army and threatened Austria. In 1245, desperate to learn as much as possible about Mongol intentions, Pope Innocent IV sent a mission to the Mongols. For this important task, he sent two Franciscan monks — one of whom was John of Plano Carpini — with two letters addressed to the Emperor of the Tartars (a compounded error that changed the Tatars, the Mongols' enemy, into the denizens of Tartarus, or Hell).

In May, the barefoot sixty-five-year-old Friar John reached Batu's camp on the Volga River, from which he was relayed to Mongolia by five fresh horses a day in order to reach the capital at Karakorum in time for the installation of the third Great Khan, Guyuk (r. 1246–1248) in July and August.

In this selection from his *History of the Mongols,* John writes of his arrival in Mongolia for the installation of Guyuk (here written as Cuyuc). In what ways does John's account change or expand your understanding of the Mongols? Was John a good observer? How does he compensate for his ignorance (as an outside observer) of Mongol society and culture? In what ways does he remain a victim of his outsider status?

Thinking Historically

How would you characterize John's moral stance towards the Mongols? Consider your own moral judgment, if any, of the Mongols. How is it related to your historical understanding?

. . . On our arrival Cuyuc had us given a tent and provisions, such as it is the custom for the Tartars to give, but they treated us better than other envoys. Nevertheless we were not invited to visit him for he had not yet been elected, nor did he yet concern himself with the government. The translation of the Lord Pope's letter, however, and the things I had said had been sent to him by Bati. After we had stayed there for five or six days he sent us to his mother where the solemn court was assembling. By the time we got there a large pavilion had already been put up made of white velvet, and in my opinion it was so big that more than two thousand men could have got into it. Around it had been erected a wooden palisade, on which various designs were painted. On the second or third day we went with the Tartars who had been appointed to look after us and there all the chiefs were assembled and each one was riding with his followers among the hills and over the plains round about.

On the first day they were all clothed in white velvet, on the second in red — that day Cuyuc came to the tent — on the third day they were all in blue velvet, and on the fourth in the finest brocade. In the palisade round the pavilion were two large gates, through one of which the Emperor alone had the right to enter and there were no guards placed at it although it was open, for no one dare enter or leave by it; through the other gate all those who were granted admittance entered and there were guards there with swords and bows and arrows. . . . The chiefs went about everywhere armed and accompanied by a number of their men, but none, unless their group of ten was complete, could go as far as the horses; indeed those who attempted to do so were severely beaten. There were many of them who had, as far as I could judge, about twenty marks' worth of gold on their bits, breastplates, saddles, and cruppers. The chiefs held their conference inside the tent and, so I believe, conducted the election. All the other people however were a long way away outside the aforementioned palisade. There they remained until almost midday and then they began to drink mare's milk and they drank until the evening, so much that it was amazing to see. We were invited inside and they gave us mead as we would not take mare's milk. They did this to show us great honour, but they kept on plying us with drinks to such an extent that we could not possibly stand it, not being used to it, so we gave them to understand that it was disagreeable to us and they left off pressing us.

Outside were Duke Jerozlaus of Susdal in Russia and several chiefs of the Kitayans and Solangi, also two sons of the King of Georgia, the ambassador of the Caliph of Baghdad, who was a Sultan, and more than ten other Sultans of the Saracens, so I believe and so we were told by the stewards. There were more than four thousand envoys there, counting those who were carrying tribute, those who were bringing gifts, the Sultans and other chiefs who were coming to submit to them, those summoned by the Tartars and the governors of territories. All these were put together outside the palisade and they were given drinks at the same time, but when we were outside with them we and Duke Jerozlaus were always given the best places. I think, if I remember rightly, that we had been there a good four weeks when, as I believe, the election took place; the result however was not made public at that time; the chief ground for my supposition was that whenever Cuyuc left the tent they sang before him and as long as he remained outside they dipped to him beautiful rods on the top of which was scarlet wool, which they did not do for any of the other chiefs. They call this court the Sira Orda.

Leaving there we rode all together for three or four leagues to another place, where on a pleasant plain near a river among the mountains another tent had been set up, which is called by them the Golden Orda, it was here that Cuyuc was to be enthroned on the feast of the Assumption of Our Lady. . . .

At that place we were summoned into the presence of the Emperor, and Chingay the protonotary wrote down our names and the names of those who had sent us, also the names of the chief of the Solangi and of others, and then calling out in a loud voice he recited them before the Emperor and all the chiefs. When this was finished each one of us genuflected four times on the left knee and they warned us not to touch the lower part of the threshold. After we had been most thoroughly searched for knives and they had found nothing at all, we entered by a door on the east side, for no one dare enter from the west with the sole exception of the Emperor or, if it is a chief's tent, the chief; those of lower rank do not pay much attention to such things. This was the first time since Cuyuc had been made Emperor that we had entered his tent in his presence. He also received all the envoys in that place, but very few entered his tent.

So many gifts were bestowed by the envoys there that it was marvellous to behold — gifts of silk, samite, velvet, brocade, girdles of silk threaded with gold, choice furs, and other presents. The Emperor was also given a sunshade or little awning such as is carried over his head, and it was all decorated with precious stones. . . .

Leaving there we went to another place where a wonderful tent had been set up all of red velvet, and this had been given by the Kitayans; there also we were taken inside. Whenever we went in we were given mead and wine to drink, and cooked meat was offered us if we wished to have it. A lofty platform of boards had been erected, on which the Emperor's throne was placed. The throne, which was of ivory, was wonderfully carved and there was also gold on it, and precious stones, if I remember rightly, and pearls. Steps led up to it and it was rounded behind. Benches were also placed round the throne, and here the ladies sat in their seats on the left; nobody, however, sat on the right, but the chiefs were on benches in the middle and the rest of the people sat beyond them. Every day a great crowd of ladies came.

Finally, after some time, John was to be brought again before the Emperor. When he heard from them that we had come to him he ordered us to go back to his mother, the reason being that he wished on the following day to raise his banner against the whole of the Western world — we were told this definitely by men who knew . . . — and he wanted us to be kept in ignorance of this. On our return we stayed for a few days, then we went back to him again and remained with him for a good month, enduring such hunger and thirst that we could scarcely keep alive, for the food provided for four was barely sufficient for one, moreover, we were unable to find anything to buy, for the market was a very long way off. If the Lord had not sent us a certain Russian, by name Cosmas, a goldsmith and a great favourite of the Emperor, who supported us to some extent, we would, I believe, have died, unless the Lord had helped us in some other way. . . .

After this the Emperor sent for us, and through Chingay his protonotary told us to write down what we had to say and our business, and give it to him. We did this and wrote out for him all that we said earlier to Bati. . . . A few days passed by; then he had us summoned again and told us through Kadac, the procurator of the whole empire, in the presence of Bala and Chingay his protonotaries and many other scribes, to say all we had to say: We did this willingly and gladly. Our interpreter on this as on the previous occasion was Temer, a knight of Jerozlaus': and there were also present a cleric who was with him and another cleric who was with the Emperor. On this occasion we were asked if there were any people with the Lord Pope who understood the writing of the Russians or Saracens or even of the Tartars. We gave answer that we used neither the Ruthenian nor Saracen writing; there were however Saracens in the country but they were a long way from the Lord Pope; but we said that it seemed to us that the most expedient course would be for them to write in Tartar and translate it for us, and we would write it down carefully in our own script and we would take both the letter and the translation to the Lord Pope. Thereupon they left us to go to the Emperor.

On St. Martin's day we were again summoned, and Kadac, Chingay, and Bala, the aforementioned secretaries, came to us and translated the letter for us word by word. When we had written it in Latin, they had it translated so that they might hear a phrase at a time, for they wanted to know if we had made a mistake in any word. When both letters were written, they made us read it once and a second time in case we had left out anything. . . .

It is the custom for the Emperor of the Tartars never to speak to a foreigner, however important he may be, except through an intermediary, and he listens and gives his answer, also through the intermediary. Whenever his subjects have any business to bring before Kadac, or while they are listening to the Emperor's reply, they stay on their knees until the end of the conversation, however important they may be. It is not possible nor indeed is it the custom for anyone to say anything about any matter after the Emperor has declared his decision. This Emperor not only has a procurator and protonotaries and secretaries, but all officials for dealing with both public and private matters, except that he has no advocates, for everything is settled according to the decision of the Emperor without the turmoil of legal trials. The other princes of the Tartars do the same in those matters concerning them.

The present Emperor may be forty or forty-five years old or more; he is of medium height, very intelligent, and extremely shrewd, and most serious and grave in his manner. He is never seen to laugh for a slight cause nor to indulge in any frivolity, so we were told by the Christians who are constantly with him. The Christians of his household also told us that they firmly believed he was about to become a Christian, and they have clear evidence of this, for he maintains Christian clerics and provides them with supplies of Christian things; in addition he always has a chapel before his chief tent and they sing openly and in public and beat the board for services after the Greek fashion like other Christians, however big a crowd of Tartars or other men be there. The other chiefs do not behave like this.

. . . on the feast of St. Brice [November 13th], they gave us a permit to depart and a letter sealed with the Emperor's seal, and sent us to the Emperor's mother. She gave each of us a fox-skin cloak, which had the fur outside and was lined inside, and a length of velvet; our Tartars stole a good yard from each of the pieces of velvet and from the piece given to our servant they stole more than half. This did not escape our notice, but we preferred not to make a fuss about it.

We then set out on the return journey. . . .

REFLECTIONS

The great Chinese artist Cheng Ssu-hsaio (1241–1318) continued to paint his delicate Chinese orchids in the years after the Mongol defeat of the Sung dynasty, under the alien rule of Khubilai Khan (r. 1260–1294), the fifth Great Khan and the founder of the Mongol Yuan dynasty of China. But when Cheng was asked why he always painted the orchids without earth around their roots, he replied that the earth had been stolen by the barbarians.

Just as it would be a mistake to see a fifth-generation Mongol ruler like Khubilai as a barbarian, it would also be a mistake to assume that Cheng's hardened resistance remained the norm. In fact, a younger generation of artists found opportunity and even freedom in Khubilai's China. Khubilai appointed some of the most famous Chinese painters of his era to positions of government — Ministries of War, Public

Works, Justice, Personnel, Imperial Sacrifices — actively recruiting the bright young men, artists and intellectuals, for his government. While some painters catered to the Mongol elite's inclination for paintings of horses, others relished the wider range of subjects allowed by a regime free of highly cultivated prejudices.

If conquest invariably brings charges of barbarism, it also eventually turns to issues of government and administration. Administrators need officials. Though Khubilai abolished the Chinese civil service examination system because it would have forced him to rely on Chinese officials, the Chinese language, and an educational system based on the Chinese classics, he actively sought ways of governing that were neither too Chinese nor too Mongolian. Typically, he promulgated a Chinese alphabet that was based on Tibetan, hoping that its phonetic symbols would make communication easier and less classical. Many of his achievements were unintended. While his officials continued to use Chinese characters and the Uighur script, the Yüan dynasty witnessed a flowering of literary culture, including theater and novels. For some, no doubt, the wind from the steppe blew away the dust and cobwebs that had accumulated for too long.

Our judgment of the Mongols depends to a great extent on the period of Mongol history we consider. But while it is easy to condemn Chingis Khan and the initial conquests and praise the later enlightened governance, two considerations come to mind. First, in the great sweep of history, many "barbarians" became benign, even indulgent, administrators. Second, the Mongols were not unique in making that transition.

Before the Mongols, the Vikings had already made the transition from raiding to trading and from conquering to colonizing. In fact, as Cunliffe points out, the Vikings had always been farmer-sailors who were as hungry for land as for plunder. Unlike the Mongols who were born on horses, continually picking up and remaking camp in new pastureland, the Vikings became nomadic in emergencies when a search for new settlements was necessary.

The memory of Viking assaults also faded faster than that of the Mongols. The Viking Rus had the Mongols to thank. The Rus of Viking cities like Novgorod became the national heroes of anti-Mongol Russian legend. The Viking Rus became the Russians. In Europe, too, the descendants of Vikings helped establish new national identities. The last great Viking king, Harald the Hard Ruler, "Thunderbolt of the North," won back his father's crown as King of Norway after preparing himself in Russian trading cities and Byzantine courts. He married a Russian princess and fought for the Byzantines in Asia Minor, Jerusalem, and the Caucasus Mountains. In 1066, this King of Norway lost his control of England when he was killed by an English earl. A few days later the new English king was killed by William Duke of

Normandy, a Viking son who had previously conquered much of France. Norman rule was to last over a hundred years, from 1066 to 1215, and create a new English identity.

In the North Atlantic and North America the Vikings traded with indigenous peoples whom they called "wretches" and later generations were to call Eskimos, Inuit, and Indians. But the land did not allow much contact and they learned very little from each other.

At the end of the day, history is neither moral nor immoral. History is what happened, for better or worse, and moralistic history is generally bad history. The Vikings and Mongols of our period were no more morally frozen in time than were the Christian and Muslim crusaders of the same era who visited such violence upon each other.

Just as the role of nomads and settlers changes over time, so does the degree to which a people are particularly aggressive or peaceful. It is hard to imagine a more fearful people than the Mongols of the thirteenth century or the Vikings of the tenth century. Yet modern Scandinavia, Iceland, and Mongolia are among the most peaceful places on the planet.

We can study societies or periods marked by unusually high levels of violence in order to understand the causes and avoid the repetition. History never offers simple lessons, but without its rich sources for explanation and reflection, we sail adrift bereft of markers or direction. Indeed, as history teaches us the consequences of our acts, we might say that without history there can hardly be morality.

12

The Black Death

Afro-Eurasia, 1346–1350 C.E.

HISTORICAL CONTEXT

The Mongol peace that made the Persian Ilkhanid dynasty (1256–1353) and the Chinese Yuan dynasty (1279–1368) sister empires nurtured a level of economic exchange and artistic communication greater than in the most cosmopolitan days of the early Roman/Han Silk Road. But the new caravan routes that spanned Central Asia could carry microbes as well as people. The plague that had long been endemic in country rats spread by fleas to city rats and other animals, including humans. As early as 1346, travelers reported millions killed in China, Central Asia, and the Middle East. In Europe and Egypt, approximately a third of the population perished. In some cities, the death toll was greater than half. This pandemic plague of 1348–1350 is sometimes called the Black Death, after the discolored wounds it caused.

THINKING HISTORICALLY
Considering Cause and Effect

The study of history, like the practice of medicine, is a process of understanding the causes of certain effects. In medicine the effects are diseases; in history they are more varied events. Nevertheless, understanding the causes of things is central to both disciplines. For medical specialists the goal of understanding causes is implicitly a part of the process of finding a cure. Historians rarely envision "cures" for social ills, but many believe that an understanding of cause and effect can improve society's chances of progress.

Still, the most hopeful medical researcher or historian would agree that the process of relating cause and effect, of finding causes and explaining effects, is fraught with difficulties. We will explore some of those difficulties in this chapter.

MARK WHEELIS

Biological Warfare at the 1346 Siege of Caffa

We are used to thinking of biological warfare as a recently developed threat. This article, published in a journal for public health professionals, suggests a longer history. According to the author, how and where did the Black Death originate? What was the significance of the Mongol siege of Caffa in 1346? The author draws on the contemporary account of the Black Death by Gabriele de Mussis. On what points does he agree and disagree with de Mussis?

Thinking Historically

The author of this selection, a professor of microbiology at the University of California, was trained as a bacterial physiologist and geneticist, but for more than the last ten years his research has concentrated on the history and control of biological weapons. Notice how he explains the causes of such events as the spread of plague and the infection at Caffa. Would you call his way of finding causes the method of a medical researcher or a historian, or does he employ the methods of both? If you see a distinction, try to note the places where he is thinking more like a medical scientist and those where he is thinking more like a historian.

The Black Death, which swept through Europe, the Near East, and North Africa in the mid-fourteenth-century, was probably the greatest public health disaster in recorded history and one of the most dramatic examples ever of emerging or reemerging disease. Europe lost an

Mark Wheelis, "Biological Warfare at the 1346 Siege of Caffa," *Emerging Infectious Diseases*, 8, no. 9 (September, 2002): 971–75. The journal is published by the U.S. Centers for Disease Control and Prevention (C.D.C.), Atlanta, and is also available online at http://www.cdc.gov/ncidod/EID/vol8no9/01-0536.htm.

estimated one quarter to one third of its population, and the mortality in North Africa and the Near East was comparable. China, India, and the rest of the Far East are commonly believed to have also been severely affected, but little evidence supports that belief.

A principal source on the origin of the Black Death is a memoir by the Italian Gabriele de' Mussis. This memoir has been published several times in its original Latin and has recently been translated into English (although brief passages have been previously published in translation). This narrative contains some startling assertions: that the Mongol army hurled plague-infected cadavers into the besieged Crimean city of Caffa, thereby transmitting the disease to the inhabitants; and that fleeing survivors of the siege spread plague from Caffa to the Mediterranean Basin. If this account is correct, Caffa should be recognized as the site of the most spectacular incident of biological warfare ever, with the Black Death as its disastrous consequence. After analyzing these claims, I have concluded that it is plausible that the biological attack took place as described and was responsible for infecting the inhabitants of Caffa; however, the event was unimportant in the spread of the plague pandemic.

Origin of the Fourteenth-Century Pandemic

The disease that caused this catastrophic pandemic has, since Hecker, generally been considered to have been a plague, a zoonotic disease caused by the gram-negative bacterium *Yersinia pestis,* the principal reservoir for which is wild rodents. The ultimate origin of the Black Death is uncertain — China, Mongolia, India, central Asia, and southern Russia have all been suggested. Known fourteenth-century sources are of little help; they refer repeatedly to an eastern origin, but none of the reports is firsthand. Historians generally agree that the outbreak moved west out of the steppes north of the Black and Caspian Seas, and its spread through Europe and the Middle East is fairly well documented (see Map 12.1). However, despite more than a century of speculation about an ultimate origin further east, the requisite scholarship using Chinese and central Asian sources has yet to be done. In any event, the Crimea clearly played a pivotal role as the proximal source from which the Mediterranean Basin was infected.

Historical Background to the Siege of Caffa

Caffa (now Feodosija, Ukraine) was established by Genoa in 1266 by agreement with the Kahn of the Golden Horde. It was the main port for the great Genoese merchant ships, which connected there to a coastal shipping industry to Tana (now Azov, Russia) on the Don

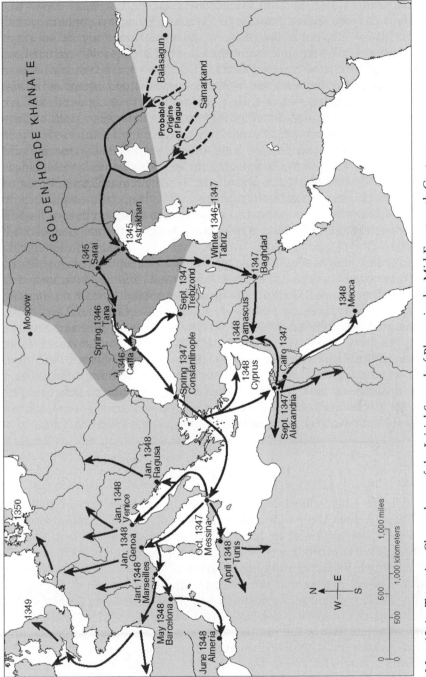

Map 12.1 Tentative Chronology of the Initial Spread of Plague in the Mid-Fourteenth Century.

River. Trade along the Don connected Tana to Central Russia, and overland caravan routes linked it to Sarai and thence to the Far East.

Relations between Italian traders and their Mongol hosts were uneasy, and in 1307 Toqtai, Kahn of the Golden Horde, arrested the Italian residents of Sarai, and besieged Caffa. The cause was apparently Toqtai's displeasure at the Italian trade in Turkic slaves (sold for soldiers to the Mameluke Sultanate). The Genoese resisted for a year, but in 1308 set fire to their city and abandoned it. Relations between the Italians and the Golden Horde remained tense until Toqtai's death in 1312.

Toqtai's successor, Özbeg, welcomed the Genoese back, and also ceded land at Tana to the Italians for the expansion of their trading enterprise. By the 1340s, Caffa was again a thriving city, heavily fortified within two concentric walls. The inner wall enclosed 6,000 houses, the outer 11,000. The city's population was highly cosmopolitan, including Genoese, Venetian, Greeks, Armenians, Jews, Mongols, and Turkic peoples.

In 1343 the Mongols under Janibeg (who succeeded Özbeg in 1340) besieged Caffa and the Italian enclave at Tana following a brawl between Italians and Muslims in Tana. The Italian merchants in Tana fled to Caffa (which, by virtue of its location directly on the coast, maintained maritime access despite the siege). The siege of Caffa lasted until February 1344, when it was lifted after an Italian relief force killed 15,000 Mongol troops and destroyed their siege machines. Janibeg renewed the siege in 1345 but was again forced to lift it after a year, this time by an epidemic of plague that devastated his forces. The Italians blockaded Mongol ports, forcing Janibeg to negotiate, and in 1347 the Italians were allowed to reestablish their colony in Tana.

Gabriele de' Mussis

Gabriele de' Mussis, born circa 1280, practiced as a notary in the town of Piacenza, over the mountains just north of Genoa. Tononi summarizes the little we know of him. His practice was active in the years 1300–1349. He is thought to have died in approximately 1356.

Although Henschel thought de' Mussis was present at the siege of Caffa, Tononi asserts that the Piacenza archives contain deeds signed by de' Mussis spanning the period 1344 through the first half of 1346. While this does not rule out travel to Caffa in late 1346, textual evidence suggests that he did not. He does not claim to have witnessed any of the Asian events he describes and often uses a passive voice for descriptions. After describing the siege of Caffa, de' Mussis goes on to say, "Now it is time that we passed from east to west to discuss all the things which we ourselves have seen. . . ."

The Narrative of Gabriele de' Mussis

The de' Mussis account is presumed to have been written in 1348 or early 1349 because of its immediacy and the narrow time period described. The original is lost, but a copy is included in a compilation of historical and geographic accounts by various authors, dating from approximately 1367. The account begins with an introductory comment by the scribe who copied the documents: "In the name of God, Amen. Here begins an account of the disease or mortality which occurred in 1348, put together by Gabrielem de Mussis of Piacenza."

The narrative begins with an apocalyptic speech by God, lamenting the depravity into which humanity has fallen and describing the retribution intended. It goes on:

". . . In 1346, in the countries of the East, countless numbers of Tartars and Saracens were struck down by a mysterious illness which brought sudden death. Within these countries broad regions, far-spreading provinces, magnificent kingdoms, cities, towns and settlements, ground down by illness and devoured by dreadful death, were soon stripped of their inhabitants. An eastern settlement under the rule of the Tartars called Tana, which lay to the north of Constantinople and was much frequented by Italian merchants, was totally abandoned after an incident there which led to its being besieged and attacked by hordes of Tartars who gathered in a short space of time. The Christian merchants, who had been driven out by force, were so terrified of the power of the Tartars that, to save themselves and their belongings, they fled in an armed ship to Caffa, a settlement in the same part of the world which had been founded long ago by the Genoese.

"Oh God! See how the heathen Tartar races, pouring together from all sides, suddenly invested the city of Caffa and besieged the trapped Christians there for almost three years. There, hemmed in by an immense army, they could hardly draw breath, although food could be shipped in, which offered them some hope. But behold, the whole army was affected by a disease which overran the Tartars and killed thousands upon thousands every day. It was as though arrows were raining down from heaven to strike and crush the Tartars' arrogance. All medical advice and attention was useless; the Tartars died as soon as the signs of disease appeared on their bodies: swellings in the armpit or groin caused by coagulating humours, followed by a putrid fever.

"The dying Tartars, stunned and stupefied by the immensity of the disaster brought about by the disease, and realizing that they had no hope of escape, lost interest in the siege. But they ordered corpses to be placed in catapults[1] and lobbed into the city in the hope that the intolerable stench would kill everyone inside.[2] What seemed like mountains of dead were thrown into the city, and the Christians could not hide or flee or escape from them, although they dumped as many of the bodies as they could in the sea. And soon the rotting corpses tainted the air and poisoned the water supply, and the stench was so overwhelming that hardly one in several thousand was in a position to flee the remains of the Tartar army. Moreover one infected man could carry the poison to others, and infect people and places with the disease by look alone. No one knew, or could discover, a means of defense.

"Thus almost everyone who had been in the East, or in the regions to the south and north, fell victim to sudden death after contracting this pestilential disease, as if struck by a lethal arrow which raised a tumor on their bodies. The scale of the mortality and the form which it took persuaded those who lived, weeping and lamenting, through the bitter events of 1346 to 1348 — the Chinese, Indians, Persians, Medes, Kurds, Armenians, Cilicians, Georgians, Mesopotamians, Nubians, Ethiopians, Turks, Egyptians, Arabs, Saracens, and Greeks (for almost all the East has been affected) — that the last judgement had come.

". . . As it happened, among those who escaped from Caffa by boat were a few sailors who had been infected with the poisonous disease. Some boats were bound for Genoa, others went to Venice and to other Christian areas. When the sailors reached these places and mixed with the people there, it was as if they had brought evil spirits with them: every city, every settlement, every place was poisoned by the contagious pestilence, and their inhabitants, both men and women, died suddenly. And when one person had contracted the illness, he poisoned his whole family even as he fell and died, so that those preparing to bury his body were seized by death in the same way. Thus death entered through the windows, and as cities and towns were depopulated their inhabitants mourned their dead neighbours."

The account closes with an extended description of the plague in Piacenza, and a reprise of the apocalyptic vision with which it begins.

---

[1]Technically trebuchets, not catapults. Catapults hurl objects by the release of tension on twisted cordage; they are not capable of hurling loads over a few dozen kilograms. Trebuchets are counter-weight-driven hurling machines, very effective for throwing ammunition weighing a hundred kilos or more.

[2]Medieval society lacked a coherent theory of disease causation. Three notions coexisted in a somewhat contradictory mixture: 1) disease was a divine punishment for individual or collective transgression: 2) disease was the result of "miasma," or the stench of decay: and 3) disease was the result of person-to-person contagion.

Commentary

In this narrative, de' Mussis makes two important claims about the siege of Caffa and the Black Death: that plague was transmitted to Europeans by the hurling of diseased cadavers into the besieged city of Caffa and that Italians fleeing from Caffa brought it to the Mediterranean ports.

Biological Warfare at Caffa

De' Mussis's account is probably secondhand and is uncorroborated; however, he seems, in general, to be a reliable source, and as a Piacenzian he would have had access to eyewitnesses of the siege. Several considerations incline me to trust his account: this was probably not the only, nor the first, instance of apparent attempts to transmit disease by hurling biological material into besieged cities; it was within the technical capabilities of besieging armies of the time; and it is consistent with medieval notions of disease causality.

Tentatively accepting that the attack took place as described, we can consider two principal hypotheses for the entry of plague into the city: it might, as de' Mussis asserts, have been transmitted by the hurling of plague cadavers; or it might have entered by rodent-to-rodent transmission from the Mongol encampments into the city.

Diseased cadavers hurled into the city could easily have transmitted plague, as defenders handled the cadavers during disposal. Contact with infected material is a known mechanism of transmission; for instance, among 284 cases of plague in the United States in 1970–1995 for which a mechanism of transmission could be reasonably inferred, 20 percent were thought to be by direct contact. Such transmission would have been especially likely at Caffa, where cadavers would have been badly mangled by being hurled, and many of the defenders probably had cut or abraded hands from coping with the bombardment. Very large numbers of cadavers were possibly involved, greatly increasing the opportunity for disease transmission. Since disposal of the bodies of victims in a major outbreak of lethal disease is always a problem, the Mongol forces may have used their hurling machines as a solution to their mortuary problem, in which case many thousands of cadavers could have been involved. de' Mussis's description of "mountains of dead" might have been quite literally true.

Thus it seems plausible that the events recounted by de' Mussis could have been an effective means of transmission of plague into the city. The alternative, rodent-to-rodent transmission from the Mongol encampments into the city, is less likely. Besieging forces must have camped at least a kilometer away from the city walls. This distance is necessary to have a healthy margin of safety from arrows and artillery and to provide space for logistical support and other military activities between the encampments and the front lines. Front-line location must have been approximately 250–300 m from the walls; trebuchets are known from modern reconstruction to be capable of hurling 100 kg more than 200 m, and historical sources claim 300 m as the working range of large machines. Thus, the bulk of rodent nests associated with the besieging armies would have been located a kilometer or more away from the cities, and none would have likely been closer than 250 m. Rats are quite sedentary and rarely venture more than a few tens of meters from their nest. It is thus unlikely that there was any contact between the rat populations within and outside the walls.

Given the many uncertainties, any conclusion must remain tentative. However, the considerations above suggest that the hurling of plague cadavers might well have occurred as de' Mussis claimed, and if so, that this biological attack was probably responsible for the transmission of the disease from the besiegers to the besieged. Thus, this early act of biological warfare, if such it were, appears to have been spectacularly successful in producing casualties, although of no strategic importance (the city remained in Italian hands, and the Mongols abandoned the siege).

Crimea as the Source of European and Near Eastern Plague

There has never been any doubt that plague entered the Mediterranean from the Crimea, following established maritime trade routes. Rat infestations in the holds of cargo ships would have been highly susceptible to the rapid spread of plague, and even if most rats died during the voyage, they would have left abundant hungry fleas that would infect humans unpacking the holds. Shore rats foraging on board recently arrived ships would also become infected, transmitting plague to city rat populations.

Plague appears to have been spread in a stepwise fashion, on many ships rather than on a few [see Map 12.1], taking over a year to reach Europe from the Crimea. This conclusion seems fairly firm, as the dates for the arrival of plague in Constantinople and more westerly cities are reasonably certain. Thus de' Mussis was probably mistaken in attributing the Black Death to fleeing survivors of Caffa, who should not have needed more than a few months to return to Italy.

Furthermore, a number of other Crimean ports were under Mongol control, making it unlikely that Caffa was the only source of infected ships heading west. And the overland caravan routes to the Middle East from Serai and Astrakhan insured that plague was also spreading south (Map 12.1), whence it would have entered Europe in any case. The siege of Caffa and its gruesome finale thus are unlikely to have been seriously implicated in the transmission of plague from the Black Sea to Europe.

Conclusion

Gabriele de' Mussis's account of the origin and spread of plague appears to be consistent with most known facts, although mistaken in its claim that plague arrived in Italy directly from the Crimea. His account of biological attack is plausible, consistent with the technology of the time, and it provides the best explanation of disease transmission into besieged Caffa. This thus appears to be one of the first biological attacks recorded and among the most successful of all time.

However, it is unlikely that the attack had a decisive role in the spread of plague to Europe. Much maritime commerce probably continued throughout this period from other Crimean ports. Overland caravan routes to the Middle East were also unaffected. Thus, refugees from Caffa would most likely have constituted only one of several streams of infected ships and caravans leaving the region. The siege of Caffa, for all of its dramatic appeal, probably had no more than anecdotal importance in the spread of plague, a macabre incident in terrifying times.

Despite its historical unimportance, the siege of Caffa is a powerful reminder of the horrific consequences when disease is successfully used as a weapon. The Japanese use of plague as a weapon in World War II and the huge Soviet stockpiles of *Y. pestis* prepared for use in an all-out war further remind us that plague remains a very real problem for modern arms control, six and a half centuries later.

$$\boxed{76}$$

GABRIELE DE' MUSSIS

Origins of the Black Death

Gabriele de' Mussis (d. 1356) was a lawyer who lived in the northern Italian city of Piacenza. The previous reading introduced you to de' Mussis and the importance of his history of the Black Death. Since Wheelis quoted abundantly from the story of the siege of Caffa, we pick up the story in de' Mussis's words of the spread of the plague to Europe where, as he wrote, he had direct evidence. How would you

The Black Death, trans. and ed. Rosemary Horrox (Manchester, England: Manchester University Press, 1994), 18–26.

rate de' Mussis as an eyewitness observer? According to his evidence, how did the Black Death spread in Italy? How deadly was it?

Thinking Historically

As in the previous selection, there are two causal chains in this account, but in this case they are not medical and historical. Rather, reminiscent of the readings on the First Crusade, they are divine and human chains of causation. What according to the author were the divine or religious causes of the Black Death? What were the human, physical, or scientific causes? What remedies does each type of cause call for?

Now it is time that we passed from east to west, to discuss all the things which we ourselves have seen, or known, or consider likely on the basis of the evidence, and, by so doing, to show forth the terrifying judgements of God. Listen everybody, and it will set tears pouring from your eyes. For the Almighty has said: "I shall wipe man, whom I created, off the face of the earth. Because he is flesh and blood, let him be turned to dust and ashes. My spirit shall not remain among man."

— "What are you thinking of, merciful God, thus to destroy your creation and the human race; to order and command its sudden annihilation in this way? What has become of your mercy; the faith of our fathers; the blessed virgin, who holds sinners in her lap; the precious blood of the martyrs; the worthy army of confessors and virgins; the whole host of paradise, who pray ceaselessly for sinners; the most precious death of Christ on the cross and our wonderful redemption? Kind God, I beg that your anger may cease, that you do not destroy sinners in this way, and, because you desire mercy rather than sacrifice, that you turn away all evil from the penitent, and do not allow the just to be condemned with the unjust."

— "I hear you, sinner, dropping words into my ears. I bid you weep. The time for mercy has passed. I, God, am called to vengeance. It is my pleasure to take revenge on sin and wickedness. I shall give my signs to the dying, let them take steps to provide for the health of their souls."

As it happened, among those who escaped from Caffa by boat were a few sailors who had been infected with the poisonous disease. Some boats were bound for Genoa, others went to Venice and to other Christian areas. . . .

— "We Genoese and Venetians bear the responsibility for revealing the judgements of God. Alas, once our ships had brought us to port we went to our homes. And because we had been delayed by tragic events, and because among us there were scarcely ten survivors from a thousand sailors, relations, kinsmen and neighbours flocked to us from all sides. But, to our anguish, we were carrying the darts of death. While they hugged and kissed us we were spreading poison from our lips even as we spoke."

When they returned to their own folk, these people speedily poisoned the whole family, and within three days the afflicted family would succumb to the dart of death. Mass funerals had to be held and there was not enough room to bury the growing numbers of dead. Priests and doctors, upon whom most of the care of the sick devolved, had their hands full in visiting the sick and, alas, by the time they left they too had been infected and followed the dead immediately to the grave. Oh fathers! Oh mothers! Oh children and wives! For a long time prosperity preserved you from harm, but one grave now covers you and the unfortunate alike. You who enjoyed the world and upon whom pleasure and prosperity smiled, who mingled joys with follies, the same tomb receives you and you are handed over as food for worms. Oh hard death, impious death, bitter death, cruel death, who divides parents, divorces spouses, parts children, separates brothers and sisters. We bewail our wretched plight. The past has devoured us, the present is gnawing our entrails, the future threatens yet greater dangers. What we laboured to amass with feverish activity, we have lost in one hour.

Where are the fine clothes of gilded youth? Where is nobility and the courage of fighters, where the mature wisdom of elders and the regal throng of great ladies, where the piles of treasure and precious stones? Alas! All have been destroyed; thrust aside by death. To whom shall we turn, who can help us? To flee is impossible, to hide futile. Cities, fortresses, fields, woods, highways and rivers are ringed by thieves — which is to say by evil spirits, the executioners of the supreme Judge, preparing endless punishments for us all.

We can unfold a terrifying event which happened when an army was camped near Genoa. Four of the soldiers left the force in search of plunder and made their way to Rivarolo on the coast, where the disease had killed all the inhabitants. Finding the houses shut up, and no one about, they broke into one of the houses and stole a fleece which they found on a bed. They then rejoined the army and on the following night the four of them bedded down under the fleece. When morning comes it finds them dead. As a result everyone panicked, and thereafter nobody would use the goods and clothes of the dead, or even handle them, but rejected them outright.

Scarcely one in seven of the Genoese survived. In Venice, where an inquiry was held into the mortality, it was found that more than 70 percent of the people had died, and that within a short period 20 out of 24 excellent physicians had died. The rest of Italy, Sicily, and Apulia and the neighbouring regions maintain that they have been virtually emptied of inhabitants. The people of Florence, Pisa, and Lucca, finding themselves bereft of their fellow residents, emphasise their losses. The Roman Curia at Avignon, the provinces on both sides of the Rhône, Spain,

France, and the Empire cry up their griefs and disasters — all of which makes it extraordinarily difficult for me to give an accurate picture.

By contrast, what befell the Saracens can be established from trust-worthy accounts. In the city of Babylon alone (the heart of the Sultan's power), 480,000 of his subjects are said to have been carried off by dis-ease in less than three months in 1348 — and this is known from the Sul-tan's register which records the names of the dead, because he receives a gold bezant for each person buried. I am silent about Damascus and his other cities, where the number of dead was infinite. In the other countries of the East, which are so vast that it takes three years to ride across them and which have a population of 10,000 for every one inhabitant of the west, it is credibly reported that countless people have died.

Everyone has a responsibility to keep some record of the disease and the deaths, and because I am myself from Piacenza I have been urged to write more about what happened there in 1348. . . .

I don't know where to begin. Cries and laments arise on all sides. Day after day one sees the Cross and the Host[1] being carried about the city, and countless dead being buried. The ensuing mortality was so great that people could scarcely snatch breath. The living made prepa-rations for their burial, and because there was not enough room for in-dividual graves, pits had to be dug in colonnades and piazzas, where nobody had ever been buried before. It often happened that man and wife, father and son, mother and daughter, and soon the whole house-hold and many neighbours, were buried together in one place. The same thing happened in Castell' Arquato and Viguzzolo and in the other towns, villages, cities, and settlements, and last of all in the Val Tidone, where they had hitherto escaped the plague.

Very many people died. One Oberto de Sasso, who had come from the infected neighbourhood around the church of the Franciscans, wished to make his will and accordingly summoned a notary and his neighbours as witnesses, all of whom, more than sixty of them, died soon after. At this time the Dominican friar Syfredo de Bardis, a man of prudence and great learning who had visited the Holy Sepulchre, also died, along with 23 brothers of the same house. There also died within a short time the Franciscan friar Bertolino Coxadocha of Piacenza, renowned for his learning and many virtues, along with 24 brothers of the same house, nine of them on one day; seven of the Augustinians; the Carmelite friar Francesco Todischi with six of his brethren; four of the order of Mary; more than sixty prelates and parish priests from the city and district of Piacenza; many nobles; countless young people; numberless women, particularly those who were pregnant. It is too dis-tressing to recite any more, or to lay bare the wounds inflicted by so great a disaster.

[1]The consecrated Eucharistic wafer. The reference is to priests taking the last sacrament to the dying.

Let all creation tremble with fear before the judgement of God. Let human frailty submit to its creator. May a greater grief be kindled in all hearts, and tears well up in all eyes as future ages hear what happened in this disaster. When one person lay sick in a house no one would come near. Even dear friends would hide themselves away, weeping. The physician would not visit. The priest, panic-stricken, administered the sacraments with fear and trembling.

Listen to the tearful voices of the sick: "Have pity, have pity, my friends. At least say something, now that the hand of God has touched me."

"Oh father, why have you abandoned me? Do you forget that I am your child?"

"Mother, where have you gone? Why are you now so cruel to me when only yesterday you were so kind? You fed me at your breast and carried me within your womb for nine months."

"My children, whom I brought up with toil and sweat, why have you run away?"

Man and wife reached out to each other, "Alas, once we slept happily together but now are separated and wretched."

And when the sick were in the throes of death, they still called out piteously to their family and neighbours, "Come here. I'm thirsty, bring me a drink of water. I'm still alive. Don't be frightened. Perhaps I won't die. Please hold me tight, hug my wasted body. You ought to be holding me in your arms."

At this, as everyone else kept their distance, somebody might take pity and leave a candle burning by the bed head as he fled. And when the victim had breathed his last, it was often the mother who shrouded her son and placed him in the coffin, or the husband who did the same for his wife, for everybody else refused to touch the dead body. . . .

I am overwhelmed, I can't go on. Everywhere one turns there is death and bitterness to be described. The hand of the Almighty strikes repeatedly, to greater and greater effect. The terrible judgement gains in power as time goes by.

— What shall we do? Kind Jesus, receive the souls of the dead, avert your gaze from our sins and blot out all our iniquities.

We know that whatever we suffer is the just reward of our sins. Now, therefore, when the Lord is enraged, embrace acts of penance, so that you do not stray from the right path and perish. Let the proud be humbled. Let misers, who withheld alms from the poor, blush for shame. Let the envious become zealous in almsgiving. Let lechers put aside their filthy habits and distinguish themselves in honest living. Let the raging and wrathful restrain themselves from violence. Let gluttons temper their appetites by fasting. Let the slaves of sloth arise and dress themselves in good works. Let adolescents and youths abandon their present delight in following fashion. Let there be good faith and equity among judges, and respect for the law among merchants. Let pettifogging lawyers study and grow wise before they put pen to paper. Let members of religious orders abandon hypocrisy. Let the dignity of prelates be put to better use. Let all of you hurry to set your feet on the way of salvation. And let the overweening vanity of great ladies, which so easily turns into voluptuousness, be bridled. It was against their arrogance that Isaiah inveighed: "Because the daughters of Sion are haughty, and have walked with stretched out necks and wanton glances of their eyes, and made a noise as they walked with their feet, and moved in a set pace. . . . Thy fairest men also shall fall by the sword: and thy valiant ones in battle. And her gates shall lament and mourn: and she shall sit desolate on the ground" [Isaiah 3.16–26]. This was directed against the pride of ladies and young people.

For the rest, so that the conditions, causes, and symptoms of this pestilential disease should be made plain to all, I have decided to set them out in writing. Those of both sexes who were in health, and in no fear of death, were struck by four savage blows to the flesh. First, out of the blue, a kind of chilly stiffness troubled their bodies. They felt a tingling sensation, as if they were being pricked by the points of arrows. The next stage was a fearsome attack which took the form of an extremely hard, solid boil. In some people this developed under the armpit and in others in the groin between the scrotum and the body. As it grew more solid, its burning heat caused the patients to fall into an acute and putrid fever, with severe headaches. As it intensified its extreme bitterness could have various effects. In some cases it gave rise to an intolerable stench. In others it brought vomiting of blood, or swellings near the place from which the corrupt humour arose: on the back, across the chest, near the thigh. Some people lay as if in a drunken stupor and could not be roused. Behold the swellings, the warning signs sent by the Lord.[2] All these people were in danger of dying. Some died on the very day the illness took possession of them, others on the next day, others — the majority — between the third and fifth day. There was no known remedy for the vomiting of blood. Those who fell into a coma, or suffered a swelling or the stink of corruption very rarely escaped. But from the fever it was sometimes possible to make a recovery. . . .

Truly, then was a time of bitterness and grief, which served to turn men to the Lord. I shall recount what happened. A warning was given by a certain holy person, who received it in a vision, that in cities, towns and other settlements, everyone, male and female alike, should gather in their parish church on three consecutive days and, each with a lighted candle in their hand, hear with great devotion the mass of the

[2]A pun: *bulla* is a swelling, but it is also the word for the papal seal, and hence for a papal document (or bull). De' Mussis is playing on the idea of the swelling characteristic of the plague being God's seal, notifying the victim of his imminent fate.

Blessed Anastasia, which is normally performed at dawn on Christmas day, and they should humbly beg for mercy, so that they might be delivered from the disease through the merits of the holy mass. Other people sought deliverance through the mediation of a blessed martyr; and others humbly turned to other saints, so that they might escape the abomination of disease. For among the aforesaid martyrs, some, as stories relate, are said to have died from repeated blows, and it was therefore the general opinion that they would be able to protect people against the arrows of death. Finally, in 1350, the most holy Pope Clement ordained a general indulgence, to be valid for a year, which remitted penance and guilt to all who were truly penitent and confessed. And as a result a numberless multitude of people made the pilgrimage to Rome, to visit with great reverence and devotion the basilicas of the blessed apostles Peter and Paul and St John.

Oh, most dearly beloved, let us therefore not be like vipers, growing ever more wicked, but let us rather hold up our hands to heaven to beg for mercy on us all, for who but God shall have mercy on us? With this, I make an end. May the heavenly physician heal our wounds — our spiritual rather than our bodily wounds. To whom be the blessing and the praise and the glory for ever and ever, Amen.

GIOVANNI BOCCACCIO

The Plague in Florence: *From* the Decameron

Giovanni Boccaccio* **(1313–1375) was a poet in Florence, Italy, when the plague struck in 1348. His *Decameron*† is a collection of a hundred tales based on his experiences during the plague years. This selection is drawn from the Introduction. What does Boccaccio add to your understanding of the Black Death?**

*boh KAH chee oh
†deh KAM uh rahn

Giovanni Boccaccio, *Decameron*, trans. G. H. McWilliam (Harmondsworth, England: Penguin, 1972), 50–58.

Thinking Historically

Compare Boccaccio's treatment of divine and human causes of the plague. Boccaccio not only muses on the causes of the plague; he also sees the plague as the cause of new forms of behavior. What were the behavioral effects of the plague according to Boccaccio?

I say, then, that the sum of thirteen hundred and forty-eight years had elapsed since the fruitful Incarnation of the Son of God, when the noble city of Florence, which for its great beauty excels all others in Italy, was visited by the deadly pestilence. Some say that it descended upon the human race through the influence of the heavenly bodies, others that it was a punishment signifying God's righteous anger at our iniquitous way of life. But whatever its cause, it had originated some years earlier in the East, where it had claimed countless lives before it unhappily spread westward, growing in strength as it swept relentlessly on from one place to the next.

In the face of its onrush, all the wisdom and ingenuity of man were unavailing. Large quantities of refuse were cleared out of the city by officials specially appointed for the purpose, all sick persons were forbidden entry, and numerous instructions were issued for safeguarding the people's health, but all to no avail. Nor were the countless petitions humbly directed to God by the pious, whether by means of formal processions or in any other guise, any less ineffectual. For in the early spring of the year we have mentioned, the plague began, in a terrifying and extraordinary manner, to make its disastrous effects apparent. It did not take the form it had assumed in the East, where if anyone bled from the nose it was an obvious portent of certain death. On the contrary, its earliest symptom, in men and women alike, was the appearance of certain swellings in the groin or the armpit, some of which were egg-shaped whilst others were roughly the size of the common apple. Sometimes the swellings were large, sometimes not so large, and they were referred to by the populace as *gavòccioli*. From the two areas already mentioned, this deadly *gavòcciolo* would begin to spread, and within a short time it would appear at random all over the body. Later on, the symptoms of the disease changed, and many people began to find dark blotches and bruises on their arms, thighs, and other parts of the body, sometimes large and few in number, at other times tiny and closely spaced. These, to anyone unfortunate enough to contract them, were just as infallible a sign that he would die as the *gavòcciolo* had been earlier, and as indeed it still was.

Against these maladies, it seemed that all the advice of physicians and all the power of medicine were profitless and unavailing. Perhaps the nature of the illness was such that it allowed no remedy; or perhaps those people who were treating the illness (whose numbers had increased enormously because the ranks of the qualified were invaded by people, both men and women, who had never received any training in medicine), being ignorant of its causes, were not prescribing the appropriate cure. At all events, few of those who caught it ever recovered, and in most cases death occurred within three days from the appearance of the symptoms we have described, some people dying more rapidly than others, the majority without any fever or other complications.

But what made this pestilence even more severe was that whenever those suffering from it mixed with people who were still unaffected, it would rush upon these with the speed of a fire racing through dry or oily substances that happened to be placed within its reach. Nor was this the full extent of its evil, for not only did it infect healthy persons who conversed or had any dealings with the sick, making them ill or visiting an equally horrible death upon them, but it also seemed to transfer the sickness to anyone touching the clothes or other objects which had been handled or used by its victims. . . .

Some people were of the opinion that a sober and abstemious mode of living considerably reduced the risk of infection. They therefore formed themselves into groups and lived in isolation from everyone else. Having withdrawn to a comfortable abode where there were no sick persons, they locked themselves in and settled down to a peaceable existence, consuming modest quantities of delicate foods and precious wines and avoiding all excesses. They refrained from speaking to outsiders, refused to receive news of the dead or sick, and entertained themselves with music and whatever other amusements they were able to devise.

Others took the opposite view, and maintained that an infallible way of warding off this appalling evil was to drink heavily, enjoy life to the full, go round singing and merrymaking, gratify all of one's cravings whenever the opportunity offered, and shrug the whole thing off as one enormous joke. Moreover, they practised what they preached to the best of their ability, for they would visit one tavern after another, drinking all day and night to immoderate excess; or alternatively (and this was their more frequent custom), they would do their drinking in various private houses, but only in the ones where the conversation was restricted to subjects that were pleasant or entertaining. Such places were easy to find, for people behaved as though their days were numbered, and treated their belongings and their own persons with equal abandon. Hence most houses had become common property, and any passing stranger could make himself at home as naturally as though he were the rightful owner. But for all their riotous manner of living, these people always took good care to avoid any contact with the sick.

In the face of so much affliction and misery, all respect for the laws of God and man had virtually broken down and been extinguished in our city. For like everybody else, those ministers and executors of the laws who were not either dead or ill were left with so few subordinates that they were unable to discharge any of their duties. Hence everyone was free to behave as he pleased.

There were many other people who steered a middle course between the two already mentioned, neither restricting their diet to the same degree as the first group, nor indulging so freely as the second in drinking and other forms of wantonness, but simply doing no more than satisfy their appetite. Instead of incarcerating themselves, these people moved about freely, holding in their hands a posy of flowers, or fragrant herbs, or one of a wide range of spices, which they applied at frequent intervals to their nostrils, thinking it an excellent idea to fortify the brain with smells of that particular sort; for the stench of dead bodies, sickness, and medicines seemed to fill and pollute the whole of the atmosphere.

Some people, pursuing what was possibly the safer alternative, callously maintained that there was no better or more efficacious remedy against a plague than to run away from it. Swayed by this argument, and sparing no thought for anyone but themselves, large numbers of men and women abandoned their city, their homes, their relatives, their estates, and their belongings, and headed for the countryside, either in Florentine territory or, better still, abroad. It was as though they imagined that the wrath of God would not unleash this plague against men for their iniquities irrespective of where they happened to be, but would only be aroused against those who found themselves within the city walls; or possibly they assumed that the whole of the population would be exterminated and that the city's last hour had come.

Of the people who held these various opinions, not all of them died. Nor, however, did they all survive. On the contrary, many of each different persuasion fell ill here, there, and everywhere, and having themselves, when they were fit and well, set an example to those who were as yet unaffected, they languished away with virtually no one to nurse them. It was not merely a question of one citizen avoiding another, and of people almost invariably neglecting their neighbours and rarely or never visiting their relatives, addressing them only from a distance; this scourge had implanted so great a terror in the hearts of men and women that brothers abandoned brothers, uncles their nephews, sisters their brothers, and in many cases wives deserted their husbands. But even worse, and almost incredible, was the fact that fathers and mothers refused to nurse and assist their own children, as though they did not belong to them.

Hence the countless numbers of people who fell ill, both male and female, were entirely dependent upon either the charity of friends (who were few and far between) or the greed of servants, who remained in short supply despite the attraction of high wages out of all proportion to the services they performed. Furthermore, these latter were men and women of coarse intellect and the majority were unused to such duties, and they did little more than hand things to the invalid when asked to do so and watch over him when he was dying. And in performing this kind of service, they frequently lost their lives as well as their earnings.

As a result of this wholesale desertion of the sick by neighbours, relatives, and friends, and in view of the scarcity of servants, there grew up a practice almost never previously heard of, whereby when a woman fell ill, no matter how gracious or beautiful or gently bred she might be, she raised no objection to being attended by a male servant, whether he was young or not. Nor did she have any scruples about showing him every part of her body as freely as she would have displayed it to a woman, provided that the nature of her infirmity required her to do so; and this explains why those women who recovered were possibly less chaste in the period that followed.

Moreover a great many people died who would perhaps have survived had they received some assistance. And hence, what with the lack of appropriate means for tending the sick, and the virulence of the plague, the number of deaths reported in the city whether by day or night was so enormous that it astonished all who heard tell of it, to say nothing of the people who actually witnessed the carnage. . . .

As for the common people and a large proportion of the bourgeoisie, they presented a much more pathetic spectacle, for the majority of them were constrained, either by their poverty or the hope of survival, to remain in their houses. Being confined to their own parts of the city, they fell ill daily in their thousands, and since they had no one to assist them or attend to their needs, they inevitably perished almost without exception. Many dropped dead in the open streets, both by day and by night, whilst a great many others, though dying in their own houses, drew their neighbours' attention to the fact more by the smell of their rotting corpses than by any other means. And what with these, and the others who were dying all over the city, bodies were here, there, and everywhere. . . .

[T]here were no tears or candles or mourners to honour the dead; in fact, no more respect was accorded to dead people than would nowadays be shown towards dead goats. For it was quite apparent that the one thing which, in normal times, no wise man had ever learned to accept with patient resignation (even though it struck so seldom and unobtrusively), had now been brought home to the feeble-minded as well, but the scale of the calamity caused them to regard it with indifference.

Such was the multitude of corpses (of which further consignments were arriving every day and almost by the hour at each of the churches), that there was not sufficient consecrated ground for them to be buried in, especially if each was to have its own plot in accordance with long-established custom. So when all the graves were full, huge trenches were excavated in the churchyards, into which new arrivals were placed in their hundreds, stowed tier upon tier like ships' cargo, each layer of corpses being covered over with a thin layer of soil till the trench was filled to the top.

But rather than describe in elaborate detail the calamities we experienced in the city at that time, I must mention that, whilst an ill wind was blowing through Florence itself, the surrounding region was no less badly affected. In the fortified towns, conditions were similar to those in the city itself on a minor scale; but in the scattered hamlets and the countryside proper, the poor unfortunate peasants and their families had no physicians or servants whatever to assist them, and collapsed by the wayside, in their fields, and in their cottages at all hours of the day and night, dying more like animals than human beings. Like the townspeople, they too grew apathetic in their ways, disregarded their affairs, and neglected their possessions. Moreover, they all behaved as though each day was to be their last, and far from making provision for the future by tilling their lands, tending their flocks, and adding to their previous labours, they tried in every way they could think of to squander the assets already in their possession. Thus it came about that oxen, asses, sheep, goats, pigs, chickens, and even dogs (for all their deep fidelity to man) were driven away and allowed to roam freely through the fields, where the crops lay abandoned and had not even been reaped, let alone gathered in. And after a whole day's feasting, many of these animals, as though possessing the power of reason, would return glutted in the evening to their own quarters without any shepherd to guide them.

But let us leave the countryside and return to the city. What more remains to be said, except that the cruelty of heaven (and possibly, in some measure, also that of man) was so immense and so devastating that between March and July of the year in question, what with the fury of the pestilence and the fact that so many of the sick were inadequately cared for or abandoned in their hour of need because the healthy were too terrified to approach them, it is reliably thought that over a hundred thousand human lives were extinguished within the walls of the city of Florence? Yet before this lethal catastrophe fell upon the city, it is doubtful whether anyone would have guessed it contained so many inhabitants.

78

Images of the Black Death

Contemporary accounts testify to the plague's terrifying physical, social, and psychological impact. Images from the period document the ravages of the epidemic as well, sometimes in gruesome detail. The engraving in Figure 12.1, for example, shows a plague victim covered in the dark blotches characteristic of the disease. The town in the back-

Figure 12.1   Plague Victim with Maiden, 1348.

Source: The Bridgeman Art Library International.

ground appears to be going up in flames while lightning flares in the sky above. What else do you think is going on in this image? Who is the woman depicted and what is she doing? If this is a group fleeing with their belongings from the burning town, do you think the plague victim is part of their entourage? What might be the significance of the flag they carry?

Figures 12.2 and 12.3 show two well-documented phenomena of the plague years: The first depicts a group of flagellants, members of a movement who wandered from town to town beating themselves with whips studded with iron nails in an effort to do penance for the sins they believed had brought on the plague. Written accounts confirm many elements in this picture: Flagellants usually carried crosses or banners with crosses on them, wore long pleated skirts, and went around bare-chested, the better to make their scourging as painful as possible. Figure 12.3 illustrates a similar impulse toward punishment as a means of coping with the plague, but this time the violence is

Figure 12.2 Flagellants, from a Fifteenth-Century Chronicle from Constance, Switzerland.

Source: © Bettmann/CORBIS.

Figure 12.3 The Burning of Jews in an Early Printed Woodcut.

Source: © Christel Gerstenberg/CORBIS.

directed outward, against Jews, so often the scapegoats in troubled times. Baseless accusations that Jews poisoned wells to spread the plague resulted in many such attacks against them during the period.

The final image, Figure 12.4, is one of a transi tomb from 1390. Transi tombs, which emerged during and after the plague era, were a major departure from standard funerary monuments that typically offered an idealized depiction of the deceased. Instead these tombs showed decaying or skeletal corpses covered with worms and other emblems of bodily corruption. Scholars differ over their meaning. How might you explain them?

Thinking Historically

What can these images tell us about fourteenth-century people's beliefs about the possible causes — medical or religious — of the plague? Think about the social and religious changes wrought by the plague recounted in the de' Mussis and Boccaccio readings. What evidence, if any, do you see in these images of these changes?

Figure 12.4 François de la Sarra, Tomb at La Sarraz, Switzerland, c. 1390.
Source: Reproduced courtesy of Harry N. Abrams, Inc.

79

AHMAD AL-MAQRIZI
The Plague in Cairo

Ahmad al-Maqrizi* (1364–1442) became a historian after pursuing a career as an administrator in post-plague Cairo. While he wrote his history of the plague period more than fifty years after the event, he probably had access to contemporary sources that are now lost to us. Compare al-Maqrizi's account of the plague in Cairo with the prior accounts of the plague in Italy. How was the experience of the Black Death in Cairo similar to, and different from, the experience in Florence?

Thinking Historically

Like Boccaccio, al-Maqrizi devotes more attention to the effects than to the causes of the Black Death. What effects were similar in Florence and Cairo? Al-Maqrizi discusses certain effects that were not mentioned in the Italian accounts. Which, if any, of these effects do you think also probably occurred in Italy?

In January 1349, there appeared new symptoms that consisted of spitting up of blood. The disease caused one to experience an internal fever, followed by an uncontrollable desire to vomit; then one spat up blood and died. The inhabitants of a house were stricken one after the other, and in one night or two, the dwelling became deserted. Each individual lived with this fixed idea that he was going to die in this way. He prepared for himself a good death by distributing alms; he arranged for scenes of reconciliation and his acts of devotion multiplied. . . .

By January 21, Cairo had become an abandoned desert, and one did not see anyone walking along the streets. A man could go from the Port Zuwayla to Bāb al-Nasr[1] without encountering a living soul. The dead were very numerous, and all the world could think of nothing else. Debris piled up in the streets. People went around with worried faces. Everywhere one heard lamentations, and one could not pass by any house without being overwhelmed by the howling. Cadavers

---

*ahk MAHD   ahl mah KREE zee
[1]This was apparently the busiest boulevard in medieval Cairo.

John Aberth, *The Black Death: The Great Mortality of 1348–1350, A Brief History with Documents* (Boston: Bedford/St. Martin's, 2005), 84–87.

formed a heap on the public highway, funeral processions were so many that they could not file past without bumping into each other, and the dead were transported in some confusion. . . .

One began to have to search for readers of the Koran for funeral ceremonies, and a number of individuals quit their usual occupations in order to recite prayers at the head of funeral processions. In the same way, some people devoted themselves to smearing crypts with plaster; others presented themselves as volunteers to wash the dead or carry them. These latter folk earned substantial salaries. For example, a reader of the Koran took ten *dirhams*.[2] Also, hardly had he reached the oratory when he slipped away very quickly in order to go officiate at a new [funeral]. Porters demanded 6 *dirhams* at the time they were engaged, and then it was necessary to match it [at the grave]. The gravedigger demanded fifty *dirhams* per grave. Most of the rest of these people died without having taken any profit from their gains. . . . Also families kept their dead on the bare ground, due to the impossibility of having them interred. The inhabitants of a house died by the tens and, since there wasn't a litter ready to hand, one had to carry them away in stages. Moreover, some people appropriated for themselves without scruple the immovable and movable goods and cash of their former owners after their demise. But very few lived long enough to profit thereby, and those who remained alive would have been able to do without. . . .

Family festivities and weddings had no more place [in life]. No one issued an invitation to a feast during the whole time of the epidemic, and one did not hear any concert. The *vizier*[3] lifted a third of what he was owed from the woman responsible [for collecting] the tax on singers. The call to prayer was canceled in various places, and in the exact same way, those places [where prayer] was most frequent subsisted on a *muezzin*[4] alone. . . .

The men of the [military] troop and the cultivators took a world of trouble to finish their sowing [of fields]. The plague emerged at the end of the season when the fields were becoming green. How many times did one see a laborer, at Gaza, at Ramleh, and along other points of the Syrian littoral,[5] guide his plow being pulled by oxen suddenly fall down dead, still holding in his hands his plow, while the oxen stood at their place without a conductor.

It was the same in Egypt: When the harvest time came, there remained only a very small number of *fellahs*.[6] The soldiers and their

---

[2]A silver coin used in the Muslim world.

[3]The chief minister of the caliph, or leader of the Muslim community.

[4]An official of the mosque who called the faithful to prayer from the minaret.

[5]The coastal plain of southern Palestine, where the most fertile land was located.

[6]Arabic word for ploughman or tiller, which also denoted the peasantry of Egypt and is the origin of the modern term, *fellahin*.

valets left for the harvest and attempted to hire workers, promising them half of the crop, but they could not find anyone to help them reap it. They loaded the grain on their horses, did the mowing themselves, but, being powerless to carry out the greatest portion of the work, they abandoned this enterprise.

The endowments[7] passed rapidly from hand to hand as a consequence of the multiplicity of deaths in the army. Such a concession passed from one to the other until the seventh or eighth holder, to fall finally [into the hands] of artisans, such as tailors, shoemakers, or public criers, and these mounted the horse, donned the [military] headdress, and dressed in military tunics.

Actually, no one collected the whole revenue of his endowment, and a number of holders harvested absolutely nothing. During the flooding of the Nile[8] and the time of the sprouting of vegetation, one could procure a laborer only with difficulty: On half the lands only did the harvest reach maturity. Moreover, there was no one to buy the green clover [as feed] and no one sent their horses to graze over the field. This was the ruin of royal properties in the suburbs of Cairo, like Matarieh, Hums, Siryaqus, and Bahtit. In the canton [administrative district] of Nay and Tanan, 1,500 *feddans*[9] of clover were abandoned where it stood: No one came to buy it, either to pasture their beasts on the place or to gather it into barns and use it as fodder.

The province of Upper Egypt was deserted, in spite of the vast abundance of cultivable terrain. It used to be that, after the land surface was cultivated in the territory of Asyūt,[10] 6,000 individuals were subject to payment of the property tax; now, in the year of the epidemic [1348–49], one could not count on more than 106 contributors. Nevertheless, during this period, the price of wheat did not rise past fifteen *dirhams* per *ardeb*.[11]

Most of the trades disappeared, for a number of artisans devoted themselves to handling the dead, while the others, no less numerous, occupied themselves in selling off to bidders [the dead's] movable goods and clothing, so well that the price of linen and similar objects fell by a fifth of their real value, at the very least, and still further until one found customers. . . .

Thus the trades disappeared: One could no longer find either a water carrier, or a laundress, or a domestic. The monthly salary of a

---

[7]Mamluk commanders and elite soldiers, like their Ayyubid predecessors, were paid out of the revenues of land grants, known as *iqtas* (similar to fiefs in Europe). With the dearth of labor caused by the Black Death, it became far more difficult to extract income from these estates.

[8]This usually took place between September and November of every year.

[9]A *feddan* is equivalent to 1.038 acres.

[10]Located along the Nile in Upper Egypt, about midway between Cairo and Aswan.

[11]An *ardeb* is equivalent to 5.62 bushels.

groom rose from thirty *dirhams* to eighty. A proclamation made in Cairo invited the artisans to take up their old trades, and some of the recalcitrants reformed themselves. Because of the shortage of men and camels, a goatskin of water reached the price of eight *dirhams,* and in order to grind an *ardeb* of wheat, one paid fifteen *dirhams.*

80

WILLIAM H. McNEILL

Consequences of the Black Death in Europe

In this selection, William H. McNeill, a leading world historian (see selection 10), explores the psychological, cultural, and economic consequences of the Black Death in Europe. What, according to McNeill, were these consequences? Which do you think were most important?

Thinking Historically

McNeill uses the term *consequences* rather than *effects.* Do the words mean the same thing, or are his "consequences" too general to be attached to specific causes? In fact, he lists some of the major changes that occurred in European culture and economy in the centuries after the Black Death. Which of these consequences was likely caused by the Black Death? In the last sentence of this selection, McNeill makes a distinction between effects that depend on a single cause "alone" and on causes that "contributed" to a broader effect. What does he mean by this distinction?

Before pursuing this theme, however, it seems worth venturing a few remarks about the psychological, economic, and cultural consequences of Europe's encounter with the plague in the fourteenth and succeeding centuries; and then we must survey as best we can the disease consequences for Asia and Africa of the Mongol opening of the steppelands to regular transit.

William H. McNeill, *Plagues and Peoples* (Garden City, N.Y.: Anchor Books, 1976), 161–65.

At the psychological and cultural level European reactions were obvious and varied. In face of intense and immediate crisis, when an outbreak of plague implanted fear of imminent death in an entire community, ordinary routines and customary restraints regularly broke down. In time, rituals arose to discharge anxiety in socially acceptable ways; but in the fourteenth century itself, local panic often provoked bizarre behavior. The first important effort at ritualizing responses to the plague took extreme and ugly forms. In Germany and some adjacent parts of Europe companies of Flagellants aimed at propitiating God's wrath by beating each other bloody and attacking Jews, who were commonly accused of spreading the pestilence. The Flagellants disdained all established authorities of church and state and, if accounts are to be believed, their rituals were well-nigh suicidal for the participants.

Attacks on German-Jewish communities inspired by Flagellants and others probably accelerated an eastward shift of centers of Jewish population in Europe. Poland escaped the first round of plague almost entirely, and though popular rioting against Jews occurred there too, royal authorities welcomed German Jews for the urban skills they brought into the country. The subsequent development of east European Jewry was therefore significantly affected (and the rise in the Vistula and Nieman valleys of a market-oriented agriculture, largely under Jewish management, was probably accelerated) by the fourteenth-century pattern of popular reaction to plague.

These and other violent episodes attest the initial impact of the plague on European consciousness. In time, the fear and horror of the first onset relaxed. Writers as diverse as Boccaccio, Chaucer, and William Langland all treated the plague as a routine crisis of human life — an act of God, like the weather. Perhaps the plague had other, more lasting, consequences for literature: scholars have suggested, for instance, that the rise of vernacular tongues as a medium for serious writing and the decay of Latin as a *lingua franca* among the educated men of western Europe was hastened by the die-off of clerics and teachers who knew enough Latin to keep that ancient tongue alive. Painting also responded to the plague-darkened vision of the human condition provoked by repeated exposure to sudden, inexplicable death. Tuscan painters, for instance, reacted against Giotto's serenity, preferring sterner, hieratic portrayals of religious scenes and figures. The "Dance of Death" became a common theme for art; and several other macabre motifs entered the European repertory. The buoyancy and self-confidence, so characteristic of the thirteenth century, when Europe's great cathedrals were abuilding, gave way to a more troubled age. Acute social tensions between economic classes and intimate acquaintance with sudden death assumed far greater importance for almost everyone than had been true previously.

The economic impact of the Black Death was enormous, though local differences were greater than an earlier generation of scholars assumed. In highly developed regions like northern Italy and Flanders, harsh collisions between social classes manifested themselves as the boom times of the thirteenth century faded into the past. The plague, by disrupting wage and price patterns sharply, exacerbated these conflicts, at least in the short run. Some ninety years ago Thorold Rogers argued that the Black Death had improved the lot of the lower classes and advanced freedom by destroying serfdom. His idea was that labor shortage caused by plague deaths allowed wage earners to bargain among rival would-be employers and thus improve their real wages. This view is no longer widely believed. Local circumstances differed widely. Employers died as well as laborers; and manpower shortages proved evanescent in those towns where a vigorous market economy did effect a short-term rise in real wages.

In time, of course, the initial perturbations created by the plague tended to diminish. All the same, two general displacements of European culture and society can be discerned in the latter fourteenth and fifteenth centuries that seem plausibly related to the terrifying, constantly renewed experience of plague.

When the plague was raging, a person might be in full health one day and die miserably within twenty-four hours. This utterly discredited any merely human effort to explain the mysteries of the world. The confidence in rational theology, which characterized the age of Aquinas (d. 1274), could not survive such experiences. A world view allowing ample scope to arbitrary, inexplicable catastrophe alone was compatible with the grim reality of plague. Hedonism and revival of one or another form of fatalistic pagan philosophy were possible reactions, though confined always to a few. Far more popular and respectable was an upsurge of mysticism, aimed at achieving encounter with God in inexplicable, unpredictable, intense, and purely personal ways. Hesychasm[1] among the Orthodox, and more variegated movements among Latin Christians — e.g., the practices of the so-called Rhineland mystics, of the Brethren of the Common Life, and of heretical groups like the Lollards of England — all gave expression to the need for a more personal, antinomian access to God than had been offered by Thomist theology and the previously recognized forms of piety. Recurrence of plague refreshed this psychological need until the mid-seventeenth century; hence it is no accident that all branches of organized Christianity — Orthodox, Catholic, and Protestant — made more room for personal mysticism and other forms of communion with God, even though ecclesiastical

---

[1]Mystical religious practice by Orthodox monks which involved certain repetitive movements and recitation of prayer. [Ed.]

authorities always remained uncomfortable when confronting too much private zeal.

Secondly, the inadequacy of established ecclesiastical rituals and administrative measures to cope with the unexampled emergency of plague had pervasively unsettling effects. In the fourteenth century, many priests and monks died; often their successors were less well trained and faced more quizzical if not openly antagonistic flocks. God's justice seemed far to seek in the way plague spared some, killed others; and the regular administration of God's grace through the sacraments (even when consecrated priests remained available) was an entirely inadequate psychological counterpoise to the statistical vagaries of lethal infection and sudden death. Anticlericalism was of course not new in Christian Europe; after 1346, however, it became more open and widespread, and provided one of the elements contributing to Luther's later success.

Because sacred rituals remained vigorously conservative, it took centuries for the Roman Church to adjust to the recurrent crises created by outbreaks of plague. Hence it was mainly in the period of the Counter-Reformation that psychologically adequate ceremonies and symbols for coping with recurrent lethal epidemics defined themselves. Invocation of St. Sebastian, who in early Christian centuries had already attracted to himself many of the attributes once assigned to Apollo, became central in Catholic rituals of prophylaxis against the plague. The suffering saint, whose death by arrows was symbolic of deaths dealt by the unseen arrows of pestilential infection, began to figure largely in religious art as well. A second important figure was St. Roch. He had a different character, being an exemplar and patron of the acts of public charity and nursing that softened the impact of plague in those cities of Mediterranean Europe that were most exposed to the infection.

Protestant Europe never developed much in the way of special rituals for meeting epidemic emergencies. The Bible had little to say about how to cope with massive outbreaks of infectious disease, and since plague seldom affected the North (though when it came it was sometimes exceptionally severe), Protestants lacked sufficient stimulus to such a development.

In contrast to the rigidities that beset the church, city governments, especially in Italy, responded rather quickly to the challenges presented by devastating disease. Magistrates learned how to cope at the practical level, organizing burials, safeguarding food deliveries, setting up quarantines, hiring doctors, and establishing other regulations for public and private behavior in time of plague. The ability of city authorities to react in these more or less effective ways was symptomatic of their general vigor — a vigor that made the centuries between 1350 and 1550 a sort of golden age for European city-states, especially Germany and Italy, where competition with any superior secular government was minimal.

Italian and German city governments and businessmen not only managed their own local affairs with general success, but also pioneered the development of a far more closely integrated inter-regional market economy that ran throughout all of Europe. Ere long these same cities also defined a more secularized style of life and thought that by 1500 attracted the liveliest attention throughout the continent. The shift from medieval to renaissance cultural values, needless to say, did not depend on the plague alone; yet the plague, and the generally successful way city authorities managed to react to its ravages, surely contributed something to the general transformation of European sensibility.

When we turn attention from Europe and ask what the new plague pattern may have meant elsewhere in the Old World, a troublesome void presents itself. Scholarly discussion of the Black Death in Europe, its course and consequences, is more than a century old; nothing remotely comparable exists for other regions of the earth. Yet it is impossible to believe that the plague did not affect China, India, and the Middle East; and it is even more implausible to think that human life on the steppe was not also brought under new and unexampled stress by the establishment of a persistent reservoir of bubonic infection among the rodents of the Eurasian grasslands all the way from Manchuria to the Ukraine.

To be sure, there is ample evidence that plague became and remained, as in Europe, a dreaded recurrent affliction throughout the Islamic world. Egypt and Syria shared the plague experience of other parts of the Mediterranean coastlands with which they remained always in close contact. About a third of Egypt's population seems to have died in the first attack, 1347–1349, and the plague returned to the Nile Valley at frequent intervals thereafter, appearing there most recently in the 1940s.

REFLECTIONS

History is always written backwards. We study the rearview mirror to see where we are going. What can the Black Death tell us about the possibility of pandemic disease in the future? Historians who are sometimes embarrassed by their present-mindedness can take refuge in the conventions of the discipline: Histories begin in the past and work chronologically toward the present; narratives seem to only tell the story, just as it happened. But both chronological and narrative presentations imply a chain of cause and effect where analysis might reveal chance or no relationship at all.

We can all easily fall prey to the logical fallacy called in Latin "*post hoc, ergo propter hoc*" (meaning literally "after this, therefore because of this"). Just because "B" came after "A" doesn't mean that "B" was caused by "A." Still it is only natural to cast around for this sort of simple, uncomplicated causation when your world is falling apart. Consider how de' Mussis, Boccaccio, or the Flagellants and Europeans shown in Figures 12.2 and 12.3 and discussed in the McNeill reading explained what was happening to them. Nevertheless, in our lives, as in our understanding of history, we can only see the past from the standpoint of the immediate present, and all roads seem to lead inexorably to Now. Though most of us like to think we can shape our future, we gain some comfort from believing that we couldn't have changed our past.

At least for the purposes of historical accuracy, how do we break this mindset? We have already suggested (in our introduction to the reading by McNeill) the importance of recognizing multiple causation. Rarely if ever is any event the result of a single cause. Even a single premeditated act of an individual can be usefully understood in terms of a myriad of factors. Anything as complex as a social movement, economic trend, political revolution, or cultural style results from a profound web of causes. When we ask about the causes of the Protestant Reformation or the Communist Revolution in China, we are clearly dealing with multiple factors, all of which were imporant to some degree in these developments.

Finally, it is important to keep in mind that historical causation always underplays the role of chance or accident. We know our personal lives are full of chance events. Do these unpredictable events become more predictable in larger social groups or over longer time periods? Sometimes we realize later that an event we thought was chance actually had causes. Might this be true more generally? Are chance events merely those we have not yet been able to explain?

We end, perhaps, with more questions than answers. This is because the study of history involves nothing less than the study of everything that has happened to all of the very complex creatures we call human beings. We can formulate certain scientific methods for studying the past. We can even use these methods to improve our understanding of the past. But we never have a single or final explanation of any of it.

On Cities

European, Chinese, Islamic,
and Mexican Cities, 1000–1550 C.E.

HISTORICAL CONTEXT

During the last five thousand years, cities have grown and multiplied, the world becoming increasingly urbanized. There have been interruptions in this process, however: the period of the Mongol invasions in the first half of the thirteenth century and the era of the Black Death, the plague that wiped out urban populations in the middle of the fourteenth century, for instance. But, by and large, the general course of world history has promoted the rise and expansion of cities and of urban over rural populations.

In this chapter, we ask what this increasing urbanization meant for those who lived in the cities and for those who did not. We compare cities in various parts of the world between 1000 and 1550. We will study primary and secondary sources, and you will be asked to note the ways in which these cities are similar and different.

THINKING HISTORICALLY
Evaluating a Comparative Thesis

Many of the chapters, even individual readings, in this volume have been comparative. Making comparisons is a critical skill in any disciplined thinking process. In the study of world history, comparisons are particularly important and potentially fruitful, since until recently the historical profession tended to study different nations' histories somewhat in isolation from each other or without reference to a broader comparative context.

Comparisons are not useful in and of themselves. They are merely a first step toward a thesis that attempts to explain the differences or similarities noticed. To say that something is bigger or smaller, hotter or colder, than something else, that one country is more densely populated or more religious than another, may or may not be obvious or interesting, but the observation is not meaningful in and of itself. The comparative observation becomes meaningful when it is explained by some general rule that covers both cases. Human behavior is too complex to attain what some call "covering laws" in science, but the effort to reach an explanation that covered both cases might be called a comparative thesis.

In history, there are many comparative theses. An example of one might run something like this: Canada has a more universal health care system than the United States because it has a longer tradition of mutual aid and trust in government. Now, one might agree or disagree with either the comparison or the explanation. If one disagrees with the comparison there is no need to go further. But if one agrees with the comparison, then one has to evaluate the comparative thesis.

In this chapter you will be asked to consider a comparative thesis about cities that is offered in the first reading. The other readings in the chapter will enable you to consider what evidence they offer for or against the initial comparison and its explanatory thesis.

81

FERNAND BRAUDEL

Towns and Cities

Fernand Braudel* (1902–1985) was one of the great historians of the twentieth century, and the following selection, which provides a broad overview of medieval towns and cities throughout the world, is from one of his interpretative works of world history. According to Braudel, what were some of the distinctive characteristics of Western, or European, towns? Why did Western towns acquire these character-

*broh DELL

Fernand Braudel, *The Structures of Everyday Life: The Limits of the Possible* (London: Collins, 1983), 509–15, 518–25.

istics? How does Braudel describe Chinese and Islamic cities? Why
and how did these towns develop differently?

Thinking Historically

Braudel begins with a comparative judgment—that European towns
"were marked by an unparalleled freedom." How does he explain this
supposed difference between European towns and those of other societies? He offers a kind of covering law in the form of a "Western
model" that relates urban freedom to a number of other features. He
says these towns were autonomous, self-governing, bodies of largely
middle-class citizens who thought of themselves as a community. They
were not governed by a king, emperor, or territorial state, but, rather,
governed themselves through a number of organizations. In addition to
governing councils and militaries, these organizations included guilds,
church groups, and various other voluntary societies in which citizens
exercised real power over their lives. On an even broader level, Braudel
attributes these differences to the long history of European feudalism
and weak states, and to the rise of capitalism and a middle class.

As you read Braudel, try to weigh his evidence for both the comparison and the larger model. Does it appear from the reading that inhabitants of European towns had greater freedom than the people of
other towns? If you agree with his comparison, try to evaluate his
model. Do the elements of the model fit together? Was there a
complex of features in Western society that did not occur elsewhere?
What is his evidence for that comparative thesis? What else would you
want to learn to challenge or confirm his thesis?

The Originality of Western Towns

. . . What were Europe's differences and original features? Its towns
were marked by an unparalleled freedom. They had developed as autonomous worlds and according to their own propensities. They had
outwitted the territorial state, which was established slowly and then
only grew with their interested co-operation—and was moreover only
an enlarged and often insipid copy of their development. They ruled
their countrysides autocratically, regarding them exactly as later powers regarded their colonies, and treating them as such. They pursued an
economic policy of their own via their satellites and the nervous system
of urban relay points; they were capable of breaking down obstacles
and creating or recreating protective privileges. Imagine what would
happen if modern states were suppressed so that the Chambers of Commerce of the large towns were free to act as they pleased!

Even without resort to doubtful comparisons these long-standing
realities leap to the eye. And they lead us to a key problem which can
be formulated in two or three different ways: What stopped the other

cities of the world from enjoying the same relative freedom? Or to take another aspect of the same problem, why was change a striking feature of the destiny of Western towns (even their physical existence was transformed) while the other cities have no history by comparison and seem to have been shut in long periods of immobility? Why were some cities like steam-engines while the others were like clocks, to parody Lévi-Strauss? Comparative history compels us to look for the reason for these differences and to attempt to establish a dynamic "model" of the turbulent urban evolution of the West, whereas a model representing city life in the rest of the world would run in a straight and scarcely broken line across time.

Free Worlds

Urban freedom in Europe is a classic and fairly well documented subject; let us start with it.

In a simplified form we can say:

1. The West well and truly lost its urban framework with the end of the Roman Empire. Moreover the towns in the Empire had been gradually declining since before the arrival of the barbarians. The very relative animation of the Merovingian period was followed, slightly earlier in some places, slightly later in others, by a complete halt.

2. The urban renaissance from the eleventh century was precipitated by and superimposed on a rise in rural vigour, a growth of fields, vineyards, and orchards. Towns grew in harmony with villages and clearly outlined urban law often emerged from the communal privileges of village groups. The town was often simply the country revived and remodeled. The names of a number of streets in Frankfurt (which remained very rural until the sixteenth century) recall the woods, clumps of trees, and marshland amid which the town grew up.

This rural rearrangement naturally brought to the nascent city the representatives of political and social authority: nobles, lay princes, and ecclesiastics.

3. None of this would have been possible without a general return to health and a growing monetary economy. Money, a traveler from perhaps distant lands (from Islam, according to Maurice Lombard), was the active and decisive force. Two centuries before Saint Thomas Aquinas, Alain de Lille said: "Money, not Caesar, is everything now." And money meant towns.

Thousands of towns were founded at this time, but few of them went on to brilliant futures. Only certain regions, therefore, were urbanized in depth, thus distinguishing themselves from the rest and playing a vitalizing role: such was the region between the Loire and the Rhine, for instance, or northern and central Italy, and certain key points on Mediterranean coasts. Merchants, craft guilds, industries, long-distance trade, and banks were quick to appear there, as well as a certain kind of bourgeoisie and even some sort of capitalism. The destinies of these very special cities were linked not only to the progress of the surrounding countryside but to international trade. Indeed, they often broke free of rural society and former political ties. The break might be achieved violently or amicably, but it was always a sign of strength, plentiful money, and real power.

Soon there were no states around these privileged towns. This was the case in Italy and Germany, with the political collapses of the thirteenth century. The hare beat the tortoise for once. Elsewhere—in France, England, Castile, even in Aragon—the earlier rebirth of the territorial state restricted the development of the towns, which in addition were not situated in particularly lively economic areas. They grew less rapidly than elsewhere.

But the main, the unpredictable thing was that certain towns made themselves into autonomous worlds, city-states, buttressed with privileges (acquired or extorted) like so many juridical ramparts. Perhaps in the past historians have insisted too much on the legal factors involved, for if such considerations were indeed sometimes more important than, or of equal importance to, geographical, sociological, and economic factors, the latter did count to a large extent. What is privilege without material substance?

In fact the miracle in the West was not so much that everything sprang up again from the eleventh century, after having been almost annihilated with the disaster of the fifth. History is full of examples of secular revivals, of urban expansion, of births and rebirths: Greece from the fifth to the second century B.C.E.; Rome perhaps; Islam from the ninth century; China under the Sungs. But these revivals always featured two runners, the state and the city. The state usually won and the city then remained subject and under a heavy yoke. The miracle of the first great urban centuries in Europe was that the city won hands down, at least in Italy, Flanders, and Germany. It was able to try the experiment of leading a completely separate life for quite a long time. This was a colossal event. Its genesis cannot be pinpointed with certainty, but its enormous consequences are visible.

Towns as Outposts of Modernity

It was on the basis of this liberty that the great Western cities, and other towns they influenced and to which they served as examples, built up a distinctive civilization and spread techniques which were new, or had been revived or rediscovered after centuries—it matters little which. The important thing is that these cities had the rare privilege of following through an unusual political, social, and economic experience.

In the financial sphere, the towns organized taxation, finances, public credit, customs, and excise. They invented public loans: the first issues of the Monte Vecchio in Venice could be said to go back to 1167, the first formulation of the Casa di San Giorgio to 1407. One after another, they reinvented gold money, following Genoa which may have minted the *genovino* as early as the late twelfth century. They organized industry and the guilds; they invented long-distance trade, bills of exchange, the first forms of trading companies and accountancy. They also quickly became the scene of class struggles. For if the towns were "communities" as has been said, they were also "societies" in the modern sense of the word, with their tensions and civil struggles: nobles against bourgeois; poor against rich ("thin people" *popolo magro* against "fat people" *popolo grosso*). The struggles in Florence were already more deeply akin to those of the industrial early nineteenth century than to the faction-fights of ancient Rome, as the drama of the Ciompi (1378) demonstrates.

This society divided from within also faced enemies from without— the worlds of the noble, prince, or peasant, of everybody who was not a citizen. The cities were the West's first focus for patriotism—and the patriotism they inspired was long to be more coherent and much more conscious than the territorial kind, which emerged only slowly in the first states. . . .

A new state of mind was established, broadly that of an early, still faltering, Western capitalism—a collection of rules, possibilities, calculations, the art both of getting rich and of living. It also included gambling and risk: the key words of commercial language, *fortuna*, *ventura*, *ragione*, *prudenza*, *sicurta*, define the risks to be guarded against. No question now of living from day to day as noblemen did, always putting up their revenues to try to meet the level of their expenditure, which invariably came first—and letting the future take care of itself. The merchant was economical with his money, calculated his expenditure according to his returns, his investments according to their yield. The hour-glass had turned back the right way. He would also be economical with his time: A merchant could already say that *chi tempo ha e tempo aspetta tempo perde*, which means much the same thing as "time is money."

Capitalism and towns were basically the same thing in the West. Lewis Mumford humorously claimed that capitalism was the cuckoo's egg laid in the confined nests of the medieval towns. By this he meant to convey that the bird was destined to grow inordinately and burst its tight framework (which was true), and then link up with the state, the conqueror of towns but heir to their institutions and way of thinking and completely incapable of dispensing with them. The important thing was that even when it had declined as a city the town continued to rule the roost all the time it was passing into the actual or apparent service of the prince. The wealth of the state would still be the wealth of the town: Portugal converged on Lisbon, the Netherlands on Amsterdam, and English primacy was London's primacy (the capital modelled England in its own image after the peaceful revolution of 1688). The latent defect in the Spanish imperial economy was that it was based on Seville—a controlled town rotten with dishonest officials and long dominated by foreign capitalists—and not on a powerful free town capable of producing and carrying through a really individual economic policy. Likewise, if Louis XIV did not succeed in founding a "royal bank," despite various projects (1703, 1706, 1709), it was because faced with the power of the monarch, Paris did not offer the protection of a town free to do what it wanted and accountable to no one.

Urban Patterns

Let us imagine we are looking at a comprehensive history of the towns of Europe covering the complete series of their forms from the Greek city-state to an eighteenth-century town—everything Europe was able to build at home and overseas, from Muscovy in the East to America in the West. . . .

Simplifying, one could say that the West has had three basic types of town in the course of its evolution: open towns, that is to say not differentiated from their hinterland, even blending into it (A); towns closed in on themselves in every sense, their walls marking the boundaries of an individual way of life more than a territory (B); finally towns held in subjection, by which is meant the whole range of known controls by prince or state (C).

Roughly, A preceded B, and B preceded C. But there is no suggestion of strict succession about this order. It is rather a question of directions and dimensions shaping the complicated careers of the Western towns. They did not all develop at the same time or in the same way. Later we will see if this "grid" is valid for classifying all the towns of the world.

Type A: the ancient Greek or Roman city was open to the surrounding countryside and on terms of equality with it. Athens accepted inside its walls as rightful citizens the Eupatrid horse-breeders as well as the vine-growing peasants so dear to Aristophanes. As soon as the smoke rose above the Pnyx, the peasant responded to the signal and attended the Assembly of the People, where he sat among his equals. At the beginning of the Peloponnesian war, the entire population of the Attic countryside evacuated itself to Athens where it took refuge while the Spartans ravaged the fields, olive groves, and houses. When the Spartans fell back at the approach of winter, the country people returned to their homes. The Greek city was in fact the sum of the town and its surrounding countryside. . . . Likewise, if one explores the ruins of Roman cities, one is in open country immediately outside the gates: There are no suburbs, which is as good as saying no industry or active and organized trades in their duly allotted place.

Type B: the closed city: the medieval town was the classic example of a closed city, a self-sufficient unit, an exclusive, Lilliputian empire. Entering its gates was like crossing one of the serious frontiers of the world today. You were free to thumb your nose at your neighbour from the other side of the barrier. He could not touch you. The peasant who uprooted himself from his land and arrived in the town was immediately another man. He was free—or rather he had abandoned a known and hated servitude for another, not always guessing the extent of it beforehand. But this mattered little. If the town had adopted him, he could snap his fingers when his lord called for him. And though obsolete elsewhere, such calls were still frequently to be heard in Silesia in the eighteenth century and in Muscovy up to the nineteenth.

Though the towns opened their gates easily it was not enough to walk through them to be immediately and really part of them. Full citizens were a jealous minority, a small town inside the town itself. A citadel of the rich was built up in Venice in 1297 thanks to the *serrata*, the closing of the Great Council to new members. The *nobili* of Venice became a closed class for centuries. Very rarely did anyone force its gates. The category of ordinary *cittadini*—at a lower level—was probably more hospitable. But the Signoria very soon created two types of citizen, one *de intus*, the other *de intus et extra*, the latter full, the former partial. Fifteen years' residence were still required to be allowed to apply for the first, twenty-five years for the second. A decree by the Senate in 1386 even forbade new citizens (including those who were full citizens) from trading directly in Venice with German merchants at the Fondego dei Todeschi or outside it. The ordinary townspeople were no less mistrustful or hostile to newcomers. According to Marin Sanudo, in June 1520, the street people attacked the peasants who had arrived from the mainland as recruits for the galleys or the army, crying *"Poltroni ande arar!"* "Back to the plough, shirkers!"

Of course Venice was an extreme example. Moreover, it owed the preservation of its own constitution until 1797 to an aristocratic and extremely reactionary regime, as well as to the conquest at the beginning of the fifteenth century of the Terra Firma, which extended its authority as far as the Alps and Brescia. It was the last *polis* in the West. But citizenship was also parsimoniously granted in Marseilles in the sixteenth century; it was necessary to have "ten years of domicile, to possess property, to have married a local girl." Otherwise the man remained amongst the masses of non-citizens of the town. This limited conception of citizenship was the general rule everywhere.

The main source of contention can be glimpsed throughout this vast process: to whom did industry and craft, their privileges and profits, belong? In fact they belonged to the town, to its authorities and to its merchant entrepreneurs. They decided if it were necessary to deprive, or to try to deprive, the rural area of the city of the right to spin, weave, and dye, or if on the contrary it would be advantageous to grant it these rights. Everything was possible in these interchanges, as the history of each individual town shows.

As far as work inside the walls was concerned (we can hardly call it industry without qualification), everything was arranged for the benefit of the craft guilds. They enjoyed exclusive contiguous monopolies, fiercely defended along the imprecise frontiers that so easily led to absurd conflicts. The urban authorities did not always have the situation under control. Sooner or later, with the help of money, they were to allow obvious, acknowledged, honorary superiorities, consecrated by money or power, to become apparent. The "Six Corps" (drapers, grocers, haberdashers, furriers, hosiers, goldsmiths) were the commercial aristocracy of Paris from 1625. In Florence it was the *arte dela lana* and the *Arte di Calimala* (engaged in dyeing fabric imported from the north, unbleached). But town museums in Germany supply the best evidence of these old situations. In Ulm, for example, each guild owned a picture hinged in triptych form. The side panels represented characteristic scenes of the craft. The centre, like a treasured family album, showed innumerable small portraits recalling the successive generations of masters of the guild over the centuries.

An even more telling example was the City of London and its annexes (running along its walls) in the eighteenth century, still the domain of fussy, obsolete, and powerful guilds. If Westminster and the suburbs were growing continually, noted a well-informed economist (1754), it was for obvious reasons: "These suburbs are free and present a clear field for every industrious citizen, while in its bosom London nourishes ninety-two of all sorts of those exclusive companies [guilds], whose numerous members can be seen adorning the Lord Mayor's Show every year with immoderate pomp." . . .

Type C: subjugated towns, of early modern times. Everywhere in Europe, as soon as the state was firmly established it disciplined the towns with instinctive relentlessness, whether or not it used violence. The Habsburgs did so just as much as the Popes, the German princes as much as the Medicis or the kings of France. Except in the Netherlands and England, obedience was imposed.

Take Florence as an example: The Medicis had slowly subjugated it, almost elegantly in Lorenzo's time. But after 1532 and the return of the Medicis to power the process accelerated. Florence in the seventeenth century was no more than the Grand Duke's court. He had seized every-thing—money, the right to govern, and to distribute honours. From the Pitti Palace, on the left bank of the Arno, a gallery—a secret passage in fact—allowed the prince to cross the river and reach the Uffizi. This ele-gant gallery, still in existence today on the Ponte Vecchio, was the thread from which the spider at the extremity of his web supervised the imprisoned town. . . .

Different Types of Development

But we know, of course, that urban development does not happen of its own accord: It is not an endogenous phenomenon produced under a bell-jar. It is always the expression of a society which controls it from within, but also from without, and in this respect, our classification is, I repeat, too simple. That said, how does it work when applied outside the narrow confines of Western Europe?

1. *Towns in colonial America.* We should say "in Latin America," be-cause the English towns remained a separate case. They had to live by their own resources and emerge from their wilderness to find a place in the vast world; the real parallel for them is the medieval city. The towns in Iberian America had a much simpler and more limited career. Built like Roman camps inside four earth walls, they were garrisons lost in the midst of vast hostile expanses, linked together by communica-tions which were slow because they stretched across enormous empty spaces. Curiously, at a period when the privileged medieval town had spread over practically the whole of Europe, the ancient rule prevailed in all Hispano-Portuguese America, apart from the large towns of the viceroys: Mexico City, Lima, Santiago de Chile, San Salvador (Bahia)—that is to say the official, already parasitical organisms.

There were scarcely any purely commercial towns in this part of America, or if there were they were of minor importance. For example, Recife—the merchants' town—stood next to aristocratic Olinda, town of great plantation owners, *senhores de engenhos*,[1] and slave owners. It was rather like Piraeus or Phalera in relation to Pericles' Athens. Buenos Aires after its second foundation (the successful one in 1580) was still a small market village—like Megara or Aegina. It had the mis-fortune to have nothing but Indian *bravos* round about, and its inhabi-tants complained of being forced to earn "their bread by the sweat of their brow" in this America where the whites were *rentiers*.[2] But cara-vans of mules or large wooden carts arrived there from the Andes, from

[1] Men of talent. [Ed.]
[2] Property owners. [Ed.]

Lima, which was a way of acquiring Potosi silver. Sugar, and soon gold, came by sailing ship from Brazil. And contact with Portugal and Africa was maintained through the smuggling carried on by sailing ships bringing black slaves. But Buenos Aires remained an exception amidst the "barbarism" of nascent Argentina.

The American town was generally tiny, without these gifts from abroad. It governed itself. No one was really concerned with its fate. Its masters were the landowners who had their houses in the town, with rings for tethering their horses fixed on the front walls overlooking the street. These were the "men of property," *os homes bons* of the municipalities of Brazil, or the *hacendados* of the Spanish *cabildos*.[3] These towns were so many miniature versions of Sparta or of Thebes in the time of Epaminondas. It could safely be said that the history of the Western towns in America began again from zero. Naturally there was no separation between the towns and the hinterland and there was no industry to be shared out. Wherever industry appeared—in Mexico city, for example—it was carried on by slaves or semi-slaves. The medieval European town would not have been conceivable if its artisans had been serfs.

2. *How should Russian towns be classified?* One can tell at a glance that the towns that survived or grew up again in Muscovy after the terrible catastrophes of the Mongol invasion no longer lived according to the Western pattern. Although there were great cities among them, like Moscow or Novgorod, they were kept in hand sometimes brutally. In the sixteenth century a proverb still asked: "Who can set his face against God and the mighty Novgorod?" But the proverb was wrong. The town was harshly brought to heel in 1427 and again in 1477 (it had to deliver 300 cartloads of gold). Executions, deportations, confiscations followed in quick succession. Above all, these towns were caught up in the slow circulation of traffic over an immense, already Asiatic, still wild expanse. In 1650, as in the past, transport on the rivers or overland by sledge or by convoys of carts moved with an enormous loss of time. It was often dangerous even to go near villages, and a halt had to be called every evening in open country—as on the Balkan roads—deploying the carriages in a circle, with everyone on the alert to defend himself.

For all these reasons the Muscovy towns did not impose themselves on the vast surrounding countryside; quite the reverse. They were unable to dictate their wishes to a peasant world which was biologically extraordinarily strong, although poverty-stricken, restless, and perpetually on the move. The important fact was that "harvests per hectare in

---

[3]Town councils. [Ed.]

the European countries of the East remained constant on average, from the sixteenth to the nineteenth century"—at a low level. There was no healthy rural surplus and therefore no really prosperous town. Nor did the Russian towns have serving them those secondary towns that were a characteristic of the West and its lively trade.

Consequently, there were innumerable peasant serfs practically without land, insolvent in the eyes of their lords and even the state. It was of no importance whether they went to towns or to work in the houses of rich peasants. In the town they became beggars, porters, craftsmen, poor tradesmen, or very rarely merchants who got rich quickly. They might also stay put and become craftsmen in their own villages, or seek the necessary supplement to their earnings by becoming carriers or travelling pedlars. This irresistible tide of mendicancy could not be stemmed, and indeed it often served the interests of the landlord who gave it his blessing: All such artisans and traders remained his serfs whatever they did and however great their social success; they still owed him their dues.

These examples and others indicate a fate resembling what may after all have happened at the beginning of Western urbanization. Though a clearer case, it is comparable to the caesura[4] between the eleventh and thirteenth centuries, that interlude when almost everything was born of the villages and peasant vitality. We might call it an intermediate position between A and C, without the B type (the independent city) ever having arisen. The prince appeared too quickly, like the ogre in a fairy tale.

3. *Imperial towns in the East and Far East.* The same problems and ambiguities—only deeper—arise when we leave Europe and move east.

Towns similar to those in medieval Europe—masters of their fate for a brief moment—only arose in Islam when the empires collapsed. They marked some outstanding moments in Islamic civilization. But they only lasted for a time and the main beneficiaries were certain marginal towns like Cordoba, or the cities which were urban republics by the fifteenth century, like Ceuta before the Portuguese occupation in 1415, or Oran before the Spanish occupation in 1509. The usual pattern was the huge city under the rule of a prince or a Caliph: a Baghdad or a Cairo.

Towns in distant Asia were of the same type: imperial or royal cities, enormous, parasitical, soft, and luxurious—Delhi and Vijnayanagar, Peking and to some extent Nanking, though this was rather different. The great prestige enjoyed by the prince comes as no surprise to us.

[4]Pause. [Ed.]

And if one ruler was swallowed up by the city or more likely by his palace, another immediately took his place and the subjection continued. Neither will it surprise us to learn that these towns were incapable of taking over the artisanal trades from the countryside: They were both open towns and subject towns simultaneously. Besides, in India as in China, social structures already existing hampered the free movement of the towns. If the town did not win its independence, it was not only because of the bastinadoes[5] ordered by the mandarins or the cruelty of the prince to merchants and ordinary citizens. It was because society was prematurely fixed, crystallized in a certain mould.

In India, the caste system automatically divided and broke up every urban community. In China, the cult of the *gentes*[6] on the one hand was confronted on the other by a mixture comparable to that which created the Western town: Like the latter it acted as a melting-pot, breaking old bonds and placing individuals on the same level. The arrival of immigrants created an "American" environment, where those already settled set the tone and the way of life. In addition, there was no independent authority representing the Chinese town as a unit, in its dealings with the State or with the very powerful countryside. The rural areas were the real heart of living, active, and thinking China.

The town, residence of officials and nobles, was not the property of either guilds or merchants. There was no gradual "rise of the bourgeoisie" here. No sooner did a bourgeoisie appear than it was tempted by class betrayal, fascinated by the luxurious life of the mandarins. The towns might have lived their own lives, filled in the contours of their own destiny, if individual initiative and capitalism had had a clear field. But the tutelary State hardly lent itself to this. It did occasionally nod, intentionally or not: At the end of the sixteenth century a bourgeoisie seems to have emerged with a taste for business enterprise, and we can guess what part it played in the large iron-works near Peking, in the private porcelain workshops that developed in King-te-chen, and even more in the rise of the silk trade in Su-Chu, the capital of Kiang-tsu. But this was no more than a flash in the pan. With the Manchu conquest, the Chinese crisis was resolved in the seventeenth century in a direction completely opposed to urban freedoms.

Only the West swung completely over in favour of its towns. The towns caused the West to advance. It was, let us repeat, an enormous event, but the deep-seated reasons behind it are still inadequately explained. What would the Chinese towns have become if the junks had discovered the Cape of Good Hope at the beginning of the fifteenth century, and had made full use of such a chance of world conquest?

---

[5] Beatings (often on soles of the feet). [Ed.]
[6] People. [Ed.]

82

Charter of Henry I
for London, 1130–1133

In the last century types of cities have been distinguished by historians and sociologists who have recognized that European cities in the late Middle Ages were relatively independent of rulers and other cities due to charters of freedom. Town and city charters were frequently drawn up between European lords, princes, and kings, on the one hand, and the inhabitants, owners, or burghers, on the other. These charters, which were granted to the town for a fee, brought needed income to the lord or ruler while ensuring the ruler access to an active class of artisans, merchants, specialists, and luxury providers.

In this charter, for London, England, what does the king give to the townspeople? What powers does the king retain? What seems to have been the main concerns of the townspeople and king that are settled here?

Thinking Historically

Does this charter reflect King Henry's strength or his weakness? Would this sort of arrangement be more likely to develop in a feudal society like Europe than it would in a Mongol or Chinese empire? Why or why not? Does the charter support Braudel's comparative thesis?

Henry, by the grace of God, king of the English, to the archbishop of Canterbury, and to the bishops and abbots, and earls and barons and justices and sheriffs, and to all his liegemen, both French and English, of the whole of England, greeting. Know that I have granted to my citizens of London that they shall hold middlesex at "farm" for three hundred pounds "by tale" for themselves and their heirs from me and my heirs, so that the citizens shall appoint as sheriff from themselves whomsoever they may choose, and shall appoint from among themselves as justice whomsoever they choose to look after the pleas of my crown and the pleadings which arise in connexion with them. No other shall be justice over the same men of London. And the citizens shall not plead outside the walls of the city in respect of any plea; and they shall

Charter of Henry I for London (1130–1133), from *English Historical Documents*, vol. II, ed. David C. Douglas and George W. Greenaway (London: Eyre and Spottiswoode, Ltd., 1955), 945–46.

be quit of scot and of Danegeld[1] and the murder-fine. Nor shall any of them be compelled to offer trial by battle. And if any one of the citizens shall be impleaded in respect of the pleas of the crown, let him prove himself to be a man of London by an oath which shall be judged in the city. Let no one be billeted within the walls of the city, either of my household, or by the force of anyone else. And let all the men of London and their property be quit and free from toll and passage and lestage[2] and from all other customs throughout all England and at the seaports. And let the churches and barons and citizens hold and have well and in peace their sokes,[3] with all their customs, so that those who dwell in these sokes shall pay no customs except to him who possesses the soke, or to the steward whom he has placed there. And a man of London shall not be fined at mercy except according to his "were," that is to say, up to one hundred shillings: This applies to an offence which can be punished by a fine. And there shall no longer be "miskenning"[4] in the hustings court,[5] nor in the folk-moot,[6] nor in other pleas within the city. And the hustings court shall sit once a week, to wit, on Monday. I will cause my citizens to have their lands and pledges and debts within the city and outside it. And in respect of the lands about which they make claim to me, I will do them right according to the law of the city. And if anyone has taken toll or custom from the citizens of London, then the citizens of London may take from the borough or village where toll or custom has been levied as much as the man of London gave for toll, and more also may be taken for a penalty. And let all debtors to the citizens of London discharge their debts, or prove in London that they do not owe them; and if they refuse either to pay, or to come and make such proof, then the citizens to whom the debts are due may take pledges within the city either from the borough or from the village or from the county in which the debtor lives. And the citizens shall have their hunting chases, as well and fully as had their predecessors, to wit, in Chiltern and Middlesex and Surrey.

---

[1]A medieval land tax, originally levied to buy off raiding Danes (literally, "Dane's money"). First levied in England in 868, but generally discontinued in the twelfth century. [Ed.]

[2]Sometimes "lastage": a toll payable by traders attending fairs and markets. [Ed.]

[3]A right of local jurisdiction. [Ed.]

[4]A verbal error in making a formal oath. [Ed.]

[5]King's court or court of king's representatives. [Ed.]

[6]A general assembly of the people. [Ed.]

83

GREGORIO DATI

Corporations and Community in Florence

This is an account of the Italian city of Florence and its inhabitants from 1380 to 1405. While family identity was primary, residents of Florence were also members of many corporate organizations that served to channel their loyalty to the larger urban community. Among these were guilds and parish churches, as well as political, welfare, and religious organizations. On public holidays like the feast day of St. John the Baptist, the patron saint of Florence, these various groups would come together in a display of communal solidarity that was often more fraternal than the deliberations in the political arena. What seems to motivate people to participate in public acts and parades in Florence?

Thinking Historically

Would a chartered city be more or less likely than a city run by a king to hold these sorts of festivities? In what ways would you expect the politics of Florence to be similar to and different from those of London? What aspects of this account support Braudel's thesis?

When springtime comes and the whole world rejoices, every Florentine begins to think about organizing a magnificent celebration on the feast day of St. John the Baptist [June 24]. . . . For two months in advance, everyone is planning marriage feasts or other celebrations in honor of the day. There are preparations for the horse races, the costumes of the retinues, the flags, and the trumpets; there are the pennants and the wax candles and other things which the subject territories offer to the Commune. Messengers are sent to obtain provisions for the banquets, and horses come from everywhere to run in the races. The whole city is engaged in preparing for the feast, and the spirits of the young people and the women [are animated] by these preparations. . . . Everyone is filled with gaiety; there are dances and concerts and songfests and tournaments and other joyous activities. Up to the eve of the holiday, no one thinks about anything else.

Gregorio Dati, "*Istoria di Firenze dall'anno MCCCLXXX all'anno MCCCCV*" (History of Florence from 1380 to 1405) (Florence, 1735), in *The Society of Renaissance Florence*, ed. and trans. Gene Brucker (New York: Harper & Row, 1971), 75–78.

Early on the morning of the day before the holiday, each guild has a display outside of its shops of its fine wares, its ornaments, and jewels. There are cloths of gold and silk sufficient to adorn ten kingdoms. . . . Then at the third hour, there is a solemn procession of clerics, priests, monks, and friars, and there are so many [religious] orders, and so many relics of saints, that the procession seems endless. [It is a manifestation] of great devotion, on account of the marvelous richness of the adornments . . . and clothing of gold and silk with embroidered figures. There are many confraternities of men who assemble at the place where their meetings are held, dressed as angels, and with musical instruments of every kind and marvelous singing. They stage the most beautiful representations of the saints, and of those relics in whose honor they perform. They leave from S. Maria del Fiore [the cathedral] and march through the city and then return.

Then, after midday, when the heat has abated before sunset, all of the citizens assemble under [the banner of] their district, of which there are sixteen. Each goes in the procession in turn, the first, then the second, and so on with one district following the other, and in each group the citizens march two by two, with the oldest and most distinguished at the head, and proceeding down to the young men in rich garments. They march to the church of St. John [the Baptistery] to offer, one by one, a wax candle weighing one pound. . . . The walls along the streets through which they pass are all decorated, and there are . . . benches on which are seated young ladies and girls dressed in silk and adorned with jewels, pearls, and precious stones. This procession continues until sunset, and after each citizen has made his offering, he returns home with his wife to prepare for the next morning.

Whoever goes to the Piazza della Signoria on the morning of St. John's Day witnesses a magnificent, marvelous, and triumphant sight, which the mind can scarcely grasp. Around the great piazza are a hundred towers which appear to be made of gold. Some were brought on carts and others by porters. . . . [These towers] are made of wood, paper, and wax [and decorated] with gold, colored paints, and with figures. . . . Next to the rostrum of the palace [of the Signoria] are standards . . . which belong to the most important towns which are subject to the Commune: Pisa, Arezzo, Pistoia, Volterra, Cortona, Lucignano. . . .

First to present their offering, in the morning, are the captains of the Parte Guelfa, together with all of the knights, lords, ambassadors, and foreign knights. They are accompanied by a large number of the most honorable citizens, and before them, riding on a charger covered with a cloth . . . is one of their pages carrying a banner with the insignia of the Parte Guelfa. Then there follow the above-mentioned standards, each one carried by men on horseback . . . and they all go to make their offerings at the Baptistery. And these standards are given a tribute by the districts which have been acquired by the Commune of Florence. . . . The wax candles, which have the appearance of golden towers, are the tribute of the regions which in most ancient times were subject to the Florentines. In order of dignity, they are brought, one by one, to be offered to St. John, and on the following day, they are hung inside the church and there they remain for the entire year until the next feast day. . . . Then come . . . an infinite number of large wax candles, some weighing one hundred pounds and others fifty, some more and some less . . . carried by the residents of the villages [in the *contado*[1]] which offer them. . . .

Then the lord priors and their colleges come to make their offerings, accompanied by their rectors, that is, the podestà, the captain [of the *popolo*[2]], and the executor. . . . And after the lord [priors] come those who are participating in the horse race, and they are followed by the Flemings and the residents of Brabant who are weavers of woolen cloth in Florence. Then there are offerings by twelve prisoners who, as an act of mercy, have been released from prison . . . in honor of St. John, and these are poor people. . . . After all of these offerings have been made, men and women return home to dine. . . .

[1]Countryside. [Ed.]
[2]People. [Ed.]

84

MARCO POLO

From The Travels of Marco Polo

In *The Travels of Marco Polo,* the Venetian merchant recounted his travels across the Silk Road to Mongolia and China. According to his account he stayed in China from 1275 to 1292 before returning to Venice. In 1275, the Chinese Southern Song capital of Hangchou had just been conquered by Kubilai Khan, the grandson of Ghengis Khan. The Mongols were able to conquer China, but they could not radically change it. The structure and organization of towns and cities remained very much the way it had been under the Song. In addition to Hangchou, which Marco Polo calls Kinsay, he had been to the Mon-

Marco Polo, *The Travels of Marco Polo,* the Complete Yule-Currier ed., vol. 2 (New York: Dover, 1993), 185–206.

gol capital at Karakorum and to the Chinese cities of Peking and Changan. Why does he consider the city of Hangchou "the finest and the noblest in the world"? How does his description support that characterization? What do you see in this account of Hangchou that supports or challenges Braudel's comparison and thesis?

Thinking Historically

In what ways does the Hangchou that emerges from this document resemble London or Florence? In what ways was Hangchou significantly different? Does Marco Polo's description show signs that Chinese cities were autonomous or that they were not?

When you have left the city of Changan and have travelled for three days through a splendid country, passing a number of towns and villages, you arrive at the most noble city of Kinsay,[1] a name which is as much as to say in our tongue "The City of Heaven," as I told you before.

And since we have got thither I will enter into particulars about its magnificence; and these are well worth the telling, for the city is beyond dispute the finest and the noblest in the world. In this we shall speak according to the written statement which the Queen of this Realm sent to Bayan the conqueror of the country for transmission to the Great Kaan, in order that he might be aware of the surpassing grandeur of the city and might be moved to save it from destruction or injury. I will tell you all the truth as it was set down in that document. For truth it was, as the said Messer Marco Polo at a later date was able to witness with his own eyes. And now we shall rehearse those particulars.

First and foremost, then, the document stated the city of Kinsay to be so great that it hath an hundred miles of compass. And there are in it twelve thousand bridges of stone,[2] for the most part so lofty that a great fleet could pass beneath them. And let no man marvel that there are so many bridges, for you see the whole city stands as it were in the water and surrounded by water, so that a great many bridges are required to give free passage about it. [And though the bridges be so high, the approaches are so well contrived that carts and horses do cross them.]

The document aforesaid also went on to state that there were in this city twelve guilds of the different crafts, and that each guild had twelve thousand houses in the occupation of its workmen. Each of these houses contains at least twelve men, whilst some contain twenty and some forty,—not that these are all masters, but inclusive of the

[1]Kinsay simply means "capital." The current name is Hangchou. [Ed.]
[2]Generally assumed to be an exaggeration; one thousand would have been a lot. [Ed.]

journeymen who work under the masters. And yet all these craftsmen had full occupation, for many other cities of the kingdom are supplied from this city with what they require.

The document aforesaid also stated that the number and wealth of the merchants, and the amount of goods that passed through their hands, was so enormous that no man could form a just estimate thereof. And I should have told you with regard to those masters of the different crafts who are at the head of such houses as I have mentioned, that neither they nor their wives ever touch a piece of work with their own hands, but live as nicely and delicately as if they were kings and queens. The wives indeed are most dainty and angelical creatures! Moreover it was an ordinance laid down by the King that every man should follow his father's business and no other, no matter if he possessed 100,000 bezants.[3]

Inside the city there is a Lake which has a compass of some thirty miles:[4] and all round it are erected beautiful palaces and mansions, of the richest and most exquisite structure that you can imagine, belonging to the nobles of the city. There are also on its shores many abbeys and churches of the Idolaters. In the middle of the Lake are two Islands, on each of which stands a rich, beautiful, and spacious edifice, furnished in such style as to seem fit for the palace of an Emperor. And when any one of the citizens desired to hold a marriage feast, or to give any other entertainment, it used to be done at one of these palaces. And everything would be found there ready to order, such as silver plate, trenchers, and dishes [napkins and tablecloths], and whatever else was needful. The King made this provision for the gratification of his people, and the place was open to every one who desired to give an entertainment. . . .

The people are Idolaters; and since they were conquered by the Great Kaan they use paper money. [Both men and women are fair and comely, and for the most part clothe themselves in silk, so vast is the supply of that material, both from the whole district of Kinsay, and from the imports by traders from other provinces.] And you must know they eat every kind of flesh, even that of dogs and other unclean beasts, which nothing would induce a Christian to eat.

Since the Great Kaan occupied the city he has ordained that each of the twelve thousand bridges should be provided with a guard of ten men, in case of any disturbance, or of any being so rash as to plot treason or insurrection against him. [Each guard is provided with a hollow

---

[3]A gold coin struck at Byzantium (or Constantinople) and used throughout Europe from the ninth century. [Ed.]

[4]The circumference of the lake was more probably 30 li. A li was about a third of a mile, but it was sometimes used to mean a hundredth of a day's march. The entire circumference of the city could not have been more than 100 li. [Ed.]

instrument of wood and with a metal basin, and with a timekeeper to enable them to know the hour of the day or night. . . .

Part of the watch patrols the quarter, to see if any light or fire is burning after the lawful hours; if they find any they mark the door, and in the morning the owner is summoned before the magistrates, and unless he can plead a good excuse he is punished. Also if they find any one going about the streets at unlawful hours they arrest him, and in the morning they bring him before the magistrates. Likewise if in the daytime they find any poor cripple unable to work for his livelihood, they take him to one of the hospitals, of which there are many, founded by the ancient kings, and endowed with great revenues. Or if he be capable of work they oblige him to take up some trade. . . .

The Kaan watches this city with especial diligence because it forms the head of all Manzi;[5] and because he has an immense revenue from the duties levied on the transactions of trade therein, the amount of which is such that no one would credit it on mere hearsay.

All the streets of the city are paved with stone or brick, as indeed are all the highways throughout Manzi, so that you ride and travel in every direction without inconvenience. . . .

You must know also that the city of Kinsay has some three thousand baths, the water of which is supplied by springs. They are hot baths, and the people take great delight in them, frequenting them several times a month, for they are very cleanly in their persons. They are the finest and largest baths in the world; large enough for one hundred persons to bathe together.

And the Ocean Sea comes within twenty-five miles of the city at a place called Ganfu, where there is a town and an excellent haven, with a vast amount of shipping which is engaged in the traffic to and from India and other foreign parts, exporting and importing many kinds of wares, by which the city benefits. And a great river flows from the city of Kinsay to that sea-haven, by which vessels can come up to the city itself. This river extends also to other places further inland.

Know also that the Great Kaan hath distributed the territory of Manzi into nine parts, which he hath constituted into nine kingdoms. To each of these kingdoms a king is appointed who is subordinate to the Great Kaan, and every year renders the accounts of his kingdom to the fiscal office at the capital. This city of Kinsay is the seat of one of these kings, who rules over one hundred forty great and wealthy cities. For in the whole of this vast country of Manzi there are more than twelve hundred great and wealthy cities, without counting the towns and villages, which are in great numbers. And you may receive it for certain that in each of those twelve hundred cities the Great Kaan has a

[5]China. [Ed.]

garrison, and that the smallest of such garrisons musters one thousand men; whilst there are some of ten thousand, twenty thousand, and thirty thousand; so that the total number of troops is something scarcely calculable. . . . And all of them belong to the army of the Great Kaan.

I repeat that everything appertaining to this city is on so vast a scale, and the Great Kaan's yearly revenues therefrom are so immense, that it is not easy even to put it in writing, and it seems past belief to one who merely hears it told. But I *will* write it down for you. . . .

I must tell you that in this city there are 160 *tomans*[6] of fires, or in other words 160 *tomans* of houses. Now I should tell you that the *toman* is 10,000, so that you can reckon the total as altogether 1,600,000 houses, among which are a great number of rich palaces. There is one church only, belonging to the Nestorian Christians.

There is another thing I must tell you. It is the custom for every burgess of this city, and in fact for every description of person in it, to write over his door his own name, the name of his wife, and those of his children, his slaves, and all the inmates of his house, and also the number of animals that he keeps. And if any one dies in the house then the name of that person is erased, and if any child is born its name is added. So in this way the sovereign is able to know exactly the population of the city. And this is the practice also throughout all Manzi and Cathay.

And I must tell you that every hosteler who keeps an hostel for travellers is bound to register their names and surnames, as well as the day and month of their arrival and departure. And thus the sovereign hath the means of knowing, whenever it pleases him, who come and go throughout his dominions. And certes this is a wise order and a provident [one].

The position of the city is such that it has on one side a lake of fresh and exquisitely clear water (already spoken of), and on the other a very large river. The waters of the latter fill a number of canals of all sizes which run through the different quarters of the city, carry away all impurities, and then enter the Lake; whence they issue again and flow to the Ocean, thus producing a most excellent atmosphere. By means of these channels, as well as by the streets, you can go all about the city. Both streets and canals are so wide and spacious that carts on the one and boats on the other can readily pass to and fro, conveying necessary supplies to the inhabitants.

At the opposite side the city is shut in by a channel, perhaps forty miles in length, very wide, and full of water derived from the river aforesaid, which was made by the ancient kings of the country in order to relieve the river when flooding its banks. This serves also as a de-

---

[6]A *toman* is a Mongol measurement of ten thousand. [Ed.]

fence to the city, and the earth dug from it has been thrown inward, forming a kind of mound enclosing the city.

In this part are the ten principal markets, though besides these there are a vast number of others in the different parts of the town. The former are all squares of half a mile to the side, and along their front passes the main street, which is forty paces in width, and runs straight from end to end of the city, crossing many bridges of easy and commodious approach. At every four miles of its length comes one of those great squares of two miles (as we have mentioned) in compass. So also parallel to this great street, but at the back of the marketplaces, there runs a very large canal, on the bank of which toward the squares are built great houses of stone, in which the merchants from India and other foreign parts store their wares, to be handy for the markets. In each of the squares is held a market three days in the week, frequented by forty thousand or fifty thousand persons, who bring thither for sale every possible necessary of life, so that there is always an ample supply of every kind of meat and game, as of roebuck, red-deer, fallow-deer, hares, rabbits, partridges, pheasants, francolins, quails, fowls, capons, and of ducks and geese an infinite quantity; for so many are bred on the Lake that for a Venice groat of silver you can have a couple of geese and two couple of ducks. Then there are the shambles where the larger animals are slaughtered, such as calves, beeves, kids, and lambs, the flesh of which is eaten by the rich and the great dignitaries.

Those markets make a daily display of every kind of vegetables and fruits; and among the latter there are in particular certain pears of enormous size, weighing as much as ten pounds apiece, and the pulp of which is white and fragrant like a confection; besides peaches in their season both yellow and white, of every delicate flavour. . . .

All the ten marketplaces are encompassed by lofty houses, and below these are shops where all sorts of crafts are carried on, and all sorts of wares are on sale, including spices and jewels and pearls. Some of these shops are entirely devoted to the sale of wine made from rice and spices, which is constantly made fresh, and is sold very cheap.

Certain of the streets are occupied by the women of the town, who are in such a number that I dare not say what it is. They are found not only in the vicinity of the marketplaces, where usually a quarter is assigned to them, but all over the city. They exhibit themselves splendidly attired and abundantly perfumed, in finely garnished houses, with trains of waiting-women. These women are extremely accomplished in all the arts of allurement, and readily adapt their conversation to all sorts of persons, insomuch that strangers who have once tasted their attractions seem to get bewitched, and are so taken with their blandishments and their fascinating ways that they never can get these out of their heads. Hence it comes to pass that when they return home they say they have been to Kinsay or the City of Heaven, and their only desire is to get back thither as soon as possible.

Other streets are occupied by the Physicians, and by the Astrologers, who are also teachers of reading and writing; and an infinity of other professions have their places round about those squares. In each of the squares there are two great palaces facing one another, in which are established the officers appointed by the King to decide differences arising between merchants, or other inhabitants of the quarter. It is the daily duty of these officers to see that the guards are at their posts on the neighbouring bridges, and to punish them at their discretion if they are absent. . . .

The natives of the city are men of peaceful character, both from education and from the example of their kings, whose disposition was the same. They know nothing of handling arms, and keep none in their houses. You hear of no feuds or noisy quarrels or dissensions of any kind among them. Both in their commercial dealings and in their manufactures they are thoroughly honest and truthful, and there is such a degree of good will and neighbourly attachment among both men and women that you would take the people who live in the same street to be all one family.

And this familiar intimacy is free from all jealousy or suspicion of the conduct of their women. These they treat with the greatest respect, and a man who should presume to make loose proposals to a married woman would be regarded as an infamous rascal. They also treat the foreigners who visit them for the sake of trade with great cordiality, and entertain them in the most winning manner, affording them every help and advice on their business. But on the other hand they hate to see soldiers, and not least those of the Great Kaan's garrisons, regarding them as the cause of their having lost their native kings and lords.

85

S. D. GOITEIN

Cairo: An Islamic City
in Light of the Geniza

The author of this selection provides an especially detailed picture of medieval Cairo due to an unusual discovery of documents. "The Geniza" refers to a treasure trove of documents maintained by a Jewish synagogue in Cairo from the tenth to thirteenth centuries. It contains correspondence, legal documents, receipts, inventories, prescriptions, and notes—written in Hebrew characters in the Arabic language—and offers a rare opportunity to review virtually everything a community wrote over a long period of time. It is an extremely valuable resource that can answer most questions about medieval society in Cairo.

In this selection, S. D. Goitein studies the documents for the insight they provide into city life in Cairo. What do the Geniza documents tell us about city life in Cairo? What would it have been like to live in medieval Cairo?

Thinking Historically

In what ways would life in medieval Cairo have been similar to or different from life in a city of medieval Europe or medieval China? What is the significance of the lack of public buildings and guilds in Cairo? In what ways was the Muslim identity larger or more cosmopolitan than European urban identities? How does this support or challenge Braudel's thesis?

. . . It is astounding how rarely government buildings are mentioned in the Geniza documents. There were the local police stations and prisons, as well as the offices where one received the licenses occasionally needed, but even these are seldom referred to. The Mint and the Exchange are frequently referred to, but at least the latter was only semi-public in character, since the persons working there were not on the government payroll. Taxes were normally collected by tax farmers. Thus there was little direct contact between the government and the

S. D. Goitein, "Cairo: An Islamic City in Light of the Geniza," in *Middle Eastern Cities*, ed. Ira M. Lapidus (Berkeley and Los Angeles: University of California Press, 1969), 90–95.

populace and consequently not much need for public buildings. The imperial palace and its barracks formed a city by itself, occasionally mentioned in Ayyūbid times, but almost never in the Fāṭimid period.

Government, although not conspicuous by many public buildings, was present in the city in many other ways. A city was governed by a military commander called *amīr*, who was assisted by the *wālī* or superintendent of the police. Smaller towns had only a *wālī* and no *amīr*. Very powerful, sometimes more powerful than the *amīr*, was the *qāḍī*, or judge, who had administrative duties in addition to his substantial judicial functions. The chief *qāḍī* often held other functions such as the control of the taxes or of a port, as we read with regard to Alexandria or Tyre. The city was divided into small administrative units called *rabʿ* (which is not the classical *rub*, meaning quarter, but instead designates an area, or rather a compound). Each *rabʿ* had a superintendent called *ṣāḥib rabʿ* (pronounced rub), very often referred to in the Geniza papers. In addition to regular and mounted police there were plain clothesmen, or secret service men, called *aṣḥāb al-khabar*, "informants" who formed a government agency independent even of the *qāḍī*, a state of affairs for which there seem to exist parallels in more modern times.

An ancient source tells us that the vizier[1] al-Ma'mūn, mentioned above, instructed the two superintendents of the police of Fusṭāṭ[2] and Cairo, respectively, to draw up exact lists of the inhabitants showing their occupations and other circumstances and to permit no one to move from one house to another without notification of the police. This is described as an extraordinary measure aimed at locating any would-be assassins who might have been sent to the Egyptian capital by the Bāṭiniyya, an Ismāʿīlī group using murder as a political weapon. Such lists, probably with fewer details, no doubt were in regular use for the needs of taxation. In a letter from Sicily, either from its capital Palermo or from Mazara on its southwestern tip, the writer, an immigrant from Tunisia around 1063, informs his business friend in Egypt that he is going to buy a house and that he has already registered for the purpose in the *qānūn* (Greek *canon*) which must have designated an official list of inhabitants. With regard to non-Muslims, a differentiation was made between permanent residents and newcomers. Whether the same practice existed with respect to Muslims is not evident from the Geniza papers.

What were the dues that a town dweller had to pay to the government in his capacity as the inhabitant of a city, and what were the benefits that he derived from such payments? By right of conquest, the

---

[1]Prime minister. [Ed.]
[2]Old Cairo. [Ed.]

ground on which Fusṭāṭ stood belonged to the Muslims, that is, to the government (the same was the case in many other Islamic cities), and a ground rent, called *ḥikr*, had to be paid for each building. A great many deeds of sale, gift, and rent refer to this imposition. . . .

Besides the ground rent, every month a *ḥarāsa*, or "due for protection," had to be paid to the government. The protection was partly in the hands of a police force, partly in those of the superintendents of the compounds, and partly was entrusted to nightwatchmen, usually referred to as *ṭawwāfūn*, literally, "those that make the round," but known also by other designations. As we learn expressly from a Geniza source, the nightwatchmen, like the regular police, were appointed by the government (and not by a municipality or local body which did not exist). The amounts of the *ḥarāsa* in the communal accounts cannot be related to the value of the properties for which they were paid, but it is evident that they were moderate.

In a responsum[3] written around 1165, Rabbi Maimon, the father of Moses Maimonides,[4] states that the markets of Fusṭāṭ used to remain open during the nights, in contrast of course to what the writer was accustomed from having lived in other Islamic cities. In Fusṭāṭ, too, this had not been always the case. In a description of the festival of Epiphany from the year 941 in which all parts of the population took part, it is mentioned as exceptional that the streets were not closed during that particular night.

Sanitation must have been another great concern of the government, for the items "removal of rubbish" (called "throwing out of dust") and "cleaning of pipes" appear with great regularity in the monthly accounts preserved in the Geniza. One gets the impression that these hygienic measures were not left to the discretion of each individual proprietor of a house. The clay tubes bringing water (for washing purposes) to a house and those connecting it with a cesspool constantly needed clearing, and there are also many references to their construction. The amounts paid for both operations were considerable. The Geniza has preserved an autograph note by Maimonides permitting a beadle[5] to spend a certain sum on "throwing out of dust" (presumably from a synagogue). This may serve as an illustration for the fact that landlords may have found the payment of these dues not always easy.

In this context we may also draw attention to the new insights gained through the study of the documents from the Geniza about the

---

[3] A legal document. [Ed.]
[4] (1135–1204), a Jewish rabbi, physician, and philosopher in Spain and Egypt. [Ed.]
[5] A minor official. [Ed.]

social life of Cairo. Massignon[6] had asserted, and he was followed by many, that the life-unit in the Islamic city was the professional corporation, the guilds of the merchants, artisans, and scholars which had professional, as well as social and religious functions. No one would deny that this was true to a large extent for the sixteenth through the nineteenth centuries. However, there is not a shred of evidence that this was true for the ninth through the thirteenth centuries. . . .

The term "guild" designates a medieval union of craftsmen or traders which supervised the work of its members in order to uphold standards, and made arrangements for the education of apprentices and their initiation into the union. The guild protected its members against competition, and in Christian countries was closely connected with religion.

Scrutinizing the records of the Cairo Geniza or the Muslim handbooks of market supervision contemporary with them, one looks in vain for an Arabic equivalent of the term "guild." There was no such word because there was no such institution. The supervision of the quality of the artisans' work was in the hands of the state police, which availed itself of the services of trustworthy and expert assistants.

Regarding apprenticeship and admission to a profession, no formalities and no rigid rules are to be discovered in our sources. Parents were expected to have their sons learn a craft and to pay for their instruction, and the Geniza has preserved several contracts to this effect.

The protection of the local industries from the competition of newcomers and outsiders is richly documented by the Geniza records, but nowhere do we hear about a professional corporation fulfilling this task. It was the Jewish local community, the central Jewish authorities, the state police, or influential notables, Muslim and Jewish, who were active in these matters.

As to the religious aspect of professional corporation, the associations of artisans and traders in imperial Rome, or at least a part of them, bore a religious character and were often connected with the local cult of the town from which the founders of an association had originated. Similarly, the Christian guilds of the late Middle Ages had their patron saints and special rites. The fourteenth century was the heyday of Muslim corporations, especially in Anatolia (the present day Turkey), which adopted the doctrines and ceremonies of Muslim mystic brotherhoods. One looks in vain for similar combinations of artisanship and religious cult in the period and the countries under discussion. On the other hand, we find partnerships of Muslims and Jews both in workshops and in mercantile undertakings, for free partnerships were the normal form of industrial cooperation, and were common as well in commercial ventures. The classical Islamic city was a

---

[6]Louis Massignon (1883–1962), a French scholar of Islam. [Ed.]

free enterprise society, the very opposite of a community organized in rigid guilds and tight professional corporations.

Further, we have stated before that no formal citizenship existed. The question is, however, how far did people feel a personal attachment to their native towns. "Homesickness," says Professor Gibb in his translation of the famous traveler Ibn Baṭṭūṭa, "was hardly to be expected in a society so cosmopolitan as that of medieval Islam." Indeed the extent of travel and migration reflected in the Geniza is astounding. No less remarkable, however, is the frequency of expressions of longing for one's native city and the wish to return to it, as well as the fervor with which compatriots stuck together when they were abroad. On the other hand, I cannot find much of neighborhood factionalism or professional *esprit de corps*, both of which were so prominent in the later Middle Ages. Under an ever more oppressive military feudalism and government-regimented economy, life became miserable and insecure, and people looked for protection and assistance in their immediate neighborhood. In an earlier period, in a free-enterprise, competitive society, there was no place for such factionalism. A man felt himself to be the son of a city which provided him with the security, the economic possibilities, and the spiritual amenities which he needed.

86

BERNAL DÍAZ
Cities of Mexico

Bernal Díaz (1492–1580) accompanied Hernando Cortés* and the band of Spanish conquistadors who were the first Europeans to see the cities of the central Mexican plateau, dominated by the Aztec capital of Tenochtitlan,† or Mexico, in 1519. Later in life, he recalled what he saw in this account of *The Conquest of New Spain*. What impressed Díaz about the cities of Mexico? How, according to Díaz, were they different from the cities of Europe?

*kohr TEHZ
†teh NOHCH teet LAHN

Bernal Díaz, *The Conquest of New Spain*, trans. J. M. Cohen (London: Penguin Books, 1963), 214–20, 230–35.

Thinking Historically

The cities of Mexico provide the best example of how much cities could differ. Unlike the cities of Eurasia, or even Islamic Africa, the development of Mexican cities was entirely separate from and uninfluenced by the other cultures we have studied. Therefore, this description of Mexico, and the other cities of the Mexican plateau, like Iztapalapa and Coyoacan, is enormously useful to us.

In what respects were these cities different from others you have read about? What other cities do they most resemble? How does this selection support or challenge Braudel's comparison and thesis?

Next morning, we came to a broad causeway[1] and continued our march towards Iztapalapa. And when we saw all those cities and villages built in the water, and other great towns on dry land, and that straight and level causeway leading to Mexico, we were astounded. These great towns and *cues*[2] and buildings rising from the water, all made of stone, seemed like an enchanted vision from the tale of Amadis. Indeed, some of our soldiers asked whether it was not all a dream. It is not surprising therefore that I should write in this vein. It was all so wonderful that I do not know how to describe this first glimpse of things never heard of, seen, or dreamed of before.

When we arrived near Iztapalapa we beheld the splendour of the other *Caciques*[3] who came out to meet us, the lord of that city whose name was Cuitlahuac, and the lord of Culuacan, both of them close relations of Montezuma. And when we entered the city of Iztapalapa, the sight of the palaces in which they lodged us! They were very spacious and well built, of magnificent stone, cedar wood, and the wood of other sweet-smelling trees, with great rooms and courts, which were a wonderful sight, and all covered with awnings of woven cotton.

When we had taken a good look at all this, we went to the orchard and garden, which was a marvellous place both to see and walk in. I was never tired of noticing the diversity of trees and the various scents given off by each, and the paths choked with roses and other flowers, and the many local fruit-trees and rose-bushes, and the pond of fresh water. Another remarkable thing was that large canoes could come into the garden from the lake, through a channel they had cut, and their crews did not have to disembark. Everything was shining with lime and decorated with different kinds of stonework and paintings which were a marvel to gaze

[1] The causeway of Cuitlahuac, which separated the lakes of Chalco and Xochimilco.
[2] Spanish for temple; probably refers to pyramids. [Ed.]
[3] Taino for rulers. [Ed.]

on. Then there were birds of many breeds and varieties which came to
the pond. I say again that I stood looking at it, and thought that no land
like it would ever be discovered in the whole world, because at that time
Peru was neither known nor thought of. But today all that I then saw is
overthrown and destroyed; nothing is left standing.

The Entrance into Mexico

Early next day we left Iztapalapa with a large escort of these great
Caciques, and followed the causeway, which is eight yards wide and
goes so straight to the city of Mexico that I do not think it curves at all.
Wide though it was, it was so crowded with people that there was
hardly room for them all. Some were going to Mexico and others coming away, besides those who had come out to see us, and we could
hardly get through the crowds that were there. For the towers and the
cues were full, and they came in canoes from all parts of the lake. No
wonder, since they had never seen horses or men like us before!

With such wonderful sights to gaze on we did not know what to
say, or if this was real that we saw before our eyes. On the land side
there were great cities, and on the lake many more. The lake was
crowded with canoes. At intervals along the causeway there were many
bridges, and before us was the great city of Mexico [Tenochtitlan]. As
for us, we were scarcely four hundred strong, and we well remembered
the words and warnings of the people of Huexotzinco and Tlascala and
Tlamanalco, and the many other warnings we had received to beware
of entering the city of Mexico, since they would kill us as soon as they
had us inside. Let the interested reader consider whether there is not
much to ponder in this narrative of mine. What men in all the world
have shown such daring? But let us go on.

We marched along our causeway to a point where another small
causeway branches off to another city called Coyoacan, and there, beside some towerlike buildings, which were their shrines, we were met
by many more *Caciques* and dignitaries in very rich cloaks. The different chieftains wore different brilliant liveries, and the causeways were
full of them. Montezuma had sent these great *Caciques* in advance to
receive us, and as soon as they came before Cortes they told him in
their language that we were welcome, and as a sign of peace they
touched the ground with their hands and kissed it. . . .

Who could now count the multitude of men, women, and boys in
the streets, on the roof-tops and in canoes on the waterways, who had
come out to see us? It was a wonderful sight and, as I write, it all comes
before my eyes as if it had happened only yesterday.

They led us to our quarters, which were in some large houses capable of accommodating us all and had formerly belonged to the great

Montezuma's father, who was called Axayacatl. Here Montezuma now kept the great shrines of his gods, and a secret chamber containing gold bars and jewels. This was the treasure he had inherited from his father, which he never touched. Perhaps their reason for lodging us here was that, since they called us *Teules*[4] and considered us as such, they wished to have us near their idols. In any case they took us to this place, where there were many great halls, and a dais hung with the cloth of their country for our Captain, and matting beds with canopies over them for each of us.

On our arrival we entered the large court, where the great Montezuma was awaiting our Captain. Taking him by the hand, the prince led him to his apartment in the hall where he was to lodge, which was very richly furnished in their manner. Montezuma had ready for him a very rich necklace, made of golden crabs, a marvellous piece of work, which he hung round Cortes' neck. His captains were greatly astonished at this sign of honour.

After this ceremony, for which Cortes thanked him through our interpreters, Montezuma said: "Malinche,[5] you and your brothers are in your own house. Rest awhile." He then returned to his palace, which was not far off.

We divided our lodgings by companies, and placed our artillery in a convenient spot. Then the order we were to keep was clearly explained to us, and we were warned to be very much on the alert, both the horsemen and the rest of us soldiers. We then ate a sumptuous dinner which they had prepared for us in their native style.

So, with luck on our side, we boldly entered the city of Tenochtitlan or Mexico on 8 November in the year of our Lord 1519. . . .

I must now speak of the skilled workmen whom Montezuma employed in all the crafts they practised, beginning with the jewellers and workers in silver and gold and various kinds of hollowed objects, which excited the admiration of our great silversmiths at home. Many of the best of them lived in a town called Atzcapotzalco, three miles from Mexico. There were other skilled craftsmen who worked with precious stones and *chalchihuites*, and specialists in feather-work, and very fine painters and carvers. We can form some judgement of what they did then from what we can see of their work today. There are three Indians now living in the city of Mexico, named Marcos de

---

[4]Gods. [Ed.]

[5]mah LEEN cheh   Also known as Malintzin and Doña Marina. According to Díaz, she was a daughter of a cacique who was given away as a slave after her mother remarried. She had learned Nahuatl as a youth and Yucatec Mayan as a slave. Thus, with the help of a Spanish sailor who had learned Mayan, Cortés could initially translate between Nahuatl and Spanish. Malinche also learned Spanish and became Cortés's translator and mistress, eventually giving birth to Cortés's son, Martin. [Ed.]

Aquino, Juan de la Cruz, and El Crespillo, who are such magnificent painters and carvers that, had they lived in the age of the Apelles of old,[6] or of Michael Angelo,[7] or Berruguete[8] in our own day, they would be counted in the same rank.

Let us go on to the women, the weavers and sempstresses, who made such a huge quantity of fine robes with very elaborate feather designs. These things were generally brought from some towns in the province of Cotaxtla, which is on the north coast, quite near San Juan de Ulua. In Montezuma's own palaces very fine cloths were woven by those chieftains' daughters whom he kept as mistresses; and the daughters of other dignitaries, who lived in a kind of retirement like nuns in some houses close to the great *cue* of Huichilobos,[9] wore robes entirely of featherwork. Out of devotion for that god and a female deity who was said to preside over marriage, their fathers would place them in religious retirement until they found husbands. They would then take them out to be married.

Now to speak of the great number of performers whom Montezuma kept to entertain him. There were dancers and stilt-walkers, and some who seemed to fly as they leapt through the air, and men rather like clowns to make him laugh. There was a whole quarter full of these people who had no other occupation. He had as many workmen as he needed, too, stonecutters, masons, and carpenters, to keep his houses in repair. . . .

When we had already been in Mexico for four days, . . . Cortés said it would be a good thing to visit the large square of Tlatelolco and see the great *cue* of Huichilobos. So he sent Aguilar, Doña Marina,[10] and his own young page Orteguilla, who by now knew something of the language, to ask for Montezuma's approval of this plan. On receiving his request, the prince replied that we were welcome to go, but for fear that we might offer some offence to his idols he would himself accompany us with many of his chieftains. Leaving the palace in his fine litter, when he had gone about half way, he dismounted beside some shrines, since he considered it an insult to his gods to visit their dwelling in a litter. Some of the great chieftains then supported him by the arms, and his principal vassals walked before him, carrying two staves, like sceptres raised on high as a sign that the great Montezuma was approaching. When riding in his litter he had carried a rod, partly of gold and partly of wood, held up like a wand of justice. The prince now climbed

---

[6]Famous Ancient Greek painter. [Ed.]

[7]Michelangelo (1476–1564), Renaissance master painter and sculptor. [Ed.]

[8]Berruguete is either Pedro (1450–1504) or his son, Alonso (1488–1561), both famous Spanish painters. [Ed.]

[9]Huitzilopochtli. Aztec god of sun and war; required human sacrifice. [Ed.]

[10]Same as Malinche (footnote 5). [Ed.]

the steps of the great *cue*, escorted by many *papas*,[11] and began to burn incense and perform other ceremonies for Huichilobos. . . .

On reaching the market-place, escorted by the many *Caciques* whom Montezuma had assigned to us, we were astounded at the great number of people and the quantities of merchandise, and at the orderliness and good arrangements that prevailed, for we had never seen such a thing before. The chieftains who accompanied us pointed everything out. Every kind of merchandise was kept separate and had its fixed place marked for it.

Let us begin with the dealers in gold, silver, and precious stones, feathers, cloaks, and embroidered goods, and male and female slaves who are also sold there. They bring as many slaves to be sold in that market as the Portuguese bring Negroes from Guinea. Some are brought there attached to long poles by means of collars round their necks to prevent them from escaping, but others are left loose. Next there were those who sold coarser cloth, and cotton goods and fabrics made of twisted thread, and there were chocolate merchants with their chocolate. In this way you could see every kind of merchandise to be found anywhere in New Spain, laid out in the same way as goods are laid out in my own district of Medina del Campo, a centre for fairs, where each line of stalls has its own particular sort. So it was in this great market. There were those who sold sisal cloth and ropes and the sandals they wear on their feet, which are made from the same plant. All these were kept in one part of the market, in the place assigned to them, and in another part were skins of tigers and lions, otters, jackals, and deer, badgers, mountain cats, and other wild animals, some tanned and some untanned, and other classes of merchandise.

There were sellers of kidney-beans and sage and other vegetables and herbs in another place, and in yet another they were selling fowls, and birds with great dewlaps,[12] also rabbits, hares, deer, young ducks, little dogs, and other such creatures. Then there were the fruiterers; and the women who sold cooked food, flour and honey cake, and tripe, had their part of the market. Then came pottery of all kinds, from big water-jars to little jugs, displayed in its own place, also honey, honey-paste, and other sweets like nougat. Elsewhere they sold timber too, boards, cradles, beams, blocks, and benches, all in a quarter of their own.

Then there were the sellers of pitch-pine for torches, and other things of that kind, and I must also mention, with all apologies, that they sold many canoe-loads of human excrement, which they kept in the creeks near the market. This was for the manufacture of salt and

[11]Aztec priests. [Ed.]
[12]Turkeys.

the curing of skins, which they say cannot be done without it. I know that many gentlemen will laugh at this, but I assure them it is true. I may add that on all the roads they have shelters made of reeds or straw or grass so that they can retire when they wish to do so, and purge their bowels unseen by passers-by, and also in order that their excrement shall not be lost. . . .

We went on to the great *cue*, and as we approached its wide courts, before leaving the market-place itself, we saw many more merchants who, so I was told, brought gold to sell in grains, just as they extract it from the mines. This gold is placed in the thin quills of the large geese of that country, which are so white as to be transparent. They used to reckon their accounts with one another by the length and thickness of these little quills, how much so many cloaks or so many gourds of chocolate or so many slaves were worth, or anything else they were bartering.

Now let us leave the market, having given it a final glance, and come to the courts and enclosures in which their great *cue* stood. Before reaching it you passed through a series of large courts, bigger I think than the Plaza at Salamanca. These courts were surrounded by a double masonry wall and paved, like the whole place, with very large smooth white flagstones. Where these stones were absent everything was whitened and polished, indeed the whole place was so clean that there was not a straw or a grain of dust to be found there.

When we arrived near the great temple and before we had climbed a single step, the great Montezuma sent six *papas* and two chieftains down from the top, where he was making his sacrifices, to escort our Captain; and as he climbed the steps, of which there were one hundred and fourteen, they tried to take him by the arms to help him up in the same way as they helped Montezuma, thinking he might be tired, but he would not let them near him.

The top of the *cue* formed an open square on which stood something like a platform, and it was here that the great stones stood on which they placed the poor Indians for sacrifice. Here also was a massive image like a dragon, and other hideous figures, and a great deal of blood that had been spilled that day. Emerging in the company of two *papas* from the shrine which houses his accursed images, Montezuma made a deep bow to us all and said: "My lord Malinche, you must be tired after climbing this great *cue* of ours." And Cortes replied that none of us was ever exhausted by anything. Then Montezuma took him by the hand, and told him to look at his great city and all the other cities standing in the water, and the many others on the land round the lake; and he said that if Cortes had not had a good view of the great market-place he could see it better from where he now was. So we stood there looking, because that huge accursed *cue* stood so high that it dominated everything. We saw the three causeways that led into

Mexico: the causeway of Iztapalapa by which we had entered four days before. . . . We saw the fresh water which came from Chapultepec to supply the city, and the bridges that were constructed at intervals on the causeways so that the water could flow in and out from one part of the lake to another. We saw a great number of canoes, some coming with provisions and others returning with cargo and merchandise; and we saw too that one could not pass from one house to another of that great city and the other cities that were built on the water except over wooden drawbridges or by canoe. We saw *cues* and shrines in these cities that looked like gleaming white towers and castles: a marvellous sight. All the houses had flat roofs, and on the causeways were other small towers and shrines built like fortresses.

Having examined and considered all that we had seen, we turned back to the great market and the swarm of people buying and selling. The mere murmur of their voices talking was loud enough to be heard more than three miles away. Some of our soldiers who had been in many parts of the world, in Constantinople, in Rome, and all over Italy, said that they had never seen a market so well laid out, so large, so orderly, and so full of people.

REFLECTIONS

Our selections certainly offer support for Braudel's thesis on the European city. London was hardly unique among European cities. The chartering of cities as independent corporations with their own laws, courts, and independent citizenry was a phenomenon repeated throughout Europe, especially in the West and the Mediterranean from the eleventh to the fifteenth century. The Florentine festival demonstrates how citizens came together in so many groups to celebrate their collective identity as citizens. Europe was a world without emperors, in which kings and lords were forced to bargain freedoms for favors.

Marco Polo unwittingly points to the power of the emperor, Song or Mongol, in imperial China. The capital city especially is designed and maintained according to his specifications. City life may be vibrant. There may even be enormous markets and wealthy merchants, but it is the emperor's city, not the merchants'. Rich merchants might train their sons to govern, but only as officials of the emperor.

Neither Chinese nor Muslim urban dwellers find their primary identities as citizens or even as residents of a particular city. They may be Cairenes, but they are Muslims first. Muslims had no need for self-governing cities when they could travel and work anywhere in the vast world of Islam.

Braudel struggled with American cities. North American towns, he thought, were re-creations of European towns. In Latin America, he classified Mexico City as similar to the imperial capitals of other parts of the world. Like Hangchou, Mexico City could be astonishingly rich, but it was not an autonomous entity under Aztecs or Spaniards. The readings were selected not to stack the deck, but to show what Braudel meant. Consequently, some qualifications of Braudel's thesis might be in order.

First, we should not assume that autonomous or communal cities were limited to Europe. Rather, they were a product of a feudal, or politically weak and decentralized, society, where urban populations could bargain for special privileges. We could find similar examples of urban autonomy among, for example, Japanese port cities during the Japanese feudal era of the fourteenth to sixteenth centuries. One of these, Sakai, was called the Venice of Japan. Not until after 1600 and the re-centralization of Japan under the Tokugawa administration were these independent cities brought to heel. In many ways, Tokugawa developments paralleled those of Europe, where centralized states also subordinated the independence of commercial cities after 1700.

Second, the absence of a movement for urban autonomy in Islamic and Chinese cities—important as it was in the time and places discussed in this chapter—was not universal. Chinese cities before the Mongol Yüan dynasty, especially in the earlier Sung dynasty, had developed an extremely prosperous commercial class. And while it is true that they did not gain (or seek) urban independence, they were content to exercise sufficient influence on the local representatives of the emperor. No appointed official could think lightly of ignoring the advice of Chinese merchants, the uniquely Chinese class of civil-service exam graduates, and the many Chinese guilds (one of the more important forces for self-government in Europe).

Third, while medieval Muslim cities encouraged little urban autonomy or identity, a prosperous class of merchants—always at the core of Islam—were nourished by more enlightened sultans and emirs. The Turkish historian Halil Inalcik writes that it was "the deliberate policy" of the Ottoman government, as it founded its successive capitals at Bursa in 1326, Edirne in 1402, and Istanbul in 1453, to create commercial and industrial centers, and that it consequently used every means—from tax exemptions to force—to attract and settle merchants and artisans in the new capitals. With the same end in view, Mehmed II encouraged the Jews of Europe to migrate to his new capital at Istanbul as they were being expelled from Spain and Portugal.

Braudel's thesis emphasizes the differences among cities, but as he well knew, one could emphasize the similarities as well. All cities distinguished themselves from the countryside which they controlled and exploited. All cities built and concentrated the wealth, achievements, and opportunities of the culture within their walls. All cities were greater engines of change than were villages, farm, and pasture. And some have argued that all cities promote patriarchy and class stratification.

Today about half the world's people live in cities. In 1800 only 3 percent of the world's population lived in cities. It is expected that by 2030, 60 percent of the world's population will be urban. Does that mean the lives of so many people will change in a similar way? Does it mean increasing patriarchy? Increasing exploitation of the countryside? Increasing inequality? Do significant choices need to be made about the types of cities we inhabit? Can we find ways to make our cities of the future our own?

14

Ecology, Technology, and Science

Europe, Asia, Oceania, and Africa, 500–1550 C.E.

HISTORICAL CONTEXT

Everyone knows that the world has changed drastically since the Middle Ages. And most people would agree that the most important and far-reaching changes have occurred in the fields of ecology, technology, and science. Global population has grown tenfold. The world has become a single ecological unit where microbes, migrants, and money travel everywhere at jet speed. In most parts of the world, average life expectancy has doubled; cities have mushroomed, supplanting farm and pasture. Machines have replaced the labor of humans and animals. Powers that were only imagined in the Middle Ages — elixirs to cure disease, energy to harness rivers, machines that could fly — are now commonplace. Other aspects of life — among them religion, political behavior, music, and art — have also evolved, but even these were affected significantly by advances in modern science and technology.

Have the changes been for good or ill? The signs of environmental stress are visible everywhere. The hole in the earth's protective ozone layer over Antarctica continues to expand. The North Pole floats in the summer. Ten-thousand-year-old glaciers are disappearing. The oceans are rising two to four inches every ten years. Our atmosphere contains more carbon gasses than it has for at least 650,000 years. The stored energy of millions of years burns to service the richest members of a couple of generations. Ancient aquifers are drained to water the lawns of desert cities.

Precisely what change or changes occurred? When did the cycle of change begin and what caused it? We will examine these questions here. You will read three substantial answers. Lynn White Jr. defines the transformation to modernity in largely technological and ecological terms, but emphasizes the role of cultural causes. Lynda Shaffer discusses technological and scientific changes as spreading through contact and trade. Jared Diamond writes of cultural failures to meet new natural and technological crises.

These explanations of long-term change differ most markedly in how they explain the roots of the transformation. White, a historian of medieval European technology, focuses on the role of medieval European religion: Christianity. Shaffer, a world historian, underscores the role of India and South Asia. Diamond, a professor of geography with numerous specializations in fields like physiology, evolutionary biology, and biogeography, finds a failure of will in many societies.

THINKING HISTORICALLY
Evaluating Grand Theories

Big questions deserve big answers — or at least grand theories. Here we consider three grand theories about the origins of our technological transformation and ecological difficulties, the links between environmental decline and the growth of technology and science, and the role of Western (European and American) economic growth in undermining the environment. Grand theories are especially speculative. They give us much to question and challenge. But their scope and freshness can often suggest new insights. Grand theories almost inevitably have elements that seem partly wrong and partly right. You will be encouraged to weigh some of the many elements in these theories. Then you can evaluate the theories, decide where you agree and disagree, and, perhaps, begin to develop your own grand theory as well.

87

LYNN WHITE JR.

The Historical Roots of
Our Ecological Crisis

This classic essay first appeared in the magazine *Science* in 1967 and has since been reprinted and commented on many times. What do you think of White's linkage of ecological crisis and Christianity? Which of White's arguments and evidence do you find most persuasive? Which do you find least convincing? Imagine a continuum that includes all of the world's people, from the most ecologically minded "tree-huggers" on the left to the most damaging polluters and destroyers of the environment on the right. Where on that continuum would you place the historical majority of Christians? Buddhists? Why?

Thinking Historically

A grand theory like this — that Christianity is responsible for our environmental problems — argues far more than can be proven in such a brief essay. White concentrates on making certain kinds of connections and marshaling certain kinds of evidence. In addition to weighing the arguments he makes, consider the gaps in his argument. What sorts of evidence would you seek to make White's theory more convincing?

A conversation with Aldous Huxley[1] not infrequently put one at the receiving end of an unforgettable monologue. About a year before his lamented death he was discoursing on a favorite topic: man's unnatural treatment of nature and its sad results. To illustrate his point he told how, during the previous summer, he had returned to a little valley in England where he had spent many happy months as a child. Once it had been composed of delightful grassy glades; now it was becoming overgrown with unsightly brush because the rabbits that formerly kept such growth under control had largely succumbed to a disease, myxomatosis, that was deliberately introduced by the local farmers to reduce

---

[1]Aldous Huxley (1894–1963), British author of novels, short stories, travel books, biography, and essays. Best known for *Brave New World* (1932). [Ed.]

Lynn White Jr., "The Historical Roots of Our Ecological Crisis," *Science* 155 (March 1967): 1203–7.

the rabbits' destruction of crops. Being something of a Philistine,[2] I could be silent no longer, even in the interests of great rhetoric. I interrupted to point out that the rabbit itself had been brought as a domestic animal to England in 1176, presumably to improve the protein diet of the peasantry.

All forms of life modify their contexts. The most spectacular and benign instance is doubtless the coral polyp. By serving its own ends, it has created a vast undersea world favorable to thousands of other kinds of animals and plants. Ever since man became a numerous species he has affected his environment notably. The hypothesis that his fire-drive[3] method of hunting created the world's great grasslands and helped to exterminate the monster mammals of the Pleistocene from much of the globe is plausible, if not proved. For six millennia at least, the banks of the lower Nile have been a human artifact rather than the swampy African jungle which nature, apart from man, would have made it. The Aswan Dam, flooding five thousand square miles, is only the latest stage in a long process. In many regions terracing or irrigation, overgrazing, and the cutting of forests by Romans to build ships to fight Carthaginians or by Crusaders to solve the logistics problems of their expeditions have profoundly changed some ecologies. Observation that the French landscape falls into two basic types, the open fields of the north and the *bocage*[4] of the south and west, inspired Marc Bloch to undertake his classic study of medieval agricultural methods. Quite unintentionally, changes in human ways often affect nonhuman nature. It has been noted, for example, that the advent of the automobile eliminated huge flocks of sparrows that once fed on the horse manure littering every street.

The history of ecologic change is still so rudimentary that we know little about what really happened, or what the results were. The extinction of the European aurochs[5] as late as 1627 would seem to have been a simple case of overenthusiastic hunting. On more intricate matters it often is impossible to find solid information. For a thousand years or more the Frisians and Hollanders have been pushing back the North Sea, and the process is culminating in our own time in the reclamation

[2]An anti-intellectual (though obviously White is not; he was only impatient with Huxley's pedantry). [Ed.]

[3]Paleolithic hunters used fires to drive animals to their deaths. [Ed.]

[4]Full of groves or woodlands. Marc Bloch reasoned that the open fields north of the Loire River in France must have been plowed by teams of oxen and heavy plows because of the hard soil. In the south farmers could use scratch plows on the softer soil and therefore did not clear large fields, preserving more woodlands. [Ed.]

[5]A now extinct European wild ox believed to be the ancestor of European domestic cattle. [Ed.]

of the Zuider Zee.[6] What, if any, species of animals, birds, fish, shore life, or plants have died out in the process? In their epic combat with Neptune have the Netherlanders overlooked ecological values in such a way that the quality of human life in the Netherlands has suffered? I cannot discover that the questions have ever been asked, much less answered.

People, then, have often been a dynamic element in their own environment, but in the present state of historical scholarship we usually do not know exactly when, where, or with what effects man-induced changes came. As we enter the last third of the twentieth century, however, concern for the problem of ecologic backlash is mounting feverishly. Natural science, conceived as the effort to understand the nature of things, had flourished in several eras and among several peoples. Similarly there had been an age-old accumulation of technological skills, sometimes growing rapidly, sometimes slowly. But it was not until about four generations ago that Western Europe and North America arranged a marriage between science and technology, a union of the theoretical and the empirical approaches to our natural environment. The emergence in widespread practice of the Baconian creed that scientific knowledge means technological power over nature can scarcely be dated before about 1850, save in the chemical industries, where it is anticipated in the eighteenth century. Its acceptance as a normal pattern of action may mark the greatest event in human history since the invention of agriculture, and perhaps in nonhuman terrestrial history as well.

Almost at once the new situation forced the crystallization of the novel concept of ecology; indeed, the word *ecology* first appeared in the English language in 1873. Today, less than a century later, the impact of our race upon the environment has so increased in force that it has changed in essence. When the first cannons were fired, in the early fourteenth century, they affected ecology by sending workers scrambling to the forests and mountains for more potash, sulfur, iron ore, and charcoal, with some resulting erosion and deforestation. Hydrogen bombs are of a different order: A war fought with them might alter the genetics of all life on this planet. By 1285 London had a smog problem arising from the burning of soft coal, but our present combustion of fossil fuels threatens to change the chemistry of the globe's atmosphere as a whole, with consequences which we are only beginning to guess. With the population explosion, the carcinoma of planless urbanism, the now geological deposits of sewage and garbage, surely no creature other than man has ever managed to foul its nest in such short order.

---

[6]Once a Dutch lake, it was joined to the North Sea by a flood in the thirteenth century but has since been reclaimed by the building of a dam. [Ed.]

There are many calls to action, but specific proposals, however worthy as individual items, seem too partial, palliative, negative: Ban the bomb, tear down the billboards, give the Hindus contraceptives and tell them to eat their sacred cows. The simplest solution to any suspect change is, of course, to stop it, or, better yet, to revert to a romanticized past: Make those ugly gasoline stations look like Anne Hathaway's cottage or (in the Far West) like ghost-town saloons. The "wilderness area" mentality invariably advocates deep-freezing an ecology, whether San Gimignano or the High Sierra, as it was before the first Kleenex was dropped. But neither atavism nor prettification will cope with the ecologic crisis of our time.

What shall we do? No one yet knows. Unless we think about fundamentals, our specific measures may produce new backlashes more serious than those they are designed to remedy.

As a beginning we should try to clarify our thinking by looking, in some historical depth, at the presuppositions that underlie modern technology and science. Science was traditionally aristocratic, speculative, intellectual in intent; technology was lower-class, empirical, action-oriented. The quite sudden fusion of these two, toward the middle of the nineteenth century, is surely related to the slightly prior and contemporary democratic revolutions which, by reducing social barriers, tended to assert a functional unity of brain and hand. Our ecologic crisis is the product of an emerging, entirely novel, democratic culture. The issue is whether a democratized world can survive its own implications. Presumably we cannot unless we rethink our axioms.

The Western Traditions of Technology and Science

One thing is so certain that it seems stupid to verbalize it: Both modern technology and modern science are distinctively *Occidental*. Our technology has absorbed elements from all over the world, notably from China; yet everywhere today, whether in Japan or in Nigeria, successful technology is Western. Our science is the heir to all the sciences of the past, especially perhaps to the work of the great Islamic scientists of the Middle Ages, who so often outdid the ancient Greeks in skill and perspicacity: al-Rāzī in medicine, for example; or ibn-al-Haytham in optics; or Omar Khayyám in mathematics. Indeed, not a few works of such geniuses seem to have vanished in the original Arabic and to survive only in medieval Latin translations that helped to lay the foundations for later Western developments. Today, around the globe, all significant science is Western in style and method, whatever the pigmentation or language of the scientists.

A second pair of facts is less well recognized because they result from quite recent historical scholarship. The leadership of the West, both in technology and in science, is far older than the so-called Scientific Revolution of the seventeenth century or the so-called Industrial Revolution of the eighteenth century. These terms are in fact outmoded and obscure the true nature of what they try to describe — significant stages in two long and separate developments. By A.D. 1000 at the latest — and perhaps, feebly, as much as two hundred years earlier — the West began to apply water power to industrial processes other than milling grain. This was followed in the late twelfth century by the harnessing of wind power. From simple beginnings, but with remarkable consistency of style, the West rapidly expanded its skills in the development of power machinery, labor-saving devices, and automation. Those who doubt should contemplate that most monumental achievement in the history of automation: the weight-driven mechanical clock, which appeared in two forms in the early fourteenth century. Not in craftsmanship but in basic technological capacity, the Latin West of the later Middle Ages far outstripped its elaborate, sophisticated, and esthetically magnificent sister cultures, Byzantium and Islam. In 1444 a great Greek ecclesiastic, Bessarion, who had gone to Italy, wrote a letter to a prince in Greece. He is amazed by the superiority of Western ships, arms, textiles, glass. But above all he is astonished by the spectacle of waterwheels sawing timbers and pumping the bellows of blast furnaces. Clearly, he had seen nothing of the sort in the Near East.

By the end of the fifteenth century the technological superiority of Europe was such that its small, mutually hostile nations could spill out over all the rest of the world, conquering, looting, and colonizing. The symbol of this technological superiority is the fact that Portugal, one of the weakest states of the Occident, was able to become, and to remain for a century, mistress of the East Indies. And we must remember that the technology of Vasco da Gama and Albuquerque was built by pure empiricism, drawing remarkably little support or inspiration from science.

In the present-day vernacular understanding, modern science is supposed to have begun in 1543, when both Copernicus and Vesalius published their great works. It is no derogation of their accomplishments, however, to point out that such structures as the *Fabrica*[7] and the *De revolutionibus*[8] do not appear overnight. The distinctive Western tradition of science, in fact, began in the late eleventh century with a massive movement of translation of Arabic and Greek scientific works into Latin. A

---

[7]*De Humani Corporis Fabrica* (1543), an illustrated work on human anatomy based on dissections, was produced by Andreas Vesalius (1514–1564), a Flemish anatomist, at the University of Padua in Italy. [Ed.]

[8]*De revolutionibus orbium coelestium* (1543; On the Revolutions of Heavenly Bodies) was published by Nicolas Copernicus (1473–1543); it showed the sun as the center of a system around which the Earth revolved. [Ed.]

few notable books — Theophrastus, for example — escaped the West's avid new appetite for science, but within less than two hundred years effectively the entire corpus of Greek and Muslim science was available in Latin, and was being eagerly read and criticized in the new European universities. Out of criticism arose new observation, speculation, and increasing distrust of ancient authorities. By the late thirteenth century Europe had seized global scientific leadership from the faltering hands of Islam. It would be as absurd to deny the profound originality of Newton, Galileo, or Copernicus as to deny that of the fourteenth-century scholastic scientists like Buridan or Oresme on whose work they built. Before the eleventh century, science scarcely existed in the Latin West, even in Roman times. From the eleventh century onward, the scientific sector of Occidental culture has increased in a steady crescendo.

Since both our technological and our scientific movements got their start, acquired their character, and achieved world dominance in the Middle Ages, it would seem that we cannot understand their nature or their present impact upon ecology without examining fundamental medieval assumptions and developments.

Medieval View of Man and Nature

Until recently, agriculture has been the chief occupation even in "advanced" societies; hence, any change in methods of tillage has much importance. Early plows, drawn by two oxen, did not normally turn the sod but merely scratched it. Thus, cross-plowing was needed and fields tended to be squarish. In the fairly light soils and semiarid climates of the Near East and Mediterranean, this worked well. But such a plow was inappropriate to the wet climate and often sticky soils of northern Europe. By the latter part of the seventh century after Christ, however, following obscure beginnings, certain northern peasants were using an entirely new kind of plow, equipped with a vertical knife to cut the line of the furrow, a horizontal share to slice under the sod, and a moldboard to turn it over. The friction of this plow with the soil was so great that it normally required not two but eight oxen. It attacked the land with such violence that cross-plowing was not needed, and fields tended to be shaped in long strips.

In the days of the scratch-plow, fields were distributed generally in units capable of supporting a single family. Subsistence farming was the presupposition. But no peasant owned eight oxen: to use the new and more efficient plow, peasants pooled their oxen to form large plowteams, originally receiving (it would appear) plowed strips in proportion to their contribution. Thus, distribution of land was based no longer on the needs of a family but, rather, on the capacity of a power machine to till the earth. Man's relation to the soil was profoundly changed. Formerly man had been part of nature; now he was the exploiter of nature. Nowhere else in the world did farmers develop any analogous agricultural implement. Is it coincidence that modern technology, with its ruthlessness toward nature, has so largely been produced by descendants of these peasants of northern Europe?

This same exploitive attitude appears slightly before A.D. 830 in Western illustrated calendars. In older calendars the months were shown as passive personifications. The new Frankish calendars, which set the style for the Middle Ages, are very different: They show men coercing the world around them — plowing, harvesting, chopping trees, butchering pigs. Man and nature are two things, and man is master.

These novelties seem to be in harmony with larger intellectual patterns. What people do about their ecology depends on what they think about themselves in relation to things around them. Human ecology is deeply conditioned by beliefs about our nature and destiny — that is, by religion. To Western eyes this is very evident in, say, India or Ceylon. It is equally true of ourselves and of our medieval ancestors.

The victory of Christianity over paganism was the greatest psychic revolution in the history of our culture. It has become fashionable today to say that, for better or worse, we live in "the post-Christian age." Certainly the forms of our thinking and language have largely ceased to be Christian, but to my eye the substance often remains amazingly akin to that of the past. Our daily habits of action, for example, are dominated by an implicit faith in perpetual progress which was unknown either to Greco-Roman antiquity or to the Orient. It is rooted in, and is indefensible apart from, Judeo-Christian teleology.[9] The fact that Communists share it merely helps to show what can be demonstrated on many other grounds: that Marxism, like Islam, is a Judeo-Christian heresy. We continue today to live, as we have lived for about seventeen hundred years, very largely in a context of Christian axioms.

What did Christianity tell people about their relations with the environment?

While many of the world's mythologies provide stories of creation, Greco-Roman mythology was singularly incoherent in this respect. Like Aristotle, the intellectuals of the ancient West denied that the visible world had had a beginning. Indeed, the idea of a beginning was impossible in the framework of their cyclical notion of time. In sharp contrast, Christianity inherited from Judaism not only a concept of time as nonrepetitive and linear but also a striking story of creation. By gradual stages a loving and all-powerful God had created light and darkness, the heavenly bodies, the earth and all its plants, animals, birds, and fishes. Finally, God had created Adam and, as an afterthought,

---

[9]The Biblical idea that God's purpose is revealed in his creation, that human history can be seen as the result of God's intentions. [Ed.]

Eve to keep man from being lonely. Man named all the animals, thus establishing his dominance over them. God planned all of this explicitly for man's benefit and rule: No item in the physical creation had any purpose save to serve man's purposes. And, although man's body is made of clay, he is not simply part of nature: He is made in God's image.

Especially in its Western form, Christianity is the most anthropocentric religion the world has seen. As early as the second century both Tertullian and Saint Irenaeus of Lyons were insisting that when God shaped Adam he was foreshadowing the image of the incarnate Christ, the Second Adam. Man shares, in great measure, God's transcendence of nature. Christianity, in absolute contrast to ancient paganism and Asia's religions (except, perhaps, Zoroastrianism), not only established a dualism of man and nature but also insisted that it is God's will that man exploit nature for his proper ends.

At the level of the common people this worked out in an interesting way. In Antiquity every tree, every spring, every stream, every hill had its own *genius loci*, its guardian spirit. These spirits were accessible to men, but were very unlike men; centaurs, fauns, and mermaids show their ambivalence. Before one cut a tree, mined a mountain, or dammed a brook, it was important to placate the spirit in charge of that particular situation, and to keep it placated. By destroying pagan animism, Christianity made it possible to exploit nature in a mood of indifference to the feelings of natural objects.

It is often said that for animism the Church substituted the cult of saints. True; but the cult of saints is functionally quite different from animism. The saint is not *in* natural objects; he may have special shrines, but his citizenship is in heaven. Moreover, a saint is entirely a man; he can be approached in human terms. In addition to saints, Christianity of course also had angels and demons inherited from Judaism and perhaps, at one remove, from Zoroastrianism. But these were all as mobile as the saints themselves. The spirits *in* natural objects, which formerly had protected nature from man, evaporated. Man's effective monopoly on spirit in this world was confirmed, and the old inhibitions to the exploitation of nature crumbled.

When one speaks in such sweeping terms, a note of caution is in order. Christianity is a complex faith, and its consequences differ in differing contexts. What I have said may well apply to the medieval West, where in fact technology made spectacular advances. But the Greek East, a highly civilized realm of equal Christian devotion, seems to have produced no marked technological innovation after the late seventh century, when Greek fire was invented. The key to the contrast may perhaps be found in a difference in the tonality of piety and thought which students of comparative theology find between the Greek and the Latin Churches. The Greeks believed that sin was intellectual blindness, and that salvation was found in illumination, orthodoxy — that is, clear thinking. The Latins, on the other hand, felt that sin was moral evil, and that salvation was to be found in right conduct. Eastern theology has been intellectualist. Western theology has been voluntarist. The Greek saint contemplates; the Western saint acts. The implications of Christianity for the conquest of nature would emerge more easily in the Western atmosphere.

The Christian dogma of creation, which is found in the first clause of all the Creeds, has another meaning for our comprehension of today's ecologic crisis. By revelation, God had given man the Bible, the Book of Scripture. But since God had made nature, nature also must reveal the divine mentality. The religious study of nature for the better understanding of God was known as natural theology. In the early Church, and always in the Greek East, nature was conceived primarily as a symbolic system through which God speaks to men: The ant is a sermon to sluggards; rising flames are the symbol of the soul's aspiration. This view of nature was essentially artistic rather than scientific. While Byzantium preserved and copied great numbers of ancient Greek scientific texts, science as we conceive it could scarcely flourish in such an ambience.

However, in the Latin West by the early thirteenth century natural theology was following a very different bent. It was ceasing to be the decoding of the physical symbols of God's communication with man and was becoming the effort to understand God's mind by discovering how his creation operates. The rainbow was no longer simply a symbol of hope first sent to Noah after the Deluge: Robert Grosseteste, Friar Roger Bacon, and Theodoric of Freiberg produced startlingly sophisticated work on the optics of the rainbow, but they did it as a venture in religious understanding. From the thirteenth century onward, up to and including Leibnitz and Newton, every major scientist, in effect, explained his motivations in religious terms. Indeed, if Galileo had not been so expert an amateur theologian he would have got into far less trouble: The professionals resented his intrusion. And Newton seems to have regarded himself more as a theologian than as a scientist. It was not until the late eighteenth century that the hypothesis of God became unnecessary to many scientists.

It is often hard for the historian to judge, when men explain why they are doing what they want to do, whether they are offering real reasons or merely culturally acceptable reasons. The consistency with which scientists during the long formative centuries of Western science said that the task and the reward of the scientist was "to think God's thoughts after him" leads one to believe that this was their real motivation. If so, then modern Western science was cast in a matrix of Christian theology. The dynamism of religious devotion, shaped by the Judeo-Christian dogma of creation, gave it impetus.

An Alternative Christian View

We would seem to be headed toward conclusions unpalatable to many Christians. Since both *science* and *technology* are blessed words in our contemporary vocabulary, some may be happy at the notions, first, that, viewed historically, modern science is an extrapolation of natural theology and, second, that modern technology is at least partly to be explained as an Occidental, voluntarist realization of the Christian dogma of man's transcendence of, and rightful mastery over, nature. But, as we now recognize, somewhat over a century ago science and technology — hitherto quite separate activities — joined to give mankind powers which, to judge by many of the ecologic effects, are out of control. If so, Christianity bears a huge burden of guilt.

I personally doubt that disastrous ecologic backlash can be avoided simply by applying to our problems more science and more technology. Our science and technology have grown out of Christian attitudes toward man's relation to nature which are almost universally held not only by Christians and neo-Christians but also by those who fondly regard themselves as post-Christians. Despite Copernicus, all the cosmos rotates around our little globe. Despite Darwin, we are *not*, in our hearts, part of the natural process. We are superior to nature, contemptuous of it, willing to use it for our slightest whim. The newly elected Governor of California,[10] like myself a churchman but less troubled than I, spoke for the Christian tradition when he said (as is alleged), "when you've seen one redwood tree, you've seen them all." To a Christian a tree can be no more than a physical fact. The whole concept of the sacred grove is alien to Christianity and to the ethos of the West. For nearly two millennia Christian missionaries have been chopping down sacred groves, which are idolatrous because they assume spirit in nature.

What we do about ecology depends on our ideas of the man-nature relationship. More science and more technology are not going to get us out of the present ecologic crisis until we find a new religion, or rethink our old one. The beatniks, who are the basic revolutionaries of our time, show a sound instinct in their affinity for Zen Buddhism, which conceives of the man-nature relationship as very nearly the mirror image of the Christian view. Zen, however, is as deeply conditioned by Asian history as Christianity is by the experience of the West, and I am dubious of its viability among us.

Possibly we should ponder the greatest radical in Christian history since Christ: Saint Francis of Assisi. The prime miracle of Saint Francis is the fact that he did not end at the stake, as many of his left-wing fol-

[10]Ronald Reagan, governor from 1967 to 1975.

lowers did. He was so clearly heretical that a General of the Franciscan Order, Saint Bonaventura, a great and perceptive Christian, tried to suppress the early accounts of Franciscanism. The key to an understanding of Francis is his belief in the virtue of humility — not merely for the individual but for man as a species. Francis tried to depose man from his monarchy over creation and set up a democracy of all God's creatures. With him the ant is no longer simply a homily for the lazy, flames a sign of the thrust of the soul toward union with God; now they are Brother Ant and Sister Fire, praising the Creator in their own ways as Brother Man does in his.

Later commentators have said that Francis preached to the birds as a rebuke to men who would not listen. The records do not read so: He urged the little birds to praise God, and in spiritual ecstasy they flapped their wings and chirped rejoicing. Legends of saints, especially the Irish saints, had long told of their dealings with animals but always, I believe, to show their human dominance over creatures. With Francis it is different. The land around Gubbio in the Apennines was being ravaged by a fierce wolf. Saint Francis, says the legend, talked to the wolf and persuaded him of the error of his ways. The wolf repented, died in the odor of sanctity, and was buried in consecrated ground.

What Sir Steven Ruciman calls "the Franciscan doctrine of the animal soul" was quickly stamped out. Quite possibly it was in part inspired, consciously or unconsciously, by the belief in reincarnation held by the Cathar heretics who at that time teemed in Italy and southern France, and who presumably had got it originally from India. It is significant that at just the same moment, about 1200, traces of metempsychosis are found also in Western Judaism, in the Provençal *Cabbala*. But Francis held neither to transmigration of souls nor to pantheism. His view of nature and of man rested on a unique sort of pan-psychism of all things animate and inanimate, designed for the glorification of their transcendent Creator, who, in the ultimate gesture of cosmic humility, assumed flesh, lay helpless in a manger, and hung dying on a scaffold.

I am not suggesting that many contemporary Americans who are concerned about our ecologic crisis will be either able or willing to counsel with wolves or exhort birds. However, the present increasing disruption of the global environment is the product of a dynamic technology and science which were originating in the Western medieval world against which Saint Francis was rebelling in so original a way. Their growth cannot be understood historically apart from distinctive attitudes toward nature which are deeply grounded in Christian dogma. The fact that most people do not think of these attitudes as Christian is irrelevant. No new set of basic values has been accepted in our society to displace those of Christianity. Hence we shall continue to have a worsening ecologic crisis until we reject the Christian axiom that nature has no reason for existence save to serve man.

The greatest spiritual revolutionary in Western history, Saint Francis, proposed what he thought was an alternative Christian view of nature and man's relation to it: He tried to substitute the idea of the equality of all creatures, including man, for the idea of man's limitless rule of creation. He failed. Both our present science and our present technology are so tinctured with orthodox Christian arrogance toward nature that no solution for our ecologic crisis can be expected from them alone. Since the roots of our trouble are so largely religious, the remedy must also be essentially religious, whether we call it that or not. We must rethink and refeel our nature and destiny. The profoundly religious, but heretical, sense of the primitive Franciscans for the spiritual autonomy of all parts of nature may point a direction. I propose Francis as a patron saint for ecologists.

88

Life of Boniface:
Converting the Hessians

This story about the Christian missionary Boniface was told in the *Life of Boniface*, written between 754 and 768, by Willibald, one of his students. The Hessians, previously converted to Christianity, had reverted to paganism, and Boniface traveled from England to Germany to reconvert them. Hessians were widely regarded by the early Christian missionaries to Germany as a difficult people to convert. Boniface's success became a guide for future missions. What does this account tell us about the nature of Hessian paganism? What does Boniface do to reconvert them to Christianity? What, if anything, does the story tell us about Christianity?

Thinking Historically

How does this primary source relate to Lynn White Jr.'s article? Does it support his argument? Can a single piece like this ever prove an argument like White's, or can it only illustrate it?

The Anglo-Saxon Missionaries in Germany, trans. C. H. Talbot (London: Sheed and Ward, 1954), 45–46.

Now many of the Hessians who at that time had acknowledged the Catholic faith were confirmed by the grace of the Holy Spirit and received the laying-on of hands. But others, not yet strong in the spirit, refused to accept the pure teachings of the Church in their entirety. Moreover, some continued secretly, others openly, to offer sacrifices to trees and springs, to inspect the entrails of victims; some practised divination, legerdemain,[1] and incantations; some turned their attention to auguries, auspices, and other sacrificial rites; whilst others, of a more reasonable character, forsook all the profane practices of heathenism and committed none of these crimes. With the counsel and advice of the latter persons, Boniface in their presence attempted to cut down, at a place called Gaesmere, . . . a certain oak of extraordinary size called by the pagans of olden times the Oak of Jupiter. Taking his courage in his hands (for a great crowd of pagans stood by watching and bitterly cursing in their hearts the enemy of the gods), he cut the first notch. But when he had made a superficial cut, suddenly the oak's vast bulk, shaken by a mighty blast of wind from above, crashed to the ground shivering its topmost branches into fragments in its fall. As if by the express will of God (for the brethren present had done nothing to cause it) the oak burst asunder into four parts, each part having a trunk of equal length. At the sight of this extraordinary spectacle the heathens who had been cursing ceased to revile and began, on the contrary, to believe and bless the Lord. Thereupon the holy bishop took counsel with the brethren, built an oratory from the timber of the oak and dedicated it to St. Peter the Apostle. He then set out on a journey to Thuringia, having accomplished by the help of God all the things we have already mentioned. Arrived there, he addressed the elders and the chiefs of the people, calling on them to put aside their blind ignorance and to return to the Christian religion which they had formerly embraced. . . .

---

[1]Sleight of hand.

Image from a Cistercian Manuscript,
Twelfth Century

This image of a monk chopping down a tree while his lay servant prunes the branches is from a manuscript of the Cistercian order of monks, from the twelfth century. The Cistercians, more than other orders, spoke out in favor of conserving forest resources, but they also celebrated manual labor. Does this image indicate that the monks were in favor of forest clearance?

Thinking Historically

Does this image lend support to White's argument? Why or why not? If there were many such images, would visual evidence like this convince you of White's argument? Would it be more convincing if almost all European images of trees showed someone chopping them down and virtually no Chinese tree images showed that? In other words, how much visual evidence would convince you of White's interpretation?

Image from a Cistercian manuscript, 12th c., monk chopping tree (Dijon, Bibliothèque municipale, MS 173), duplicated in *Cambridge Illustrated History of the Middle Ages*, Robert Fossier, ed. (Cambridge: Cambridge University Press, 1997), 72.

Figure 14.1 Twelfth-Century Manuscript.
Source: Courtesy of Tresorier Principal
Municipal, Dijon.

90

Image from a French Calendar, Fifteenth Century

This French calendar scene for March is from the early fifteenth century. What sorts of activities does it show? How does it relate specifically to White's argument about the changing images of European calendars? (See p. 501.) The top half of the calendar shows a zodiac. In what ways are these images of nature different from those in the bottom half?

Thinking Historically

What technologies are shown here? Were any of these technologies particularly recent or European? Does this image merely illustrate White's argument, or does it support it to some extent? What other visual evidence would you want to see in order to be persuaded by White's argument?

From *Les trés riches heures du duc de Berry*, Giraudon, Musée de Condé.

Figure 14.2 French Calendar Scene.

Source: Bridgeman-Giraudon/Art Resource, N.Y.

91

Image of a Chinese *Feng-Shui* Master

Although the Chinese celebrated the natural landscape in their paintings, they also created drawings that showcased their advanced technologies. The Chinese made and used the compass (as well as paper, printing, and gunpowder) long before Europeans. Instead of using it to subdue the natural world, however, they used it to find harmony with nature, specifically through the practice of *feng-shui*.* *Feng-shui,* which literally means wind over water, is the Chinese art of determining the best position and placement of structures such as houses within the natural environment. In the following image we see a type of compass used in the work of a Chinese *feng-shui* master. Before building, the *feng-shui* master would use instruments like this to ascertain the flow of energy (*chi*) on the site, resulting in new buildings that would be in harmony with, rather than obstruct, this flow. How might a compass detect energy? How was the Chinese use of a compass-like device different from the modern scientific use of the compass?

Thinking Historically

An image has many elements to read. What information is revealed about Chinese society in this image, in addition to the scientific devices? What significance do you attach to the artist's depiction of humans and the natural setting? In what ways does this image support Lynn White Jr.'s argument? In what ways does it challenge his interpretation? On balance, do you find it more supportive or critical of White's position?

*fung SHWEE

Joseph Needham, *Science and Civilization in China*, vol. 2 (Cambridge: Cambridge University Press, 1956), 362.

Figure 14.3 Chinese *Feng-Shui* Master.

92

LYNDA NORENE SHAFFER

Southernization

The author of this selection began her career as a historian of China, but she is currently a world historian, having published books on Native American, Southeast Asian, and Chinese history. Shaffer coins the term *Southernization* to suggest that *Westernization* was preceded by an earlier "southern" process of technological expansion that eventually made it possible. Which of her examples of Southernization do you find most important in changing the world? Which least significant? Did India and Indian Ocean societies of the early Middle Ages play a role like that of the West today?

Thinking Historically

Shaffer did not write this essay to criticize Lynn White Jr., nor does her essay address precisely the same issues. Our exercise here is not the relatively simple task of weighing two debaters on a single issue. Rather, Shaffer's essay challenges some of the assumptions and arguments made by White and many other historians when they discuss the history of technology. What are some of the assumptions and arguments of White that Shaffer challenges? How might you use Shaffer to challenge White's grand theory? Which essay provides a more satisfying explanation of the origins of modern science and technology?

The term *Southernization* is a new one. It is used here to refer to a multifaceted process that began in Southern Asia and spread from there to various other places around the globe. The process included so many interrelated strands of development that it is impossible to do more here than sketch out the general outlines of a few of them. Among the most important that will be omitted from this discussion are the metallurgical, the medical, and the literary. Those included are the development of mathematics; the production and marketing of subtropical or tropical spices; the pioneering of new trade routes; the cultivation, processing, and marketing of southern crops such as sugar and cotton; and the development of various related technologies.

The term *Southernization* is meant to be analogous to *Westernization*. Westernization refers to certain developments that first occurred in western Europe. Those developments changed Europe and eventually

Lynda Norene Shaffer, "Southernization," *Journal of World History* 5 (Spring 1994): 1–21.

spread to other places and changed them as well. In the same way, southernization changed Southern Asia and later spread to other areas, which then underwent a process of change.

Southernization was well under way in Southern Asia by the fifth century C.E., during the reign of India's Gupta kings (320–535 C.E.). It was by that time already spreading to China. In the eighth century various elements characteristic of Southernization began spreading through the lands of the Muslim caliphates. Both in China and in the lands of the caliphate, the process led to dramatic changes, and by the year 1200 it was beginning to have an impact on the Christian Mediterranean. One could argue that within the Northern Hemisphere, by this time the process of Southernization had created an Eastern Hemisphere characterized by a rich south and a north that was poor in comparison. And one might even go so far as to suggest that in Europe and its colonies, the process of Southernization laid the foundation for Westernization.

The Indian Beginning

Southernization was the result of developments that took place in many parts of southern Asia, both on the Indian subcontinent and in Southeast Asia. By the time of the Gupta kings, several of its constituent parts already had a long history in India. Perhaps the oldest strand in the process was the cultivation of cotton and the production of cotton textiles for export. Cotton was first domesticated in the Indus River valley some time between 2300 and 1760 B.C.E., and by the second millennium B.C.E., the Indians had begun to develop sophisticated dyeing techniques. During these early millennia Indus River valley merchants are known to have lived in Mesopotamia, where they sold cotton textiles.

In the first century C.E. Egypt became an important overseas market for Indian cottons. By the next century there was a strong demand for these textiles both in the Mediterranean and in East Africa, and by the fifth century they were being traded in Southeast Asia. The Indian textile trade continued to grow throughout the next millennium. Even after the arrival of European ships in Asian ports at the turn of the sixteenth century, it continued unscathed. According to one textile expert, "India virtually clothed the world" by the mid-eighteenth century. The subcontinent's position was not undermined until Britain's Industrial Revolution, when steam engines began to power the production of cotton textiles.

Another strand in the process of Southernization, the search for new sources of bullion, can be traced back in India to the end of the Mauryan Empire (321–185 B.C.E.). During Mauryan rule Siberia had been India's main source of gold, but nomadic disturbances in Central Asia disrupted the traffic between Siberia and India at about the time that the Mauryans fell. Indian sailors then began to travel to the Malay peninsula and the islands of Indonesia in search of an alternative source, which they most likely "discovered" with the help of local peoples who knew the sites. (This is generally the case with bullion discoveries, including those made by Arabs and Europeans.) What the Indians (and others later on) did do was introduce this gold to international trade routes.

The Indians' search for gold may also have led them to the shores of Africa. Although its interpretation is controversial, some archaeological evidence suggests the existence of Indian influence on parts of East Africa as early as 300 c.e. There is also one report that gold was being sought in East Africa by Ethiopian merchants, who were among India's most important trading partners.

The sixth-century Byzantine geographer Cosmas Indicopleustes described Ethiopian merchants who went to some location inland from the East African coast to obtain gold. "Every other year they would sail far to the south, then march inland, and in return for various made-up articles they would come back laden with ingots of gold." The fact that the expeditions left every other year suggests that it took two years to get to their destination and return. If so, their destination, even at this early date, may have been Zimbabwe. The wind patterns are such that sailors who ride the monsoon south as far as Kilwa can catch the return monsoon to the Red Sea area within the same year. But if they go beyond Kilwa to the Zambezi River, from which they might go inland to Zimbabwe, they cannot return until the following year.

Indian voyages on the Indian Ocean were part of a more general development, more or less contemporary with the Mauryan Empire, in which sailors of various nationalities began to knit together the shores of the "Southern Ocean," a Chinese term referring to all the waters from the South China Sea to the eastern coast of Africa. During this period there is no doubt that the most intrepid sailors were the Malays, peoples who lived in what is now Malaysia, Indonesia, the southeastern coast of Vietnam, and the Philippines.

Sometime before 300 B.C.E. Malay sailors began to ride the monsoons, the seasonal winds that blow off the continent of Asia in the colder months and onto its shores in the warmer months. Chinese records indicate that by the third century B.C.E. "Kunlun" sailors, the Chinese term for the Malay seamen, were sailing north to the southern coasts of China. They may also have been sailing west to India, through the straits now called Malacca and Sunda. If so they may have been the first to establish contact between India and Southeast Asia.

Malay sailors had reached the eastern coast of Africa at least by the first century B.C.E., if not earlier. Their presence in East African waters is testified to by the peoples of Madagascar, who still speak a Malayo-Polynesian language. Some evidence also suggests that Malay sailors had settled in the Red Sea area. Indeed, it appears that they were the first to develop a long-distance trade in a southern spice. In the last centuries B.C.E., if not earlier, Malay sailors were delivering cinnamon from South China Sea ports to East Africa and the Red Sea.

By about 400 C.E. Malay sailors could be found two-thirds of the way around the world, from Easter Island to East Africa. They rode the monsoons without a compass, out of sight of land, and often at latitudes below the equator where the northern pole star cannot be seen. They navigated by the wind and the stars, by cloud formations, the color of the water, and swell and wave patterns on the ocean's surface. They could discern the presence of an island some thirty miles from its shores by noting the behavior of birds, the animal and plant life in the water, and the swell and wave patterns. Given their manner of sailing, their most likely route to Africa and the Red Sea would have been by way of the island clusters, the Maldives, the Chagos, the Seychelles, and the Comoros.

Malay ships used balance lug sails, which were square in shape and mounted so that they could pivot. This made it possible for sailors to tack against the wind, that is, to sail into the wind by going diagonally against it, first one way and then the other. Due to the way the sails were mounted, they appeared somewhat triangular in shape, and thus the Malays' balance lug sail may well be the prototype of the triangular lateen, which can also be used to tack against the wind. The latter was invented by both the Polynesians to the Malays' east and by the Arabs to their west, both of whom had ample opportunity to see the Malays' ships in action.

It appears that the pepper trade developed after the cinnamon trade. In the first century C.E. southern India began supplying the Mediterranean with large quantities of pepper. Thereafter, Indian merchants could be found living on the island of Socotra, near the mouth of the Red Sea, and Greek-speaking sailors, including the anonymous author of the *Periplus of the Erythraean Sea*, could be found sailing in the Red Sea and riding the monsoons from there to India.

Indian traders and shippers and Malay sailors were also responsible for opening up an all-sea route to China. The traders' desire for silk drew them out into dangerous waters in search of a more direct way to its source. By the second century C.E. Indian merchants could make the trip by sea, but the route was slow, and it took at least two years to make a round trip. Merchants leaving from India's eastern coast rounded the shores of the Bay of Bengal. When they came to the Isthmus of Kra, the narrowest part of the Malay peninsula, the ships were unloaded, and the goods were portaged across to the Gulf of Thailand. The cargo was then reloaded on ships that rounded the gulf until they reached Funan, a kingdom on what is now the Kampuchea-Vietnam border. There they had to wait for the winds to shift, before embarking upon a ship that rode the monsoon to China.

Some time before 400 C.E. travelers began to use a new all-sea route to China, a route that went around the Malay peninsula and thus avoided the Isthmus of Kra portage. The ships left from Sri Lanka and sailed before the monsoon, far from any coasts, through either the Strait of Malacca or the Strait of Sunda into the Java Sea. After waiting in the Java Sea port for the winds to shift, they rode the monsoon to southern China. The most likely developers of this route were Malay sailors, since the new stopover ports were located within their territories.

Not until the latter part of the fourth century, at about the same time as the new all-sea route began to direct commercial traffic through the Java Sea, did the fine spices — cloves, nutmeg, and mace — begin to assume importance on international markets. These rare and expensive spices came from the Moluccas, several island groups about a thousand miles east of Java. Cloves were produced on about five minuscule islands off the western coast of Halmahera; nutmeg and mace came from only a few of the Banda Islands, some ten islands with a total area of seventeen square miles, located in the middle of the Banda Sea. Until 1621 these Moluccan islands were the only places in the world able to produce cloves, nutmeg, and mace in commercial quantities. The Moluccan producers themselves brought their spices to the international markets of the Java Sea ports and created the market for them.

It was also during the time of the Gupta kings, around 350 C.E., that the Indians discovered how to crystallize sugar. There is considerable disagreement about where sugar was first domesticated. Some believe that the plant was native to New Guinea and domesticated there, and others argue that it was domesticated by Southeast Asian peoples living in what is now southern China. In any case, sugar cultivation spread to the Indian subcontinent. Sugar, however, did not become an important item of trade until the Indians discovered how to turn sugarcane juice into granulated crystals that could be easily stored and transported. This was a momentous development, and it may have been encouraged by Indian sailing, for sugar and clarified butter (ghee) were among the dietary mainstays of Indian sailors.

The Indians also laid the foundation for modern mathematics during the time of the Guptas. Western numerals, which the Europeans called Arabic since they acquired them from the Arabs, actually come from India. (The Arabs call them Hindi numbers.) The most significant feature of the Indian system was the invention of the zero as a number concept. The oldest extant treatise that uses the zero in the modern way is a mathematical appendix attached to Aryabhata's text on astronomy, which is dated 499 C.E.

The Indian zero made the place-value system of writing numbers superior to all others. Without it, the use of this system, base ten or otherwise, was fraught with difficulties and did not seem any better than alternative systems. With the zero the Indians were able to perform calculations rapidly and accurately, to perform much more complicated calculations, and to discern mathematical relationships more aptly. These numerals and the mathematics that the Indians developed with them are now universal — just one indication of the global significance of Southernization.

As a result of these developments India acquired a reputation as a place of marvels, a reputation that was maintained for many centuries after the Gupta dynasty fell. As late as the ninth century Amr ibn Bahr al Jahiz (c. 776–868), one of the most influential writers of Arabic, had the following to say about India:

> As regards the Indians, they are among the leaders in astronomy, mathematics — in particular, they have Indian numerals — and medicine; they alone possess the secrets of the latter, and use them to practice some remarkable forms of treatment. They have the art of carving statues and painted figures. They possess the game of chess, which is the noblest of games and requires more judgment and intelligence than any other. They make Kedah swords, and excel in their use. They have splendid music. . . . They possess a script capable of expressing the sounds of all languages, as well as many numerals. They have a great deal of poetry, many long treatises, and a deep understanding of philosophy and letters; the book *Kalila wa-Dimna* originated with them. They are intelligent and courageous. . . . Their sound judgment and sensible habits led them to invent pins, cork, toothpicks, the drape of clothes, and the dyeing of hair. They are handsome, attractive, and forbearing; their women are proverbial; and their country produces the matchless Indian aloes which are supplied to kings. They were the originators of the science of *fikr*, by which a poison can be counteracted after it has been used, and of astronomical reckoning, subsequently adopted by the rest of the world. When Adam descended from Paradise, it was to their land that he made his way.

The Southernization of China

These Southern Asian developments began to have a significant impact on China after 350 C.E. The Han dynasty had fallen in 221 C.E., and for more than 350 years thereafter China was ruled by an ever-changing collection of regional kingdoms. During these centuries Buddhism became increasingly important in China, Buddhist monasteries spread throughout the disunited realm, and cultural exchange between India and China grew accordingly. By 581, when the Sui dynasty reunited the empire, processes associated with Southernization had already had a major impact on China. The influence of Southernization continued during the T'ang (618–906) and Sung (960–1279) dynasties. One might even go so far as to suggest that the process of Southernization underlay the revolutionary social, political, economic, and technological developments of the T'ang and Sung.

The Chinese reformed their mathematics, incorporating the advantages of the Indian system, even though they did not adopt the Indian numerals at that time. They then went on to develop an advanced mathematics, which was flourishing by the time of the Sung dynasty. Cotton and indigo became well established, giving rise to the blue-black peasant garb that is still omnipresent in China. Also in the Sung period the Chinese first developed cotton canvas, which they used to make a more efficient sail for ocean-going ships.

Although sugar had long been grown in some parts of southern China it did not become an important crop in this region until the process of Southernization was well under way. The process also introduced new varieties of rice. The most important of these was what the Chinese called Champa rice, since it came to China from Champa, a Malay kingdom located on what is now the southeastern coast of Vietnam. Champa rice was a drought-resistant, early ripening variety that made it possible to extend cultivation up well-watered hillsides, thereby doubling the area of rice cultivation in China. . . .

In southern China the further development of rice production brought significant changes in the landscape. Before the introduction of Champa rice, rice cultivation had been confined to lowlands, deltas, basins, and river valleys. Once Champa rice was introduced and rice cultivation spread up the hillsides, the Chinese began systematic terracing and made use of sophisticated techniques of water control on mountain slopes. Between the mid-eighth and the early twelfth century the population of southern China tripled, and the total Chinese population doubled. According to Sung dynasty household registration figures for 1102 and 1110 — figures that Sung dynasty specialists have shown to be reliable — there were 100 million people in China by the first decade of the twelfth century.

Before the process of Southernization, northern China had always been predominant, intellectually, socially, and politically. The imperial center of gravity was clearly in the north, and the southern part of China was perceived as a frontier area. But Southernization changed this situation dramatically. By 600, southern China was well on its way to becoming the most prosperous and most commercial part of the empire. The most telling evidence for this is the construction of the Grand Canal, which was completed around 610, during the Sui dynasty. Even though the rulers of the Sui had managed to put the pieces of the empire back together in 581 and rule the whole of China again from a single northern capital, they were dependent on the new southern crops. Thus it is no coincidence that this dynasty felt the need to build a canal that could deliver southern rice to northern cities.

The T'ang dynasty, when Buddhist influence in China was especially strong, saw two exceedingly important technological innovations — the invention of printing and gunpowder. These developments may also be linked to Southernization. Printing seems to have developed within the walls of Buddhist monasteries between 700 and 750, and subtropical Sichuan was one of the earliest centers of the art. The invention of gunpowder in China by Taoist alchemists in the ninth century may also be related to the linkages between India and China created by Buddhism. In 644 an Indian monk identified soils in China that contained saltpeter and demonstrated the purple flame that results from its ignition. As early as 919 C.E. gunpowder was used as an igniter in a flamethrower, and the tenth century also saw the use of flaming arrows, rockets, and bombs thrown by catapults. The earliest evidence of a cannon or bombard (1127) has been found in Sichuan, quite near the Tibetan border, across the Himalayas from India.

By the time of the Sung the Chinese also had perfected the "south-pointing needle," otherwise known as the compass. Various prototypes of the compass had existed in China from the third century B.C.E., but the new version developed during the Sung was particularly well suited for navigation. Soon Chinese mariners were using the south-pointing needle on the oceans, publishing "needle charts" for the benefit of sea captains, and following "needle routes" on the Southern Ocean.

Once the Chinese had the compass they, like Columbus, set out to find a direct route to the spice markets of Java and ultimately to the Spice Islands in the Moluccas. Unlike Columbus, they found them. They did not bump into an obstacle, now known as the Western Hemisphere, on their way, since it was not located between China and the Spice Islands. If it had been so situated, the Chinese would have found it some 500 years before Columbus.

Cities on China's southern coasts became centers of overseas commerce. Silk remained an important export, and by the T'ang dynasty it had been joined by a true porcelain, which was developed in China sometime before 400 C.E. China and its East Asian neighbors had a monopoly on the manufacture of true porcelain until the early eighteenth century. Many attempts were made to imitate it, and some of the resulting imitations were economically and stylistically important. China's southern ports were also exporting to Southeast Asia large quantities of ordinary consumer goods, including iron hardware, such as needles, scissors, and cooking pots. Although iron manufacturing was concentrated in the north, the large quantity of goods produced was a direct result of the size of the market in southern China and overseas. Until the British Industrial Revolution of the eighteenth century, no other place ever equaled the iron production of Sung China.

The Muslim Caliphates

In the seventh century C.E., Arab cavalries, recently converted to the new religion of Islam, conquered eastern and southern Mediterranean shores that had been Byzantine (and Christian), as well as the Sassanian empire

(Zoroastrian) in what is now Iraq and Iran. In the eighth century they went on to conquer Spain and Turko-Iranian areas of Central Asia, as well as northwestern India. Once established on the Indian frontier, they became acquainted with many of the elements of Southernization.

The Arabs were responsible for the spread of many important crops, developed or improved in India, to the Middle East, North Africa, and Islamic Spain. Among the most important were sugar, cotton, and citrus fruits. Although sugarcane and cotton cultivation may have spread to Iraq and Ethiopia before the Arab conquests, only after the establishment of the caliphates did these southern crops have a major impact throughout the Middle East and North Africa.

The Arabs were the first to import large numbers of enslaved Africans in order to produce sugar. Fields in the vicinity of Basra, at the northern end of the Persian Gulf, were the most important sugar-producing areas within the caliphates, but before this land could be used, it had to be desalinated. To accomplish this task, the Arabs imported East African (Zanj) slaves. This African community remained in the area, where they worked as agricultural laborers. The famous writer al Jahiz, whose essay on India was quoted earlier, was a descendant of Zanj slaves. In 869, one year after his death, the Zanj slaves in Iraq rebelled. It took the caliphate fifteen years of hard fighting to defeat them, and thereafter Muslim owners rarely used slaves for purposes that would require their concentration in large numbers.

The Arabs were responsible for moving sugarcane cultivation and sugar manufacturing westward from southern Iraq into other relatively arid lands. Growers had to adapt the plant to new conditions, and they had to develop more efficient irrigation technologies. By 1000 or so sugarcane had become an important crop in the Yemen; in Arabian oases; in irrigated areas of Syria, Lebanon, Palestine, Egypt, and the Mahgrib; in Spain; and on Mediterranean islands controlled by Muslims. By the tenth century cotton also had become a major crop in the lands of the caliphate, from Iran and Central Asia to Spain and the Mediterranean islands. Cotton industries sprang up wherever the plant was cultivated, producing for both local and distant markets. . . .

Under Arab auspices, Indian mathematics followed the same routes as the crops. Al-Kharazmi (c. 780–847) introduced Indian mathematics to the Arabic-reading world in his *Treatise on Calculation with the Hindu Numerals*, written around 825. Mathematicians within the caliphates then could draw upon the Indian tradition, as well as the Greek and Persian. On this foundation Muslim scientists of many nationalities, including al-Battani (d. 929), who came from the northern reaches of the Mesopotamian plain, and the Persian Omar Khayyám (d. 1123), made remarkable advances in both algebra and trigonometry.

The Arab conquests also led to an increase in long-distance commerce and the "discovery" of new sources of bullion. Soon after the Abbasid caliphate established its capital at Baghdad, the caliph al-Mansur (r. 745–75) reportedly remarked, "This is the Tigris; there is no obstacle between us and China; everything on the sea can come to us." By this time Arab ships were plying the maritime routes from the Persian Gulf to China, and they soon outnumbered all others using these routes. By the ninth century they had acquired the compass (in China, most likely), and they may well have been the first to use it for marine navigation, since the Chinese do not seem to have used it for this purpose until after the tenth century.

. . . Thus it was that the Arabs "pioneered" or improved an existing long-distance route across the Sahara, an ocean of sand rather than water. Routes across this desert had always existed, and trade and other contacts between West Africa and the Mediterranean date back at least to the Phoenician period. Still, the numbers of people and animals crossing this great ocean of sand were limited until the eighth century when Arabs, desiring to go directly to the source of the gold, prompted an expansion of trade across the Sahara. Also during the eighth century Abdul al-Rahman, an Arab ruler of Morocco, sponsored the construction of wells on the trans-Saharan route from Sijilmasa to Wadidara to facilitate this traffic. This Arab "discovery" of West African gold eventually doubled the amount of gold in international circulation. East Africa, too, became a source of gold for the Arabs. By the tenth century Kilwa had become an important source of Zimbabwean gold.

Developments after 1200: The Mongolian Conquest and the Southernization of the European Mediterranean

By 1200 the process of Southernization had created a prosperous south from China to the Muslim Mediterranean. Although mathematics, the pioneering of new ocean routes, and "discoveries" of bullion are not inextricably connected to locations within forty degrees of the equator, several crucial elements in the process of Southernization were closely linked to latitude. Cotton generally does not grow above the fortieth parallel. Sugar, cinnamon, and pepper are tropical or subtropical crops, and the fine spices will grow only on particular tropical islands. Thus for many centuries the more southern parts of Asia and the Muslim Mediterranean enjoyed the profits that these developments brought, while locations that were too far north to grow these southern crops were unable to participate in such lucrative agricultural enterprises.

The process of Southernization reached its zenith after 1200, in large part because of the tumultuous events of the thirteenth century. During that century in both hemispheres there were major transformations in the distribution of power, wealth, and prestige. In the Western

Hemisphere several great powers went down. Cahokia (near East St. Louis, Illinois), which for three centuries had been the largest and most influential of the Mississippian mound-building centers, declined after 1200, and in Mexico Toltec power collapsed. In the Mediterranean the prestige of the Byzantine empire was destroyed when Venetians seized its capital in 1204. From 1212 to 1270 the Christians conquered southern Spain, except for Granada. In West Africa, Ghana fell to Sosso, and so did Mali, one of Ghana's allies. But by about 1230 Mali, in the process of seeking its own revenge, had created an empire even larger than Ghana's. At the same time Zimbabwe was also becoming a major power in southern Africa.

The grandest conquerors of the thirteenth century were the Central Asians. Turkish invaders established the Delhi sultanate in India. Mongolian cavalries devastated Baghdad, the seat of the Abbasid caliphate since the eighth century, and they captured Kiev, further weakening Byzantium. By the end of the century they had captured China, Korea, and parts of mainland Southeast Asia as well.

Because the Mongols were pagans at the time of their conquests, the western Europeans cheered them on as they laid waste to one after another Muslim center of power in the Middle East. The Mongols were stopped only when they encountered the Mamluks of Egypt at Damascus. In East Asia and Southeast Asia only the Japanese and the Javanese were able to defeat them. The victors in Java went on to found Majapahit, whose power and prestige then spread through maritime Southeast Asia.

Both hemispheres were reorganized profoundly during this turmoil. Many places that had flourished were toppled, and power gravitated to new locales. In the Eastern Hemisphere the Central Asian conquerors had done great damage to traditional southern centers just about everywhere, except in Africa, southern China, southern India, and maritime Southeast Asia. At the same time the Mongols' control of overland routes between Europe and Asia in the thirteenth and early fourteenth centuries fostered unprecedented contacts between Europeans and peoples from those areas that had long been southernized. Marco Polo's long sojourn in Yüan Dynasty China is just one example of such interaction.

Under the Mongols overland trade routes in Asia shifted north and converged on the Black Sea. After the Genoese helped the Byzantines to retake Constantinople from the Venetians in 1261, the Genoese were granted special privileges of trade in the Black Sea. Italy then became directly linked to the Mongolian routes. Genoese traders were among the first and were certainly the most numerous to open up trade with the Mongolian states in southern Russia and Iran. In the words of one Western historian, in their Black Sea colonies they "admitted to citizenship" people of many nationalities, including those of "strange background and questionable belief," and they "wound up christening children of the best ancestry with such uncanny names as Saladin, Hethum, or Hulugu."

Such contacts contributed to the Southernization of the Christian Mediterranean during this period of Mongolian hegemony. Although European conquerors sometimes had taken over sugar and cotton lands in the Middle East during the Crusades, not until some time after 1200 did the European-held Mediterranean islands become important exporters. Also after 1200 Indian mathematics began to have a significant impact in Europe. Before that time a few western European scholars had become acquainted with Indian numerals in Spain, where the works of al-Kharazmi, al-Battani, and other mathematicians had been translated into Latin. Nevertheless, Indian numerals and mathematics did not become important in western Europe until the thirteenth century after the book *Liber abaci* (1202), written by Leonardo Fibonacci of Pisa (c. 1170–1250), introduced them to the commercial centers of Italy. Leonardo had grown up in North Africa (in what is now Bejala, Algeria), where his father, consul over the Pisan merchants in that port, had sent him to study calculation with an Arab master.

In the seventeenth century, when Francis Bacon observed the "force and virtue and consequences of discoveries," he singled out three technologies in particular that "have changed the whole face and state of things throughout the world." These were all Chinese inventions — the compass, printing, and gunpowder. All three were first acquired by Europeans during this time of hemispheric reorganization.

It was most likely the Arabs who introduced the compass to Mediterranean waters, either at the end of the twelfth or in the thirteenth century. Block printing, gunpowder, and cannon appeared first in Italy in the fourteenth century, apparently after making a single great leap from Mongolian-held regions of East Asia to Italy. How this great leap was accomplished is not known, but the most likely scenario is one suggested by Lynn White Jr., in an article concerning how various other Southern (rather than Eastern) Asian technologies reached western Europe at about this time. He thought it most likely that they were introduced by "Tatar" slaves, Lama Buddhists from the frontiers of China whom the Genoese purchased in Black Sea marts and delivered to Italy. By 1450 when this trade reached its peak, there were thousands of these Asian slaves in every major Italian city.

Yet another consequence of the increased traffic and communication on the more northern trade routes traversing the Eurasian steppe was the transmission of the bubonic plague from China to the Black Sea. The plague had broken out first in China in 1331, and apparently rats and lice infected with the disease rode westward in the saddlebags of Mongolian post messengers, horsemen who were capable of traveling one hundred miles per day. By 1346 it had reached a Black Sea port, whence it made its way to the Middle East and Europe.

During the latter part of the fourteenth century the unity of the Mongolian empire began to disintegrate, and new regional powers began to emerge in its wake. Throughout much of Asia the chief beneficiaries of imperial disintegration were Turkic or Turko-Mongolian powers of the Muslim faith. The importance of Islam in Africa was also growing at this time, and the peoples of Southeast Asia, from the Malay peninsula to the southern Philippines, were converting to the faith.

Indeed, the world's most obvious dynamic in the centuries before Columbus was the expansion of the Islamic faith. Under Turkish auspices Islam was even spreading into eastern Europe, a development marked by the Ottoman conquest of Constantinople in 1453. This traumatic event lent a special urgency to Iberian expansion. The Iberians came to see themselves as the chosen defenders of Christendom. Ever since the twelfth century, while Christian Byzantium had been losing Anatolia and parts of southeastern Europe to Islam, they had been retaking the Iberian peninsula for Christendom.

One way to weaken the Ottomans and Islam was to go around the North African Muslims and find a new oceanic route to the source of West African gold. Before the Portuguese efforts, sailing routes had never developed off the western shore of Africa, since the winds there blow in the same direction all year long, from north to south. (Earlier European sailors could have gone to West Africa, but they would not have been able to return home.)

The Portuguese success would have been impossible without the Chinese compass, Arabic tables indicating the declination of the noonday sun at various latitudes, and the lateen sail, which was also an Arab innovation. The Portuguese caravels were of mixed, or multiple, ancestry, with a traditional Atlantic hull and a rigging that combined the traditional Atlantic square sail with the lateen sail of Southern Ocean provenance. With the lateen sail the Portuguese could tack against the wind for the trip homeward.

The new route to West Africa led to Portugal's rounding of Africa and direct participation in Southern Ocean trade. While making the voyages to West Africa, European sailors learned the wind patterns and ocean currents west of Africa, knowledge that made the Columbian voyages possible. The Portuguese moved the sugarcane plant from Sicily to Madeira, in the Atlantic, and they found new sources of gold, first in West Africa and then in East Africa. Given that there was little demand in Southern Ocean ports for European trade goods, they would not have been able to sustain their Asian trade without this African gold.

The Rise of Europe's North

The rise of the north, or more precisely, the rise of Europe's northwest, began with the appropriation of those elements of Southernization that were not confined by geography. In the wake of their southern European neighbors, they became partially southernized, but they could not engage in all aspects of the process due to their distance from the equator. Full Southernization and the wealth that we now associate with northwestern Europe came about only after their outright seizure of tropical and subtropical territories and their rounding of Africa and participation in Southern Ocean trade. . . .

Even though the significance of indigenous developments in the rise of northwestern Europe should not be minimized, it should be emphasized that many of the most important causes of the rise of the West are not to be found within the bounds of Europe. Rather, they are the result of the transformation of western Europe's relationships with other regions of the Eastern Hemisphere. Europe began its rise only after the thirteenth-century reorganization of the Eastern Hemisphere facilitated its Southernization, and Europe's northwest did not rise until it too was reaping the profits of Southernization. Thus the rise of the North Atlantic powers should not be oversimplified so that it appears to be an isolated and solely European phenomenon, with roots that spread no farther afield than Greece. Rather, it should be portrayed as one part of a hemisphere-wide process, in which a northwestern Europe ran to catch up with a more developed south — a race not completed until the eighteenth century.

93

JARED DIAMOND
Easter Island's End

In comparison with the grand theories of White and Shaffer, an essay on a small island in the Pacific might seem to be an exercise in the recent vogue of small-bore "micro-history." It is not. Jared Diamond, author of *Guns, Germs, and Steel,* uses small examples to big effect. In this selection and in his larger book-length treatment, *Collapse: How Societies Choose to Fail or Succeed,* Diamond teases a global lesson from the history of tiny Easter Island. What is that lesson? What does Diamond's essay suggest about the causes of environmental decline? Are we in danger of duplicating the fate of Easter Island? How can we avoid the fate of Easter Island?

Jared Diamond, "Easter Island's End," *Discover* 16, no. 8 (August 1995).

Thinking Historically

How does Diamond's essay challenge the thesis of Lynn White Jr.? Do you see in this essay an alternative grand theory for understanding our environmental problems? If so, what is that theory? Do you agree or disagree with it? Why or why not?

In just a few centuries, the people of Easter Island wiped out their forest, drove their plants and animals to extinction, and saw their complex society spiral into chaos and cannibalism. Are we about to follow their lead?

Among the most riveting mysteries of human history are those posed by vanished civilizations. Everyone who has seen the abandoned buildings of the Khmer, the Maya, or the Anasazi is immediately moved to ask the same question: Why did the societies that erected those structures disappear?

Their vanishing touches us as the disappearance of other animals, even the dinosaurs, never can. No matter how exotic those lost civilizations seem, their framers were humans like us. Who is to say we won't succumb to the same fate? Perhaps someday New York's skyscrapers will stand derelict and overgrown with vegetation, like the temples at Angkor Wat and Tikal.

Among all such vanished civilizations, that of the former Polynesian society on Easter Island remains unsurpassed in mystery and isolation. The mystery stems especially from the island's gigantic stone statues and its impoverished landscape, but it is enhanced by our associations with the specific people involved: Polynesians represent for us the ultimate in exotic romance, the background for many a child's, and an adult's, vision of paradise. My own interest in Easter was kindled over 30 years ago when I read Thor Heyerdahl's fabulous accounts of his Kon-Tiki voyage.

But my interest has been revived recently by a much more exciting account, one not of heroic voyages but of painstaking research and analysis. My friend David Steadman, a paleontologist, has been working with a number of other researchers who are carrying out the first systematic excavations on Easter intended to identify the animals and plants that once lived there. Their work is contributing to a new interpretation of the island's history that makes it a tale not only of wonder but of warning as well.

Easter Island, with an area of only 64 square miles, is the world's most isolated scrap of habitable land. It lies in the Pacific Ocean more than 2,000 miles west of the nearest continent (South America), 1,400 miles from even the nearest habitable island (Pitcairn). Its subtropical location and latitude — at 27 degrees south, it is approximately as far below the equator as Houston is north of it — help give it a rather mild climate, while its volcanic origins make its soil fertile. In theory, this combination of blessings should have made Easter a miniature paradise, remote from problems that beset the rest of the world.

The island derives its name from its "discovery" by the Dutch explorer Jacob Roggeveen, on Easter (April 5) in 1722. Roggeveen's first impression was not of a paradise but of a wasteland: "We originally, from a further distance, have considered the said Easter Island as sandy; the reason for that is this, that we counted as sand the withered grass, hay, or other scorched and burnt vegetation, because its wasted appearance could give no other impression than of a singular poverty and barrenness."

The island Roggeveen saw was a grassland without a single tree or bush over ten feet high. Modern botanists have identified only 47 species of higher plants native to Easter, most of them grasses, sedges, and ferns. The list includes just two species of small trees and two of woody shrubs. With such flora, the islanders Roggeveen encountered had no source of real firewood to warm themselves during Easter's cool, wet, windy winters. Their native animals included nothing larger than insects, not even a single species of native bat, land bird, land snail, or lizard. For domestic animals, they had only chickens. European visitors throughout the eighteenth and early nineteenth centuries estimated Easter's human population at about 2,000, a modest number considering the island's fertility. As Captain James Cook recognized during his brief visit in 1774, the islanders were Polynesians (a Tahitian man accompanying Cook was able to converse with them). Yet despite the Polynesians' well-deserved fame as a great seafaring people, the Easter Islanders who came out to Roggeveen's and Cook's ships did so by swimming or paddling canoes that Roggeveen described as "bad and frail." Their craft, he wrote, were "put together with manifold small planks and light inner timbers, which they cleverly stitched together with very fine twisted threads. . . . But as they lack the knowledge and particularly the materials for caulking and making tight the great number of seams of the canoes, these are accordingly very leaky, for which reason they are compelled to spend half the time in bailing." The canoes, only ten feet long, held at most two people, and only three or four canoes were observed on the entire island.

With such flimsy craft, Polynesians could never have colonized Easter from even the nearest island, nor could they have traveled far offshore to fish. The islanders Roggeveen met were totally isolated, unaware that other people existed. Investigators in all the years since his visit have discovered no trace of the islanders' having any outside contacts: not a single Easter Island rock or product has turned up elsewhere, nor has anything been found on the island that could have been brought by anyone other than the original settlers or the Europeans. Yet the people living on Easter claimed memories of visiting the uninhabited Sala y Gomez reef 260 miles away, far beyond the range of the leaky canoes seen by Roggeveen. How did the islanders' ancestors reach that reef from Easter, or reach Easter from anywhere else?

Easter Island's most famous feature is its huge stone statues, more than 200 of which once stood on massive stone platforms lining the coast. [See Figure 14.4.] At least 700 more, in all stages of completion, were abandoned in quarries or on ancient roads between the quarries and the coast, as if the carvers and moving crews had thrown down their tools and walked off the job. Most of the erected statues were carved in a single quarry and then somehow transported as far as six miles — despite heights as great as 33 feet and weights up to 82 tons. The abandoned statues, meanwhile, were as much as 65 feet tall and weighed up to 270 tons. The stone platforms were equally gigantic: up to 500 feet long and 10 feet high, with facing slabs weighing up to 10 tons.

Roggeveen himself quickly recognized the problem the statues posed: "The stone images at first caused us to be struck with astonishment," he wrote, "because we could not comprehend how it was possible that these people, who are devoid of heavy thick timber for making any machines, as well as strong ropes, nevertheless had been able to erect such images." Roggeveen might have added that the islanders had no wheels, no draft animals, and no source of power except their own muscles. How did they transport the giant statues for miles, even before erecting them? To deepen the mystery, the statues were still standing in 1770, but by 1864 all of them had been pulled down, by the islanders themselves. Why then did they carve them in the first place? And why did they stop?

The statues imply a society very different from the one Roggeveen saw in 1722. Their sheer number and size suggest a population much larger than 2,000 people. What became of everyone? Furthermore, that society must have been highly organized. Easter's resources were scattered across the island: the best stone for the statues was quarried at Rano Raraku near Easter's northeast end; red stone, used for large crowns adorning some of the statues, was quarried at Puna Pau, inland in the southwest; stone carving tools came mostly from Aroi in the northwest. Meanwhile, the best farmland lay in the south and east, and the best fishing grounds on the north and west coasts. Extracting and redistributing all those goods required complex political organization. What happened to that organization, and how could it ever have arisen in such a barren landscape?

Easter Island's mysteries have spawned volumes of speculation for more than two and a half centuries. Many Europeans were incredulous that Polynesians — commonly characterized as "mere savages" — could have created the statues or the beautifully constructed stone platforms. In the 1950s, Heyerdahl argued that Polynesia must have been settled by advanced societies of American Indians, who in turn must have received civilization across the Atlantic from more advanced societies of the Old World. Heyerdahl's raft voyages aimed to prove the feasibility of such prehistoric transoceanic contacts. In the 1960s the

Figure 14.4   Easter Island Statues.
   Source: © Westend61/Alamy.

Swiss writer Erich von Däniken, an ardent believer in Earth visits by extraterrestrial astronauts, went further, claiming that Easter's statues were the work of intelligent beings who owned ultramodern tools, became stranded on Easter, and were finally rescued.

Heyerdahl and von Däeniken both brushed aside overwhelming evidence that the Easter Islanders were typical Polynesians derived from Asia rather than from the Americas and that their culture (including their statues) grew out of Polynesian culture. Their language was Polynesian, as Cook had already concluded. Specifically, they spoke an eastern Polynesian dialect related to Hawaiian and Marquesan, a dialect isolated since about A.D. 400, as estimated from slight differences in vocabulary. Their fishhooks and stone adzes resembled early Marquesan models. Last year DNA extracted from 12 Easter Island skeletons was also shown to be Polynesian. The islanders grew bananas, taro, sweet potatoes, sugarcane, and paper mulberry — typical Polynesian crops, mostly of Southeast Asian origin. Their sole domestic animal, the chicken, was also typically Polynesian and ultimately Asian, as were the rats that arrived as stowaways in the canoes of the first settlers.

What happened to those settlers? The fanciful theories of the past must give way to evidence gathered by hardworking practitioners in three fields: archeology, pollen analysis, and paleontology. Modern archeological excavations on Easter have continued since Heyerdahl's 1955 expedition. The earliest radiocarbon dates associated with human activities are around A.D. 400 to 700, in reasonable agreement with the approximate settlement date of 400 estimated by linguists. The period of statue construction peaked around 1200 to 1500, with few if any statues erected thereafter. Densities of archeological sites suggest a large population; an estimate of 7,000 people is widely quoted by archeologists, but other estimates range up to 20,000, which does not seem implausible for an island of Easter's area and fertility.

Archeologists have also enlisted surviving islanders in experiments aimed at figuring out how the statues might have been carved and erected. Twenty people, using only stone chisels, could have carved even the largest completed statue within a year. Given enough timber and fiber for making ropes, teams of at most a few hundred people could have loaded the statues onto wooden sleds, dragged them over lubricated wooden tracks or rollers, and used logs as levers to maneuver them into a standing position. Rope could have been made from the fiber of a small native tree, related to the linden, called the hauhau. However, that tree is now extremely scarce on Easter, and hauling one statue would have required hundreds of yards of rope. Did Easter's now barren landscape once support the necessary trees? That question can be answered by the technique of pollen analysis, which involves boring out a column of sediment from a swamp or pond, with the most recent deposits at the top and relatively more ancient deposits at the bottom. The absolute age of each layer can be dated by radiocarbon methods. Then begins the hard work: examining tens of thousands of pollen grains under a microscope, counting them, and identifying the plant species that produced each one by comparing the grains with modern pollen from known plant species. For Easter Island, the bleary-eyed scientists who performed that task were John Flenley, now at Massey University in New Zealand, and Sarah King of the University of Hull in England.

Flenley and King's heroic efforts were rewarded by the striking new picture that emerged of Easter's prehistoric landscape. For at least 30,000 years before human arrival and during the early years of Polynesian settlement, Easter was not a wasteland at all. Instead, a subtropical forest of trees and woody bushes towered over a ground layer of shrubs, herbs, ferns, and grasses. In the forest grew tree daisies, the rope-yielding hauhau tree, and the toromiro tree, which furnishes a dense, mesquite-like firewood. The most common tree in the forest was a species of palm now absent on Easter but formerly so abundant that the bottom strata of the sediment column were packed with its pollen. The Easter Island palm was closely related to the still-surviving Chilean wine palm, which grows up to 82 feet tall and 6 feet in diameter. The tall, unbranched trunks of the Easter Island palm would have been ideal for transporting and erecting statues and constructing large canoes. The palm would also have been a valuable food source, since its

Chilean relative yields edible nuts as well as sap from which Chileans make sugar, syrup, honey, and wine.

What did the first settlers of Easter Island eat when they were not glutting themselves on the local equivalent of maple syrup? Recent excavations by David Steadman, of the New York State Museum at Albany, have yielded a picture of Easter's original animal world as surprising as Flenley and King's picture of its plant world. Steadman's expectations for Easter were conditioned by his experiences elsewhere in Polynesia, where fish are overwhelmingly the main food at archeological sites, typically accounting for more than 90 percent of the bones in ancient Polynesian garbage heaps. Easter, though, is too cool for the coral reefs beloved by fish, and its cliff-girded coastline permits shallow-water fishing in only a few places. Less than a quarter of the bones in its early garbage heaps (from the period 900 to 1300) belonged to fish; instead, nearly one-third of all bones came from porpoises.

Nowhere else in Polynesia do porpoises account for even 1 percent of discarded food bones. But most other Polynesian islands offered animal food in the form of birds and mammals, such as New Zealand's now extinct giant moas and Hawaii's now extinct flightless geese. Most other islanders also had domestic pigs and dogs. On Easter, porpoises would have been the largest animal available — other than humans. The porpoise species identified at Easter, the common dolphin, weighs up to 165 pounds. It generally lives out at sea, so it could not have been hunted by line fishing or spearfishing from shore. Instead, it must have been harpooned far offshore, in big seaworthy canoes built from the extinct palm tree.

In addition to porpoise meat, Steadman found, the early Polynesian settlers were feasting on seabirds. For those birds, Easter's remoteness and lack of predators made it an ideal haven as a breeding site, at least until humans arrived. Among the prodigious numbers of seabirds that bred on Easter were albatross, boobies, frigate birds, fulmars, petrels, prions, shearwaters, storm petrels, terns, and tropic birds. With at least 25 nesting species, Easter was the richest seabird breeding site in Polynesia and probably in the whole Pacific. Land birds as well went into early Easter Island cooking pots.

Steadman identified bones of at least six species, including barn owls, herons, parrots, and rail. Bird stew would have been seasoned with meat from large numbers of rats, which the Polynesian colonists inadvertently brought with them; Easter Island is the sole known Polynesian island where rat bones outnumber fish bones at archeological sites. (In case you're squeamish and consider rats inedible, I still recall recipes for creamed laboratory rat that my British biologist friends used to supplement their diet during their years of wartime food rationing.)

Porpoises, seabirds, land birds, and rats did not complete the list of meat sources formerly available on Easter. A few bones hint at the possibility of breeding seal colonies as well. All these delicacies were cooked in ovens fired by wood from the island's forests.

Such evidence lets us imagine the island onto which Easter's first Polynesian colonists stepped ashore some 1,600 years ago, after a long canoe voyage from eastern Polynesia. They found themselves in a pristine paradise. What then happened to it? The pollen grains and the bones yield a grim answer.

Pollen records show that destruction of Easter's forests was well under way by the year 800, just a few centuries after the start of human settlement. Then charcoal from wood fires came to fill the sediment cores, while pollen of palms and other trees and woody shrubs decreased or disappeared, and pollen of the grasses that replaced the forest became more abundant. Not long after 1400 the palm finally became extinct, not only as a result of being chopped down but also because the now ubiquitous rats prevented its regeneration: of the dozens of preserved palm nuts discovered in caves on Easter, all had been chewed by rats and could no longer germinate. While the hauhau tree did not become extinct in Polynesian times, its numbers declined drastically until there weren't enough left to make ropes from. By the time Heyerdahl visited Easter, only a single, nearly dead toromiro tree remained on the island, and even that lone survivor has now disappeared. (Fortunately, the toromiro still grows in botanical gardens elsewhere.)

The fifteenth century marked the end not only for Easter's palm but for the forest itself. Its doom had been approaching as people cleared land to plant gardens; as they felled trees to build canoes, to transport and erect statues, and to burn; as rats devoured seeds; and probably as the native birds died out that had pollinated the trees' flowers and dispersed their fruit. The overall picture is among the most extreme examples of forest destruction anywhere in the world: the whole forest gone, and most of its tree species extinct.

The destruction of the island's animals was as extreme as that of the forest: without exception, every species of native land bird became extinct. Even shellfish were overexploited, until people had to settle for small sea snails instead of larger cowries. Porpoise bones disappeared abruptly from garbage heaps around 1500; no one could harpoon porpoises anymore, since the trees used for constructing the big seagoing canoes no longer existed. The colonies of more than half of the seabird species breeding on Easter or on its offshore islets were wiped out.

In place of these meat supplies, the Easter Islanders intensified their production of chickens, which had been only an occasional food item. They also turned to the largest remaining meat source available: humans, whose bones became common in late Easter Island garbage heaps. Oral traditions of the islanders are rife with cannibalism; the most inflammatory taunt that could be snarled at an enemy was "The flesh of your mother sticks between my teeth." With no wood available to cook these new goodies, the islanders resorted to sugarcane scraps, grass, and sedges to fuel their fires.

All these strands of evidence can be wound into a coherent narrative of a society's decline and fall. The first Polynesian colonists found themselves on an island with fertile soil, abundant food, bountiful building materials, ample lebensraum, and all the prerequisites for comfortable living. They prospered and multiplied.

After a few centuries, they began erecting stone statues on platforms, like the ones their Polynesian forebears had carved. With passing years, the statues and platforms became larger and larger, and the statues began sporting ten-ton red crowns — probably in an escalating spiral of one-upmanship, as rival clans tried to surpass each other with shows of wealth and power. (In the same way, successive Egyptian pharaohs built ever-larger pyramids. Today Hollywood movie moguls near my home in Los Angeles are displaying their wealth and power by building ever more ostentatious mansions. Tycoon Marvin Davis topped previous moguls with plans for a 50,000-square-foot house, so now Aaron Spelling has topped Davis with a 56,000-square-foot house. All that those buildings lack to make the message explicit are ten-ton red crowns.) On Easter, as in modern America, society was held together by a complex political system to redistribute locally available resources and to integrate the economies of different areas.

Eventually Easter's growing population was cutting the forest more rapidly than the forest was regenerating. The people used the land for gardens and the wood for fuel, canoes, and houses — and, of course, for lugging statues. As forest disappeared, the islanders ran out of timber and rope to transport and erect their statues. Life became more uncomfortable — springs and streams dried up, and wood was no longer available for fires.

People also found it harder to fill their stomachs, as land birds, large sea snails, and many seabirds disappeared. Because timber for building seagoing canoes vanished, fish catches declined and porpoises disappeared from the table. Crop yields also declined, since deforestation allowed the soil to be eroded by rain and wind, dried by the sun, and its nutrients to be leeched from it. Intensified chicken production and cannibalism replaced only part of all those lost foods. Preserved statuettes with sunken cheeks and visible ribs suggest that people were starving.

With the disappearance of food surpluses, Easter Island could no longer feed the chiefs, bureaucrats, and priests who had kept a complex society running. Surviving islanders described to early European visitors how local chaos replaced centralized government and a warrior class took over from the hereditary chiefs. The stone points of spears and daggers, made by the warriors during their heyday in the 1600s and 1700s, still litter the ground of Easter today. By around 1700, the population began to crash toward between one-quarter and one-tenth of its former number. People took to living in caves for protection against their enemies. Around 1770 rival clans started to topple each other's statues, breaking the heads off. By 1864 the last statue had been thrown down and desecrated.

As we try to imagine the decline of Easter's civilization, we ask ourselves, "Why didn't they look around, realize what they were doing, and stop before it was too late? What were they thinking when they cut down the last palm tree?"

I suspect, though, that the disaster happened not with a bang but with a whimper. After all, there are those hundreds of abandoned statues to consider. The forest the islanders depended on for rollers and rope didn't simply disappear one day — it vanished slowly, over decades. Perhaps war interrupted the moving teams; perhaps by the time the carvers had finished their work, the last rope snapped. In the meantime, any islander who tried to warn about the dangers of progressive deforestation would have been overridden by vested interests of carvers, bureaucrats, and chiefs, whose jobs depended on continued deforestation. Our Pacific Northwest loggers are only the latest in a long line of loggers to cry, "Jobs over trees!" The changes in forest cover from year to year would have been hard to detect: yes, this year we cleared those woods over there, but trees are starting to grow back again on this abandoned garden site here. Only older people, recollecting their childhoods decades earlier, could have recognized a difference. Their children could no more have comprehended their parents' tales than my eight-year-old sons today can comprehend my wife's and my tales of what Los Angeles was like 30 years ago.

Gradually trees became fewer, smaller, and less important. By the time the last fruit-bearing adult palm tree was cut, palms had long since ceased to be of economic significance. That left only smaller and smaller palm saplings to clear each year, along with other bushes and treelets. No one would have noticed the felling of the last small palm.

By now the meaning of Easter Island for us should be chillingly obvious. Easter Island is Earth writ small. Today, again, a rising population confronts shrinking resources. We too have no emigration valve, because all human societies are linked by international transport, and we can no more escape into space than the Easter Islanders could flee into the ocean. If we continue to follow our present course, we shall have exhausted the world's major fisheries, tropical rain forests, fossil fuels, and much of our soil by the time my sons reach my current age.

Every day newspapers report details of famished countries — Afghanistan, Liberia, Rwanda, Sierra Leone, Somalia, the former Yugoslavia, Zaire — where soldiers have appropriated the wealth or where central government is yielding to local gangs of thugs. With the risk of nuclear war receding, the threat of our ending with a bang no longer has a chance of galvanizing us to halt our course. Our risk now is of winding down, slowly, in a whimper. Corrective action is blocked by vested interests, by well-intentioned political and business leaders, and by their electorates, all of whom are perfectly correct in not noticing big changes from year to year. Instead, each year there are just somewhat more people, and somewhat fewer resources, on Earth. It would be easy to close our eyes or to give up in despair. If mere thousands of Easter Islanders with only stone tools and their own muscle power sufficed to destroy their society, how can billions of people with metal tools and machine power fail to do worse? But there is one crucial difference. The Easter Islanders had no books and no histories of other doomed societies. Unlike the Easter Islanders, we have histories of the past — information that can save us. My main hope for my sons' generation is that we may now choose to learn from the fates of societies like Easter's.

REFLECTIONS

Grand theories are difficult to evaluate, as are these. In part the difficulty is that they cover so much. How many images or primary sources could ever establish that a particular set of Christian ideas affected the way Christians actually behaved? And yet we know, or believe, that ideas matter. How many South Asian crops, tools, skills, and ideas constitute a global technological, let alone a scientific, revolution? And yet we know past historians have overemphasized the impact of European independence and Westernization. How many histories of societal collapse do we need to understand the threats to our own? And yet, we know that the more knowledge of how others have struggled and failed or succeeded we possess, the better our own chances for survival.

At least two issues lie beneath the surface of the debate in this chapter. One is the issue of culture, specifically the importance of cultural or religious ideas in shaping human behavior. White argues that religious ideas have a profound impact on how societies behave. Shaffer's study of material things rather than ideas, and even of ideas as things, offers a different view. By her account economic growth and technological development proceed with little regard to religions, ideologies, or belief systems. For Diamond too, not only are Christian or monotheistic ideas irrelevant, but historical processes leave precious little room for thoughtful intervention.

Historians are always working between ideas and things. Historians of ideas may have a tendency to see ideas shaping history, and historians of things (economic historians, for instance) may see ideas as mere rationalizations. But good historians are not predictable. Lynn White Jr. is perhaps best known for his book *Medieval Technology and*

Social Change in which he argued, among other things, that the introduction of the stirrup into medieval Europe was the cause of the society
and culture we call feudalism. While this idea is much debated today,
one would have a hard time finding an example of a stronger argument
of how a thing created a culture. Nor does Diamond, a professor of geography and physiology, ignore the role of ideas. In addition to the case
of Easter Island, he surveys the example of Viking collapse in Greenland in his recent book, *Collapse: How Societies Choose to Fail or Succeed* (a title that suggests the power of will and ideas). The Vikings, he
suggests, failed in Greenland because they were unable to change their
culture in ways necessary to adapt to the new environment. For
Diamond, ideas and political will offer the only hope against the blind
destructiveness of entrenched interests and seemingly unstoppable historical processes.

Another issue below the surface of this debate is the relationship
between ecology and economic development. We tend to think that one
comes at the expense of the other. White criticizes Western (Christian)
environmental behavior with the same lens that has allowed others to
celebrate Western (Christian) economic development. This is a reason,
by the way, why many contemporary world historians find both views
too centered on the West or Europe. Lynda Shaffer's article on "Southernization" is in good part an effort to counter Europe-centered history
with a more global version. But if Europe was not the source of modern
technology, it was also not a source of our modern ecological predicament. Diamond is also critical of approaches that start and end in Europe. (His area of specialty is New Guinea.) Since he eliminated religious or cultural motives, his story of Easter Island can be read as an
indictment of economic growth as the cause of ecological collapse. But
the villain in Diamond's essay is not any kind of economic growth; it is
the competitive economic exploitation of different tribes without any
common plan or restraint. His message for our own predicament is to
correct the anarchy of competing greedy corporations and interest
groups with a common agenda and control.

Are not genuine economic growth and ecological balance mutually
supportive? It is difficult to imagine long-term, healthy economic growth
continuing while wrecking the environment. Similarly with environmental movements: White has us imagine that the true environmental-
ists are Buddhist mendicants and Hindu tree-huggers. But Buddhist
monks might be content to cultivate their own gardens and ignore the
rest of the world. After all, modern ecological political movements are
largely products of rich societies with threatened environments. Might
the most precarious ecologies display — by necessity — the greatest
ecological concern? If that is the case, is the renewed popularity of environmental movements in our own age at least a sign of hope?

15

Overseas Expansion
in the Early Modern Period

China and Europe, 1400–1600

HISTORICAL CONTEXT

Between 1400 and 1500, the balance between Chinese and European sea power changed drastically. Before 1434, Chinese shipbuilding was the envy of the world. Chinese ships were larger, more numerous, safer, and better outfitted than European ships. The Chinese navy made frequent trips through the South China Sea to the Spice Islands, through the Indian Ocean, and as far as East Africa and the Persian Gulf (see Map 15.1). Every island, port, and kingdom along the route was integrated into the Chinese system of tributaries. Goods were exchanged, marriages arranged, and princes taken to visit the Chinese emperor.

In the second half of the fifteenth century, the Chinese navy virtually disappeared. At the same time, the Portuguese began a series of explorations down the coast of Africa and into the Atlantic Ocean. In 1434, Portuguese ships rounded the treacherous Cape Bojador, just south of Morocco. In 1488, Bartolomeu Dias rounded the Cape of Good Hope. Vasco da Gama sailed into the Indian Ocean, arriving in Calicut the following year. And in 1500 a fortuitous landfall in Brazil by Pedro Cabral gave the Portuguese a claim from the western Atlantic to the Indian Ocean. By 1512, Portuguese ships had reached the Bandas and Moluccas — the Spice Islands of what is today eastern Indonesia.

Beginning in 1492, after the defeat of the Moors (Muslims) and the voyages of Columbus, the Spanish claimed most of the Western Hemisphere until challenged by the Dutch, English, and French. European control in the Americas penetrated far deeper than in Asia, where it was limited to enclaves on the coast, and where European nations were in an almost perpetual state of war with each other. Taken together, the nations of Western Europe dominated the seas of the world after 1500 (see Map 15.2).

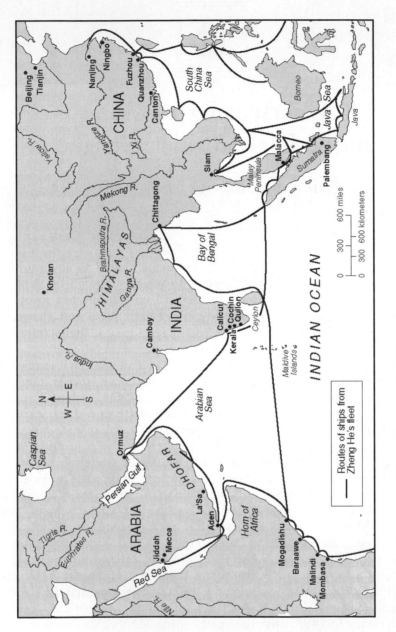

Map 15.1 Chinese Naval Expeditions, 1405–1433.

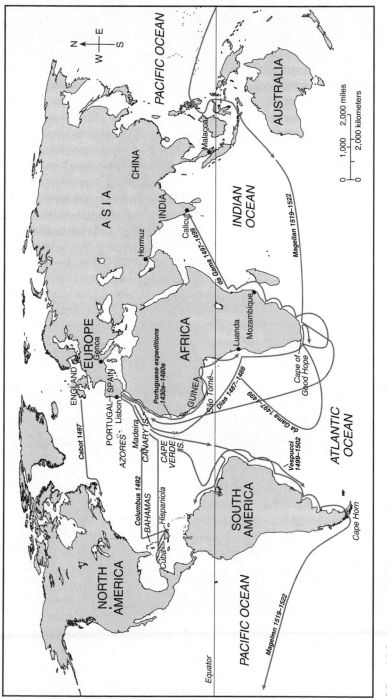

Map 15.2 European Overseas Exploration, 1430s–1530s.

What accounts for the different fortunes of China and Europe in the fifteenth century? Were the decline of China and the rise of Europe inevitable? Probably no objective observer of the time would have thought so. In what ways were the expansions of China and Europe similar? In what ways were they different? Think about these questions as you reflect on the readings in this chapter.

THINKING HISTORICALLY
Reading Primary and Secondary Sources

This chapter contains both primary and secondary sources. *Primary sources* are actual pieces of the past and include anything — art, letters, essays, and so on — from the historical period being studied. If a future historian were to study and research students in American colleges at the beginning of the twenty-first century, some primary sources might include diaries, letters, cartoons, music videos, posters, paintings, e-mail messages, blogs and Web sites, class notes, school newspapers, tests, and official and unofficial records. *Secondary sources* are usually books and articles *about* the past — interpretations of the past. These sources are "secondary" because they must be based on primary sources; therefore, a history written after an event occurs is a secondary source.

In your studies, you will be expected to distinguish primary from secondary sources. A quick glance at the introductions to this chapter's selections tells you that the first article is written by a modern journalist and the third and fifth are written by an amateur historian and an environmentalist, taken from books published in 2003 and 1991, respectively. In contrast, the second selection, an inscription ordered by Admiral Zheng He* that dates from the fifteenth century, and the fourth selection, a letter penned by Christopher Columbus more than five hundred years ago, are firsthand accounts of worlds long past.

Having determined whether selections are primary or secondary sources, we also explore some of the subtle complexities that are overlooked by such designations.

Note: Pronunciations of difficult-to-pronounce terms will be given throughout the chapter. The emphasis goes on the syllable appearing in all capital letters. [Ed.]
*jung HUH

94

JOSEPH KAHN

"China Has an Ancient Mariner to Tell You About"

In this 2005 *New York Times* article journalist Joseph Kahn, currently Beijing bureau chief for the *Times*, combines a brief history of the life of Zheng He with a critical view of recent Chinese government efforts at reviving the reputation of the fifteenth-century admiral. Who was Zheng He? Why, according to Kahn, is China focusing attention on him?

Thinking Historically

Newspaper stories are not primary sources — unless the subject is the newspaper itself, the reporter of the story, or the way in which newspapers presented the particular story. Some historians would say that a newspaper story as brief as this one is hardly even a secondary source because it tells us very little of what modern historians know about Zheng He. For an understanding of the great Chinese admiral, this might better be called a third level, or tertiary, source. Still, even a news story must rely on sources. What primary and secondary sources does this article refer to?

The captivating tale of Zheng He, a Chinese eunuch who explored the Pacific and Indian Oceans with a mighty armada almost a century before Columbus discovered America, has long languished as a tantalizing footnote in China's imperial history.

Zheng He (pronounced jung huh) fell into disfavor before he completed the last of his early 15th-century voyages, and most historical records were destroyed. Authorities protected his old family home in Nanjing, but it was often shuttered, its rooms used to store unrelated relics.

Joseph Kahn, "Letter from Asia: China Has an Ancient Mariner to Tell You About," *New York Times*, July 20, 2005, Section A, p. 4.

Now, on the 600th anniversary of Zheng He's first mission in 1405, all that is changing. Zheng He's legacy is being burnished — some critics say glossed over — to give rising China a new image on the world stage.

Books and television shows, replicas of Zheng He's ships and a new $50 million museum in Nanjing promote Zheng He as a maritime cultural ambassador for a powerful but ardently peaceful nation.

Officials have even endorsed the theory, so far unproven, that one of Zheng He's ships foundered on the rocks near Lamu island, off the coast of today's Kenya, with survivors swimming ashore, marrying locals and creating a family of Chinese-Africans that is now being reunited with the Chinese motherland.

The message is that Zheng He foreshadowed China's 21st-century emergence as a world power, though one that differs in crucial respects from Spain, Britain, France, Germany, Japan, and, most pointedly, the United States.

"In the heyday of the Ming Dynasty, China did not seek hegemony," says Wan Ming, a leading scholar of the era. "Today, we are once again growing stronger all the time, and China's style of peaceful development has been welcomed all over the world."

The Communist Party hopes to signal to its own people that it has recaptured past glory, while reassuring foreign countries that China can be strong and non-threatening at the same time.

Even within China, though, the use of poorly documented history as a modern propaganda prop has generated a backlash.

Several scholars have publicly criticized the campaign as a distortion, saying Zheng He treated foreigners as barbarians and most foreign countries as vassal states. His voyages amounted to a wasteful tribute to a maniacal emperor, some argue.

Zheng He resonates, favorably or not, in Asia. Arguably for the first time since his final voyage in 1433, China is vying to become a major maritime power.

Beijing has upgraded its navy with Russian-built Sovremenny-class guided missile destroyers, Kilo-class diesel submarines, and a new nuclear submarine equipped to carry intercontinental ballistic missiles. It has flirted with the idea of building an aircraft carrier, according to conflicting reports in state media.

Sustained double-digit increases in defense spending have helped make China one of the largest military powers in the world, though still well behind the United States. China says it aims only to defend itself. But others are skeptical.

"Since no nation threatens China, one wonders: why this growing investment?" Defense Secretary Donald H. Rumsfeld asked recently in a speech on China's buildup during a visit to Singapore last month.

Beijing clearly hopes history will help answer the question.

Zheng He was a Chinese Muslim who, following the custom of the day, was castrated so he could serve in the household of a prince, Zhu Di.*

Zhu Di later toppled the emperor, his brother, and took the throne for himself. He rewarded Zheng He, his co-conspirator, with command of the greatest naval expedition that the world had ever seen. Beginning in July 1405, Zheng He made port calls all around Southeast Asia, rounded India, explored the Middle East and reached the eastern coast of Africa.

The three ships Columbus guided across the Atlantic 87 years later, the Niña, Pinta, and Santa María, could fit inside a single large vessel in Zheng He's armada, which at its peak had up to 300 ships and 30,000 sailors. Some of China's maritime innovations at the time, including watertight compartments, did not show up on European vessels for hundreds of years.

Zheng He was China's first big ocean trader, presenting gifts from the emperor to leaders in foreign ports and hauling back crabapples, myrrh, mastic gum, and even a giraffe.

In time, though, the emperor turned against seafaring, partly because of the exorbitant cost, partly because of China's religious certitude that it had nothing to learn from the outside world. By the latter part of the 15th century the country had entered a prolonged period of self-imposed isolation that lasted into the 20th century, leaving European powers to rule the seas.

For Chinese officials today, the sudden end of China's maritime ambitions 600 years ago conveniently signals something else: that China is a gentle giant with enduring good will.

Zheng He represents China's commitment to "good neighborliness, peaceful coexistence, and scientific navigation," government-run China Central Television said during an hour-long documentary on the explorer last week.

Earlier this month, authorities opened a $50 million memorial to Zheng He. Tributes to him fill courtyard-style exhibition halls, painted in stately vermillion and imperial yellow. A hulking statue of Zheng He, his chest flung forward as in many Communist-era likenesses of Mao, decorates the main hall.

As the Zheng He anniversary approached, delegations of Chinese diplomats and scholars also traveled to Kenya to investigate the claims that islanders there could trace their roots to sailors on Zheng He's fleet.

On one remote island, called Siyu, the Chinese found a 19-year-old high school student, Mwamaka Sharifu, who claimed Chinese ancestry.

*zhoo DEE

Beijing's embassy in Nairobi arranged for her to visit China to attend Zheng He celebrations. Beijing has invited her back to study in China, tuition-free, this fall.

"My family members have round faces, small eyes, and black hair, so we long believed we are Chinese," Ms. Sharifu said in a telephone interview. "Now we have a direct link to China itself."

The outreach effort has generated positive publicity for China in Kenya and some other African countries, as well as around Southeast Asia, where Zheng He is widely admired.

But Zheng He has been more coolly received by some scholars in China and abroad.

Geoff Wade, a China specialist at the National University of Singapore, argued in an academic essay that Zheng He helped the Ming state colonize neighboring countries. His far-flung expeditions aimed at enforcing a "pax Ming" through Southeast Asia, allowing China to wrest control of trade routes dominated at that time by Arabs, he wrote.

Several Chinese experts also questioned whether Zheng He's legacy is as salutary as government officials hope.

Ye Jun, a Beijing historian, said the official contention that Zheng He was a good-will ambassador is a "one-sided interpretation that blindly ignores the objective fact that Zheng He engaged in military suppression" to achieve the emperor's goals.

"These matters should be left to scholars," Mr. Ye said.

$$\boxed{95}$$

ZHENG HE

Inscription to the Goddess

This inscription was carved on a stone erected to the Chinese Daoist goddess called the Celestial Spouse at Changle in Fujian Province of China in 1431. Zheng He left other inscriptions to other deities on his travels so it would be a mistake to read much of a religious motive in this act by the admiral who had been raised a Muslim. In fact, in

Zheng He, "Inscription to the Goddess," in *China and Africa in the Middle Ages*, ed. Teobaldo Filesi, trans. David L. Morrison (London: Frank Cass, 1972), 57–61. Americanized and slightly simplified.

1411, Zheng He erected a monument in Sri Lanka dedicated to three deities in three languages. The Chinese portion praised Buddha, a section in Tamil was dedicated to the god Tenavarai-Nayanar, and a third section in Persian was inscribed to Allah.

This selection conveys some idea of how Zheng He must have perceived his mission or wanted it to be understood. Judging from this inscription, would you call Zheng He, to use Joseph Kahn's terms, a good-will ambassador or a military oppressor?

Thinking Historically

Primary sources like this one can be difficult for a modern reader to interpret because they were not written for us, but for another audience in a different time. A modern journalist like Joseph Kahn speaks directly to us; the fifteenth-century mariner does not. This lack of "fit" between ancient source and modern ear can actually be a benefit, however, because it better enables us to distinguish fact from propaganda, truth from spin. As you read this selection, ask yourself what the author wants the reader to believe and what in his writing he could not have crafted for the purpose of persuading or fooling the audience. Your answer to the latter part of this question provides us with historical knowledge of a high degree of certainty.

For an example of how this works, look at the first sentence, the title that declares the nature of the inscription: "Record of the miraculous answer (to prayer) of the goddess the Celestial Spouse." We *do not* learn from this that the author received a miraculous answer to his prayer. We cannot even be sure that he thought he did (since he may not be telling the truth). But we do learn some things beyond doubt. We learn from this sentence that some Chinese believed in a goddess called "the Celestial Spouse." We learn that some Chinese prayed to the goddess and that some believed she could provide "miraculous answers." We learn all of these things because the inscription would make no sense otherwise. These are the assumptions rather than the arguments of the inscription. We learn from primary sources by asking about the things they *assume*. Try this exercise with the rest of the selection.

Record of the miraculous answer (to prayer) of the goddess the Celestial Spouse.

The Imperial Ming Dynasty unifying seas and continents, surpassing the three dynasties even goes beyond the Han and Tang dynasties. The countries beyond the horizon and from the ends of the earth have all become subjects and to the most western of the western or the most northern of the northern countries, however far they may be, the distance and the routes may be calculated. Thus the barbarians from beyond the seas, though their countries are truly distant, have come to audience bearing precious objects and presents.

The Emperor, approving of their loyalty and sincerity, has ordered Zheng He and others at the head of several tens of thousands of officers and flag-troops to ascend more than one hundred large ships to go and confer presents on them in order to make manifest the transforming power of the imperial virtue and to treat distant people with kindness. From the third year of Yongle (1405) till now we have seven times received the commission of ambassadors to countries of the western ocean. The barbarian countries which we have visited are: by way of Zhancheng (Champa), Zhaowa (Java), Sanfoqi (Palembang) and Xianle (Siam) crossing straight over to Xilanshan (Ceylon) in South India, Guli (Calicut), and Kezhi (Cochin), we have gone to the western regions Hulumosi (Hormuz), Adan (Aden), Mugudushu (Mogadishu), altogether more than thirty countries large and small. We have traversed more than one hundred thousand li[1] of immense water spaces and have beheld in the ocean huge waves like mountains rising sky-high, and we have set eyes on barbarian regions far away hidden in a blue transparency of light vapors, while our sails loftily unfurled like clouds day and night continued their course rapid like a star, traversing those savage waves as if we were treading a public thoroughfare. Truly this was due to the majesty and the good fortune of the Court and moreover we owe it to the protecting virtue of the divine Celestial Spouse.

The power of the goddess having indeed been manifested in previous times has been abundantly revealed in the present generation. In the midst of the rushing waters it happened that, when there was a hurricane, suddenly there was a divine lantern shining in the mast, and as soon as this miraculous light appeared the danger was appeased, so that even in the danger of capsizing one felt reassured that there was no cause for fear. When we arrived in the distant countries we captured alive those of the native kings who were not respectful and exterminated those barbarian robbers who were engaged in piracy, so that consequently the sea route was cleansed and pacified and the natives put their trust in it. All this is due to the favors of the goddess.

It is not easy to enumerate completely all the cases where the goddess has answered prayers. Previously in a memorial to the Court we have requested that her virtue be registered in the Court of Sacrificial Worship and a temple be built at Nanking on the bank of the dragon river where regular sacrifices should be transmitted forever. We have respectfully received an Imperial commemorative composition exalting the miraculous favors, which is the highest recompense and praise in-

---

[1]A li = ⅓ mile. [Ed.]

deed. However, the miraculous power of the goddess resides wherever one goes. As for the temporary palace on the southern mountain at Changle, I have, at the head of the fleet, frequently resided there awaiting the favorable wind to set sail for the ocean.

We, Zheng He and others, on the one hand have received the high favor of a gracious commission of our Sacred Lord, and on the other hand carry to the distant barbarians the benefits of respect and good faith. Commanding the multitudes on the fleet and being responsible for a quantity of money and valuables, in the face of the violence of the winds and the nights, our one fear is not to be able to succeed; how should we then dare not to serve our dynasty with exertion of all our loyalty and the gods with the utmost sincerity? How would it be possible not to realize what is the source of the tranquility of the fleet and the troops and the salvation on the voyage both going and returning? Therefore we have made manifest the virtue of the goddess on stone and have moreover recorded the years and months of the voyages to the barbarian countries and the return in order to leave the memory for ever.

I. In the third year of Yongle (1405) commanding the fleet we went to Guli (Calicut) and other countries. At that time the pirate Chen Zuyi had gathered his followers in the country of Sanfoqi (Palembang), where he plundered the native merchants. When he also advanced to resist our fleet, supernatural soldiers secretly came to the rescue so that after one beating of the drum he was annihilated. In the fifth year (1407) we returned.

II. In the fifth year of Yongle (1407) commanding the fleet we went to Zhaowa (Java), Guli (Calicut), Kezhi (Cochin), and Xianle (Siam). The kings of these countries all sent as tribute precious objects, precious birds, and rare animals. In the seventh year (1409) we returned.

III. In the seventh year of Yongle (1409) commanding the fleet we went to the countries visited before and took our route by the country of Xilanshan (Ceylon). Its king Yaliekunaier (Alagakkonara) was guilty of a gross lack of respect and plotted against the fleet. Owing to the manifest answer to prayer of the goddess the plot was discovered and thereupon that king was captured alive. In the ninth year (1411) on our return the king was presented to the throne as a prisoner; subsequently he received the Imperial favor of returning to his own country.

IV. In the eleventh year of Yongle (1413) commanding the fleet we went to Hulumosi (Ormuz) and other countries. In the country of Sumendala (Samudra)[2] there was a false king Suganla (Sekandar) who was marauding and invading his country. Its king Cainu-liabiding

---

[2]Kerala, India. [Ed.]

(Zaynu-'l-Abidin) had sent an envoy to the Palace Gates in order to lodge a complaint. We went thither with the official troops under our command and exterminated some and arrested other rebels, and owing to the silent aid of the goddess we captured the false king alive. In the thirteenth year (1415) on our return he was presented to the Emperor as a prisoner. In that year the king of the country of Manlajia (Malacca) came in person with his wife and son to present tribute.

V. In the fifteenth year of Yongle (1417) commanding the fleet we visited the western regions. The country of Hulumosi (Ormuz) presented lions, leopards with gold spots, and large western horses. The country of Adan (Aden) presented qilin of which the native name is culafa (giraffe), as well as the long-horned animal maha (oryx). The country of Mugudushu (Mogadishu) presented huafu lu ("striped" zebras) as well as lions. The country of Bulawa (Brava)[3] presented camels which run one thousand li as well as camel-birds (ostriches). The countries of Zhaowa (Java) and Guli (Calicut) presented the animal miligao. They all vied in presenting the marvelous objects preserved in the mountains or hidden in the seas and the beautiful treasures buried in the sand or deposited on the shores. Some sent a maternal uncle of the king, others a paternal uncle or a younger brother of the king in order to present a letter of homage written on gold leaf as well as tribute.

VI. In the nineteenth year of Yongle (1421) commanding the fleet we conducted the ambassadors from Hulumosi (Ormuz) and the other countries that had been in attendance at the capital for a long time back to their countries. The kings of all these countries prepared even more tribute than previously.

VII. In the sixth year of Xuande (1431) once more commanding the fleet we have left for the barbarian countries in order to read to them (an Imperial edict) and to confer presents.

We have anchored in this port awaiting a north wind to take the sea, and recalling how previously we have on several occasions received the benefits of the protection of the divine intelligence we have thus recorded an inscription in stone.

---

[3]Baraawe, Somalia. [Ed.]

GAVIN MENZIES

From 1421: The Year China Discovered America

Writer Gavin Menzies has recently caused a stir among historians by arguing in his book *1421: The Year China Discovered America* that Zheng He's ships actually reached America. This selection from that same work contains the author's more reliable discussion of the preparations for the great Chinese naval expedition of 1421, Zheng He's sixth, setting events in the broader context of Chinese imperial history and its tribute system.

As Zheng He indicated in the "Inscription to the Goddess" (selection 95), the 1421 voyage was intended to return a number of foreign ambassadors to their home countries after they had participated in the inauguration of the emperor Zhu Di's new capital city at Beijing. How was such a voyage part of the Chinese system of trade and diplomacy? What did the Chinese stand to gain by such a system? What did those tribute-paying countries gain? Does Menzies's description support the Chinese government claim that the tribute system was peaceful, or does it seem to be the "military suppression" charged by at least one historian (see selection 94)?

Thinking Historically

This is clearly a secondary source. It depends on many primary and other secondary sources. As indicated in the first selection of this chapter, the gathering of primary sources about the Chinese treasure ships suffers from severe limitations. Most of the imperial archives as well as the ships were destroyed by the successor Ming emperors after 1435. Persuaded by the traditional Confucian bureaucracy to abandon the naval ventures favored by palace eunuchs, later emperors even banned Chinese habitation along the coastal corridor of the China Sea.

For this selection, however, on the preparations for the voyage of 1421, Gavin Menzies is able to use available primary and secondary sources on various aspects of Ming Chinese society and culture. Notice also how he uses information from other cultures and other periods to

Gavin Menzies, *1421: The Year China Discovered America* (New York: HarperCollins, 2003), 60–71.

help the reader understand the scale of these Ming treasure ships. The ordinary reader cannot distinguish Menzies's assumptions from his arguments as easily as with a primary source. One tends to read a secondary source less critically than a primary source. Nevertheless, what are the advantages of a secondary source like this? Without checking the footnotes (and Menzies provides very few), which of the details or interpretations in this selection are you most inclined to question? Why?

Chinese foreign policy was quite different from that of the Europeans who followed them to the Indian Ocean many years later. The Chinese preferred to pursue their aims by trade, influence, and bribery rather than by open conflict and direct colonization. Zhu Di's policy was to despatch huge armadas every few years throughout the known world, bearing gifts and trade goods; the massive treasure ships carrying a huge array of guns and a travelling army of soldiers were also a potent reminder of his imperial might: China alone had the necessary firepower to protect friendly countries from invasion and quash insurrections against their rulers. The treasure ships returned to China with all manner of exotic items: "dragon saliva [ambergris], incense and golden amber" and "lions, gold spotted leopards and camel-birds [ostriches] which are six or seven feet tall" from Africa; gold cloth from Calicut in south-west India, studded with pearls and precious stones; elephants, parrots, sandalwood, peacocks, hardwood, incense, tin, and cardamom from Siam (modern Thailand).

Those rulers who accepted the emperor's overlordship were rewarded with titles, protection, and trade missions. In south-east Asia, Malacca was rewarded for its loyalty by being promoted as a trading port at the expense of Java and Sumatra; the emperor even personally composed a poem for the Malaccan sultan, and can be said to have been the founder of Malaysia. The subservient Siamese were also extended trading privileges to the detriment of the truculent Cambodians. Korea was especially important to China: Zhu Di lost no time in despatching an envoy to the King of Korea, Yi Pang-Won, granting him an honorary Chinese title. The Koreans needed Chinese medicine, books, and astronomical instruments, and in return they agreed to set up an observatory to co-operate with Zhu Di in charting the world. They traded leopards, seals, gold, silver and horses — one thousand of them in 1403, ten thousand the next year. Despite some reluctance, they also found it expedient to comply with Chinese requests to fill Zhu Di's harem with virgins. Many Korean ships were to join the Chinese fleets when they left to sail the world.

As soon as he had expelled the last Mongols from China in 1382, Zhu Di had despatched his eunuch Isiha to the perennially troublesome region of Manchuria in the far north-east, and in 1413 the Jurchen people of Manchuria responded by sending a prestigious mission to Beijing, where its members were showered with titles, gifts, and trading rights. Japan was also assiduously courted. The third Ashikaga Shogun Yoshimitsu was a Sinophile[1]; he lost no time in kow-towing as "your subject, the King of Japan." His reward was a string of special ports opened to promote trade with Japan, at Ningbo, Quanzhou, and Guangdong (Canton). Like Korea, Japan also set up an observatory to aid Zhu Di's astronomical research, and Japanese ships also joined the globetrotting Chinese convoys.

Having pacified Manchuria and brought Korea and Japan into the Chinese tribute system, Zhu Di next turned his attention to Tibet. Another court eunuch, Hau-Xian, led a mission to court the famous holy man the Karmapa, leader of one of the four sects of Tibetan Buddhism, and bring him to China. When he arrived, a procession of Buddhist monks met him outside the city and Zhu Di bestowed upon him the title "Divine Son of India Below the Sky and Upon the Earth, Inventor of the Alphabet, Incarnated Buddha, Maintainer of the Kingdom's Prosperity, Source of Rhetoric." The emperor then presented the Karmapa with a square black hat bearing a diamond-studded emblem. It has been worn by successive incarnations of the Karmapa ever since.

Joining China's tribute system also gave rulers and their envoys the opportunity to visit the capital of the oldest and finest civilization in the world. The traditional imperial capital of Nanjing had received dignitaries from around the world, and now the new capital of Beijing began to welcome the latest arrivals. Although the emperor's main concern was to awe all countries into becoming tribute-bearing states, great efforts were also made to learn about their history, geography, manners, and customs. Beijing was to be not only the world's greatest city but its intellectual capital, with encyclopedias and libraries covering every subject known to man. In December 1404, Zhu Di had appointed two long-time advisers, Yao Guang Xiao and Lui Chi'ih, assisted by 2,180 scholars, to take charge of a project, the Yong-le-Dadian, to preserve all known literature and knowledge. It was the largest scholarly enterprise ever undertaken. The result, a massive encyclopedia of four thousand volumes containing some fifty million characters, was completed just before the Forbidden City was inaugurated.

In parallel with this great endeavour, Zhu Di ordered the opinions of 120 philosophers and sages of the Song dynasty to be collated and stored in the Forbidden City together with the complete commentaries of thinkers from the eleventh to the thirteenth centuries. In addition to this wealth of academic knowledge, hundreds of printed novels could be bought from Beijing market stalls. There was nothing remotely

[1]A lover of China and things Chinese. [Ed.]

comparable anywhere in the world. Printing was unknown in Europe — Gutenberg did not complete his printed Bible for another thirty years — and though Europe was on the eve of the Renaissance that was to transform its culture and scientific knowledge, it lagged far behind China. The library of Henry V (1387–1422) comprised six handwritten books, three of which were on loan to him from a nunnery, and the Florentine Francesco Datini, the wealthiest European merchant of the same era, possessed twelve books, eight of which were on religious subjects.

The voyage to the intellectual paradise of Beijing also offered foreign potentates and envoys many earthly delights. Carried in sumptuous comfort aboard the leviathan ships, they consumed the finest foods and wines, and pleasured themselves with the concubines whose only role was to please these foreign dignitaries. The formal inauguration of the Forbidden City was followed by a sumptuous banquet. Its scale and opulence emphasized China's position at the summit of the civilized world. In comparison, Europe was backward, crude, and barbaric. Henry V's marriage to Catherine of Valois took place in London just three weeks after the inauguration of the Forbidden City. Twenty-six thousand guests were entertained in Beijing, where they ate a ten-course banquet served on dishes of the finest porcelain; a mere six hundred guests attended Henry's nuptials and they were served stockfish (salted cod) on rounds of stale bread that acted as plates. Catherine de Valois wore neither knickers nor stockings at her wedding; Zhu Di's favourite concubine was clad in the finest silks and her jewellery included cornelians from Persia, rubies from Sri Lanka, Indian diamonds and jade from Kotan (in Chinese Turkestan). Her perfume contained ambergris from the Pacific, myrrh from Arabia, and sandalwood from the Spice Islands. China's army numbered one million men, armed with guns; Henry V could put five thousand men in the field, armed only with longbows, swords, and pikes. The fleet that would carry Zhu Di's guests home numbered over a hundred ships with a complement of thirty thousand men; when Henry went to war against France in June of that year, he ferried his army across the Channel in four fishing boats, carrying a hundred men on each crossing and sailing only in daylight hours.

For a further month after the inauguration of the Forbidden City, the rulers and envoys in Beijing were provided with lavish imperial hospitality — the finest foods and wines, the most splendid entertainments and the most beautiful concubines, skilled in the arts of love. Finally, on 3 March 1421, a great ceremony was mounted to commemorate the departure of the envoys for their native lands. A vast honour guard was assembled: "First came commanders of ten thousands, next commanders of thousands, all numbering about one hundred thousand men. . . . Behind them stood troops in serried ranks, two hundred thousand strong. . . . The whole body . . . stood so silent it seemed there was not a breathing soul there." At noon precisely, cymbals clashed, elephants lowered their trunks, and clouds of smoke wafted from incense-holders in the shape of tortoises and cranes. The emperor appeared, striding through the smoke to present the departing ambassadors with their farewell gifts — crates of blue and white porcelain, rolls of silk, bundles of cotton cloth, and bamboo cases of jade. His great fleets stood ready to carry them back to Hormuz, Aden, La'Sa, and Dhofar in Arabia; to Mogadishu, Brava, Malindi, and Mombasa in Africa; to Sri Lanka, Calicut, Cochin, and Cambay in India; to Japan, Vietnam, Java, Sumatra, Malacca, and Borneo in south-east Asia, and elsewhere.

Admiral Zheng He, dressed in his formal uniform — a long red robe and a tall black hat — presented the emperor with his compliments and reported that an armada comprising four of the emperor's great fleets was ready to set sail; the fifth, commanded by Grand Eunuch Yang Qing, had put to sea the previous month. The return of the envoys to their homelands was only the first part of this armada's overall mission. It was then to "proceed all the way to the end of the earth to collect tribute from the barbarians beyond the seas . . . to attract all under heaven to be civilised in Confucian harmony." Zheng He's reward for his lifelong, devoted service to his emperor had been the command of five previous treasure fleets tasked with promoting Chinese trade and influence in Asia, India, Africa, and the Middle East. Now he was to lead one of the largest armadas the world had ever seen. Zhu Di had also rewarded other eunuchs for their part in helping him to liberate China. Many of the army commanders in the war against the Mongols were now admirals and captains of his treasure fleets. Zheng He had become a master of delegation. By the fourth voyage fleets were sailing separately. On this great sixth voyage loyal eunuchs would command separate fleets. Zheng He would lead them to the Indian Ocean then return home confident that they would handle their fleets as he had taught them.

The envoys' parting gifts were packed into their carriages, the emperor made a short speech, and then, after kow-towing one last time, the envoys embarked and the procession moved off. Servants ran behind the carriages as they rumbled down to the Grand Canal a mile to the east of the city. There, a fleet of barges decked with silk awnings awaited them. Teams of horses, ten to twelve for each barge, stood on the banks, bamboo poles tied to their harnesses. When the envoys were aboard, whips cracked and the sturdy animals began to drag the barges on their slow journey down to the coast.

Two days and thirty-six locks later, they arrived at Tanggu (near the modern city of Tianjin) on the Yellow Sea. The sight that greeted the envoys at Tanggu was one that must have lingered long in their minds. More than one hundred huge junks rode at anchor, towering above the watchers on the quayside — the ships were taller by far than the thatched houses lining the bay. Surrounding them was a fleet of smaller merchant ships. Each capital ship was about 480 feet in length (444 *chi*, the standard Chinese unit of measurement, equivalent to about 12.5 inches or 32 centimetres) and 180 feet across — big enough to swallow fifty fishing boats. On the prow, glaring serpents' eyes served to frighten away evil spirits. Pennants streamed from the tips of a forest of a thousand masts; below them great sails of red silk, light but immensely strong, were furled on each ship's nine masts. "When their sails are spread, they are like great clouds in the sky."

The armada was composed very much like a Second World War convoy. At the centre were the great leviathan flagships, surrounded by a host of merchant junks, most 90 feet long and 30 feet wide. Around the perimeters were squadrons of fast, manoeuvrable warships. As the voyage progressed, trading ships of several other nations, especially Japan, Korea, Burma, Vietnam, and India, joined the convoy, taking advantage of the protection afforded by the warships and the opportunities offered as the magnificent armada, almost a trading country in its own right, swept over the oceans. By the time it reached Calicut, it comprised more than eight hundred vessels whose combined population exceeded that of any city between China and India. Each treasure ship had sixteen internal watertight compartments, any two of which could be flooded without sinking the ship. Some internal compartments could also be partially flooded to act as tanks for the trained sea-otters used in fishing, or for use by divers entering and leaving the sea. The otters, held on long cords, were employed to herd shoals of fish into nets, a method still practised in parts of China, Malaysia, and Bengal today. The admiral's sea cabin was above the stern of his flagship. Below were sixty staterooms for foreign ambassadors, envoys and their entourages. Their concubines were housed in adjacent cabins and most had balconies overlooking the sea. Chinese ambassadors, one for each country to be visited, were housed in less grand but nonetheless spacious apartments. Each ambassador had ten assistants as *chefs de protocol* and a further fifty-two eunuchs served as secretaries. The crewmen's quarters were on the lower decks.

In 1407, Zheng He had established a language school in Nanjing, the Ssu-i-Quan (Si Yi Guan), to train interpreters, and sixteen of its finest graduates travelled with the fleets, enabling the admirals to communicate with rulers from India to Africa in Arabic, Persian, Swahili, Hindi, Tamil, and many other languages. Zhu Di and Zheng He also actively sought out foreign navigators and cartographers; the diaries of one of them, an Indonesian by the name of Master Bentun, have survived. Religious tolerance was one of Zhu Di's great virtues, and the junks also habitually carried Islamic, Hindu, and Buddhist savants to provide advice and guidance. Buddhism, with its teachings of universal compassion and tolerance, had been the religion of the majority of the Chinese people for centuries. Buddhism in no way conflicted with Confucianism, which could be said to be a code of civic values rather than a religion. On this sixth and final voyage of the treasure fleets which would last until 1423, the Buddhist monk Sheng Hui and the religious leaders Ha San and Pu He Ri were aboard. After the inauguration of the Forbidden City and the dedication of the awesome encyclopedia the Yong-le-Dadian, thousands of scholars found themselves without an obvious role. It would have been natural for Zhu Di to send them overseas on the great voyages of exploration. Through interpreters, Chinese mathematicians, astronomers, navigators, engineers, and architects would have been able to converse with and learn from their counterparts throughout the Indian Ocean. Once the ambassadors and their entourages had disembarked, the vast ships with their labyrinths of cabins would have been well suited to use as laboratories for scientific experiments. Metallurgists could prospect for minerals in the countries the Chinese visited, physicians could search out new healing plants, medicines, and treatments that might help to combat plagues and epidemics, and botanists could propagate valuable food plants. Chinese agricultural scientists and farmers had millennia of experience of developing and propagating hybrids.

The native Chinese flora is perhaps the richest in the world: "In wealth of its endemic species and in the extent of the genus and species potential of its cultivated plants, China is conspicuous among other centres of origin of plant forms. Moreover the species are usually represented by enormous numbers of botanical varieties and hereditary forms." In Europe, a long period of economic and agricultural decline followed the fall of the Roman Empire. The plant forms known to the Western world from Theophrastus to the German fathers of botany show that European knowledge had slumped, but there was no corresponding "dark age" in Chinese scientific history. Botanical knowledge, and the number of plant species recorded by the Chinese, grew steadily as the centuries passed. The contrast between the voyages of discovery of the Chinese and those of the Europeans cannot be overestimated. The only interest of the Spanish and Portuguese was in gathering sustenance, gold, and spices, while warding off attacks from the natives. The great Chinese fleets undertook scientific expeditions the Europeans could not even begin to equal in scale or scope until Captain Cook set sail three and a half centuries later.

As the admirals and envoys embarked, and the armada was readied for sea, the water around the great ships was still black with smaller craft shuttling from ship to shore. For days the port had been in turmoil as cartloads of vegetables and dried fish and hundreds of tons of water were hauled aboard to provision this armada of thirty thousand men for their voyage. Even at this late hour, barges were still bringing final supplies of fresh water and rice. The great armada's ships could remain at sea for over three months and cover at least 4,500 miles without making landfall to replenish food or water, for separate grain ships and water tankers sailed with them. The grain ships also carried an array of flora the Chinese intended to plant in foreign lands, some as further benefits of the tribute system and others to provide food for the Chinese colonies that would be created in new lands. Dogs were also taken aboard as pets, others to be bred for food and to hunt rats, and there were coops of Asiatic chickens as valuable presents for foreign dignitaries. The larger ships even kept sties of Chinese pigs. Separate horse-ships carried the mounts for the cavalry.

The staggering size of the individual ships, not to mention the armada itself, can best be understood by comparison with other navies of the same era. In 1421, the next most powerful fleet afloat was that of Venice. The Venetians possessed around three hundred galleys — fast, light, thin-skinned ships built with soft-wood planking, rowed by oarsmen and only suitable for island-hopping in the calm of a Mediterranean summer. The biggest Venetian galleys were some 150 feet long and 20 feet wide and carried at best 50 tons of cargo. In comparison, Zhu Di's treasure ships were ocean-going monsters built of teak. The rudder of one of these great ships stood 36 feet high — almost as long as the whole of the flagship the *Niña* in which Columbus was later to set sail for the New World. Each treasure ship could carry more than two thousand tons of cargo and reach Malacca in five weeks, Hormuz in the Persian Gulf in twelve. They were capable of sailing the wildest oceans of the world, in voyages lasting years at a time. That so many ships were lost on the Chinese voyages of discovery testifies not to any lack of strength in their construction but rather to the perilous, uncharted waters they explored and the hurricanes and tsunami they encountered along rocky coasts and razor-sharp coral reefs to the ice-strewn oceans of the far north and far south. Venetian galleys were protected by archers; Chinese ships were armed with gunpowder weapons, brass and iron cannon, mortars, flaming arrows, and exploding shells that sprayed excrement over their adversaries. In every single respect — construction, cargo capacity, damage control, armament, range, communications, the ability to navigate in the trackless ocean and to repair and maintain their ships at sea for months on end — the Chinese were centuries ahead of Europe. Admiral Zheng He would have had no difficulty in destroying any fleet that crossed his path. A battle between this Chinese armada and the other navies of the world combined would have resembled one between a pack of sharks and a shoal of sprats.

By the end of the middle watch — four in the morning — the last provisions had been lashed down and the armada weighed anchor. A prayer was said to Ma Tsu, Taoist goddess of the sea, and then, as their red silk sails slowly filled, the ships, resembling great houses, gathered way before the winds of the north-east monsoon. As they sailed out across the Yellow Sea, the last flickering lights of Tanggu faded into the darkness while the sailors clustered at the rails, straining for a last sight of their homeland. In the long months they would spend travelling the oceans, their only remaining links to the land would be memories, keepsakes, and the scented roses many brought with them, growing them in pots and even sharing their water rations with them. The majority of those seamen at the rails would never see China again. Many would die, many others would be shipwrecked or left behind to set up colonies on foreign shores. Those who eventually returned after two and a half years at sea would find their country convulsed and transformed beyond all recognition.

CHRISTOPHER COLUMBUS
Letter to King Ferdinand and Queen Isabella

Christopher Columbus sent this letter to his royal backers, King Ferdinand and Queen Isabella of Spain, on his return in March 1493 from his first voyage across the Atlantic. (See Map 15.3.)

   An Italian sailor from Genoa, Columbus, in 1483–1484, tried to convince King John II of Portugal to underwrite his plan to sail across the western ocean to the spice-rich East Indies. Relying on a Florentine map that used Marco Polo's overstated distance from Venice to Japan across Asia and an understated estimate of the circumference of the globe, Columbus believed that Japan lay only 2,500 miles west of the Portuguese Azores. King John II rejected the proposal because more accurate estimates indicated that sailing around Africa was the shorter route, a feat achieved in 1488 by Portuguese navigator Bartolomeu Dias.

   Less knowledgeable about navigation, the new Spanish monarchs, Ferdinand and Isabella, supported Columbus and financed his plan to sail west to Asia. In four voyages, Columbus touched a number of Caribbean islands and the coast of Central America, settled Spaniards on Hispaniola (Española), and began to create one of the largest

"First Voyage of Columbus," in *The Four Voyages of Columbus*, ed. Cecil Jane (New York: Dover, 1988), 1–18.

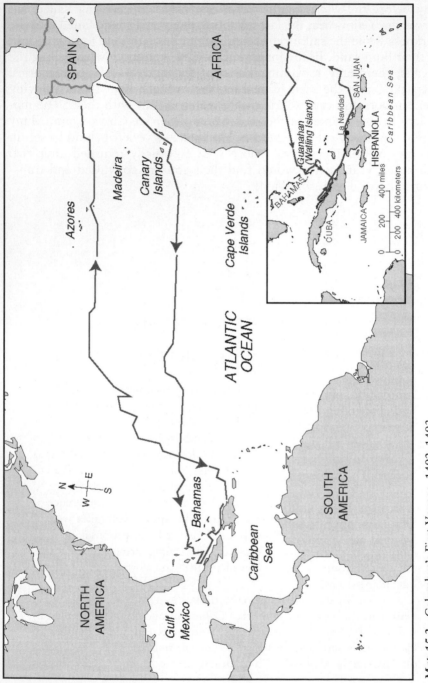

Map 15.3 Columbus's First Voyage, 1492–1493.
Source: Lawrence V. Mott.

empires in world history for Spain — all the while thinking he was near China and Japan, in the realm of the Great Khan whom Marco Polo had met and who had died hundreds of years earlier.

In what ways was the voyage of Columbus similar to that of Zheng He? In what ways was it different? How were the relationships of the explorers with their kings similar and different? Were the motives driving Chinese and European expansion more alike or different?

Thinking Historically

Because this document comes from the period we are studying and is written by Columbus himself, it is a primary source. Primary sources, like this letter and Zheng He's inscription, have a great sense of immediacy and can often "transport" us to the past intellectually. However, involvement when reading does not always lead to understanding, so it is important to think critically about the source and the writer's intended audience as you read. First we must determine the source of the document. Where does it come from? Is it original? If not, is it a copy or a translation? Next, we must determine who wrote it, when it was written, and for what purpose. After answering these questions, we are able to read the document with a critical eye, which leads to greater understanding.

The original letter by Columbus has been lost. This selection is an English translation based on three different printed Spanish versions of the letter. So this text is a reconstruction, not an original, though it is believed to be quite close to the original.

The original letter was probably composed during a relaxed time on the return voyage before its date of February 15, 1493 — possibly as early as the middle of January — and sent to the Spanish monarchs from Lisbon in order to reach them by the time Columbus arrived in Barcelona.

What does Columbus want to impart to Ferdinand and Isabella? First and foremost, he wants them to know that he reached the Indies, that the voyage was a success. And so, the letter's opening sentence tells us something that Columbus certainly did not intend or know. We learn that on his return in 1493, Columbus thought he had been to the Indies when in fact he had not. (It is due to Columbus's confusion that we call the islands he visited the West Indies and Native Americans "Indians.")

Knowing what the author wants a reader to believe is useful information because it serves as a point of reference for other statements the author makes. The success of Columbus's voyage is a case in point. Columbus does not admit to the loss of one of his ships in his letter, nor does he explain fully why he had to build a fort at Navidad and leave some of his crew there, returning home without them. Clearly, Columbus had reason to worry that his voyage would be viewed as a failure. He had not found the gold mines he sought or the Asian cities described by Marco Polo. He thought he had discovered many spices, though only the chili peppers were new. Notice, as you read this letter, how Columbus presents his voyage in the best light.

Aside from what Columbus intends, what facts do you learn from the letter about Columbus, his first voyage, and his encounter with the New World? What seems to drive Columbus to do what he does? What is Columbus's attitude toward the "Indians"? What does Columbus's letter tell us about the society and culture of the Taino* — the people he met in the Caribbean?

Sir, As I know that you will be pleased at the great victory with which Our Lord has crowned my voyage, I write this to you, from which you will learn how in thirty-three days, I passed from the Canary Islands to the Indies with the fleet which the most illustrious king and queen, our sovereigns, gave to me. And there I found very many islands filled with people innumerable, and of them all I have taken possession for their highnesses, by proclamation made and with the royal standard unfurled, and no opposition was offered to me. To the first island which I found, I gave the name *San Salvador*, in remembrance of the Divine Majesty, Who has marvellously bestowed all this; the Indians call it "Guanahani."† To the second, I gave the name *Isla de Santa María de Concepción*; to the third, *Fernandina*; to the fourth, *Isabella*; to the fifth, *Isla Juana*, and so to each one I gave a new name.

When I reached Juana, I followed its coast to the westward, and I found it to be so extensive that I thought that it must be the mainland, the province of Catayo. And since there were neither towns nor villages on the seashore, but only small hamlets, with the people which I could not have speech, because they all fled immediately, I went forward on the same course, thinking that I should not fail to find great cities and towns. And, at the end of many leagues, seeing that there was no change and that the coast was bearing me northwards, which I wished to avoid, since winter was already beginning and I proposed to make from it to the south, and as moreover the wind was carrying me forward, I determined not to wait for a change in the weather and retraced my path as far as a certain harbour known to me. And from that point, I sent two men inland to learn if there were a king or great cities. They travelled three days' journey and found an infinity of small hamlets and people without number, but nothing of importance. For this reason, they returned.

I understood sufficiently from other Indians, whom I had already taken, that this land was nothing but an island. And therefore I fol-

*TY noh
†gwah nah HAH nee

lowed its coast eastwards for one hundred and seven leagues to the point where it ended. And from that cape, I saw another island, distant eighteen leagues from the former, to the east, to which I at once gave the name "Española." And I went there and followed its northern coast, as I had in the case of Juana, to the eastward for one hundred and eighty-eight great leagues in a straight line. This island and all the others are very fertile to a limitless degree, and this island is extremely so. In it there are many harbours on the coast of the sea, beyond comparison with others which I know in Christendom, and many rivers, good and large, which is marvellous. Its lands are high, and there are in it very many sierras and very lofty mountains, beyond comparison with the island of Teneriffe. All are most beautiful, of a thousand shapes, and all are accessible and filled with trees of a thousand kinds and tall, and they seem to touch the sky. And I am told that they never lose their foliage, as I can understand, for I saw them as green and as lovely as they are in Spain in May, and some of them were flowering, some bearing fruit, and some in another stage, according to their nature. And the nightingale was singing and other birds of a thousand kinds in the month of November there where I went. There are six or eight kinds of palm, which are a wonder to behold on account of their beautiful variety, but so are the other trees and fruits and plants. In it are marvellous pine groves, and there are very large tracts of cultivatable lands, and there is honey, and there are birds of many kinds and fruits in great diversity. In the interior are mines of metals, and the population is without number. Española is a marvel.

The sierras and mountains, the plains and arable lands and pastures, are so lovely and rich for planting and sowing, for breeding cattle of every kind, for building towns and villages. The harbours of the sea here are such as cannot be believed to exist unless they have been seen, and so with the rivers, many and great, and good waters, the majority of which contain gold. In the trees and fruits and plants, there is a great difference from those of Juana. In this island, there are many spices and great mines of gold and of other metals.

The people of this island, and of all the other islands which I have found and of which I have information, all go naked, men and women, as their mothers bore them, although some women cover a single place with the leaf of a plant or with a net of cotton which they make for the purpose. They have no iron or steel or weapons, nor are they fitted to use them, not because they are not well built men and of handsome stature, but because they are very marvellously timorous. They have no other arms than weapons made of canes, cut in seeding time, to the ends of which they fix a small sharpened stick. And they do not dare to make use of these, for many times it has happened that I have sent ashore two or three men to some town to have speech, and countless people have come out to them, and as soon as they have seen my men approaching they have fled, even a father not waiting for his son. And this, not because ill has been done to anyone; on the contrary, at every point where I have been and have been able to have speech, I have given to them of all that I had, such as cloth and many other things, without receiving anything for it; but so they are, incurably timid. It is true that, after they have been reassured and have lost their fear, they are so guileless and so generous with all they possess, that no one would believe it who has not seen it. They never refuse anything which they possess, if it be asked of them; on the contrary, they invite anyone to share it, and display as much love as if they would give their hearts, and whether the thing be of value or whether it be of small price, at once with whatever trifle of whatever kind it may be that is given to them, with that they are content. I forbade that they should be given things so worthless as fragments of broken crockery and scraps of broken glass, and ends of straps, although when they were able to get them, they fancied that they possessed the best jewel in the world. So it was found that a sailor for a strap received gold to the weight of two and a half *castellanos*, and others much more for other things which were worth much less. As for new *blancas*, for them they would give everything which they had, although it might be two or three *castellanos'* weight of gold or an *arroba* or two of spun cotton. . . . They took even the pieces of the broken hoops of the wine barrels and, like savages, gave what they had, so that it seemed to me to be wrong and I forbade it. And I gave a thousand handsome good things, which I had brought, in order that they might conceive affection, and more than that, might become Christians and be inclined to the love and service of their highnesses and of the whole Castilian nation, and strive to aid us and to give us of the things which they have in abundance and which are necessary to us. And they do not know any creed and are not idolaters; only they all believe that power and good are in the heavens, and they are very firmly convinced that I, with these ships and men, came from the heavens, and in this belief they everywhere received me, after they had overcome their fear. And this does not come because they are ignorant; on the contrary, they are of a very acute intelligence and are men who navigate all those seas, so that it is amazing how good an account they give of everything, but it is because they have never seen people clothed or ships of such a kind.

And as soon as I arrived in the Indies, in the first island which I found, I took by force some of them, in order that they might learn and give me information of that which there is in those parts, and so it was that they soon understood us, and we them, either by speech or signs, and they have been very serviceable. I still take them with me, and they are always assured that I come from Heaven, for all the intercourse which they have had with me; and they were the first to announce this wherever I went, and the others went running from house to house and to the neighbouring towns, with loud cries of, "Come! Come to see the people from Heaven!" So all, men and women alike, when their minds were set at rest concerning us, came, so that not one, great or small, remained behind, and all brought something to eat and drink, which they gave with extraordinary affection. In all the island, they have very many canoes, like rowing *fustas*, some larger, some smaller, and some are larger than a *fusta* of eighteen benches. They are not so broad, because they are made of a single log of wood, but a *fusta* would not keep up with them in rowing, since their speed is a thing incredible. And in these they navigate among all those islands, which are innumerable, and carry their goods. One of these canoes I have seen with seventy and eighty men in her, and each one with his oar.

In all these islands, I saw no great diversity in the appearance of the people or in their manners and language. On the contrary, they all understand one another, which is a very curious thing, on account of which I hope that their highnesses will determine upon their conversion to our holy faith, towards which they are very inclined.

I have already said how I have gone one hundred and seven leagues in a straight line from west to east along the seashore of the island Juana, and as a result of that voyage, I can say that this island is larger than England and Scotland together, for, beyond these one hundred and seven leagues, there remain to the westward two provinces to which I have not gone. One of these provinces they call "Avan," and there the people are born with tails; and these provinces cannot have a length of less than fifty or sixty leagues, as I could understand from those Indians whom I have and who know all the islands.

The other, Española, has a circumference greater than all Spain, from Colibre, by the sea-coast, to Fuenterabia in Vizcaya, since I voyaged along one side one hundred and eighty-eight great leagues in a straight line from west to east. It is a land to be desired and, seen, it is never to be left. And in it, although of all I have taken possession for their highnesses and all are more richly endowed than I know how, or am able, to say, and I hold them all for their highnesses, so that they may dispose of them as, and as absolutely as, of the kingdoms of Castile, in this Española, in the situation most convenient and in the best position for the mines of gold and for all intercourse as well with the mainland here as with that there, belonging to the Grand Khan, where will be great trade and gain, I have taken possession of a large town, to which I gave the name *Villa de Navidad*, and in it I have made fortifications and a fort, which now will by this time be entirely finished, and I have left in it sufficient men for such a purpose with arms and artillery and provisions for more than a year, and a *fusta*, and one, a master of all seacraft, to build others, and great friendship with the king of that land, so much so, that he was proud to call me, and to treat me as, a brother. And even if he were to change his attitude to one of hostility towards these men, he and his do not know what arms are and they go naked, as I have already said, and are the most timorous people that there are in the world, so that the men whom I have left there alone would suffice to destroy all that land, and the island is without danger for their persons, if they know how to govern themselves.

In all these islands, it seems to me that all men are content with one woman, and to their chief or king they give as many as twenty. It appears to me that the women work more than the men. And I have not been able to learn if they hold private property; what seemed to me to appear was that, in that which one had, all took a share, especially of eatable things.

In these islands I have so far found no human monstrosities, as many expected, but on the contrary the whole population is very well-formed, nor are they negros as in Guinea, but their hair is flowing, and they are not born where there is intense force in the rays of the sun; it is true that the sun has there great power, although it is distant from the equinoctial line twenty-six degrees. In these islands, where there are high mountains, the cold was severe this winter, but they endure it, being used to it and with the help of meats which they eat with many and extremely hot spices. As I have found no monsters, so I have had no report of any, except in an island "Quaris," the second at the coming into the Indies, which is inhabited by a people who are regarded in all the islands as very fierce and who eat human flesh. They have many canoes with which they range through all the islands of India and pillage and take as many as they can. They are no more malformed than the others, except that they have the custom of wearing their hair long like women, and they use bows and arrows of the same cane stems, with a small piece of wood at the end, owing to lack of iron which they do not possess. They are ferocious among these other people who are cowardly to an excessive degree, but I make no more account of them than of the rest. These are those who have intercourse with the women of "Matinino," which is the first island met on the way from Spain to the Indies, in which there is not a man. These women engage in no feminine occupation, but use bows and arrows of cane, like those already mentioned, and they arm and protect themselves with plates of copper, of which they have much.

In another island, which they assure me is larger than Española, the people have no hair. In it, there is gold incalculable, and from it and from the other islands, I bring with me Indians as evidence.

In conclusion, to speak only of that which has been accomplished on this voyage, which was so hasty, their highnesses can see that I will give them as much gold as they may need, if their highnesses will render me very slight assistance; moreover, spice and cotton, as much as their highnesses shall command; and mastic, as much as they shall order to be shipped and which, up to now, has been found only in Greece, in the island of Chios, and the Seignory sells it for what it pleases; and aloe wood, as much as they shall order to be shipped, and slaves, as many as they shall order to be shipped and who will be from the idolaters. And I believe that I have found rhubarb and cinnamon, and I shall find a thousand other things of value, which the people whom I have left there will have discovered, for I have not delayed at any point, so far as the wind allowed me to sail, except in the town of Navidad, in order to leave it secured and well established, and in truth, I should have done much more, if the ships had served me, as reason demanded.

This is enough . . . and the eternal God, our Lord, Who gives to all those who walk in His way triumph over things which appear to be impossible, and this was notably one; for, although men have talked or have written of these lands, all was conjectural, without suggestion of ocular evidence, but amounted only to this, that those who heard for the most part listened and judged it to be rather a fable than as having any vestige of truth. So that, since Our Redeemer has given this victory to our most illustrious king and queen, and to their renowned kingdoms, in so great a matter, for this all Christendom ought to feel delight and make great feasts and give solemn thanks to the Holy Trinity with many solemn prayers for the great exaltation which they shall have, in the turning of so many peoples to our holy faith, and afterwards for temporal benefits, for not only Spain but all Christians will have hence refreshment and gain.

This, in accordance with that which has been accomplished, thus briefly.

Done in the caravel,[1] off the Canary Islands, on the fifteenth of February, in the year one thousand four hundred and ninety-three.

At your orders.   El Almirante.

After having written this, and being in the sea of Castile, there came on me so great a south-south-west wind, that I was obliged to lighten ship. But I ran here to-day into this port of Lisbon, which was the greatest marvel in the world, whence I decided to write to their highnesses. In all the Indies, I have always found weather like May; where I went in thirty-three days and I had returned in twenty-eight, save for these storms which have detained me for fourteen days, beating about in this sea. Here all the sailors say that never has there been so bad a winter nor so many ships lost.

Done on the fourth day of March.

---

[1]Sailing ship, in this case the *Santa María*. [Ed.]

KIRKPATRICK SALE

From The Conquest of Paradise

In this selection from his popular study of Columbus, Sale is concerned with Columbus's attitude toward nature in the New World.
Do you think Sale's comments are accurate? Are they insightful? Do
they help us understand Columbus?

Sale regards Columbus as a symbol of European expansion. Let us
for the moment grant him that. If Columbus is distinctly European,
what is Sale saying about European expansion? How and what does
Sale add to your understanding of the similarities and differences between Chinese and European expansion?

Was Columbus much different from Zheng He? Or were the areas
and peoples they visited causes for different responses?

Thinking Historically

Clearly, this selection is a secondary source; Sale is a modern writer,
not a fifteenth-century contemporary of Columbus. Still, you will not
have to read very far into the selection to realize that Sale has a distinct point of view. Secondary sources, like primary ones, should be
analyzed for bias and perspective and should identify the author's interpretation.

Sale is an environmentalist and a cultural critic. Do his beliefs and
values hinder his understanding of Columbus, or do they inform and
illuminate aspects of Columbus that might otherwise be missed? Does
Sale help you recognize things you would not have seen on your own,
or does he persuade you to see things that might not truly be there?

Notice how Sale uses primary sources in his text. He quotes from
Columbus's journal and his letter to King Ferdinand and Queen Isabella. Do these quotes help you understand Columbus, or do they
simply support Sale's argument? What do you think about Sale's use
of the Spanish "Colón"* for "Columbus"? Does Sale "take possession" of Columbus by, in effect, "renaming" him for modern readers?
Is the effect humanizing or debunking?

*koh LOHN

Kirkpatrick Sale, *The Conquest of Paradise* (New York: Penguin, 1991), 92–104.

Notice how Sale sometimes calls attention to what the primary
source did *not* say rather than what it did say. Is this a legitimate way
to understand someone, or is Sale projecting a twentieth-century perspective on Columbus to make a point?

Toward the end of the selection, Sale extends his criticism beyond
Columbus to include others. Who are the others? What is the effect of
this larger criticism?

Admiral Colón spent a total of ninety-six days exploring the lands he
encountered on the far side of the Ocean Sea — four rather small
coralline islands in the Bahamian chain and two substantial coastlines
of what he finally acknowledged were larger islands — every one of
which he "took possession of" in the name of his Sovereigns.

The first he named San Salvador, no doubt as much in thanksgiving
for its welcome presence after more than a month at sea as for the Son
of God whom it honored; the second he called Santa María de la Con-
cepcíon, after the Virgin whose name his flagship bore; and the third
and fourth he called Fernandina and Isabela, for his patrons, honoring
Aragon before Castile for reasons never explained (possibly protocol,
possibly in recognition of the chief sources of backing for the voyage).
The first of the two large and very fertile islands he called Juana, which
Fernando [Columbus's son] says was done in honor of Prince Juan, heir
to the Castilian throne, but just as plausibly might have been done in
recognition of Princess Juana, the unstable child who eventually carried
on the line; the second he named la Ysla Española, the "Spanish Island," because it resembled (though he felt it surpassed in beauty) the
lands of Castile.

It was not that the islands were in need of names, mind you, nor indeed that Colón was ignorant of the names that native peoples had already given them, for he frequently used those original names before
endowing them with his own. Rather, the process of bestowing new
names went along with "taking possession of" those parts of the world
he deemed suitable for Spanish ownership, showing the royal banners,
erecting various crosses, and pronouncing certain oaths and pledges. If
this was presumption, it had an honored heritage: It was Adam who
was charged by his Creator with the task of naming "every living creature," including the product of his own rib, in the course of establishing
"dominion over" them.

Colón went on to assign no fewer than sixty-two other names on
the geography of the islands — capes, points, mountains, ports — with
a blithe assurance suggesting that in his (and Europe's) perception the
act of name-giving was in some sense a talisman of conquest, a rite that
changed raw neutral stretches of far-off earth into extensions of

Europe. The process began slowly, even haltingly — he forgot to record, for example, until four days afterward that he named the land-fall island San Salvador — but by the time he came to Española at the end he went on a naming spree, using more than two-thirds of all the ti-tles he concocted on that one coastline. On certain days it became al-most a frenzy: on December 6 he named six places, on the nineteenth six more, and on January 11 no fewer than ten — eight capes, a point, and a mountain. It is almost as if, as he sailed along the last of the islands, he was determined to leave his mark on it the only way he knew how, and thus to establish his authority — and by extension Spain's — even, as with baptism, to make it thus sanctified, and real, and official. . . .

This business of naming and "possessing" foreign islands was by no means casual. The Admiral took it very seriously, pointing out that "it was my wish to bypass no island without taking possession" (Octo-ber 15) and that "in all regions [I] always left a cross standing" (No-vember 16) as a mark of Christian dominance. There even seem to have been certain prescriptions for it (the instructions from the Sovereigns speak of "the administering of the oath and the performing of the rites prescribed in such cases"), and Rodrigo de Escobedo was sent along as secretary of the fleet explicitly to witness and record these events in de-tail.

But consider the implications of this act and the questions it raises again about what was in the Sovereigns' minds, what in Colón's. Why would the Admiral assume that these territories were in some way *un*-possessed — even by those clearly inhabiting them — and thus available for Spain to claim? Why would he not think twice about the possibility that some considerable potentate — the Grand Khan of China, for ex-ample, whom he later acknowledged (November 6) "must be" the ruler of Española — might descend upon him at any moment with a greater military force than his three vessels commanded and punish him for his territorial presumption? Why would he make the ceremony of posses-sion his very first act on shore, even before meeting the inhabitants or exploring the environs, or finding out if anybody there objected to being thus possessed — particularly if they actually owned the great treasures he hoped would be there? No European would have imagined that anyone — three small boatloads of Indians, say — could come up to a European shore or island and "take possession" of it, nor would a European imagine marching up to some part of North Africa or the Middle East and claiming sovereignty there with impunity. Why were these lands thought to be different?

Could there be any reason for the Admiral to assume he had reached "unclaimed" shores, new lands that lay far from the domains of any of the potentates of the East? Can that really have been in his mind — or can it all be explained as simple Eurocentrism, or Eurosupe-riority, mixed with cupidity and naiveté? . . .

Once safely "possessed,"[1] San Salvador was open for inspection. Now the Admiral turned his attention for the first time to the "naked people" staring at him on the beach — he did not automatically give them a name, interestingly enough, and it would be another six days before he decided what he might call them — and tried to win their favor with his trinkets.

> They all go around as naked as their mothers bore them; and also the women, although I didn't see more than one really young girl. All that I saw were young people [*mancebos*], none of them more than 30 years old. They are very well built, with very handsome bodies and very good faces; their hair [is] coarse, almost like the silk of a horse's tail, and short. They wear their hair over their eyebrows, except for a little in the back that they wear long and never cut. Some of them paint themselves black (and they are the color of the Canary Islanders, neither black nor white), and some paint themselves white, and some red, and some with what they find. And some paint their faces, and some of them the whole body, and some the eyes only, and some of them only the nose.

It may fairly be called the birth of American anthropology.

A crude anthropology, of course, as superficial as Colón's descriptions always were when his interest was limited, but simple and straightforward enough, with none of the fable and fantasy that characterized many earlier (and even some later) accounts of new-found peoples. There was no pretense to objectivity, or any sense that these people might be representatives of a culture equal to, or in any way a model for, Europe's. Colón immediately presumed the inferiority of the natives, not merely because (a sure enough sign) they were naked, but because (his society could have no surer measure) they seemed so technologically backward. "It appeared to me that these people were very poor in everything," he wrote on that first day, and, worse still, "they have no iron." And they went on to prove their inferiority to the Admiral by being ignorant of even such a basic artifact of European life as a sword: "They bear no arms, nor are they acquainted with them," he wrote, "for I showed them swords and they grasped them by the blade and cut themselves through ignorance." Thus did European arms spill the first drops of native blood on the sands of the New World, accompanied not with a gasp of compassion but with a smirk of superiority.

Then, just six sentences further on, Colón clarified what this inferiority meant in his eyes:

[1]Given Spanish names. [Ed.]

They ought to be good servants and of good intelligence [*ingenio*]. . . .
I believe that they would easily be made Christians, because it seemed
to me that they had no religion. Our Lord pleasing, I will carry off six
of them at my departure to Your Highnesses, in order that they may
learn to speak.

No clothes, no arms, no possessions, no iron, and now no religion —
not even speech: hence they were fit to be servants, and captives. It may
fairly be called the birth of American slavery.

Whether or not the idea of slavery was in Colón's mind all along is
uncertain, although he did suggest he had had experience as a slave
trader in Africa (November 12) and he certainly knew of Portuguese
plantation slavery in the Madeiras and Spanish slavery of Guanches in
the Canaries. But it seems to have taken shape early and grown ever
firmer as the weeks went on and as he captured more and more of the
helpless natives. At one point he even sent his crew ashore to kidnap
"seven head of women, young ones and adults, and three small children"; the expression of such callousness led the Spanish historian Salvador de Madariaga to remark, "It would be difficult to find a starker
utterance of utilitarian subjection of man by man than this passage
[whose] form is no less devoid of human feeling than its substance."

To be sure, Colón knew nothing about these people he encountered
and considered enslaving, and he was hardly trained to find out very
much, even if he was moved to care. But they were in fact members of
an extensive, populous, and successful people whom Europe, using its
own peculiar taxonomy, subsequently called "Taino" (or "Taíno"),
their own word for "good" or "noble," and their response when asked
who they were. They were related distantly by both language and culture to the Arawak people of the South American mainland, but it is
misleading (and needlessly imprecise) to call them Arawaks, as historians are wont to do, when the term "Taino" better establishes their ethnic and historical distinctiveness. They had migrated to the islands from
the mainland at about the time of the birth of Christ, occupying the
three large islands we now call the Greater Antilles and arriving at
Guanahani (Colón's San Salvador) and the end of the Bahamian chain
probably sometime around A.D. 900. There they displaced an earlier
people, the Guanahacabibes (sometimes called Guanahatabeys), who
by the time of the European discovery occupied only the western third
of Cuba and possibly remote corners of Española; and there, probably
in the early fifteenth century, they eventually confronted another people
moving up the islands from the mainland, the Caribs, whose culture
eventually occupied a dozen small islands of what are called the Lesser
Antilles.

The Tainos were not nearly so backward as Colón assumed from
their lack of dress. (It might be said that it was the Europeans, who

generally kept clothed head to foot during the day despite temperatures regularly in the eighties, who were the more unsophisticated in garmenture — especially since the Tainos, as Colón later noted, also used their body paint to prevent sunburn.) Indeed, they had achieved a means of living in a balanced and fruitful harmony with their natural surroundings that any society might well have envied. They had, to begin with, a not unsophisticated technology that made exact use of their available resources, two parts of which were so impressive that they were picked up and adopted by the European invaders: *canoa* (canoes) that were carved and fire-burned from large silk-cotton trees, "all in one piece, and wonderfully made" (October 13), some of which were capable of carrying up to 150 passengers; and *hamaca* (hammocks) that were "like nets of cotton" (October 17) and may have been a staple item of trade with Indian tribes as far away as the Florida mainland. Their houses were not only spacious and clean — as the Europeans noted with surprise and appreciation, used as they were to the generally crowded and slovenly hovels and huts of south European peasantry — but more apropos, remarkably resistant to hurricanes; the circular walls were made of strong cane poles set deep and close together ("as close as the fingers of a hand," Colón noted), the conical roofs of branches and vines tightly interwoven on a frame of smaller poles and covered with heavy palm leaves. Their artifacts and jewelry, with the exception of a few gold trinkets and ornaments, were based largely on renewable materials, including bracelets and necklaces of coral, shells, bone, and stone, embroidered cotton belts, woven baskets, carved statues and chairs, wooden and shell utensils, and pottery of variously intricate decoration depending on period and place.

Perhaps the most sophisticated, and most carefully integrated, part of their technology was their agricultural system, extraordinarily productive and perfectly adapted to the conditions of the island environment. It was based primarily on fields of knee-high mounds, called *conucos*, planted with *yuca* (sometimes called manioc), *batata* (sweet potato), and various squashes and beans grown all together in multi-crop harmony: The root crops were excellent in resisting erosion and producing minerals and potash, the leaf crops effective in providing shade and moisture, and the mound configurations largely resistant to erosion and flooding and adaptable to almost all topographic conditions including steep hillsides. Not only was the *conuco* system environmentally appropriate — "conuco agriculture seems to have provided an exceptionally ecologically well-balanced and protective form of land use," according to David Watts's recent and authoritative *West Indies* — but it was also highly productive, surpassing in yields anything known in Europe at the time, with labor that amounted to hardly more than two or three hours a week, and in continuous yearlong harvest. The pioneering American geographical scholar Carl Sauer calls

Taino agriculture "productive as few parts of the world," giving the "highest returns of food in continuous supply by the simplest methods and modest labor," and adds, with a touch of regret, "The white man never fully appreciated the excellent combination of plants that were grown in conucos."

In their arts of government the Tainos seem to have achieved a parallel sort of harmony. Most villages were small (ten to fifteen families) and autonomous, although many apparently recognized loose allegiances with neighboring villages, and they were governed by a hereditary official called a *kaseke* (*cacique*,* in the Spanish form), something of a cross between an arbiter and a prolocutor, supported by advisers and elders. So little a part did violence play in their system that they seem, remarkably, to have been a society without war (at least we know of no war music or signals or artifacts, and no evidence of intertribal combats) and even without overt conflict (Las Casas reports that no Spaniard ever saw two Tainos fighting). And here we come to what was obviously the Tainos' outstanding cultural achievement, a proficiency in the social arts that led those who first met them to comment unfailingly on their friendliness, their warmth, their openness, and above all — so striking to those of an acquisitive culture — their generosity.

"They are the best people in the world and above all the gentlest," Colón recorded in his *Journal* (December 16), and from first to last he was astonished at their kindness:

> They became so much our friends that it was a marvel. . . . They traded and gave everything they had, with good will [October 12].
>
> I sent the ship's boat ashore for water, and they very willingly showed my people where the water was, and they themselves carried the full barrels to the boat, and took great delight in pleasing us [October 16].
>
> They are very gentle and without knowledge of what is evil; nor do they murder or steal [November 12].
>
> Your Highnesses may believe that in all the world there can be no better or gentler people . . . for neither better people nor land can there be. . . . All the people show the most singular loving behavior and they speak pleasantly [December 24].
>
> I assure Your Highnesses that I believe that in all the world there is no better people nor better country. They love their neighbors as themselves, and they have the sweetest talk in the world, and are gentle and always laughing [December 25].

Even if one allows for some exaggeration — Colón was clearly trying to convince Ferdinand and Isabella that his Indians could be easily

*kah SEEK

conquered and converted, should that be the Sovereigns' wish — it is obvious that the Tainos exhibited a manner of social discourse that quite impressed the rough Europeans. But that was not high among the traits of "civilized" nations, as Colón and Europe understood it, and it counted for little in the Admiral's assessment of these people. However struck he was with such behavior, he would not have thought that it was the mark of a benign and harmonious society, or that from it another culture might learn. For him it was something like the wondrous behavior of children, the naive guilelessness of prelapsarian[2] creatures who knew no better how to bargain and chaffer and cheat than they did to dress themselves: "For a lacepoint they gave good pieces of gold the size of two fingers" (January 6), and "They even took pieces of the broken hoops of the wine casks and, like beasts [*como besti*], gave what they had" (Santangel Letter)[3]. Like beasts; such innocence was not human.

It is to be regretted that the Admiral, unable to see past their nakedness, as it were, knew not the real virtues of the people he confronted. For the Tainos' lives were in many ways as idyllic as their surroundings, into which they fit with such skill and comfort. They were well fed and well housed, without poverty or serious disease. They enjoyed considerable leisure, given over to dancing, singing, ballgames, and sex, and expressed themselves artistically in basketry, woodworking, pottery, and jewelry. They lived in general harmony and peace, without greed or covetousness or theft. . . .

It is perhaps only natural that Colón should devote his initial attention to the handsome, naked, naive islanders, but it does seem peculiar that he pays almost no attention, especially in the early days, to the spectacular scenery around them. Here he was, in the middle of an old-growth tropical forest the likes of which he could not have imagined before, its trees reaching sixty or seventy feet into the sky, more varieties than he knew how to count much less name, exhibiting a lushness that stood in sharp contrast to the sparse and denuded lands he had known in the Mediterranean, hearing a melodious multiplicity of bird songs and parrot calls — why was it not an occasion of wonder, excitement, and the sheer joy at nature in its full, arrogant abundance? But there is not a word of that: He actually said nothing about the physical surroundings on the first day, aside from a single phrase about "very green trees" and "many streams," and on the second managed only that short sentence about a big island with a big lake and green trees. Indeed, for the whole two weeks of the first leg of his voyage through the Bahamas to Cuba, he devoted only a third of the lines of descrip-

---

[2]Before the Fall. In other words, before the time, according to the Old Testament, when Adam and Eve sinned and were banished by God from the Garden of Eden. [Ed.]

[3]Santangel was the minister of Ferdinand and Isabella who received the letter (see selection 4).

tion to the phenomena around him. And there are some natural sights he seems not to have noticed at all: He did not mention (except in terms of navigation) the nighttime heavens, the sharp, glorious configurations of stars that he must have seen virtually every night of his journey, many for the first time.

Eventually Colón succumbed to the islands' natural charms as he sailed on — how could he not? — and began to wax warmly about how "these islands are very green and fertile and the air very sweet" (October 15), with "trees which were more beautiful to see than any other thing that has ever been seen" (October 17), and "so good and sweet a smell of flowers or trees from the land" (October 19). But his descriptions are curiously vapid and vague, the language opaque and lifeless:

> The other island, which is very big [October 15] . . . this island is very large [October 16] . . . these islands are very green and fertile [October 15] . . . this land is the best and most fertile [October 17] . . . in it many plants and trees . . . if the others are very beautiful, this is more so [October 19] . . . here are some great lagoons . . . big and little birds of all sorts . . . if the others already seen are very beautiful and green and fertile, this one is much more so [October 21] . . . full of very good harbors and deep rivers [October 28].

You begin to see the Admiral's problem: He cares little about the features of nature, at least the ones he doesn't use for sailing, and even when he admires them he has little experience in assessing them and less acquaintance with a vocabulary to describe them. To convey the lush density and stately grandeur of those tropical forests, for example, he had little more than the modifiers "green" and "very": "very green trees" (October 12), "trees very green" (October 13), "trees . . . so green and with leaves like those of Castile" (October 14), "very green and very big trees" (October 19), "large groves are very green" (October 21), "trees . . . beautiful and green" (October 28). And when he began to be aware of the diversity among those trees, he was still unable to make meaningful distinctions: "All the trees are as different from ours as day from night" (October 17), "trees of a thousand kinds" (October 21), "a thousand sorts of trees" (October 23), "trees . . . different from ours" (October 28), "trees of a thousand sorts" (November 14), "trees of a thousand kinds" (December 6).

Such was his ignorance — a failing he repeatedly bemoaned ("I don't recognize them, which gives me great grief," October 19) — that when he did stop to examine a species he often had no idea what he was looking at. "I saw many trees very different from ours," he wrote on October 16, "and many of them have branches of many kinds, and all on one trunk, and one twig is of one kind and another of another, and so different that it is the greatest wonder in the world how much diversity there is of one kind from the other. That is to say, one branch has leaves like a cane, and another like mastic, and thus on one tree five or six kinds, and all so different." There is no such tree in existence, much less "many of them," and never was: Why would anyone imagine, or so contrive, such a thing to be?

Colón's attempts to identify species were likewise frequently wrongheaded, usually imputing to them commercial worth that they did not have, as with the worthless "aloes" he loaded such quantities of. The "amaranth" he identified on October 28 and the "oaks" and "arbutus" of November 25 are species that do not grow in the Caribbean; the "mastic" he found on November 5 and loaded on board to sell in Spain was gumbo-limbo, commercially worthless. (On the other hand, one of the species of flora he deemed of no marketable interest — "weeds [*tizon*] in their hands to drink in the fragrant smoke" [November 6] — was tobacco.) Similarly, the "whales" he spotted on October 16 must have been simply large fish, the "geese" he saw on November 6 and again on December 22 were ducks, the "nightingales" that kept delighting him (November 6; December 7, 13) do not exist in the Americas, and the skulls of "cows" he identified on October 29 were probably not those of land animals but of manatees.

This all seems a little sad, revealing a man rather lost in a world that he cannot come to know, a man with a "geographic and naturalistic knowledge that doesn't turn out to be very deep or nearly complete," and "a limited imagination and a capacity for comparisons conditioned by a not very broad geographic culture," in the words of Gaetano Ferro, a Columbus scholar and professor of geography at the University of Genoa. One could not of course have expected that an adventurer and sailor of this era would also be a naturalist, or necessarily even have some genuine interest in or curiosity about the natural world, but it is a disappointment nonetheless that the Discoverer of the New World turns out to be quite so simple, quite so inexperienced, in the ways of discovering his environment.

Colón's limitations, I hasten to say, were not his alone; they were of his culture, and they would be found in the descriptions of many others — Vespucci, Cortés, Hawkins, Juet, Cartier, Champlain, Ralegh — in the century of discovery to follow. They are the source of what the distinguished English historian J. H. Elliott has called "the problem of description" faced by Europeans confronting the uniqueness of the New World: "So often the physical appearance of the New World is either totally ignored or else described in the flattest and most conventional phraseology. This off-hand treatment of nature contrasts strikingly with the many precise and acute descriptions of the native inhabitants. It is as if the American landscape is seen as no more than a backcloth against which the strange and perennially fascinating peoples of the New World are dutifully grouped." The reason, Elliott thinks, and this is telling, may be "a lack of interest among sixteenth-century

Europeans, and especially those of the Mediterranean world, in landscape and in nature." This lack of interest was reflected in the lack of
vocabulary, the lack of that facility common to nature-based peoples
whose cultures are steeped in natural imagery. Oviedo, for example,
setting out to write descriptions for his *Historia general* in the next century, continually threw his hands up in the air: "Of all the things I have
seen," he said at one point, "this is the one which has most left me
without hope of being able to describe it in words"; or at another, "It
needs to be painted by the hand of a Berruguete or some other excellent
painter like him, or by Leonardo da Vinci or Andrea Mantegna, famous painters whom I knew in Italy." Like Colón, visitor after visitor
to the New World seemed mind-boggled and tongue-tied trying to convey the wonders before them, and about the only color they seem to
have eyes for is green — and not very many shades of that, either. . . .

REFLECTIONS

It is difficult to ignore moral issues when considering explorations and
explorers. The prefix *great* is used liberally, and words like *discovery*
and *courage* readily fit when describing "firsts" and "unknowns."
However, celebratory images, national myths, and heroic biographies
inevitably engender the reverse. Ye Jun and a new breed of Beijing historians condemn Zheng He for military suppression. Kirkpatrick Sale
charges Columbus with arrogance, ignorance, and insufficient curiosity.

On the matter of preparation, the difference between the Chinese
and Columbian voyages is especially striking. The floating Chinese scientific laboratories, traveling experts, sages, and interpreters contrast
starkly with the lack of a single artist or naturalist on board Columbus's ships. But the inability to distinguish shades of green is not a
moral failure. We might say that Columbus's voyage was premature,
Zheng He's meticulously planned and prepared. Like the designers of a
modern aircraft, the Chinese built in redundancies: separate compartments that could fill with water without sinking the ship, more rice and
fresh water than they would need, experts to find plants that might
cure diseases yet unknown. By contrast, Columbus seems like a loose
cannon, unaware of where he was going or where he had been, capable
of lighting a match inside a dark powder shed.

These were, and in many ways still are, the differences between
Chinese and European (now Western) scientific innovation. No European could (or can) organize an enterprise on the scale of Zhu Di. No
Chinese emperor had reason to sanction an experimental voyage into
the unknown. In the same book from which we excerpted a noncontro-
versial section, Gavin Menzies argues that Zheng He's voyage of 1421

led eventually around Africa and across the Atlantic to the Americas. But in addition to the weakness of the evidence that Zheng He reached the Americas, this would have been out of character for Chinese imperial tribute missions. There were, no doubt, Chinese sailors who came upon unknown lands, possibly even across the great Pacific Ocean; but the domain of the emperor was the known world, of which he was the center. In the Europe of closely competing princes, a Columbus could hatch a personal scheme with minimal supervision and barely sufficient funding and the consequences could still be — indeed, were — momentous. (See Chapter 16.) Was such a system irresponsible? Today, as we begin to probe the heavens around us, even as we tamper with technologies that change the balance of natural forces on earth, we might consider whether the Confucian scholars of six hundred years ago were on to something when they burned the ships and destroyed all of the records of their age of great discovery.

Primary sources are not limited to written records, however. When the Chinese recently revived the memory of Zheng He, Joseph Kahn tells us, they drew on an unlikely record of Chinese settlement in east Africa: the young woman from Kenya, Mwamaka Sharifu, who claimed Chinese ancestry. Chinese-African faces on the coast of East Africa are evidence of contact, but not of contact in 1421. Combined, however, with family stories, DNA tests, local histories, archaeological finds, a single living primary source may become the basis for a new interpretation of a broader history. In the case of Mwamaka Sharifu, members of her family, and other residents of coastal Somalia and Kenya, the evidence has proved convincing.

Lawyers are fond of saying that the absence of evidence is not the same as the evidence of absence. Still, the absence of primary evidence, despite Gavin Menzies's Herculean but ultimately fruitless efforts at finding evidence of Chinese settlement in the Americas, seriously challenges his secondary interpretation. The absence of any fifteenth-century Chinese remains in the Western Hemisphere contrasts starkly with the archaeological and genetic record of the Indian Ocean. Primary sources, then, reveal by their silences as well as their inclusions. As Menzies himself notes, Zheng He's account of his voyages dots the Indian Ocean ports from Ceylon to India to Arabia to East Africa, as far as the Somali ports of Mogadishu and Brava — but no further (see Map 15.1). Sometimes primary sources are more reliable than secondary ones, if the Zheng He and Menzies selections are any indication. But both kinds of sources are necessary to develop the historical sensibility required to engage the difficult moral issues that the past and, of course, the future confront us with.

16

Atlantic World Encounters

*Europeans, Americans,
and Africans, 1500–1750*

HISTORICAL CONTEXT

European expansion in the Atlantic that began with Portuguese voyages along the African coast in the 1440s and Columbus's discovery of the Americas in 1492 had by 1750 created a new Atlantic zone of human contact and communication that embraced four continents and one ocean. Until this point, nothing — neither the Chinese contacts with Africa in the early fifteenth century, nor the expansion of Islam throughout Eurasia in the almost thousand years since the Prophet Muhammad's death in 632 — had so thoroughly and so permanently changed the human and ecological balance of the world.

Sub-Saharan Africa had already been integrated into the world of Eurasia by 1450. African populations became more mixed, as peoples from the Niger River area migrated east and south throughout the continent during the fifteen hundred years before the arrival of the Portuguese. Muslims from North Africa and the Middle East had aided or established Muslim states and trading ports south of the Sahara in East and West Africa after 1000. Cultural and technical innovations of the Middle East, like the literacy that came with Islam, penetrated slowly, and the spread of the many plants and animals of the northern hemisphere was slowed by the Sahara and equator. However, microbes traveled swiftly and easily from Eurasia to Africa, creating a single set of diseases and immunities for the peoples of the Afro-Eurasian Old World.

The peoples of the Americas, having been isolated ecologically for more than a thousand years, were not so fortunate. The arrival of Europeans and Africans in the Americas after 1492 had devastating consequences for Native American populations. Old World diseases like smallpox were responsible for millions of Native American deaths — a tragedy far worse in scope than the casualties caused by wars. To work the mines and plantations of the New World, Europeans used Indian labor, but increasingly, especially for lowland plantations, they used African slaves (see Map 16.1). By 1750, the combination of Indian "die off" and African and European migration resulted in vastly different populations in the Americas. On some Caribbean islands and in plantation areas like northeastern Brazil, Indian populations were entirely replaced by Africans. At the same time, European animals (for example, goats, cattle, horses) multiplied in the absence of natural predators.

The new Atlantic ecological system was not a uniform zone, however. Coastal regions in Western Europe and towns on the eastern seaboard of the Americas prospered, while American interiors and African populations in Africa stagnated or declined. The Atlantic Ocean became a vast lake that united port cities and plantations with sailing ships that carried African slaves to the Caribbean, Caribbean sugar and rum to North American and European industrial ports, and guns, pots, and liquor to the African "Slave Coast."

Thus, the Atlantic world was integrated with the Old World. Trade routes that began in Boston or Bahia, Brazil, stretched across Eurasia and around southern Africa into the Indian Ocean and the China Sea. Crops that had previously been known only to Native Americans — corn, potatoes, and tomatoes — fueled population explosions from Ireland to China and graced the tables of peasants and princes in between. What began as an effort by European merchants to import Asian spices directly became after 1650 (as European tastes for pepper and Asian spices moderated) a new global pantry of possibilities.

In this chapter, we will read selections that describe some of the first contacts that led to this new global dynamic. We will read of Europeans in Mexico, North America, and West Africa and examine European depictions of natives from both North and South America. We will also explore some of the African and American responses to this European expansion. When studying these accounts and images, notice how these individuals at the frontier of a new age understand and treat each other. Consider how these initial exchanges, so apparently fortuitous and transitory at the time, changed the face of the world.

THINKING HISTORICALLY
Comparing Primary Sources

By comparing and contrasting one thing with another, we learn more about each, and by examining related works in their proper context, we learn more about the whole of which they are part. In the last chapter we compared China and Europe or Chinese and European (mainly

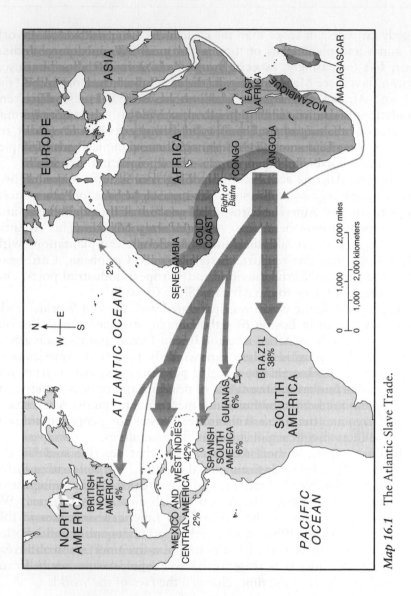

Map 16.1　The Atlantic Slave Trade.

Spanish) expansion in the fifteenth century. In this chapter we look at the Atlantic world, specifically at Europeans in Africa and the Americas. We begin with three views of the Spanish conquest of Mexico — separate accounts by the Spanish conquistadors, by the Mexicans, and by a Dominican friar. The fourth selection juxtaposes two European depictions of Native Americans. The fifth selection recounts the Dutch conquest of the Algonquin nation in North America (in what is today New York City), and allows us to compare Dutch and Spanish colonial policies.

The final three readings examine encounters between Europeans and Africans and the development of the Atlantic slave trade. Did Europeans treat Native Americans and Africans differently? If so, why?

BERNAL DÍAZ

From The Conquest of New Spain

Bernal Díaz del Castillo was born in Spain in 1492, the year Columbus sailed to America. After participating in two explorations of the Mexican coast, Díaz joined the expedition of Hernán Cortés to Mexico City in 1519. He wrote this history of the conquest much later, when he was in his seventies; he died circa 1580, a municipal official with a small estate in Guatemala.

The conquest of Mexico did not automatically follow from the first Spanish settlements in Santo Domingo, Hispaniola, and then Cuba in the West Indies. The Spanish crown had given permission for trade and exploration, not colonization. But many Spaniards, from fortune-seeking peasant-soldiers to minor nobility, were eager to conquer their own lands and exploit the populations of dependent Indians.

Cortés, of minor noble descent, sailed to the Indies at the age of nineteen, where he established a sizeable estate on the island of Hispaniola. When he heard stories of Montezuma's gold, he was determined to find the fabled capital of the Aztec empire, Tenochtitlán*

---

*teh nohch teet LAHN

Bernal Díaz, *The Conquest of New Spain*, trans. J. M. Cohen (Baltimore: Penguin Books, 1963), 217–19, 221–25, 228–38, 241–43.

(modern Mexico City). He gathered more than five hundred amateur soldiers, eleven ships, sixteen horses, and several pieces of artillery, then sailed across the Caribbean and Gulf of Mexico and there began the long march from the coast up to the high central plateau of Mexico.

The Aztecs were new to central Mexico, arriving from the North American desert only about two hundred years before the Spanish, around 1325. By 1500 they had established dominion over almost all other city-states of Mexico, ruling an empire that stretched as far south as Guatemala and as far east as the Mayan lands of the Yucatan Peninsula.

Aztec power relied on a combination of old and new religious ideas and a military system that conquered through terror. The older religious tradition that the Aztecs adopted from Toltec culture centered on Quetzalcoatl[*] — the feathered serpent, god of creation and brotherhood, whose nurturing forces continued in Aztec society in a system of universal education and in festivals dedicated to life, creativity, and procreation. But the Aztecs also worshipped Huitzilopochtli,[†] a warrior god primed for death and sacrifice, who was given dominant status in the Aztec pantheon. Huitzilopochtli (rendered "Huichilobos"[‡] in this selection) was a force for building a powerful Aztec empire. Drawing on the god's need for human sacrifice — a need not unknown among religions of central Mexico (or Christians) — Montezuma's predecessors built altars to Huitzilopochtli at Tenochtitlán, Cholula, and other sites. The war god required a neverending supply of human hearts, a need that prompted armies to evermore remote sections of Central America in search of sacrificial victims and creating an endless supply of enemies of the Aztecs, among these, the Tlaxcalans.

With the help of his Indian captive and companion Doña Marina — called La Malinche[§] by some of the Indians (thus, Montezuma sometimes calls Cortés "Lord Malinche" in the selection) — Cortés was able to communicate with the Tlaxcalans and other Indians who were tired of Aztec domination. On his march toward Tenochtitlán, Cortés stopped to join forces with the Tlaxcalans, perhaps cementing the relationship and demonstrating his resolve through a brutal massacre of the people of Cholula, an Aztec ally and arch enemy of the Tlaxcalans. By the time Cortés arrived at Tenochtitlán, Montezuma knew of the defeat of his allies at Cholula.

This selection from Bernal Díaz begins with the Spanish entry into Tenochtitlán. What impresses Díaz, and presumably other Spanish

[*]keht zahl koh AH tuhl
[†]wheat zee loh poácht lee
[‡]wee chee LOH bohs
[§]La Malinche (lah   mah LEEN cheh). A variation on "Marina." In contemporary Mexico a traitor is often called a "Malinchisto."

conquistadors, about the Mexican capital city? What parts of the city attract his attention the most? What conclusions does he draw about Mexican (or Aztec) civilization? Does he think Spanish civilization is equal, inferior, or superior to that of Mexico?

Thinking Historically

Díaz gives us a dramatic account of the meeting of Cortés and Montezuma. What do you think each is thinking and feeling? Do you see any signs of tension in their elaborate greetings? Why are both behaving so politely? What do they want from each other?

Notice how the initial hospitality turns tense. What causes this? Is either side more to blame for what happens next? Was conflict inevitable? Could the encounter have ended in some sort of peaceful resolution?

Remember, we are going to compare Díaz's view with a Mexican view of these events. From your reading of Díaz, does he seem able to understand the Mexican point of view? Would you call him a sympathetic observer?

When Cortes saw, heard, and was told that the great Montezuma was approaching, he dismounted from his horse, and when he came near to Montezuma each bowed deeply to the other. Montezuma welcomed our Captain, and Cortes, speaking through Doña Marina, answered by wishing him very good health. Cortes, I think, offered Montezuma his right hand, but Montezuma refused it and extended his own. Then Cortes brought out a necklace which he had been holding. It was made of those elaborately worked and coloured glass beads called *margaritas*, . . . and was strung on a gold cord and dipped in musk to give it a good odour. This he hung round the great Montezuma's neck, and as he did so attempted to embrace him. But the great princes who stood round Montezuma grasped Cortes' arm to prevent him, for they considered this an indignity.

Then Cortes told Montezuma that it rejoiced his heart to have seen such a great prince, and that he took his coming in person to receive him and the repeated favours he had done him as a high honour. After this Montezuma made him another complimentary speech, and ordered two of his nephews who were supporting him, the lords of Texcoco and Coyoacan, to go with us and show us our quarters. Montezuma returned to the city with the other two kinsmen of his escort, the lords of Cuitlahuac and Tacuba; and all those grand companies of *Caciques*[1] and dignitaries who had come with him returned also in his train. . . .

[1]Chiefs. Kah SEEK [Ed.]

On our arrival we entered the large court, where the great Montezuma was awaiting our Captain. Taking him by the hand, the prince led him to his apartment in the hall where he was to lodge, which was very richly furnished in their manner. Montezuma had ready for him a very rich necklace, made of golden crabs, a marvellous piece of work, which he hung round Cortes' neck. His captains were greatly astonished at this sign of honour.

After this ceremony, for which Cortes thanked him through our interpreters, Montezuma said: "Malinche, you and your brothers are in your own house. Rest awhile." He then returned to his palace, which was not far off.

We divided our lodgings by companies, and placed our artillery in a convenient spot. Then the order we were to keep was clearly explained to us, and we were warned to be very much on the alert, both the horsemen and the rest of us soldiers. We then ate a sumptuous dinner which they had prepared for us in their native style.

So, with luck on our side, we boldly entered the city of Tenochtitlán or Mexico on 8 November in the year of our Lord 1519.

The Stay in Mexico

. . . Montezuma had ordered his stewards to provide us with everything we needed for our way of living: maize, grindstones, women to make our bread, fowls, fruit, and plenty of fodder for the horses. He then took leave of us all with the greatest courtesy, and we accompanied him to the street. However, Cortes ordered us not to go far from our quarters for the present until we knew better what conduct to observe.

Next day Cortes decided to go to Montezuma's palace. But first he sent to know whether the prince was busy and to inform him of our coming. He took four captains with him: Pedro de Alvarado, Juan Velazquez de Leon, Diego de Ordaz, and Gonzalo de Sandoval, and five of us soldiers.

When Montezuma was informed of our coming, he advanced into the middle of the hall to receive us, closely surrounded by his nephews, for no other chiefs were allowed to enter his palace or communicate with him except upon important business. Cortes and Montezuma exchanged bows, and clasped hands. Then Montezuma led Cortes to his own dais, and setting him down on his right, called for more seats, on which he ordered us all to sit also.

Cortes began to make a speech through our interpreters, saying that we were all now rested, and that in coming to see and speak with such a great prince we had fulfilled the purpose of our voyage and the orders of our lord the King. The principal things he had come to say on behalf of our Lord God had already been communicated to Montezuma through his three ambassadors, on that occasion in the sand-hills when he did us the favour of sending us the golden moon and sun. We had then told him that we were Christians and worshipped one God alone, named Jesus Christ, who had suffered His passion and death to save us; and that what they worshipped as gods were not gods but devils, which were evil things, and if they were ugly to look at, their deeds were uglier. But he had proved to them how evil and ineffectual their gods were, as both the prince and his people would observe in the course of time, since, where we had put up crosses such as their ambassadors had seen, they had been too frightened to appear before them.

The favour he now begged of the great Montezuma was that he should listen to the words he now wished to speak. Then he very carefully expounded the creation of the world, how we are all brothers, the children of one mother and father called Adam and Eve; and how such a brother as our great Emperor, grieving for the perdition of so many souls as their idols were leading to hell, where they burnt in living flame, had sent us to tell him this, so that he might put a stop to it, and so that they might give up the worship of idols and make no more human sacrifices — for all men are brothers — and commit no more robbery or sodomy. He also promised that in the course of time the King would send some men who lead holy lives among us, much better than our own, to explain this more fully, for we had only come to give them warning. Therefore he begged Montezuma to do as he was asked.

As Montezuma seemed about to reply, Cortes broke off his speech, saying to those of us who were with him: "Since this is only the first attempt, we have now done our duty."

"My lord Malinche," Montezuma replied, "these arguments of yours have been familiar to me for some time. I understand what you said to my ambassadors on the sandhills about the three gods and the cross, also what you preached in the various towns through which you passed. We have given you no answer, since we have worshipped our own gods here from the beginning and know them to be good. No doubt yours are good also, but do not trouble to tell us any more about them at present. Regarding the creation of the world, we have held the same belief for many ages, and for this reason are certain that you are those who our ancestors predicted would come from the direction of the sunrise. As for your great King, I am in his debt and will give him of what I possess. For, as I have already said, two years ago I had news of the Captains who came in ships, by the road that you came, and said they were servants of this great king of yours. I should like to know if you are all the same people."

Cortes answered that we were all brothers and servants of the Emperor, and that they had come to discover a route and explore the seas and ports, so that when they knew them well we could follow, as we had done. Montezuma was referring to the expeditions of Francisco

Hernandez de Cordoba and of Grijalva, the first voyages of discovery. He said that ever since that time he had wanted to invite some of these men to visit the cities of his kingdom, where he would receive them and do them honour, and that now his gods had fulfilled his desire, for we were in his house, which we might call our own. Here we might rest and enjoy ourselves, for we should receive good treatment. If on other occasions he had sent to forbid our entrance into his city, it was not of his own free will, but because his vassals were afraid. For they told him we shot out flashes of lightning, and killed many Indians with our horses, and that we were angry *Teules*, and other such childish stories. But now that he had seen us, he knew that we were of flesh and blood and very intelligent, also very brave. Therefore he had a far greater esteem for us than these reports had given him, and would share with us what he had.

We all thanked him heartily for his . . . good will, and Montezuma replied with a laugh, because in his princely manner he spoke very gaily: "Malinche, I know that these people of Tlascala with whom you are so friendly have told you that I am a sort of god or *Teule*, and keep nothing in any of my houses that is not made of silver and gold and precious stones. But I know very well that you are too intelligent to believe this and will take it as a joke. See now, Malinche, my body is made of flesh and blood like yours, and my houses and palaces are of stone, wood, and plaster. It is true that I am a great king, and have inherited the riches of my ancestors, but the lies and nonsense you have heard of us are not true. You must take them as a joke, as I take the story of your thunders and lightnings."

Cortes answered also with a laugh that enemies always speak evil and tell lies about the people they hate, but he knew he could not hope to find a more magnificent prince in that land, and there was good reason why his fame should have reached our Emperor.

While this conversation was going on, Montezuma quietly sent one of his nephews, a great *Cacique*, to order his stewards to bring certain pieces of gold, which had apparently been set aside as a gift for Cortes, and ten loads of fine cloaks which he divided: the gold and cloaks between Cortes and the four captains, and for each of us soldiers two gold necklaces, each worth ten pesos, and two loads of cloaks. The gold that he then gave us was worth in all more than a thousand pesos, and he gave it all cheerfully, like a great and valiant prince.

As it was now past midday and he did not wish to be importunate, Cortes said to Montezuma: "My lord, the favours you do us increase, load by load, every day, and it is now the hour of your dinner." Montezuma answered that he thanked us for visiting him. We then took our leave with the greatest courtesy, and returned to our quarters, talking as we went of the prince's fine breeding and manners and deciding to show him the greatest respect in every way, and to remove our quilted caps in his presence, which we always did.

The great Montezuma was about forty years old, of good height, well proportioned, spare and slight, and not very dark, though of the usual Indian complexion. He did not wear his hair long but just over his ears, and he had a short black beard, well-shaped and thin. His face was rather long and cheerful, he had fine eyes, and in his appearance and manner could express geniality or, when necessary, a serious composure. He was very neat and clean, and took a bath every afternoon. He had many women as his mistresses, the daughters of chieftains, but two legitimate wives who were *Caciques* in their own right, and when he had intercourse with any of them it was so secret that only some of his servants knew of it. He was quite free from sodomy. The clothes he wore one day he did not wear again till three or four days later. He had a guard of two hundred chieftains lodged in rooms beside his own, only some of whom were permitted to speak to him. When they entered his presence they were compelled to take off their rich cloaks and put on others of little value. They had to be clean and walk barefoot, with their eyes downcast, for they were not allowed to look him in the face, and as they approached they had to make three obeisances, saying as they did so, "Lord, my lord, my great lord!" Then, when they had said what they had come to say, he would dismiss them with a few words. They did not turn their backs on him as they went out, but kept their faces towards him and their eyes downcast, only turning round when they had left the room. Another thing I noticed was that when other great chiefs came from distant lands about disputes or on business, they too had to take off their shoes and put on poor cloaks before entering Montezuma's apartments; and they were not allowed to enter the palace immediately but had to linger for a while near the door, since to enter hurriedly was considered disrespectful. . . .

Montezuma had two houses stocked with every sort of weapon; many of them were richly adorned with gold and precious stones. There were shields large and small, and a sort of broadsword, and two-handed swords set with flint blades that cut much better than our swords, and lances longer than ours, with five-foot blades consisting of many knives. Even when these are driven at a buckler or a shield they are not deflected. In fact they cut like razors, and the Indians can shave their heads with them. They had very good bows and arrows, and double and single-pointed javelins as well as their throwing-sticks and many slings and round stones shaped by hand, and another sort of shield that can be rolled up when they are not fighting, so that it does not get in the way, but which can be opened when they need it in battle and covers their bodies from head to foot. There was also a great deal of cotton armour richly worked on the outside with different coloured feathers, which they used as devices and distinguishing marks, and they had casques and helmets made of wood and bone which were also highly decorated with feathers on the outside. They had other arms of different kinds which I will not mention through fear of prolixity, and workmen skilled in the manufacture of such things, and stewards who were in charge of these arms. . . .

I have already described the manner of their sacrifices. They strike open the wretched Indian's chest with flint knives and hastily tear out the palpitating heart which, with the blood, they present to the idols in whose name they have performed the sacrifice. Then they cut off the arms, thighs, and head, eating the arms and thighs at their ceremonial banquets. The head they hang up on a beam, and the body of the sacrificed man is not eaten but given to the beasts of prey. They also had many vipers in this accursed house, and poisonous snakes which have something that sounds like a bell in their tails. These, which are the deadliest snakes of all, they kept in jars and great pottery vessels full of feathers, in which they laid their eggs and reared their young. They were fed on the bodies of sacrificed Indians and the flesh of the dogs that they bred. We know for certain, too, that when they drove us out of Mexico and killed over eight hundred and fifty of our soldiers, they fed those beasts and snakes on their bodies for many days, as I shall relate in due course. These snakes and wild beasts were dedicated to their fierce idols, and kept them company. As for the horrible noise when the lions and tigers roared, and the jackals and foxes howled, and the serpents hissed, it was so appalling that one seemed to be in hell. . . .

When our Captain and the Mercedarian friar realized that Montezuma would not allow us to set up a cross at Huichilobos' *cue*[2] or build a church there, it was decided that we should ask his stewards for masons so that we could put up a church in our own quarters. For every time we had said mass since entering the city of Mexico we had had to erect an altar on tables and dismantle it again.

The stewards promised to tell Montezuma of our wishes, and Cortes also sent our interpreters to ask him in person. Montezuma granted our request and ordered that we should be supplied with all the necessary material. We had our church finished in two days, and a cross erected in front of our lodgings, and mass was said there each day until the wine gave out. For as Cortes and some other captains and a friar had been ill during the Tlascalan campaign, there had been a run on the wine that we kept for mass. Still, though it was finished, we still went to church every day and prayed on our knees before the altar and images, firstly because it was our obligation as Christians and a good habit, and secondly so that Montezuma and all his captains should observe us and, seeing us worshipping on our knees before the cross — especially when we intoned the Ave Maria — might be inclined to imitate us.

---

[2] The temple of the sun god who demanded human sacrifice. [Ed.]

It being our habit to examine and inquire into everything, when we were all assembled in our lodging and considering which was the best place for an altar, two of our men, one of whom was the carpenter Alonso Yañez, called attention to some marks on one of the walls which showed that there had once been a door, though it had been well plastered up and painted. Now as we had heard that Montezuma kept his father's treasure in this building, we immediately suspected that it must be in this room, which had been closed up only a few days before. Yañez made the suggestion to Juan Velazquez de Leon and Francisco de Lugo, both relatives of mine, to whom he had attached himself as a servant; and they mentioned the matter to Cortes. So the door was secretly opened, and Cortes went in first with certain captains. When they saw the quantity of golden objects — jewels and plates and ingots — which lay in that chamber they were quite transported. They did not know what to think of such riches. The news soon spread to the other captains and soldiers, and very secretly we all went in to see. The sight of all that wealth dumbfounded me. Being only a youth at the time and never having seen such riches before, I felt certain that there could not be a store like it in the whole world. We unanimously decided that we could not think of touching a particle of it, and that the stones should immediately be replaced in the doorway, which should be blocked again and cemented just as we had found it. We resolved also that not a word should be said about this until times changed, for fear Montezuma might hear of our discovery.

Let us leave this subject of the treasure and tell how four of our most valiant captains took Cortes aside in the church, with a dozen soldiers who were in his trust and confidence, myself among them, and asked him to consider the net or trap in which we were caught, to look at the great strength of the city and observe the causeways and bridges, and remember the warnings we had received in every town we had passed through that Huichilobos had counselled Montezuma to let us into the city and kill us there. We reminded him that the hearts of men are very fickle, especially among the Indians, and begged him not to trust the good will and affection that Montezuma was showing us, because from one hour to another it might change. If he should take it into his head to attack us, we said, the stoppage of our supplies of food and water, or the raising of any of the bridges, would render us helpless. Then, considering the vast army of warriors he possessed, we should be incapable of attacking or defending ourselves. And since all the houses stood in the water, how could our Tlascalan allies come in to help us? We asked him to think over all that we had said, for if we wanted to preserve our lives we must seize Montezuma immediately, without even a day's delay. We pointed out that all the gold Montezuma had given us, and all that we had seen in the treasury of his father Axayacatl, and all the food we ate was turning to poison in our bodies, for we could not sleep by night or day or take any rest while these thoughts were in our minds. If any of our soldiers gave him less drastic advice, we concluded, they would be senseless beasts charmed by the gold and incapable of looking death in the eye.

When he had heard our opinion, Cortes answered: "Do not imagine, gentlemen, that I am asleep or that I do not share your anxiety. You must have seen that I do. But what strength have we got for so bold a course as to take this great lord in his own palace, surrounded as he is by warriors and guards? What scheme or trick can we devise to prevent him from summoning his soldiers to attack us at once?"

Our captains (Juan Velazquez de Leon, Diego de Ordaz, Gonzalo de Sandoval, and Pedro de Alvarado) replied that Montezuma must be got out of his palace by smooth words and brought to our quarters. Once there, he must be told that he must remain as a prisoner, and that if he called out or made any disturbance he would pay for it with his life. If Cortes was unwilling to take this course at once, they begged him for permission to do it themselves. With two very dangerous alternatives before us, the better and more profitable thing, they said, would be to seize Montezuma rather than wait for him to attack us. Once he did so, what chance would we have? Some of us soldiers also remarked that Montezuma's stewards who brought us our food seemed to be growing insolent, and did not serve us as politely as they had at first. Two of our Tlascalan allies had, moreover, secretly observed to Jeronimo de Aguilar that for the last two days the Mexicans had appeared less well disposed to us. We spent a good hour discussing whether or not to take Montezuma prisoner, and how it should be done. But our final advice, that at all costs we should take him prisoner, was approved by our Captain, and we then left the matter till next day. All night we prayed God to direct events in the interests of His holy service. . . .

From The Broken Spears:
The Aztec Account of
the Conquest of Mexico

This Aztec account of the encounter between the Spanish and the Indians of Mexico was written some years after the events described.
Spanish Christian monks helped a postconquest generation of Aztec
Nahuatl* speakers translate the illustrated manuscripts of the conquest period. According to this account, how did Montezuma respond
to Cortés? Was Montezuma's attitude toward the Spanish shared by
other Aztecs? How reliable is this account, do you think, in describing
Montezuma's thoughts, motives, and behavior?

Thinking Historically

How does the Aztec account of the conquest differ from that of the
Spanish, written by Díaz? Is this difference merely a matter of perspective, or do the authors disagree about what happened? To the extent
to which there are differences, how do you decide which account to
believe and accept?

Speeches of Motecuhzoma and Cortes

When Motecuhzoma[1] had given necklaces to each one, Cortes asked
him: "Are you Motecuhzoma? Are you the king? Is it true that you are
the king Motecuhzoma?"

And the king said: "Yes, I am Motecuhzoma." Then he stood up to
welcome Cortes; he came forward, bowed his head low and addressed
him in these words: "Our lord, you are weary. The journey has tired
you, but now you have arrived on the earth. You have come to your
city, Mexico. You have come here to sit on your throne, to sit under its
canopy.

"The kings who have gone before, your representatives, guarded it
and preserved it for your coming. The kings Itzcoatl, Motecuhzoma the
Elder, Axayacatl, Tizoc, and Ahuitzol ruled for you in the City of

*nah WAH tuhl
[1]Original Indian spelling of Montezuma. [Ed.]

The Broken Spears: The Aztec Account of the Conquest of Mexico, ed. Miguel Leon-Portilla
(Boston: Beacon Press, 1990), 64–76.

Mexico. The people were protected by their swords and sheltered by their shields.

"Do the kings know the destiny of those they left behind, their posterity? If only they are watching! If only they can see what I see!

"No, it is not a dream. I am not walking in my sleep. I am not seeing you in my dreams. . . . I have seen you at last! I have met you face to face! I was in agony for five days, for ten days, with my eyes fixed on the Region of the Mystery. And now you have come out of the clouds and mists to sit on your throne again.

"This was foretold by the kings who governed your city, and now it has taken place. You have come back to us; you have come down from the sky. Rest now, and take possession of your royal houses. Welcome to your land, my lords!"

When Motecuhzoma had finished, La Malinche translated his address into Spanish so that the Captain could understand it. Cortes replied in his strange and savage tongue, speaking first to La Malinche: "Tell Motecuhzoma that we are his friends. There is nothing to fear. We have wanted to see him for a long time, and now we have seen his face and heard his words. Tell him that we love him well and that our hearts are contented."

Then he said to Motecuhzoma: "We have come to your house in Mexico as friends. There is nothing to fear."

La Malinche translated this speech and the Spaniards grasped Motecuhzoma's hands and patted his back to show their affection for him.

Attitudes of the Spaniards and the Native Lords

The Spaniards examined everything they saw. They dismounted from their horses, and mounted them again, and dismounted again, so as not to miss anything of interest.

The chiefs who accompanied Motecuhzoma were: Cacama, king of Tezcoco; Tetlepanquetzaltzin, king of Tlacopan; Itzcuauhtzin the Tlacochcalcatl, lord of Tlatelolco; and Topantemoc, Motecuhzoma's treasurer in Tlatelolco. These four chiefs were standing in a file.

The other princes were: Atlixcatzin [chief who has taken captives];[2] Tepeoatzin, the Tlacochcalcatl; Quetzalaztatzin, the keeper of the chalk; Totomotzin; Hecateupatiltzin; and Cuappiatzin.

When Motecuhzoma was imprisoned, they all went into hiding. They ran away to hide and treacherously abandoned him!

---

[2]Military title given to a warrior who had captured four enemies.

The Spaniards Take Possession of the City

When the Spaniards entered the Royal House, they placed Motecuhzoma under guard and kept him under their vigilance. They also placed a guard over Itzcuauhtzin, but the other lords were permitted to depart.

Then the Spaniards fired one of their cannons, and this caused great confusion in the city. The people scattered in every direction; they fled without rhyme or reason; they ran off as if they were being pursued. It was as if they had eaten the mushrooms that confuse the mind, or had seen some dreadful apparition. They were all overcome by terror, as if their hearts had fainted. And when night fell, the panic spread through the city and their fears would not let them sleep.

In the morning the Spaniards told Motecuhzoma what they needed in the way of supplies: tortillas, fried chickens, hens' eggs, pure water, firewood, and charcoal. Also: large, clean cooking pots, water jars, pitchers, dishes, and other pottery. Motecuhzoma ordered that it be sent to them. The chiefs who received this order were angry with the king and no longer revered or respected him. But they furnished the Spaniards with all the provisions they needed — food, beverages, and water, and fodder for the horses.

The Spaniards Reveal Their Greed

When the Spaniards were installed in the palace, they asked Motecuhzoma about the city's resources and reserves and about the warriors' ensigns and shields. They questioned him closely and then demanded gold.

Motecuhzoma guided them to it. They surrounded him and crowded close with their weapons. He walked in the center, while they formed a circle around him.

When they arrived at the treasure house called Teucalco, the riches of gold and feathers were brought out to them: ornaments made of quetzal feathers, richly worked shields, disks of gold, the necklaces of the idols, gold nose plugs, gold greaves, and bracelets and crowns.

The Spaniards immediately stripped the feathers from the gold shields and ensigns. They gathered all the gold into a great mound and set fire to everything else, regardless of its value. Then they melted down the gold into ingots. As for the precious green stones, they took only the best of them; the rest were snatched up by the Tlaxcaltecas. The Spaniards searched through the whole treasure house, questioning and quarreling, and seized every object they thought was beautiful.

The Seizure of
Motecuhzoma's Treasures

Next they went to Motecuhzoma's storehouse, in the place called Toto-calco [Place of the Palace of the Birds],[3] where his personal treasures were kept. The Spaniards grinned like little beasts and patted each other with delight.

When they entered the hall of treasures, it was as if they had arrived in Paradise. They searched everywhere and coveted everything; they were slaves to their own greed. All of Motecuhzoma's possessions were brought out: fine bracelets, necklaces with large stones, ankle rings with little gold bells, the royal crowns, and all the royal finery — everything that belonged to the king and was reserved to him only. They seized these treasures as if they were their own, as if this plunder were merely a stroke of good luck. And when they had taken all the gold, they heaped up everything else in the middle of the patio.

La Malinche called the nobles together. She climbed up to the palace roof and cried: "Mexicanos, come forward! The Spaniards need your help! Bring them food and pure water. They are tired and hungry; they are almost fainting from exhaustion! Why do you not come forward? Are you angry with them?"

The Mexicans were too frightened to approach. They were crushed by terror and would not risk coming forward. They shied away as if the Spaniards were wild beasts, as if the hour were midnight on the blackest night of the year. Yet they did not abandon the Spaniards to hunger and thirst. They brought them whatever they needed, but shook with fear as they did so. They delivered the supplies to the Spaniards with trembling hands, then turned and hurried away.

The Preparations for the Fiesta

The Aztecs begged permission of their king to hold the fiesta of Huitzilopochtli.[3] The Spaniards wanted to see this fiesta to learn how it was celebrated. A delegation of the celebrants came to the palace where Motecuhzoma was a prisoner, and when their spokesman asked his permission, he granted it to them.

As soon as the delegation returned, the women began to grind seeds of the *chicalote*.[4] These women had fasted for a whole year. They ground the seeds in the patio of the temple.

The Spaniards came out of the palace together, dressed in armor and carrying their weapons with them. They stalked among the women

---

[3]The zoological garden attached to the royal palaces.
[4]Edible plants also used in medicines.

and looked at them one by one; they stared into the faces of the women who were grinding seeds. After this cold inspection, they went back into the palace. It is said that they planned to kill the celebrants if the men entered the patio.

The Statue of Huitzilopochtli

On the evening before the fiesta of Toxcatl, the celebrants began to model a statue of Huitzilopochtli. They gave it such a human appearance that it seemed the body of a living man. Yet they made the statue with nothing but a paste made of the ground seeds of the chicalote, which they shaped over an armature of sticks.

When the statue was finished, they dressed it in rich feathers, and they painted crossbars over and under its eyes. They also clipped on its earrings of turquoise mosaic; these were in the shape of serpents, with gold rings hanging from them. Its nose plug, in the shape of an arrow, was made of gold and was inlaid with fine stones.

They placed the magic headdress of hummingbird feathers on its head. They also adorned it with an *anecuyotl*, which was a belt made of feathers, with a cone at the back. Then they hung around its neck an ornament of yellow parrot feathers, fringed like the locks of a young boy. Over this they put its nettle-leaf cape, which was painted black and decorated with five clusters of eagle feathers.

Next they wrapped it in its cloak, which was painted with skull and bones, and over this they fastened its vest. The vest was painted with dismembered human parts: skulls, ears, hearts, intestines, torsos, breasts, hands, and feet. They also put on its *maxtlatl*, or loincloth, which was decorated with images of dissevered limbs and fringed with amate paper. This *maxtlatl* was painted with vertical stripes of bright blue.

They fastened a red paper flag at its shoulder and placed on its head what looked like a sacrificial flint knife. This too was made of red paper; it seemed to have been steeped in blood.

The statue carried a *tehuehuelli*, a bamboo shield decorated with four clusters of fine eagle feathers. The pendant of this shield was blood-red, like the knife and the shoulder flag. The statue also carried four arrows.

Finally, they put the wristbands on its arms. These bands, made of coyote skin, were fringed with paper cut into little strips.

The Beginning of the Fiesta

Early the next morning, the statue's face was uncovered by those who had been chosen for that ceremony. They gathered in front of the idol in single file and offered it gifts of food, such as round seedcakes or perhaps human flesh. But they did not carry it up to its temple on top of the pyramid.

All the young warriors were eager for the fiesta to begin. They had sworn to dance and sing with all their hearts, so that the Spaniards would marvel at the beauty of the rituals.

The procession began, and the celebrants filed into the temple patio to dance the Dance of the Serpent. When they were all together in the patio, the songs and the dance began. Those who had fasted for twenty days and those who had fasted for a year were in command of the others; they kept the dancers in file with their pine wands. (If anyone wished to urinate, he did not stop dancing, but simply opened his clothing at the hips and separated his clusters of heron feathers.)

If anyone disobeyed the leaders or was not in his proper place they struck him on the hips and shoulders. Then they drove him out of the patio, beating him and shoving him from behind. They pushed him so hard that he sprawled to the ground, and they dragged him outside by the ears. No one dared to say a word about this punishment, for those who had fasted during the year were feared and venerated; they had earned the exclusive title "Brothers of Huitzilopochtli."

The great captains, the bravest warriors, danced at the head of the files to guide the others. The youths followed at a slight distance. Some of the youths wore their hair gathered into large locks, a sign that they had never taken any captives. Others carried their headdresses on their shoulders; they had taken captives, but only with help.

Then came the recruits, who were called "the young warriors." They had each captured an enemy or two. The others called to them: "Come, comrades, show us how brave you are! Dance with all your hearts!"

The Spaniards Attack the Celebrants

At this moment in the fiesta, when the dance was loveliest and when song was linked to song, the Spaniards were seized with an urge to kill the celebrants. They all ran forward, armed as if for battle. They closed the entrances and passageways, all the gates of the patio: the Eagle Gate in the lesser palace, the Gate of the Canestalk and the Gate of the Serpent of Mirrors. They posted guards so that no one could escape, and then rushed into the Sacred Patio to slaughter the celebrants. They came on foot, carrying their swords and their wooden or metal shields.

They ran in among the dancers, forcing their way to the place where the drums were played. They attacked the man who was drumming and cut off his arms. Then they cut off his head, and it rolled across the floor.

They attacked all the celebrants, stabbing them, spearing them, striking them with their swords. They attacked some of them from behind, and these fell instantly to the ground with their entrails hanging out. Others they beheaded: they cut off their heads, or split their heads to pieces.

They struck others in the shoulders, and their arms were torn from their bodies. They wounded some in the thigh and some in the calf. They slashed others in the abdomen, and their entrails all spilled to the ground. Some attempted to run away, but their intestines dragged as they ran; they seemed to tangle their feet in their own entrails. No matter how they tried to save themselves, they could find no escape.

Some attempted to force their way out, but the Spaniards murdered them at the gates. Others climbed the walls, but they could not save themselves. Those who ran into the communal houses were safe there for a while; so were those who lay down among the victims and pretended to be dead. But if they stood up again, the Spaniards saw them and killed them.

The blood of the warriors flowed like water and gathered into pools. The pools widened, and the stench of blood and entrails filled the air. The Spaniards ran into the communal houses to kill those who were hiding. They ran everywhere and searched everywhere; they invaded every room, hunting and killing.

$$\boxed{101}$$

BARTOLOMEO DE LAS CASAS

From The Devastation of the Indies

Las Casas (1484–1566) emigrated with his father from Spain to the island of Hispaniola in 1502. Eight years later he became a priest, served as a missionary to the Taino of Cuba (1512), attempted to create a utopian society for the Indians of Venezuela, and became a Dominican friar in 1522. Repelled by his early experience among the conquistadors, Las Casas the priest and friar devoted his adult life to aiding the Indians in the Americas and defending their rights in the Spanish court. This selection is drawn from his brief history, *The Devastation of the Indies*, published in 1555. The work for this book and

Bartolomeo de Las Casas, *The Devastation of the Indies: A Brief Account*, trans. Herma Briffault (Baltimore: Johns Hopkins University Press, 1992), 32–35, 40–41.

a larger volume, *In Defense of the Indians*, presented his case against Indian slavery in the great debate at the Spanish court at Valladolid in 1550. Along with his monumental *History of the Indies*, published after his death, the writings of Las Casas constituted such an indictment of Spanish colonialism that Protestant enemies were able to argue that Catholic slavery and exploitation of the "New World" was worse than their own, a dubious proposition that became known as "the Black Legend." What do you make of this account by Las Casas? Does he exaggerate, or is it likely that these events happened?

Thinking Historically

Compare this account with the two previous selections. Do you think the Spanish treated the people of Hispaniola and Mexico differently? Do these three readings offer different interpretations of the role of Christianity in the Americas?

This [Hispaniola][1] was the first land in the New World to be destroyed and depopulated by the Christians, and here they began their subjection of the women and children, taking them away from the Indians to use them and ill use them, eating the food they provided with their sweat and toil. The Spaniards did not content themselves with what the Indians gave them of their own free will, according to their ability, which was always too little to satisfy enormous appetites, for a Christian eats and consumes in one day an amount of food that would suffice to feed three houses inhabited by ten Indians for one month. And they committed other acts of force and violence and oppression which made the Indians realize that these men had not come from Heaven. And some of the Indians concealed their foods while others concealed their wives and children and still others fled to the mountains to avoid the terrible transactions of the Christians.

And the Christians attacked them with buffets and beatings, until finally they laid hands on the nobles of the villages. Then they behaved with such temerity and shamelessness that the most powerful ruler of the islands had to see his own wife raped by a Christian officer.

From that time onward the Indians began to seek ways to throw the Christians out of their lands. They took up arms, but their weapons were very weak and of little service in offense and still less in defense. (Because of this, the wars of the Indians against each other are little more than games played by children.) And the Christians, with their horses and swords and pikes began to carry out massacres and strange

[1]The island that today includes the Dominican Republic and Haiti. [Ed.]

cruelties against them. They attacked the towns and spared neither the children nor the aged nor pregnant women nor women in childbed, not only stabbing them and dismembering them but cutting them to pieces as if dealing with sheep in the slaughter house. They laid bets as to who, with one stroke of the sword, could split a man in two or could cut off his head or spill out his entrails with a single stroke of the pike. They took infants from their mothers' breasts, snatching them by the legs and pitching them headfirst against the crags or snatched them by the arms and threw them into the rivers, roaring with laughter and saying as the babies fell into the water, "Boil there, you offspring of the devil!" Other infants they put to the sword along with their mothers and anyone else who happened to be nearby. They made some low wide gallows on which the hanged victim's feet almost touched the ground, stringing up their victims in lots of thirteen, in memory of Our Redeemer and His twelve Apostles, then set burning wood at their feet and thus burned them alive. To others they attached straw or wrapped their whole bodies in straw and set them afire. With still others, all those they wanted to capture alive, they cut off their hands and hung them round the victim's neck, saying, "Go now, carry the message," meaning, Take the news to the Indians who have fled to the mountains. They usually dealt with the chieftains and nobles in the following way: they made a grid of rods which they placed on forked sticks, then lashed the victims to the grid and lighted a smoldering fire underneath, so that little by little, as those captives screamed in despair and torment, their souls would leave them.

I once saw this, when there were four or five nobles lashed on grids and burning; I seem even to recall that there were two or three pairs of grids where others were burning, and because they uttered such loud screams that they disturbed the captain's sleep, he ordered them to be strangled. And the constable, who was worse than an executioner, did not want to obey that order (and I know the name of that constable and know his relatives in Seville), but instead put a stick over the victims' tongues, so they could not make a sound, and he stirred up the fire, but not too much, so that they roasted slowly, as he liked. I saw all these things I have described, and countless others.

And because all the people who could do so fled to the mountains to escape these inhuman, ruthless, and ferocious acts, the Spanish captains, enemies of the human race, pursued them with the fierce dogs they kept which attacked the Indians, tearing them to pieces and devouring them. And because on few and far between occasions, the Indians justifiably killed some Christians, the Spaniards made a rule among themselves that for every Christian slain by the Indians, they would slay a hundred Indians. . . .

Because the particulars that enter into these outrages are so numerous they could not be contained in the scope of much writing, for in

truth I believe that in the great deal I have set down here I have not revealed the thousandth part of the sufferings endured by the Indians, I
now want only to add that, in the matter of these unprovoked and destructive wars, and God is my witness, all these acts of wickedness I
have described, as well as those I have omitted, were perpetrated
against the Indians without cause, without any more cause than could
give a community of good monks living together in a monastery. And
still more strongly I affirm that until the multitude of people on this island of Hispaniola were killed and their lands devastated, they committed no sin against the Christians that would be punishable by man's
laws, and as to those sins punishable by God's law, such as vengeful
feelings against such powerful enemies as the Christians have been,
those sins would be committed by the very few Indians who are hard-
hearted and impetuous. And I can say this from my great experience
with them: their hardness and impetuosity would be that of children, of
boys ten or twelve years old. I know by certain infallible signs that the
wars waged by the Indians against the Christians have been justifiable
wars and that all the wars waged by the Christians against the Indians
have been unjust wars, more diabolical than any wars ever waged anywhere in the world. This I declare to be so of all the many wars they
have waged against the peoples throughout the Indies.

After the wars and the killings had ended, when usually there survived only some boys, some women, and children, these survivors were
distributed among the Christians to be slaves. The *repartimiento* or distribution was made according to the rank and importance of the Christian to whom the Indians were allocated, one of them being given
thirty, another forty, still another, one or two hundred, and besides the
rank of the Christian there was also to be considered in what favor he
stood with the tyrant they called Governor. The pretext was that these
allocated Indians were to be instructed in the articles of the Christian
Faith. As if those Christians who were as a rule foolish and cruel and
greedy and vicious could be caretakers of souls! And the care they took
was to send the men to the mines to dig for gold, which is intolerable
labor, and to send the women into the fields of the big ranches to hoe
and till the land, work suitable for strong men. Nor to either the men
or the women did they give any food except herbs and legumes, things
of little substance. The milk in the breasts of the women with infants
dried up and thus in a short while the infants perished.

102

Two European Views of Native Americans

Las Casas's sympathetic view of the Indians was hardly one shared by the average Frenchman, Italian, or Scot. Indeed, many Europeans harbored fantastical and negative notions about the inhabitants of the "New World," envisioning them as wild and cannibalistic, savage and ruthless toward their enemies. Reinforcing this impression were images that circulated throughout Europe during the sixteenth and seventeenth centuries, such as this engraving from the 1590s, part of a series by Flemish engraver Theodore de Bry, based on paintings by an artist who had accompanied a French expedition to Florida a few decades earlier. Figure 16.1 shows the cannibalistic practices by natives supposedly witnessed by the explorers. What is going on in this picture? It is likely that de Bry made adjustments to his engravings from the originals to please potential buyers. If so, what does this tell us about the expectations of European audiences about the Americas and their inhabitants?

Almost seventy-five years later, a very different set of no less remarkable images emerged from a Dutch colony in northeastern Brazil. Count Johan Maurits, the humanist governor general of the colony from 1636 to 1644, brought several artists and scientists with him to observe and record the region's flora and fauna as well as its inhabitants. Johan Maurits, who was fascinated by the local peoples and their cultures, commissioned from artist Albert Eckhout a number of still-lifes and group and individual portraits, including one showing a female Tapuya Indian (see Figure 16.2). According to Dutch accounts, the Tapuya were more warlike and less "civilized" than some of the other local peoples — for example, they sometimes consumed their dead instead of burying them. Aside from the body parts this woman carries in her hand and in her bag, what other signs of this warlike tendency do you see in Figure 16.2? Look closely at the many interesting details in this painting. What does the artist seem to be interested in showing?

Thinking Historically

What are the differences in style and content between Figures 16.1 and 16.2, and how do you account for them? Which of the following factors do you think is most important in explaining their differences: chronology, agenda of the artist, the potential audience for the image, the setting in which they were produced? What might be the pitfalls for students of history in comparing these two images? How do you reconcile Las Casas's account in the previous source with the scene

Figure 16.1   Cannibalism, Engraving by Theodore de Bry.
Source: Service Historique de la Marine, Vincennes, France, Giraudon/The Bridgeman Art Library International.

portrayed in Figure 16.1? Which source would you consider more reliable and why? Which source would a sixteenth-century Spaniard have considered more reliable and why? Consider how women (or woman) are depicted in these works. What differences and similarities do you see? What might that tell us about European notions of women and gender in the New World?

Figure 16.2 Tapuya Indian, by Albert Eckhout.
Source: National Museum of Denmark.

103

DAVID PIETERZEN DeVRIES

A Dutch Massacre of the Algonquins

David Pieterzen DeVries was a ship's captain who became a landlord or "patroonship" holder in the Dutch colony of New Amsterdam (now New York). After a disastrous venture to establish a farming and whaling colony, Swanendael on the Delaware River (near modern Philadelphia), he was granted the first patroonship on Staten Island. There he had frequent contact with the Algonquin and Raritan Indians. He was a member of the Board of Directors (the Twelve Men), responsible to the Dutch West India Company for the governance of New Amsterdam. When in 1642, a new governor, Dutch merchant Willem Kieft, urged increased settlement and Indian removal, DeVries urged caution. He described what happened in February 1643 in his book, *Voyages from Holland to America*.

Why did DeVries oppose the governor's plan to attack the Algonquins? What does his story suggest about Dutch-Indian relations before 1643? What were the consequences of the massacre?

Thinking Historically

How is the Dutch treatment of the Algonquins different from the Spanish treatment of the Native Americans? What accounts for these differences? Consider this source in light of the images in the previous document. How might seventeenth-century Europeans reconcile the scene in Figure 16.1 with what DeVries describes in his account?

Do you think an Algonquin account of this encounter would be significantly different from that of DeVries? How might it differ?

The 24th of February, sitting at a table with the Governor, he began to state his intentions, that he had a mind to *wipe the mouths* of the savages; that he had been dining at the house of Jan Claesen Damen, where Maryn Adriaensen and Jan Claesen Damen, together with Jacob Planck, had presented a petition to him to begin this work. I answered him that they were not wise to request this; that such work could not

David Pieterzen DeVries, *Voyages from Holland to America*, A.D. 1632–1644, trans. H. C. Murphy (New York: Billing Brothers, 1853), 114–17.

be done without the approbation of the Twelve Men; that it could not take place without my assent, who was one of the Twelve Men; that moreover I was the first patroon, and no one else hitherto had risked there so many thousands, and also his person, as I was the first to come from Holland or Zeeland to plant a colony; and that he should consider what profit he could derive from this business, as he well knew that on account of trifling with the Indians we had lost our colony in the South River at Swanendael, in the Hoere-kil, with thirty-two men, who were murdered in the year 1630; and that in the year 1640, the cause of my people being murdered on Staten Island was a difficulty which he had brought on with the Raritan Indians, where his soldiers had for some trifling thing killed some savages. . . . But it appeared that my speaking was of no avail. He had, with his comurderers, determined to commit the murder, deeming it a Roman deed, and to do it without warning the inhabitants in the open lands that each one might take care of himself against the retaliation of the savages, for he could not kill all the Indians. When I had expressed all these things in full, sitting at the table, and the meal was over, he told me he wished me to go to the large hall, which he had been lately adding to his house. Coming to it, there stood all his soldiers ready to cross the river to Pavonia to commit the murder. Then spoke I again to Governor Willem Kieft: "Let this work alone; you wish to break the mouths of the Indians, but you will also murder our own nation, for there are none of the settlers in the open country who are aware of it. My own dwelling, my people, cattle, corn, and tobacco will be lost." He answered me, assuring me that there would be no danger; that some soldiers should go to my house to protect it. But that was not done. So was this business begun between the 25th and 26th of February in the year 1643. I remained that night at the Governor's, sitting up. I went and sat by the kitchen fire, when about midnight I heard a great shrieking, and I ran to the ramparts of the fort, and looked over to Pavonia. Saw nothing but firing, and heard the shrieks of the savages murdered in their sleep. I returned again to the house by the fire. Having sat there awhile, there came an Indian with his squaw, whom I knew well, and who lived about an hour's walk from my house, and told me that they two had fled in a small skiff, which they had taken from the shore at Pavonia; that the Indians from Fort Orange had surprised them; and that they had come to conceal themselves in the fort. I told them that they must go away immediately; that this was no time for them to come to the fort to conceal themselves; that they who had killed their people at Pavonia were not Indians, but the Swannekens, as they call the Dutch, had done it. They then asked me how they should get out of the fort. I took them to the door, and there was no sentry there, and so they betook themselves to the woods. When it was day the soldiers returned to the fort, having

massacred or murdered eighty Indians, and considering they had done
a deed of Roman valor, in murdering so many in their sleep; where infants were torn from their mothers' breasts, and hacked to pieces in the
presence of the parents, and the pieces thrown into the fire and in the
water, and other sucklings, being bound to small boards, were cut,
stuck, and pierced, and miserably massacred in a manner to move a
heart of stone. Some were thrown into the river, and when the fathers
and mothers endeavored to save them, the soldiers would not let them
come on land but made both parents and children drown — children
from five to six years of age, and also some old and decrepit persons.
Those who fled from this onslaught, and concealed themselves in the
neighboring sedge, and when it was morning, came out to beg a piece
of bread, and to be permitted to warm themselves, were murdered in
cold blood and tossed into the fire or the water. Some came to our people in the country with their hands, some with their legs cut off, and
some holding their entrails in their arms, and others had such horrible
cuts and gashes, that worse than they were could never happen. And
these poor simple creatures, as also many of our own people, did not
know any better than that they had been attacked by a party of other
Indians — the Maquas. After this exploit, the soldiers were rewarded
for their services, and Director Kieft thanked them by taking them by
the hand and congratulating them. At another place, on the same night,
on Corler's Hook near Corler's plantation, forty Indians were in the
same manner attacked in their sleep, and massacred there in the same
manner. Did the Duke of Alva[1] in the Netherlands ever do anything
more cruel? This is indeed a disgrace to our nation, who have so generous a governor in our Fatherland as the Prince of Orange, who has always endeavored in his wars to spill as little blood as possible. As soon
as the savages understood that the Swannekens had so treated them, all
the men whom they could surprise on the farmlands, they killed; but
we have never heard that they have ever permitted women or children
to be killed. They burned all the houses, farms, barns, grain, haystacks,
and destroyed everything they could get hold of. So there was an open
destructive war begun. They also burnt my farm, cattle, corn, barn, to-
bacco-house, and all the tobacco. My people saved themselves in the
house where I alone lived, which was made with embrasures, through
which they defended themselves. Whilst my people were in alarm the
savage whom I had aided to escape from the fort in the night came
there, and told the other Indians that I was a good chief, that I had
helped him out of the fort, and that the killing of the Indians took place

---

[1]Spanish tyrant who ruled over the Netherlands before the Dutch gained their independence in 1581. [Ed.]

contrary to my wish. Then they all cried out together to my people that they would not shoot them; that if they had not destroyed my cattle they would not do it, nor burn my house; that they would let my little brewery stand, though they wished to get the copper kettle, in order to make darts for their arrows; but hearing now that it had been done contrary to my wish, they all went away, and left my house unbesieged. When now the Indians had destroyed so many farms and men in revenge for their people, I went to Governor Willem Kieft, and asked him if it was not as I had said it would be, that he would only effect the spilling of Christian blood. Who would now compensate us for our losses? But he gave me no answer. He said he wondered that no Indians came to the fort. I told him that I did not wonder at it; "why should the Indians come here where you have so treated them?"

104

NZINGA MBEMBA

Appeal to the King of Portugal

Europeans were unable to conquer Africa as they did the Americas until the end of the nineteenth century. Rivers that fell steeply to the sea, military defenses, and diseases like malaria proved insurmountable to Europeans before the age of the steamship, the machine gun, and quinine pills. Before the last half of the nineteenth century, Europeans had to be content with alliances with African kings and rulers. The Portuguese had been the first to meet Africans in the towns and villages along the Atlantic coast, and they became the first European missionaries and trading partners.

Nzinga Mbemba, whose Christian name was Affonso, was king of the west African state of Congo (comprising what is today parts of Angola as well as the two Congo states) from about 1506 to 1543. He succeeded his father, King Nzinga a Kuwu who, shortly after their first Portuguese contact in 1483, sent officials to Lisbon to learn European ways. In 1491 father and son were baptized, and Portuguese

---

Basil Davidson, *The African Past* (Boston: Little, Brown, and Company, 1964), 191–94.

priests, merchants, artisans, and soldiers were provided with a coastal settlement.

What exactly is the complaint of the King of Congo? What seems to be the impact of Portuguese traders (factors) in the Congo? What does King Affonso want the King of Portugal to do?

Thinking Historically

This selection offers an opportunity to compare European expansion in the Americas and Africa. Portuguese contact with Nzinga Mbemba of the Congo was roughly contemporaneous with Spanish colonialism in the Americas. What differences do you see between these two cases of early European expansion? Can you think of any reasons that Congo kings converted to Christianity while Mexican kings did not?

Compare the European treatment of Africans with their treatment of Native Americans. Why did Europeans enslave Africans and not, for the most part, American Indians?

Sir, Your Highness [of Portugal] should know how our Kingdom is being lost in so many ways that it is convenient to provide for the necessary remedy, since this is caused by the excessive freedom given by your factors and officials to the men and merchants who are allowed to come to this Kingdom to set up shops with goods and many things which have been prohibited by us, and which they spread throughout our Kingdoms and Domains in such an abundance that many of our vassals, whom we had in obedience, do not comply because they have the things in greater abundance than we ourselves; and it was with these things that we had them content and subjected under our vassalage and jurisdiction, so it is doing a great harm not only to the service of God, but to the security and peace of our Kingdoms and State as well.

And we cannot reckon how great the damage is, since the mentioned merchants are taking every day our natives, sons of the land and the sons of our noblemen and vassals and our relatives, because the thieves and men of bad conscience grab them wishing to have the things and wares of this Kingdom which they are ambitious of; they grab them and get them to be sold; and so great, Sir, is the corruption and licentiousness that our country is being completely depopulated, and Your Highness should not agree with this nor accept it as in your service. And to avoid it we need from those [your] Kingdoms no more than some priests and a few people to teach in schools, and no other goods except wine and flour for the holy sacrament. That is why we beg of Your Highness to help and assist us in this matter, commanding your factors that they should not send here either merchants or wares, because it is *our will that in these Kingdoms there should not be any trade of slaves nor outlet for them.*[1] Concerning what is referred above, again we beg of Your Highness to agree with it, since otherwise we cannot remedy such an obvious damage. Pray Our Lord in His mercy to have Your Highness under His guard and let you do for ever the things of His service. I kiss your hands many times.

At our town of Congo, written on the sixth day of July.
João Teixeira did it in 1526.
The King. Dom Affonso.
[On the back of this letter the following can be read:
To the most powerful and excellent prince Dom João, King our Brother.]

Moreover, Sir, in our Kingdoms there is another great inconvenience which is of little service to God, and this is that many of our people [*naturaes*], keenly desirous as they are of the wares and things of your Kingdoms, which are brought here by your people, and in order to satisfy their voracious appetite, seize many of our people, freed and exempt men; and very often it happens that they kidnap even noblemen and the sons of noblemen, and our relatives, and take them to be sold to the white men who are in our Kingdoms; and for this purpose they have concealed them; and others are brought during the night so that they might not be recognized.

And as soon as they are taken by the white men they are immediately ironed and branded with fire, and when they are carried to be embarked, if they are caught by our guards' men the whites allege that they have bought them but they cannot say from whom, so that it is our duty to do justice and to restore to the freemen their freedom, but it cannot be done if your subjects feel offended, as they claim to be.

And to avoid such a great evil we passed a law so that any white man living in our Kingdoms and wanting to purchase goods in any way should first inform three of our noblemen and officials of our court whom we rely upon in this matter, and these are Dom Pedro Manipanza and Dom Manuel Manissaba, our chief usher, and Gonçalo Pires our chief freighter, who should investigate if the mentioned goods are captives or free men, and if cleared by them there will be no further doubt nor embargo for them to be taken and embarked. But if the white men do not comply with it they will lose the aforementioned goods. And if we do them this favor and concession it is for the part Your Highness has in it, since we know that it is in your service too that these goods are taken from our Kingdom, otherwise we should not consent to this. . . .

---

[1]Emphasis in the original.

Sir, Your Highness has been kind enough to write to us saying that we should ask in our letters for anything we need, and that we shall be provided with everything, and as the peace and the health of our Kingdom depend on us, and as there are among us old folks and people who have lived for many days, it happens that we have continuously many and different diseases which put us very often in such a weakness that we reach almost the last extreme; and the same happens to our children, relatives, and natives owing to the lack in this country of physicians and surgeons who might know how to cure properly such diseases. And as we have got neither dispensaries nor drugs which might help us in this forlornness, many of those who had been already confirmed and instructed in the holy faith of Our Lord Jesus Christ perish and die; and the rest of the people in their majority cure themselves with herbs and breads and other ancient methods, so that they put all their faith in the mentioned herbs and ceremonies if they live, and believe that they are saved if they die; and this is not much in the service of God.

And to avoid such a great error and inconvenience, since it is from God in the first place and then from your Kingdoms and from Your Highness that all the goods and drugs and medicines have come to save us, we beg of you to be agreeable and kind enough to send us two physicians and two apothecaries and one surgeon, so that they may come with their drug-stores and all the necessary things to stay in our kingdoms, because we are in extreme need of them all and each of them. We shall do them all good and shall benefit them by all means, since they are sent by Your Highness, whom we thank for your work in their coming. We beg of Your Highness as a great favor to do this for us, because besides being good in itself it is in the service of God as we have said above.

WILLIAM BOSMAN

Slave Trader

William Bosman was the chief agent of the Dutch West India Company on the African coast where he lived from 1686 to 1702. Here he explains how slaves were brought to Whydah, an English fort on the coast of Dahomey (between the Gold Coast of Ghana and the slave coast of Nigeria). Bosman discusses various ways in which he received slaves. What were these ways? Which does he seem to prefer?

Thinking Historically

Compare Bosman's description of the slave trade with that of Nzinga Mbemba in the preceding selection. How do you account for the differences? Are they due to Dutch and Portuguese practice, to policies of the Congo and Dahomey, or to the passage of time between 1526 and 1700?

The author, a Dutchman, makes certain comparisons between Dutch slave ships and those of other Europeans. Do you see any evidence for his claims?

The first business of one of our factors [agents] when he comes to Fida [Whydah], is to satisfy the customs of the king and the great men, which amounts to about a hundred pounds in Guinea value, as the goods must yield there. After which we have free license to trade, which is published throughout the whole land by the crier.

But yet before we can deal with any person, we are obliged to buy the king's whole stock of slaves at a set price, which is commonly one third or one fourth higher than ordinary; after which, we obtain free leave to deal with all his subjects, of what rank soever. But if there happen to be no stock of slaves, the factor must then resolve to run the risk of trusting the inhabitants with goods to the value of one or two hundred slaves; which commodities they send into the inland country, in

William Bosman, *A New and Accurate Description of the Coast of Guinea, Divided into the Gold, the Slave, and the Ivory Coasts,* 2nd ed., trans. from Dutch (London: 1721), Barnes & Noble, 1967, pp. 363a–365a.

order to buy with them slaves at all markets, and that sometimes two hundred miles deep in the country. For you ought to be informed, that markets of men are here kept in the same manner as those of beasts with us.

Not a few in our country fondly imagine that parents here sell their children, men their wives, and one brother the other. But those who think so, do deceive themselves; for this never happens on any other account but that of necessity, or some great crime; but most of the slaves that are offered to us, are prisoners of war, which are sold by the victors as their booty.

When these slaves come to Fida, they are put in prison all together; and when we treat concerning buying them, they are all brought out together in a large plain; where, by our surgeons, whose province it is, they are thoroughly examined, even to the smallest member, and that naked, both men and women, without the least distinction or modesty. Those that are approved as good, are set on one side; and the lame or faulty are set by as invalids, which are here called *mackrons*: these are such as are above five and thirty years old, or are maimed in the arms, legs, or feet; have lost a tooth, are grey-haired, or have films over their eyes; as well as all those which are affected with any venereal distemper, or several other diseases.

The invalids and the maimed being thrown out, as I have told you, the remainder are numbered, and it is entered who delivered them. In the meanwhile, a burning iron, with the arms or name of the companies, lies in the fire, with which ours are marked on the breast. This is done that we may distinguish them from the slaves of the English, French, or others (which are also marked with their mark), and to prevent the Negroes exchanging them for worse, at which they have a good hand. I doubt not but this trade seems very barbarous to you, but since it is followed by mere necessity, it must go on; but we yet take all possible care that they are not burned too hard, especially the women, who are more tender than the men.

We are seldom long detained in the buying of these slaves, because their price is established, the women being one fourth or fifth part cheaper than the men. The disputes which we generally have with the owners of these slaves are, that we will not give them such goods as they ask for them, especially the *boesies* [cowry shells] (as I have told you, the money of this country) of which they are very fond, though we generally make a division on this head, in order to make one part of the goods help off another; because those slaves which are paid for in *boesies*, cost the company one half more than those bought with other goods. . . .

When we have agreed with the owners of the slaves, they are returned to their prison; where, from that time forwards, they are kept at our charge, cost us two pence a day a slave; which serves to subsist them, like our criminals, on bread and water: so that to save charges, we send them on board our ships with the very first opportunity, before which their masters strip them of all they have on their backs; so that they come to us stark-naked, as well women as men: in which condition they are obliged to continue, if the master of the ship is not so charitable (which he commonly is) as to bestow something on them to cover their nakedness.

You would really wonder to see how these slaves live on board; for though their number sometimes amounts to six or seven hundred, yet by the careful management of our masters of ships, they are so [well] regulated, that it seems incredible. And in this particular our nation exceeds all other Europeans; for as the French, Portuguese, and English slave-ships are always foul and stinking; on the contrary, ours are for the most part clean and neat.

The slaves are fed three times a day with indifferent good victuals, and much better than they eat in their own country. Their lodging place is divided into two parts; one of which is appointed for the men, the other for the women, each sex being kept apart. Here they lie as close together as it is possible for them to be crowded.

We are sometimes sufficiently plagued with a parcel of slaves which come from a far inland country, who very innocently persuade one another, that we buy them only to fatten, and afterwards eat them as a delicacy. When we are so unhappy as to be pestered with many of this sort, they resolve and agree together (and bring over the rest of their party) to run away from the ship, kill the Europeans, and set the vessel ashore; by which means they design to free themselves from being our food.

I have twice met with this misfortune; and the first time proved very unlucky to me, I not in the least suspecting it; but the uproar was timely quashed by the master of the ship and myself, by causing the abettor to be shot through the head, after which all was quiet.

But the second time it fell heavier on another ship, and that chiefly by the carelessness of the master, who having fished up the anchor of a departed English ship, had laid it in the hold where the male slaves were lodged, who, unknown to any of the ship's crew, possessed themselves of a hammer, with which, in a short time they broke all their fetters in pieces upon the anchor: After this, they came above deck, and fell upon our men, some of whom they grievously wounded, and would certainly have mastered the ship, if a French and English ship had not very fortunately happened to lie by us; who perceiving by our firing a distressed-gun, that something was in disorder on board, immediately came to our assistance with shallops and men, and drove the slaves under deck: notwithstanding which, before all was appeased, about twenty of them were killed.

The Portuguese have been more unlucky in this particular than we; for in four years time they lost four ships in this manner.

OLAUDAH EQUIANO

Enslaved Captive

The Interesting Narrative of the Life of Olaudah Equiano,* or Gustavus Vassa the African, written by himself was published in 1789. It tells the story of a young boy sold into slavery in Africa and transported to the Americas, who after winning his freedom became a spokesman for the abolition of slavery in England and America. Recent research suggests that the author, Equiano, may have actually been born a slave in South Carolina and that his tale of earlier African slavery may be a composite of the stories of others. If *The Interesting Narrative* is less autobiographical than once believed, it is no less interesting, and still conveys a wealth of useful information about African experiences of slavery. How was slavery in Africa different from slavery in America? What were the worst aspects of the Atlantic slave trades according to the author? Why does Equiano address his audience as "nominal Christians"?

Thinking Historically

Compare Equiano's attitude toward slavery with that of another author in this chapter. Is Equiano opposed to all forms of slavery or only to certain kinds of slavery? How does Equiano's attitude towards Europeans compare with that of other authors in this chapter?

I hope the reader will not think I have trespassed on his patience in introducing myself to him with some account of the manners and customs of my country. They had been implanted in me with great care, and made an impression on my mind, which time could not erase, and which all the adversity and variety of fortune I have since experienced, served only to rivet and record: for, whether the love of one's country be real or imaginary, or a lesson of reason, or an instinct of nature, I still look back with pleasure on the first scenes of my life, though that pleasure has been for the most part mingled with sorrow.

*oh law OO dah eh kwee AH noh

"Olaudah Equiano of the Niger Ibo," ed. G. I. Jones, in *Africa Remembered,* ed. Philip D. Curtin (Madison: University of Wisconsin Press, 1967), 60–98.

I have already acquainted the reader with the time and place of my birth. My father, besides many slaves, had a numerous family, of which seven lived to grow up, including myself and sister, who was the only daughter. As I was the youngest of the sons, I became, of course, the greatest favorite with my mother, and was always with her; and she used to take particular pains to form my mind. I was trained up from my earliest years in the art of war: my daily exercise was shooting and throwing javelins, and my mother adorned me with emblems, after the manner of our greatest warriors. In this way I grew up till I had turned the age of eleven, when an end was put to my happiness in the following manner: Generally, when the grown people in the neighborhood were gone far in the fields to labor, the children assembled together in some of the neighboring premises to play; and commonly some of us used to get up a tree to look out for any assailant, or kidnapper, that might come upon us — for they sometimes took those opportunities of our parents' absence, to attack and carry off as many as they could seize. . . . Alas! ere long it was my fate to be thus attacked, and to be carried off, when none of the grown people were nigh.

One day, when all our people were gone out to their works as usual, and only I and my dear sister were left to mind the house, two men and a woman got over our walls, and in a moment seized us both, and, without giving us time to cry out, or make resistance, they stopped our mouths, and ran off with us into the nearest wood. Here they tied our hands, and continued to carry us as far as they could, till night came on, when we reached a small house, where the robbers halted for refreshment, and spent the night. We were then unbound, but were unable to take any food; and, being quite overpowered by fatigue and grief, our only relief was some sleep, which allayed our misfortune for a short time. The next morning we left the house, and continued travelling all the day. For a long time we had kept the woods, but at last we came into a road which I believed I knew. I had now some hopes of being delivered; for we had advanced but a little way before I discovered some people at a distance, on which I began to cry out for their assistance; but my cries had no other effect than to make them tie me faster and stop my mouth, and then they put me into a large sack. They also stopped my sister's mouth, and tied her hands; and in this manner we proceeded till we were out of sight of these people. When we went to rest the following night, they offered us some victuals, but we refused it; and the only comfort we had was in being in one another's arms all that night, and bathing each other with our tears. But alas! we were soon deprived of even the small comfort of weeping together.

The next day proved a day of greater sorrow than I had yet experienced; for my sister and I were then separated, while we lay clasped in each other's arms. It was in vain that we besought them not to part us; she was torn from me, and immediately carried away, while I was left in a state of distraction not to be described. I cried and grieved continually; and for several days did not eat anything but what they forced into my mouth. At length, after many days' travelling, during which I had often changed masters, I got into the hands of a chieftain, in a very pleasant country. This man had two wives and some children, and they all used me extremely well, and did all they could do to comfort me; particularly the first wife, who was something like my mother. Although I was a great many days' journey from my father's house, yet these people spoke exactly the same language with us. This first master of mine, as I may call him, was a smith, and my principal employment was working his bellows, which were the same kind as I had seen in my vicinity. They were in some respects not unlike the stoves here in gentlemen's kitchens, and were covered over with leather; and in the middle of that leather a stick was fixed, and a person stood up, and worked it in the same manner as is done to pump water out of a cask with a hand pump. I believe it was gold he worked, for it was of a lovely bright yellow color, and was worn by the women on their wrists and ankles. . . .

Soon after this, my master's only daughter, and child by his first wife, sickened and died, which affected him so much that for some time he was almost frantic, and really would have killed himself, had he not been watched and prevented. However, in a short time afterwards he recovered, and I was again sold. I was now carried to the left of the sun's rising, through many dreary wastes and dismal woods, amidst the hideous roarings of wild beasts. The people I was sold to used to carry me very often, when I was tired, either on their shoulders or on their backs. I saw many convenient well-built sheds along the road, at proper distances, to accommodate the merchants and travellers, who lay in those buildings along with their wives, who often accompany them; and they always go well armed. . . .

After travelling a considerable time. I came to a town called Tinmah, in the most beautiful country I had yet seen in Africa. It was extremely rich, and there were many rivulets which flowed through it, and supplied a large pond in the centre of the town, where the people washed. Here I saw for the first time cocoanuts, which I thought superior to any nuts I had ever tasted before; and the trees, which were loaded, were also interspersed among the houses, which had commodious shades adjoining, and were in the same manner as ours, the insides being neatly plastered and whitewashed. Here I also saw and tasted for the first time, sugar-cane. Their money consisted of little white shells, the size of the fingernail. I was sold here for one hundred and seventy-two of them, by a merchant who lived and brought me there.

I had been about two or three days at his house, when a wealthy widow, a neighbor of his, came there one evening, and brought with her an only son, a young gentleman about my own age and size. Here they saw me; and, having taken a fancy to me, I was bought of the merchant, and went home with them. Her house and premises were situated close to one of those rivulets I have mentioned, and were the finest I ever saw in Africa: they were very extensive, and she had a number of slaves to attend her. The next day I was washed and perfumed, and when meal time came, I was led into the presence of my mistress, and ate and drank before her with her son. This filled me with astonishment; and I could scarce help expressing my surprise that the young gentleman should suffer me, who was bound, to eat with him who was free; and not only so, but that he would not at any time either eat or drink till I had taken first, because I was the eldest, which was agreeable to our custom. Indeed, every thing here, and all their treatment of me, made me forget that I was a slave. The language of these people resembled ours so nearly, that we understood each other perfectly. They had also the very same customs as we. There were likewise slaves daily to attend us, while my young master and I, with other boys, sported with our darts and bows and arrows, as I had been used to do at home. In this resemblance to my former happy state, I passed about two months; and I now began to think I was to be adopted into the family, and was beginning to be reconciled to my situation, and to forget by degrees my misfortunes, when all at once the delusion vanished; for, without the least previous knowledge, one morning early, while my dear master and companion was still asleep, I was awakened out of my reverie to fresh sorrow, and hurried away. . . .

Thus, at the very moment I dreamed of the greatest happiness, I found myself most miserable; and it seemed as if fortune wished to give me this taste of joy only to render the reverse more poignant. The change I now experienced was as painful as it was sudden and unexpected. It was a change indeed, from a state of bliss to a scene which is inexpressible by me, as it discovered to me an element I had never before beheld, and till then had no idea of, and wherein such instances of hardship and cruelty continually occurred, as I can never reflect on but with horror. . . .

Thus I continued to travel, sometimes by land, sometimes by water, through different countries and various nations, till, at the end of six or seven months after I had been kidnapped, I arrived at the sea coast. . . .

The first object which saluted my eyes when I arrived on the coast was the sea, and a slave ship, which was then riding at anchor, and waiting for its cargo. These filled me with astonishment, which was soon converted into terror, when I was carried on board. I was immediately handled, and tossed up to see if I were sound, by some of the crew; and I was now persuaded that I had gotten into a world of bad spirits, and that they were going to kill me. Their complexions, too, differing so much from ours, their long hair, and the language they spoke (which was very different from any I had ever heard), united to confirm me in this belief. . . . When I looked round the ship too, and saw a large furnace of copper boiling, and a multitude of black people of every description chained together, every one of their countenances expressing dejection and sorrow, I no longer doubted of my fate; and, quite overpowered with horror and anguish, I fell motionless on the deck and fainted. . . .

I now saw myself deprived of all chance of returning to my native country, or even the least glimpse of hope of gaining the shore, which I now considered as friendly; and I even wished for my former slavery in preference to my present situation, which was filled with horrors of every kind, still heightened by my ignorance of what I was to undergo. I was not long suffered to indulge my grief; I was soon put down under the decks, and there I received such a salutation in my nostrils as I had never experienced in my life: so that, with the loathsomeness of the stench, and crying together, I became so sick and low that I was not able to eat, nor had I the least desire to taste anything. I now wished for the last friend, death, to relieve me; but soon, to my grief, two of the white men offered me eatables; and, on my refusing to eat, one of them held me fast by the hands, and laid me across, I think, the windlass, and tied my feet, while the other flogged me severely. I had never experienced anything of this kind before, and, although not being used to the water, I naturally feared that element the first time I saw it, yet, nevertheless, could I have got over the nettings, I would have jumped over the side, but I could not; and besides, the crew used to watch us very closely who were not chained down to the decks, lest we should leap into the water; and I have seen some of these poor African prisoners most severely cut for attempting to do so, and hourly whipped for not eating. This indeed was often the case with myself.

In a little time after, amongst the poor chained men, I found some of my own nation, which in a small degree gave ease to my mind. I inquired of them what was to be done with us? They gave me to understand we were to be carried to these white people's country to work for them. I then was a little revived, and thought, if it were no worse than working, my situation was not so desperate: but still I feared I should be put to death, the white people looked and acted, as I thought, in so savage a manner; for I had never seen among any people such instances of brutal cruelty; and this not only shown towards us blacks, but also to some of the whites themselves. One white man in particular I saw, when we were permitted to be on deck, flogged so unmercifully with a large rope near the foremast, that he died in consequence of it; and they tossed him over the side as they would have done a brute. This made me fear these people the more; and I expected nothing less than to be treated in the same manner. I could not help expressing my fears and apprehensions to some of my countrymen: I asked them if these people had no country, but lived in this hollow place the ship? They told me they did not, but came from a distant one. "Then," said I, "how comes it in all our country we never heard of them?" They told me, because they lived so very far off. I then asked, where were their women? Had they any like themselves? I was told they had. "And why," said I, "do we not see them?" They answered, because they were left behind. I asked how the vessel could go? They told me they could not tell; but that there were cloth put upon the masts by the help of the ropes I saw, and then the vessel went on; and the white men had some spell or magic they put in the water when they liked in order to stop the vessel. I was exceedingly amazed at this account, and really thought they were spirits. I therefore wished much to be from amongst them, for I expected they would sacrifice me: but my wishes were vain — for we were so quartered that it was impossible for any of us to make our escape. . . .

At last, when the ship we were in had got in all her cargo, they made ready with many fearful noises, and we were all put under deck, so that we could not see how they managed the vessel. But this disappointment was the least of my sorrow. The stench of the hold while we were on the coast was so intolerably loathsome, that it was dangerous to remain there for any time, and some of us had been permitted to stay on the deck for the fresh air; but now that the whole ship's cargo were confined together, it became absolutely pestilential. The closeness of the place, and the heat of the climate, added to the number in the ship, which was so crowded that each had scarcely room to turn himself, almost suffocated us. This produced copious perspirations, so that the air soon became unfit for respiration, from a variety of loathsome smells, and brought on a sickness amongst the slaves, of which many died — thus falling victims to the improvident avarice, as I may call it, of their purchasers. This wretched situation was again aggravated by the galling of the chains, now become insupportable; and the filth of the necessary tubs, into which the children often fell, and were almost suffocated. The shrieks of the women, and the groans of the dying, rendered the whole a scene of horror almost inconceivable. Happily perhaps for myself I was soon reduced so low here that it was thought necessary to keep me almost always on deck; and from my extreme youth I was not put in fetters. In this situation I expected every hour to share the fate of my companions, some of whom were almost daily brought upon deck at the point of death, which I began to hope would soon put an end to my miseries. Often did I think many of the inhabitants of the deep much more happy than myself; I envied them the freedom they enjoyed, and as often wished I could change my condition for theirs. Every circumstance I met with served only to render my state more painful, and heighten my apprehensions and my opinion of the cruelty of the whites.

One day they had taken a number of fishes; and when they had killed and satisfied themselves with as many as they thought fit, to our astonishment who were on the deck, rather than give any of them to us to eat, as we expected, they tossed the remaining fish into the sea again, although we begged and prayed for some as well as we could, but in vain; and some of my countrymen, being pressed by hunger, took an opportunity, when they thought no one saw them, of trying to get a little privately; but they were discovered, and the attempt procured them some very severe floggings.

One day, when we had a smooth sea, and moderate wind, two of my wearied countrymen, who were chained together (I was near them at the time), preferring death to such a life of misery, somehow made through the nettings, and jumped into the sea; immediately another quite dejected fellow, who, on account of his illness, was suffered to be out of irons, also followed their example; and I believe many more would very soon have done the same, if they had not been prevented by the ship's crew, who were instantly alarmed. Those of us that were the most active were in a moment put down under the deck; and there was such a noise and confusion amongst the people of the ship as I never heard before, to stop her, and get the boat out to go after the slaves. However, two of the wretches were drowned, but they got the other, and afterwards flogged him unmercifully, for thus attempting to prefer death to slavery. In this manner we continued to undergo more hardships than I can now relate; hardships which are inseparable from this accursed trade. Many a time we were near suffocation, from the want of fresh air, which we were often without for whole days together. This, and the stench of the necessary tubs, carried off many.

During our passage I first saw flying fishes, which surprised me very much: They used frequently to fly across the ship, and many of them fell on the deck. I also now first saw the use of the quadrant. I had often with astonishment seen the mariners make observations with it, and I could not think what it meant. They at last took notice of my surprise; and one of them, willing to increase it, as well as to gratify my curiosity, made me one day look through it. The clouds appeared to me to be land, which disappeared as they passed along. This heightened my wonder, and I was now more persuaded than ever that I was in another world, and that every thing about me was magic.

At last, we came in sight of the island of Barbadoes, at which the whites on board gave a great shout, and made many signs of joy to us. We did not know what to think of this; but, as the vessel drew nearer, we plainly saw the harbour, and other ships of different kinds and sizes; and we soon anchored amongst them off Bridge Town. Many merchants and planters now come on board, though it was in the evening. They put us in separate parcels, and examined us attentively.

They also made us jump, and pointed to the land, signifying we were to go there. We thought by this we should be eaten by these ugly men, as they appeared to us; and when, soon after we were all put down under the deck again, there was much dread and trembling among us, and nothing but bitter cries to be heard all the night from these apprehensions, insomuch that at last the white people got some old slaves from the land to pacify us. They told us we were not to be eaten, but to work, and were soon to go on land where we should see many of our country people. This report eased us much; and sure enough, soon after we landed, there came to us Africans of all languages.

We were conducted immediately to the merchant's yard, where we were all pent up together like so many sheep in a fold, without regard to sex or age. As every object was new to me, everything I saw filled me with surprise. What struck me first was, that the houses were built with bricks, in stories, and in every other respect different from those I have seen in Africa; but I was still more astonished on seeing people on horseback. I did not know what this could mean; and indeed I thought these people were full of nothing but magical arts. . . .

We were not many days in the merchant's custody, before we were sold after their usual manner, which is this: On a signal given (as the beat of a drum), the buyers rush at once into the yard where the slaves are confined, and make choice of that parcel they like best. The noise and clamor with which this is attended, and the eagerness visible in the countenances of the buyers, serve not a little to increase the apprehension of the terrified Africans, who may well be supposed to consider them as the ministers of that destruction to which they think themselves devoted. In this manner, without scruple, are relations and friends separated, most of them never to see each other again.

I remember in the vessel in which I was brought over, in the men's apartment, there were several brothers who, in the sale, were sold in different lots; and it was very moving on this occasion to see and hear their cries at parting. O, ye nominal Christians! Might not an African ask you — learned you this from your God, who says unto you, Do unto all men as you would men should do unto you. Is it not enough that we are torn from our country and friends to toil for your luxury and lust of gain? Must every tender feeling be likewise sacrificed to your avarice? Are the dearest friends and relations, now rendered more dear by their separation from their kindred, still to be parted from each other, and thus preventing from cheering the gloom of slavery with the small comfort of being together, and mingling their sufferings and sorrows? Why are parents to love their children, brothers their sisters, or husbands their wives? Surely this is a new refinement in cruelty, which, while it has no advantage to atone for it, thus aggravates distress, and adds fresh horrors even to the wretchedness of slavery.

REFLECTIONS

This chapter asks you to compare European encounters with Native Americans and Africans. Why did Europeans enslave Africans and not, for the most part, American Indians? Because so many Africans were brought to the Americas to work on plantations, this topic is especially compelling.

Initially, of course, Indians *were* enslaved. Recall the letter of Columbus (selection 97). Part of the reason this enslavement did not continue was the high mortality of Native Americans exposed to smallpox and other Old World diseases. In addition, Native Americans who survived the bacterial onslaught had the "local knowledge" and support needed to escape from slavery.

Above and beyond this were the humanitarian objections of Spanish priests like Bartolomeo de Las Casas and the concerns of the Spanish monarchy that slavery would increase the power of the conquistadors at the expense of the crown. In 1542, the enslavement of Indians was outlawed in Spanish dominions of the New World. Clearly, these "New Laws" were not always obeyed by Spaniards in the Americas or by the Portuguese subjects of the unified Spanish-Portuguese crown between 1580 and 1640. Still, the different legal positions of Africans and Indians in the minds of Europeans require further explanation.

Some scholars have suggested that the difference in treatment lies in the differing needs of the main European powers involved in the encounter. The anthropologist Marvin Harris makes the argument this way:

> The most plausible explanation of the New Laws [of 1542] is that they represented the intersection of the interests of three power groups: the Church, the Crown, and the colonists. All three of these interests sought to maximize their respective control over the aboriginal populations. Outright enslavement of the Indians was the method preferred by the colonists. But neither the Crown nor the Church could permit this to happen without surrendering their own vested and potential interests in the greatest resource of the New World — its manpower.

Why then did they permit and even encourage the enslavement of Africans? In this matter all three power groups stood to gain. Africans who remained in Africa were of no use to anybody, since effective military and political domination of that continent by Europeans was not achieved until the middle of the nineteenth century. To make use of African manpower, Africans had to be removed from their homelands. The only way to accomplish this was to buy them as slaves from dealers on the coast. For both the Crown and the Church, it was better to have Africans under the control of the New World colonists than to leave Africans under the control of Africans.[1]

But of course the Atlantic world slave trade was just one of the lasting outcomes of Atlantic world encounters. Towards the end of his dramatic account of the Spanish conquest of Mexico (selection 99), Bernal Díaz describes a grizzly discovery made by the victorious conquistadors:

> I solemnly swear that all the houses and stockades in the lake were full of heads and corpses. I do not know how to describe it but it was the same in the streets and courts of Tlatelolco. We could not walk without treading on the bodies and heads of dead Indians. (Díaz, 1963, 405)

After two years of continual and heavy warfare, the fortunes of the Spanish turned in their favor and they seized a ravaged city where, according to Bernal Díaz, "the stench was so bad, no one could endure it." Díaz assumed that the Mexicans had been starved and denied fresh water, but we now know that at least part of the cause was the spread of smallpox, a disease which the Spanish carried from the Old World and for which the Native Americans had no immunities. Because of thousands of years of contact, Africans shared many of the same immunities as Europeans, but Native Americans, having inhabited a separate biological realm for over ten thousand years, were completely vulnerable to the new diseases and perished in droves.

Ultimately, slavery came to an end, even if in some cases — the work of Italians on Brazilian sugar plantations, Chinese rail workers, or free African day laborers — it was hard to tell the difference. In any case, the long-term impact of the "Columbian exchange" was more ecological than economic. The potatoes of South America and the corn of Mexico fed more families in Afro-Eurasia than had ever existed in the Americas. The flora and fauna of the New World became new again, through the introduction of the grasses, trees, fruits, grains, horses, cattle, pigs, and chickens that the Old World had known for centuries.

---

[1]Marvin Harris, *Patterns of Race in the Americas* (New York: W. W. Norton, 1964), 17.

17

State and Religion

Asian, Islamic, and Christian States,
1500–1800

HISTORICAL CONTEXT

The relationship between state and religion is a matter of concern and debate almost everywhere in the modern world. In the United States, the issue of the separation of church and state engenders conflicts about the legality of abortion, prayer in the schools, government vouchers for religious schools, and the public display of religious symbols like the Ten Commandments, Nativity scenes, and Chanukah menorahs. Governments in countries as diverse as France and Turkey have recently debated the wearing of headscarves and the display of religious symbols in public schools and other public spaces.

Few states in the world today are dedicated to a single religion as are Saudi Arabia, Israel, and the Vatican. Yet even such places where religious devotion is extreme allow citizenship, residence, and rights in some measure for people of other religions. A few other states have official religions: Brazil is officially Roman Catholic, as was Italy until 1984; Iran is officially Muslim. But, with some notable exceptions, these designations often have little effect on what people believe or how they behave.

While the role of religion in public life and the relationship between church and state are important current issues, from the long-term historical view, the state has only become more important in peoples' lives while religion has become less influential. In the period before 1500, with the notable exception of China, many religious organizations were more important in people's lives than political entities. But, in much of the world, the story of the last five hundred years has been the replacement of religious authority by that of the state.

From the shortened perspective of the last fifty years, such changes may seem negligible. In some places in the world — the United States and the Middle East — religious commitment and fundamentalism have been on the rise in recent decades, becoming more pervasive than fifty years ago, if not more than five hundred years ago. In this chapter, we look at religion and the state in three parts of the world two to five hundred years ago to see how different things were but also to locate the roots of present church-state conflicts. We look first at China where state formation began over two thousand years ago and official Confucianism supported the authority of the emperor. Japan, by contrast, emerged from feudalism to begin state formation only after 1600. Both East Asian societies struggled with the claims of Buddhists, Christians, Muslims, and popular religious sects. Next we look at India, conquered by the Muslim Mughals after 1500, many of whom were remarkably tolerant of Hindus and Hinduism. We conclude with the West, Europe, and colonial America to understand how Christian states struggled with some of the challenges posed by religion. Ultimately, we will be looking for the roots of religious toleration.

Kings and political leaders are almost all more comfortable with some kind of orthodoxy (conventional belief and practice) than with heterodoxy (dissident or heretical belief and practice). But one person's orthodox belief is another's heterodoxy. Most Muslim states, for instance, see Iran's Shi'ism as heterodox, but for most Iranian governments Shi'ism has been the orthodox norm and Sunni Islam more heretical. Orthodoxy frequently undermines religious toleration, but toleration is not the same as heterodoxy. In modern society, we see toleration as a product of secularism. In fact, its history suggests something very different.

THINKING HISTORICALLY
Relating Past and Present

"The past," novelist L. P. Hartley famously wrote, "is a foreign country. They do things differently there." Understanding the past can be like learning a foreign language or exercising muscles gone slack from the daily grind of the commonplace and predictable. These are the muscles that help us imagine and tolerate differences, accept the strange as a possible norm, and allow us to hold conflicting ideas together without forcing agreement or rushing to judgment.

The issue of "state and religion" or "church and state" is a very modern one. We are invoking that modern concern in framing our study of the period between 1500 and 1800. But we should be wary of how past ideas of state and religion may differ from our own. Even the words we use reflect our modern vocabulary and understanding. For the most part, before the sixteenth century, the world's people did not make a distinction between state and religion. Not only were states few and far between, but religious life was not separated from politics or other aspects of life.

In this chapter we ask questions about the history of religious toleration. This too is a modern question. Toleration is a modern idea, but, as we shall see, that does not mean that emperors or governments did not practice it. Various empires throughout history have allowed a variety of beliefs and practices among their subjects, not because they believed it was morally the right thing to do, but because it made good practical political sense.

As you read the following selections, you will be asked to flex your imaginative muscles and reflect on how our modern conceptions of an apparently familiar topic are often different from those of our "foreign" predecessors. Then we can ask how those differences affect our ability to use the past to understand the present.

JONATHAN SPENCE

The Ming Chinese State and Religion

In this brief introduction to China of the Ming dynasty (1368–1644), a leading modern historian of China paints a picture of an advanced civilization where a confident government need not "tolerate other centers of authority." What were the elements of Chinese state authority? What religious authorities might have challenged these? Why was the Chinese state able to control these challenges?

Thinking Historically

Spence uses architectural imagery to describe China in 1600. Architecture can tell us much about a society's priorities and values, if only because building represents such a large investment in resources and labor. What does Ming architecture tell us about state and religion in China? What priorities and values might you deduce from our own society's architecture?

Jonathan D. Spence, *The Search for Modern China* (New York: W. W. Norton, 1990), 7–9.

Architectural monuments and buildings offer a constant reminder of the past. But because construction continues from one generation to the next and some buildings last longer than others, we rarely see a single period of the past on a city street or even a single building. We must "read" the architectural styles and details to separate the various layers of the past found in any city or complex settlement.

Oddly, our interest in imagining the past is evoked more by ruins. We cannot help imagining how people might have lived in an ancient city ruin, its building blocks askew, like the Roman Forum or the Mayan remains at Tulum on the Yucatán Peninsula. We are less likely to imagine what a place that has been rebuilt over the generations, such as a modern city, was like in past ages. In such "living museums" the past is drowned out by current distractions. The study of history is based on evidence and facts, but it is nourished by imagination. Look around. Imagine what your surroundings looked like fifty years ago and five hundred years ago.

In the year A.D. 1600, the empire of China was the largest and most sophisticated of all the unified realms on earth. The extent of its territorial domains was unparalleled at a time when Russia was only just beginning to coalesce as a country, India was fragmented between Mughal and Hindu rulers, and a grim combination of infectious disease and Spanish conquerors had laid low the once great empires of Mexico and Peru. And China's population of some 120 million was far larger than that of all the European countries combined.

There was certainly pomp and stately ritual in capitals from Kyoto to Prague, from Delhi to Paris, but none of these cities could boast of a palace complex like that in Peking, where, nestled behind immense walls, the gleaming yellow roofs and spacious marble courts of the Forbidden City symbolized the majesty of the Chinese emperor. Laid out in a meticulous geometrical order, the grand stairways and mighty doors of each successive palace building and throne hall were precisely aligned with the arches leading out of Peking to the south, speaking to all comers of the connectedness of things personified in this man the Chinese termed the Son of Heaven.

Rulers in Europe, India, Japan, Russia, and the Ottoman Empire were all struggling to develop systematic bureaucracies that would expand their tax base and manage their swelling territories effectively, as well as draw to new royal power centers the resources of agriculture and trade. But China's massive bureaucracy was already firmly in place, harmonized by a millennium of tradition and bonded by an immense body of statutory laws and provisions that, in theory at least, could offer pertinent advice on any problem that might arise in the daily life of China's people.

One segment of this bureaucracy lived in Peking, serving the emperor in an elaborate hierarchy that divided the country's business among six ministries dealing respectively with finance and personnel, rituals and laws, military affairs and public works. Also in Peking were the senior scholars and academicians who advised the emperor on ritual matters, wrote the official histories, and supervised the education of the imperial children. This concourse of official functionaries worked in uneasy proximity with the enormous palace staff who attended to the emperor's more personal needs: the court women and their eunuch watchmen, the imperial children and their nurses, the elite bodyguards, the banquet-hall and kitchen staffs, the grooms, the sweepers, and the water carriers.

The other segment of the Chinese bureaucracy consisted of those assigned to posts in the fifteen major provinces into which China was divided during the Ming dynasty. These posts also were arranged in elaborate hierarchies, running from the provincial governor at the top, down through the prefects in major cities to the magistrates in the countries. Below the magistrates were the police, couriers, militiamen, and tax gatherers who extracted a regular flow of revenue from China's farmers. A group of officials known as censors kept watch over the integrity of the bureaucracy both in Peking and in the provinces.

The towns and cities of China did not, in most cases, display the imposing solidity in stone and brick of the larger urban centers in post-Renaissance Europe. Nor, with the exception of a few famous pagodas, were Chinese skylines pierced by towers as soaring as those of the greatest Christian cathedrals or the minarets of Muslim cities. But this low architectural profile did not signify an absence of wealth or religion. There were many prosperous Buddhist temples in China, just as there were Daoist temples dedicated to the natural forces of the cosmos, ancestral meeting halls, and shrines to Confucius, the founding father of China's ethical system who had lived in the fifth century B.C. A scattering of mosques dotted some eastern cities and the far western areas, where most of China's Muslims lived. There were also some synagogues, where descendants of early Jewish travelers still congregated, and dispersed small groups with hazy memories of the teachings of Nestorian Christianity, which had reached China a millennium earlier. The lesser grandeur of China's city architecture and religious centers represented not any absence of civic pride or disesteem of religion, but rather a political fact: The Chinese state was more effectively centralized than those elsewhere in the world; its religions were more effectively controlled; and the growth of powerful, independent cities was prevented by a watchful government that would not tolerate rival centers of authority.

108

MATTEO RICCI

Jesuit Missionaries in Ming China

Matteo Ricci (1555–1610) was born in Italy, studied law and mathematics, entered the Jesuit monastic order (founded by the Spaniard Ignatius Loyola in 1540), and sailed to Portuguese Goa in India where he was ordained into the priesthood, learned Chinese, and directed a Jesuit expedition to China. After living in the southern capital of Nanking, Ricci was expelled and set up a mission in the secondary city of Nanchang (referred to in the following document as "Nancian"), where the events described in this selection took place in 1606 and 1607. Ricci went on to live in the northern capital of Peking for the rest of his life. There he gained the attention of the emperor with his fluent Chinese, his incomparable memory, and his work in astronomy and mathematics. He published a remarkably accurate map of the world, translated the books of Euclid, the Greek mathematician, into Chinese, and published a number of other books in Chinese.

The following selection is excerpted from Ricci's journals, published posthumously by one of his fellow Jesuits in 1615. What does this selection tell you about Jesuit missionary life in China at this time? How would you describe Chinese attitudes toward Christianity? What does this selection tell you about Chinese ideas regarding religion and the state?

Thinking Historically

Parts of this story evoke the feeling that "some things never change." Consider for instance, the envy generated by the Jesuit purchase of a larger house, or the conflict between two intellectual elites: the new Bachelors (Confucian literati who have passed their exams) and the foreign Jesuit community. What other elements in the story strike you as fairly universal or constant throughout history? Are there elements of the story that strike you as foreign or strange, suggesting a very different way of doing things in the Chinese Ming dynasty?

When we get to the point where we can feel somewhat "at home" in a particular past, we may also find elements in a primary source that surprise us because they run counter to our expectations. In this story do any elements that you would have expected to be very different turn

China in the Sixteenth Century: The Journals of Matthew Ricci: 1583–1610, trans. Louis J. Gallagher, S.J. (New York: Random House, 1953), 522–30.

out to be very similar to modern ways of doing things? How do you account for that "strange familiarity"?

During 1606 and the year following, the progress of Christianity in Nancian was in no wise retarded, . . .

Through the efforts of Father Emanuele Dias another and a larger house was purchased, in August of 1607, at a price of a thousand gold pieces. This change was necessary, because the house he had was too small for his needs and was situated in a flood area. Just as the community was about to change from one house to the other, a sudden uprising broke out against them. It happened that some of the pedants among the lettered Bachelors[1] had become dissatisfied with the growing popularity of the Christian faith. So they wrote out a complaint against the Fathers and took it to the governing Pimpithau, the Mayor, who had charge of all city affairs. They were neither well received nor patiently listened to, and he answered them saying, "If this Christian law, against which you are complaining, does not seem good to you, then do not accept it. I have not as yet heard that anyone has been forced into it. If the house which they have bought happens to be large, you are not the ones who are paying for it, and they will never interfere with your property." This answer only aroused their anger, and they went to the Governor of the metropolitan district. It happened that this man, whose name was Lu, was a friend of Father Ricci, with whom he had become acquainted, some years before, in Pekin. He accepted their complaint and then disregarded it, and the lawyers who presented it could not persuade him to give them an answer. This second rebuff also had its effect on their impatience.

At the beginning of each month, the Magistrates hold a public assembly, together with the Bachelors in Philosophy, in the temple of their great Philosopher.[2] When the rites of the new-moon were completed in the temple, and these are civil rather than religious rites, one of those present took advantage of the occasion to speak on behalf of the others, and to address the highest Magistrate present, the Pucinsu. "We wish to warn you," he said, "that there are certain foreign priests in this royal city, who are preaching a law, hitherto unheard of in this kingdom, and who are holding large gatherings of people in their house." Having said this, he referred them to their local Magistrate, called Ticho, who was also head of the school to which the speaker was attached, and he in turn ordered the plaintiffs to present their case in

---

[1] The Confucian literati. [Ed.]
[2] Confucius. [Ed.]

writing, assuring them that he would support it with all his authority, in an effort to have the foreign priests expelled. The complaint was written out that same day and signed with twenty-seven signatures. They gave one copy to the Director of the school and one to the Supreme Magistrate. The content of the document was somewhat as follows.

"Matthew Ricci, Giovanni Soeiro, Emanuele Dias, and certain other foreigners from western kingdoms, men who are guilty of high treason against the throne, are scattered amongst us, in five different provinces. They are continually communicating with each other and are here and there practicing brigandage on the rivers, collecting money, and then distributing it to the people, in order to curry favor with the multitudes. They are frequently visited by the Magistrates, by the high nobility and by the Military Prefects, with whom they have entered into a secret pact, binding unto death.

"These men teach that we should pay no respect to the images of our ancestors, a doctrine which is destined to extinguish the love of future generations for their forebears. Some of them break up the idols, leaving the temples empty and the gods to be pitied, without any patronage. In the beginning they lived in small houses, but by this time they have bought up large and magnificent residences. The doctrine they teach is something infernal. It attracts the ignorant into its fraudulent meshes, and great crowds of this class are continually assembled at their houses. Their doctrine gets beyond the city walls and spreads itself through the neighboring towns and villages and into the open country, and the people become so wrapt up in its falsity, that students are not following their courses, laborers are neglecting their work, farmers are not cultivating their acres, and even the women have no interest in their housework. The whole city has become disturbed, and, whereas in the beginning there were only a hundred or so professing their faith, now there are more than twenty thousand. These priests distribute pictures of some Tartar or Saracen, who they say is God, who came down from heaven to redeem and to instruct all of humanity, and who alone according to their doctrine, can give wealth and happiness; a doctrine by which the simple people are very easily deceived. These men are an abomination on the face of the earth, and there is just ground for fear that once they have erected their own temples, they will start a rebellion, as they did in recent years, according to report, in the provinces of Fuchian and Nankin. Wherefore, moved by their interest in the maintenance of the public good, in the conservation of the realm, and in the preservation, whole and entire, of their ancient laws, the petitioners are presenting this complaint and demanding, in the name of the entire province, that a rescript of it be forwarded to the King, asking that these foreigners be sentenced to death, or banished from the realm, to some deserted island in the sea."

Such, in brief, was the content of the complaint, eloquently worded, with alleged proofs and testimony, and couched in a persuasive style, at which the quasi-literati are very adept. Each of the Magistrates to whom the indictment was presented asserted that the spread of Christianity should be prohibited, and that the foreign priests should be expelled from the city, if the Mayor saw fit, after hearing the case, and notifying the foreigners. All those who knew nothing about the method of conducting affairs in the Chinese kingdom, were fairly well persuaded that the Fathers would at least be chased out of the metropolitan city, and as a result their many friends hesitated to come to their assistance, in what looked like a hopeless case. But the Fathers, themselves, were not too greatly disturbed, placing their confidence in Divine Providence, which had always been present to assist them on other such dangerous occasions. Their first problem was to decide upon the initial step to be taken in a matter of so grave importance.

Many of their friends thought they should seek out an intercessor, who might be induced for a consideration to have the sentence of the Magistrates revoked, as a favor to him. Instead, Father Emanuele, in his own defense, wrote out a request for justice, which he began with an instant petition to the Magistrates to make an exact inquiry into the crimes of which they had been accused, and if they were found guilty, to punish them to the full extent of the law. The Mayor and the same Magistrate, Director of the Schools, received copies of this document, and after the Chief Justice had heard the Fathers and kept them a long time on their knees, clad as criminals, he broke forth with the following questions: "Why is it that you have not left the city, after arousing the hatred of the Baccalaureates? What is this law that you are promulgating? What is this crime you have committed? Why do you forbid the people to honor their ancestors? What infernal image is this that you honor? Where did you get the money to buy these houses?" These and more questions were hurled at them, with little show of civility. Father Emanuele undertook to answer these questions with one of his Lay Brothers acting as an interpreter. First he gave a brief outline of the Christian doctrine. Then he showed that according to the divine law, the first to be honored, after God, were a man's parents. But the judge had no mind to hear or to accept any of this and he made it known that he thought it was all false. After that repulse, with things going from bad to worse, it looked as if they were on the verge of desperation, so much so, indeed, that they increased their prayers, their sacrifices and their bodily penances, in petition for a favorable solution of their difficulty. Their adversaries appeared to be triumphantly victorious. They were already wrangling about the division of the furniture of the Mission residences, and to make results doubly certain, they stirred up the flames anew with added accusations and indictments. They persuaded the civil leaders to urge on the Magistrates. One of the minor Magistrates to whom a copy of the new indictment was given, in order to flatter their zeal, said there was no need to inquire, as to whether or not the Christian law was true. The fact that it was being preached by foreigners was sufficient reason for suppressing it, adding that he himself would exterminate such men, if the complaint had not been handed on to the higher court.

The Mayor, who was somewhat friendly with the Fathers, realizing that there was much in the accusation that was patently false, asked the Magistrate Director of the Schools, if he knew whether or not this man Emanuele was a companion of Matthew Ricci, who was so highly respected at the royal court, and who was granted a subsidy from the royal treasury, because of the gifts he had presented to the King. Did he realize that the Fathers had lived in Nankin for twelve years, and that no true complaint had ever been entered against them for having violated the laws. Then he asked him if he had really given full consideration as to what was to be proven in the present indictment. To this the Director of the Schools replied that he wished the Mayor to make a detailed investigation of the case and then to confer with him. The Chief Justice then ordered the same thing to be done. Fortunately, it was this same Justice who was in charge of city affairs when Father Ricci first arrived in Nancian. It was he who first gave the Fathers permission, with the authority of the Viceroy, to open a house there. After that, through a series of promotions he returned to Nancian, to occupy the highest position in this metropolis. He exercised great prudence in handling the public rebuff the Fathers had received, being careful not to favor either side in the case. He was set on making the truth appear, and yet he did not wish to throw out the case of the quasi-literati because he himself was at one time the Director of their schools.

At that time, some of the accusing element, feeling certain that they had gained a victory, went into the houses of the neophytes looking for pictures of the Saviour, two or three of which they tore to pieces. Father Emanuele then advised the new Christians to hide the pictures from these bandits and, for the time being, not to hang them in their living rooms. He told them that in so doing they were not denying their faith but just preventing further sacrilege. He told them also that they could carry their rosaries in public if they wished to, but that there was no obligation to do so.

After the Mayor had examined the charges of the plaintiffs and the reply of the defendants, he subjected the quasi-literati to an examination in open court, and taking the Fathers under his patronage, he took it upon himself to refute the calumnies of their accusers. He said he was fully convinced that these strangers were honest men, and that he knew that there were only two of them in their local residence and not twenty, as had been asserted. To this they replied that the Chinese were becoming their disciples. To which the Justice in turn replied: "What of it? Why should we be afraid of our own people? Perhaps you are un-aware of the fact that Matthew Ricci's company is cultivated by every-one in Pekin, and that he is being subsidized by the royal treasury. How dare the Magistrates who are living outside of the royal city, expel men who have permission to live at the royal court? These men here have lived peacefully in Nankin for twelve years. I command," he added, "that they buy no more large houses, and that the people are not to fol-low their law." Then in the presence of the court he addressed the Fa-thers, very kindly, saying that there were some in the city who were angry because they had bought the larger house, when the smaller one would have served their needs.

Relative to the Christian law, he told Father Emanuele that he had no objection whatsoever to its observance by him and by his own people, but that he should not teach it to the people of this country, be-cause in this respect they are not trustworthy. He warned him, that even if the people did accept his religion, in the beginning, they would afterwards turn against it. All this he told them, calmly, and more of a similar nature, and what he said was accepted by all as being quite fa-vorable. Afterwards, while speaking with one of his associates, in open court, he told them that the law which this man professed was quite in keeping with right reason, and that Father Emanuele was a good ex-ample of a man who lived according to what he preached. He ex-plained that the Baccalaureates were bold enough to enter charges against Father Emanuele because he was a foreigner and, as they thought, unprotected by any patronage. The Chief Justice then told the Director of the Schools not to make any trouble for the Father, because it was evident that the general charges made by the Baccalaureates were fictitious and trumped up for the purpose of securing bribe money. He said the people of Nancian were a hard lot to please, and that he would give Father Emanuele permission to buy the house because, formerly, when he was Mayor, he gave Father Ricci permission to buy whatever house he wished.

109

Japanese Edicts Regulating Religion

The history of the state in Japan was very different from that of China. Between 1200 and 1600 Japan went through a period in which the state was eclipsed by aristocratic, warrior, and religious groups. When the Tokugawa Shogunate reasserted the authority of a central state in 1600, the memory of monk-soldiers and numerous independent armies called for a series of measures directed at controlling religious institutions and other independent powers. In one measure, all farmers were forbidden to have swords. Another regulated all religious temples. Between 1633 and 1639 the Tokugawa government took the further step of closing the country to all foreign religions, a move directed mainly at the influence previously enjoyed by Portuguese Catholic missionaries.

The first of the two documents in this selection is a vow by which Japanese Christians renounced their faith in 1645. The second document is a government edict regulating temples, mainly Buddhist temples, in 1665. What do these documents tell you about the relationship between the state and religion in Tokugawa Japan?

Thinking Historically

We tend to think of religions as fixed phenomena: eternal and unchanging. In fact, religious ideas and behavior change over time. Religious change is particularly striking in cases where missionaries convert people from a foreign culture. Inevitably, the religion that the convert accepts is different from the religion the missionary preaches. Can you identify some of the changes Christianity underwent in Japan?

Similarly, the regulation of Buddhist temples by the new centralizing Tokugawa government brought changes in Buddhism. How would you expect the edict of 1665 to have changed Japanese Buddhism?

Much in these documents will strike the modern reader as very foreign, even to the extent of requiring an imaginative leap to understand how people might have thought. Choose one of these passages and explain how and why it is so strange to you. Try also to explain how you might understand it.

Yosaburo Takekoshi, *The Economic Aspects of the History of the Civilization of Japan*, vol. 2 (New York: Macmillan, 1930), 88–89. Reprinted in *Japan: A Documentary History*, vol. I, ed. David J. Lu (Armonk, N.Y.: M. E. Sharpe, 2005), 224–25.
Japan: A Documentary History, vol. I, ed. David J. Lu (Armonk, N.Y.: M. E. Sharpe, 2005), 219–20.

Renouncing the Kirishitan Faith, 1645

Vow of Namban (Southern Barbarians): We have been Kirishitans for many years. But the more we learn of the Kirishitan doctrines the greater becomes our conviction that they are evil. In the first place, we who received instructions from the padre regarding the future life were threatened with excommunication which would keep us away from association with the rest of humanity in all things in the present world, and would cast us into hell in the next world. We were also taught that, unless a person committing a sin confesses it to the padre and secures his pardon, he shall not be saved in the world beyond. In that way the people were led into believing in the padres. All that was for the purpose of taking the lands of others.

When we learned of it, we "shifted" from Kirishitan and became adherents of Hokkekyō while our wives became adherents of Ikkōshō. We hereby present a statement in writing to you, worshipful Magistrate, as a testimony.

Hereafter we shall not harbor any thought of the Kirishitan in our heart. Should we entertain any thought of it at all, we shall be punished by Deus Paternus (God the Father), Jesus (His Son), Spirito Santo (the Holy Ghost), as well as by Santa Maria (St. Mary), various angels, and saints.

The grace of God will be lost altogether. Like Judas Iscariot, we shall be without hope, and shall be mere objects of ridicule to the people. We shall never rise. The foregoing is our Kirishitan vow.

Japanese Pledge: We have no thought of the Kirishitan in our hearts. We have certainly "shifted" our faith. If any falsehood be noted in our declaration now or in the future, we shall be subject to divine punishment by Bonten, Taishaku, the four deva kings, the great or little gods in all the sixty or more provinces of Japan, especially the Mishima Daimyōjin, the representatives of the god of Izu and Hakone, Hachiman Daibosatsu, Temman Daijizai Tenjin, especially our own family gods, Suwa Daimyōjin, the village people, and our relatives. This is to certify to the foregoing.

The second year of Shōhō [1645]
Endorsement.

Regulations for Buddhist Temples, 1665

1. The doctrines and rituals established for different sects must not be mixed and disarranged. If there is anyone who does not behave in accordance with this injunction, an appropriate measure must be taken expeditiously.

2. No one who does not understand the basic doctrines or rituals of a given sect is permitted to become the chief priest of a temple. Addendum: If a new rite is established, it must not preach strange doctrines.

3. The regulations which govern relationships between the main temple and branch temples must not be violated. However, even the main temple cannot take measures against branch temples in an unreasonable manner.

4. Parishioners of the temples can choose to which temple they wish to belong and make contributions. Therefore priests must not compete against one another for parishioners.

5. Priests are enjoined from engaging in activities unbecoming of priests, such as forming groups or planning to fight one another.

6. If there is anyone who has violated the law of the land, and that fact is communicated to a temple, it must turn him away without question.

7. When making repairs to a temple or a monastery, do not make them ostentatiously. Addendum: Temples must be kept clean without fail.

8. The estate belonging to a temple is not subject to sale, nor can it be mortgaged.

9. Do not allow anyone who has expressed a desire to become a disciple but is not of good lineage to enter the priesthood freely. If there is a particular candidate who has an improper and questionable background, the judgment of the domanial lord or magistrate of his domicile must be sought and then act accordingly.

The above articles must be strictly observed by all the sects. . . .

Fifth year of Kanbun [1665], seventh month, 11th day.

110

BADA'UNI

Akbar and Religion

At the same time the Chinese and Japanese confronted Christian missionaries, the descendents of Muslim Turkic and Mongol peoples of central Asia were conquering the Hindu kingdoms of northern India. Babur (1483–1530), the first of these Mughal rulers, swept into India from Afghanistan in 1525. Successive Mughal emperors enlarged the empire so that by the time of Akbar (r. 1556–1605) it included all of northern India. Like his contemporaries Philip II of Spain (r. 1556–1598) and Elizabeth of England (r. 1558–1603), Akbar created an elaborate and enduring administrative bureaucracy. But unlike Philip and Elizabeth, who waged religious wars against each other and forcibly converted their domestic subjects and newly conquered peoples, Akbar reached out to his Hindu subjects in ways that would have astonished his European contemporaries. In fact, he angered many of his own Muslim advisors, including Bada'uni, the author of the following memoir. What bothered Bada'uni about Akbar? What does this selection tell you about Akbar's rule? What factors might have motivated his toleration of heterodoxy?

Thinking Historically

What strikes the modern reader here is Akbar's evident curiosity about religious ideas and his lack of doctrinal rigidity. These are not qualities most people expect from a Muslim ruler, perhaps especially a premodern one. Why are we modern readers surprised by this? How might our ideas about Islam and Hinduism in the modern world influence our understanding of these religious traditions in the past?

We know from other sources that Akbar made special efforts to include Hindus in his administration. About a third of his governing bureaucracy were Hindus and he gave Hindu-governed territories a large degree of self-rule — allowing them to retain their own law and courts. Various taxes normally paid by non-Muslims were abolished. Among Akbar's five thousand wives his favorite was the mother of his

Bada'uni, 'Abdul Qadir. *Muntakhab ut-Tawarikh*, vol. 2, trans. G. S. A. Ranking and W. H. Lowe (Calcutta: Asiatic Society of Bengal 1895–1925), 200–201, 255–61 *passim*, 324. Edited and reprinted in *Sources of Indian Tradition*, ed. Ainslie T. Embree (New York: Columbia University Press, 1988), 465–68.

successor, Jahangir (r. 1605–1628). Akbar's policy of toleration continued under his son and grandson, Jahangir and Shah Jahan (r. 1628–1658), but was largely reversed by his great grandson, Aurangzeb (r. 1658–1707). How does this understanding of a particular past affect our ideas about the present? Does it make conflict seem less inevitable?

In the year nine hundred and eighty-three [1605] the buildings of the 'Ibādatkhāna[1] were completed. The cause was this. For many years previously the emperor had gained in succession remarkable and decisive victories. The empire had grown in extent from day to day; everything turned out well, and no opponent was left in the whole world. His Majesty had thus leisure to come into nearer contact with ascetics and the disciples of his reverence [the late] Mu'īn, and passed much of his time in discussing the word of God and the word of the Prophet. Questions of Sufism,[2] scientific discussions, inquiries into philosophy and law, were the order of the day.

And later that day the emperor came to Fatehpur. There he used to spend much time in the Hall of Worship in the company of learned men and shaikhs and especially on Friday nights, when he would sit up there the whole night continually occupied in discussing questions of religion, whether fundamental or collateral. The learned men used to draw the sword of the tongue on the battlefield of mutual contradiction and opposition, and the antagonism of the sects reached such a pitch that they would call one another fools and heretics. The controversies used to pass beyond the differences of Sunni, and Shī'a, of Hanafī and Shāfi'ī, of lawyer and divine, and they would attack the very bases of belief. And Makhdūm-ul-Mulk wrote a treatise to the effect that Shaikh 'Abd-al-Nabī had unjustly killed Khizr Khān Sarwānī, who had been suspected of blaspheming the Prophet [peace be upon him!], and Mīr Habsh, who had been suspected of being a Shī'a, and saying that it was not right to repeat the prayers after him, because he was undutiful toward his father, and was himself afflicted with hemorrhoids. Shaikh 'Abd-al-Nabī replied to him that he was a fool and a heretic. Then the mullās [Muslim theologians] became divided into two parties, and one party took one side and one the other, and became very Jews and Egyptians for hatred of each other. And persons of

---

[1]Hall of Religious Discussions. [Ed.]
[2]Mystical, poetic Islamic tradition. [Ed.]

novel and whimsical opinions, in accordance with their pernicious ideas and vain doubts, coming out of ambush, decked the false in the garb of the true, and wrong in the dress of right, and cast the emperor, who was possessed of an excellent disposition, and was an earnest searcher after truth, but very ignorant and a mere tyro, and used to the company of infidels and base persons, into perplexity, till doubt was heaped upon doubt, and he lost all definite aim, and the straight wall of the clear law and of firm religion was broken down, so that after five or six years not a trace of Islam was left in him: and everything was turned topsy-turvy. . . .

And samanas [Hindu or Buddhist ascetics] and brāhmans (who as far as the matter of private interviews is concerned gained the advantage over everyone in attaining the honor of interviews with His Majesty, and in associating with him, and were in every way superior in reputation to all learned and trained men for their treatises on morals, and on physical and religious sciences, and in religious ecstasies, and stages of spiritual progress and human perfections) brought forward proofs, based on reason and traditional testimony, for the truth of their own, and the fallacy of our religion, and inculcated their doctrine with such firmness and assurance, that they affirmed mere imaginations as though they were self-evident facts, the truth of which the doubts of the sceptic could no more shake "Than the mountains crumble, and the heavens be cleft!" And the Resurrection, and Judgment, and other details and traditions, of which the Prophet was the repository, he laid all aside. And he made his courtiers continually listen to those revilings and attacks against our pure and easy, bright and holy faith. . . .

Some time before this a brāhman, named Puruk'hotam, who had written a commentary on the Book, *Increase of Wisdom* (Khirad-afzā), had had private interviews with him, and he had asked him to invent particular Sanskrit names for all things in existence. And at one time a brāhman, named Debi, who was one of the interpreters of the *Mahābhārata*, was pulled up the wall of the castle sitting on a bedstead till he arrived near a balcony, which the emperor had made his bedchamber. Whilst thus suspended he instructed His Majesty in the secrets and legends of Hinduism, in the manner of worshiping idols, the fire, the sun and stars, and of revering the chief gods of these unbelievers, such as Brahma, Mahadev [Shiva], Bishn [Vishnu], Kishn [Krishna], Ram, and Mahama (whose existence as sons of the human race is a supposition, but whose nonexistence is a certainty, though in their idle belief they look on some of them as gods, and some as angels). His Majesty, on hearing further how much the people of the country prized their institutions, began to look upon them with affection. . . .

Sometimes again it was Shaikh Tāj ud-dīn whom he sent for. This shaikh was son of Shaikh Zakarīya of Ajodhan. . . . He had been a pupil of Rashīd Shaikh Zamān of Panipat, author of a commentary on the *Paths* (*Lawā'ih*), and of other excellent works, was most excellent in Sufism, and in the knowledge of theology second only to Shaikh Ibn 'Arabī and had written a comprehensive commentary on the *Joy of the Souls* (*Nuzhat ul-Arwāh*). Like the preceding he was drawn up the wall of the castle in a blanket, and His Majesty listened the whole night to his Sufic obscenities and follies. The shaikh, since he did not in any great degree feel himself bound by the injunctions of the law, introduced arguments concerning the unity of existence, such as idle Sufis discuss, and which eventually lead to license and open heresy. . . .

Learned monks also from Europe, who are called *Padre*, and have an infallible head, called *Papa*,[3] who is able to change religious ordinances as he may deem advisable for the moment, and to whose authority kings must submit, brought the Gospel, and advanced proofs for the Trinity. His Majesty firmly believed in the truth of the Christian religion, and wishing to spread the doctrines of Jesus, ordered Prince Murād to take a few lessons in Christianity under good auspices, and charged Abū'l Fazl to translate the Gospel. . . .

Fire worshipers also came from Nousarī in Gujarat, proclaimed the religion of Zardusht [Zarathustra] as the true one, and declared reverence to fire to be superior to every other kind of worship. They also attracted the emperor's regard, and taught him the peculiar terms, the ordinances, the rites and ceremonies of the Kaianians [a pre-Muslim Persian dynasty]. At last he ordered that the sacred fire should be made over to the charge of Abū'l Fazl, and that after the manner of the kings of Persia, in whose temples blazed perpetual fires, he should take care it was never extinguished night or day, for that it is one of the signs of God, and one light from His lights. . . .

His Majesty also called some of the yogis, and gave them at night private interviews, inquiring into abstract truths; their articles of faith; their occupation; the influence of pensiveness; their several practices and usages; the power of being absent from the body; or into alchemy, physiognomy, and the power of omnipresence of the soul.

[3]The Roman Catholic Pope. [Ed.]

111

DONALD QUATAERT

Ottoman Inter-communal Relations

Between 1500 and 1922 the Ottoman Empire, centered in Turkey, embraced a greater variety of religious and ethnic groups than any other state in world history. Many of these peoples, like the Jews expelled from Spain in 1492, came as exiles. According to this history of the empire by modern historian Donald Quataert, Ottoman administration of this incredibly diverse empire was remarkably tolerant. The degree of intercommunal peace and cooperation declined in later centuries, however. What evidence does the author offer of a generally cooperative interchange in the early centuries? Why, according to the author, did this situation change after 1800?

Thinking Historically

As the author points out in the beginning of this selection, the number of recent conflicts occurring in the territory of the old Ottoman Empire has engendered much interest in this topic. It is common to imagine that intractable contemporary conflicts have an ancient history. Often the participants in a conflict have a stake in overemphasizing the longevity of the conflict. But in this selection, the author argues that the roots of these conflicts are not nearly so deep. The causes are more recent than ancient. If he is right, how does that change our present understanding of these conflicts? How might it change our ability to deal with these conflicts?

The subject of historical intergroup relations in the Ottoman empire looms large because of the many conflicts that currently plague the lands it once occupied. Recall, for example, the Palestinian-Israeli struggle, the Kurdish issue, the Armenian question, as well as the horrific events that have befallen Bosnia and Kossovo. All rage in lands once Ottoman. What then, is the connection between these struggles of today and the inter-communal experiences of the Ottoman past?

Donald Quataert, *The Ottoman Empire, 1700–1922* (Cambridge: Cambridge University Press, 2000), 172–77.

There was nothing inevitable about these conflicts — all were historically conditioned. Other outcomes historically were possible but did not happen because of a particular unfolding of events. Nor are any of these struggles ancient ones reflecting millennia-old hatreds. Rather, each of them can be explained with reference to the nineteenth and twentieth centuries, through the unfolding of specific events rather than racial animosities. But because these contemporary struggles loom so large and because we assume that present-day hostilities have ancient and general rather than recent and specific causes, our understanding of the Ottoman inter-communal record has been profoundly obscured.

Despite all stereotypes and preconceptions to the contrary, inter-group relations during most of Ottoman history were rather good relative to the standards of the age. For many centuries, persons who were of minority status enjoyed fuller rights and more legal protection in the Ottoman lands than, for example, did minorities in the realm of the French king or of the Habsburg emperor. It is also true that Ottoman inter-communal relations worsened in the eighteenth and nineteenth centuries. In large part, this chapter argues, the deterioration derives directly from the explosive mixture of Western capital, Great Power interference in internal Ottoman affairs, and the transitional nature of an Ottoman polity struggling to establish broader political rights. Such an assessment does *not* aim to idealize the Ottoman record of inter-communal relations, which was hardly unblemished, or explain away the major injustices and atrocities inflicted on Ottoman subjects.

Nonetheless, the goal is to replace the stereotypes that too long have prevailed regarding relations among the religious and ethnic Ottoman communities. One's religion — as Muslim, Christian, or Jew — was an important means of differentiation in the Ottoman world. Indeed, ethnic terms confusingly often described what actually were religious differences. In the Balkan and Anatolian lands, Ottoman Christians informally spoke of "Turks" when in fact they meant Muslims. "Turk" was a kind of shorthand for referring to Muslims of every sort, whether Kurds, Turks, or Albanians (but not Arabs). Today's Bosnian Muslims are called Turks by the Serbian Christians even though they actually have a common Slavic ethnicity. In the Arab world, Muslim Arabs used "Turk" when sometimes they meant Albanian or Circassian Muslim, one who had come from outside the region.

Stereotypes present distorted pictures of Ottoman subjects living apart, in sharply divided, mutually impenetrable religious communities called *millets* that date back to the fifteenth century. In this incorrect view, each community lived in isolation from one another, adjacent but separate. And supposedly implacable hatreds prevailed: Muslims hated Christians who hated Jews who hated Christians who hated Muslims. Recent scholarship shows this view to be fundamentally wrong on almost every score. To begin with, the term *millet* as a designator for

Ottoman non-Muslims is not ancient but dates from the reign of Sultan Mahmut II, in the early nineteenth century. Before then, *millet* in fact meant Muslims within the empire and Christians *outside* it.

Let us continue this exploration of inter-communal relations with two different versions of the past in Ottoman Bulgaria during the 1700–1922 era. In the first version, we hear the voices of Father Paissiy (1722–1773) and S. Vrachanski (1739–1813) calling their Ottoman overlords "ferocious and savage infidels," "Ishmaelites," "sons of infidels," "wild beasts," and "loathsome barbarians." Somewhat later, another Bulgarian Christian writer Khristo Botev (1848–1876) wrote of the Ottoman administration:

> And the tyrant rages
> and ravages our native home:
> impales, hangs, flogs, curses
> and fines the people thus enslaved.

In the first quotation are the words of Bulgarian emigré intelligentsia who were seeking to promote a Bulgarian nation state and break from Ottoman rule.[1] To justify this separation, they invented a new past in which the Ottomans had brought an abrupt end to the Bulgarian cultural renaissance of the medieval era, destroying its ties to the West and preventing Bulgaria from participating in and contributing to western civilization.

And yet, hear two other Bulgarian Christian voices speaking about Bulgarian Muslims, the first during the period just before formal independence in 1908 and the other a few years later:

> Turks and Bulgarians lived together and were good neighbors. On holidays they exchanged pleasantries. We sent the Turks *kozunak* and red eggs at Easter, and they sent us baklava at Bayram. And on these occasions we visited each other.[2]
>
> In Khaskovo, our neighbors were Turks. They were good neighbors. They got on well together. They even had a little gate between their gardens. Both my parents knew Turkish well. My father was away fighting [during the Balkan Wars]. My mother was alone with four children. And the neighbors said: "You're not going anywhere. You'll stay with us. . . ." So Mama stayed with the Turks. . . . What I'm trying to tell you is that we lived well with these people."[3]

---

[1] The quotations provided from the oral interviews conducted in Bulgaria by Barbara Reeves-Ellington, Binghamton University.

[2] Interview with Simeon Radev, 1879–1967, describing his childhood before 1900, provided by Barbara Reeves-Ellington.

[3] Interview with Iveta Gospodarova, personal narrative, Sofia, January 19, 1995, provided by Barbara Reeves-Ellington.

Concepts of the "other" abound in history. The ancient Greeks divided the world into that of the civilized Greek and of the barbarian others. Barbarians could be brave and courageous but they did not possess civilization. For Jews, there are the *goyim* — the non-Jew, the other — whose lack of certain characteristics keeps them outside the chosen, Jewish, community. For Muslims, the notion of the *dhimmi* is another way of talking about difference. In this case, Muslims regard Christians and Jews as "the People of the Book" (*dhimmi*), who received God's revelation before Muhammad and therefore only incompletely. Thus, *dhimmi* have religion, civilization, and God's message. But since they received only part of that message, they are inherently different from and inferior to Muslims.

In the Ottoman world, people were acutely aware of differences between Muslims and non-Muslims. Muslims, as such, shared their religious beliefs with the dynasty and most members of the Ottoman state apparatus. The state itself, among its many attributes, called itself an Islamic one and many sultans included the term "*gazi*," warrior for the Islamic faith, among their titles. Later on, as seen, they revived the title of caliph, one with deep roots in the early Islamic past. Further, for many centuries military service primarily was carried out as a Muslim duty, although there were always some non-Muslims in the military service such as Christian Greeks serving as sailors in the navy during the 1840s. Yet, in a real sense, the military obligation had become a Muslim one. Even when an 1856 law required Ottoman Christian military service, the purchase of exemption quickly became institutionalized as a special tax. A 1909 law ended this loophole but then hundreds of thousands of Ottoman Christians fled the empire rather than serve. Thus, subjects understood that Muslims needed to fight but non-Muslims did not.

A variety of mechanisms maintained difference and distinction. Clothing laws . . . distinguished among the various religious communities, delineating the religious allegiance of passersby. They reassured maintenance of the differences not simply as instruments of discipline but useful markers of community boundaries, immediately identifying outsiders and insiders. Apparel gave a sense of group identity to members of the specific community.

Until the nineteenth century, the legal system was predicated on religious distinctions. Each religious community maintained its own courts, judges, and legal principles for the use of coreligionists. Since Muslims theologically were superior, so too, in principle, was their court system. Muslim courts thus held sway in cases between Muslims and non-Muslims. The latter, moreover, simply did not possess the necessary authority (*velayet*) and so, with a few exceptions, could not testify against Muslims. The state used the religious authorities and courts to announce decrees and taxes and, more generally, as instruments of imperial control. The ranking government official of an area, for example, the governor, received an imperial order and summoned the various religious authorities. They in turn informed their communities which negotiated within themselves over enforcement of the order or distribution of the taxes being imposed.

Muslim courts often provided rights to Christians and Jews that were unavailable in their own courts. And so non-Muslims routinely sought out Muslim courts when they were under no obligation to do so. Once they appeared before the Islamic court, its decisions took precedence. They often appealed to Muslim courts to gain access to the provisions of Islamic inheritance laws which absolutely guaranteed certain shares of estates to relatives — daughters, fathers, uncles, sisters. Thus, persons who feared disinheritance or a smaller share in the will of a Christian or Jew placed themselves under Islamic law. Christian widows frequently registered in the Islamic courts because these provided a greater share to the wife of the deceased than did ecclesiastical law. Or, take the case of *dhimmi* girls being forced into arranged marriages by fellow Christians or Jews. Since Islamic law required the female's consent to the marriage contract, the young woman in question could go to the Muslim court that took her side, thus preventing the unwanted arranged marriage.

With the Tanzimat reforms,[4] the old system of differentiation and distinction and of Muslim legal superiority formally disappeared. Equality of status meant equality of obligation and military service for all. The clothing laws disappeared and, while the religious courts remained, many of their functions vanished. New courts appeared: so-called mixed courts at first heard commercial, criminal, and then civil cases involving persons of different religious communities. Then, beginning in 1869, secular courts (*nizamiye*) presided over civil and criminal cases involving Muslim and non-Muslim. Whether or not these changes automatically and always improved the rights and status of individuals — Christian, Jew, or Muslim — currently is being debated by scholars. Some, for example, argue that women's legal rights overall declined with the replacement of Islamic by secular law, but others disagree.

So, how equal were Ottoman subjects and how well were non-Muslims treated? Quite arbitrarily, I offer the testimony of the Jewish community of Ottoman Salonica, as recorded in the "Annual Report of the Jews of Turkey" of the *Bulletin de l'Alliance Israélite Universelle* in 1893. French Jews had founded the Alliance Israélite Universelle in 1860 to work for Jewish emancipation and combat discrimination all over the world. The organization placed great stress on schools and education as a liberating device, establishing its first Ottoman school in 1867 and within a few decades, some fifty more. It published a journal,

---

[4]1839–1876. [Ed.]

the *Bulletin*, in Paris, to which Jewish communities from all over the world sent letters reporting on local conditions. Here then is the statement which the Jewish community of Salonica sent to the *Bulletin* in 1893:

> There are but few countries, even among those which are considered the most enlightened and the most civilized, where Jews enjoy a more complete equality than in Turkey [the Ottoman Empire]. H. M. the sultan and the government of the Porte display towards Jews a spirit of largest toleration and liberalism.

To place these words in context, we need to consider several points. First of all, the statement likely can be read at face value since it was not prepared for circulation within the empire. Second, Ottoman Jewish-Muslim relations were better than Muslim-Christian (or Jewish-Christian) relations. Nonetheless, this statement likely represents the sentiments of large numbers of Ottoman non-Muslim subjects, Christian and Jewish alike during the eighteenth and nineteenth centuries.

112

MARTIN LUTHER

Law and the Gospel: Princes and Turks

Martin Luther (1483–1546) launched the Protestant Reformation when he published his "95 Theses" in 1517, challenging the domination of Christianity by Rome and the Papacy. Luther's immediate complaint centered on the authority of the Pope and his agents to sell indulgences, which promised lessened time in purgatory for deceased loved ones on receipt of a contribution to a building fund for St. Peter's Cathedral. As Luther's criticism of papal practices reached the point of a breach, Luther turned to the German princes to support churches independent of Rome.

The issue of religious and political authority has long been debated and negotiated in Christian Europe. Unlike Islam, which was founded

The Table-Talk of Martin Luther, trans. William Hazlitt, Esq. (Philadelphia: The Lutheran Publication Society, 1997).

by a prophet who also governed, Christianity was founded and grew in an anti-Roman and even antipolitical environment. Typically, Christianity settled on an ambiguous or dualistic relationship between government and God. "Render to Caesar the things that are Caesar's, and to God the things that are God's," Jesus declared according to Mark (12:17) and Matthew (22:21). St. Augustine distinguished between the two cities: the city of God and the city of Man. In the Middle Ages, the doctrine of the two swords, temporal and spiritual, suggested a similar duality. Periodically one force asserted superiority over the other. In 800 Charlemagne took the coronation crown from the hands of the Pope. In 1054, the Holy Roman Emperor was said to crawl through the snow on his hands and knees to beg forgiveness from the Pope. The popes of the Italian Renaissance lived like kings, but in the sixteenth century, secular princes increased the power of the state.

Martin Luther's initial break with Rome encouraged other protests against both secular and religious authorities. His stress on individual interpretation of scripture and the power of following one's own conscience inspired more radical groups like the German Anabaptists to defy all worldly authority. In the wake of a peasant's revolt throughout Germany in 1523–1525, Luther joined forces with the German princes and voiced approval of the authority of the state.

This selection is drawn from a collection of conversational statements by Luther that were recorded by his followers and published under the title *Table-Talk* in 1566, after Luther's death.

What was Luther's attitude toward law and the state? What role did he think princes or governments ought to have in enforcing religious doctrine or behavior? What did he think of the Ottoman Turks?

Thinking Historically

Luther's ideas live on today in the minds of modern Protestants, especially Lutherans. Even the words Luther used — *law, conscience, government* — are as familiar now as they were in the sixteenth century. But Luther's ideas are also the product of a sixteenth-century thinker in sixteenth-century circumstances. Consequently, we can never assume that when we use these words or express these ideas we mean what Luther meant.

Notice, for instance, how Martin Luther dealt with the laws of the state and the call of conscience or the Gospel in the selections on "Law and the Gospel." What did "law" mean for the first Protestant? How did "conscience" or "the Gospel" provide better footing for Luther's challenge of the church? How do people compare or contrast law and conscience today? Would Luther have understood a modern appeal to conscience that led to civil disobedience?

In the selections on "Princes and Potentates" Luther turns his attention to the laws that would be enforced by his allies, the German princes. What vision of religion and politics is implied in these selections? What role did Luther leave for conscience or nonconformity? Would we want to allow a greater freedom of conscience today? Do we?

In what ways are Luther's ideas of the Ottoman Turks similar to European ideas of Muslim countries today? Was Luther poorly informed or prejudiced? Are we?

Of the Law and the Gospel

CCLXXI

We must reject those who so highly boast of Moses' laws, as to temporal affairs, for we have our written imperial and country laws, under which we live, and unto which we are sworn. Neither Naaman the Assyrian, nor Job, nor Joseph, nor Daniel, nor many other good and godly Jews, observed Moses' laws out of their country, but those of the Gentiles among whom they lived. Moses' law bound and obliged only the Jews in that place which God made choice of. Now they are free. If we should keep and observe the laws and rites of Moses, we must also be circumcised, and keep the mosaical ceremonies; for there is no difference; he that holds one to be necessary, must hold the rest so too. Therefore let us leave Moses to his laws, excepting only the *Moralia*,[1] which God has planted in nature, as the ten commandments, which concern God's true worshipping and service, and a civil life. . . .

CCLXXXVIII

In what darkness, unbelief, traditions, and ordinances of men have we lived, and in how many conflicts of the conscience we have been ensnared, confounded, and captivated under popedom, is testified by the books of the papists, and by many people now living. From all which snares and horrors we are now delivered and freed by Jesus Christ and his Gospel, and are called to the true righteousness of faith; insomuch that with good and peaceable consciences we now believe in God the Father, we trust in him, and have just cause to boast that we have sure and certain remission of our sins through the death of Christ Jesus, dearly bought and purchased. Who can sufficiently extol these treasures of the conscience, which everywhere are spread abroad, offered, and presented merely by grace? We are now conquerors of sin, of the

[1]Moral code. [Ed.]

law, of death, and of the devil; freed and delivered from all human traditions. If we would but consider the tyranny of auricular confession,[2] one of the least things we have escaped from, we could not show ourselves sufficiently thankful to God for loosing us out of that one snare. When popedom stood and flourished among us, then every king would willingly have given ten hundred thousand guilders, a prince one hundred thousand, a nobleman one thousand, a gentleman one hundred, a citizen or countryman twenty or ten, to have been freed from that tyranny. But now seeing that such freedom is obtained for nothing, by grace, it is not much regarded, neither give we thanks to God for it.

CCLXXXIX

. . . We must make a clear distinction; we must place the Gospel in heaven, and leave the law on earth; we must receive of the Gospel a heavenly and a divine righteousness; while we value the law as an earthly and human righteousness, and thus directly and diligently separate the righteousness of the gospel from the righteousness of the law, even as God has separated and distinguished heaven from earth, light from darkness, day from night, etc., so that the righteousness of the Gospel be the light and the day, but the righteousness of the law, darkness and night. Therefore all Christians should learn rightly to discern the law and grace in their hearts, and know how to keep one from the other, in deed and in truth, not merely in words, as the pope and other heretics do, who mingle them together, and, as it were, make thereout a cake not fit to eat. . . .

Of Princes and Potentates

DCCXI

Government is a sign of the divine grace, of the mercy of God, who has no pleasure in murdering, killing, and strangling. If God left all things to go where they would, as among the Turks and other nations, without good government, we should quickly dispatch one another out of this world.

DCCXII

Parents keep their children with greater diligence and care than rulers and governors keep their subjects. Fathers and mothers are masters naturally and willingly; it is a self-grown dominion; but rulers and magis-

---

[2]Catholic confession to a priest. [Ed.]

trates have a compulsory mastery; they act by force, with a prepared dominion; when father and mother can rule no more, the public police must take the matter in hand. Rulers and magistrates must watch over the sixth commandment.

DCCXIII

The temporal magistrate is even like a fish net, set before the fish in a pond or a lake, but God is the plunger, who drives the fish into it. For when a thief, robber, adulterer, murderer, is ripe, he hunts him into the net, that is, causes him to be taken by the magistrate, and punished; for it is written: "God is judge upon earth." Therefore repent, or thou must be punished.

DCCXIV

Princes and rulers should maintain the laws and statues, or they will be condemned. They should, above all, hold the Gospel in honor, and bear it ever in their hands, for it aids and preserves them, and ennobles the state and office of magistracy, so that they know where their vocation and calling is, and that with good and safe conscience they may execute the works of their office. At Rome, the executioner always craved pardon of the condemned malefactor, when he was to execute his office, as though he were doing wrong, or sinning in executing the criminal; whereas 'tis his proper office, which God has set.

St. Paul says: "He beareth not the sword in vain"; he is God's minister, a revenger, to execute wrath upon him that does evil. When the magistrate punishes, God himself punishes.

On the Turks

DCCCXXVII

The power of the Turk is very great; he keeps in his pay, all the year through, hundreds of thousands of soldiers. He must have more than two millions of florins annual revenue. We are far less strong in our bodies, and are divided out among different masters, all opposed the one to the other, yet we might conquer these infidels with only the Lord's prayer, if our own people did not spill so much blood in religious quarrels, and in persecuting the truths contained in that prayer. God will punish us as he punished Sodom and Gomorrah, but I would fain 'twere by the hand of some pious potentate, and not by that of the accursed Turk. . . .

DCCCXXX

News came from Torgau that the Turks had led out into the great square at Constantinople twenty-three Christian prisoners, who, on their refusing to apostatize, were beheaded. Dr. Luther said: Their blood will cry up to heaven against the Turks, as that of John Huss[3] did against the papists. 'Tis certain, tyranny and persecution will not avail to stifle the Word of Jesus Christ. It flourishes and grows in blood. Where one Christian is slaughtered, a host of others arise. 'Tis not on our walls or our arquebusses[4] I rely for resisting the Turk, but upon the *Pater Noster*. 'Tis that will triumph. The Decalogue is not, of itself, sufficient. I said to the engineers at Wittenberg: Why strengthen your walls — they are trash; the walls with which a Christian should fortify himself are made, not of stone and mortar, but of prayer and faith. . . .

DCCCXXXV

. . . The Turks pretend, despite the Holy Scriptures, that they are the chosen people of God, as descendants of Ishmael. They say that Ishmael was the true son of the promise, for that when Issac was about to be sacrificed, he fled from his father, and from the slaughter knife, and, meanwhile, Ishmael came and truly offered himself to be sacrificed, whence he became the child of the promise; as gross a lie as that of the papists concerning one kind in the sacrament. The Turks make a boast of being very religious, and treat all other nations as idolaters. They slanderously accuse the Christians of worshipping three gods. They swear by one only God, creator of heaven and earth, by his angels, by the four evangelists, and by the eighty heaven-descended prophets, of whom Mohammed is the greatest. They reject all images and pictures, and render homage to God alone. They pay the most honorable testimony to Jesus Christ, saying that he was a prophet of preeminent sanctity, born of the Virgin Mary, and an envoy from God, but that Mohammed succeeded him, and that while Mohammed sits, in heaven, on the right hand of the Father, Jesus Christ is seated on his left. The Turks have retained many features of the law of Moses, but, inflated with the insolence of victory, they have adopted a new worship; for the glory of warlike triumphs is, in the opinion of the world, the greatest of all.

Luther complained of the emperor Charles's[5] negligence, who, taken up with other wars, suffered the Turk to capture one place after

---

[3]In Czech, known as Jan Hus. Hus (1369–1415) was a Czech forerunner of the Protestant Reformation. [Ed.]

[4]Primitive firearms used from the fifteenth to the seventeenth centuries. [Ed.]

[5]Charles V (1500–1558), the Habsburg Emperor, fought the French as well as the Ottomans. [Ed.]

another. 'Tis with the Turks as heretofore with the Romans, every subject is a soldier, as long as he is able to bear arms, so they have always a disciplined army ready for the field; whereas we gather together ephemeral bodies of vagabonds, untried wretches, upon whom is no dependence. My fear is, that the papists will unite with the Turks to exterminate us. Please God, my anticipation come not true, but certain it is, that the desperate creatures will do their best to deliver us over to the Turks.

113

ROGER WILLIAMS

The Bloody Tenent of Persecution
for Cause of Conscience

Roger Williams (1603–1683), a minister of the Church of England sympathetic to its puritan reformist wing, sailed from England in 1630 to join the newly founded Massachusetts Bay Colony. But for Williams the colony remained too close to the Church of England, especially in its continuing legacies of Catholicism: bishops, infant baptism, ritual kneeling, and making the sign of the cross. Williams moved on to the more separatist Pilgrim colony in Plymouth and to a church in Salem in 1633. There he became engaged in a series of conflicts with the General Court of Massachusetts for defaming the churches and the civil authority of the colony. For his "dangerous opinions" he was given six weeks to leave. In the howling winter of 1635, he brought his small band of followers south to Narragansett Bay where he bought a tract of land from the Indians which he called Providence and which would later become Rhode Island.

The Bloody Tenent, written sometime between 1636 and 1644 when it was finally published (and then burned) in London, summarized the disagreements that Williams had with the Massachusetts authorities, the Church of England, and, one might add, the long history of Catholicism. What did Williams mean by the "bloody tenent"

Roger Williams, *The Bloody Tenent of Persecution for Cause of Conscience, Discussed in a Conference between Truth and Peace*, ed. Richard Groves (Macon, Ga.: Mercer University Press, 2001)

(tenet or doctrine) of persecution for conscience? Why does he call
this doctrine bloody? According to Williams, what should be the relationship between church and state? Why? How is Williams's idea of
this relationship different from Luther's? How do you account for
that difference?

Thinking Historically

In Protestant America of the 1630s the more fervent advocates of religious purity rallied around symbols and signs that more mainstream
Protestants dismissed as unimportant. But the religious purists and the
mainstreamers of the American seventeenth century argued the exact
opposite of what we might expect to hear today. Roger Williams and
his Separatist followers objected to the display of the most sacred
Christian symbol, the cross, on the English flag. For them the cross on
the flag was a sacrilegious confusion of nation and church, politics
and faith. Some of the Separatists of Salem got into trouble with the
Massachusetts government for desecrating the flag by cutting out the
cross. Williams and the Separatists also objected to political officials
taking an oath of office saying "so help me God." The judges and officials of the state should not presume to act for God, Williams argued, and nonbelievers should not be forced to take the name of "the
Lord thy God" in vain. Nothing good could come from governments
policing faith or from communities of the faithful mucking about in
worldly affairs. What do you think Roger Williams would have
thought of prayer in the public schools, the idea that America was a
"Christian nation," or politicians saying "God Bless America"?

In this selection, Williams makes reference to a number of different
historical periods. First he refers to the religious wars between
Catholics and Protestants that had ravaged Europe. Like Luther, he
also refers to two of the most important historical markers for Christians: Ancient Israel of the Old Testament and the coming of Christ.
Why does he say what he says about ancient Israel? What is his attitude toward Jews and non-Christians alike after the coming of Christ?
Christian theology was (and is) highly historical. It envisions a timeline that stretches into the future as well. What future developments
does Williams envision?

First, that the blood of so many hundred thousand souls of Protestants
and papists, spilled in the wars of present and former ages for their respective consciences, is not required nor accepted by Jesus Christ the
Prince of Peace.

Secondly, pregnant scriptures and arguments are throughout the work proposed against the doctrine of persecution for cause of conscience.

Thirdly, satisfactory answers are given to scriptures and objections produced by Mr. Calvin, Beza,[1] Mr. Cotton, and the ministers of the New English churches, and others former and later, tending to prove the doctrine of persecution for cause of conscience.

Fourthly, the doctrine of persecution for cause of conscience is proved guilty of all the blood of the souls crying for vengeance under the altar.

Fifthly, all civil states, with their officers of justice, in their respective constitutions and administrations, are proved essentially civil, and therefore not judges, governors, or defenders of the spiritual, or Christian, state and worship.

Sixthly, it is the will and command of God that, since the coming of his Son the Lord Jesus, a permission of the most paganish, Jewish, Turkish, or anti-Christian consciences and worships be granted to all men in all nations and countries, and they are only to be fought against with that sword which is only, in soul matters, able to conquer, to wit, the sword of God's Spirit, the word of God.

Seventhly, the state of the land of Israel, the kings and people thereof, in peace and war, is proved figurative and ceremonial, and no pattern nor precedent for any kingdom or civil state in the world to follow.

Eighthly, God requires not a uniformity of religion to be enacted and enforced in any civil state; which enforced uniformity, sooner or later, is the greatest occasion of civil war, ravishing of conscience, persecution of Christ Jesus in his servants, and of the hypocrisy and destruction of millions of souls.

Ninthly, in holding an enforced uniformity of religion in a civil state, we must necessarily disclaim our desires and hopes of the Jews' conversion to Christ.

Tenthly, an enforced uniformity of religion throughout a nation or civil state confounds the civil and religious, denies the principles of Christianity and civility, and that Jesus Christ is come in the flesh.

Eleventhly, the permission of other consciences and worships that a state professes only can, according to God, procure a firm and lasting peace; good assurance being taken, according to the wisdom of the civil state, for uniformity of civil obedience from all sorts.

Twelfthly, lastly, true civility and Christianity may both flourish in a state or kingdom, notwithstanding the permission of divers and contrary consciences, either of Jew or Gentile.

---

[1]Theodore Beza (1519–1605), John Calvin's successor. [Ed.]

REFLECTIONS

School prayer, abortion, the public display of religious symbols — what is the proper relationship of government and religion? Roger Williams reminds us that the principle of the separation of church and state, a pillar of modern civic society, originated not as a secular humanist denigration of religion but as an effort by the most fervent Protestant Separatists to preserve their religion's purity and independence.

Luther's discussion of government and religion strikes a more expected tone. The great reformer was able to dismiss thousands of years of law from ancient Israel and the Roman papacy, but he gave German princes far greater authority over religious matters than most Christians would allow today. How do we account for the differences between Martin Luther and Roger Williams on this issue? Is it simply a matter of each preaching the politics of their position — the privileged versus the persecuted?

The Christian debate was unique. Muslims also quarreled about who had the truth, but they lacked a tradition of separating religious and secular authority. In the Ottoman Empire the sultan issued edicts on matters that were not covered in the Koran, but this body of secular law merely supplemented Koranic law, and both were administered by the same judges and officials. There was neither the theoretical possibility that the two systems would disagree nor that separate judicial institutions might come into conflict. Nevertheless, the Ottomans developed a tolerance for differences that would have struck many Catholics and Protestants, in their less accommodating moods, as sheer folly. In the Ottoman Empire, non-Muslims were subject to the religious law of their own communities, and when they violated the secular law of the states, Muslims often suffered more severe punishment on the principle that Muslims should set a better example.

Like Christians, however, Muslims held religious truths that they believed applied to all people. As a consequence both Christian and Muslim society gave rise to religious zealots who wanted the state to enshrine God's Truth. In that way, Christians and Muslims were very different from the rulers, subjects, and thinkers of China and Japan.

Neither the Chinese nor Japanese traditions held religious orthodoxies. But both required proper observance of certain social and political proprieties. Strong governments, as in most of Chinese history, turned principles like Confucian filial piety into virtual religions but they had the force of law and made little appeal to conscience or individual choice. Daoism and Buddhism appealed to the inner lives of Chinese and Japanese devotees, but posed no conflict to state power. Only in periods of unrest, feudalism, or the breakdown of the state did Buddhist or Daoist priests and monks exercise political power. Even then, however, they did not challenge the state as much as they filled the vacuum left by its disappearance. In both Japan and Europe, the post-feudal age was one in which the state's rise depended, in part, on the reclamation and monopolization of powers previously exercised by religious institutions.

Three pasts, but increasingly one present. As cultural differences meld with the force of rockets and the speed of the Internet, one might well ask what separate histories matter to a common present. Increasingly principles of toleration are enshrined by international organizations in declarations of human rights and the proceedings of international tribunals. Whether we see the roots of modern principles of tolerance in Confucian secularism, Christian separation of church and state, or Muslim cosmopolitanism, we live in a world where intolerance is widely condemned and legitimately prosecuted.

And yet, fanaticism and intolerance have not disappeared. Religious fundamentalists of various stripes declare their missions to take over governments, convert populations, and bring about the rule of God. History has shown that tolerance need not be secular. Indeed even the aggressively secular regimes of the twentieth and twenty-first centuries have demonstrated and continue to demonstrate a capacity for brutal persecution of dissidents, religious and otherwise.

The study of the past may be more proficient at telling us what we want than how we can achieve it. But the knowledge of how to get there from here begins with the knowledge of where we are and where we have been. At the very least, the knowledge of how things have changed from the past to the present holds the key to unlocking the future.

18

Gender and Family

China, Southeast Asia,
Europe, and "New Spain," 1600–1750

HISTORICAL CONTEXT

Women are half of humanity. The family is the oldest and most important social institution. Marriage is one of the most important passages in one's life. Yet up until the last few decades these subjects rarely registered as important topics in world history. There were at least two reasons for this: One was the tendency to think of history as the story of public events only — the actions of political officials, governments, and their representatives — instead of the private and domestic sphere. The second was the assumption that the private or domestic sphere had no history, and that it had always been the same. As the documents in this chapter will show, nothing could be further from the truth.

Since the urban revolution five thousand years ago most societies have been patriarchal. The laws, social codes, and dominant ideas have enshrined the power and prestige of men over women, husbands over wives, fathers over children, gods over goddesses, even brothers over sisters. Double standards for adultery, inheritance laws that favor sons, and laws that deny women property or political rights all attest to the power of patriarchal culture and norms. Almost everywhere patriarchies have limited women to the domestic sphere while granting men public and political power. Nevertheless, we will see in this chapter that not all patriarchies were alike. Some were less stringent than others, and in many societies during this period, women, individually, in families, and even in larger groups, discovered ways both large and small to assert their social, cultural, and economic independence. As you read about women in China, Southeast Asia, Europe, and the Americas, consider how women's lives varied from one patriarchal society to another and how women found openings to express themselves and create their own worlds.

THINKING HISTORICALLY
Making Comparisons

We learn by making comparisons. Every new piece of knowledge we acquire leads to a comparison with what we already know. For example, we arrive in a new town and we are struck by something that we have not seen before. The town has odd street lamps, flowerpots on the sidewalks, or lots of trucks on the street. We start to formulate a theory about the differences between what we observe in the new town and what we already know about our old town. We think we're on to something, but our theory falls apart when we make more observations by staying in the new town another day, or traveling on to the next town, or going halfway across the world. As we gain more experience and make more observations, our original theory explaining an observed difference is supplanted by a much more complex theory about *types* of towns.

History is very much like travel. We learn by comparison, one step at a time, and the journey is never ending. On this trip we begin in China and then move on to other regions of the world. We begin with primary sources, but make comparisons based on secondary sources as well. In fact, we conclude with a secondary source that will allow us to draw upon our previous readings to make increasingly informed and complex comparisons. Welcome aboard. Next stop, China.

$$\boxed{114}$$

Family Instructions for the Miu Lineage

Chinese families in Ming times (1368–1644) often organized themselves into groups by male lineage. These groups often shared common land, built ancestral halls, published genealogies, honored their common ancestors, and ensured the success and well-being of future generations. To accomplish the last of these, lineage groups frequently compiled lists of family rules or instructions. This particular example, from the various lines of the Miu family of the Guangdong province

---

"Family Instructions for the Miu Lineage, Late Sixteenth Century," trans. Clara Yu, in *Chinese Civilization: A Sourcebook*, 2nd ed., ed. Patricia Ebrey (New York: Free Press, 1993), 238–40, 241–43.

in the south, shows how extensive these instructions could be. What values did these family instructions encourage? What activities did the Miu lineage regulate? What kind of families, and what kind of individuals, were these rules intended to produce? How would these rules have had a different impact on women and men?

Thinking Historically

It is difficult to read this selection without thinking of one's own family and of families in one's own society. How many of the Miu lineage's concerns are concerns of families you know? Family instructions and lineage organizations are not common features of modern American society, even among Chinese Americans who may have a sense of their lineage and family identity. What institutions in modern American society regulate the activities addressed by these family instructions? Or are these activities allowed to regulate themselves or to go unregulated? From reading this document, what do you think are some of the differences between Ming-era Chinese families and modern American families?

Work Hard at One of the Principal Occupations

1. To be filial to one's parents, to be loving to one's brothers, to be diligent and frugal — these are the first tenets of a person of good character. They must be thoroughly understood and faithfully carried out.

One's conscience should be followed like a strict teacher and insight should be sought through introspection. One should study the words and deeds of the ancients to find out their ultimate meanings. One should always remember the principles followed by the ancients, and should not become overwhelmed by current customs. For if one gives in to cruelty, pride, or extravagance, all virtues will be undermined, and nothing will be achieved.

Parents have special responsibilities. *The Book of Changes*[1] says: "The members of a family have strict sovereigns." The "sovereigns" are the parents. Their position in a family is one of unique authority, and they should utilize their authority to dictate matters to maintain order, and to inspire respect, so that the members of the family will all be obedient. If the parents are lenient and indulgent, there will be many troubles which in turn will give rise to even more troubles. Who is to blame for all this? The elders in a family must demand discipline of themselves, following all rules and regulations to the letter, so that the younger members emulate their good behavior and exhort each other

---

[1]The *I Ching*, a Chinese classic. [Ed.]

to abide by the teachings of the ancient sages. Only in this way can the family hope to last for generations. If, however, the elders of a family should find it difficult to abide by these regulations, the virtuous youngsters of the family should help them along. Because the purpose of my work is to make such work easier, I am not afraid of giving many small details. . . .

2. Those youngsters who have taken Confucian scholarship as their hereditary occupation should be sincere and hard-working, and try to achieve learning naturally while studying under a teacher. Confucianism is the only thing to follow if they wish to bring glory to their family. Those who know how to keep what they have but do not study are as useless as puppets made of clay or wood. Those who study, even if they do not succeed in the examinations, can hope to become teachers or to gain personal benefit. However, there are people who study not for learning's sake, but as a vulgar means of gaining profit. These people are better off doing nothing.

Youngsters who are incapable of concentrating on studying should devote themselves to farming; they should personally grasp the ploughs and eat the fruit of their own labor. In this way they will be able to support their families. If they fold their hands and do nothing, they will soon have to worry about hunger and cold. If, however, they realize that their forefathers also worked hard and that farming is a difficult way of life, they will not be inferior to anyone. In earlier dynasties, officials were all selected because they were filial sons, loving brothers, and diligent farmers. This was to set an example for all people to devote themselves to their professions, and to ensure that the officials were familiar with the hardships of the common people, thereby preventing them from exploiting the commoners for their own profit.

3. Farmers should personally attend to the inspection, measurement, and management of the fields, noting the soil as well as the terrain. The early harvest as well as the grain taxes and the labor service obligations should be carefully calculated. Anyone who indulges in indolence and entrusts these matters to others will not be able to distinguish one kind of crop from another and will certainly be cheated by others. I do not believe such a person could escape bankruptcy.

4. The usual occupations of the people are farming and commerce. If one tries by every possible means to make a great profit from these occupations, it usually leads to loss of capital. Therefore it is more profitable to put one's energy into farming the land; only when the fields are too far away to be tilled by oneself should they be leased to others. One should solicit advice from old farmers as to one's own capacity in farming.

Those who do not follow the usual occupations of farming or business should be taught a skill. Being an artisan is a good way of life and will also shelter a person from hunger and cold. All in all, it is important to remember that one should work hard when young, for when youth expires one can no longer achieve anything. Many people learn this lesson only after it is too late. We should guard against this mistake.

5. Fish can be raised in ponds by supplying them with grass and manure. Vegetables need water. In empty plots one can plant fruit trees such as the pear, persimmon, peach, prune, and plum, and also beans, wheat, hemp, peas, potatoes, and melons. When harvested, these vegetables and fruits can sustain life. During their growth, one should give them constant care, nourishing them and weeding them. In this way, no labor is wasted and no fertile land is left uncultivated. On the contrary, to purchase everything needed for the morning and evening meals means the members of the family will merely sit and eat. Is this the way things should be?

6. Housewives should take full charge of the kitchen. They should make sure that the store of firewood is sufficient, so that even if it rains several days in succession, they will not be forced to use silver or rice to pay for firewood, thereby impoverishing the family. Housewives should also closely calculate the daily grocery expenses, and make sure there is no undue extravagance. Those who simply sit and wait to be fed only are treating themselves like pigs and dogs, but also are leading their whole households to ruin. . . .

Exercise Restraint

1. Our young people should know their place and observe correct manners. They are not permitted to gamble, to fight, to engage in lawsuits, or to deal in salt[2] privately. Such unlawful acts will only lead to their own downfall.

2. If land or property is not obtained by righteous means, descendants will not be able to enjoy it. When the ancients invented characters, they put gold next to two spears to mean "money," indicating that the danger of plunder or robbery is associated with it. If money is not accumulated by good means, it will disperse like overflowing water; how could it be put to any good? The result is misfortune for oneself as well as for one's posterity. This is the meaning of the saying: "The way of Heaven detests fullness, and only the humble gain." Therefore, accumulation of great wealth inevitably leads to great loss. How true are the words of Laozi![3]

---

[2]Get involved in the salt trade, a state monopoly. Salt was used as a preservative for fish, meat, and other foods. [Ed.]

[3]Lao Tzu, legendary Chinese philosopher and author of the *Dao de Jing*, the Daoist classic. [Ed.]

A person's fortune and rank are predestined. One can only do one's best according to propriety and one's own ability; the rest is up to Heaven. If one is easily contented, then a diet of vegetables and soups provides a lifetime of joy. If one does not know one's limitations and tries to accumulate wealth by immoral and dishonest means, how can one avoid disaster? To be able to support oneself through life and not leave one's sons and grandsons in hunger and cold is enough; why should one toil so much?

3. Pride is a dangerous trait. Those who pride themselves on wealth, rank, or learning are inviting evil consequences. Even if one's accomplishments are indeed unique, there is no need to press them on anyone else. "The way of Heaven detests fullness, and only the humble gain." I have seen the truth of this saying many times.

4. Taking concubines in order to beget heirs should be a last resort, for the sons of the legal wife and the sons of the concubine are never of one mind, causing innumerable conflicts between half brothers. If the parents are in the least partial, problems will multiply, creating misfortune in later generations. Since families have been ruined because of this, it should not be taken lightly.

5. Just as diseases are caused by what goes into one's mouth, misfortunes are caused by what comes out of one's mouth. Those who are immoderate in eating and unrestrained in speaking have no one else to blame for their own ruin.

6. Most men lack resolve and listen to what their women say. As a result, blood relatives become estranged and competitiveness, suspicion, and distance arise between them. Therefore, when a wife first comes into a family, it should be made clear to her that such things are prohibited. "Start teaching one's son when he is a baby; start teaching one's daughter-in-law when she first arrives." That is to say, preventive measures should be taken early.

7. "A family's fortune can be foretold from whether its members are early risers" is a maxim of our ancient sages. Everyone, male and female, should rise before dawn and should not go to bed until after the first drum. Never should they indulge themselves in a false sense of security and leisure, for such behavior will eventually lead them to poverty.

8. Young family members who deliberately violate family regulations should be taken to the family temple, have their offenses reported to the ancestors, and be severely punished. They should then be taught to improve themselves. Those who do not accept punishment or persist in their wrongdoings will bring harm to themselves.

9. As a preventive measure against the unpredictable, the gates should be closed at dusk, and no one should be allowed to go out. Even when there are visitors, dinner parties should end early, so that there will be no need for lighting lamps and candles. On very hot or very cold days, one should be especially considerate of the kitchen servants.

10. For generations this family had dwelt in the country, and everyone has had a set profession; therefore, our descendants should not be allowed to change their place of residence. After living in the city for three years, a person forgets everything about farming; after ten years, he does not even know his lineage. Extravagance and leisure transform people, and it is hard for anyone to remain unaffected. I once remarked that the only legitimate excuse to live in a city temporarily is to flee from bandits.

11. The inner and outer rooms, halls, doorways, and furniture should be swept and dusted every morning at dawn. Dirty doorways and courtyards and haphazardly placed furniture are sure signs of a declining family. Therefore, a schedule should be followed for cleaning them, with no excuses allowed.

12. Those in charge of cooking and kitchen work should make sure that breakfast is served before nine o'clock in the morning and dinner before five o'clock in the afternoon. Every evening the iron wok and other utensils should be washed and put away, so that the next morning, after rising at dawn, one can expect tea and breakfast to be prepared immediately and served on time. In the kitchen no lamps are allowed in the morning or at night. This is not only to save the expense, but also to avoid harmful contamination of food. Although this is a small matter, it has a great effect on health. Furthermore, since all members of the family have their regular work to do, letting them toil all day without giving them meals at regular hours is no way to provide comfort and relief for them. If these rules are deliberately violated, the person in charge will be punished as an example to the rest.

13. On the tenth and twenty-fifth days of every month, all the members of this branch, from the honored aged members to the youngsters, should gather at dusk for a meeting. Each will give an account of what he has learned, by either calling attention to examples of good and evil, or encouraging diligence, or expounding his obligations, or pointing out tasks to be completed. Each member will take turns presenting his own opinions and listening attentively to others. He should examine himself in the matters being discussed and make efforts to improve himself. The purpose of these meetings is to encourage one another in virtue and to correct each other's mistakes.

The members of the family will take turns being the chairman of these meetings, according to schedule. If someone is unable to chair a meeting on a certain day, he should ask the next person in line to take his place. The chairman should provide tea, but never wine. The meetings may be canceled on days of ancestor worship, parties, or other such occasions, or if the weather is severe. Those who are absent from these meetings for no reason are only doing themselves harm.

There are no set rules for where the meeting should be held, but the place should be convenient for group discussions. The time of the meeting should always be early evening, for this is when people have free time. As a general precaution the meeting should never last until late at night.

14. Women from lower-class families who stop at our houses tend to gossip, create conflicts, peek into the kitchens, or induce our women to believe in prayer and fortune-telling, thereby cheating them out of their money and possessions. Consequently, one should question these women often and punish those who come for no reason, so as to put a stop to the traffic.

15. Blood relatives are as close as the branches of a tree, yet their relationships can still be differentiated according to importance and priority: Parents should be considered before brothers, and brothers should be considered before wives and children. Each person should fulfill his own duties and share with others profit and loss, joy and sorrow, life and death. In this way, the family will get along well and be blessed by Heaven. Should family members fight over property or end up treating each other like enemies, then when death or misfortune strikes they will be of even less use than strangers. If our ancestors have consciousness, they will not tolerate these unprincipled descendants who are but animals in man's clothing. Heaven responds to human vices with punishments as surely as an echo follows a sound. I hope my sons and grandsons take my words seriously.

16. To get along with patrilineal relatives, fellow villages, and relatives through marriage, one should be gentle in speech and mild in manners. When one is opposed by others, one may remonstrate with them; but when others fall short because of their limitations, one should be tolerant. If one's youngsters or servants get into fights with others, one should look into oneself to find the blame. It is better to be wronged than to wrong others. Those who take affront and become enraged, who conceal their own shortcomings and seek to defeat others, are courting immediate misfortune. Even if the other party is unbearably unreasonable, one should contemplate the fact that the ancient sages had to endure much more. If one remains tolerant and forgiving, one will be able to curb the other party's violence.

MAO XIANG

How Dong Xiaowan Became My Concubine

Mao Xiang* (1611–1693) was one of the great poets, artists, and calligraphers of the late Ming dynasty and, after its demise in 1644, a persistent critic of the succeeding Manchu or Ching dynasty. He was also known for his love of beautiful women, especially three famous courtesans who were also talented artists: Dong Xiaowan† (1625–1651), Cai Han (1647–1686), and Qin Yue (c. 1660–1690). (Note what these dates reveal.) Whether or not this is a reliable account of how Dong Xiaowan became his concubine, what does this piece from Mao Xiang's memoir tell you about his society's attitudes towards women, marriage, and family?

Thinking Historically

If comparisons originate in our recognition of institutions and ideas that are foreign to our own, certainly the acceptance of concubines in seventeenth-century Chinese society is a sharp contrast to modern American family values. Concubines were mainly an indulgence of upper-class Chinese men, but concubinage was an institution that touched all classes of Chinese society. Poor peasants knew that they could sell their daughters into the trade, if need be. And even middle-class wives worried that a concubine might be waiting in the wings should they prove to be infertile, unable to bear a son, or otherwise displeasing to their husband or mother-in-law.

We might also compare this selection with the previous one. How does the blatant acceptance of concubinage in this selection compare to the emphasis on family stability in the Miu lineage rules? Are these documents from two different Chinas, or are they compatible? Does this selection force you to modify the contrast you drew between Ming China and modern America from the previous selection?

*mow   zhee ANG
†dong   zhow AHN

"How Dong Xiaowan Became My Concubine," in *Chinese Civilization: A Sourcebook*, 2nd ed., ed. Patricia Ebrey (New York: Free Press, 1993), 246–49.

I was rather depressed that evening, so I got a boat and went with a friend on an excursion to Tiger Hill. My plan was to send a messenger to Xiangyang the next morning and then set out for home. As our boat passed under a bridge, I saw a small building by the bank. When I asked who lived there, my friend told me that this was [the singing girl] Dong's home. I was wildly happy with memories of three years before. I insisted on the boat's stopping, wanting to see Xiaowan at once. My friend, however, restrained me, saying, "Xiaowan has been terrified by the threat of being kidnapped by a powerful man and has been seriously ill for eighteen days. Since her mother's death,[1] she is said to have locked her door and refrained from receiving any guests." I nevertheless insisted on going ashore.

Not until I had knocked two or three times did the door open. I found no light in the house and had to grope my way upstairs. There I discovered medicine all over the table and bed.

Xiaowan, moaning, asked where I had come from and I told her I was the man she once saw beside a winding balustrade, intoxicated.

"Well, Sir," she said, recalling the incident, "I remember years ago you called at my house several times. Even though she only saw you once, my mother often spoke highly of you and considered it a great pity that I never had the chance to wait on you. Three years have passed. Mother died recently, but on seeing you now, I can hear her words in my ears. Where are you coming from this time?"

With an effort, she rose to draw aside the curtains and inspected me closely. She moved the lamp and asked me to sit on her bed. After talking awhile, I said I would go, not wanting to tire her. She, however, begged me to remain, saying, "During the past eighteen days I have had no appetite for food, nor have I been able to sleep well. My soul has been restless, dreaming almost all the time. But on seeing you, I feel as if my spirit has revived and my vigor returned." She then had her servant serve wine and food at her bedside, and kept refilling my cup herself.

Several times I expressed my desire to leave, but each time she urged me to stay. . . . The following morning, I was eager to set off on the trip home, but my friend and my servant both asked me not to be ungrateful for Xiaowan's kindness as she had had only a brief chance to talk with me the previous night. Accordingly I went to say goodbye to her. I found her, fresh from her toilet, leaning against a window upstairs quite composed. On seeing my boat approaching the bank, she hurried aboard to greet me. I told her that I had to leave immediately,

---

[1]The "mother" here may well be the woman who managed her, rather than her natural mother.

but she said that she had packed up her belongings and would accompany me. I felt unable to refuse her.

We went from Hushuguan to Wuxi, and from there to Changzhou, Yixing, and Jiangyin, finally arriving at Jinjiang. All this took twenty-seven days, and twenty-seven times I asked her to go back, but she was firm in her desire to follow me. On climbing Golden Hill, she pointed to the river and swore, "My body is as constant as the direction of the Yangzi River. I am determined never to go back to Suzhou!"

On hearing her words, I turned red and reiterated my refusal, "The provincial examination is coming up soon. Because my father's recent posts have been dangerous ones, I have failed to attend to family affairs and have not been able to look after my mother on a daily basis. This is my first chance to go back and take care of things. Moreover, you have so many creditors in Suzhou and it will take a lot to redeem your singing-girl's contract in Nanjing. So please go back to Suzhou for the time being. After I have taken the examination at the end of summer, I will send word and meet you in Nanjing. At any rate, I must await the result of the examination before I even think about these matters. Insisting on it now will do neither of us any good."

She, however, still hesitated. There were dice on the table, and one of my friends said to her jokingly, "If you are ever going to get your wish [to become his concubine], they will land with the same side up." She then bowed toward the window, said a prayer, and tossed the dice. They all landed on six. All on board expressed their amazement, and I said to her, "Should Heaven really be on our side, I'm afraid we might bungle the whole thing if we proceed too hurriedly. You had better leave me temporarily, and we'll see what we can do by and by." Thus against her wishes she said goodbye, concealing her tearstained face with her hands.

I had pity for her plight but at the same time once I was on my own felt relieved of a heavy burden. Upon arrival at Taizhou, I sat for the examination. When I got home in the sixth month, my wife said to me, "Xiaowan sent her father to bring word that since her return to Suzhou, she has kept to a vegetarian diet and confined herself to her home, waiting on tiptoe for you to bring her to Nanjing as you promised. I felt awkward and gave her father ten taels[2] of silver, asking him to tell her that I am in sympathy with her and consent to her request, but she must wait till you finish the examination."

I appreciated the way my wife had handled Xiaowan's request. I then directly proceeded to Nanjing without keeping my promise to send someone to fetch her, planning to write to her after I had finished the examination. However, scarcely had I come out of the examination hall

---

[2]A tael is equivalent to about 1¼ ounce. [Ed.]

on the morning of the 15th of the eighth month when she suddenly called at my lodgings at Peach Leaf Ferry. It turned out that after waiting in vain for news from me, she had hired a boat, setting out from Suzhou and proceeding along the river with an old woman as her companion. She met with robbers on the way, and her boat had to hide among reeds and rushes. With the rudder broken, the boat could not proceed, and she had had practically nothing to eat for three days. She arrived at Sanshan Gate of Nanjing on the 8th, but not wanting to disturb my thoughts during the examination, she delayed entering the city for two days.

Though delighted to see me, she looked and sounded rather sad as she vividly described what had happened during the hundred days of our separation, including her confinement at home on vegetarian fare, her encounter with robbers on the river, and her other experiences of a voyage fraught with danger. Now she was more insistent than ever on getting her wish. The men in my literary society from Kashan, Sungjiang, Fujian, and Henan all admired her farsightedness and sincerity and encouraged her with their verses and paintings.

When the examination was over, I thought I might pass it, so hoped I would soon be able to settle my affairs and gratify her desire to become my concubine. Unexpectedly, on the 17th I was informed that my father had arrived by boat. . . . I had not seen him for two years and was overjoyed that he had returned alive from the battlefront. Without delaying to tell Xiaowan, I immediately went to meet him. . . . Before long she set out by boat in pursuit of me from the lodging house at Peach Leaf Ferry. A storm at Swallow's Ledge nearly cost her her life. At Shierhui she came on board and stayed with me again for seven days.

When the results of the examination were announced, I found my name on the list of the not quite successful candidates. I then traveled day and night to get home, while she followed weeping, unwilling to part. I was, however, well aware that I could not by myself settle her affairs in Suzhou and that her creditors would, on discovering her departure, increase their demands. Moreover, my father's recent return and my disappointment in the exams had made it all the more difficult to gratify her desire at once. On arrival at Puchao on the outskirts of my native city, I had to put on a cold face and turn ironhearted to part from her, telling her to go back to Suzhou to set her creditors at ease and thus pave the way for our future plans.

In the tenth month, while passing Jinjiang, I went to visit Mr. Zheng, the man who had been my examiner. At that time, Liu Daxing of Fujian had arrived from the capital. During a drinking party in his boat with General Chen, my friend Prefect Liu, and myself, my servant returned from seeing Xiaowan home. He reported that on arrival at Suzhou she did not change out of her autumn clothing, saying that she intended to die of cold if I did not see my way to settle her affairs promptly. On hearing this, Liu Daxing pointed to me and said, "Pijiang, you are well known as a man of honor. Could you really betray a girl like this?"

"Surely scholars are not capable of the gallant deeds of Huang Shanke and Gu Yaya," I replied.

The prefect raised his cup, and with a gesture of excitement exclaimed, "Well, if I were given a thousand taels of silver to pay my expenses, I'd start right away today!"

General Chen at once lent me several hundred taels, and Liu Daxing helped with a present of several catties[3] of ginseng. But how could it have been anticipated that the prefect, on arrival at Suzhou, failed to carry out his mission, and that when the creditors had kicked up a row and the matter had been brought to a deadlock, he fled to Wujiang? I had no chance to make further inquiries, as I returned home shortly afterwards.

Xiaowan was left in an awkward position, with little she could do. On hearing of her trouble, Qian Qianyi of Changshu went to Bantang himself and brought her to his boat. He approached her creditors, from the gentry to the townsmen, and within three days managed to clear every single debt of hers, the bills redeemed piling up a foot in height. This done, he arranged a farewell banquet on a pleasure boat and entertained her at the foot of Tiger Hill. He then hired a boat and sent someone to see her to Rugao.

On the evening of the 15th of the eleventh month when I was drinking wine with my father in our Zhuocun Hall, I was suddenly informed that Xiaowan had arrived at the jetty. After reading Qian's long interesting letter, I learned how she had gotten here. I also learned that Qian had written to a pupil of his, Zhang of the ministry of rites, asking him to redeem her singing girl's contract at once. Her minor problems at Suzhou were later settled by Mr. Zhou of the bureau of ceremonies while Mr. Li, formerly attached to that bureau, had also rendered her great assistance in Nanjing.

Ten months thereafter, her desire was gratified [and she became my concubine]. After the endless tangle of troubles and emotional pain, we had what we wanted.

---

[3]One catty is equivalent to 16 taels, 20 ounces, or a British pound. [Ed.]

KENNETH POMERANZ

How the Other Half Traded

The "other half" of this recent essay, written by historian Kenneth Pomeranz, refers not only to women, but to the women who were the Southeast Asian trading partners of Portuguese and then Dutch merchants in the sixteenth and seventeenth centuries. Why did these women play such an important role in European trade with Southeast Asia? How did both Europeans and Southeast Asians benefit socially and economically from these alliances?

Thinking Historically

Pomeranz enables us to make a number of comparisons about gender and family. How, for instance, was the role of women in Southeast Asia different from that of their sisters in China? How did the role and rights of women in Europe differ from those in Southeast Asia? Were gender relations more alike in Europe and Southeast Asia, or in Europe and China? How would you expect European trade with China to be different from European trade with Southeast Asia?

Even today, companies often find that keeping up the morale of employees sent overseas is difficult. But consider an earlier multinational: the Dutch East India Company (VOC) of the seventeenth and eighteenth centuries. Its outposts in India, Southeast Asia, Japan, and Taiwan were places where few Dutchwomen were willing to live; and while most men working for the company were quite willing to seek mates among indigenous women, this brought complications of its own. Given the cultural gulf separating these couples, it may be no great surprise that the private letters of these men are full of references to how hard it was to "tame" these women into the kinds of wives they expected. What may be more surprising is how hard the VOC, the Dutch Reformed Church, and other Europeans in Southeast Asia found it to break the *commercial* power of these women, many of whom were substantial traders in their own right.

Kenneth Pomeranz, "How the Other Half Traded," in Kenneth Pomeranz and Steven Topik, eds., *The World That Trade Created* (Armonk, N.Y.: M. E. Sharpe, 2006), 27–30.

Long before Europeans arrived, maritime Southeast Asia (including present-day Malaysia, Indonesia, and the Philippines) carried on a substantial long-distance trade. Many of the merchants were women — in some cases because commerce was thought too base an occupation for upper-class men, but too lucrative for elite families to abstain from completely. (Some elites carried this snobbery a step further, and held that noble women were also too lofty to barter in the marketplace or to visit the Chinese settlements where much long-distance trading was arranged; they were not, however, too noble to supervise a team of servants who carried out these businesses.) Malay proverbs of the 1500s spoke of the importance of teaching daughters how to calculate and make a profit.

More generally, these societies typically allowed women to control their own property, gave them considerable voice in the choice of husbands, and were often quite tolerant of other liaisons. The long journeys away from home that some of these women took even made it necessary to allow them, within the crude limits of available technology, to control their own fertility. (Herbal medicines, jumping from rocks to induce miscarriages, and even occasional infanticides were among the methods used.) Both the Islamic missionaries who swept through the area in the 1400s and the Christians who followed a hundred years later were appalled, and hoped to bring such women to heel.

But despite these qualms, the Portuguese, the first Europeans to establish themselves in this world, had found intermarrying with such women to be an indispensable part of creating profitable and defensible colonies. When the VOC gave up on importing Dutchwomen — having sometimes found "willing" candidates only in the orphanages or even brothels of Holland, and facing discontent among the intended husbands of these women — it turned to the daughters of these earlier Portuguese-Asian unions: they at least spoke a Western language, and were at least nominally Christian. Many had also learned from their mothers how useful a European husband could be for protecting their business interests in an increasingly multinational and often violent trading world. Councillors of the Dutch court in Batavia (present-day Jakarta), who were rarely rich themselves, but were very well placed to prevent the VOC's rules and monopoly claims from interfering with their wives' trade, were often particularly good matches for the richest of these women. Thus, arranging elite interracial marriages proved relatively easy: but making the resulting families conform to visions hatched in Amsterdam proved harder.

The VOC's principal goal, of course, was profit, and profit was best secured by monopolizing the export of all sorts of Asian goods — from pepper to porcelain — back to Europe. In theory, the Company also claimed — at least intermittently — the right to license and tax (or sink) all the ships participating in the much larger intra-Asian trade, including those of Southeast Asia's women traders. But the realities of huge oceans and numerous rivals made enforcing such a system impossible, and the VOC also faced powerful enemies within. Most Company servants soon discovered that while smuggling goods back to Holland was risky and difficult, they could earn sums by trading illegally (or semi-legally) within Asia that dwarfed their official salaries. Here their wives were a perfect vehicle for making a fortune: they were well connected in and knowledgeable about local markets, often possessed of considerable capital, and able to manage the family business continuously without being susceptible to sudden transfer by the Company.

And for some particularly unscrupulous Dutchmen there was the possibility of a kind of lucrative cultural arbitrage: after profiting from the relatively high status of Southeast Asian women, one might take advantage of their low status in Dutch law to gain sole control of the family fortune, and then perhaps even return to the Netherlands to settle down with a "proper" wife. (Though even with the law on the man's side, such a process could be very complex if the woman used her informal influence cleverly and hid her assets — in one such case the man eventually won control of most of his wife's profits, but the legal proceedings took nineteen years.)

But if men had powerful allies in the Dutch law and church, women had the climate on their side. Foreigners tended to die young in India and Southeast Asia, leaving behind wealthy widows. Such women were often eagerly sought after by the next wave of incoming European adventurers, enabling them to strike marriage bargains that safeguarded at least some of their independence; many wed and survived three or four husbands. The rare Dutchman who did live a long life in Batavia was likely to rise quite high in the VOC, become very wealthy, and marry more than once himself; but since such men (not needing a particularly well-connected or rich spouse once they'd risen this high) often chose a last wife much younger than themselves, they tended to leave behind a small circle of very wealthy widows, whose behavior often scandalized those Dutchmen who took their Calvinism seriously.

From the founding of Batavia in 1619 until the late 1800s, Dutch moralists and monopolists waged an endless battle to "tame" these women, and at least partially succeeded; later generations, for instance, seem to have conformed much more than earlier ones to European sexual mores. And as the scale of capital and international contacts needed to succeed in long-distance trade grew larger, European companies and their Chinese or Indian merchant allies — all of them male — did increasingly shrink the sphere in which these women operated.

Eventually, when late nineteenth-century innovations — the Suez Canal, telegraphs, refrigerated shipping, vaccinations, and so on — made it more and more possible to live a truly European life-style in Southeast Asia, a new generation of Dutch officials chose to bring wives with them, or to assume they would quickly return to Holland and marry there.

Even so, trade managed by Eurasian women remained a crucial part of local and regional economies: many, for instance, managed commercial real estate and money-lending operations through which they funneled profits from their husbands' activities into local development around the fringes of Southeast Asian trading cities. (Ironically, this niche may have been kept for them in part through the racism of many of their husbands, who preferred to deal with the locals as little as possible.)

As late as the turn of the twentieth century, this sphere and those who managed it refused to disappear — the Indonesian novelist Pramoedaya Toer has painted a powerful portrait of one such woman, who waged a running battle to hold on to the businesses (and children) she had handled for years against her half-mad Dutch consort and his "legal" family back in Holland. Along with most of her real-life counterparts, this fictional woman was ultimately defeated; but for three centuries, women like her had built and sustained much of the world their husbands claimed was theirs.

$$\boxed{117}$$

JOHN E. WILLS JR.

Sor Juana Inés de la Cruz

After the conquest of the Aztecs, the Spanish attempted to govern Mexico by converting the surviving Indians to Roman Catholicism and exploiting their labor. In addition, they encouraged fellow Spaniards to settle in the colony and imported African slaves, creating a mixed society of Europeans, Indians, and Africans. As in the rest of North America, the dividing line between slave and free was the most important social distinction. But unlike their English counterparts to the north, New Spain's colonists also distinguished between *Peninsulares*, colonists who were born in Spain, and Creoles, colonists who were born of Spanish parents in the Americas.

In the following selection a modern historian evokes the life of Sor Juana Inés de la Cruz* (1651–1695), a poet, artist, and nun who lived

*sohr hoo AH nah   ee NEZ   duh lah CROOZ

John E. Wills Jr., "Sor Juana Inés de la Cruz," in *1688: A Global History* (New York: W. W. Norton, 2001), 13–19.

in Mexico City in "New Spain." Sister Juana was a Creole woman and the author argues she was distinctly a product of Mexican Creole society. In what ways was she Spanish? In what ways was she Mexican? How do you think the life of a Creole woman, born and raised in the colony, would be different from that of a woman born in Spain?

Thinking Historically

The previous selection reminds us that some societies, like Southeast Asia, were less patriarchal than others. The arrival of Europeans sometimes enhanced the wealth and influence of women traders in Southeast Asia. The widows and daughters of mixed marriages often benefited from both worlds.

The daughters of Spanish settlers in the Americas had fewer opportunities for financial advancement than did the daughters of Dutch settlers in Java, and the Spanish patriarchy was as unyielding as any in Europe. Nevertheless, the culture that the Old World imported into the New provided alternatives for women that were absent in the East Indies. What were these alternatives? Were they a product of Europe, America, or the intermixture of the two?

On April 28, 1688, a long procession moved out of Mexico City, along the causeways that crossed the nearby lakes, and through the small towns and farms of the plateau, on its way toward the pass between the two volcanoes Iztaccihuatl and Popocatépetl, both more than sixteen thousand feet high, and down to the tropical port of Vera Cruz. The farmers in their villages and fields were used to a good deal of such coming and going, but this time they stopped their work to look and to call out to each other in Nahuatl, the main indigenous language, for this was no ordinary procession. Cavalry outriders and a huge coach were followed by many baggage wagons and a long line of fine coaches. The marquis of Laguna had served as viceroy of New Spain from 1680 to 1686. With their wealth, powerful connections in Madrid, and a taste for elegance and the arts, he and his wife had given the viceregal court a few years of splendor and sophistication comparable, if not to Madrid, certainly to many of the lesser courts of Europe. Now their wealthy Spanish friends were riding in their coaches as far as the Villa de Guadalupe, seeing the marquis and marchioness off on their voyage home to Spain.

> A child born of a slave shall be received,
> according to our Law, as property
> of the owner to whom fealty
> is rendered by the mother who conceived.

The harvest from a grateful land retrieved,
the finest fruit, offered obediently,
is for the lord, for its fecundity
is owing to the care it has received.

So too, Lysis divine, these my poor lines:
as children of my soul, born of my heart,
they must in justice be to you returned;

Let not their defects cause them to be spurned,
for of your rightful due they are a part,
as concepts of a soul to yours consigned.

These lines were written sometime later in 1688 and sent off from Mexico to the marchioness of Laguna in Spain. They make use of metaphors and classical conceits to express and conceal the feelings of the author, who had lost, with the marchioness's departure, the object of the nearest thing she had ever known to true love and, with the marquis's departure, her ultimate protection from those who found her opinions and her way of life scandalous. The trouble was not that the author was lesbian — although her feelings toward men and women were unusually complicated and unconventional, anything approaching a physical relation or even passion is most unlikely — but that she was a cloistered Hieronymite nun, who read and studied a wide range of secular books, held long intellectual conversations with many friends, wrote constantly in a variety of religious and secular styles, and betrayed in her writings sympathy for Hermetic and Neoplatonic views that were on the edge of heresy if not beyond it. Her name in religion was Sor Juana Inés de la Cruz. She is recognized today as one of the great poets in the history of the Spanish language.

Mexico in the 1680s was a society of dramatic contradictions. The elegant viceregal court and the opulent ecclesiastical hierarchy looked toward Europe for style and ideas. The vast majority of the population sought to preserve as much as possible of the language, beliefs, and ways of life that had guided them before the coming of the Spaniards; the worship of the Virgin of Guadalupe, for example, owed much to the shrine of an Aztec goddess that had been the setting of the original appearance of the Virgin to a Mexican peasant. In between the "peninsular" elite and the "Indians," the native-born "creoles" of Spanish language and culture managed huge cattle ranches and sought constantly new veins of profitable silver ore and new techniques to exploit old ones. Neither "Spanish" nor "Indian," they experienced the full force of the contradictions of Mexican society and culture.

The literary world in which Sor Juana was such an anomalous eminence thrived on these contradictions of society and culture. This was a baroque culture. The word *baroque*, originating as a Portuguese term for the peculiar beauty of a deformed, uneven pearl, suggests a range of artistic styles in which the balance and harmony of the Renaissance styles are abandoned for imbalance, free elaboration of form, playful gesture, and surprising allusion, through which the most intense of emotions and the darkest of realities may be glimpsed, their power enhanced by the glittering surface that partially conceals them. Contradiction and its partial, playful reconciliation are the stuff of the baroque style. So is the layering of illusion on illusion, meaning upon meaning. And what more baroque conceit could be imagined than the literary eminence of a cloistered nun in a rough frontier society, with a church and state of the strongest and narrowest male supremacist prejudices? Look again at the poem quoted earlier: The chaste nun refers to her poem as her child or the harvest from a grateful land. She declares her love once again to the departed marchioness.

Sor Juana was a product of Mexican creole society, born on a ranch on the shoulder of the great volcano Popocatépetl. Her mother was illiterate and very probably had not been married to her father. But some of the family branches lived in the city, with good books and advantageous connections. As soon as she discovered the books in her grandfather's library, she was consumed with a thirst for solitude and reading. Her extraordinary talents for literature and learning were recognized. When she was fifteen, in 1664, she was taken into the household of a newly arrived viceroy, as his wife's favorite and constant companion. She must have enjoyed the attention, the luxury, the admiration of her cleverness. She no doubt participated in the highly stylized exchange of "gallantries" between young men and young women. But she had no dowry. Solitude was her natural habitat. As a wife and mother, what chance would she have to read, to write, to be alone? In 1668 she took her vows in the Hieronymite convent of an order named after Saint Jerome, cloistered and meditative by rule.

This was a big decision, but less drastic than one might think. Certainly she was a believing Catholic. Her new status did not require total devotion to prayer and extinction of self. It did not imply that she was abandoning all the friendships and secular learning that meant so much to her. The nuns had a daily round of collective devotions; but many rules were not fully honored, and the regimen left her much free time for reading and writing. Each of the nuns had comfortable private quarters, with a kitchen, room for a bathtub, and sleeping space for a servant and a dependent or two; Sor Juana usually had one slave and one or two nieces or other junior dependents living in her quarters. The nuns visited back and forth in their quarters to the point that Sor Juana complained of the interruptions to her reading and writing, but outsiders spoke to the nuns only in the locutory especially provided for that purpose. From the beginning she turned the locutory into an elegant salon, as the viceroy and his lady and other fashionable people came to visit her and they passed hours in learned debate, literary improvisation, and gossip.

One of Sor Juana's most constant friends and supporters was Carlos de Sigüenza y Góngora, professor of mathematics at the University of Mexico, an eminently learned creole scholar whose position was almost as anomalous as hers. He had been educated by the Jesuits and had longed to be one of them but had been expelled from their college. He had managed to obtain his position, without a university degree, by demonstrating his superior knowledge of his subject. He had added Góngora to his name to emphasize his distant kinship, through his mother's family, with the most famous of Spain's baroque poets. But he always felt insecure among the European-born professors, churchmen, and high officials. He wrote a great deal, much of it about the history of Mexico. He was in no way Sor Juana's equal as a writer, but he probably was responsible for most of her smattering of knowledge of modern science and recent philosophy.

There was a rule of poverty among the Hieronymites, but it was generally ignored. Sor Juana received many gifts, some of them substantial enough to enable the former dowerless girl to invest money at interest. By gift and purchase she built up a library of about four thousand volumes and a small collection of scientific instruments, probably provided by Sigüenza. Her reading was broad but not very systematic, contributing to the stock of ideas and allusions she drew on constantly in her writings but giving her little sense of the intellectual tensions and transformations that were building up in Europe. She wrote constantly, in a wide variety of complex and exacting forms. Voluntarily or upon commission or request, she wrote occasional poems of all kinds for her friends and patrons. A celebration might call for a *loa*, a brief theatrical piece in praise of a dignitary. In one of hers, for example, a character "clad in sunrays" declares:

> I am a reflection
> of that blazing sun
> who, among shining rays
> numbers brilliant sons:
> when his illustrious rays
> strike a speculum,
> on it is portrayed
> the likeness of his form.

Sor Juana's standing in society reached a new height with the arrival in 1680 of the marquis and marchioness of Laguana. Even in the public festivities celebrating their arrival, she outdid herself in baroque elaborations of texts and conceits for a temporary triumphal arch erected at the cathedral. It was an allegory on Neptune, in which the deeds of the Greek god were compared to the real or imaginary deeds of the marquis. Much was made of the echoes among the marquis's title of Laguna, meaning *lake*, Neptune's reign over the oceans, and the origins of Mexico City as the Aztec city of Tenochtitlán in the middle of its great lake: an elaborate union of sycophancy to a ruler, somewhat strained classical allusion, and a creole quest for a Mexican identity. In parts of the text the author even drew in Isis as an ancestor of Neptune, and in others of her works from this time she showed a great interest in Egyptian antiquity as it was then understood, including the belief that the god Hermes Trismegistus had revealed the most ancient and purest wisdom and anticipated the Mosaic and Christian revelations. These ideas, the accompanying quasi-Platonic separation of soul and body, and her use of them to imply that a female or androgynous condition was closer to the divine wisdom than the male took her to the edge of heresy or beyond and was turned against her in later years.

Sor Juana soon established a close friendship with the marchioness of Laguna. Some of the poems she sent her are among her very finest, and they are unmistakably love poems. Some of them accompanied a portrait of the author. Several portraits in which a very handsome woman gazes boldly at us, her black-and-white habit simply setting off her own strength and elegance, have come down to us. [See Figure 18.1.]

> And if it is that you should rue
> the absence of a soul in me [the portrait],
> you can confer one, easily,
> from the many rendered you:
> and as my soul I [Sor Juana] tendered you,
> and though my being yours obeyed,
> and though you look on me amazed
> in this insentient apathy,
> you are the soul of this body,
> and are the body of this shade.

The marquis of Laguna stepped down as viceroy in 1686 but remained in Mexico until 1688. In that year Sor Juana was very busy. The marchioness was taking texts of her poems back to Spain, where they soon would be published. She added to them a play, *The Divine Narcissus*, interweaving the legend of Narcissus and the life of Jesus, which probably was performed in Madrid in 1689 or 1690. Her niece took her vows in the convent in 1688. Late in the year, after her noble friends had left, she wrote the poem quoted earlier as well as a romantic comedy, *Love Is the Greater Labyrinth*, which was performed in Mexico City early in 1689.

A large collection of her poetry was published in Madrid in 1689. The next year in Mexico she published a letter taking abstruse issue with a sermon preached decades before by the famous Portuguese Jesuit

Figure 18.1 Portrait of Sor Juana Inés de la Cruz, 1750.
This portrait of Sor Juana was done by one of Mexico's most famous
painters, Miguel Cabrera (1695–1768), the official painter of the Archbishop of Mexico. The nun sits surrounded by the emblems of her literary
life, including quill pens, inkwell, and an open volume from her enormous
library. In the original portrait, the viewer can discern a host of classical
authors lining the shelves, including Hippocrates, Virgil, and Cicero.
Source: Schalkwijk/Art Resource, N.Y.

Antonio Vieira. Her casual way with the rules of the religious life, her
flirtings with heresy, her many writings in secular forms with intima-
tions of understanding of love inappropriate to her profession had
made her many enemies, but they could do nothing while the marquis
of Laguna and his lady were on hand to protect her. Now they closed

in. In 1694 she was forced formally to renounce all writing and humane studies and to relinquish her library and collection of scientific instruments. In 1695 she devotedly cared for her sisters in the convent during an epidemic, caught the disease, and died.

$$\boxed{118}$$

ANNA BIJNS

"Unyoked Is Best! Happy the Woman without a Man"

Anna Bijns* (1494–1575) was a Flemish poet who lived in Antwerp, taught in a Catholic school in that city, wrote biting criticism of Martin Luther and the Protestant Reformation, and in her many works helped shape the Dutch language. The impact of Luther, and Protestantism more generally, on the lives of women has been the subject of much debate. Luther opposed nunneries and monasticism, believing that it was the natural duty of all women to marry and bear children. At the same time, he encouraged a level of reciprocal love and respect in marriage that was less emphasized in Catholicism. The Protestant translations of the Bible from Latin also opened a pathway for individuals, including educated women, to participate in the religious life, though not as nuns. Whether or not the sentiments of this poem are more Catholic than Protestant, are they more European than Chinese? Why or why not?

Thinking Historically

No one should imagine that the ideas conveyed in this poem were typical or representative of European thought in the sixteenth century. This was obviously an extreme view that ran counter to traditional and commonly accepted ideas. Note how some phrases of the poem convey the recognition that most people will disagree with the sentiments being expressed.

*bynz

Anna Bijns, "Unyoked Is Best," trans. Kristiaan P. G. Aercke, in *Women and Writers of the Renaissance and Reformation*, ed. Katharina M. Wilson (Athens: The University of Georgia Press, 1987), 382–83.

When we are comparing documents from different cultures, we must always try to understand how representative they are of the views of the larger population. The Miu family document (selection 114) expresses the views of a single family, but lineage regulations were common in sixteenth-century China, and their ubiquity reflected an even greater consensus on the importance of the family. Anna Bijns's poem is a personal view that expresses a minority opinion. But in what sense is this a European, rather than Chinese, minority view? What sort of extreme minority views might Southeast Asian or European-American cultures produce? Do you think Anna Bijns's view might appeal to more people today than it did in the sixteenth century? If so, why?

How good to be a woman, how much better to be a man!
Maidens and wenches, remember the lesson you're about to hear.
Don't hurtle yourself into marriage far too soon.
The saying goes: "Where's your spouse? Where's your honor?"
But one who earns her board and clothes
Shouldn't scurry to suffer a man's rod.
So much for my advice, because I suspect —
Nay, see it sadly proven day by day —
'T happens all the time!
However rich in goods a girl might be,
Her marriage ring will shackle her for life.
If however she stays single
With purity and spotlessness foremost,
Then she is lord as well as lady, Fantastic, not?
Though wedlock I do not decry:
Unyoked is best! Happy the woman without a man.

Fine girls turning into loathly hags —
'Tis true! Poor sluts! Poor tramps! Cruel marriage!
Which makes me deaf to wedding bells.
Huh! First they marry the guy, luckless dears,
Thinking their love just too hot to cool.
Well, they're sorry and sad within a single year.
Wedlock's burden is far too heavy.
They know best whom it harnessed.
So often is a wife distressed, afraid.
When after troubles hither and thither he goes
In search of dice and liquor, night and day,
She'll curse herself for that initial "yes."
So, beware ere you begin.
Just listen, don't get yourself into it.
Unyoked is best! Happy the woman without a man.

A man oft comes home all drunk and pissed
Just when his wife had worked her fingers to the bone
(So many chores to keep a decent house!),
But if she wants to get in a word or two,
She gets to taste his fist — no more.
And that besotted keg she is supposed to obey?
Why, yelling and scolding is all she gets,
Such are his ways — and hapless his victim.
And if the nymphs of Venus he chooses to frequent,
What hearty welcome will await him home.
Maidens, young ladies: learn from another's doom,
Ere you, too, end up in fetters and chains,
Please don't argue with me on this,
No matter who contradicts, I stick to it:
Unyoked is best! Happy the woman without a man.

A single lady has a single income,
But likewise, isn't bothered by another's whims.
And I think: that freedom is worth a lot.
Who'll scoff at her, regardless what she does,
And though every penny she makes herself,
Just think of how much less she spends!
An independent lady is an extraordinary prize —
All right, of a man's boon she is deprived,
But she's lord and lady of her very own hearth.
To do one's business and no explaining sure is lots of fun!
Go to bed when she list,[1] rise when she list, all as she will,
And no one to comment! Grab tight your independence then.
Freedom is such a blessed thing.
To all girls: though the right Guy might come along:
Unyoked is best! Happy the woman without a man.

Regardless of the fortune a woman might bring,
Many men consider her a slave, that's all.
Don't let a honeyed tongue catch you off guard,
Refrain from gulping it all down. Let them rave,
For, I guess, decent men resemble white ravens.
Abandon the airy castles they will build for you.
Once their tongue has limed[2] a bird:
Bye bye love — and love just flies away.
To women marriage comes to mean betrayal

[1]Wants. [Ed.]
[2]Caught. [Ed.]

And the condemnation to a very awful fate.
All her own is spent, her lord impossible to bear.
It's *peine forte et dure*[3] instead of fun and games.
Oft it was the money, and not the man
Which goaded so many into their fate.
Unyoked is best! Happy the woman without a man.

---

[3]Long and forceful punishment; a form of torture whereby the victim was slowly crushed by heaping rocks on a board laid over his or her body. [Ed.]

119

MARY JO MAYNES
AND ANN WALTNER

Women and Marriage in Europe and China

This article is the product of a rich collaboration between historians of China and Europe who show us how a study of women and marriage is anything but peripheral to a study of these areas. Rather it can help us answer a major historical question: How do we explain the dramatic rise of Western Europe after 1500, especially in the wake of prodigious Chinese growth that continued into the sixteenth century?

The authors begin by comparing the role of religion, the state, and the family in setting marriage patterns in both China and Europe. Did Christianity allow European women more independence than Confucianism allowed women in China? In which society was the patriarchal family more powerful, and what was the relative impact of patriarchy on women in both societies? How did the age and rate at which people married in each society compare? What was the importance of Chinese concubinage and Christian ideals of chastity?

Thinking Historically

The authors' questions about marriage in Europe and China lead finally to a consideration of one of the most frequently asked comparative questions: Why did Europe industrialize before China? Do the dif-

---

Mary Jo Maynes and Ann Waltner, "Childhood, Youth, and the Female Life Cycle: Women's Life-Cycle Transitions in a World-Historical Perspective: Comparing Marriage in China and Europe," *Journal of Women's History*, 12, no. 4 (Winter 2001), 11–19.

ferent European and Chinese marriage patterns answer this question? What other comparative questions would we have to ask to arrive at a full answer?

Comparing Marriage Cross-Culturally

A number of years ago, we were involved in organizing a comparative historical conference on gender and kinship (our areas of specialization are Chinese and European family and women's history). Conversations that began at the conference resulted in a collection of coedited articles, but they also spurred the two of us to collaboratively teach a world history course in which family and women's history play key roles. We introduce students in that course to historical comparison by talking about marriage. In particular, we begin with a pointed comparison between the history of marriage in China and Europe based on research presented at the kinship conference.

Beginning in the late 1500s, women in northern Italy began to appeal to legal courts run by the Catholic Church when they got into disputes with their families over arranged marriages. Within the early modern Italy family system the father held a great deal of authority over his children and it was usual for the parents to determine when and whom sons and daughters married. Women and children held little power in comparison with adult men. But the Catholic Church's insistence that both parties enter into the marriage willingly gave some women an out — namely, an appeal to the Church court, claiming that the marriage their family wanted was being forced upon them without their consent. Surprisingly, these young women often won their cases against their fathers. In early modern China, by way of contrast, state, religion, and family were bound together under the veil of Confucianism. Paternal authority echoed and reinforced the political and the moral order. Religious institutions could rarely be called upon to intervene in family disputes. Therefore, young women (or young men, for that matter) had no clearly established institutional recourse in situations of unwanted marriage. So, despite the fact that paternal power was very strong in both early modern Italy and early modern China, specific institutional differences put young women at the moment of marriage in somewhat different positions.

We began with the presumption that however different the institution of "marriage" was in Italy and China, it nevertheless offered enough similarities that it made sense to speak comparatively about a category called "marriage." Parallels in the two cultures between the institution of marriage and the moment in the woman's life course that it represented make comparison useful. Nevertheless, this particular comparison also isolates some of the variable features of marriage systems that are especially significant in addressing gender relations in a world-historical context. In China, the rules of family formation and family governance were generally enforced within the bounds of each extended family group. State and religious influences were felt only indirectly through family leaders as mediators or enforcers of state and religious law. Throughout Europe, beginning in the Middle Ages, the institution of marriage was altered first by the effort of the Catholic Church to wrest some control over marriage from the family by defining it as a sacrament, and then eventually by the struggle between churches and state authorities to regulate families.

This contest among church, state, and family authorities over marriage decisions turns out to have been a particular feature of European history that had consequences for many aspects of social life. A focus on the moment of marriage presents special opportunities for understanding connections between the operation of gender relations in everyday life and in the realm of broader political developments. Marriage is a familial institution, of course, but, to varying degrees, political authorities also have a stake in it because of its implications for property transfer, reproduction, religion, and morality — in short, significant aspects of the social order. In this essay, we compare one dimension of marriage — its timing in a woman's life cycle — in two contexts, Europe and China. We argue that variations in marriage timing have world-historical implications. We examine how a woman's status and situation shifted at marriage and then suggest some implications of comparative differences in the timing and circumstances of this change of status.

The Moment of Marriage in European History

One striking peculiarity of Central and Western European history between 1600 and 1850 was the relatively late age at first marriage for men and women compared with other regions of the world. The so-called "Western European marriage pattern" was marked by relatively late marriage — that is, relative to other regions of the world where some form of marriage usually occurred around the time of puberty. In much of Europe, in contrast, men did not typically marry until their late twenties and women their mid-twenties. This practice of relatively late marriage was closely connected with the custom of delaying marriage until the couple commanded sufficient resources to raise a family. For artisans this traditionally meant having a shop and master status. For merchants it entailed saving capital to begin a business. In the case of peasant couples, this meant having a house and land and basic farming equipment. It was the responsibility of the family and the community to oversee courtship, betrothal, and marriage to assure that these conditions were met. This phenomenon was also rooted in the common practice of neolocality — the expectation that a bride and groom would set up their own household at or soon after marriage. This "delayed" marriage has attracted the attention of European historical demographers. The delay of marriage meant, quite significantly, that most European women did not begin to have children until their twenties. But this marriage pattern also has significance in other realms as well. In particular, young people of both sexes experienced a relatively long hiatus between puberty and marriage.

Unmarried European youth played a distinctive role in economic, social, cultural, and political life through such institutions as guilds, village youth groups, and universities. For the most part, historians' attention to European youth has centered on young men. Major works on the history of youth in Europe, like theories of adolescent development, tend to center on the male experience as normative. Only when gender differences in youth are recognized and the history of young women is written will the broad historical significance of the European marriage pattern become clear. Contrast between European demographic history and that of other world regions suggests a comparative pattern of particular significance for girls: Delayed marriage and childbearing meant that teenage girls were available for employment outside the familial household (either natal or marital) to a degree uncommon elsewhere. Household divisions of labor according to age and gender created constant demand for servants on larger farms; typically, unmarried youth who could be hired in from neighboring farms as servants filled this role. A period of service in a farm household, as an apprentice, or as a domestic servant in an urban household characterized male and female European youth in the lifecycle phase preceding marriage. Historians have noted but never fully explored the role young women played in European economic development, and in particular their role in the early industrial labor force.

Late marriage had gender-specific cultural ramifications as well. Whereas it was considered normal and even appropriate for teenage men to be initiated into heterosexual intercourse at brothels, in most regions of Europe, young women were expected to remain chaste until marriage. Delay of marriage heightened anxiety over unmarried women's sexuality, especially the dangers to which young women were increasingly exposed as the locus of their labor shifted from home and village to factory and city. Premarital or extramarital sexuality was uncommon, and was rigorously policed especially in the period following the religious upheavals of the Reformation in the sixteenth century. In rural areas, church and community, in addition to the family, exerted control over sexuality. Moreover, the unmarried male youth cohort of many village communities often served, in effect, as "morals police," enforcing local customs. These young men regulated courtship rituals,

organized dances that young people went to, and oversaw the formation of couples. Sometimes, judging and public shaming by the youth
group was the fate of couples who were mismatched by age or wealth
or who violated sexual taboos. Some customs, at least symbolically,
punished young men from far away who married local women, removing them from the marriage pool. Often, such a bridegroom had to pay
for drinks in each village that the bridal couple passed through as they
moved from the bride's parish church to their new abode — the longer
the distance, the more expensive his bill.

Once married, a couple would usually begin having children immediately. Demographic evidence suggests that for most of Central and
Western Europe there was virtually no practice of contraception among
lower classes prior to the middle of the nineteenth century. Women had
babies about every two years (more or less frequently according to region and depending on such local customs as breast-feeding length and
intercourse taboos). Even though completed family sizes could be large
by modern standards, the number of children most women bore was
still less than if they had married in their teens. And prevailing high
mortality rates further reduced the number of children who survived to
adulthood.

The Moment of Marriage in Chinese History

The Chinese marriage system was traditionally characterized by early
age at marriage, nearly universal marriage for women, virilocal residence (a newly married couple resided with the groom's parents), concubinage for elite men, and norms that discouraged widow remarriage.
From the sixteenth through twentieth centuries, Chinese men and
women married much younger on average than did their European
counterparts — late teens or early twenties for women and a bit later
for men. A bride typically moved to her husband's family home, which
was often in a different village from her own. The moment of marriage
not only meant that a girl would leave her parents but that she would
also leave her network of kin and friends, all that was familiar. Families
chose marriage partners, and a matchmaker negotiated the arrangements. Nothing resembling courtship existed; the bride and groom
would often first meet on their wedding day.

Because a newly married Chinese couple would typically reside in
an already-existing household, it was not necessary for an artisan to become established, a merchant to accumulate capital, or a peasant to
own a farm before marrying. Newly married couples participated in
ongoing domestic and economic enterprises that already supported the
groom's family. New households were eventually established by a
process of household division, which typically happened at the death of

the father rather than the moment of marriage (although it could happen at other points in the family cycle as well).

Daughters were groomed from birth for marriage. They were taught skills appropriate to their social class or the social class into which their parents aspired to marry them. (In the ideal Chinese marriage, the groom was in fact supposed to be of slightly higher social status than the bride.) The feet of upper-class girls (and some who were not upper class) were bound, since Chinese men found this erotic. Bound feet also symbolically, if not actually, restricted upper-class women's movement. Thus bound feet simultaneously enhanced the sexual desirability of upper-class women and served to contain their sexuality within domestic bounds.

Virtually all Chinese girls became brides, though not all of them married as principal wives. (This contrasts with the European pattern where a substantial minority of women in most regions never married.) Upper-class men might take one or more concubines in addition to a principal wife. The relationship between a man and his concubine was recognized legally and ritually, and children born of these unions were legitimate. A wife had very secure status: divorce was almost nonexistent. A concubine's status, in contrast, was much more tenuous. She could be expelled at the whim of her "husband"; her only real protection was community sentiment. Although only a small percentage of Chinese marriages (no more than 5 percent) involved concubines, the practice remained an important structural feature of the Chinese marriage system until the twentieth century. Concubinage also provides a partial explanation of why, despite the fact that marriage was nearly universal for women, a substantial proportion of men (perhaps as high as 10 percent) never married. Also contributing to this apparent anomaly was the practice of sex-selective infanticide, a common practice that discriminated against girl babies and, ultimately, reduced the number of potential brides.

Once married, Chinese couples began to have children almost immediately, generally spacing births at longer intervals than did European couples. The reasons for this are not yet completely understood, although infanticide, extended breast-feeding, and the fairly large number of days on which sexual intercourse was forbidden all seem to have played a role in lowering Chinese family size.

Early marriage in China meant that the category of "youth," which has been so significant for European social and economic history, has no precise counterpart in Chinese history. Young Chinese women labored, to be sure, but the location of their work was domestic — either in the household of their father or husband. Female servants existed in China, but their servitude was normally of longer duration than the life-cycle servitude common in Europe. The domestic location of young women's labor in the Chinese context also had implications for the particular ways in which Chinese industries were organized, as we suggest below.

Patterns of Marriage in Europe and China

To sum up, then, there are differences of both timing of and residency before and after marriage that are particularly germane to the comparative history of young women. As demographic historians James Z. Lee and Wang Feng also have argued, "in China, females have always married universally and early . . . in contrast to female marriage in Western Europe, which occurred late or not at all." Whereas, in the nineteenth century, all but 20 percent of young Chinese women were married by age twenty, among European populations, between 60 and 80 percent of young women remained single at this age. In traditional China, only 1 or 2 percent of women remained unmarried at age thirty, whereas between 15 and 25 percent of thirty-year-old Western European women were still single. (For men, the differences though in the same direction are far less stark.) As for residence, in the Western European neolocal pattern, norms and practices in many regions resulted in a pattern whereby newly married couples moved into a separate household at marriage; but concomitant with this was their delaying marriage until they could afford a new household. In China, newly married couples generally resided in the groom's father's household. In Western Europe, the majority of postpubescent young men and many young women left home in their teenage years for a period of employment. In the early modern era, such employment was often as a servant or apprentice in either a craft or a farm household, but, over time, that employment was increasingly likely to be in a nondomestic work setting, such as a factory, store, or other urban enterprise. "Youth" was a distinctive phase in the life course of young men and increasingly of young women in Europe, although there were important gender distinctions. Such a period of postpubescent semiautonomy from parental households did not exist for Chinese youth, especially not for young women in traditional China. Young men more typically remained in their father's household and young women moved at marriage in their late teens from their own father's household to that of their husband's father.

Comparing the Moment of Marriage: Implications and Cautions

We would now like to discuss some of the world-historical implications of this important (if crude) comparison in the marriage systems of China and Western Europe. There are obviously many possible realms for investigation. For example, these patterns imply differences in young women's education, intergenerational relationships among women (especially between mothers and daughters and mothers-in-law and daughters-in-law), and household power relations. Here, we restrict our discussion to two areas of undoubted world-historical significance, namely economic development, on the one hand, and sexuality and reproduction, on the other.

The question of why the Industrial Revolution, or, alternatively, the emergence of industrial capitalism, occurred first in Europe, has been and remains salient for both European and world historians. R. Bin Wong explores this question in his innovative comparative study of economic development in Europe and China. Wong argues that there were rough parallels in the dynamics linking demographic expansion and economic growth in China and Europe until the nineteenth century. Both economies were expanding on the basis of growth of rural industrial enterprises in which peasant families supplemented agricultural work and income with part-time industrial production. What the Chinese case demonstrates, Wong argues, is that this so-called protoindustrial form of development may be viewed as an alternative route to industrialization rather than merely a precursor of factory production. Indeed, Charles Tilly has suggested that a prescient contemporary observer of the European economy in 1750 would likely have predicted such a future — that is "a countryside with a growing proletariat working in both agriculture and manufacturing."

While Wong's study is devoted to comparative examination of the economic roots and implications of varying paths to industrial development, he also connects economic and demographic growth. In particular, Wong mentions the link between marriage and economic opportunity: "in both China and Europe, rural industry supported lower age at marriage and higher proportions of ever married than would have been plausible in its absence. This does not mean that ages at marriage dropped in Europe when rural industry appeared, but the possibility was present. For China, the development of rural industry may not have lowered ages at marriage or raised proportions married as much as it allowed previous practices of relatively low ages at marriage and high proportions of women ever married to continue." What Wong does not explore is the way in which these "previous practices" that connected the low age at marriage with both virilocality and a relatively high commitment to the domestic containment of daughters and wives also had implications for patterns of economic development. In a comparative account of why Chinese industrial development relied heavily on domestic production, the fact that the young female labor force in China was to an extent far greater than that of Europe both married and "tied" to the male-headed household needs to be part of the story. This pattern of female marriage and residency held implications for entrepreneurial choice that helped to determine the different paths toward industrialization in Europe and China. World-historical comparison, taking into account aspects of gender relations and marriage and kinship systems, highlights their possible significance for economic development, a significance that has not been given proper attention by economic historians. Indeed, it is arguable that the family and marital status of the young women who played so significant a role in the workforce (especially those employed in the textile industry, which was key to early industrial development in both Europe and China) were major factors in the varying paths to development followed in China and Europe in the centuries of protoindustrial growth and industrialization.

A second set of implications concerns sexuality and reproduction. Again, we are aided by another recent study, which, in a fashion parallel to Wong's, uses Chinese historical evidence to call into question generalizations about historical development based on a European model. In their book on Chinese demographic history, Lee and Wang argue against the hegemonic Malthusian (mis)understandings according to which the family and population history to China has been seen as an example of a society's failure to curb population growth by any means other than recurrent disaster (by "positive" rather than "preventive" checks in Malthusian terms). They note the important difference in marriage systems that we have just described, but they dispute conclusions too often drawn from the Chinese historical pattern concerning overpopulation. Instead, according to Lee and Wang "persistently high nuptiality . . . did not inflate Chinese fertility, because of . . . the low level of fertility within marriage."

This second example points to another important realm for which the age at which women marry has great consequences. But the findings reported by Lee and Wang also caution scholars against leaping to comparative conclusions about one society on the basis of models established in another, even while their claims still suggest the value of comparison. We should not presume that since Chinese women were married universally and young, they therefore had more children or devoted a greater proportion of their time and energy to childbearing and child rearing than did their later married counterparts in Europe. Although the evidence is far from definitive, it nevertheless indicates that total marital fertility may have been somewhat lower in China than in Europe until the late nineteenth or early twentieth centuries. The factors in China that produced this pattern included relatively high rates of infanticide, especially of female infants, as well as different beliefs and practices about child care and sexuality. For example, babies were apparently breast-fed longer in China than in Europe (a pattern in turn related to the domestic location of women's work), which would have both increased infants' chances of survival and also lengthened the intervals between births. In the realm of sexuality, pertinent factors include both prescriptions for men against overly frequent intercourse, and coresidence with a parental generation whose vigilance included policing young couples' sexual behavior.

These two examples are meant to suggest how looking at women's life cycles comparatively both enhances our understanding of the implications of varying patterns for women's history and also suggests the very broad ramifications, indeed world-historical significance, of different ways of institutionalizing the female life cycle.

REFLECTIONS

Women's history has entered the mainstream during the last few decades. An older view, still pervasive in the academic world forty years ago, assumed women's history was adequately covered by general history, which was largely the story of the exploits of men. Political, military, and diplomatic history took precedence over historical fields seen as less resolutely masculine, such as social and cultural history.

Today, women's history not only stands independently in college and university curriculums, it has helped open doors to a wide range of new fields in social history — gender, family, childhood, sexuality, domesticity, and health, to name but a few. These new research fields have also contributed significantly to issues of general history, as the authors of the last reading show. In fact, the growth and development of new fields of research and teaching in social and cultural history have had the effect of relegating the study of presidents, wars, and treaties to the periphery of the profession. The 2006 meeting of the American Historical Association, where historians came together to talk about their work, had more sessions on women, gender, and sexuality than on politics, diplomacy, military, war, World War I, World War II, and the American Civil War, combined.

Some more traditional historians complain that this is a fad, and that sooner or later the profession will get back to the more "important" topics. But others respond that it is hard to think of anything more important than the history of half of humanity or the history of human health. This debate leads to questions about the importance of particular individuals in history. Who had a greater impact, for instance, thirtieth U.S. president Calvin Coolidge (1872–1933) or Marie Curie (1867–1934), who won the Nobel Prize for isolating radium for therapeutic purposes?

What role do individuals play on the historical canvas anyway? A president or Nobel laureate works according to social norms, available resources, supporting institutions, and the work of hundreds or thousands of others, living and dead. Forty years ago, historians put greater stress on institutions, movements, and perceived forces than they do today. In recent years, historians have looked for the "agency" of individuals and groups, perhaps in an effort to see how people can have an impact on their world. The power of slavery and the impact of imperialism have been balanced with the tales of slave revolts, the stories of successful collaborators, adapters, and resisters, and the voices of slaves and indigenous and colonized peoples. We see this in the study of women's history as well.

We began this chapter with the observation that we live in a patriarchy. Even if we are dismantling it in the twenty-first century, it was a powerful force between 1500 and 1800: a historical force, not natural, but a product of the urban revolution, perhaps, beginning about five thousand years ago. It is useful to understand its causes, describe its workings, and relate its history. But does doing so only hamper our capacity for change? Does it ignore the stories of women who have made a difference? Conversely, are women empowered, humanity enriched, by knowing how individual women were able to work within the system, secure their needs, engage, negotiate, compromise? Do the stories of a Sor Juana or the poems of an Anna Bijns inspire us? Or do they misrepresent the past and, by consequence, delude us?

Perhaps there are no easy answers to those questions, but our exercise in comparison might come in handy. The rich and varied detail of the human past should warn us against absolute declarations. We may emphasize patriarchy or emphasize women's power, but we would be foolish to deny either. In consequence, it may be most useful to ask more specific questions and to compare. Can women own property here? Is there more restriction on women's movement in this society or that? Only then can we begin to understand why here and not there, why then and not now. And only then can we use our understanding of the past to improve the present.

19

The Scientific Revolution

Europe, the Ottoman Empire, China, Japan,
and the Americas, 1600–1800

HISTORICAL CONTEXT

Modern life is unthinkable apart from science. We surround ourselves with its products, from cars and computers to telephones and televisions; we are dependent on its institutions — hospitals, universities, and research laboratories; and we have internalized the methods and procedures of science in every aspect of our daily lives, from balancing checkbooks to counting calories. Even on social and humanitarian questions, the scientific method has become almost the exclusive model of knowledge in modern society.

We can trace the scientific focus of modern society to the "scientific revolution" of the seventeenth century. The seventeenth-century scientific revolution was a European phenomenon, with such notables as Nicolas Copernicus (1473–1543) in Poland, Galileo Galilei (1564–1642) in Tuscany, and Isaac Newton (1642–1727) in England. But it was also a global event, prompted initially by Europe's new knowledge of Asia, Africa, and the Americas, and ultimately spread as a universal method for understanding and manipulating the world.

What was the scientific revolution? How revolutionary was it? How similar, or different, was European science from that practiced elsewhere in the world? And how much did the European revolution affect scientific traditions elsewhere? These are some of the issues we will study in this chapter.

THINKING HISTORICALLY
Distinguishing Change from Revolution

The world is always changing; it always has been changing. Sometimes, however, the change seems so formidable, extensive, important, or quick that we use the term *revolution*. In fact, we will use the term in this and the next two chapters. In this chapter we will examine what historians call the scientific revolution. The next chapter will deal with political revolutions and the chapter following with the industrial revolution. In each of these cases there are some historians who object that the changes were not really revolutionary, that they were more gradual or limited. Thus, we ask the question, how do we distinguish between mere change and revolutionary change?

In this chapter you will be asked, how revolutionary were the changes that are often called the scientific revolution? The point, however, is not to get your vote, pro or con, but to get you to think about how you might answer such a question. Do we, for instance, compare "the before" with "the after" and then somehow divide by the time it took to get from one to the other? Do we look at what people said at the time about how things were changing? Are we gauging speed of change or extent of change? What makes things change at different speeds? What constitutes a revolution?

$\boxed{120}$

FRANKLIN LE VAN BAUMER
The Scientific Revolution in the West

In this selection, an intellectual historian of Europe summarizes the scientific revolution. Without enumerating the achievements of European science in the seventeenth century, Baumer finds evidence of the "revolutionary" nature of the transformation by referring to the popularity of scientific societies and the powerful appeal of the new scien-

---

Franklin Le Van Baumer, "The Scientific Revolution in the West," in *Main Currents of Western Thought*, ed. F. Le Van Baumer (New Haven: Yale University Press, 1978).

tific mentality. How does he define the scientific revolution? How does he date it? Why does he believe that it was a revolution?

Thinking Historically

What intellectual or cultural changes did the scientific revolution bring about, according to Baumer? What ideas did Europeans have about nature before the scientific revolution? Baumer suggests that we can see the scientific revolution in new intellectual institutions, educational reforms, and new careers. What were these changes? How rapid, extensive, or important were they?

In his book *The Origins of Modern Science* Professor [Herbert] Butterfield of Cambridge writes that the "scientific revolution" of the sixteenth and seventeenth centuries "outshines everything since the rise of Christianity and reduces the Renaissance and Reformation to the rank of mere episodes, mere internal displacements, within the system of medieval Christendom." "It looms so large as the real origin both of the modern world and of the modern mentality that our customary periodisation of European history has become an anachronism and an encumbrance." This view can no longer be seriously questioned. The scientific achievements of the century and a half between the publication of Copernicus's *De Revolutionibus Orbium Celestium* (1543) and Newton's *Principia* (1687) marked the opening of a new period of intellectual and cultural life in the West, which I shall call the Age of Science. What chiefly distinguished this age from its predecessor was that science — meaning by science a body of knowledge, a method, an attitude of mind, a metaphysic (to be described below) — became the directive force of Western civilization, displacing theology and antique letters. Science made the world of the spirit, of Platonic Ideas, seem unreliable and dim by comparison with the material world. In the seventeenth century it drove revealed Christianity out of the physical universe into the region of history and private morals; to an ever growing number of people in the two succeeding centuries it made religion seem outmoded even there. Science invaded the schools, imposed literary canons, altered the world-picture of the philosophers, suggested new techniques to the social theorists. It changed profoundly man's attitude toward custom and tradition, enabling him to declare his independence of the past, to look down condescendingly upon the "ancients," and to envisage a rosy future. The Age of Science made the intoxicating discovery that melioration depends, not upon "change from within" (St. Paul's birth of the new man), but upon "change from without" (scientific and social mechanics).

1

Some people will perhaps object that there was no such thing as "scientific revolution" in the sixteenth and seventeenth centuries. They will say that history does not work that way, that the new science was not "revolutionary," but the cumulative effect of centuries of trial and error among scientists. But if by "scientific revolution" is meant the occasion when science became a real intellectual and cultural force in the West, this objection must surely evaporate. The evidence is rather overwhelming that sometime between 1543 and 1687, certainly by the late seventeenth century, science captured the interest of the intellectuals and upper classes. Francis Bacon's ringing of a bell to call the wits of Europe together to advance scientific learning did not go unheeded. Note the creation of new intellectual institutions to provide a home for science — the *Academia del Cimento* at Florence (1661), the Royal Society at London (1662), the *Académie des Sciences* at Paris (1666), the Berlin Academy (1700), to mention only the most important. These scientific academies signified the advent of science as an organized activity. Note the appearance of a literature of popular science, of which Fontenelle's *Plurality of Worlds* is only one example, and of popular lectures on scientific subjects. Note the movement for educational reform sponsored by Bacon and the Czech John Amos Comenius, who denounced the traditional education for its exclusive emphasis upon "words rather than things" (literature rather than nature itself). Evidently, by the end of the seventeenth century the prejudice against "mechanical" studies as belonging to practical rather than high mental life had all but disappeared. Bacon complained in 1605 that "matters mechanical" were esteemed "a kind of dishonour unto learning to descend to inquiry or meditation upon." But the Royal Society included in its roster a number of ecclesiastics and men of fashion. The second marquis of Worcester maintained a laboratory and published a book of inventions in 1663. Not a few men appear to have been "converted" from an ecclesiastical to a scientific career, and, as Butterfield notes, to have carried the gospel into the byways, with all the zest of the early Christian missionaries.

To account historically for the scientific revolution is no easy task. The problem becomes somewhat more manageable, however, if we exclude from the discussion the specific discoveries of the scientists. Only the internal history of science can explain how Harvey, for example, discovered the circulation of the blood, or Newton the universal law of gravitation.

But certain extrascientific factors were plainly instrumental in causing so many people to be simultaneously interested in "nature," and, moreover, to think about nature in the way they did. Professor [Alfred North] Whitehead reminds us that one of these factors was medieval Christianity itself and medieval scholasticism. Medieval Christianity sponsored the Greek, as opposed to the primitive, idea of a rationally ordered universe which made the orderly investigation of nature seem possible. Scholasticism trained western intellectuals in exact thinking. The Renaissance and the Protestant Reformation also prepared the ground for the scientific revolution — not by design, but as an indirect consequence of their thinking. . . . [H]umanism and Protestantism represented a movement toward the concrete. Erasmus preferred ethics to the metaphysical debates of the philosophers and theologians. The Protestants reduced the miraculous element in institutional Christianity and emphasized labor in a worldly calling. Furthermore, by attacking scholastic theology with which Aristotle was bound up, they made it easier for scientists to think about physics and astronomy in un-Aristotelian terms. As [philosopher] E. A. Burtt has noted of Copernicus, these men lived in a mental climate in which people generally were seeking new centers of reference. Copernicus, the architect of the heliocentric theory of the universe, was a contemporary of Luther and Archbishop Cranmer, who moved the religious center from Rome to Wittenberg and Canterbury. In the sixteenth century the economic center of gravity was similarly shifting from the Mediterranean to the English Channel and the Atlantic Ocean. The revival of ancient philosophies and ancient texts at the Renaissance also sharpened the scientific appetite. The Platonic and Phythagorean revival in fifteenth-century Italy undoubtedly did a good deal to accustom scientists to think of the universe in mathematical, quantitative terms. The translation of Galen and Archimedes worked the last rich vein of ancient science, and made it abundantly clear that the ancients had frequently disagreed on fundamentals, thus necessitating independent investigation. By their enthusiasm for natural beauty, the humanists helped to remove from nature the medieval stigma of sin, and thus to make possible the confident pronouncement of the scientific movement that God's Word could be read not only in the Bible but in the great book of nature.

But no one of these factors, nor all of them together, could have produced the scientific revolution. One is instantly reminded of Bacon's statement that "by the distant voyages and travels which have become frequent in our times, many things in nature have been laid open and discovered which may let in new light upon philosophy." The expansion of Europe, and increased travel in Europe itself, not only stimulated interest in nature but opened up to the West the vision of a "Kingdom of Man" upon earth. Much of Bacon's imagery was borrowed from the geographical discoveries: He aspired to be the Columbus of a new intellectual world, to sail through the Pillars of Hercules (symbol of the old knowledge) into the Atlantic Ocean in search of new and more useful knowledge. Bacon, however, failed to detect the coincidence of the scientific revolution with commercial prosperity and the rise of the middle class. Doubtless, the Marxist Professor Hessen greatly oversimplified when he wrote that "Newton was the typical representative of the rising bourgeoisie, and in his philosophy he embodies the characteristic features of his class." The theoretical scientists had mixed motives. Along with a concern for technology, they pursued truth for its own sake, and they sought God in his great creation. All the same, it is not stretching the imagination too far to see a rough correspondence between the mechanical universe of the seventeenth-century philosophers and the bourgeois desire for rational, predictable order. Science and business were a two-way street. If science affected business, so did business affect science — by its businesslike temper and its quantitative thinking, by its interest in "matter" and the rational control of matter.

2

The scientific revolution gave birth to a new conception of knowledge, a new methodology, and a new worldview substantially different from the old Aristotelian-Christian worldview. . . .

Knowledge now meant exact knowledge: what you know for certain, and not what may possibly or even probably be. Knowledge is what can be clearly apprehended by the mind, or measured by mathematics, or demonstrated by experiment. Galileo came close to saying this when he declared that without mathematics "it is impossible to comprehend a single word of (the great book of the universe);" likewise Descartes when he wrote that "we ought never to allow ourselves to be persuaded of the truth of anything unless on the evidence of our Reason." The distinction between "primary" and "secondary qualities" in seventeenth-century metaphysics carried the same implication. To Galileo, Descartes, and Robert Boyle those mathematical qualities that inhered in objects (size, weight, position, etc.) were "primary," i.e., matters of real knowledge; whereas all the other qualities that our senses tell us are in objects (color, odor, taste, etc.) were "secondary," less real because less amenable to measurement. The inference of all this is plain: Knowledge pertains to "natural philosophy" and possibly social theory, but not to theology or the older philosophy or poetry which involve opinion, belief, faith, but not knowledge. The Royal Society actually undertook to renovate the English language, by excluding from it metaphors and pulpit eloquence which conveyed no precise meaning. The "enthusiasm" of the religious man became suspect as did the "sixth sense" of the poet who could convey pleasure but not knowledge.

The odd thing about the scientific revolution is that for all its avowed distrust of hypotheses and systems, it created its own system of nature, or worldview. "I perceive," says the "Countess" in Fontenelle's popular dialogue of 1686, "Philosophy is now become very Mechanical." "I value (this universe) the more since I know it resembles a Watch, and the whole order of Nature the more plain and easy it is, to me it appears the more admirable." Descartes and other philosophers of science in the seventeenth century constructed a mechanical universe which resembled the machines — watches, pendulum clocks, steam engines — currently being built by scientists and artisans. However, it was not the observation of actual machines but the new astronomy and physics that made it possible to picture the universe in this way. The "Copernican revolution" destroyed Aristotle's "celestial world" of planets and stars which, because they were formed of a subtle substance having no weight, behaved differently from bodies on earth and in the "sublunary world." The new laws of motion formulated by a succession of physicists from Kepler to Newton explained the movement of bodies, both celestial and terrestrial, entirely on mechanical and mathematical principles. According to the law of inertia, the "natural" motion of bodies was in a straight line out into Euclidean space. The planets were pulled into their curvilinear orbits by gravitation which could operate at tremendous distances, and which varied inversely as the square of the distance.

Thus, the universe pictured by Fontenelle's Countess was very different from that of Dante in the thirteenth, or Richard Hooker in the sixteenth century. Gone was the Aristotelian-Christian universe of purposes, forms, and final causes. Gone were the spirits and intelligences which had been required to push the skies daily around the earth. The fundamental features of the new universe were numbers (mathematical quantities) and invariable laws. It was an economical universe in which nature did nothing in vain and performed its daily tasks without waste. In such a universe the scientist could delight and the bourgeois could live happily ever after — or at least up to the time of Darwin. The fact that nature appeared to have no spiritual purpose — Descartes said that it would continue to exist regardless of whether there were any human beings to think it — was more than compensated for by its dependability. Philosophy had indeed become very mechanical. Descartes kept God to start his machine going, and Newton did what he could to save the doctrine of providence. But for all practical purposes, God had become the First Cause, "very well skilled in mechanics and geometry." And the rage for mechanical explanation soon spread beyond the confines of physics to encompass the biological and social sciences. Thus did Descartes regard animals as a piece of clockwork, Robert Boyle the human body as a "matchless engine."

Under the circumstances, one would logically expect there to have been warfare between science and religion in the seventeenth century. But such was not the case. To be sure, some theologians expressed dismay at the downfall of Aristotelianism, and the Roman Church took steps to suppress Copernicanism when Giordano Bruno interpreted it to mean an infinite universe and a plurality of worlds. But the majority of

the scientists and popularizers of science were sincerely religious men —
not a few were actually ecclesiastics — who either saw no conflict or else
went to some lengths to resolve it. Science itself was commonly regarded
as a religious enterprise. . . .

In the final analysis, however, the new thing in seventeenth-century
thought was the dethronement of theology from its proud position as
the sun of the intellectual universe. Bacon and Descartes and Newton
lived in an age that was finding it increasingly difficult to reconcile science and religion. To save the best features of both they effected a
shaky compromise. For all practical purposes they eliminated religious
purpose from nature — thus allowing science to get on with its work,
while leaving religion in control of private belief and morals. By their
insistence that religious truth itself must pass the tests of reason and reliable evidence, John Locke and the rationalists further reduced theology's prerogatives. Bacon was prepared to believe the word of God
"though our reason be shocked at it." But not Locke: "'I believe because it is impossible,' might," he says, "in a good man, pass for a sally
of zeal, but would prove a very ill rule for men to choose their opinions
or religion by." Good Christian though Locke might be, his teaching
had the effect of playing down the supernatural aspects of religion, of
equating religion with simple ethics. . . .

121

GALILEO GALILEI

Letter to the Grand Duchess Christina

One reason for thinking of European scientific developments in the
seventeenth century as a revolution lies in their condemnation by established authority, particularly religious authority. Both Protestants
and Catholics condemned the sun-centered model of the universe proposed by Copernicus and modified by Tycho Brahe (1546–1601) and
Johannes Kepler (1571–1630). Giordano Bruno, a religious philosopher and Copernican, was burned at the stake in 1600 by the Catholic

Galileo's Letter to the Grand Duchess Christina (1615), in *The Galileo Affair: A Documentary History*, ed. and trans. Maurice A. Finocchiaro (Berkeley and Los Angeles: University of
California Press, 1989), 87–90, 114–18.

Church. Galileo was investigated in 1615 and 1616 for work that gave added weight to Copernicus's theory. His use of the telescope revealed more stars than the fixed number seen by the naked eye or shown on the accepted model of the heavenly spheres of the ancient authority, Ptolemy. Galileo, by assuming that the Earth revolved around the sun (and the moon around the Earth), conceived orbits that were neater and closer to what had been observed.

This letter to the Grand Duchess Christina in 1615 shows Galileo already under siege. He had received a letter in 1613 from a supporter, Benedetto Castelli, who had been questioned by Christina (of Lorraine), the mother of the Grand Duke of Tuscany, Cosimo II de' Medici, about Galileo's views. Having left his twenty-year post at the University of Padua, Galileo was in 1613 philosopher and mathematician to the Duchy of Tuscany, and so he was in the delicate and precarious position of receiving notice of his employer's dissatisfaction with his views. This letter is his attempt to explain himself and to prevent the initiation of an inquisition. His efforts were unsuccessful. In 1633 Galileo was tried, condemned, forced to recant his views, and placed under house arrest. (The condemnation was retracted by the papacy in 1992.)

What seem to be Grand Duchess Christina's objections? How does Galileo try to answer them? How convincing would you find Galileo if you were the Grand Duchess?

Thinking Historically

What claims to new discoveries did Galileo make in this letter? In what respect did Galileo claim his work was not new? On balance, what did he perceive to be the differences between himself and his contemporaries? How is his argument "modern" or scientific? Does this letter support Baumer's interpretation of the scientific revolution?

T o the Most Serene Ladyship the Grand Duchess Dowager:

As Your Most Serene Highness knows very well, a few years ago I discovered in the heavens many particulars which had been invisible until our time. Because of their novelty, and because of some consequences deriving from them which contradict certain physical propositions[1] commonly accepted in philosophical schools, they roused against

---

[1]In *The Starry Messenger* (Venice, 1610) Galileo had described his discovery, through telescopic observation, of lunar mountains, four satellites of Jupiter (which he named "Medicean planets"), the stellar composition of the Milky Way and of nebulas, and the existence of thousands of previously invisible fixed stars. Within a few years, Galileo added to these his observations of sunspots, the phases of Venus, and Saturn's rings.

me no small number of such professors, as if I had placed these things in heaven with my hands in order to confound nature and the sciences. These people seemed to forget that a multitude of truths contribute to inquiry and to the growth and strength of disciplines rather than to their diminution or destruction, and at the same time they showed greater affection for their own opinions than for the true ones; thus they proceeded to deny and to try to nullify those novelties, about which the senses themselves could have rendered them certain, if they had wanted to look at those novelties carefully. To this end they produced various matters, and they published some writings full of useless discussions and sprinkled with quotations from the Holy Scripture, taken from passages which they do not properly understand and which they inappropriately adduce.[2] . . .

These people are aware that in my astronomical and philosophical studies, on the question of the constitution of the world's parts, I hold that the sun is located at the center of the revolution of the heavenly orbs and does not change place, and that the earth rotates on itself and moves around it. Moreover, they hear how I confirm this view not only by refuting Ptolemy's and Aristotle's arguments, but also by producing many for the other side, especially some pertaining to physical effects whose causes perhaps cannot be determined in any other way, and other astronomical ones dependent on many features of the new celestial discoveries; these discoveries clearly confute the Ptolemaic system, and they agree admirably with this other position and confirm it. Now, these people are perhaps confounded by the known truth of the other

[2]Galileo has been notified that Cardinal Bellarmine finds the Copernican theory heretical because the sun must go around the Earth according to Psalm 19:

The heavens declare the glory of God;
. . . .
In them hath he set a tabernacle for the sun,
Which is as a bridegroom coming out of his chamber,
And rejoiceth as a strong man to run a race.
His going forth is from the end of the heaven,
And his circuit unto the ends of it:
And there is nothing hid from the heat thereof. (19:1, 4–6 King James Version)

The Grand Duchess mentioned to Castelli the passage in Joshua 10:12–13 (KJV):

Then spake Joshua to the Lord in the day when the Lord delivered the Amorites before the children of Israel, and he said in the sight of Israel, Sun, stand thou still upon Gibeon; and thou, Moon, in the valley of Ajalon. And the sun stood still, and the moon stayed, until the people had avenged themselves upon their enemies. Is not this written in the book of Jasher? So the sun stood still in the midst of heaven, and hastened not to go down about a whole day.

Thus, the Bible seemed to indicate that the sun revolved around the Earth. [Ed.]

propositions different from the ordinary which I hold, and so they may lack confidence to defend themselves as long as they remain in the philosophical field. Therefore, since they persist in their original self-appointed task of beating down me and my findings by every imaginable means, they have decided to try to shield the fallacies of their arguments with the cloak of simulated religiousness and with the authority of Holy Scripture, unintelligently using the latter for the confutation of arguments they neither understand nor have heard.

At first, they tried on their own to spread among common people the idea that such propositions are against Holy Scripture, and consequently damnable and heretical. Then they realized how by and large human nature is more inclined to join those ventures which result in the oppression of other people (even if unjustly) than those which result in their just improvement, and so it was not difficult for them to find someone who with unusual confidence did preach even from the pulpit that it is damnable and heretical; and this was done with little compassion and with little consideration of the injury not only to this doctrine and its followers, but also to mathematics and all mathematicians. Thus, having acquired more confidence, and with the vain hope that the seed which first took root in their insincere minds would grow into a tree and rise toward the sky, they are spreading among the people the rumor that it will shortly be declared heretical by the supreme authority. They also know that such a declaration not only would uproot these two conclusions, but also would render damnable all the other astronomical and physical observations and propositions which correspond and are necessarily connected with them; hence, they alleviate their task as much as they can by making it look, at least among common people, as if this opinion were new and especially mine, pretending not to know that Nicolaus Copernicus was its author or rather its reformer and confirmer. Now, Copernicus was not only a Catholic but also a clergyman and a canon, and he was so highly regarded that he was called to Rome from the remotest parts of Germany[3] when under Leo X the Lateran Council was discussing the reform of the ecclesiastical calendar; at that time this reform remained unfinished only because there was still no exact knowledge of the precise length of the year and the lunar month. Thus he was charged by the Bishop of Fossombrone,[4] who was then supervising this undertaking, to try by repeated studies and efforts to acquire more understanding and certainty about those celestial motions; and so he undertook this study, and, by truly Herculean labor and by his admirable mind, he made so much progress in this science and acquired such an exact knowledge of the periods of celestial

---

[3] Actually Poland.
[4] Paul of Middelburg (1445–1533).

motions that he earned the title of supreme astronomer; then in accordance with his doctrine not only was the calendar regularized,[5] but tables of all planetary motions were constructed. Having expounded this doctrine in six parts, he published it at the request of the Cardinal of Capua[6] and the Bishop of Kulm;[7] and since he had undertaken this task and these labors on orders from the Supreme Pontiff, he dedicated his book *On Heavenly Revolutions* to the successor of the latter, Paul III. Once printed this book was accepted by the Holy Church, and it was read and studied all over the world without anyone ever having had the least scruple about its doctrine.[8] Finally, now that one is discovering how well founded upon clear observations and necessary demonstrations this doctrine is, some persons come along who, without having even seen the book, give its author the reward of so much work by trying to have him declared a heretic; this they do only in order to satisfy their special animosity, groundlessly conceived against someone else who has no greater connection with Copernicus than the endorsement of his doctrine.

Now, in matters of religion and reputation I have the greatest regard for how common people judge and view me; so, because of the false aspersions my enemies so unjustly try to cast upon me, I have thought it necessary to justify myself by discussing the details of what they produce to detest and abolish this opinion, in short, to declare it not just false but heretical. They always shield themselves with a simulated religious zeal, and they also try to involve Holy Scripture and to make it somehow subservient to their insincere objectives; against the intention of Scripture and the Holy Fathers (if I am not mistaken), they want to extend, not to say abuse, its authority, so that even for purely physical conclusions which are not matters of faith one must totally abandon the senses and demonstrative arguments in favor of any scriptural passage whose apparent words may contain a different indication. . . .

---

[5]Though the Copernican system did play a role in the reform of the calendar, the new Gregorian calendar was constructed on the basis of non-Copernican ideas.

[6]Cardinal Nicolaus von Schoenberg (1472–1537), archbishop of Capua.

[7]Tiedemann Giese (1480–1550), Polish friend of Copernicus.

[8]Of course, Galileo had no way of knowing that one Giovanni Maria Tolosani had had quite a few scruples about it.

122

NATALIE ZEMON DAVIS

Metamorphoses: Maria Sibylla Merian

Davis, a modern historian, writes here of a woman scientist and artist, Maria Sibylla Merian* (1647–1717), whose work graphically illustrates the new approaches to nature in the seventeenth century. What did Merian accomplish? What do her accomplishments suggest about the history of science?

Thinking Historically

What aspects of Merian's work were radically new or revolutionary? What elements were continuations of traditional ideas? How might the idea of metamorphoses apply to her work and the scientific revolution?

In June 1699, . . . Maria Sibylla Merian and her daughter Dorothea were boarding a boat in Amsterdam, bound for America. Their destination was Suriname, where they intended to study and paint the insects, butterflies, and plants of that tropical land.

At age fifty-two, Maria Sibylla Merian was a person of some reputation. As early as 1675, when she was a young mother living with her husband in Nuremberg, the learned painter Joachim Sandrart had included her in his *German Academy*, as he called his history of German art. Not only was she skilled in watercolor and oils, in painting textiles and engraving copperplates; not only could she render flowers, plants, and insects with perfect naturalness; but she also was a knowing observer of the habits of caterpillars, flies, spiders, and other such creatures. A virtuous woman and a fine housekeeper (despite all the insects), Merian, said Sandrart, could be likened to the goddess Minerva. A few years later, when she published the two volumes of her *Wonderful Transformation and Singular Plant-Food of Caterpillars*, a Nuremberg luminary, Christopher Arnold, sang in verse of all the men who were being equaled by this ingenious woman. Her work was "*verwunderns*" — "amazing."

*ma REE ah   sih BIHL ah   meh ree AHN

Natalie Zemon Davis, *Women on the Margins: Three Seventeenth-Century Lives* (Cambridge: Harvard University Press, 1995), 140–41, 147–48, 149–50, 154–56, plate 23.

Then, in 1692, another kind of singularity was noted about Maria Sibylla Merian, for a different set of readers. Petrus Dittelbach, a disaffected member of the Labadists (a radical Protestant community in the Dutch province of Friesland) published an exposé of the conduct of his former coreligionists. Among them was "a woman of Frankfurt am Main" who had left her husband, the painter Johann Andreas Graff, in Germany to find peace among the Labadists of Wieuwerd. When Graff came to get her back, he was informed by the leading Brothers that a believer like Maria Sibylla was freed from marital obligations toward an unbeliever like him. Refused entry into the community, the husband stayed around for a time doing construction work outside its walls, and then left. Dittelbach had heard that he was going to break his matrimonial tie, and indeed, about the time *The Decline and Fall of the Labadists* appeared in print, Graff was asking the Nuremberg town council for a divorce from Maria Sibylla so that he could marry someone else.

These accounts suggest the turnings in the life of the artist-naturalist Maria Sibylla Merian. And there were more changes to come. She sailed back from America laden with specimens, published her great work *Metamorphosis of the Insects of Suriname*, amplified her *European Insects*, and was an important figure in the circle of Amsterdam botanists, scientists, and collectors till her death in 1717. . . .

. . . Her *Raupen* of 1679, or (to give the title in English) the *Wonderful Transformation and Singular Flower-Food of Caterpillars . . . Painted from Life and Engraved in Copper*, [was] followed by a second volume in 1683. In each of the hundred copperplates (fifty per volume, available in black and white or handcolored, depending on the buyer's wish and purse), one or more species of insect were depicted from life, in their various stages: caterpillar or larva; pupa with or without cocoon; and moth, butterfly, or fly, in flight or at rest (sometimes in both states). Many of the plates included the egg stage as well. Each picture was organized around a single plant, represented most often in the flowering stage and sometimes in the fruit stage; the plant was selected to show the leaves upon which the caterpillar fed and the places on the leaves or stem (or on the ground nearby) where the female laid its eggs. Each plant was identified by its German and Latin names, and a page or two of German text facing the picture gave Maria Sibylla's observations on how her insect specimen had looked and behaved at each stage, often with exact dates, and her reactions to its appearance. She did not give names to individual species of moths and butterflies — in fact, her contemporaries had names for only a small number of them — but her descriptions yielded individual life histories.

Here is what she said of an insect shown in its stages from egg to moth on a cherry plant (pictured in the illustrations in this volume):

Many years ago when I first saw this large moth, so prettily marked by nature, I could not marvel enough over its beautiful gradation of color and varying hue, and I made use of it often in my painting. Later, as through God's grace I discovered the metamorphosis of caterpillars, a long time went by until this beautiful moth appeared. When I caught sight of it, I was enveloped in such great joy and so gratified in my wishes that I can hardly describe it. Then for several years in a row I got hold of its caterpillars and maintained them until July on the leaves of sweet cherries, apples, pears, and plums. They have a beautiful green color, like the young grass of spring, and a lovely straight black stripe the length of the back, and across each segment also a black stripe out of which four little white round beads glisten like pearls. Among them is a yellow-gold oval spot and under them a white pearl. Underneath the first three segments they have three red claws on each side, then two empty segments, after which there are four little green feet of the same color as the caterpillars, and at the end again a foot on both sides. Sprouting out of each pearl are long black hairs, together with other, smaller ones, so stiff that one could almost be pricked by them. Strange to note, when they have no food, this variety of caterpillars devour each other, so great is their hunger; but so soon as they obtain [food], they leave off [eating each other].

When such a caterpillar attains its full size, as you can see [in my picture] on the green leaf and stem, then it makes a tough and lustrous cocoon, bright as silver and oval round, wherein it first sheds and expels its entire skin and changes itself into a liver-colored date stone [*Dattelkern*, her usual word for pupa], which stays together with the cast-off skin over the caterpillar. It remains thus motionless until the middle of August, when finally the moth of such laudable beauty comes out and takes flight. It is white and has gray spotted patches, two yellow eyes, and two brown feelers (Hörner). On each of the four wings are a few round circles in and about each other, which are black and white as well as yellow. The ends of the wings are brown, but near the tips (by which I mean only the ends of the moth's two outer wings) are two beautiful rose-colored spots. By day the moth is quiet, but at night very restless.

Her concern with beauty linked her to the still-life tradition in which she had been formed, and she herself acknowledged in her 1679 preface that her juxtaposition of plants and insects owed something to the artist's concern for adornment. She was also building on earlier efforts to achieve "naturalistic" or "mimetic" representations of flora and fauna. Detailed and lifelike pictures of insects and plants can be found in the margins of Netherlandish prayerbooks as early as the late fifteenth century, well before they surfaced in Dutch still-lifes in watercolor and oil. To give an example of the quest for precision close to home, Georg Flegel, Jacob Marrel's first teacher in Frankfurt, did small, careful studies of insects (one of them followed a silkworm from egg to moth); and flies, dragonflies, beetles, and butterflies appear among the foods, fruits, sugars, birds, and wines of Flegel's larger oil paintings.

But Maria Sibylla Merian had something else in mind when she did her insect studies from life. The moths and caterpillars of her *Raupen* did not just add to the "lively" ("*lebendig*") quality of flower pictures, as in the bouquets and wreaths painted by her stepfather Marrel and his student Abraham Mignon. The insects were there for themselves. When necessary, Merian sacrificed verisimilitude (the way things might look to an observer) for a decorative portrayal of the stripes and spikes and legs the caterpillar actually had (what a nature lover must know about an insect).

Above all, her insects and plants were telling a life story. Time moved in her pictures not to suggest the general transience of things or the year's round of the most precious blossoms, but to evoke a particular and interconnected process of change. Her insects were not placed to convey metaphorical messages, as was the practice of many still-life painters and specifically of her step-father's Utrecht teacher, Jan Davidsz de Heem (the butterfly as the symbol of the resurrected soul, the fly as the symbol of sinfulness, and so on). The *Ignis* of Joris Hoefnagel, a remarkable collection of insect watercolors by an artist-naturalist of the late sixteenth century, was designed like an emblem book, each picture preceded by a biblical quote or adage and followed by a poem. Merian's work was infused with religious spirit, as we shall see, but, except for a nod at the goodness of the bee, there were no allegorical comments in her texts.

If Maria Sibylla recentered flower painting around the life cycle of moths and butterflies and the plant hosts of their caterpillars, how different were her volumes of 1679 and 1683 from the more narrowly scientific insect books of her day? The 1660s were important years for the history of entomology: sustained observation and improved magnification allowed much new understanding of the anatomy and molting of insects and laid to rest among naturalists the belief in abiogenesis (that is, spontaneous generation of certain insects from decaying matter). New systems of classification were tried out, quite different from those used in Renaissance encyclopedias such as the one the Merian brothers had illustrated and published in 1653. There Jan Jonston had followed Thomas Mouffet (and Aristotle) in making the possession of wings a major criterion for classification: wingless caterpillars were treated along with worms in chapters separate from butterflies and moths, and metamorphosis was accordingly slighted. . . .

Merian's goal was simply ill-served by boundary classifications. Her subject was a set of events — "you'll find in this volume more than a hundred transformations [*Verwandlungen*]," she said in 1683 — and to represent them properly meant crossing the line between orders and putting the plant and animal kingdoms in the same picture. Yet even while lacking the logic of classification, her sequence was not "tumultuous." Emerging from the sensibility of two artists, Merian and her publisher-husband Graff, the books moved the reader's eye through the transformations by a visually striking and pleasurable path. The "method" of the *Raupen* — highly particular pictures and accounts strung together by an aesthetic link — had scientific importance quite apart from the new species contained on its pages. It made the little-studied process of metamorphosis easy to visualize and remember, and insisted on nature's connections, a long-term contribution. It also fractured older classification systems by its particularism and surprising mixtures, and so cleared the ground for those like Swammerdam who were proposing a replacement.

Publishing the Raupen was "remarkable" for a woman, as Christopher Arnold told readers in his opening poem of 1679 — "remarkable that women also venture to write for you / with care / what has given flocks of scholars so much to do." Merian herself drew on her female status only once, perhaps disingenuously: in the midst of her description of the insects on the goose-foot plant, she imagined her readers asking whether the thousands of exceptionally large caterpillars during that year of 1679 would not lead to much damage. "Whereupon, following my womanly simplicity [*meiner Weiblichen Einfalt*] I give this answer: the damage is already evident in empty fruit trees and defective plants."

But can we go deeper than Arnold's "beyond-her-sex" topos and Maria Sibylla's modesty topos? Can we ask whether her experience or cultural habits as a seventeenth-century woman helped generate her ecological vision of nature and the crossing of boundaries in her particular narratives?

For the seventeenth century, Maria Sibylla Merian is a sample of one. Other women still-life painters of her day, such as Margaretha de Heer from Friesland, included insects in their pictures, but did not go so far as to breed and study them (Merian's daughters would do so under her influence, but only much later). Other women of her day collected butterflies, moths, and caterpillars, but did not write about or represent them. John Ray's four daughters all brought him specimens, but it was only he who wrote down the observations, naming each caterpillar after the daughter who had collected it. Moreover, Ray had been attentive to the habitat of insects in his early observations, even while making classification his most important goal, and continued to include metamorphoses in his descriptions of individual insects when he was aware of them.

Still Merian was a pioneer, crossing boundaries of education and gender to acquire learning on insects and nurturing daughters as she observed, painted, and wrote. Her focus on breeding, habitat, and metamorphosis fits nicely with the domestic practice of a seventeenth-century mother and housewife. We have here not a female mind uneasy with analysis or timelessly connected to the organic (images that have been thoroughly challenged in recent scholarship), but a woman perched for scientific enterprise on a creative margin — for her a buzzing ecosystem — between domestic workshop and learned academy.

More explicitly important to Maria Sibylla Merian than her gender was the legitimation, nay, the sanctification of her entomological task by religion: "These wondrous transformations," she wrote in her 1679 preface to the reader, "have happened so many times that one is full of praise for God's mysterious power and his wonderful attention to such insignificant little creatures and unworthy flying things . . . Thus I am moved to present God's miracles such as these to the world in a little book. But do not praise and honor me for it; praise God alone, glorifying Him as the creator of even the smallest and most insignificant of these worms.". . .

Maria Sibylla had not yet undergone her conversion experience when she began to publish the *Raupen*, but her stress on God's creativity in nature and her "enthusiasm" in talking about insects and their beauty surely prepared her ears for the prophetic and lyrical cadences that soon were to fill her world. As Jean de Labadie had said some years before: "Everything we hear or see announces God or figures him. The song of a bird, the bleating of a lamb, the voice of a man. The sight of heaven and its stars, the air and its birds, the sea and its fish, the land and its plants and animals . . . Everything tells of God, everything represents him, but few ears and eyes try to hear or see him." Maria Sibylla was one of those trying to see.

123

LADY MARY WORTLEY MONTAGUE
Letter on Turkish Smallpox Inoculation

Lady Mary Wortley Montague, an English aristocrat, came down with smallpox in 1715. She survived, but was badly scarred by the rash that accompanied the often-fatal disease. Her younger brother died from smallpox, one of the tens of thousands who succumbed in epidemics across Europe and around the world in the eighteenth and nineteenth centuries. Two years after her recovery Montague traveled to Istanbul with her husband, who was the British ambassador to the Ottoman Empire. There, she witnessed a new approach to warding off smallpox infections, as she described in the following letter to a friend in England. What process does Montague describe in her letter? What was her response to the events she witnessed in Turkey?

Thinking Historically

This letter provides a clear example of how scientific observation can change the material world in which we live. After observing the Turkish smallpox inoculation Montague had her son and daughter inoculated. In fact, she became an advocate for smallpox inoculation in England and played an important role in persuading the English medical profession to support the innovative procedure. Montague paved the way for a safer vaccine, developed by Edward Jenner in 1796, that would eventually eradicate the disease from the planet.

Despite her admirable efforts, it was difficult to convince Europeans to embrace smallpox inoculation, which had been practiced in Asia for centuries. Even though the effectiveness of this technology came to be recognized in England during Montague's lifetime, the French and other Europeans, according to Voltaire, thought that the English were "fools and madmen" for experimenting with inoculation. What does this suggest about the nature of scientific discovery? Besides lack of knowledge, what other obstacles need to be overcome?

Letters of Lady Mary Wortley Montague, written during her travels in Europe, Asia, and Africa, to which are added poems by the same author (Bordeaux, J. Pinard, 1805). The UCLA Louis M. Darling Biomedical Library, History and Special Collections Division.

To Mrs. S. C., Adrianople, April 1, O.S.

A Propos of distempers, I am going to tell you a thing, that will make you wish yourself here. The small pox, so fatal, and so general amongst us, is here entirely harmless, by the invention of ingrafting, which is the term they give it. There is a set of old women, who make it their business to perform the operation, every autumn, in the month of september, when the great heat is abated. People send to one another to know if any of their family has a mind to have the small-pox; they make parties for this purpose, and when they are met (commonly fifteen or sixteen together) the old woman comes with a nut-shell full of the matter of the best sort of small pox, and asks what vein you please to have opened. She immediately rips open than you offer to her, with a large needle (which gives you no more pain than a common scratch), and puts into the vein as much matter as can lie upon the head of her needle, and after that, binds up the little wound with a hollow bit of shell, and in this manner opens four or five veins. The Grecians have commonly the superstition of opening one in the middle of the forehead, one in each arm, and one in the breast, to mark the sign of the cross; but this has a very ill effect, all these wounds leaving little scars, and is not done by those that are not superstitious, who choose to have them in the legs, or that part of the arm that is concealed. The children or young patients play together all the rest of the day, and are in perfect health to the eighth.

Then the fever begins to seize them, and they keep their beds two days, very seldom three. They have very rarely above twenty or thirty in their faces, which never mark, and in eight days time they are as well as before their illness. Where they are wounded, there remains running sores during the distemper, which I don't doubt is a great relief to it. Every year thousands undergo this operation, and the French ambassador says pleasantly that they take the small-pox here by way of diversion, as they take the waters in other countries. There is no example of any one that has died in it, and you may believe I am well satisfied of the safety of this experiment, since I intend to try it on my dear little son. I am patriot enough to take pains to bring this useful invention into fashion in England, and I should not fail to write to some of our doctors very particularly about it, if I knew any one of them that I thought had virtue enough to destroy such a considerable branch of their revenue, for the good of mankind. But that distemper is too beneficial to them, not to expose to all their resentment the hardy wight[1] that should undertake to put an end to it. Perhaps if I live to return, I may, however have the courage to war with them. Upon this occasion, admire the heroism in the heart of

Your friend, etc. etc.

[1]Creature.

124

LYNDA NORENE SHAFFER

China, Technology, and Change

In this essay an important contemporary world historian asks us to
compare the revolutionary consequences of scientific and technological changes that occurred in China and Europe before the seventeenth
century. What is Shaffer's argument? In what ways was the European
scientific revolution different from the changes in China she describes
here?

Thinking Historically

What exactly was the impact of printing, the compass, and gunpowder in Europe? What was the "before" and "after" for each of these
innovations? What, according to Shaffer, was the situation in China
before and after each of these innovations? Were these innovations as
revolutionary in China as they were in Europe?

Francis Bacon (1561–1626), an early advocate of the empirical
method, upon which the scientific revolution was based, attributed
Western Europe's early modern take-off to three things in particular:
printing, the compass, and gunpowder. Bacon had no idea where these
things had come from, but historians now know that all three were invented in China. Since, unlike Europe, China did not take off onto a
path leading from the scientific to the Industrial Revolution, some historians are now asking why these inventions were so revolutionary in
Western Europe and, apparently, so unrevolutionary in China.

In fact, the question has been posed by none other than Joseph
Needham, the foremost English-language scholar of Chinese science
and technology. It is only because of Needham's work that the Western
academic community has become aware that until Europe's take-off,
China was the unrivaled world leader in technological development.
That is why it is so disturbing that Needham himself has posed this apparent puzzle. The English-speaking academic world relies upon him
and repeats him; soon this question and the vision of China that it im-
plies will become dogma. Traditional China will take on supersociety

Lynda Norene Shaffer, "China, Technology and Change," *World History Bulletin,* 4, no. 1
(Fall/Winter, 1986–1987), 1–6.

qualities — able to contain the power of printing, to rein in the potential of the compass, even to muffle the blast of gunpowder.

The impact of these inventions on Western Europe is well known. Printing not only eliminated much of the opportunity for human copying errors, it also encouraged the production of more copies of old books and an increasing number of new books. As written material became both cheaper and more easily available, intellectual activity increased. Printing would eventually be held responsible, at least in part, for the spread of classical humanism and other ideas from the Renaissance. It is also said to have stimulated the Protestant Reformation, which urged a return to the Bible as the primary religious authority.

The introduction of gunpowder in Europe made castles and other medieval fortifications obsolete (since it could be used to blow holes in their walls) and thus helped to liberate Western Europe from feudal aristocratic power. As an aid to navigation the compass facilitated the Portuguese- and Spanish-sponsored voyages that led to Atlantic Europe's sole possession of the Western Hemisphere, as well as the Portuguese circumnavigation of Africa, which opened up the first all-sea route from Western Europe to the long-established ports of East Africa and Asia.

Needham's question can thus be understood to mean, Why didn't China use gunpowder to destroy feudal walls? Why didn't China use the compass to cross the Pacific and discover America, or to find an all-sea route to Western Europe? Why didn't China undergo a Renaissance or Reformation? The implication is that even though China possessed these technologies, it did not change much. Essentially Needham's question is asking, What was wrong with China?

Actually, there was nothing wrong with China. China was changed fundamentally by these inventions. But in order to see the changes, one must abandon the search for peculiarly European events in Chinese history, and look instead at China itself before and after these breakthroughs.

To begin, one should note that China possessed all three of these technologies by the latter part of the Tang dynasty (618–906) — between four and six hundred years before they appeared in Europe. And it was during just that time, from about 850, when the Tang dynasty began to falter, until 960, when the Song dynasty (960–1279) was established, that China underwent fundamental changes in all spheres. In fact, historians are now beginning to use the term *revolution* when referring to technological and commercial changes that culminated in the Song dynasty, in the same way that they refer to the changes in eighteenth- and nineteenth-century England as the Industrial Revolution. And the word might well be applied to other sorts of changes in China during this period.

For example, the Tang dynasty elite was aristocratic, but that of the Song was not. No one has ever considered whether the invention of gunpowder contributed to the demise of China's aristocrats, which occurred between 750 and 960, shortly after its invention. Gunpowder may, indeed, have been a factor although it is unlikely that its importance lay in blowing up feudal walls. Tang China enjoyed such internal peace that its aristocratic lineages did not engage in castle-building of the sort typical in Europe. Thus, China did not have many feudal fortifications to blow up.

The only wall of significance in this respect was the Great Wall, which was designed to keep steppe nomads from invading China. In fact, gunpowder may have played a role in blowing holes in this wall, for the Chinese could not monopolize the terrible new weapon, and their nomadic enemies to the north soon learned to use it against them. The Song dynasty ultimately fell to the Mongols, the most formidable force ever to emerge from the Eurasian steppe. Gunpowder may have had a profound effect on China — exposing a united empire to foreign invasion and terrible devastation — but an effect quite opposite to the one it had on Western Europe.

On the other hand, the impact of printing on China was in some ways very similar to its later impact on Europe. For example, printing contributed to a rebirth of classical (that is, preceding the third century A.D.) Confucian learning, helping to revive a fundamentally humanistic outlook that had been pushed aside for several centuries.

After the fall of the Han dynasty (206 B.C. – A.D. 220), Confucianism had lost much of its credibility as a world view, and it eventually lost its central place in the scholarly world. It was replaced by Buddhism, which had come from India. Buddhists believed that much human pain and confusion resulted from the pursuit of illusory pleasures and dubious ambitions: Enlightenment and, ultimately, salvation would come from a progressive disengagement from the real world, which they also believed to be illusory. This point of view dominated Chinese intellectual life until the ninth century. Thus the academic and intellectual comeback of classical Confucianism was in essence a return to a more optimistic literature that affirmed the world as humans had made it.

The resurgence of Confucianism within the scholarly community was due to many factors, but printing was certainly one of the most important. Although it was invented by Buddhist monks in China, and at first benefited Buddhism, by the middle of the tenth century, printers were turning out innumerable copies of the classical Confucian corpus. This return of scholars to classical learning was part of a more general movement that shared not only its humanistic features with the later Western European Renaissance, but certain artistic trends as well.

Furthermore, the Protestant Reformation in Western Europe was in some ways reminiscent of the emergence and eventual triumph of Neo-Confucian philosophy. Although the roots of Neo-Confucianism can be found in the ninth century, the man who created what would become its most orthodox synthesis was Zhu Xi (Chu Hsi, 1130–1200). Neo-Confucianism was significantly different from classical Confucianism, for it had undergone an intellectual (and political) confrontation with Buddhism and had emerged profoundly changed. It is of the utmost importance to understand that not only was Neo-Confucianism new, it was also heresy, even during Zhu Xi's lifetime. It did not triumph until the thirteenth century, and it was not until 1313 (when Mongol conquerors ruled China) that Zhu Xi's commentaries on the classics became the single authoritative text against which all academic opinion was judged.

In the same way that Protestantism emerged out of a confrontation with the Roman Catholic establishment and asserted the individual Christian's autonomy, Neo-Confucianism emerged as a critique of Buddhist ideas that had taken hold in China, and it asserted an individual moral capacity totally unrelated to the ascetic practices and prayers of the Buddhist priesthood. In the twelfth century Neo-Confucianists lifted the work of Mencius (Meng Zi, 370–290 B.C.) out of obscurity and assigned it a place in the corpus second only to that of the *Analects of Confucius*. Many facets of Mencius appealed to the Neo-Confucianists, but one of the most important was his argument that humans by nature are fundamentally good. Within the context of the Song dynasty, this was an assertion that morality could be pursued through an engagement in human affairs, and that the Buddhist monks' withdrawal from life's mainstream did not bestow upon them any special virtue.

The importance of these philosophical developments notwithstanding, printing probably had its greatest impact on the Chinese political system. The origin of the civil service examination system in China can be traced back to the Han dynasty, but in the Song dynasty government-administered examinations became the most important route to political power in China. For almost a thousand years (except the early period of Mongol rule), China was governed by men who had come to power simply because they had done exceedingly well in examinations on the Neo-Confucian canon. At any one time thousands of students were studying for the exams, and thousands of inexpensive books were required. Without printing such a system would not have been possible.

The development of this alternative to aristocratic rule was one of the most radical changes in world history. Since the examinations were ultimately open to 98 percent of all males (actors were one of the few groups excluded), it was the most democratic system in the world prior to the development of representative democracy and popular suffrage in Western Europe in the eighteenth and nineteenth centuries. (There were some small-scale systems, such as the classical Greek city-states, which might be considered more democratic, but nothing comparable in size to Song China or even the modern nation-states of Europe.)

Finally we come to the compass. Suffice it to say that during the Song dynasty, China developed the world's largest and most technologically sophisticated merchant marine and navy. By the fifteenth century its ships were sailing from the north Pacific to the east coast of Africa. They could have made the arduous journey around the tip of Africa and on into Portuguese ports; however, they had no reason to do so. Although the Western European economy was prospering, it offered nothing that China could not acquire much closer to home at much less cost. In particular, wool, Western Europe's most important export, could easily be obtained along China's northern frontier.

Certainly, the Portuguese and the Spanish did not make their unprecedented voyages out of idle curiosity. They were trying to go to the Spice Islands, in what is now Indonesia, in order to acquire the most valuable commercial items of the time. In the fifteenth century these islands were the world's sole suppliers of the fine spices, such as cloves, nutmeg, and mace, as well as a source for the more generally available pepper. It was this spice market that lured Columbus westward from Spain and drew Vasco Da Gama around Africa and across the Indian Ocean.

After the invention of the compass, China also wanted to go to the Spice Islands and, in fact, did go, regularly — but Chinese ships did not have to go around the world to get there. The Atlantic nations of Western Europe, on the other hand, had to buy spices from Venice (which controlled the Mediterranean trade routes) or from other Italian city-states; or they had to find a new way to the Spice Islands. It was necessity that mothered those revolutionary routes that ultimately changed the world.

Gunpowder, printing, the compass — clearly these three inventions changed China as much as they changed Europe. And it should come as no surprise that changes wrought in China between the eighth and tenth centuries were different from changes wrought in Western Europe between the thirteenth and fifteenth centuries. It would, of course, be unfair and ahistorical to imply that something was wrong with Western Europe because the technologies appeared there later. It is equally unfair to ask why the Chinese did not accidentally bump into the Western Hemisphere while sailing east across the Pacific to find the wool markets of Spain.

125

SUGITA GEMPAKU

A Dutch Anatomy Lesson in Japan

Sugita Gempaku* (1733–1817) was a Japanese physician who, as he tells us here in his memoir, suddenly discovered the value of Western medical science when he chanced to witness a dissection shortly after he obtained a Dutch anatomy book.

What was it that Sugita Gempaku learned on that day in 1771? What were the differences between the treatments of anatomy in the Chinese *Book of Medicine* and the Dutch medical book? What accounts for these differences?

Thinking Historically

How might the Dutch book have changed the way the author practiced medicine? How did it change his knowledge of the human body? How did it change the relevance of his knowledge of the human body to the medicine he practiced? How revolutionary was the new knowledge for Sugita Gempaku?

Whenever I met Hiraga Gennai (1729–1779), we talked to each other on this matter: "As we have learned, the Dutch method of scholarly investigation through field work and surveys is truly amazing. If we can directly understand books written by them, we will benefit greatly. However, it is pitiful that there has been no one who has set his mind on working in this field. Can we somehow blaze this trail? It is impossible to do it in Edo. Perhaps it is best if we ask translators in Nagasaki to make some translations. If one book can be completely translated, there will be an immeasurable benefit to the country." Every time we spoke in this manner, we deplored the impossibility of imple-

*SOO gee tah   gehm PAH koo

Sugita Gempaku, *Ranto Kotohajime* (The Beginning of Dutch Studies in the East), in David J. Lu, ed., *Japan: A Documentary History*, vol. I (Armonk, N.Y.: M. E. Sharpe, 2005), 264–66. Iwanami Shoten, *Nihon Koten Bunka Taikei* (Major Compilation of Japanese Classics), vol. 95 (Tokyo: Iwanami Shoten, 1969), 487–93.

menting our desires. However, we did not vainly lament the matter for long.

Somehow, miraculously I obtained a book on anatomy written in that country. It may well be that Dutch studies in this country began when I thought of comparing the illustrations in the book with real things. It was a strange and even miraculous happening that I was able to obtain that book in that particular spring of 1771. Then at the night of the third day of the third month, I received a letter from a man by the name of Tokuno Bambei, who was in the service of the then Town Commissioner, Magaribuchi Kai-no-kami. Tokuno stated in his letter that "A post-mortem examination of the body of a condemned criminal by a resident physician will be held tomorrow at Senjukotsukahara. You are welcome to witness it if you so desire." At one time my colleague by the name of Kosugi Genteki had an occasion to witness a post-mortem dissection of a body when he studied under Dr. Yamawaki Tōyō of Kyoto. After seeing the dissection firsthand, Kosugi remarked that what was said by the people of old was false and simply could not be trusted. "The people of old spoke of nine internal organs, and nowadays, people divide them into five viscera and six internal organs. That [perpetuates] inaccuracy," Kosugi once said. Around that time (1759) Dr. Tōyō published a book entitled *Zōshi* (*On Internal Organs*). Having read that book, I had hoped that some day I could witness a dissection. When I also acquired a Dutch book on anatomy, I wanted above all to compare the two to find out which one accurately described the truth. I rejoiced at this unusually fortunate circumstance, and my mind could not entertain any other thought. However, a thought occurred to me that I should not monopolize this good fortune, and decided to share it with those of my colleagues who were diligent in the pursuit of their medicine. . . . Among those I invited was one [Maeno] Ryōtaku (1723–1803). . . .

The next day, when we arrived at the location . . . Ryōtaku reached under his kimono to produce a Dutch book and showed it to us. "This is a Dutch book of anatomy called *Tabulae Anatomicae*. I bought this a few years ago when I went to Nagasaki, and kept it." As I examined it, it was the same book I had and was of the same edition. We held each other's hands and exclaimed: "What a coincidence!" Ryōtaku continued by saying: "When I went to Nagasaki, I learned and heard," and opened his book. "These are called *long* in Dutch, they are lungs," he taught us. "This is *hart*, or the heart. When it says *maag* it is the stomach, and when it says *milt* it is the spleen." However, they did not look like the heart given in the Chinese medical books, and none of us were sure until we could actually see the dissection.

Thereafter we went together to the place which was especially set for us to observe the dissection in Kotsukahara. . . . The regular man who performed the chore of dissection was ill, and his grandfather, who was ninety years of age, came in his place. He was a healthy old man. He had experienced many dissections since his youth, and boasted that he dissected a number of bodies. Those dissections were performed in those days by men of the *eta*[1] class. . . . That day, the old butcher pointed to this and that organ. After the heart, liver, gall bladder, and stomach were identified, he pointed to other parts for which there were no names. "I don't know their names. But I have dissected quite a few bodies from my youthful days. Inside of everyone's abdomen there were these parts and those parts." Later, after consulting the anatomy chart, it became clear to me that I saw an arterial tube, a vein, and the suprarenal gland. The old butcher again said, "Every time I had a dissection, I pointed out to those physicians many of these parts, but not a single one of them questioned 'what was this?' or 'what was that?'" We compared the body as dissected against the charts both Ryōtaku and I had, and could not find a single variance from the charts. The Chinese *Book of Medicine* (*Yi Jing*) says that the lungs are like the eight petals of the lotus flower, with three petals hanging in front, three in back, and two petals forming like two ears and that the liver has three petals to the left and four petals to the right. There were no such divisions, and the positions and shapes of intestines and gastric organs were all different from those taught by the old theories. The official physicians, Dr. Okada Yōsen and Dr. Fujimoto Rissen, have witnessed dissection seven or eight times. Whenever they witnessed the dissection, they found that the old theories contradicted reality. Each time they were perplexed and could not resolve their doubts. Every time they wrote down what they thought was strange. They wrote in their books. "The more we think of it, there must be fundamental differences in the bodies of Chinese and of the eastern barbarians [i.e., Japanese]." I could see why they wrote this way.

That day, after the dissection was over, we decided that we also should examine the shape of the skeletons left exposed on the execution ground. We collected the bones, and examined a number of them. Again, we were struck by the fact that they all differed from the old theories while conforming to the Dutch charts.

The three of us, Ryōtaku, [Nakagawa] Junan (1739–1786), and I went home together. On the way home we spoke to each other and felt the same way. "How marvelous was our actual experience today. It is a shame that we were ignorant of these things until now. As physicians who serve their masters through medicine, we performed our duties in complete ignorance of the true form of the human body. How disgraceful it is. Somehow, through this experience, let us investigate further the truth about the human body. If we practice medicine with this knowledge behind us, we can make contributions for people under heaven

---

[1]The eta were an untouchable caste in Japan, defined by their restriction to certain occupations associated with death — tanning or working with hides, cremating the dead, butchering meat, and, thus, doing autopsies. They could not be physicians. [Ed.]

and on this earth." Ryōtaku spoke to us. "Indeed, I agree with you wholeheartedly." Then I spoke to my two companions. "Somehow if we can translate anew this book called *Tabulae Anatomicae*, we can get a clear notion of the human body inside out. It will have great benefit in the treatment of our patients. Let us do our best to read it and understand it without the help of translators." Ryōtaku responded: "I have been wanting to read Dutch books for some time, but there has been no friend who would share my ambitions. I have spent days lamenting it. If both of you wish, I have been in Nagasaki before and have retained some Dutch. Let us use it as a beginning to tackle the book together." After hearing it, I answered, "This is simply wonderful. If we are to join our efforts, I shall also resolve to do my very best." . . .

The next day, we assembled at the house of Ryōtaku and recalled the happenings of the previous day. When we faced that *Tabulae Anatomicae*, we felt as if we were setting sail on a great ocean in a ship without oars or a rudder. With the magnitude of the work before us, we were dumbfounded by our own ignorance. However, Ryōtaku had been thinking of this for some time, and he had been in Nagasaki. He knew some Dutch through studying and hearing, and knew some sentence patterns and words. He was also ten years older than I, and we decided to make him head of our group and our teacher. At that time I did not know the twenty-five letters of the Dutch alphabet. I decided to study the language with firm determination, but I had to acquaint myself with letters and words gradually.

126

BENJAMIN FRANKLIN

Letter on a Balloon Experiment in 1783

Benjamin Franklin (1706–1790) was the preeminent statesman, diplomat, and spokesman for the British colonies that became the United States during his long lifetime. Trained as a candle maker and printer, he became a journalist, publisher, merchant, homespun philosopher, and inveterate inventor. He invented the lightning rod, the Franklin stove, bifocals, and the medical catheter, among other things. His

---

Nathan G. Goodman, ed., *The Ingenious Dr. Franklin, Selected Scientific Letters of Benjamin Franklin* (Philadelphia: University of Pennsylvania Press, 1931), 99–102.

inventions sprang from a gift of immense curiosity and an exhaustive reading in the science of his day.

Franklin, sometimes called "the first American," represented the fledging Republic in France during the Revolution, ensuring French participation against the British. In 1783 he signed the second Treaty of Paris, by which the British recognized the independence of the United States. Franklin was the only founding father to sign the Declaration of Independence (1776), the Treaty of Paris (1783), and the Constitution of the United States (1789). Throughout his life Franklin furthered his interest in scientific experiment and invention. In December of 1783, he wrote to a friend about a recent invention that fascinated him: an early experiment in air travel in a balloon. What did Franklin see and what did it mean to him?

Thinking Historically

What evidence do you see in this letter that the scientific revolution was a genuinely revolutionary change? What was revolutionary about it? What evidence do you see that the people of the time thought they were living in a revolutionary age? How would you compare their attitudes with those of people today toward modern technological innovations?

TO

Sᴉʀ Jᴏsᴇᴘʜ Bᴀɴᴋs

Passy, Dec. 1, 1783.

Dear Sir: —

In mine of yesterday I promised to give you an account of Messrs. Charles & Robert's experiment, which was to have been made this day, and at which I intended to be present. Being a little indisposed, and the air cool, and the ground damp, I declined going into the garden of the Tuileries, where the balloon was placed, not knowing how long I might be obliged to wait there before it was ready to depart, and chose to stay in my carriage near the statue of Louis XV, from whence I could well see it rise, and have an extensive view of the region of air through which, as the wind sat, it was likely to pass. The morning was foggy, but about one o'clock the air became tolerably clear, to the great satisfaction of the spectators, who were infinite, notice having been given of the intended experiment several days before in the papers, so that all Paris was out, either about the Tuileries, on the quays and bridges, in the fields, the streets, at the windows, or on the tops of houses, besides the inhabitants of all the towns and villages of the environs. Never before was a philosophical experiment so magnificently attended. Some guns were fired to give notice that the departure of the balloon was near, and a small one was discharged, which went to an amazing height, there being but little wind to make it deviate from its perpendicular course, and at length the sight of it was lost. Means were used, I am told, to prevent the great balloon's rising so high as might endanger its bursting. Several bags of sand were taken on board before the cord that held it down was cut, and the whole weight being then too much to be lifted, such a quantity was discharged as to permit its rising slowly. Thus it would sooner arrive at that region where it would be in equilibrio with the surrounding air, and by discharging more sand afterwards, it might go higher if desired. Between one and two o'clock, all eyes were gratified with seeing it rise majestically from among the trees, and ascend gradually above the buildings, a most beautiful spectacle. When it was about two hundred feet high, the brave adventurers held out and waved a little white pennant, on both sides [of] their car, to salute the spectators, who returned loud claps of applause. The wind was very little, so that the object though moving to the northward, continued long in view; and it was a great while before the admiring people began to disperse. The persons embarked were Mr. Charles, professor of experimental philosophy, and a zealous promoter of that science; and one of the Messieurs Robert, the very ingenious constructors of the machine. When it arrived at its height, which I suppose might be three or four hundred toises, it appeared to have only horizontal motion. I had a pocket-glass, with which I followed it, till I lost sight first of the men, then of the car, and when I last saw the balloon, it appeared no bigger than a walnut. I write this at seven in the evening. What became of them is not yet known here. I hope they descended by daylight, so as to see and avoid falling among trees or on houses, and that the experiment was completed without any mischievous accident, which the novelty of it and the want of experience might well occasion. I am the more anxious for the event, because I am not well informed of the means provided for letting themselves down, and the loss of these very ingenious men would not only be a discouragement to the progress of the art, but be a sensible loss to science and society.

I shall inclose one of the tickets of admission, on which the globe was represented, as originally intended, but is altered by the pen to show its real state when it went off. When the tickets were engraved the car was to have been hung to the neck of the globe, as represented by a little drawing I have made in the corner.

I suppose it may have been an apprehension of danger in straining too much the balloon or tearing the silk, that induced the constructors to throw a net over it, fixed to a hoop which went round its middle, and to hang the car to that hoop.

Tuesday morning, December 2d. — I am relieved from my anxiety by hearing that the adventurers descended well near L'Isle Adam before sunset. This place is near seven leagues from Paris. Had the wind blown fresh they might have gone much farther.

If I receive any further particulars of importance, I shall communicate them hereafter.

With great esteem, I am, dear sir, your most obedient and most humble servant,

FRANKLIN

P.S. *Tuesday evening.* — Since writing the above I have received the printed paper and the manuscript containing some particulars of the experiment, which I enclose. I hear further that the travellers had perfect command of their carriage, descending as they pleased by letting some of the inflammable air escape, and rising again by discharging some sand; that they descended over a field so low as to talk with the labourers in passing, and mounted again to pass a hill. The little balloon falling at Vincennes shows that mounting higher it met with a current of air in a contrary direction, an observation that may be of use to future aerial voyagers.

REFLECTIONS

Was there a scientific revolution in the seventeenth and eighteenth century? By most measures we would have to say "yes." There were new polished-glass instruments with which to observe and measure; books, theories, diagrams, debates, and discoveries emerged at a dizzying pace. Age-old authorities — Aristotle, Ptolemy, even the Bible — were called into question. The wisdom of the ages was interrogated for evidence and forced to submit to tests by experiment. But these changes would not have constituted a revolution if they occurred in a vacuum.

Maria Sibylla Merian's metaphor is perhaps most appropriate. There was a metamorphosis — a change from one way of looking at the world to another. We might even say it was a change from a medieval manner of wearing the world like a robe to a modern view of the world as a stage, as a reality seen through a window, something separate that could be touched, weighed, measured, even bought and sold.

However we choose to characterize the changes in scientific thinking during this period, it is important to emphasize the revolutionary impact of the European scientific revolution of the seventeenth century without slighting the scientific and technological achievements of other civilizations. Many of the scientific developments in Europe sprang from foreign innovations, and in some fields Europe was not as advanced as other societies. Yet the scientific revolution's unique combination of observation and generalization, experimentation and mathematics, induction and deduction established a body of knowledge and a method for research that proved lasting and irreversible.

Why was it that China, so scientifically and technologically adept during the Sung dynasty, pictured hearts and lungs as flower petals in the late-Ming and early-Ch'ing seventeenth century? Was it that Chinese science lost momentum or changed direction? Or does such a question, as Lynda Shaffer warns, judge China unfairly by Western standards? Do the petal hearts reflect a different set of interests rather than a failure of Chinese science?

Chinese scientists excelled in acupuncture, massage, and herbal medicine, while European scientists excelled in surgery. It turned out that the inner workings of the human body were better revealed in surgical dissection than in muscle manipulation or in oral remedies. And, as Sugita Gempaku reminds us, the Europeans not only cut and removed, they also named what they found and tried to understand how it worked. Perhaps the major difference between science in Europe and that in India, China, and Japan in the seventeenth century was one of perspective: Europeans were beginning to imagine the human body as a machine and asking how it worked. In some respects, the metaphor of man as a machine proved more fruitful than organic metaphors of humans as plants or animals.

Asking probing questions and testing the answers also changed our understanding of the heavens. If mathematical calculations indicated that a star would appear at a particular spot in the heavens and it did not, Galileo might just as soon have questioned the observation as the math. From the seventeenth century on, scientists would check one or the other on the assumption that observation and mathematics could be brought together to understand the same event, that they would have to be in agreement, and that such agreement could lead to laws that could then be tested and proved or disproved.

It is this method of inquiry, not the discoveries, that was new. For the scientific method that emerged during this period constituted a systematic means of inquiry based on agreed-upon rules of hypothesis, experimentation, theory testing, law, and dissemination. This scientific inquiry was a social process in two important ways: First, any scientific discovery had to be reproducible and recognized by other scientists to gain credence. Second, a community of scientists was needed to question, dismiss, or validate the work of its members.

Finally, we return to Baumer's emphasis on the societies of seventeenth-century science. The numerous organizations in Europe are testaments not only to a growing interest in science but to a continuing public conversation. Science in Europe thus became a matter of public concern, a popular endeavor. Compare the masses of Parisians Ben Franklin described who turned out to view the balloon experiment with the few physicians gathered around Sugita Gempaku who could learn from the expertise of outcast butchers.

Ultimately, then, the difference between European science and that of India or China in the seventeenth century may have had more to do with society than with culture. The development of modern scientific methods relied on the numerous debates and discussions of a self-conscious class of gentlemen scientists in a Europe where news traveled quickly and ideas could be translated and tested with confidence across numerous borders. To what extent does science everywhere today demonstrate the hallmarks of the seventeenth-century scientific revolution?

Enlightenment and Revolution

Europe and the Americas, 1650–1850

HISTORICAL CONTEXT

The modern world puts its faith in science, reason, and democracy. The seventeenth-century scientific revolution established reason as the key to understanding nature, and its application-directed thought, organized society, and measured governments during the eighteenth-century Enlightenment. Most — though, as we shall see, not all — people believed that reason would eventually lead to freedom. Freedom of thought, religion, and association, and political liberties and representative governments were hailed as hallmarks of the Age of Enlightenment.

For some, enlightened society meant a more controlled rather than a more democratic society. Philosophers like Immanuel Kant and Jean-Jacques Rousseau wanted people to become free but thought most people were incapable of achieving such a state. Rulers who were called "enlightened despots" believed that the application of reason to society would make people happier, not necessarily freer.

Ultimately, however, the Enlightenment's faith in reason led to calls for political revolution as well as for schemes of order. In England in the seventeenth century, in America and France at the end of the eighteenth century, and in Latin America shortly thereafter, revolutionary governments were created according to rational principles of liberty and equality that dispatched monarchs and enshrined the rule of the people. In this chapter we will concentrate on the heritage of the Enlightenment, examining competing tendencies toward order and revolution, stability and liberty, equality and freedom. We will also compare the American and the French Revolutions, and these with the later revolutions in Latin America. Finally, in reflection, we will briefly compare these distinctly European and American developments with processes in other parts of the world.

THINKING HISTORICALLY
Close Reading and
Interpretation of Texts

At the core of the Enlightenment was a trust in reasoned discussion, a belief that people could understand each other, even if they were not in agreement. Such understanding demanded clear and concise communication in a world where the masses were often swayed by fiery sermons and flamboyant rhetoric. But the Enlightenment also put its faith in the written word and a literate public. Ideas were debated face to face in the salons and coffeehouses of Europe and in the meeting halls of America, but it was through letters, diaries, the new world of newspapers, and the burgeoning spread of printed books that the people of the Enlightenment learned what they and their neighbors thought.

It is appropriate then for us to read the selections in this chapter — all primary sources — in the spirit in which they were written. We will pay special attention to the words and language that the authors use and will attempt to understand exactly what they meant, even why they chose the words they did. Such explication is a twofold process; we must understand the words first and foremost; then we must strive to understand the words in their proper context, as they were intended by the author. To achieve our first goal, we will paraphrase, a difficult task because the eighteenth-century writing style differs greatly from our own: Sentences are longer and arguments are often complex. Vocabularies were broad during this period, and we may encounter words that are used in ways unknown to us. As to our latter goal, we must try to make the vocabulary and perspective of the authors our own. Grappling with what makes the least sense to us and trying to understand why it was said is the challenge.

127

DAVID HUME
On Miracles

The European Enlightenment of the eighteenth century was the expression of a new class of intellectuals, independent of the clergy but allied with the rising middle class. Their favorite words were *reason*, *nature*, and *progress*. They applied the systematic doubt of René Descartes (1596–1650) and the reasoning method of the scientific revolution to human affairs, including religion and politics. With caustic wit and good humor, they asked new questions and popularized new points of view that would eventually revolutionize Western politics and culture. While the French *philosophes* and Voltaire (1694–1778) may be the best known, the Scottish philosopher David Hume (1711–1776) may have been the most brilliant. What does Hume argue in this selection? Does he prove his point to your satisfaction? How does he use reason and nature to make his case? Is reason incompatible with religion?

Thinking Historically

The first step in understanding what Hume means in this essay must come from a careful reading — a sentence-by-sentence exploration. Try to paraphrase each sentence, putting it into your own words. For example, you might paraphrase the first sentence like this: "I've found a way to disprove superstition; this method should be useful as long as superstition exists, which may be forever." Notice the content of such words as *just* and *check*. What does Hume mean by these words and by *prodigies*?

The second sentence is a concise definition of the scientific method. How would you paraphrase it? The second and third sentences summarize the method Hume has discovered to counter superstition. What is the meaning of the third sentence?

In the rest of the essay, Hume offers four proofs, or reasons, why miracles do not exist. How would you paraphrase each of these? Do you find these more or less convincing than his more general opening and closing arguments? What does Hume mean by *miracles*?

The Philosophical Works of David Hume (Edinburgh: A. Black and W. Tait, 1826).

I flatter myself that I have discovered an argument . . . , which, if just, will, with the wise and learned, be an everlasting check to all kinds of superstitious delusion, and consequently will be useful as long as the world endures; for so long, I presume, will the accounts of miracles and prodigies be found in all history, sacred and profane. . . .

A wise man proportions his belief to the evidence. . . .

A miracle is a violation of the laws of nature; and as a firm and unalterable experience has established these laws, the proof against a miracle, from the very nature of the fact, is as entire as any argument from experience can possibly be imagined. . . . Nothing is esteemed a miracle, if it ever happens in the common course of nature. It is no miracle that a man, seemingly in good health, should die on a sudden; because such a kind of death, though more unusual than any other, has yet been frequently observed to happen. But it is a miracle that a dead man should come to life; because that has never been observed in any age or country. There must, therefore, be an uniform experience against every miraculous event, otherwise the event would not merit that appellation. And as an uniform experience amounts to a proof, there is here a direct and full *proof*, from the nature of the fact, against the existence of any miracle. . . .

(Further) there is not to be found, in all history, any miracle attested by a sufficient number of men, of such unquestioned good sense, education, and learning, as to secure us against all delusion in themselves; of such undoubted integrity, as to place them beyond all suspicion of any design to deceive others; of such credit and reputation in the eyes of mankind, as to have a great deal to lose in case of their being detected in any falsehood. . . .

Secondly, We may observe in human nature a principle which, if strictly examined, will be found to diminish extremely the assurance, which we might, from human testimony, have in any kind of prodigy. . . . The passion of *surprise* and *wonder*, arising from miracles, being an agreeable emotion, gives a sensible tendency towards the belief of those events from which it is derived. . . .

With what greediness are the miraculous accounts of travellers received, their descriptions of sea and land monsters, their relations of wonderful adventures, strange men, and uncouth manners? But if the spirit of religion join itself to the love of wonder, there is an end of common sense; and human testimony, in these circumstances, loses all pretensions to authority. A religionist may be an enthusiast, and imagine he sees what has no reality: He may know his narrative to be false, and yet persevere in it, with the best intentions in the world, for the sake of promoting so holy a cause: Or even where this delusion has not place, vanity, excited by so strong a temptation, operates on him more powerfully than on the rest of mankind in any other circumstances; and self-interest with equal force. . . .

The many instances of forged miracles and prophecies and supernatural events, which, in all ages, have either been detected by contrary evidence, or which detect themselves by their absurdity, prove sufficiently the strong propensity of mankind to the extraordinary and marvellous, and ought reasonably to beget a suspicion against all relations of this kind.[1] . . .

Thirdly, It forms a strong presumption against all supernatural and miraculous relations, that they are observed chiefly to abound among ignorant and barbarous nations; or if a civilized people has ever given admission to any of them, that people will be found to have received them from ignorant and barbarous ancestors, who transmitted them with that inviolable sanction and authority which always attend received opinions. . . .

I may add, as a *fourth* reason, which diminishes the authority of prodigies, that there is no testimony for any, even those which have not been expressly detected, that is not opposed by any infinite number of witnesses; so that not only the miracle destroys the credit of testimony, but the testimony destroys itself. To make this the better understood, let us consider, that in matters of religion, whatever is different is contrary; and that it is impossible the religions of ancient Rome, of Turkey, of Siam, and of China, should all of them be established on any solid foundation. Every miracle, therefore, pretended to have been wrought in any of these religions (and all of them abound in miracles), as its direct scope is to establish the particular system to which it is attributed; so has it the same force, though more indirectly, to overthrow every other system. In destroying a rival system, it likewise destroys the credit of those miracles on which that system was established, so that all the prodigies of different religions are to be regarded as contrary facts, and the evidences of these prodigies, whether weak or strong, as opposite to each other. . . .

Upon the whole, then, it appears, that no testimony for any kind of miracle has ever amounted to a probability, much less to a proof; and that, even supposing it amounted to proof, it would be opposed by another proof, derived from the very nature of the fact which it would endeavour to establish. It is experience only which gives authority to human testimony; and it is the same experience which assures us of the laws of nature. When, therefore, these two kinds of experience are contrary, we have nothing to do but to subtract the one from the other, and embrace an opinion either on one side or the other, with that assurance which arises from the remainder. But according to the principle here explained, this subtraction with regard to all popular religions amounts to an entire annihilation; and therefore we may establish it as a maxim, that no human testimony can have such force as to prove a miracle, and make it a just foundation for any such system of religion.

[1]Accounts of miracles. [Ed.]

128

DENIS DIDEROT

Supplement to the Voyage of Bougainville

French *philosophe* Denis Diderot* (1713–1784) personified the Enlightenment with his literary wit, faith in reason, passion for universal knowledge, and constant challenge to custom, convention, and censorship. He wrote his great *Encyclopedia* of seventeen volumes, a compendium of the wisdom of the eighteenth century, amidst a life of philosophical treatises, provocative popular essays, numerous marriages and affairs, and periods of imprisonment for his writings.

His *Supplement to the Voyage of Bougainville*† (1772) is a literary invention presented as if it were a recently discovered addition to the famous 1768 account of the voyage to Tahiti by the French explorer, Louis-Antoine de Bougainville. Bougainville's very popular *Voyage around the World* spread the idea of the South Sea Islanders as "noble savages," untarnished by civilization, free to lead a life in tune with nature. Such accounts became a literary model for European self-criticism.

In this passage, Diderot uses the departure of the French from Tahiti as an opportunity for an old Tahitian to wish them good riddance. What criticisms does Diderot's old Tahitian make of the French and their civilization?

Thinking Historically

The idea of presenting one's philosophical ideas in a "long-lost" book or in the voice of "the native" was an old technique in the eighteenth century, possibly initiated as early as 1516 in Thomas More's classic work in which a traveller describes an ideal world called *Utopia*. For both Diderot and More, the use of the foreigner's voice provided the author with a bit of distance for protection from the censor, or worse, the police and jailer. Under the guise of "only reporting what others said," the author could try out new and sometimes radical ideas. It is likely, however, that the speech Diderot put in the mouth of the old Tahitian in this section represented Diderot's own ideas about French civilization.

*dee duh ROH
†boo gan VEEL

Denis Diderot, *Supplement to the Voyage of Bougainville*, Part II, "The Old Man's Farewell" (Essex, U.K.: Project Gutenberg, University of Essex, 2006), http://courses.essex.ac.uk/cs/cs101/txframe.htm.

Bear in mind that Diderot is writing on the eve of the French Revolution, which broke out in 1789. While no one foresaw the future in 1772, the strains of the old regime were evident to many philosophers of the Enlightenment like Diderot: an indifferent monarchy; a depleted treasury to be worsened by aid to the American Revolution; a creakingly inequitable Parliament where the nobility and clergy each had as much representation as everyone else. What evidence do you see of Diderot's concern about these issues? In addition, thinkers like Voltaire and Diderot were critical of French colonialism and slavery. What evidence do you see of this critique in this document? What other criticisms does Diderot make of French civilization?

Part II, "The Old Man's Farewell"

He was the father of a large family. On the arrival of the Europeans, he cast looks of disdain at them, showing neither astonishment, fright, nor curiosity. [The presence of this old man and his attitude to the Europeans are mentioned by Bougainville.] They came up to him: he turned his back on them and retired into his cabin. His silence and his anxiety revealed his thoughts too well. He groaned within himself over the happy days of his country, now for ever eclipsed. On the departure of Bougainville, as the inhabitants rushed in a crowd on to the beach, attached themselves to his clothing, hugged his comrades in their arms and wept, this old man advanced, severe in mien, and said: "Weep, luckless Tahitiens weep, but for the arrival not for the departure of these ambitious and wicked men. One day you will know them better. One day they will return, holding in one hand the morsel of wood you see attached to this man's belt, in the other, the iron which hangs from that man's side: they will return to throw you into chains, to cut your throats, or to subject you to their extravagance and vices: one day you will serve under them, as corrupted, as vile, as luckless as they. One consolation I have. My life is drawing to its close. And the calamity I announce to you, *I* shall not see. O Tahitiens, my friends, there is one method which might save you from your tragic future. But I would rather die than advise it. Let them withdraw and live."

Then addressing Bougainville, he added:

"And thou, chief of the brigands who obey thee, quickly push off thy vessel from our shore. We are innocent; we are happy: and thou canst not but spoil our happiness. We follow the pure instinct of nature: thou hast sought to efface its character from our souls. Here all things belong to all men. Thou hast preached some strange distinction between thine and mine. Our daughters and our wives were held in common by us all: thou hast shared this privilege with us, and thou hast come and inflamed them with frenzies unknown before. They have lost their reason in thy arms. Thou hast become ferocious in theirs. They have come to hate each other. You have slaughtered each other for them: they have come back stained with your blood. We are free: and see thou hast planted in our earth the title of our future slavery. Thou art neither god nor demon. Who art thou then to make slaves? Orou! thou who understandest the language of these men, tell us all as thou hast told me, what they have written on this metal blade! *This country is ours.* This country is thine! And why? Because thou hast set foot there? If a Tahitien disembarked one day upon your shores, and graved upon one of your stones or on the bark of one of your trees: *This country belongs to the inhabitants of Tahiti,* what wouldst thou think of such a proceeding? Thou art the stronger! But what of that? When someone took from you one of those rubbishy trifles with which your hut is filled, thou didst cry out and take thy revenge. Yet at that moment thou wast projecting in the depth of thy heart the theft of a whole country. Thou art not a slave. Thou wouldst suffer death rather than become one, yet us thou wouldst enslave. Thinkest thou then that the Tahitien cannot defend his liberty and die? He, whom thou wishest to seize like an animal, the Tahitien, is thy brother. You are both children of nature. What right hast thou over him that he has not over thee? Thou art come. Did we fall upon thee? Did we pillage thy ship? Did we seize thee and expose thee to the arrows of our enemies? Did we yoke thee to our animals toiling in the fields? No. We have respected our image in thee. Leave us our customs. They are wiser and more honourable than thine. We have no wish to barter what thou callest our ignorance against thy useless knowledge. We possess all that is necessary and good for us. Do we deserve contempt because we have not known how to fabricate for ourselves wants in superfluity? When we are hungry we have enough to eat; when we are cold the means to clothe ourselves. Thou hast entered our cabins. What, in thy opinion, is lacking? Pursue as long as thou wilt what thou callest the commodities of life. But permit sensible beings to stop, when by continuing their painful labour they will gain but imaginary good. If thou persuadest us to cross the narrow limit of necessity, when shall we stop working? What time will be left over for enjoying ourselves? We have reduced to the smallest possible the sum of our annual and daily toil, because to us nothing seems better than repose. Go back to thine own country to trouble and torment thyself as much as thou wilt. Trouble us neither with thy artificial needs, nor thy imaginary virtues. Look at these men: how straight, healthy, and robust they are! Look at these women. How straight, healthy, fresh, and fair they are. Take this bow. It is mine. Call to help thee, one, two, three, four of thy comrades and try to bend it. I bend it myself alone. I plough the earth. I climb the mountain. I pierce the forest. I cover a league of the plain in less than an hour. Thy young companions can scarcely follow me, and I am ninety years old and more. Woe to this island! Woe to all Tahitiens present and to come for the day of this thy visit! We only know one illness that to which man, animal, and plant have been condemned, old age: and thou hast brought to us another. Thou hast infected our blood. Perhaps we shall have to exterminate with our own hands, our daughters, our wives, our children: the men who have approached thy women: the women who have approached thy men. Our fields will be damp with the impure blood which has passed from thy veins into ours: else our children will be condemned to nourish and perpetuate the ill thou hast given to their fathers and mothers and to transmit it for ever to their descendants. Wretch! thou wilt be guilty of the ravages that follow thy fatal embraces or of the murders we shall commit to check the poison! Thou speakest of crimes! Knowest thou a greater than thine own? What with thee is the punishment for the man who kills his neighbour? Death by iron. And what for the coward who poisons him? Death by fire. Compare thy crime to this latter one, and tell us, poisoner of nations, the punishment thou deservest. A moment ago the young Tahitien maiden abandoned herself with transport to the embraces of the Tahitien boy: she waited with impatience till her mother (authorized by her reaching the nubile age), raised her veil and bared her throat. She was proud to excite the desires or to fix the amorous gaze of the stranger, her parents or her brother. She accepted fearlessly and shamelessly, in our presence, midst a circle of innocent Tahitiens, to the sound of flutes, between the dances, the caresses of him her young heart and the secret voice of her senses had chosen. The idea of crime and the danger of disease have come with thee amongst us. Our pleasures, formerly so sweet, are accompanied by remorse and terror. That man in black, next you, who listens to me, has spoken to our boys. I know not what he has said to our girls. But our boys hesitate: our girls blush. Plunge if thou wilt into the dark forest with the perverse partner of thy pleasures, but allow the good and simple Tahitiens to reproduce without shame, in the face of heaven and the open day. What sentiment more honourable and greater couldst thou find to replace the one we have breathed into them and which animates their lives? They think the moment has come to enrich the nation and the family with a new citizen and they glory in it. They eat to live and grow. They grow to multiply, they find there neither vice nor shame. Listen to the succession of thy crimes. Scarcely hadst thou appeared among them, but they turn thieves. Scarcely hadst thou descended on our soil, but it smoked blood. That Tahitien who ran to meet thee, who greeted thee, who received thee crying *Taio*, *friend*, *friend*: you killed him. And why, did you kill him? Because he had been seduced by the glitter of thy little serpents' eggs. He gave thee his fruits: he offered thee his wife and daughter: he yielded thee his cabin. And thou hast killed him for a handful of these grains, which he took from thee without asking. And this people? At the sound of thy deadly firearms, terror seized them and they fled into the mountain. But understand they would have speedily come down again. Without me you may be sure you would all have perished in an instant. Why have I calmed, why have I restrained them? Why do I restrain them even now? I do not know. For thou deservest no sentiment of pity. Thou hast a ferocious soul which never felt it. Thou didst walk, thou and thine, in our island: thou hast been respected: thou hast enjoyed everything: thou hast found in thy way neither barrier nor refusal: thou wast invited in: thou sattest down: there was laid out before thee the abundance of the country. Didst thou wish for our young girls? Save for these, who have not yet the privilege of showing face and throat, their mothers presented thee them all quite naked. Thine the tender victim of hostly duty. For her and for thee the ground hast been scattered with leaves and flowers: the musicians have tuned their instruments: nothing has troubled the sweetness nor hindered the liberty of her caresses or thine. The hymn was chanted, the hymn which exhorted thee to be a man and our child to be a woman, a woman yielding and voluptuous. There was dancing round your bed, and it is on leaving the arms of this woman, after feeling on her breast the sweetest rapture, that thou hast killed her brother, her friend, her father perhaps. Thou hast done worse still. Look this way. See this enclosure stiff with arms: these arms which had only menaced our enemies, they are turned against our own children: see the wretched companions of our pleasures: see their sadness. See the grief of their fathers: the despair of their mothers. In that place they have been condemned to perish by our hands or by the ills that thou hast done them. Withdraw unless thy cruel eyes take pleasure in spectacles of death: withdraw, go, and may the guilty seas which have spared thee in thy voyage gain their own absolution and avenge us by swallowing thee up before thy return. And you, Tahitiens, return to your cabins every one of you and let these unworthy strangers hear on their departure but the moaning wave, and see but the foam whose fury whitens a deserted beach."

He had scarcely finished, but the crowd of inhabitants had disappeared. A vast silence reigned over all the island. Nothing was heard but the shrill whistle of the winds and the dull noise of the water along all the coast. One might have thought that air and water, responsive to the old man's voice, were happy to obey him.

129

The American Declaration of Independence

If anyone had taken a poll of Americans in the thirteen colonies as late as 1775, independence would not have won a majority vote anywhere. Massachusetts might have come close, perhaps, but nowhere in the land was there a definitive urge to separate from the British Empire. Still, three thousand miles was a long way for news, views, appointees, and petitions to travel and tensions between the colonies and Britain had been growing.

Of course, each side looked at the cost of colonial administration differently. The British believed that they had carried a large part of the costs of migration, administration of trade, and control of the sea, while the colonists resented the humiliation resulting from their lack of political representation and the often inept royal officials and punitive legislation imposed on them from afar by the Parliament and the king.

By the spring of 1775, events were rapidly pushing the colonies toward independence. In April, British troops engaged colonial forces at Lexington and Concord, instigating a land war that was to last until 1781. In the midst of other urgent business, most notably raising an army, the Continental Congress asked a committee that included Thomas Jefferson, Benjamin Franklin, and John Adams to compose a statement outlining these and other reasons for separation from Britain. Jefferson wrote the first draft, the bulk of which became the final version accepted by the Continental Congress on July 4, 1776.

The Declaration of Independence was preeminently a document of the Enlightenment. Its principal author, Thomas Jefferson, exemplified the Enlightenment intellectual. Conversant in European literature, law, and political thought, he made significant contributions to eighteenth-century knowledge in natural science and architecture. Benjamin Franklin and other delegates to the Congress in Philadelphia were similarly accomplished.

It is no wonder, then, that the Declaration and the establishment of an independent United States of America should strike the world as the realization of the Enlightenment's basic tenets. That a wholly new country could be created by people with intelligence and foresight, according to principles of reason, and to realize human liberty was heady stuff.

A Documentary History of the United States, ed. Richard D. Heffner (New York: Penguin Books, 1991), 15–18.

Enlightenment and Revolution

What were the goals of the authors of this document? In what ways was the Declaration a call for democracy? In what ways was it not?

Thinking Historically

Before interpreting any document, we must read it carefully and put it into context — that is, determine the what, where, and why. Some of this information may be available in the text itself. For instance, whom is the Declaration addressed to? What is the reason given for writing it?

We interpret or extract meaning from documents by asking questions, that emerge from the reading. These questions may arise from passages we do not understand, from lack of clarity in the text, or from an incongruence between the text and our expectations. It may surprise some readers, for example, that the Declaration criticizes the king so sharply. To question this might lead us to explore the need for American colonists to defend their actions in terms of British legal tradition. For years, the American colonists blamed the king's ministers for their difficulties; in July 1776 they blamed the king — a traditional sign of revolutionary intent in England, which meant efforts toward independence were imminent.

Consider also the disparity between the lofty sentiments of liberty and independence and the existence of slavery in the Americas. How is it possible that Jefferson and some of the signers of the Declaration could own slaves while declaring it "self-evident that all men are created equal"? To whom did this statement apply?

In Congress, July 4, 1776, the Unanimous Declaration of the Thirteen United States of America

When in the course of human events, it becomes necessary for one people to dissolve the political bands which have connected them with another, and to assume among the powers of the earth, the separate and equal station to which the Laws of Nature and of Nature's God entitle them, a decent respect to the opinions of mankind requires that they should declare the causes which impel them to the separation.

We hold these truths to be self-evident, that all men are created equal, that they are endowed by their Creator with certain unalienable rights, that among these are life, liberty, and the pursuit of happiness. That to secure these rights, governments are instituted among men, deriving their just powers from the consent of the governed. That whenever any form of government becomes destructive of these ends, it is the right of the people to alter or to abolish it, and to institute new government, laying its foundation on such principles and organizing its powers in such form, as to them shall seem most likely to effect their safety and happiness. Prudence, indeed, will dictate that governments long established should not be changed for light and transient causes; and accordingly all experience hath shown, that mankind are more disposed to suffer, while evils are sufferable, than to right themselves by abolishing the forms to which they are accustomed. But when a long train of abuses and usurpations, pursuing invariably the same object evinces a design to reduce them under absolute despotism, it is their right, it is their duty, to throw off such government, and to provide new guards for their future security. Such has been the patient sufferance of these Colonies; and such is now the necessity which constrains them to alter their former systems of government. The history of the present King of Great Britain is a history of repeated injuries and usurpations, all having in direct object the establishment of an absolute tyranny over these States. To prove this, let facts be submitted to a candid world.

He has refused his assent to laws, the most wholesome and necessary for the public good.

He has forbidden his Governors to pass laws of immediate and pressing importance, unless suspended in their operation till his assent should be obtained; and when so suspended, he has utterly neglected to attend to them.

He has refused to pass other laws for the accommodation of large districts of people, unless those people would relinquish the right of representation in the Legislature, a right inestimable to them and formidable to tyrants only.

He has called together legislative bodies at places unusual, uncomfortable, and distant from the depository of their public records, for the sole purpose of fatiguing them into compliance with his measures.

He has dissolved representative houses repeatedly, for opposing with manly firmness his invasions on the rights of the people.

He has refused for a long time, after such dissolutions, to cause others to be elected; whereby the legislative powers, incapable of annihilation, have returned to the people at large for their exercise; the State remaining in the meantime exposed to all the dangers of invasion from without and convulsions within.

He has endeavoured to prevent the population of these states; for that purpose obstructing the laws of naturalization of foreigners; refusing to pass others to encourage their migration hither, and raising the conditions of new appropriations of lands.

He has obstructed the administration of justice, by refusing his assent to laws for establishing judiciary powers.

He has made judges dependent on his will alone, for the tenure of their offices, and the amount and payment of their salaries.

He has erected a multitude of new offices, and sent hither swarms of officers to harass our people, and eat out their substance.

He has kept among us, in times of peace, standing armies without the consent of our legislatures.

He has affected to render the military independent of and superior to the civil power.

He has combined with others to subject us to a jurisdiction foreign to our constitution, and unacknowledged by our laws; giving his assent to their acts of pretended legislation:

For quartering large bodies of armed troops among us:

For protecting them, by a mock trial, from punishment for any murders which they should commit on the inhabitants of these States:

For cutting off our trade with all parts of the world:

For imposing taxes on us without our consent:

For depriving us in many cases, of the benefits of trial by jury:

For transporting us beyond seas to be tried for pretended offences:

For abolishing the free system of English laws in a neighbouring Province, establishing therein an arbitrary government, and enlarging its boundaries so as to render it at once an example and fit instrument for introducing the same absolute rule into these Colonies:

For taking away our Charters, abolishing our most valuable laws, and altering fundamentally the forms of our governments:

For suspending our own Legislatures, and declaring themselves invested with power to legislate for us in all cases whatsoever.

He has abdicated government here, by declaring us out of his protection and waging war against us.

He has plundered our seas, ravaged our coasts, burnt our towns, and destroyed the lives of our people.

He is at this time transporting large armies of foreign mercenaries to complete the works of death, desolation, and tyranny, already begun with circumstances of cruelty and perfidy scarcely paralleled in the most barbarous ages, and totally unworthy the head of a civilized nation.

He has constrained our fellow citizens taken captive on the high seas to bear arms against their country, to become the executioners of their friends and brethren, or to fall themselves by their hands.

He has excited domestic insurrections amongst us, and has endeavoured to bring on the inhabitants of our frontiers, the merciless Indian savages, whose known rule of warfare, is an undistinguished destruction of all ages, sexes, and conditions.

In every state of these oppressions we have petitioned for redress in the most humble terms: our repeated petitions have been answered only by repeated injury. A prince whose character is thus marked by every act which may define a tyrant is unfit to be the ruler of a free people.

Nor have we been wanting in attention to our British brethren. We have warned them from time to time of attempts by their legislature to extend an unwarrantable jurisdiction over us. We have reminded them of the circumstances of our emigration and settlement here. We have appealed to their native justice and magnanimity, and we have conjured them by the ties of our common kindred to disavow these usurpations, which would inevitably interrupt our connections and correspondence. They too have been deaf to the voice of justice and of consanguinity. We must, therefore, acquiesce in the necessity, which denounces our separation, and hold them, as we hold the rest of mankind, enemies in war, in peace friends.

We, therefore, the Representatives of the United States of America, in General Congress assembled, appealing to the Supreme Judge of the world for the rectitude of our intentions, do, in the name, and by authority of the good people of these Colonies, solemnly publish and declare, That these United Colonies are, and of right ought to be Free and Independent States; that they are absolved from all allegiance to the British Crown, and that all political connection between them and the State of Great Britain, is and ought to be totally dissolved; and that as Free and Independent States, they have full power to levy war, conclude peace, contract alliances, establish commerce, and to do all other acts and things which Independent States may of right do. And for the support of this declaration, with a firm reliance on the protection of Divine Province, we mutually pledge to each other our lives, our fortunes, and our sacred honor.

$$\boxed{130}$$

The French Declaration of the Rights of Man and Citizen

The founding of the Republic of the United States of America provided a model for other peoples chafing under oppressive rule to emulate. Not surprisingly then, when the French movement to end political injustices turned to revolution in 1789 and the revolutionaries convened at the National Assembly, the Marquis de Lafayette (1757–1834), hero of the American Revolution, proposed a Declaration of the Rights of Man and Citizen. Lafayette had the American Declaration in

A Documentary History of the French Revolution, ed. John Hall Stewart (London: Macmillan, 1979).

mind, and he had the assistance of Thomas Jefferson, present in Paris as the first United States ambassador to France.

While the resulting document appealed to the French revolutionaries, the French were not able to start afresh as the Americans had done. In 1789 Louis XVI was still king of France: He could not be made to leave by a turn of phrase. Nor were men created equal in France in 1789. Those born into the nobility led lives different from those born into the Third Estate (the 99 percent of the population who were not nobility or clergy), and they had different legal rights as well. This disparity was precisely what the revolutionaries and the Declaration sought to change. Inevitably, though, such change would prove to be a more violent and revolutionary proposition than it had been in the American colonies.

In what ways did the Declaration of the Rights of Man and Citizen resemble the American Declaration of Independence? In what ways was it different? Which was more democratic?

Thinking Historically

The French Declaration is full of abstract, universal principles. But notice how such abstractions can claim our consent by their rationality without informing us as to how they will be implemented. What is meant by the first right, for instance? What does it mean to say that men are "born free"? Why is it necessary to distinguish between "born" and "remain"? What is meant by the phrase "general usefulness"? Do statements like these increase people's liberties, or are they intentionally vague so they can be interpreted at will?

The slogan of the French Revolution was "Liberty, Equality, Fraternity." Which of the rights in the French Declaration emphasize liberty, which equality? Can these two goals be opposed to each other? Explain how.

The representatives of the French people, organized in National Assembly, considering that ignorance, forgetfulness, or contempt of the rights of man are the sole causes of public misfortunes and of the corruption of governments, have resolved to set forth in a solemn declaration the natural, inalienable, and sacred rights of man, in order that such declaration, continually before all members of the social body, may be a perpetual reminder of their rights and duties; in order that the acts of the legislative power and those of the executive power may constantly be compared with the aim of every political institution and may accordingly be more respected; in order that the demands of the citizens, founded henceforth upon simple and incontestable principles, may always be directed towards the maintenance of the Constitution and the welfare of all.

Accordingly, the National Assembly recognizes and proclaims, in the presence and under the auspices of the Supreme Being, the following rights of man and citizen.

1. Men are born and remain free and equal in rights; social distinctions may be based only upon general usefulness.

2. The aim of every political association is the preservation of the natural and inalienable rights of man; these rights are liberty, property, security, and resistance to oppression.

3. The source of all sovereignty resides essentially in the nation; no group, no individual may exercise authority not emanating expressly therefrom.

4. Liberty consists of the power to do whatever is not injurious to others; thus the enjoyment of the natural rights of every man has for its limits only those that assure other members of society the enjoyment of those same rights; such limits may be determined only by law.

5. The law has the right to forbid only actions which are injurious to society. Whatever is not forbidden by law may not be prevented, and no one may be constrained to do what it does not prescribe.

6. Law is the expression of the general will; all citizens have the right to concur personally, or through their representatives, in its formation; it must be the same for all, whether it protects or punishes. All citizens, being equal before it, are equally admissible to all public offices, positions, and employments, according to their capacity, and without other distinction than that of virtues and talents.

7. No man may be accused, arrested, or detained except in the cases determined by law, and according to the forms prescribed thereby. Whoever solicit, expedite, or execute arbitrary orders, or have them executed, must be punished; but every citizen summoned or apprehended in pursuance of the law must obey immediately; he renders himself culpable by resistance.

8. The law is to establish only penalties that are absolutely and obviously necessary; and no one may be punished except by virtue of a law established and promulgated prior to the offence and legally applied.

9. Since every man is presumed innocent until declared guilty, if arrest be deemed indispensable, all unnecessary severity for securing the person of the accused must be severely repressed by law.

10. No one is to be disquieted because of his opinions, even religious, provided their manifestation does not disturb the public order established by law.

11. Free communication of ideas and opinions is one of the most precious of the rights of man. Consequently, every citizen may speak,

write, and print freely, subject to responsibility for the abuse of such liberty in the cases determined by law.

12. The guarantee of the rights of man and citizen necessitates a public force; therefore, is instituted for the advantage of all and not for the particular benefit of those to whom it is entrusted.

13. For the maintenance of the public force and for the expenses of administration a common tax is indispensable; it must be assessed equally on all citizens in proportion to their means.

14. Citizens have the right to ascertain, by themselves or through their representatives, the necessity of the public tax, to consent to it freely, to supervise its use, and to determine its quota, assessment, payment, and duration.

15. Society has the right to require of every public agent an accounting of his administration.

16. Every society in which the guarantee of rights is not assured or the separation of powers not determined has no constitution at all.

17. Since property is a sacred and inviolate right, no one may be deprived thereof unless a legally established public necessity obviously requires it, and upon condition of a just and previous indemnity.

$$\boxed{131}$$

MARY WOLLSTONECRAFT

A Vindication of the Rights of Woman

Mary Wollstonecraft (1759–1797) lived a short but influential life as a writer in England and France in the midst of the French Revolution. She wrote *A Vindication of the Rights of Woman* (1792) in response to the radical changes that were occurring in France. She also lent support to Thomas Paine's radical *Rights of Man* (1791) which challenged conservative Edmund Burke's critical *Reflections on the Revolution in France* (1790).

The American and French revolutions enshrined many of the ideas and much of the language of the eighteenth-century Enlightenment. The very success of these revolutions demonstrated the power of En-

Mary Wollstonecraft, *A Vindication of the Rights of Woman* (Boston: Peter Edes, 1792). Spelling Americanized.

lightenment ideas about freedom and equality and, thus, inspired other marginalized groups to wonder about their own rights. If all men were created equal, then what about slaves? If kings and their governments could be overthrown and replaced by the rule of "the people," why, then, did women have no power politically — they were people too, weren't they? Mary Wollstonecraft, sometimes called the first feminist, was one of those who wondered about this, and who took Enlightenment reasoning a step further.

The male thinkers of the Enlightenment had been content to declare the "rights of man" as sufficient protection for women, assuming that "man" stood for mankind. Wollstonecraft forced them to confront that when they declared that "all men" are created equal, they did not mean to include women. In fact, they believed that women did not have the same rational faculties as men, and that women were principally meant to attend to their appearance and the service of the naturally dominant sex. Wollstonecraft pointed out that women were trained by society to accept these insults as part of the "natural" state of things.

Modern feminists sometimes distinguish between two types of demands: political/legal and cultural. Generally political and legal demands are easier to identify and label — like the right to vote or the right to own property — and the only requirement for these rights to become available to women is that legislation be enacted. Cultural demands are often more subtle and complicated and require changes in the way people think. Which of Wollstonecraft's demands are political or legal? Which are cultural? Which of her demands have been realized since 1792? Which have not?

Thinking Historically

When Jefferson wrote that "all men are created equal," he was writing in the language of eighteenth-century enlightened universalism. But he did not imagine that any of his contemporaries would think the document included women or African slaves. Notice how Mary Wollstonecraft speaks of man in general in most of the first chapter and then turns to "men" in most of the rest of the selection. Why do you think she changes her focus from mankind to men?

In addition to the enormous differences between eighteenth-century and modern vocabulary and writing styles, both the questions and the answers of the eighteenth century were different from our own. Most people today would answer eighteenth-century questions very differently from the way they were answered then. If asked, few people today, for instance, would say that men alone should be educated. The idea that both men and women should be educated is an example of an idea that was new in 1792, but is now almost universally accepted. What other ideas does Wollstonecraft express that have since become fairly universal?

In addition, we no longer ask some of the questions that were asked in the eighteenth century. What examples do you see here of questions that are generally no longer asked? What other kinds of questions have we stopped asking? Why?

Chap. I. The Rights and Involved Duties of Mankind Considered

In the present state of society it appears necessary to go back to first principles in search of the most simple truths, and to dispute with some prevailing prejudice every inch of ground. To clear my way, I must be allowed to ask some plain questions, and the answers will probably appear as unequivocal as the axioms on which reasoning is built; though, when entangled with various motives of action, they are formally contradicted, either by the words or conduct of men.

In what does man's pre-eminence over the brute creation consist? The answer is as clear as that a half is less than the whole; in Reason.

What acquirement exalts one being above another? Virtue, we spontaneously reply.

For what purpose were the passions implanted? That man by struggling with them might attain a degree of knowledge denied to the brutes, whispers Experience.

Consequently the perfection of our nature and capability of happiness must be estimated by the degree of reason, virtue, and knowledge that distinguish the individual, and direct the laws which bind society: and that from the exercise of reason, knowledge and virtue naturally flow is equally undeniable, if mankind be viewed collectively.

The rights and duties of man thus simplified, it seems almost impertinent to attempt to illustrate truths that appear so incontrovertible; yet such deeply rooted prejudices have clouded reason, and such spurious qualities have assumed the name of virtues, that it is necessary to pursue the course of reason as it has been perplexed and involved in error, by various adventitious circumstances, comparing the simple axiom with casual deviations.

Men, in general, seem to employ their reason to justify prejudices, which they have imbibed, they cannot trace how, rather than to root them out. The mind must be strong that resolutely forms its own principles; for a kind of intellectual cowardice prevails which makes many men shrink from the task, or only do it by halves. Yet the imperfect conclusions thus drawn, are frequently very plausible, because they are built on partial experience, on just, though narrow, views. . . .

Chap. II. The Prevailing Opinion
of a Sexual Character Discussed

To account for, and excuse the tyranny of man, many ingenious arguments have been brought forward to prove, that the two sexes, in the acquirement of virtue, ought to aim at attaining a very different character: or, to speak explicitly, women are not allowed to have sufficient strength of mind to acquire what really deserves the name of virtue. Yet it should seem, allowing them to have souls, that there is but one way appointed by Providence to lead *mankind* to either virtue or happiness.

If then women are not a swarm of ephemeron triflers, why should they be kept in ignorance under the specious name of innocence? Men complain, and with reason, of the follies and caprices of our sex, when they do not keenly satirize our headstrong passions and groveling vices. Behold, I should answer, the natural effect of ignorance! The mind will ever be unstable that has only prejudices to rest on, and the current will run with destructive fury when there are no barriers to break its force. Women are told from their infancy, and taught by the example of their mothers, that a little knowledge of human weakness, justly termed cunning, softness of temper, *outward* obedience, and a scrupulous attention to a puerile kind of propriety, will obtain for them the protection of man; and should they be beautiful, every thing else is needless, for, at least, twenty years of their lives. . . .

How grossly do they insult us who thus advise us only to render ourselves gentle, domestic brutes! For instance, the winning softness so warmly, and frequently, recommended, that governs by obeying. What childish expressions, and how insignificant is the being — can it be an immortal one? who will condescend to govern by such sinister methods! "Certainly," says Lord Bacon,[1] "man is of kin to the beasts by his body; and if he be not of kin to God by his spirit, he is a base and ignoble creature!" Men, indeed, appear to me to act in a very unphilosophical manner when they try to secure the good conduct of women by attempting to keep them always in a state of childhood. . . .

Chap. IV. Observations on the State of Degradation
to Which Woman Is Reduced by Various Causes

. . . The power of generalizing ideas, of drawing comprehensive conclusions from individual observations, is the only acquirement, for an immortal being, that really deserves the name of knowledge. Merely to observe, without endeavoring to account for any thing, may (in a very

---

[1]Francis Bacon (1561–1626), English philosopher, writer, and statesman. [Ed.]

incomplete manner) serve as the common sense of life; but where is the store laid up that is to clothe the soul when it leaves the body?

This power has not only been denied to women; but writers have insisted that it is inconsistent, with a few exceptions, with their sexual character. Let men prove this, and I shall grant that woman only exists for man. I must, however, previously remark, that the power of generalizing ideas, to any great extent, is not very common amongst men or women. But this exercise is the true cultivation of the understanding; and every thing conspires to render the cultivation of the understanding more difficult in the female than the male world.

I am naturally led by this assertion to the main subject of the present chapter, and shall now attempt to point out some of the causes that degrade the sex, and prevent women from generalizing their observations. . . .

Ah! why do women, I write with affectionate solicitude, condescend to receive a degree of attention and respect from strangers, different from that reciprocation of civility which the dictates of humanity and the politeness of civilization authorize between man and man? And, why do they not discover, when "in the noon of beauty's power," that they are treated like queens only to be deluded by hollow respect, till they are led to resign, or not assume, their natural prerogatives? Confined then in cages like the feathered race, they have nothing to do but to plume themselves, and stalk with mock majesty from perch to perch. It is true they are provided with food and raiment, for which they neither toil nor spin; but health, liberty, and virtue, are given in exchange. But, where, amongst mankind has been found sufficient strength of mind to enable a being to resign these adventitious prerogatives; one who, rising with the calm dignity of reason above opinion, dared to be proud of the privileges inherent in man? And it is vain to expect it whilst hereditary power chokes the affections and nips reason in the bud. . . .

"I have endeavoured," says Lord Chesterfield,[2] "to gain the hearts of twenty women, whose persons I would not have given a fig for." . . .

I lament that women are systematically degraded by receiving the trivial attentions, which men think it manly to pay to the sex, when, in fact, they are insultingly supporting their own superiority. It is not condescension to bow to an inferior. So ludicrous, in fact, do these ceremonies appear to me, that I scarcely am able to govern my muscles, when I see a man start with eager, and serious solicitude to lift a handkerchief, or shut a door, when the *lady* could have done it herself, had she only moved a pace or two. . . .

---

[2]Philip Dormer Stanhope, fourth earl of Chesterfield (1694–1773), English statesman, diplomat, and wit. [Ed.]

Mankind, including every description, wish to be loved and respected for *something*; and the common herd will always take the nearest road to the completion of their wishes. The respect paid to wealth and beauty is the most certain, and unequivocal; and, of course, will always attract the vulgar eye of common minds. Abilities and virtues are absolutely necessary to raise men from the middle rank of life into notice; and the natural consequence is notorious; the middle rank contains most virtue and abilities. Men have thus, in one station, at least, an opportunity of exerting themselves with dignity, and of rising by the exertions which really improve a rational creature; but the whole female sex are, till their character is formed, in the same condition as the rich: for they are born, I now speak of a state of civilization, with certain sexual privileges, and whilst they are gratuitously granted them, few will ever think of works of supererogation,[3] to obtain the esteem of a small number of superior people. . . .

Women, commonly called Ladies, are not to be contradicted in company, are not allowed to exert any manual strength; and from them the negative virtues only are expected, when any virtues are expected, patience, docility, good-humor, and flexibility; virtues incompatible with any vigorous exertion of intellect. Besides, by living more with each other, and being seldom absolutely alone, they are more under the influence of sentiments than passions. Solitude and reflection are necessary to give to wishes the force of passions, and to enable the imagination to enlarge the object, and make it the most desirable. The same may be said of the rich; they do not sufficiently deal in general ideas, collected by impassioned thinking, or calm investigation, to acquire that strength of character on which great resolves are built.

Chap. XII. On National Education

The good effects resulting from attention to private education will ever be very confined, and the parent who really puts his own hand to the plow, will always, in some degree, be disappointed, till education becomes a grand national concern. A man cannot retire into a desert with his child, and if he did he could not bring himself back to childhood, and become the proper friend and play-fellow of an infant or youth. And when children are confined to the society of men and women, they very soon acquire that kind of premature manhood which stops the growth of every vigorous power of mind or body. In order to open their faculties they should be excited to think for themselves; and this

---

[3]More than is necessary. [Ed.]

can only be done by mixing a number of children together, and making them jointly pursue the same objects.

Let an enlightened nation then try what effect reason would have to bring them back to nature, and their duty; and allowing them to share the advantages of education and government with man, see whether they will become better, as they grow wiser and become free. They cannot be injured by the experiment; for it is not in the power of man to render them more insignificant than they are at present.

To render this practicable, day schools, for particular ages, should be established by government, in which boys and girls might be educated together. The school for the younger children, from five to nine years of age, ought to be absolutely free and open to all classes. . . .

After the age of nine, girls and boys, intended for domestic employments, or mechanical trades, ought to be removed to other schools, and receive instruction, in some measure appropriated to the destination of each individual, the two sexes being still together in the morning; but in the afternoon, the girls should attend a school, where plain-work, mantua-making, millinery, etc. would be their employment.

The young people of superior abilities, or fortune, might now be taught, in another school, the dead and living languages, the elements of science, and continue the study of history and politics, on a more extensive scale, which would not exclude polite literature.

Girls and boys still together? I hear some readers ask: yes. And I should not fear any other consequence than that some early attachment might take place; which, whilst it had the best effect on the moral character of the young people, might not perfectly agree with the views of the parents, for it will be a long time, I fear, before the world is so far enlightened that parents, only anxious to render their children virtuous, will let them choose companions for life themselves. . . .

In short, in whatever light I view the subject, reason and experience convince me that the only method of leading women to fulfill their peculiar duties, is to free them from all restraint by allowing them to participate in the inherent rights of mankind.

Make them free, and they will quickly become wise and virtuous, as men become more so; for the improvement must be mutual, or the injustice which one half of the human race are obliged to submit to, retorting on their oppressors, the virtue of man will be worm-eaten by the insect whom he keeps under his feet.

Let men take their choice, man and woman were made for each other, though not to become one being; and if they will not improve women, they will deprave them!

132

TOUSSAINT L'OUVERTURE
Letter to the Directory

When the French revolutionaries proclaimed the Declaration of the Rights of Man and Citizen in 1789, the French colony of Saint-Domingue[1] (now Haiti) contained a half million African slaves, most of whom worked on the sugar plantations that made France one of the richest countries in the world. Thus, the French were confronted with the difficult problem of reconciling their enlightened principles with the extremely profitable, but fundamentally unequal, institution of slavery.

French revolutionaries remained locked in debate about this issue when in 1791, the slaves of Saint-Domingue organized a revolt that culminated in establishing Haiti's national independence twelve years later. François Dominique Toussaint L'Ouverture,* a self-educated Haitian slave, led the revolt and the subsequent battles against the French planter class and French armies, as well as the Spanish forces of neighboring Santo Domingo, now the other half of the island known as the Dominican Republic and the antirevolutionary forces of Britain, all of whom vied for control of the island at the end of the eighteenth century.

At first Toussaint enjoyed the support of the revolutionary government in Paris; in the decree of 16 Pluviôse (1794) the National Convention abolished slavery in the colonies. But after 1795, the revolution turned on itself and Toussaint feared the new conservative government, called the Directory, might send troops to restore slavery on the island.

In 1797 he wrote the Directory the letter that follows. Notice how Toussaint negotiated a difficult situation. How did he try to reassure the government of his allegiance to France? At the same time, how did

---

[1]san doh MANG   Santo Domingo was the Spanish name for the eastern half of Hispaniola (now the Dominican Republic). Saint-Domingue was the French name for the western half of the island, now Haiti. San Domingo, which is used in the text, is a nineteenth-century abbreviation for Saint-Domingue. To further complicate matters, both the Spanish and French sometimes used their term for the whole island of Hispaniola. Spain controlled the entire island until 1697 when the Spanish recognized French control of the west. [Ed.]

*too SAN   loo vehr TUR

Toussaint L'Ouverture, "Letter to the Directory, November 5, 1797," in *The Black Jacobins*, ed. C. L. R. James (New York: Vintage Books, 1989), 195–97.

he attempt to convince the Directory that a return to slavery was unthinkable?

Thinking Historically

Notice how the author is torn between the ideals of the French Revolution and the interests of the people of Saint-Domingue. Where did Toussaint's true loyalty lie? At the time he wrote this letter events had not yet forced him to declare the independence of Saint-Domingue (Haiti); this would not happen until January 1, 1804. But, according to the letter, how and why did Toussaint regard the principles of the French Revolution as more important than his loyalty to France?

. . . The impolitic and incendiary discourse of Vaublanc has not affected the blacks nearly so much as their certainty of the projects which the proprietors of San Domingo are planning: insidious declarations should not have any effect in the eyes of wise legislators who have decreed liberty for the nations. But the attempts on that liberty which the colonists propose are all the more to be feared because it is with the veil of patriotism that they cover their detestable plans. We know that they seek to impose some of them on you by illusory and specious promises, in order to see renewed in this colony its former scenes of horror. Already perfidious emissaries have stepped in among us to ferment the destructive leaven prepared by the hands of liberticides. But they will not succeed. I swear it by all that liberty holds most sacred. My attachment to France, my knowledge of the blacks, make it my duty not to leave you ignorant either of the crimes which they meditate or the oath that we renew, to bury ourselves under the ruins of a country revived by liberty rather than suffer the return of slavery.

It is for you, Citizens Directors, to turn from over our heads the storm which the eternal enemies of our liberty are preparing in the shades of silence. It is for you to enlighten the legislature, it is for you to prevent the enemies of the present system from spreading themselves on our unfortunate shores to sully it with new crimes. Do not allow our brothers, our friends, to be sacrificed to men who wish to reign over the ruins of the human species. But no, your wisdom will enable you to avoid the dangerous snares which our common enemies hold out for you. . . .

I send you with this letter a declaration which will acquaint you with the unity that exists between the proprietors of San Domingo who are in France, those in the United States, and those who serve under the English banner. You will see there a resolution, unequivocal and carefully constructed, for the restoration of slavery; you will see there that their determination to succeed has led them to envelop themselves in the mantle of liberty in order to strike it more deadly blows. You will see that they are counting heavily on my complacency in lending myself to their perfidious views by my fear for my children. It is not astonishing that these men who sacrifice their country to their interests are unable to conceive how many sacrifices a true love of country can support in a better father than they, since I unhesitatingly base the happiness of my children on that of my country, which they and they alone wish to destroy.

I shall never hesitate between the safety of San Domingo and my personal happiness; but I have nothing to fear. It is to the solicitude of the French Government that I have confided my children. . . . I would tremble with horror if it was into the hands of the colonists that I had sent them as hostages; but even if it were so, let them know that in punishing them for the fidelity of their father, they would only add one degree more to their barbarism, without any hope of ever making me fail in my duty. . . . Blind as they are! They cannot see how this odious conduct on their part can become the signal of new disasters and irreparable misfortunes, and that far from making them regain what in their eyes liberty for all has made them lose, they expose themselves to a total ruin and the colony to its inevitable destruction. Do they think that men who have been able to enjoy the blessing of liberty will calmly see it snatched away? They supported their chains only so long as they did not know any condition of life more happy than that of slavery. But to-day when they have left it, if they had a thousand lives they would sacrifice them all rather than be forced into slavery again. But no, the same hand which has broken our chains will not enslave us anew. France will not revoke her principles, she will not withdraw from us the greatest of her benefits. She will protect us against all our enemies; she will not permit her sublime morality to be perverted, those principles which do her most honour to be destroyed, her most beautiful achievement to be degraded, and her Decree of 16 Pluviôse which so honours humanity to be revoked. *But if, to re-establish slavery in San Domingo, this was done, then I declare to you it would be to attempt the impossible: we have known how to face dangers to obtain our liberty, we shall know how to brave death to maintain it.*

This, Citizens Directors, is the morale of the people of San Domingo, those are the principles that they transmit to you by me.

My own you know. It is sufficient to renew, my hand in yours, the oath that I have made, to cease to live before gratitude dies in my heart, before I cease to be faithful to France and to my duty, before the god of liberty is profaned and sullied by the liberticides, before they can snatch from my hands that sword, those arms, which France confided to me for the defence of its rights and those of humanity, for the triumph of liberty and equality.

133

SIMÓN BOLÍVAR
A Constitution for Venezuela

As we have seen, the Enlightenment principles of reason, human rights, and equality ignited revolutions on both sides of the Atlantic. In Europe, these revolutions overturned kings and tyrannies, marshaling national citizen armies and creating parliamentary democracies. In the American colonies, the revolutions took shape as anticolonial struggles for independence. Sometimes the effort to create both an independent nation *and* a democracy proved overwhelming.

Simón Bolívar* (1783–1830), called "the Liberator," successfully led the Latin American revolution for independence from Spain between 1810 and 1824. (See Map 20.1.) In 1819, he became president of Venezuela and of what is today Colombia, Ecuador, and Panama, and he gave the speech on the Constitution of Venezuela that follows.

What does Bolívar see as the difference between the independence of Spanish-American colonies and that of the American colonies? What does he mean when he says that Latin Americans have been denied "domestic tyranny"? Would you call Bolívar a "democrat"? Is he more or less democratic than the French or North American revolutionaries? What kind of society do you think would result from the constitution he envisions?

Thinking Historically

How does Bolívar characterize the revolutionary population of South America? How does he think this population differs from the North American revolutionaries? What do you think accounts for this difference?

In what ways did the revolutionaries of South America, North America, and France see their problems and needs differently? How did Bolívar propose to solve what he perceived to be the unique problems of South America? What do you think of his solution?

*see MOHN   boh LEE vahr

Selected Writings of Bolívar, comp. Vincent Lecuna, ed. Harold A. Bierck Jr., 2 vols. (New York: Colonial Press, 1951), 175–91.

Map 20.1   Latin American Independence, 1804–1830

Let us review the past to discover the base upon which the Republic of Venezuela is founded.

America, in separating from the Spanish monarchy, found herself in a situation similar to that of the Roman Empire when its enormous framework fell to pieces in the midst of the ancient world. Each Roman division then formed an independent nation in keeping with its location or interests; but this situation differed from America's in that those members proceeded to reestablish their former associations. We, on the contrary, do not even retain the vestiges of our original being. We are not Europeans; we are not Indians; we are but a mixed species of aborigines and Spaniards. Americans by birth and Europeans by law, we find ourselves engaged in a dual conflict: We are disputing with the natives for titles of ownership, and at the same time we are struggling to maintain ourselves in the country that gave us birth against the opposition of the invaders. Thus our position is most extraordinary and complicated. But there is more. As our role has always been strictly passive and political existence nil, we find that our quest for liberty is now even more difficult of accomplishment; for we, having been placed in a state lower than slavery, had been robbed not only of our freedom but also of the right to exercise an active domestic tyranny. Permit me to explain this paradox.

In absolute systems, the central power is unlimited. The will of the despot is the supreme law, arbitrarily enforced by subordinates who take part in the organized oppression in proportion to the authority that they wield. They are charged with civil, political, military, and religious functions; but, in the final analysis, the satraps of Persia are Persian, the pashas of the Grand Turk are Turks, and the sultans of Tartary are Tartars. China does not seek her mandarins in the homeland of Genghis Khan, her conqueror. America, on the contrary, received everything from Spain, who, in effect, deprived her of the experience that she would have gained from the exercise of an active tyranny by not allowing her to take part in her own domestic affairs and administration. This exclusion made it impossible for us to acquaint ourselves with the management of public affairs; nor did we enjoy that personal consideration, of such great value in major revolutions, that the brilliance of power inspires in the eyes of the multitude. In brief, Gentlemen, we were deliberately kept in ignorance and cut off from the world in all matters relating to the science of government.

Subject to the three-fold yoke of ignorance, tyranny, and vice, the American people have been unable to acquire knowledge, power, or [civic] virtue. The lessons we received and the models we studied, as pupils of such pernicious teachers, were most destructive. We have been ruled more by deceit than by force, and we have been degraded more by vice than by superstition. Slavery is the daughter of darkness: An ignorant people is a blind instrument of its own destruction. Ambition and intrigue abuse the credulity and experience of men lacking all political, economic, and civic knowledge; they adopt pure illusion as reality; they take license for liberty, treachery for patriotism, and vengeance for justice. This situation is similar to that of the robust blind man who, beguiled by his strength, strides forward with all the assurance of one who can see, but, upon hitting every variety of obstacle, finds himself unable to retrace his steps.

If a people, perverted by their training, succeed in achieving their liberty, they will soon lose it, for it would be of no avail to endeavor to explain to them that happiness consists in the practice of virtue; that the rule of law is more powerful than the rule of tyrants, because, as the laws are more inflexible, every one should submit to their beneficent austerity; that proper morals, and not force, are the bases of law; and that to practice justice is to practice liberty. Therefore, Legislators, your work is so much the more arduous, inasmuch as you have to reeducate men who have been corrupted by erroneous illusions and false incentives. Liberty, says Rousseau, is a succulent morsel, but one difficult to digest. Our weak fellow-citizens will have to strengthen their spirit greatly before they can digest the wholesome nutriment of freedom. Their limbs benumbed by chains, their sight dimmed by the darkness of dungeons, and their strength sapped by the pestilence of servitude, are they capable of marching toward the august temple of Liberty without faltering? Can they come near enough to bask in its brilliant rays and to breathe freely the pure air which reigns therein? . . .

The more I admire the excellence of the federal Constitution of Venezuela, the more I am convinced of the impossibility of its application to our state. And to my way of thinking, it is a marvel that its prototype in North America endures so successfully and has not been overthrown at the first sign of adversity or danger. Although the people of North America are a singular model of political virtue and moral rectitude; although the nation was cradled in liberty, reared on freedom, and maintained by liberty alone; and — I must reveal everything — although those people, so lacking in many respects, are unique in the history of mankind, it is a marvel, I repeat, that so weak and complicated a government as the federal system has managed to govern them in the difficult and trying circumstances of their past. But, regardless of the effectiveness of this form of government with respect to North America, I must say that it has never for a moment entered my mind to compare the position and character of two states as dissimilar as the English-American and the Spanish-American. Would it not be most difficult to apply to Spain the English system of political, civil, and religious liberty? Hence, it would be even more difficult to adapt to Venezuela the laws of North America. Does not *L'Esprit des Lois* state that laws should be suited to the people for whom they are made; that it would be a major coincidence if those of one nation could be adapted to another; that laws must take into account the physical conditions of the country, climate, character of the land, location, size, and mode of living of the people; that they should be in keeping with the degree of liberty that the Constitution can sanction respecting the religion of the inhabitants, their inclinations, resources, number, commerce, habits, and customs? This is the code we must consult, not the code of Washington! . . .

Venezuela had, has, and should have a republican government. Its principles should be the sovereignty of the people, division of powers, civil liberty, proscription of slavery, and the abolition of monarchy and privileges. We need equality to recast, so to speak, into a unified nation, the classes of men, political opinions, and public customs.

Among the ancient and modern nations, Rome and Great Britain are the most outstanding. Both were born to govern and to be free and both were built not on ostentatious forms of freedom, but upon solid institutions. Thus I recommend to you, Representatives, the study of the British Constitution, for that body of laws appears destined to bring about the greatest possible good for the peoples that adopt it; but, however perfect it may be, I am by no means proposing that you imitate it slavishly. When I speak of the British government, I only refer to its republican features; and, indeed, can a political system be labelled a monarchy when it recognizes popular sovereignty, division and balance of powers, civil liberty, freedom of conscience and of press, and all that is politically sublime? Can there be more liberty in any other type of republic? Can more be asked of any society? I commend this Constitution to you as that most worthy of serving as model for those who aspire to the enjoyment of the rights of man and who seek all the political happiness which is compatible with the frailty of human nature.

Nothing in our fundamental laws would have to be altered were we to adopt a legislative power similar to that held by the British Parliament. Like the North Americans, we have divided national representation into two chambers; that of Representatives and the Senate. The first is very wisely constituted. It enjoys all its proper functions, and it requires no essential revision, because the Constitution, in creating it, gave it the form and powers which the people deemed necessary in order that they might be legally and properly represented. If the Senate were hereditary rather than elective, it would, in my opinion, be the basis, the tie, the very soul of our republic. In political storms this body would arrest the thunderbolts of the government and would repel any violent popular reaction. Devoted to the government because of a natural interest in its own preservation, a hereditary senate would always oppose any attempt on the part of the people to infringe upon the jurisdiction and authority of their magistrates. It must be confessed that most men are unaware of their best interests, and that they constantly endeavor to assail them in the hands of their custodians — the individual clashes with the mass, and the mass with authority. It is necessary, therefore, that in all governments there be a neutral body to protect the injured and disarm the offender. To be neutral, this body must not owe its origin to appointment by the government or to election by the people, if it is to enjoy a full measure of independence which neither fears nor expects anything from these two sources of authority. The hereditary senate, as a part of the people, shares its interests, its sentiments, and its spirit. For this reason it should not be presumed that a hereditary senate would ignore the interests of the people or forget its legislative duties. The senators in Rome and in the House of Lords in London have been the strongest pillars upon which the edifice of political and civil liberty has rested.

At the outset, these senators should be elected by Congress. The successors to this Senate must command the initial attention of the government, which should educate them in a *colegio* designed especially to train these guardians and future legislators of the nation. They ought to

learn the arts, sciences, and letters that enrich the mind of a public figure. From childhood they should understand the career for which they
have been destined by Providence, and from earliest youth they should
prepare their minds for the dignity that awaits them.

The creation of a hereditary senate would in no way be a violation
of political equality. I do not solicit the establishment of a nobility, for
as a celebrated republican has said, that would simultaneously destroy
equality and liberty. What I propose is an office for which the candidates must prepare themselves, an office that demands great knowledge
and the ability to acquire such knowledge. All should not be left to
chance and the outcome of elections. The people are more easily deceived than is Nature perfected by art; and, although these senators, it
is true, would not be bred in an environment that is all virtue, it is
equally true that they would be raised in an atmosphere of enlightened
education. Furthermore, the liberators of Venezuela are entitled to occupy forever a high rank in the Republic that they have brought into
existence. I believe that posterity would view with regret the effacement
of the illustrious names of its first benefactors. I say, moreover, that it
is a matter of public interest and national honor, of gratitude on
Venezuela's part, to honor gloriously, until the end of time, a race of
virtuous, prudent, and persevering men who, overcoming every obstacle, have founded the Republic at the price of the most heroic sacrifices. And if the people of Venezuela do not applaud the elevation of
their benefactors, then they are unworthy to be free, and they will never
be free.

A hereditary senate, I repeat, will be the fundamental basis of the
legislative power, and therefore the foundation of the entire government. It will also serve as a counterweight to both government and
people; and as a neutral power it will weaken the mutual attacks of
these two eternally rival powers. In all conflicts the calm reasoning of a
third party will serve as the means of reconciliation. Thus the Venezue-
lan senate will give strength to this delicate political structure, so sensitive to violent repercussions; it will be the mediator that will lull the
storms and it will maintain harmony between the head and the other
parts of the political body.

REFLECTIONS

The Enlightenment and its political legacies — secular order and revolutionary republicanism — were European in origin but global in impact. In this chapter, we have touched on just a few of the crosscurrents
of what some historians call an "Atlantic Revolution." A tide of revolutionary fervor swept through France, the United States, and Latin

America, found sympathy in Russia in 1825, and echoed in the Muslim heartland, resulting in secular, modernizing regimes in Turkey and Egypt in the next century.

The appeal of the Enlightenment, of rationally ordered society, and of democratic government continues. Elements of this eighteenth-century revolution — the rule of law; regular, popular elections of representatives; the separation of church and state, of government and politics, and of civil and military authority — are widely recognized ideals and emerging global realities. Like science, the principles of the Enlightenment are universal in their claims and often seem universal in their appeal. Nothing is simpler, more rational, or easier to follow than a call to reason, law, liberty, justice, or equality. And yet every society has evolved its own guidelines under different circumstances, often with lasting results. France had its king and still has a relatively centralized state. The United States began with slavery and still suffers from racism. South American states became free of Europe only to dominate Native Americans, and they continue to do so. One democratic society has a king, another a House of Lords, another a national church. Are these different adaptations of the Enlightenment ideal? Or are these examples of incomplete revolution, cases of special interests allowing their governments to fall short of principle?

The debate continues today as more societies seek to realize responsive, representative government and the rule of law while oftentimes respecting conflicting traditions. Muslim countries and Israel struggle with the competing demands of secular law and religion, citizenship and communalism. Former communist countries adopt market economies and struggle with traditions of collective support and the appeal of individual liberty.

Perhaps these are conflicts within the Enlightenment tradition itself. How is it possible to have both liberty and equality? How can we claim inalienable rights on the basis of a secular, scientific creed? How does a faith in human reason lead to revolution? And how can ideas of order or justice avoid the consequences of history and human nature?

The great revolutionary declarations of the Enlightenment embarrass the modern skeptic with their naïve faith in natural laws, their universal prescriptions to cure all ills, and their hypocritical avoidance of slaves, women, and the colonized. The selections by Diderot, Toussaint, and Wollstonecraft, however, remind us that Enlightenment universalism was based not only on cool reason and calculation and the blind arrogance of the powerful. At least some of the great Enlightenment thinkers based their global prescription on the *felt* needs, even the sufferings, of others. For Diderot, Toussaint, and perhaps especially, Wollstonecraft, the recognition of human commonality began with a capacity for empathy that the Enlightenment may have bequeathed to the modern world.

21

Capitalism and the Industrial Revolution

Europe and the World, 1750–1900

HISTORICAL CONTEXT

Two principal forces have shaped the modern world: capitalism and the industrial revolution. As influential as the transformations discussed in Chapters 19 and 20 (the rise of science and the democratic revolution), these two forces are sometimes considered to be one and the same, because the industrial revolution occurred first in capitalist countries such as England, Belgium, and the United States. In fact, the rise of capitalism preceded the industrial revolution by centuries.

Capitalism denotes a particular economic organization of a society, whereas *industrial revolution* refers to a particular transformation of technology. Specifically, in capitalism market forces (supply and demand) set money prices that determine how goods are distributed. Before 1500, most economic behavior was regulated by family, religion, tradition, and political authority rather than by markets. Increasingly after 1500 in Europe, feudal dues were converted into money rents, periodic fairs became institutionalized, banks were established, modern bookkeeping procedures were developed, and older systems of inherited economic status were loosened. After 1800, new populations of urban workers had to work for money to buy food and shelter; after 1850 even clothing had to be purchased in the new "department stores." By 1900, the market had become the operating metaphor of society: One sold oneself; everything had its price. Viewed positively, a capitalist society is one in which buyers and sellers, who together compose the market, make most decisions about the production and distribution of resources. Viewed less favorably, it is the capitalists — those who own the resources of the society — who make the decisions about production and distribution. The democratic process of one person, one vote is supplanted by one dollar, one vote.

The industrial revolution made mass production possible with the use of power-driven machines. Mills driven by waterwheels existed in ancient times, but the construction of identical, replaceable machinery — the machine production of machines — revolutionized industry and enabled the coordination of production on a vast scale, occurring first in England's cotton textile mills at the end of the eighteenth century. The market for such textiles was capitalist, though the demand for many early mass-produced goods, such as muskets and uniforms, was government-driven.

The origins of capitalism are hotly debated among historians. Because the world's first cities, five thousand years ago, created markets, merchants, money, and private ownership of capital, some historians refer to an ancient capitalism. In this text, *capitalism* refers to those societies whose markets, merchants, money, and private ownership became central to the way society operated. As such, ancient Mesopotamia, Rome, and Sung dynasty China, which had extensive markets and paper money a thousand years ago, were not among the first capitalist societies. Smaller societies in which commercial interests and merchant classes took hold to direct political and economic matters were the capitalist forerunners. Venice, Florence, Holland, and England, the mercantile states of the fifteenth to seventeenth centuries, exemplify *commercial capitalism* or mercantile capitalism. Thus, the shift to industrial capitalism was more than a change in scale; it was also a transition from a trade-based economy to a manufacturing-based economy, a difference that meant an enormous increase in productivity, profits, and prosperity.

THINKING HISTORICALLY
Distinguishing Causes of Change

Because industry and capitalism are so closely associated, it is difficult to distinguish the effects of one from the other. Still, such a distinction is necessary if we are to understand historical change.

Try to make an analytical distinction between capitalism and industrialization, even when the sources in this chapter do not. By determining what changes can be attributed to each, you will come to understand the changes that capitalism and industrialization might bring to other societies and the impact they may have had in other time periods.

134

ARNOLD PACEY

Asia and the Industrial Revolution

Here a modern historian of technology demonstrates how Indian and East Asian manufacturing techniques were assimilated by Europeans, particularly by the English successors of the Mughal Empire, providing a boost to the industrial revolution in Britain. In what ways was Indian technology considered superior prior to the industrial revolution? How did European products gain greater markets than those of India?

Thinking Historically

Notice how the author distinguishes between capitalism and the industrial revolution. Was India more industrially advanced than capitalistic? Did the British conquest of India benefit more from capitalism, industry, or something else?

Deindustrialization

During the eighteenth century, India participated in the European industrial revolution through the influence of its textile trade, and through the investments in shipping made by Indian bankers and merchants. Developments in textiles and shipbuilding constituted a significant industrial movement, but it would be wrong to suggest that India was on the verge of its own industrial revolution. There was no steam engine in India, no coal mines, and few machines. . . . [E]xpanding industries were mostly in coastal areas. Much of the interior was in economic decline, with irrigation works damaged and neglected as a result of the breakup of the Mughal Empire and the disruption of war. Though political weakness in the empire had been evident since 1707, and a Persian army heavily defeated Mughal forces at Delhi in 1739, it was the British who most fully took advantage of the collapse of the empire. Between 1757 and 1803, they took control of most of India except the Northwest. The result was that the East India Company now administered major sectors of the economy, and quickly reduced the role of the big Indian bankers by changes in taxes and methods of collecting them.

Arnold Pacey, *Technology in World Civilization* (Cambridge: MIT Press, 1990), 128–35.

Meanwhile, India's markets in Europe were being eroded by competition from machine-spun yarns and printed calicoes made in Lancashire, and high customs duties were directed against Indian imports into Britain. Restrictions were also placed on the use of Indian-built ships for voyages to England. From 1812, there were extra duties on any imports they delivered, and that must be one factor in the decline in shipbuilding. A few Indian ships continued to make the voyage to Britain, however, and there was one in Liverpool Docks in 1839 when Herman Melville arrived from America. It was the *Irrawaddy* from Bombay and Melville commented: "Forty years ago, these merchantmen were nearly the largest in the world; and they still exceed the generality." They were "wholly built by the native shipwrights of India, who . . . surpassed the European artisans." Melville further commented on a point which an Indian historian confirms, that the coconut fibre rope used for rigging on most Indian ships was too elastic and needed constant attention. Thus the rigging on the *Irrawaddy* was being changed for hemp rope while it was in Liverpool. Sisal rope was an alternative in India, used with advantage on some ships based at Calcutta.

Attitudes to India changed markedly after the subcontinent had fallen into British hands. Before this, travellers found much to admire in technologies ranging from agriculture to metallurgy. After 1803, however, the arrogance of conquest was reinforced by the rapid development of British industry. This meant that Indian techniques which a few years earlier seemed remarkable could now be equalled at much lower cost by British factories. India was then made to appear rather primitive, and the idea grew that its proper role was to provide raw materials for western industry, including raw cotton and indigo dye, and to function as a market for British goods. This policy was reflected in 1813 by a relaxation of the East India Company's monopoly of trade so that other British companies could now bring in manufactured goods freely for sale in India. Thus the textile industry, iron production, and shipbuilding were all eroded by cheap imports from Britain, and by handicaps placed on Indian merchants.

By 1830, the situation had become so bad that even some of the British in India began to protest. One exclaimed, "We have destroyed the manufactures of India," pleading that there should be some protection for silk weaving, "the last of the expiring manufactures of India." Another observer was alarmed by a "commercial revolution" which produced "so much present suffering to numerous classes in India."

The question that remains is the speculative one of what might have happened if a strong Mughal government had survived. Fernand Braudel argues that although there was no lack of "capitalism" in India, the economy was not moving in the direction of home-grown industrialization. The historian of technology inevitably notes the lack of development of machines, even though there had been some increase in the use of water-wheels during the eighteenth century both in the iron industry and at gunpowder mills. However, it is impossible not to be struck by the achievements of the shipbuilding industry, which produced skilled carpenters and a model of large-scale organizations. It also trained up draughtsmen and people with mechanical interests. It is striking that one of the Wadia shipbuilders installed gas lighting in his home in 1834 and built a small foundry in which he made parts for steam engines. Given an independent and more prosperous India, it is difficult not to believe that a response to British industrialization might well have taken the form of a spread of skill and innovation from the shipyards into other industries.

As it was, such developments were delayed until the 1850s and later, when the first mechanized cotton mill opened. It is significant that some of the entrepreneurs who backed the development of this industry were from the same Parsi families as had built ships in Bombay and invested in overseas trade in the eighteenth century.

Guns and Rails: Asia, Britain, and America

Asian Stimulus

Britain's "conquest" of India cannot be attributed to superior armaments. Indian armies were also well equipped. More significant was the prior breakdown of Mughal government and the collaboration of many Indians. Some victories were also the result of good discipline and bold strategy, especially when Arthur Wellesley, the future Duke of Wellington, was in command. Wellesley's contribution also illustrates the distinctive western approach to the organizational aspect of technology. Indian armies might have had good armament, but because their guns were made in a great variety of different sizes, precise weapons drill was impossible and the supply of shot to the battlefield was unnecessarily complicated. By contrast, Wellesley's forces standardized on just three sizes of field gun, and the commander himself paid close attention to the design of gun carriages and to the bullocks which hauled them, so that his artillery could move as fast as his infantry, and without delays due to wheel breakages.

Significantly, the one major criticism regularly made of Indian artillery concerned the poor design of gun carriages. Many, particularly before 1760, were little better than four-wheeled trolleys. But the guns themselves were often of excellent design and workmanship. Whilst some were imported and others were made with the assistance of foreign craftworkers, there was many a brass cannon and mortar of Indian design, as well as heavy muskets for camel-mounted troops. Captured field guns were often taken over for use by the British, and after capturing ninety guns in one crucial battle, Wellesley wrote that seventy were "the finest brass ordnance I have ever seen." They were probably made in northern India, perhaps at the great Mughal arsenal at Agra.

Whilst Indians had been making guns from brass since the sixteenth century, Europeans could at first only produce this alloy in relatively small quantities because they had no technique for smelting zinc. By the eighteenth century, however, brass was being produced in large quantities in Europe, and brass cannon were being cast at Woolwich Arsenal near London. Several European countries were importing metallic zinc from China for this purpose. However, from 1743 there was a smelter near Bristol in England producing zinc, using coke[1] as fuel, and zinc smelters were also developed in Germany. At the end of the century, Britain's imports of zinc from the Far East were only about forty tons per year. Nevertheless, a British party which visited China in 1797 took particular note of zinc smelting methods. These were similar to the process used in India, which involved vaporizing the metal and then condensing it. There is a suspicion that the Bristol smelting works of 1743 was based on Indian practice, although the possibility of independent invention cannot be excluded.

A much clearer example of the transfer of technology from India occurred when British armies on the subcontinent encountered rockets, a type of weapon of which they had no previous experience. The basic technology had come from the Ottoman Turks or from Syria before 1500, although the Chinese had invented rockets even earlier. In the 1790s, some Indian armies included very large infantry units equipped with rockets. French mercenaries in Mysore had learned to make them, and the British Ordnance Office was enquiring for somebody with expertise on the subject. In response, William Congreve, whose father was head of the laboratory at Woolwich Arsenal, undertook to design a rocket on Indian lines. After a successful demonstration, about two hundred of his rockets were used by the British in an attack on Boulogne in 1806. Fired from over a kilometre away, they set fire to the town. After this success, rockets were adopted quite widely by European armies, though some commanders, notably the Duke of Wellington, frowned on such imprecise weapons, and they tended to drop out of use later in the century. What happened next, however, was typical of the whole British relationship with India. William Congreve set up a factory to manufacture the weapons in 1817, and part of its output was exported to India to equip rocket troops operating there under British command.

Yet another aspect of Asian technology in which eighteenth-century Europeans were interested was the design of farm implements. Reports on seed drills and ploughs were sent to the British Board of Agriculture from India in 1795. A century earlier the Dutch had found much of

---

[1]Fuel from soft coal. [Ed.]

interest in ploughs and winnowing machines of a Chinese type which they saw in Java. Then a Swedish party visiting Guangzhou (Canton) took a winnowing machine back home with them. Indeed, several of these machines were imported into different parts of Europe, and similar devices for cleaning threshed grain were soon being made there. The inventor of one of them, Jonas Norberg, admitted that he got "the initial idea" from three machines "brought here from China," but had to create a new type because the Chinese machines "do not suit our kinds of grain." Similarly, the Dutch saw that the Chinese plough did not suit their type of soil, but it stimulated them to produce new designs with curved metal mould-boards in contrast to the less efficient flat wooden boards used in Europe hitherto.

In most of these cases, and especially with zinc smelting, rockets, and winnowing machines, we have clear evidence of Europeans studying Asian technology in detail. With rockets and winnowers, though perhaps not with zinc, there was an element of imitation in the European inventions which followed. In other instances, however, the more usual course of technological dialogue between Europe and Asia was that European innovation was challenged by the quality or scale of Asian output, but took a different direction, as we have seen in many aspects of the textile industry. Sometimes, the dialogue was even more limited, and served mainly to give confidence in a technique that was already known. Such was the case with occasional references to China in the writings of engineers designing suspension bridges in Britain. The Chinese had a reputation for bridge construction, and before 1700 Peter the Great had asked for bridge-builders to be sent from China to work in Russia. Later, several books published in Europe described a variety of Chinese bridges, notably a long-span suspension bridge made with iron chains.

Among those who developed the suspension bridge in the West were James Finley in America, beginning in 1801, and Samuel Brown and Thomas Telford in Britain. About 1814, Brown devised a flat, wrought-iron chain link which Telford later used to form the main structural chains in his suspension bridges. But beyond borrowing this specific technique, what Telford needed was evidence that the suspension principle was applicable to the problem he was then tackling. Finley's two longest bridges had spanned seventy-four and ninety-three metres, over the Merrimac and Schuylkill Rivers in the eastern United States. Telford was aiming to span almost twice the larger distance with his 176-metre Menai Bridge. Experiments at a Shropshire ironworks gave confidence in the strength of the chains. But Telford may have looked for reassurance even further afield. One of his notebooks contains the reminder, "Examine Chinese bridges." It is clear from the wording which follows that he had seen a recent booklet advocating a "bridge of chains," partly based on a Chinese example, to cross the Firth of Forth in Scotland.

135

ADAM SMITH

From The Wealth of Nations

An Inquiry into the Nature and Causes of the Wealth of Nations
might justly be called the bible of free-market capitalism. Written in
1776 in the context of the British (and European) debate over the
proper role of government in the economy, Smith's work takes aim at
mercantilism, or government supervision of the economy. Mercan-
tilists believed that national economies required government assistance and direction to prosper.

Smith argues that free trade will produce greater wealth than mer-
cantilist trade and that free markets allocate resources more efficiently
than the government. His notion of *laissez-faire* (literally "let do")
capitalism assumes neither that capitalists are virtuous nor that governments should absent themselves entirely from the economy. However, Smith does believe that the greed of capitalists generally negates
itself and produces results that are advantageous to, but unimagined
by, the individual. "It is not from the benevolence of the butcher, the
brewer, or the baker, that we expect our dinner," Smith wrote, "but
from their regard of their own interest. We address ourselves not to
their humanity, but to their self-love, and never talk to them of our
own necessities, but of their advantage."[1] Each person seeks to maxi-
mize his or her own gain, thereby creating an efficient market in
which the cost of goods is instantly adjusted to exploit changes in supply and demand, while the market provides what is needed at the
price people are willing to pay "as if by an invisible hand."

What would Smith say to a farmer or manufacturer who wanted to
institute tariffs or quotas to limit the number of cheaper imports entering the country and to minimize competition? What would he say
to a government official who wanted to protect an important domestic industry? What would he say to a worker who complained about
low wages or boring work?

[1]Book I, chapter 2.

Adam Smith, *The Wealth of Nations* (London: Everyman's Library, M. Dent & Sons, Ltd., 1910).

Thinking Historically

The Wealth of Nations was written in defense of free capitalism at a moment when the industrial revolution was just beginning. Some elements of Smith's writing suggest a preindustrial world, as in the quotation about the butcher, brewer, and baker mentioned earlier. Still, Smith was aware how new industrial methods were transforming age-old labor relations and manufacturing processes. In some respects, Smith recognized that capitalism could create wealth, not just redistribute it, because he appreciated the potential of industrial technology.

As you read this selection, note when Smith is discussing capitalism, the economic system, and the power of the new industrial technology. In his discussion of the division of labor, what relationship does Smith see between the development of a capitalistic market and the rise of industrial technology? According to Smith, what is the relationship between money and industry, and which is more important? What would Smith think about a "postindustrial" or "service" economy in which few workers actually make products? What would he think of a prosperous country that imported more than it exported?

Book I: Of the Causes of Improvement in the Productive Powers of Labour, and of the Order According to Which Its Produce Is Naturally Distributed among the Different Ranks of the People

Chapter 1: Of the Division of Labour

The greatest improvement in the productive powers of labour, and the greater part of the skill, dexterity, and judgment with which it is anywhere directed, or applied, seem to have been the effects of the division of labour.

The effects of the division of labour, in the general business of society, will be more easily understood by considering in what manner it operates in some particular manufactures. . . .

To take an example, therefore, from a very trifling manufacture; but one in which the division of labour has been very often taken notice of, the trade of the pin-maker; a workman not educated to this business (which the division of labour has rendered a distinct trade), nor acquainted with the use of the machinery employed in it (to the invention of which the same division of labour has probably given occasion), could scarce, perhaps, with his utmost industry, make one pin in a day, and certainly could not make twenty. But in the way in which this business is now carried on, not only the whole work is a peculiar trade, but it is divided into a number of branches, of which the greater part are likewise peculiar trades. One man draws out the wire, another straights it, a third cuts it, a fourth points it, a fifth grinds it at the top for receiving the head; to make the head requires two or three distinct operations; to put it on is a peculiar business, to whiten the pins is another; it is even a trade by itself to put them into the paper; and the important business of making a pin is, in this manner, divided into about eighteen distinct operations, which, in some manufactories, are all performed by distinct hands, though in others the same man will sometimes perform two or three of them. I have seen a small manufactory of this kind where ten men only were employed, and where some of them consequently performed two or three distinct operations. But though they were very poor, and therefore but indifferently accommodated with the necessary machinery, they could, when they exerted themselves, make among them about twelve pounds of pins in a day. There are in a pound upwards of four thousand pins of a middling size. Those ten persons, therefore, could make among them upwards of forty-eight thousand pins in a day. Each person, therefore, making a tenth part of forty-eight thousand pins, might be considered as making four thousand eight hundred pins in a day. But if they had all wrought separately and independently, and without any of them having been educated to this peculiar business, they certainly could not each of them have made twenty, perhaps not one pin in a day; that is, certainly, not the two hundred and fortieth, perhaps not the four thousand eight hundredth part of what they are at present capable of performing, in consequence of a proper division and combination of their different operations.

In every other art and manufacture, the effects of the division of labour are similar to what they are in this very trifling one; though, in many of them, the labour can neither be so much subdivided, nor reduced to so great a simplicity of operation. . . .

Chapter 3: That the Division of Labour Is Limited by the Extent of the Market

As it is the power of exchanging that gives occasion to the division of labour, so the extent of this division must always be limited by the extent of that power, or, in other words, by the extent of the market. When the market is very small, no person can have any encouragement to dedicate himself entirely to one employment, for want of the power to exchange all that surplus part of the produce of his own labour, which is over and above his own consumption, for such parts of the produce of other men's labour as he has occasion for.

There are some sorts of industry, even of the lowest kind, which can be carried on nowhere but in a great town. A porter, for example, can find employment and subsistence in no other place. A village is by much too narrow a sphere for him. . . .

Chapter 5: Of the Real and Nominal Price of Commodities, or Their Price in Labour, and Their Price in Money

Every man is rich or poor according to the degree in which he can afford to enjoy the necessaries, conveniences, and amusements of human life. But after the division of labour has once thoroughly taken place, it is but a very small part of these with which a man's own labour can supply him. The far greater part of them he must derive from the labour of other people, and he must be rich or poor according to the quantity of that labour which he can command, or which he can afford to purchase. The value of any commodity, therefore, to the person who possesses it, and who means not to use or consume it himself, but to exchange it for other commodities, is equal to the quantity of labour which it enables him to purchase or command. Labour, therefore, is the real measure of the exchangeable value of all commodities. . . .

Chapter 7: Of the Natural and Market Price of Commodities

. . . When the quantity of any commodity which is brought to market falls short of the effectual demand, all those who are willing to pay the whole value of the rent, wages, and profit, which must be paid in order to bring it thither, cannot be supplied with the quantity which they want. Rather than want[1] it altogether, some of them will be willing to give more. A competition will immediately begin among them, and the market price will rise more or less above the natural price, according as either the greatness of the deficiency, or the wealth and wanton luxury of the competitors, happen to animate more or less the eagerness of the competition. Among competitors of equal wealth and luxury the same deficiency will generally occasion a more or less eager competition, according as the acquisition of the commodity happens to be of more or less importance to them. Hence the exorbitant price of the necessaries of life during the blockade of a town or in a famine.

When the quantity brought to market exceeds the effectual demand, it cannot be all sold to those who are willing to pay the whole value of the rent, wages, and profit, which must be paid in order to bring it thither. Some part must be sold to those who are willing to pay less, and the low price which they give for it must reduce the price of the whole. The market price will sink more or less below the natural price, according as the greatness of the excess increases more or less the competition of the sellers, or according as it happens to be more or less important to them to get immediately rid of the commodity. The same excess in the importation of perishables will occasion a much greater

[1]Be without it. [Ed.]

competition than in that of durable commodities; in the importation of oranges, for example, than in that of old iron.

When the quantity brought to market is just sufficient to supply the effectual demand, and no more, the market price naturally comes to be either exactly, or as nearly as can be judged of, the same with the natural price. The whole quantity upon hand can be disposed of for this price, and cannot be disposed of for more. The competition of the different dealers obliges them all to accept of this price, but does not oblige them to accept of less.

The quantity of every commodity brought to market naturally suits itself to the effectual demand. It is the interest of all those who employ their land, labour, or stock, in bringing any commodity to market, that the quantity never should exceed the effectual demand; and it is the interest of all other people that it never should fall short of that demand.

Book IV: *Of Systems of Political Economy*

Chapter 1: Of the Principle of the Commercial or Mercantile System

I thought it necessary, though at the hazard of being tedious, to examine at full length this popular notion that wealth consists in money, or in gold and silver. Money in common language, as I have already observed, frequently signifies wealth, and this ambiguity of expression has rendered this popular notion so familiar to us that even they who are convinced of its absurdity are very apt to forget their own principles, and in the course of their reasonings to take it for granted as a certain and undeniable truth. Some of the best English writers upon commerce set out with observing that the wealth of a country consists, not in its gold and silver only, but in its lands, houses, and consumable goods of all different kinds. In the course of their reasonings, however, the lands, houses, and consumable goods seem to slip out of their memory, and the strain of their argument frequently supposes that all wealth consists in gold and silver, and that to multiply those metals is the great object of national industry and commerce. . . .

Chapter 2: Of Restraints upon the Importation from Foreign Countries of Such Goods as Can Be Produced at Home

. . . The produce of industry is what it adds to the subject or materials upon which it is employed. In proportion as the value of this produce is great or small, so will likewise be the profits of the employer. But it is only for the sake of profit that any man employs a capital in the support of industry; and he will always, therefore, endeavour to employ it in the support of that industry of which the produce is likely to be of the greatest value, or to exchange for the greatest quantity either of money or of other goods.

But the annual revenue of every society is always precisely equal to the exchangeable value of the whole annual produce of its industry, or rather is precisely the same thing with that exchangeable value. As every individual, therefore, endeavours as much as he can both to employ his capital in the support of domestic industry, and so to direct that industry that its produce may be of the greatest value; every individual necessarily labours to render the annual revenue of the society as great as he can. He generally, indeed, neither intends to promote the public interest, nor knows how much he is promoting it. By preferring the support of domestic to that of foreign industry, he intends only his own security; and by directing that industry in such a manner as its produce may be of the greatest value, he intends only his own gain, and he is in this, as in many other cases, led by an invisible hand to promote an end which was no part of his intention. Nor is it always the worse for the society that it was no part of it. By pursuing his own interest he frequently promotes that of the society more effectually than when he really intends to promote it. I have never known much good done by those who affected to trade for the public good. It is an affectation, indeed, not very common among merchants, and very few words need be employed in dissuading them from it.

What is the species of domestic industry which his capital can employ, and of which the produce is likely to be of the greatest value, every individual, it is evident, can, in his local situation, judge much better than any statesman or lawgiver can do for him. The statesman who should attempt to direct private people in what manner they ought to employ their capitals would not only load himself with a most unnecessary attention, but assume an authority which could safely be trusted, not only to no single person, but to no council or senate whatever, and which would nowhere be so dangerous as in the hands of a man who had folly and presumption enough to fancy himself fit to exercise it.

To give the monopoly of the home market to the produce of domestic industry, in any particular art or manufacture, is in some measure to direct private people in what manner they ought to employ their capitals, and must, in almost all cases, be either a useless or a hurtful regulation. If the produce of domestic can be brought there as cheap as that of foreign industry, the regulation is evidently useless. If it cannot, it must generally be hurtful. It is the maxim of every prudent master of a family never to attempt to make at home what it will cost him more to make than to buy. The tailor does not attempt to make his own shoes, but buys them of the shoemaker. The shoemaker does not attempt to make his own clothes, but employs a tailor. The farmer attempts to make neither the one nor the other, but employs those different artificers. All of them find it for their interest to employ their whole industry in a way in which they have some advantage over their neighbours, and to purchase with a part of its produce, or what is the same thing, with the price of a part of it, whatever else they have occasion for.

What is prudence in the conduct of every private family can scarce be folly in that of a great kingdom. If a foreign country can supply us with a commodity cheaper than we ourselves can make it, better buy it of them with some part of the produce of our own industry employed in a way in which we have some advantage. The general industry of the country, being always in proportion to the capital which employs it, will not thereby be diminished, no more than that of the above-mentioned artificers; but only left to find out the way in which it can be employed with the greatest advantage. It is certainly not employed to the greatest advantage when it is thus directed towards an object which it can buy cheaper than it can make. . . .

$$136$$

From The Sadler Report of
the House of Commons

Although children were among the ideal workers in the factories of the industrial revolution, according to many factory owners, increasingly their exploitation became a concern of the British Parliament. One important parliamentary investigation, chaired by Michael Sadler, took volumes of testimony from child workers and older people who had worked as children in the mines and factories. The following is a sample of the testimony gathered in the Sadler Report. The report led to child-labor reform in the Factory Act of 1833.

What seem to be the causes of Crabtree's distress? How could they have been alleviated?

From *The Sadler Report: Report from the Committee on the Bill to Regulate the Labour of Children in the Mills and Factories of the United Kingdom* (London: The House of Commons, 1832).

Thinking Historically

To what extent are the problems faced by Matthew Crabtree the inevitable results of machine production? To what extent are his problems caused by capitalism? How might the owner of this factory have addressed these issues?

If you asked the owner why he didn't pay more, shorten the workday, provide more time for meals, or provide medical assistance when it was needed, how do you think he would have responded? Do you think Crabtree would have been in favor of reduced hours if it meant reduced wages?

Friday, 18 May 1832 — Michael Thomas Sadler, Esquire, in the Chair

Mr. Matthew Crabtree, *called in; and Examined.*

What age are you? — Twenty-two.

What is your occupation? — A blanket manufacturer.

Have you ever been employed in a factory? — Yes.

At what age did you first go to work in one? — Eight.

How long did you continue in that occupation? — Four years.

Will you state the hours of labour at the period when you first went to the factory, in ordinary times? — From 6 in the morning to 8 at night.

Fourteen hours? — Yes.

With what intervals for refreshment and rest? — An hour at noon.

Then you had no resting time allowed in which to take your breakfast, or what is in Yorkshire called your "drinking"? — No.

When trade was brisk what were your hours? — From 5 in the morning to 9 in the evening.

Sixteen hours? — Yes.

With what intervals at dinner? — An hour.

How far did you live from the mill? — About two miles.

Was there any time allowed for you to get your breakfast in the mill? — No.

Did you take it before you left your home? — Generally.

During those long hours of labour could you be punctual; how did you awake? — I seldom did awake spontaneously; I was most generally awoke or lifted out of bed, sometimes asleep, by my parents.

Were you always in time? — No.

What was the consequence if you had been too late? — I was most commonly beaten.

Severely? — Very severely, I thought.

In whose factory was this? — Messrs. Hague & Cook's, of Dewsbury.

Will you state the effect that those long hours had upon the state of your health and feelings? — I was, when working those long hours, commonly very much fatigued at night, when I left my work; so much so that I sometimes should have slept as I walked if I had not stumbled and started awake again; and so sick often that I could not eat, and what I did eat I vomited.

Did this labour destroy your appetite? — It did.

In what situation were you in that mill? — I was a piecener.

Will you state to this Committee whether piecening is a very laborious employment for children, or not? — It is a very laborious employment. Pieceners are continually running to and fro, and on their feet the whole day.

The duty of the piecener is to take the cardings from one part of the machinery, and to place them on another? — Yes.

So that the labour is not only continual, but it is unabated to the last? — It is unabated to the last.

Do you not think, from your own experience, that the speed of the machinery is so calculated as to demand the utmost exertions of a child supposing the hours were moderate? — It is as much as they could do at the best; they are always upon the stretch, and it is commonly very difficult to keep up with their work.

State the condition of the children toward the latter part of the day, who have thus to keep up with the machinery. — It is as much as they can do when they are not very much fatigued to keep up with their work, and toward the close of the day, when they come to be more fatigued, they cannot keep up with it very well, and the consequence is that they are beaten to spur them on.

Were you beaten under those circumstances? — Yes.

Frequently? — Very frequently.

And principally at the latter end of the day? — Yes.

And is it your belief that if you had not been so beaten, you should not have got through the work? — I should not if I had not been kept up to it by some means.

Does beating then principally occur at the latter end of the day, when the children are exceedingly fatigued? — It does at the latter end of the day, and in the morning sometimes, when they are very drowsy, and have not got rid of the fatigue of the day before.

What were you beaten with principally? — A strap.

Anything else? — Yes, a stick sometimes; and there is a kind of roller which runs on the top of the machine called a billy, perhaps two or three yards in length, and perhaps an inch and a half, or more in diameter; the circumference would be four or five inches; I cannot speak exactly.

Were you beaten with that instrument? — Yes.

Have you yourself been beaten, and have you seen other children struck severely with that roller? — I have been struck very severely with it myself, so much so as to knock me down, and I have seen other children have their heads broken with it.

You think that it is a general practice to beat the children with the roller? — It is.

You do not think then that you were worse treated than other children in the mill? — No, I was not, perhaps not so bad as some were.

In those mills is chastisement towards the latter part of the day going on perpetually? — Perpetually.

So that you can hardly be in a mill without hearing constant crying? — Never an hour, I believe.

Do you think that if the overlooker were naturally a humane person it would be still found necessary for him to beat the children, in order to keep up their attention and vigilance at the termination of those extraordinary days of labour? — Yes, the machine turns off a regular quantity of cardings, and of course they must keep as regularly to their work the whole of the day; they must keep with the machine, and therefore however humane the slubber may be, as he must keep up with the machine or be found fault with, he spurs the children to keep up also by various means but that which he commonly resorts to is to strap them when they become drowsy.

At the time when you were beaten for not keeping up with your work, were you anxious to have done it if you possibly could? — Yes; the dread of being beaten if we could not keep up with our work was a sufficient impulse to keep us to it if we could.

When you got home at night after this labour, did you feel much fatigued? — Very much so.

Had you any time to be with your parents, and to receive instruction from them? — No.

What did you do? — All that we did when we got home was to get the little bit of supper that was provided for us and go to bed immediately. If the supper had not been ready directly, we should have gone to sleep while it was preparing.

Did you not, as a child, feel it a very grievous hardship to be roused so soon in the morning? — I did.

Were the rest of the children similarly circumstanced? — Yes, all of them; but they were not all of them so far from their work as I was.

And if you had been too late you were under the apprehension of being cruelly beaten? — I generally was beaten when I happened to be too late; and when I got up in the morning the apprehension of that was so great, that I used to run, and cry all the way as I went to the mill.

That was the way by which your punctual attendance was secured? — Yes.

And you do not think it could have been secured by any other means? — No.

Then it is your impression from what you have seen, and from your own experience, that those long hours of labour have the effect of rendering young persons who are subject to them exceedingly unhappy? — Yes.

You have already said it had a considerable effect upon your health? — Yes.

Do you conceive that it diminished your growth? — I did not pay much attention to that; but I have been examined by some persons who said they thought I was rather stunted, and that I should have been taller if I had not worked at the mill.

What were your wages at that time? — Three shillings (per week).

And how much a day had you for overwork when you were worked so exceedingly long? — A halfpenny a day.

Did you frequently forfeit that if you were not always there to a moment? — Yes; I most frequently forfeited what was allowed for those long hours.

You took your food to the mill; was it in your mill, as is the case in cotton mills, much spoiled by being laid aside? — It was very frequently covered by flues from the wool; and in that case they had to be blown off with the mouth, and picked off with the fingers before it could be eaten.

So that not giving you a little leisure for eating your food, but obliging you to take it at the mill, spoiled your food when you did get it? — Yes, very commonly.

And that at the same time that this over-labour injured your appetite? — Yes.

Could you eat when you got home? — Not always.

What is the effect of this piecening upon the hands? — It makes them bleed; the skin is completely rubbed off, and in that case they bleed in perhaps a dozen parts.

The prominent parts of the hand? — Yes, all the prominent parts of the hand are rubbed down till they bleed; every day they are rubbed in that way.

All the time you continue at work? — All the time we are working. The hands never can be hardened in that work, for the grease keeps them soft in the first instance, and long and continual rubbing is always wearing them down, so that if they were hard they would be sure to bleed.

It is attended with much pain? — Very much.

Do they allow you to make use of the back of the hand? — No; the work cannot be so well done with the back of the hand, or I should have made use of that.

137

KARL MARX AND FRIEDRICH ENGELS

From The Communist Manifesto

The Communist Manifesto was written in 1848 in the midst of European upheaval, a time when capitalist industrialization had spread from England to France and Germany. Marx and Engels were Germans who studied and worked in France and England. In the *Manifesto*, they imagine a revolution that will transform all of Europe. What do they see as the inevitable causes of this revolution? How, according to their analysis, is the crisis of "modern" society different from previous crises? Were Marx and Engels correct?

Thinking Historically

Notice how Marx and Engels describe the notions of capitalism and industrialization without using those words. The term *capitalism* developed later from Marx's classic *Das Kapital* (1859), but the term *bourgeoisie*,* as Engels notes in this selection, stands for the capitalist class. For Marx and Engels, the industrial revolution (another later phrase) is the product of a particular stage of capitalist development. Thus, if Marx and Engels were asked whether capitalism or industry was the principal force that created the modern world, what would their answer be?

   The Communist Manifesto is widely known as the classic critique of capitalism, but a careful reading reveals a list of achievements of capitalist or "bourgeois civilization." What are these achievements? Did Marx and Engels consider them to be achievements? How could Marx and Engels both praise and criticize capitalism?

Bourgeois and Proletarians[1]

The history of all hitherto existing society is the history of class struggles.

*bohr zhwah ZEE

[1]In French *bourgeois* means a town-dweller. *Proletarian* comes from the Latin, *proletarius*, which meant a person whose sole wealth was his offspring (*proles*). [Ed.]

   [Note by Engels] By "bourgeoisie" is meant the class of modern capitalists, owners of the means of social production and employers of wage-labor; by "proletariat," the class of modern wage-laborers who, having no means of production of their own, are reduced to selling their labor power in order to live.

Karl Marx and Friedrich Engels, *Manifesto of the Communist Party* (Arlington Heights, Ill.: Harlan Davidson, 1955). Reprinted in the Crofts Classics Series.

Freeman and slave, patrician and plebeian, lord and serf, guildmaster and journeyman, in a word, oppressor and oppressed, stood in constant opposition to one another, carried on an uninterrupted, now hidden, now open fight, a fight that each time ended, either in a revolutionary reconstitution of society at large, or in the common ruin of the contending classes.

In the earlier epochs of history, we find almost everywhere a complicated arrangement of society into various orders, a manifold gradation of social rank. In ancient Rome we have patricians, knights, plebeians, slaves; in the Middle Ages, feudal lords, vassals, guildmasters, journeymen, apprentices, serfs; in almost all of these classes, again, subordinate gradations.

The modern bourgeois society that has sprouted from the ruins of feudal society, has not done away with class antagonisms. It has but established new classes, new conditions of oppression, new forms of struggle in place of the old ones.

Our epoch, the epoch of the bourgeoisie, possesses, however, this distinctive feature: It has simplified the class antagonisms. Society as a whole is more and more splitting up into the two great hostile camps, into two great classes directly facing each other — bourgeoisie and proletariat.

From the serfs of the Middle Ages sprang the chartered burghers of the earliest towns. From these burgesses the first elements of the bourgeoisie were developed.

The discovery of America, the rounding of the Cape, opened up fresh ground for the rising bourgeoisie. The East-Indian and Chinese markets, the colonization of America, trade with the colonies, the increase in the means of exchange and in commodities generally, gave to commerce, to navigation, to industry, an impulse never before known, and thereby, to the revolutionary element in the tottering feudal society, a rapid development.

The feudal system of industry, in which industrial production was monopolized by closed guilds, now no longer sufficed for the growing wants of the new markets. The manufacturing system took its place. The guildmasters were pushed aside by the manufacturing middle class; division of labor between the different corporate guilds vanished in the face of division of labor in each single workshop.

Meantime the markets kept ever growing, the demand ever rising. Even manufacture[2] no longer sufficed. Thereupon, steam and machin-

---

[2]By *manufacture* Marx meant the system of production which succeeded the guild system but which still relied mainly upon direct human labor for power. He distinguished it from modern industry which arose when machinery driven by water and steam was introduced. [Ed.]

ery revolutionized industrial production. The place of manufacture was taken by the giant, modern industry, the place of the industrial middle class, by industrial millionaires — the leaders of whole industrial armies, the modern bourgeois.

Modern industry has established the world market, for which the discovery of America paved the way. This market has given an immense development to commerce, to navigation, to communication by land. This development has, in its turn, reacted on the extension of industry; and in proportion as industry, commerce, navigation, railways extended, in the same proportion the bourgeoisie developed, increased its capital, and pushed into the background every class handed down from the Middle Ages.

We see, therefore, how the modern bourgeoisie is itself the product of a long course of development, of a series of revolutions in the modes of production and of exchange.

Each step in the development of the bourgeoisie was accompanied by a corresponding political advance of that class. An oppressed class under the sway of the feudal nobility, it became an armed and self-governing association in the medieval commune; here independent urban republic (as in Italy and Germany), there taxable "third estate" of the monarchy (as in France); afterwards, in the period of manufacture proper, serving either the semifeudal or the absolute monarchy as a counterpoise against the nobility, and, in fact, cornerstone of the great monarchies in general — the bourgeoisie has at last, since the establishment of modern industry and of the world market, conquered for itself, in the modern representative state, exclusive political sway. The executive of the modern state is but a committee for managing the common affairs of the whole bourgeoisie.

The bourgeoisie has played a most revolutionary role in history.

The bourgeoisie, wherever it has got the upper hand, has put an end to all feudal, patriarchal, idyllic relations. It has pitilessly torn asunder the motley feudal ties that bound man to his "natural superiors," and has left no other bond between man and man than naked self-interest, than callous "cash payment." It has drowned the most heavenly ecstasies of religious fervor, of chivalrous enthusiasm, of philistine sentimentalism, in the icy water of egotistical calculation. It has resolved personal worth into exchange value, and in place of the numberless indefensible chartered freedoms, has set up that single, unconscionable freedom — Free Trade. In one word, for exploitation, veiled by religious and political illusions, it has substituted naked, shameless, direct, brutal exploitation.

The bourgeoisie has stripped of its halo every occupation hitherto honored and looked up to with reverent awe. It has converted the physician, the lawyer, the priest, the poet, the man of science, into its paid wage-laborers.

The bourgeoisie has torn away from the family its sentimental veil, and has reduced the family relation to a mere money relation.

The bourgeoisie has disclosed how it came to pass that the brutal display of vigor in the Middle Ages, which reactionaries so much admire, found its fitting complement in the most slothful indolence. It has been the first to show what man's activity can bring about. It has accomplished wonders far surpassing Egyptian pyramids, Roman aqueducts, and Gothic cathedrals; it has conducted expeditions that put in the shade all former migrations of nations and crusades.

The bourgeoisie cannot exist without constantly revolutionizing the instruments of production, and thereby the relations of production, and with them the whole relations of society. Conservation of the old modes of production in unaltered form, was, on the contrary, the first condition of existence for all earlier industrial classes. Constant revolutionizing of production, uninterrupted disturbance of all social conditions, everlasting uncertainty and agitation distinguished the bourgeois epoch from all earlier ones. All fixed, fast-frozen relations, with their train of ancient and venerable prejudices and opinions, are swept away, all new-formed ones become antiquated before they can ossify. All that is solid melts into air, all that is holy is profaned, and man is at last compelled to face with sober senses his real conditions of life and his relations with his kind.

The need of a constantly expanding market for its products chases the bourgeoisie over the whole surface of the globe. It must nestle everywhere, settle everywhere, establish connections everywhere.

The bourgeoisie has through its exploitation of the world market given a cosmopolitan character to production and consumption in every country. To the great chagrin of reactionaries, it has drawn from under the feet of industry the national ground on which it stood. All old-established national industries have been destroyed or are daily being destroyed. They are dislodged by new industries, whose introduction becomes a life and death question for all civilized nations, by industries that no longer work up indigenous raw material, but raw material drawn from the remotest zones; industries whose products are consumed, not only at home, but in every quarter of the globe. In place of the old wants, satisfied by the production of the country, we find new wants, requiring for their satisfaction the products of distant lands and climes. In place of the old local and national seclusion and self-sufficiency, we have intercourse in every direction, universal interdependence of nations. And as in material, so also in intellectual production. The intellectual creations of individual nations become common property. National one-sidedness and narrow-mindedness become more and more impossible, and from the numerous national and local literatures there arises a world literature.

The bourgeoisie, by the rapid improvement of all instruments of production, by the immensely facilitated means of communication, draws all nations, even the most barbarian, into civilization. The cheap prices of its commodities are the heavy artillery with which it batters down all Chinese walls, with which it forces the barbarians' intensely obstinate hatred for foreigners to capitulate. It compels all nations, on pain of extinction, to adopt the bourgeois mode of production; it compels them to introduce what it calls civilization into their midst, i.e., to become bourgeois themselves. In a word, it creates a world after its own image.

The bourgeoisie has subjected the country to the rule of the towns. It has created enormous cities, has greatly increased the urban population as compared with the rural, and has thus rescued a considerable part of the population from the idiocy of rural life. Just as it has made the country dependent on the towns, so it has made barbarian and semi-barbarian countries dependent on the civilized ones, nations of peasants on nations of bourgeois, the East on the West,

More and more the bourgeoisie keeps doing away with the scattered state of the population, of the means of production, and of property. It has agglomerated population, centralized means of production, and has concentrated property in a few hands. The necessary consequence of this was political centralization. Independent, or but loosely connected provinces, with separate interests, laws, governments and systems of taxation, became lumped together into one nation, with one government, one code of laws, one national class interest, one frontier and one customs tariff.

The bourgeoisie, during its rule of scarce one hundred years, has created more massive and more colossal productive forces than have all preceding generations together. Subjection of nature's forces to man, machinery, application of chemistry to industry and agriculture, steam-navigation, railways, electric telegraphs, clearing of whole continents for cultivation, canalization of rivers, whole populations conjured out of the ground — what earlier century had even a presentiment that such productive forces slumbered in the lap of social labor?

We see then that the means of production and of exchange, which served as the foundation for the growth of the bourgeoisie, were generated in feudal society. At a certain stage in the development of these means of production and of exchange, the conditions under which feudal society produced and exchanged, the feudal organization of agriculture and manufacturing industry, in a word, the feudal relations of property became no longer compatible with the already developed productive forces; they became so many fetters. They had to be burst asunder; they were burst asunder.

Into their place stepped free competition, accompanied by a social and political constitution adapted to it, and by the economic and political sway of the bourgeois class.

A similar movement is going on before our own eyes. Modern bourgeois society with its relations of production, of exchange and of property, a society that has conjured up such gigantic means of production and exchange, is like the sorcerer who is no longer able to control the powers of the nether world whom he has called up by his spells. For many a decade past the history of industry and commerce is but the history of the revolt of modern productive forces against modern conditions of production, against the property relations that are the conditions for the existence of the bourgeoisie and of its rule. It is enough to mention the commercial crises that by their periodical return put the existence of the entire bourgeoisie society on trial, each time more threateningly. In these crises a great part not only of the existing products, but also of the previously created productive forces, are periodically destroyed. In these crises there breaks out an epidemic that, in all earlier epochs, would have seemed an absurdity — the epidemic of overproduction. Society suddenly finds itself put back into a state of momentary barbarism; it appears as if a famine, a universal war of devastation had cut off the supply of every means of subsistence; industry and commerce seem to be destroyed. And why? Because there is too much civilization, too much means of subsistence, too much industry, too much commerce. The productive forces at the disposal of society no longer tend to further the development of the conditions of bourgeois property; on the contrary, they have become too powerful for these conditions, by which they are fettered, and no sooner do they overcome these fetters than they bring disorder into the whole of bourgeois society, endanger the existence of bourgeois property. The conditions of bourgeois society are too narrow to comprise the wealth created by them. And how does the bourgeoisie get over these crises? On the one hand by enforced destruction of a mass of productive forces; on the other, by the conquest of new markets, and by the more thorough exploitation of the old ones. That is to say, by paving the way for more extensive and more destructive crises, and by diminishing the means whereby crises are prevented.

The weapons with which the bourgeoisie felled feudalism to the ground are now turned against the bourgeoisie itself.

But not only has the bourgeoisie forged the weapons that bring death to itself; it has also called into existence the men who are to wield those weapons — the modern working class — the proletarians.

In proportion as the bourgeoisie, i.e., capital, is developed, in the same proportion is the proletariat, the modern working class, developed — a class of labourers, who live only so long as they find work, and who find work only so long as their labour increases capital. These labourers, who must sell themselves piece-meal, are a commodity, like every other article of commerce, and are consequently exposed to all the vicissitudes of competition, to all the fluctuations of the market.

Owing to the extensive use of machinery and to division of labour, the work of the proletarians has lost all individual character, and consequently, all charm for the workman. He becomes an appendage of the machine, and it is only the most simple, most monotonous, and most easily acquired knack, that is required of him. Hence, the cost of production of a workman is restricted, almost entirely, to the means of subsistence that he requires for his maintenance, and for the propagation of his race. But the price of a commodity, and therefore also of labour, is equal to its cost of production. In proportion therefore, as the repulsiveness of the work increases, the wage decreases. Nay more, in proportion as the use of machinery and division of labour increases, in the same proportion the burden of toil also increases, whether by prolongation of the working hours, by increase of the work exacted in a given time or by increased speed of the machinery, etc.

Modern industry has converted the little workshop of the patriarchal master into the great factory of the industrial capitalist. Masses of labourers, crowded into the factory, are organised like soldiers. As privates of the industrial army they are placed under the command of a perfect hierarchy of officers and sergeants. Not only are they slaves of the bourgeois class, and of the bourgeois State; they are daily and hourly enslaved by the machine, by the over-looker, and, above all, by the individual bourgeois manufacturer himself. The more openly this despotism proclaims gain to be its end and aim, the more petty, the more hateful and the more embittering it is.

The less the skill and exertion of strength implied in manual labour, in other words, the more modern industry becomes developed, the more is the labour of men superseded by that of women. Differences of age and sex have no longer any distinctive social validity for the working class. All are instruments of labour, more or less expensive to use, according to their age and sex.

No sooner is the exploitation of the labourer by the manufacturer, so far, at an end, that he receives his wages in cash, than he is set upon by the other portions of the bourgeoisie, the landlord, the shopkeeper, the pawnbroker, etc.

The lower strata of the middle class — the small tradespeople, shopkeepers, retired tradesmen generally, the handicraftsmen and peasants — all these sink gradually into the proletariat, partly because their diminutive capital does not suffice for the scale on which Modern Industry is carried on, and is swamped in the competition with the large capitalists, partly because their specialized skill is rendered worthless by the new methods of production. Thus the proletariat is recruited from all classes of the population.

138

PETER N. STEARNS

The Industrial Revolution Outside the West

Stearns, a modern historian, discusses the export of industrial machinery and techniques outside the West (Europe and North America) in the nineteenth century. Again and again, he finds that initial attempts at industrialization — in Russia, India, Egypt, and South America — led to increased production of export crops and resources but failed to stimulate true industrial revolutions. Consequently, as producers of raw materials, these countries became more deeply dependent on Western markets for their products, while at the same time importing from the West more valuable manufactured products like machinery. What common reasons can you find for these failures?

Thinking Historically

Did nineteenth-century efforts to ignite industrial revolutions outside the West fail because these societies neglected to develop capitalism, or did they fail because their local needs were subordinated to those of Western capitalists? Explain.

Before the 1870s no industrial revolution occurred outside Western society. The spread of industrialization within western Europe, while by no means automatic, followed from a host of shared economic, cultural, and political features. The quick ascension of the United States was somewhat more surprising — the area was not European and had been far less developed economically during the eighteenth century. Nevertheless, extensive commercial experience in the northern states and the close mercantile and cultural ties with Britain gave the new nation advantages for its rapid imitation of the British lead. Abundant natural resources and extensive investments from Europe kept the process going, joining the United States to the wider dynamic of industrialization in the nineteenth-century West.

Elsewhere, conditions did not permit an industrial revolution, an issue that must be explored in dealing with the international context for this first phase of the world's industrial experience. Yet the West's in-

Peter N. Stearns, *The Industrial Revolution in World History* (Boulder, Colo.: Westview Press, 1993), 71–79.

dustrial revolution did have substantial impact. It led to a number of pilot projects whereby initial machinery and factories were established under Western guidance. More important, it led to new Western demands on the world's economies that instigated significant change without industrialization; indeed, these demands in several cases made industrialization more difficult.

Pilot Projects

Russia's contact with the West's industrial revolution before the 1870s offers an important case study that explains why many societies could not follow the lead of nations like France or the United States in imitating Britain. Yet Russia did introduce some new equipment for economic and military-political reasons, and these initiatives did generate change — they were not mere window dressing.

More than most societies not directly part of Western civilization, Russia had special advantages in reacting to the West's industrial lead and special motivation for paying attention to this lead. Russia had been part of Europe's diplomatic network since about 1700. It saw itself as one of Europe's great powers, a participant in international conferences and military alliances. The country also had close cultural ties with western Europe, sharing in artistic styles and scientific developments — though Russian leadership had stepped back from cultural alignment because of the shock of the French Revolution in 1789 and subsequent political disorders in the West. Russian aristocrats and intellectuals routinely visited western Europe. Finally, Russia had prior experience in imitating Western technology and manufacturing: importation of Western metallurgy and shipbuilding had formed a major part of Peter the Great's reform program in the early eighteenth century.

Contacts of this sort explain why Russia began to receive an industrial outreach from the West within a few decades of the advent of the industrial revolution. British textile machinery was imported beginning in 1843. Ernst Knoop, a German immigrant to Britain who had clerked in a Manchester cotton factory, set himself up as export agent to the Russians. He also sponsored British workers who installed the machinery in Russia and told any Russian entrepreneur brash enough to ask not simply for British models but for alterations or adaptations: "That is not your affair; in England they know better than you." Despite the snobbism, a number of Russian entrepreneurs set up small factories to produce cotton, aware that even in Russia's small urban market they could make a substantial profit by underselling traditional manufactured cloth. Other factories were established directly by Britons.

Europeans and Americans were particularly active in responding to calls by the tsar's government for assistance in establishing railway and steamship lines. The first steamship appeared in Russia in 1815, and by 1820 a regular service ran on the Volga River. The first public railroad, joining St. Petersburg to the imperial residence in the suburbs, opened in 1837. In 1851 the first major line connected St. Petersburg and Moscow, along a remarkably straight route desired by Tsar Nicholas I himself. American engineers were brought in, again by the government, to set up a railroad industry so that Russians could build their own locomotives and cars. George Whistler, the father of the painter James McNeill Whistler (and thus husband of Whistler's mother), played an important role in the effort. He and some American workers helped train Russians in the needed crafts, frequently complaining about their slovenly habits but appreciating their willingness to learn.

Russian imports of machinery increased rapidly; they were over thirty times as great in 1860 as they had been in 1825. While in 1851 the nation manufactured only about half as many machines as it imported, by 1860 the equation was reversed, and the number of machine-building factories had quintupled (from nineteen to ninety-nine). The new cotton industry surged forward with most production organized in factories using wage labor.

These were important changes. They revealed that some Russians were alert to the business advantages of Western methods and that some Westerners saw the great profits to be made by setting up shop in a huge but largely agricultural country. The role of the government was vital: The tsars used tax money to offer substantial premiums to Western entrepreneurs, who liked the adventure of dealing with the Russians but liked their superior profit margins even more.

But Russia did not then industrialize. Modern industrial operations did not sufficiently dent established economic practices. The nation remained overwhelmingly agricultural. High percentage increases in manufacturing proceeded from such a low base that they had little general impact. Several structural barriers impeded a genuine industrial revolution. Russia's cities had never boasted a manufacturing tradition; there were few artisans skilled even in preindustrial methods. Only by the 1860s and 1870s had cities grown enough for an artisan core to take shape — in printing, for example — and even then large numbers of foreigners (particularly Germans) had to be imported. Even more serious was the system of serfdom that kept most Russians bound to agricultural estates. While some free laborers could be found, most rural Russians could not legally leave their land, and their obligation to devote extensive work service to their lords' estates reduced their incentive even for agricultural production. Peter the Great had managed to adapt serfdom to a preindustrial metallurgical industry by allowing landlords to sell villages and the labor therein for expansion of ironworks. But this mongrel system was not suitable for change on a grander scale, which is precisely what the industrial revolution entailed.

Furthermore, the West's industrial revolution, while it provided tangible examples for Russia to imitate, also produced pressures to develop more traditional sectors in lieu of structural change. The West's growing cities and rising prosperity claimed rising levels of Russian timber, hemp, tallow, and, increasingly, grain. These were export goods that could be produced without new technology and without altering the existing labor system. Indeed, many landlords boosted the work-service obligations of the serfs in order to generate more grain production for sale to the West. The obvious temptation was to lock in an older economy — to respond to new opportunity by incremental changes within the traditional system and to maintain serfdom and the rural preponderance rather than to risk fundamental internal transformation.

The proof of Russia's lag showed in foreign trade. It rose but rather modestly, posting a threefold increase between 1800 and 1860. Exports of raw materials approximately paid for the imports of some machinery, factory-made goods from abroad, and a substantial volume of luxury products for the aristocracy. And the regions that participated most in the growing trade were not the tiny industrial enclaves (in St. Petersburg, Moscow, and the iron-rich Urals) but the wheat-growing areas of southern Russia where even industrial pilot projects had yet to surface. Russian manufacturing exported nothing at all to the West, though it did find a few customers in Turkey, central Asia, and China.

The proof of Russia's lag showed even more dramatically in Russia's new military disadvantage. Peter the Great's main goal had been to keep Russian military production near enough to Western levels to remain competitive, with the huge Russian population added into the equation. This strategy now failed, for the West's industrial revolution changed the rules of the game. A war in 1854 pitting Russia against Britain and France led to Russia's defeat in its own backyard. The British and French objected to new Russian territorial gains (won at the expense of Turkey's Ottoman Empire) that brought Russia greater access to the Black Sea. The battleground was the Crimea. Yet British and French steamships connected their armies more reliably with supplies and reinforcements from home than did Russia's ground transportation system with its few railroads and mere three thousand miles of first-class roads. And British and French industry could pour out more and higher-quality uniforms, guns, and munitions than traditional Russian manufacturing could hope to match. The Russians lost the Crimean War, surrendering their gains and swallowing their pride in 1856. Patchwork change had clearly proved insufficient to match the military, much less the economic, power the industrial revolution had generated in the West.

After a brief interlude, the Russians digested the implications of their defeat and launched a period of basic structural reforms. The linchpin was the abolition of serfdom in 1861. Peasants were not entirely freed, and rural discontent persisted, but many workers could now leave the land; the basis for a wage labor force was established. Other reforms focused on improving basic education and health, and while change in these areas was slow, it too set the basis for a genuine commitment to industrialization. A real industrial revolution lay in the future, however. By the 1870s Russia's contact with industrialization had deepened its economic gap vis-à-vis the West but had yielded a few interesting experiments with new methods and a growing realization of the need for further change.

Societies elsewhere in the world — those more removed from traditional ties to the West or more severely disadvantaged in the ties that did exist — saw even more tentative industrial pilot projects during the West's industrialization period. The Middle East and India tried some industrial imitation early on but largely failed — though not without generating some important economic change. Latin America also launched some revealingly limited technological change. Only eastern Asia and sub-Saharan Africa were largely untouched by any explicit industrial imitations until the late 1860s or beyond; they were too distant from European culture to venture a response so quickly.

Prior links with the West formed the key variable, as Russia's experience abundantly demonstrated. Societies that had some familiarity with Western merchants and some preindustrial awareness of the West's steady commercial gains mounted some early experiments in industrialization. Whether they benefited as a result compared with areas that did nothing before the late nineteenth century might be debated.

One industrial initiative in India developed around Calcutta, where British colonial rule had centered since the East India Company founded the city in 1690. A Hindu Brahman family, the Tagores, established close ties with many British administrators. Without becoming British, they sponsored a number of efforts to revivify India, including new colleges and research centers. Dwarkanath Tagore controlled tax collection in part of Bengal, and early in the nineteenth century he used part of his profit to found a bank. He also bought up a variety of commercial landholdings and traditional manufacturing operations. In 1834 he joined with British capitalists to establish a diversified company that boasted holdings in mines (including the first Indian coal mine), sugar refineries, and some new textile factories; the equipment was imported from Britain. Tagore's dominant idea was a British-Indian economic and cultural collaboration that would revitalize his country. He enjoyed a high reputation in Europe and for a short time made a success of his economic initiatives. Tagore died on a trip abroad, and his financial empire declined soon after.

This first taste of Indian industrialization was significant, but it brought few immediate results. The big news in India, even as Tagore launched his companies, was the rapid decline of traditional textiles under the bombardment of British factory competition; millions of Indian villagers were thrown out of work. Furthermore, relations between Britain and the Indian elite worsened after the mid-1830s as British officials sought a more active economic role and became more intolerant of Indian culture. One British official, admitting no knowledge of Indian scholarship, wrote that "all the historical information" and science available in Sanskrit was "less valuable than what may be found in the most paltry abridgements used at preparatory schools in England." With these attitudes, the kind of collaboration that might have aided Indian appropriation of British industry became impossible.

The next step in India's contact with the industrial revolution did not occur until the 1850s when the colonial government began to build a significant railroad network. The first passenger line opened in 1853. Some officials feared that Hindus might object to traveling on such smoke-filled monsters, but trains proved very popular and there ensued a period of rapid economic and social change. The principal result, however, was not industrial development but further extension of commercial agriculture (production of cotton and other goods for export) and intensification of British sales to India's interior. Coal mining did expand, but manufacturing continued to shrink. There was no hint of an industrial revolution in India.

Imitation in the Middle East was somewhat more elaborate, in part because most of this region, including parts of North Africa, retained independence from European colonialism. Muslims had long disdained Western culture and Christianity, and Muslim leaders, including the rulers of the great Ottoman Empire, had been very slow to recognize the West's growing dynamism after the fifteenth century. Some Western medicine was imported, but technology was ignored. Only in the eighteenth century did this attitude begin, haltingly, to change. The Ottoman government imported a printing press from Europe and began discussing Western-style technical training, primarily in relationship to the military.

In 1798 a French force briefly seized Egypt, providing a vivid symbol of Europe's growing technical superiority. Later an Ottoman governor, Muhammed Ali, seized Egypt from the imperial government and pursued an ambitious agenda of expansionism and modernization. Muhammed Ali sponsored many changes in Egyptian society in imitation of Western patterns, including a new tax system and new kinds of schooling. He also destroyed the traditional Egyptian elite. The government encouraged agricultural production by sponsoring major irrigation projects and began to import elements of the industrial revolution from the West in the 1830s. English machinery and technicians were brought in to build textile factories, sugar refineries, paper mills, and weapons shops. Muhammed Ali clearly contemplated a sweeping reform program in which industrialization would play a central role in making Egypt a powerhouse in the Middle East and an equal to the European powers. Many of his plans worked well, but the industrialization effort failed. Egyptian factories could not in the main compete with European imports, and the initial experiments either failed or stagnated. More durable changes involved the encouragement to the production of cash crops like sugar and cotton, which the government required in order to earn tax revenues to support its armies and its industrial imports. Growing concentration on cash crops also enriched a new group of Egyptian landlords and merchants. But the shift actually formalized Egypt's dependent position in the world economy, as European businesses and governments increasingly interfered with the internal economy. The Egyptian reaction to the West's industrial revolution, even more than the Russian response, was to generate massive economic redefinition without industrialization, a strategy that locked peasants into landlord control and made a manufacturing transformation at best a remote prospect.

Spurred by the West's example and by Muhammed Ali, the Ottoman government itself set up some factories after 1839, importing equipment from Europe to manufacture textiles, paper, and guns. Coal and iron mining were encouraged. The government established a postal system in 1834, a telegraph system in 1855, and steamships and the beginning of railway construction from 1866 onward. These changes increased the role of European traders and investors in the Ottoman economy and produced no overall industrial revolution. Again, the clearest result of improved transport and communication was a growing emphasis on the export of cash crops and minerals to pay for necessary manufactured imports from Europe. An industrial example had been set, and, as in Egypt, a growing though still tiny minority of Middle Easterners gained some factory experience, but no fundamental transformation occurred. . . .

Developments of preliminary industrial trappings — a few factories, a few railroads — nowhere outside Europe converted whole economies to an industrialization process until late in the nineteenth century, though they provided some relevant experience on which later (mainly after 1870) and more intensive efforts could build. A few workers became factory hands and experienced some of the same upheaval as their Western counterparts in terms of new routines and pressures on work pace. Many sought to limit their factory experience, leaving for other work or for the countryside after a short time; transience was a problem for much the same reasons as in the West: the clash with traditional work and leisure values. Some technical and business expertise also developed. Governments took the lead in most attempts to imitate the West, which was another portent for the future; with some exceptions, local merchant groups had neither the capital nor the motivation to undertake such ambitious and uncertain projects. By the 1850s a number of governments were clearly beginning to realize that some policy response to the industrial revolution was absolutely essential, lest Western influence become still more overwhelming. On balance, however, the principal results of very limited imitation tended to heighten the economic imbalance with western Europe, a disparity that made it easier to focus on nonindustrial exports. This too was a heritage for the future. . . .

$$139$$

JOHN H. COATSWORTH
Economic Trajectories in Latin America

In this selection, John Coatsworth, a modern economic historian of Latin America, looks at the long-term economic histories of a number of Latin American countries and compares them to those of the United States. What are the main differences between the economic histories of Latin America and the United States? How were Latin American economic histories different, one from the other? What is the significance of those differences?

Thinking Historically

The author is a proponent of two recent trends in economic history. One is called neoclassical and the other is statistical. You can see the importance of statistics in this selection. Coatsworth maintained that an earlier generation of Latin American economic historians made some mistaken assumptions because they lacked the basic data that was necessary to understand the broad changes or trajectories (pathways) of Latin American economic history. How do the statistics presented here change or reinforce any of your assumptions about Latin American history? The neoclassical economic historians used data to measure the kinds of forces that Adam Smith and classical economists had emphasized. How does this essay support Smith's argument about

John H. Coatsworth, "Economic and Institutional Trajectories in Nineteenth-Century Latin America," in *Latin America and the World Economy Since 1800*, ed. John H. Coatsworth and Alan M. Taylor (Cambridge: Harvard University Press, 1998), 23–31.

the "wealth of nations"? Notice that Coatsworth says nothing about the industrial revolution and very little about technology. How can an economic history of Latin America ignore the industrial revolution?

Latin America fell into relative backwardness between roughly 1700 and 1900. At the beginning of this period, the economies of the Iberian colonies in the New World were roughly as productive as those of the British. For most of the ensuing 200 years, the Latin American economies stagnated while those of the North Atlantic achieved sustained increases in productivity. As early as 1800, most of the Latin American economies had already fallen well behind the United States. A century later, most had fallen far enough behind to qualify as "less" (or "under-") developed by contemporary standards.

In the twentieth century, the Latin American economies have achieved respectable rates of economic growth, equal on average to that of the United States. Thus, the relative gap between Latin America and the United States has not changed at all in the past 100 years, though the relative positions of individual countries have shifted. To understand how the Latin American economies fell into relative backwardness, therefore, it is crucial to look at the region's pre-1900 economic history.

Latin America stagnated for most of two crucial centuries because economic institutions distorted incentives and high transport costs left most of the region's abundant natural resources beyond the frontier of profitable exploitation. Early in the colonial era, comparatively high *levels* of productivity were achieved in economies that managed, despite these constraints, to specialize in export production. The successful cases were those that combined relatively scarce supplies of free or slave labor with accessible natural resources and a favorable policy environment. In contrast, colonial economies that relied on relatively cheap indigenous or slave labor to produce exportables in less accessible regions with high tax and regulatory burdens tended to have smaller export sectors and to be less productive. Cycles of export growth and decline, linked to market fluctuations or to freshly discovered and subsequently depleted natural resources, produced variations on these patterns well into the twentieth century in some areas.

Once the opportunities created by more (or less) favorable initial conditions were seized and exploited in a given colony, further economic *growth* usually depended on some combination of institutional modernization and transport innovation. Not until the late nineteenth century did liberalism (or, in some cases, modernizing conservative regimes) and railroads remove the two fundamental obstacles to growth in Latin America and push most of the region's economies onto new trajectories. . . .

Colonial and Nineteenth-Century Trends

As the first permanent English settlers in North America set about chopping down trees to make crude cabins in December of 1620, the Spanish and Portuguese empires in the New World had already passed their first century. It would take the English more than 200 years to catch up to the most prosperous of Spain's possessions. In 1650, Cuba had a gross domestic product (GDP) per capita of roughly $60; the British North American colonies did not reach that level until more than a century later. By 1800, Cuba's GDP per capita was near $90, whereas that of the United States had barely reached $80. The United States did not close the gap with Cuba until the 1830s.

The U.S. performance looks much better in comparison with Spain's mainland colonies. The 13 British colonies probably caught up to Mexico before 1700. Over the eighteenth century, Mexico stagnated as the U.S. economy grew at perhaps a half a percent a year. In 1800, Mexico's per capita GDP of $40 stood at half that of the United States. Brazil, recovering finally from the collapse of its short-lived gold boom (1750–1780), had fallen well behind.

The race ended long before the nineteenth century was over. By 1900, the United States had become a formidable economic power with a GDP per capita, adjusted for purchasing power parity (PPP), nearly four times higher than the mean of Latin America's eight largest economies. Even Argentina, slightly ahead of the United States in 1800 and growing rapidly by the 1870s, had fallen far behind, with a GDP per capita not much more than half that of the United States. . . .

The estimates in Table 21.1 show a consistent pattern of failure from as early as 1700 until at least the end of the nineteenth century. Every Latin American country for which we have estimates grew more slowly on average than the United States for the two centuries up to 1900. Most simply stagnated; some, like Mexico, experienced prolonged periods of economic decline. There is no reason to believe that this record would look any less dismal with more data. The twentieth-century pattern, however, is more mixed. While Argentina declined toward the regional mean of about 27 percent of U.S. GDP per capita in 1994, Brazil and Venezuela rose to meet or surpass it. . . .

In summary, the available quantitative evidence shows that Latin America became an underdeveloped region between the early eighteenth and the late nineteenth centuries. Although all of the Latin American economies fell further behind in this period, the Argentine performance was consistently better than the rest until the twentieth century, that of Brazil almost as consistently the worst. In the twentieth century, these two economies reversed positions, with Brazil consistently outperforming the rest of the region and Argentina far behind. Cuba, with the highest GDP per capita in relation to the United States

Table 21.1   GDP per Capita as Percentage of the U.S. Level, 1700–1994

Country	1700	1800	1850	1900	1913	1950	1994
Argentina		102		52	55	41	37
Brazil		36	39	10	11	15	22
Chile		46		38	40	33	34
Colombia				18	18	19	24
Cuba	167	112	78		39		
Mexico	89	50	37	35	35	27	23
Peru		41		20	20	24	14
Venezuela				10	10	38	37
Mean	128	66	51	27	28	29	27

Note: The last row reports the arithmetic mean of the countries for which there are data for each year. If each country were assigned a weight equal to its share of population, the mean for each year would be lower, since the high-income cases (Argentina and Cuba, for example) had smaller populations. In 1800, the unweighted mean in the table is 66 but the population-weighted mean of the six reported cases would be 51.

in 1700, fell furthest in relative terms over this period, though the lack of GDP estimates for the rest of Latin America (except Mexico) for 1700 makes this conclusion more tentative.

Factor Endowments

The New World factor endowments encountered by the first European entrepreneurs did not matter much. Most of Latin America's potentially exploitable natural resources lay dormant and remained inaccessible throughout the colonial era. Most of the New World's indigenous population died.

Europeans transformed the natural and human resource base of the entire New World, including vast areas they never conquered or even visited. They did so by bringing in pathogens, people, plants, animals, technologies, and institutions hitherto unknown to the Western Hemisphere. The pathogens destroyed most of the New World's inhabitants by the end of the sixteenth century, so the Europeans repopulated the hemisphere with African slaves. Old World plants and animals displaced indigenous species in many areas and in doing so transformed entire landscapes. European technologies and organizational forms, from transoceanic navigation and deep-shaft mining to metal coinage and commercial credit, transformed production and commerce. The Europeans adopted and adapted Amerindian organization, products, and technologies as well, pushing them toward patterns that facilitated money-making in all its forms.

The Europeans did not distribute themselves evenly over the landscape. "Spanish society in the Indies," James Lockhart reminds us, "was import-export oriented at the very base and in every aspect." So, too, was the great Portuguese adventure in Brazil. Publicly licensed but privately financed, the Iberian entrepreneurs who set out to conquer the New World mainly wanted to get rich. Officials and priests in both empires followed them about, careful not to miss any reasonable opportunity to collect a tax, impose a fee, or save a soul. Any exploitable resource, natural or human, that could profitably be turned into silver or gold attracted both private greed and official attention. But vast areas of these New World empires remained unexploited and ungoverned by Europeans or their descendants until long after independence. The "empty spaces" (that is, empty of Europeans) where little or no money could be made added up to more territory than Spain and Portugal actually managed to control or govern in the three centuries after the conquest.

Location determined which of the New World's people and resources the invaders rushed to exploit. The cost of overland transportation proved to be prohibitive for most commodities, even in the relatively easy terrain of plateaus and pampas. Thus, the Europeans and the slaves they brought in from Africa hardly ever settled far from navigable rivers or the seacoast. Since navigable rivers were few (and the few there were, like the Amazon, did not run past much tradable wealth), they eventually settled mainly on islands in the Caribbean and along coastlines. There they produced a variety of plantation products for European markets, including sugar, cacao, tobacco, rice, cotton, and, later in the nineteenth century, coffee, henequen, and bananas. Not until the advent of the railroad did agricultural production for export shift from seacoasts to the interior of the continent.

When Europeans settled further inland during the colonial era, as in central Mexico and parts of the Andes, it was generally to exploit opportunities to profit from the production of commodities with high value-to-bulk ratios or to supply the producers of these commodities with inputs and consumption goods. High transport costs limited the interior regions of the continent to exporting precious metals, gems (like emeralds and diamonds), and dyestuffs such as cochineal and indigo. Local markets took nearly everything else. Where export production generated market demand for food and other inputs and yielded taxes to support the royal bureaucracy, Europeans specialized in these ancillary activities. In the rest of the Americas, they had to make do with whatever they could extort from indigenous populations whose productivity was too low to generate much surplus.

At the time of the Columbus voyages, as many as 50 million Amerindians lived in the vast territories that became Latin America. By the end of the colonial era, more than half of Latin America's population of perhaps 15 million people consisted of Europeans, Africans, and the descendants of Europeans and Africans. Amerindians and mestizos, most of whom lived in Mexico, constituted less than half of the Latin American population in 1820.

The demographic and economic reorganization of New World spaces caused by Latin America's integration into the two Iberian empires with their links to the developing world market can be glimpsed from the data in Table 21.2 on population densities and productivity in 1800. Argentina, a settlement colony with a huge territory and tiny population, was the most thinly populated. Mexico and Cuba were the most densely populated. In Mexico, as in the Andes, the population figures reflect the partial recovery of the indigenous populations, though at comparatively low levels of per capita GDP. In Cuba, the high population density reflects the importation of large numbers of slaves toward the end of the eighteenth century, spurred by the island's high export-based GDP per capita.

As the table suggests, African slaves did not always end up where the marginal product of their labor was highest. Backward Brazil, with a low per capita GDP, imported nearly a third of all slaves that came to the New World, whereas the more productive Spanish islands like Cuba imported far fewer until the end of the eighteenth century. This difference was due in part to Portuguese commercial access to slave-exporting regions of Africa and Spanish restrictions on imports (including slaves) from outside the empire. Slaves were far more costly in the Spanish colonies than anywhere else until the crown relaxed restrictions on slave imports beginning in the late 1760s. In the seventeenth century, the Portuguese brought slaves to Brazil and set them to work in activities where their productivity was low, because slaves cost so little. When slave prices rose in response to Caribbean demand in the eighteenth century, Brazilian production declined. In Cuba, where slaves cost two to three times as much as in Jamaica, Europeans purchased them only when certain that they would be productive enough to compensate for their high price.

Europeans migrated to the New World in much smaller numbers than the Africans they forced to come. Migration to the Spanish colonies from Spain reached a peak at the end of the sixteenth century, but revived somewhat in the eighteenth. Throughout the colonial era, Spain tried to control and limit immigration to the New World and re-

Table 21.2   Population Densities and GDP, 1800

Colony	Area (1000s sq km)	Population (1000s)	Density (Pop. per 1000 sq km)	Total GDP (1000s) (1998 dollars)	GDP per Capita
Argentina	2,777	329	118	26,978	82
Brazil	8,457	3,250	384	94,250	29
Chile	757	535	707	19,795	37
Cuba	115	272	2,365	24,480	90
Mexico	1,967	6,000	3,050	240,340	40
Peru	1,280	1,300	1,016	2,900	33

fused permission for the citizens of other countries (except for natural-
ized Irish Catholics) to settle in its possessions. By the eighteenth century, low wages on the Spanish American mainland and rising slave imports to the islands kept the flow of Europeans low and made Spain's
efforts at controlling immigration fairly easy. Portuguese emigration to
Brazil followed a somewhat different trajectory. Like Spanish emigration, that of the Portuguese fell during the seventeenth-century depression, but revived more strongly in the eighteenth century due to the pull
of high earnings in the gold and diamond booms in the interior.

In the nineteenth century, slaves continued to arrive in large numbers only in Brazil and Cuba. British pressure finally helped to end the
slave trade in the 1850s. Meanwhile, European immigration to Latin
America slowed after 1800, reversed during the independence wars
from 1810 to the 1820s, and in some cases virtually ceased for up to
half a century after independence despite the end of Spanish and Portuguese restrictions. The persistence of slavery tended to discourage European migration to Brazil and Cuba. Low wages compounded by political instability and international war kept numbers down everywhere
else. When the slave trade ended, Cuba (for sugar) and Peru (for guano
mining as well as sugar) imported large numbers of indentured Chinese
laborers. Mass European migration did not begin until the 1870s and
1880s and when it did, most of the immigrants went to Argentina and
the southern half of Brazil.

Paradoxically, the most productive economies in Latin America at
the beginning of the nineteenth century were the two, Cuba and Argentina, where labor was most costly. No free person would go to Argentina without some assurance of gain; the few that went were not
disappointed (especially in high-wage Buenos Aires). In Cuba, no one
bought slaves at the high prices prevailing for most of the colonial era
without some highly productive use to make of them. The high cost of
labor in these two colonies resembled the pattern established in British
North America. Most of Latin America, however, consisted of far less
productive, low-wage territories with limited access to the sea. None of
the Iberian colonies or the nation states that succeeded them, not even
the most prosperous in 1800 like Cuba and Argentina, managed to
achieve rates of growth comparable to the United States until the nineteenth century had nearly ended.

Access to Trade

Great debates once raged over the impact of trade on the colonial
economies. Recent scholarship has tended to reverse the once widely
held notion that external trade is necessarily (or even often) harmful to
backward economies. Of course, colonial restrictions on trade, such as

the commercial monopolies that prohibited direct trade with foreign countries, did impose costs on colonies throughout the New World, but did so precisely because they reduced the gains such regions would otherwise have enjoyed from external trade.

The Latin American case suggests that the static gains from trade can be large, even in economies that experience little or no sustained economic growth. The cross-section data in Table 21.3 compare the export performance of the six major colonial economies in 1800. Note that the colonies are listed in the table in rank order of GDP per capita. The data demonstrate that the Latin American colonial economies with the largest export sectors tended to have the highest GDP per capita. This is because productivity was higher in export industries than in other sectors of the colonial economies, though the gap between export and domestic-use agriculture and industry must have varied considerably. The colonial economies that managed to specialize more did better. . . .

Cuba and Argentina were the most successful exporters in per capita terms by 1800. Argentina also had the largest export sector in relation to GDP, followed by Brazil and Cuba. The mainland economies that produced mainly silver for export (or, in the case of Chile, foodstuffs for export to mining colonies) had much smaller export sectors both in per capita terms and in relation to total output.

Mexico's relative failure as an exporter is perhaps the most surprising. For most of the eighteenth century, Mexico served as the cash cow of the Spanish American empire, regularly exporting huge quantities of silver along with substantial amounts of cochineal and other products. In per capita terms, however, only Chile had a smaller export sector. Although the income generated by the mining industries in Mexico and Peru was substantial, the productivity effect was limited by the relatively small proportion of the labor force employed in mining and the relatively slow growth of silver production even during boom periods.

Throughout the Caribbean, by contrast, exports accounted for a relatively high proportion of GDP. Brazil's export sector was also quite

Table 21.3   Export Performance, circa 1800

Colony	Total Exports	Exports per Capita (current dollars)	Exports as % of GDP	GDP per Capita (current dollars)
Cuba	5,000,000	18.35	20.4	90
Argentina	3,300,000	10.03	12.2	82
Mexico	12,640,800	2.11	5.2	40
Chile	874,072	1.63	4.4	37
Peru	2,998,000	2.31	7.0	33
Brazil	15,526,750	4.78	16.4	29

large, despite its regional concentration in the northeast (except during the gold and diamond export booms further south). The most striking aspect of Brazil's performance, however, is the low level of per capita exports and GDP per capita in comparison with Cuba. This may be explained in part, as mentioned above, by lower slave prices that may have encouraged more marginal producers to enter the market. By the early nineteenth century, Brazil's sugar plantations were notoriously inefficient producers in comparison with those in the Caribbean. In addition, Brazilian sugar was excluded from the markets of the European countries with sugar islands of their own.

Perhaps most surprising is the relative success of Argentina. Table 21.3 includes exports from Buenos Aires that were produced within what became the national territory. They consisted chiefly of cattle hides and salted beef, derived mainly from exploiting the wild herds of the pampas. . . .

In sum, Argentina and Cuba managed to prosper in the colonial era, despite high labor costs, in part because their well-located natural resources allowed them to specialize in export production. The less successful agricultural economies like Brazil managed to substitute cheaper labor for location, pushing export production further from the sea by using low-cost labor to compensate for higher transport costs. The remaining colonies produced small quantities (in relation to GDP) of high-value metals in primitive surroundings, especially in the Andes. Even in ostensibly opulent Mexico, at least 80 percent of the population in 1800 worked in domestic-use agriculture at low levels of productivity.

47

IWASAKI YATARO
Mitsubishi Letter to Employees

Japan was the first country outside the West to undergo an industrial revolution. After 1854 when American Commodore Perry forced Japan to open its ports to the West, Japanese society underwent a wide range of changes. In 1868, the Meiji (Enlightened) Restoration government proceeded to mobilize the population to learn Western methods of industrial production and many other facets of Western culture and society. Many Japanese were educated in the United States and Europe, especially in Germany. Japanese industry was organized along the German model, with considerable government direction and power vested in leading families. Politics was not democratic, and the economy was not capitalist. In 1870, for example, the Meiji government launched a major railroad construction plan. It hoped to raise capital from private sources, but when none was offered, the government went ahead on its own. Gradually, with the help of foreign loans and Japanese capitalists, a mixed public and private economy developed.

One of the entrepreneurs who directed Japanese industrialization was Iwasaki Yataro* (1835–1885), a clerk for a feudal lord, who used his ability and connections to create a steamship company that in 1873 took the name Mitsubishi. In 1876, the British Peninsular and Oriental Steam Navigation Company challenged Mitsubishi's growing dominance in Japanese coastal trade. Mitsubishi responded by halving its coastal fares and cutting employee wages by one-third. In this letter to his employees, Iwasaki asks for their support.

Notice Iwasaki's appeal to national security and pride. Does the appeal strike you as genuine or contrived? What would Adam Smith or Karl Marx have said about this appeal?

Thinking Historically

Iwasaki Yataro was both a capitalist and an industrialist. While Japanese industrialization enjoyed greater state sponsorship than did British or American industrialization, entrepreneurs like Iwasaki played a crucial role. In this letter, does Iwasaki speak more as a capi-

*ee wah SAH kee   yah TAH roh

David John Lu, *Sources of Japanese History*, vol. 2 (New York: McGraw-Hill, 1974), 80–82.

talist or industrialist? Is there any disparity between these two roles, or are they woven together inextricably?

Many people have expressed differing opinions concerning the principles to be followed and advantages to be obtained in engaging foreigners or Japanese in the task of coastal trade. Granted, we may permit a dissenting voice, which suggests that in principle both foreigners and Japanese must be permitted to engage in coastal trade, but once we look into the question of advantages, we know that coastal trade is too important a matter to be given over to the control of foreigners. If we allow the right of coastal navigation to fall into the hands of foreigners in peacetime, it means a loss of business and employment opportunities for our own people, and in wartime it means yielding the vital right of gathering information to foreigners. In fact, this is not too different from abandoning the rights of our country as an independent nation.

Looking back into the past, at the time when we abandoned the policy of seclusion and entered into an era of friendly intercourse and commerce with foreign nations, we should have been prepared for this very task. However, due to the fact that our people lack knowledge and wealth, we have yet to assemble a fleet sufficient to engage in coastal navigation. Furthermore, we have neither the necessary skills for navigation nor a plan for developing a maritime transportation industry. This condition has attracted foreign shipping companies to occupy our maritime transport lines. Yet our people show not a sense of surprise at it. Some people say that our treaties with foreign powers contain an express provision allowing foreign ships to proceed from Harbor A to Harbor B, and others claim that such a provision must not be regarded as granting foreign ships the right to coastal navigation inasmuch as it is intended not to impose unduly heavy taxes on them. I am not qualified to discuss its legal merit, but the issue remains an important one.

I now propose to do my utmost, and along with my 35 million compatriots, perform my duty as a citizen of this country. That is to recover the right of coastal trade in our hands and not to delegate that task to foreigners. Unless we propose to do so, it is useless for our government to revise the unequal treaties[1] or to change our entrenched customs. We need people who can respond, otherwise all the endeavors of the government will come to naught. This is the reason why the

---

[1]*Unequal treaties* was a term the Chinese used to designate the treaties that were forced upon them by the opium wars; they were "unequal" in the sense that the superior power of the British forced the defeated Chinese to comply with British demands. Here the term refers to the commercial agreements that Japan was made to sign after Admiral Perry's arrival. [Ed.]

government protects our company, and I know that our responsibilities are even greater than the full weight of Mt. Fuji thrust upon our shoulders. There have been many who wish to hinder our progress in fulfilling our obligations. However, we have been able to eliminate one of our worst enemies, the Pacific Mail Company of the United States, from contention by applying appropriate means available to us. Now another rival has emerged. It is the Peninsular & Oriental Steam Navigation Company of Great Britain, which is setting up a new line between Yokohama and Shanghai and is attempting to claim its rights over the ports of Nagasaki, Kobe, and Yokohama. The P & O Company is backed by its massive capital, its large fleet of ships, and by its experiences of operating in Oriental countries. In competing against this giant, what methods can we employ?

I have thought about this problem very carefully and have come to one conclusion. There is no other alternative but to eliminate unnecessary positions and unnecessary expenditures. This is a time-worn solution and no new wisdom is involved. Even though it is a familiar saying, it is much easier said than done, and this indeed has been the root cause of difficulties in the past and present times. Therefore, starting immediately, I propose that we engage in this task. By eliminating unnecessary personnel from the payroll, eliminating unnecessary expenditures, and engaging in hard and arduous tasks, we shall be able to solidify the foundation of our company. If there is a will, there is a way. Through our own efforts, we shall be able to repay the government for its protection and answer our nation for its confidence shown in us. Let us work together in discharging our obligations and let us not be ashamed of ourselves. Whether we succeed or fail, whether we can gain profit or sustain loss, we cannot anticipate at this time. Hopefully, all of you will join me in a singleness of heart to attain this cherished goal, forbearing and undaunted by setbacks, to restore to our own hands the right to our own coastal trade. If we succeed it will not only be an accomplishment for our company but also a glorious event for our Japanese Empire, which shall let its light shine to all four corners of the earth. We may succeed and we may fail, and it depends on your effort or lack of it. Do your utmost in this endeavor!

REFLECTIONS

> It was because of certain traits in private capitalism that the machine —
> which was a neutral agent — has often seemed, and in fact has some-
> times been, a malicious element in society, careless of human life, indif-
> ferent to human interests. The machine has suffered for the sins of
> capitalism; contrariwise, capitalism has often taken credit for the
> virtues of the machine.[1]

Our chapter turns writer Lewis Mumford's proposition into a series of
questions: What has been the impact of capitalism? Is the machine only
neutral, or does it have its own effects? How can we distinguish between the economic and the technological chains of cause and effect?

Capitalism and industrialization are difficult concepts to distinguish. Adam Smith illustrated the power of the market and the division
of labor by imagining their impact not on a shop or trading firm, but
on a pin factory, an early industrial enterprise. Karl Marx summarized
the achievements of the capitalist age by enumerating "wonders far surpassing Egyptian pyramids," which included chemical industries, steam
navigation, railroads, and electric telegraphs. Neither Smith nor Marx
used the terms *capitalism* or *industrial revolution*, although such vari-
ants as *capitalist* and *industrial* were already in circulation. Modern
historians fought over their meaning and relevance as explanations of
change through most of the last century. To understand the great transformation into modernity, some emphasized the expansion of market
capitalism; others emphasized the power of the machine. The rise of
state-capitalist and communist industrial societies politicized the debate, but even after the fall of communism, the historical questions remained. Peter Stearns looks for the forces that spread or retarded industrialization. John Coatsworth sees the root cause of change in trade
and markets.

After 1900 the industrial revolution spread throughout the world,
but its pace was not always revolutionary. Even today some societies
are still largely rural with a majority of workers engaged in subsistence
farming or small-scale manufacturing by hand. But over the long course
of history people have always tried to replace human labor with machines and increase the production of machine-made goods. In some
cases, the transformation has been dramatic. Malaysia, once a languid
land of tropical tea and rubber plantations, sprouted enough microchip
and electronics factories after 1950 to account for 60 percent of its exports by the year 2000. By the 1990s an already highly industrialized
country like Japan could produce luxury cars in factories that needed

---

[1]Lewis Mumford, *Technics and Civilization* (New York: Harcourt Brace, 1963), 27.

only a handful of humans to monitor the work of computer-driven robots. Despite occasional announcements of the arrival of a "postindustrial" society, the pressure to mechanize continues unabated in the
twenty-first century.

The fate of capitalism in the twentieth century was more varied.
The second wave of industrial revolutions — beginning with Germany
after 1850 and Japan after 1880 — was directed by governments as
much as capitalists. Socialist parties won large support in industrial
countries in the first half of the twentieth century, creating welfare
states in some after World War II. In Russia after 1917, the Communist
party pioneered a model of state-controlled industrialization that attracted imitators from China to Chile and funded anticapitalist movements throughout the world.

The Cold War (1947–1991) between the United States and the Soviet Union, though largely a power struggle between two superpowers,
was widely seen as an ideological contest between capitalism and socialism. Thus, the demise of the Soviet Union and its Communist party
in 1991 was heralded as the victory of capitalism over socialism. As
Russia, China, and other previously communist states embraced market
economies, socialism was declared dead.

But could proclaiming the death of socialism be as premature as
heralding the end of industrial society? *The Communist Manifesto* of
1848 long predates the Russian revolution of 1917. Karl Marx died in
1883. Socialists like Rosa Luxembourg criticized Lenin and the Russian
communists for misinterpreting Marxism in their impatience to transform Russian society. Socialists, even Marxists, continue to write, advise, and govern today, often urging restraints on the spread of global
capital markets and the threat of unregulated capitalism on the global
environment. Rarely are they willing to relinquish the advantages of industrial technology. Rather they seek to release the "virtues of the machine."

Colonized and Colonizers

Europeans in Africa and Asia,
1850–1930

HISTORICAL CONTEXT

The first stage of European colonialism, beginning with Columbus, was a period in which Europeans — led by the Spanish and Portuguese — settled in the Western Hemisphere and created plantations with African labor. From 1492 to 1776, European settlement in Asia was limited to a few coastal port cities where merchants and missionaries operated. The second stage — the years between 1776, when Britain lost most of its American colonies, and 1880, when the European scramble for African territory began — has sometimes been called a period of *free-trade imperialism*. This term refers to the desire by European countries in general and by Britain in particular to expand their zones of free trade. It also refers to a widespread opposition to the expense of colonization, a conviction held especially among the British, who garnered all of the advantages of political empire without the costs of occupation and outright ownership.

The British used to quip that their second global empire was created in the nineteenth century "in a fit of absentmindedness." But colonial policy in Britain and the rest of Europe was more planned and continuous than that comment might suggest. British control of India (including Burma) increased throughout the nineteenth century, as did British control of South Africa, Australia, the Pacific, and parts of the Americas. At the same time, France, having lost most of India to the British, began building an empire that included parts of North Africa, Southeast Asia, and the Pacific.

Thus, a third stage of colonialism, beginning in the mid-nineteenth century, reached a fever pitch with the partition of Africa after 1880. The period between 1888 and 1914 spawned renewed settlement and massive population transfers, with most European migrants settling in

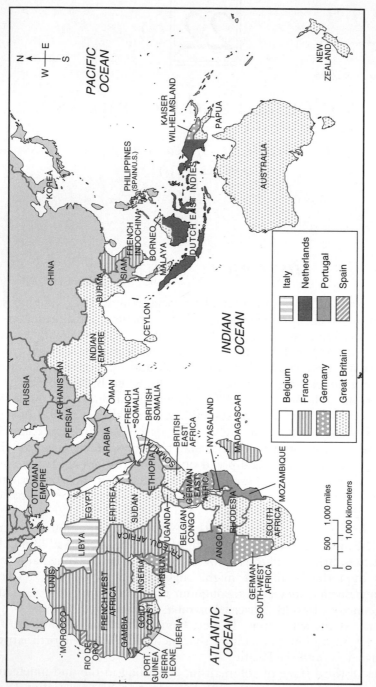

Map 22.1 European Colonialism in Africa and Asia, 1880–1914.

the older colonies of the Americas (as well as in South Africa and Australia), where indigenous populations had been reduced. Even where settlement remained light, however, Europeans took political control of large areas of the Earth's surface (see Map 22.1).

In the first reading in this chapter, a historian offers a brief history of this second stage of European colonialism and describes what the renewed era of colonization meant, both for the colonizers and the colonized. Subsequent readings examine aspects of colonial society across the globe.

THINKING HISTORICALLY
Using Literature in History

This chapter also explores whether literature can and should be used in the quest to better understand history. Beginning with some basic questions about the differences between literary and historical approaches, we examine a number of fictional accounts of colonialism, some written by the colonizers, others by the colonized or their descendants. How do these literary accounts add to, or detract from, a historical understanding of colonialism? The rich, evocative literature of the colonial period aids us in determining how we separate fact from fiction, construct historical knowledge, and appreciate the past in all its dimensions.

$\boxed{141}$

JURGEN OSTERHAMMEL
From Colonialism

In this selection, modern historian Jurgen Osterhammel provides us with an overview of European colonialism. In the first part, "Colonial Epochs," the author discusses ways in which European colonialism changed from the late eighteenth to the early twentieth century. In the second section, "Colonial Societies," he discusses the special character of the colonial social order throughout this period.

Jurgen Osterhammel, *Colonialism*, trans. Shelly Frisch (Princeton: Markus Wiener, 1997), 32–34, 86–89.

How, according to Osterhammel, did colonialism change between 1760 and 1930? How were these changes reflected in the evolution of "colonial society"?

Thinking Historically

Unlike philosophy, which tends to deal with general principles, history studies specific details. Yet as this general overview of colonialism shows, history can include summaries of long-term change and generalizations about different parts of the world over entire centuries as well as specific names and dates. What sorts of generalizations are made in this excerpt?

History, like fiction, is a form of storytelling. Fictional storytelling tends to be far more specific than history, usually documenting minutes or hours in the amount of space that it takes many historians to cover years and Osterhammel to cover centuries. Does this selection tell you a story in any sense, or is it too general to do that?

Colonial Epochs

The most important colonial advance of the period [1760–1830] was the extension of the British position in *India*. The British East India Company (EIC) originally conducted trade from port cities. Later on, it becomes increasingly involved in Indian domestic politics, which were determined by the antagonisms of regional powers in the declining phase of the Mughal empire. Unlike the Spanish in Central America, the British in India at first pursued no plans to conquer and certainly no plans to proselytize. They were far from possessing military advantages over the Indian states until about the middle of the century. In Bengal, where British trade interests were increasingly concentrated, a mutually advantageous agreement was reached with the regional prince, the Nabob. Only when a collapse of this "collaboration" was brought about by a concatenation of causes did the idea of territorial rule originate. In 1755, Robert Clive, the future conqueror of Bengal, expressed a hitherto unthinkable idea: "We must indeed become the Nabobs ourselves." From then on the British pursued a strategy of subjugation within a polycentric Indian state system, interrupted repeatedly by phases of deadlock and consolidation. Until the end of the colonial period in 1947, hundreds of seemingly autonomous principalities continued to exist, but after 1818 the British could consider themselves the "paramount power" on the subcontinent.

The East India Company continued to play its double role as business enterprise and state organization. Under constant supervision of the government in London it accompanied the military expansion of its sphere of power with the gradual establishment of colonial structures, which, in rough schematic terms, passed through a characteristic sequence of steps: (1) securing an effective trade monopoly, (2) securing military dominance and disarmament of any subjugated indigenous powers, (3) achieving a tax collection system, (4) stabilizing government by comprehensive legal regulations and the establishment of a bureaucratic administration, and (5) intervening in the indigenous society for purposes of social and humanitarian reform. This fifth stage was reached in the early 1830s. Not only did the age of European rule over highly civilized Asian societies begin in India, but India also became the prototype of an exploitation colony without settlers, a model for British expansion in other parts of Asia and Africa.

The period between 1830 and 1880 was certainly not a calm interlude in the history of European expansion. Only the Caribbean, once so rich, became a "forgotten derelict corner of the world." In an age of "free trade imperialism," China, Japan, Siam (Thailand) and, to a greater extent than was previously the case, the Ottoman Empire as well as Egypt, now de facto independent from it, were forced to open their economies. Sovereignty limitations characteristic of "informal empires" were imposed on them. Latin America, which was *no longer* colonial, and West Africa, which was rid of the slave trade but *not yet* colonized, were integrated into the world economy more closely than ever. On Java, the major island of the Netherlands East Indies, direct colonial intervention in the utilization of land began after 1830; the outer Indonesian islands were gradually subjugated in the period to follow. Foreign encroachment on continental Southeast Asia began after about 1820. First the lowlands near the coast fell into foreign hands: in 1852–1853 Lower Burma, and in 1857 Cochin China. By 1870, the later colonial borders could be distinguished clearly. During the entire period, the Tsarist Empire advanced in the Caucasus and Central Asia with military force, and shortly thereafter in the Far East with somewhat more diplomatic means, thereby intensifying the so-called "Great Game," a sustained cold war between the two Asiatic Great Powers Russia and Great Britain.

Despite these continuities of European world conquest and of ties between classic European diplomacy and "high imperialism," there is something to be said for marking a new epoch around 1870–1880. Most of the reasons can be found in the broader imperialist environment of colonialism, that is, in the structural changes of the world economy and international system. In terms of *colonial* history, the chief development over the last two decades of the nineteenth century was the European occupation of Africa, a singularly condensed expropriation of an entire continent termed the "partition of Africa." On the eve of this process, only South Africa and Algeria had been regions of European colonization, South Africa since 1652 and Algeria since

1830. Elsewhere the Portuguese (Angola, Mozambique), French (Senegal), and British (Sierra Leone, Lagos) made their presence felt in a more limited way. After all, by 1870 over 270,000 white people were already living in Algeria and about 245,000 in South Africa (including the two Boer Republics). The further expansion of these early cores of colonization was also an impetus for the occupation of Africa in the last quarter of the century. The discovery of diamond deposits in 1867 and of gold in 1886 unleashed a development that changed South Africa into a capitalist center of growth and a magnet for international capital. At the same time, it strengthened white supremacy. In Algeria the same result was achieved simultaneously under almost purely agrarian conditions by extensive land transfers from the Arabs to a rapidly growing settlement population.

The actual "partition" of Africa in the years between the occupation of Tunis by the French in 1881 and of Egypt by the British in 1882 on the one hand and the Boer War of the years 1899–1902 on the other was initially a somewhat symbolic process. With treaties *amongst themselves,* the European Great Powers committed themselves to mutual recognition of colonies, protectorates, and spheres of influence. "Paper partition" was only slowly and incompletely transformed into effective occupation, "partition on the ground." However, the borders that were drawn endured with the later establishment of independent African national states. For Africans, the so-called partition of their continent often meant the brutal disruption of bonds and established ways of life. However, partition could also result in the exact opposite: "a ruthless act of political amalgamation, whereby something of the order of ten thousand units was reduced to a mere forty." Particularly in Islamic North Africa (Egypt, Morocco, Tunisia, and Algeria) as well as in parts of Asia (Vietnam, Korea, and Burma), colonialism encountered fairly complex proto-nation-states. Colonial rule in these countries was considered even less legitimate than elsewhere.

Colonial Societies

. . . Characteristic of the social and cultural history of modern colonialism, especially in Asia, was the increasing alienation between two societies that had shared the bond of a colonial relationship since the late eighteenth century. While the status scale in Iberian America was rapidly refined, thereby placing renewed emphasis on racial criteria, the dualization of the colonial social landscape intensified in Asia and Africa. Only in Portuguese Asia was there significant progress in societal interaction, especially where native clergy were concerned, owing to the enlightened politics of the crown under the Marquis de Pombal in the 1760s and 1770s. The sealing off of the European communities from the indigenous environment had many causes, which were manifested in varying combinations: (1) Although Portugal and the Netherlands in particular had officially encouraged marriage between European men and Asian women at first, and the other colonial powers had tolerated it tacitly, immigration of European women raised the sexual autarky of the colonial societies. (2) The transition from trade to rule and often to direct production with dependent workers transformed the "age of partnership" into an age of subordination. (3) Violent resistance by the natives, such as the Native American massacre of colonists in Virginia in 1622 and the Indian rebellion of 1857–1858, strengthened the resolve of white minorities to shield themselves for self-protection. (4) A European attitude of superiority over the rest of the world, stemming from the Christian Eurocentrism of early encounters, made it appear increasingly "unreasonable" to Europeans to maintain close egalitarian relationships with non-Europeans and to make cultural accommodations to them. (5) After the gradual abolition of slave trade and slavery, racist thought lived in the less blatant, but now "scientifically" legitimated forms. It bears pointing out, however, that racism is often not the *cause* of segregation, but the *effect*. Racism has often been used to justify segregation after the fact.

Ethnosocial distancing was an outgrowth of societal interaction and was not always based on discriminatory laws. A telling example was Batavia, the most populous and resplendent city in Asia that was governed by Europe. In the first half of the seventeenth century, a mixed society was formed based on house slavery and the expansion of "Creole" family and patronage networks with relatively high tolerance for interracial family relationships. This society resembled its counterpart in Mexico and was even more akin to Portuguese colonization in Asia (Goa). In the manner of living of its upper class, the mixed society of Batavia conformed almost as closely to its Javanese surroundings as it did to Holland. A distinct demarcation between the European and Asian spheres commenced with the British interregnum of 1811–1816. In the eyes of the British, the Batavian Dutch were appallingly infected by their contact with Asians. Cultural decontamination was decreed. The whites in the city and their mestizo relatives were told to develop an identity as civilized Europeans and clearly display it in their appearances before the Javanese public.

The English in India had always been somewhat more detached from the indigenous environment than the Dutch in Indonesia. After the 1780s, their isolation gradually intensified and became obvious with the decline in status of Eurasian Anglo-Indians, even though some influential Indian politicians in 1830 were still dreaming of a racially mixed India modelled on Mexico. The club became the center of British social life in India and the other Asian colonies during the Victorian era. In clubs, one could feel like a gentleman among other gentlemen while being served by a native staff. In Kuala Lumpur, very few non-Europeans were admitted before 1940; in Singapore no non-Europeans were allowed in at all. The large clubs of Calcutta remained closed to Indians until 1946. This type of color bar was especially disturbing because it excluded from social recognition the very people who had carried their self-Anglicizing the furthest and loyally supported British rule. Even Indian members of the Indian Civil Service were excluded.

In most regions of Africa, the colonial period began at a time when exclusionist thought and action were most pronounced. In Africa there was virtually no history of intercultural proximity and therefore no need for policies enforcing detachment. The Europeans saw themselves as foreign rulers separated from the African cultures by an abyss. This absolute aloofness extended even to Islam, which they certainly did not consider "primitive," but rather historically obsolete. Color bars in Africa varied in height; they were lowest in West Africa and highest in the settlement colonies of the far north and the deep south. A process of great symptomatic significance was the rejection of the highly educated West Africans who had worked with the early mission. They had envisioned the colonial takeover as an opportunity for a joint European-African effort to modernize and civilize Africa. Instead, they were now, as "white Negroes," despised by all.

$$\boxed{142}$$

GEORGE ORWELL

From Burmese Days

This selection, from one of the great novels on colonialism, captures the life of the British colonial class in a remote "upcountry" town in Burma in the 1920s. The chapter is set in the European club. Flory, the principal character, is the only Englishman at all sympathetic to the Burmese. Though he has befriended the Indian physician, Dr. Veraswami, Flory is too weak to propose him as the first "native" member of the club. The other main characters are Westfield, District Superintendent of Police; Ellis, local company manager and the most racist of the group; Lackersteen, local manager of a timber company

---

George Orwell, *Burmese Days* (1934; reprint, San Diego: Harcourt Brace, 1962), 17–27.

who is usually drunk; Maxwell, a forest officer; and Macgregor, Deputy Commissioner and secretary of the club.

Why does the club loom so large in the lives of these Englishmen? If they complain so much, why are they in Burma? How do you account for the virulent racism of these men? Why does Ellis "correct" the butler's English? What does this story suggest about women in the colonial world?

Thinking Historically

As different as this selection is from Osterhammel's historical overview, both touch on the subjects of dual society, the European club, and colonial racism. How does this selection from Orwell support some of Osterhammel's generalizations? How does it deepen your understanding of these subjects?

The structure of a novel like this one bears certain similarities to history — a description of a place, proper names and biographies, descriptions of human interactions, an accounting of change, and a story. There are also structural differences in a novel — a lot of dialogue, greater attention to physical appearance and character, and a more prominent narrative. Do the fictional constructs in this selection detract from our historical understanding? Can such elements add to our understanding of what actually happened?

Of course, the problem with structural elements such as dialogue and story is that they are fiction. The author of a novel makes no pretense of telling the truth. Nevertheless, an author draws on what he or she knows to create a plausible scenario that is recognizable and consistent. Interestingly, Orwell knew Burma quite well. He was born in India in 1903. His father worked in the Opium Department of the Indian Civil Service. After attending school at Eton in England, Orwell returned to Burma, where he spent five years as a member of the Indian Imperial Police. Orwell, therefore, had a broad knowledge of Burma on which to base his story. Is there any way to determine what Orwell invented and what he merely described in this account?

Orwell was politically engaged throughout his life. Would political ideas make him better or worse as a historian or novelist? How so?

Flory's house was at the top of the maidan,[1] close to the edge of the jungle. From the gate the maidan sloped sharply down, scorched and khaki-coloured, with half a dozen dazzling white bungalows scattered round it. All quaked, shivered in the hot air. There was an English

---

[1]Parade-ground. [Ed.]

cemetery within a white wall half-way down the hill, and nearby a tiny tin-roofed church. Beyond that was the European Club, and when one looked at the Club — a dumpy one-storey wooden building — one looked at the real centre of the town. In any town in India the European Club is the spiritual citadel, the real seat of the British power, the Nirvana for which native officials and millionaires pine in vain. It was doubly so in this case, for it was the proud boast of Kyauktada Club that, almost alone of Clubs in Burma, it had never admitted an Oriental to membership. Beyond the Club, the Irrawaddy flowed huge and ochreous, glittering like diamonds in the patches that caught the sun; and beyond the river stretched great wastes of paddy fields, ending at the horizon in a range of blackish hills.

The native town, and the courts and the jail, were over to the right, mostly hidden in green groves of peepul trees. The spire of the pagoda rose from the trees like a slender spear tipped with gold. Kyauktada was a fairly typical Upper Burma town, that had not changed greatly between the days of Marco Polo and 1910, and might have slept in the Middle Ages for a century more if it had not proved a convenient spot for a railway terminus. In 1910 the Government made it the headquarters of a district and a seat of Progress — interpretable as a block of law courts, with their army of fat but ravenous pleaders, a hospital, a school, and one of those huge, durable jails which the English have built everywhere between Gibraltar and Hong Kong. The population was about four thousand, including a couple of hundred Indians, a few score Chinese and seven Europeans. There were also two Eurasians named Mr. Francis and Mr. Samuel, the sons of an American Baptist missionary and a Roman Catholic missionary respectively. The town contained no curiosities of any kind, except an Indian fakir who had lived for twenty years in a tree near the bazaar, drawing his food up in a basket every morning.

Flory yawned as he came out of the gate. He had been half drunk the night before, and the glare made him feel liverish. "Bloody, bloody hole!" he thought, looking down the hill. And, no one except the dog being near, he began to sing aloud, "Bloody, bloody, bloody, oh, how thou art bloody" to the tune of "Holy, holy, holy, oh how Thou art holy," as he walked down the hot red road, switching at the dried-up grasses with his stick. It was nearly nine o'clock and the sun was fiercer every minute. The heat throbbed down on one's head with a steady, rhythmic thumping, like blows from an enormous bolster. Flory stopped at the Club gate, wondering whether to go in or to go farther down the road and see Dr. Veraswami. Then he remembered that it was "English mail day" and the newspapers would have arrived. He went in, past the big tennis screen, which was overgrown by a creeper with starlike mauve flowers.

In the borders beside the path swathes of English flowers, phlox and larkspur, hollyhock and petunia, not yet slain by the sun, rioted in vast size and richness. The petunias were huge, like trees almost. There was no lawn, but instead a shrubbery of native trees and bushes — gold mohur trees like vast umbrellas of blood-red bloom, frangipanis with creamy, stalkless flowers, purple bougainvillea, scarlet hibiscus, and the pink, Chinese rose, bilious-green crotons, feathery fronds of tamarind. The clash of colours hurt one's eyes in the glare. A nearly naked *mali*,[2] watering-can in hand, was moving in the jungle of flowers like some large nectar-sucking bird.

On the Club steps a sandy-haired Englishman, with a prickly moustache, pale grey eyes too far apart, and abnormally thin calves to his legs, was standing with his hands in the pockets of his shorts. This was Mr. Westfield, the District Superintendent of Police. With a very bored air he was rocking himself backwards and forwards on his heels and pouting his upper lip so that his moustache tickled his nose. He greeted Flory with a slight sideways movement of his head. His way of speaking was clipped and soldierly, missing out every word that well could be missed out. Nearly everything he said was intended for a joke, but the tone of his voice was hollow and melancholy.

"Hullo, Flory me lad. Bloody awful morning, what?"

"We must expect it at this time of year, I suppose," Flory said. He had turned himself a little sideways, so that his birthmarked cheek was away from Westfield.

"Yes, dammit. Couple of months of this coming. Last year we didn't have a spot of rain till June. Look at that bloody sky, not a cloud in it. Like one of those damned great blue enamel saucepans. God! What'd you give to be in Piccadilly now, eh?"

"Have the English papers come?"

"Yes. Dear old *Punch, Pink'un,* and *Vie Parisienne.* Makes you homesick to read 'em, what? Let's come in and have a drink before the ice all goes. Old Lackersteen's been fairly bathing in it. Half pickled already."

They went in, Westfield remarking in his gloomy voice, "Lead on, Macduff." Inside, the Club was a teak-walled place smelling of earth-oil, and consisting of only four rooms, one of which contained a forlorn "library" of five hundred mildewed novels, and another an old and mangy billiard-table — this, however, seldom used, for during most of the year hordes of flying beetles came buzzing round the lamps and littered themselves over the cloth. There were also a card-room and a "lounge" which looked towards the river, over a wide veranda; but at

[2]Gardener. [Ed.]

this time of day all the verandas were curtained with green bamboo chicks. The lounge was an unhomelike room, with coco-nut matting on the floor, and wicker chairs and tables which were littered with shiny illustrated papers. For ornament there were a number of "Bonzo" pictures, and the dusty skulls of sambhur. A punkah,[3] lazily flapping, shook dust into the tepid air.

There were three men in the room. Under the punkah a florid, fine-looking, slightly bloated man of forty was sprawling across the table with his head in his hands, groaning in pain. This was Mr. Lackersteen, the local manager of a timber firm. He had been badly drunk the night before, and he was suffering for it. Ellis, local manager of yet another company, was standing before the notice board studying some notice with a look of bitter concentration. He was a tiny wiry-haired fellow with a pale, sharp-featured face and restless movements. Maxwell, the acting Divisional Forest Officer, was lying in one of the long chairs reading the *Field,* and invisible except for two large-boned legs and thick downy forearms.

"Look at this naughty old man," said Westfield, taking Mr. Lackersteen half affectionately by the shoulders and shaking him. "Example to the young, what? There, but for the grace of God and all that. Gives you an idea what you'll be like at forty."

Mr. Lackersteen gave a groan which sounded like "brandy."

"Poor old chap," said Westfield; "regular martyr to booze, eh? Look at it oozing out of his pores. Reminds me of the old colonel who used to sleep without a mosquito net. They asked his servant why and the servant said: 'At night, master too drunk to notice mosquitoes; in the morning, mosquitoes too drunk to notice master.' Look at him — boozed last night and then asking for more. Got a little niece coming to stay with him, too. Due tonight, isn't she, Lackersteen?"

"Oh, leave that drunken sot alone," said Ellis without turning round. He had a spiteful cockney voice. Mr. Lackersteen groaned again, "— the niece! Get me some brandy, for Christ's sake."

"Good education for the niece, eh? Seeing uncle under the table seven times a week. — Hey, butler! Bringing brandy for Lackersteen master!"

The butler, a dark, stout Dravidian[4] with liquid, yellow-irised eyes like those of a dog, brought the brandy on a brass tray. Flory and Westfield ordered gin. Mr. Lackersteen swallowed a few spoonfuls of brandy and sat back in his chair, groaning in a more resigned way. He had a beefy, ingenuous face, with a toothbrush moustache. He was re-

---

[3]Large cloth panel fan hanging from the ceiling, usually pulled by a rope to move the air. [Ed.]

[4]Dated racial term used to refer to darker skinned inhabitants of southern India. [Ed.]

ally a very simple-minded man, with no ambitions beyond having what he called "a good time." His wife governed him by the only possible method, namely, by never letting him out of her sight for more than an hour or two. Only once, a year after they were married, she had left him for a fortnight, and had returned unexpectedly a day before her time, to find Mr. Lackersteen, drunk, supported on either side by a naked Burmese girl, while a third up-ended a whisky bottle into his mouth. Since then she had watched him, as he used to complain, "like a cat over a bloody mousehole." However, he managed to enjoy quite a number of "good times," though they were usually rather hurried ones.

"My Christ, what a head I've got on me this morning," he said. "Call that butler again, Westfield. I've got to have another brandy before my missus gets here. She says she's going to cut my booze down to four pegs a day when our niece gets here. God rot them both!" he added gloomily.

"Stop playing the fool, all of you, and listen to this," said Ellis sourly. He had a queer wounding way of speaking, hardly ever opening his mouth without insulting somebody. He deliberately exaggerated his cockney accent, because of the sardonic tone it gave to his words. "Have you seen this notice of old Macgregor's? A little nosegay for everyone. Maxwell, wake up and listen!"

Maxwell lowered the *Field*. He was a fresh-coloured blond youth of not more than twenty-five or six — very young for the post he held. With his heavy limbs and thick white eyelashes he reminded one of a carthorse colt. Ellis nipped the notice from the board with a neat, spiteful little movement and began reading it aloud. It had been posted by Mr. Macgregor, who, besides being Deputy Commissioner, was secretary of the Club.

"Just listen to this. 'It has been suggested that as there are as yet no Oriental members of this club, and as it is now usual to admit officials of gazetted rank, whether native or European, to membership of most European Clubs, we should consider the question of following this practice in Kyauktada. The matter will be open for discussion at the next general meeting. On the one hand it may be pointed out' — oh, well, no need to wade through the rest of it. He can't even write out a notice without an attack of literary diarrhœa. Anyway, the point's this. He's asking us to break all our rules and take a dear little nigger-boy into this Club. *Dear* Dr. Veraswami, for instance. Dr. Very-slimy, I call him. That *would* be a treat, wouldn't it? Little pot-bellied niggers breathing garlic in your face over the bridge-table. Christ, to think of it! We've got to hang together and put our foot down on this at once. What do you say, Westfield? Flory?"

Westfield shrugged his thin shoulders philosophically. He had sat down at the table and lighted a black, stinking Burma cheroot.

"Got to put up with it, I suppose," he said. "B_____s of natives are getting into all the Clubs nowadays. Even the Pegu Club, I'm told. Way this country's going, you know. We're about the last Club in Burma to hold out against 'em."

"We are; and what's more, we're damn well going to go on holding out. I'll die in the ditch before I'll see a nigger in here." Ellis had produced a stump of pencil. With the curious air of spite that some men can put into their tiniest action, he re-pinned the notice on the board and pencilled a tiny, neat "B. F." against Mr. Macgregor's signature — "There, that's what I think of his idea. I'll tell him so when he comes down. What do *you* say, Flory?"

Flory had not spoken all this time. Though by nature anything but a silent man, he seldom found much to say in Club conversations. He had sat down at the table and was reading G. K. Chesterton's article in the *London News*, at the same time caressing Flo's [his dog] head with his left hand. Ellis, however, was one of those people who constantly nag others to echo their own opinions. He repeated his question, and Flory looked up, and their eyes met. The skin round Ellis's nose suddenly turned so pale that it was almost grey. In him it was a sign of anger. Without any prelude he burst into a stream of abuse that would have been startling, if the others had not been used to hearing something like it every morning.

"My God, I should have thought in a case like this, when it's a question of keeping those black, stinking swine out of the only place where we can enjoy ourselves, you'd have the decency to back me up. Even if that pot-bellied, greasy little sod of a nigger doctor *is* your best pal. *I* don't care if you choose to pal up with the scum of the bazaar. If it pleases you to go to Veraswami's house and drink whisky with all his nigger pals, that's your look-out. Do what you like outside the Club. But, by God, it's a different matter when you talk of bringing niggers in here. I suppose you'd like little Veraswami for a Club member, eh? Chipping into our conversation and pawing everyone with his sweaty hands and breathing his filthy garlic breath in our faces. By God, he'd go out with my boot behind him if ever I saw his black snout inside that door. Greasy, pot-bellied little ——— !" etc.

This went on for several minutes. It was curiously impressive, because it was so completely sincere. Ellis really did hate Orientals — hated them with a bitter, restless loathing as of something evil or unclean. Living and working, as the assistant of a timber firm must, in perpetual contact with the Burmese, he had never grown used to the sight of a black face. Any hint of friendly feeling towards an Oriental seemed to him a horrible perversity. He was an intelligent man and an able servant of his firm, but he was one of those Englishmen — common, unfortunately — who should never be allowed to set foot in the East.

Flory sat nursing Flo's head in his lap, unable to meet Ellis's eyes. At the best of times his birthmark made it difficult for him to look people straight in the face. And when he made ready to speak, he could feel his voice trembling — for it had a way of trembling when it should have been firm; his features, too, sometimes twitched uncontrollably.

"Steady on," he said at last, sullenly and rather feebly. "Steady on. There's no need to get so excited. *I* never suggested having any native members in here."

"Oh, didn't you? We all know bloody well you'd like to, though. Why else do you go to that oily little babu's house every morning, then? Sitting down at table with him as though he was a white man, and drinking out of glasses his filthy black lips have slobbered over — it makes me spew to think of it."

"Sit down, old chap, sit down," Westfield said. "Forget it. Have a drink on it. Not worth while quarrelling. Too hot."

"My God," said Ellis a little more calmly, taking a pace or two up and down, "my God, I don't understand you chaps. I simply don't. Here's that old fool Macgregor wanting to bring a nigger into this Club for no reason whatever, and you all sit down under it without a word. Good God, what are we supposed to be doing in this country? If we aren't going to rule, why the devil don't we clear out? Here we are, supposed to be governing a set of damn black swine who've been slaves since the beginning of history, and instead of ruling them in the only way they understand, we go and treat them as equals. And all you silly b———s take it for granted. There's Flory, makes his best pal of a black babu who calls himself a doctor because he's done two years at an Indian so-called university. And you, Westfield, proud as Punch of your knock-kneed, bribe-taking cowards of policemen. And there's Maxwell, spends his time running after Eurasian tarts. Yes, you do, Maxwell; I heard about your goings-on in Mandalay with some smelly little bitch called Molly Pereira. I supposed you'd have gone and married her if they hadn't transferred you up here? You all seem to *like* the dirty black brutes. Christ, I don't know what's come over us all. I really don't."

"Come on, have another drink," said Westfield. "Hey, butler! Spot of beer before the ice goes, eh? Beer, butler!"

The butler brought some bottles of Munich beer. Ellis presently sat down at the table with the others, and he nursed one of the cool bottles between his small hands. His forehead was sweating. He was sulky, but not in a rage any longer. At all times he was spiteful and perverse, but his violent fits of rage were soon over, and were never apologised for. Quarrels were a regular part of the routine of Club life. Mr. Lackersteen was feeling better and was studying the illustrations in *La Vie Parisienne*. It was after nine now, and the room, scented with the acrid smoke of Westfield's cheroot, was stifling hot. Everyone's shirt stuck to his back with the first sweat of the day. The invisible *chokra*[5] who pulled the punkah rope outside was falling asleep in the glare.

"Butler!" yelled Ellis, and as the butler appeared, "go and wake that bloody *chokra* up!"

"Yes, master."

"And butler!"

"Yes, master?"

"How much ice have we got left?"

"'Bout twenty pounds, master. Will only last to-day, I think. I find it very difficult to keep ice cool now."

"Don't talk like that, damn you — 'I find it very difficult!' Have you swallowed a dictionary? 'Please, master, can't keeping ice cool' — that's how you ought to talk. We shall have to sack this fellow if he gets to talk English too well. I can't stick servants who talk English. D'you hear, butler?"

"Yes, master," said the butler, and retired.

"God! No ice till Monday," Westfield said. "You going back to the jungle, Flory?"

"Yes. I ought to be there now. I only came in because of the English mail."

"Go on tour myself, I think. Knock up a spot of Travelling Allowance. I can't stick my bloody office at this time of year. Sitting there under the damned punkah, signing one chit after another. Paper-chewing. God, how I wish the war was on again!"

"I'm going out the day after to-morrow," Ellis said. "Isn't that damned padre coming to hold his service this Sunday? I'll take care not to be in for that, anyway. Bloody knee-drill."

"Next Sunday," said Westfield. "Promised to be in for it myself. So's Macgregor. Bit hard on the poor devil of a padre, I must say. Only gets here once in six weeks. Might as well get up a congregation when he does come."

"Oh, hell! I'd snivel psalms to oblige the padre, but I can't stick the way these damned native Christians come shoving into our church. A pack of Madrassi servants and Karen school-teachers. And then those two yellow-bellies, Francis and Samuel — they call themselves Christians too. Last time the padre was here they had the nerve to come up and sit on the front pews with the white men. Someone ought to speak to the padre about that. What bloody fools we were ever to let those missionaries loose in this country! Teaching bazaar sweepers they're as good as we are. 'Please, sir, me Christian same like master.' Damned cheek."

[5]Person who pulls the punkah rope that moves a large panel to let in a breeze. [Ed.]

DAVID CANNADINE

From Ornamentalism

In the following selection from his work *Ornamentalism*, David Cannadine, a modern historian, challenges a traditional interpretation of the British Empire. What is that traditional interpretation? What view does the author propose instead? Do you find his new interpretation convincing?

Thinking Historically

Does your reading of *Burmese Days* support or contradict Cannadine's interpretation of British imperialism? What evidence do you see in *Burmese Days* that social distinctions were more important than racial ones? What literary evidence does Cannadine present to support his thesis?

Nations, it has recently become commonplace to observe, are in part imagined communities, depending for their credibility and identity both on the legitimacy of government and the apparatus of the state, and on invented traditions, manufactured myths, and shared perceptions of the social order that are never more than crude categories and oversimplified stereotypes. If this has been true (as indeed it has) of a relatively compact and contained country like Britain, then how much more true must this have been of the empire that the British conquered and peopled, administered, and ruled? At its territorial zenith, shortly after the end of the First World War, it consisted of naval stations and military bases extending from Gibraltar to Hong Kong, the four great dominions of settlement, the Indian Empire that occupied an entire subcontinent, the crown colonies in Asia, Africa, and the Caribbean, and the League of Nations Mandates, especially in the Middle East. But, as with all such transoceanic realms, the British Empire was not only a geopolitical entity: it was also a culturally created and imaginatively constructed artifact. How, then, in the heyday of its existence, did Britons imagine and envisage their unprecedentedly vast and varied imperium, not so much geographically as sociologically? How did they try

David Cannadine, *Ornamentalism: How the British Saw Their Empire* (Oxford: Oxford University Press, 2001), 3–10.

to organize and to arrange their heterogeneous imperial society, as they settled and conquered, governed and ruled it, and what did they think the resulting social order looked like?

To the extent that they tried to conceive of these diverse colonies and varied populations beyond the seas as "an entire interactive system, one vast interconnected world," most Britons followed the standard pattern of human behaviour when contemplating and comprehending the unfamiliar. Their "inner predisposition" was to begin with what they knew — or what they thought they knew — namely, the social structure of their own home country. But what sort of a starting point was this, and what were the implications and consequences of British perceptions of their domestic social order for British perceptions of their imperial social order? From Hegel to Marx, and from Engels to Said, it has been commonplace to suggest that Britons saw their own society (and, by extension, that of what became their settler dominions) as dynamic, individualistic, egalitarian, modernizing — and thus superior. By comparison with such a positive and progressive metropolitan perception, this argument continues, Britons saw society in their "tropical" and "oriental" colonies as enervated, hierarchical, corporatist, backward — and thus inferior. But among its many flaws, this appealingly simplistic (and highly influential) contrast is based on a mistaken premise, in that it fundamentally misunderstands most Britons' perceptions of their domestic social world when their nation was at its zenith as an imperial power.

Far from seeing themselves as atomized individuals with no rooted sense of identity, or as collective classes coming into being and struggling with each other, or as equal citizens whose modernity engendered an unrivalled sense of progressive superiority, Britons generally conceived of themselves as belonging to an unequal society characterized by a seamless web of layered gradations, which were hallowed by time and precedent, which were sanctioned by tradition and religion, and which extended in a great chain of being from the monarch at the top to the humblest subject at the bottom. That was how they saw themselves, and it was from that starting point that they contemplated and tried to comprehend the distant realms and diverse society of their empire. This in turn meant that for the British, their overseas realms were at least as much about sameness as they were about difference. For insofar as they regarded their empire as "one vast interconnected world," they did not necessarily do so in disadvantaged or critical contrast to the way they perceived their own metropolitan society. Rather, they were at least as likely to envisage the social structure of their empire — as their predecessors had done before them — by analogy to what they knew of "home," or in replication of it, or in parallel to it, or in extension of it, or (sometimes) in idealization of it, or (even, and increasingly) in nostalgia for it.

This means that we need to be much more attentive to the varied —
sometimes, even, contradictory — ways in which the British understood, visualized, and imagined their empire hierarchically. To be sure,
one of the ways in which they did so was in racial terms of superiority
and inferiority. Like all post-Enlightenment imperial powers, only more
so, Britons saw themselves as the lords of all the world and thus of humankind. They placed themselves at the top of the scale of civilization
and achievement, they ranked all other races in descending order beneath them, according to their relative merits (and de-merits), and during the period 1780 to 1830 they increasingly embodied these views in
imperial institutions and codes. And when it came to the systematic settlement of Canada, Australia, New Zealand, and South Africa, they did
not hesitate to banish the indigenous peoples to the margins of the new,
imperial society. By the end of the nineteenth century these notions of
racial hierarchy, supremacy, and stereotyping had become more fully
developed, and stridently hardened, as exemplified in Cecil Rhodes's
remark that "the British are the finest race in the world, and the more
of the world they inhabit, the better it will be for mankind," or in Lord
Cromer's belief that the world was divided between those who were
British and those who were merely "subject races."

In short, and as Peter Marshall has observed, "Empire reinforced
a hierarchical view of the world, in which the British occupied a pre-
eminent place among the colonial powers, while those subjected to
colonial rule were ranged below them, in varying degrees of supposed
inferiority." These facts are familiar and incontrovertible. But this
mode of imperial ranking and imaging was not just based on the Enlightenment view of the intrinsic inferiority of dark-skinned peoples: it
was also based on notions of metropolitan–peripheral analogy and
sameness. For as the British contemplated the unprecedented numbers
massed together in their new industrial cities, they tended to compare
these great towns at home with the "dark continents" overseas, and
thus equate the workers in factories with coloured peoples abroad. The
"shock cities" of the 1830s and 1840s were seen as resembling "darkest Africa" in their distant, unknown, and unfathomable menaces; and
during the third quarter of the nineteenth century London's newly discovered "residuum" and "dangerous classes" were likened — in their
character and their conduct — to the "negroes" of empire. And these
domestic–imperial analogies were worked and extended in the opposite
direction as well: one additional reason why "natives" in the empire
were regarded as collectively inferior was that they were seen as the
overseas equivalent of the "undeserving poor" in Britain.

To some degree, then, these analogies and comparisons that Britons
drew and made between domestic and overseas societies, from the
eighteenth to the twentieth centuries, served to reinforce the prevailing

Enlightenment notions of racial superiority and inferiority. And it is from this premise that the British Empire has been viewed by contemporaries and by historians as an enterprise that was built and maintained on the basis of the collective, institutionalized, and politicized ranking of races. But, as these analogies and comparisons also suggest, this was not the only way in which Britons envisioned their empire, and its imperial society, as an essentially hierarchical organism. For there was another vantage-point from which they regarded the inhabitants of their far-flung realms, which was also built around notions of superiority and inferiority, but which frequently cut across, and sometimes overturned and undermined, the notion that the British Empire was based solely and completely on a hierarchy of race. This alternative approach was, indeed, the conventional way in which the English (and latterly the British) had regarded the inhabitants of other, alien worlds, for it was a perspective that long antedated the Enlightenment.

It has certainly been traced back to the sixteenth and seventeenth centuries, for when the English first encountered the native peoples of North America, they did not see them collectively as a race of inferior savages; on the contrary, they viewed them individually as fellow human beings. It was from this pre-Enlightenment perspective that the English concluded that North American society closely resembled their own: a carefully graded hierarchy of status, extending in a seamless web from chiefs and princes at the top to less worthy figures at the bottom. Moreover, these two essentially hierarchical societies were seen as coexisting, not in a relationship of (English) superiority and (North American) inferiority, but in a relationship of equivalence and similarity: princes in one society were the analogues to princes in another, and so on and so on, all the way down these two parallel social ladders. In short, when the English initially contemplated native Americans, they saw them as social equals rather than as social inferiors, and when they came to apply their conventionally hierarchical tools of observation, their prime grid of analysis was individual status rather than collective race.

It is the argument of this book that these attitudes, whereby social ranking was as important as (perhaps more important than?) colour of skin in contemplating the extra-metropolitan world, remained important for the English and, latterly, for the British long after it has been generally supposed they ceased to matter. To be sure, the Enlightenment brought about a new, collective way of looking at peoples, races, and colours, based on distance and separation and otherness. But it did not subvert the earlier, individualistic, analogical way of thinking, based on the observation of status similarities and the cultivation of affinities, that projected domestically originated perceptions of the social order overseas. On the contrary, this essentially pre-racial way of seeing things lasted for as long as the British Empire lasted. Here is one example. In the summer of 1881 King Kalakaua of Hawaii was visiting England and, in the course of an extensive round of social engagements, he found himself the guest at a party given by Lady Spencer. Also attending were the prince of Wales, who would eventually become King Edward VII, and the German crown prince, who was his brother-in-law and the future kaiser. The prince of Wales insisted that the king should take precedence over the crown prince, and when his brother-in-law objected, he offered the following pithy and trenchant justification: "Either the brute is a king, or he's a common or garden nigger; and if the latter, what's he doing here?"

Read one way, this is, to our modern sensibilities, a deeply insensitive and offensively racist observation; read from another viewpoint, this was, by the conventions of its own time, a very *un*racist remark. The traditional, pre-Enlightenment freemasonry based on the shared recognition of high social rank — a freemasonry to which Martin Malia has suggestively given the name "aristocratic internationalism" — both trumped and transcended the alternative and more recent freemasonry based on the unifying characteristic of shared skin colour. From *this* perspective, the hierarchical principle that underlay Britons' perceptions of their empire was not exclusively based on the collective, colour-coded ranking of social groups, but depended as much on the more venerable colour-blind ranking of individual social prestige. This means there were at least two visions of empire that were essentially (and elaborately) hierarchical: one centred on colour, the other on class. So, in the *Raj Quartet*, Major Ronald Merrick, whose social background was relatively lowly, believed that "the English were superior to all other races, especially black." But the Cambridge-educated Guy Perron feels a greater affinity with the Indian Hari Kumar, who went to the same public school as he did, than he does with Merrick, who is very much his social inferior.

The British Empire has been extensively studied as a complex *racial* hierarchy (and also as a less complex *gender* hierarchy); but it has received far less attention as an equally complex *social* hierarchy or, indeed, as a social organism, or construct, of any kind. This constant (and largely unquestioned) privileging of colour over class, of race over rank, of collectivities over individualities, in the scholarly literature has opened up many important new lines of inquiry. But it has also meant that scarcely any attention has been paid to empire as a functioning social structure and as an imagined social entity, in which, as Karen Ordahl Kupperman puts it, "status is fundamental to all other categories." Yet throughout its history, the views expressed by the prince of Wales reflected generally held opinions about the social arrangements existing in the empire. These attitudes and perceptions were certainly still in existence in the late eighteenth and early nineteenth centuries. But they were no less important between the 1850s and the 1950s, when the ideal of social hierarchy was seen as the model towards which the great dominions should approximate, when it formed the basis of the fully elaborated Raj in India, when it provided the key to the doctrine of "indirect rule" in Africa, when it formed the template for the new nations created in the British Middle East, when it was codified and rationalized by the imperial honours system, and when it was legitimated and unified by the imperial monarchy. In all these ways, the theory and the practice of social hierarchy served to eradicate the differences, and to homogenize the heterogeneities, of empire. . . .

We should never forget that the British Empire was first and foremost a class act, where individual social ordering often took precedence over collective racial othering.

$$\boxed{144}$$

JOSEPH CONRAD

From Heart of Darkness

Although his native tongue was Polish (and French his second language), Joseph Conrad (1857–1924) became one of the leading English novelists of the era of British imperialism. Drawing on his experience as a mariner and ship captain, he secured a post as an officer on river steamboats on the Congo River in 1890. Nine years later he published *Heart of Darkness*, a novel which has introduced generations since to Africa, the Congo, the era of colonialism, and European ideas of "the other."

In this selection from the novel, Conrad's narrator, Marlow, tells of his voyage up the Congo to meet the enigmatic European Kurtz who has secured prodigious amounts of ivory for his Belgian employer but (we learn at the end of the novel) lost his mind in the process.

What impression does *Heart of Darkness* give of Africa and of European exploration of Africa?

Joseph Conrad, *Heart of Darkness*, A Norton Critical Edition (New York: Norton, 1988), 35–39. Originally published by *Blackwood's Magazine* (London, 1899, 1902).

Thinking Historically

Like many novels, *Heart of Darkness* is based on the actual experiences of the author. Despite the basis in fact, however, it is very different from historical writing. Imagine Conrad writing a history of the events described in this selection. How would it be different? Would one account be truer, or merely reveal different truths?

Going up that river was like travelling back to the earliest beginnings of the world, when vegetation rioted on the earth and the big trees were kings. An empty stream, a great silence, an impenetrable forest. The air was warm, thick, heavy, sluggish. There was no joy in the brilliance of sunshine. The long stretches of the waterway ran on, deserted, into the gloom of overshadowed distances. On silvery sandbanks hippos and alligators sunned themselves side by side. The broadening waters flowed through a mob of wooded islands. You lost your way on that river as you would in a desert and butted all day long against shoals trying to find the channel till you thought yourself bewitched and cut off for ever from everything you had known once — somewhere — far away — in another existence perhaps. There were moments when one's past came back to one, as it will sometimes when you have not a moment to spare to yourself; but it came in the shape of an unrestful and noisy dream remembered with wonder amongst the overwhelming realities of this strange world of plants and water and silence. And this stillness of life did not in the least resemble a peace. It was the stillness of an implacable force brooding over an inscrutable intention. It looked at you with a vengeful aspect. I got used to it afterwards. I did not see it any more. I had no time. I had to keep guessing at the channel; I had to discern, mostly by inspiration, the signs of hidden banks; I watched for sunken stones; I was learning to clap my teeth smartly before my heart flew out when I shaved by a fluke some infernal sly old snag that would have ripped the life out of the tin-pot steamboat and drowned all the pilgrims; I had to keep a look-out for the signs of dead wood we could cut up in the night for next day's steaming. When you have to attend to things of that sort, to the mere incidents of the surface, the reality — the reality I tell you — fades. The inner truth is hidden — luckily, luckily. But I felt it all the same; I felt often its mysterious stillness watching me at my monkey tricks. . . .

"I managed not to sink that steamboat on my first trip. It's a wonder to me yet. Imagine a blindfolded man set to drive a van over a bad road. I sweated and shivered over that business considerably, I can tell you. After all, for a seaman, to scrape the bottom of the thing that's supposed to float all the time under his care is the unpardonable sin.

No one may know of it, but you never forget the thump — eh? A blow on the very heart. You remember it, you dream of it, you wake up at night and think of it — years after — and go hot and cold all over. I don't pretend to say that steamboat floated all the time. More than once she had to wade for a bit, with twenty cannibals splashing around and pushing. We had enlisted some of these chaps on the way for a crew. Fine fellows — cannibals — in their place. They were men one could work with, and I am grateful to them. And, after all, they did not eat each other before my face: they had brought along a provision of hippo-meat which went rotten and made the mystery of the wilderness stink in my nostrils. Phoo! I can sniff it now. I had the Manager on board and three or four pilgrims with their staves — all complete. Sometimes we came upon a station close by the bank clinging to the skirts of the unknown, and the white men rushing out of a tumble-down hovel with great gestures of joy and surprise and welcome seemed very strange, had the appearance of being held there captive by a spell. The word 'ivory' would ring in the air for a while — and on we went again into the silence, along empty reaches, round the still bends, between the high walls of our winding way, reverberating in hollow claps the ponderous beat of the stern-wheel. Trees, trees, millions of trees, massive, immense, running up high, and at their foot, hugging the bank against the stream, crept the little begrimed steamboat like a slug-gish beetle crawling on the floor of a lofty portico. It made you feel very small, very lost, and yet it was not altogether depressing, that feel-ing. After all, if you were small, the grimy beetle crawled on — which was just what you wanted it to do. Where the pilgrims imagined it crawled to I don't know. To some place where they expected to get something, I bet! For me it crawled towards Kurtz — exclusively; but when the steam-pipes started leaking we crawled very slow. The reaches opened before us and closed behind, as if the forest had stepped leisurely across the water to bar the way for our return. We penetrated deeper and deeper into the heart of darkness. It was very quiet there. At night sometimes the roll of drums behind the curtain of trees would run up the river and remain sustained faintly, as if hovering in the air high over our heads till the first break of day. Whether it meant war, peace, or prayer we could not tell. The dawns were heralded by the descent of a chill stillness. The woodcutters slept, their fires burned low, the snap-ping of a twig would make you start. We were wanderers on a prehis-toric earth, on an earth that wore the aspect of an unknown planet. We could have fancied ourselves the first of men taking possession of an ac-cursed inheritance, to be subdued at the cost of profound anguish and of excessive toil. But suddenly as we struggled round a bend there would be a glimpse of rush walls, of peaked grass-roofs, a burst of yells, a whirl of black limbs, a mass of hands clapping, of feet stamp-ing, of bodies swaying, of eyes rolling under the droop of heavy and motionless foliage. The steamer toiled along slowly on the edge of a black and incomprehensible frenzy. The prehistoric man was cursing us, praying to us, welcoming us — who could tell? We were cut off from the comprehension of our surroundings; we glided past like phantoms, wondering and secretly appalled, as sane men would be before an enthusiastic outbreak in a madhouse. We could not understand because we were too far and could not remember because we were travelling in the night of first ages, of those ages that are gone, leaving hardly a sign — and no memories.

"The earth seemed unearthly. We are accustomed to look upon the shackled form of a conquered monster, but there — there you could look at a thing monstrous and free. It was unearthly and the men were. . . . No they were not inhuman. Well, you know that was the worst of it — this suspicion of their not being inhuman. It would come slowly to one. They howled and leaped and spun and made horrid faces, but what thrilled you was just the thought of their humanity — like yours — the thought of your remote kinship with this wild and passionate uproar. Ugly. Yes, it was ugly enough, but if you were man enough you would admit to yourself that there was in you just the faintest trace of a response to the terrible frankness of that noise, a dim suspicion of there being a meaning in it which you — you so remote from the night of first ages — could comprehend. And why not? The mind of man is capable of anything — because everything is in it, all the past as well as all the future. What was there after all? Joy, fear, sorrow, devotion, valour, rage — who can tell? — but truth — truth stripped of its cloak of time. Let the fool gape and shudder — the man knows and can look on without a wink. But he must at least be as much of a man as these on the shore. He must meet that truth with his own true stuff — with his own inborn strength. Principles? Principles won't do. Acquisitions, clothes, pretty rags — rags that would fly off at the first good shake. No. You want a deliberate belief. An appeal to me in this fiendish row — is there? Very well. I hear, I admit, but I have a voice too, and for good or evil mine is the speech that cannot be silenced. Of course, a fool, what with sheer fright and fine sentiments, is always safe. Who's that grunting? You wonder I didn't go ashore for a howl and a dance? Well, no — I didn't. Fine sentiments, you say? Fine sentiments be hanged! I had no time. I had to mess about with white-lead and strips of woollen blanket helping to put bandages on those leaky steam-pipes — tell you. I had to watch the steering and circumvent those snags and get the tin-pot along by hook or by crook. There was surface-truth enough in these things to save a wiser man. And between whiles I had to look after the savage who was fireman. He was an improved specimen; he could fire up a vertical boiler. He was there below me and, upon my word, to look at him was as edifying as seeing a dog in a parody of breeches and a feather hat walking on his hind legs. A few months of training had done for that really fine chap. He squinted at the steam-gauge and at the water-gauge with an evident effort of intrepidity — and he had filed teeth too, the poor devil, and the wool of his pate shaved into queer patterns, and three ornamental scars on each of his cheeks. He ought to have been clapping his hands and stamping his feet on the bank, instead of which he was hard at work, a thrall to strange witchcraft, full of improving knowledge. He was useful because he had been instructed; and what he knew was this — that should the water in that transparent thing disappear the evil spirit inside the boiler would get angry through the greatness of his thirst and take a terrible vengeance. So he sweated and fired up and watched the glass fearfully (with an impromptu charm, made of rags, tied to his arm and a piece of polished bone as big as a watch stuck flatways through his lower lip) while the wooded banks slipped past us slowly, the shore noise was left behind, the interminable miles of silence — and we crept on, towards Kurtz.

CHINUA ACHEBE

An Image of Africa: Racism in Conrad's *Heart of Darkness*

Chinua Achebe* is modern Africa's most read novelist. His *Things Fall Apart*, about the impact of European missionaries in his native Nigeria at the end of the nineteenth century, is a classic that is as widely read as *Heart of Darkness*. In this selection, which first took form as an address to an American college audience in 1975, Achebe tackles *Heart of Darkness*. What is his argument? Are you persuaded? How, if at all, does this reading change your evaluation of the selection from David Cannadine's *Ornamentalism*?

*chih NOO ah   ah CHEH bay

Chinua Achebe, "An Image of Africa: Racism in Conrad's *Heart of Darkness*," an emended version (1987) of the second Chancellor's Lecture at the University of Massachusetts, Amherst, February 18, 1975; later published in the *Massachusetts Review*, 18 (1977). Reprinted in *Heart of Darkness*, A Norton Critical Edition (New York: Norton, 1988), 252–54, 257–60.

Thinking Historically

Achebe is a novelist criticizing another novelist for distorting history. What are the responsibilities of a novelist to historical accuracy?

Heart of Darkness projects the image of Africa as "the other world," the antithesis of Europe and therefore of civilization, a place where man's vaunted intelligence and relinement are finally mocked by triumphant bestiality. The book opens on the River Thames, tranquil, resting, peacefully "at the decline of day after ages of good service done to the race that peopled its banks." But the actual story will take place on the River Congo, the very antithesis of the Thames. The River Congo is quite decidedly not a River Emeritus. It has rendered no service and enjoys no old-age pension. We are told that "Going up that river was like travelling back to the earliest beginnings of the world."

Is Conrad saying then that these two rivers are very different, one good, the other bad? Yes, but that is not the real point. It is not the differentness that worries Conrad but the lurking hint of kinship, of common ancestry. For the Thames too "has been one of the dark places of the earth." It conquered its darkness, of course, and is now in daylight and at peace. But if it were to visit its primordial relative, the Congo, it would run the terrible risk of hearing grotesque echoes of its own forgotten darkness, and falling victim to an avenging recrudescence of the mindless frenzy of the first beginnings.

These suggestive echoes comprise Conrad's famed evocation of the African atmosphere in *Heart of Darkness*. In the final consideration his method amounts to no more than a steady, ponderous, fake-ritualistic repetition of two antithetical sentences, one about silence and the other about frenzy. We can inspect samples of this on pages 36 and 37 of the present edition: a) *It was the stillness of an implacable force brooding over an inscrutable intention* and b) *The steamer toiled along slowly on the edge of a black and incomprehensible frenzy.* Of course there is a judicious change of adjective from time to time, so that instead of *inscrutable,* for example, you might have *unspeakable,* even plain *mysterious,* etc., etc.

The eagle-eyed English critic F. R. Leavis drew attention long ago to Conrad's "adjectival insistence upon inexpressible and incomprehensible mystery." That insistence must not be dismissed lightly, as many Conrad critics have tended to do, as a mere stylistic flaw; for it raises serious questions of artistic good faith. When a writer while pretending to record scenes, incidents, and their impact is in reality engaged in inducing hypnotic stupor in his readers through a bombardment of emotive words and other forms of trickery much more has to be at stake than stylistic felicity. Generally normal readers are well armed to detect and resist such underhand activity. But Conrad chose his subject well — one which was guaranteed not to put him in conflict with the psychological pre-disposition of his readers or raise the need for him to contend with their resistance. He chose the role of purveyor of comforting myths.

The most interesting and revealing passages in *Heart of Darkness* are, however, about people. I must crave the indulgence of my reader to quote almost a whole page from about the middle of the story when representatives of Europe in a steamer going down the Congo encounter the denizens of Africa.

> We were wanderers on a prehistoric earth, on an earth that wore the aspect of an unknown planet. We could have fancied ourselves the first of men taking possession of an accursed inheritance, to be subdued at the cost of profound anguish and of excessive toil. But suddenly as we struggled round a bend there would be a glimpse of rush walls, of peaked grass-roofs, a burst of yells, a whirl of black limbs, a mass of hands clapping, of feet stamping, of bodies swaying, of eyes rolling under the droop of heavy and motionless foliage. The steamer toiled along slowly on the edge of a black and incomprehensible frenzy. The prehistoric man was cursing us, praying to us, welcoming us — who could tell? We were cut off from the comprehension of our surroundings; we glided past like phantoms, wondering and secretly appalled, as sane men would be before an enthusiastic outbreak in a madhouse. We could not understand because we were too far and could not remember, because we were travelling in the night of first ages, of those ages that are gone, leaving hardly a sign — and no memories.
>
> The earth seemed unearthly. We are accustomed to look upon the shackled form of a conquered monster, but there — there you could look at a thing monstrous and free. It was unearthly and the men were. . . . No they were not inhuman. Well, you know that was the worst of it — this suspicion of their not being inhuman. It would come slowly to one. They howled and leaped and spun and made horrid faces, but what thrilled you was just the thought of their humanity — like yours — the thought of your remote kinship with this wild and passionate uproar. Ugly. Yes, it was ugly enough, but if you were man enough you would admit to yourself that there was in you just the faintest trace of a response to the terrible frankness of that noise, a dim suspicion of there being a meaning in it which you — you so remote from the night of first ages — could comprehend.

Herein lies the meaning of *Heart of Darkness* and the fascination it holds over the Western mind: "What thrilled you was just the thought of their humanity — like yours. . . . Ugly."

Having shown us Africa in the mass, Conrad then zeros in, half a page later, on a specific example, giving us one of his rare descriptions of an African who is not just limbs or rolling eyes:

And between whiles I had to look after the savage who was fireman. He was an improved specimen; he could fire up a vertical boiler. He was there below me and, upon my word, to look at him was as edifying as seeing a dog in a parody of breeches and a feather hat walking on his hind legs. A few months of training had done for that really fine chap. He squinted at the steam-gauge and at the water-gauge with an evident effort of intrepidity — and he had filed his teeth too, the poor devil, and the wool of his pate shaved into queer patterns, and three ornamental scars on each of his cheeks. He ought to have been clapping his hands and stamping his feet on the bank, instead of which he was hard at work, a thrall to strange witchcraft, full of improving knowledge.

As everybody knows, Conrad is a romantic on the side. He might not exactly admire savages clapping their hands and stamping their feet but they have at least the merit of being in their place, unlike this dog in a parody of breeches. For Conrad things being in their place is of the utmost importance.

"Fine fellows — cannibals — in their place," he tells us pointedly. Tragedy begins when things leave their accustomed place, like Europe leaving its safe stronghold between the policeman and the baker to take a peep into the heart of darkness. . . .

The point of my observations should be quite clear by now, namely that Joseph Conrad was a thoroughgoing racist. That this simple truth is glossed over in criticisms of his work is due to the fact that white racism against Africa is such a normal way of thinking that its manifestations go completely unremarked. Students of *Heart of Darkness* will often tell you that Conrad is concerned not so much with Africa as with the deterioration of one European mind caused by solitude and sickness. They will point out to you that Conrad is, if anything, less charitable to the Europeans in the story than he is to the natives, that the point of the story is to ridicule Europe's civilizing mission in Africa. A Conrad student informed me in Scotland that Africa is merely a setting for the disintegration of the mind of Mr. Kurtz.

Which is partly the point. Africa as setting and backdrop which eliminates the African as human factor. Africa as a metaphysical battlefield devoid of all recognizable humanity, into which the wandering European enters at his peril. Can nobody see the preposterous and perverse arrogance in thus reducing Africa to the role of props for the break-up of one petty European mind? But that is not even the point. The real question is the dehumanization of Africa and Africans which this age-long attitude has fostered and continues to foster in the world. And the question is whether a novel which celebrates this dehumanization, which depersonalizes a portion of the human race, can be called a great work of art. My answer is: No, it cannot. I do not doubt Conrad's great talents. Even *Heart of Darkness* has its memorably good passages and moments:

> The reaches opened before us and closed behind, as if the forest had stepped leisurely across the water to bar the way for our return.

Its exploration of the minds of the European characters is often penetrating and full of insight. But all that has been more than fully discussed in the last fifty years. His obvious racism has, however, not been addressed. And it is high time it was!

Conrad was born in 1857, the very year in which the first Anglican missionaries were arriving among my own people in Nigeria. It was certainly not his fault that he lived his life at a time when the reputation of the black man was at a particularly low level. But even after due allowances have been made for all the influences of contemporary prejudice on his sensibility there remains still in Conrad's attitude a residue of antipathy to black people which his peculiar psychology alone can explain. His own account of his first encounter with a black man is very revealing:

> A certain enormous buck nigger encountered in Haiti fixed my conception of blind, furious, unreasoning rage, as manifested in the human animal to the end of my days. Of the nigger I used to dream for years afterwards.

Certainly Conrad had a problem with niggers. His inordinate love of that word itself should be of interest to psychoanalysts. Sometimes his fixation on blackness is equally interesting as when he gives us this brief description:

> A black figure stood up, strode on long black legs, waving long black arms. . . .

as though we might expect a black figure striding along on black legs to wave white arms! But so unrelenting is Conrad's obsession. . . .

Whatever Conrad's problems were, you might say he is now safely dead. Quite true. Unfortunately his heart of darkness plagues us still. Which is why an offensive and deplorable book can be described by a serious scholar as "among the half dozen greatest short novels in the English language." And why it is today perhaps the most commonly prescribed novel in twentieth-century literature courses in English Departments of American universities.

There are two probable grounds on which what I have said so far may be contested. The first is that it is no concern of fiction to please people about whom it is written. I will go along with that. But I am not talking about pleasing people. I am talking about a book which parades in the most vulgar fashion prejudices and insults from which a section of mankind has suffered untold agonies and atrocities in the past and continues to do so in many ways and many places today. I am talking about a story in which the very humanity of black people is called in question.

Secondly, I may be challenged on the grounds of actuality. Conrad, after all, did sail down the Congo in 1890 when my own father was still a babe in arms. How could I stand up more than fifty years after his death and purport to contradict him? My answer is that as a sensible man I will not accept just any traveller's tales solely on the grounds that I have not made the journey myself. I will not trust the evidence even of a man's very eyes when I suspect them to be as jaundiced as Conrad's. And we also happen to know that Conrad was, in the words of his biographer, Bernard C. Meyer, "notoriously inaccurate in the rendering of his own history."

But more important by far is the abundant testimony about Conrad's savages which we could gather if we were so inclined from other sources and which might lead us to think that these people must have had other occupations besides merging into the evil forest or materializing out of it simply to plague Marlow and his dispirited band. For as it happened, soon after Conrad had written his book an event of far greater consequence was taking place in the art world of Europe. This is how Frank Willett, a British art historian, describes it:

> Gaugin had gone to Tahiti, the most extravagant individual act of turning to a non-European culture in the decades immediately before and after 1900, when European artists were avid for new artistic experiences, but it was only about 1904–5 that African art began to make its distinctive impact. One piece is still identifiable; it is a mask that had been given to Maurice Vlaminck in 1905. He records that Derain was "speechless" and "stunned" when he saw it, bought it from Vlaminck and in turn showed it to Picasso and Matisse, who were also greatly affected by it. Ambroise Vollard then borrowed it and had it cast in bronze. . . . The revolution of twentieth century art was under way!

The mask in question was made by other savages living just north of Conrad's River Congo. They have a name too: the Fang people, and are without a doubt among the world's greatest masters of the sculptured form. The event Frank Willett is referring to marked the beginning of cubism and the infusion of new life into European art, which had run completely out of strength.

The point of all this is to suggest that Conrad's picture of the peoples of the Congo seems grossly inadequate even at the height of their subjection to the ravages of King Leopold's International Association for the Civilization of Central Africa.

RUDYARD KIPLING

The White Man's Burden

This poem, written by Rudyard Kipling (1865–1936), is often presented as the epitome of colonialist sentiment, though some readers see in it a critical, satirical attitude toward colonialism. Do you find the poem to be for or against colonialism? Can it be both?

Thinking Historically

"The White Man's Burden" is a phrase normally associated with European colonialism in Africa. In fact, however, Kipling wrote the poem in response to the annexation of the Philippines by the United States. How does this historical context change the meaning of the poem for you? Does the meaning of a literary work depend on the motives of the writer, the historical context in which it is written, or both?

Take up the White Man's burden —
Send forth the best ye breed —
Go, bind your sons to exile
To serve your captives' need;
To wait, in heavy harness,
On fluttered folk and wild —
Your new-caught sullen peoples,
Half devil and half child.

Take up the White Man's burden —
In patience to abide,
To veil the threat of terror
And check the show of pride;
By open speech and simple,
An hundred times made plain,
To seek another's profit
And work another's gain.

Rudyard Kipling, "The White Man's Burden," *McClure's Magazine* 12, no. 4 (February 1899): 290–91.

Take up the White Man's burden —
The savage wars of peace —
Fill full the mouth of Famine,
And bid the sickness cease;
And when your goal is nearest
(The end for others sought)
Watch sloth and heathen folly
Bring all your hope to nought.

Take up the White Man's burden —
No iron rule of kings,
But toil of serf and sweeper —
The tale of common things.
The ports ye shall not enter,
The roads ye shall not tread,
Go, make them with your living
And mark them with your dead.

Take up the White Man's burden,
And reap his own reward —
The blame of those ye better
The hate of those ye guard —
The cry of hosts ye humour
(Ah, slowly!) toward the light: —
"Why brought ye us from bondage,
Our loved Egyptian night?"

Take up the White Man's burden —
Ye dare not stoop to less —
Nor call too loud on Freedom
To cloke your weariness.
By all ye will or whisper,
By all ye leave or do,
The silent sullen peoples
Shall weigh your God and you.

Take up the White Man's burden!
Have done with childish days —
The lightly-proffered laurel,
The easy ungrudged praise:
Comes now, to search your manhood
Through all the thankless years,
Cold, edged with dear-bought wisdom,
The judgment of your peers.

REFLECTIONS

Many of the selections within this chapter as well as its title point to the dual character of colonial society. There are the colonized and the colonizers, the "natives" and the Europeans, and as racial categories hardened in the second half of the nineteenth century, the blacks and the whites. Colonialism centered on the construction of an accepted inequality. The dominant Europeans invested enormous energy in keeping the double standards, dual pay schedules, separate rules and residential areas — the two castes.

One problem with maintaining a neat division between the colonized and the colonizers is that the Europeans were massively outnumbered by the indigenous people. Thus, the colonizers needed a vast class of middle-status people to staff the army, police, and bureaucracy. These people who Osterhammel reminds us were often unkindly seen as "white negroes," might be educated in Paris or London, raised in European culture, and encouraged to develop a sense of pride in their similarity to the Europeans ("me Christian, same like master") and their differences from the other "natives." Often, like the Indian Dr. Veraswami, they were chosen for their ethnic or religious differences from the rest of the colonized population.

In short, colonialism created a whole class of people who were neither fully colonized nor colonizers. They were in between. To the extent that the colonial enterprise was an extension of European conceits of social class, as Cannadine argues, these in-between people could be British as well as Indian. Orwell's Flory is only one of the characters in *Burmese Days* caught between two inhospitable worlds. One of the most notorious of this class of Europeans "gone native" is the Mr. Kurtz that Conrad's crew will meet upriver. Achebe's point that Africa becomes a setting for the breakup of a European mind might be generalized to apply to the European perception of the colonial experience. It is certainly one of the dominant themes of the European colonial novel. Even the great ones often center on the real or imagined rape, ravishing, or corruption of the European by the seething foreign unknown. This attitude also helps us understand how Kipling could be both anti-imperialist and racist. Imperialism could seem like a thankless act to those who tried to carry civilization to "sullen peoples, half devil and half child."

All the novels and poetry excerpted in this chapter are well worth reading in their entirety, and many other excellent colonial novels can be chosen from this period as well as from the 1930s and 1940s. E. M. Forster's *A Passage to India* and Paul Scott's *The Raj Quartet* stand out as fictional introductions to British colonialism in India. (Both have also received excellent adaptations to film, the latter as the series for television called *The Jewel in the Crown*.) In addition to Chinua Achebe, Amos Tutuola and Wole Soyinka have written extensively on Nigeria; as well, Francis Bebey, Ferdinand Oyono, and Mongo Beti address French colonialism in Africa. On South Africa, the work of Alan Payton, Andre Brink, J. M. Coetzee, Peter Abrams, and James McClure, among many others, stands out.

The advantage of becoming engrossed in a novel is that we feel part of the story and have a sense that we are learning something firsthand. Of course, we are reading a work of fiction, not gaining firsthand experience or reading an accurate historical account of events. A well-made film poses an even greater problem. Its visual and aural impact imparts a psychological reality that becomes part of our experience. If it is about a subject of which we know little, the film quickly becomes our "knowledge" of the subject, and this knowledge may be incomplete or inaccurate.

On the other hand, a well-written novel or film can whet our appetite and inspire us to learn more. Choose and read a novel about colonialism or some other historical subject. Then read a biography of the author or research his or her background to determine how much the author knew about the subject. Next, read a historical account of the subject. How much attention does the historian give to the novelist's subject? How does the novel add depth to the historical account? How does the historical account place the novel in perspective? Finally how does the author's background place the novel in historical context?

23

Nationalism and Westernization

Japan, India, and the Americas, 1880–1930

HISTORICAL CONTEXT

As peoples of Asia, Africa, and the Americas adapted to Western colonialism or struggled to free themselves from it, they inevitably faced the issue of Westernization. To become Westernized was to accept and adopt the ways of the powerful colonial powers of the West: Western Europe and its more distant western offshoot, the United States. All colonized peoples were exposed to some degree of Western education, indoctrination, or control. As they sought their independence and worked to create their own national identities, they frequently revived older indigenous traditions, languages, and religions — ideas that had fallen into disuse or had been replaced by Western culture. This rebirth of traditional culture often meant a specific and determined rejection of Western ways.

This chapter explores a number of responses to Westernization at the end of the nineteenth and the beginning of the twentieth century. The first selection gives an overall picture of how these societies came to grips with the West, culturally as well as politically. In every case, a people who sought its own national identity had to determine the degree of Westernization, if any, it desired to retain.

We examine Westernization in Japan, a country that was never colonized but that experienced cultural discord as it strove to "catch up" with the West. Japan's economic and industrial Westernization was so successful that many other countries were inspired by its example. What was the range of attitudes toward the West in Japan, and how strong was the impact of Westernization on its people?

We then turn to India for comparison. While Japan adopted Western ways in its successful effort to escape Western colonization, India's

846

colonization by the British led to various forms of Westernization. However, the Westernization of India was not a monolithic process. There were both English colonials who opposed it and Indians who favored it. India was more fully Westernized than Japan, but its opposition to Westernization was more intense and eventually provided a foundation for rejecting British rule.

The North America of European immigrants joined the club of rich and powerful Western nations in the nineteenth century. Others in the Western hemisphere — Native Americans, African Americans, and many Latin Americans — struggled with the same issues of nationalist versus Western identity as did the colonized and former colonized peoples of Asia. Native Americans, in North and South America, experienced a European colonial expansion very much like that of colonized peoples in Asia. In South America, many states gained their political independence early in the nineteenth century, but often the political and military power of Spain was replaced by the dominance of the United States. In Cuba and New York, political activist José Martí looked to a free Cuba and a more global American identity.

What accounted for the appeal of the West in these different settings? Did the intellectuals of Japan and India mean the same thing by "the West"? Did the Westernizers seek to imitate different aspects of the West? And what motivated those who rejected the West? Did they have similar or different agendas?

THINKING HISTORICALLY
Appreciating Contradictions

The process of Westernization, like the experience of conquest and colonization that often preceded it, was fraught with conflict and led to frequent contradictions. Often, the struggle for national independence meant the borrowing of Western practices and ideologies: both Marxist and liberal. Indeed, the idea of national self-determination was a product of the French and American revolutions, as we have seen. Even the words and languages employed in the debate reflected Western origins as English or French was often the only common language of educated colonized peoples. Therefore, it is not surprising that contradictory behavior and ambivalent relationships were endemic in the postcolonial world, just as they had been under colonialism. These contradictions usually manifested themselves in an individual's cultural identity. How do colonized persons adopt Western ways, embrace traditional culture, and not feel as though their identity has been divided between the two? Such individuals may not fit entirely into either world and so may be torn between who they were and who they have become. The somewhat anguished experiences of these colonized people are difficult to understand. We typically want to accept one view or another, to praise or to blame. But as we have learned, the history of peoples and nations is rarely that clear. In examining some of the fundamental contradictions in the history of Westernization, we might better understand how people were variously affected.

The historical thinking skill one learns in reading documents from people torn between different ideals is the appreciation of contradictions. This operates on a number of levels. We learn that people can hold two contradictory ideas in their minds at the same time; and, in consequence, we learn to do it ourselves. This prevents us from jumping to conclusions or oversimplifying the historical process. In addition, we learn how the struggle over contradictory goals, whether internalized or expressed in group conflict, moves history forward.

147

THEODORE VON LAUE

From The World Revolution of Westernization

Western colonialism, according to von Laue, a modern historian, brought about a "world revolution of Westernization," the victory of Western culture that accompanied Western political domination. What, according to von Laue, are these Western ideas that spread throughout the world during the nineteenth century? Did these ideas spread peacefully or were they forced on non-Western peoples? What groups of people were most attracted to Western ideas? Why did some non-Western people prefer Western culture to their own?

Does von Laue believe that this "world revolution" was a good thing? Does he believe it is over? What, according to von Laue, must still be done?

Theodore von Laue, *The World Revolution of Westernization* (New York: Oxford University Press, 1987), 27–34.

Thinking Historically

Von Laue is particularly interested in the plight of what he calls the "Westernized non-Western intelligentsia." Who are these people? What is their problem? What does von Laue mean when he says that "as a result of their Westernization they became anti-Western nationalists"? How could Westernization make people anti-Western?

Throughout this selection, von Laue discusses paradoxical or ironic behavior. He writes of people learning lessons that were not formally taught and of psychological conflicts or love-hate attitudes. At one point he generalizes this phenomenon of seemingly contradictory behavior by quoting an eighteenth-century maxim that states, "To do just the opposite is also a form of imitation." Is von Laue describing some paradoxical aspect of human nature, or are these conflicts a particular product of colonialism?

While the world revolution of Westernization created a political world order radically above the horizons of all past human experience, it also unhinged, in the revolutionary manner sensed by Lord Lytton,[1] the depths of non-Western societies constituting the bulk of humanity. As he had said, "The application of the most refined principles of European government and some of the most artificial institutions of European society to a . . . vast population in whose history, habits, and traditions they have had no previous existence" was a risky enterprise, perhaps more than he had anticipated.

Examining the history of colonial expansion, one can discern a rough but generally applicable pattern for the revolutionary subversion of non-Western societies. Subversion began at the apex, with the defeat, humiliation, or even overthrow of traditional rulers. The key guarantee of law, order, and security from external interference was thus removed. With it went the continuity of tradition, whether of governance or of all other social institutions down to the subtle customs regulating the individual psyche. Thus ended not only political but also cultural self-determination. Henceforth, the initiatives shaping collective existence came from without, "mysterious formulas of a foreign and more or less uncongenial system" not only of administration but also of every aspect of life.

Once the authority of the ruler (who often was the semi-divine intermediary between Heaven and Earth) was subverted, the Western attack on the other props of society intensified. Missionaries, their

[1]British viceroy of India from 1876 to 1880.

security guaranteed by Western arms, discredited the local gods and their guardians, weakening the spiritual foundations of society. At the same time, colonial administrators interfered directly in indigenous affairs by suppressing hallowed practices repulsive to them, including human sacrifice, slavery, and physical cruelty in its many forms. Meanwhile, Western businessmen and their local agents redirected the channels of trade and economic life, making local producers and consumers dependent on a world market beyond their comprehension and control. In a thousand ways the colonial administration and its allies, though not necessarily in agreement with each other, introduced a new set of rewards and punishments, of prestige and authority. The changeover was obvious even in the externals of dress. Africans became ashamed of their nudity, women covered their breasts; Chinese men cut off their queues and adopted Western clothes. The boldest even tried to become like Westerners "in taste, in opinion, in morals, and intellect."

The pathways of subversion here outlined indicate the general pattern and the directions which it followed over time. Its speed depended on Western policy and the resilience of local society. Things seemingly fell apart quickly in the case of the most vulnerable small-scale societies of Africa and much more slowly in India or China, if at all in Japan. Often the colonial administration itself, under the policy of "indirect rule," slowed the Western impact for fear of causing cultural chaos and making trouble for itself. In all cases, tradition (however subverted) persisted in a thousand forms, merely retreating from the external world into the subliminally conditioned responses of the human psyche, its last refuge. It is still lurking in the promptings of "soul" today.

And did things really fall apart? The world revolution of Westernization prevailed by the arts of both war and peace. Certain aspects of Western power possessed an intrinsic appeal which, even by indigenous judgment, enhanced life. New crops often brought ampler food; European rule often secured peace. Through their command of the seas and of worldwide trade Europeans and Americans opened access to survival and opportunity in foreign lands to countless millions of people in China and India. Or take even the persuasion of raw power: Once convinced of the superiority of European weapons, who would not crave possession of them too? And more generally, being associated with European power also carried weight; it patently held the keys to the future. More directly perhaps, doing business with Westerners promised profit. If they played it right, compradors would get rich.

More subtly, certain categories of the local population eagerly took to foreign ways. Missionaries sheltered outcasts: slaves held for sacrifice, girls to be sold into prostitution or abandoned, or married women feeling abused and oppressed. The struggle for sexual equality is still raging in our midst, yet by comparison even Victorian England offered hope to women in Africa or East Asia. Regarding Japan, Fukuzawa[2] related the story of a highborn dowager lady who "had had some unhappy trials in earlier days." She was told of "the most remarkable of all the Western customs . . . the relations between men and women," where "men and women had equal rights, and monogamy was the strict rule in any class of people. . . ." It was, Fukuzawa reported, "as if her eyes were suddenly opened to something new. . . ." As a messenger of women's rights he certainly had Japanese women, "especially the ladies of the higher society," on his side. In China liberated women rushed to unbind their feet.

In addition, the Westerners introduced hospitals and medicines that relieved pain and saved lives, a fact not unappreciated. Besides, whose greed was not aroused by the plethora of Western goods, all fancier than local products: stronger liquor, gaudier textiles, faster transport? Simple minds soon preferred Western goods merely because they were Western. Given the comparative helplessness of local society, was it surprising that everything Western tended to be judged superior?

The Westerners with their sense of mission also introduced their education. It was perhaps not enough, according to anti-Western nationalists suspicious of European desires, to keep the natives down, yet it offered access to Western skills at some sacrifice on the part of teachers willing to forgo the easier life in their own culture. Privileged non-Westerners even attended schools and universities in the West. Thus, as part of the general pattern of Westernization, a new category of cultural half-breeds was created, the Westernized non-Western intelligentsia. It differed somewhat according to cultural origins, but shared a common predicament. Product of one culture, educated in another, it was caught in invidious comparison. As [philosopher] Thomas Hobbes observed "Man, whose Joy consisteth in comparing himselfe with other men, can relish nothing but what is eminent." Riveted to Western preeminence, this intelligentsia struggled for purpose, identity, and recognition in the treacherous no-man's-land in between — and most furiously in lands where skin color added to its disabilities. Talented and industrious, these intellectuals threw themselves heroically into the study of Western society and thought so alien to their own.

Along the way they soon acquired a taste for the dominant ideals of the West, foremost the liberal plea for equality, freedom, and self-determination and the socialists' cry of social justice for all exploited and oppressed peoples and classes. They were delighted by the bitter self-criticism they discovered among Westerners — Western society produced many doubters, especially among its fringes in central and eastern Europe. At the same time, non-Western intellectuals quickly perceived

[2]See selection 55. [Ed.]

the pride that lurked behind Western humanitarianism. They might be treated as equals in London or Paris, but "east of Aden" on the Indian circuit or anywhere in the colonies, they were "natives" — natives hypersensitive to the hypocrisy behind the Western mission of exporting high ideals without the congenital ingredient of equality. Thus they learned the lessons of power not formally taught by their masters. They needed power — state power — not only to carry the Western vision into practice on their own but also to make equality real.

Inevitably, the non-Western intellectuals turned their lessons to their own use. The ideals of freedom and self-determination justified giving free rein not only to the promptings of their own minds and souls, but also to protests over the humiliation of their countries and cultures. As a result of their Westernization they became anti-Western nationalists, outwardly curtailing, in themselves and their compatriots, the abject imitation of the West. Yet, as an 18th-century German wag had said, "To do just the opposite is also a form of imitation." Anti-Western self-assertion was a form of Westernization copying the cultural self-assertion of the West. Moreover, limiting Western influence in fact undercut any chance of matching Western power (and the issue of power was never far from their minds). Thus anti-Western intellectuals were caught in a love-hate attitude toward the West, anti-Western purveyors of further Westernization.

Take Mohandas Gandhi,[3] perhaps the greatest among the Westernized non-Western intellectuals. Born into a prominent tradition-oriented Hindu family and of a lively, ambitious mind, he broke with Hindu taboo and studied English law in London, fashionably dressed and accepted in the best society, though by preference consorting with vegetarians and students of Eastern religion. After his return he confessed that "next to India, [he] would rather live in London than in any other place in the world." From 1892 to 1914, however, he lived in South Africa, using his legal training for defending the local Indian community against white discrimination. There he put together from Indian and Western sources a philosophy as well as a practice of nonviolent resistance, strengthening the self-confidence and civil status of his clients. . . .

One of Gandhi's precursors, Narendranath Datta, better known as Swami Vivekananda, had gone even further. At a lecture in Madras he exhorted his audience: "This is the great ideal before us, and everyone must be ready for it — the conquest of the whole world by India — nothing less than that. . . . Up India and conquer the world with your spirituality." Western globalized nationalism, obviously, was working its way around the world, escalating political ambition and cultural messianism to novel intensity. . . .

[3]See selection 57. [Ed.]

... [T]he run of Westernized non-Western intellectuals led awkward lives — "in a free state," as [Indian novelist] V. S. Naipaul has put it — forever in search of roots, and certitude; inwardly split, part backward, part Western, camouflaging their imitation of the West by gestures of rejection; forever aspiring to build lofty halfway houses that bridged the disparate cultural universes, often in all-embracing designs, never admitting the fissures and cracks in their lives and opinions; and always covering up their unease with a compensating presumption of moral superiority based on the recognition that the promptings of heart and soul are superior to the dictates of reason. Knowing their own traditions and at least some of the essentials of the West, they sensed that they had a more elevated grasp of human reality; the future belonged to them rather than to the "decadent" West. Out of that existential misery of "heightened consciousness" (as [Russian novelist] Dostoyevsky called it) have come some of the most seminal contributions to the intellectual and political developments of the 20th century, including the anti-Western counterrevolutions.

... Let it be said first that the relations between the colonized and the colonizer are exceedingly subtle and complex, subject to keen controversy among all observers, all of them partisans, all of them now judging not by indigenous but by Westernized standards. Western ideals and practices have shaped and intensified the protests of Westernized non-Western intellectuals taking full advantage of the opportunities offered by Western society. Their protests, incidentally, were hardly ever turned against past inhumanities committed by their own kind (because traditionally they were not considered as such).

Next, having already surveyed the not inconsiderable side benefits of Western domination, let us ask: Did the Westerners in their expansion behave toward the non-Westerners worse than they behaved toward themselves? While they never treated their colonial subjects as equals, they never killed as many people in all their colonial campaigns as they did in their own wars at home (the brutality of Europe's cultural evolution has been carefully rinsed out of all current historical accounts). And in their peaceful intercourse with non-Westerners we find the whole range of emotions common in Western society. It was darkness at heart on one extreme and saintliness on the other, and every mix in between, with the balance perhaps tending toward darkness. As one colonial officer in East Africa confided to his diary: "It is but a small percentage of white men whose characters do not in one way or another undergo a subtle process of deterioration when they are compelled to live for any length of time among savage races and under conditions as exist in tropical climates." The colonial district commissioner, isolated among people whose ways sharply contradicted his own upbringing, often suffering from tropical sickness, and scared at heart, found himself perhaps in a worse dilemma than the Westernized non-Western intellectuals. Some of them, no doubt, were unscrupulous opportunists seeking escape from the trammels of civic conformity at home; they turned domineering sadists in the colonies. On the other hand, missionaries often sacrificed their lives, generally among uncomprehending local folk. It was perhaps a credit to the Westerners that the victims of imperialism found considerable sympathy in their own midst. The evils stood out while the good intentions were taken for granted.

Yet — to take a longer view — even compassionate Western observers generally overlook the fact that among all the gifts of the West the two most crucial boons were missing: cultural equality as the basis for political equality and reasonable harmony in the body politic. The world revolution of Westernization perpetuated inequality and ruinous cultural subversion while at the same time improving the material conditions of life. More people survived, forever subject to the agonies of inequality and disorientation resulting from enforced change originating beyond their ken. Collectively and individually, they straddled the border between West and non-West, on the one side enjoying the benefits of Western culture, on the other feeling exploited as victims of imperialism. Indigenous populations always remained backward and dependent, unable to match the resources and skills of a fast-advancing West.

What we should weigh, then, in any assessment of Western colonial expansion before World War I is perhaps not only the actions, good or evil, of the colonial powers, but also the long-run consequences thereafter. The victims of Western colonialism do not include only the casualties of colonial wars but also the far greater multitudes killed or brutalized in the civil commotions in the emerging modern nation-states. Whatever the mitigating circumstances, the anti-Western fury has its justifications indeed.

And yet, in the all-inclusive global perspective, is it morally justified? Was the outreach with all its outrages planned by the Westerners? Was it based on a deliberate design of conquest? Or was it the accidental result of stark imbalances in the resources of power for both war and peace which had come about through circumstances beyond human control? Why were the Westerners so powerful? Their stock answer has been: because of their ideals embedded in their religion, culture, and political institutions, adding up to their overwhelming material superiority. That answer, however, will not suffice for the overview appropriate to this age. In the enlarged contexts of global interaction human beings appear far more helpless than in their smaller settings, where they may claim a measure of control. As argued above, it was merely by historical and geographic accident that the Europeans were enabled to create the cultural hothouse that made them uniquely powerful in the world.

. . . As we now see the grand connections more clearly, we also understand that the burden of responsibility for bringing about cultural equality falls more heavily on those who have been so privileged, so spoiled, by circumstances beyond their control. They have furnished the energies behind the world revolution of Westernization; they carry the obligation to complete it according to their ideals of freedom, equality, and human dignity and in a manner beneficial to all humanity.

$$\boxed{148}$$

FUKUZAWA YUKICHI
Good-bye Asia

Fukuzawa* Yukichi (1835–1901) was one of the most important Japanese Westernizers during Japan's late-nineteenth-century rush to catch up with the West. The son of a lower samurai (military) family, Fukuzawa's pursuit of Western knowledge took him to a Dutch school in Osaka, where he studied everything from the Dutch language to chemistry, physics, and anatomy, and to Yedo where he studied English. Due to his privileged background and Western schooling, he was naturally included in the first Japanese mission to the United States in 1860 as well as in the first diplomatic mission to Europe in 1862. After Fukuzawa returned to Japan, he spent many years teaching and writing the books that would make him famous. The best known of these was *Seiyo Jijo* (*Things Western*), which in 1866 introduced Japanese readers to the daily life and typical institutions of Western society. According to Fukuzawa, the main obstacle that prevented Japanese society from catching up with the West was a long heritage of Chinese Confucianism, which stifled educational independence.

In the years after the Meiji Restoration of 1868, in which feudalism was abolished and power was restored to the emperor, Fukuzawa

*foo koo ZAH wah

Fukuzawa Yukichi, "Datsu-a Ron" ("On Saying Good-bye to Asia"), in *Japan: A Documentary History*, vol. II, ed. David J. Lu (Armonk, NY: M. E. Sharpe, 1997), 351–53. From Takeuchi Yoshimi, ed., *Azia Shugi* (*Asianism*) *Gendai Nihon Shisō Taikei* (*Great Compilation of Modern Japanese Thought*), vol. 8 (Tokyo: Chikuma Shobō, 1963), 38–40.

became the most popular spokesman for the Westernizing policies of the new government. In this essay, "Good-bye Asia," written in 1885, Fukuzawa describes the spread of Western civilization in Japan. Does he believe that it is both inevitable and desirable? Why? What do you make of Fukuzawa's attitude toward Chinese and Korean civilizations?

Thinking Historically

Does this selection from Fukuzawa display any of the contradictions, ambivalence, or love-hate feelings that von Laue describes as common among Westernized non-Western intellectuals? Were such conflicts inevitable? How might someone like Fukuzawa avoid this conflict, ambivalence, or uncertainty?

Transportation has become so convenient these days that once the wind of Western civilization blows to the East, every blade of grass and every tree in the East follow what the Western wind brings. Ancient Westerners and present-day Westerners are from the same stock and are not much different from one another. The ancient ones moved slowly, but their contemporary counterparts move vivaciously at a fast pace. This is possible because present-day Westerners take advantage of the means of transportation available to them. For those of us who live in the Orient, unless we want to prevent the coming of Western civilization with a firm resolve, it is best that we cast our lot with them. If one observes carefully what is going on in today's world, one knows the futility of trying to prevent the onslaught of Western civilization. Why not float with them in the same ocean of civilization, sail the same waves, and enjoy the fruits and endeavors of civilization?

The movement of a civilization is like the spread of measles. Measles in Tokyo start in Nagasaki and come eastward with the spring thaw. We may hate the spread of this communicable disease, but is there any effective way of preventing it? I can prove that it is not possible. In a communicable disease, people receive only damages. In a civilization, damages may accompany benefits, but benefits always far outweigh them, and their force cannot be stopped. This being the case, there is no point in trying to prevent their spread. A wise man encourages the spread and allows our people to get used to its ways.

The opening to the modern civilization of the West began in the reign of Kaei (1848–58). Our people began to discover its utility and gradually and yet actively moved toward its acceptance. However, there was an old-fashioned and bloated government that stood in the way of progress. It was a problem impossible to solve. If the government were allowed to continue, the new civilization could not enter. The modern civilization and Japan's old conventions were mutually exclusive. If we were to discard our old conventions, that government also had to be abolished. We could have prevented the entry of this civilization, but it would have meant loss of our national independence. The struggles taking place in the world civilization were such that they would not allow an Eastern island nation to slumber in isolation. At that point, dedicated men (*shijin*) recognized the principle of "the country is more important than the government," relied on the dignity of the Imperial Household, and toppled the old government to establish a new one. With this, public and the private sectors alike, everyone in our country accepted the modern Western civilization. Not only were we able to cast aside Japan's old conventions, but we also succeeded in creating a new axle toward progress in Asia. Our basic assumptions could be summarized in two words: "Good-bye Asia (*Datsu-a*)."

Japan is located in the eastern extremities of Asia, but the spirit of her people have already moved away from the old conventions of Asia to the Western civilization. Unfortunately for Japan, there are two neighboring countries. One is called China and another Korea. These two peoples, like the Japanese people, have been nurtured by Asiatic political thoughts and mores. It may be that we are different races of people, or it may be due to the differences in our heredity or education; significant differences mark the three peoples. The Chinese and Koreans are more like each other and together they do not show as much similarity to the Japanese. These two peoples do not know how to progress either personally or as a nation. In this day and age with transportation becoming so convenient, they cannot be blind to the manifestations of Western civilization. But they say that what is seen or heard cannot influence the disposition of their minds. Their love affairs with ancient ways and old customs remain as strong as they were centuries ago. In this new and vibrant theater of civilization when we speak of education, they only refer back to Confucianism. As for school education, they can only cite [Chinese philosopher Mencius's] precepts of humanity, righteousness, decorum, and knowledge. While professing their abhorrence to ostentation, in reality they show their ignorance of truth and principles. As for their morality, one only has to observe their unspeakable acts of cruelty and shamelessness. Yet they remain arrogant and show no sign of self-examination.

In my view, these two countries cannot survive as independent nations with the onslaught of Western civilization to the East. Their concerned citizens might yet find a way to engage in a massive reform, on the scale of our Meiji Restoration, and they could change their governments and bring about a renewal of spirit among their peoples. If that could happen they would indeed be fortunate. However, it is more likely that would never happen, and within a few short years they will be wiped out from the world with their lands divided among the civilized nations. Why is this so? Simply at a time when the spread of civilization and enlightenment (*bummei kaika*) has a force akin to that of measles, China and Korea violate the natural law of its spread. They forcibly try to avoid it by shutting off air from their rooms. Without air, they suffocate to death. It is said that neighbors must extend helping hands to one another because their relations are inseparable. Today's China and Korea have not done a thing for Japan. From the perspectives of civilized Westerners, they may see what is happening in China and Korea and judge Japan accordingly, because of the three countries' geographical proximity. The governments of China and Korea still retain their autocratic manners and do not abide by the rule of law. Westerners may consider Japan likewise a lawless society. Natives of China and Korea are deep in their hocus pocus of nonscientific behavior. Western scholars may think that Japan still remains a country dedicated to the *yin* and *yang* and five elements.[1] Chinese are mean-spirited and shameless, and the chivalry of the Japanese people is lost to the Westerners. Koreans punish their convicts in an atrocious manner, and that is imputed to the Japanese as heartless people. There are many more examples I can cite. It is not different from the case of a righteous man living in a neighborhood of a town known for foolishness, lawlessness, atrocity, and heartlessness. His action is so rare that it is always buried under the ugliness of his neighbors' activities. When these incidents are multiplied, that can affect our normal conduct of diplomatic affairs. How unfortunate it is for Japan.

What must we do today? We do not have time to wait for the enlightenment of our neighbors so that we can work together toward the development of Asia. It is better for us to leave the ranks of Asian nations and cast our lot with civilized nations of the West. As for the way of dealing with China and Korea, no special treatment is necessary just because they happen to be our neighbors. We simply follow the manner of the Westerners in knowing how to treat them. Any person who cherishes a bad friend cannot escape his bad notoriety. We simply erase from our minds our bad friends in Asia.

---

[1] *Yin* and *yang* is a traditional Chinese duality (hot/cold, active/passive, male/female) illustrated by a circle divided by an "s" to show unity within duality. The five elements suggest another traditional, prescientific idea that everything is made of five basic ingredients.

149

Images from Japan: Views of Westernization

This selection consists of three prints by Japanese artists. The first print, Figure 23.1, called *Beef Eater*, illustrates a character in Kanagaki Robun's *Aguranabe* (1871). The author, a popular newspaper humorist, parodies a new class of urban Westernized Japanese who carry watches and umbrellas and eat beef (banned by Buddhist law for centuries but added to the Japanese diet by Westerners). What response in the viewer does the artist seek to evoke?

The second piece, Figure 23.2, is called *Monkey Show Dressing Room* (1879), by Honda Kinkachiro. What is this print's message? What is the artist's attitude toward Westernization?

The third piece, Figure 23.3, *The Exotic White Man*, shows a child born to a Western man and a Japanese woman. What is the artist's message? Does the artist favor such unions? What does the artist think of Westerners?

Thinking Historically

Prints, like cartoons, are a shorthand that must capture an easily recognizable trait. What, evidently, were the widely understood Japanese images of the West? Where do you think these stereotypes of the West came from? Do you see any signs in these prints of ambivalence on the part of the artist?

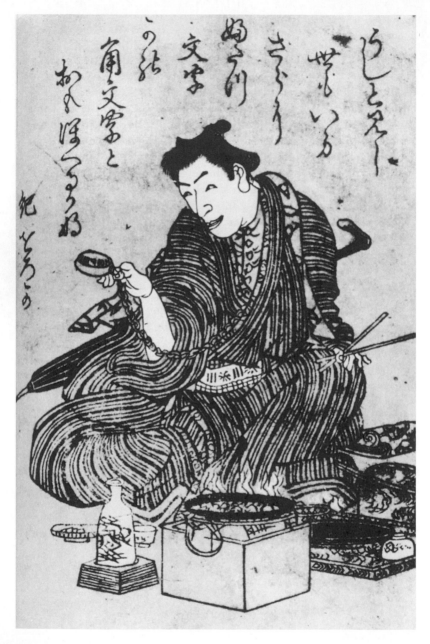

Figure 23.1 Beef Eater.

Source: Beef Eater, from Kanagaki Robun, *Aguranabe* (1871) in G. B. Sansom, *The Western World and Japan* (Tokyo: Charles E. Tuttle Co., 1977).

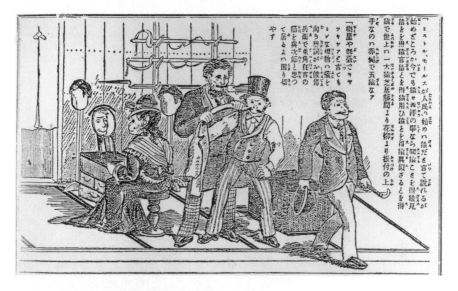

Figure 23.2 Monkey Show Dressing Room.

Source: Honda Kinkachiro, *Monkey Show Dressing Room*, in Julia Meech-Pekarik, *The World of the Meiji Print* (New York: John Weatherhill, 1986).

Figure 23.3   The Exotic White Man.

Source: Japanese color print, late 19th c., Dutch private collection, in C. A. Burland, *The Exotic White Man* (New York: McGraw-Hill, 1969), fig. 38.

150

MOHANDAS K. GANDHI

From Hind Swaraj

Mohandas K. Gandhi (1869–1948), the father of Indian independence, combined the education of an English lawyer with the tempera-
ment of an Indian ascetic to lead a national resistance movement
against the British. In the century that followed British-supported reforms to the Indian education system (in the early nineteenth century),
British rule had become far more pervasive and increasingly hostile toward Indian culture. Unlike Indian educational reformers, who had
embraced Western culture as a means to uplift Indians, Gandhi was
extremely critical of Western culture as he witnessed the havoc British
rule wreaked on his country.

Gandhi began to develop his ideas of *Hind Swaraj,** or Indian
Home Rule, while he sailed from England to South Africa in 1909
where he served as a lawyer for fellow Indians. An early version of
this essay, published then, was reissued in its present form in 1921,
two years after he returned to his birthplace, India, and again in 1938,
in the last years of struggle against British rule.

After Gandhi's introduction, the essay takes the form of questions
and answers. The questions are posed by a presumed "reader" of
Gandhi's pamphlet. As "editor," Gandhi explains what he means.
How does Gandhi compare life in Europe and India? What does he
think of the possibility of Hindus and Muslims living together? What
does he mean by passive resistance or soul-force (Satyagraha)? Why
does he think it is preferable to violence, or body-force? Gandhi was
assassinated by a Hindu extremist in 1948 before he had a chance to
shape the new nation. What kind of India would Gandhi have tried to
create had he lived?

Thinking Historically

Some historians have argued that Gandhi's contradictory roles —
Hindu philosopher espousing secular nationalism and anti-modernist
revolutionary — were ultimately unbridgeable. Notice how Gandhi
makes a lawyer's case for traditional Indian values. How does he combine both religious and secular goals for India? How does he combine
Hindu religious ideas with respect for Muslims? Were Gandhi's contradictions a fatal flaw, or could they have been his strength?

*hihnd   swah RAHJ

M. K. Gandhi, *Hind Swaraj* (Ahmedabad, India: Navajivan, 1938), 15–16, 26–27, 28, 30–31,
32–33, 58–60, 69–71, 82–85.

Civilization

READER: Now you will have to explain what you mean by civilization.

EDITOR: Let us first consider what state of things is described by the word "civilization." Its true test lies in the fact that people living in it make bodily welfare the object of life. We will take some examples. The people of Europe today live in better-built houses than they did a hundred years ago. This is considered an emblem of civilization, and this is also a matter to promote bodily happiness. Formerly, they wore skins, and used spears as their weapons. Now, they wear long trousers, and, for embellishing their bodies, they wear a variety of clothing, and, instead of spears, they carry with them revolvers containing five or more chambers. If people of a certain country, who have hitherto not been in the habit of wearing much clothing, boots, etc., adopt European clothing, they are supposed to have become civilized out of savagery. Formerly, in Europe, people ploughed their lands mainly by manual labour. Now, one man can plough a vast tract by means of steam engines and can thus amass great wealth. This is called a sign of civilization. Formerly, only a few men wrote valuable books. Now, anybody writes and prints anything he likes and poisons people's minds. Formerly, men travelled in waggons. Now, they fly through the air in trains at the rate of four hundred and more miles per day. This is considered the height of civilization. It has been stated that, as men progress, they shall be able to travel in airship and reach any part of the world in a few hours. Men will not need the use of their hands and feet. They will press a button, and they will have their clothing at their side. They will press another button, and they will have their newspaper. A third, and motor-car will be in waiting for them. They will have a variety of delicately dished up food. Everything will be done by machinery. Formerly, when people wanted to fight with one another, they measured between them their bodily strength; now it is possible to take away thousands of lives by one man working behind a gun from a hill. This is civilization. Formerly, men worked in the open air only as much as they liked. Now thousands of workmen meet together and for the sake of maintenance work in factories or mines. Their condition is worse than that of beasts. They are obliged to work, at the risk of their lives, at most dangerous occupations, for the sake of millionaires. Formerly, men were made slaves under physical compulsion. Now they are enslaved by temptation of money and of the luxuries that money can buy. There are now diseases of which people never dreamt before, and an army of doctors is engaged in finding out their cures, and so hospitals have increased. This is a test of civilization. Formerly, special messengers were required and much expense was incurred in order to send letters; today, anyone can abuse his fellow by means of a letter for one penny. True, at the same cost, one can send one's thanks also. Formerly, people had two or three meals consisting of home-made bread and vegetables; now, they require something to eat every two hours so that they have hardly leisure for anything else. What more need I say? . . . Even a child can understand that in all I have described above there can be no inducement to morality.

The Hindus and the Mahomedans

READER: Has the introduction to Mahomedanism [Islam] not unmade the nation?

EDITOR: India cannot cease to be one nation because people belonging to different religions live in it. The introduction of foreigners does not necessarily destroy the nation; they merge in it. A country is one nation only when such a condition obtains in it. That country must have a faculty for assimilation. India has ever been such a country. In reality there are as many religions as there are individuals; but those who are conscious of the spirit of nationality do not interfere with one another's religion. If they do, they are not fit to be considered a nation. If the Hindus believe that India should be peopled only by Hindus, they are living in dreamland. The Hindus, the Mahomedans, the Parsis and the Christians who have made India their country are fellow-countrymen, and they will have to live in unity, if only for their own interest. In no part of the world are one nationality and one religion synonymous terms; nor has it ever been so in India.

READER: But what about the inborn enmity between Hindus and Mahomedans?

EDITOR: That phrase has been invented by our mutual enemy. When the Hindus and Mahomedans fought against one another, they certainly spoke in that strain. They have long since ceased to fight. How, then, can there be any inborn enmity? Pray remember this too, that we did not cease to fight only after British occupation. The Hindus flourished under Moslem sovereigns and Moslems under the Hindu. Each party recognized that mutual fighting was suicidal, and that neither party would abandon its religion by force of arms. Both parties, therefore, decided to live in peace. With the English advent quarrels recommenced. . . .

How Can India Become Free?

READER: If Indian civilization is, as you say, the best of all, how do you account for India's slavery?

EDITOR: This civilization is unquestionably the best, but it is to be observed that all civilizations have been on their trial. That civilization which is permanent outlives it. Because the sons of India were found wanting, its civilization has been placed in jeopardy. But its strength is to be seen in its ability to survive the shock. Moreover, the whole of India is not touched. Those alone who have been affected by Western civilization have become enslaved. We measure the universe by our own miserable foot-rule. When we are slaves, we think that the whole universe is enslaved. Because we are in an abject condition, we think that the whole of India is in that condition. As a matter of fact, it is not so, yet it is as well to impute our slavery to the whole of India. But if we bear in mind the above fact, we can see that if we become free, India is free. And in this thought you have a definition of Swaraj. It is Swaraj when we learn to rule ourselves. It is, therefore, in the palm of our hands. Do not consider this Swaraj to be like a dream. There is no idea of sitting still. The Swaraj that I wish to picture is such that, after we have once realized it, we shall endeavour to the end of our life-time to persuade others to do likewise. But such Swaraj has to be experienced, by each one for himself. One drowning man will never save another. Slaves ourselves, it would be a mere pretension to think of freeing others. Now you will have seen that it is not necessary for us to have as our goal the expulsion of the English. If the English become Indianized, we can accommodate them. If they wish to remain in India along with their civilization, there is no room for them. It lies with us to bring about such a state of things. . . .

Passive Resistance

READER: Is there any historical evidence as to the success of what you have called soul-force or truth-force? No instance seems to have happened of any nation having risen through soul-force. I still think that the evil-doers will not cease doing evil without physical punishment.

EDITOR: The [Hindu] poet Tulsidas [1532–1623] has said: "Of religion, pity, or love, is the root, as egotism of the body. Therefore, we should not abandon pity so long as we are alive." This appears to me to be a scientific truth. We have evidence of its working at every step. The universe would disappear without the existence of that force. . . .

The fact that there are so many men still alive in the world shows that it is based not on the force of arms but on the force of truth or love. Therefore, the greatest and most unimpeachable evidence of the success of this force is to be found in the fact that, in spite of the wars of the world, it still lives on.

Thousands, indeed tens of thousands, depend for their existence on a very active working of this force. Little quarrels of millions of families in their daily lives disappear before the exercise of this force. Hundreds of nations live in peace. History does not and cannot take note of this fact. History is really a record of every interruption of the even working of the force of love or of the soul. Two brothers quarrel; one of them repents and re-awakens the love that was lying dormant in him; the two again begin to live in peace; nobody takes note of this. But if the two brothers, through the intervention of solicitors or some other reason take up arms or go to law — which is another form of the exhibition of brute force, — their doings would be immediately noticed in the press, they would be the talk of their neighbours and would probably go down to history. And what is true of families and communities is true of nations. There is no reason to believe that there is one law for families and another for nations. History, then, is a record of an interruption of the course of nature. Soul-force, being natural, is not noted in history.

READER: According to what you say, it is plain that instances of this kind of passive resistance are not to be found in history. It is necessary to understand this passive resistance more fully. It will be better, therefore, if you enlarge upon it.

EDITOR: Passive resistance is a method of securing rights by personal suffering; it is the reverse of resistance by arms. When I refuse to do a thing that is repugnant to my conscience, I use soul-force. For instance, the Government of the day has passed a law which is applicable to me. I do not like it. If by using violence I force the Government to repeal the law, I am employing what may be termed body-force. If I do not obey the law and accept the penalty for its breach, I use soul-force. It involves sacrifice of self.

$$\boxed{151}$$

JAWAHARLAL NEHRU

Gandhi

Mohandas K. Gandhi and Jawaharlal Nehru* were the two most important leaders of India's national independence movement. In 1942, Nehru published his autobiography, excerpted here, in which he had much to say about the importance of Gandhi in his life. Though they worked together and Nehru was Gandhi's choice as the first Indian prime minister, they expressed in their personalities and ideas two

*jah wah HAHR lahl   NAY roo

J. Nehru, *Toward Freedom: The Autobiography of Jawaharlal Nehru* (New York: John Day Company, 1942).

very different Indias. How would you describe these two Indias? Was it Gandhi's or Nehru's vision of the future that was realized? Who do you think was a better guide for India?

Thinking Historically

Think of Gandhi and Nehru as the two sides of the Indian struggle for independence. Did India benefit from having both of these sides represented? What would have happened if there had been only Gandhi's view or only Nehru's?

How was the debate in India about the influence of the West different from the debate in Japan?

I imagine that Gandhiji[1] is not so vague about the objective as he sometimes appears to be. He is passionately desirous of going in a certain direction, but this is wholly at variance with modern ideas and conditions, and he has so far been unable to fit the two, or to chalk out all the intermediate steps leading to his goal. Hence the appearance of vagueness and avoidance of clarity. But his general inclination has been clear enough for a quarter of a century, ever since he started formulating his philosophy in South Africa. I do not know if those early writings still represent his views. I doubt if they do so in their entirety, but they do help us to understand the background of his thought.

"India's salvation consists," he wrote in 1909, "in unlearning what she has learned during the last fifty years. The railways, telegraphs, hospitals, lawyers, doctors, and suchlike have all to go; and the so-called upper classes have to learn consciously, religiously, and deliberately the simple peasant life, knowing it to be a life giving true happiness." And again: "Every time I get into a railway car or use a motor bus I know that I am doing violence to my sense of what is right"; "to attempt to reform the world by means of highly artificial and speedy locomotion is to attempt the impossible."

All this seems to me utterly wrong and harmful doctrine, and impossible of achievement. Behind it lies Gandhiji's love and praise of poverty and suffering and the ascetic life. For him progress and civilization consist not in the multiplication of wants, of higher standards of living, "but in the deliberate and voluntary restriction of wants, which promotes real happiness and contentment, and increases the capacity for service." If these premises are once accepted, it becomes easy to follow the rest of Gandhiji's thought and to have a better understanding of his activities. But most of us do not accept those premises, and yet we complain later on when we find that his activities are not to our liking.

---

[1]Term of endearment. [Ed.]

Personally I dislike the praise of poverty and suffering. I do not think they are at all desirable, and they ought to be abolished. Nor do I appreciate the ascetic life as a social ideal, though it may suit individuals. I understand and appreciate simplicity, equality, self-control; but not the mortification of the flesh. Just as an athlete requires to train his body, I believe that the mind and habits have also to be trained and brought under control. It would be absurd to expect that a person who is given to too much self-indulgence can endure much suffering or show unusual self-control or behave like a hero when the crisis comes. To be in good moral condition requires at least as much training as to be in good physical condition. But that certainly does not mean asceticism or self-mortification.

Nor do I appreciate in the least the idealization of the "simple peasant life." I have almost a horror of it, and instead of submitting to it myself I want to drag out even the peasantry from it, not to urbanization, but to the spread of urban cultural facilities to rural areas. Far from his life's giving me true happiness, it would be almost as bad as imprisonment for me. What is there in "The Man with the Hoe" to idealize over? Crushed and exploited for innumerable generations, he is only little removed from the animals who keep him company.

> Who made him dead to rapture and despair,
> A thing that grieves not and that never hopes,
> Stolid and stunned, a brother to the ox?

This desire to get away from the mind of man to primitive conditions where mind does not count, seems to me quite incomprehensible. The very thing that is the glory and triumph of man is decried and discouraged, and a physical environment which will oppress the mind and prevent its growth is considered desirable. Present-day civilization is full of evils, but it is also full of good; and it has the capacity in it to rid itself of those evils. To destroy it root and branch is to remove that capacity from it and revert to a dull, sunless, and miserable existence. But even if that were desirable it is an impossible undertaking. We cannot stop the river of change or cut ourselves adrift from it, and psychologically we who have eaten of the apple of Eden cannot forget that taste and go back to primitiveness.

LUTHER STANDING BEAR
From Land of the Spotted Eagle

Most European-Americans accepted the idea of the magazine editor John O'Sullivan, writing in 1845, that "Our manifest destiny [is] to overspread the continent allotted by Providence for the free development of our yearly multiplying millions." Most Americans of European ancestry were not used to thinking of White settlement of Indian lands as colonialism. But manifest destiny, or not, Whites won the west by force, and the Indians who survived were herded into reservations where they lived like colonial subjects.

The American Indian confrontation with the ways of the West was not that different from that of the people of India or other European colonies. Each struggled with the conflict between Western advantage and traditional cultural identity, and each shaped a personal identity from that conflict.

Luther Standing Bear (1868–1939), born Plenty Kill, son of Standing Bear, describes his own struggle for identity in his years at boarding school in Carlisle, Pennsylvania, after he had been separated from his Lakota people. What did he see as the advantages and disadvantages of his education at Carlisle?

Thinking Historically

Would you describe the author's attitude toward Westernization as conflicted, ambiguous, compromising, practical, or something else? How does the author show us that assimilation to Western values or "civilizing" was not just an intellectual process? Change, whether or not we choose it, can have physical manifestations. Can you recall an experience where you struggled over two competing or contradictory pulls to your identity? Do you remember any physical manifestation of the conflict?

I grew up leading the traditional life of my people, learning the crafts of hunter, scout, and warrior from father, kindness to the old and feeble from mother, respect for wisdom and council from our wise men, and was trained by grandfather and older boys in the devotional rites to the Great Mystery. This was the scheme of existence as followed by my

Luther Standing Bear, *Land of the Spotted Eagle* (Lincoln: University of Nebraska Press, 1933), 229–37.

forefathers for many centuries, and more centuries might have come and gone in much the same way had it not been for a strange people who came from a far land to change and reshape our world.

At the age of eleven years, ancestral life for me and my people was most abruptly ended without regard for our wishes, comforts, or rights in the matter. At once I was thrust into an alien world, into an environment as different from the one into which I had been born as it is possible to imagine, to remake myself, if I could, into the likeness of the invader.

By 1879, my people were no longer free, but were subjects confined on reservations under the rule of agents. One day there came to the agency a party of white people from the East. Their presence aroused considerable excitement when it became known that these people were school teachers who wanted some Indian boys and girls to take away with them to train as were white boys and girls.

Now, father was a "blanket Indian,"[1] but he was wise. He listened to the white strangers, their offers and promises that if they took his son they would care well for him, teach him how to read and write, and how to wear white man's clothes. But to father all this was just "sweet talk," and I know that it was with great misgivings that he left the decision to me and asked if I cared to go with these people. I, of course, shared with the rest of my tribe a distrust of the white people, so I know that for all my dear father's anxiety he was proud to hear me say "Yes." That meant that I was brave.

I could think of no reason why white people wanted Indian boys and girls except to kill them, and not having the remotest idea of what a school was, I thought we were going East to die. But so well had courage and bravery been trained into us that it became a part of our unconscious thinking and acting, and personal life was nothing when it came time to do something for the tribe. . . . Thus, in giving myself up to go East I was proving to my father that he was honored with a brave son. In my decision to go, I gave up many things dear to the heart of a little Indian boy, and one of the things over which my child mind grieved was the thought of saying good-bye to my pony. I rode him as far as I could on the journey, which was to the Missouri River, where we took the boat. There we parted from our parents, and it was a heart-breaking scene, women and children weeping. Some of the children changed their minds and were unable to go on the boat, but for many who did go it was a final parting.

On our way to school we saw many white people, more than we ever dreamed existed, and the manner in which they acted when they saw us quite indicated their opinion of us. It was only about three years

---

[1]An Indian who prefers traditional ideas, dress, ways. [Ed.]

after the Custer battle, and the general opinion was that the Plains people merely infested the earth as nuisances. . . . At one place we were taken off the train and marched a distance down the street to a restaurant. We walked down the street between two rows of uniformed men whom we called soldiers, though I suppose they were policemen. This must have been done to protect us, for it was surely known that we boys and girls could do no harm. Back of the rows of uniformed men stood the white people craning their necks, talking, laughing, and making a great noise. They yelled and tried to mimic us by giving what they thought were war-whoops. We did not like this, and some of the children were naturally very much frightened. . . . In my mind I often recall that scene — eighty-odd blanketed boys and girls marching down the street surrounded by a jeering, unsympathetic people whose only emotions were those of hate and fear; the conquerors looking upon the conquered. And no more understanding us than if we had suddenly been dropped from the moon.

At last at Carlisle the transforming, the "civilizing" process began. It began with clothes. Never, no matter what our philosophy or spiritual quality, could we be civilized while wearing the moccasin and blanket. The task before us was not only that of accepting new ideas and adopting new manners, but actual physical changes and discomfort has to be borne uncomplainingly until the body adjusted itself to new tastes and habits. Our accustomed dress was taken and replaced with clothing that felt cumbersome and awkward. Against trousers and handkerchiefs we had a distinct feeling — they were unsanitary and the trousers kept us from breathing well. High collars, stiff-bosomed shirts, and suspenders fully three inches in width were uncomfortable, while leather boots caused actual suffering. We longed to go barefoot, but were told that the dew on the grass would give us colds. . . . red flannel undergarments were given us for winter wear, and for me, at least, discomfort grew into actual torture. I used to endure it as long as possible, then run upstairs and quickly take off the flannel garments and hide them. . . . I still remember those horrid, sticky garments which we had to wear next to the skin, and I still squirm and itch when I think of them. Of course, our hair was cut, and then there was much disapproval. But that was part of the transformation process and in some mysterious way long hair stood in the path of our development. For all the grumbling among the bigger boys, we soon had our heads shaven. How strange I felt! Involuntarily, time and time again, my hands went to my head, and that night it was a long time before I went to sleep. If we did not learn much at first, it will not be wondered at, I think. Everything was queer, and it took a few months to get adjusted to the new surroundings.

Almost immediately our names were changed to those in common use in the English language. Instead of translating our names into English and calling Zinkcaziwin, Yellow Bird, and Wanbli K'leska, Spotted Eagle, which in itself would have been educational, we were just John, Henry, or Maggie, as the case might be. I was told to take a pointer and select a name for myself from the list written on the blackboard. I did, and since one was just as good as another, and as I could not distinguish any difference in them, I placed the pointer on the name Luther. I then learned to call myself by that name and got used to hearing others call me by it, too. By that time we had been forbidden to speak our mother tongue, which is the rule in all boarding-schools. This rule is uncalled for, and today is not only robbing the Indian, but America of a rich heritage. The language of a people is part of their history. Today we should be perpetuating history instead of destroying it, and this can only be effectively done by allowing and encouraging the young to keep it alive. . . .

Of all the changes we were forced to make, that of diet was doubtless the most injurious, for it was immediate and drastic. White bread we had for the first meal and thereafter, as well as coffee and sugar. Had we been allowed our own simple diet of meat, either boiled with soup or dried, and fruit, with perhaps a few vegetables, we should have thrived. But the change in clothing, housing, food, and confinement combined with lonesomeness was too much, and in three years nearly one half of the children from the Plains were dead and through with all earthly schools. In the graveyard at Carlisle most of the graves are those of little ones.

I am now going to confess that I had been at Carlisle a full year before I decided to learn all I could of the white man's ways, and then the inspiration was furnished by my father, the man who has been the greatest influence in all my life. When I had been in school a year, father made his first trip to see me. After I had received permission to speak to him, he told me that on his journey he had seen that the land was full of "Long Knives." "They greatly outnumber us and are here to stay," he said, and advised me, "Son, learn all you can of the white man's ways and try to be like him." From that day on I tried. Those few words of my father I remember as if we talked but yesterday, and in the maturity of my mind I have thought of what he said. He did not say that he thought the white man's ways better than our own; neither did he say that I could be like a white man. He said, "Son, try to be like a white man." So, in two more years I had been "made over." I was Luther Standing Bear wearing the blue uniform of the school, shorn of my hair, and trying hard to walk naturally and easily in stiff-soled cowhide boots. I was now "civilized" enough to go to work in John Wanamaker's fine store in Philadelphia.

I returned from the East at about the age of sixteen, after five years' contact with the white people, to resume life upon the reservation. But I returned, to spend some thirty years before again leaving, just as I had gone — a Lakota.

Outwardly I lived the life of the white man, yet all the while I kept in direct contact with tribal life. While I had learned all that I could of the white man's culture, I never forgot that of my people. I kept the language, tribal manners and usages, sang the songs and danced the dances. I still listened to and respected the advice of the older people of the tribe. I did not come home so "progressive" that I could not speak the language of my father and mother. I did not learn the vices of chewing tobacco, smoking, drinking, and swearing, and for all this I am grateful. I have never, in fact, "progressed" that far.

But I soon began to see the sad sight, so common today, of returned students who could not speak their native tongue, or, worse yet, some who pretended they could no longer converse in the mother tongue. They had become ashamed and this led them into deception and trickery. The boys came home wearing stiff paper collars, tight patent-leather boots, and derby hats on heads that were meant to be clothed in the long hair of the Lakota brave. The girls came home wearing muslin dresses and long ribbon sashes in bright hues which were very pretty. But they were trying to squeeze their feet into heeled shoes of factory make and their waists into binding apparatuses that were not garments — at least they served no purpose of a garment, but bordered on some mechanical device. However, the wearing of them was part of the "civilization" received from those who were doing the same thing. So we went to school to copy, to imitate; not to exchange languages and ideas, and not to develop the best traits that had come out of uncountable experiences of hundreds and thousands of years living upon this continent. Our annals, all happenings of human import, were stored in our song and dance rituals, our history differing in that it was not stored in books, but in the living memory. So, while the white people had much to teach us, we had much to teach them, and what a school could have been established upon that idea! However, this was not the attitude of the day, though the teachers were sympathetic and kind, and some came to be my lifelong friends. But in the main, Indian qualities were undivined and Indian virtues not conceded. And I can well remember when Indians in those days were stoned upon the streets as were the dogs that roamed them. We were "savages," and all who had not come under the influence of the missionary were "heathen," and Wakan Tanka [the Great Mystery], who had since the beginning watched over the Lakota and his land, was denied by these men of God. Should we not have been justified in thinking them heathen? And so the "civilizing" process went on, killing us as it went.

JOSÉ MARTÍ
Letters from New York

José Martí* (1853–1895) is the national hero of Cuba. As poet, journalist, and organizer, he devoted his life to Cuban independence. He fought Spain during the Ten Year War, 1868–1878, and directed the independence movement to the successful war of 1895–1898 but was killed in one of the first battles. Because of his revolutionary activities, Martí spent much of his life in exile in Spain, Mexico, Guatemala, and the United States. In the last fifteen years of his life he lived in New York, where he represented various Latin American governments and wrote widely for Latin American publications. This selection includes excerpts from two of his "Letters from New York." The first, an early one published in Colombia, describes the new Coney Island amusement park to Latin American readers. The second, published in the Spanish *Illustrated Review of New York*, lays out his larger nationalist vision for Cuba and the other countries of Latin America. What in New York appeals to Martí? What bothers him about North American life? What does Martí mean by "our America"? What most concerns him about Latin America in 1891? What does he think needs to be done?

Thinking Historically

Martí's life embodied the contradictions of the nationalist in exile. Living in New York from 1880 to the end of his life, he continually interpreted each America to the other. But his stance was hardly neutral. How did he balance the ways of North America and Latin America? How was Martí both pro–United States and pro–Latin American? In what ways was he both a nationalist and a globalist?

*hoh SAY   mahr TEE

José Martí, "Coney Island," trans. Esther Allen, in *Selected Writings* (New York: Penguin Books, 2002), 89–94. Originally published in *La Pluma* (Bogota, Colombia), December 3, 1881. José Martí, "Our America," is edited from the Web site of the Cuban ministry of foreign affairs, http://www.cubaminrex.cu/English/index.asp. Originally published as "Nuestra América" in *La Revista Ilustrada de Nueva York*, January 1, 1891.

Coney Island (1881)

Nothing in the annals of humanity can compare to the marvelous prosperity of the United States of the North. Does the country lack deep roots? Are ties of sacrifice and shared suffering more lasting within countries than those of common interest? Does this colossal nation contain ferocious and terrible elements? Does the absence of the feminine spirit, source of artistic sensibility and complement to national identity, harden and corrupt the heart of this astonishing people? Only time will tell.

For now it is certain that never has a happier, more joyous, better equipped, more densely packed, more jovial, or more frenetic multitude lived in such useful labor in any land on earth, or generated and enjoyed greater wealth, or covered rivers and seas with more gaily bedecked steamers, or spread out with more bustling order and naive merriment across gentle coastlines, gigantic piers, and fantastical, glittering promenades.

The North American newspapers are full of hyperbolic descriptions of the original beauties and unique attractions of one of those summer resorts, overflowing with people, dotted with sumptuous hotels, crosshatched by an aerial tramway, and colored in with gardens, kiosks, small theaters, saloons, circuses, tents, droves of carriages, picturesque assemblies, bathing machines, auctioneers, fountains.

Echoes of its fame have reached the French newspapers.

From the farthest reaches of the American Union, legions of intrepid ladies and gallant rustics arrive to admire the splendid landscapes, the unrivaled wealth, the bedazzling variety, the Herculean effort, the astonishing sight of the now world-famous Coney Island. Four years ago it was a barren heap of dirt, but today it is a spacious place of relaxation, shelter, and amusement for the hundred thousand or so New Yorkers who repair to its glad beaches each day.

[Martí goes on to describe the town and beach of Gable where Coney Island was located.] But the main attraction of the island is not far-off Rockaway or monotonous Brighton or grave and aristocratic Manhattan Beach: it is Gable, laughing Gable, with its elevator that goes higher than the spire of Trinity Church in New York — twice as high as the spire of our cathedral — and allows travelers to rise to the dizzying heights of its summit, suspended in a tiny, fragile cage. Gable, with its two iron piers that advance on elegant pillars for three blocks out over the sea, and its Sea Beach Palace, which is only a hotel now but was the famous Agricultural Building at the Philadelphia Centennial Exposition, transported to New York as if by magic and rebuilt in its original form down to the last shingle on the coast of Coney Island. Gable, with its fifty-cent museums exhibiting human freaks, preposterous fish, bearded ladies, melancholy dwarves, and stunted elephants grandiloquently advertised as the largest on earth; Gable, with its hundred orchestras, its mirthful dances, its battalions of baby carriages, its gigantic cow, perpetually milked and perpetually giving milk, its twenty-five-cent glasses of fresh cider, its innumerable pairs of amorous wanderers. . . .

Gable, where families gather to seek respite from the rank, unwholesome New York air in the healthy and invigorating seaside breeze; where impoverished mothers — as they empty the enormous box containing the family's lunch onto one of the tables provided without cost in vast pavilions. . . .

Ferries come and go; trains blow their whistles, belch smoke, depart, and arrive, their serpentine bosoms swollen with families they disgorge onto the beach. The women rent blue flannel bathing costumes and rough straw hats that they tie under their chins; the men, in less complicated garments, hold the women's hands and go into the sea, while barefoot children wait along the shore for the roaring wave to drench them, and flee as it reaches them, hiding their terror behind gales of laughter, then return in bands — the better to defy the enemy — to this game of which these innocents, prostrate an hour earlier from the terrible heat, never tire. . . . The amazing thing here is the size, the quantity, this sudden result of human activity, this immense valve of pleasure opened to an immense people, these dining rooms that, seen from afar, look like the encampments of armies, these roads that from two miles away are not roads at all but long carpets of heads, the daily surge of a prodigious people onto a prodigious beach, this mobility, this faculty for progress, this enterprise, this altered form, this fevered rivalry in wealth, the monumentality of the whole, which makes this seaside resort comparable in majesty to the earth that bears it, the sea that caresses it, and the sky that crowns it, this rising tide, this overwhelming and invincible, constant and frenetic drive to expand, and the taking for granted of these very wonders — that is the amazing thing here.

Other peoples — ourselves among them — live in prey to a sublime inner demon that drives us to relentless pursuit of an ideal of love or glory. And when, with the joy of grasping an eagle, we seize the degree of ideal we were pursuing, a new zeal inflames us, a new ambition spurs us on, a new aspiration catapults us into a new and vehement longing, and from the captured eagle goes a free, rebellious butterfly, as if defying us to follow it and chaining us to its restless flight.

Not so these tranquil spirits, disturbed only by their eagerness to possess wealth. The eyes travel across these reverberating beaches; the traveler goes in and out of these dining rooms, vast as the pampas, and climbs to the tops of these colossal buildings, high as mountains; seated in a comfortable chair by the sea, the passerby fills his lungs with that powerful and salubrious air, and yet it is well known that a sad melancholy steals over the men of our Hispanoamerican peoples who live here. They seek each other in vain, and however much the first impressions may have gratified their senses, enamored their eyes, and dazzled and befuddled their minds, the anguish of solitude possesses them in the end. Nostalgia for a superior spiritual world invades and afflicts them; they feel like lambs with no mother or shepherd, lost from the flock, and though their eyes may be dry, the frightened spirit breaks into a torrent of the bitterest tears because this great land is devoid of spirit.

But what comings and goings! What spendings of money! What opportunities for every pleasure! What absolute absence of any visible sadness or poverty! Everything is out in the open: the noisy groups, the vast dining rooms, the peculiar courtship of the North Americans — almost wholly devoid of the elements that comprise the bashful, tender, and elevated courtship of our lands — the theater, the photographer, the bathhouse — all of it out in the open. Some weigh themselves, because for the North Americans it is a matter of positive joy or real grief to weigh a pound more or less; others, for fifty cents, receive from the hands of a robust German girl an envelope containing their fortune; others, with incomprehensible delight, drink unpalatable mineral waters from glasses as long and narrow as artillery shells.

Our America (1891)

The conceited villager believes the entire world to be his village. Provided that he can be mayor, humiliate the rival who stole his sweetheart, or add to the savings in his strongbox, he considers the universal order good, unaware of those giants with seven-league boots who can crush him underfoot, or of the strife in the heavens between comets that go through the air asleep, gulping down worlds. What remains of the village in America must rouse itself. These are not the times for sleeping in a nightcap, but with weapons for a pillow, like the warriors of Juan de Castellanos[1]: weapons of the mind, which conquer all others. Barricades of ideas are worth more than barricades of stones.

There is no prow that can cut through a cloudbank of ideas. A powerful idea, waved before the world at the proper time, can stop a squadron of iron-clad ships, like the mystical flag of the last judgment. Nations that do not know one another should quickly become acquainted, as men who are to fight a common enemy. Those who shake their fists, like jealous brothers coveting the same tract of land, or like the modest cottager who envies the esquire his mansion, should clasp hands and become one. . . . We can no longer be a people of leaves, liv-

---

[1] (1522–1607), chronicler and participant in Spanish conquest of Colombia. [Ed.]

ing in the air, our foliage heavy with blooms and crackling or humming at the whim of the sun's caress, or buffeted and tossed by the storms. The trees must form ranks to keep the giant with seven-league boots from passing! It is the time of mobilization, of marching together, and we must go forward in close ranks, like silver in the veins of the Andes.

. . . Those born in America who are ashamed of the mother that reared them, because she wears an Indian apron, and, who disown their sick mothers, the scoundrels, abandoning her on her sickbed! Then who is a real man? He who stays with his mother and nurses her in her illness, or he who puts her to work out of sight, and lives at her expense on decadent lands, sporting fancy neckties, cursing the womb that carried him, displaying the sign of the traitor on the back of his paper frockcoat? These sons of our America, which will be saved by its Indians in blood and is growing better; these deserters who take up arms in the army of a North America that drowns its Indians in blood and is growing worse! . . .

For in what lands can men take more pride than in our long-suffering American republics, raised up among the silent Indian masses by the bleeding arms of a hundred apostles, to the sound of battle between the book and processional candle? Never in history have such advanced and united nations been forged in so short a time from such disorganized elements. The presumptuous man feels that the earth was made to serve as his pedestal, because he happens to have a facile pen or colorful speech, and he accuses his native land of being worthless and beyond redemption because its virgin jungles fail to provide him with a constant means of traveling over the world, driving Persian ponies and lavishing champagne like a tycoon. The incapacity does not lie with the emerging country in quest of suitable forms and utilitarian greatness; it lies rather with those who attempt to rule nations of a unique and violent character by means of laws inherited from four centuries of freedom in the United States and nineteen centuries of monarchy in France. A decree by Hamilton does not halt the charge of a gaucho's horse. A phrase by Sieyes[2] does nothing to quicken the stagnant blood of the Indian race. To govern well, one must see things as they are. And the able governor in America is not the one who knows how to govern the Germans or the French; he must know the elements that make up his own country, and how to bring them together, using methods and institutions originating within the country, to reach that desirable state where each man can attain self-realization and all may enjoy the abundance that Nature has bestowed on everyone in the nation to enrich with their toil and defend with their lives. Government must

[2]French priest whose question "What is the third estate, if not the entire nation?" was said to spark the French Revolution of 1789. [Ed.]

originate in the country. The spirit of government must be that of the country. Its structure must conform to rules appropriate to the country. Good government is nothing more than the balance of the country's natural elements.

That is why in America the imported book has been conquered by the natural man. Natural men have conquered learned and artificial men. The native half-breed has conquered the exotic Creole. The struggle is not between civilization and barbarity, but between false erudition and Nature. The natural man is good, and he respects and rewards superior intelligence as long as his humility is not turned against him. . . . Republics have paid with oppression for their inability to recognize the true elements of their countries, to derive from them the right kind of government, and to govern accordingly. In a new nation a government means a creator.

In nations composed of both cultured and uncultured elements, the uncultured will govern because it is their habit to attack and resolve doubts with their fists in cases where the cultured have failed in the art of governing. The uncultured masses are lazy and timid in the realm of intelligence, and they want to be governed well. But if the government hurts them, they shake it off and govern themselves. How can the universities produce governors if not a single university in America teaches the rudiments of the art of government, the analysis of elements peculiar to the peoples of America? The young go out into the world wearing Yankee or French spectacles, hoping to govern a people they do not know. . . . To know one's country and govern it with that knowledge is the only way to free it from tyranny. The European university must bow to the American university. The history of America, from the Incas to the present, must be taught in clear detail and to the letter, even if the archons of Greece are overlooked. Our Greece must take priority over the Greece which is not ours. We need it more. Nationalist statement must replace foreign statement. Let the world be grafted onto our republics, but the trunk must be our own. And let the vanquished pedant hold his tongue, for there are no lands in which a man may take greater pride than in our long-suffering American republics. . . .

We were a phenomenon with the chest of an athlete, the hands of a dandy, and the brain of a child. We were a masquerader in English breeches, Parisian vest, North American jacket, and Spanish cap. The Indian hovered near us in silence, and went off to hills to baptize his children. The Negro, pursued from afar, poured out the songs of his heart at night, alone and unrecognized between the waves and wild beasts. The peasant, the creator, turned in blind indignation against the disdainful city, against his own child. We wore epaulets and judges' robes in countries that came into the world wearing hemp sandals and headbands. . . . Neither the Europeans nor the Yankee could provide the key to the Spanish American riddle. So the people tried hatred instead, and every year the countries amounted to less. Exhausted by useless hatred, by the senseless struggle between the book and the lance, between reason and the processional candle, between the city and the country, weary of the impossible rule by rival urban cliques over the natural nation tempestuous or inert by turns, we are beginning almost unconsciously to try love. Nations stand up and greet one another. "What are we?" is the mutual question, and little by little they furnish answers. When a problem arises in Cojímar,[3] they do not seek its solution in Danzig. The frockcoats are still French, but thought begins to be American. The youth of America are rolling up their sleeves, digging their hands in the dough, and making it rise with the sweat of their brows. They realize that there is too much imitation, and that creation holds the key to salvation. "Create" is the password of this generation. Make wine from plantains; it may be sour, but it is our own wine! . . . Thaw out frozen America with the fire of your hearts! Make the natural blood of the nations course vigorously through their veins! The new Americans are on their feet, saluting each other from nation to nation, the eyes of the laborers shining with joy. The natural statesman arises, schooled in the direct study of Nature. He reads to apply his knowledge, not to imitate. Economists study the problems at their point of origin. Speakers begin a policy of moderation. Playwrights bring native characters to the stage. Academies discuss practical subjects. Poetry shears off its . . . locks and hangs its red vest on the glorious tree. Selective and sparkling prose is filled with ideas. In the Indian republics, the governors are learning Indian languages. . . .

There can be no racial animosity, because there are no races. The theorist and feeble thinkers string together and warm over the bookshelf races which the well-disposed observer and the fair-minded traveler vainly seek in the justice of Nature where man's universal identity springs forth from triumphant love and the turbulent hunger for life. The soul, equal and eternal, emanates from bodies of different shapes and colors. Whoever foments and spreads antagonism and hate between the races, sins against humanity. With a single voice the hymn is already being sung; the present generation is carrying industrious America along the road enriched by their sublime fathers; from Rio Grande to the strains of Magellan, the Great Cemi,[4] astride its condor, has scattered the seeds of the new America over the romantic nations of the continent and the sorrowful islands of the sea!

[3]Near Havana, Cuba. [Ed.]
[4]Spirit worshipped by the Taino people of the Caribbean. [Ed.]

REFLECTIONS

We have looked at the conflict between Westernization and nationalism through windows on three different societies: Japan, India, and the
Americas. For the Japanese, the borrowing of Western institutions and
ideas provided an escape from colonization. By the time India gained
political independence in 1947, it had become partially Westernized by
three hundred years of colonialism. Yet in both countries, as in the
countries of the Americas, there were those who resisted Western ways,
those who embraced them, and others still who developed what von
Laue called (after Dostoyevski) "heightened consciousness" from the
contrary experiences or "love-hate" feelings within their own hearts.

This last response — accepting the contradictions: treasuring the
traditional while trying the new — may have been the most difficult,
but ultimately the most useful. It must have been far easier to cast off
everything Asian, as Fukuzawa urged, or make fun of any contact with
the West as buffoonery, monkeying around, or frightful miscegenation,
as the Japanese cartoons suggested. Japan may have made the most
successful non-Western transition to industrial modernity because it
steered a path between Fukuzawa's prescription for wholesale cultural
capitulation and the cartoonists' blanket rejection of anything new and
foreign.

India, with older indigenous traditions than Japan, but also a
longer period confronting the influence of Western culture, approached
independence in 1947 with a political elite trained in English law, liberal and Marxist political parties, a literate English-speaking middle
class, and a long-suppressed hunger for economic freedom and material
well-being. Gandhi feared violence, anticolonial in 1909 and anti-
Muslim in 1947, more than the repressions of the old society. While he
sought a new social cohesion in traditional religious spiritualism,
Nehru hoped to forge a new solidarity along the Western industrial socialist model.

In America, when the ideal of assimilation was not just a sham (as
it was for many Africans and Native Americans), it required a cultural
whitewashing in exchange for material success. Few could condemn
themselves or their countrymen to economic dependence, but Martí,
and others among the best and brightest, could insist on the need to
find their own way.

Our brief summary of Westernization raises many questions. Why
do so many nationalist leaders emerge from outside their native countries? Did Gandhi become more Indian in England or South Africa?
Were Indians who lived overseas more free to express themselves, better able to contribute financially, or more optimistic about changing societies? Did Martí become a Cuban and first citizen of all the Americas

through his travels, or his life in Nueva York? We cannot overlook the international aspects of nationalist movements in the twentieth century; Westernizers and anti-Westernizers seem to have been profoundly influenced by their foreign travel experiences. Is the history of Westernization, and of the opposition to Westernization, ultimately a global story? And are the global processes such that the story eventually becomes irrelevant?

In his book *The Birth of the Modern World, 1780–1914*, historian C. A. Bayly observes that at the beginning of the twenty-first century, it is difficult to distinguish Westernization from globalization, as the forces that threaten the national economies or cultures of Asia, Africa, and Latin America tend to come from every direction. Perhaps future generations will see Westernization as only the initial stage of a larger process of economic and cultural integration, which we now call globalization.

World War I and Its Consequences

Europe and the Soviet Union, 1914–1920

HISTORICAL CONTEXT

The Europe that so many non-European intellectuals sought to imitate or reject between 1880 and 1920 came very close to self-destructing between 1914 and 1918, and bringing many of the world's peoples from Asia, Africa, and the Americas down with it. The orgy of bloodletting, then known as the "Great War," put seventy million men in uniform, of whom ten million were killed and twenty million were wounded. Most of the soldiers were Western European, though Russia contributed more soldiers than France or Germany, while Japan enlisted as many as the Austro-Hungarian empire that began the war. Enlisted men also came from the United States, Canada, Australia, New Zealand, South Africa, and the colonies: India, French West Africa, German East Africa, among others. The majority of soldiers were killed in Europe, especially along the German Western front — four hundred miles of trenches that spanned from Switzerland to the English Channel, across northeastern France. But battles were also fought along the borders of German, French, and English colonies in Africa, and there were high Australian casualties on the coast of Gallipoli in Ottoman Turkey.

The readings in this chapter focus on the lives and deaths of the soldiers, as well as the efforts of some of their political leaders to redefine the world around them. We examine the experiences of soldiers and how the war changed the lives of those who survived its devastating toll. We compare the accounts of those who fought on both sides of the great divide. Germany and the Austro-Hungarian empire, joined by the Ottoman Empire, formed an alliance called the Central Powers (see Map 24.1). In opposition, England, France, and Russia, the Allied Powers, were later joined by Italy, Greece, Japan, and the United

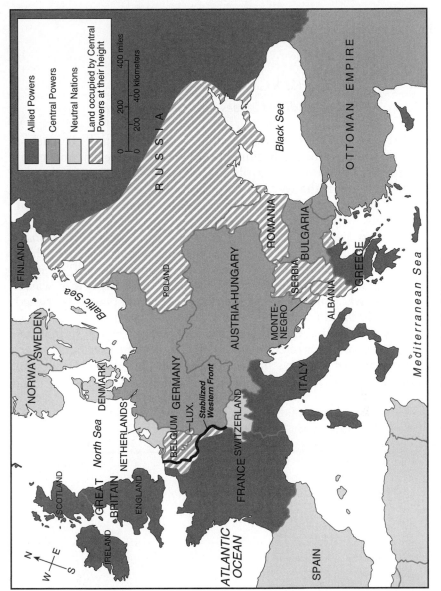

Map 24.1 Allied Powers and Central Powers in World War I.

Legend

- Allied Powers
- Central Powers
- Neutral Nations
- Land occupied by Central Powers at their height

0   200   400 miles
0   200   400 kilometers

NORWAY

SWEDEN

FINLAND

Baltic Sea

DENMARK

NETHERLANDS

BELGIUM
GERMANY
LUX.

Stabilized Western Front

FRANCE

SWITZERLAND

GREAT BRITAIN

SCOTLAND

IRELAND

ENGLAND

North Sea

ATLANTIC OCEAN

SPAIN

ITALY

AUSTRIA-HUNGARY

POLAND

RUSSIA

Black Sea

ROMANIA

BULGARIA

SERBIA

MONTE-NEGRO

ALBANIA

GREECE

OTTOMAN EMPIRE

Mediterranean Sea

N
W — E
S

States. We compare views across the generational divide as well as from the trenches and government offices.

THINKING HISTORICALLY
Understanding Causes and Consequences

From 1914 to 1920, the greatest divide was the war itself. It marked the end of one era and the beginning of another. Few events have left the participants with such a profound sense of fundamental change. And so our study of the war is an appropriate place to ask two of the universal questions of major historical change: What caused it? What were the consequences?

The *causes* are those events or forces that came before; the *consequences* are the results, what the war itself prompted to occur. Thus, causes and consequences are part of the same continuum. Still, we must remember that not everything that happened before the war was a cause of the war. Similarly, not everything that happened afterward was a result of the war.

In this chapter we explore specific ideas about cause and consequence. Our goal is not to compile a definitive list of either but, rather, to explore some of the ways that historians and thoughtful readers can make sense of the past.

154

SALLY MARKS

The Coming of the First World War

Sally Marks, a modern scholar, begins the following selection by declaring that, after much debate, historians have recently come to agree that Germany was the country primarily responsible for causing the First World War. Other countries were not blameless, however, and waging war in the twentieth century required willing recruits and popular support on all sides. Further, as Marks notes, there were secondary or background causes that precipitated the outbreak of war. What were these secondary causes? How important were they?

Thinking Historically

In studying the causes of major historical events, historians distinguish between structural or long-term causes, direct or immediate causes, and contingent events or accidents. Which events and circumstances leading up to the First World War would you place in each of these categories? Marks writes mainly of political decisions made by governments, which are often the most immediate causes of war. She also writes of long-term historic developments, however, such as competition for colonies, the difference between "young" and "old" states, the balance of power in international politics, the development of nationalism, as well as more personal factors such as leaders' fears and miscalculations. Were any of these long-term developments "causes" of war? How important does Marks think they were? Why does she think German political decisions were more important?

There is little that historians debate more endlessly than causation, and certainly much ink has been expended in arguing the origins of World War I. In recent years, however, a degree of consensus has emerged, even among German scholars, that primary responsibility should be assigned to the Second Reich, though debate continues about German motives and intentions. It now seems clear that Germany's

Sally Marks, *The Ebbing of European Ascendancy: An International History of the World, 1914–1945* (New York: Oxford University Press, 2002), 19–22, 25, 26, 31–36.

power, policies, actions, and diplomatic style provided a continual factor between its creation in 1870–1871 and the great collision of 1914.

Germany's unification, coupled with its industrial and demographic growth, brought a young but very strong power to the center of the European stage, hitherto a comparatively weak area. The power balance was at once implicitly altered. But Prince Otto von Bismarck, Chancellor of the new Germany until 1890, chose not to make this explicit in Europe or elsewhere. Preferring to build the Reich's institutions and industry, he restored the Concert of Europe, used it to settle quarrels threatening the peace and his new empire, and eschewed colonies. Between 1894 and 1914, however, a series of political, economic, and diplomatic events contributed to a gradual coalescing of the great power alliances — Russia, France, Great Britain (and later Italy) on the one side, and Germany, Austria-Hungary, and Turkey on the other — that would confront each other in World War I. Other key developments in this period and leading up to 1914 included Germany's growing policy of expansion, hunger for colonies, and military buildup, this last evolving into a fast-escalating naval race with Great Britain.

Although the old Concert was not quite moribund, all European powers of consequence were thus aligned in the two blocs, the Triple Alliance down the center of Europe, and the Triple Entente on the edges. Germany saw the Entente policy of containment as encirclement, and its fears in this respect only increased "the amalgam of insecurity and self-assertion in her make-up. . .". Thus its diplomacy became more bullying, which had the effect of driving Britain and France together, causing the Triple Entente to solidify. Both Germany's insistent claims and Russia's return from East Asia to compete with Austria in the Balkans contributed to growing conflict and tension between the two alignments.

Most of the conflicts concerned imperial matters although a European power struggle underlay them all. Part of the trouble was that the days when there were plenty of colonies available for everybody had passed, and as the powers bumped into each other, the latecomers were dissatisfied. Timing proved crucial to the imperial race; those who did not seize the moment encountered difficulties in doing later what other powers had done earlier. The latecomers were Germany, Japan, and Italy, impatient youngsters who remained dissatisfied, always seeking more until they went down to decisive defeat in World War II. But in the decade before the First World War, the collisions were not only in Africa and Asia, but also in the Balkans, as Russia turned to Austria's sole remaining sphere. Wherever confrontations occurred they brought with them the risk of a major conflagration, not merely a local conflict between two states, but a global struggle between two alignments of powers.

War among the major powers was avoided for a decade despite a series of crises, but only at the price of exhausting options and reducing flexibility, thus rendering resolution more difficult for the future. Great powers, especially the more precarious ones, could not repeatedly accept defeat and humiliation and still remain great powers. Another option which several states exhausted was that of not supporting an ally. With Europe divided into two camps, both of which were arming briskly, retaining one's allies was vital. However, one can desert an ally only so often and still keep it as an ally. Equally, the need for allies meant that both crises and atonements for desertion tended to solidify the two rival alignments, further reducing flexibility.

During the decade before 1914 the Anglo-German naval competition continued, despite British efforts to come to terms, and crises, often entailing lack of support from allies or diplomatic defeat, were too numerous to recount briefly. Though all depleted the reservoirs of good will and elasticity, only a few were so serious that they brought the risk of a pan-European war. Nonetheless, the fact that Europe came to the brink of a great war five or six times in ten short years is indicative of the instability and tension which were mounting.

Part of the problem was that Europe's power system was increasingly out of balance. The Habsburg Empire was no longer really a great power, while France was fading in comparative terms. Russia's vast size did not fully compensate for technological and organizational weakness, especially after the regime was shaken by defeat and revolution in 1905, while at the other end of the continent, Britain's economic lead was less commanding than before. In the middle of Europe Germany was becoming comparatively something of a superpower, already dominant economically, especially in relation to its neighbours, and aspiring to a comparable political and world position. And this young, thrustingly ambitious Reich pursued a high-risk policy of confrontation which created or aggravated crises, contributing to ten years of international tension. . . .

In the chanceries of Europe, a major war was anticipated before long. Some leaders thought that sooner rather than later would be more advantageous for their countries. All assumed that a pan-European war would be short — for economic and technological reasons. But despite the decade of crises and mounting tension, the situation seemed more serene in 1914. In particular, Anglo-German relations appeared improved. The two countries had worked together at the conference of ambassadors in London in 1913 to prevent an Austro-Serbian war, though the German calculations and hope was that if war came, Russia would be blamed and Britain would remain neutral. But that was not public knowledge. However, the citizenry did know that there had not been a major European war for a hundred years; collisions between the great powers had been short and snappy, especially since mid-century, and the last one had occurred nearly 45 years before. A widespread assumption had developed that wars were something which occurred only overseas or in the backward Balkans among quarrelsome infant states. Even Anglo-German naval relations were now less tense, and in July of 1914 the two countries reached an agreement about the Berlin to Baghdad railway. For these and other reasons, the prospects for peace looked better than in the recent past as the spectacularly beautiful summer of 1914 opened.

The sunny calm was shattered on 28 June 1914 by the assassination of the heir to the Austrian throne and his wife in Sarajevo, the capital of Bosnia, by young Bosnian nationalists backed by Unification or Death,[1] a secret Serbian society in which key Serbian army officers were dominant. Their complicity is clear; members of the Serbian cabinet may have had partial foreknowledge as well. The chanceries of Europe anticipated an Austrian reaction directed against Serbia, whose involvement was widely assumed, but not a major war. However, the assassination led to the July crisis of 1914, culminating in World War I. . . .

Austria's actions played a substantial contributory role, and the Habsburg monarchy is usually assigned secondary responsibility for causing World War I, but only secondary, because Austria's actions were obviously contingent. It is beyond serious doubt that it would not have acted against Serbia or risked war with Russia without solid German support. Berlin not only gave that support and repeatedly urged Austria on but also decided upon war now and declared it against Russia and France without any direct provocation from either. A leading German scholar of the July crisis has concluded that "the German Government opened Pandora's box in an act of sheer political and ideological despair."

One must ask what brought the European continent's strongest power to such despair and created a situation where it almost desperately opted to set off a continental war with the risk of world war. Some of the answers lie within German domestic politics and the psychological frame of reference of its leaders. Additional answers lie, as do the contributory errors from other powers, in broader aspects of the European scene in 1914.

For example, there were both men and nations which could ill afford to back down. Too often in the past, the Russian foreign minister, his Austrian counterpart, and the German Kaiser had all displayed timidity, hesitation, and reluctance to commit themselves to firm action. Kaiser Wilhelm in particular was determined to prove that he was not a coward, and, like the Russian foreign minister, he was rather unstable. Similarly, it was doubtful whether the Austrian and Russian regimes could survive major diplomatic defeats. Austria was internally

---

[1] Popularly known as the Black Hand.

so precarious and Russia had sustained so many recent humiliations that disintegration of the one and revolution in the other were real possibilities. This factor loomed large in the calculations of leaders in Vienna, St. Petersburg, and Berlin. Paris concentrated more on retaining its Russian ally. Moreover, the intensity of public opinion in most countries made backing down almost impossible for weak regimes and politicians who wished to retain office. Under the circumstances, it was easy to hope that a strong stand would deter others and solve the problem.

The stronger great powers feared that their allies would cease to be great powers and, to varying degrees, felt a need to bolster them. There was also a widespread fear of losing an ally altogether. Both Britain and France had worried in past crises about losing Russia: France because she compensated for her own deficiencies with the Russian tie, Britain from fear of adding Russia to its enemies. Austria and Germany feared losing each other: Austria because its need was great, Germany from a sense of isolation. Both France and Germany worried that Russia and Austria would fight only if their own interests were involved. Each concluded that it was better for war to come on an issue where the ally's concerns were directly engaged.

Most states feared losing prestige and great power status. This was of intense concern to Austria and Russia, and in both instances was focused primarily on the Balkans, which impacted on domestic concerns and where the situation had changed so rapidly with the removal of Turkey. Yet dread of the results of backing down was widespread and extended even to Britain, master of the seas and of the world's greatest empire. On 31 July 1914, a senior British official argued for action by saying, "The theory that England cannot engage in a big war means her abdication as an independent state. . . . A balance of power cannot be maintained by a State that is incapable of fighting and consequently carries no weight."

Threats to prestige, authority, and vital interests were almost universally perceived. Britain had long recognized a German challenge on and beyond the seas; the invasion of Belgium seemed to be striking at the British heartland. France, aside from other considerations, could hardly hand over her border forts without becoming a defenceless laughing stock. Russia felt its future in the Balkans and among the Slavs was at stake. Austria saw Serbia as a danger to its very existence, whereas Germany perceived a Russian threat and perhaps was as obsessed by Russia as Britain had been in the mid-nineteenth century and the United States would be in the mid-twentieth century. Clearly, some threats were more real and immediate than others, but leaders acted upon their perceptions, even if erroneous.

Nationalism, whether unifying or divisive, and imperialism contributed to the crises and tensions of the pre-war years, if they did not themselves directly cause the war. And certainly Austria-Hungary's ageing, archaic multinational empire, trying to maintain itself against mounting nationalist pressures, was a major contributing factor, as was the Austro-Russian rivalry among the infant national states of the Balkans. The pre-war arms race contributed to the international tension of the era but of itself was not a direct causal factor, despite the beliefs of a later generation, particularly of Americans.

More important, probably, was a widespread pseudo-Darwinian view of international politics, an assumption that it was a question of dog eat dog with the strongest and speediest dog surviving. Furthermore, crises had become the norm, so much so that some leaders expected war before long. Especially in Germany, there was a belief that war and Darwinian struggle were unavoidable, which perhaps explains the preoccupation with an assumed Russian threat and a fatalistic view that a Russo-German war was inevitable soon. Nowhere was there any awareness of what a war would be like; as a result there was scant caution about the dangers war would bring. The short war illusion was widespread and had contributed to the arms race on the assumption that the war would be fought with what equipment one had at the outset. The businessmen would see to it that the war was brief (if they did not prevent it altogether, as some believed, but not those determining national policies). Few in power had much appreciation of what the industrialization, nationalization, and democratization of war signified. Indeed, it was widely held that war was good and glorious and cleansing.

In some countries, military men and military plans played a considerable role. The military plans were rigid, too few in number, and had tight timetables; the military men were wedded to them. The generals tended to be more eager for war than the civilian leaders; even where they were not, there was a fear that any delay in mobilization would be catastrophic. Initially there was often lack of co-ordination between civilian and military leaders, thanks to administrative inadequacy at the top, especially in Germany and Russia, and then tugs-of-war ensued, particularly to sway the autocrat. At a more fundamental level, appreciations in various countries of the military balance of power, then and as it would be in the future, clearly contributed to the pressures toward war.

The alliance system did not of itself cause any war, local, continental, or world. But it constituted a substantial reason why a local crisis became a world war, and partially explains why a murder in Bosnia caused Germany to invade Belgium and why that event in turn led to a world war, with Japan occupying Germany's Asian colonies. This is particularly true in view of the suddenness and speed of the crisis. Peace movements collapsed, and little time was left for diplomacy. Furthermore, previous crises had made the alliances more rigid. Europe had managed to edge past the abyss repeatedly in recent years, but only at the price of expending options and losing flexibility. Now governments felt they had few choices left. . . .

In the end, the debate always comes back to Germany. Clearly, Austria intended to start nothing without Germany at its side, and none of the Entente powers actively wanted a war in 1914. There was no Entente equivalent to Wilhelm's "Now or never." Thus, one must ask whether Germany wanted war in 1914, if so why, and what its reasons and motives were. Why did it encourage local war, accept continental war, and risk world war? The answers are contradictory, thanks to illogic, conflicts, and differing perceptions within Berlin's upper echelons, where policy-making was disorganized. . . .

War came when it did primarily because Germany opted for a war, if not necessarily for the war which eventuated. There has been a good deal of debate about why Germany did so and to what end. Was it largely a matter of miscalculation? Had there been a systematic two-year German plan for world conquest? Was Germany running a calculated risk, hoping to get its way without intent of war? Was the goal a preventive war, to deter future Russian aggression, or was Germany itself engaging in an opportunistic war of aggression?

The answers to these questions are a matter of opinion and the object of heated historical debate. Certainly there was miscalculation aplenty, and repeated gambles constituted calculated or miscalculated risks. It is perhaps begging the question to say that little German policy formulation was systematic, but, despite conferences debating war in December 1912 and thereafter, evidence for a conscious systematic two-year drive toward a world war depends heavily on interpretation and is hotly disputed. Clearly, Germany seized the opportunity for a war of aggression, but the question is why it thought it should.

Perhaps it is best to let German leaders speak for themselves. In February 1918 Bethmann Hollweg, who had been Chancellor in 1914, explained privately, "Yes, my god, in a certain sense it was a preventive war. But when war was hanging above us, when it had to come in two years even more dangerously and more inescapably, and when the generals said, now it is still possible, without defeat, but not in two years time." And in August 1916, Bethmann's close aide and confidante, who himself propounded the theory of the calculated risk, explained that the purpose of the war was "defence against present-day France, preventive war against the Russia of the future, struggle with Britain for world domination."

155

ERICH MARIA REMARQUE

From All Quiet on the Western Front

In this selection, the beginning of one of the most famous war novels ever written, we are introduced to the main characters and to the daily routines of the German army on "the Western Front," the long line of trenches that stretched across northern France from Switzerland to the English Channel for most of the war between 1914 and 1918. What does this selection suggest about the types of people recruited to serve in the army? How does Remarque view friendship, authority, and discipline in the army? Do you imagine these German soldiers behaved very differently from French or English soldiers?

Thinking Historically

Remarque's novel is not intended as an explanation of the causes of war, but this excerpt offers an explanation of how young men were recruited to fight and gives us some idea of their mental state. How might you use material from this novel, assuming that it is factual, to propose at least one cause of World War I?

   In this brief selection, the author also suggests something about the consequences of the war. What, according to Remarque, are the war's likely outcomes? The consequences described here are arrived at very early in the war. Is it likely that they will change significantly as the war continues?

Kantorek had been our schoolmaster, a stern little man in a grey tail-coat, with a face like a shrew mouse. He was about the same size as Corporal Himmelstoss, the "terror of Klosterberg." It is very queer that the unhappiness of the world is so often brought on by small men. They are so much more energetic and uncompromising than the big fellows. I have always taken good care to keep out of sections with small company commanders. They are mostly confounded little martinets.

   During drill-time Kantorek gave us long lectures until the whole of our class went, under his shepherding, to the District Commandant and

Erich Maria Remarque, *All Quiet on the Western Front*, trans. A. W. Wheen (New York: Fawcett Books, 1929), 1–18.

volunteered. I can see him now, as he used to glare at us through his spectacles and say in a moving voice: "Won't you join up, Comrades?"

These teachers always carry their feelings ready in their waistcoat pockets, and trot them out by the hour. But we didn't think of that then.

There was, indeed, one of us who hesitated and did not want to fall into line. That was Joseph Behm, a plump, homely fellow. But he did allow himself to be persuaded, otherwise he would have been ostracized. And perhaps more of us thought as he did, but no one could very well stand out, because at that time even one's parents were ready with the word "coward"; no one had the vaguest idea what we were in for. The wisest were just the poor and simple people. They knew the war to be a misfortune, whereas those who were better off, and should have been able to see more clearly what the consequences would be, were beside themselves with joy.

Katczinsky said that was a result of their upbringing. It made them stupid. And what Kat said, he had thought about.

Strange to say, Behm was one of the first to fall. He got hit in the eye during an attack, and we left him lying for dead. We couldn't bring him with us, because we had to come back helter-skelter. In the afternoon suddenly we heard him call, and saw him crawling about in No Man's Land. He had only been knocked unconscious. Because he could not see, and was mad with pain, he failed to keep under cover, and so was shot down before anyone could go and fetch him in.

Naturally we couldn't blame Kantorek for this. Where would the world be if one brought every man to book? There were thousands of Kantoreks, all of whom were convinced that they were acting for the best — in a way that cost them nothing.

And that is why they let us down so badly.

For us lads of eighteen they ought to have been mediators and guides to the world of maturity, the world of work, of duty, of culture, of progress — to the future. We often made fun of them and played jokes on them, but in our hearts we trusted them. The idea of authority, which they represented, was associated in our minds with a greater insight and a more humane wisdom. But the first death we saw shattered this belief. We had to recognize that our generation was more to be trusted than theirs. They surpassed us only in phrases and in cleverness. The first bombardment showed us our mistake, and under it the world as they had taught it to us broke in pieces.

While they continued to write and talk, we saw the wounded and dying. While they taught that duty to one's country is the greatest thing, we already knew that death-throes are stronger. But for all that we were no mutineers, no deserters, no cowards — they were very free with all these expressions. We loved our country as much as they; we went courageously into every action; but also we distinguished the false from true, we had suddenly learned to see. And we saw that there was nothing of their world left. We were all at once terribly alone; and alone we must see it through.

Before going over to see Kemmerich we pack up his things: He will need them on the way back.

In the dressing station there is great activity: It reeks as ever of carbolic, pus, and sweat. We are accustomed to a good deal in the billets, but this makes us feel faint. We ask for Kemmerich. He lies in a large room and receives us with feeble expressions of joy and helpless agitation. While he was unconscious someone had stolen his watch.

Müller shakes his head: "I always told you that nobody should carry as good a watch as that."

Müller is rather crude and tactless, otherwise he would hold his tongue, for anybody can see that Kemmerich will never come out of this place again. Whether he finds his watch or not will make no difference, at the most one will only be able to send it to his people.

"How goes it, Franz?" asks Kropp.

Kemmerich's head sinks.

"Not so bad . . . but I have such a damned pain in my foot."

We look at his bed covering. His leg lies under a wire basket. The bed covering arches over it. I kick Müller on the shin, for he is just about to tell Kemmerich what the orderlies told us outside: that Kemmerich has lost his foot. The leg is amputated. He looks ghastly, yellow and wan. In his face there are already the strained lines that we know so well, we have seen them now hundreds of times. They are not so much lines as marks. Under the skin the life no longer pulses, it has already pressed out the boundaries of the body. Death is working through from within. It already has command in the eyes. Here lies our comrade, Kemmerich, who a little while ago was roasting horse flesh with us and squatting in the shellholes. He it is still and yet it is not he any longer. His features have become uncertain and faint, like a photographic plate from which two pictures have been taken. Even his voice sounds like ashes.

I think of the time when we went away. His mother, a good plump matron, brought him to the station. She wept continually, her face was bloated and swollen. Kemmerich felt embarrassed, for she was the least composed of all; she simply dissolved into fat and water. Then she caught sight of me and took hold of my arm again and again, and implored me to look after Franz out there. Indeed he did have a face like a child, and such frail bones that after four weeks' pack-carrying he already had flat feet. But how can a man look after anyone in the field!

"Now you will soon be going home," says Kropp. "You would have had to wait at least three or four months for your leave."

Kemmerich nods. I cannot bear to look at his hands, they are like wax. Under the nails is the dirt of the trenches, it shows through blue-black like poison. It strikes me that these nails will continue to grow like lean fantastic cellar-plants long after Kemmerich breathes no more. I see the picture before me. They twist themselves into corkscrews and grow and grow, and with them the hair on the decaying skull, just like grass in a good soil, just like grass, how can it be possible ———

Müller leans over. "We have brought your things, Franz."

Kemmerich signs with his hands. "Put them under the bed."

Müller does so. Kemmerich starts on again about the watch. How can one calm him without making him suspicious?

Müller reappears with a pair of airman's boots. They are fine English boots of soft, yellow leather which reach to the knees and lace up all the way — they are things to be coveted.

Müller is delighted at the sight of them. He matches their soles against his own clumsy boots and says: "Will you be taking them with you then, Franz?"

We all three have the same thought; even if he should get better, he would be able to use only one — they are no use to him. But as things are now it is a pity that they should stay here; the orderlies will of course grab them as soon as he is dead.

"Won't you leave them with us?" Müller repeats.

Kemmerich doesn't want to. They are his most prized possessions.

"Well, we could exchange," suggests Müller again. "Out here one can make some use of them." Still Kemmerich is not to be moved.

I tread on Müller's foot; reluctantly he puts the fine boots back again under the bed.

We talk a little more and then take our leave.

"Cheerio, Franz."

I promise him to come back in the morning. Müller talks of doing so, too. He is thinking of the lace-up boots and means to be on the spot.

Kemmerich groans. He is feverish. We get hold of an orderly outside and ask him to give Kemmerich a dose of morphia.

He refuses. "If we were to give morphia to everyone we would have to have tubs full ———"

"You only attend to officers properly," says Kropp viciously.

I hastily intervene and give him a cigarette. He takes it.

"Are you usually allowed to give it, then?" I ask him.

He is annoyed. "If you don't think so, then why do you ask?"

I press a few more cigarettes into his hand. "Do us the favour ———"

"Well, all right," he says.

Kropp goes in with him. He doesn't trust him and wants to see. We wait outside.

Müller returns to the subject of the boots. "They would fit me perfectly. In these boots I get blister after blister. Do you think he will last till tomorrow after drill?" If he passes out in the night, we know where the boots ———"

Kropp returns. "Do you think ——?" he asks.

"Done for," said Müller emphatically.

We go back to the huts. I think of the letter that I must write to-morrow to Kemmerich's mother. I am freezing. I could do with a tot of rum. Müller pulls up some grass and chews it. Suddenly little Kropp throws his cigarette away, stamps on it savagely, and looking around him with a broken and distracted face, stammers "Damned shit, the damned shit!"

We walk on for a long time. Kropp has calmed himself; we understand, he saw red; out there every man gets like that sometime.

"What has Kantorek written to you?" Müller asks him.

He laughs. "We are the Iron Youth."

We all three smile bitterly, Kropp rails: He is glad that he can speak.

Yes, that's the way they think, these hundred thousand Kantoreks! Iron Youth! Youth! We are none of us more than twenty years old. But young? Youth? That is long ago. We are old folk.

$$\boxed{156}$$

World War I Propaganda Posters

Posters were the communication medium of the First World War. In an age when governments had still not taught most people how to read but increasingly needed their consent or compliance, images often spoke louder than words, but those images had to be *persuasive*.

The American poster from 1917 and the German poster from 1915–1916 (Figures 24.1 and 24.3) implore men to enlist in the army; the Italian poster from 1917 (Figure 24.2) encourages people to buy war bonds. What do you think accounts for the similar graphic style used in these three posters? How effective do you think they were and why?

Another strategy for promoting loyalty, patriotism, and support for a war that was lasting far longer than anyone had anticipated was to demonize or ridicule the enemy. What feelings does the U.S. anti-German poster from 1916 (Figure 24.4) attempt to provoke in viewers and how does the scene shown achieve this? Compare this portrayal of German brutishness to the narrator of *All Quiet on the Western Front* and his soldier companions. Why is it often essential to dehumanize the enemy in wartime? Figure 24.5, a German propaganda

Figure 24.1   Recruiting Poster for U.S. Army.

poster, takes a different tack, depicting the Allied Powers as a series of ineffectual toy soldiers. The caption in German mockingly confirms this notion: "You six aren't worth the waste of shot and powder." Although it may be difficult to discern, each soldier bears a letter above or next to his head indicating his country of origin. Viewing them left to right the soldiers are Montenegrin, Serbian, Russian, English, French, and Belgian. What cultural and ethnic stereotypes do these figures reveal?

The signing of the armistice in 1918 did not mean the end of propaganda, as Figure 24.6, a lithograph from 1920 exhorting French citizens to help repay the war debt, shows. The female figure striding optimistically forward is the goddess Victory holding aloft an olive branch, a symbol of peace. What do you make of the other elements in this print? What sentiments does this picture appeal to?

Figure 24.2 Italian Poster for National War Loan, 1917.
Source: Snark/Art Resource, N.Y.

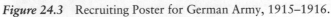

Figure 24.3   Recruiting Poster for German Army, 1915–1916.

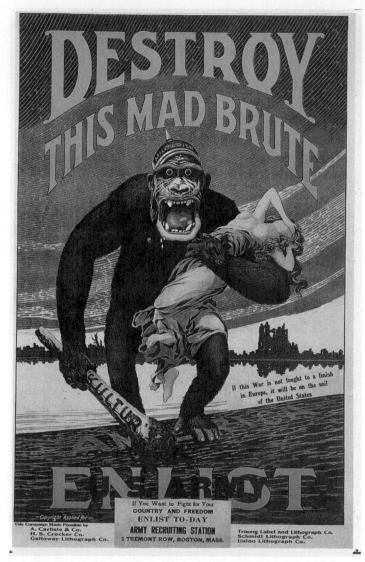

Figure 24.4   Propaganda Poster, United States, 1916.

Figure 24.5 German Propaganda Poster, 1916.

Figure 24.6 French War Loan Poster, 1920.
Source: The Image Works.

Thinking Historically

When war broke out overseas, President Woodrow Wilson declared it a European matter that had nothing to do with the United States and most Americans agreed. Indeed, the United States did not join the war and throw its crucial weight behind the Allied Powers until April 1917. What role do you think propaganda such as Figure 24.4 played in swaying public opinion? This and the other posters illustrate both sides' efforts to promote and sustain the cause of war. But do they reveal anything about the changes wrought by the war?

$$157$$

SIEGFRIED SASSOON

Base Details

An English gentleman and pastoral poet before the war, Siegfried Sassoon (1886–1967) enlisted with a noble innocence soon challenged on the battlefield. In addition to his own sobering experiences, his brother and a fellow officer were among the many slaughtered in the failed Allied effort of 1915 to conquer Turkish defenses at Gallipoli. What is the message of this poem?

Thinking Historically

Poems are not, of course, exercises in historical explanation. Nevertheless, there is here a partial explanation of the continuation, if not the cause, of the war. What is that explanation? How is it similar to, or different from, others you have read in this chapter?

Siegfried Sassoon, *Counter-Attack and Other Poems* (London: W. Heinemann, 1918).

If I were fierce, and bald, and short of breath,
	I'd live with scarlet Majors at the Base,
And speed glum heroes up the line to death.
	You'd see me with my puffy petulant face,
Guzzling and gulping in the best hotel,
	Reading the Roll of Honour. "Poor young chap,"
I'd say — "I used to know his father well;
	Yes, we've lost heavily in this last scrap."
And when the war is done and youth stone dead,
	I'd toddle safely home and die — in bed.

$$\boxed{158}$$

WILFRED OWEN

Dulce et Decorum Est

Wilfred Owen (1893–1918) enlisted in the British Army in 1915, was wounded in 1917, and was hospitalized, released, and sent back to the front, where he died on November 4, 1918, one week before the end of the war. In this poem, he describes a poison gas attack. Like the machine gun and the airplane, gas was a common element of the new mechanized mass warfare. Owen describes how physically debilitating the effects of gas were. Why was gas such an effective and deadly weapon? How, according to Owen, had the nature of war changed?

Thinking Historically

The concluding phrase, which means "Sweet and proper it is to die for one's country," was a Latin declaration of patriotic duty that English students repeated as a lesson, not only in Latin classes but, more important, in their political education as subjects of the British empire. How does Owen portray this lesson as a cause of the war? What does he imagine to be the consequences of fighting a war with such patriotic slogans in mind?

Wilfred Owen, *Poems*, ed. Siegfried Sassoon (London: Chatto and Windus, 1920).

Dulce et Decorum Est

Bent double, like old beggars under sacks,
Knock-kneed, coughing like hags, we cursed
    through sludge,
Till on the haunting flares we turned our backs
And towards our distant rest began the trudge.
Men marched asleep. Many had lost their boots
But limped on, blood-shod. All went lame; all
    blind;
Drunk with fatigue; deaf even to the hoots
Of tired, outstripped Five-Nines[1] that dropped
    behind.

Gas! GAS! Quick, boys! — An ecstasy of
    fumbling,
Fitting the clumsy helmets just in time;
But someone still was yelling out and stumbling,
And flound'ring like a man in fire or lime. . . .
Dim, through the misty panes and thick green
    light,
As under a green sea, I saw him drowning.

In all my dreams, before my helpless sight,
He plunges at me, guttering, choking,
    drowning.

If in some smothering dreams you too could
    pace
Behind the wagon that we flung him in,
And watch the white eyes writhing in his face,
His hanging face, like a devil's sick of sin;
If you could hear, at every jolt, the blood
Come gargling from the froth-corrupted lungs,
Obscene as cancer, bitter as the cud
Of vile, incurable sores on innocent tongues,
My friend, you would not tell with such high
    zest,
To children ardent for some desperate glory,
The old Lie: Dulce et decorum est
Pro patria mori.

---

[1] German artillery shells. [Ed.]

159

ROSA LUXEMBURG
The Junius[1] Pamphlet

Many Europeans greeted the onset of war with enthusiasm, expecting a quick victory. Before 1914 the socialist parties of Europe were among the few voices for peace and international cooperation. But when war came, the socialist parties of Germany, England, and France were swept up in the nationalist furor for war, like everyone else. Rosa Luxemburg (1871–1919), a Polish refugee who had earned a doctorate in Switzerland and became a leader of German socialism, feared their capitulation. When it happened she broke with the German Social Democratic party and founded the more radical Spartacus League. Because of her activities, she spent most of the war in jail. There she wrote the Junius Pamphlet in 1915. What reasons did she give for opposing the war?

Thinking Historically

Rosa Luxemburg's opposition to the war was based on a Marxist interpretation of history according to which the wars of capitalist societies were products of particular causes. What were these causes? What, according to this view, would be the consequences of capitalist wars?

The scene has changed fundamentally. The six weeks' march to Paris has grown into a world drama.[2] Mass slaughter has become the tiresome and monotonous business of the day and the end is no closer. Bourgeois statecraft is held fast in its own vise. The spirits summoned up can no longer be exorcised.

Gone is the euphoria. Gone the patriotic noise in the streets, the chase after the gold-colored automobile, one false telegram after another, the wells poisoned by cholera, the Russian students heaving

---

[1]Perhaps a reference to Lucius Junius Brutus, a republican hero of ancient Rome, legendary founder of the Roman Republic, c. 509 B.C.E. [Ed.]

[2]Six weeks was the time allotted for victory on the Western Front by the Schlieffen Plan. The general staff was forced to scrap the plan in October 1914, as the war of movement swiftly devolved into grinding trench warfare. [Ed.]

"Die Krise der Sozialdemokratie (Junius-Broschüre)," trans. Richard S. Levy, in Rosa Luxemburg, *Politische Schriften*, Günter Radczun, ed. (Leipzig, 1970), 229–43, 357–72. Also available on-line at http://h-net.org/~german/gtext/kaiserreich/lux.html.

bombs over every railway bridge in Berlin, the French airplanes over Nuremberg, the spy hunting public running amok in the streets, the swaying crowds in the coffee shops with ear-deafening patriotic songs surging ever higher, whole city neighborhoods transformed into mobs ready to denounce, to mistreat women, to shout hurrah and to induce delirium in themselves by means of wild rumors. . . .

The spectacle is over. German scholars, those "stumbling lemurs," have been whistled off the stage long ago. The trains full of reservists are no longer accompanied by virgins fainting from pure jubilation. They no longer greet the people from the windows of the train with joyous smiles. Carrying their packs, they quietly trot along the streets where the public goes about its daily business with aggrieved visages.

In the prosaic atmosphere of pale day there sounds a different chorus — the hoarse cries of the vulture and the hyenas of the battlefield. Ten thousand tarpaulins guaranteed up to regulations! A hundred thousand kilos of bacon, cocoa powder, coffee-substitute — c.o.d., immediate delivery! Hand grenades, lathes, cartridge pouches, marriage bureaus for widows of the fallen, leather belts, jobbers for war orders — serious offers only! The cannon fodder loaded onto trains in August and September is moldering in the killing fields of Belgium, the Vosges, and Masurian Lakes where the profits are springing up like weeds. It's a question of getting the harvest into the barn quickly. Across the ocean stretch thousands of greedy hands to snatch it up.

Business thrives in the ruins. Cities become piles of ruins; villages become cemeteries; countries, deserts; populations are beggared; churches, horse stalls. International law, treaties and alliances, the most sacred words and the highest authority have been torn in shreds. Every sovereign "by the grace of God" is called a rogue and lying scoundrel by his cousin on the other side. Every diplomat is a cunning rascal to his colleagues in the other party. Every government sees every other as dooming its own people and worthy only of universal contempt. There are food riots in Venice, in Lisbon, Moscow, Singapore. There is plague in Russia, and misery and despair everywhere.

Violated, dishonored, wading in blood, dripping filth — there stands bourgeois society. This is it [in reality]. Not all spic and span and moral, with pretense to culture, philosophy, ethics, order, peace, and the rule of law — but the ravening beast, the witches' sabbath of anarchy, a plague to culture and humanity. Thus it reveals itself in its true, its naked form.

In the midst of this witches' sabbath a catastrophe of world-historical proportions has happened: International Social Democracy has capitulated. To deceive ourselves about it, to cover it up, would be the most foolish, the most fatal thing the proletariat could do. . . .

Friedrich Engels once said: "Bourgeois society stands at the crossroads, either transition to socialism or regression into barbarism.". . .

This world war is a regression into barbarism. The triumph of imperialism leads to the annihilation of civilization. . . .

The war means ruin for all the belligerents, although more so for the defeated. On the day after the concluding of peace, preparations for a new world war will be begun under the leadership of England in order to throw off the yoke of Prusso-German militarism burdening Europe and the Near East. A German victory would be only a prelude to a soon-to-follow second world war; and this would be the signal for a new, feverish arms race as well as the unleashing of the blackest reaction in all countries, but first and foremost in Germany itself. . . . from this side, too, [an Anglo-French] victory would lead to a new feverish armaments race among all the states — with defeated Germany obviously in the forefront. An era of unalloyed militarism and reaction would dominate all Europe with a new world war as its ultimate goal. . . .

The world war today is demonstrably not only murder on a grand scale; it is also suicide of the working classes of Europe. The soldiers of socialism, the proletarians of England, France, Germany, Russia, and Belgium have for months been killing one another at the behest of capital. They are driving the cold steel of murder into each other's hearts. Locked in the embrace of death, they tumble into a common grave.

"*Deutschland, Deutschland über Alles!* Long live democracy! Long live the Tsar and Slav-dom! Ten thousand tarpaulins guaranteed up to regulations! A hundred thousand kilos of bacon, coffee-substitute for immediate delivery!" . . . Dividends are rising, and the proletarians are falling. And with every one there sinks into the grave a fighter of the future, a soldier of the revolution, mankind's savior from the yoke of capitalism.

The madness will cease and the bloody demons of hell will vanish only when workers in Germany and France, England and Russia finally awake from their stupor, extend to each other a brotherly hand, and drown out the bestial chorus of imperialist war-mongers and the shrill cry of capitalist hyenas with labor's old and mighty battle cry: Proletarians of all lands, unite!

160

V. I. LENIN

From War and Revolution

One of the great casualties of the First World War was the Russian empire, including the czar, his family, many of the members of their class, and its centuries-old autocratic system. The burden of war was simply too much for Russian society to bear. The disillusionment in the army and civilian society, along with the overwhelming costs of war, fueled uprisings among civilians and the army and Czar Nicholas II was forced to abdicate in February of 1917. The government that emerged, under Alexander Kerensky, proved unable to satisfy the growing demands of peasants, veterans, and urban workers for "land, peace, and bread," a slogan that V. I. Lenin (1870–1924) and the communists exploited, successfully seizing power from the moderate parliamentarians in October of that year.

As a Marxist, Lenin believed that he could establish a socialist society in Russia, but he argued that Russian conditions (e.g., economic underdevelopment; the devastation of war; the opposition of Europe, the United States, and Russian nobles to the revolution) made a democratic transition impossible. According to Lenin, a self-appointed government acting in the interests of the working class was the only way to a socialist Soviet Union. Lenin called this government "the dictatorship of the proletariat." Rosa Luxemburg was one of Lenin's fiercest critics on this point, arguing that capitalism in Russia was not sufficiently developed to allow for a democratic socialist revolution, and that dictatorial means would result in dictatorial ends.

Lenin delivered his "War and Revolution" address in May of 1917, during the fateful summer that followed the liberal February revolution and preceded the Bolshevik revolution in October. How did Lenin view the First World War and Russia's continued participation in it? What did he hope to accomplish in the summer of 1917? How did he hope to accomplish it? The most important news for Russia's allies, England and France, in the summer of 1917 was the United States' entry into the war on their behalf. What was Lenin's reaction to this development?

V. I. Lenin, *Collected Works*, vol. 24, 4th English ed. (Moscow: Progress Publishers, 1964), 398–421.

Thinking Historically

According to Lenin, what were the causes of the First World War? What did he believe to be the main cause of the Russian revolution that occurred in February? What were the consequences of that revolution? What did he think would be the causes of a new revolution in Russia?

What we have at present is primarily two leagues, two groups of capitalist powers. We have before us all the world's greatest capitalist powers — Britain, France, America, and Germany — who for decades have doggedly pursued a policy of incessant economic rivalry aimed at achieving world supremacy, subjugating the small nations, and making threefold and tenfold profits on banking capital, which has caught the whole world in the net of its influence. That is what Britain's and Germany's policies really amount to. . . .

These policies show us just one thing — continuous economic rivalry between the world's two greatest giants, capitalist economies. On the one hand we have Britain, a country which owns the greater part of the globe, a country which ranks first in wealth, which has created this wealth not so much by the labour of its workers as by the exploitation of innumerable colonies, by the vast power of its banks which have developed at the head of all the others into an insignificantly small group of some four or five super-banks handling billions of rubles, and handling them in such a way that it can be said without exaggeration that there is not a patch of land in the world today on which this capital has not laid its heavy hand, not a patch of land which British capital has not enmeshed by a thousand threads. . . .

On the other hand, opposed to this, mainly Anglo-French group, we have another group of capitalists, an even more rapacious, even more predatory one, a group who came to the capitalist banqueting table when all the seats were occupied, but who introduced into the struggle new methods for developing capitalist production, improved techniques, and superior organization, which turned the old capitalism, the capitalism of the free-competition age, into the capitalism of giant trusts, syndicates, and cartels. This group introduced the beginnings of state-controlled capitalist production, combining the colossal power of capitalism with the colossal power of the state into a single mechanism and bringing tens of millions of people within the single organization of state capitalism. Here is economic history, here is diplomatic history, covering several decades, from which no one can get away. It is the one and only guide-post to a proper solution of the problem of war; it leads you to the conclusion that the present war, too, is the outcome of the policies of the classes who have come to grips in it, of the two supreme giants, who, long before the war, had caught the whole world, all countries, in the net of financial exploitation and economically divided the globe up among themselves. They were bound to clash, because a redivision of this supremacy, from the point of view of capitalism, had become inevitable. . . .

The present war is a continuation of the policy of conquest, of the shooting down of whole nationalities, of unbelievable atrocities committed by the Germans and the British in Africa, and by the British and the Russians in Persia — which of them committed most it is difficult to say. It was for this reason that the German capitalists looked upon them as their enemies. Ah, they said, you are strong because you are rich? But we are stronger, therefore we have the same "sacred" right to plunder. That is what the real history of British and German finance capital in the course of several decades preceding the war amounts to. That is what the history of Russo-German, Russo-British, and German-British relations amounts to. There you have the clue to an understanding of what the war is about. That is why the story that is current about the cause of the war is sheer duplicity and humbug. Forgetting the history of finance capital, the history of how this war had been brewing over the issue of redivision, they present the matter like this: Two nations were living at peace, then one attacked the other, and the other fought back. All science, all banks are forgotten, and the peoples are told to take up arms, and so are the peasants, who know nothing about politics. . . .

. . . What revolution did we make? We overthrew Nicholas. The revolution was not so very difficult compared with one that would have overthrown the whole class of landowners and capitalists. Who did the revolution put in power? The landowners and capitalists — the very same classes who have long been in power in Europe. . . . The [February] Russian revolution has not altered the war, but it has created organizations which exist in no other country and were seldom found in revolutions in the West. . . . We have all over Russia a network of Soviets of Workers', Soldiers', and Peasants' Deputies. Here is a revolution which has not said its last word yet. . . .

. . . In the two months following the revolution the industrialists have robbed the whole of Russia. Capitalists have made staggering profits; every financial report tells you that. And when the workers, two months after the revolution, had the "audacity" to say they wanted to live like human beings, the whole capitalist press throughout the country set up a howl.

On the question of America entering the war I shall say this. People argue that America is a democracy, America has the White House. I say: Slavery was abolished there half a century ago. The anti-slave war ended in 1865. Since then multimillionaires have mushroomed. They have the whole of America in their financial grip. They are making ready to subdue Mexico and will inevitably come to war with Japan over a carve-up of the Pacific. This war has been brewing for several decades. All literature speaks about it. America's real aim in entering the war is to prepare for this future war with Japan. The American people do enjoy considerable freedom and it is difficult to conceive them standing for compulsory military service, for the setting up of an army pursuing any aims of conquest — a struggle with Japan, for instance. The Americans have the example of Europe to show them what this leads to. The American capitalists have stepped into this war in order to have an excuse, behind a smoke-screen of lofty ideals championing the rights of small nations, for building up a strong standing army. . . .

. . . Tens of millions of people are facing disaster and death; safeguarding the interests of the capitalists is the last thing that should bother us. The only way out is for all power to be transferred to the Soviets, which represent the majority of the population. Possibly mistakes may be made in the process. No one claims that such a difficult task can be disposed of offhand. We do not say anything of the sort. We are told that we want the power to be in the hands of the Soviets, but they don't want it. We say that life's experience will suggest this solution to them, and the whole nation will see that there is no other way out. We do not want a "seizure" of power, because the entire experience of past revolutions teaches us that the only stable power is the one that has the backing of the majority of the population. "Seizure" of power, therefore, would be adventurism, and our Party will not have it. . . .

Nothing but a workers' revolution in several countries can defeat this war. The war is not a game, it is an appalling thing taking a toll of millions of lives, and it is not to be ended easily.

. . . The war has been brought about by the ruling classes and only a revolution of the working class can end it. Whether you will get a speedy peace or not depends on how the revolution will develop.

Whatever sentimental things may be said, however much we may be told: Let us end the war immediately — this cannot be done without the development of the revolution. When power passes to the Soviets the capitalists will come out against us. Japan, France, Britain — the governments of all countries will be against us. The capitalists will be against, but the workers will be for us. That will be the end of the war which the capitalists started. There you have the answer to the question of how to end the war.

161

WOODROW WILSON

Fourteen Points

Woodrow Wilson (1856–1924) was president of the United States during the First World War. He presented these "Fourteen Points" to Congress in January 1918 as a basis for a just peace treaty to end the war.

You may wish to compare these proposals with the actual peace settlement. Only points VII, VIII, X, and XIV were realized. Point IV was applied only to the defeated nations. The Versailles Treaty, which the defeated Germans were forced to sign on June 28, 1919, contained much harsher terms, including the famous "war guilt" clause (Article 231):

> The Allied and Associated Governments affirm and Germany accepts the responsibility of Germany and her allies for causing all the loss and damage to which the Allied and Associated Governments and their nationals have been subjected as a consequence of the war imposed upon them by the aggression of Germany and her allies.

Why do you think there was such a gap between Wilson's ideals and the actual treaty? How might Wilson have improved on these Fourteen Points? Could he reasonably expect all of them to be accepted?

Thinking Historically

What does the first paragraph suggest Wilson thought was one cause of the war? What does the beginning of the second paragraph suggest about the cause for U.S. entry into the war? What would have been the consequences of a peace fashioned along the lines Wilson envisioned in his Fourteen Points?

It will be our wish and purpose that the processes of peace, when they are begun, shall be absolutely open, and that they shall involve and permit henceforth no secret understandings of any kind. The day of

---

Woodrow Wilson, *War and Peace: Presidential Messages, Addresses, and Public Papers (1917–1924)*, vol. 1, ed. Ray Stannard Baker and William E. Dodd (New York: Harper Brothers, 1927).

conquest and aggrandizement is gone by; so is also the day of secret covenants entered into in the interest of particular Governments and likely at some unlooked-for moment to upset the peace of the world. It is this happy fact, now clear to the view of every public man whose thoughts do not still linger in an age that is dead and gone, which makes it possible for every nation whose purposes are consistent with justice and the peace of the world to avow now or at any other time the objects it has in view.

We entered this war because violations of right had occurred which touched us to the quick and made the life of our own people impossible unless they were corrected and the world secured once for all against their recurrence. What we demand in this war, therefore, is nothing peculiar to ourselves. It is that the world be made fit and safe to live in; and particularly that it be made safe for every peace-loving nation which, like our own, wishes to live its own life, determine its own institutions, be assured of justice and fair dealing by the other peoples of the world as against force and selfish aggression. All the peoples of the world are in effect partners in this interest, and for our own part we see very clearly that unless justice be done to others it will not be done to us. The program of the world's peace, therefore, is our program; and that program, the only possible program, as we see it, is this:

I. Open covenants of peace, openly arrived at, after which there shall be no private international understandings of any kind but diplomacy shall proceed always frankly and in the public view.

II. Absolute freedom of navigation upon the seas, outside territorial waters, alike in peace and in war, except as the seas may be closed in whole or in part by international action. . . .

III. The removal, so far as possible, of all economic barriers and the establishment of an equality of trade conditions among all the nations consenting to the peace and associating themselves for its maintenance.

IV. Adequate guarantees given and taken that national armaments will be reduced to the lowest point consistent with domestic safety.

V. A free, open-minded, and absolutely impartial adjustment of all colonial claims, based upon a strict observance of the principle that in determining all such questions of sovereignty the interests of the populations concerned must have equal weight with the equitable claims of the government whose title is to be determined.

VI. The Evacuation of all Russian territory and such a settlement of all questions affecting Russia as will secure the best and freest cooperation of the other nations of the world in obtaining for her an unhampered and unembarrassed opportunity for the independent determination of her own political development and national policy and assure her of a sincere welcome into the society of free nations under institutions of her own choosing; and, more than a welcome, assistance also of every kind that she may need and may herself desire. The treatment accorded Russia by her sister nations in the months to come will be the acid test of their good will, of their comprehension of her needs as distinguished from their own interests, and of their intelligent and unselfish sympathy.

VII. Belgium, the whole world will agree, must be evacuated and restored, without any attempt to limit the sovereignty which she enjoys in common with all other free nations. No other single act will serve to restore confidence among the nations in the laws which they have themselves set and determined for the government of their relations with one another. Without this healing act the whole structure and validity of international law is forever impaired.

VIII. All French territory should be freed and the invaded portions restored, and the wrong done to France by Prussia in 1871 in the matter of Alsace-Lorraine, which has unsettled the peace of the world for nearly fifty years, should be righted, in order that peace may once more be made secure in the interest of all.

IX. A readjustment of the frontiers of Italy should be effected along clearly recognizable lines of nationality.

X. The peoples of Austria-Hungary, whose place among the nations we wish to see safeguarded and assured, should be accorded the freest opportunity of autonomous development.

XI. Rumania, Serbia, and Montenegro should be evacuated; occupied territories restored; Serbia accorded free and secure access to the sea; and the relations of the several Balkan states to one another determined by friendly counsel along historically established lines of allegiance and nationality; and international guarantees of the political and economic independence and territorial integrity of the several Balkan states should be entered into.

XII. The Turkish portions of the present Ottoman Empire should be assured a secure sovereignty, but the other nationalities which are now under Turkish rule should be assured an undoubted security of life and an absolutely unmolested opportunity of autonomous development, and the Dardanelles should be permanently opened as a free passage to the ships and commerce of all nations under international guarantees.

XIII. An independent Polish state should be erected which should include the territories inhabited by indisputably Polish populations, which should be assured a free and secure access to the sea, and whose political and economic independence and territorial integrity should be guaranteed by international covenant.

XIV. A general association of nations must be formed under specific covenants for the purpose of affording mutual guarantees of political independence and territorial integrity to great and small states alike.

In regard to these essential rectifications of wrong and assertions of right we feel ourselves to be intimate partners of all the governments and peoples associated together against the Imperialists. We cannot be separated in interest or divided in purpose. We stand together until the end.

For such arrangements and covenants we are willing to fight and to continue to fight until they are achieved; but only because we wish the right to prevail and desire a just and stable peace such as can be secured only by removing the chief provocations to war, which this program does remove. We have no jealousy of German greatness, and there is nothing in this program that impairs it. We grudge her no achievement or distinction of learning or of pacific enterprise such as have made her record very bright and very enviable. We do not wish to injure her or to block in any way her legitimate influence or power. We do not wish to fight her either with arms or with hostile arrangements of trade if she is willing to associate herself with us and the other peace-loving nations of the world in covenants of justice and law and fair dealing. We wish her only to accept a place of equality among the peoples of the world, — the new world in which we now live — instead of a place of mastery.

. . . An evident principle runs through the whole program I have outlined. It is the principle of justice to all peoples and nationalities, and their right to live on equal terms of liberty and safety with one another, whether they be strong or weak. Unless this principle be made its foundation no part of the structure of international justice can stand. The people of the United States could act upon no other principle; and to the vindication of this principle they are ready to devote their lives, their honor, and everything that they possess. The moral climax of this the culminating and final war for human liberty has come, and they are ready to put their own strength, their own highest purpose, their own integrity and devotion to the test.

REFLECTIONS

By studying causes and consequences of world events, we learn how things change but more important we learn how to avoid repeating past mistakes. History is full of lessons that breed humility as well as confidence. In *The Origins of the First World War*,[1] historian James Joll points out how unprepared people were for the war as late as the summer of 1914. Even after the Austrian ultimatum to Serbia was issued on July 23 (almost a month after the assassination of the Archduke Franz Ferdinand on June 28), diplomats across Europe left for their summer holidays. By August, all of Europe was at war, though as Sally Marks noted, the expectation was that it would be over in a month.

---

[1]James Joll, *The Origins of the First World War* (London: Longman, 1992), 200.

We could make a good case for diplomatic blundering as an important cause of the First World War. It is safe to say that few statesmen had any inkling of the consequences of their actions in 1914. And yet, if we concentrate on the daily decisions of diplomats that summer, we may pay attention only to the tossing of lit matches by people sitting on powder kegs rather than on the origins of the powder kegs themselves.

President Wilson blamed secret diplomacy, the international system of alliances, and imperialism as the chief causes of the war. On the importance of imperialism, Wilson's conclusion was the same as that of Lenin and Luxemburg, though he certainly did not share their conviction that capitalism was the root cause of imperialism and, in 1919, neither alliances nor imperialism were regarded as un-American or likely to end any time soon. Still, Wilson's radical moral aversion to reviving Old World empires might have prevented a new stage of imperialism in the League of Nations mandate system. One of the consequences of a Wilsonian peace might have been the creation of independent states in the Middle East and Africa a generation earlier.

The principle of the "self-determination of nations" that Wilson espoused, however, was a double-edged sword. The fact that the war had been "caused" by a Bosnian Serb nationalist assassin in 1914 might have been a warning that national self-determination could become an infinite regress in which smaller and smaller units sought to separate themselves from "foreign" domination. On the issue of nationalism versus internationalism, Wilson might have benefited from listening to Rosa Luxemburg. When asked about anti-Semitism, Luxemburg, a Jew from Russian Poland, answered:

> What do you want with this particular suffering of the Jews? The poor victims of the rubber plantations of Putumayo, the Negroes of Africa with whose bodies the Europeans play a game of catch are just as near to me. . . . I have no special corner of my heart reserved for the ghetto: I am at home wherever in the world there are clouds, birds, and human tears.[2]

Woodrow Wilson was a historian and president of Princeton University before he became president of the United States. Rosa Luxemburg was a professional revolutionary — perhaps the leading socialist theorist in Europe. Both were trained to think historically. Which of the two better understood the causes and consequences of the First World War? Which of the two had a better appreciation of the problems of nationalism that were to continue to haunt the twentieth century?

---

[2]Jay Winter and Blaine Baggett, *The Great War* (New York: Penguin, 1996), 248, quoting Rosa Luxemburg.

The rise of nationalist movements and international organizations were only two consequences of the First World War. Historians have attributed many other aspects of the twentieth century to the war. In an engaging account of his own search for the evidence of war along the Western Front, Stephen O'Shea writes:

> It is generally accepted that the Great War and its fifty-two months of senseless slaughter encouraged, or amplified, among other things: the loss of a belief in progress, a mistrust of technology, the loss of religious faith, the loss of a belief in Western cultural superiority, the rejection of class distinctions, the rejection of traditional sexual roles, the birth of the Modern [in art], the rejection of the past, the elevation of irony to a standard mode of apprehending the world, the unbuttoning of moral codes, and the conscious embrace of the irrational.[3]

What evidence can you find of any of these consequences in the accounts of this chapter?

[3]Stephen O'Shea, *Back to the Front: An Accidental Historian Walks the Trenches of World War I* (New York: Avon Books, 1996), 9.

World War II and Genocide

Europe, Japan, China, Rwanda,
and Guatemala, 1931–1994

HISTORICAL CONTEXT

It is easier to understand the causes of the Second World War than of the First World War. In 1914, we might have pointed to Serbia or Austria, Germany or England, even the bellicosity of Russia and France. But in 1939, it was Hitler's invasion of Poland that led to war with France (which was occupied by the Germans along with most of Europe in 1940), England, and the nations of the British Commonwealth, followed by the Soviet Union after 1940 and the United States after 1941. As in 1914, Germany was allied with Austria (a remnant of the former empire annexed by Germany after 1937) and the new Axis alliance of Japan and Italy.

World War II was even more of a global conflict than World War I. That conflict began with the Japanese invasion of Manchuria in 1931, continuing with Japan's conquest of most of China in 1937 and of Southeast Asia and the Pacific in 1941. For Africans, the war began with the Italian invasion of Ethiopia in 1935. After 1940, North Africa became an increasingly important battleground. As in World War I, soldiers were drawn from all over the world, from Africa and India, the Caribbean and Middle East, but especially in the end, from the United States, Canada, Australia, and New Zealand.

The death toll from World War II may have approached one hundred million, soldiers and civilians combined. Civilian casualties in an age of lightning tank attacks, military occupation of cities, and aerial bombing were enormous. World War I blurred the distinction between soldiers and civilians; World War II ended it. Millions of civilians died in Eastern Europe — along the paths of invading armies — in the great cities of China, and in the bombed-out cities of Germany and Japan. The numbers of wounded, mentally or physically, cannot be counted and the hunger, disease, and deprivation continued long after the end of the war in 1945.

Death tolls offer a crude glimpse of war, and clearly World War II was one of the worst. This chapter focuses on a terrifying aspect of this and more recent conflicts: genocide. Hitler's attempt to rid the world of Jews was genocide. The systematic roundup and murder of the Roma and Sinti peoples,[1] homosexuals, and psychiatric patients, among others, was part of his larger attempt at racial "cleansing" and "Aryan" domination for which the war was little more than a pretext. In addition, Hitler undertook the mass slaughter of all leaders and educated civilians in occupied Poland and Russia for the express purpose of turning those nations into docile armies of brute labor for German industry.

The Nazis' gross indifference to human life, their sadistic killing of defenseless civilians — among them women and children, the helpless, infirm, and aged — reached unimagined heights. Whether or not this was due to factors that distinguish the twentieth century from earlier eras (e.g., the anonymity of mass society, the rise of racist ideas, economic depression, the rise of fascism, the militarization of political life) we do not know. We do know that the Nazi experience was not singular. Imperial Japan, run by a militaristic fascist government in the 1930s, encouraged similar racist and inhumane behavior in its troops in Manchuria, China, and Southeast Asia. Were such barbarities limited to these two countries and this particular era? Certainly not, for aspects of earlier twentieth-century conflicts prepared the ground for mid-century genocide. During the Boer War (1899–1902) British troops in South Africa burned the homes of Dutch "Boer" settlers, forcing women and children into refugee or concentration camps where many died. Shortly thereafter in neighboring German South-West Africa, as recounted in selection 166, German colonial officials put the indigenous Herero people in work camps and concentration camps as part of a policy of extermination and control. During World War I, hundreds of thousands of Armenians in Eastern Turkey were evacuated and massacred. Hitler famously commented: "Who, after all, remembers the Armenians?"

Nor, unfortunately, did genocide end with the Second World War. We will look at two recent examples from the early 1990s — Rwanda and Guatemala — where genocide was committed. We might just as readily explore the cases of ethnic cleansing in the breakup of Yugoslavia in the same period, the annihilation of urban Cambodians in the 1970s, or more recent ethnic conflicts in Darfur, Sudan. One might have thought that the horrendous revelation of the Nazi holocaust

---

[1]The West commonly refers to the Roma and Sinti as "Gypsies" — a misnomer based on the mistaken belief that they were from Egypt. These peoples consider this a pejorative term.

would have ensured a global "Amen" to the declaration: "Never Again." We will do our best to understand why it did not.

THINKING HISTORICALLY
Understanding and Explaining the Unforgivable

Occasionally when we learn of something horrendous, we simply say, "I don't believe it." Our disbelief harbors two feelings: first, our sense of outrage and anger, a rejection of what was done; second, our unwillingness to believe that such a thing could happen or did happen. Our choice of words expresses the difficulty we have making sense of the senseless.

We must try, however, to understand such catastrophes so that we can help to prevent similar horrors in the future. Understanding requires a level of empathy that is often difficult to arouse when we find someone's actions reprehensible. As you read these selections, you will be encouraged to understand and explain, not to forgive.

JOACHIM C. FEST
The Rise of Hitler

World War II had its origins in World War I. The peace terms imposed by the victors demanded the removal of the kaiser, the demilitarization of Germany, the transfer of Germany's industrial heartland to France, and the payment of enormous sums in reparation for the war. In addition, the revolutionary establishment of a republic by the German socialist party was followed by the unsuccessful uprising by the far more radical Spartacus League, which had raised the specter of a Bolshevik coup that would later turn Germany into a communist state.

In this essay, historian Joachim Fest explores the response of German conservative, nationalist, and middle-class groups to these developments. The National Socialists (the Nazi party) was just one of many fascist groups in Germany. Initiated by Mussolini in Italy in

Joachim C. Fest, *Hitler*, trans. Clara and Richard Winston (New York: Harcourt Brace and Co., 1974), 89–91, 92–93, 99–102, 104–5.

1922, fascism was a movement that spread throughout Europe. As defined by Mussolini, in fascism the state dominates everything else:

> For the Fascist the state is all-embracing; outside it no human or spiritual values exist, much less have worth. In this sense Fascism is totalitarian, and the Fascist State — a synthesis and a unity of all values — interprets, develops, and gives power to the whole life of the people.[1]

Why did fascism appeal more to the middle class than to the working class? Was Hitler typical of those who were attracted to fascism? Was Hitler out of touch with reality, or was he tuned in to the feelings of many?

Thinking Historically

Fest helps us understand some of the appeal of fascism by putting it into the context of Germany's defeat in World War I and the real or imagined threat of a Bolshevik revolution. Can you imagine empathizing with antirevolutionary fears if you lived then? Imagine how you might have responded to some of the other fascist appeals: fewer politicians, more police? The nobility of sacrificing for higher purposes; challenging the gray ordinariness of modern life; following instinct rather than reason; and war as authentic experience?

At the end of the First World War the victory of the democratic idea seemed beyond question. Whatever its weaknesses might be, it rose above the turmoil of the times, the uprisings, the dislocations, and the continual quarrels among nations as the unifying principle of the new age. For the war had not only decided a claim to power. It had at the same time altered a conception of government. After the collapse of virtually all the governmental structures of Central and Eastern Europe, many new political entities had emerged out of turmoil and revolution. And these for the most part were organized on democratic principles. In 1914 there had been only three republics alongside of seventeen monarchies in Europe. Four years later there were as many republics as monarchies. The spirit of the age seemed to be pointing unequivocally toward various forms of popular rule.

Only Germany seemed to be opposing this mood of the times, after having been temporarily gripped and carried along by it. Those who would not acknowledge the reality created by the war organized into a fantastic swarm of *völkisch* (racist-nationalist) parties, clubs, and free

---

[1] *Enciclopedia Italiana*, vol. xiv, s.v. "fascism," signed by Mussolini but actually written by the philosopher Giovanni Gentile (1932), 847.

corps. To these groups the revolution had been an act of treason; parliamentary democracy was something foreign and imposed from without, merely a synonym for "everything contrary to the German political will," or else an "institution for pillaging created by Allied capitalism."

Germany's former enemies regarded the multifarious symptoms of nationalistic protest as the response of an inveterately authoritarian people to democracy and civic responsibility. To be sure, the Germans were staggering beneath terrible political and psychological burdens: There was the shock of defeat, the moral censure of the Versailles Treaty, the loss of territory and the demand for reparations, the impoverishment and spiritual undermining of much of the population. Nevertheless, the conviction remained that a great moral gap existed between the Germans and most of their neighbours. Full of resentment, refusing to learn a lesson, this incomprehensible country had withdrawn into its reactionary doctrines, made of them a special virtue, abjured Western rationality and humanity, and in general set itself against the universal trend of the age. For decades this picture of Germany dominated the discussion of the reasons for the rise of National Socialism.

But the image of democracy victorious was also deceptive. The moment in which democracy seemed to be achieving historic fulfillment simultaneously marked the beginning of its crisis. Only a few years later the idea of democracy was challenged in principle as it had never been before. Only a few years after it had celebrated its triumph it was overwhelmed or at least direly threatened by a new movement that had sprung to life in almost all European countries.

This movement recorded its most lasting successes in countries in which the war had aroused considerable discontent or made it conscious of existing discontent, and especially in countries in which the war had been followed by leftist revolutionary uprisings. In some places these movements were conservative, harking back to better times when men were more honorable, the valleys more peaceable, and money had more worth; in others these movements were revolutionary and vied with one another in their contempt for the existing order of things. Some attracted chiefly the petty bourgeois elements, others the peasants, others portions of the working class. Whatever their strange compound of classes, interests, and principles, all seemed to be drawing their dynamic force from the less conscious and more vital lower strata of society. National Socialism was merely one variant of this widespread European movement of protest and opposition aimed at overturning the general order of things.

National Socialism rose from provincial beginnings, from philistine clubs, as Hitler scornfully described them, which met in Munich bars over a few rounds of beer to talk over national and family troubles. No one would have dreamed that they could ever challenge, let alone outdo, the powerful, highly organized Marxist parties. But the following years proved that in these clubs of nationalistic beer drinkers, soon swelled by disillusioned homecoming soldiers and proletarianized members of the middle class, a tremendous force was waiting to be awakened, consolidated, and applied.

In Munich alone there existed, in 1919, nearly fifty more or less political associations, whose membership consisted chiefly of confused remnants of the prewar parties that had been broken up by war and revolution. . . . What united them all and drew them together theoretically and in reality was nothing but an overwhelming feeling of anxiety.

First of all, and most immediate, there was the fear of revolution, that *grande peur* which after the French Revolution had haunted the European-bourgeoisie throughout the nineteenth century. The notion that revolutions were like forces of nature, elemental mechanisms operating without reference to the will of the actors in them, following their own logic and leading perforce to reigns of terror, destruction, killing, and chaos — that notion was seared into the public mind. That was the unforgettable experience, not [German philosopher Immanuel] Kant's belief that the French Revolution had also shown the potentiality for betterment inherent in human nature. For generations, particularly in Germany, this fear stood in the way of any practical revolutionary strivings and produced a mania for keeping things quiet, with the result that every revolutionary proclamation up to 1918 was countered by the standard appeal to law and order.

This old fear was revived by the pseudorevolutionary events in Germany and by the menace of the October Revolution in Russia. Diabolical traits were ascribed to the Reds. The refugees pouring into Munich described bloodthirsty barbarians on a rampage of killing. Such imagery had instant appeal to the nationalists. . . .

This threat dominated Hitler's speeches of the early years. In garish colors he depicted the ravages of the "Red squads of butchers," the "murderous communists," the "bloody morass of Bolshevism." In Russia, he told his audiences, more than thirty million persons had been murdered, "partly on the scaffold, partly by machine guns and similar means, partly in veritable slaughterhouses, partly, millions upon millions, by hunger; and we all know that this wave of hunger is creeping on . . . and see that this scourge is approaching, that it is also coming upon Germany." The intelligentsia of the Soviet Union, he declared, had been exterminated by mass murder, the economy utterly smashed. Thousands of German prisoners-of-war had been drowned in the Neva or sold as slaves. Meanwhile, in Germany the enemy was boring away at the foundations of society "in unremitting, ever unchanging undermining work." The fate of Russia, he said again and again, would soon be ours! . . .

National Socialism owed a considerable part of its emotional appeal, its militancy, and its cohesion to this defensive attitude toward the threat of Marxist revolution. The aim of the National Socialist Party, Hitler repeatedly declared, "is very brief: Annihilation and extermination of the Marxist world view." This was to be accomplished by an "incomparable, brilliantly orchestrated propaganda and information organization" side by side with a movement "of the most ruthless force and most brutal resolution, prepared to oppose all terrorism on the part of the Marxists with tenfold greater terrorism." At about the same time, for similar reasons, Mussolini was founding his Fasci di combattimento [battle group]. Henceforth, the new movements were to be identified by the general name of "Fascism."

But the fear of revolution would not have been enough to endow the movement with that fierce energy, which for a time seemed to stem the universal trend toward democracy. After all, for many people revolution meant hope. A stronger and more elemental motivation had to be added. And in fact Marxism was feared as the precursor of a far more comprehensive assault upon all traditional ideas. It was viewed as the contemporary political aspect of a metaphysical upheaval, as a "declaration of war upon the European . . . idea of culture." Marxism itself was only the metaphor for something dreaded that escaped definition. . . .

This first phase of the postwar era was characterized both by fear of revolution and anticivilizational resentments; these together, curiously intertwined and reciprocally stimulating each other, produced a syndrome of extraordinary force. Into the brew went the hate and defense complexes of a society shaken to its foundations. German society had lost its imperial glory, its civil order, its national confidence, its prosperity, and its familiar authorities. The whole system had been turned topsy-turvy, and now many Germans blindly and bitterly wanted back what they thought had been unjustly taken from them. These general feelings of unhappiness were intensified and further radicalized by a variety of unsatisfied group interests. The class of white-collar workers, continuing to grow apace, proved especially susceptible to the grand gesture of total criticism. For the industrial revolution had just begun to affect office workers and was reducing the former "non-commissioned officers of capitalism" to the status of last victims of "modern slavery." It was all the worse for them because unlike the proletarians they had never developed a class pride of their own or imagined that the breakdown of the existing order was going to lead to their own apotheosis. Small businessmen were equally susceptible because of their fear of being crushed by corporations, department stores, and rationalized competition. Another unhappy group consisted of farmers who, slow to change and lacking capital, were fettered to backward modes of production. Another group were the academics and formerly solid bourgeois who felt themselves caught in the tremendous suction of proletarianization. Without outside support you found yourself "at once despised, declassed; to be unemployed is the same as being a communist," one victim stated in a questionnaire of the period. No statistics, no figures on rates of inflation, bankruptcies, and suicides can describe the feelings of those threatened by unemployment or poverty, or can express the anxieties of those others who still possessed some property and feared the consequences of so much accumulated discontent. . . .

The vigilante groups and the free corps that were being organized in great numbers, partly on private initiative, partly with covert government support, chiefly to meet the threat of Communist revolution, formed centers of bewildered but determined resistance to the *status quo*. The members of these paramilitary groups were vaguely looking around for someone to lead them into a new system. At first there was another reservoir of militant energies alongside the parliamentary groups: the mass of homecoming soldiers. Many of these stayed in the barracks dragging out a pointless military life, baffled and unable to say good-bye to the warrior dreams of their recent youth. In the front-line trenches they had glimpsed the outlines of a new meaning to life; in the sluggishly resuming normality of the postwar period they tried in vain to find that meaning again. They had not fought and suffered for years for the sake of this weakened regime with its borrowed ideals which, as they saw it, could be pushed around by the most contemptible of their former enemies. And they also feared, after the exalting sense of life the war had given them, the ignobility of the commonplace bourgeois world.

It remained for Hitler to bring together these feelings and to appoint himself their spearhead. Indeed, Hitler regarded as a phenomenon seems like the synthetic product of all the anxiety, pessimism, nostalgia, and defensiveness we have discussed. For him, too, the war had been education and liberation. If there is a "Fascistic" type, it was embodied in him. More than any of his followers he expressed the underlying psychological, social, and ideological motives of the movement. He was never just its leader; he was also its exponent.

His early years had contributed their share to that experience of overwhelming anxiety which dominated his intellectual and emotional constitution. That lurking anxiety can be seen at the root of almost all his statements and reactions. It had everyday as well as cosmic dimensions. Many who knew him in his youth have described his pallid, "timorous" nature, which provided the fertile soil for his lush fantasies. His "constant fear" of contact with strangers was another aspect of that anxiety, as was his extreme distrust and his compulsion to wash frequently, which became more and more pronounced in later life. The same complex is apparent in his oft-expressed fear of venereal disease and his fear of contagion in general. He knew that "microbes are rushing at me." He was ridden by the Austrian Pan-German's fear of being overwhelmed by alien races, by fear of the "locust-like immigration of

Russian and Polish Jews," by fear of "the niggerizing of the Germans," by fear of the Germans' "expulsion from Germany," and finally by fear that the Germans would be "exterminated." He had the *Völkische Boebachter* print an alleged French soldier's song whose refrain was: "Germans, we will possess your daughters!" Among his phobias were American technology, the birth rate of the Slavs, big cities, "industrialization as unrestricted as it is harmful," the "economization of the nation," corporations, the "morass of metropolitan amusement culture," and modern art, which sought "to kill the soul of the people" by painting meadows blue and skies green. Wherever he looked he discovered the "signs of decay of a slowly ebbing world." Not an element of pessimistic anticivilizational criticism was missing from his imagination.

What linked Hitler with the leading Fascists of other countries was the resolve to halt this process of degeneration. What set him apart from them, however, was the manic single-mindedness with which he traced all the anxieties he had ever felt back to a single source. For at the heart of the towering structure of anxiety, black and hairy, stood the figure of the Jew: evil-smelling, smacking his lips, lusting after blonde girls, eternal contaminator of the blood, but "racially harder" than the Aryan, as Hitler uneasily declared as late as the summer of 1942. A prey to his psychosis, he saw Germany as the object of a worldwide conspiracy, pressed on all sides by Bolshevists, Freemasons, capitalists, Jesuits, all hand in glove with each other and directed in their nefarious projects by the "bloodthirsty and avaricious Jewish tyrant." *The* Jew had 75 per cent of world capital at his disposal. He dominated the stock exchanges and the Marxist parties, the Gold and Red Internationals. He was the "advocate of birth control and the idea of emigration." He undermined governments, bastardized races, glorified fratricide, fomented civil war, justified baseness, and poisoned nobility: "the wirepuller of the destinies of mankind." The whole world was in danger, Hitler cried imploringly; it had fallen "into the embrace of this octopus." He groped for images in which to make his horror tangible, saw "creeping venom," "belly-worms," and "adders devouring the nation's body." . . .

The appearance of Hitler signaled a union of those forces that in crisis conditions had great political potential. The Fascistic movements all centered on the charismatic appeal of a unique leader. The leader was to be the resolute voice of order controlling chaos. He would have looked further and thought deeper, would know the despairs but also the means of salvation. This looming giant had already been given established form in a prophetic literature that went back to German folklore. Like the mythology of many other nations unfortunate in their history, that of the Germans has its sleeping leaders dreaming away the centuries in the bowels of a mountain, but destined some day to return to rally their people and punish the guilty world. . . .

The success of Fascism in contrast to many of its rivals was in large part due to its perceiving the essence of the crisis, of which it was itself the symptom. All the other parties affirmed the process of industrialization and emancipation, whereas the Fascists, evidently sharing the universal anxiety, tried to deal with it by translating it into violent action and histrionics. . . .

$$\boxed{163}$$

HEINRICH HIMMLER

Speech to the SS

Heinrich Himmler (1900–1945) was one of the most powerful leaders of Nazi Germany. He was the head of the SS, or *Schutzstaffel*, an elite army that was responsible for, among other things, running the many concentration camps. Hitler gave Himmler the task of implementing the "final solution of the Jewish question": killing the Jewish population of Germany and the other countries the Nazis occupied. The horror that resulted is today often referred to by the biblical word *holocaust*.

The following reading is an excerpt from a speech Himmler gave to SS leaders on October 4, 1943. What was Himmler's concern in this speech? What kind of general support for the extermination of the Jews does this excerpt suggest existed?

Thinking Historically

Psychiatrists say that people use various strategies to cope when they must do something distasteful. We might summarize these strategies as denial, distancing, compartmentalizing, ennobling, rationalizing, and scapegoating. *Denial* is pretending that something has not happened. *Distancing* removes the idea, memory, or reality from the mind, placing it at a distance. *Compartmentalizing* separates one action, memory, or idea from others, allowing one to "put away" certain feelings. *Ennobling* makes the distasteful act a matter of pride rather than guilt, nobility rather than disgrace. *Rationalizing* creates

Heinrich Himmler, "Secret Speech at Posen," *A Holocaust Reader*, ed. Lucy S. Dawidowicz (New York: Behrman House, 1976), 132–33.

"good" reasons for doing something, while *scapegoating* puts blame on someone else.

What evidence do you see of these strategies in Himmler's speech? Judging from the speech, which of these strategies do you think his listeners used to rationalize their actions?

I also want to make reference before you here, in complete frankness, to a really grave matter. Among ourselves, this once, it shall be uttered quite frankly; but in public we will never speak of it. Just as we did not hesitate on June 30, 1934, to do our duty as ordered, to stand up against the wall comrades who had transgressed,[1] and shoot them, so we have never talked about this and never will. It was the tact which I am glad to say is a matter of course to us that made us never discuss it among ourselves, never talk about it. Each of us shuddered, and yet each one knew that he would do it again if it were ordered and if it were necessary.

I am referring to the evacuation of the Jews, the annihilation of the Jewish people. This is one of those things that are easily said. "The Jewish people is going to be annihilated," says every party member. "Sure, it's in our program, elimination of the Jews, annihilation — we'll take care of it." And then they all come trudging, 80 million worthy Germans, and each one has his one decent Jew. Sure, the others are swine, but this one is an A-1 Jew. Of all those who talk this way, not one has seen it happen, not one has been through it. Most of you must know what it means to see a hundred corpses lie side by side, or five hundred, or a thousand. To have stuck this out — excepting cases of human weakness — to have kept our integrity, that is what has made us hard. In our history, this is an unwritten and never-to-be-written page of glory, for we know how difficult we would have made it for ourselves if today — amid the bombing raids, the hardships, and the deprivations of war — we still had the Jews in every city as secret saboteurs, agitators, and demagogues. If the Jews were still ensconced in the body of the German nation, we probably would have reached the 1916–17 stage by now.[2]

The wealth they had we have taken from them. I have issued a strict order, carried out by SS-Obergruppenfuhrer Pohl, that this wealth in its entirety is to be turned over to the Reich as a matter of course.

---

[1]A reference to the "Night of the Long Knives," when Hitler ordered the SS to murder the leaders of the SA, a Nazi group he wished to suppress. [Ed.]

[2]Here Himmler is apparently referring to the stalemate on Germany's western front in World War I. [Ed.]

We have taken none of it for ourselves. Individuals who transgress will be punished in accordance with an order I issued at the beginning, threatening that whoever takes so much as a mark of it for himself is a dead man. A number of SS men — not very many — have transgressed, and they will die, without mercy. We had the moral right, we had the duty toward our people, to kill this people which wanted to kill us. But we do not have the right to enrich ourselves with so much as a fur, a watch, a mark, or a cigarette, or anything else. Having exterminated a germ, we do not want, in the end, to be infected by the germ, and die of it. I will not stand by and let even a small rotten spot develop or take hold. Wherever it may form, we together will cauterize it. All in all, however, we can say that we have carried out this heaviest of our tasks in a spirit of love for our people. And our inward being, our soul, our character has not suffered injury from it.

164

JEAN-FRANÇOIS STEINER

From Treblinka

Treblinka, in Poland, was one of several Nazi death camps. (Auschwitz was the largest camp.) (See Map 25.1.) In these "death factories," the Nazis murdered millions of Jews as well as many thousands of Roma and Sinti, socialists, Soviet prisoners of war, and other people. In this selection, Steiner, who lost his father at Treblinka, reveals how "rational" and "scientific" mass murder can be. How could this happen? Can it happen again?

Thinking Historically

Try to imagine what went through the mind of Lalka as he designed the extermination process at Treblinka. How did concerns for efficiency and humanity enter into his deliberations? Do you think he found his work distasteful? If so, which of the strategies mentioned in the previous selection did he adopt?

Jean-François Steiner, *Treblinka* (New York: Simon & Schuster, 1967), 153–54, 155–58, 159–60.

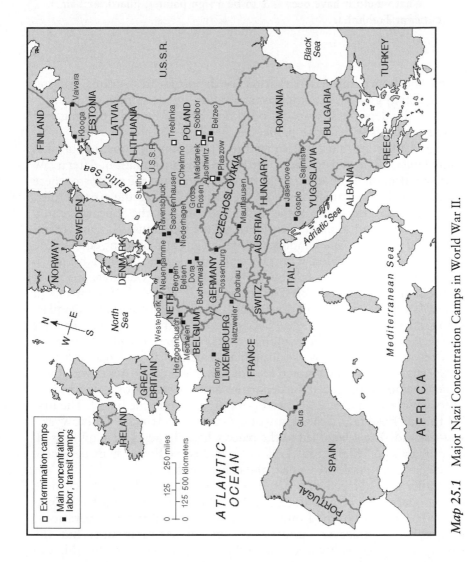

Map 25.1 Major Nazi Concentration Camps in World War II.

What would it have been like to be a sign-painter, guard, or hair-cutter at Treblinka?

Each poorly organized debarkation [of deportees from trains arriving at Treblinka] gave rise to unpleasant scenes — uncertainties and confusion for the deportees, who did not know where they were going and were sometimes seized with panic.

So, the first problem was to restore a minimum of hope. Lalka[1] had many faults, but he did not lack a certain creative imagination. After a few days of reflection he hit upon the idea of transforming the platform where the convoys [trains] arrived into a false station. He had the ground filled in to the level of the doors of the cars in order to give the appearance of a train platform and to make it easier to get off the trains. . . . On [a] wall Lalka had . . . doors and windows painted in gay and pleasing colors. The windows were decorated with cheerful curtains and framed by green blinds which were just as false as the rest. Each door was given a special name, stencilled at eye level: "Stationmaster," "Toilet," "Infirmary" (a red cross was painted on this door). Lalka carried his concern for detail so far as to have his men paint two doors leading to the waiting rooms, first and second class. The ticket window, which was barred with a horizontal sign reading, "Closed," was a little masterpiece with its ledge and false perspective and its grill, painted line for line. Next to the ticket window a large timetable announced the departure times of trains for Warsaw, Bialystok, Wolkowysk, etc. . . . Two doors were cut into the [wall]. The first led to the "hospital," bearing a wooden arrow on which "Wolkowysk" was painted. The second led to the place where the Jews were undressed; that arrow said "Bialystok." Lalka also had some flower beds designed, which gave the whole area a neat and cheery look. . . .

Lalka also decided that better organization could save much time in the operations of undressing and recovery of the [deportees'] baggage. To do this you had only to rationalize the different operations, that is, to organize the undressing like an assembly line. But the rhythm of this assembly line was at the mercy of the sick, the old, and the wounded, who, since they were unable to keep the pace, threatened to bog down the operation and make it proceed even more slowly than before. . . . Individuals of both sexes over the age of ten, and children under ten, at a maximum rate of two children per adult, were judged fit to follow the complete circuit,[2] as long as they did not show

---

[1]Kurt Franz, whom the prisoners called Lalka, designed the highly efficient system of extermination at Treblinka. [Ed.]

[2]The "complete" circuit was getting off the train, walking along the platform through the door to the men's or women's barracks, undressing, and being led to the gas chamber "showers." [Ed.]

serious wounds or marked disability. Victims who did not correspond to the norms were to be conducted to the "hospital" by members of the blue commando and turned over to the Ukrainians [guards] for special treatment. A bench was built all around the ditch of the "hospital" so that the victims would fall of their own weight after receiving the bullet in the back of the head. This bench was to be used only when Kurland[3] was swamped with work. On the platform, the door which these victims took was surmounted by the Wolkowysk arrow. In the Sibylline language of Treblinka, "Wolkowysk" meant the bullet in the back of the neck or the injection. "Bialystok" meant the gas chamber.

Beside the "Bialystok" door stood a tall Jew whose role was to shout endlessly, "Large bundles here, large bundles here!" He had been nicknamed "Groysse Pack." As soon as the victims had gone through, Groysse Pack and his men from the red commando carried the bundles at a run to the sorting square, where the sorting commandos immediately took possession of them. As soon as they had gone through the door came the order, "Women to the left, men to the right." This moment generally gave rise to painful scenes.

While the women were being led to the left-hand barracks to undress and go to the hairdresser, the men, who were lined up double file, slowly entered the production line. This production line included five stations. At each of these a group of "reds" shouted at the top of their lungs the name of the piece of clothing that it was in charge of receiving. At the first station the victim handed over his coat and hat. At the second, his jacket. (In exchange, he received a piece of string.) At the third he sat down, took off his shoes, and tied them together with the string he had just received. Until then the shoes were not tied together in pairs, and since the yield was at least fifteen thousand pairs of shoes per day, they were all lost, since they could not be matched up again.) At the fourth station the victim left his trousers, and at the fifth his shirt and underwear.

After they had been stripped, the victims were conducted, as they came off the assembly line, to the right-hand barracks and penned in until the women had finished: ladies first. However, a small number, chosen from among the most able-bodied, were singled out at the door to carry the clothing to the sorting square. They did this while running naked between two rows of Ukrainian guards. Without stopping once they threw their bundles onto the pile, turned around, and went back for another.

Meanwhile the women had been conducted to the barracks on the left. This barracks was divided into two parts: a dressing room and a

[3]Kurland was a Jew assigned to the "hospital," where he gave injections of poison to those who were too ill or crippled to make the complete circuit. [Ed.]

beauty salon. "Put your clothes in a pile so you will be able to find them after the shower," they were ordered in the first room. The "beauty salon" was a room furnished with six benches, each of which could seat twenty women at a time. Behind each bench twenty prisoners of the red commando, wearing white tunics and armed with scissors, waited at attention until all the women were seated. Between hair-cutting sessions they sat down on the benches and, under the direction of a *kapo* [prisoner guard] who was transformed into a conductor, they had to sing old Yiddish melodies.

Lalka, who had insisted on taking personal responsibility for every detail, had perfected the technique of what he called the "Treblinka cut." With five well-placed slashes the whole head of hair was trans-ferred to a sack placed beside each hairdresser for this purpose. It was simple and efficient. How many dramas did this "beauty salon" see? From the very beautiful young woman who wept when her hair was cut off, because she would be ugly, to the mother who grabbed a pair of scissors from one of the "hairdressers" and literally severed a Ukrain-ian's arm; from the sister who recognized one of the "hairdressers" as her brother to the young girl, Ruth Dorfman, who, suddenly under-standing and fighting back her tears, asked whether it was difficult to die and admitted in a small brave voice that she was a little afraid and wished it were all over.

When they had been shorn the women left the "beauty salon" double file. Outside the door, they had to squat in a particular way also specified by Lalka, in order to be intimately searched. Up to this point, doubt had been carefully maintained. Of course, a discriminating eye might have observed that . . . the smell was the smell of rotting bodies. A thousand details proved that Treblinka was not a transient camp, and some realized this, but the majority had believed in the impossible for too long to begin to doubt at the last moment. The door of the bar-racks, which opened directly onto the "road to heaven," represented the turning point. Up to here the prisoners had been given a minimum of hope, from here on this policy was abandoned.

This was one of Lalka's great innovations. After what point was it no longer necessary to delude the victims? This detail had been the sub-ject of rather heated controversy among the Technicians. At the Nurem-berg trials, Rudolf Höss, Commandant of Auschwitz, criticized Tre-blinka where, according to him, the victims knew that they were going to be killed. Höss was an advocate of the towel distributed at the door to the gas chamber. He claimed that this system not only avoided disor-der, but was more humane, and he was proud of it. But Höss did not invent this "towel technique"; it was in all the manuals, and it was uti-lized at Treblinka until Lalka's great reform.

Lalka's studies had led to what might be called the "principle of the cutoff." His reasoning was simple: Since sooner or later the victims must realize that they were going to be killed, to postpone this moment was only false humanity. The principle "the later the better" did not apply here. Lalka had been led to make an intensive study of this problem upon observing one day completely by chance, that winded victims died much more rapidly than the rest. The discovery had led him to make a clean sweep of accepted principles. Let us follow his industrialist's logic, keeping well in mind that his great preoccupation was the saving of time. A winded victim dies faster. Hence, a saving of time. The best way to wind a man is to make him run — another saving of time. Thus Lalka arrived at the conclusion that you must make the victims run. A new question had then arisen: At what point must you make the victims run and thus create panic (a further aid to breathlessness)? The question had answered itself: As soon as you have nothing more to make them do. Franz located the exact point, the point of no return: the door of the barracks.

The rest was merely a matter of working out the details. Along the "road to heaven" and in front of the gas chambers he stationed a cordon of guards armed with whips, whose function was to make the victims run, to make them rush into the gas chambers of their own accord in search of refuge. One can see that this system is more daring than the classic system, but one can also see the danger it represents. Suddenly abandoned to their despair, realizing that they no longer had anything to lose, the victims might attack the guards. Lalka was aware of this risk, but he maintained that everything depended on the pace. "It's close work," he said, "but if you maintain a very rapid pace and do not allow a single moment of hesitation, the method is absolutely without danger." There were still further elaborations later on, but from the first day, Lalka had only to pride himself on his innovation: It took no more than three quarters of an hour, by the clock, to put the victims through their last voyage, from the moment the doors of the cattle cars were unbolted to the moment the great trap doors of the gas chamber were opened to take out the bodies. . . .

But let us return to the men. The timing was worked out so that by the time the last woman had emerged from the left-hand barracks, all the clothes had been transported to the sorting square. The men were immediately taken out of the right-hand barracks and driven after the women into the "road to heaven," which they reached by way of a special side path. By the time they arrived at the gas chambers the toughest, who had begun to run before the others to carry the bundles, were just as winded as the weakest. Everyone died in perfect unison for the greater satisfaction of that great Technician Kurt Franz, the Stakhanovite [model worker] of extermination.

165

IRIS CHANG
From The Rape of Nanking

Nazi genocide was not the only systematic murder of civilian populations during World War II. The military government of Japan, a German ally during the war, engaged in some of the same tactics of brutal and indiscriminate mass murder of civilians. In fact, atrocities in Japan preceded those in Germany.

While for Europeans World War II began with the German invasion of Poland on September 1, 1939, and for Americans with the Japanese attack at Pearl Harbor, Hawaii, on December 7, 1941, for the Chinese it began ten years earlier with the Japanese invasion of Manchuria in 1931. By 1937, Japanese troops occupied Peking and Shanghai as well as the old imperial capital of Nanking. It is estimated that more than twenty-five thousand civilians were killed by Japanese soldiers in the months after the fall of Nanking on December 13, 1937. But it was the appalling brutality of Japanese troops that foreign residents remembered, even those who could recall the brutality of the Chinese nationalist troops who captured the city in 1927. In the Introduction to *The Rape of Nanking*, Iris Chang writes:

> The Rape of Nanking should be remembered not only for the number of people slaughtered but for the cruel manner in which many met their deaths. Chinese men were used for bayonet practice and in decapitation contests. An estimated 20,000 to 80,000 Chinese women were raped. Many soldiers went beyond rape to disembowel women, slice off their breasts, nail them alive to walls. Fathers were forced to rape their daughters, and sons their mothers, as other family members watched. Not only did live burials, castration, the carving of organs, and the roasting of people become routine, but more diabolical tortures were practiced, such as hanging people by their tongues on iron hooks or burying people to their waist and watching them get torn apart by German shepherds. So sickening was the spectacle that even the Nazis in the city were horrified, one declaring the massacre to be the work of "bestial machinery." (p. 6)

In the selection that follows, the author asks how Japanese soldiers were capable of such offenses. What is her answer?

Iris Chang, *The Rape of Nanking* (New York: Basic Books, 1997), 55–59.

Thinking Historically

What would have happened to these recruits if they had refused an order to kill a prisoner or noncombatant? Once they had killed one prisoner, why did they find it easier to kill another? Did they eventually enjoy it, feel pride, or think it insignificant? The last informant, Nagatomi, says he had been a "devil." Had he been possessed? By whom?

How then do we explain the raw brutality carried out day after day after day in the city of Nanking? Unlike their Nazi counterparts, who have mostly perished in prisons and before execution squads or, if alive, are spending their remaining days as fugitives from the law, many of the Japanese war criminals are still alive, living in peace and comfort, protected by the Japanese government. They are therefore some of the few people on this planet who, without concern for retaliation in a court of international law, can give authors and journalists a glimpse of their thoughts and feelings while committing World War II atrocities.

Here is what we learn. The Japanese soldier was not simply hardened for battle in China; he was hardened for the task of murdering Chinese combatants and noncombatants alike. Indeed, various games and exercises were set up by the Japanese military to numb its men to the human instinct against killing people who are not attacking.

For example, on their way to the capital, Japanese soldiers were made to participate in killing competitions, which were avidly covered by the Japanese media like sporting events. The most notorious one appeared in the December 7 issue of the *Japan Advertiser* under the headline "Sub-Lieutenants in Race to Fell 100 Chinese Running Close Contest."

> Sub-Lieutenant Mukai Toshiaki and Sub-Lieutenant Noda Takeshi, both of the Katagiri unit at Kuyung, in a friendly contest to see which of them will first fell 100 Chinese in individual sword combat before the Japanese forces completely occupy Nanking, are well in the final phase of their race, running almost neck to neck. On Sunday [December 5] . . . the "score," according to the Asahi, was: Sub-Lieutenant Mukai, 89, and Sub-Lieutenant Noda, 78.

A week later the paper reported that neither man could decide who had passed the 100 mark first, so they upped the goal to 150. "Mukai's blade was slightly damaged in the competition," the *Japan Advertiser* reported. "He explained that this was the result of cutting a Chinese in half, helmet and all. The contest was 'fun' he declared. " . . .

For new soldiers, horror was a natural impulse. One Japanese wartime memoir describes how a group of green Japanese recruits

failed to conceal their shock when they witnessed seasoned soldiers torture a group of civilians to death. Their commander expected this reaction and wrote in his diary: "All new recruits are like this, but soon
they will be doing the same things themselves."

But new officers also required desensitization. A veteran officer
named Tominaga Shozo recalled vividly his own transformation from
innocent youth to killing machine. Tominaga had been a fresh second
lieutenant from a military academy when assigned to the 232nd Regiment of the 39th Division from Hiroshima. When he was introduced to
the men under his command, Tominaga was stunned. "They had evil
eyes," he remembered. "They weren't human eyes, but the eyes of leopards or tigers."

On the front Tominaga and other new candidate officers underwent intensive training to stiffen their endurance for war. In the program an instructor had pointed to a thin, emaciated Chinese in a detention center and told the officers: "These are the raw materials for your
trial of courage." Day after day the instructor taught them how to cut
off heads and bayonet living prisoners.

> On the final day, we were taken out to the site of our trial. Twenty-
> four prisoners were squatting there with their hands tied behind
> their backs. They were blindfolded. A big hole had been dug — ten
> meters long, two meters wide, and more than three meters deep. The
> regimental commander, the battalion commanders, and the company
> commanders all took the seats arranged for them. Second Lieutenant
> Tanaka bowed to the regimental commander and reported, "We shall
> now begin." He ordered a soldier on fatigue duty to haul one of the
> prisoners to the edge of the pit; the prisoner was kicked when he re-
> sisted. The soldiers finally dragged him over and forced him to his
> knees. Tanaka turned toward us and looked into each of our faces in
> turn. "Heads should be cut off like this," he said, unsheathing his
> army sword. He scooped water from a bucket with a dipper, then
> poured it over both sides of the blade. Swishing off the water, he raised
> his sword in a long arc. Standing behind the prisoner, Tanaka steadied
> himself, legs spread apart, and cut off the man's head with a shout,
> "Yo!" The head flew more than a meter away. Blood spurted up in
> two fountains from the body and sprayed into the hole.
> The scene was so appalling that I felt I couldn't breathe.

But gradually, Tominaga Shozo learned to kill. And as he grew
more adept at it, he no longer felt that his men's eyes were evil. For
him, atrocities became routine, almost banal. Looking back on his experience, he wrote: "We made them like this. Good sons, good daddies,
good elder brothers at home were brought to the front to kill each
other. Human beings turned into murdering demons. Everyone became
a demon within three months."

Some Japanese soldiers admitted it was easy for them to kill because they had been taught that next to the emperor, all individual life — even their own — was valueless. Azuma Shiro, the Japanese soldier who witnessed a series of atrocities in Nanking, made an excellent point about his comrades' behavior in his letter to me. During his two years of military training in the 20th Infantry Regiment of Kyoto-fu Fukuchi-yama, he was taught that "loyalty is heavier than a mountain, and our life is lighter than a feather." He recalled that the highest honor a soldier could achieve during war was to come back dead: To die for the emperor was the greatest glory, to be caught alive by the enemy the greatest shame. "If my life was not important," Azuma wrote to me, "an enemy's life became inevitably much less important. . . . This philosophy led us to look down on the enemy and eventually to the mass murder and ill treatment of the captives."

In interview after interview, Japanese veterans from the Nanking massacre reported honestly that they experienced a complete lack of remorse or sense of wrongdoing, even when torturing helpless civilians. Nagatomi Hakudo spoke candidly about his emotions in the fallen capital:

> I remember being driven in a truck along a path that had been cleared through piles of thousands and thousands of slaughtered bodies. Wild dogs were gnawing at the dead flesh as we stopped and pulled a group of Chinese prisoners out of the back. Then the Japanese officer proposed a test of my courage. He unsheathed his sword, spat on it, and with a sudden mighty swing he brought it down on the neck of a Chinese boy cowering before us. The head was cut clean off and tumbled away on the group as the body slumped forward, blood spurting in two great gushing fountains from the neck. The officer suggested I take the head home as a souvenir. I remember smiling proudly as I took his sword and began killing people.

After almost sixty years of soul-searching, Nagatomi is a changed man. A doctor in Japan, he has built a shrine of remorse in his waiting room. Patients can watch videotapes of his trial in Nanking and a full confession of his crimes. The gentle and hospitable demeanor of the doctor belies the horror of his past, making it almost impossible for one to imagine that he had once been a ruthless murderer.

"Few know that soldiers impaled babies on bayonets and tossed them still alive into pots of boiling water," Nagatomi said. "They gang-raped women from the ages of twelve to eighty and then killed them when they could no longer satisfy sexual requirements. I beheaded people, starved them to death, burned them, and buried them alive, over two hundred in all. It is terrible that I could turn into an animal and do these things. There are really no words to explain what I was doing. I was truly a devil."

166

MAHMOOD MAMDANI
Thinking about Genocide

On December 11, 1946, the General Assembly of the United Nations declared genocide a crime under international law. In 1948 the international body defined genocide as "acts committed with intent to destroy, in whole or in part, a national, ethnical, racial, or religious group." Before the signatures dried on the second document, the world witnessed the bloody partition of British India between Hindus and Muslims and the beginnings of an international balance of terror depending on the threat of mutual nuclear destruction. By and large, the ethnic, national, and religious violence of the immediate post-war was not called genocide. The term was limited to the Nazi attempt to exterminate Jews.

In the early 1990s, the specter of genocide returned in the breakup of Yugoslavia and in the African state of Rwanda. (See Map 25.2.) While Yugoslavia died a slow death, the outburst of killing in Rwanda in 1994 was remarkable for its suddenness. Within a matter of months, the majority Hutu population slaughtered almost a million of the minority Tutsis. Under German and then Belgian colonialism, the Tutsis had been designated a superior race and given special power and privileges. This was a common divide-and-rule tactic of European colonial control. In the period of independence (1959–1962), Hutu resentment against Tutsis came to a boil. Thousands of Tutsis were killed and hundreds of thousands were expelled. Hutus took their place and controlled the government and resources. Over the next decades, Tutsis came back to the densely populated country, formed a political party, and became stronger. By 1994, the Hutu president and many of his supporters feared a return of Tutsi rule. When the president and many of his advisors were killed in a plane crash, the Hutu media and militant groups marshaled a campaign of extermination.

In this selection, Mahmood Mamdani, born in Uganda and currently director of the Institute of African Studies at Columbia University, reflects on the meaning of that genocide committed so soon after the world community had declared "never again." How, according to the author, was the Hutu genocide different from that of the Nazis? What is the significance of that difference? Does it matter?

Mahmood Mamdani, *When Victims Become Killers: Colonialism, Nativism and Genocide in Rwanda* (Princeton, N.J.: Princeton University Press, 2001), 3–14.

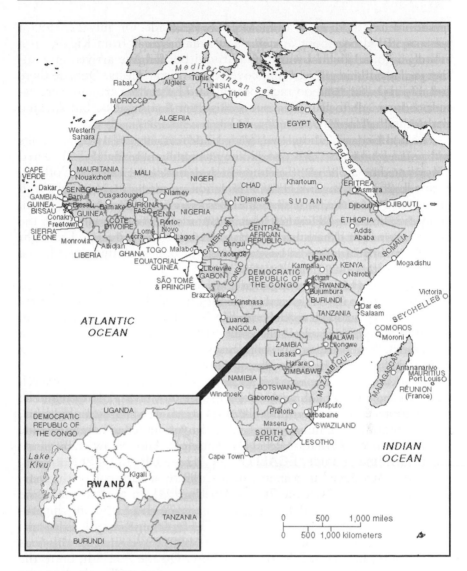

Map 25.2   Rwanda in Africa.

Thinking Historically

The author says that the "violence cannot be understood as rational: yet we need to understand it as thinkable" (p. 947). What does he mean? Do you agree? How does he help you to understand it as thinkable?

I visited Rwanda roughly a year after the genocide. On July 22, 1995, I went to Ntarama, about an hour and a half by car from Kigali, on a dirt road going south toward the Burundi border. We arrived at a village church, made of brick and covered with iron sheets. Outside there was a wood and bamboo rack, bearing skulls. On the ground were assorted bones, collected and pressed together inside sacks, but sticking out of their torn cloth. . . .

The church was about twenty by sixty feet. Inside, wooden planks were placed on stones. I supposed they were meant as benches. I peered inside and saw a pile of belongings — shoulder sacks, tattered clothing, a towel, a wooden box, a *suferia* (cooking pot), plastic mugs and plates, straw mats and hats — the worldly goods of the poor. Then, amidst it all, I saw bones, and then entire skeletons, each caught in the posture in which it had died. Even a year after the genocide, I thought the air smelled of blood, mixed with that of bones, clothing, earth — a human mildew.

I scanned the walls with their gaping holes. The guide explained these were made by the Interahamwe (youth militia of the ruling party) so they could throw grenades into the building. He said that those in the church were lucky. They died, almost instantly. Those outside had a protracted, brutal death, in some cases drawn out over as long as a week, with one part of the body cut daily.

I raised my eyes, away from the skeletons, to look at the church wall. Much of it was still covered with some old posters. They read like exhortations common to radical regimes with a developmental agenda, regimes that I was familiar with and had lived under for decades. One read: "Journée Internationale de la Femme." And below it, was another, this time in bold: "ÉGALITÉ — PAIX — DÉVELOPPEMENT."

I was introduced to a man called Callixte, a survivor of the massacre in Ntarama. "On the 7th of April [1994], in the morning," he explained, "they started burning houses over there and moving towards here. Only a few were killed. The burning pushed us to this place. Our group decided to run to this place. We thought this was God's house, no one would attack us here. On the 7th, 8th, up to the 10th, we were fighting them. We were using stones. They had *pangas* (machetes), spears, hammers, grenades. On the 10th, their numbers were increased. On the 14th, we were being pushed inside the church. The church was attacked on the 14th and the 15th. The actual killing was on the 15th.

"On the 15th, they brought Presidential Guards. They were supporting Interahamwe, brought in from neighboring communes. I was not in the group here. Here, there were women, children, and old men. The men had formed defense units outside. I was outside. Most men died fighting. When our defense was broken through, they came and killed everyone here. After that, they started hunting for those hiding in the hills. I and others ran to the swamp."

I asked about his *secteur,* about how many lived in it, how many Tutsi, how many Hutu, who participated in the killing. "In my *secteur,* Hutu were two-thirds, Tutsi one-third. There were about 5,000 in our *secteur.* Of the 3,500 Hutu, all the men participated. It was like an order, except there were prominent leaders who would command. The rest followed."

I asked whether there were no intermarriages in the *secteur.* "Too many. About one-third of Tutsi daughters would be married to Hutu. But Hutu daughters married to Tutsi men were only 1 per cent: Hutu didn't want to marry their daughters to Tutsi who were poor and it was risky. Because the Tutsi were discriminated against, they didn't want to give their daughters where there was no education, no jobs . . . risky. Prospects were better for Tutsi daughters marrying Hutu men. They would get better opportunities.

"Tutsi women married to Hutu were killed. I know only one who survived. The administration forced Hutu men to kill their Tutsi wives before they go to kill anyone else — to prove they were true Interahamwe. One man tried to refuse. He was told he must choose between the wife and himself. He then chose to save his own life. Another Hutu man rebuked him for having killed his Tutsi wife. That man was also killed. Kallisa — the man who was forced to kill his wife — is in jail. After killing his wife, he became a convert. He began to distribute grenades all around.

"The killing was planned, because some were given guns. During the war with the RPF, many young men were taken in the reserves and trained and given guns. Those coming from training would disassociate themselves from Tutsi. Some of my friends received training. When they returned, they were busy mobilizing others. They never came to see me. I am fifty-seven. Even people in their sixties joined in the killing, though they were not trained. The trained were Senior 6 or Technical School leavers." I asked how such killers could have been his friends. "I was a friend to their fathers. It was a father-son relationship. I think the fathers must have known."

Who were the killers in Ntarama? Units of the Presidential Guard came from Kigali. The Interahamwe were brought in from neighboring communes. Youth who had been trained in self-defense units after the civil war began provided the local trained force. But the truth is that everybody participated, at least all men. And not only men, women, too: cheering their men, participating in auxiliary roles, like the second line in a street-to-street battle.

No one can say with certainty how many Tutsi were killed between March and July of 1994 in Rwanda. In the fateful one hundred days that followed the downing of the presidential plane — and the coup d'état thereafter — a section of the army and civilian leadership organized the Hutu majority to kill all Tutsi, even babies. In the process, they also killed not only the Hutu political opposition, but also many nonpolitical Hutu who showed reluctance to perform what was touted as a "national" duty. The estimates of those killed vary: between ten and fifty thousand Hutu, and between 500,000 and a million Tutsi. Whereas the Hutu were killed as individuals, the Tutsi were killed as a group, recalling German designs to extinguish the country's Jewish population. This explicit goal is why the killings of Tutsi between March and July of 1994 must be termed "genocide." This single fact underlines a crucial similarity between the Rwandan genocide and the Nazi Holocaust.

In the history of genocide, however, the Rwandan genocide raises a difficult political question. Unlike the Nazi Holocaust, the Rwandan genocide was not carried out from a distance, in remote concentration camps beyond national borders, in industrial killing camps operated by agents who often did no more than drop Zyklon B crystals into gas chambers from above. The Rwandan genocide was executed with the slash of machetes rather than the drop of crystals, with all the gruesome detail of a street murder rather than the bureaucratic efficiency of a mass extermination. The difference in technology is indicative of a more significant social difference. The technology of the holocaust allowed a few to kill many, but the machete had to be wielded by a single pair of hands. It required not one but many hacks of a machete to kill even one person. With a machete, killing was hard work; that is why there were often several killers for every single victim. Whereas Nazis made every attempt to separate victims from perpetrators, the Rwandan genocide was very much an intimate affair. It was carried out by hundreds of thousands, perhaps even more, and witnessed by millions. . . .

The Rwandan genocide unfolded in just a hundred days. "It was not just a small group that killed and moved," a political commissar in the police explained to me in Kigali in July 1995. "Because genocide was so extensive, there were killers in every locality — from ministers to peasants — for it to happen in so short a time and on such a large scale." Opening the international conference on Genocide, Impunity and Accountability in Kigali in late 1995, the country's president, Pasteur Bizimungu, spoke of "hundreds of thousands of criminals" evenly spread across the land:

> Each village of this country has been affected by the tragedy, either because the whole population was mobilized to go and kill elsewhere, or

because one section undertook or was pushed to hunt and kill their fellow villagers. The survey conducted in Kigali, Kibungo, Byumba, Gitarama, and Butare Préfectures showed that genocide had been characterized by torture and utmost cruelty. About forty-eight methods of torture were used countrywide. They ranged from burying people alive in graves they had dug up themselves, to cutting and opening wombs of pregnant mothers. People were quartered, impaled or roasted to death.

On many occasions, death was the consequence of ablation of organs, such as the heart, from alive people. In some cases, victims had to pay fabulous amounts of money to the killers for a quick death. The brutality that characterised the genocide has been unprecedented. . . .

The violence of the genocide was the result of both planning and participation. The agenda imposed from above became a gruesome reality to the extent it resonated with perspectives from below. Rather than accent one or the other side of this relationship and thereby arrive at either a state-centered or a society-centered explanation, a complete picture of the genocide needs to take both sides into account. For this was neither just a conspiracy from above that only needed enough time and suitable circumstance to mature, nor was it a popular *jacquerie* gone berserk. If the violence from below could not have spread without cultivation and direction from above, it is equally true that the conspiracy of the tiny fragment of *génocidaires* could not have succeeded had it not found resonance from below. The design from above involved a tiny minority and is easier to understand. The response and initiative from below involved multitudes and presents the true moral dilemma of the Rwandan genocide.

In sum, the Rwandan genocide poses a set of deeply troubling questions. Why did hundreds of thousands, those who had never before killed, take part in mass slaughter? Why did such a disproportionate number of the educated — not just members of the political elite but, as we shall see, civic leaders such as doctors, nurses, judges, human rights activists, and so on — play a leading role in the genocide? Similarly, why did places of shelter where victims expected sanctuary — churches, hospitals, and schools — turn into slaughterhouses where innocents were murdered in the tens and hundreds, and sometimes even thousands? . . .

We may agree that genocidal violence cannot be understood as rational; yet, we need to understand it as thinkable. Rather than run away from it, we need to realize that it is the "popularity" of the genocide that is its uniquely troubling aspect. In its social aspect, Hutu/Tutsi violence in the Rwandan genocide invites comparison with Hindu/Muslim violence at the time of the partition of colonial India. Neither can be explained as simply a state project. One shudders to put the words "popular" and "genocide" together, therefore I put "popularity" in quotation marks. And yet, one needs to explain the large-scale civilian involvement in the genocide. To do so is to contextualize it, to understand the logic of its development. . . .

Colonialism and Genocide

The genocidal impulse to eliminate an enemy may indeed be as old as organized power. Thus, God instructed his Old Testament disciples through Moses, saying:

> Avenge the children of Israel of the Medianites: afterward shalt thou be gathered unto thy people. And Moses spake unto the people saying, Arm ye men from among you for the war, that they may go against Median, to execute the LORD's vengeance on Median. . . . And they warred against Median, as the LORD commanded Moses, and they slew every male. . . . And the children of Israel took captive the women of Median and their little ones; and all their cattle, and all their flocks, and all their goods, they took for a prey. And all their cities in the places wherein they dwelt, and all their encampments, they burnt with fire. And they took all the spoil, and all the prey, both of man and of beast. . . . And Moses said unto them, Have you saved all the women alive? Behold, these caused the children of Israel, through the counsel of Balaam, to commit trespass against the LORD in the matter of Peor, and so the plague was among the congregation of the LORD. Now therefore kill every male among the little ones, and kill every woman that hath known man by lying with him. But all the women children that have not known man by lying with him, keep alive for yourselves.

If the genocidal impulse is as old as the organization of power, one may be tempted to think that all that has changed through history is the technology of genocide. Yet, it is not simply the technology of genocide that has changed through history, but surely also how that impulse is organized and its target defined. Before you can try and eliminate an enemy, you must first define that enemy. The definition of the political self and the political other has varied through history. The history of that variation is the history of political identities, be these religious, national, racial, or otherwise.

I argue that the Rwandan genocide needs to be thought through within the logic of colonialism. The horror of colonialism led to two types of genocidal impulses. The first was the genocide of the native by the settler, to become a reality where the violence of colonial pacification took on extreme proportions. The second was the native impulse to eliminate the settler. Whereas the former was obviously despicable, the latter was not. The very political character of native violence made it difficult to think of it as an impulse to genocide. Because it was derivative of settler violence, the natives' violence appeared less of an outright aggression and more a self defense in the face of continuing aggression. Faced with the violent denial of his humanity by the settler, the native's violence began as a counter to violence. It even seemed more like the affirmation of the native's humanity than the brutal extinction of life that it came to be. When the native killed the settler, it was violence by yesterday's victims. More of a culmination of anticolonial resistance than a direct assault on life and freedom, this violence of victims-turned-perpetrators always provoked a greater moral ambiguity than did the settlers' violence. . . .

Settlers' Genocide

It is more or less a rule of thumb that the more Western settlement a colony experienced, the greater was the violence unleashed against the native population. The reason was simple: settler colonization led to land deprivation. Whereas the prototype of settler violence in the history of modern colonialism is the near-extermination of Amerindians in the New World, the prototype of settler violence in the African colonies was the German annihilation of over 80 percent of the Herero population in the colony of German South West Africa in a single year, 1904. Its context was Herero resistance to land and cattle appropriation by German settlers and their *Schutztruppe* allies. Faced with continuing armed resistance by the Herero, German opinion divided between two points of views, one championed by General Theodor Leutwein, who commanded the army in the colony, and the other by General Lothar von Trotha, who took over the military command when General Leutwein failed to put down native resistance. The difference between them illuminates the range of political choice in a colonial context.

General Trotha explained the difference in a letter:

> Now I have to ask myself how to end the war with the Hereros. The views of the Governor and also a few old Africa hands [*alte Afrikaner*] on the one hand, and my views on the other, differ completely. The first wanted to negotiate for some time already and regard the Herero nation as necessary labour material for the future development of the country. I believe that the nation as such should be annihilated, or, if this was not possible by tactical measures, have to be expelled from the country by operative means and further detailed treatment. This will be possible if the water-holes from Grootfontein to Gobabis are occupied. The constant movement of our troops will enable us to find the small groups of the nation who have moved back westwards and destroy them gradually.

Equally illuminating is General Trotha's rationale for the annihilation policy: "My intimate knowledge of many central African tribes (Bantu and others) has everywhere convinced me of the necessity that the Negro does not respect treaties but only brute force."

The plan Trotha laid out in the letter is more or less the fate he meted to the Herero on the ground. To begin with, the army exterminated as many Herero as possible. For those who fled, all escape routes except the one southeast to the Omeheke, a waterless sandveld in the Kalahari Desert, were blocked. The fleeing Herero were forcibly separated from their cattle and denied access to water holes, leaving them with but one option: to cross the desert into Botswana, in reality a march to death. This, indeed, is how the majority of the Herero perished. It was a fate of which the German general staff was well aware, as is clear from the following gleeful entry in its official publication, *Der Kampf*: "No efforts, no hardships were spared in order to deprive the enemy of his last reserves of resistance; like a half-dead animal he was hunted from water-hole to water-hole until he became a lethargic victim of the nature of his own country. The waterless Omaheke was to complete the work of the German arms: the annihilation of the Herero people."

Lest the reader be tempted to dismiss General Lothar von Trotha as an improbable character come to life from the lunatic fringe of the German officer corps, one given a free hand in a distant and unimportant colony, I hasten to point out that the general had a distinguished record in the annals of colonial conquest, indeed the most likely reason he was chosen to squash a protracted rebellion. Renowned for his brutal involvement in the suppression of the Chinese Boxer Rebellion in 1900, and a veteran of bloody suppression of African resistance to German occupation in Rwanda, Burundi, and Tanzania, General Trotha often enthused about his own methods of colonial warfare: "The exercise of violence with crass terrorism and even with gruesomeness was and is my policy. I destroy the African tribes with streams of blood and streams of money. Only following this cleansing can something new emerge, which will remain."

Opposition to Trotha's annihilation policy had come from two sources: colonial officials who looked at the Herero as potential labor, and church officials who saw them as potential converts. Eventually, the Herero who survived were gathered by the German army with the help of missionary societies and were put in concentration camps, also run by missionaries along with the German army. By 1908, inmates of these concentration camps were estimated at 15,000. Put to slave labor, overworked, hungry, and exposed to diseases such as typhoid and smallpox, more Herero men perished in these camps. Herero women, meanwhile, were turned into sex slaves. At the same time, those who survived were converted en masse to Christianity. When the camps were closed in 1908, the Herero were distributed as laborers among the settlers. Henceforth, all Herero over the age of seven were expected to carry around their necks a metal disk bearing their labor registration number.

The genocide of the Herero was the first genocide of the twentieth century. The links between it and the Holocaust go beyond the building of concentration camps and the execution of an annihilation policy and are worth exploring. It is surely of significance that when General Trotha wrote, as above, of destroying "African tribes with streams of blood," he saw this as some kind of a Social Darwinist "cleansing" after which "something new" would "emerge." It is also relevant that, when the general sought to distribute responsibility for the genocide, he accused the missions of inciting the Herero with images "of the blood-curdling Jewish history of the Old Testament." . . . It seems to me that Hannah Arendt erred when she presumed a relatively uncomplicated relationship between settlers' genocide in the colonies and the Nazi Holocaust at home: When Nazis set out to annihilate Jews, it is far more likely that they thought of themselves as natives, and Jews as settlers. Yet, there is a link that connects the genocide of the Herero and the Nazi Holocaust to the Rwandan genocide. That link is *race branding*, whereby it became possible not only to set a group apart as an enemy, but also to exterminate it with an easy conscience.

Natives' Genocide

In the annals of colonial history, the natives' genocide never became a historical reality. Yet, it always hovered on the horizon as a historical possibility. None sensed it better than Frantz Fanon, whose writings now read like a foreboding. For Fanon, the native's violence was not life denying, but life affirming: "For he knows that he is not an animal; and it is precisely when he realizes his humanity that he begins to sharpen the weapons with which he will secure its victory." What distinguished native violence from the violence of the settler, its saving grace, was that it was the violence of yesterday's victims who have turned around and decided to cast aside their victimhood and become masters of their own lives. "He of whom they have never stopped saying that the only language he understands is that of force, decides to give utterance by force." Indeed, "the argument the native chooses has been furnished by the settler, and by an ironic turning of the tables it is the native who now affirms that the colonialist understands nothing but force." What affirmed the natives' humanity for Fanon was not that they were willing to take the settler's life, but that they were willing to risk their own: "The colonized man finds his freedom in and through violence." If its outcome would be death, of settlers by natives, it would need to be understood as a derivative outcome, a result of a prior logic, the genocidal logic of colonial pacification and occupation infecting anticolonial resistance. "The settler's work is to make even dreams of liberty impossible for the native. The native's work is to imagine all possible methods for destroying the settler. . . . For the native, life can only spring up again out of the rotting corpse of the settler . . . for the colonized people, this violence, because it constitutes their only work, invests their character with positive and creative qualities. The practice of violence binds them together as a whole, since each individual forms a violent link in the great chain, a part of the great organism of violence which has surged upwards in reaction to the settler's violence in the beginning."

The great crime of colonialism went beyond expropriating the native, the name it gave to the indigenous population. *The greater crime was to politicize indigeneity in the first place*: first negatively, as a settler libel of the native; but then positively, as a native response, as a self-assertion. The dialectic of the settler and the native did not end with colonialism and political independence. To understand the logic of genocide, I argue, it is necessary to think through the political world that colonialism set into motion. This was the world of the settler and the native, a world organized around a binary preoccupation that was as compelling as it was confining. It is in this context that Tutsi, a group with a privileged relationship to power before colonialism, got constructed as a privileged *alien settler* presence, first by the great nativist revolution of 1959, and then by Hutu Power propaganda after 1990.

In its motivation and construction, I argue that the Rwandan genocide needs to be understood as a natives' genocide. It was a genocide by those who saw themselves as sons — and daughters — of the soil, and their mission as one of clearing the soil of a threatening *alien* presence. This was not an "ethnic" but a "racial" cleansing, not a violence against one who is seen as a neighbor but against one who is seen as a foreigner; not a violence that targets a transgression across a boundary into home but one that seeks to eliminate a foreign presence from home soil, literally and physically. From this point of view, we need to distinguish between racial and ethnic violence: ethnic violence can result in massacres, but not genocide. Massacres are about transgressions, excess; genocide questions the very legitimacy of a presence as alien. For the Hutu who killed, the Tutsi was a settler, not a neighbor. Rather than take these identities as a given, as a starting point of analysis, I seek to ask: When and how was Hutu made into a native identity and Tutsi into a settler identity? The analytical challenge is to understand the historical dynamic through which Hutu and Tutsi came to be synonyms for native and settler.

167

GLENN GARVIN AND EDWARD HEGSTROM

Report: Maya Indians Suffered Genocide

In 1994, the United Nations–brokered Accord of Oslo brought an end to the civil war that had wracked Guatemala for almost four decades. The Accord created a Guatemalan truth commission, the Commission for Historical Clarification, "in order to clarify with objectivity, equity and impartiality, the human rights violations and acts of violence connected with the armed confrontation that caused suffering among the Guatemalan people."[1] The commission examined 42,275 cases of human rights abuses, including the destruction of over 400 villages and more than 626 massacres. It concluded that 93 percent of the abuses were committed by the U.S.-backed military and paramilitary forces and 3 percent were committed by the rebels. (The cause of 4 percent could not be determined.) The report, issued in 1999, concluded that genocide had occurred.

Major U.S. involvement in Guatemala dates back to the early 1950s in the aftermath of the country's first free election. In 1950, Jacobo Arbenz Guzman, a reformer, won 60 percent of the vote and became president of Guatemala. His efforts to redistribute about 1 percent of the land to the poor raised fears in the Eisenhower administration of the spread of communism in the hemisphere. In 1954, the CIA organized a coup that ousted Arbenz and installed a military junta that plunged the country into thirty-six years of political turbulence. (See Map 25.3.) During that period the U.S. government maintained close relations with the junta and trained and aided its army.

This was the first time a United Nations–sponsored report reached the conclusion that events in a Latin American country constituted genocide. Using the categories of genocide suggested by Mahmood Mamdani in the previous selection, what kind of genocide was committed in Guatemala? One commentator, Andrew Reding, writing in the *Journal of Commerce*[2] declared Guatemala America's Rwanda and urged the creation of a United Nations–sponsored genocide

---

[1] Guatemala Memory of Silence: Report of the Commission for Historical Clarification, Conclusions and Recommendations; Prologue. See http://shr.aaas.org/guatemala/ceh/report/english/prologue.html.

[2] March 18, 1999.

Glenn Garvin and Edward Hegstrom, "Report: Maya Indians Suffered Genocide," *Miami Herald*, February 25, 1999.

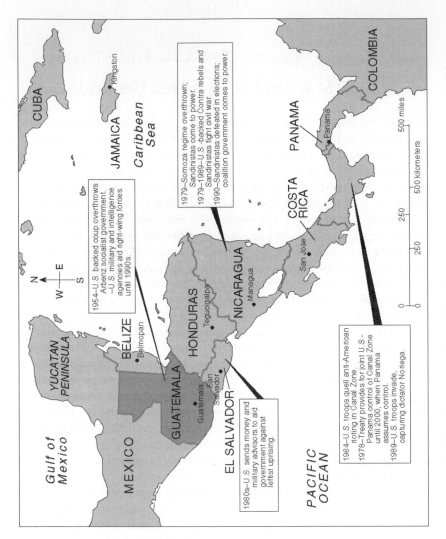

CUBA

Kingston •

JAMAICA

Caribbean Sea

1979–Somoza regime overthrown; Sandinistas come to power. 1979–1989–U.S.-backed Contra rebels and Sandinistas fight civil war. 1990–Sandinistas defeated in elections; coalition government comes to power.

COLOMBIA

PANAMA

Panama •

COSTA RICA

San José •

NICARAGUA

Managua •

1954–U.S. backed coup overthrows Arbenz socialist government. –U.S. military and intelligence agencies aid right-wing forces until 1990s.

N
W — E
S

HONDURAS

Tegucigalpa •

BELIZE

Belmopan •

YUCATAN PENINSULA

GUATEMALA

Guatemala •
San Salvador •

EL SALVADOR

1980s–U.S. sends money and military advisors to aid government against leftist uprising.

MEXICO

Gulf of Mexico

1964–U.S. troops quell anti-American rioting in Canal Zone. 1978–Treaty provides for joint U.S.-Panama control of Canal Zone until 2000, when Panama assumes control. 1989–U.S. troops invade, capturing dictator Noriega.

PACIFIC OCEAN

0   250   500 miles
0   250   500 kilometers

Map 25.3   U.S. Involvement in Central America.

tribunal, similar to that for Rwanda. What do you think of this idea? Should government officials of the United States be held to international laws?

Thinking Historically

How should one respond to charges of genocide? When the report was released, President Clinton apologized to the people of Guatemala. He said: "It is important that I state clearly that support for military forces or intelligence units which engaged in violent and widespread repression of the kind described in the report was wrong. And the United States must not repeat that mistake. We must, and we will, instead continue to support the peace and reconciliation process in Guatemala." What do you think of Clinton's characterization of these events as a "mistake"? Compare his response to that of the diplomats described in the news article. How would you describe the attitude of the reporters for the *Miami Herald*? If the actions of the United States do not appear to be rational, how were they "thinkable"? In other words, how did this happen?

GUATEMALA CITY — A Guatemalan truth commission investigating the country's vicious 36-year civil war issued a final report Thursday placing the blame for most of the 200,000 deaths on a "racist" Guatemalan government that received considerable support from the United States. Guatemala's Maya Indian population, which suffered "acts of genocide," bore the brunt of the government's repression, the report said. More than 80 percent of the victims of human rights abuses during the war were Indians, the Commission for Historical Clarification concluded.

"The massacres, scorched-earth operations, forced disappearances, and executions of Maya authorities, leaders, and spiritual guides were not only an attempt to destroy the social base of the guerrillas," the report said, "but above all, to destroy the cultural values that ensured cohesion and collective action in Maya communities."

Although the report was couched in relatively moderate language when it came to assigning blame to non-Guatemalan participants, Commission Chairman Christian Tomuschat accused the United States of being responsible for much of the bloodshed. As seething U.S. diplomats looked on, Tomuschat said the Guatemalan army carried out hundreds of massacres of civilians at a time when "the United States government and U.S. private companies exercised pressure to maintain the country's archaic and unjust socioeconomic structure."

Tomuschat said the CIA and other U.S. agencies "lent direct and indirect support to some illegal state operations." This encouraged a

Guatemalan military government that was committing genocide against
the country's Indian population, he added.

Tomuschat spoke at the unveiling of the commission's 3,600-page
report on human rights abuses during the civil war that ended in 1996.
The report took 18 months to assemble. Hundreds of spectators —
many of them former Marxist guerrillas who battled the government —
burst into wild applause after Tomuschat, a German law professor, finished his attack on the United States.

A contingent of U.S. diplomats, including Ambassador Donald
Planty and Mark Schneider, an assistant administrator of the Agency
for International Development (USAID), stared stonily ahead during
Tomuschat's speech. Afterward, a clearly furious Planty said the attack
was unfair. "Everyone knows the historical context in which the conflict took place," Planty said. "But that doesn't obscure the fact that the
violence was committed by Guatemalans against Guatemalans."

The surprise of Planty and other U.S. diplomats was compounded
by the fact that USAID financed much of the commission's work with a
donation of $1.5 million. One of the three members of the commission,
bilingual education expert Otilia Lux de Coti, is a USAID employee
who took a leave of absence to work on the report.

Cold War Impact Cited

The report's 100-page executive summary, while noting that Cold War
policies in both the United States and Cuba "had a bearing" on the war,
said the Guatemalan government used a relatively small Marxist insur-
gency as an excuse for the "physical annihilation" of all its political opponents in a war that claimed 200,000 lives, the vast majority of them
civilians. "The inclusion of all opponents under one banner, democratic
or otherwise, pacifist or guerrilla, legal or illegal, communist or noncom-
munist, served to justify numerous and serious crimes," the report said.

Coup Attempt Sparked War

The Guatemalan civil war began in November 1960, when leftist officers attempted a coup against the country's right-wing military government. When they failed, many of the officers went into the countryside
to form guerrilla groups. Many political analysts, however, say the
roots of the war lay in the 1950s, when a coup supported by the CIA
toppled the Marxist government of President Jacobo Arbenz and put in
place the first of a series of military governments.

Tomuschat's searing comments on the United States clearly delighted many Guatemalan human rights activists. "Today, Tomuschat

spoke the truth about Guatemala as it has never been spoken before," said Frank La Rue, who runs a human rights legal foundation.

Others, however, said Guatemalans might be trying to let themselves off the hook, pretending they were merely pawns in the Cold War rather than enthusiastic participants. "Blaming the U.S. is a national pastime here," said David Holiday, an American political consultant based in Guatemala. "That unjustly exonerates the Guatemala players."

Offenders Not Named

The report does not include names of individual human rights offenders. It does single out a handful of senior officials for blame — like former military strongman Efrain Rios Montt — who already have been excoriated in numerous other human rights reports.

The last time a highly publicized human rights report was unveiled in Guatemala, it was followed 48 hours later by the murder of its principal author. Bishop Juan Gerardi was beaten to death two days after the Roman Catholic Church's human rights office issued a report similar to the one released Thursday.

Gerardi's killing remains unsolved and it has not been determined that it was related to the bishop's human rights work. Nonetheless, all three members of the Commission for Historical Clarification are reportedly leaving Guatemala for lengthy stays overseas.

REFLECTIONS

Short of war, the world community has adopted three strategies to counter genocide and mass murder. The first is trial of war criminals. At the conclusion of World War II, war-crime trials of Nazis and Japanese were conducted. The terms *war crimes* and *war criminals* are unfortunate misnomers because they suggest a criminalization of military activities. In fact, the crimes recounted in this chapter were not crimes of the battlefield but, rather, massive crimes against civilian populations.

Developing and refining international laws respecting human rights is the second strategy. The "Declaration of Human Rights" passed by the United Nations, itself a shaper and guardian of international law, offers a recognized standard and continuing process for defining and preventing genocide, mass murder, and "crimes against humanity."

The third strategy, one in which all of us can participate, is the dissemination of information and concerted efforts toward understanding.

To promote understanding, archives must be opened, and laws such as the Freedom of Information Act must be used aggressively. We must develop sensitivity to the plight of victims, knowledge of the victimizers' motives, and understanding about the ways that the horrendous can happen.

In recent years "truth and reconciliation" commissions have been formed in South Africa and El Salvador to enable those countries to get beyond years of government-sponsored terrorism. In cases like these, when such governments have relinquished power but their personnel are either too powerful or too numerous to be brought to justice, the new democratic governments and their truth and reconciliation commissions have asked for a complete and remorseful accounting of past crimes. Some say these commissions have been able to accept truth instead of revenge; others find it to be truth instead of justice. The cases of Yugoslavia and Rwanda, which have followed the route of international trials rather than truth and justice commissions, continue in the International Court of Justice at the Hague and the International Criminal Tribunal for Rwanda in Tanzania as this is written. The case of Guatemala has gone no further than the United Nations report issued in 1999. It is the U.S. position that international tribunals are not appropriate for its citizens or officials. Do you think U.S. citizens should be exempt from international law or immune from prosecution in international courts? If so, how would you make that case to citizens of other countries? If international criminal courts are not appropriate, should the United States form a truth and reconciliation commission for events in Guatemala? Truth can be an amazing restorative, especially when it is linked with genuine contrition. The price of amnesty can hardly be less. Forgiveness may be much more. Which, if any, of the crimes recalled in this chapter would you be willing to forgive? What should be necessary for acquittal or amnesty? How do we prevent such things from occurring again and again?

Religion and Politics

Israel, Palestine, and the West,
1896 to the Present

HISTORICAL CONTEXT

Many of the political conflicts of the mid- to late twentieth century turned on, or were expressed in, the language of religion: Catholics and Protestants in Northern Ireland; Hindus and Muslims in India, Pakistan, and the disputed areas of Kashmir; Jews and Muslims in Palestine and Israel. None of these conflicts were new to the twentieth century but were continuations of conflicts hundreds or thousands of years old. Yet the post–World War II end of European colonialism unleashed sectarian religious forces that were dormant or suppressed for centuries.

The great colonial empires were not above favoring one religion or ethnic group over another. The British invented their "martial races"[1] to serve as elite enforcers; the Austro-Hungarian Empire favored Austrians and Hungarians over Slavs, Serbs, and almost everyone else. But ethnic or religious sectarianism could be the death of empires. In the case of the Austro-Hungarian Empire, it was. Consequently most great empires attempted to stress more universal identities: the Islamic brotherhood of the Ottomans or the Socialist unity of the Soviets. The demise of the great empires left kindling resentments that could be blown into full flame.

This chapter will explore one of these post–World War II political conflicts fueled by religious nationalism. The conflict between Israel and Palestine may not be representative of other struggles, like those between Catholics and Protestants, or Muslims and Hindus. In some ways the creation of a Jewish homeland in the Arab Middle East was a unique event. But nothing under the sun is entirely new, and no two cases are the same. We will study the role of religion and politics in a particular place

---

[1]Sikhs in India, Nepali Gurkhas, Hausas in West Africa, and the Kamba in East Africa were thought to be naturally warlike and were selected for police or army overrepresentation.

at a particular time, but it is a place that has appeared at the very center of world maps for millennia and its conflicts still shake our world.

THINKING HISTORICALLY
Making Use of the Unexpected

The most lasting learning comes from making our own meanings. We do that to a certain extent when we read something and put it in our own words. But most of what we read washes over us. We remember it or not, but generally we do not make our own meaning out of information and ideas that are expected or unexceptional.

Sometimes, however, we come across details, ideas, or statements that surprise us. They stop us in our tracks because they are unexpected: They seem wrong, unbelievable, or senseless. The most common response to the unexpected may be to ignore it and move on, but by doing so we may miss an opportunity to learn something new. The unexpected can provide an entry point into a document, period, culture, or movement that opens up a whole new realm of understanding. In this chapter, you will be encouraged to reflect on the unexpected so that you might use it as an opportunity to create new meaning and deepen your understanding.

168

THEODOR HERZL
From The Jewish State

Born and raised in an assimilated Hungarian family, Theodor Herzl* (1860–1904) first experienced anti-Semitism as a student at the University of Vienna, but he was most profoundly shaken by the Dreyfus Affair in France. In 1894, Captain Alfred Dreyfus†, a Jewish officer in the French army, was falsely convicted of treason on a wave of public

*HAYR tzuhl
†DRY fuhs

Theodor Herzl, *The Jewish State*, trans. Sylvie D'Avigdor (American Zionist Emergency Council, 1946), selections from Chapters 2 and 5. Originally published in German in 1896. Also available online at http://www.jewishvirtuallibrary.org/jsource/Zionism/herzl2e.html.

hostility toward Jews. Herzl, a reporter in Paris at the time, was shocked to hear French mobs shouting "Death to the Jews." The events, he later wrote, radically transformed him. In 1896 he published *The Jewish State*. What reasons did he give for forming a Jewish state? How and where did he intend to create this Jewish state? How "religious" was this state to be? What did he see as the potential problems of a Jewish state and how did he propose to solve those problems?

Thinking Historically

Different details may surprise different readers. The more we know, perhaps the smaller or less obvious the surprise. Nevertheless, even the least knowledgeable student of modern history will likely be surprised by the appearance in this text of the word "Argentine." Why is that a surprise? What does its presence in the text tell you about Herzl or early Zionism? (Uganda, too, was an early candidate for a Jewish homeland.)

Details like this seem unlikely from the perspective of the present. Our contemporary association of Israel as "the home of the Jews" is so strong, it is difficult to imagine the possibility of a different historical outcome. And perhaps there was not. But clearly, the possibilities of the early twentieth century were more fluid than those of today. What other unexpected details do you see in the document? How might they lead to new ways of thinking about the subject?

Chapter 2

The Jewish Question

No one can deny the gravity of the situation of the Jews. Wherever they live in perceptible numbers, they are more or less persecuted. Their equality before the law, granted by statute, has become practically a dead letter. They are debarred from filling even moderately high positions, either in the army, or in any public or private capacity. And attempts are made to thrust them out of business also: "Don't buy from Jews!"

Attacks in Parliaments, in assemblies, in the press, in the pulpit, in the street, on journeys — for example, their exclusion from certain hotels — even in places of recreation, become daily more numerous. The forms of persecution vary according to the countries and social circles in which they occur. In Russia, imposts are levied on Jewish villages; in Rumania, a few persons are put to death; in Germany, they get a good beating occasionally; in Austria, Anti-Semites exercise terrorism over all public life; in Algeria, there are traveling agitators; in Paris, the Jews are shut out of the so-called best social circles and excluded from clubs. Shades of anti-Jewish feeling are innumerable. But this is not to be an attempt to make out a doleful category of Jewish hardships.

I do not intend to arouse sympathetic emotions on our behalf. That would be a foolish, futile, and undignified proceeding. I shall content myself with putting the following questions to the Jews: Is it not true that, in countries where we live in perceptible numbers, the position of Jewish lawyers, doctors, technicians, teachers, and employees of all descriptions becomes daily more intolerable? Is it not true, that the Jewish middle classes are seriously threatened? Is it not true, that the passions of the mob are incited against our wealthy people? Is it not true, that our poor endure greater sufferings than any other proletariat? I think that this external pressure makes itself felt everywhere. In our economically upper classes it causes discomfort, in our middle classes continual and grave anxieties, in our lower classes absolute despair.

Everything tends, in fact, to one and the same conclusion, which is clearly enunciated in that classic Berlin phrase: "Juden Raus" (Out with the Jews!).

I shall now put the Question in the briefest possible form: Are we to "get out" now and where to? . . .

The Plan

The whole plan is in its essence perfectly simple, as it must necessarily be if it is to come within the comprehension of all.

Let the sovereignty be granted us over a portion of the globe large enough to satisfy the rightful requirements of a nation; the rest we shall manage for ourselves.

The creation of a new State is neither ridiculous nor impossible. We have in our day witnessed the process in connection with nations which were not largely members of the middle class, but poorer, less educated, and consequently weaker than ourselves. The Governments of all countries scourged by Anti-Semitism will be keenly interested in assisting us to obtain the sovereignty we want.

The plan, simple in design, but complicated in execution, will be carried out by two agencies: The Society of Jews and the Jewish Company.

The Society of Jews will do the preparatory work in the domains of science and politics, which the Jewish Company will afterwards apply practically.

The Jewish Company will be the liquidating agent of the business interests of departing Jews, and will organize commerce and trade in the new country.

We must not imagine the departure of the Jews to be a sudden one. It will be gradual, continuous, and will cover many decades. The poorest will go first to cultivate the soil. In accordance with a preconceived plan, they will construct roads, bridges, railways, and telegraph installations; regulate rivers; and build their own dwellings; their labor will create trade, trade will create markets, and markets will attract new settlers, for every man will go voluntarily, at his own expense and his own risk. The labor expended on the land will enhance its value, and the Jews will soon perceive that a new and permanent sphere of operation is opening here for that spirit of enterprise which has heretofore met only with hatred and obloquy. . . .

The emigrants standing lowest in the economic scale will be slowly followed by those of a higher grade. Those who at this moment are living in despair will go first. They will be led by the mediocre intellects which we produce so superabundantly and which are persecuted everywhere.

This pamphlet will open a general discussion on the Jewish Question, but that does not mean that there will be any voting on it. Such a result would ruin the cause from the outset, and dissidents must remember that allegiance or opposition is entirely voluntary. He who will not come with us should remain behind.

Let all who are willing to join us, fall in behind our banner and fight for our cause with voice and pen and deed.

Those Jews who agree with our idea of a State will attach themselves to the Society, which will thereby be authorized to confer and treat with Governments in the name of our people. The Society will thus be acknowledged in its relations with Governments as a State-creating power. This acknowledgment will practically create the State.

Should the Powers declare themselves willing to admit our sovereignty over a neutral piece of land, then the Society will enter into negotiations for the possession of this land. Here two territories come under consideration, Palestine and Argentine. In both countries important experiments in colonization have been made, though on the mistaken principle of a gradual infiltration of Jews. An infiltration is bound to end badly. It continues till the inevitable moment when the native population feels itself threatened, and forces the Government to stop a further influx of Jews. Immigration is consequently futile unless we have the sovereign right to continue such immigration.

The Society of Jews will treat with the present masters of the land, putting itself under the protectorate of the European Powers, if they prove friendly to the plan. We could offer the present possessors of the land enormous advantages, assume part of the public debt, build new roads for traffic, which our presence in the country would render necessary, and do many other things. The creation of our State would be beneficial to adjacent countries, because the cultivation of a strip of land increases the value of its surrounding districts in innumerable ways.

Palestine or Argentine?

Shall we choose Palestine or Argentine? We shall take what is given us, and what is selected by Jewish public opinion. The Society will determine both these points.

Argentine is one of the most fertile countries in the world, extends over a vast area, has a sparse population and a mild climate. The Argentine Republic would derive considerable profit from the cession of a portion of its territory to us. The present infiltration of Jews has certainly produced some discontent, and it would be necessary to enlighten the Republic on the intrinsic difference of our new movement.

Palestine is our ever-memorable historic home. The very name of Palestine would attract our people with a force of marvelous potency. If His Majesty the Sultan were to give us Palestine, we could in return undertake to regulate the whole finances of Turkey. We should there form a portion of a rampart of Europe against Asia, an outpost of civilization as opposed to barbarism. We should as a neutral State remain in contact with all Europe, which would have to guarantee our existence. The sanctuaries of Christendom would be safeguarded by assigning to them an extra-territorial status such as is well-known to the law of nations. We should form a guard of honor about these sanctuaries, answering for the fulfillment of this duty with our existence. This guard of honor would be the great symbol of the solution of the Jewish question after eighteen centuries of Jewish suffering.

Chapter 5

Language

It might be suggested that our want of a common current language would present difficulties. We cannot converse with one another in Hebrew. Who amongst us has a sufficient acquaintance with Hebrew to ask for a railway ticket in that language! Such a thing cannot be done. Yet the difficulty is very easily circumvented. Every man can preserve the language in which his thoughts are at home. Switzerland affords a conclusive proof of the possibility of a federation of tongues. We shall remain in the new country what we now are here, and we shall never cease to cherish with sadness the memory of the native land out of which we have been driven.

We shall give up using those miserable stunted jargons, those Ghetto languages which we still employ, for these were the stealthy tongues of prisoners. Our national teachers will give due attention to this matter; and the language which proves itself to be of greatest utility for general intercourse will be adopted without compulsion as our national tongue. Our community of race is peculiar and unique, for we are bound together only by the faith of our fathers.

Theocracy

Shall we end by having a theocracy? No, indeed. Faith unites us, knowledge gives us freedom. We shall therefore prevent any theocratic tendencies from coming to the fore on the part of our priesthood. We shall keep our priests within the confines of their temples in the same way as we shall keep our professional army within the confines of their barracks. Army and priesthood shall receive honors high as their valuable functions deserve. But they must not interfere in the administration of the State which confers distinction upon them, else they will conjure up difficulties without and within.

Every man will be as free and undisturbed in his faith or his disbelief as he is in his nationality. And if it should occur that men of other creeds and different nationalities come to live amongst us, we should accord them honorable protection and equality before the law. We have learnt toleration in Europe. This is not sarcastically said; for the Anti-Semitism of today could only in a very few places be taken for old religious intolerance. It is for the most part a movement among civilized nations by which they try to chase away the spectres of their own past. . . .

The Army

The Jewish State is conceived as a neutral one. It will therefore require only a professional army, equipped, of course, with every requisite of modern warfare, to preserve order internally and externally.

The Flag

We have no flag, and we need one. If we desire to lead many men, we must raise a symbol above their heads.

I would suggest a white flag, with seven golden stars. The white field symbolizes our pure new life; the stars are the seven golden hours of our working-day. For we shall march into the Promised Land carrying the badge of honor.

169

DAVID FROMKIN

On the Balfour Declaration

In a brief note, dated November 2, 1917, British Foreign Secretary Lord Balfour declared that Britain was in favor of the creation of a "national home" for Jews in Palestine. The note, delivered to Lord Rothschild, a leading British Zionist, marked a crucial turning point in British policy. It suddenly turned Zionism from a quixotic dream to a strategic movement. Yet, as the following selection from a history of the Middle East reveals, the Balfour Declaration was issued despite considerable domestic opposition and numerous British misconceptions about the needs and beliefs of its allies and enemies. Recall that the Great War of 1914–1918 pitted England, France, and Russia against Germany, Austria, and the Ottoman Empire. Palestine was part of the Ottoman Empire until taken from Turkey by British troops and Arab allies shortly after the Declaration was issued. The Arabs expected to govern the land themselves. Neither they nor the French or Russians were consulted or advised of Balfour's plans.

According to Fromkin's history, what were the reasons for the British and American support of a Jewish homeland in Palestine? Who was in favor of a creation of a Jewish homeland in Palestine, and who was opposed? What did the British government expect to gain? Were they successful?

Thinking Historically

Here you have the actual document and a modern historian's account of the political considerations that finally led to passage of the Balfour Declaration. What elements in either the Declaration or Fromkin's history surprise you? What do you make of such surprises? How, if at all, are they related to the surprises in the other selections?

The Prime Minister had always planned to carry through a Zionist program; and while he did not express an interest in declaring Britain's intentions in advance, neither did he place any obstacle in the way of his government's doing so once his colleagues thought it useful.

Yet the proposal that Balfour should issue his pro-Zionist declaration suddenly encountered opposition that brought it to a halt. The op-

David Fromkin, *A Peace to End All Peace* (New York: Avon Books, 1989), 294–330.

position came from leading figures in the British Jewish community. Edwin Montagu, Secretary of State for India, led the opposition group within the Cabinet. He, along with his cousin, Herbert Samuel, and Rufus Isaacs (Lord Reading) had broken new ground for their co-religionists: they had been the first Jews to sit in a British Cabinet.[1] The second son of a successful financier who had been ennobled, Montagu saw Zionism as a threat to the position in British society that he and his family had so recently, and with so much exertion, attained. Judaism, he argued, was a religion, not a nationality, and to say otherwise was to say that he was less than 100 percent British.

Montagu was regarded as by far the most capable of the younger men in the Liberal ranks, and it was deemed a political masterstroke for the Prime Minister to have taken him and Churchill away from Asquith. Yet a typical political comment at the time (from Lord Derby, the War Minister) was, "The appointment of Montagu, a Jew, to the India Office has made, as far as I can judge, an uneasy feeling both in India and here"; though Derby added that "I, personally, have a very high opinion of his capability and I expect he will do well." It bothered Montagu that, despite his lack of religious faith, he could not avoid being categorized as a Jew. He was the millionaire son of an English lord, but was driven to lament that "I have been striving all my life to escape from the Ghetto."

The evidence suggested that in his non-Zionism, Montagu was speaking for a majority of Jews. As of 1913, the last date for which there were figures, only about one percent of the world's Jews had signified their adherence to Zionism. British Intelligence reports indicated a surge of Zionist feeling during the war in the Pale of Russia, but there were no figures either to substantiate or to quantify it. In Britain, the Conjoint Committee, which represented British Jewry in all matters affecting Jews abroad, had been against Zionism from the start and remained so.

Montagu's opposition brought all matters to a halt. In disgust, Graham reported that the proposed declaration was "hung up" by Montagu, "who represents a certain section of the rich Jews and who seems to fear that he and his like will be expelled from England and asked to cultivate farms in Palestine."

The sub-Cabinet officials who were pushing for a pro-Zionist commitment attempted to allay such fears. Amery, who was helping Milner redraft the proposed Declaration, explained the concept behind it to a Cabinet member as not really being addressed to British subjects of the Jewish faith, but to Jews who resided in countries that denied them real citizenship. "Apart from those Jews who have become citizens of this

---

[1]Disraeli, of course, though of Jewish ancestry, was baptized a Christian.

or any other country in the fullest sense, there is also a large body, more particularly of the Jews in Poland and Russia . . . who are still in a very real sense a separate nation. . . ." Denied the right to become Russians, they would be offered a chance to rebuild their own homeland in Palestine.

Montagu, however, took little interest in the position of Jews in other countries. It was the position of Jews in British society that concerned him; feeling threatened, he fought back with a ferocity that brought the Cabinet's deliberations on the matter to a standstill.

Montagu was aided by Lord Curzon, who argued that Palestine was too meagre in resources to accommodate the Zionist dream. More important, he was aided by Andrew Bonar Law — leader of the dominant party in the Coalition government and the Prime Minister's powerful political partner — who urged delay. Bonar Law argued that the time was not yet ripe for a consideration of the Zionist issue.

Montagu was also aided by the United States, which, until mid-October 1917, cautiously counselled delay. President Wilson was sympathetic to Zionism, but suspicious of British motives; he favored a Jewish Palestine but was less enthusiastic about a British Palestine. As the British Cabinet considered issuing the Balfour Declaration, it solicited the advice, and by implication the support, of President Wilson. The proposed Declaration was described by the Cabinet to the American government as an expression of sympathy for Zionist aspirations, as though it were motivated solely by concern for the plight of persecuted Jews. Wilson's foreign policy adviser, Colonel House, translated this as follows: "The English naturally want the road to Egypt and India blocked, and Lloyd George is not above using us to further this plan."

This was a fair interpretation of the views of the Prime Minister and of the Milner circle which advised him. According to Chaim Weizmann, Philip Kerr (the former Milner aide who served as Lloyd George's secretary) "saw in a Jewish Palestine a bridge between Africa, Asia, and Europe on the road to India." It was not, however, a fair interpretation of the views of the Foreign Office, which had been won over by the argument that a pro-Zionist declaration would prove a crucial weapon against Germany in the war and afterward. The Foreign Office believed that the Jewish communities in America and, above all, Russia, wielded great power. The British ambassador in Petrograd, well aware that Jews were a weak and persecuted minority in imperial Russia and of no political consequence, reported that Zionists could not affect the outcome of the struggle for power in Russia. His home government persisted in believing, however, that the Jewish community in Russia could keep the government that ruled them in the Allied camp. As the crisis in Russia deepened, the Foreign Office was seized by a sense of urgency in seeking Jewish support.

IV

Fear begets fear. In Germany the press was aroused by rumors of what the British Foreign Office intended to do. In June 1917 Sir Ronald Graham received from Chaim Weizmann an issue of a Berlin newspaper known for its close relationship to the government, reporting that the British were flirting with the idea of endorsing Zionism in order to acquire the Palestinian land bridge on the road from Egypt to India, and proposing that Germany forestall the maneuver by endorsing Zionism first. (Though the British did not know it, the German government took little interest in adopting a pro-Zionist stance; it was the German press that took an interest in it.)

That summer Graham communicated his fears to Balfour. In his minute, Graham wrote that he had heard there was to be another postponement which he believed would "jeopardise the whole Jewish situation." This endangered the position in Russia where, he asserted, the Jews were all anti-Ally and, to a lesser extent, it would antagonize public opinion in the United States. Warning that Britain must not "throw the Zionists into the arms of the Germans," he argued that "We might at any moment be confronted by a German move on the Zionist question and it must be remembered that Zionism was originally if not a German Jewish at any rate an Austrian Jewish idea."

Graham attached to his minute a list of dates showing how extensive the government's delays had been in dealing with the Zionist matter. In October, Balfour forwarded the minute to the Prime Minister, along with the list of dates which he said showed that the Zionists had reasonable cause to complain, to which he added his own recommendation that the question be taken up by the Cabinet as soon as possible.

On 26 October 1917, *The Times* published a leading article attacking the continuing delay. Stating that it was no secret that British and Allied governments had been considering a statement about Palestine, *The Times* argued that the time had come to make one.

> Do our statesmen fail to see how valuable to the Allied cause would be the hearty sympathy of the Jews throughout the world which an unequivocal declaration of British policy might win? Germany has been quick to perceive the danger to her schemes and to her propaganda that would be involved in the association of the Allies with Jewish national hopes, and she has not been idle in attempting to forestall us.

On 31 October 1917 the Cabinet overrode the opposition of Montagu and Curzon and authorized the Foreign Secretary to issue a much-diluted version of the assurance of support that Weizmann had requested. An ebullient Sykes rushed over with the news, "Dr. Weizmann, it's a boy"; but the Zionist leader was unhappy that the original language had been so watered down.

Addressed to the most illustrious name in British Jewry, the Foreign
Secretary's letter of 2 November 1917 stated:

> Dear Lord Rothschild,
> I have much pleasure in conveying to you, on behalf of His Majesty's
> Government, the following declaration of sympathy with Jewish Zion-
> ist aspirations which has been submitted to, and approved by, the Cab-
> inet: "His Majesty's Government view with favour the establishment
> in Palestine of a national home for the Jewish people, and will use their
> best endeavours to facilitate the achievement of this object, it being
> clearly understood that nothing shall be done which may prejudice the
> civil and religious rights of existing non-Jewish communities in Pales-
> tine, or the rights and political status enjoyed by Jews in any other
> country." I should be grateful if you would bring this declaration to
> the knowledge of the Zionist Federation.

Britain's leaders anticipated no adverse reaction from their Arab allies; they had seen France as their only problem in this connection, and
that had been resolved. The Prime Minister later wrote of the Arab
leaders that "Palestine did not seem to give them much anxiety." He
pointed out that his government had informed King Hussein and Prince
Feisal of its plans to re-create a Jewish homeland in the Holy Land. He
caustically added that "We could not get in touch with the Palestinian
Arabs as they were fighting against us."

The public announcement of the Balfour Declaration was delayed
until the following Friday, the publication date of the weekly *Jewish
Chronicle*. By then the news was overshadowed by reports from Petrograd that Lenin and Trotsky had seized power. The Foreign Office had
hoped the Balfour Declaration would help to swing Russian Jewish
support to the Allied side and against Bolshevism. This hope remained
alive until the Bolsheviks decisively won the Russian Civil War in the
early 1920s. In November of 1917 the battle against Bolshevism in
Russia had just begun, and those Britons who supported the Balfour
Declaration, because they mistakenly believed Russian Jews were powerful and could be valuable allies, were driven to support it all the more
by the dramatic news from Petrograd.

It was not until 9 November that *The Times* was able to report the
announcement of the Balfour Declaration, and not until 3 December
that it published comments approving it. The comments followed upon
a celebration at the London Opera House on 2 December organized by
the British Zionist Federation. In addition to the Zionist leaders, speakers included Lord Robert Cecil, Sir Mark Sykes, and William Ormsby-
Gore, as well as a Syrian Christian, an Arab nationalist, and spokesmen
for Armenia. The theme of the meeting, eloquently pursued by many of
the speakers, was the need for Jews, Arabs, and Armenians to help one
another and to move forward in harmony. The opinion of *The Times*

was that "The presence and the words of influential representatives of the Arab and Armenian peoples, and their assurances of agreement and cooperation with the Jews, would alone have sufficed to make the meeting memorable."

Of the meeting, *The Times* wrote that "its outstanding features were the Old Testament spirit which pervaded it and the feeling that, in the somewhat incongruous setting of a London theatre, the approaching fulfillment of ancient prophecy was being celebrated with faith and fervour." It was appropriate that it should be so: Biblical prophecy was the first and most enduring of the many motives that led Britons to want to restore the Jews to Zion.

The Prime Minister planned to foster a Jewish home in Palestine, in any event, and later wrote that the peace treaty would have provided that Palestine should be a homeland for the Jews "even had there been no previous pledge or promise." The importance of the Balfour Declaration, he wrote, was its contribution to the war effort. He claimed that Russian Jews had given invaluable support to the war against Germany because of it. The grateful Zionist leaders had promised to work toward an Allied victory — and had done so. Writing two decades later, as the British government was about to abandon the Balfour Declaration, he said that the Zionists "kept their word in the letter and the spirit, and the only question that remains now is whether we mean to honour ours."

The Prime Minister underestimated the effect of the Balfour Declaration on the eventual peace settlement. Its character as a public document — issued with the approval of the United States and France and after consultation with Italy and the Vatican, and greeted with approval by the public and the press throughout the western world — made it a commitment that was difficult to ignore when the peace settlement was being negotiated. It took on a life and momentum of its own.

V

The Declaration also played a role in the development of the Zionist movement in the American Jewish community. American Zionism had been a tiny movement when the war began. Of the roughly three million Jews who then lived in the United States, only 12,000 belonged to the often ephemeral groups loosely bound together in the amateurishly led Zionist Federation. The movement's treasury contained 15,000 dollars; its annual budget never exceeded 5,200 dollars. The largest single donation the Federation ever received prior to 1914 was 200 dollars. In New York the movement had only 500 members.

Louis D. Brandeis, an outstanding Boston lawyer not previously identified with specifically Jewish causes, had become a Zionist in 1912 and took over leadership of the movement in 1914. As the intellectual giant of the Progressive movement in American politics, he was believed to exert great influence over President Wilson. Brandeis was perhaps the first Jew to play an important part in American politics since the Civil War. Only one Jew had ever been a member of a president's cabinet,[2] and Brandeis himself was to become the first Jewish member of the U.S. Supreme Court.

The great waves of Jewish immigration into the United States were recent, and most immigrants were anxious to learn English, to shed their foreign accents and ways, and to become American. American-born Jews, too, wanted to distance themselves from any foreign taint and feared that attachment to Zionism on their part might make them seem less than wholehearted in their loyalty to the United States.

It was this issue, above all, that Brandeis set out to address. As he saw it, American Jews lacked something important that other Americans possessed: a national past. Others could point to an ancestral homeland and take pride in it and in themselves. Brandeis especially admired Irish-Americans in this respect and for manifesting their opposition to continued British rule in Ireland.

Arguing that this kind of political concern and involvement is entirely consistent with American patriotism, and indeed enhances it, he proclaimed that "Every Irish-American who contributed towards advancing home rule was a better man and a better American for the sacrifice he made. Every American Jew who aids in advancing the Jewish settlement in Palestine . . . will likewise be a better man and a better American for doing so."

The ethical idealism of Brandeis made a powerful impression on Arthur Balfour when the British Foreign Secretary visited the United States in 1917 and discussed the future of Palestine. In turn, the Balfour Declaration vindicated the arguments that Brandeis had used in his appeals to the American Jewish community. It showed that Zionism was in harmony with patriotism in wartime because a Jewish Palestine was an Allied war goal. Soon afterward it also became an officially supported American goal. On the occasion of the Jewish New Year in September 1918, President Wilson endorsed the principles of the Balfour Declaration in a letter of holiday greetings to the American Jewish community.

Whether because of the Balfour Declaration or because of Brandeis's effective and professional leadership, support for Zionism within the Jewish community grew dramatically. In 1919 membership of the Zionist Federation grew to more than 175,000, though Zionist supporters remained a minority group within American Jewry and still en-

[2]Oscar Straus, Secretary of Commerce and Labor from 1906 to 1909.

countered fierce opposition from the richer and more established Jews — opposition that was not really overcome until the 1940s. But Brandeis had made American Zionism into a substantial organization along the lines pioneered by Irish-Americans who supported independence for Ireland; and the Balfour Declaration had helped him to do so — even though the Foreign Office had issued the declaration in part because they supposed such a force was already in existence and needed to be appeased.

$$\boxed{170}$$

The Zionist and Arab Cases to the Anglo-American Committee of Inquiry

After World War I, the victorious allies transferred control of Palestine from defeated Turkey to Britain. The new League of Nations sanctioned the mandate system as a preparatory stage to eventual independence. Jewish immigration to Palestine continued, but in response to Arab rebellions from 1936 to 1939, Britain effectively rescinded the Balfour Declaration and ended Jewish immigration in 1939. In 1942, in the midst of World War II, leading figures in the Zionist movement gathered at the Biltmore Hotel in New York City. Their "Biltmore Program" demanded renewed immigration, a British return to the policy of the Balfour Declaration, and the establishment of Palestine not only as "a home" for Jews, but as a Jewish state.

In the immediate aftermath of the Second World War, in November 1945, the new United Nations established the Anglo-American Committee of Inquiry to find a solution. The committee took testimony from Jews and Arabs, in Europe, America, Palestine, and the Middle East. In the following selections the committee's report, published in May 1946, summarized what it called "The Jewish Attitude" and "The Arab Attitude" towards the British Mandate of Palestine. What were the arguments of both sides in 1946? Were these two sides reconcilable?

Reports of the Anglo-American Committee of Inquiry, Confidential Files, Re, Palestine, 1944–1946, Chapter 5, "The Jewish Attitude," and Chapter 6, "The Arab Attitude." Available online at http://www.mideastweb.org/angloamerican.htm.

The report purports to present the two sides to the Palestine debate in an evenhanded way. Clearly, the committee interviewed many people, official and otherwise. Yet, the debate is filtered through the committee's lens. Even the terms *Jewish* and *Arab* focus the issue in a particular way. What do these terms capture, and what do they miss? How balanced does the report seem? How can you tell? Do you see any signs that the committee favors a particular political outcome? The Committee recommended the immediate acceptance of 100,000 Jewish refugees and the development of a binational state (including Jews and Arabs) under United Nations auspices. (See Map 26.1.) Which groups would have accepted, which opposed, a binational state?

Thinking Historically

It is difficult, if not impossible, to view this debate apart from the knowledge of what later occurred. This report was issued only two years before Israel declared, fought for, and won its independence. Yet one is struck by the lack of unanimity on this issue among the Jews of Palestine as well as the West. Why did some Jews object to Zionism? Are there other arguments from either side that surprise you? Are there any arguments for or against a Jewish state in Palestine that you would expect to find here, but do not? If so, how do you account for the absence of these arguments?

The Jewish Attitude

1. The Committee heard the Jewish case, presented at full length and with voluminous written evidence, in three series of public hearings — in Washington by the American Zionists, in London by the British Zionists, and finally and most massively by the Jewish Agency in Jerusalem. The basic policy advocated was always the same, the so-called Biltmore Program of 1942, with the additional demand that 100,000 certificates for immigration into Palestine should be issued immediately to relieve the distress in Europe. This policy can be summed up in three points: (1) that the Mandatory should hand over control of immigration to the Jewish Agency; (2) that it should abolish restrictions on the sale of land; and (3) that it should proclaim as its ultimate aim the establishment of a Jewish State as soon as a Jewish majority has been achieved. It should be noted that the demand for a Jewish State goes beyond the obligations of either the Balfour Declaration or the Mandate, and was expressly disowned by the Chairman of the Jewish Agency as late as 1932.

2. In all the hearings, although evidence was given by those sections of the Zionist movement which are critical of the Biltmore Program, most

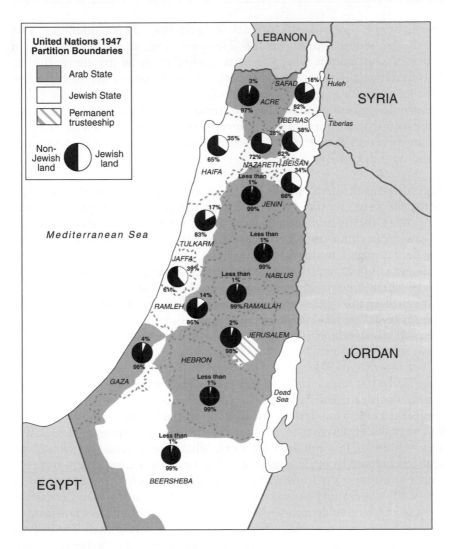

Map 26.1 The 1947 United Nations Partition Plan as a Reflection of Patterns of Land Ownership in Palestine by Subdistrict.

of the witnesses took the official Zionist line. The Committee also heard the Jewish opponents of Zionism: first, the small groups in America and Britain who advocate assimilation as an alternative to Jewish nationalism; second, Agudath Israel, an organization of orthodox Jews which supports unrestricted Jewish immigration into Palestine while objecting to the secular tendencies of Zionism; and third, representatives of important sections of Middle Eastern Jewry, many of whom fear that their friendly relations with the Arabs are being endangered by political Zionism.

3. As the result of the public hearings and of many private conversations, we came to the conclusion that the Biltmore Program has the support of the overwhelming majority of Zionists. Though many Jews have doubts about the wisdom of formulating these ultimate demands, the program has undoubtedly won the support of the Zionist movement as a whole, chiefly because it expresses the policy of Palestinian Jewry which now plays a leading role in the Jewish-Agency.

   Whether this almost universal support for the demand for a Jewish State is based on full knowledge of the implications of the policy and of the risks involved in carrying it out is, of course, quite another matter.

4. The position in Palestine itself is somewhat different. Here, where the issue is not the achievement of a remote idea, but is regarded as a matter of life and death for the Jewish nation, the position is naturally more complex. Palestinian Jewry is riddled with party differences. The number of political newspapers and periodicals bears witness to the variety and vitality of this political life, and, apart from pressure exerted on Jews considered to be disloyal to the National Home, we found little evidence to support the rumors that it was dangerous to advocate minority views. Of the major political parties, Mapai (the Labor Party) is far the biggest and largely determines the official line. Opposed to the Agency's policy are two main groups. On the one side stand two small but important parties: the Conservative Aliyah Hadashah (New Settlers), drawn chiefly from colonists of German and western European extraction, and Hashomer Hatzair, a socialist party which, while demanding the right of unrestricted immigration and land settlement, challenges the concept of the Jewish State and particularly emphasizes the need for cooperation with the Arabs. Hashomer Hatzair, though it did not appear before us, published shortly before we left Jerusalem a striking pamphlet in support of bi-nationalism. Very close to Hashomer Hatzair, but without its socialist ideology, stands Dr. Magnes and his small Thud group, whose importance is far greater than its numbers. Taken altogether, these Palestinian critics of the Biltmore Program certainly do not exceed at the moment one quarter of the Jewish population in Palestine. But they represent a constructive minority.

5. On the other side stands the Revisionist Party, numbering some one percent of the Jewish community, and beyond it the various more extreme groups, which call for active resistance to the White Paper[1] and participate in and openly support the present terrorist campaign. This wing of Palestinian Jewry derives its inspiration and its methods from the revolutionary traditions of Poland and eastern Europe. Many of these extremists are boys and girls under twenty, of good education, filled with a political fanaticism as self-sacrificing as it is pernicious.

6. The Biltmore Program can only be fully understood if it is studied against this background of Palestinian life. Like all political platforms, it is a result of conflicting political pressures, an attempt by the leadership to maintain unity without sacrificing principle. The Jew who lives and works in the National Home is deeply aware both of his achievements and of how much more could have been achieved with whole-hearted support by the Mandatory Power. His political outlook is thus a mixture of self-confident pride and bitter frustration: pride that he has turned the desert and the swamp into a land flowing with milk and honey; frustration because he is denied opportunity of settlement in nine-tenths of that Eretz Israel which he considers his own by right; pride that he has disproved the theory that the Jews cannot build a healthy community based on the tilling of the soil; frustration that the Jew is barred entry to the National Home, where that community is now in being; pride that he is taking part in a bold collective experiment; frustration because he feels himself hampered by British officials whom he often regards as less able than himself; pride because in Palestine he feels himself at last a free member of a free community; frustration because he lives, not under a freely elected government, but under an autocratic if humane regime.

7. The main complaint of the Jews of Palestine is that, since the White Paper of 1930, the Mandatory Power has slowed up the development of the National Home in order to placate Arab opposition. The sudden rise of immigration after the Nazi seizure of power had as its direct result the three and a half years of Arab revolt, during which the Jew had to train himself for self-defence, and to accustom himself to the life of a pioneer in an armed stockade. The high barbed wire and the watchtowers, manned by the settlement police day and night, strike the eye of the visitor as he approaches every collective colony. They are an outward symbol of the new attitude to life and politics which developed among the Palestinian Jews between 1936 and 1938. As a Jewish settler said to a member of the Committee: "We are the vanguard of a great army, de-

---

[1]The White Paper of 1939 rescinded British support of the Balfour Declaration. Instead Britain promised to create a Palestinian Arab state and reduce the immigration of Jews. [Ed.]

fending the advanced positions until the reinforcements arrive from Europe."

8. The Jews in Palestine are convinced that Arab violence paid [off]. Throughout the Arab rising, the Jews in the National Home, despite every provocation, obeyed the orders of their leaders and exercised a remarkable self-discipline. They shot, but only in self-defence; they rarely took reprisals on the Arab population. They state bitterly that the reward for this restraint was the Conference and the White Paper of 1939. The Mandatory Power, they argue, yielded to force, cut down immigration, and thus caused the death of thousands of Jews in Hitler's gas chambers. The Arabs, who had recourse to violence, received substantial concessions, while the Jews, who had put their faith in the Mandatory, were compelled to accept what they regard as a violation of the spirit and the letter of the Mandate.

The Arab Attitude

1. The Committee heard a brief presentation of the Arab case in Washington, statements made in London by delegates from the Arab States to the United Nations, a fuller statement from the Secretary General and other representatives of the Arab League in Cairo, and evidence given on behalf of the Arab Higher (committee) and the Arab Office in Jerusalem. In addition, subcommittees visited Baghdad, Riyadh, Damascus, Beirut, and Amman, where they were informed of the views of Government and of unofficial spokesmen.

2. Stripped to the bare essentials, the Arab case is based upon the fact that Palestine is a country which the Arabs have occupied for more than a thousand years, and a denial of the Jewish historical claims to Palestine. In issuing the *Balfour Declaration,* the Arabs maintain, the British Government were giving away something that did not belong to Britain, and they have consistently argued that the Mandate conflicted with the Covenant of the League of Nations from which it derived its authority. The Arabs deny that the part played by the British in freeing them from the Turks gave Great Britain a right to dispose of their country. Indeed, they assert that Turkish was preferable to British rule, if the latter involves their eventual subjection to the Jews. They consider the Mandate a violation of their right of self-determination since it is forcing upon them an immigration which they do not desire and will not tolerate — an invasion of Palestine by the Jews.

3. The Arabs of Palestine point out that all the surrounding Arab States have now been granted independence. They argue that they are just as

advanced as are the citizens of the nearby States, and they demand independence for Palestine now. The promises which have been made to them in the name of Great Britain, and the assurances concerning Palestine given to Arab leaders by Presidents Roosevelt and Truman, have been understood by the Arabs of Palestine as a recognition of the principle that they should enjoy the same rights as those enjoyed by the neighboring countries. Christian Arabs unite with Moslems in all of these contentions. They demand that their independence should be recognized at once, and they would like Palestine, as a self-governing country, to join the Arab League.

4. The Arabs attach the highest importance to the fulfillment of the promises made by the British Government in the White Paper of 1939. King Abdul Aziz ibn Saud, when he spoke with three members of the Committee at Riyadh, made frequent reference both to these promises and to the assurances given him by the late President Roosevelt at their meeting in February, 1945. His Majesty made clear the strain which would be placed upon Arab friendship with Great Britain and the United States by any policy which Arabs regarded as a betrayal of these pledges. The same warning was repeated by an Arab witness in Jerusalem, who said that "Zionism for the Arabs has become a test of Western intentions."

5. The suggestion that self-government should be withheld from Palestine until the Jews have acquired a majority seems outrageous to the Arabs. They wish to be masters in their own house. The Arabs were opposed to the idea of a Jewish National Home even before the Biltmore Program and the demand for a Jewish State. Needless to say, however, their opposition has become more intense and more bitter since that program was adopted.

6. The Arabs maintain that they have never been anti-Semitic; indeed, they are Semites themselves. Arab spokesmen profess the greatest sympathy for the persecuted Jews of Europe, but they point out that they have not been responsible for this persecution and that it is not just that they should be compelled to atone for the sins of Western peoples by accepting into their country hundreds of thousands of victims of European anti-Semitism. Some Arabs even declare that they might be willing to do their share in providing for refugees on a quota basis if the United States, the British Commonwealth, and other Western countries would do the same.

ABBA EBAN
The Refugee Problem

The United Nations did not create a binational state as the Anglo-American committee recommended. By 1947 the immigration of Jewish European refugees, many who were survivors of the Nazi holocaust, had increased the Jewish population of Palestine to 600,000, but the Arab population had risen to 1.2 million. A single state would have been two-thirds Arab and one-third Jewish. Zionists wanted a state where Jews were in the majority. With U.S. support, the United Nations passed a resolution in November 1947 that partitioned Palestine into separate Jewish and Arab states, to be established when the British Mandate ended in 1948. (See Map 26.2.) Immediately Palestinian Arabs went on strike in protest. Zionist forces readily took over towns and cities, forcing Arabs to leave. The conflict came to a head in May 1948, when Israel declared its independence and the armies of surrounding Arab states went to war to prevent it. By the time of the armistice in 1949, Israel had increased its territory by 20 percent. Arabs numbering 750,000 had left their homes and become refugees. The conditions of their departure became a matter of contention in future years.

In 1958, Abba Eban, who later became Israeli foreign minister, gave the following explanation in his address to the United Nations. What, according to Eban, were the reasons why so many Palestinian Arabs left their homes in 1948? Who was responsible?

Thinking Historically

Diplomatic speeches before the United Nations rarely contain big surprises, and this is no exception. There may be, however, elements of Abba Eban's address that raise questions. Does he give you a clear idea of how these refugees were created? Could he be clearer about the process? What questions would you want to ask if you were in the audience?

Walter Laqueur and Barry Rubin, eds., *The Israel-Arab Reader* (New York: Penguin Books, 1995), 129–32.

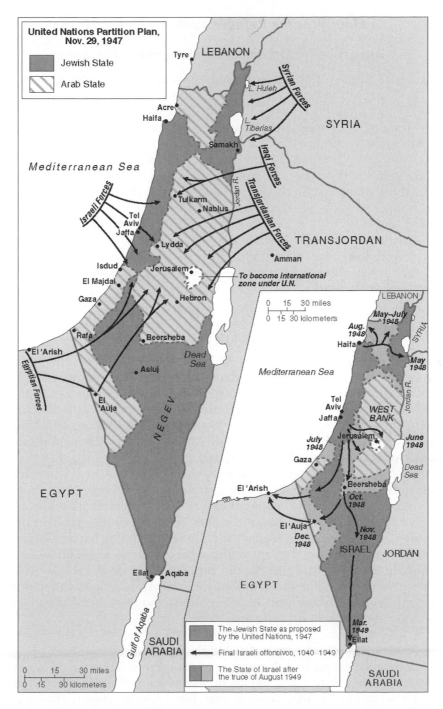

Map 26.2 1948 War and Israeli Expansion beyond the Partition Lines to 1949.

How Was the Refugee Problem Caused?

Aggression by Arab States Created Refugee Problem

The Arab refugee problem was caused by a war of aggression, launched by the Arab States against Israel in 1947 and 1948. Let there be no mistake. If there had been no war against Israel, with its consequent harvest of bloodshed, misery, panic, and flight, there would be no problem of Arab refugees today. Once you determine the responsibility for that war, you have determined the responsibility for the refugee problem. Nothing in the history of our generation is clearer or less controversial than the initiative of Arab governments for the conflict out of which the refugee tragedy emerged. The historic origins of that conflict are clearly defined by the confessions of Arab governments themselves: "This will be a war of extermination," declared the Secretary General of the Arab League speaking for the governments of six Arab States; "It will be a momentous massacre to be spoken of like the Mongolian massacre and the Crusades."

Palestine Arabs Urged to Flee by Arab Leaders

The assault began on the last day of November 1947. From then until the expiration of the British Mandate in May 1948 the Arab States, in concert with Palestine Arab leaders, plunged the land into turmoil and chaos. On the day of Israel's Declaration of Independence, on May 14, 1948, the armed forces of Egypt, Jordan, Syria, Lebanon, and Iraq, supported by contingents from Saudi Arabia and the Yemen, crossed their frontiers and marched against Israel. The perils which then confronted our community; the danger which darkened every life and home; the successful repulse of the assault and the emergence of Israel into the life of the world community are all chapters of past history, gone but not forgotten. But the traces of that conflict still remain deeply inscribed upon our region's life. Caught up in the havoc and tension of war; demoralized by the flight of their leaders; urged on by irresponsible promises that they would return to inherit the spoils of Israel's destruction — hundreds of thousands of Arabs sought the shelter of Arab lands. A survey by an international body in 1957 described these violent events in the following terms:

> As early as the first months of 1948 the Arab League issued orders exhorting the people to seek a temporary refuge in neighboring countries, later to return to their abodes in the wake of the victorious Arab armies and obtain their share of abandoned Jewish property (Research Group for European Migration Problems Bulletin, Vol. V, No. 1, 1957, p. 10).

Contemporary statements by Arab leaders fully confirm this version. On 16 August 1948 Msgr. George Hakim, the Greek Catholic Archbishop of Galilee, recalled:

> The refugees had been confident that their absence from Palestine would not last long; that they would return within a few days — within a week or two; their leaders had promised them that the Arab armies would crush the "Zionist gangs" very quickly and that there would be no need for panic or fear of a long exile.

A month later on September 15, 1948, Mr. Emile Ghoury who had been the Secretary of the Arab Higher Committee at the time of the Arab invasion of Israel declared:

> I do not want to impugn anyone but only to help the refugees. The fact that there are these refugees is the direct consequence of the action of the Arab States in opposing partition and the Jewish State. The Arab States agreed upon this policy unanimously and they must share in the solution of the problem.

Misery Is Result of Unlawful Resort to Force by Arabs

No less compelling than these avowals by Arab leaders are the judgments of United Nations organs. In April 1948, when the flight of the refugees was in full swing, the United Nations Palestine Commission inscribed its verdict on the tablets of history:

> Arab opposition to the plan of the Assembly of 29 November 1947 has taken the form of organized efforts by strong Arab elements, both inside and outside Palestine, to prevent its implementation and to thwart its objectives by threats and acts of violence, including repeated armed incursions into Palestine territory. The Commission has had to report to the Security Council that powerful Arab interests, both inside and outside Palestine, are defying the resolution of the General Assembly and are engaged in a deliberate effort to alter by force the settlement envisaged therein.

This is a description of the events between November 1947 and May 1948 when the Arab exodus began. Months later, when the tide of battle rolled away, its consequences of bereavement, devastation and panic were left behind. At the General Assembly meetings in 1948 the United Nations Acting Mediator recorded a grave international judgment:

> The Arab States had forcibly opposed the existence of the Jewish State in Palestine in direct opposition to the wishes of two-thirds of the members of the Assembly. Nevertheless their armed intervention proved useless. The [Mediator's] report was based solely on the fact

that the Arab States had no right to resort to force and that the United Nations should exert its authority to prevent such a use of force.

The significance of the Arab assault upon Israel by five neighboring States had been reflected in a letter addressed by the Secretary General of the United Nations to representatives of the permanent members of the Security Council on 16 May 1948: —

"The Egyptian Government," wrote the Secretary-General, "has declared in a cablegram to the President of the Security Council on 15 May that Egyptian armed forces have entered Palestine and it has engaged in 'armed intervention' in that country. On 16 May I received a cablegram from the Arab League making similar statements on behalf of the Arab States. I consider it my duty to emphasize to you that *this is the first time since the adoption of the Charter that Member States have openly declared that they have engaged in armed intervention outside their own territory.*"

Arab Governments Must Accept Responsibility

These are only a few of the documents which set out the responsibility of the Arab Governments for the warfare of which the refugees are the main surviving victims. Even after a full decade it is difficult to sit here with equanimity and listen to Arab representatives disengaging themselves from any responsibility for the travail and anguish which they caused. I recall this history not for the purpose of recrimination, but because of its direct bearing on the Committee's discussion. Should not the representatives of Arab States, as the authors of this tragedy, come here in a mood of humility and repentance rather than in shrill and negative indignation? Since these governments have, by acts of policy, created this tragic problem, *does it not follow that the world community has an unimpeachable right to claim their full assistance in its solution?* How can governments create a vast humanitarian problem by their action — then wash their hands of all responsibility for its alleviation? The claim of the world community on the cooperation of Arab governments is all the more compelling when we reflect that these States, in their vast lands, command all the resources and conditions which would enable them to liberate the refugees from their plight, in full dignity and freedom.

With this history in mind the Committee should not find it difficult to reject the assertion that the guilt for the refugee problem lies with the United Nations itself. The refugee problem was not created by the General Assembly's recommendation for the establishment of Israel. It was created by the attempts of Arab governments to destroy that recommendation by force. The crisis arose not as Arab spokesmen have said because the United Nations adopted a resolution eleven years ago; it arose because Arab governments attacked that resolution by force. If the United Nations proposal had been peacefully accepted, there would be no refugee problem today hanging as a cloud upon the tense horizons of the Middle East.

The next question is — why has the problem endured?

Why Does the Refugee Problem Endure?

Refugee Problem Cannot Be Solved by Repatriation

In his statement to the Committee on November 10, 1958, the representative of the United States said:

> In our view it is not good enough consciously to perpetuate for over a decade the dependent status of nearly a million refugees.

Other speakers in this debate have echoed a similar sense of frustration.

Apart from the question of its origin, the perpetuation of this refugee problem is an unnatural event, running against the whole course of experience and precedent. Since the end of the Second World War, problems affecting forty million refugees have confronted Governments in various parts of the world. In no case, except that of the Arab refugees, amounting to less than two percent of the whole, has the international community shown constant responsibility and provided lavish aid. In every other case a solution has been found by the integration of refugees into their host countries. Nine million Koreans; 900,000 refugees from the conflict in Viet Nam; 8½ million Hindus and Sikhs leaving Pakistan for India; 6½ million Moslems fleeing India to Pakistan; 700,000 Chinese refugees in Hong Kong; 13 million Germans from the Sudetenland, Poland, and other East European States reaching West and East Germany; thousands of Turkish refugees from Bulgaria; 440,000 Finns separated from their homeland by a change of frontier; 450,000 refugees from Arab lands arrived destitute in Israel; and an equal number converging on Israel from the remnants of the Jewish holocaust in Europe — these form the tragic procession of the world's refugee population in the past two decades. *In every case but that of the Arab refugees now in Arab lands the countries in which the refugees sought shelter have facilitated their integration.* In this case alone has integration been obstructed.

The paradox is the more astonishing when we reflect that the kinship of language, religion, social background and national sentiment existing between the Arab refugees and their Arab host countries has been at least as intimate as those existing between any other host countries and any other refugee groups. It is impossible to escape the conclusion that the integration of Arab refugees into the life of the

Arab world is an objectively feasible process which has been resisted for political reasons.

In a learned study on refugee problems published by the Carnegie Endowment for International Peace in November 1957 under the title "Century of the Homeless Man" Dr. Elfan Rees, Advisor on Refugees to the World Council of Churches, sums up the international experience in the following terms:

> No large scale refugee problem has ever been solved by repatriation, and there are certainly no grounds for believing that this particular problem can be so solved. Nothing can bring it about except wars which in our time would leave nothing to go back to. War has never solved a refugee problem and it is not in the books that a modern war would.

$$\boxed{172}$$

ARI SHAVIT

An Interview with Benny Morris

Benny Morris is the leader of the academic Israeli "New History," which has challenged many of the founding myths of Israel and the Zionist movement. His book *The Birth of the Palestinian Refugee Problem* (1987) showed that Palestinian Arabs did not leave voluntarily in 1948, but were terrorized and forced from their villages by militarized Zionists. His upending of some of the sacred Israeli founding myths gave Morris the reputation of a radical anti-Zionist, but in this interview in the Israeli newspaper *Ha'aretz* in January 2004, Morris revealed he was not.

How did Morris's research challenge older Israeli views like that of Abba Eban in the previous selection? How were Morris's conclusions from that research different from what you might expect?

Ari Shavit, "Survival of the Fittest: An Interview with Benny Morris," *Ha'aretz*, 9 (January 2004). Available online at http://www.haaretzdaily.com/hasen/pages/ShArt.jhtml?itemNo=380986.

Thinking Historically

In this selection, the interviewer, Ari Shavit, cues the surprises for us. They are on both the factual level of Benny Morris's research and the personal level of Morris's response to his research. What do you find surprising or unexpected in this interview? How do those unexpected discoveries deepen your understanding of the conflict?

*B*enny Morris, *in the month ahead the new version of your book on the birth of the Palestinian refugee problem is due to be published. Who will be less pleased with the book — the Israelis or the Palestinians?*

"The revised book is a double-edged sword. It is based on many documents that were not available to me when I wrote the original book, most of them from the Israel Defense Forces Archives. What the new material shows is that there were far more Israeli acts of massacre than I had previously thought. To my surprise, there were also many cases of rape. In the months of April-May 1948, units of the Haganah [the pre–state defense force that was the precursor of the IDF] were given operational orders that stated explicitly that they were to uproot the villagers, expel them, and destroy the villages themselves.

"At the same time, it turns out that there was a series of orders issued by the Arab Higher Committee and by the Palestinian intermediate levels to remove children, women, and the elderly from the villages. So that on the one hand, the book reinforces the accusation against the Zionist side, but on the other hand it also proves that many of those who left the villages did so with the encouragement of the Palestinian leadership itself."

According to your new findings, how many cases of Israeli rape were there in 1948?

"About a dozen. In Acre four soldiers raped a girl and murdered her and her father. In Jaffa, soldiers of the Kiryati Brigade raped one girl and tried to rape several more. At Hunin, which is in the Galilee, two girls were raped and then murdered. There were one or two cases of rape at Tantura, south of Haifa. There was one case of rape at Qula, in the center of the country. At the village of Abu Shusha, near Kibbutz Gezer [in the Ramle area] there were four female prisoners, one of whom was raped a number of times. And there were other cases. Usually more than one soldier was involved. Usually there were one or two Palestinian girls. In a large proportion of the cases the event ended with murder. Because neither the victims nor the rapists liked to report these events, we have to assume that the dozen cases of rape that were reported, which I found, are not the whole story. They are just the tip of the iceberg."

According to your findings, how many acts of Israeli massacre were perpetrated in 1948?

"Twenty-four. In some cases four or five people were executed, in others the numbers were 70, 80, 100. There was also a great deal of arbitrary killing. Two old men are spotted walking in a field — they are shot. A woman is found in an abandoned village — she is shot. There are cases such as the village of Dawayima [in the Hebron region], in which a column entered the village with all guns blazing and killed anything that moved.

"The worst cases were Saliha (70–80 killed), Deir Yassin (100–110), Lod (250), Dawayima (hundreds), and perhaps Abu Shusha (70). There is no unequivocal proof of a large-scale massacre at Tantura, but war crimes were perpetrated there. At Jaffa there was a massacre about which nothing had been known until now. The same at Arab al Muwasi, in the north. About half of the acts of massacre were part of Operation Hiram [in the north, in October 1948]: at Safsaf, Saliha, Jish, Eilaboun, Arab al Muwasi, Deir al Asad, Majdal Krum, Sasa. In Operation Hiram there was a unusually high concentration of executions of people against a wall or next to a well in an orderly fashion.

"That can't be chance. It's a pattern. Apparently, various officers who took part in the operation understood that the expulsion order they received permitted them to do these deeds in order to encourage the population to take to the roads. The fact is that no one was punished for these acts of murder. Ben-Gurion silenced the matter. He covered up for the officers who did the massacres."

What you are telling me here, as though by the way, is that in Operation Hiram there was a comprehensive and explicit expulsion order. Is that right?

"Yes. One of the revelations in the book is that on October 31, 1948, the commander of the Northern Front, Moshe Carmel, issued an order in writing to his units to expedite the removal of the Arab population. Carmel took this action immediately after a visit by Ben-Gurion to the Northern Command in Nazareth. There is no doubt in my mind that this order originated with Ben-Gurion. Just as the expulsion order for the city of Lod, which was signed by Yitzhak Rabin, was issued immediately after Ben-Gurion visited the headquarters of Operation Dani [July 1948]."

Are you saying that Ben-Gurion was personally responsible for a deliberate and systematic policy of mass expulsion?

"From April 1948, Ben-Gurion is projecting a message of transfer. There is no explicit order of his in writing, there is no orderly comprehensive policy, but there is an atmosphere of [population] transfer. The transfer idea is in the air. The entire leadership understands that this is the idea. The officer corps understands what is required of them. Under Ben-Gurion, a consensus of transfer is created."

Ben-Gurion was a "transferist"?

"Of course. Ben-Gurion was a transferist. He understood that there could be no Jewish state with a large and hostile Arab minority in its midst. There would be no such state. It would not be able to exist."

I don't hear you condemning him.

"Ben-Gurion was right. If he had not done what he did, a state would not have come into being. That has to be clear. It is impossible to evade it. Without the uprooting of the Palestinians, a Jewish state would not have arisen here."

When Ethnic Cleansing Is Justified

Benny Morris, for decades you have been researching the dark side of Zionism. You are an expert on the atrocities of 1948. In the end, do you in effect justify all this? Are you an advocate of the transfer of 1948?

"There is no justification for acts of rape. There is no justification for acts of massacre. Those are war crimes. But in certain conditions, expulsion is not a war crime. I don't think that the expulsions of 1948 were war crimes. You can't make an omelet without breaking eggs. You have to dirty your hands."

We are talking about the killing of thousands of people, the destruction of an entire society.

"A society that aims to kill you forces you to destroy it. When the choice is between destroying or being destroyed, it's better to destroy."

There is something chilling about the quiet way in which you say that.

"If you expected me to burst into tears, I'm sorry to disappoint you. I will not do that."

So when the commanders of Operation Dani are standing there and observing the long and terrible column of the 50,000 people expelled from Lod walking eastward, you stand there with them? You justify them?

"I definitely understand them. I understand their motives. I don't think they felt any pangs of conscience, and in their place I wouldn't have felt pangs of conscience. Without that act, they would not have won the war and the state would not have come into being."

You do not condemn them morally?

"No."

They perpetrated ethnic cleansing.

"There are circumstances in history that justify ethnic cleansing. I know that this term is completely negative in the discourse of the twenty-first century, but when the choice is between ethnic cleansing and genocide — the annihilation of your people — I prefer ethnic cleansing."

And that was the situation in 1948?

"That was the situation. That is what Zionism faced. A Jewish state would not have come into being without the uprooting of 700,000 Palestinians. Therefore it was necessary to uproot them. There was no choice but to expel that population. It was necessary to cleanse the hinterland and cleanse the border areas and cleanse the main roads. It was necessary to cleanse the villages from which our convoys and our settlements were fired on."

The term "to cleanse" is terrible.

"I know it doesn't sound nice but that's the term they used at the time. I adopted it from all the 1948 documents in which I am immersed."

What you are saying is hard to listen to and hard to digest. You sound hard-hearted.

"I feel sympathy for the Palestinian people, which truly underwent a hard tragedy. I feel sympathy for the refugees themselves. But if the desire to establish a Jewish state here is legitimate, there was no other choice. It was impossible to leave a large fifth column in the country. From the moment the Yishuv [pre-1948 Jewish community in Palestine] was attacked by the Palestinians and afterward by the Arab states, there was no choice but to expel the Palestinian population. To uproot it in the course of war.

"Remember another thing: the Arab people gained a large slice of the planet. Not thanks to its skills or its great virtues, but because it conquered and murdered and forced those it conquered to convert during many generations. But in the end the Arabs have 22 states. The Jewish people did not have even one state. There was no reason in the world why it should not have one state. Therefore, from my point of view, the need to establish this state in this place overcame the injustice that was done to the Palestinians by uprooting them."

And morally speaking, you have no problem with that deed?

"That is correct. Even the great American democracy could not have been created without the annihilation of the Indians. There are cases in which the overall, final good justifies harsh and cruel acts that are committed in the course of history."

And in our case it effectively justifies a population transfer.

"That's what emerges."

And you take that in stride? War crimes? Massacres? The burning fields and the devastated villages of the Nakba? [catastrophe]

"You have to put things in proportion. These are small war crimes. All told, if we take all the massacres and all the executions of 1948, we come to about 800 who were killed. In comparison to the massacres that were perpetrated in Bosnia, that's peanuts. In comparison to the massacres the Russians perpetrated against the Germans at Stalingrad, that's chicken feed. When you take into account that there was a bloody civil war here and that we lost an entire 1 percent of the population, you find that we behaved very well."

The Next Transfer

You went through an interesting process. You went to research Ben-Gurion and the Zionist establishment critically, but in the end you actually identify with them. You are as tough in your words as they were in their deeds.

"You may be right. Because I investigated the conflict in depth, I was forced to cope with the in-depth questions that those people coped with. I understood the problematic character of the situation they faced and maybe I adopted part of their universe of concepts. But I do not identify with Ben-Gurion. I think he made a serious historical mistake in 1948. Even though he understood the demographic issue and the need to establish a Jewish state without a large Arab minority, he got cold feet during the war. In the end, he faltered."

I'm not sure I understand. Are you saying that Ben-Gurion erred in expelling too few Arabs?

"If he was already engaged in expulsion, maybe he should have done a complete job. I know that this stuns the Arabs and the liberals and the politically correct types. But my feeling is that this place would be quieter and know less suffering if the matter had been resolved once and for all. If Ben-Gurion had carried out a large expulsion and cleansed the whole country — the whole Land of Israel, as far as the Jordan River. It may yet turn out that this was his fatal mistake. If he had carried out a full expulsion — rather than a partial one — he would have stabilized the State of Israel for generations."

I find it hard to believe what I am hearing.

"If the end of the story turns out to be a gloomy one for the Jews, it will be because Ben-Gurion did not complete the transfer in 1948. Because he left a large and volatile demographic reserve in the West Bank and Gaza and within Israel itself."

In his place, would you have expelled them all? All the Arabs in the country?

"But I am not a statesman. I do not put myself in his place. But as an historian, I assert that a mistake was made here. Yes. The non-completion of the transfer was a mistake."

And today? Do you advocate a transfer today?

"If you are asking me whether I support the transfer and expulsion of the Arabs from the West Bank, Gaza, and perhaps even from Galilee and the Triangle, I say not at this moment. I am not willing to be a partner to that act. In the present circumstances it is neither moral nor realistic. The world would not allow it, the Arab world would not allow it; it would destroy the Jewish society from within. But I am ready to tell you that in other circumstances, apocalyptic ones, which are liable to be realized in five or ten years, I can see expulsions. If we find ourselves with atomic weapons around us, or if there is a general Arab attack on us and a situation of warfare on the front with Arabs in the rear shooting at convoys on their way to the front, acts of expulsion will be entirely reasonable. They may even be essential."

Including the expulsion of Israeli Arabs?

"The Israeli Arabs are a time bomb. Their slide into complete Palestinization has made them an emissary of the enemy that is among us. They are a potential fifth column. In both demographic and security terms they are liable to undermine the state. So that if Israel again finds itself in a situation of existential threat, as in 1948, it may be forced to act as it did then. If we are attacked by Egypt (after an Islamist revolution in Cairo) and by Syria, and chemical and biological missiles slam into our cities, and at the same time Israeli Palestinians attack us from behind, I can see an expulsion situation. It could happen. If the threat to Israel is existential, expulsion will be justified."

Cultural Dementia

Besides being tough, you are also very gloomy. You weren't always like that, were you?

"My turning point began after 2000. I wasn't a great optimist even before that. True, I always voted Labor or Meretz or Sheli [a dovish party of the late 1970s], and in 1988 I refused to serve in the territories and was jailed for it, but I always doubted the intentions of the Palestinians. The events of Camp David and what followed in their wake turned the doubt into certainty. When the Palestinians rejected the proposal of [prime minister Ehud] Barak in July 2000 and the Clinton proposal in December 2000, I understood that they are unwilling to accept the two-state solution. They want it all. . . .

The situation as you describe it is extremely harsh. You are not entirely convinced that we can survive here, are you?

"The possibility of annihilation exists."

Would you describe yourself as an apocalyptic person?

"The whole Zionist project is apocalyptic. It exists within hostile surroundings and in a certain sense its existence is unreasonable. It wasn't reasonable for it to succeed in 1881 and it wasn't reasonable for it to succeed in 1948 and it's not reasonable that it will succeed now. Nevertheless, it has come this far. In a certain way it is miraculous. I live the events of 1948, and 1948 projects itself on what could happen here. Yes, I think of Armageddon. It's possible. Within the next 20 years there could be an atomic war here."

If Zionism is so dangerous for the Jews and if Zionism makes the Arabs so wretched, maybe it's a mistake?

"No, Zionism was not a mistake. The desire to establish a Jewish state here was a legitimate one, a positive one. But given the character of Islam and given the character of the Arab nation, it was a mistake to think that it would be possible to establish a tranquil state here that lives in harmony with its surroundings."

Which leaves us, nevertheless, with two possibilities: either a cruel, tragic Zionism, or the forgoing of Zionism.

"Yes. That's so. You have pared it down, but that's correct."

Would you agree that this historical reality is intolerable, that there is something inhuman about it?

"Yes. But that's so for the Jewish people, not the Palestinians. A people that suffered for 2,000 years, that went through the Holocaust, arrives at its patrimony but is thrust into a renewed round of bloodshed, that is perhaps the road to annihilation. In terms of cosmic justice, that's terrible. It's far more shocking than what happened in 1948 to a small part of the Arab nation that was then in Palestine."

So what you are telling me is that you live the Palestinian Nakba of the past less than you live the possible Jewish Nakba of the future?

"Yes. Destruction could be the end of this process. It could be the end of the Zionist experiment. And that's what really depresses and scares me."

The title of the book you are now publishing in Hebrew is "Victims." In the end, then, your argument is that of the two victims of this conflict, we are the bigger one.

"Yes. Exactly. We are the greater victims in the course of history and we are also the greater potential victim. Even though we are oppressing the Palestinians, we are the weaker side here. We are a small minority in a large sea of hostile Arabs who want to eliminate us. So it's possible that when their desire is realized, everyone will understand what I am saying to you now. Everyone will understand we are the true victims. But by then it will be too late."

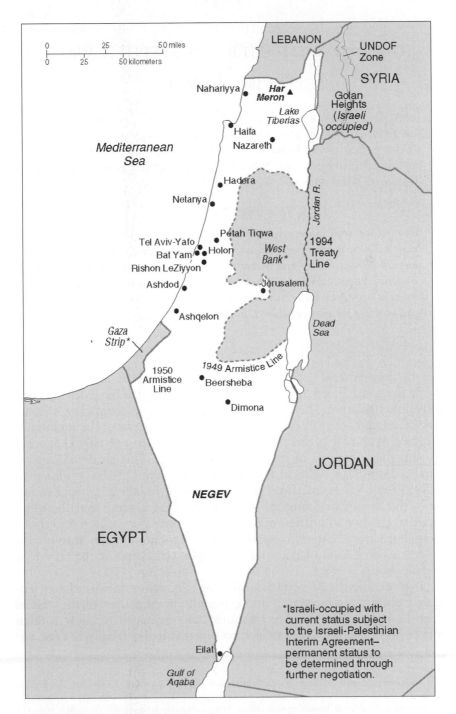

0   25   50 miles
0   25   50 kilometers

LEBANON

UNDOF
Zone

SYRIA

Nahariyya

*Har
Meron* ▲

Lake
Tiberias

Golan
Heights
(*Israeli
occupied*)

Haifa

Nazareth

*Mediterranean
Sea*

Hadera

Netanya

Petah Tiqwa

Tel Aviv-Yafo

Holon

Bat Yam

Rishon LeZiyyon

*West
Bank**

Jordan R.

1994
Treaty
Line

Ashdod

Jerusalem

Ashqelon

Dead
Sea

*Gaza
Strip**

1949 Armistice Line

1950
Armistice
Line

Beersheba

Dimona

JORDAN

NEGEV

EGYPT

*Israeli-occupied with
current status subject
to the Israeli-Palestinian
Interim Agreement–
permanent status to
be determined through
further negotiation.

Eilat

*Gulf of
Aqaba*

Map 26.3   Israel and Palestine, 2006.

JOHN MEARSHEIMER AND STEPHEN WALT

The Israel Lobby

John Mearsheimer and Stephen Walt are American political scientists, not historians, but in this excerpt from a paper they present a history of U.S. policy toward Israel since 1967 that is different from the more traditional interpretations. What is their argument? How might you dispute it? What do you find convincing?

Thinking Historically

This paper was extremely controversial when it was published in March 2006. Even today you are likely to find the claims the authors make well outside the mainstream of public opinion about Israel and the United States. Which of these claims do you find most surprising? On reflection, are there any which you are prone to dismiss? Which lead you to new ways of thinking about the subject?

For the past several decades, and especially since the Six-Day War in 1967, the centrepiece of U.S. Middle Eastern policy has been its relationship with Israel. The combination of unwavering support for Israel and the related effort to spread "democracy" throughout the region has inflamed Arab and Islamic opinion and jeopardised not only U.S. security but that of much of the rest of the world. This situation has no equal in American political history. Why has the U.S. been willing to set aside its own security and that of many of its allies in order to advance the interests of another state? One might assume that the bond between the two countries was based on shared strategic interests or compelling moral imperatives, but neither explanation can account for the remarkable level of material and diplomatic support that the U.S. provides.

Instead, the thrust of U.S. policy in the region derives almost entirely from domestic politics, and especially the activities of the "Israel Lobby." Other special-interest groups have managed to skew foreign policy, but no lobby has managed to divert it as far from what the na-

John Mearsheimer and Stephen Walt, "The Israel Lobby," *London Review of Books,* 28, no. 6 (March 23, 2006). Available online at http://www.lrb.co.uk/v28/n06/print/mear01_ .html. Also available at http://ksgnotes1.harvard.edu/Research/wpaper.nsf/rwp/RWP06-011 as Working Paper Number: RWP06-011. Submitted: March 13, 2006, Harvard University, Kennedy School of Government, Faculty Research Working Paper Series.

tional interest would suggest, while simultaneously convincing Americans that U.S. interests and those of the other country — in this case, Israel — are essentially identical.

Since the October War in 1973, Washington has provided Israel with a level of support dwarfing that given to any other state. It has been the largest annual recipient of direct economic and military assistance since 1976, and is the largest recipient in total since World War Two, to the tune of well over $140 billion (in 2004 dollars). Israel receives about $3 billion in direct assistance each year, roughly one-fifth of the foreign aid budget, and worth about $500 a year for every Israeli. This largesse is especially striking since Israel is now a wealthy industrial state with a per capita income roughly equal to that of South Korea or Spain. . . .

Beginning in the 1990s, and even more after 9/11, U.S. support has been justified by the claim that both states are threatened by terrorist groups originating in the Arab and Muslim world, and by "rogue states" that back these groups and seek weapons of mass destruction. This is taken to mean not only that Washington should give Israel a free hand in dealing with the Palestinians and not press it to make concessions until all Palestinian terrorists are imprisoned or dead, but that the U.S. should go after countries like Iran and Syria. Israel is thus seen as a crucial ally in the war on terror, because its enemies are America's enemies. In fact, Israel is a liability in the war on terror and the broader effort to deal with rogue states.

"Terrorism" is not a single adversary, but a tactic employed by a wide array of political groups. The terrorist organisations that threaten Israel do not threaten the United States, except when it intervenes against them (as in Lebanon in 1982). Moreover, Palestinian terrorism is not random violence directed against Israel or "the West"; it is largely a response to Israel's prolonged campaign to colonise the West Bank and Gaza Strip.

More important, saying that Israel and the U.S. are united by a shared terrorist threat has the causal relationship backwards: The U.S. has a terrorism problem in good part because it is so closely allied with Israel, not the other way around. Support for Israel is not the only source of anti-American terrorism, but it is an important one, and it makes winning the war on terror more difficult. There is no question that many al-Qaida leaders, including Osama bin Laden, are motivated by Israel's presence in Jerusalem and the plight of the Palestinians. Unconditional support for Israel makes it easier for extremists to rally popular support and to attract recruits.

As for so-called rogue states in the Middle East, they are not a dire threat to vital U.S. interests, except inasmuch as they are a threat to Israel. Even if these states acquire nuclear weapons — which is obviously undesirable — neither America nor Israel could be blackmailed, because the blackmailer could not carry out the threat without suffering over-whelming retaliation. The danger of a nuclear handover to terrorists is equally remote, because a rogue state could not be sure the transfer would go undetected or that it would not be blamed and punished after-wards. The relationship with Israel actually makes it harder for the U.S. to deal with these states. Israel's nuclear arsenal is one reason some of its neighbours want nuclear weapons, and threatening them with regime change merely increases that desire.

A final reason to question Israel's strategic value is that it does not behave like a loyal ally. Israeli officials frequently ignore U.S. requests and renege on promises (including pledges to stop building settlements and to refrain from "targeted assassinations" of Palestinian leaders). Is-rael has provided sensitive military technology to potential rivals like China, in what the State Department inspector-general called "a sys-tematic and growing pattern of unauthorised transfers." According to the General Accounting Office, Israel also "conducts the most aggres-sive espionage operations against the U.S. of any ally." In addition to the case of Jonathan Pollard, who gave Israel large quantities of classi-fied material in the early 1980s (which it reportedly passed on to the Soviet Union in return for more exit visas for Soviet Jews), a new con-troversy erupted in 2004 when it was revealed that a key Pentagon offi-cial called Larry Franklin had passed classified information to an Israeli diplomat. Israel is hardly the only country that spies on the U.S., but its willingness to spy on its principal patron casts further doubt on its strategic value.

Israel's strategic value isn't the only issue. Its backers also argue that it deserves unqualified support because it is weak and surrounded by enemies; it is a democracy; the Jewish people have suffered from past crimes and therefore deserve special treatment; and Israel's con-duct has been morally superior to that of its adversaries. On close in-spection, none of these arguments is persuasive. There is a strong moral case for supporting Israel's existence, but that is not in jeopardy. Viewed objectively, its past and present conduct offers no moral basis for privileging it over the Palestinians.

Israel is often portrayed as David confronted by Goliath, but the converse is closer to the truth. Contrary to popular belief, the Zionists had larger, better equipped, and better led forces during the 1947–49 War of Independence, and the Israel Defence Forces won quick and easy victories against Egypt in 1956 and against Egypt, Jordan, and Syria in 1967 — all of this before large-scale U.S. aid began flowing. Today, Israel is the strongest military power in the Middle East. Its conventional forces are far superior to those of its neighbours and it is the only state in the region with nuclear weapons. Egypt and Jordan have signed peace treaties with it, and Saudi Arabia has offered to do so. Syria has lost its Soviet patron, Iraq has been devastated by three disastrous wars, and Iran is hundreds of miles away. The Palestinians barely have an effective police force, let alone an army that could pose a threat to Israel. According to a 2005 assessment by Tel Aviv University's Jaffee Centre for Strategic Studies, "the strategic balance decidedly favours Israel, which has continued to widen the qualitative gap between its own military capability and deterrence powers and those of its neighbours." If backing the underdog were a compelling motive, the United States would be supporting Israel's opponents.

That Israel is a fellow democracy surrounded by hostile dictatorships cannot account for the current level of aid: there are many democracies around the world, but none receives the same lavish support. The U.S. has overthrown democratic governments in the past and supported dictators when this was thought to advance its interests — it has good relations with a number of dictatorships today.

Some aspects of Israeli democracy are at odds with core American values. Unlike the U.S., where people are supposed to enjoy equal rights irrespective of race, religion, or ethnicity, Israel was explicitly founded as a Jewish state and citizenship is based on the principle of blood kinship. Given this, it is not surprising that its 1.3 million Arabs are treated as second-class citizens, or that a recent Israeli government commission found that Israel behaves in a "neglectful and discriminatory" manner towards them. Its democratic status is also undermined by its refusal to grant the Palestinians a viable state of their own or full political rights.

A third justification is the history of Jewish suffering in the Christian West, especially during the Holocaust. Because Jews were persecuted for centuries and could feel safe only in a Jewish homeland, many people now believe that Israel deserves special treatment from the United States. The country's creation was undoubtedly an appropriate response to the long record of crimes against Jews, but it also brought about fresh crimes against a largely innocent third party: the Palestinians.

This was well understood by Israel's early leaders. David Ben-Gurion told Nahum Goldmann, the president of the World Jewish Congress:

> If I were an Arab leader I would never make terms with Israel. That is natural: we have taken their country . . . We come from Israel, but two thousand years ago, and what is that to them? There has been anti-semitism, the Nazis, Hitler, Auschwitz, but was that their fault? They only see one thing: we have come here and stolen their country. Why should they accept that?

Since then, Israeli leaders have repeatedly sought to deny the Palestinians' national ambitions. When she was prime minister, Golda Meir famously remarked that "there is no such thing as a Palestinian." Pressure from extremist violence and Palestinian population growth has forced subsequent Israeli leaders to disengage from the Gaza Strip and consider other territorial compromises, but not even Yitzhak Rabin was willing to offer the Palestinians a viable state. Ehud Barak's purportedly generous offer at Camp David would have given them only a disarmed set of Bantustans under de facto Israeli control. The tragic history of the Jewish people does not obligate the U.S. to help Israel today no matter what it does.

Israel's backers also portray it as a country that has sought peace at every turn and shown great restraint even when provoked. The Arabs, by contrast, are said to have acted with great wickedness. Yet on the ground, Israel's record is not distinguishable from that of its opponents. Ben-Gurion acknowledged that the early Zionists were far from benevolent towards the Palestinian Arabs, who resisted their encroachments — which is hardly surprising, given that the Zionists were trying to create their own state on Arab land. In the same way, the creation of Israel in 1947–48 involved acts of ethnic cleansing, including executions, massacres, and rapes by Jews, and Israel's subsequent conduct has often been brutal, belying any claim to moral superiority. Between 1949 and 1956, for example, Israeli security forces killed between 2700 and 5000 Arab infiltrators, the overwhelming majority of them unarmed. The IDF murdered hundreds of Egyptian prisoners of war in both the 1956 and 1967 wars, while in 1967, it expelled between 100,000 and 260,000 Palestinians from the newly conquered West Bank, and drove 80,000 Syrians from the Golan Heights.

During the first intifada, the IDF distributed truncheons to its troops and encouraged them to break the bones of Palestinian protesters. The Swedish branch of Save the Children estimated that "23,600 to 29,900 children required medical treatment for their beating injuries in the first two years of the intifada." Nearly a third of them were aged ten or under. The response to the second intifada has been even more violent, leading *Ha'aretz* to declare that "the IDF . . . is turning into a killing machine whose efficiency is awe-inspiring, yet shocking." The IDF fired one million bullets in the first days of the uprising. Since then, for every Israeli lost, Israel has killed 3.4 Palestinians, the majority of whom have been innocent bystanders; the ratio of Palestinian to Israeli children killed is even higher (5.7:1). It is also worth bearing in mind that the Zionists relied on terrorist bombs to drive the British from Palestine, and that Yitzhak Shamir, once a terrorist and later prime minister, declared that "neither Jewish ethics nor Jewish tradition can disqualify terrorism as a means of combat."

The Palestinian resort to terrorism is wrong but it isn't surprising. The Palestinians believe they have no other way to force Israeli concessions. As Ehud Barak once admitted, had he been born a Palestinian, he "would have joined a terrorist organisation."

So if neither strategic nor moral arguments can account for America's support for Israel, how are we to explain it?

The explanation is the unmatched power of the Israel Lobby. We use "the Lobby" as shorthand for the loose coalition of individuals and organisations who actively work to steer U.S. foreign policy in a pro-Israel direction. This is not meant to suggest that "the Lobby" is a unified movement with a central leadership, or that individuals within it do not disagree on certain issues. Not all Jewish Americans are part of the Lobby, because Israel is not a salient issue for many of them. In a 2004 survey, for example, roughly 36 per cent of American Jews said they were either "not very" or "not at all" emotionally attached to Israel.

Jewish Americans also differ on specific Israeli policies. Many of the key organisations in the Lobby, such as the American-Israel Public Affairs Committee (AIPAC) and the Conference of Presidents of Major Jewish Organisations, are run by hardliners who generally support the Likud Party's expansionist policies, including its hostility to the Oslo peace process. The bulk of U.S. Jewry, meanwhile, is more inclined to make concessions to the Palestinians, and a few groups — such as Jewish Voice for Peace — strongly advocate such steps. Despite these differences, moderates and hardliners both favour giving steadfast support to Israel. . . .

In its basic operations, the Israel Lobby is no different from the farm lobby, steel or textile workers' unions, or other ethnic lobbies. There is nothing improper about American Jews and their Christian allies attempting to sway U.S. policy: the Lobby's activities are not a conspiracy of the sort depicted in tracts like the *Protocols of the Elders of Zion*. For the most part, the individuals and groups that comprise it are only doing what other special interest groups do, but doing it very much better. By contrast, pro-Arab interest groups, in so far as they exist at all, are weak, which makes the Israel Lobby's task even easier.

The Lobby pursues two broad strategies. First, it wields its significant influence in Washington, pressuring both Congress and the executive branch. Whatever an individual lawmaker or policymaker's own views may be, the Lobby tries to make supporting Israel the "smart" choice. Second, it strives to ensure that public discourse portrays Israel in a positive light, by repeating myths about its founding and by promoting its point of view in policy debates. The goal is to prevent critical comments from getting a fair hearing in the political arena. Controlling the debate is essential to guaranteeing U.S. support, because a candid discussion of U.S.-Israeli relations might lead Americans to favour a different policy.

A key pillar of the Lobby's effectiveness is its influence in Congress, where Israel is virtually immune from criticism. This in itself is remarkable, because Congress rarely shies away from contentious issues.

Where Israel is concerned, however, potential critics fall silent. One reason is that some key members are Christian Zionists like Dick Armey, who said in September 2002: "My No. 1 priority in foreign policy is to protect Israel." One might think that the No. 1 priority for any congressman would be to protect America. There are also Jewish senators and congressmen who work to ensure that U.S. foreign policy supports Israel's interests. . . .

The bottom line is that AIPAC, a de facto agent for a foreign government, has a stranglehold on Congress, with the result that U.S. policy towards Israel is not debated there, even though that policy has important consequences for the entire world. In other words, one of the three main branches of the government is firmly committed to supporting Israel. As one former Democratic senator, Ernest Hollings, noted on leaving office, "you can't have an Israeli policy other than what AIPAC gives you around here." Or as Ariel Sharon once told an American audience, "when people ask me how they can help Israel, I tell them: 'Help AIPAC.'"

Thanks in part to the influence Jewish voters have on presidential elections, the Lobby also has significant leverage over the executive branch. Although they make up fewer than 3 per cent of the population, they make large campaign donations to candidates from both parties. The *Washington Post* once estimated that Democratic presidential candidates "depend on Jewish supporters to supply as much as 60 per cent of the money." And because Jewish voters have high turn-out rates and are concentrated in key states like California, Florida, Illinois, New York, and Pennsylvania, presidential candidates go to great lengths not to antagonise them. . . .

During the Clinton administration, Middle Eastern policy was largely shaped by officials with close ties to Israel or to prominent pro-Israel organisations; among them, Martin Indyk, the former deputy director of research at AIPAC and co-founder of the pro-Israel Washington Institute for Near East Policy (WINEP); Dennis Ross, who joined WINEP after leaving government in 2001; and Aaron Miller, who has lived in Israel and often visits the country. These men were among Clinton's closest advisers at the Camp David summit in July 2000. Although all three supported the Oslo peace process and favoured the creation of a Palestinian state, they did so only within the limits of what would be acceptable to Israel. The American delegation took its cues from Ehud Barak, coordinated its negotiating positions with Israel in advance, and did not offer independent proposals. Not surprisingly, Palestinian negotiators complained that they were "negotiating with two Israeli teams — one displaying an Israeli flag, and one an American flag."

The situation is even more pronounced in the Bush administration, whose ranks have included such fervent advocates of the Israeli cause as Elliot Abrams, John Bolton, Douglas Feith, I. Lewis ("Scooter") Libby, Richard Perle, Paul Wolfowitz, and David Wurmser. As we shall see, these officials have consistently pushed for policies favoured by Israel and backed by organisations in the Lobby.

The Lobby doesn't want an open debate, of course, because that might lead Americans to question the level of support they provide. Accordingly, pro-Israel organisations work hard to influence the institutions that do most to shape popular opinion.

The Lobby's perspective prevails in the mainstream media: the debate among Middle East pundits, the journalist Eric Alterman writes, is "dominated by people who cannot imagine criticising Israel." He lists 61 "columnists and commentators who can be counted on to support Israel reflexively and without qualification." Conversely, he found just five pundits who consistently criticise Israeli actions or endorse Arab positions. Newspapers occasionally publish guest op-eds challenging Israeli policy, but the balance of opinion clearly favours the other side. It is hard to imagine any mainstream media outlet in the United States publishing a piece like this one. . . .

No discussion of the Lobby would be complete without an examination of one of its most powerful weapons: the charge of anti-semitism. Anyone who criticises Israel's actions or argues that pro-Israel groups have significant influence over U.S. Middle Eastern policy — an influence AIPAC celebrates — stands a good chance of being labelled an anti-semite. Indeed, anyone who merely claims that there *is* an Israel Lobby runs the risk of being charged with anti-semitism, even though the Israeli media refer to America's "Jewish Lobby." In other words, the Lobby first boasts of its influence and then attacks anyone who calls attention to it. It's a very effective tactic: anti-semitism is something no one wants to be accused of. . . .

Critics are also accused of holding Israel to an unfair standard or questioning its right to exist. But these are bogus charges too. Western critics of Israel hardly ever question its right to exist: they question its behaviour towards the Palestinians, as do Israelis themselves. Nor is Israel being judged unfairly. Israeli treatment of the Palestinians elicits criticism because it is contrary to widely accepted notions of human rights, to international law, and to the principle of national self-determination. And it is hardly the only state that has faced sharp criticism on these grounds.

In the autumn of 2001, and especially in the spring of 2002, the Bush administration tried to reduce anti-American sentiment in the Arab world and undermine support for terrorist groups like al-Qaida by halting Israel's expansionist policies in the Occupied Territories and advocating the creation of a Palestinian state. Bush had very significant means of persuasion at his disposal. He could have threatened to reduce economic and diplomatic support for Israel, and the American people would almost certainly have supported him. A May 2003 poll reported that more than 60 per cent of Americans were willing to withhold aid if Israel resisted U.S. pressure to settle the conflict, and that number rose to 70 per cent among the "politically active." Indeed, 73 per cent said that the United States should not favour either side.

Yet the administration failed to change Israeli policy, and Washington ended up backing it. Over time, the administration also adopted Israel's own justifications of its position, so that U.S. rhetoric began to mimic Israeli rhetoric. By February 2003, a *Washington Post* headline summarised the situation: "Bush and Sharon Nearly Identical on Mideast Policy." The main reason for this switch was the Lobby. . . .

Maintaining U.S. support for Israel's policies against the Palestinians is essential as far as the Lobby is concerned, but its ambitions do not stop there. It also wants America to help Israel remain the dominant regional power. The Israeli government and pro-Israel groups in the United States have worked together to shape the administration's policy towards Iraq, Syria, and Iran, as well as its grand scheme for reordering the Middle East.

Pressure from Israel and the Lobby was not the only factor behind the decision to attack Iraq in March 2003, but it was critical. Some Americans believe that this was a war for oil, but there is hardly any direct evidence to support this claim. Instead, the war was motivated in good part by a desire to make Israel more secure. According to Philip Zelikow, a former member of the president's Foreign Intelligence Advisory Board, the executive director of the 9/11 Commission, and now a counsellor to Condoleezza Rice, the "real threat" from Iraq was not a threat to the United States. The "unstated threat" was the "threat against Israel," Zelikow told an audience at the University of Virginia in September 2002. "The American government," he added, "doesn't want to lean too hard on it rhetorically, because it is not a popular sell." . . .

Within the U.S., the main driving force behind the war was a small band of neo-conservatives, many with ties to Likud. But leaders of the Lobby's major organisations lent their voices to the campaign. "As President Bush attempted to sell the . . . war in Iraq," the *Forward* reported, "America's most important Jewish organisations rallied as one to his defence. In statement after statement community leaders stressed the need to rid the world of Saddam Hussein and his weapons of mass destruction." The editorial goes on to say that "concern for Israel's safety rightfully factored into the deliberations of the main Jewish groups."

Although neo-conservatives and other Lobby leaders were eager to invade Iraq, the broader American Jewish community was not. Just after the war started, Samuel Freedman reported that "a compilation of nationwide opinion polls by the Pew Research Center shows that Jews are less supportive of the Iraq war than the population at large, 52 per cent to 62 per cent." Clearly, it would be wrong to blame the war in Iraq on "Jewish influence." Rather, it was due in large part to the Lobby's influence, especially that of the neo-conservatives within it. . . .

Given the neo-conservatives' devotion to Israel, their obsession with Iraq, and their influence in the Bush administration, it isn't surprising that many Americans suspected that the war was designed to further Israeli interests. Last March, Barry Jacobs of the American Jewish Committee acknowledged that the belief that Israel and the neo-conservatives had conspired to get the U.S. into a war in Iraq was "pervasive" in the intelligence community. Yet few people would say so publicly, and most of those who did — including Senator Ernest Hollings and Representative James Moran — were condemned for raising the issue. Michael Kinsley wrote in late 2002 that "the lack of public discussion about the role of Israel . . . is the proverbial elephant in the room." The reason for the reluctance to talk about it, he observed, was fear of being labelled an anti-semite. There is little doubt that Israel and the Lobby were key factors in the decision to go to war. It's a decision the U.S. would have been far less likely to take without their efforts. And the war itself was intended to be only the first step. A front-page headline in the *Wall Street Journal* shortly after the war began says it all: "President's Dream: Changing Not Just Regime but a Region: A Pro-US, Democratic Area Is a Goal That Has Israeli and Neo-Conservative Roots."

REFLECTIONS

We began the chapter by asking how representative the Israel/Palestine conflict was of other conflicts over religion and politics at the end of the twentieth century. It is almost commonplace today to describe the conflict between Israel and Palestine as an eternal struggle between two implacably opposed religions: Judaism and Islam. We do this with other contemporary conflicts where religion plays a role: We call the conflict in Northern Ireland one between Catholics and Protestants, that of India and Pakistan a conflict between Hindus and Muslims. But in all of these cases, religion is only part of the story. There is also a conflict over land, ethnic and class differences, and political alliances that have nothing to do with religion (Pakistan and China, for instance), and often secular military leaders play a major role.

One of the greatest surprises in our investigation of the background of the conflict between Israel and Palestine might be how unimportant religion was at many stages. For Herzl and the early Zionists, religion as nationality was important, but most Jews were more intent on assimilating into their European or American cultures. David Fromkin notes that before World War I only about 1 percent of the world's Jews were Zionists, a proportion also roughly true for Jews in the United States. After the Balfour Declaration, and far more after World War II and the Holocaust, the number of Jews who chose to emigrate to Israel increased considerably, as did those who supported Israel.

Many Jewish immigrants to Israel, however, were secular in culture and belief. Herzl imagined a flag with seven stars not to evoke the days of creation and the Sabbath day of rest but to symbolise the hope of Jewish socialists for a seven-hour day. The model form of early Jewish colonization was the communal settlement or *kibbutz*. European and Russian refugees came to Israel for land and political autonomy, many from communities which were not religious. Even today many Israelis describe themselves as secular Jews.

Similarly on the Palestinian side, we read complaints in the documents of Jewish immigrants buying and taking Arab land and of changing the character of Palestine, but not of animosity to Judaism as a faith or practice. In fact, one of the central Palestinian fears from 1917 to 1948 was that the creation of a Jewish state — as opposed to a binational state — would make Palestinians unwelcome in their own land. There appears to be little conflict between the faiths of Judaism and Islam in these documents. Jews and the international inquiries speak of Arabs, not Muslims. From 1948 until 2000 the dominant parties of the Palestinian resistance movement were all rigorously secular. Hamas and Muslim fundamentalist or Islamicist groups gained popular support only after the failure of the secular movement sensed in the collapse of the Camp David peace talks in 2000 and the death of Yassir Arafat and defeat of his Fatah party shortly thereafter. Notice how deeply disillusioned Benny Morris became after 2000.

Recent years have witnessed increased religious motivation and more widespread religious fundamentalism on the part of Jews and Christians as well as Muslims. Hamas fundamentalists have their counterparts in Israeli settlers who believe God calls them to claim all of Biblical Israel regardless of current state boundaries and Christian evangelicals who foment strife in Israel to realize Armageddon.

The last reading, however, suggests that the religious fervor of Jews and Christians has been exploited and channeled by more political interests in the United States and Israel. If our analysis is correct, the local and global political powers play a dangerous game manipulating popular religious extremism to temporary advantages. When the great powers of 1914 used nationalist extremists in the same way, the disastrous consequences were felt globally and lasted for generations.

Women's World

1950 to the Present

HISTORICAL CONTEXT

Today, historians both male and female try not to restrict their work to the activities or testimonies of men. Yet, because men dominated politics, war, and industry for many years, oftentimes important historical studies have ignored women. Historians now attempt to research and write more complete, balanced historical accounts, addressing topics in which women have played important roles. Such topics include the history of the family, sexuality, privacy, popular culture, domesticity, and work, among others. In recent years, women's history and women's studies have become vibrant fields of specialization and discovery.

This chapter offers readings that, taken together, constitute a history of women since 1950. We will read women's accounts from various parts of the world, as they describe aspects of their lives and those of other women. We begin, however, with the Chinese Marriage Law of 1950 so we might consider the new legal baseline for one-fifth of the world's population. (This law was replicated in many other countries as well.) We then turn to the emerging women's movement in the United States, spearheaded by a far-reaching book, *The Feminine Mystique* (1963). Next, an Algerian novelist reflects on youth, adolescence, and family. Then an unemployed Brazilian talks about her life. Finally, we move from the personal to the political, with letters from Aung San Suu Kyi of Burma, a U.N. document on women in politics, and an unusual news story.

All of the women featured in this chapter are articulate, literate, self-conscious writers. Their eloquence allows us to reflect on the power of words for women, as well as for men.

THINKING HISTORICALLY
Constructing Theory

The notion of "constructing theory" may seem much more demanding than it is. It is little more than bringing together ideas that explain phenomena in history. Put simply, a theory offers a possible answer to a question or an explanation of a problem. Theories are not necessarily true; they are guesses, called hypotheses, and have to be tested and supported with evidence. Theories might come to us from reading either primary or secondary sources, but ultimately a theory must make sense of the primary sources, the raw experience of history. A theory organizes experience in a way that makes it more comprehensible. It seeks patterns or an explanation of patterns: causes, consequences, connections, relationships, reasons.

Ultimately, of course, a theory must be tested with new evidence. A good theory will interpret or incorporate new evidence without needing much change. In this chapter, you are asked only to focus on constructing theory. Occasionally, you will be reminded of the limitations of the sources included here, but our emphasis will be on conceiving and expressing theories that give meaning to the material at hand.

As you read these selections, try to construct a theory about the history of women over the last fifty or sixty years. You might begin with the very basic question: Did the lives of women improve during this period? If you think they have, or have not, you might develop a theory as to why. It could be more modest than that. You might, for instance, develop a theory about why women's lives improved in a particular kind of society, but not in some other type of society. It might be something unrelated to the larger question of improvements for women. You might have a theory about particular kinds of women, or gender relations somewhere, or voting for women, or whatever springs from the readings and answers some question that the readings pose for you.

174

The Marriage Law of the People's Republic of China

Chinese revolutionaries in the twentieth century frequently called for women's rights and equality. The "women question" was at the forefront of the Nationalist revolution of 1911 and, again, of the Communist revolution of 1949. Women who had been active in the revolution of 1911 sought women's suffrage and an end to such patriarchal practices as foot-binding, the concubine system, child marriage, and prostitution. But the visions of Chinese revolutionaries often remained promises in word only.

The government of Chiang Kai-shek passed major resolutions in 1924 and 1926 to enact laws that would codify many of the aspirations of the women's movement: legal equality, right to own property, freely entered marriage, right to divorce, even equal pay for equal work. But in 1927, Chiang's Nationalist party broke its alliance with the communists and identified them with women's issues to smear them. In fact, many of the founders of the Communist party, including Mao Zedong, were proponents of family reform (free marriage and free love) before they were Marxists. Despite this, as they sought supporters and volunteers throughout China after 1927, especially in the more traditional and male-dominated countryside, they quickly dropped their calls for reform of the marriage and family laws.

When the Communists came to power in China in 1949, marriage reform again surfaced as a high priority in constructing a new society. The 1950 Marriage Law, excerpted here, led to a widespread debate on the role of women in Chinese communist society. What practices did the Chinese Communists seek to curb with this law?

Thinking Historically

Construct a theory about how different groups of people in China might respond to this law. Among the groups you might consider are rich men, poor men, rich women, poor women, young and old, city and country people.

The Marriage Law of the People's Republic of China (Peking: Foreign Languages Press, 1959).

Chapter I. General Principles

Article 1. The arbitrary and compulsory feudal marriage system, which is based on the superiority of man over woman and which ignores the children's interests, shall be abolished.

The new democratic marriage system, which is based on free choice of partners, on monogamy, on equal rights for both sexes, and on protection of the lawful interests of women and children, shall be put into effect.

Article 2. Bigamy, concubinage, child betrothal, interference with the remarriage of widows, and the exaction of money or gifts in connection with marriage shall be prohibited. . . .

Chapter III. Rights and Duties of Husband and Wife

Article 7. Husband and wife are companions living together and shall enjoy equal status in the home.

Article 8. Husband and wife are in duty bound to love, respect, assist, and look after each other, to live in harmony, to engage in production, to care for the children, and to strive jointly for the welfare of the family and for the building up of a new society.

Article 9. Both husband and wife shall have the right to free choice of occupation and free participation in work or in social activities.

Article 10. Both husband and wife shall have equal right in the possession and management of family property.

175

BETTY FRIEDAN

From The Feminine Mystique

This book elicited an enormous response from women in the United States and around the world when it was published in 1963. What Friedan* called "the problem that has no name" was immediately understood and widely discussed. What name would you give to the problem? What were its causes? Do women still feel it today?

Thinking Historically

In what ways were the needs of American women after World War II like those of Chinese women? In what ways were they different? Which do you find more striking, the similarities or the differences? What theories would explain why Chinese and American women had different problems in the 1950s and 1960s?

The problem lay buried, unspoken, for many years in the minds of American women. It was a strange stirring, a sense of dissatisfaction, a yearning that women suffered in the middle of the twentieth century in the United States. Each suburban wife struggled with it alone. As she made the beds, shopped for groceries, matched slipcover material, ate peanut butter sandwiches with her children, chauffeured Cub Scouts and Brownies, lay beside her husband at night — she was afraid to ask even of herself the silent question — "Is this all?"

For over fifteen years there was no word of this yearning in the millions of words written about women, for women, in all the columns, books, and articles by experts telling women their role was to seek fulfillment as wives and mothers. Over and over women heard in voices of tradition and of Freudian sophistication that they could desire no greater destiny than to glory in their own femininity. Experts told them how to catch a man and keep him, how to breastfeed children and handle their toilet training, how to cope with sibling rivalry and adolescent rebellion; how to buy a dishwasher, bake bread, cook gourmet snails, and build a swimming pool with their own hands; how to dress, look, and act more feminine and make marriage more exciting; how to

*free DAN

Betty Friedan, *The Feminine Mystique* (New York: Dell, 1963), 11–12, 14, 15–16, 27.

keep their husbands from dying young and their sons from growing into delinquents. They were taught to pity the neurotic, unfeminine, unhappy women who wanted to be poets or physicists or presidents. They learned that truly feminine women do not want careers, higher education, political rights — the independence and the opportunities that the old-fashioned feminists fought for. Some women, in their forties and fifties, still remembered painfully giving up those dreams, but most of the younger women no longer even thought about them. A thousand expert voices applauded their femininity, their adjustment, their new maturity. All they had to do was devote their lives from earliest girlhood to finding a husband and bearing children. . . .

In the fifteen years after World War II, this mystique of feminine fulfillment became the cherished and self-perpetuating core of contemporary American culture. Millions of women lived their lives in the image of those pretty pictures of the American suburban housewife, kissing their husbands goodbye in front of the picture window, depositing their stationwagonsful of children at school, and smiling as they ran the new electric waxer over the spotless kitchen floor. They baked their own bread, sewed their own and their children's clothes, kept their new washing machines and dryers running all day. They changed the sheets on the beds twice a week instead of once, took the rug-hooking class in adult education, and pitied their poor frustrated mothers, who had dreamed of having a career. Their only dream was to be perfect wives and mothers; their highest ambition to have five children and a beautiful house, their only fight to get and keep their husbands. They had no thought for the unfeminine problems of the world outside the home; they wanted the men to make the major decisions. They gloried in their role as women, and wrote proudly on the census blank: "Occupation: housewife." . . .

If a woman had a problem in the 1950s and 1960s, she knew that something must be wrong with her marriage, or with herself. Other women were satisfied with their lives, she thought. What kind of a woman was she if she did not feel this mysterious fulfillment waxing the kitchen floor? She was so ashamed to admit her dissatisfaction that she never knew how many other women shared it. If she tried to tell her husband, he didn't understand what she was talking about. She did not really understand it herself. For over fifteen years women in America found it harder to talk about this problem than about sex. Even the psychoanalysts had no name for it. When a woman went to a psychiatrist for help, as many women did, she would say, "I'm so ashamed," or "I must be hopelessly neurotic." "I don't know what's wrong with women today," a suburban psychiatrist said uneasily. "I only know something is wrong because most of my patients happen to be women. And their problem isn't sexual." Most women with this problem did not go to see a psychoanalyst, however. "There's nothing wrong really," they kept telling themselves. "There isn't any problem."

But on an April morning in 1959, I heard a mother of four, having coffee with four other mothers in a suburban development fifteen miles from New York, say in a tone of quiet desperation, "the problem." And the others knew, without words, that she was not talking about a problem with her husband, or her children, or her home. Suddenly they realized they all shared the same problem, the problem that has no name. They began, hesitantly, to talk about it. Later, after they had picked up their children at nursery school and taken them home to nap, two of the women cried, in sheer relief, just to know they were not alone.

Gradually I came to realize that the problem that has no name was shared by countless women in America. As a magazine writer I often interviewed women about problems with their children, or their marriages, or their houses, or their communities. But after a while I began to recognize the telltale signs of this other problem. I saw the same signs in suburban ranch houses and split-levels on Long Island and in New Jersey and Westchester County; in colonial houses in a small Massachusetts town; on patios in Memphis; in suburban and city apartments; in living rooms in the Midwest. Sometimes I sensed the problem, not as a reporter, but as a suburban housewife, for during this time I was also bringing up my own three children in Rockland County, New York. I heard echoes of the problem in college dormitories and semi-private maternity wards, at PTA meetings and luncheons of the League of Women Voters, at suburban cocktail parties, in station wagons waiting for trains, and in snatches of conversation overheard at Schrafft's.[1] The groping words I heard from other women, on quiet afternoons when children were at school or on quiet evenings when husbands worked late, I think I understood first as a woman long before I understood their larger social and psychological implications.

Just what was this problem that has no name? What were the words women used when they tried to express it? Sometimes a woman would say "I feel empty somehow . . . incomplete." Or she would say, "I feel as if I don't exist." Sometimes she blotted out the feeling with a tranquilizer. Sometimes she thought the problem was with her husband, or her children, or that what she really needed was to redecorate her house, or move to a better neighborhood, or have an affair, or another baby. Sometimes, she went to a doctor with symptoms she could hardly describe: "A tired feeling . . . I get so angry with the children it

---

[1]A popular restaurant. [Ed.]

scares me . . . I feel like crying without any reason." (A Cleveland doctor called it "the housewife's syndrome.") A number of women told me
about great bleeding blisters that break out on their hands and arms.
"I call it the housewife's blight," said a family doctor in Pennsylvania.
"I see it so often lately in these young women with four, five, and six
children who bury themselves in their dishpans. But it isn't caused by
detergent and it isn't cured by cortisone." . . .

If I am right, the problem that has no name stirring in the minds of
so many American women today is not a matter of loss of femininity or
too much education, or the demands of domesticity. It is far more important than anyone recognizes. It is the key to these other new and old
problems which have been torturing women and their husbands and
children, and puzzling their doctors and educators for years. It may
well be the key to our future as a nation and a culture. We can no
longer ignore that voice within women that says: "I want something
more than my husband and my children and my home."

$$\boxed{176}$$

ASSIA DJEBAR

Growing Up in Algeria

Excerpted from a novel by Algerian author Assia Djebar*, this selection is about growing up in Algeria just before the revolution for independence from France, which began in 1954. To the extent to which
her account is autobiographical, what do you think it was like to
grow up in Algeria as a young teenage girl around 1950? How typical
do you think this girl's life and concerns were?

The author discusses how her experiences in the French and Koranic
religious school pulled her in different directions. What were they?
Writing and reading were very important to her, but they both meant
different things in Arabic Muslim culture and French culture. In the Koranic schools, young people learn the Koran by reciting and memorizing
it (just as Mohammed did). What was the meaning of reading in French

*AHS yuh   jeh BAHR

Assia Djebar, "Growing Up in Algeria," in *Fantasia: An Algerian Cavalcade*, trans. Dorothy
S. Blair (Portsmouth, N.H.: Heinemann, 1993), 179–85.

for the author? What were the different meanings of writing for her? Do you think this exposure to both languages was making her more Arabic or French? Which identity was more real for her?

In what ways were the needs and interests of this teenage girl similar to, or different from, those of an American teenage girl in the same period? Do you think their lives have become more alike since then?

Thinking Historically

Construct a theory that answers one of the questions posed above. Keep in mind that a theory is not an answer — it is a guiding principle for an answer. So, for instance, if you choose to consider the question, "Which identity was more real for her?" an answer might be "Arabic," and a theory could be that "a person's mother tongue determines who she is." A theory is a general principle supported by evidence. (For example, you could interview bilingual people to find out if their first language played a greater role than their second in shaping their identities.) Keep in mind that many different theories are possible in answer to each question.

At the age when I should be veiled already, I can still move about freely thanks to the French school: Every Monday the village bus takes me to the boarding school in the nearby town, and brings me back on Saturday to my parents' home.

I have a friend who is half Italian and who goes home every weekend to a fishing port on the coast; we go together to catch our respective buses and are tempted by all sorts of escapades . . . With beating hearts we make our way into the centre of the town; to enter a smart cake-shop, wander along the edge of the park, stroll along the boulevard, which only runs alongside common barracks, seems the acme of freedom, after a week of boarding school! Excited by the proximity of forbidden pleasures, we eventually each catch our bus; the thrill lay in the risk of missing it!

As a young teenager I enjoy the exhilarating hours spent every Thursday in training on the sports field. I only have one worry: fear that my father might come to visit me! How can I tell him that it's compulsory for me to wear shorts, in other words, I have to show my legs? I keep this fear a secret, unable to confide in any of my schoolfriends; unlike me, they haven't got cousins who do not show their ankles or their arms, who do not even expose their faces. My panic is also compounded by an Arab woman's "shame." The French girls whirl around me; they do not suspect that my body is caught in invisible snares.

"Doesn't your daughter wear a veil yet?" asks one or other of the matrons, gazing questioningly at my mother with suspicious kohl-rimmed eyes, on the occasion of one of the summer weddings. I must be thirteen, or possibly fourteen.

"She reads!" my mother replies stiffly.

Everyone is swallowed up in the embarrassed silence that ensues. And in my own silence.

"She reads," that is to say in Arabic, "she studies." I think now that this command "to read" was not just casually included in the Quranic revelation made by the Angel Gabriel in the cave ... "She reads" is tantamount to saying that writing to be read, including that of the unbelievers, is always a source of revelation: in my case of the mobility of my body, and so of my future freedom.

When I am growing up — shortly before my native land throws off the colonial yoke — while the man still has the right to four legitimate wives, we girls, big and little, have at our command four languages to express desire before all that is left for us is sighs and moans: French for secret missives; Arabic for our stifled aspirations towards God-the-Father, the God of the religions of the Book; Lybico-Berber which takes us back to the pagan idols — mother-gods — of pre-Islamic Mecca. The fourth language, for all females, young or old, cloistered or half-emancipated, remains that of the body: the body which male neighbours' and cousins' eyes require to be deaf and blind, since they cannot completely incarcerate it; the body which, in trances, dances or vociferations, in fits of hope or despair, rebels, and unable to read or write, seeks some unknown shore as destination for its message of love.

In our towns, the first woman-reality is the voice, a dart which flies off into space, an arrow which slowly falls to earth; next comes writing with the scratching pointed quill forming amorous snares with its liana letters. By way of compensation, the need is felt to blot out women's bodies and they must be muffled up, tightly swathed, swaddled like infants or shrouded like corpses. Exposed, a woman's body would offend every eye, be an assault on the dimmest of desires, emphasize every separation. The voice, on the other hand, acts like a perfume, a draft of fresh water for the dry throat; and when it is savoured, it can be enjoyed by several simultaneously; a secret, polygamous pleasure ...

When the hand writes, slow positioning of the arm, carefully bending forward or leaning to one side, crouching, swaying to and fro, as in an act of love. When reading, the eyes take their time, delight in caressing the curves, while the calligraphy suggests the rhythm of the scansion: as if the writing marked the beginning and the end of possession.

Writing: Everywhere, a wealth of burnished gold and in its vicinity there is no place for other imagery from either animal or vegetable kingdom; it looks in the mirror of its scrolls and curlicues and sees itself as woman, not the reflection of a voice. It emphasizes by its presence alone where to begin and where to retreat; it suggests, by the song that smoulders in its heart, the dance floor for rejoicing and hair-shirt for the ascetic; I speak of the Arabic script; to be separated from it is to be separated from a great love. This script, which I mastered only to write the sacred words, I see now spread out before me cloaked in innocence and whispering arabesques — and ever since, all other scripts (French, English, Greek) seem only to babble, are never cathartic; they may contain truth, indeed, but a blemished truth.

Just as the pentathlon runner of old needed the starter, so, as soon as I learned the foreign script, my body began to move as if by instinct.

As if the French language suddenly had eyes, and lent them me to see into liberty; as if the French language blinded the peeping-toms of my clan and, at this price, I could move freely, run headlong down every street, annex the outdoors for my cloistered companions, for the matriarchs of my family who endured a living death. As if . . . Derision! I know that every language is a dark depository for piled-up corpses, refuse, sewage, but faced with the language of the former conquerer, which offers me its ornaments, its jewels, its flowers, I find they are the flowers of death — chrysanthemums on tombs!

Its script is a public unveiling in front of sniggering onlookers . . . A queen walks down the street, white, anonymous, draped, but when the shroud of rough wool is torn away and drops sudddenly at her feet, which a moment ago were hidden, she becomes a beggar again, squatting in the dust, to be spat at, the target of cruel comments.

In my earliest childhood — from the age of five to ten — I attended the French school in the village, and every day after lessons there I went on to the Quranic school.

Classes were held in a back room lent by a grocer, one of the village notables. I can recall the place, and its dim light: Was it because the time for the lessons was just before dark, or because the lighting of the room was so parsimonious? . . .

The master's image has remained singularly clear: delicate features, pale complexion, a scholar's sunken cheeks; about forty families supported him. I was struck by the elegance of his bearing and his traditional attire: A spotless light muslin was wrapped around his head-dress and floated behind his neck; his serge tunic was dazzling white. I never saw this man except sitting.

In comparison, the horde of misbehaving little urchins squatting on straw mats — sons of *fellaheen* [peasants] for the most part — seemed crude riffraff, from whom I kept my distance.

We were only four or five little girls. I suppose that our sex kept us apart, rather than my supercilious amazement at their behaviour. In spite of his aristocratic bearing, the *taleb* [teacher] did not hesitate to lift his cane and bring it down on the fingers of a recalcitrant or slow-witted lad. (I can still hear it whistle through the air.) We girls were spared this regular punishment.

I can remember the little impromptu parties my mother devised in our flat when I brought home (as later my brother was to do) the walnut table decorated with arabesques. This was the master's reward when we had learnt a long *sura* by heart. My mother and our village nanny, who was a second mother to us, then let out that semi-barbaric "you-you." That prolonged, irregular, spasmodic cooing, which in our building reserved for teachers' families — all European except for ours — must have appeared incongruous, a truly primitive cry. My mother considered the circumstances (the study of the Quran undertaken by her children) sufficiently important for her to let out this ancestral cry of jubilation in the middle of the village where she nevertheless felt herself an exile.

At every prize-giving ceremony at the French school, every prize I obtained strengthened my solidarity with my own family; but I felt there was more glory in this ostentatious clamour. The Quranic school, that dim cavern in which the haughty figure of the Sheikh was enthroned above the poor village children, this school became, thanks to the joy my mother demonstrated in this way, an island of bliss — Paradise regained.

Back in my native city, I learned that another Arab school was being opened, also funded by private contributions. One of my cousins attended it; she took me there. I was disappointed. The buildings, the timetable, the modern appearance of the masters, made it no different from a common-or-garden French school . . .

I understood later that in the village I had participated in the last of popular, secular teaching. In the city, thanks to the Nationalist movement of "Modernist Muslims," a new generation of Arab culture was being forged.

Since then these *medrasas* have sprung up everywhere. If I had attended one of them (if I'd grown up in the town where I was born) I would have found it quite natural to swathe my head in a turban, to hide my hair, to cover my arms and calves, in a word to move about out of doors like a Muslim nun!

After the age of ten or eleven, shortly before puberty, I was no longer allowed to attend the Quranic school. At this age, boys are suddenly excluded from the women's Turkish bath — that emollient world of naked bodies stifling in a whirl of scalding steam . . . The same thing happened to my companions, the little village girls, one of whom I would like to describe here.

The daughter of the Kabyle baker must, like me, have attended the French school simultaneously with the Quranic school. But I can only recall her presence squatting at my side in front of the Sheikh: side by side, half smiling to each other, both already finding it uncomfortable to sit cross-legged! . . . My legs must have been too long, because of my height: It wasn't easy for me to hide them under my skirt.

For this reason alone I think that I would in any case have been weaned from Quranic instruction at this age: There is no doubt that it's easier to sit cross-legged when wearing a *seroual*; a young girl's body that is beginning to develop more easily conceals its form under the ample folds of the traditional costume. But my skirts, justified by my attendance at the French school, were ill adapted to such a posture.

When I was eleven I started secondary school and became a boarder. What happened to the baker's daughter? Certainly veiled, withdrawn overnight from school: betrayed by her figure. Her swelling breasts, her slender legs, in a word, the emergence of her woman's personality transformed her into an incarcerated body!

I remember how much this Quranic learning, as it is progressively acquired, is linked to the body.

The portion of the sacred verse, inscribed on both sides of the walnut tablet, had to be wiped off at least once a week, after we had shown that we could recite it off by heart. We scrubbed the piece of wood thoroughly, just like other people wash their clothes: The time it took to dry seemed to ensure the interval that the memory needed to digest what it had swallowed . . .

The learning was absorbed by the fingers, the arms, through the physical effort. The act of cleaning the tablet seemed like ingesting a portion of the Quranic text. The writing — itself a copy of writing which is considered immutable — could only continue to unfold before us if it relied, clause by clause, on this osmosis . . .

As the hand traces the liana-script, the mouth opens to repeat the words, obedient to their rhythm, partly to memorize, partly to relieve the muscular tension . . . The shrill voices of the drowsy children rise up in a monotonous, sing-song chorus.

Stumbling on, swaying from side to side, care taken to observe the tonic accents, to differentiate between long and short vowels, attentive to the rhythm of the chant; muscles of the larynx as well as the torso moving in harmony. Controlling the breath to allow the correct emission of the voice, and letting the understanding advance precariously along its tight-rope. Respecting the grammar by speaking it aloud, making it part of the chant.

This language which I learn demands the correct posture for the body, on which the memory rests for its support. The childish hand, spurred on — as in training for some sport — by willpower worthy of an adult, begins to write. "Read!" The fingers labouring on the tablet send back the signs to the body, which is simultaneously reader and servant. The lips having finished their muttering, the hand will once more do the washing, proceeding to wipe out what is written on the tablet: This is the moment of absolution, like touching the hem of death's garment. Again, it is the turn of writing, and the circle is completed.

And when I sit curled up like this to study my native language it is as though my body reproduces the architecture of my native city: the *medinas* with their tortuous alleyways closed off to the outside world, living their secret life. When I write and read the foreign language, my body travels far in subversive space, in spite of the neighbours and suspicious matrons; it would not need much for it to take wing and fly away!

As I approach a marriageable age, these two different apprenticeships, undertaken simultaneously, land me in a dichotomy of location. My father's preference will decide for me: light rather than darkness. I do not realize that an irrevocable choice is being made: the outdoors and the risk, instead of the prison of my peers. This stroke of luck brings me to the verge of breakdown.

I write and speak French outside: The words I use convey no flesh-and-blood reality. I learn the names of birds I've never seen, trees I shall take ten years or more to identify, lists of flowers and plants that I shall never smell until I travel north of the Mediterranean. In this respect, all vocabulary expresses what is missing in my life, exoticism without mystery, causing a kind of visual humiliation that it is not seemly to admit to ... Settings and episodes in children's books are nothing but theoretical concepts; in the French family the mother comes to fetch her daughter or son from school; in the French street, the parents walk quite naturally side by side ... So, the world of the school is expunged from the daily life of my native city, as it is from the life of my family. The latter is refused any referential rôle.

My conscious mind is here, huddled against my mother's knees, in the darkest corners of the flat which she never leaves. The ambit of the school is elsewhere: My search, my eyes are fixed on other regions. I do not realize, no-one around me realizes, that, in the conflict between these two worlds, lies an incipient vertigo.

CAROLINA MARIA DE JESUS

From Child of the Dark:
The Diary of Carolina Maria de Jesus

This selection is from the diary of a common — and extraordinary — woman in Brazil in 1958. Carolina Maria de Jesus* was born in 1913 in a small town in the interior of Brazil. Her mother, unmarried and unemployed, insisted that Carolina attend school, which she hated until the day she learned to read. She remembers reading out loud every sign and label she could find. It was the beginning of a lifetime fascination with words, but she was forced to leave school after the second grade.

When Carolina was sixteen, her mother moved to the suburbs of São Paulo.† Carolina worked in a hospital, ran away to sing in a circus, and was employed in a long succession of jobs as cleaning woman and maid when, in 1947, she became pregnant. Her lover had abandoned her, and the family she worked for refused to let her into their house. Desperate, she moved into a *favela*‡ (slum) in São Paulo, building her own shack with cardboard and cans taken from a Church construction site. In the next ten years she had two more children. In order to keep from thinking of her troubles, she wrote. Poems, plays, novels, "anything and everything, for when I was writing I was in a golden palace, with crystal windows and silver chandeliers." She also kept a diary that reveals the actual details of her daily life. It is a life still lived by many women in the *favelas* of Brazil.

What does the diary tell you about the lives of the poor in Brazil?

Thinking Historically

Carolina Maria de Jesus is an articulate and thoughtful woman whose writing has helped her shape her own ideas. If you asked her what caused such poverty in her country, what might she say? Does she offer any theories about this? What is your theory for the existence of such poverty? How do you think she would respond to *The Feminine Mystique*? Do you have a theory about that?

---

*kah rol LEE nah   mah REE ah   duh jay SOOS
†sown   POW loh
‡fah VEL uh

Carolina Maria de Jesus, *Child of the Dark: The Diary of Carolina Maria de Jesus*, trans. David St. Clair (New York: NAL Penguin, 1962), 32–34, 42–47.

May 2, 1958 I'm not lazy. There are times when I try to keep up my diary. But then I think it's not worth it and figure I'm wasting my time.

I've made a promise to myself. I want to treat people that I know with more consideration. I want to have a pleasant smile for children and the employed.

I received a summons to appear at 8 P.M. at police station number 12. I spent the day looking for paper. At night my feet pained me so I couldn't walk. It started to rain. I went to the station and took José Carlos with me. The summons was for him. José Carlos is nine years old.

May 3 I went to the market at Carlos de Campos Street looking for any old thing. I got a lot of greens. But it didn't help much, for I've got no cooking fat. The children are upset because there's nothing to eat.

May 6 In the morning I went for water. I made João carry it. I was happy, then I received another summons. I was inspired yesterday and my verses were so pretty, I forgot to go to the station. It was 11:00 when I remembered the invitation from the illustrious lieutenant of the 12th precinct.

My advice to would-be politicians is that people do not tolerate hunger. It's necessary to know hunger to know how to describe it.

They are putting up a circus here at Araguaia Street. The Nilo Circus Theater.

May 9 I looked for paper but I didn't like it. Then I thought: I'll pretend that I'm dreaming.

May 10 I went to the police station and talked to the lieutenant. What a pleasant man! If I had known he was going to be so pleasant, I'd have gone on the first summons. The lieutenant was interested in my boys' education. He said the *favelas* have an unhealthy atmosphere where the people have more chance to go wrong than to become useful to state and country. I thought: If he knows this why doesn't he make a report and send it to the politicians? . . . Now he tells me this, I a poor garbage collector. I can't even solve my own problems.

Brazil needs to be led by a person who has known hunger. Hunger is also a teacher.

Who has gone hungry learns to think of the future and of the children.

May 11 Today is Mother's Day. The sky is blue and white. It seems that even nature wants to pay homage to the mothers who feel unhappy because they can't realize the desires of their children.

The sun keeps climbing. Today it's not going to rain. Today is our day.

Dona Teresinha came to visit me. She gave me 15 *cruzeiros* and said it was for Vera to go to the circus. But I'm going to use the money to buy bread tomorrow because I only have four *cruzeiros*.

Yesterday I got half a pig's head at the slaughterhouse. We ate the meat and saved the bones. Today I put the bones on to boil and into the broth I put some potatoes. My children are always hungry. When they are starving they aren't so fussy about what they eat.

Night came. The stars are hidden. The shack is filled with mosquitoes. I lit a page from a newspaper and ran it over the walls. This is the way the *favela* dwellers kill mosquitoes.

May 13 At dawn it was raining. Today is a nice day for me, it's the anniversary of the Abolition. The day we celebrate the freeing of the slaves. In the jails the Negroes were the scapegoats. But now the whites are more educated and don't treat us any more with contempt. May God enlighten the whites so that the Negroes may have a happier life.

It continued to rain and I only have beans and salt. The rain is strong but even so I sent the boys to school. I'm writing until the rain goes away so I can go to Senhor Manuel and sell scrap. With that money I'm going to buy rice and sausage. The rain has stopped for a while. I'm going out.

I feel so sorry for my children. When they see the things to eat that I come home with they shout:

"Viva Mama!"

Their outbursts please me. I've lost the habit of smiling. Ten minutes later they want more food. I sent João to ask Dona Ida for a little pork fat. She didn't have any. I sent her a note:

"Dona Ida, I beg you to help me get a little pork fat, so I can make soup for the children. Today it's raining and I can't go looking for paper. Thank you, Carolina."

It rained and got colder. Winter had arrived and in winter people eat more. Vera asked for food, and I didn't have any. It was the same old show. I had two *cruzeiros* and wanted to buy a little flour to make a *virado*.[1] I went to ask Dona Alice for a little pork. She gave me pork and rice. It was 9 at night when we ate.

And that is the way on May 13, 1958, I fought against the real slavery — hunger!

May 15 On the nights they have a party they don't let anybody sleep. The neighbors in the brick houses near by have signed a petition to get rid of the *favelados*. But they won't get their way. The neighbors in the brick houses say:

"The politicians protect the *favelados*."

Who protects us are the public and the Order of St. Vincent Church. The politicians only show up here during election campaigns. Senhor Candido Sampaio, when he was city councilman in 1953, spent his Sundays here in the *favela*. He was so nice. He drank our coffee, drinking right out of our cups. He made us laugh with his jokes. He played with our children. He left a good impression here

---

[1]A dish of black beans, manioc flour, pork, and eggs.

and when he was candidate for state deputy, he won. But the Chamber of Deputies didn't do one thing for the *favelados*. He doesn't visit us any more. . . .

May 22 Today I'm sad. I'm nervous. I don't know if I should start crying or start running until I fall unconscious. At dawn it was raining. I couldn't go out to get any money. I spent the day writing. I cooked the macaroni and I'll warm it up again for the children. I cooked the potatoes and they ate them. I have a few tin cans and a little scrap that I'm going to sell to Senhor Manuel. When João came home from school I sent him to sell the scrap. He got 13 *cruzeiros*. He bought a glass of mineral water: two *cruzeiros*. I was furious with him. Where had he seen a *favelado* with such highborn tastes?

The children eat a lot of bread. They like soft bread but when they don't have it, they eat hard bread.

Hard is the bread that we eat. Hard is the bed on which we sleep. Hard is the life of the *favelado*.

Oh, São Paulo! A queen that vainly shows her skyscrapers that are her crown of gold. All dressed up in velvet and silk but with cheap stockings underneath — the *favela*.

The money didn't stretch far enough to buy meat, so I cooked macaroni with a carrot. I didn't have any grease, it was horrible. Vera was the only one who complained yet asked for more.

"Mama, sell me to Dona Julita, because she has delicious food."

I know that there exist Brazilians here inside São Paulo who suffer more than I do. In June of '57 I felt sick and passed through the offices of the Social Service. I had carried a lot of scrap iron and got pains in my kidneys. So as not to see my children hungry I asked for help from the famous Social Service. It was there that I saw the tears slipping from the eyes of the poor. How painful it is to see the dramas that are played out there. The coldness in which they treat the poor. The only things they want to know about them is their name and address.

I went to the Governor's Palace.[2] The Palace sent me to an office at Brigadeiro Luis Antonio Avenue. They in turn sent me to the Social Service at the Santa Casa charity hospital. There I talked with Dona Maria Aparecida, who listened to me, said many things yet said nothing. I decided to go back to the Palace. I talked with Senhor Alcides. He is not Japanese yet is as yellow as rotten butter. I said to Senhor Alcides:

"I came here to ask for help because I'm ill. You sent me to Brigadeiro Luis Antonio Avenue, and I went. There they sent me to the Santa Casa. And I spent all the money I have on transportation."

"Take her!"

---

[2]Like most Brazilians, Carolina believes in going straight to the top to make her complaints.

They wouldn't let me leave. A soldier put his bayonet at my chest. I looked the soldier in the eyes and saw that he had pity on me. I told him:

"I am poor. That's why I came here."

Dr. Osvaldo de Barros entered, a false philanthropist in São Paulo who is masquerading as St. Vincent de Paul. He said:

"Call a squad car!"

The policeman took me back to the *favela* and warned me that the next time I made a scene at the welfare agency I would be locked up.

Welfare agency! Welfare for whom? . . .

May 27 It seems that the slaughterhouse threw kerosene on their garbage dump so the *favelados* would not look for meat to eat. I didn't have any breakfast and walked around half dizzy. The daze of hunger is worse than that of alcohol. The daze of alcohol makes us sing, but the one of hunger makes us shake. I know how horrible it is to only have air in the stomach.

I began to have a bitter taste in my mouth. I thought: Is there no end to the bitterness of life? I think that when I was born I was marked by fate to go hungry. I filled one sack of paper. When I entered Paulo Guimarães Street, a woman gave me some newspapers. They were clean and I went to the junk yard picking up everything that I found. Steel, tin, coal, everything serves the *favelado*. Leon weighed the paper and I got six *cruzeiros*.

I wanted to save the money to buy beans but I couldn't because my stomach was screaming and torturing me.

I decided to do something about it and bought a bread roll. What a surprising effect food has on our organisms. Before I ate, I saw the sky, the trees, and the birds all yellow, but after I ate, everything was normal to my eyes.

Food in the stomach is like fuel in machines. I was able to work better. My body stopped weighing me down. I started to walk faster. I had the feeling that I was gliding in space. I started to smile as if I was witnessing a beautiful play. And will there ever be a drama more beautiful than that of eating? I felt that I was eating for the first time in my life.

The Radio Patrol arrived. They came to take the two Negro boys who had broken into the power station. Four and six years old. It's easy to see that they are of the *favela. Favela* children are the most ragged children in the city. What they can find in the streets they eat. Banana peels, melon rind, and even pineapple husks. Anything that is too tough to chew, they grind. These boys had their pockets filled with aluminum coins, that new money in circulation.

May 28 It dawned raining. I only have three *cruzeiros* because I loaned Leila five so she could get her daughter in the hospital. I'm confused and don't know where to begin. I want to write, I want to work, I want to wash clothes. I'm cold and I don't have any shoes to wear. The children's shoes are worn out.

The worst thing in the *favela* is that there are children here. All the children of the *favela* know what a woman's body looks like. Because when the couples that are drunk fight, the woman, so as not to get a beating, runs naked into the street. When the fights start the *favelados* leave whatever they are doing to be present at the battle. So that when the woman goes running naked it's a real show for Joe Citizen. Afterward the comments begin among the children:

"Fernanda ran out nude when Armin was hitting her."

"Oh, I didn't see it. Damn!"

"What does a naked woman look like?"

And then the other, in order to tell him, puts his mouth near his ear. And the loud laughter echoes. Everything that is obscene or pornographic the *favelado* learns quickly.

There are some shacks where prostitutes play their love scenes right in front of the children.

The rich neighbors in the brick houses say we are protected by the politicians. They're wrong. The politicians only show up here in the Garbage Dump at election time. This year we had a visit from a candidate for deputy, Dr. Paulo de Campos Moura, who gave us beans and some wonderful blankets. He came at an opportune moment, before it got cold.

What I want to clear up about the people who live in the *favela* is the following: The only ones who really survive here are the *nordestinos*.[3] They work and don't squander. They buy a house or go back up north.

Here in the *favela* there are those who build shacks to live in and those who build them to rent. And the rents are from 500 to 700 *cruzeiros*. Those who make shacks to sell spend 4,000 *cruzeiros* and sell them for 11,000. Who made a lot of shacks to sell was Tiburcio.

May 29 It finally stopped raining. The clouds glided toward the horizon. Only the cold attacked us. Many people in the *favela* don't have warm clothing. When one has shoes he won't have a coat. I choke up watching the children walk in the mud. It seems that some new people have arrived in the *favela*. They are ragged with undernourished faces. They improvised a shack. It hurts me to see so much pain, reserved for the working class. I stared at my new companion in misfortune. She looked at the *favela* with its mud and sickly children. It was the saddest look I'd ever seen. Perhaps she has no more illusions. She had given her life over to misery.

[3]Forced by land-parching droughts and almost no industry, the poor of the north swarm into cities like São Paulo and Rio looking for work. Needing a place to live, they choose the *favelas* and end up worse off than they were before.

There will be those who reading what I write will say — this is untrue. But misery is real.

What I revolt against is the greed of men who squeeze other men as if they were squeezing oranges.

$$178$$

AUNG SAN SUU KYI*

From Letters from Burma

The author of these letters heads the democratic political party that won election in Burma in 1980. In consequence, she was placed under house arrest by the brutal military junta (SLORC, for State Law and Order Restoration Council), which has continued to rule. Despite her receipt of the Nobel Prize in 1991 and continued devotional support from the Burmese people, the generals have refused to let this daughter of Aung San — Burma's national hero who was assassinated in 1947 just before Burma achieved independence — take office and sometimes even leave her house.

In these letters, written to a Japanese newspaper in 1996, Suu Kyi reveals an unusual combination of the personal and political, some might say the patriotic without the patriarchal. Is this a view of politics that a male politician would be unlikely to hold?

Thinking Historically

Is there such a thing as women's politics? Do women vote differently than men? If so, what is that difference? Construct a theory that explains it.

Some people have pointed to the relatively large number of women presidents and prime ministers in South Asia in recent years. Women have been elected to govern India, Pakistan, Sri Lanka, as well as Burma. Can you formulate a theory that might explain this?

Many would say that particular women who have governed South Asia — Indira Gandhi of India, Benazir Bhutto of Pakistan, Sirimavo Bandaranaike of Sri Lanka — have not governed any differently from

---

*ong sahn   soo KYEE

Aung San Suu Kyi, *Letters from Burma* (New York: Penguin, 1996), 19–21, 55–57.

men. Perhaps politics has more to do with social background, interests, wealth, and class than it does with gender. Try to formulate a theory about women in politics that is based on the readings of this chapter.

The Peacock and the Dragon

The tenth day of the waning moon of the month of Tazaungdine marks National Day in Burma. It is the anniversary of the boycott against the 1920 Rangoon University Act which was seen by the Burmese as a move to restrict higher education to a privileged few. This boycott, which was initiated by university students, gained widespread support and could be said to have been the first step in the movement for an independent Burma. National Day is thus a symbol of the intimate and indissoluble link between political and intellectual freedom and of the vital role that students have played in the politics of Burma.

This year the seventy-fifth anniversary of National Day fell on 16 November. A committee headed by elder politicians and prominent men of letters was formed to plan the commemoration ceremony. It was decided that the celebrations should be on a modest scale in keeping with our financial resources and the economic situation of the country. The programme was very simple: some speeches, the presentation of prizes to those who had taken part in essay competitions organized by the National League for Democracy, and the playing of songs dating back to the days of the independence struggle. There was also a small exhibition of photographs, old books, and magazines.

An unseasonable rain had been falling for several days before the sixteenth but on the morning of National Day itself the weather turned out to be fine and dry. Many of the guests came clad in *pinni*, a hand-woven cotton cloth that ranges in colour from a flaxen beige through varying shades of apricot and orange to burnt umber. During the independence struggle *pinni* had acquired the same significance in Burma as *khaddi* in India, a symbol of patriotism and a practical sign of support for native goods.

Since 1988 it has also become the symbol of the movement for democracy. A *pinni* jacket worn with a white collarless shirt and a Kachin sarong (a tartan pattern in purple, black, and green) is the unofficial uniform for "democracy men." The dress for "democracy women" is a *pinni aingyi* (Burmese style blouse) with a traditional hand-woven sarong. During my campaign trip to the state of Kachin in 1989 I once drove through an area considered unsafe because it was within a zone where insurgents were known to be active. For mile upon mile men clad in *pinni* jackets on which the red badge of NLD [National League for Democracy] gleamed bravely stood as a "guard of honour" along the route, entirely unarmed. It was a proud and joyous sight.

The seventy-fifth anniversary of National Day brought a proud and joyous sight too. The guests were not all clad in *pinni* but there was about them a brightness that was pleasing to both the eye and the heart. The younger people were full of quiet enthusiasm and the older ones seemed rejuvenated. A well-known student politician of the 1930s who had become notorious in his mature years for the shapeless shirt, shabby denim trousers, scuffed shoes (gum boots during the monsoons), and battered hat in which he would tramp around town was suddenly transformed into a dapper gentleman in full Burmese national costume. All who knew him were stunned by the sudden picture of elegance he presented and our photographer hastened to record such an extraordinary vision.

The large bamboo and thatch pavilion that had been put up to receive the thousand guests was decorated with white banners on which were printed the green figure of a dancing peacock. As a backdrop to the stage there was a large dancing peacock, delicately executed on a white disc. This bird is the symbol of the students who first awoke the political consciousness of the people of Burma. It represents a national movement that culminated triumphantly with the independence of the country.

The orchestra had arrived a little late as there had been an attempt to try to "persuade" the musicians not to perform at our celebration. But their spirits were not dampened. They stayed on after the end of the official ceremony to play and sing nationalist songs from the old days. The most popular of these was *Nagani*, "Red Dragon." *Nagani* was the name of a book club founded by a group of young politicians in 1937 with the intention of making works on politics, economics, history, and literature accessible to the people of Burma. The name of the club became closely identified with patriotism and a song was written about the prosperity that would come to the country through the power of the Red Dragon.

Nagani was sung by a young man with a strong, beautiful voice and we all joined in the chorus while some of the guests went up on stage and performed Burmese dances. But beneath the light-hearted merriment ran a current of serious intent. The work of our national movement remains unfinished. We have still to achieve the prosperity promised by the dragon. It is not yet time for the triumphant dance of the peacock. . . .

A Baby in the Family

A couple of weeks ago some friends of mine became grandparents for the first time when their daughter gave birth to a little girl. The husband accepted his new status as grandfather with customary joviality, while the wife, too young-looking and pretty to get into the conventional idea of a cosily aged grandmother, found it a somewhat startling experience. The baby was the first grandchild for the "boy's side" as well, so she was truly a novel addition to the family circle, the subject of much adoring attention. I was told the paternal grandfather was especially pleased because the baby had been born in the Burmese month of *Pyatho* — an auspicious time for the birth of a girl child.

In societies where the birth of a girl is considered a disaster, the atmosphere of excitement and pride surrounding my friends' granddaughter would have caused astonishment. In Burma there is no prejudice against girl babies. In fact, there is a general belief that daughters are more dutiful and loving than sons and many Burmese parents welcome the birth of a daughter as an assurance that they will have somebody to take care of them in their old age.

My friends' granddaughter was only twelve days old when I went to admire her. She lay swaddled in pristine white on a comfortable pile of blankets and sheets spread on the wooden floor of my friends' bungalow, a small dome of mosquito netting arched prettily over her. It had been a long time since I had seen such a tiny baby and I was struck by its miniature perfection. I do not subscribe to the Wodehousian view that all babies look like poached eggs. Even if they do not have clearly defined features, babies have distinct expressions that mark them off as individuals from birth. And they certainly have individual cries, a fact I learned soon after the birth of my first son. It took me a few hours to realize that the yells of each tiny vociferous inmate of the maternity hospital had its own unique pitch, cadence, range, and grace-notes.

My friends' grandchild, however, did not provide me with a chance to familiarize myself with her particular milk call. Throughout my visit she remained as inanimate and still as a carved papoose on display in a museum, oblivious of the fuss and chatter around her. At one time her eyelids fluttered slightly and she showed signs of stirring but it was a false alarm. She remained resolutely asleep even when I picked her up and we all clustered around to have our photograph taken with the new star in our firmament.

Babies, I have read somewhere, are specially constructed to present an appealingly vulnerable appearance aimed at arousing tender, protective instincts: only then can tough adults be induced to act as willing slaves to demanding little beings utterly incapable of doing anything for themselves. It is claimed that there is something about the natural smell of a baby's skin that invites cuddles and kisses. Certainly I like both the shape and smell of babies, but I wonder whether their attraction does not lie in something more than merely physical attributes. Is it not the thought of a life stretching out like a shining clean slate on which might one day be written the most beautiful prose and poetry of existence that engenders such joy in the hearts of the parents and grandparents of a newly born child? The birth of a baby is an occasion for weaving hopeful dreams about the future.

However, in some families parents are not able to indulge in long dreams over their children. The infant mortality rate in Burma is 94 per 1000 live births, the fourth highest among the nations of the East Asia and Pacific Region. The mortality rate for those under the age of five too is the fourth highest in the region, 147 per 1000. And the maternal mortality rate is the third highest in the region at the official rate of 123 per 100 000 live births. (United Nations agencies surmise that the actual maternal mortality rate is in fact higher, 140 or more per 100 000.)

The reasons for these high mortality rates are malnutrition, lack of access to safe water and sanitation, lack of access to health services, and lack of caring capacity, which includes programmes for childhood development, primary education, and health education. In summary, there is a strong need in Burma for greater investment in health and education. Yet government expenditure in both sectors, as a proportion of the budget, has been falling steadily. Education accounted for 5.9 per cent of the budget in 1992–3, 5.2 per cent in 1993–4, and 5 per cent in 1994–5. Similarly, government spending on health care has dropped from 2.6 per cent in 1992–3, to 1.8 per cent in 1993–4, and 1.6 per cent in 1994–5.

Some of the best indicators of a country developing along the right lines are healthy mothers giving birth to healthy children who are assured of good care and a sound education that will enable them to face the challenges of a changing world. Our dreams for the future of the children of Burma have to be woven firmly around a commitment to better health care and better education.

179

UNFPA

Gender Inequality in National Parliaments

The United Nations Population Fund known by the acronym UNFPA (because it was established in 1969 as the United Nations Fund for Population Activities) works with governments and nongovernmental organizations in over 140 countries. As the largest international source for funding of population and reproductive health programs, the Fund is particularly concerned with the lives and needs of women. This reading is drawn from UNFPA's *State of the World 2005 Fact Sheet*, which summarizes the global dimensions of women's health, employment, education, and, in this particular selection, political participation. What do these charts and accompanying explanations tell you about women's political power in the governments of our contemporary world?

Thinking Historically

Theory construction almost always begins with questions. Look over the numbers in the two charts (Tables 27.1 and 27.2) in this selection and see what questions these numbers raise in your mind. Construct a theory based on the numbers in one or both of the charts. Notice how the accompanying explanations to the charts pose or answer questions. What theories do these explanations offer? How is your theory similar or different from those suggested by the explanations? What other types of sources (aside from this fact sheet and tables) would you look to to reinforce your theory?

Gender Inequality in National Parliaments

The number of women in national parliaments continues to increase, but no country in the world has yet reached gender parity.

A number of factors continue to present challenges to women's parliamentary representation:

- The type of electoral system in place in a country
- The role and discipline of political parties

United Nations Population Fund, Gender Equality Fact Sheet UNFPA, in *State of the World 2005 Fact Sheet*. Available on-line at http://www.unfpa.org/swp/2005/presskit/factsheets/facts_gender.htm.

- Women's social and economic status
- Socio-cultural traditions and beliefs about a woman's place in the family and society.
- Women's double burden of work and family responsibilities.

Since the early 1990s, women's share of *seats in parliament* has steadily increased. Nevertheless, women still hold only 16 per cent of seats worldwide.

Share of Women in Single or Lower Houses of Parliament, 1990–2005[1]

Table 27.1 Percentage of Parliamentary Seats Held by Women (single or lower house only),* 1990–2005

Regions	1990	1997	2005
World	12.4	11.4	15.9
Developed regions	15.4	15.6	20.9
Commonwealth of Independent States	—	6.2	10.5
Commonwealth of Independent States, Asia	—	7.0	11.5
Commonwealth of Independent States, Europe	—	5.4	10.5
Developing regions	10.4	10.1	14.3
Northern Africa	2.6	1.8	8.5
Sub-Saharan Africa	7.2	9.0	14.2
Latin America and the Caribbean	11.9	12.4	19.0
Eastern Asia	20.2	19.3	19.4
Southern Asia	5.7	5.9	8.3
South-Eastern Asia	10.4	10.8	15.5
Western Asia	4.6	3.0	5.0
Oceania	1.2	1.6	3.0
Least developed countries	7.3	7.3	12.7
Landlocked developing countries	14.0	6.6	13.2
Small island developing states	14.4	11.0	17.3

*Data refer to 1 January of each year.

Source: United Nations Statistics Division, "World and Regional Trends," Millennium Indicators Database, http://millenniumindicators.un.org (accessed June 2005) based on data provided by the Inter-Parliamentary Union.

The largest relative increases in the proportion of women in parliament have been in Northern Africa — where the percentage of women in parliaments tripled since 1990 — followed by Latin America and the Caribbean and sub-Saharan Africa.

---

[1]Statistics and charts are based on Department of Economic and Social Affairs. Statistics Division. Progress towards the Millennium Development Goals, 1990–2005. Available on-line at http://unstats.un.org/unsd/mi/goals_2005/goal_3.pdf. [Ed.]

There was significant progress also in the developed regions and in Southern and South-Eastern Asia.

In moving towards multiparty democracies, countries in the CIS (former Soviet Union) saw a significant decrease in the number of women in the political arena in the early 1990s. Previously, women's political participation was guaranteed, and their representation was frequently over 30 per cent.

Nordic countries have experienced a sustained and exceptionally high level of women's participation in the political arena, with the percentage of women in parliament well above 30 per cent.

Strategies for Increased Political Participation of Women

Many post-conflict countries have recognized the importance of including women in peace-building and reconstruction and have instituted measures to ensure women's participation in new democratic institutions.

- The national constitutions of Rwanda and Burundi now include provisions to reserve seats for women.
- In 2003, elections in Rwanda saw the greatest proportion of women elected to any parliament in history. These elections were the first since the internal conflict of 1994.
- The Rwandan parliament has come closest to reaching an equal number of men and women in parliament.
- In South Africa and Mozambique, the introduction of quota mechanisms by political parties meant that, in 2004, post-conflict and post-crisis countries ranked among the highest in the world in terms of women's representation.
- In Eritrea, Mozambique, and South Africa women comprise between 22 per cent to 35 per cent of the legislature.

The increase in women's parliamentary representation in Latin America and the Caribbean is also attributable to the introduction of affirmative action measures. Various quotas for women's political participation exist in 17 countries in this region. Similar efforts have been made in the Arab world.

In Morocco, the electoral law was amended prior to the 2002 parliamentary elections to reserve 30 seats for women. Thirty-five women were subsequently elected. In Tunisia, the President's party allocated 25 per cent of positions on its electoral list for women, winning them 22.7 per cent of the seats in the Chamber of Deputies in 2004. Consequently, Tunisia leads the regional ranking for women in Arab parliaments. See http://unstats.un.org/unsd/mi/goals_2005/goal_3.pdf.

Table 27.2 Countries That Have Reached 30 Per Cent Representation by Women in Parliament, as of 1 January 2005

	Percentage of seats held by women	Number of seats held by women	Total number of seats
Rwanda	48.8	39	80
Sweden	45.3	158	349
Norway	38.2	63	165
Denmark	38.0	68	179
Finland	37.5	75	200
Netherlands	36.7	55	150
Cuba	36.0	219	609
Spain	36.0	126	350
Costa Rica	35.1	20	57
Mozambique	34.8	87	250
Belgium	34.7	52	150
Austria	33.9	62	183
Argentina	33.7	86	255
Germany	32.8	197	601
South Africa	32.8	131	400
Guyana	30.8	20	65
Iceland	30.2	19	63

Source: United Nations Statistics Division, "World and Regional Trends," Millennium Indicators Database, http://millenniumindicators.un.org (accessed June 2005), based on data provided by the Inter-Parliamentary Union.

180

DIANE DIXON

Michelle, Top Woman in a Macho World

On March 11, 2005, Michelle Bachelet* became the first woman president of Chile, a victory made even more impressive by the fact that she was a socialist, an agnostic, and an unwed mother in a traditionally Catholic conservative country. Nor was she the daughter or widow of a previous president. In fact, she had been imprisoned and tortured by the Pinochet government that toppled the socialist

*bah chel LEHT

Diane Dixon, "Michelle, Top Woman in a Macho World," *The Observer*, April 2, 2006, n.p. Also available on-line at http://observer.guardian.co.uk/world/story/0,,1744947,00.html.

Salvador Allende* in 1973. Like Allende, she is also a medical doctor. This selection is drawn from *The Observer,* the Sunday magazine, from the British newspaper *The Guardian.* How would you explain Michelle Bachelet's popularity and political success? Is there a pattern in the success of the twelve heads of state profiled here?

Thinking Historically

This selection presents the stories of Michelle Bachelet and those of the eleven other women recently elected heads of state. Collectively they suggest various theories about a wide range of issues. We might ask how women attain such an office, what conditions or cultures make the success of women more or less likely, whether women in office pursue significantly different policies than men, whether women officials significantly improve the lives of women, and many other questions. Choose one of these questions, or ask another, and then suggest a theory to answer it. How would you try to find out if your theory was accurate or mistaken?

Michelle Bachelet remembers the day of her inauguration as Chile's first woman leader with pride: "They were very beautiful moments. I remember the feeling of joy. In the streets, thousands of women and children put on presidential sashes. It meant everyone was going to La Moneda [the Presidential Palace] together with me."

With that bright display of solidarity on a warm March day three weeks ago Bachelet became the world's 11th female elected leader. On Thursday the inauguration of Portia Simpson-Miller in Jamaica made her the 12th, and just over 6 per cent of countries are led by women. Discounting the crowned heads of the past, it is a small but unprecedented number.

What these dozen women have in common — with the exception perhaps of Bangladesh's Begum Khaleda Zia, who was projected into premiership by her husband's death — is beating intensely male-dominated odds to achieve power in some fairly conservative societies. As Bachelet said in her victory speech: "Who would have thought, friends . . . 20, 10, or five years ago, that Chile would elect a woman as president?"

And who would have thought that a Catholic country that only legalised divorce a few years ago would elect an agnostic, single mother who promised equality — exactly half of her cabinet appointees are women.

It is an undoubted phenomenon that this immensely popular multilingual mother-of-three was able to slash through the bonds of male

*ah YEHN day

political party politics to become Minister of Health and, subsequently, South America's first woman Minister of Defence. But, in an exclusive interview with *The Observer*, Bachelet said she believes the credit does not go so much to the willing patronage of her male politicians as to that of the Chilean people, who commonly call their president by her first name and sing the Beatles tune of the same name to her.

"It was said that Chile was not ready to vote for a woman, it was traditionally a sexist country. In the end, the reverse happened: The fact of being a woman became a symbol of the process of cultural change the country was undergoing. Men voted for me in their majority, but, for the first time, the Concertación [the Centre Left Coalition of which Bachelet was the candidate] also won extensively among women."

"The possibility of my presidential candidacy emerged spontaneously in public opinion polls. For my part, I noticed people's affection when I was doing work on the ground. I think the important thing is that my candidacy was born from citizens themselves, driven by the people and which the parties picked up favourably."

She is the daughter of an air force general, Alberto Bachelet, who, because he remained loyal to Salvador Allende, was killed by his own comrades after the coup that brought Augusto Pinochet to power in September 1973. She herself was a victim, along with her archaeologist mother, Angela Jeria, of the worst abuses of the Pinochet dictatorship, jailed and tortured and exiled first to Australia and then to Germany. Her only brother, Alberto, died in 2001.

In difficult circumstances under the dictatorship, she qualified as a doctor and paediatrician, going on to work with child victims of human rights abuses. But politics were always close to her. Bachelet joined Chile's Young Socialists in her teens, rising through the ranks and campaigning for the return to democracy in Chile, which was achieved in the 1988 plebiscite that ousted the Pinochet regime. When the opposition lambasted Bachelet for being overweight in the physical sense and lightweight in the political, her mother's retort was: "Have they ever looked at her CV!"

Bachelet the girl was renowned for her insistence on having her views heard and, according to Jeria, "was very firm and defended her ideas forcefully. She never accepted being told that no you can't do that. She always demanded an explanation. But at the same time she was a sweet child whose intelligence was noticeable in thousands of details."

And it was in her youth, Bachelet says, that "her most intense moments" came. "Having experienced personally and through my family the tragedy of Chile is something always present in my memory. I do not want events of that nature ever to happen again, and I have dedicated an important part of my life to ensuring that and to the reunion of all Chileans."

By the mid-1990s, she was established as an adviser in the Ministry of Health and started studies in military strategy at Chile's National

Academy for Political and Military Strategy on a course normally the reserve of military commanders. Having graduated, she was awarded a presidential grant of honour which took her to Washington to take an elite course at the Inter-American Defence College, where once again she came first.

"During the transition to democracy, I felt there was a necessity to unite two worlds, the military and the civic. I felt political leaders didn't know or understand the military world and that it was fundamentally important that political leaders got inside the world of defence to establish a bridge between the two worlds. Given political history in Chile, it seemed to me that there was a critical task of consolidating a democracy and creating healthy civic-military and political-military relationships."

In 2000, Bachelet was made minister of health by President Ricardo Lagos and handed the task of ending within three months the queues for appointments in health centres: "It was about giving a very clear signal of making people the central focus of state services. The state is at the service of people, not the opposite. My impression is that people understood the message very well, they realised the effort that we made."

In January 2002 came another challenge. Lagos took the bold step in macho Latin America of naming her minister of defence: "The truth is that I confronted it with a great deal of calm. My relationship with the armed forces was proper and normal from the beginning, despite the fact I was a woman, a socialist, and a victim of human rights abuses. But I must be honest: There was never any improper attitude towards me in the armed forces for these reasons, quite the contrary. I believe it is important to highlight this.

"In respect of political achievements, the most important thing for me is to have contributed to the consolidation of the first process of reunion between the Armed Forces and society in Chile's modern history. For many decades the military had aligned themselves to an ideology that was not shared by the whole country. Today, the Chilean military have embraced a democratic vision of their profession and are committed to a democratic state of law. I am pleased to have contributed to this process."

Having made the appointment, Lagos asked a close collaborator of Bachelet's, Carlos Ominami, if he thought she would do well. The response was: "If only we had 20 like Michelle."

Bachelet is also the mother of three children, Sebastián, Francisca, and Sofía, the youngest, who is 12. Two are by her former husband, architect Jorge Davalos, one by a subsequent boyfriend, Dr. Anibal Henriquez. Her mother gave up her own political activities to help with the grandchildren and has become a celebrity in her own right. "Once it took me five minutes to go to the supermarket," she told *The Observer*. "Now everyone wants to chat and it takes five times that."

And Bachelet recognises the support: "It is undeniable that my current responsibilities demand some changes in my life, but I aspire to maintaining the most normal family life possible. I hope that not much changes now that I am president. I would like Chileans to remember me as a transparent woman, who always said what she thought and did what she said."

Other Female Leaders

The Philippines: Undaunted Coup Survivor

The President of the Philippines may be on the *Forbes* list as the fourth most powerful woman in the world, but Gloria Arroyo, 58, is fighting calls for her resignation after narrowly escaping impeachment for allegedly rigging last year's presidential election, in which she defeated a popular film star, Fernando Poe. During her first term, she overcame a coup attempt and a Senate investigation of her lawyer husband, Jose Miguel, into alleged money laundering and keeping excess campaign funds. Arroyo, the daughter of former president Diosdado Macapagal and a trained economist, was elected to the Senate in 1992. She came to power in the rollercoaster world of Philippines politics when former film star President Joseph Estrada was toppled in a "people's revolution."

Germany: East Berlin's "Thatcher"

Often described as the German Margaret Thatcher, Angela Merkel* is the first female Chancellor of Germany. She is also the first former citizen of the old communist East Germany to head the reunited country. Fluent in Russian and English, she grew up in the countryside north of Berlin. She became involved in the pro-democracy movements that helped bring down the Berlin wall in 1989 and then entered national German politics after reunification. Her old East German party merged with the conservative CDU. She became Chancellor by defeating Gerhard Schroeder in 2005's narrow elections. After a shaky start, one poll in January showed that Merkel's popularity ratings were the highest for any German chancellor since 1949. But it has been a long hard struggle all the way for the woman whose childlessness became an election issue for her when critics attacked her for being "incomplete."

Liberia: After Exile and Prison,
the Chance to Rebuild a Nation

Liberia's new 68-year-old female president faces one of the biggest tasks of any world leader: rebuilding her shattered homeland after

*AHN gel ah   MAYR kuhl

decades of civil war. Ellen Johnson Sirleaf has said the problems are so great that even just restoring electricity to the capital Monrovia will be an achievement. She also faces a country deeply divided ethnically, flooded with guns and traumatised child soldiers.

Sirleaf has a German grandfather who married a Liberian market-woman from a rural village. She went to college in Liberia and then studied in America, including Harvard. She entered Liberian politics in 1979 and became an assistant minister of finance. During the country's multiple civil wars in the 1980s and 1990s Sirleaf spent time in jail, was exiled to Kenya, and ended up working for the World Bank. She returned with the overthrow of warlord Charles Taylor and won countrywide elections last year, defeating footballer George Weah. She was inaugurated in January.

Jamaica: "Sista P" Breaks Male Monopoly as She Guns for the Drug Gangs

Portia Simpson Miller, 60, who was sworn in as Jamaica's new Prime Minister last Thursday, has become the first female leader of a nation with a very male political culture. She launched her bid to head first the People's National Party and then the country by ignoring her critics. She was ridiculed in some parts of the island nation's media as a "serial kisser" at rallies and an intellectual lightweight. Yet Miller confounded the nay-sayers, and her genuine popularity at the grassroots level of politics saw her swept into office.

Known to many as "Sista P," Miller is seen as someone who can crack down on crime, especially the drugs trade, and bring greater economic development to a country still mired in poverty and drug violence. She has promised to enlist her friend, star athlete Asafa Powell, in the quest to end drug-related killings, especially in the slums of the capital, Kingston.

Miller first entered parliament in 1976. In a male-dominated culture she fought her way to the top, earning several ministerial portfolios including labour, welfare, and sports. She is married to Errald Miller, a former chief executive of the Jamaica arm of Cable and Wireless. She is a keen fan of boxing and golf.

Miller has criticised some aspects of Jamaica's tourist industry, saying the behaviour of some visitors clashes with the island's traditional morals.

Finland: Radical Leftist Goes on with 90 Per Cent Approval

Finland's president Tarja Halonen, 61, has just begun her second term in office. When it expires in 2012, she will have been the Scandinavian nation's head of state for 12 years. Raised in a working-class area of

Helsinki, she represents a radical leftist strand of Finnish politics. She was an unmarried mother — although has since wed her partner.

Her time in office has put a strong emphasis on pacifism, human rights, and international co-operation. Despite initially coming to office after a narrow election victory, she has become extremely popular with Finns of every political persuasion, regularly enjoying approval ratings in excess of 90 per cent. In 2004 she was the only living person to be placed in the top 10 of a television programme dedicated to the country's greatest public and historic figures.

Bangladesh: Widow Who Inherited the Mantle of Leadership

As the widow of assassinated president Ziaur Rahman, Bangladesh's first woman Prime Minister, Khaleda Zia is among the women who have had leadership foisted on them because of their marriage and subsequent widowhood. She was premier from 1991 to 1996 and again from 2001 to the present. Until her husband's death in a 1981 attempted military coup, Zia had little role in politics. But afterwards she became a senior figure in her husband's old party, the Bangladesh Nationalist Party. She has made education for girls, particularly those from poor rural families, one of her government's top priorities.

Others

Vaira Vike-Freiberga, aged 68, President of Latvia. Has been in power since 1999.

Mary McAleese, 54, President of Ireland since 1997.

Luisa Diogo, 47, Prime Minister of Mozambique since 2004.

Helen Clark, 55, Prime Minister of New Zealand since 1999.

Chandrika Kumaratunga, 60, President of Sri Lanka, in power since 1994.

Women on the Verge

Hillary Clinton, 59, hopes to run as Democratic party candidate in America's 2008 presidential race.

Ségolène Royal, 52, front runner to be chosen as the Socialist candidate to fight France's presidential elections next year.

Yulia Tymoshenko, 45, was dismissed as Prime Minister of Ukraine last September. But the results of last month's parliamentary elections, which brought her success, have brought pressure on President Viktor Yushchenko to reinstate her in a coalition government. He needs her support after suffering a setback.

REFLECTIONS

Can there be a history of women, even a history of women during the last half of the twentieth century? Or are the lives of women too diverse — globally, economically, politically, culturally — to make a single, coherent story? Is the history of women during the last fifty years markedly different from the history of men or the history of humanity?

This chapter gives only a hint of the diversity of women's lives. We included China's hopeful marriage law at the beginning of the chapter but nothing about the failures to observe it, or about women who were forced out of work to make room for men, or about girls who were sold into virtual slavery, or about young women forced to work long hours in sweatshops. Nor did we include any discussion of glamorous models in Shanghai, rich capitalists and poor sex workers in Hong Kong, or ordinary mothers, wives, and workers for whom the law of 1950 *did* make a difference.

While Betty Friedan verbalized the feelings of many American women in 1963, how many women today, exhausted by working long hours that barely cover the costs of child care and commuting, would consider returning to a fifties world of motherhood and housework? How important are national differences? In what sense, if any, does an Algerian woman who is Muslim speak for a Muslim woman in Egypt or Iran or Pakistan, or for a Christian woman in Algeria? We have not even considered women from the Middle East, India, Russia, and Europe. These questions are intended to point to the enormous variety of women's experiences. Of course, the historian is forever seeking patterns and process, but finding even the general direction of change is not as simple as it might seem.

Have the lives of women improved over the course of the last hundred or the last fifty years? It is commonly thought that the twentieth century was extremely important in freeing women from the bonds of patriarchal limitations. Often, this process is divided into two stages, the first consisting of gaining the vote in the early decades of the century in Europe and America, and the second, the successes of the women's movement since 1960. This second wave broadened the feminist critique from concerns about elections to issues of equality in the workplace and patriarchy as a social and cultural force, ultimately resulting in a cohesive movement, improved public awareness, and specific legislation regarding women's rights. In this way, the movement of the sixties became public policy.

Patriarchies continue to oppress women in many parts of the world. Women in Africa, Asia, and Latin America suffer from higher rates of illiteracy, child marriage, spousal abuse, and mortality in child birth than women in the developed world, but recent increases in parliamentary representation by women in the developing world must inevitably redress these imbalances. If the campaign for women's political rights came first to the developed world, some of the countries in the developing world have left Europe and North America far behind. Nor is the second wave or "cultural revolution" for women limited to the rich countries of the West. The success of women like Aung San Suu Kyi in Burma and Michelle Bachelet in Chile suggest that the United States and Europe might still have far to go in achieving true social and political equality for women.

For most women today, the world has been shaped less by political struggles and more by the expanding global market. Poor women in Brazil, Indonesia, China, and the Philippines have seized the opportunity to escape the authority of fathers and village elders to work in modern factories that pay far more than they ever imagined, but barely enough to survive in distant cities after sending money home. The victory of market forces in former "command economies," like Russia, Poland, and Lithuania (countries where most doctors were women), has been accompanied by drastic declines in the employment of women and men, as well as declines in the percentage of professional women.

If there is not a single history of women that is different from a single history of humanity, there are millions, indeed billions, of histories of women, women's acts, women's worlds. The selections in this chapter hint at just a few of those histories. Perhaps the most useful service our brief discussions here can serve is to encourage you to explore women's stories further.

Globalization
and Planetary Health

1960 to the Present

HISTORICAL CONTEXT

Globalization is a term used by historians, economists, politicians, religious leaders, social reformers, business people, and average citizens to describe large-scale changes and trends in the world today. It is often defined as a complex phenomenon whereby individuals, nations, and regions of the world become increasingly integrated and interdependent, and national and traditional identities are diminished. Although it is a widely used term, globalization is also a controversial and widely debated topic. Is globalization really a new phenomenon or is it a continuation of earlier trends? Is it driven by technological forces or economic forces, or both? Does it enrich or impoverish? Is it democratizing or antidemocratic? Is it generally a positive or negative thing?

Some limit the definition of globalization to the global integration driven by the development of the international market economy in the last twenty to forty years. Worldwide integration dates back much further, however, and has important technological, cultural, and political causes as well. In fact, all of human history can be understood as the story of increased interaction on a limited planet. Ancient empires brought diverse peoples from vast regions of the world together under single administrations. These empires, connected by land or maritime routes, interacted with each other through trade and exploration, exchanging goods as well as ideas. The unification of the Eastern and Western hemispheres after 1492 was a major step in the globalization of crops, peoples, cultures, and diseases. The industrial revolution joined countries and continents in ever vaster and faster transportation and communication networks. The great colonial empires that developed during the eighteenth and nineteenth centuries integrated the populations of far-flung areas of the world. The commercial aspects of these developments cannot be divorced from religious zeal, technological innovations, and political motives, which were often driving factors.

The current era of economic globalization is largely a product of the industrial capitalist world, roughly dating back to the middle of the nineteenth century. We might call the period between 1850 and 1914 the first great age of globalization in the modern sense. It was the age of ocean liners, mass migrations, undersea telegraph cables, transcontinental railroads, refrigeration, and preserved canned foods, when huge European empires dramatically reduced the number of sovereign states in the world. The period ended with World War I, which not only dug trenches between nations and wiped out a generation of future migrants and visitors, but also planted seeds of animosity that festered for decades, strangling the growth of international trade, interaction, and immigration.

Since the conclusion of World War II in 1945, and increasingly since the end of the Cold War in 1989, political and technological developments have enabled economic globalization on a wider scale and at a faster pace than occurred during the previous age of steamships and telegraphs. The collapse of the Soviet Union and international communism unleashed the forces of market capitalism as never before. Jet travel, satellite technology, mobile phones, and the World Wide Web have revived global integration and enabled the global marketplace. The United States, the World Bank, and the International Monetary Fund led in the creation of regional and international free-trade agreements, the reduction of tariffs, and the removal of national trade barriers, touting these changes as agents of material progress and democratic transformation. Yet these changes have also elicited wide-ranging resistance in peaceful protests, especially against the West's economic dominance, and violent ones against the West's political and cultural domination, protest that has taken the form of terrorist attacks like those of September 11, 2001.

Multinational companies are now able to generate great wealth by moving capital, labor, raw materials, and finished products through international markets at increasing speeds and with lasting impact. This economic globalization has profound cultural ramifications; increasingly the peoples of the world are watching the same films and television programs, speaking the same languages, wearing the same clothes, enjoying the same amusements, and listening to the same music. Whether free-market capitalism lifts all boats, or only yachts, is a hotly debated issue today.

Global health may or may not benefit from globalization, but recent developments suggest the well-being of the planet and the welfare of its inhabitants may be in jeopardy. The very integration of the world makes it possible for a virus, whether organic or cyber, to travel fast and infect the most distant areas of the planet. The uniformity of modern life makes it possible to share our dreams and inventions but also our nightmares and mistakes, and with a global and instantaneous effect as September 11th and subsequent terrorist attacks made abundantly clear. The technology of nuclear energy and war and the impact of our fossil fuel binge on the very atmosphere that supports us are causes of great concern, as are the perceived political and cultural dominance of the West.

THINKING HISTORICALLY
Understanding Process

What are the most important ways in which the world is changing? What are the most significant and powerful forces of change? What is the engine that is driving our world? These are the big questions raised at the end of historical investigation. They also arise at the beginning, as the assumptions that shape our specific investigations. Globalization is one of the words most frequently used to describe the big changes that are occurring in our world. All of the readings in this chapter assume or describe some kind of global integration as a dominant driver of the world in which we live. This chapter asks you to think about large-scale historical processes. It asks you to examine globalization as one of the most important of these processes. It asks you to reflect on what globalization means, and what causes it. How does each of these authors use the term? Do the authors see this process as primarily commercial and market-driven, or do they view it as a matter of culture or politics? Does globalization come from one place or many, from a center outwards, from one kind of society to another? Is globalization linear or unidirectional, or does it have differing, even opposite effects? What do these writers, thinkers, and activists believe about the most important changes transforming our world? And what do you think?

SHERIF HETATA

Dollarization

Sherif Hetata is an Egyptian intellectual, novelist, and activist who was originally trained as a medical doctor. He and his wife, the prominent feminist writer Nawal El-Saadawi, have worked together to promote reform in Egypt and the larger Arab world. In the following address Hetata outlines the global economy's homogenizing effects on culture. Through what historic lens does Hetata view globalization? What links does he make between globalization and imperialism? What do you think of his argument?

Thinking Historically

What, according to Hetata, is the main process that is changing the world? Does he think the engine of world change is primarily technological, commercial, or cultural?

As a young medical student, born and brought up in a colony, like many other people in my country, Egypt, I quickly learned to make the link between politics, economics, culture, and religion. Educated in an English school, I discovered that my English teachers looked down on us. We learned Rudyard Kipling by heart, praised the glories of the British Empire, followed the adventures of Kim in India, imbibed the culture of British supremacy, and sang carols on Christmas night.

At the medical school in university, when students demonstrated against occupation by British troops it was the Moslem Brothers who beat them up, using iron chains and long curved knives, and it was the governments supported by the king that shot at them or locked them up.

When I graduated in 1946, the hospital wards taught me how poverty and health are linked. I needed only another step to know that poverty had something to do with colonial rule, with the king who supported it, with class and race, with what was called imperialism at the time, with cotton prices falling on the market, with the seizure of land by foreign banks. These things were common talk in family gatherings,

Sherif Hetata, "Dollarization, Fragmentation, and God," in *The Cultures of Globalization*, ed. Fredric Jameson and Masao Miyoshi (Durham, N.C.: Duke University Press, 1998), 273–74, 276–80.

expressed in a simple, colorful language without frills. They were the facts of everyday life. We did not need to read books to make the links: They were there for us to see and grasp. And every time we made a link, someone told us it was time to stop, someone in authority whom we did not like: a ruler or a father, a policeman or a teacher, a landowner, a *maulana* (religious leader or teacher), a Jesuit, or a God.

And if we went on making these links, they locked us up.

For me, therefore, coming from this background, cultural studies and globalization open up a vast horizon, one of global links in a world where things are changing quickly. It is a chance to learn and probe how the economics, the politics, the culture, the philosophical thought of our days connect or disconnect, harmonize or contradict.

Of course, I will not even try to deal with all of that. I just want to raise a few points to discuss under the title of my talk, "Dollarization, Fragmentation, and God." Because I come from Egypt, my vantage point will be that of someone looking at the globe from the part we now call South, rather than "third world" or something else.

A New Economic Order: Gazing North at the Global Few

Never before in the history of the world has there been such a concentration and centralization of capital in so few nations and in the hands of so few people. The countries that form the Group of Seven, with their 800 million inhabitants, control more technological, economic, informatics, and military power than the rest of the approximately 430 billion who live in Asia, Africa, Eastern Europe, and Latin America.

Five hundred multinational corporations account for 80 percent of world trade and 75 percent of investment. Half of all the multinational corporations are based in the United States, Germany, Japan, and Switzerland. The OECD (Organization for Economic Cooperation and Development) group of countries contributes 80 percent of world production. . . .

A Global Culture for a Global Market

To expand the world market, to globalize it, to maintain the New Economic Order, the multinational corporations use economic power and control politics and the armed forces. But this is not so easy. People will always resist being exploited, resist injustice, struggle for their freedom, their needs, security, a better life, peace.

However, it becomes easier if they can be convinced to do what the masters of the global economy want them to do. This is where the issue of culture comes in. Culture can serve in different ways to help the global economy reach out all over the world and expand its markets to the most distant regions. Culture can also serve to reduce or destroy or prevent or divide or outflank the resistance of people who do not like what is happening to them, or have their doubts about it, or want to think. Culture can be like cocaine, which is going global these days: from Kali in Colombia to Texas, to Madrid, to the Italian mafiosi in southern Italy, to Moscow, Burma, and Thailand, a worldwide network uses the methods and the cover of big business, with a total trade of $5 billion a year, midway between oil and the arms trade.

At the disposal of global culture today are powerful means that function across the whole world: the media, which, like the economy, have made it one world, a bipolar North/South world. If genetic engineering gives scientists the possibility of programming embryos before children are born, children, youth, and adults are now being programmed after they are born in the culture they imbibe mainly through the media, but also in the family, in school, at the university, and elsewhere. Is this an exaggeration? an excessively gloomy picture of the world?

To expand the global market, increase the number of consumers, make sure that they buy what is sold, develop needs that conform to what is produced, and develop the fever of consumerism, culture must play a role in developing certain values, patterns of behavior, visions of what is happiness and success in the world, attitudes toward sex and love. Culture must model a global consumer.

In some ways, I was a "conservative radical." I went to jail, but I always dressed in a classical, subdued way. When my son started wearing blue jeans and New Balance shoes, I shivered with horror. He's going to become like some of those crazy kids abroad, the disco generation, I thought! Until the age of twenty-five he adamantly refused to smoke. Now he smokes two packs of Marlboros a day (the ones that the macho cowboy smokes). That does not prevent him from being a talented film director. But in the third-world, films, TV, and other media have increased the percentage of smokers. I saw half-starved kids in a marketplace in Mali buying single imported Benson & Hedges cigarettes and smoking.

But worse was still to come. Something happened that to me seemed impossible at one time, more difficult than adhering to a left-wing movement. At the age of seventy-one, I have taken to wearing blue jeans and Nike shoes. I listen to rock and reggae and sometimes rap. I like to go to discos and I sometimes have other cravings, which so far I have successfully fought! And I know these things have crept into our lives through the media, through TV, films, radio, advertisements, newspapers, and even novels, music, and poetry. It's a culture and it's reaching out, becoming global.

In my village, I have a friend. He is a peasant and we are very close. He lives in a big mud hut, and the animals (buffalo, sheep, cows, and donkeys) live in the house with him. Altogether, in the household, with the wife and children of his brother, his uncle, the mother, and his own family, there are thirty people. He wears a long *galabeya* (robe), works in the fields for long hours, and eats food cooked in the mud oven.

But when he married, he rode around the village in a hired Peugeot car with his bride. She wore a white wedding dress, her face was made up like a film star, her hair curled at the hairdresser's of the provincial town, her finger and toe nails manicured and polished, and her body bathed with special soap and perfumed. At the marriage ceremony, they had a wedding cake, which she cut with her husband's hand over hers. Very different from the customary rural marriage ceremony of his father. And all this change in the notion of beauty, of femininity, of celebration, of happiness, of prestige, of progress happened to my peasant friend and his bride in one generation.

The culprit, or the benevolent agent, depending on how you see it, was television.

In the past years, television has been the subject of numerous studies. In France, such studies have shown that before the age of twelve a child will have been exposed to an average 100,000 TV advertisements. Through these TV advertisements, the young boy or girl will have assimilated a whole set of values and behavioral patterns, of which he or she is not aware, of course. They become a part of his or her psychological (emotional and mental) makeup. Linked to these values are the norms and ways in which we see good and evil, beauty and ugliness, justice and injustice, truth and falseness, and which are being propagated at the same time. In other words, the fundamental values that form our aesthetic and moral vision of things are being inculcated, even hammered home, at this early stage, and they remain almost unchanged throughout life.

The commercial media no longer worry about the truthfulness or falsity of what they portray. Their role is to sell: beauty products, for example, to propagate the "beauty myth" and a "beauty culture" for both females and males alike and ensure that it reaches the farthest corners of the earth, including my village in the Delta of the Nile. Many of these beauty products are harmful to the health, can cause allergic disorders or skin infections or even worse. They cost money, work on the sex drives, and transform women and men, but especially women, into sex objects. They hide the real person, the natural beauty, the process of time, the stages of life, and instill false values about who we are, can be, or should become.

Advertisements do not depend on verifiable information or even rational thinking. They depend for their effect on images, colors, smart technical production, associations, and hidden drives. For them, attracting the opposite sex or social success or professional achievement and promotion or happiness do not depend on truthfulness or hard work or character, but rather on seduction, having a powerful car, buying things or people. . . .

Thus the media produce and reproduce the culture of consumption, of violence and sex to ensure that the global economic powers, the multinational corporations can promote a global market for themselves and protect it. And when everything is being bought or sold everyday and at all times in this vast supermarket, including culture, art, science, and thought, prostitution can become a way of life, for everything is priced. The search for the immediate need, the fleeting pleasure, the quick enjoyment, the commodity to buy, excess, pornography, drugs keeps this global economy rolling, for to stop is suicide.

PHILIPPE LEGRAIN

Cultural Globalization Is Not Americanization

Philippe Legrain, an economist, journalist, and former advisor to the World Trade Organization, takes aim at what he calls the myths of globalization in the following article. He argues that globalization brings cultural enrichment, not monotonous conformity, and that the intermixing of cultures is an old story with many happy results. What do you think of his argument? How might Sherif Hetata respond to it?

Thinking Historically

Does the author believe the driving force of globalization is economic or cultural? How important does he think globalization is? How, according to the author, is globalization changing the world? What examples does he cite? How does Legrain's view of America differ from Hetata's?

Philippe Legrain, "Cultural Globalization Is Not Americanization," *The Chronicle of Higher Education*, 49, no. 35 (May 9, 2003): B7.

Fears that globalization is imposing a deadening cultural uniformity are as ubiquitous as Coca-Cola, McDonald's, and Mickey Mouse. Europeans and Latin Americans, left-wingers and right, rich and poor — all of them dread that local cultures and national identities are dissolving into a crass All-American consumerism. That cultural imperialism is said to impose American values as well as products, promote the commercial at the expense of the authentic, and substitute shallow gratification for deeper satisfaction.

. . . If critics of globalization were less obsessed with "Coca-colonization," they might notice a rich feast of cultural mixing that belies fears about Americanized uniformity. Algerians in Paris practice Thai boxing; Asian rappers in London snack on Turkish pizza; Salman Rushdie delights readers everywhere with his Anglo-Indian tales. Although — as with any change — there can be downsides to cultural globalization, this cross-fertilization is overwhelmingly a force for good.

The beauty of globalization is that it can free people from the tyranny of geography. Just because someone was born in France does not mean they can only aspire to speak French, eat French food, read French books, visit museums in France, and so on. A Frenchman — or an American, for that matter — can take holidays in Spain or Florida, eat sushi or spaghetti for dinner, drink Coke or Chilean wine, watch a Hollywood blockbuster or an Almodóvar, listen to bhangra or rap, practice yoga or kickboxing, read *Elle* or *The Economist*, and have friends from around the world. That we are increasingly free to choose our cultural experiences enriches our lives immeasurably. We could not always enjoy the best the world has to offer.

Globalization not only increases individual freedom, but also revitalizes cultures and cultural artifacts through foreign influences, technologies, and markets. Thriving cultures are not set in stone. They are forever changing from within and without. Each generation challenges the previous one; science and technology alter the way we see ourselves and the world; fashions come and go; experience and events influence our beliefs; outsiders affect us for good and ill.

Many of the best things come from cultures mixing: V. S. Naipaul's Anglo-Indo-Caribbean writing, Paul Gauguin painting in Polynesia, or the African rhythms in rock 'n' roll. Behold the great British curry. Admire the many-colored faces of France's World Cup–winning soccer team, the ferment of ideas that came from Eastern Europe's Jewish diaspora, and the cosmopolitan cities of London and New York. Western numbers are actually Arabic; zero comes most recently from India; Icelandic, French, and Sanskrit stem from a common root.

John Stuart Mill was right: "The economical benefits of commerce are surpassed in importance by those of its effects which are intellectual and moral. It is hardly possible to overrate the value, for the improvement of human beings, of things which bring them into contact with persons dissimilar to themselves, and with modes of thought and action unlike those with which they are familiar. . . . It is indispensable to be perpetually comparing [one's] own notions and customs with the experience and example of persons in different circumstances. . . . There is no nation which does not need to borrow from others."

It is a myth that globalization involves the imposition of Americanized uniformity, rather than an explosion of cultural exchange. For a start, many archetypal "American" products are not as all-American as they seem. Levi Strauss, a German immigrant, invented jeans by combining denim cloth (or "serge de Nîmes," because it was traditionally woven in the French town) with Genes, a style of trousers worn by Genoese sailors. So Levi's jeans are in fact an American twist on a European hybrid. Even quintessentially American exports are often tailored to local tastes. MTV in Asia promotes Thai pop stars and plays rock music sung in Mandarin. CNN en Español offers a Latin American take on world news. McDonald's sells beer in France, lamb in India, and chili in Mexico.

In some ways, America is an outlier, not a global leader. Most of the world has adopted the metric system born from the French Revolution; America persists with antiquated measurements inherited from its British-colonial past. Most developed countries have become intensely secular, but many Americans burn with fundamentalist fervor — like Muslims in the Middle East. Where else in the developed world could there be a serious debate about teaching kids Bible-inspired "creationism" instead of Darwinist evolution?

America's tastes in sports are often idiosyncratic, too. Baseball and American football have not traveled well, although basketball has fared rather better. Many of the world's most popular sports, notably soccer, came by way of Britain. Asian martial arts — judo, karate, kickboxing — and pastimes like yoga have also swept the world.

People are not only guzzling hamburgers and Coke. Despite Coke's ambition of displacing water as the world's drink of choice, it accounts for less than 2 of the 64 fluid ounces that the typical person drinks a day. Britain's favorite takeaway is a curry, not a burger: Indian restaurants there outnumber McDonald's six to one. For all the concerns about American fast food trashing France's culinary traditions, France imported a mere $620 million in food from the United States in 2000, while exporting to America three times that. Nor is plonk[1] from America's Gallo displacing Europe's finest: Italy and France together account for three-fifths of global wine exports, the United States for only a twentieth. Worldwide, pizzas are more popular than burgers, Chinese

---

[1]British slang for cheap, low-quality alcohol. [Ed.]

restaurants seem to sprout up everywhere, and sushi is spreading fast. By far the biggest purveyor of alcoholic drinks is Britain's Diageo, which sells the world's best-selling whiskey (Johnnie Walker), gin (Gordon's), vodka (Smirnoff), and liqueur (Baileys).

In fashion, the ne plus ultra is Italian or French. Trendy Americans wear Gucci, Armani, Versace, Chanel, and Hermès. On the high street and in the mall, Sweden's Hennes & Mauritz (H&M) and Spain's Zara vie with America's Gap to dress the global masses. Nike shoes are given a run for their money by Germany's Adidas, Britain's Reebok, and Italy's Fila.

In pop music, American crooners do not have the stage to themselves. The three artists who were featured most widely in national Top Ten album charts in 2000 were America's Britney Spears, closely followed by Mexico's Carlos Santana and the British Beatles. Even tiny Iceland has produced a global star: Björk. Popular opera's biggest singers are Italy's Luciano Pavarotti, Spain's José Carreras, and the Spanish-Mexican Placido Domingo. Latin American salsa, Brazilian lambada, and African music have all carved out global niches for themselves. In most countries, local artists still top the charts. According to the IFPI, the record-industry bible, local acts accounted for 68 percent of music sales in 2000, up from 58 percent in 1991.

One of the most famous living writers is a Colombian, Gabriel García Márquez, author of *One Hundred Years of Solitude*. Paulo Coelho, another writer who has notched up tens of millions of global sales with *The Alchemist* and other books, is Brazilian. More than 200 million Harlequin romance novels, a Canadian export, were sold in 1990; they account for two-fifths of mass-market paperback sales in the United States. The biggest publisher in the English-speaking world is Germany's Bertelsmann, which gobbled up America's largest, Random House, in 1998.

Local fare glues more eyeballs to TV screens than American programs. Although nearly three-quarters of television drama exported worldwide comes from the United States, most countries' favorite shows are homegrown.

Nor are Americans the only players in the global media industry. Of the seven market leaders that have their fingers in nearly every pie, four are American (AOL Time Warner, Disney, Viacom, and News Corporation), one is German (Bertelsmann), one is French (Vivendi), and one Japanese (Sony). What they distribute comes from all quarters: Bertelsmann publishes books by American writers; News Corporation broadcasts Asian news; Sony sells Brazilian music.

The evidence is overwhelming. Fears about an Americanized uniformity are over-blown: American cultural products are not uniquely dominant; local ones are alive and well.

183

MIRIAM CHING YOON LOUIE

From Sweatshop Warriors: Immigrant Women Workers Take On the Global Factory

Sherif Hetata and Philippe Legrain highlight the impact of globalization on consumers, but it is also important to examine how it affects workers. Free-trade policies have removed barriers to international trade, with global consequences. An example of such change can be witnessed along the border between Mexico and the United States, especially in the export factories, or *maquiladoras*,* that are run by international corporations on both the U.S. and Mexican side of the border. In the following excerpt, Miriam Ching Yoon Louie, a writer and activist, interviews Mexican women who work in these factories and explores both the challenges they face and the strength they show in overcoming these challenges. What is the impact of liberalized trade laws on women who work in the *maquiladoras*? What is neoliberalism and how is it tied to globalization? Why are women particularly vulnerable to these policies?

Thinking Historically

According to Louie, how far back do neoliberalism and economic globalization date? How does Louie's assessment of economic globalization differ from the views expressed by Legrain? How might they both be right?

M any of today's *nuevas revolucionarias* started working on the global assembly line as young women in northern Mexico for foreign transnational corporations. Some women worked on the U.S. side as "commuters" before they moved across the border with their families. Their stories reveal the length, complexity, and interpenetration of the U.S. and Mexican economies, labor markets, histories, cultures, and race relations. The women talk about the devastating impact of globalization, including massive layoffs and the spread of sweatshops on both sides of

---

*mah kee lah DOH rahs

Miriam Ching Yoon Louie, *Sweatshop Warriors: Immigrant Women Workers Take On the Global Factory* (Cambridge, Mass.: South End Press, 2001), 65–71, 87–89.

the border. *Las mujeres* recount what drove them to join and lead movements for economic, racial, and gender justice, as well as the challenges they faced within their families and communities to assert their basic human rights. . . .

Growing Up Female and Poor

Mexican women and girls were traditionally expected to do all the cooking, cleaning, and serving for their husbands, brothers, and sons. For girls from poor families, shouldering these domestic responsibilities proved doubly difficult because they also performed farm, sweatshop, or domestic service work simultaneously. . . .

Petra Mata, a former seamstress for Levi's whose mother died shortly after childbirth, recalls the heavy housework she did as the only daughter:

> Aiyeee, let me tell you! It was very hard. In those times in Mexico, I was raised with the ideal that you have to learn to do everything — cook, make tortillas, wash your clothes, and clean the house — just the way they wanted you to. My grandparents were very strict. I always had to ask their permission and then let them tell me what to do. I was not a free woman. Life was hard for me. I didn't have much of a childhood; I started working when I was 12 or 13 years old.

Neoliberalism and Creeping Maquiladorization

These women came of age during a period of major change in the relationship between the Mexican and U.S. economies. Like Puerto Rico, Hong Kong, South Korea, Taiwan, Malaysia, Singapore, and the Philippines, northern Mexico served as one of the first stations of the global assembly line tapping young women's labor. In 1965 the Mexican government initiated the Border Industrialization Program (BIP) that set up export plants, called *maquiladoras* or *maquilas*, which were either the direct subsidiaries or subcontractors of transnational corporations. Mexican government incentives to U.S. and other foreign investors included low wages and high productivity; infrastructure; proximity to U.S. markets, facilities, and lifestyles; tariff loopholes; and pliant, pro-government unions. . . .

Describing her quarter-century-long sewing career in Mexico, Celeste Jiménez ticks off the names of famous U.S. manufacturers who hopped over the border to take advantage of cheap wages:

> I sewed for twenty-four years when I lived in Chihuahua in big name factories like Billy the Kid, Levi Strauss, and Lee *maquiladoras.* Every-

one was down there. Here a company might sell under the brand name of Lee; there in Mexico it would be called Blanca García.

Transnational exploitation of women's labor was part of a broader set of policies that critical opposition movements in the Third World have dubbed "neoliberalism," i.e., the new version of the British Liberal Party's program of laissez faire capitalism espoused by the rising European and U.S. colonial powers during the late eighteenth and nineteenth centuries. The Western powers, Japan, and international financial institutions like the World Bank and International Monetary Fund have aggressively promoted neoliberal policies since the 1970s. Mexico served as an early testing ground for such standard neoliberal policies as erection of free trade zones; commercialization of agriculture; currency devaluation; deregulation; privatization; outsourcing; cuts in wages and social programs; suppression of workers', women's, and indigenous people's rights; free trade; militarization; and promotion of neoconservative ideology.

Neoliberalism intersects with gender and national oppression. Third World women constitute the majority of migrants seeking jobs as maids, vendors, maquila operatives, and service industry workers. Women also pay the highest price for cuts in education, health and housing programs, and food and energy subsidies and increases in their unpaid labor. . . .

The deepening of the economic crisis in Mexico, especially under the International Monetary Fund's pressure to devaluate the peso in 1976, 1982, and 1994, forced many women to work in both the formal and informal economy to survive and meet their childbearing and household responsibilities. María Antonia Flores was forced to work two jobs after her husband abandoned the family, leaving her with three children to support. She had no choice but to leave her children home alone, *solitos,* to look after themselves. Refugio Arrieta straddled the formal and informal economy because her job in an auto parts assembly *maquiladora* failed to bring in sufficient income. To compensate for the shortfall, she worked longer hours at her *maquila* job and "moonlighted" elsewhere:

> We made chassis for cars and for the headlights. I worked lots! I worked 12 hours more or less because they paid us so little that if you worked more, you got more money. I did this because the schools in Mexico don't provide everything. You have to buy the books, notebooks, *todos, todos* [everything]. And I had five kids. It's very expensive. I also worked out of my house and sold ceramics. I did many things to get more money for my kids.

In the three decades following its humble beginnings in the mid-1960s, the *maquila* sector swelled to more than 2,000 plants employing an estimated 776,000 people, over 10 percent of Mexico's labor force. In 1985, *maquiladoras* overtook tourism as the largest source of foreign exchange. In 1996, this sector trailed only petroleum-related industries in economic importance and accounted for over U.S. $29 billion in export earnings annually. The *maquila* system has also penetrated the interior of the country, as in the case of Guadalajara's electronics assembly industry and Tehuacán's jeans production zones. Although the proportion of male *maquila* workers has increased since 1983, especially in auto-transport equipment assembly, almost 70 percent of the workers continue to be women.

As part of a delegation of labor and human rights activists, this author met some of Mexico's newest proletarians — young indigenous women migrant workers from the Sierra Negra to Tehuacán, a town famous for its refreshing mineral water springs in the state of Puebla, just southeast of Mexico City. Standing packed like cattle in the back of the trucks each morning the women headed for jobs sewing for name brand manufacturers like Guess?, VF Corporation (producing Lee brand clothing), Gap, Sun Apparel (producing brands such as Polo, Arizona, and Express), Cherokee, Ditto Apparel of California, Levi's, and others. The workers told U.S. delegation members that their wages averaged U.S. $30 to $50 a week for 12-hour work days, six days a week. Some workers reported having to do *veladas* [all-nighters] once or twice a week. Employees often stayed longer without pay if they did not finish high production goals.

Girls as young as 12 and 13 worked in the factories. Workers were searched when they left for lunch and again at the end of the day to check that they weren't stealing materials. Women were routinely given urine tests when hired and those found to be pregnant were promptly fired, in violation of Mexican labor law. Although the workers had organized an independent union several years earlier, Tehuacán's Human Rights Commission members told us that it had collapsed after one of its leaders was assassinated.

Carmen Valadez and Reyna Montero, long-time activists in the women's and social justice movements, helped found Casa de La Mujer Factor X in 1977, a workers' center in Tijuana that organizes around women's workplace, reproductive, and health rights, and against domestic violence. Valadez and Montero say that the low wages and dangerous working conditions characteristic of the *maquiladoras* on the Mexico-U.S. border are being "extended to all areas of the country and to Central America and the Caribbean. NAFTA represents nothing but the '*maquiladorization*' of the region."

Elizabeth "Beti" Robles Ortega, who began working in the *maquilas* at the age of fourteen and was blacklisted after participating in independent union organizing drives on Mexico's northern border, now works as an organizer for the Servicio, Desarrollo y Paz, AC

(SEDEPAC) [Service, Development and Peace organization]. Robles described the erosion of workers' rights and women's health under NAFTA:

> NAFTA has led to an increase in the workforce, as foreign industry has grown. They are reforming labor laws and our constitution to favor even more foreign investment, which is unfair against our labor rights. For example, they are now trying to take away from us free organization which was guaranteed by Mexican law. Because foreign capital is investing in Mexico and is dominating, we must have guarantees. The government is just there with its hands held out; it's always had them out but now even more shamelessly. . . . Ecological problems are increasing. A majority of women are coming down with cancer — skin and breast cancer, leukemia, and lung and heart problems. There are daily deaths of worker women. You can see and feel the contamination of the water and the air. As soon as you arrive and start breathing the air in Acuña and Piedras Negras [border cities between the states of Coahuila and Texas], you sense the heavy air, making you feel like vomiting.

. . .

Joining the Movement

Much of the education and leadership training the women received took place "on the job." The women talked about how much their participation in the movement had changed them. They learned how to analyze working conditions and social problems, who was responsible for these conditions, and what workers could do to get justice. They learned to speak truth to power, whether this was to government representatives, corporate management, the media, unions, or co-ethnic gatekeepers. They built relations with different kinds of sectors and groups and organized a wide variety of educational activities and actions. Their activism expanded their world view beyond that of their immediate families to seeing themselves as part of peoples' movements fighting for justice. . . .

. . . Through her participation in the movement, [María del Carmen Domínguez] developed her skills, leadership, and awareness:

> When I stayed at work in the factory, I was only thinking of myself and how am I going to support my family — nothing more, nothing less. And I served my husband and my son, my girl. But when I started working with La Mujer Obrera I thought, "I need more respect for myself. We need more respect for ourselves." (laughs) . . .
>
> . . . I learned about the law and I learned how to organize classes with people, whether they were men or women like me.

184

BENJAMIN BARBER

From Jihad vs. McWorld

Not everyone views the world as coming together, for better or worse, under the umbrella of globalization. Benjamin Barber, a political scientist, uses the terms *Jihad* and *McWorld* to refer to what he sees as the two poles of the modern global system. *McWorld* is the force of Hollywood, fast-food outlets, jeans, and Americanization. *Jihad* (the Arab word for "struggle") is used to symbolize all the nationalist, fundamentalist, ethnocentric, and tribal rejections of McWorld. Barber's argument is that these forces have largely shaped modern culture and that despite their opposition to each other, they both prevent the development of civic society and democracy: Jihad by terrorist opposition to discussion and debate, and McWorld by turning everyone into complacent, unthinking robots. What do you think of his argument? Is it persuasive? What sort of future does he predict?

Thinking Historically

Barber argues that Jihad originated in opposition to McWorld and that the two play off each other in a way that gives them both substance and support. Jihad thrives on the insensitivity, blandness, and oppression of McWorld; McWorld needs ethnic realities to give substance and soul to its theme parks and entertainments. Thus, according to Barber, they make each other stronger by struggling against each other. The gains of these two extreme positions come at the expense of a genuine, democratic civic culture. How useful is Barber's model for understanding how the world has changed?

History is not over. Nor are we arrived in the wondrous land of techné[1] promised by the futurologists. The collapse of state communism has not delivered people to a safe democratic haven, and the past, fratricide and civil discord perduring, still clouds the horizon just behind us. Those who look back see all of the horrors of the ancient slaughterbench reenacted in disintegral nations like Bosnia, Sri Lanka,

---

[1]Technology.

Benjamin Barber, *Jihad vs. McWorld: How Globalism and Tribalism Are Reshaping the World* (New York: Ballantine, 1995), 3–8.

Ossetia, and Rwanda and they declare that nothing has changed. Those who look forward prophesize commercial and technological interdependence — a virtual paradise made possible by spreading markets and global technology — and they proclaim that everything is or soon will be different. The rival observers seem to consult different almanacs drawn from the libraries of contrarian planets.

Yet anyone who reads the daily papers carefully, taking in the front page accounts of civil carnage as well as the business page stories on the mechanics of the information superhighway and the economics of communication mergers, anyone who turns deliberately to take in the whole 360-degree horizon, knows that our world and our lives are caught between what [Irish poet] William Butler Yeats called the two eternities of race and soul: that of race reflecting the tribal past, that of soul anticipating the cosmopolitan future. Our secular eternities are corrupted, however, race reduced to an insignia of resentment, and soul sized down to fit the demanding body by which it now measures its needs. Neither race nor soul offers us a future that is other than bleak, neither promises a polity that is remotely democratic.

The first scenario rooted in race holds out the grim prospect of a retribalization of large swaths of humankind by war and bloodshed: a threatened balkanization of nation-states in which culture is pitted against culture, people against people, tribe against tribe, a Jihad in the name of a hundred narrowly conceived faiths against every kind of interdependence, every kind of artificial social cooperation and mutuality: against technology, against pop culture, and against integrated markets; against modernity itself as well as the future in which modernity issues. The second paints that future in shimmering pastels, a busy portrait of onrushing economic, technological, and ecological forces that demand integration and uniformity and that mesmerize peoples everywhere with fast music, fast computers, and fast food — MTV, Macintosh, and McDonald's — pressing nations into one homogenous global theme park, one McWorld tied together by communications, information, entertainment, and commerce. Caught between Babel and Disneyland, the planet is falling precipitously apart and coming reluctantly together at the very same moment.

Some stunned observers notice only Babel, complaining about the thousand newly sundered "peoples" who prefer to address their neighbors with sniper rifles and mortars; others — zealots in Disneyland — seize on futurological platitudes and the promise of virtuality, exclaiming "It's a small world after all!" Both are right, but how can that be?

We are compelled to choose between what passes as "the twilight of sovereignty" and an entropic end of all history, or a return to the past's most fractious and demoralizing discord; to "the menace of global anarchy," to [John] Milton's capital of hell, Pandaemonium; to a world totally "out of control."

The apparent truth, which speaks to the paradox at the core of this book, is that the tendencies of both Jihad *and* McWorld are at work, both visible sometimes in the same country at the very same instant. Iranian zealots keep one ear tuned to the mullahs urging holy war and the other cocked to [Australian media mogul] Rupert Murdoch's Star television beaming in *Dynasty, Donahue,* and *The Simpsons* from hovering satellites. Chinese entrepreneurs vie for the attention of party cadres in Beijing and simultaneously pursue KFC franchises in cities like Nanjing, Hangzhou, and Xian where twenty-eight outlets serve over 100,000 customers a day. The Russian Orthodox church, even as it struggles to renew the ancient faith, has entered a joint venture with California businessmen to bottle and sell natural waters under the rubric Saint Springs Water Company. Serbian assassins wear Adidas sneakers and listen to Madonna on Walkman headphones as they take aim through their gunscopes at scurrying Sarajevo civilians looking to fill family watercans. Orthodox Hasids and brooding neo-Nazis have both turned to rock music to get their traditional messages out to the new generation, while fundamentalists plot virtual conspiracies on the Internet.

Now neither Jihad nor McWorld is in itself novel. History ending in the triumph of science and reason or some monstrous perversion thereof (Mary Shelley's Doctor Frankenstein) has been the leitmotiv of every philosopher and poet who has regretted the Age of Reason since the Enlightenment. [W. B.] Yeats lamented "the center will not hold, mere anarchy is loosed upon the world," and observers of Jihad today have little but historical detail to add. The Christian parable of the Fall and of the possibilities of redemption that it makes possible captures the eighteenth-century ambivalence — and our own — about past and future. I want, however, to do more than dress up the central paradox of human history in modern clothes. It is not Jihad and McWorld but the relationship between them that most interests me. For, squeezed between their opposing forces, the world has been sent spinning out of control. Can it be that what Jihad and McWorld have in common is anarchy: the absence of common will and that conscious and collective human control under the guidance of law we call democracy?

Progress moves in steps that sometimes lurch backwards; in history's twisting maze, Jihad not only revolts against but abets McWorld, while McWorld not only imperils but re-creates and reinforces Jihad. They produce their contraries and need one another. My object here then is not simply to offer sequential portraits of McWorld and Jihad, but while examining McWorld, to keep Jihad in my field of vision, and while dissecting Jihad, never to forget the context of McWorld. Call it a dialectic of McWorld: a study in the cunning of reason that does honor to the radical differences that distinguish Jihad and McWorld yet that acknowledges their powerful and paradoxical interdependence.

There is a crucial difference, however, between my modest attempt at dialectic and that of the masters of the nineteenth century. Still seduced by the Enlightenment's faith in progress, both [G. W. F.] Hegel and [Karl] Marx believed reason's cunning was on the side of progress. But it is harder to believe that the clash of Jihad and McWorld will issue in some overriding good. The outcome seems more likely to pervert than to nurture human liberty. The two may, in opposing each other, work to the same ends, work in apparent tension yet in covert harmony, but democracy is not their beneficiary. In East Berlin, tribal communism has yielded to capitalism. In Marx-Engelsplatz, the stolid, overbearing statues of Marx and [Friedrich] Engels face east, as if seeking distant solace from Moscow: but now, circling them along the streets that surround the park that is their prison are chain eateries like T.G.I. Friday's, international hotels like the Radisson, and a circle of neon billboards mocking them with brand names like Panasonic, Coke, and GoldStar. New gods, yes, but more liberty?

What then does it mean in concrete terms to view Jihad and McWorld dialectically when the tendencies of the two sets of forces initially appear so intractably antithetical? After all, Jihad and McWorld operate with equal strength in opposite directions, the one driven by parochial hatreds, the other by universalizing markets, the one recreating ancient subnational and ethnic borders from within, the other making national borders porous from without. Yet Jihad and McWorld have this in common: They both make war on the sovereign nation-state and thus undermine the nation-state's democratic institutions. Each eschews civil society and belittles democratic citizenship, neither seeks alternative democratic institutions. Their common thread is indifference to civil liberty. Jihad forges communities of blood rooted in exclusion and hatred, communities that slight democracy in favor of tyrannical paternalism or consensual tribalism. McWorld forges global markets rooted in consumption and profit, leaving to an untrustworthy, if not altogether fictitious, invisible hand issues of public interest and common good that once might have been nurtured by democratic citizenries and their watchful governments. Such governments, intimidated by market ideology, are actually pulling back at the very moment they ought to be aggressively intervening. What was once understood as protecting the public interest is now excoriated as heavy-handed regulatory browbeating. Justice yields to markets, even though, as [New York banker] Felix Rohatyn has bluntly confessed, "there is a brutal Darwinian logic to these markets. They are nervous and greedy. They look for stability and transparency, but what they reward is not always our preferred form of democracy." If the traditional conservators of freedom were democratic constitutions and Bills of Rights, "the new temples to liberty," [literary critic and philosopher] George Steiner suggests, "will be McDonald's and Kentucky Fried Chicken."

In being reduced to a choice between the market's universal church and a retribalizing politics of particularist identities, peoples around the globe are threatened with an atavistic return to medieval politics where local tribes and ambitious emperors together ruled the world entire, women and men united by the universal abstraction of Christianity even as they lived out isolated lives in warring fiefdoms defined by involuntary (ascriptive) forms of identity. This was a world in which princes and kings had little real power until they conceived the ideology of nationalism. Nationalism established government on a scale greater than the tribe yet less cosmopolitan than the universal church and in time gave birth to those intermediate, gradually more democratic institutions that would come to constitute the nation-state. Today, at the far end of this history, we seem intent on re-creating a world in which our only choices are the secular universalism of the cosmopolitan market and the everyday particularism of the fractious tribe.

In the tumult of the confrontation between global commerce and parochial ethnicity, the virtues of the democratic nation are lost and the instrumentalities by which it permitted peoples to transform themselves into nations and seize sovereign power in the name of liberty and the commonweal are put at risk. Neither Jihad nor McWorld aspires to resecure the civic virtues undermined by its denationalizing practices; neither global markets nor blood communities service public goods or pursue equality and justice. Impartial judiciaries and deliberate assemblies play no role in the roving killer bands that speak on behalf of newly liberated "peoples," and such democratic institutions have at best only marginal influence on the roving multinational corporations that speak on behalf of newly liberated markets. Jihad pursues a bloody politics of identity, McWorld a bloodless economics of profit. Belonging by default to McWorld, everyone is a consumer; seeking a repository for identity, everyone belongs to some tribe. But no one is a citizen. Without citizens, how can there be democracy?

185

Global Snapshots

Cartogram of Global Warming

The Earth at Night

Population Density of the World, 2004

GDP per Capita Growth, 1990–2001

At the heart of many debates surrounding globalization is the natural environment. It is difficult to ignore the vast problems endangering the planet — global warming, acid rain, species extinction, rainforest depletion. These environmental issues require global cooperation to be solved, and they also require a certain global consciousness, or understanding, that all people are part of a global community and that what people do in one part of the world affects those in another part.

These four images provide a graphic measure of the integration and imbalances of the world today. Specifically, they show how the consumption of energy resources — heat and light — is distributed throughout the world, population density across the planet, and nattural differences in economic growth, or GDP.

Figure 28.1 is a cartogram, which is a stylized map in which countries are not represented to scale, but are sized to reflect a specific measurement. This cartogram measures relative emissions of greenhouse gases by country, so the largest countries on the map emit the most gases, and the smallest emit the fewest. Which countries produce the most greenhouse gases? Which countries produce the least? What accounts for these differences?

Figure 28.2, a satellite photograph of the Earth at night, shows that energy use is no more uniform within countries than it is from one country to another. What areas of countries use the most light? Why? Does the photograph correspond to the cartogram in every respect? What does the photograph tell you about the relationship between energy use, transportation routes, urban centers, and general population density? What else can you deduce about global energy use from the photograph?

Figure 28.1 Cartogram of Global Warming. Emissions of carbon dioxide, one of the main greenhouse gases.

Source: Courtesy Mark Newman.

Figure 28.2   Satellite Photo of the Earth at Night.
Source: NASA.

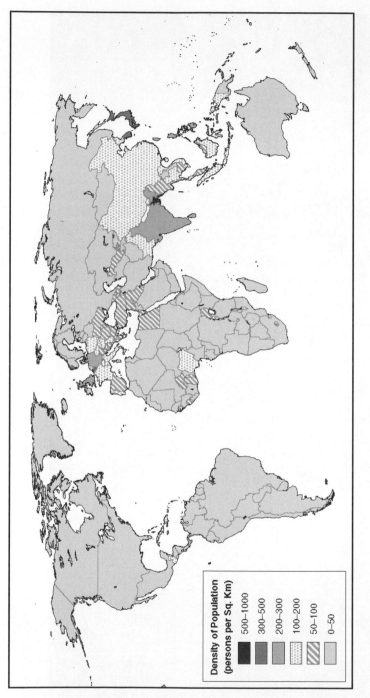

Map 28.1 Population Density of the World, 2004.

Source: © 2004 Compare Infobase Pvt. Ltd.

Density of Population
(persons per Sq. Km)

500–1000
300–500
200–300
100–200
50–100
0–50

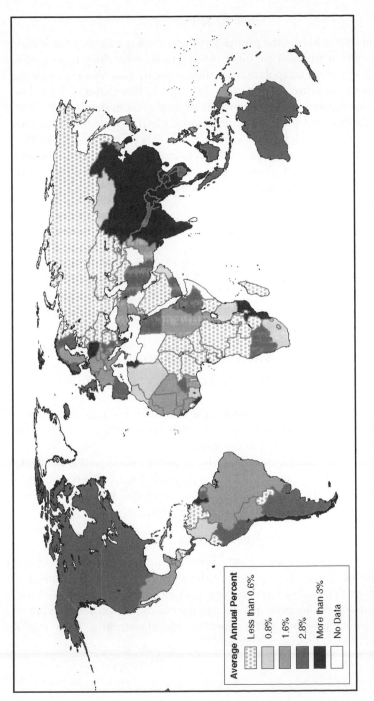

Map 28.2 GDP per Capita Growth, 1990–2001.

Source: © 2003–2004 Compare Infobase Pvt. Ltd.

Average Annual Percent

- Less than 0.6%
- 0.8%
- 1.6%
- 2.8%
- More than 3%
- No Data

Thinking Historically

A snapshot is hardly the proper format to display change since it captures only a moment in time. Nevertheless, what long-term global trends can you extrapolate from these images? Can you see evidence of any of the historical processes discussed in this chapter? What historical processes do these snapshots capture most dramatically? Compare the maps of population density and of GDP with the cartogram and the satellite photo and with each other. Is there a correlation between energy use and population? Between density of population and wealth? What conclusions might you draw from comparing these maps with each other, and with previous images?

JOHN ROACH

By 2050 Warming to Doom Million Species, Study Says

Global warming looms as perhaps the most serious threat to planetary health ever. What according to this article are the likely consequences of global warming? What are its causes?

What does the cartogram in the previous selection (Figure 28.1) suggest about the causes of global warming? What is the relationship between the places most responsible for global warming and the places where the most species are disappearing?

Thinking Historically

According to the author, some scientists think that the loss of 15–35 percent of the earth's species by the year 2050 may be optimistic. They say that global warming sets in motion other processes — habitat destruction, invasive species, and the buildup of carbon dioxide in the landscape — that further increase global warming. How might these different processes be related?

John Roach, "By 2050 Warming to Doom Million Species, Study Says," *National Geographic News* (July 12, 2004), http://nationalgeographic.com/news/2004/01/0107_040107_extinction.html.

By 2050, rising temperatures exacerbated by human-induced belches of carbon dioxide and other greenhouse gases could send more than a million of Earth's land-dwelling plants and animals down the road to extinction, according to a recent study.

"Climate change now represents at least as great a threat to the number of species surviving on Earth as habitat-destruction and modification," said Chris Thomas, a conservation biologist at the University of Leeds in the United Kingdom.

Thomas is the lead author of the study published earlier this year in the science journal *Nature*. His co-authors included 18 scientists from around the world, making this the largest collaboration of its type.

Townsend Peterson, an evolutionary biologist at the University of Kansas in Lawrence and one of the study's co-authors, said the paper allows scientists for the first time to "get a grip" on the impact of climate change as far as natural systems are concerned. "A lot of us are in this to start to get a handle on what we are talking about," he said. "When we talk about the difference between half a percent and one percent of carbon dioxide emissions what does that mean?"

The researchers worked independently in six biodiversity-rich regions around the world, from Australia to South Africa, plugging field data on species distribution and regional climate into computer models that simulated the ways species' ranges are expected to move in response to temperature and climate changes. "We later met and decided to pool results to produce a more globally relevant look at the issue," said Lee Hannah, a climate change biologist with Conservation International's Center for Applied Biodiversity Science in Washington, D.C.

Study Results

According to the researchers' collective results, the predicted range of climate change by 2050 will place 15 to 35 percent of the 1,103 species studied at risk of extinction. The numbers are expected to hold up when extrapolated globally, potentially dooming more than a million species. "These are first-pass estimates, but they put the problem in the right ballpark . . . I expect more detailed studies to refine these numbers and to add data for additional regions, but not to change the general import of these findings," said Hannah.

Writing in an accompanying commentary to the study in *Nature*, J. Alan Pounds of the Monteverde Cloud Forest Reserve in Costa Rica, and Robert Puschendorf, a biologist at the University of Costa Rica, say these estimates "might be optimistic." As global warming interacts with other factors such as habitat-destruction, invasive species, and the build up of carbon dioxide in the landscape, the risk of extinction increases even further, they say.

In agreement with the study authors, Pounds and Puschendorf say taking immediate steps to reduce greenhouse gas emissions is imperative to constrain global warming to the minimum predicted levels and thus prevent many of the extinctions from occurring. "The threat to life on Earth is not just a problem for the future. It is part of the here and now," they write.

Climate Scenarios

The researchers based their study on minimum, mid-range, and maximum future climate scenarios based on information released by the United Nations Intergovernmental Panel on Climate Change (IPCC) in 2001.

According to the IPCC, temperatures are expected to rise from somewhere between 1.5 and more than 4 degrees Fahrenheit (0.8 and more than 2 degrees Celsius) by the year 2050. "Few climate scientists around the world think that 2050 temperatures will fall outside those bounds," said Thomas. "In some respects, we have been conservative because almost all future climate projections expect more warming and hence more extinction between 2050 and 2100."

In addition, the researchers accounted for the ability of species to disperse or successfully move to a new area, thus preventing climate change-induced extinction. They used two alternatives: one where species couldn't move at all, the other assuming unlimited abilities for movement. "We are trying to bracket the truth," said Peterson. "If you bracket the truth and look at the two endpoints and they give the same general message, then you can start to believe it."

Outside of the small group of researchers working directly on the impacts of climate change to species diversity, "the numbers will come as a huge shock," said Thomas.

Extinction Prevention

The researchers point out that there is a significant gap between the low and high ends of the species predicted to be on the road to extinction by 2050. Taking action to ensure the climate ends up on the low end of the range is vital to prevent catastrophic extinctions. "We need to start thinking about the fullest of costs involved with our activities, the real costs of what we do in modern society," said Peterson.

Thomas said that since there may be a large time lag between the climate changing and the last individual of a doomed species dying off, rapid reductions of greenhouse gas emissions may allow some of these species to hang on. "The only conservation action that really makes sense, at a global scale, is for the international community to minimize warming through reduced emissions and the potential establishment of carbon-sequestration programs," he said.

ANDREW C. REVKIN

Climate Data Hint at Irreversible Rise in Seas

This is another news story on global warming, reporting another set of scientific studies. But the danger presented here is rising sea levels rather than the extinction of species. What according to the author are the threats to coastal areas from the kind of global warming projected over the next one hundred years? In what ways are these conclusions similar to that of the previous article?

Thinking Historically

We might add rising sea levels to the list of factors that would interact to cause the depletion of species. Studies of global warming show us the extent of interrelationship among natural processes. This selection also warns us that natural processes can suddenly speed up or reach a tipping point of no return. Yet both of these studies suggest a fairly obvious remedy: reducing the carbon dioxide and other greenhouse gases produced by humans. What should be done? If humans can cause long-term changes in nature, can humans also prevent them?

Within the next 100 years, the growing human influence on Earth's climate could lead to a long and irreversible rise in sea levels by eroding the planet's vast polar ice sheets, according to new observations and analysis by several teams of scientists.

One team, using computer models of climate and ice, found that by about 2100, average temperatures could be four degrees higher than today and that over the coming centuries, the oceans could rise 13 to

Andrew C. Revkin, "Climate Data Hint at Irreversible Rise in Seas," *New York Times*, March 24, 2006, p. A-12.

20 feet — conditions last seen 129,000 years ago, between the last two ice ages. The findings, being reported today in the journal *Science,* are consistent with other recent studies of melting and erosion at the poles. Many experts say there are still uncertainties about timing, extent, and causes.

But Jonathan T. Overpeck of the University of Arizona, a lead author of one of the studies, said the new findings made a strong case for the danger of failing to curb emissions of carbon dioxide and other gases that trap heat in a greenhouselike effect. "If we don't like the idea of flooding out New Orleans, major portions of South Florida, and many other valued parts of the coastal U.S.," Dr. Overpeck said, "we will have to commit soon to a major effort to stop most emissions of carbon to the atmosphere."

According to the computer simulations, the global nature of the warming from greenhouse gases, which diffuse around the atmosphere, could amplify the melting around Antarctica beyond that of the last warm period, which was driven mainly by extra sunlight reaching the Northern Hemisphere.

The researchers also said that stains from dark soot drifting from power plants and vehicles could hasten melting in the Arctic by increasing the amount of solar energy absorbed by ice. The rise in sea levels, driven by loss of ice from Greenland and West Antarctica, would occur over many centuries and be largely irreversible, but could be delayed by curbing emissions of the greenhouse gases, said Dr. Overpeck and his fellow lead author, Bette L. Otto-Bliesner of the National Center for Atmospheric Research in Boulder, Colo.

In a second article in *Science,* researchers say they have detected a rising frequency of earthquakelike rumblings in the bedrock beneath Greenland's two-mile-thick ice cap in late summer since 1993. They say there is no obvious explanation other than abrupt movements of the overlying ice caused by surface melting. The jostling of that giant ice-cloaked island is five times more frequent in summer than in winter, and has greatly intensified since 2002, the researchers found. The data mesh with recent satellite readings showing that the ice can lurch toward the sea during the melting season. The analysis was led by Goran Ekstrom of Harvard and Meredith Nettles of the Lamont-Doherty Earth Observatory in Palisades, N.Y., part of Columbia University.

H. Jay Zwally, a NASA scientist studying the polar ice sheets with satellites, said the seismic signals from ice movement were consistent with his discovery in 2002 that summer melting on the surface of Greenland's ice sheets could almost immediately spur them to shift measurably. The meltwater apparently trickles through fissures and lubricates the interface between ice and underlying rock. "Models are important, but measurements tell the real story," Dr. Zwally said. "During the last 10 years, we have seen only about 10 percent of the greenhouse warming expected during the next 100 years, but already the polar ice sheets are responding in ways we didn't even know about only a few years ago."

In both Antarctica and Greenland, it appears that warming waters are also at work, melting the protruding tongues of ice where glaciers flow into the sea or intruding beneath ice sheets, like those in western Antarctica, that lie mostly below sea level. Both processes can cause the ice to flow more readily, scientists say. Many experts on climate and the poles, citing evidence from past natural warm periods, agreed with the general notion that a world much warmer than today's, regardless of the cause of warming, will have higher sea levels.

But significant disagreements remain over whether recent changes in sea level and ice conditions cited in the new studies could be attributed to rising concentrations of the greenhouse gases and temperatures linked by most experts to human activities.

Sea levels have been rising for thousands of years as an aftereffect of the warming and polar melting that followed the last ice age, which ended about 10,000 years ago. Discriminating between that residual effect and any new influence from human actions remains impossible for the moment, many experts say.

Satellites and tide gauges show that seas rose about eight inches over the last century and the pace has picked up markedly since the 1990's. Dr. Overpeck, the co-author of the paper on rising sea levels, acknowledged the uncertainties about the causes. But he said that in a world in which humans, rich and poor, increasingly clustered on coasts, the risks were great enough to justify prompt action.

"People driving big old S.U.V.'s to their favorite beach or coastal golf course," he said, should "start to think twice about what they might be doing."

LARRY ROHTER

With Big Boost from Sugar Cane, Brazil Is Satisfying Its Fuel Needs

Because modern industrial technologies bear so much responsibility for global warming, pessimists often blame technology itself or even Man the Toolmaker. Optimists, on the other hand, see hope in green technologies, which they expect to be developed by the cutting-edge, science-based, rich, competitive economies. This article gives reason to question both those who envision no technological solutions and those who look for the contemporary masters of the industrial world to go green.

How has Brazil been able to do something as important as this? What can the United States learn from Brazil?

Thinking Historically

This is a story about human, not natural, processes. Human processes frequently involve various political and economic motivations and decisions. What are some of the political and economic decisions that Brazil and the United States made in their different responses to the need for renewable energy? Why did the two countries go different ways?

At the dawn of the automobile age, Henry Ford predicted that "ethyl alcohol is the fuel of the future." With petroleum about $65 a barrel, President Bush has now embraced that view, too. But Brazil is already there. . . .

This country expects to become energy self-sufficient this year, meeting its growing demand for fuel by increasing production from petroleum and ethanol. Already the use of ethanol, derived in Brazil from sugar cane, is so widespread that some gas stations have two sets of pumps, marked A for alcohol and G for gas.

In his State of the Union address in January, Mr. Bush backed financing for "cutting-edge methods of producing ethanol, not just from corn but wood chips and stalks or switch grass" with the goal of making ethanol competitive in six years.

Larry Rohter, "With Big Boost from Sugar Cane, Brazil Is Satisfying Its Fuel Needs," *New York Times*, April 10, 2006, p. 1.

But Brazil's path has taken 30 years of effort, required several billion dollars in incentives and involved many missteps. While not always easy, it provides clues to the real challenges facing the United States' ambitions.

Brazilian officials and scientists say that, in their country at least, the main barriers to the broader use of ethanol today come from outside. Brazil's ethanol yields nearly eight times as much energy as corn-based options, according to scientific data. Yet heavy import duties on the Brazilian product have limited its entry into the United States and Europe.

Brazilian officials and scientists say sugar cane yields are likely to increase because of recent research.

"Renewable fuel has been a fantastic solution for us," Brazil's minister of agriculture, Roberto Rodrigues, said in a recent interview in São Paulo, the capital of São Paulo State, which accounts for 60 percent of sugar production in Brazil. "And it offers a way out of the fossil fuel trap for others as well."

Here, where Brazil has cultivated sugar cane since the 16th century, green fields of cane, stalks rippling gently in the tropical breeze, stretch to the horizon, producing a crop that is destined to be consumed not just as candy and soft drinks but also in the tanks of millions of cars.

The use of ethanol in Brazil was greatly accelerated in the last three years with the introduction of "flex fuel" engines, designed to run on ethanol, gasoline, or any mixture of the two. (The gasoline sold in Brazil contains about 25 percent alcohol, a practice that has accelerated Brazil's shift from imported oil.)

But Brazilian officials and business executives say the ethanol industry would develop even faster if the United States did not levy a tax of 54 cents a gallon on all imports of Brazilian cane-based ethanol.

With demand for ethanol soaring in Brazil, sugar producers recognize that it is unrealistic to think of exports to the United States now. But Brazilian leaders complain that Washington's restrictions have inhibited foreign investment, particularly by Americans.

As a result, ethanol development has been led by Brazilian companies with limited capital. But with oil prices soaring, the four international giants that control much of the world's agribusiness — Archer Daniels Midland, Bunge and Born, Cargill, and Louis Dreyfus — have recently begun showing interest.

Brazil says those and other outsiders are welcome. Aware that the United States and other industrialized countries are reluctant to trade their longstanding dependence on oil for a new dependence on renewable fuels, government and industry officials say they are willing to share technology with those interested in following Brazil's example.

"We are not interested in becoming the Saudi Arabia of ethanol," said Eduardo Carvalho, director of the National Sugarcane Agro-Industry

Union, a producer's group. "It's not our strategy because it doesn't produce results. As a large producer and user, I need to have other big buyers and sellers in the international market if ethanol is to become a commodity, which is our real goal."

The ethanol boom in Brazil, which took off at the start of the decade after a long slump, is not the first. The government introduced its original "Pro-Alcohol" program in 1975, after the first global energy crisis, and by the mid-1980's, more than three quarters of the 800,000 cars made in Brazil each year could run on cane-based ethanol.

But when sugar prices rose sharply in 1989, mill owners stopped making cane available for processing into alcohol, preferring to profit from the hard currency that premium international markets were paying.

Brazilian motorists were left in the lurch, as were the automakers who had retooled their production lines to make alcohol-powered cars. Ethanol fell into discredit, for economic rather than technical reasons.

Consumers' suspicions remained high through the 1990's and were overcome only in 2003, when automakers, beginning with Volkswagen, introduced the "flex fuel" motor in Brazil. Those engines gave consumers the autonomy to buy the cheapest fuel, freeing them from any potential shortages in ethanol's supply. Also, ethanol-only engines can be slower to start when cold, a problem the flex fuel owners can bypass.

"Motorists liked the flex-fuel system from the start because it permits them free choice and puts them in control," said Vicente Lourenço, technical director at General Motors do Brasil.

Today, less than three years after the technology was introduced, more than 70 percent of the automobiles sold in Brazil, expected to reach 1.1 million this year, have flex fuel engines, which have entered the market generally without price increases.

"The rate at which this technology has been adopted is remarkable, the fastest I have ever seen in the motor sector, faster even than the airbag, automatic transmission or electric windows," said Barry Engle, president of Ford do Brasil. "From the consumer standpoint, it's wonderful, because you get flexibility and you don't have to pay for it."

Yet the ethanol boom has also brought the prospect of distortions that may not be as easy to resolve. The expansion of sugar production, for example, has come largely at the expense of pasture land, leading to worries that the grazing of cattle, another booming export product, could be shifted to the Amazon, encouraging greater deforestation.

Industry and government officials say such concerns are unwarranted. Sugar cane's expanding frontier is, they argue, an environmental plus, because it is putting largely abandoned or degraded pasture land back into production. And of course, ethanol burns far cleaner than fossil fuels.

Human rights and worker advocacy groups also complain that the boom has led to more hardships for the peasants who cut sugar cane. "You used to have to cut 4 tons a day, but now they want 8 or 10, and if you can't make the quota, you'll be fired," said Silvio Donizetti Palvequeres, president of the farmworkers union in Ribeirão Preto, an important cane area north of here. "We have to work a lot harder than we did 10 years ago, and the working conditions continue to be tough."

Producers say that problem will be eliminated in the next decade by greater mechanization. A much more serious long-term worry, they say, is Brazil's lack of infrastructure, particularly its limited and poorly maintained highways.

Ethanol can be made through the fermentation of many natural substances, but sugar cane offers advantages over others, like corn. For each unit of energy expended to turn cane into ethanol, 8.3 times as much energy is created, compared with a maximum of 1.3 times for corn, according to scientists at the Center for Sugarcane Technology here and other Brazilian research institutes.

"There's no reason why we shouldn't be able to improve that ratio to 10 to 1," said Suani Teixeira Coelho, director of the National Center for Biomass at the University of São Paulo. "It's no miracle. Our energy balance is so favorable not just because we have high yields, but also because we don't use any fossil fuels to process the cane, which is not the case with corn."

Brazilian producers estimate that they have an edge over gasoline as long as oil prices do not drop below $30 a barrel. But they have already embarked on technical improvements that promise to lift yields and cut costs even more.

In the past, the residue left when cane stalks are compressed to squeeze out juice was discarded. Today, Brazilian sugar mills use that residue to generate the electricity to process cane into ethanol, and use other byproducts to fertilize the fields where cane is planted.

Some mills are now producing so much electricity that they sell their excess to the national grid. In addition, Brazilian scientists, with money from São Paulo State, have mapped the sugar cane genome. That opens the prospect of planting genetically modified sugar, if the government allows, that could be made into ethanol even more efficiently.

"There is so much biological potential yet to be developed, including varieties of cane that are resistant to pesticides and pests and even drought," said Tadeu Andrade, director of the Center for Sugarcane Technology. "We've already had several qualitative leaps without that, and we are convinced there is no ceiling on productivity, at least theoretically."

REFLECTIONS

Understanding the process of change is the most useful "habit of mind" we gain from studying the past. Although the facts are many and the details overwhelming, process only appears through the study of the specific. And we must continually check our theories of change with the facts, and revise them to conform to new information.

More important, understanding change does not necessarily mean that we must submit to it. Of the processes of globalization discussed in this chapter — trade and technological transfers, cultural homogenization and competition, commercialization, and market expansion — some may seem inevitable, some merely strong, some even reversible. Intelligent action requires an appreciation of the possible as well as the identification of the improbable.

The process of global warming poses the threat of a far greater catastrophe than globalization. For the first time, humans threaten to permanently unbalance nature. We do not know when human action will push nature to a tipping point that is irreversible. The results for hundreds of millions of people living in coastal zones, the extinction of species, and the unleashing of violent weather patterns would constitute the greatest multiple disasters of human history. We would have only ourselves to blame.

History is not an exact science. Fortunately, human beings are creators, as well as subjects, of change. Even winds that cannot be stopped can be deflected and harnessed. Which way is the world moving? What are we becoming? What can we do? What kind of world can we create? These are questions that can only be answered by studying the past, both distant and recent, and trying to understand the overarching changes that are shaping our world. Worlds of history converge upon us, but only one world will emerge from our wishes, our wisdom, and our will.

Acknowledgments

John Aberth. "Ahmad al-Maqrizi, the Plague in Cairo." From *The Black Death: The Great Mortality of 1348–1350* by John Aberth. Copyright © 2005 by Bedford/St. Martin's. Reproduced by permission of Bedford/St. Martin's.

Chinua Achebe. "An Image of Africa: Racism in Conrad's *Heart of Darkness*." First published in *Massachusetts Review* 18 (1977): 782–94. Copyright © by Chinua Achebe. Reprinted by permission of David Higham Associates, Limited.

S. A. M. Adshead. "China and Rome Compared." Excerpts from *China in World History*. Copyright © 2000. Reprinted by permission of Palgrave Macmillan.

Natalie Angier. "Furs for Evening, But Cloth Was the Stone Age Standby." From *The New York Times*, December 14, 1999. Copyright © 1999 by The New York Times. Reprinted with permission.

Anonymous. Excerpt from "Chandogya Upanishad." In *The Upanishads: Breath of the Eternal*, translated by Juan Mascaro. Copyright © by Juan Mascaro. Reprinted with permission of Penguin Books, Ltd.

Anonymous. Excerpt from *The Bhagavad-Gita: Caste and Self* translated by Barbara Stoler Miller. Copyright © 1986 by Barbara Stoler Miller. Used by permission of Bantam Books, a division of Random House, Inc.

Anonymous. Excerpt from *The Epic of Gilgamesh*, translated by N. K. Sanders. Copyright © 1972 by N. K. Sanders. Reprinted with the permission of Penguin Books, Ltd.

Anonymous. "The Rig-Veda: Sacrifice as Creation." Excerpt from *Sources of Indian Tradition*, Second Edition, by Ainslie T. Embree. Copyright © 1988 by Columbia University Press. Reprinted with the permission of the publisher.

Anonymous. "Svetasvatara Upanished." From *The Upanishads: Breath of the Eternal*, translated by Swami Prabhavananda and Frederick Manchester. Copyright © 1948, 1957 by The Vedanta Society of Southern California. Reprinted with permission.

Anonymous. "The Upanishads: Karma and Reincarnation." Excerpt from *The Hindu Tradition: Readings in Oriental Thought*, edited by Ainslie T. Embree. Copyright © 1966 by Random House, Inc. Used by permission of Random House, Inc.

Aristophanes. Excerpt from *Lysistrata*, edited by William Arrowsmith, translated by Douglass Parker. Copyright © 1964 by William Arrowsmith. Used by permission of Dutton Signet, a division of Penguin Group (USA) Inc.

Aristotle. "The Athenian Constitution." From *Aristotle, Politics and the Athenian Constitution*, translated by John Warrington. Copyright © 1959 by John Warrington. Reprinted with the permission of David Campbell Publishers, Ltd.

Aung San Suu Kyi. Excerpt from *Letters from Burma*. Introduction by Fergal Keane, translated by Graeme Wilson (Penguin Books Ltd. 1997). Text copyright © Aung San Suu Kyi, 1997. Illustrations copyright © Kyaw Zura, 1997. Reprinted by permission of Penguin Books, UK.

"Aztec Account of the Conquest." From *The Broken Spears: The Atzec Account of the Conquest of Mexico*, by Miguel Leon-Portilla. Copyright © 1962, 1990 by Miguel Leon-Portilla. Expanded and Updated Edition © 1992 by Miguel Leon-Portilla. Reprinted by permission of Beacon Press, Boston.

Ban Zhao. "Lessons for Women." From *Pan Chao: Foremost Woman Scholar of China, First Century A.D.: Background, Ancestry, Life and Writings of the Most*

Celebrated Chinese Woman of Letters, translated by Nancy Lee Swann. Copyright © The East Asian Library and the Gest Collection, Princeton University. Reprinted by permission of Princeton University.

William Theodore De Bary. Excerpts from "The Buddha's First Sermon," "Buddhism and Caste," and "Buddhism in China" (Hung-ming chi, in Taisho daizokyo, LII, 1-7). From *The Buddhist Tradition in India, China and Japan* by William Theodore De Bary. Copyright © 1969 by William Theodore De Bary. Used by permission of Random House, Inc.

Jerry H. Bentley. "The Spread of World Religions." From *Old World Encounters: Cross-Cultural Contacts and Exchanges in Pre-Modern Times.* Copyright 1992 by Oxford University Press, Inc. Used by permission of Oxford University Press, Inc.

Benjamin Barber. Excerpt from *Jihad vs. McWorld: How Globalism and Tribalism Are Reshaping the World.* Copyright © 1995 by Benjamin R. Barber. Used by permission of Times Books, a division of Random House, Inc.

Franklin Le Van Baumer. "The Scientific Revolution in the West." From *Main Currents of Western Thought,* edited by Franklin Le Van Baumer. Copyright © 1978 by Franklin Le Van Baumer. Reprinted by permission of Yale University Press.

Anna Bijns. "Unyoked Is Best! Happy Is the Woman without a Man." From *Women Writers of the Renaissance and Reformation,* edited by Katharina M. Wilson. Copyright 1987 by The University of Georgia Press. Reprinted by permission of The University of Georgia Press.

Giovanni Boccaccio. Excerpt from *The Decameron* by Boccaccio, translated by G. H. McWilliam (Penguin Classics 1972, Second Edition, 1995). Copyright © G. H. McWilliam 1972, 1995. Reprinted by permission of Penguin Books Ltd.

Elise Boulding. "Women and the Agricultural Revolution." From *The Underside of History: A View of Women through Time* (Boulder, Colo.: Westview Press, 1976). Copyright © 1976 by Elise Boulding. Reprinted by permission of the author.

Fernand Braudel. "Towns and Cities." Excerpt from *The Structures of Everyday Life: The Limits of the Possible* by Fernand Braudel (London: Collins, 1983). Copyright © 1983. Reprinted by permission Armand Colin Foreign Rights.

David Cannadine. Excerpt from *Ornamentalism: How the British Saw Their Empire.* Copyright © 2005. Reprinted by permission of Oxford University Press.

Andreas Capellanus. Excerpt from *The Art of Courtly Love,* translated by John J. Parry. Copyright © 1990 by Columbia University Press. Reprinted with the permission of the publisher.

Iris Chang. Excerpt from *The Rape of Nanking: The Forgotten Holocaust of World War II.* Copyright © 1997 by Iris Chang. Reprinted with the permission of Basic Books, a member of Perseus Books, LLC.

"Chronicle of Solomon bar Simon." From *The Jews and the Crusaders: The Hebrew Chronicles of the First and Second Crusades* by Schlomo Eidelberg, editor and translator (The University of Wisconsin Press, 1977). © 1977. Reprinted with the permission of Schlomo Eidelberg.

Cicero. "Against Verres." From *On Government,* translated by Michael Grant. Copyright © Michael Grant Publications, Ltd. 1993. Reprinted with permission of Penguin Books Ltd.

John H. Coatsworth. "Economic Trajectories in Nineteenth-Century Latin America." From *Latin America and the World Economy since 1800,* edited by John H. Coatsworth and Alan M. Taylor. Copyright © 1998 by Harvard University Press. Reprinted by permission.

Anna Comnena. Excerpt from *The Alexiad of Princess Anna Comnena*, translated by Elizabeth A. S. Dawes. Reprinted with the permission of Barnes and Noble Books, Totowa, New Jersey, 07512.

Barry Cunliffe. "The Western Vikings." Excerpts from *Facing the Ocean: The Atlantic and Its Peoples.* Copyright © 2001 Oxford University Press. Reprinted with permission.

Natalie Zemon Davis. Excerpted text from *Women on the Margins: Three Seventeenth-Century Lives* by Natalie Zemon Davis. The Belknap Press of Harvard University Press. Copyright © 1995 by the President and Fellows of Harvard College. Reprinted by permission of the publisher.

Carolina Maria de Jesus. Excerpts from *Child of the Dark: The Diary of Carolina Maria de Jesus* by Carolina Maria de Jesus, translated by David St. Clair. Translation copyright © 1962 by E. P. Dutton & Co., Inc., New York and Souvenir Press Ltd., London. Used by permission of Dutton, a division of Penguin Group (USA) Inc.

Jared Diamond. "Easter Island's End." From *Discover*, volume 16, No. 8, August 1995. Copyright © 1995. Reprinted by permission of the author.

Bernal Díaz. Excerpt from *The Conquest of New Spain*, translated by J. M. Cohen. Copyright 1963 by J. M. Cohen. Reprinted with the permission of Penguin Books, Ltd.

Bernal Díaz. Excerpt from *The Conquest of New Spain* by Bernal Díaz. Translated by J. M. Cohen (Penguin Classics, 1963). Copyright © J. M. Cohen, 1963. Reprinted by permission of Penguin Group, UK.

Diane Dixon. "Michelle, Top Woman in a Macho World." From *The Observer*, Sunday, April 2, 2006. Copyright © Guardian Newspapers Limited, 2006. Reprinted with permission.

Assia Djebar. "Growing Up in Algeria." From *Fantasia: An Algerian Cavalcade*, translated by Dorothy S. Blair. Copyright © 1993 Dorothy S. Blair. Reprinted by permission of Heinemann (Portsmouth, NH).

Abba Eban. "The Refugee Problem." From *The Arab-Israeli Reader* by Walter Laqueur and Barry Rubin. Copyright © 1969, 1970 by B. L. Mazel, Inc. Copyright © 1976 by Walter Laqueur. Copyright © 1984, 1995, 2000 by Walter Laqueur and Barry Rubin. Used by permission of Viking Penguin, a division of Penguin Group (USA) Inc.

Patricia Buckley Ebrey. "The Debate on Salt and Iron." Excerpt translated by Patricia Buckley Ebrey, in *Chinese Civilization: A Sourcebook*, Second Edition. Copyright © 1993 by Patricia Buckley Ebrey. Reprinted with the permission of The Free Press, a Division of Simon & Schuster Adult Publishing Group. All rights reserved.

Patricia Buckley Ebrey. "Family Instructions for the Miu Lineage," and "How Dong Xiaowan Became My Concubine." From *Chinese Civilization: A Sourcebook*, Second Edition by Patricia Buckley Ebrey, ed. Copyright © 1993 by Patricia Buckley Ebrey. Reprinted with the permission of The Free Press, a division of Simon & Schuster Adult Publishing Group. All rights reserved.

Ainslee T. Embree. "Bada'uni, Akbar and Religion." From *Sources of Indian Tradition* by Ainslee T. Embree. Copyright © 1988 by Ainslee T. Embree. Reprinted by permission of Columbia University Press.

Olaudah Equiano. "Enslaved Captive." From *Africa Remembered: Narratives by West Africans from the Era of the Slave Trade.* by Phillip D. Curtin, ed. Waveland Press, Inc., 1967 (reissued 1997). All rights reserved.

Sarah Shaver Hughes and Brady Hughes. Excerpt from "Women in Ancient Civilizations." As published in *Women's History in Global Perspective*, vol. 2, pp. 26–30 and 36–40. Copyright © 1998 by Sarah Shaver Hughes and Brady Hughes. Reprinted with permission of the American Historical Association and the authors.

G. W. B. Huntingford. Excerpt from *The Glorious Victories of 'Āmda Seyon: King of Ethiopia.* Translated by G. W. B. Huntingford. Copyright © 1965. Published by Oxford University Press. Reprinted by permission.

Ibn al-Athir. "The Conquest of Jerusalem." Excerpt from *Arab Historians of the Crusades: Selected and Translated from the Arabic Sources*, edited and translated by E. J. Costello. Islamic World Series, 1969. Copyright © 1969 Routledge & Kegan Paul, Ltd. Reprinted by permission of Copyright Clearance Center, via the format Textbook.

John of Plano Carpini. Excerpt from *History of the Mongols*; Guyuk Khan, "Letter to Pope Innocent IV," excerpts from "Narrative of Brother Benedict the Pole," and excerpt from *The Journey of William of Rubrick* from *Mission to Asia: Narratives and Letters of the Franciscan Missionaries to Mongolia and China in the Thirteenth and Fourteenth Centuries*, translated by a nun of Stanbrook Abbey, edited by Christopher Dawson. Copyright © 1955. Reprinted with permission of The Continuum International Publishing Group.

Joseph Kahn. "Letter from Asia: China Has an Ancient Mariner to Tell You About." From *The New York Times*, July 20, 2005. Copyright © 2005 by The New York Times Company. Reprinted by permission.

Kalidasa. Excerpt from *Shakuntala*. Translated by Barbara Stoler Miller. From *Theatre of Memory: The Plays of Kalidasa*, edited by Barbara Stoler Miller. Copyright © 1984 Columbia University Press. Reprinted with permission.

Bartolomeo de Las Casas. Excerpt from *Bartolomeo de Las Casas: A Selection of His Writings* by Bartolomeo de Las Casas, translated by George Sanderlin. Copyright © 1971 by Alfred A. Knopf, a division of Random House, Inc. Used by permission of Alfred A. Knopf, a division of Random House, Inc.

Bartolomeo de Las Casas. "Hispaniola." From *The Devastation of the Indies: A Brief Account*, translated by Herma Briffault. Copyright © 1974. Reprinted by permission of The Continuum International Publishing Group.

Philippe Legrain. "Cultural Globalization Is Not Americanization." Originally published in *The Chronicle of Higher Education*, Volume 49, Issue 35, p. B7. Reprinted by permission.

Gerda Lerner. "The Urban Revolution: Origins of Patriarchy." From *The Creation of Patriarchy*. Copyright © 1986, 1987 by Gerda Lerner. Used by permission of Oxford University Press, Inc.

Richard S. Levy. "Die Krise der Sozialdemokratie (Junius-Broschure)," in Rosa Luxemburg, *Politische Schriften* (Leipzig, 1970). Edited by Gunter Radezun and translated by Richard S. Levy. Reprinted by Richard S. Levy.

Bernard Lewis. "Peace Terms with Jerusalem," from "Al Tabari, Tarik al-Rusulcwa'I muluk" (Lciden: Brill), published in *Islam from the Prophet Muhammad to the Conquest of Constantinople*, edited and translated by Bernard Lewis. Vol. I: Politics and War. Excerpt from Vol II: Religion and Society. Published by Harper & Row, 1974.

Miriam Lichtheim. "Advice to the Young Egyptian: Be a Scribe." From *Ancient Egyptian Literature: A Book of Readings, Volume 2; The New Kingdom* by Miriam Lichtheim. Copyright © 1976 by the University of California Press

Books. Reproduced with permission of University of California Press Books in the format Textbook via Copyright Clearance Center.

Liu Tsung-yuan. "Camel Kuo the Gardner" from *An Anthology of Chinese Literature: From Early Times to the Fourteenth Century,* edited by Cyril Birch. Copyright © 1965 by Grove Press, Inc. Used by permission of Grove/Atlantic, Inc.

Livy. Excerpt from *Women's Life in Greece and Rome,* Second Edition. Mary R. Lefkowitz and Maureen B. Fant, eds. Copyright © 1992. Reprinted with the permission of The Johns Hopkins University Press.

G. E. R. Lloyd. "Chinese and Greco-Roman Innovation." Excerpts from *The Ambitions of Curiosity* by G. E. R. Lloyd. Copyright © 2002 by G. E. R. Lloyd. Reprinted with the permission of Cambridge University Press.

Miriam Ching Yoon Louie. Excerpted text from *Sweatshop Warriors: Immigrant Workers Take On the Global Factory.* Copyright © 2001. Reprinted by permission of South End Press.

Toussaint L'Ouverture. "Letter to the Directory, November 5, 1797." From *The Black Jacobins* by C. L. R. James. Copyright © 1989. Published by Seeker & Warburg. Used by permission of The Random House Group Limited.

Magnus Magnusson and Hermann Palsson. "Eiric's Saga." From *The Vinland Sagas: The Norse Discover America,* translated with an introduction by Magnus Magnusson and Hermann Palsson (Penguin Classics, 1965). Copyright © Magnus Magnusson and Hermann Palsson, 1965. Reprinted by permission of Penguin Books Ltd.

Mahmood Mamdani. "Thinking about Genocide." Excerpt from *When Victims Become Killers.* Copyright © 2002 by Mahmood Mamdani. Reprinted by permission of Princeton University Press.

Marco Polo. Excerpt from *Marco Polo: The Travels,* translated by Ronald Latham. Copyright © 1958 by Ronald Latham. Reprinted with the permission of Penguin Books, Ltd.

Sally Marks. "The Coming of the First World War." Excerpts from *The Ebbing of European Ascendancy: An International History of the World 1914–1945,* co-published in the U.S. by Oxford University Press. Copyright 2002. Reprinted by permission of Hodder Arnold (UK).

José Martí. "Coney Island." From *José Martí: Selected Writings* by José Martí. Introduction by Roberto Gonzalez Echevarria. Edited by Esther Allen. Translated by Esther Allen. Copyright © 2002 by Esther Allen. Used by permission of Viking Penguin, a division of Penguin Group (USA) Inc.

Karl Marx and Friedrich Engels. Excerpt from *The Communist Manifesto* edited by Samuel H. Beer. Crofts Classics Series. Copyright © 1955 by Harlan Davidson, Inc. Reprinted with permission.

Mary Jo Maynes and Ann Waltner. "Women and Marriage in Europe and China" and "Childhood, Youth, and the Female Life Cycle: Women's Life Cycle Transitions in a World-Historical Perspective: Comparing Marriage in China and Europe." Excerpt from *Journal of Women's History,* 12, no. 4 (Winter 2001). Copyright © 2001. Reprinted by permission of Indiana University Press.

John Mearsheimer and Stephen Walt. "The Israel Lobby." An edited version of an article which first appeared in *The London Review of Books,* vol. 28, no. 6, March 23, 2006. Reprinted by permission of London Review of Books. www.lrb.co.uk.

Gavin Menzies. Selection from *1421: The Year China Discovered America* by Gavin Menzies. Copyright © 2003 by Gavin Menzies. Reprinted with permission of HarperCollins Publishers.

Nzinga Mbemba. "Appeal to the King of Portugal." From *The African Past* by Basil Davidson. Copyright © 1964 by Basil Davidson. Reprinted by permission of Curtis Brown, Ltd.

William H. McNeill. "Greek and Indian Civilization." From *A World History*, Second Edition. Copyright © 1971 by Oxford University Press. Reprinted by permission of the author. "Consequences of the Black Death in Europe." From *Plagues and Peoples* by William H. McNeill. Copyright © 1976 by William H. McNeill. Used by permission of Doubleday, a division of Random House, Inc.

Mirabai. Excerpt from Bhakti poems, from *Sources of Indian Tradition*, Volume I: From the Beginning to 1800, 2nd edition. Edited by Ainslee Embree. Copyright © 1988 Columbia University Press. Reprinted with permission.

Ichisada Miyazaki. "The Chinese Civil Service Exam System." From *China's Examination Hell*, translated by Conrad Schirokauer. Copyright 1976. Reprinted by permission of the publishers, Weatherhill, Inc.

Gabriele de' Mussis. "Origins of the Black Death." From *The Black Death* by Rosemary Horrox. Copyright © 1994 Manchester University Press, Manchester, UK. Reprinted by permission.

R. K. Narayan. Excerpt from *The Ramayana* by R. K. Narayan. Copyright © R. K. Narayan 1972. Used by permission of the Wallace Literary Agency, Inc.

Jawaharlal Nehru. "Gandhi." From *Toward Freedom: The Autobiography of Jawaharlal Nehru*. Reprinted by permission of the Jawaharlal Nehru Memorial Fund.

George Orwell. Excerpt from *Burmese Days* by George Orwell. Copyright © by George Orwell and renewed 1962 by Sonia Pitt-Rivers. Reprinted by permission of Harcourt, Inc. and Bill Hamilton as the Literary Executor of the Estate of the Late Sonia Brownell Orwell and Seeker & Warburg, Ltd.

Jurgen Osterhammel. Excerpt from *Colonialism*, translated by Shelly Frisch. Copyright © 1997 by Shelly L. Frisch. Reprinted with the permission of Markus Weiner Publishers.

Arnold Pacey. "Asia and the Industrial Revolution." From *Technology in World Civilizations: A Thousand Year History*. Copyright 1990. Reprinted by permission of MIT Press, Cambridge, Mass.

Pliny. "Pliny Consults the Emperor Trajan." [Letters 10: 96-97] From *Pliny Secundus: Letters and Panegyricus*, Volume II, Loeb Classical Library, Volume 59, translated by Betty Radice. Copyright © 1969 by the President and Fellows of Harvard College. The Loeb Classical Library ® is a registered trademark of the President and Fellows of Harvard College. Reprinted by permission of the publishers and the Trustees of the Loeb Classical Library.

Kenneth Pomeranz. "How the Other Side Traded." From *The World That Trade Created: Society, Culture, and the World Economy, 1400 to the Present*, 2nd edition by Kenneth Pomeranz and Steven Topik. Copyright © 2006 by M. E. Sharpe, Inc. Reprinted with permission.

Roxanne Prazniak. "Ban Zhao and the End of Chinese Feudalism." From *Dialogues Across Civilizations* by Roxanne Prazniak. Copyright © 1996 Westview Press. Reprinted by permission of Copyright Clearance Center.

Donald Quataert. Excerpts from *The Ottoman Empire, 1700–1922.* Copyright © 2000 by Donald Quataert. Reprinted with the permission of Cambridge University Press.

Kevin Reilly. "Cities and Civilizations," and "Love in Medieval Europe, India, and Japan." From *The West and the World: A History of Civilization*, Second Edition. Copyright © 1989 by Kevin Reilly. Reprinted by the permission of Pearson Education Inc.

Erich Maria Remarque. Excerpt from *All Quiet on the Western Front* by Erich Maria Remarque. "Im Western Nichts Neues." Copyright 1928 by Ullstein A. G.; Copyright renewed © 1956 by Erich Maria Remarque. "All Quiet on The Western Front." Copyright 1929, 1930 by Little, Brown and Company. Copyright renewed © 1957, 1958 by Erich Maria Remarque. All rights reserved. Reprinted by permission of Pryor Cashman Sherman and Flynn LLP.

Andrew C. Revkin. "Climate Data Hint at Irreversible Rise in Seas." From *The New York Times*, March 24, 2006. Copyright © 2006 by The New York Times Company. Reprinted with permission.

Matteo Ricci. "Jesuit Missionaries in Ming China." From *China in the Sixteenth Century* by Matteo Ricci, translated by Louis J. Gallagher. Copyright © 1942, 1953 and renewed 1970 by Louis J. Gallagher, S.J. Used by permission of Random House, Inc.

John Roach. "By 2050 Warming to Doom Million Species, Study Says." From *National Geographic News*, July 12, 2004. Copyright © 2004 by National Geographic Society. Reprinted with permission.

Larry Rohter. "With Big Boost from Sugar Cane, Brazil Is Satisfying Its Fuel Needs." From *The New York Times*, April 10, 2006. Copyright © 2006 by The New York Times Company. Reprinted with permission.

Kirkpatrick Sale. Excerpt from *The Conquest of Paradise.* Copyright © 1990 Kirkpatrick Sale. Used by permission of Alfred A. Knopf, a division of Random House, Inc.

Lynda Norene Shaffer. "China, Technology and Change." From *World History Bulletin* 4, no. 1 (Fall/Winter, 1986–87): 1–6. Copyright © 1987. Reprinted with permission.

Lynda Shaffer. "Southernization." From *Journal of World History* 5, no. 1, Spring 1994. Copyright © 1994 by the University of Hawaii Press. Reprinted with the permission of the publishers. All rights reserved.

Ari Shavit. "An Interview with Benny Morris." From *Ha'aretz*, January 9, 2004. Copyright © 2004 by Ari Shavit. Reprinted with permission of Ha'aretz Syndication Service.

Murasaki Shikibu. Excerpts from *The Tale of Genji*, Volume 1, by Lady Murasaki. Translated by Arthur Waley. Originally published by Houghton Mifflin Company. Copyright © by permission of The Arthur Waley Estate. All rights reserved.

Marjorie Shostak. "Memories of a !Kung Girlhood." From *Nisa: The Life and Words of a !Kung Woman.* Copyright © 1981 by Marjorie Shostak. Reprinted with the permission of Harvard University Press.

Jonathan Spence. "The Late Ming Empire." From *The Search for Modern China.* Copyright © 1990 by Jonathan Spence. Used by permission of W. W. Norton & Company, Inc. Includes Tang Xianzu, excerpts from *The Peony Pavilion*, translated by Cyril Birch. Copyright © 1980 by Indiana University Press. Reprinted with the permission of the publishers.

Luther Standing Bear. Excerpt from *Land of the Spotted Eagle* by Luther Standing Bear. Copyright © 1933 by Luther Standing Bear. Renewal Copyright 1960 by May Jones. Reprinted by permission of the University of Nebraska Press.

Peter N. Stearns. "The Industrial Revolution Outside the West." From *Industrial Revolution in World History* by Peter N. Stearns. Copyright © 1998 by Westview Press. Reprinted by permission of Westview Press, a member of Perseus Books, LLC.

Jean-François Steiner. Excerpt from *Treblinka*. English translation copyright © 1967 by Simon & Schuster, Inc. Reprinted with the permission of Simon & Schuster Adult Publishing Group.

J. W. Thomas. Excerpt from *Ulrich von Liechtenstein's The Service of Ladies*, translated by J.W. Thomas. Copyright © 1969. Published by arrangement with North Carolina Press (1969). Reprinted with permission.

Theodore von Laue. Excerpt from *The World Revolution of Westernization: The Twentieth Century in Global Perspective.* Copyright 1987 by Oxford University Press, Inc. Used by permission of Oxford University Press, Inc.

Burton Watson. Excerpt from *The Lotus Sutra*, translated by Burton Watson. Copyright © 1993 by Burton Watson. Reprinted by permission of Columbia University Press.

Lynn White Jr. The Historical Roots of Our Ecological Crisis." From *Science* 155: 1203-07 (1967). Copyright © 1967 AAAS. Reprinted by permission.

John E. Wills Jr. "Sor Juana Inés de la Cruz." From *1688: A Global History.* Copyright © 2001 John E. Wills Jr. Used by permission of W. W. Norton & Company, Inc.

Iwasaki Yataro. "Letter to Employees of the Mitsubishi Company." From *Sources of Japanese History,* Volume II, by David Lu, ed. Copyright © 1974 (McGraw-Hill). Reprinted by permission of David Lu.

Fukuzawa Yukichi. "Datsu-a Ron (On Saying Good-bye to Asia)." From *Japan: A Documentary History*, Vol II: *The Late Tokugawa Period to the Present* by David J. Lu, ed. Translation copyright © 1997 by David J. Lu. Reprinted by permission of M. E. Sharpe, Inc.

Zheng He. "Inscription to the Goddess." From *China and Africa in the Middle Ages*, ed. Teobaldo Filesi, translated and inscribed by David Morrison. Copyright © 1972 by David Morrison. Reprinted with permission of the publisher.